For Tom Tanselle

STRONG ON MUSIC

The New York Music Scene in the Days of George Templeton Strong

VOLUME II

REVERBERATIONS 1850–1856

Vera Brodsky Lawrence

THE UNIVERSITY OF CHICAGO PRESS
Chicago and London

STRONG ON MUSIC
The New York Music Scene
in the Days of George Templeton Strong

VOLUME I: RESONANCES, 1836–1849

VOLUME II: REVERBERATIONS, 1850–1856

The University of Chicago Press, Chicago 60637
The University of Chicago Press, Ltd., London

Printed in the United States of America

04 03 02 01 00 99 98 97 96 95 5 4 3 2 1

ISBN (cloth): 0-226-47010-5
ISBN (paper): 0-226-47011-3

This publication has been supported by a grant from the National Endowment for the Humanities, an independent federal agency.

Library of Congress Cataloging-in-Publication Data

Lawrence, Vera Brodsky.
Reverberations, 1850–1856 / Vera Brodsky Lawrence.
p. cm.—(Strong on music ; v. 2)
Includes index.
ISBN 0-226-47010-5. — ISBN 0-226-47011-3 (pbk.)
1. Music—New York (N.Y.)—19th century—History and criticism.
2. Strong, George Templeton, 1820–1875—Diaries. 3. Musicians—New York (N.Y.)—Diaries. 4. New York (N.Y.)—Intellectual life.
I. Strong, George Templeton, 1820–1875. II. Title. III. Series:
Lawrence, Vera Brodsky. Strong on music ; v. 2.
ML200.8.N5L4 1995 vol. 2
780′.9747′109034—dc20 91-14828
CIP
MN

♾ The paper used in this publication meets the minimum requirements of the American National Standard for Information Sciences—Permanence of Paper for Printed Library Materials, ANSI Z39.48-1984.

New York, say the professionals, is to the rest of the United States what Europe is to New York, namely, the place where the reputation is made; or, in other words, it is the dog on which the physic is tried.

Home Journal
September 10, 1853

This journal, though it means to be truthful, is no picture of my inner life. I'm a case of chronic dualism, *beyond Homeopathy—or any other 'pathy.*

George Templeton Strong
Private Journal, October 11, 1853

CONTENTS

6

7

PREFACE

Continuing to explore the musical *terra incognita* discovered in the first volume of *Strong on Music, Reverberations* proceeds into the 1850s, a time when New York was rapidly progressing from small town to sophisticated metropolis. Notoriously an amusement-loving community, New York—as it gained in world importance—became a mecca for visiting musicians from abroad. In 1850 the memorable opera season performed by an unprecedentedly superb Italian company from Havana, followed by Jenny Lind's legendary visit, master-minded by Phineas T. Barnum, irrevocably propelled New York into the musical big time.

Because the Barnum/Lind legend has been told and retold, always portraying Lind as the supremely adored, flawless, all-time Goddess of Song, it was revealing, indeed shocking, to discover—in the enormous mass of contemporary newspaper coverage of her visit—that a goodly amount of adverse criticism had been leveled against Lind; that she was not the angel contrived by Barnum to mesmerize the American public; and that she eventually departed from the United States in a cloud of bitterness. Amazingly, it is Barnum's promotional wizardry rather than Lind's perfections that—after the passage of more than a century and a half—still continues to preserve the legend.

Although remarkable, this circumstance is regrettable, not only because the facts of the Lind/Barnum story are even more fascinating than the fiction, but because it indicates the strange lack of scholarly curiosity and gumption that has impeded and dwarfed the study-in-depth of our lively musical evolution during the formative early and middle years of the nineteenth century. It is both frustrating and puzzling that—although nineteenth-century European composers and critics continue to be widely studied and celebrated—no biographies exist of such important early champions of American music as Ureli Corelli Hill, Charles Jerome Hopkins, and George Frederick Bristow. No one has yet undertaken to supplant the inadequate existing biographies of William Henry Fry and Anthony Philip Heinrich. Shrouded in silence are the critical thunderbolts hurled against the baffling new music of Schumann, Brahms, Berlioz, Schubert, Liszt, Wagner, and particularly Verdi (as well as the boring music of the old-fogy composers Mozart and Bach) by such unsung critics as Nathaniel Parker Willis, Richard Storrs Willis, Hermann Saroni, Richard Grant White, Charles Bailey Seymour, Henry C. Watson, Charles Burkhardt, Oliver Dyer, George William Curtis, and Theodore Hagen (to say nothing of hordes of pseudonymous critics). Yet they helped shape the world of music that we have inherited. Although their often idiosyncratic writings constitute an important body of music criticism crucial to the understanding of our musical foundations (and an object lesson for present-day reception of new music), they remain largely ignored. A serious lack.

The beguiling exploits of the ferociously competitive, mutually destructive, trio of pioneering opera impresarios Bernard Ullman, Maurice Strakosch, and Max Maretzek—with their cabals and plots and ploys and perpetual feuds and expedient reconciliations—have sunk into undeserved oblivion. (It is an indication of what passes for scholarship in this neglected field that a recent, shockingly errata-laden history, so-called, of opera in America omits even to mention Ullman, an omission as unthinkable as a history of American show business without Barnum, or a history of American films without D. W. Griffith.)

We remain woefully uninformed, too, about the American careers of the armies of divas and divos who thrilled opera-loving New Yorkers of the 1850s: Teresa Parodi, Balbina Steffanone, Angiolina Bosio, Fortunata Tedesco, Anna de Lagrange, Marietta Alboni, Henriette Sontag, Felicita Vestvali, Grisi and Mario, Anna Bishop, and Catherine Hayes; the Americans Elise Biscaccianti, Elise Hensler, Adelaide Phillips, Cora de Wilhorst, and the phenomenal Black Swan, Elizabeth Taylor Greenfield; also Pasquale Brignoli, Alessandro Amodio, Ignazio Marini, Cesare Badiali, Lorenzo Salvi, and scores of others deserving biographical notice. Little has been written of the important early Philharmonic conductors, George Loder, Theodore Eisfeld, and Carl Bergmann, or the spectacular American tour of Louis Antoine Jullien, or the pianists Richard Hoffman, Gustav Satter, and Sebastian Bach Mills, or of Eisfeld's archetypal yearly series of chamber music concerts, or the violinists Joseph Burke, Paul Julien, and the American career of Henri Vieuxtemps, or the bandleading Dodworths, to name only a few of the myriad important musicians waiting to be resurrected.

My purpose in writing *Strong on Music* is twofold: to bring to life the lost world that these musicians inhabited and to kindle the desire in scholarly bosoms to carry forward what has been begun here. Despite its somewhat misleading title (I just couldn't resist the tempting pun), *Strong on Music* is primarily concerned with New York's predilection for music, not Strong's. Although the music entries in his journal—and all of them are found here—constitute an important element of the work, by no means should they be construed as its primary subject. Serving instead as a passport to a bygone world, Strong's journal provides an invaluable perspective on one aspect of that world's stratified socio-cultural climate.

In the following pages, the tiny superior eighth-note (♪) acts as a symbol for "see volume one." As in the first volume, the GTS chapters—setting forth Strong's pungent dictums—alternate with the OBBLIGATO chapters, which investigate the thousand-and-one concurrent music happenings outside (often beneath) Strong's notice. Together they embrace many of the diverse musics that made up the fascinating and complex New York music scene of the 1850s.

New York
January 1995

VERA BRODSKY LAWRENCE

ACKNOWLEDGMENTS

For enabling me—over a period of years—single-mindedly to devote myself to *Strong on Music,* and for their assistance in making possible the publication of this, its second volume, I am eternally indebted to the National Endowment for the Humanities. I wish to express, too, my special thanks to Elizabeth Arndt, my program officer at the NEH, for her unfailing kindness, helpfulness, solicitude, and her valued friendship.

To the John Simon Guggenheim Memorial Foundation I am deeply grateful, once again, for their generous subvention for the illustrations and index of this volume and for their continuing interest in this project, begun—with their assistance—some two decades ago.

I am profoundly appreciative of the cooperation and splendid assistance, through thick and thin, of the gallant staff members of the New-York Historical Society, May Stone and Mariam Touba in the Library and Wendy Shadwell and Dale Neighbors in the Prints and Photographs Division.

I am beholden to Jean Bowen, chief of the Music Division of the New York Public Library, for her continuing interest and assistance; to Leslie Foss, a member of her staff, for his willing help; to Barbara Haws, archivist/historian of the New York Philharmonic, for permitting me to study the fragile copybooks containing the minutes of Philharmonic directors' meetings in the nineteenth century, an invaluable resource; to Larry E. Sullivan, chief of the Rare Book and Special Collections Division at the Library of Congress, for his assistance in finding the unfindable; to Wallace Bjorke of the University of Michigan Library at Ann Arbor for supplying me with materials that were unavailable elsewhere; and to Mark Piel, librarian of the New York Society Library for his unfailing willingness to assist.

For their generous permission to reproduce items in their pictorial collections, my thanks again to Jean Bowen at the New York Public Library; also to the New-York Historical Society; to the National Portrait Gallery; to Robert Tuggle, director of the Metropolitan Opera Archives, who kindly permitted me to use items in his personal collection; and to Dr. Girvice Archer, Jr., who most generously put his extraordinary collection of nineteenth-century iconography at my disposal.

I am greatly obliged to Douglas F. Bauer for his beautiful translation of Aristophanes; to Charles Suttoni for his guidance in esoteric matters of the nineteenth century in Europe; to Rena Mueller for information about the non-existence of a song attributed to Franz Liszt; to Thomas G. Kaufman for so willingly sharing his encyclopedic knowledge of Italian operas and opera singers; to D. W. Fostle for inside information on nineteenth-century members of the Steinway family; and to Dorothy Arnof, Robin Hicks, and Barbara Schneider for invaluable moral support.

My special thanks are offered to John G. Doyle for so graciously sharing his prodigious knowledge of Louis Moreau Gottschalk; and to S. Frederick Starr, Gottschalk's biographer, to whom I am eternally obliged for his enthusiastic support and his wonderful assistance in helping this volume see the light of day.

I am obliged, too, to Wayne Shirley for his invaluable comments on *Reverberations*, to Marilyn Bliss for her creative index making, and to Pauline Fox for her meticulous copyediting. To my synergetic editor, Kathleen Hansell, and her colleagues at the University of Chicago Press I offer my appreciation for an uncommonly pleasant publishing experience.

And to G. Thomas Tanselle, I offer this book, with my deepest gratitude for his encouragement, advice, and his treasured friendship.

VBL

ILLUSTRATIONS

In the listing below, publishing information is given in parentheses.

Reverberations

I

GTS: 1850

. . . we may well be surprised if the present season should not make this city a perfect musical Mecca, bringing in the lovers of sweet sounds, like so many pilgrims, to render the coming season in the metropolis a continuous festival.

New York Herald
September 3, 1850

TOWARD THE END OF JANUARY 1850, George Templeton Strong at last broke the self-imposed musical fast that he had rigorously maintained since the previous May, when his wife, Ellen, had suffered her lamentable (and interminably lamented) miscarriage.♪ Throughout the months of Ellen's convalescence—relentlessly prolonged by her overzealous young husband—no attendance at a concert or an opera was recorded in the pages of Strong's private journal.

Not that there had been a dearth of musical activity. Particularly at the Astor Place Opera House,♪ where the Strongs had concentrated their fashionable music-going after their marriage in 1848, the canny and resourceful maestro/impresario Max Maretzek♪ had presented an uninterrupted flow of opera performances, a phenomenon without precedent in the turbulent history of Italian opera in New York. It was Maretzek's proud boast that under his management "sixty performances took place without the slightest disappointment to the public" (Maretzek, *Crotchets,* pp. 87–88). Strong, however, as he never tired of reminding his journal, had no fondness for the popular Italian opera repertory—the ceaselessly repeated *Lucia*s, *Lucrezia*s, and *Ernani*s—that constituted the fare at the Astor Place Opera House. True, it was Maretzek's policy to present a "novelty," in some instances a long-neglected work masquerading as a first performance in New York. The latest of these disguised revivals was Donizetti's *Anna Bolena,* locally given in Italian for the first time on January 7, 1850, but previously heard—in French in 1843 and in English in 1844—as Mordecai M. Noah♪ informed the readers of his *Sunday Times and Noah's Weekly Messenger* (January 13, 1850).

Now performed by the fair-to-middling stars of the Astor Place opera company—Apollonia Bertucca♪ in the title role, Amalia Patti♪ as Jane Seymour, Pietro Novelli♪ as Henry VIII, and Giuseppe Forti♪ as Lord Percy—*Anna Bolena,* despite a reported "most magnificent production," achieved only a lukewarm success. It was played six times to the Astor Place subscribers, then shelved.

New-York Historical Society

Main entrance to the Astor Place Opera House.

The critics, as usual, differed widely on the merits of the work and the performers.[1] The *Herald* (January 8, 1850) exuberantly pronounced *Anna Bolena* to be Donizetti's most glorious creation and Signorina Bertucca "almost too charming—for Henry would never have spurned so charming an Anna." Henry C. Watson,♪ a supporter of Maretzek if not of Donizetti, pointed out in the *Albion* (January 12, 1850, p. 20) that although *Anna Bolena* was regarded by the European cognoscenti as Donizetti's best work, the composer, without plagiarizing actual tunes, had cribbed from all the best composers—Rossini, Mozart, Meyerbeer, and even Beethoven. It was, nonetheless—or perhaps for this very reason—Donizetti's best score; in it he observed a proper balance between singer and orchestra, in contrast to Verdi, who used both his voices and instruments "like an ill-educated giant." In the role of Anne Boleyn, proclaimed Watson, an inveterate name-dropper, Bertucca was "every inch a queen," and, as he weightily informed his readers, he had seen a few queens in his day.

But the ultra-precious editor of the *Home Journal,* Nathaniel P. Willis,♪ hotly pursuing his vendetta against Maretzek, attacked him for his "stubborn partisanship of the wound-up and wooden Bertucca [the imminent Mrs. Maretzek], whose throat and

[1] "To cavil appears the goal, the beginning, and the end of every would-be critic of this well-conducted establishment" (the Astor Place Opera House), wrote the newly arrived English composer and cellist Frederick Nicholls Crouch (1808–1896)♪ in the *Message Bird* (March 1, 1850, p. 248).

chin," he cruelly wrote, "collapse like a shut-up umbrella when the sound has passed from under." In general: "To a poorer Operatic effort we never were witness" (*Home Journal,* January 5, 12, 1850).[2]

Willis's persistent needling of Maretzek at last erupted into full-scale warfare when an exasperated Maretzek released to the press—and put on public display at the Astor Place box office—an arrogant note he had received from Willis. Ostensibly written to request a replacement for his accidentally destroyed season ticket to the Astor Place Opera, Willis had disingenuously taken the opportunity to trust that "my dear Maretzek" accepted his incessant disparagement in the *Home Journal* for what it was worth—merely a playful desire to introduce a little variety, a spicy "*basso* of criticism"—to relieve the "excess of *alto*" (the unanimous critical approval) in the other newspapers. Had the general tone of the reviews been adverse, Willis blandly assured Maretzek, he might just as easily have adopted the opposite point of view. Later attempting, once the cat was out of the bag, to justify this professionally unjustifiable assertion, Willis defensively wrote: "There are two ways of criticizing—one to point out and dwell on the beauties of a performance—the other to point out and dwell on its defects. Both may be done with perfect truth" (*Home Journal,* January 19, 26, 1850).

The episode provided New York's mutually hostile journalistic community with material for delectable gossip. Referring to the Willis/Maretzek feud as a "chapter of blunders" on the parts of both belligerents, the *Evening Mirror* (January 19, 1850), presumably its editor Hiram Fuller,[♪] dryly observed that Willis, a former editor of the *Mirror,* had "made the first blunder when he ventured to write about music—or any art at all. His ignorance of the true principles of art, and particularly of music, is astoundingly profound and complete." He had made his next blunder, the *Mirror* went on, in "attacking the person of that accomplished artist Bertucca"; his third blunder was the assumption that with his "twaddle . . . he had any influence upon 'opera-going circles'"; his fourth was that "after having abused the person of Max Maretzek's principal artist and sneered at his company generally, he wrote a note—and such a note—to the manager, which showed that his praise or blame is worth literally nothing. . . . He was thus silly enough to put himself completely in the power of a man whose interests he had done his best to injure."

Maretzek, continued the *Mirror,* had committed the fifth blunder by publishing Willis's personal note, however abusive.[3] "We do not justify the manager in the publication of Willis's *sub rosa* note, in which the critic confesses himself utterly destitute of principles; but at the same time the offense is not greater than the publications of *private conversation* picked up at dinner parties and retailed at a penny a line through the columns of Magazines and Newspapers" (*Mirror,* January 26, 1850). Although the delicious hubbub vastly increased both the circulation of the *Home Journal* and the sale of tickets at the Astor Place Opera House (*Crotchets,* p. 85), Strong was not tempted to

[2] The *New York Herald,* a pro-Maretzek paper, on January 18 accused Willis of being at the head of an Italian clique "which conspired against Bertucca and killed her *Anna Bolena* by withdrawing its applause" (quoted in the *Evening Mirror,* January 19, 1850).

[3] Maretzek discloses that "an excellent lawyer" had dissuaded him from suing Willis for libel after Willis accused him in print of having "robbed the subscribers of their money." It was at this point, writes Maretzek, that he conceived the idea of waging war on Willis in the press (*Crotchets,* pp. 84–85).

New-York Historical Society

Apollonia Bertucca and Max Maretzek, and (below) their abuser, Nathaniel Parker Willis

return to the opera. Not until it was announced that *Don Giovanni* was in preparation did his old appetite for music show signs of reviving. That is, for music not composed by Verdi.

January 26, 1850. . . . They play *Don Giovanni* Tuesday night [January 29]!!!!!!!!! I'll hear it, unless something particularly special happens to prevent. *Non sperai—Batti, batti—Là ci darem—Vedrai, carino*!!!! If those be fair examples, what must the whole lot be! But Niminy will call it "quaint," and Piminy will say it's very bad unless it's sung by first-rate artistes. And so they'll cackle and bray, according to their several gifts, and admit that it's very fine, and sigh in their hearts for the fleshpots of Egypt, or the inanities of Donizetti, or the delicious unisons of Mr. Verdi. Verdi!!!!!

A good deal of *Ernani* is written with a degree of effort that justifies one in putting Rabelais, a little transposed, into the lips of Mr. Verdi: "I cannot ordinarily write music without gnashing my teeth and making filthy faces, for of my brain I am naturally costive."

~

Strong's repugnance toward Verdi reflected current musical attitudes as faithfully as did his elation over the return of Mozart's *Don Giovanni* a quarter-century after its legendary first performance in New York by the Garcias.♪[4] During the interim, in 1840 and 1849, it had been presented in a doubtfully "authentic" English adaptation by the Seguins.♪[5] Strong had attended none of these productions: in 1826 he was too young to have heard the Garcias—and in any case he had virtuously avoided the contaminating influences of the theatre (opera included) until 1845, when he was twenty-five years old. His familiarity—such as it was—with the score of *Don Giovanni* had come from music-making around the parlor piano and from an occasional excerpt performed at an occasional concert. Like his contemporaries, Strong regarded the work with an almost religious awe, looking upon it as the supreme pinnacle of all musical creation.[6] Indeed, among New York's musical cognoscenti, familiarity with *Don Giovanni* had come to be regarded as a kind of cultural status symbol.

To guide the general public in the proper appreciation of this esoteric work, a goodly amount of preliminary instruction was dispensed in the press, together with a flood of reminiscences of its fabled performances by the Garcias in 1826. As the *Mirror* observed (January 29, 1850), they had been so much talked about over the intervening two and a half decades that "many people who were in the nursery then have quite a vivid impression that they actually heard the *Don Giovanni* of the Garcias."

This did not apply to the music critic of Horace Greeley's *New-York Daily Tribune,* possibly young Richard Storrs Willis,♪ whose local memory was necessarily short. Born in Boston in 1819, educated at Yale and in Germany, Willis had somehow re-

[4] The historic American premiere of *Don Giovanni* took place at the Park Theatre on May 23, 1826.

[5] Although well staged and a success, *Don Giovanni* in English reportedly did not satisfy the cognoscenti: "Not a little of the spirit of the opera has evaporated in its passage from the Italian flask to the English decanter," wrote the *Mirror* (January 29, 1850). "'Chide me, chide me' was not *'Batti, batti'*; and so the craving for the genuine and only *Don Giovanni* remained unsatisfied."

[6] His worship of the musical score continued unabated; but soon, like his contemporaries, he came to regard the libretto as a moral abomination.

mained unaware of the mythic Garcia performances. The forthcoming production, he misinformed his readers, would offer the first authentic presentation of *Don Giovanni* ever to have been performed in the United States. "The English versions occasionally given of the great *chef d'oeuvre* of the great composer," he explained, had been "either paraphrase or burlesque, inadequate to convey the slightest idea of the original." Reflecting his Germanic orientation, he added: "It is necessary to say only one thing to those who are but slightly acquainted with music theoretically: the constant ding-dong of heavy brass accompaniments of the operas of Rossini, Donizetti, and especially Verdi, will be missed in *Don Giovanni,* which will, to the person of whom we speak, consequently seem tame and meager. To those, however, who understand music and know how to appreciate its most exquisite and beautiful effects, the production of *Don Giovanni,* as we know it will be produced, will be the commencement of a new and delightful epoch in the history of their musical experience" (*Tribune,* January 29, 1850).

Mordecai M. Noah, who on the other hand possessed the longest memory in the New York press and loved nothing better than to rummage in its dusty corridors, ridiculed the critic of the *New-York Express* (most probably James F. Otis)♪ for being similarly unaware of the Garcias' *Don Giovanni.* This lapse offered Noah a perfect excuse for embarking on another of his luxurious rambles into the past. Not only did he blissfully recall the elder Manuel Garcia as the Don and his enchanting, eighteen-year-old daughter Maria Felicità, the eternally idolized "Signorina," as Zerlina, but he further provided a lengthy and worshipful essay on Mozart and his miraculous operas *Don Giovanni, Die Zauberflöte,* and *Le nozze di Figaro.* In vivid words, Noah expressed his emotions on again hearing the Overture to *Don Giovanni:* "The blood creeps and the frame almost trembles on hearing it," he wrote in the *Times and Messenger* (February 3, 1850).[7]

Henry C. Watson, who, of course, had frequently heard *Don Giovanni* magnificently performed in Europe, as he "would never hear it again," by such legendary artists as Grisi, Persiani, Tamburini, Lablache, and Mario, surprisingly professed to be "most pleasurably disappointed" with everything and everybody connected with Maretzek's excellent production of the work (*Albion,* January 5, p. 8; February 2, 1850, p. 56).[8]

With minor differences the press, however, generally tended to agree with Hermann Saroni,♪ the saber-toothed critic and publisher of *Saroni's Musical Times,* who pronounced Federico Beneventano,♪ the Don Giovanni, to be "too rough, too boisterous, too vulgar." As for the other singers, Teresa Truffi,♪ the Donna Anna, looked the part but her singing was superficial; Antonio Sanquirico, with his overdone buffoonery, completely mistook the part of Leporello; Pietro Novelli, the Masetto, was vocally acceptable but he had no clue to the character he was portraying; and Bertucca, the Zerlina, was indifferent in both her acting and singing. Only young Amalia Patti, the Donna Elvira, and Giuseppe Forti, the Don Ottavio, seemed to understand the music and how to perform it.

[7] But Philip Hone,♪ who also sentimentally remembered the Garcias, found this new production of *Don Giovanni* to be "not the same exhibition with which I was formerly delighted in operatic days. I do not pretend to enjoy, because I cannot understand, the music and the dialogue; it is all heathen Greek to me" (Hone, MS Diary, February 13, 1850).

[8] Watson did take issue, however, with Sanquirico,♪ an "otherwise perfect Leporello," for playing to the gallery with his silly substitution of "one thousand and three" for *mille e tre,* a tactic that Watson termed "mere nonsense and entirely out of place" (*Albion,* February 2, 1850, p. 561).

Saroni was dissatisfied, too, with the orchestra: "Here an impertinent *roulade* was cut short by the dissonant interval of a clarionet; there a brilliant cadenza came to an untimely end by the unmerciful blast of a red-hot, republican trumpet. Wherever the frightened singers turned, abysses and precipices met them, and it required on the part of the leader all the skillful guidance of a practiced muleteer to preserve a sure footing for those entrusted to his charge." In Saroni's opinion the effort was to be regarded not as a first performance but a last rehearsal (*Musical Times,* February 2, 1850, p. 218).

The *Herald,* chiefly concerned with the sociopolitical implications of a nonsubscription audience in proletarian garb at Astor Place, commented approvingly on the "democratic" absence of full evening dress and white kids. Democratically garbed, perhaps, but musically uninformed, for "More than one *scena,* excellently rendered, was passed over without much applause, as the cause of opera is a sealed book to hundreds, and is only now heard for the first time by many of our music-loving citizens" (*Herald,* January 10; February 7, 1850).

The *Tribune* (January 30, 1850), on the contrary, "ventured" to state that "no operatic first performance in the United States of so important a work as *Don Giovanni* was ever received with more decided, more earnest, or more discriminating applause. Several of the choicest pieces of the opera were encored. . . . From the moment the first phrase of the introduction fell upon the ear until the last echo of the wild and unearthly finale died away, the genius of the great enchanter Mozart asserted itself, and his spell was acknowledged by every palpitating heart." After hearing this sublime work, it would be "as unthinkable to listen patiently to the sing-song of modern [Italian] opera" as to go back to "Newark cider after genuine champagne." (A startling observation from a newspaper aggressively committed to temperance!)

The *Message Bird,* whose rigid moral principles exceeded even the *Tribune*'s—and who consequently disapproved of opera in general—attributed the infrequent performances of *Don Giovanni* to its unpopularity among singers because of its vocal difficulties. And impresarios avoided it because it demanded a large cast and did not lend itself to switching arias from one character to another, to save on singers. Although Maretzek deserved credit for producing it at all, no matter how, with the best will in the world this writer could not praise the company. Yet, a month later, in the same journal, the recently emigrated Frederick Nicholls Crouch (then a cellist in the Astor Place orchestra and therefore perhaps not the most unbiased of critics) pronounced the *Don Giovanni* production "the most perfect musical representation ever given in these States" (*Message Bird,* February 15, p. 231; March 15, 1850, p. 249).

But Nathaniel Willis, a wasp in butterfly's clothing, viciously attacked Maretzek and his singers—Bertucca, Forti, and the contralto Giulietta Perrini—on the incriminating grounds that they were "Hebrews." Willis had deduced this damaging information from their recent participation in a benefit performance (January 22 at the Broadway Tabernacle) for the Young Men's Hebrew Benevolent Association, when Maretzek and Forti had each been presented with a handsome gold snuff box to express the Association's gratitude for their services (*Albion,* February 9, 1850, p. 68).

Of the *Don Giovanni* production, sneered Willis: "Our little Hebrews are scarcely to blame for failing when put to work that is altogether beyond them."[9] He fervently

[9] Willis had apparently forgotten that Lorenzo da Ponte, the librettist of *Don Giovanni,* had started out in life as Emanuele Conegliano, a "little Hebrew."

"prayed" for their "banishment" from Astor Place and a "coming in of the Gentiles" to replace them, in the persons of his protégés Teresa Truffi, Sesto Benedetti,♪ Settimio Rosi,♪ and Francesco Taffanelli♪ (*Home Journal,* February 16, 1850).

In the *Times and Messenger* (February 17, 1850) Noah attempted to carry off the whole disgraceful episode with his customary urbanity, but he nonetheless managed to admonish Willis in telling and timeless terms: "Do not you, who have attained an honorable name in the Republic of Letters, sanction opinions which would carry us back to the darkest ages of bigotry and superstition, and extinguish those lights of learning and civilization which lead a free country with liberal laws to the heights of honor, power, and prosperity."

Strong, who had attended the opening night performance and doubtless had read a fair number of the reviews, shared the prevailing opinion of the *Don Giovanni* production.

February 1. . . . *Don Giovanni* Tuesday night. Glorious composition, but much damaged and defaced in the performance. The Don is a gentleman (in the George the Fourth sense), whereas Beneventano enacts a rank and unmitigated brute Bowery roué, and suggests no ideas but those of adultery and fornication and all manner of uncleanness. Bertucca is but a mechanical sort of Zerlina, and Donna Anna gives Truffi nothing to do that allows of her showing her strong points. As to Ottavio [Forti], he's a stick, or dolt, or clod, and sings and acts with as little feeling of life as an automaton.

Notwithstanding his disapproval of the cast, Strong returned twice to hear *Don Giovanni*—on February 5 and 11. Surprisingly, for once he did not record his innermost reactions to a momentous musical experience. After his second hearing he wrote, on February 10: "It's too late for me to set about discussing *Don Giovanni,*" and uncharacteristically dropped the subject then and there.

Critical cavils notwithstanding, *Don Giovanni* enjoyed an unprecedented popular success, to the everlasting wonderment of the reviewers themselves. Some ascribed the phenomenon to the perpetually celebrated "improvement" in the great American musical taste; some to the overpowering magnificence of the work; some congratulated themselves on their edifying influence upon the public.[10] But the production's success was mostly (and probably justly) credited to Maretzek's unorthodox and "democratic" act of valor in directly addressing the production to a wider, less fashionable, perhaps more music-oriented, audience than the gilded subscribers who preempted the Astor Place edifice on opera nights—Mondays, Wednesdays, and Fridays—primarily for purposes of sartorial display and social ritual. As we have seen, Maretzek first presented *Don Giovanni* on a Tuesday, an "off night," and a benefit performance (for Beneventano) besides. Heresy!

Maretzek's audacity—dictated, as he frankly admits, by financial desperation—paid off. He blissfully relates how *Don Giovanni,* a work that had been promised "regu-

[10]"Musical criticism, too, is now established on a higher and surer footing than it ever was. . . . At all events, it must now appear certain that music has entered on a new career of success among us, and that a very general appetite has been created for musical performances of an exalted order" (*Musical Times,* March 16, 1850, p. 290).

larly by all Managers for . . . fifteen years,"[11] but invariably set aside by the opera-house hierarchy, saved his entrepreneurial skin. Bypassing his "Upper Ten" subscribers, he appealed directly to "that public which I had been managed into the neglect of. Nor did they fail me. The Opera of *Don Giovanni* brought me support from all classes and attracted persons of all professions and every description to the Opera House. Fourteen consecutive evenings was it played to crowded houses. This Opera alone has enabled me to conclude the season and satisfy all demands upon my exchequer. . . . [It] had the greatest success of any Opera . . . brought forward, in my time, in America" (*Crotchets,* pp. 98, 102).

Despite Maretzek's claim of an uninterrupted run of *Don Giovanni* performances until the end of the season, several other operas were performed at the season-end benefits—*Anna Bolena, Otello, Lucia di Lammermoor, Ernani, La favorita, Lucrezia Borgia* (together with a single act of Mercadante's *Il giuramento*), and, of particular interest, *Norma.* Given for Amalia Patti's benefit, the title role was sung by her mother, the aging but still potent Caterina Barili-Patti,♪ matriarch of the phenomenal clan of Barilis and Pattis who so significantly inhabited the musical nineteenth century. As Watson reported, although her voice was gone, Barili-Patti still gave "an overwhelming, dramatic performance of *Norma,* vivid and powerful." She could still compete with many of her younger rivals (*Albion,* February 16, 1850, p. 80).[12]

The Astor Place opera season closed on March 7 with Maretzek's benefit, fittingly a gala performance of *Don Giovanni.* Probably due to the doubled ticket prices, the opera house was less crowded than expected, but the occasion was nonetheless sufficiently festive. Backstage, after the second act, Maretzek received from his orchestra, represented by F. N. Crouch, a "massive and elegant silver goblet, with appropriate inscriptions."[13] The actor/playwright John Brougham,♪ on behalf of the Dramatic Fund, then came forward with a "superb" silver pitcher and salver, to express the Fund's gratitude for Maretzek's unfailingly generous assistance to that organization. After a brief, trilateral exchange of graceful compliments, the opera was resumed, and in the ensuing banquet scene the trophies were displayed to the delighted audience.[14]

At the conclusion of the performance, reported Watson (*Albion,* March 9, 1850,

[11] ". . . every manager who has undertaken to give Italian opera for the benefit of the public and his own destruction has deemed it indispensable to announce that 'in the course of the season, Mozart's *Don Giovanni* will be performed with a powerful cast.' But somehow or other, the promise has never been kept" (*Mirror,* January 29, 1850).

[12] "The audience was taken by surprise by the excellence of the performance," reported the *New-York Evening Post* (February 18, 1850). "Madame Patti, who it was understood had retired from the stage, on the contrary, acted and sang the part of Norma with an energy, a feeling, and a correctness that created more enthusiasm than we have seen evinced for a long period." Indeed, the reviewer preferred this production of *Norma* to that of *Don Giovanni.*

[13] The conductor George Loder,♪ too, played in the Astor Place orchestra during the run of *Don Giovanni.* As the *Mirror* observed in a follow-up review on February 4: ". . . one of the great pleasures of the evening was to see so distinguished a musician as Mr. George Loder playing first contrabass under the baton of his rival. An honor to Mozart, we presume."

[14] The *Herald* (February 15, 1850) protested the slipshod stage-direction of the banquet scene, wherein "a little more care in opening the champagne" would have been advisable. It was repugnant to the feelings of the audience "to see a bottle broken and afterward drank [*sic*] from, as serious accidents have resulted from swallowing small fibers of glass on such occasions."

p. 116), Maretzek made a "brief and telling" curtain speech in his heavily accented English, expressing his gratification at the public's support of his first complete season at Astor Place and their acceptance of Italian opera, which he felt was at last firmly established in New York.[15] Indeed, Maretzek had renewed his lease of the Astor Place Opera House for another year. As he later wryly remembered (*Crotchets,* pp. 104–7), he had no choice, finding himself (despite his claims of fiscal deliverance by *Don Giovanni*) in debt at the end of the season to the tune of $3600. That he could expect no help from the Astor Place proprietors was made abundantly clear the morning after his benefit, when an embarrassed representative of the Committee of Five-Year Subscribers—in effect, the Astor Place landlords—delivered to him an, alas, non-negotiable token of their esteem—a copy of the minutes of their recent Annual Meeting. In this document was recorded, among other items of business, their agreement to the renewal of his lease and a list of twelve resolutions, of which five commended Maretzek for his efforts to keep Astor Place afloat. Copies had been sent to the various newspapers.[16]

In reporting the Maretzek gala, Watson summarized the opera adventure at Astor Place from the time of its origin in 1847. A dismal failure under its first directors Antonio Sanquirico and Salvatore Patti,♪ the Astor Place venture had fallen into complete disarray under the ensuing directorship of Edward P. Fry.♪ With the house under a stigma after the grisly Forrest/Macready riots in 1849,♪ it had become virtually impossible to find reputable singers willing to perform there. "Indeed, it was thought by many that [the Astor Place Theatre] could never again be used for operatic purposes." Yet, Maretzek had conquered, despite all hardships—among them a grievous personal loss of $500, due to the inept handling of an overpretentious opera ball foisted on him by the Astor Place proprietors. With his taste, tact, and talent, he had courageously risen above seemingly insurmountable trials and difficulties and emerged triumphant.

During the just-concluded season Maretzek's company had comprised a large and capable cast of singers: Apollonia Bertucca, Teresa Truffi, Eufrasia Borghese,♪ Giulietta Perrini, Giuseppina and Emilio Rossi Corsi,♪ Amalia Patti, Signora Caterina Barili-Patti, Giuseppe Forti, Giuseppe Guidi,♪ Federico Beneventano, Augusto Giubilei,♪ Pietro Novelli, and Antonio Sanquirico. Maretzek had enlarged the chorus and tamed the orchestra; and under his able management a copious repertory had been presented: *Lucia di Lammermoor, Otello, Ernani, Maria di Rohan, Don Pasquale, Anna Bolena, La favorita,* and *Don Giovanni.* In addition to current repertory, one new opera—or a revival of an old one—had been presented each week of the season, a heroic feat unprecedented in New York. Great credit was due as well to I. Kreutzer, the leader (concertmaster) of the orchestra, and Frederic Hensler, the chorus master. But above all, the greatest possible credit accrued to Maretzek, who had achieved this veritable miracle.

[15] Watson reported that Maretzek's father, only recently arrived from Europe, was deeply moved by the success of his sons Max and Albert in the United States (*Albion,* March 5, 1850, p. 116). Shortly after, Albert Maretzek was dispatched to Europe on a double mission: to engage a new contralto and *basso profundo* for Astor Place and to bring his mother back with him (*Tribune,* May 28, 1850).

[16] The publication of this document induced further gnashing of teeth by N. P. Willis in the *Home Journal.*

Although Strong had resumed his opera- and concert-going to a limited degree in 1850, he remained surprisingly aloof from the recurrent tidal waves of musical excitement that drenched the city during this prodigious musical year. He continued, however, to record in his private journal his sometimes obscure reactions to the little music he did hear.

March 4. . . . Took Ellie to the Philharmonic♪ [on March 2]—first I've attended in two years. It was that well-remembered, dark *A-Symphony* [Beethoven's Seventh], the most essentially Beethovenish production extant, so far as I know, and selections from Mendelssohn's lovely *Midsummer Night's Dream* music [1842]: Overture, *Hochzeitsmarsch* and so forth. As to the Symphony in A, I hold it to be an immoral composition—immoral just as *Childe Harold* is immoral, from the absence of good rather than the presence of evil. *Doesn't* that sound like puppyism?

But let anyone compare it with the C-minor. Think of the deepening gloom and the sorrow that grows more passionate—the abrupt, discordant transitions into feverish exultation and wild, unhealthy joy—the progress of the successive movements by a downward *crescendo* into the universal frenzy and chaos and desperation that are embodied in the finale of *this* composition—and then remember the purity and the

New-York Historical Society

The Firemen's Ball at the Astor Place Opera House.

strength of the C-minor—the glorious march of that symphony through ever nobler and more exalted feeling, from the *Kyrie eleison* of the first movement to the triumphant *Gloria in Excelsis* of the fourth, and then say if there be not the same difference between the two that there is between darkness and light—Byron and Schiller. Say if Right and Wrong—Truth and Falsehood—cannot be predicated on Music.

This was the third concert of the Philharmonic's eighth season and the second given in 1850. Conducted by Theodore Eisfeld,♪ the vocal excerpts from *A Midsummer Night's Dream* were sung by Mrs. Laura A. Jones,♪ Miss Emmeline De Luce,♪ and some "amateur ladies," probably members of the emerging Harmonic Society, of which Eisfeld was the conductor. "It was the universal opinion of all present," wrote an uncommonly benign Watson, "that this was the best [Philharmonic] concert given this season—the best, indeed, for years past." But although the performance had been "exquisite," Watson was withholding his more detailed comments on the performance of Mendelssohn's wonderful score for his review of the approaching concert of the Musical Fund Society,♪ to take place on March 21 at the Astor Place Opera House. On that occasion the *Midsummer Night's Dream* music, again performed by the Philharmonic under Eisfeld and with the same soloists, would be illuminated by readings from the play by Fanny Kemble.[17]

In the meantime, however, Watson wanted to register his good will: "We are glad of an opportunity of giving credit to the Philharmonic where it is due" (*Albion,* March 9, 1850, p. 116).

Despite his professed solicitude for the Philharmonic, Watson had neglected to review their preceding concert, on January 12, when George Loder had conducted a program consisting of Spohr's by-now familiar *Die Weihe der Töne,* op. 86, and the first American performance of Mendelssohn's *Meeresstille und glückliche Fahrt* ("Calm Sea and Prosperous Voyage"), op. 27 (1832). Also, William Scharfenberg♪ had played Mendelssohn's *Capriccio brillant,* op. 22, for piano and orchestra; Lindpaintner's *Sinfonia concertante,* op. 2, for flute, oboe, clarinet, bassoon, horn, and orchestra was played, respectively, by the Philharmonic musicians Rietzel, Wiese, Starck, Eltz, and Schmitz; and Meyerbeer's Overture to *The Huguenots* had completed the program.

Reviewing this earlier concert, *Saroni's Musical Times* (January 12, 1850, p. 195) had observed that Loder was not to blame that the concert was not up to the highest standard. It was the fault of the constant shuffling and reshuffling of conductors and orchestra personnel at the Philharmonic: "We believe there have not been three concerts in succession without a change in the orchestra. Such a system—or want of system—cannot fail to be injurious to the interests of the art."

The *Message Bird* (February 1, 1850, pp. 216–17) complained sharply of the Philharmonic's everlasting programing of *Die Weihe der Töne,* an overrated and endlessly

[17] Frances Kemble (1809–1893), the celebrated English actress, was currently giving one of her highly regarded seasons of Shakespeare readings at Stuyvesant Hall.♪ Often donating her talents to charitable causes, her participation in the Musical Fund Society's fourth concert was reported in the *Herald* (March 22, 1850) to have attracted a huge audience and enriched the Society's coffers by some $2000.

boring work with which the reviewer had been "afflicted" too often to "have any wish for again doing so."[18]

Neither Strong nor Watson attended the two remaining Philharmonic concerts of 1850—on April 20, conducted by Eisfeld, and on November 23, when Loder made another of his dwindling appearances with the Society. At the April 20 concert Eisfeld conducted Mendelssohn's Third ("Scotch") Symphony, op. 56 (1842); Weber's *Euryanthe* Overture (1823); Hummel's *Oberons Zauberhorn,* op. 116, the piano part played by Henry C. Timm;♪ a *Concertante* for four violins and orchestra, op. 55 (1838), by the German composer Ludwig Maurer (1789–1878), played by Joseph Noll, G. F. Bristow,♪ Henry Reyer, and Michele Rapetti's♪ brilliant young pupil James W. Perkins;♪ and Rossini's Overture to *La gazza ladra.*

Although Saroni attributed the Philharmonic's splendid performances—again their best yet, particularly the Mendelssohn symphony—to Eisfeld's "untiring watchfulness and efficiency as a leader," (*Saroni's Musical Times,* April 27, 1850, pp. 363–64), the *Message Bird* (May 1, 1850, pp. 313–14) thunderously disapproved of a surfeit of Mendelssohn at the Philharmonic. The embattled reviewer, apparently a recently arrived Briton (most probably F. N. Crouch) complained of the Society's incessant reiteration of Mendelssohn, in his opinion "not the greatest composer of symphonies." After all, "Mozart and Beethoven have existed, and this season we have had little other than Mendelssohn's music in some shape or other from the Society."[19] The writer complained, too, of the audience's indiscriminate applause after each movement of each symphony. This was a deplorable and destructive custom, for it led the performers to think too highly of themselves.

It was all the fault of the conductor, wrote this Anglophile critic, who then launched into an attack on the heavily German bias of the Philharmonic. With Eisfeld conducting three Philharmonic concerts this season to Loder's one, "the strong clannish feeling which may be remarked in the German musician in this country will probably install [Eisfeld] in the approaching season as the conductor of all four." This would indeed come to pass, but not until two years later, by which time Loder, perhaps having read the handwriting on the wall, had departed for San Francisco.

On November 23, 1850, at the first concert of the Philharmonic's ninth season, Loder conducted his own *Marmion* Overture♪ and Niels Gade's Symphony No. 1 in C minor,♪ works that he had introduced, respectively, in 1846 and 1848. His program also included the Concertino, op. 29, for two pianos and orchestra, by Julius Benedict,♪ Jenny Lind's conductor for the first phase of her current sensational concert tour of the United States (discussed later in this chapter). With Benedict and Timm performing splendidly at the two pianos, the work was pronounced "an elaborate and learned production, which might possibly be considered a little dry by a popular audience." During the short time he had been in New York, Benedict had acquired many friends and admirers in the music community, and his imminent departure on the next leg of the Lind tour was "universally regretted"; his memory would be "cherished by

[18] This stern critic congratulated himself on, at least, having improved the manners of the Philharmonic subscribers: "We are almost tempted," he wrote, "to give ourselves the credit for having produced so desirable a reform as inducing the audience to sit out the end of the performance."

[19] In the past the critics had complained of too much Beethoven at the Philharmonic.

those to whom his talents and estimable qualities [had] become known" (*Message Bird,* December 2, 1859, p. 546).

Appearing on the same program, the Philharmonic hornist Henry Schmitz♪ gave a brilliant performance of a so-called Concertino for French horn and orchestra by one H. Fuchs, a work that turned out to be a set of virtuosic variations on "Weber's Last Waltz" by Reissiger;♪ the program ended with the Overture to Lindpaintner's (not Marschner's) opera *Der Vampyr* (1828).

All told, 1850 was not the Philharmonic's most lustrous year: "We hear, by accident," sardonically noted the lively new weekly *Figaro!*[20] (December 21, 1850, p. 231), "that this Society still exists and actually gives a concert occasionally, taking great pains to keep the fact as much as possible from the knowledge of the public, in order to prevent anything like an increase of patronage to the institution, or improvement in the public taste for music. We learn that in these efforts the managers are succeeding to their hearts' content, that the list of subscribers is in a rapid decline, and at their last concert the Apollo Room was about one-third full! Go on, gentlemen, and in another year or two the Philharmonic Society will be altogether unheard and unheard of."

In April, on the heels of the Astor Place company's departure for Boston, Don Francisco Martí's♪ latest and greatest opera company arrived from Havana—his first company to visit New York since 1847.♪ With a minimum of advance fanfare, they opened at Niblo's Garden♪ and proceeded, with their extraordinary performances, to expand the American opera experience to unprecedented dimensions. No less an authority than Maretzek unequivocally states that they were not only "the greatest troupe which had ever been heard in America,[21] [but] in point of integral talent, number, and excellence of the artists composing it, it must be admitted that it has seldom been excelled in any part of the old world" (*Crotchets,* p. 156).

With even greater prodigality than before, Martí had sent a group of artists of past, present, and future international renown, comprising not one, but three superb *prima donnas*: the sopranos Balbina Steffanone (1825–?) and Angiolina Bosio (1830–1859), and the contralto Fortunata Tedesco;♪ a fine contralto Carolina Vietti (later known as Carolina Vietti-Vertiprach); three first tenors: Lorenzo Salvi (1810–1879), ranked in Europe as second only to the matchless Mario,[22] Domenico Lorini, and (later) Adelindo Vietti;♪ two top-ranking baritones, Cesare Badiali (1810–1865) and Domenico Coletti; and two basses, Corradi-Setti (more a baritone than a bass) and Ignazio Marini (1811–1873), the last regarded in Europe as nearly the equal, if not the full equal, of the fabled Luigi Lablache.[23] They were supplemented by a lavish number of secondary singers, a chorus of forty, and an orchestra of fifty—or so the

[20] *Figaro! or Corbyn's Chronicle of Amusements, Devoted to Music, Theatre, Literature, and the Arts,* was co-edited by the theatrical agent Wardle Corbyn♪ and J. W. S. Hows, a Columbia College professor of rhetoric, who for many years wrote dramatic criticism for the *Albion.*

[21] On hearing them, Maretzek realized that competition with a company of this caliber was impossible. Thus: "I made up my mind, if it were by any means possible, to secure them for this city" (*Crotchets,* p. 157). This would come to pass the following year.

[22] Liszt, who had heard Salvi in Genoa in 1838, wrote that he possessed a "remarkable voice," and that his singing was "moving, his voice production big and pure, and his delivery and gestures [had] a faultless ease and nobility about them" (Liszt, *An Artist's Journey,* p. 175).

[23] Lablache (1794–1858) was regarded as the supreme opera basso of the nineteenth century.

Balbina Steffanone and Ignazio Marini, shining stars in the Havana Opera Company galaxy.

advertisements read. Federico Badiali (Cesare's brother) managed the company and, as before, Giovanni Bottesini and Luigi Arditi were in charge of musical matters—Bottesini as maestro and director of the company and Arditi as conductor of the orchestra (*Herald,* April 8, 1850).

Opening with *Norma* on April 11, the performances of Steffanone as Norma and Marini as Oroveso electrified critics and public alike. As the reviewer *G* wrote in the *Mirror*[24] (April 13, 1850): "We are weary of *Norma*—weary, weary, weary—and have been any time these ten years almost. . . . But weary as we are of the music, we of course made up our minds to undergo it for the first night of a new Opera company, and so did about 1500 other people who were present, the ladies in hats and demi-toilettes and the gentlemen in frock coats, for it is understood as a matter of course that this is to be an undress opera season. We and the other 1500 were well paid for our self-sacrificing determination: we experienced a new sensation and a delightful one—two, in fact—the Norma and Oroveso of the evening. The former, particularly, more than satisfied our rather elegant expectations."

Steffanone (persistently spelled "Steffanoni" in the New York papers) was "really a superb Norma, we have seen none such here. . . . She is large, stately, and fine looking without being decidedly handsome.[25] Her face, in some positions, and when ex-

[24] The writer might have been Richard Grant White, who acted as a freelance music and drama critic for the *Mirror* during the early months of 1850, as we learn from the anonymously published pamphlet *Squints Through an Opera Glass* (pp. 16–17).

[25] N. P. Willis, too, reported that she was large and beautiful—not the kind of beauty that would photograph well, but beautiful in person. However, being Willis, he could not resist adding: "Her

pressing certain emotions, is very classical, quite Niobe-like in its expression, and her gesture is always graceful and impressive. Her manner is full of repose, quiet and *insouciant* almost even to sluggishness, save when she is roused by a scene of violent emotion, and then her energies flash out so suddenly as to astonish and almost bewilder." At first underplaying her role, "when her anger and scorn burst upon Pollione the effect was instantaneous, electric. It broke forth like the sharp crack of thunder from a cloud which has but faintly muttered before, and startled the whole house." Last, but not least, her voice, although a soprano, reminded the writer of Tedesco's contralto, but it was "sympathetic," which in his opinion Tedesco's was not. All in all, she was "a *prima donna* of high rank, the first of her class who has visited us for a long time."

As for Marini (elsewhere described as a "semi-giant"): "His figure is good, his head fine, and his carriage dignified, though in his attempts at dramatic effect his spirited action did occasionally verge on excess." *G* was willing to forgive him this little self-indulgence, for Marini shed "such a feeling of comfort the moment he opened his mouth. . . . His voice is a pure, sonorous, sympathetic bass—a quality rarely heard. . . . He delivers it freely and purely, without the slightest trick, affectation, impediment, or peculiarity, and this, after the mouthing and bellowing of various kinds to which we have been subjected for some years past, gives indeed, in itself, no insignificant pleasure."

The "very acceptable Pollione" was Lorini, a tenor who had appeared uneventfully with the Havana company of 1847, but who had improved since his last visit. The orchestra performed under the dual direction of Bottesini, who played his "admirable contrabass" in the pit, and Arditi, who led (or wielded the baton). *G* heartily welcomed the return of Bottesini and his marvelous playing, but the orchestra, although not large (despite the advertisements it apparently consisted of thirty-two players), was "very noisy, and the same may be said for the chorus [now reported to be twenty-four men and thirteen women]. There were no *pianissimos* last evening." *G* blamed Arditi for this excessive loudness and tactlessly suggested that he "take a few lessons from Maretzek."

The *Herald* (April 12, 1850), in the untrammeled prose that characterized its vivid editor James Gordon Bennett,[♪] loudly proclaimed: "By the Eternal! We have got the Italian opera at last in New York, and no mistake." Steffanone displayed the "highest order of genius—the most perfect, both as a singer and as an actress, that we have ever seen since the time of Malibran, and [heresy of heresies!] even far more matured than what Malibran was when she visited New York." Steffanone epitomized the "elements of Giulia Grisi, Jenny Lind, and Fanny Kemble, all mixed and compounded most exquisitely together. The other artists were perfect in their parts. . . . The orchestra was superb and the whole Opera complete. . . . So, at last we have got a real, true, undoubted *prima donna* of the Italian school." She was "a splendid woman—a brilliant artist, and [would] create a perfect *furore* in fashionable circles in this metropolis." Lorini, too, was "superb in his character. The basso Marini equally so—all—all—all—all most complete. We say again, at last we have got the grand Italian opera in New York, and no, no, no mistake."

---

upper lip is unfinished on the inside and—during impassive singing—does not play well upon the teeth" (*Home Journal,* April 20, 1850).

Watson was thrilled to have Bottesini back and so unspoiled by his great successes in England. It might seem odd to some that an Opera Director played the contrabass in the orchestra pit, "but then, he plays as no other man can play."

Steffanone was the greatest Norma that Watson had ever seen in the United States, except, of course, Madame Anna Bishop,♪ whose perfections he unflaggingly and eternally heralded. But among the other great Normas he had heard, Steffanone reminded him of Grisi. She possessed the same "tremendous physique" as Grisi and the same passions, which "seem to sweep like whirlwinds, or to labor like the upheaving of a volcano."

Still and all, Madame Bishop was superior, being "much more the priestess and more the woman." Although it was also true that Steffanone's "grand physique, corporeal and vocal, admits of greater transitions and affects the mind with greater wonder." Yet, her *Casta diva* lacked the inspiration of Madame Bishop's. And up and down, and back and forth, went the Watsonian teeter-totter.

Lorini was a fine tenor, possessing energy and much taste, but his voice was "incapable of those inflections which speak to the heart, or rather, through which the heart speaks." Marini had a "stunning voice which rattles out like a discharge of ordinance, to the great danger of our aural faculties." Though enormous in power, it was, however, "lacking in profundity, but he [used] it like an artist." Watson recognized in him "unmistakable talent, if not positive genius."

The orchestra was admirably drilled, with excellent strings, but the winds were "coarse and unsympathetic." The male part of the chorus was as fine as any Watson had ever heard, but the female part was only so-so. But they were all too loud—they let out in this moderate-sized theatre as if they were in their Havana wilderness[26] (*Albion,* April 13, 1850, p. 176).

Saroni stated that *Norma* had never been better produced on any American stage, and he listed in loving detail its many felicities (*Musical Times,* April 20, 1850, p. 351), but Noah perversely contended that the Havana company had been overpraised, that the opening night audience had responded very coldly. True, the orchestra, smaller than the one at Astor Place, had played too loudly; on the other hand, the chorus was the greatest Noah had ever heard in this country, even if the ladies were too fat. Of the ladies in the parquette and boxes, however, Noah approvingly noted that they were "very neatly dressed and generally wore bonnets and *negligées* and few opera dresses" (*Times and Messenger,* April 14, 1850).

After a single repetition of *Norma* to a packed house, on April 15 the Havana company presented the first performance in the United States of Verdi's *Attila* (Venice 1846), a work composed for Marini. The critics were generally torn between their admiration of the performers and their loathing of the composer. In the customarily harsh opinion of the *Courier and Enquirer* (April 17, 1850), *Attila* was, "with the exception of one or two brilliant pieces . . . the most unmitigated, unqualified piece of stupidity both in plot and music, that we ever had the ill fortune to hear. There was some hearty applause after the first act . . . which Signor Marini appropriated to himself en-

[26]Located just outside the city walls, Havana's Grand Tacón Theatre, with five tiers of boxes and a parquette holding 600 stalls, had a capacity of about 5000 seats (*Message Bird,* March 1, 1850, p. 248).

tirely, and the applause being kept up, he reappeared four or five times until laughter, hisses, and calls for Tedesco [the second of the Havana company's *prime donne* to appear] and Lorini opened his eyes to the state of the case, and he brought them forward to receive what was at first intended equally for all. The finale of the opera," the anonymous critic concluded, "is contemptibly puerile, and the curtain fell upon dead silence and surprise." This critic found Tedesco's voice to be as fresh and brilliant as ever, but Marini was "evidently not the man he was when he made his reputation."

N. P. Willis, on the other hand, reported that Marini, "a magnificent fellow of six-foot-two, [sang] as if he could call up an earthquake at the shortest notice, and his cloak of lion's skin, with the paws sweeping the ground, [seemed] to have a movement like a cloud stirring up the thunder in his lungs." But no matter how savage the character he portrayed, Marini was always a gentleman, unlike Beneventano, whom Willis shuddered even to imagine in the role. Willis granted that the "pulpy and plumptitudinous" Tedesco sang "sweetly," but in no way did she suggest Verdi's "warrior girl" (*Home Journal,* April 27, 1850).

The *Tribune* (April 17, 1850) found Marini's performance of Attila to be "worthy of his reputation and of the applause it received—voice, execution, and acting alike bespoke the great artist—[but] of his costume we cannot speak in terms of commendation. His face was a mixture of Indian and Tartar,[27] which ill accorded with the fine French boots that graced his shapely leg." Corradi-Setti was an excellent bass/baritone and actor, but at a disadvantage next to Marini; Lorini had a fine but rather soulless tenor voice and Tedesco was warmly greeted on her return. But "the opera itself cannot be the object of any extravagant admiration, and judging by its success last night, the manager will hardly keep it long upon the stage."

Saroni pronounced each of Verdi's successive operas to be "but a *crescendo* from noise to thunder." Despite some "very good airs," his music contained "such a chasing after rhythmical and harmonical effects that melody is sometimes entirely forgotten." Although Verdi was often accused of imitating the German school, Saroni, a German, indignantly considered it "far from German" when a simple melody was "broken into by a crash of brazen instruments loud enough to make the walls of Jericho tumble into ruins." Nor did he consider it German "when one single dissonance is kept for twenty or more bars, with only a change of position, and without the slightest pretension of melody." Nor was it German "to make all kinds of earthly and unearthly noises for no other purpose than just to make noise."

After a sparsely attended second performance, *Attila* was withdrawn, as most of the critics had urged, and on April 18 the third female star in the company's firmament, Angiolina Bosio, sensationally made her bow in *Lucrezia Borgia.* Although she was billed as *seconda donna,* it was instantly recognized that Bosio was of the stuff of which great *prime donne* are made (as her subsequent, alas too short, career in Europe proved). The *Mirror* (April 19, 1850) described her voice as a soprano of "exquisite beauty, and although not possessing the power of Steffanone's, the tones fell with such liquid sweetness upon the ear, her execution was so faultless, her method so finished, that the audience were perfectly enraptured; throughout the piece she was loudly ap-

[27] Noah reported that Marini surely looked and acted the rough Goth—"or was he a Visigoth?" With his "giant build, bushy hair, eyes ringed with black, and his bearskin [not lion skin] robe," he was an "object of terror" (*Times and Messenger,* April 21, 1850).

Girvice Archer, Jr.

Angiolina Bosio, the surprise sensation of the Havana Opera season.

plauded. The lady," added the *Mirror,* "has a slender and graceful figure, a pleasing face, and large, dark, expressive eyes."[28]

Carolina Vietti, making her New York debut in the breeches role of Maffio Orsini, possessed a contralto voice of "extended register" with, however, "somewhat defective" lower notes. "But we must do her the justice to say," admitted the *Mirror,* "that we have rarely heard the drinking song so well given; it received a vehement encore.[29]

"Signor Marini looked, acted, and sang the part of the Duke Alfonso superbly. . . . But we should find it an endless task almost, to point out the many excellent points of this performance, which, taken altogether, we have rarely heard excelled. We have seen *prima donna*s of more brilliant quality than Bosio in the role of Lucrezia, a more finished artist than Vietti in that of Orsini. We have seen Rubini[30] as Gennaro and Lablache as Alfonso," boasted the critic (sounding more and more like Watson), "but still, we have seldom witnessed an opera with more pleasure and satisfaction than we experienced last night."

Amid the mounting opera fervor, on April 20 the *Tribune* published a perceptive and thoughtful editorial on the important role music had come to assume in contem-

[28] N. P. Willis thought Bosio "too delicate looking for the stage," but she convincingly created the impression of being a real duchess. Indeed, with her "thoroughbred, high-conditioned, and race-horse-y carriage and performance," she soon shared a "divided empire" with Steffanone (*Home Journal,* April 27; May 4, 1850).

[29] Noah described Vietti as a typical Italian, "with bronze complexion, large, lustrous eyes, and a substantial person." To Willis she was less memorable for her voice than for the "beauty of her locomotives" (*Times and Messenger,* April 21; *Home Journal,* May 11, 1850).

[30] Giovanni-Battista Rubini (1795–1854), the tenor of the legendary quartet comprising Luigi Lablache, the baritone Antonio Tamburini (1800–1876), and the soprano Giulia Grisi (1811–1869).

New-York Historical Society

The Celebrated Trio in Lucrezia Borgia, *sung by Bosio, Marini, and Domenico Lorini.*

porary American life: "During the past few years so many musical people, celebrated in their art, have visited us and resided among us that the subject of Music has become of permanent and positive interest. It enters so largely into the realities of life, its influence is so widely extended, it is so mixed up with our social relations and with our public amusements, that it demands as searching a scrutiny, as close a supervision by the Press as any other subject of general public interest."

The presence of the Havana company was an event of no small significance, continued the editorial. Ten years ago the company would have found many more worshipers, but few, very few, "appreciators." If the public awareness of music had progressed slowly, the progress had nonetheless been steady. "Suffice it to say that musical people of this City have been drilled into a tolerably correct taste by a ten years' succession of excellent Artists in the various branches of the Musical Science—some of whom flashed into our horizon like brilliant meteors, and so departed, while others remained with us, to our positive and permanent benefit. . . . This advancement of taste has not been confined to certain circles but has been pretty generally disseminated."

The reason the masses did not support opera, the *Tribune* claimed, was because the upper classes had "arrogated the almost exclusive right to enjoy its charms." Twenty years earlier, when the country was more democratic, the masses had loved and supported musical entertainments from sheer love of melody. "Now," the writer observed, "the patronage is confined to the exclusive few." But music was not a restricted commodity to be addressed to a single social set. The artists of the Havana company, by far the greatest we had ever had, were happily not dependent upon patrons, but were supported by the public at large (and, as the writer failed to mention, by solid contractual safeguards guaranteed by the fabulously wealthy Don Francisco Martí).

Following a detailed, person-by-person evaluation of the Havana company, their strengths and weaknesses (their scenery really was "detestable"), the *Tribune* editorial turned to their future presentations, particularly the debut of the celebrated tenor Lorenzo Salvi, delayed because of illness, and to the forthcoming production of *Macbeth,* by the "obstreperous Verdi." The writer winced in advance at the prospect of "our Shakespeare" being reduced to the level of crass Italian operatics, but at least everybody would know the plot, which was better than to know neither plot nor Italian—too often the case.

But first, on April 22, Salvi made his delayed debut as Fernando in Donizetti's *La favorita,* and George Templeton Strong was there to hear him.

April 22. . . . Just from hearing the *Favorita* by the Havana Company at Niblo's. Tremendous house, immense enthusiasm, and an undeniably admirable performance. Steffanone falls a little short of my expectations, but the power and expression and cultivation of the tenor (Salvi) triumphed over all deficiencies in the rest, and gave a tone and character to the whole performance quite beyond anything in the way of opera I've ever heard. Of course, I speak merely of the execution, not of the music executed, for the *Favorita,* though more to my taste than anything of Donizetti's I've heard, and full of passages that actually mean something beyond mere vocalization (not a great deal, to be sure), is but a weak and watery treatment to sit under for three hours.

~

Unable to attend the performance, Henry C. Watson reported by hearsay that Salvi had created a furor, not least at the box office, which on the day of his debut had taken in a record-breaking $3000, and the following day some $2000 for the scheduled second performance of *La favorita*. But again the tenor did not appear, "in consequence of a return of his indisposition" (*Albion,* April 27, 1850, p. 200).

Hearing a subsequent performance of *La favorita* with Steffanone and Salvi, Watson, for once unmindful of Madame Bishop's perfections, was obliged to admit that Steffanone's Leonora was, "without exception, the most brilliant vocal effort we have heard on this side of the great waters. In purity of intonation, in justness of expression, in sterling and brilliant execution, in method, style, delivery, and passion, it was admirable. There was nothing wanting; the whole scope and meaning of the music was filled up, and we could hardly desire any change."

As for Salvi, he stood "first in the list of our American recollections. We have had *voices,* plenty of voices, but of *brains* there has been a plentiful scarcity." Watson preened himself on his unceasing labors to "awaken our singers to the fact that there is much more necessary besides singing the notes merely as they are written." Until now Benedetti had been the nearest approach to what We had wanted, but while he had physical energy, he was sadly lacking in the understanding of the beautiful and truthful in music. Salvi possessed both qualities: "He is a *mental* singer"; his rendition of the *Spirito gentil* was "the most finished and perfect singing that we have listened to from the lips of a man in the last ten years" (*Albion,* May 4, 1850, p. 212).

But in the following issue of the *Albion* (May 11, 1850, p. 224), Watson reversed his opinion of Salvi. True, he was by far the greatest singer we had ever heard in this country, but he was an in-and-outer, great only in fits and starts. Like Marini, Salvi labored under the impediment of an impaired voice. Where Salvi had once used art to embellish nature, he now used it to conceal nature (a favorite Watsonism). He used exaggerated contrasts of loud and soft to get his effects. Watson longed once again for Sesto Benedetti and one of his great outbursts of genuine manly feeling. With Salvi one got nothing but art, art, art, and absolutely no nature.[31]

Aside from a few minor differences, it was more or less unanimously agreed among the critical fraternity that Cesare Badiali as Don Alfonso gave a masterly performance. Noah, who was disappointed in Salvi, approved mightily of Badiali, whose voice was so "colossal" that it positively made one's ears ring (*Times and Messenger,* April 28, 1850).

The first performance in America, on April 24, of Verdi's *Macbeth* (Florence 1847) called forth a more than ordinarily curious medley of contrasting reactions from the press. Most of the critics resented Verdi's effrontery in daring to drag Shakespeare down to his own detestable level, although some admitted that his score possessed—in spots—unexpected merit. The *Tribune* (April 26, 1850), which like the other papers had voiced dire forebodings, admitted to being agreeably surprised. The work was more simple and severe, less noisy, and on a higher plane than might have been expected from Verdi. But it was "an Italian *Macbeth* from beginning to end, with an Italian Lady Macbeth [Bosio] and Italian witches. The contrast of the tragedy with the opera was continually and painfully kept before us by the close imitation of the original," complained the writer (Richard Storrs Willis). Rather than approving the libretto's faithful adherence to the text, Willis condemned it, but all the same conceded that some of the music was really fine. The singers were admirable; "if we cannot make up our minds to like the opera, it is no fault of theirs."

The *Mirror* (April 26, 1850) contended that although the libretto closely followed the original text, even using some of the speeches, "the operatic *Macbeth* is far from the Shakespeare original."[32]

The writer was "outrageously shocked at the dagger scene done into recitative, and the occurrence of a regular Italian *aria,* with the stereotyped tum-ti-tum-ti-tum accompaniment, immediately upon the murder, and while [Macbeth's] hands were still reeking with the blood of the good old King Malcolm [*sic*]."

Although it was admittedly the best Verdi score yet—at least insofar as it displayed unusual care in balancing the recitatives with their instrumental accompaniments—the

[31] Saroni proclaimed Salvi to be a true artist in the highest sense of the word: he possessed a perfect knowledge of singing, his acting always served the character he was portraying, he excelled in *sostenuto* passages, his *portamento* was graceful, and his scales had none of that "ha-ha-ha which mars the singing of even more reputed artists than he" (*Musical Times,* May 11, 1850, pp. 386–87).

[32] The reviewer was probably Richard Grant White, an authority on Shakespeare.

Cesare Badiali, a splendid, albeit Italianate, Macbeth

reviewer was "constantly annoyed by the incongruities, unnatural and exaggerated to the last degree. . . . When [Verdi] comes to the arias he revels in his usual outrageous style, constructing after his own fashion, which is a bad one, mere vocal exercises, without regard to the character or the sentiment of the subject.

"Verdi's music is an anomaly," the writer continued. "We can never tell what prevents us from hissing it, and yet, while we detect at a glance the flimsiness of the materials from which it was constructed, there is a certain management, an underneath peculiarity, which holds back the half-spoken, utter condemnation. Deep passion, intense sensibility he has none. But he understands the *crescendo;* he understands how to fill up the noise upon a climax, and he makes as many climaxes as possible, being well aware that the surest way to secure admiration is to go entirely beyond the comprehension of his hearers—and how can he better accomplish that than by substituting sound for sense."

As to the witches: "Verdi has also attempted to paint Shakespearean witches. . . . He has made the music queer and peculiar, but his Southern imagination was not equal to the conception of the character of the wild, haggard, fiendish witches of the bleak North. . . . We can forgive him the failure, for it would take the mind of a Beethoven or a Weber to render such a character musically."

The finales, unwillingly admitted this detractor, "took the audience by storm." Bosio was a "charming person," but unequal to the role of Lady Macbeth: her music is "truly frightful in its demands upon the physical powers, and is far more than the slight and very beautiful voice of Signora Bosio can give." Nonetheless, her performance was marvelous.

Cesare Badiali, the Macbeth, was splendid; he had a rich and melodious voice, and his exaggeration on this occasion was not offensive. The others—Lorini as Macduff and Coletti as Banquo—were excellent, and the "choruses were sung in the finest possible style; we have heard no such chorus singing on the New-York stage for years." The "band," too, was splendid and the production magnificent. Everybody in New York was advised to see it.

And in the *Albion* (May 4, 1850, p. 212), Watson, who had "expected little of *Macbeth* and was not disappointed," stated that in this work Verdi was far out of his depth: "The subject was too grand for his mental capacity, and we soon found out that he was floundering about helpless." Some strong effects were achieved by a "reckless and unmusician-like use of the brass instruments, but no heart is moved by a thrill of terror or by a softer emotion, as is the case in the truthful simplicity of *Don Giovanni*. . . . The finales exceed in unmitigated noise anything that we have heard in the shape of operatic music, and although the unthinking public may be filled with a sense of its grandeur—for they only hear and do not reflect—we cannot, in justice to the art we love, concede that it is music."

But Noah enthusiastically pronounced *Macbeth* to be Verdi's best opera, indeed, *the* opera of the season. The music really did fit the drama, he wrote, and although Bosio was too fragile for Lady Macbeth (they should have cast Steffanone in the role), Badiali was totally tremendous as Macbeth (*Times and Messenger,* April 28, 1850).

Macbeth provided N. P. Willis with some "charming surprises," and had it not been the "inevitable caricature of the *Macbeth* one was brought up with, it would be a noble and unexceptionable opera." Willis was willing to admit that Badiali sang the role well, "but the parallel with Macready[♪] [not Forrest][♪] was always in the mind" (*Home Journal,* May 4, 1850).

The *Message Bird* appreciated Badiali's excellence as Macbeth, but flatly stated: "We never wish to hear an operatic version of Shakespeare's plays, and this is the least fit for such a purpose" (May 1, 1850, p. 314).

George Templeton Strong echoed the prevailing critical judgments, but with his own embellishments.

April 28. . . . Went to Niblo's Friday night with Ellie, Charley *et ux.,* and her cousin Miss Watson from Providence. *Macbeth,* almost scene-for-scene with the tragedy—and absurd enough is the attempt to marry northern legend to modern Italian music, even were the legend not canonized and beatified by Shakespeare and the music not that of Verdi. The music is Verdiesque. Screaming unisons everywhere and all the melodies of that peculiar style, the parallel whereof is rope-dancing: first a swing and flourish hanging on by the hands, then a somerset, and then another swing to an erect position on the rope, a few shines cut there, and then down again. The unfortunate man is incapable of real melody; his airs are such as a man born deaf would compare by calculation of the distance of musical notes and the intervals between them.

His *supernatural* music in this opera is especially comical. Like very many of his brethren of this day, the deluded author has no means whatever of expressing *feeling* in music, except by a coarse daubing of *color.* Passion is typified and portrayed by a musical phrase instrumented with the brass; softer emotion by the same phrase written for the oboes and flutes; terror by ditto through the medium of the brasses judiciously heightened with the big drum and the ophicleide—and so of every other subject of musical expression.

It is music in the same stage of early infancy with the painting of the more brutal races of savages who are incapable of nice definitions by means of *form,* and give effect in their pictures by gaudy coloring. The one only merit that it professes is that it shows off the capabilities of the human lungs and bronchia for the emission of sound—that it requires labor and cultivation to sing the notes which Verdi has written.

And it is as much like real music as the phrase, "Six slim, slick saplings," or "Peter Piper picked a peck of pickled peppers," etc., is to poetry or eloquence.

~

On May 6, Strong went with Ellen to hear Bosio, Salvi, and Marini in *Lucrezia Borgia* but, suffering from one of his recurrent headaches, he stayed for only one act, then "handed [Ellen] over to her father and went home." N. P. Willis, who apparently stayed through the performance, lauded it in his most idiosyncratic terms: its remembrance, he wrote, would be "boned, potted, and put away by all who heard it" (*Home Journal,* May 11, 1850).

As the Havana company neared the end of their season, the opera excitement escalated, and on May 9, at their closing performance—*Lucia di Lammermoor*—they drew the largest audience that had ever attended an opera in New York, estimated at some 3500. According to N. P. Willis: "The crowd standing in the street and awaiting the opening of the doors at seven o'clock was impearled with a sprinkling of the most fashionable belles of New-York, and when the passage was opened, the tremendous pressure played the crowd like a bagpipe—the screams of the ladies and the exclamations of the men rising above the roll of omnibusses with startling vehemence." Once inside the theatre, even the corridors and staircases were jammed (*Home Journal,* May 18; *Times and Messenger,* May 12, 1850).

"We do not ever remember to have heard the opera of 'Lucia' so effectively given as on this occasion," at last chirped the heretofore silent *Message Bird* (May 15, 1850, p. 335). It was masterly; everything—chorus, orchestra, and principals—exceeded anything that had ever been known in New York. If Steffanone, who sang that evening, had not become ill, *Lucia* could have run forever.

After the Havana company completed their engagement at Niblo's and departed for Boston (where they aroused the natives to an even higher pitch of frenzy), the New York critics looked back on their season with the perverse intermingling of praise and faultfinding endemic to music critics through the ages.

The *Message Bird,* now that it had come around to accepting opera, was no exception. In a long and detailed retrospection on the Havana season, their English-oriented critic, from his eminence as a veteran opera-goer in the old country, submitted the various singers to minute—not always charitable—scrutiny. Although the tenors were "remarkably good," Salvi was far superior to Lorini, even though his (Salvi's) voice was now greatly inferior to what it had been some eight years earlier when he had been the superb first tenor at both Her Majesty's Theatre and the Italian Opera in London. Unhappily, though he still had his moments of supremacy, he was now definitely on the wane.

Badiali was a good enough baritone, but the music of Verdi, especially *Macbeth,* demanded greater musical judgment than he possessed. A pity, for it prevented him from doing justice to his fine voice.

Marini was one of the greatest basses alive and was now at the peak of his magnificent powers. His Oroveso in *Norma* was fully the equal of Lablache's, and the power of his thunderous tones in *Attila* had almost induced this critic to forgive the sins of the composer. But Marini could never approach the style and finish of Salvi—although one could almost forgive him this shortcoming when under the influence of his tremendous sound.

The critic was far less pleased with Steffanone than were his colleagues. Her Norma was merely acceptable to one who had heard most of the legendary Normas—and here the writer trotted out the *Norma* pantheon: Grisi, Viardot-Garcia, Schroeder-Devrient, and Adelaide Kemble, omitting only Pasta and Lind. Steffanone, he said, was accepted as a *prima donna* only because of her insoluble tie with Marini, "as wherever he is engaged Steffanone must also appear," much to Marini's professional detriment. The writer grudgingly supposed that her "having filled the nominal place of a first soprano at Covent Garden," when she had accompanied Marini to London, accounted for her being engaged as a *prima cantatrice* in Havana and New York.

Tedesco, in his opinion, far outshone Steffanone as a vocalist "without anything like the same crude and somewhat vulgarly educated strength of lungs which distinguished her rival." Bosio he dismissed as a pleasant and very agreeable singer, who, like her colleagues, had been suffering from a cold ever since reaching this forbidding northern clime. In sum, they were surely the best opera company to have come to the United States since the hallowed days of the Garcias, and the writer hoped they would return (*Message Bird,* May 15, 1850, p. 330).

In fact, their return had been announced before they went to Boston; they had secured the Astor Place Opera House for the month of June and would open there in about three weeks. But even three weeks without them, moaned the *Herald,* would seem an eternity!

On May 10 the Strongs attended the debut of the New-York Harmonic Society, the choral group organized in late 1849 to fill the gap left by the virtually simultaneous dissolution of the city's two major singing societies, the New-York Sacred Music Society♪ and the American Musical Institute.♪

May 17. . . . We had quite a nice time at the Tabernacle last Friday. Ellen bore the *Messiah* much better than I expected.[33] The performance was not very satisfactory, but an improvement on any I've listened to—orchestra and chorus good enough, and some of the solo parts respectable. One Mrs. L. A. Jones sang "He shall feed his flock like a shepherd" very effectively.

[33] Undoubtedly a reference to Ellen's "delicate health," not the endurableness of Handel's *Messiah*. In fact, Ellen had been able to engage in music-making with the talented Maurans♪ at the Strongs' on May 16. In Strong's opinion, "it would be hard to match among the amateurs of this town those three young damosels, being, in their several ways, among the best and most thoroughly educated musicians we have, and Ellen being, notwithstanding a cold, able to work with them" (Private Journal, May 17, 1850).

Girvice Archer, Jr.

Fortunata Tedesco, Steffanone's rival.

The ruthless rivalry that had brought about the mutual collapse of the two earlier singing societies was in no small way attributable to the machinations of Henry C. Watson, whose ambition it was to become a supreme power in the New York world of music. Now, apparently chagrined at being excluded from the board of governors of the new Harmonic Society,[34] he wrote a transparently vengeful review in the *Albion* of the Harmonic Society's first concert, reminiscent of his persecution in 1842 of the newly formed Philharmonic for failing to elect him a member.♪ "A sacred music society was greatly needed in this city," he wrote, "and if we were not much in favor of the class of persons into whose hands the [Harmonic Society's] government [had] fallen—and if we *did* feel that cant and white neckcloths would overpower all liberal feeling, and [that] cliquing and clanning would prove the order of the day—still we wished it good success for the sake of its cause, hoping that it would be for the benefit of music and for the honor of the Art." Whether or not they would succeed in realiz-

[34] Watson promptly announced a (short-lived) singing society of his own, the Mendelssohn Vocal Society, "for the practice of Vocal Music, Glees, Motettes, Madrigals, and Solos, with Chorusses both operatic and oratorial," all under Watson's conductorship (*Herald,* January 5; *Tribune,* January 11, 1850).

ing this goal would be decided only by time, "but if we are again to judge by their performance last week, [they] will effect but little for the honor of the Art."

Although the Society was newly organized, he pointed out, its members were by no means "untried hands." They comprised the "most efficient portions of the choral strength" of the defunct Sacred Music Society, the New-York Vocal Society,♪ and the American Musical Institute. "We" had a right to expect an expert performance from them, especially as they had been rehearsing *Messiah* for the past three months. Besides, the tickets were one dollar, reason enough to expect excellence.

Always the staunch Briton, Watson proceeded to praise the superior system practiced by English singing societies, who paid generous fees for the best singers but charged little for tickets. Here, singers were "begged" for no pay, yet exorbitant prices of admission were exacted. And for that meager orchestra and chorus! "*Quite* a difference, we should think!" And, by the way, what did the Society ever do with the $5000 they had raised before they began operations if they did not use it to pay their singers?

As for their performance of *Messiah:* "We attended it and have regretted having done so ever since." The audience was miserably small, due to the high price of tickets and inadequate advertising. The score had been mercilessly cut, but perhaps that was a kindness, considering the performance. In several sections the orchestra had been omitted and replaced by a melodion. What a desecration! Next, *Messiah* would be accompanied by a Jew's harp!

Marcus Colburn,♪ the veteran oratorio tenor from Boston (more recently a hotel-keeper in Albany) "opened his attack on Handel splendidly: he hit him right and left, and destroyed his style, meaning, and matter, leaving the Father of Sacred Music a perfect wreck." It was an awful thing to be assaulted by that "horrid nasal twang and conventicle whine, though it was positively asserted that Mr. Colburn was sent for from a long distance to edify and enlighten New-York upon the subject of sacred music. If they were really liberal enough to pay him for coming hither . . . we suggest that a like amount of money be appropriated before the next concert to ensure his being kept at a considerable distance from this city."

As for the remainder of the cast, Mrs. Charles E. Horn♪ was most unsuitable; Stephen Leach♪ might have been tolerable if he had displayed more sustained power; Mrs. Emma Gillingham Bostwick♪ was a relic of an outmoded style—"drawling and conventicle"—and displayed a lamentable "absence of dignity and want of execution and of impulse and nature"; Miss Anna Stone,♪ the well-known Boston vocalist now transplanted to New York, with her "faulty shake on whole tones where they were inadmissable," was utterly beneath discussion. Only Mrs. Laura A. Jones offered comparative relief in this generally dismal proceeding, not that she possessed the requisite "education," but that she had "few vices in the style" and sang "naturally and with all her heart." Watson did not stay to hear Edward Sheppard,♪ but was later told that he had run a race with the orchestra, conducted by Eisfeld—it was uncertain who had won. Heaping abuse on the unfortunate chorus, Watson concluded with the fervent hope never again to hear another such *Messiah* (*Albion,* May 18, 1850, p. 236).

In less devastating terms—indeed, brimming over with good will—Saroni benignly disapproved of the Harmonic Society's maiden flight. If this performance was less than good, it nonetheless held promise of better things to come, and Saroni hoped that their second concert would "permit us to bestow upon it all the encomiums at our command" (*Musical Times,* May 18, 1850, pp. 398–99).

On the other hand, the *Message Bird,* which had been instrumental in forming the Harmonic Society and was their most ardent supporter, proudly reported (May 15, 1850, pp. 330–31) that "we have never heard as a whole the choruses of this sublime Oratorio sung throughout with so much fullness, unity, and precision." Indeed, the Hallelujah Chorus was "boisterously *encored,*" perhaps gratifying as a manifestation of the audience's untrammeled delight, but most improper and irreverent behavior at a performance of so solemn a work. It was a practice firmly to be discouraged.

The orchestra, almost exclusively composed of Philharmonic players, received a mild slap on the wrist for their defective light and shade—but it was the conductor's fault; the solo singers, except for a few inconsequential flaws here and there, were generally praised, particularly Mrs. Jones. But the trumpet player, in his obbligato to "The trumpet shall sound," succeeded in showing up the "absurdity of . . . associating the tones of a petty military trumpet with those sublime words." It was a "profane burlesque which ought to be suppressed, if by no other means, by legislative enactment."

The substitution of a melodion for the organ, the *Message Bird* explained, had unfortunately been necessary because the brass instruments were "too sharp" for the Tabernacle organ.[35] It was hoped that the new music hall, then being built, would "contain an instrument worthy the requirements of the city." As it turned out the new music hall contained no organ at all.

Despite the unprecedented profusion of excellent music events, it was not until October that Strong heard his next concert—he appears not to have attended another opera for the remainder of the year. Preoccupied with his developing law practice, his growing social life, and above all, obsessed by what he considered his wife's precarious health (complemented by his own increasing hypochondria), Strong seems to have had little time or inclination left for music.

In the meantime, the Havana opera company had returned from their triumphs in Boston,[36] and on June 3 they opened at the Astor Place Opera House with *Lucrezia Borgia,* sung by the same cast that had performed it so wonderfully during their earlier sojourn—Bosio, Carolina Vietti, Salvi, and Marini.[37] It was followed on June 5 by *Norma,* again with Steffanone, Marini, and Lorini. Then, dropping *Attila,* the company proceeded to perform their previous repertory with rearranged casts. Steffanone, Bosio, and Tedesco interchangeably appeared in *Ernani, Lucrezia, Lucia,* and *La favorita,* as did their male counterparts. It was a startling innovation, ostensibly "aimed at satis-

[35] In an aggrieved footnote the *Message Bird* further explained: "The elevation of pitch for the last century or two may be judged of from the fact that the Great Bell of St. Paul's, London, which in the reign of Queen Anne was C concert pitch, is now A. Where is this ever to stop? If not checked in its career, the compositions of Handel must soon be laid aside, or recomposed: no voices will be able to reach the altitude required. Besides destroying the original inspiration and sublimity of these writings, it is producing the same results upon the scale of the Organ, which will indeed become a 'box of whistles,' if the progressive nonsense is allowed the latitude of a few more centuries" (*Message Bird,* May 15, 1850, p. 331).

[36] Tickets had been in such great demand in Boston that they were sold at auction, with premiums of 50 cents to $1 paid on single tickets (*Mirror,* May 20, 1850).

[37] With the last-minute substitution of *Lucrezia Borgia* for *La favorita,* originally announced for the opening, some people had been disappointed to get Bosio instead of Steffanone, reported the *Spirit of the Times* (June 8, 1850, p. 192).

fying all listeners," but more realistically designed to stimulate additional opera-going "for purposes of comparison."[38] Watson disapproved of the practice.

On June 24, postponed from June 21 to permit extra rehearsals, the Havana company presented Meyerbeer's *Gli Ugonotti* (*Les Huguenots*), erroneously announced as its first performance in the United States. As Henry C. Watson reminded his readers, it had been brilliantly performed in French in 1845 by the visiting opera company from New Orleans.♪

In Watson's opinion, the plot, which he characterized as "dramatic but revolting," worked better in French than in Italian. At any rate, Meyerbeer was an overrated composer, inferior to Bellini—the one being all Art, the other all Nature. Watson neglected to say which was which. "How rarely Meyerbeer touches the soul," he wrote, then proceeded to devote the greater part of his review to an elaborate hatchet job on Meyerbeer in all his aspects, but especially on his faulty orchestration. If we were to accept this sort of orchestration, wrote Watson, "then we must also honor such outlandish apparitions as Berlioz, Verdi, and such." Bosio, Steffanone, Salvi, Marini, Carolina Vietti, and the remainder of the cast were in varying degrees splendid. Notwithstanding the score's deficiencies, Watson pronounced the performance "worth half a day's journey to hear" (*Albion,* June 29, 1850, p. 308).

The *Herald* (June 25, 1850), taking a more liberal view of Meyerbeer's score, observed that its style was new, "blending the graces of the three great schools of music and running independent of one single *motivo*." Long though the review was, the *Herald* critic bemoaned the insufficient space at his disposal properly to enumerate the separate excellences of the huge cast, not excepting the prompter.

Without doubt, the Havana company had again taken the city by storm. So enormous had been the demand for opening night seats for *Gli Ugonotti* that the company manager, now one Antonio Pader, was forced personally to assure the mob clamoring for tickets that every seat in the house was taken; he suggested that they try for the next performance two nights later. If the crowds continued at this rate, commented the *Herald,* we would soon need to emulate the Bostonians and hold auctions for opera tickets.

On July 1 the company presented Rossini's *Semiramide*♪ as their final production at the Astor Place Opera House, then moved on to Castle Garden♪ for the third and most successful phase of their New York adventure.

Although no great lover of Rossini, Watson joyously greeted the announcement of *Semiramide,* which, as he put it, would "afford a musical ecstasy after Verdi's row-di-dow."[39] But he was less than ecstatic over the management's "peculiar" casting of the opera. The title role had been entrusted to Tedesco, a sluggish Semiramide, and the remaining roles—with the exception of Carolina Vietti, the best Arsace we ever had in New York—were sung by second-stringers: Corradi-Setti, Coletti, and the sweet-voiced, but listless, tenor Adelindo Vietti. "It was a mortifying disappointment," wrote Watson (not that he wished to disparage the artists), and almost more than he could endure to sit it through (*Albion,* June 15, p. 284; June 16, 1850, p. 320).

[38] "Those who cared nothing for the music cared much for the pleasure of . . . appearing to decide that Steffanone was better than Tedesco, and Tedesco better than Steffanone" (*Message Bird,* June 15, 1850, p. 362).

[39] Verdi's most recently heard "row-di-dow" was *Ernani,* given on June 7, with Steffanone as Elvira, switching roles with Tedesco.

Noah, too, was disappointed with the casting. Steffanone, not the "phlegmatic" Tedesco, should have sung the leading role (*Times and Messenger*, July 7, 1850). But the *Tribune* (July 2) rated *Semiramide* as one of the finest productions of the season and Tedesco's performance superior to anything she had yet done: "Her general indolence of demeanor, relieved now and then by a burst of impassioned vocalization, was no inappropriate personation of the Assyrian queen." Next to Tedesco, the greatest success was scored by Carolina Vietti, whose energy and spirit "aroused the sweltering enthusiasm of the house," a large one despite "the intense sultriness of the evening."

On July 8, the Havana company began their triumphant final engagement, at Castle Garden. "Our Havana Opera Company travels about New-York city so independently, changing their locality every now and then, that we are compelled to keep a bright lookout, lest we lose track of them," buoyantly commented the *Albion* (July 13, 1850, p. 332). "From Niblo's public resort they visited the aristocratically exclusive Astor Place Opera House, and . . . now we find them in democratic quarters, at Castle Garden, where, at fifty cents a head, from three to four thousand persons visit nightly."[40] Originally announced for a six-week season, they were, indeed, so fervently received that they continued there until September, leaving only when they were evicted by the arrival of Jenny Lind.

The *Albion* predicted astronomical profits for the opera management, even with the low ticket prices.[41] Not only was New York crowded with summer visitors who flocked by the thousands to Castle Garden, but even for those natives who were not away on summer holiday "the cool breezes and pleasant lounge are attractions not to be resisted in this weather." Indeed, "flesh and blood could not stand four hours of music in a shut-up theatre, with the thermometer at 90, and everyone looking overheated and tired to death."

Performing six nights a week, the company at first appeared in operas on Mondays, Wednesdays, and Fridays, and on the alternate nights in promenade concerts, accompanied by George Loder and a handpicked orchestra combining the opera musicians and the best available local talent. On Sunday evenings Loder presented "sacred concerts" in which the opera singers did not participate. After three highly praised, but poorly attended, promenade concerts the company reverted to a six-nights-a-week schedule of operas, except on evenings when the Garden was closed—sometimes because of bad weather,[42] sometimes for what were called rehearsals.

To their previous repertory—*Norma, Semiramide, Ernani, Lucrezia, La favorita,*

[40]This was, of course, journalistic license. Such audiences—and even larger ones—were known to attend the opera at Castle Garden, but not nightly, as a comparison of the press figures with those in the Castle Garden day book will show.

[41]But according to Maretzek: ". . . it was a matter of the purest indifference to Martí whether they made him money, or whether they did not make him money, during their summer season. Their salaries were provided for out of the receipts of the winter performances in Havana." Martí's principal purpose in sending his opera to the United States was to keep the company intact, occupied, and at a safe distance from the yellow fever that plagued Havana in the summer (*Crotchets*, p. 157).

[42]"The storms of the preceding week have been fatal to the opera," wrote Noah in the *Times and Messenger* on July 21. "No place in the world can equal the calm beauties of Castle Garden on a mild summer night, but when the waves are lashed in a foam and break with violence over the turrets of the Castle, they drown in their hoarse surges the most bewitching melodies of the Havana troupe."

Music Division, The New York Public Library

Giovanni Bottesini, unsurpassed master of the "violone."

Lucia, and *Macbeth*—they added Verdi's *I due Foscari,* Donizetti's *L'elisir d'amore,* Bellini's *I puritani,* and Pacini's *Saffo,*♪ each (with the exception of *Saffo*) eliciting ever more ecstatic reviews. The audiences, which were generally large, increased as the season progressed. For the first performance of *I puritani,* on August 2, an audience of more than three thousand was logged in the Castle Garden day book; the *Herald* reported six thousand, maybe seven. Except for occasional cavils over last-minute cancellations of performers or performances, disappointing untold numbers of people, the reviews continued at white heat until the company departed.[43]

According them a radiant valedictory editorial, the *Message Bird* (September 14, 1850, p. 461) wrote: "As the season of the company drew towards its termination, our citizens appeared to awaken to the fact that there was a constellation of artists among them such as is rarely the privilege of any city to possess in combination. . . . This sudden and unprecedented enthusiasm . . . induced the manager to prolong the season an additional week," during which the various singers' benefits produced "the gratifica-

[43] All told, the company gave thirty-four opera performances and three concerts during their 1850 sojourn at Castle Garden.

tion and recompense of crowded houses." For example, at Steffanone's benefit—*I puritani* on August 28—"sixty-five hundred tickets were received at the door." ("Between three and four thousand present," records the Castle Garden day book.)

Once again enumerating each singer's excellences, the *Message Bird* concluded with a eulogy of the company's two *maestri,* who throughout the engagement had received remarkably sparse attention from the critics: "It is true that Bottesini and Arditi added to the general attraction the aid of their wonderful skill on their favorite instruments, the Double Bass and Violin [playing solos and duets during opera intermissions]. And now, without any disparagement to Arditi's excellence, let us recur a moment to the wonderful Bottesini—without doubt and beyond all rivalry, the greatest performer on the *violone* in the world. At Salvi's benefit he gave Paganini's 'Carnival of Venice' on this huge instrument, with all the ease of the most accomplished violinist. The harmonic tones which he draws so gracefully from the upper, or G, string of his instrument are singularly powerful and beautiful, his shake is firm and faultless. . . . It is needless, though gratifying, to add that the honors awarded this great artist were such as became such a performance. Bottesini, however, seems instinctively to shrink from notice, with that modesty which frequently accompanies superior genius."

Bottesini was a splendid, but unsung, composer as well, and the writer went on to

New-York Historical Society

A concert at Castle Garden.

praise "an ever fresh and strangely spiritual solo for the clarionette" that he had composed as an introduction to act one, scene four, of *Lucia*. Audiences generally credited it to Donizetti, although in this critic's opinion Donizetti never in his happiest moments attained half the purity and originality of this prelude of Bottesini's.

The writer regretted that "such eminent talent should not be permanently retained in the United States. . . . How much we are in want of a music school in which the genius of such men as Bottesini . . . should be thoroughly appreciated by the world!" Reluctantly the writer bade his "final *addio* to this excellent company." He hoped they would be properly appreciated in Philadelphia, where they were stopping off on their way back to Havana.

In addition to the excitement over the Havana company, by September 1, when Jenny Lind (1830–1887) arrived, the populace had been goaded to a state of near-frenzy by the spells and incantations of that supreme necromancer Phineas T. Barnum (1810–1891).♪ From the time of his announcement some eight months earlier that, at last, after complex negotiations in Europe by his agent John Hall Wilton,[44] Lind had agreed to come to the United States, her name had not been allowed to slip from the public consciousness—not even for a day. Making his momentous first announcement in a letter to the press, appearing in all the New York papers on February 22, 1850, and promptly reprinted throughout the country, Barnum had "confided" the startling financial details of his agreement with Lind, involving sums so prodigious as to numb contemporary comprehension.

He would pay Lind $1000 a concert for 150 concerts and/or oratorio appearances but no operas. (To the dismay of her overseas worshipers, the twenty-nine-year-old Lind, for reasons attributed to her celebrated piety, had recently renounced the opera stage, whereon she had particularly triumphed.)[45] Should Barnum's profits reach $75,000 after seventy-five concerts, Lind would then receive, in addition, one-fifth of all future profits. Exclusive of their contract, Lind would be free, after two concerts in any given place, to appear on her own in as many charity concerts as she pleased.

Barnum would pay all traveling expenses for Lind and her party, to include, in addition to her supporting artists, a traveling companion and a secretary; he would provide her with appropriately luxurious living quarters, a maidservant, and, in every city she would visit, which included Havana, a carriage and pair of horses "with their necessary attendants." Julius Benedict, her conductor, accompanist, and music director, would be paid $25,000 for his participation in the tour, and her assisting artist, the well-known opera baritone Giovanni Belletti (1813–1890), $12,500.

[44] Wilton, an Englishman, had managed the Distin Family's American tour in 1849.♪ Although it was believed that he had originated the idea of bringing Lind to America, four other impresarios, among them the formidable Chevalier Wikoff,♪ are said to have competed with Barnum at the time (see Saxon, *Selected Letters of P. T. Barnum*, p. 165).

[45] From her tenth year, Lind, an illegitimate child with an extraordinary voice, had been educated for the stage at State expense at the School of the Royal Theatre in Stockholm. Her spectacular gesture of self-denial in renouncing opera at the peak of her sweeping operatic triumphs—together with her colossal philanthropies, her unimpeachable virtue, her rigid piety—might have signified a confusion of compulsions to atone, and at the same time to retaliate, for her shameful origin. Or was it all a form of inverted hubris?

As security, before her departure for the United States, Barnum was required to deposit with Lind's London bankers the full, staggering sum of $187,500, which with great difficulty he managed to raise.[46] He wished it understood, however, that profit was not his primary motive in bringing the "Swedish Nightingale" to America. He stood cheerfully ready, Barnum piously asserted, to lose money on Lind's tour for the "blessing" she would bring to the country, not only with her glorious singing, but with her simplicity, her modesty, her spotless virtue, her saintly benevolence.[47]

Since Lind's debut in England (in 1847), as Barnum informed the press, "she has given to the poor from her own private purse more than the whole amount which I have engaged to pay her, and the proceeds of concerts for charitable purposes in Great Britain, where she has sung gratuitously, have realized more than ten times that amount" (cited in Barnum, *Life of Barnum,* p. 307).[48]

Thus did Phineas T. Barnum lay the groundwork for his epical selling of Jenny Lind to the American public. Keenly responsive to the heady fragrance of box-office gold, Barnum had acutely assessed the special nature of the Lind phenomenon abroad. In England and on the Continent she was as universally idolized for her spectacular private charities and public benefactions as for her astounding vocal virtuosity.[49]

No sooner was his deal with Lind consummated than Barnum proceeded to devote his formidable gifts to fashioning for American consumption an outsized image of Lind the Angel. "I may as well state," Barnum confesses in his autobiography, "that although I relied prominently upon Jenny Lind's reputation as a great musical *artiste,* I also took largely into my estimate of her success with all classes of the American public her character for extraordinary benevolence and generosity. Without this peculiarity in her disposition, I would never have dared to make the engagement which I did, as I

[46] Unable to raise the final $5000 of this sum after exhausting every possibility, Barnum was rescued at the last moment by his friend the Universalist minister Abel C. Thomas, who loaned him the money.

[47] The Austrian/French pianist and composer Henri Herz,♪ touring throughout the United States and Latin America since 1846, claims that Barnum sought to engage him as an assisting artist for Lind's forthcoming tour. Herz states, probably with hindsight, that Barnum confided his strategy to make Lind "pass as an angel descended from the skies," and to present her as "a pure and radiant symbol for young America." "No one will believe it at first," Barnum was supposed to have said, "but I will say it and have it repeated so many times, and so well, that everyone will believe it" (Herz, pp. 31–32). Foolishly, Herz declined Barnum's offer, and Richard Hoffman♪ was engaged in his stead.

[48] The complete press release is quoted in the various editions of Barnum's seductively "candid," perennially fluid, variously titled autobiography. Published as *The Life of P. T. Barnum* in 1855, when he was forty-five years old, it was brought up to date and, retitled *Struggles and Triumphs: or, Forty Years' Recollections,* was issued in 1869 by subscription and in 1871 for the edification of the general public. Thereafter, and until 1889, *Struggles and Triumphs* reappeared virtually annually in updated editions. At Barnum's behest, after his death his widow issued the ultimate edition, titled *The Last Chapter.* Barnum claimed a sale of more than a million copies of his book during his lifetime. More than a vastly entertaining, unblushingly apocryphal, chronicle of an extraordinary life, Barnum's autobiography, as his biographer Neil Harris felicitously puts it, is "a text on the social functions of illusion and the role of the deceiver in an egalitarian society" (Harris, p. 231).

[49] Benjamin Lumley (1811–1875), the English impresario who brought Lind to London in 1847 and engineered her phenomenal successes in England, later wrote: "The report of her unblemished character, of her unbounded charities, and of her modesty . . . added greatly to the favour with which she was received by the English public, and gave increased lustre to her professional reputation" (Lumley, p. 187).

felt sure that there were multitudes of individuals in America who would be prompted to attend her concerts by this feeling alone" (*Life of Barnum,* p. 307).

Sensitively attuned to the nuances of the American psyche, Barnum proceeded artfully to "put innumerable means and appliances into operation for the furtherance of my object, and little did the public see of the hand that indirectly pulled at their heart-strings, preparatory to a relaxation of their purse-strings" (*ibid.,* p. 315).

As Max Maretzek, with heartstrings impervious, tells it: "Reputation was manufactured for [Lind] by wholesale. It was not merely made by the inch, but was prepared by the cart-load. 'Letters from England' were written in New York anterior to the arrival of each steamer, and by the highly moral Phineas were passed into the columns of the newspapers as genuine epistles from the other side of the Atlantic. These letters were received and published by the New York press with a *bonhomie* and readiness to oblige which I have never seen manifested by any other press in the world."

Barnum's "gigantic system of eulogy" had little to do with Lind's "actual qualities as an artist," claims Maretzek. "He [Barnum] exaggerated her virtues *à la Munchausen:* he proclaimed her a ventriloquist, romanced about [Queen] Victoria's adoration of her excellencies [*sic*], and fabricated charities by the bushelful" (*Crotchets,* pp. 121–22, 124).

In selling Lind, Barnum creatively expanded and elaborated upon the inspired techniques by which he had earlier bewitched hordes of Americans with his dwarfs and giants, his Fejee Mermaid, his Woolly Horse, and his thousand and one other freaks and wonders. "The show business has all phases of dignity," he declared, "from the exhibition of a monkey to the exposition of [the] highest art in music or the drama." In Barnum's democratic canon all were equally "merchantable . . . from the highest art to the lowest" (*Struggles and Triumphs* [1871], pp. 71–72). After the passage of more than a century, Phineas T. Barnum, the self-styled "Prince of Humbug," vibrantly remains the True Prophet and Patron Saint of Media Hype, as we have come to know it.

Barnum's "means and appliances" were implemented by a corps of copywriters who, under the Master's guidance, ceaselessly devised titillating "news" items about Lind and fed them to the voracious daily press.[50] "I worked by setting others to work," he writes. "Biographies of the Swedish Nightingale were largely [commissioned and] circulated; 'Foreign Correspondence' glorified her talents and triumphs by narratives of her benevolence; and 'printers' ink' was invoked in every possible form to put and keep Jenny Lind before the people" (*Life of Barnum,* p. 316).

Exposed to this relentless, day-after-day, month-after-month *ostinato,* the public that so frenetically greeted Jenny Lind upon her arrival on September 1 had been conditioned to act as a kind of automatic, self-perpetuating public-relations apparatus programed to do the wizard's every bidding.

Barnum's mass mesmerism spawned as well a thriving subsidiary industry in Jenny Lind memorabilia, to rival, if not surpass, the vast output of Lindish objects that had signalized the Lind furor overseas. Not only did Jenny Lind fashions from bonnets to boots become the rage, but a plethora of unlikely "Lind" articles flooded the market;

[50] Most of the newspapers ran daily columns devoted solely to Lind chitchat. The *Mirror* chose to head its daily dose of Lindiana with such punning captions as "Jenny-flexions," and "Jenny-sis," and to employ such locutions as "Jennywine," "Jennyral," and "Jenny-sais-quoi."

to name only a few: Jenny Lind Hair Gloss, Jenny Lind Pens, Jenny Lind Chewing Tobacco, Jenny Lind Canes, and Jenny Lind "Fuzees" (mechanical contraptions for out-of-doors lighting of cigars—preferably "Jenny Lind Segars"). Printers reaped a golden harvest with Jenny Lind biographies; lithographers enjoyed a huge boom in Jenny Lind portraits; and music publishers mined a veritable bonanza in Jenny Lind sheet music—not only her legendary arias and songs, but also a torrent of locally composed Jenny Lind "songs, quadrilles, and polkas," usually displaying on their covers portraits of varying resemblance to the Nightingale.[51] Even the illustrious A. P. Heinrich♪ contributed to the musical output with an ill-starred *Divertissement* for Grand Orchestra titled "Jenny Lind's Musical Journey Across the Atlantic" and a *Concertante* for Piano Forte called "Barnum's Invitation to Jenny Lind; The Museum Polka" (see APPENDIX 1).

Lind's prospective presence exerted more consequential influences as well. Under the heading "New Musical Hall—Jenny Lind," the *Herald* on February 21, 1850, "threw out" a provocative "hint to capitalists": "The great thing now wanted in this city by the musical public is a large Musical Hall, capable of seating some 4000 to 5000 and built with an eye, or an ear, to sound. No proper place at present exists in New-York for giving a good concert. . . . Such a building put up anywhere between Canal Street and Niblo's [Broadway and Prince Street] would be a great investment and an honor to our city.[52] If some enterprising person would undertake this at once," the *Herald* urged, "it might be finished by the first of September next and be christened the 'Jenny Lind,'[53] as undoubtedly Barnum would gladly engage it some fifteen to twenty nights for her concerts." (That's not exactly the way it turned out.)

The enterprise progressed rapidly. Before a month had passed, a builder (A. B. Tripler) had been found, and a tenant for the projected new hall was being sought, ostensibly by Barnum: "The Jenny Lind Music Hall. A rare chance. It is proposed, and will be erected immediately in Broadway, a magnificent, commodious Concert Hall, in which Mlle. Jenny Lind will make her first appearance. The hall will be built from plans combining every modern improvement for sound, elegance, and structure; to contain a spacious Concert Room, Ball and Supper Room, with every adjacent convenience, provided some responsible person will lease it for a term of years at a moderate rent, the builder being willing to erect but not to trouble himself with the immediate charge of it. Applications by letter on the subject to be addressed to P. T. Barnum, American Museum, without delay" (*Herald,* March 19, 1850).

Continuing to hold public fervor at white heat, in April the press reported that

[51] Furious rivalry prevailed among New York music publishers, some of whom claimed unique authenticity for their editions of the Jenny Lind repertory. In July the rival firms of S. C. Jollie and Firth, Pond and Company, in a rare collaboration, announced that they had acquired the rights to publish anything Jenny Lind would sing in the United States. "She has got an entirely new and beautiful repertoire, which has been sent out, song by song, to the above enterprising publishers," they advertised, and claimed furthermore, "These songs are authenticated by her and contain her exquisite ornaments and graces" (*Albion,* July 20, 1850, p. 344).

[52] In 1849, Hermann Saroni had energetically campaigned for a proper concert hall in New York.♪

[53] As far away as gold-rush San Francisco, a place she never visited, a Jenny Lind Theatre, seating 2000, was erected; a *Jenny Lind* steamer plied the Pacific coast; and delicacies were dispensed at a Jenny Lind bakery.

Barnum had engaged a splendid suite of apartments for Jenny Lind at the Irving House (Broadway at Chambers Street). After her arrival all the newspapers would not only describe its sumptuous furnishings—from draperies to bedspreads to wallpaper—but would report the cost of each item as well.[54]

In June a lavishly engraved, prospective "souvenir ticket" for the Jenny Lind concerts-to-be was put on display. Designed by the "celebrated engraver of Broadway, Mr. [James] Everdell," the ticket was described in the *Mirror* (June 7, 1850) as an item of "exquisite beauty. As everything relating to the Queen of Song and her forthcoming engagement with Mr. Barnum must be eagerly sought after by the public, we will give a brief description of the design for this elegant ticket, which it is intended, we believe, that each spectator shall retain as a memento of having seen and heard this extraordinary singer." The "splendidly engraved" item was 6½ by 4 inches in size and sported a medallion portrait of Jenny Lind in the center, surrounded by scrolls, leaves, and flowers, and flanked by two "celestials."

In July, work on Jenny Lind Hall (now a reality) suffered a setback when the construction crew struck for an increase in their wages of nine shillings ($1.12½) a day. "In consequence of non-compliance by the builder, work is stationary," reported the socially conscious *Tribune* (July 10, 1850). But only temporarily.

In August—amid such news items as the public exhibition of a piano with the Dolce Campana attachment, specially constructed for Jenny Lind,[55] and of Barnum's shopping for a horse for his diva, who reportedly was fond of a morning canter—a major new excitement was launched. On August 14, Barnum announced a competition open to American "first-rate literary men" for a "Welcome to America" (or, as it turned out, "Greeting to America") song text, to be set to music by Julius Benedict and sung by Lind at her first concert. At first offering a prize of $100, Barnum, on being twitted for niggardliness, quickly doubled the sum. In a convoluted way—via a letter pretending to have been written by Benedict in Germany but carelessly misdated August 24—the idea for the prize song was attributed to Lind herself.

M. M. Noah facetiously predicted that the offer would arouse the enthusiasm of "the tuneful nine hundred ninety-nine poets . . . engaged in the rhyming business from Maine to Georgia" (*Times and Messenger,* August 18, 1850). And indeed, a distinguished committee of judges, comprising two editors—the illustrious former Brook Farmer, George Ripley, now of the *Tribune,* and Lewis Gaylord Clark of the *Knickerbocker*—two publishers—Justus Starr Redfield (Barnum's future publisher) and George Palmer Putnam—and Julius Benedict, who appears miraculously to have crossed the Atlantic before posting his letter in Germany, were soon hurriedly examining not 999, but 753 submissions "from all over the country."

[54] It was gossiped that throughout Lind's tour Barnum made personally advantageous deals with hotelkeepers eager to receive the Nightingale. Not only did her presence, however fleeting, provide an enduring magnet to sensation-hungry travelers, but the special furnishings purchased for her sojourns were usually auctioned off at a neat profit, in which Barnum reportedly shared equally.

[55] The Dolce Campana attachment was another of the endless parade of devices intended to make pianos sound like something else. It was manufactured and energetically promoted by the Albany piano firm of Boardman and Gray. As it turned out, pianos unequipped with the Dolce Campana—Chickerings and Érards (the latter imported by Boardman and Gray)—were used in the Lind concerts.

The prize was awarded, amid angry charges of favoritism, to the minor poet and travel writer Bayard Taylor (1825–1878), a Putnam author and currently an assistant editor in the *Tribune* office. "The committee state in their report," Philip Hone gleefully observed, "that a large proportion of the [entries] were not fit to feed the pigs" (Hone, *Diary,* September 5, 1850); even Barnum later characterized the general quality of the submissions as "doggerel trash" (*Life of Barnum,* p. 309). Despite general agreement that Taylor's poem was beneath mediocrity, it was immediately published in newspapers and journals throughout the land.[56]

Beyond the mighty discontent it engendered in 752 defeated bardic bosoms,[57] the episode inspired considerable public controversy, several satirical parodies, and limitless "notoriety," as Barnum fondly termed it—precious beyond price.[58]

Descriptions of Lind's sensational welcome filled the newspapers for days, then later—with the daily press panting to keep up with Barnum's latest post-arrival Lindiana—the biweekly *Message Bird,* on September 14, 1855 (p. 458), came forth with its own vivid account not only of the pandemonium that had greeted the Swedish Nightingale but of the special role played by the New York music community in welcoming Lind on her first day in the United States: "On Sunday, the 1st instant, at about half-past one P.M., the booming of two distant, but heavy, guns announced the arrival of [her ship] the *Atlantic* at Quarantine. The news soon circulated through the city, and presently all the streets and avenues communicating with the dock of the steamer began to contribute their living streams to the immense aggregation of human beings which thronged the foot of Canal Street and adjacent piers."

Long before the *Atlantic* berthed, the pier—festive with a "bower of green trees" and not one, but two triumphal arches decked in flags and flowers and messages of welcome—was so jammed with people that at least one unfortunate welcomer had to be fished out of the river. The mass of humanity, estimated (perhaps apocryphally) at

[56] Given her choice between Taylor's poem and the runner-up "Salutation to America," composed by the local man-of-letters Epes Sargent (1813–1880), Lind is reported to have chosen Taylor's effort because it was shorter. And even so, she sang only two of its three stilted stanzas:

> I greet with a full heart the Land of the West
>   Whose Banner of Stars o'er a world is unrolled;
> Whose empire o'ershadows Atlantic's wide breast,
>   And opens to sunset its gateway of gold!
> The land of the mountain, the land of the lake.
>   And rivers that roll in magnificent tide—
> Where the souls of the mighty from slumbers awake,
>   And hallow the soil for whose freedom they died.

[57] The *Tribune* (September 10, 1850) reported that the preacher and dental pioneer, Solyman Brown (1790–1876), himself a poet, proposed to publish all 752 of the rejected "Welcome to America" lyrics.

[58] Saroni regretted that Barnum had not offered a companion prize to an American composer for the music, but it's never too late "for such a patriotic enterprise" (*Musical Times,* August 17, 1850, p. 556). Accordingly, Saroni, himself no mean hand at promotion, soon announced a prize-song competition of his own, and in November his committee—Benedict, Scharfenberg, and Timm—awarded a prize of $25 to Otto Dresel♪ (only a recent American).

30,000 to 40,000 in number, covered neighboring rooftops, piers, and ships, hung from windows and lampposts, and clung to spars and riggings, to bulkheads, and even to the fenders of the Hoboken Ferry House (Rosenberg, pp. 8–9).

A beaming Barnum stood at Lind's side as the *Atlantic* docked. Having spent an anxious night on Staten Island, he had climbed aboard the ship at Quarantine, huge bouquet tucked into white vest, and for the first time set eyes on his Nightingale.

What he saw (according to the *Tribune,* September 2, 1850) was a young woman "twenty-nine years of age," with "very frank, engaging manners" and an "expression of habitual good humor in her clear blue eye, which would win the heart of a crowd by a single glance." Lind was "rather more robust in face and person than her portraits would indicate. Her forehead is finely formed, shaded by waves of pale brown hair [others described it as yellow]; her eyes . . . light blue and joyous; her nose and mouth, though molded on the large, Swedish type, convey an impression of benevolence and sound goodness of heart, which is thoroughly in keeping with the many stories we have heard of her charitable doings."

And for the feminine readership: "Miss Lind was dressed with great taste and simplicity. She wore a *visite* [a cape or short coat] of rich black cashmere over a dress of silver-gray silk, with a pale blue silk hat and black veil." At her feet lay a floppy-eared, silky lap dog of a "rare breed," purportedly a gift from Queen Victoria.

New-York Historical Society

The dockside welcome to Jenny Lind.

THE LANDING OF JENNY LIND.

About one o'clock on Sunday, the report of a gun announced to the half-frantic population of New York, that the Steamer Atlantic was puffiing and blowing her way up to the good city of Gotham, and within her wooden walls were confined the Sweedish Nightingale, as passenger. Then came the rush of tag-rag and bobtail :—

Corns were jam'd, and shins were skin'd,
To get a glimpse of Jenny Lind,
Many could'nt bear the shock,
Fell, pell-mell into the dock.
The fences broke, and there was Mose,
Giving a chap a bloody nose.
M. P's. were seen among the crowd,
Children bawling, some quite loud,
Mothers from their children torn,
Ladies, over heads were bourne.
And many of them in the tussel,
Lost their shoes, some their bustle.
Men were queer from drinking rum,
Some gals were hit upon the bum.
Old Atlanta too, on the Steamer,
Sounded his horn, and such a screamer.
Some will get their eyes well skinn'd,
Before she quits, sweet Jenny Lind.
Perhaps you also will be a ninny,
For a Jackass is sure to run after a Jenny.

Once the ship docked, it was "only through the desperate exertions of the police" that Lind was safely brought ashore and into a carriage waiting on the pier; but it was beyond their ability to control the stampeding mob that blocked the exit from the pier, and several injuries were reported.

"Smothered in bouquets, and suffocated by the crowd that pressed around and climbed upon the wheels of the vehicle, and even upon its top, in their eagerness to catch a glimpse of her, [Lind was] literally engulphed [*sic*] in a sea of human beings," continues the *Message Bird*. Through all this she responded with "inimitable grace—bowing, waving her pocket handkerchief, and wafting, with both hands, kisses to the crowd."[59]

Along Lind's route to the Irving House, streets, windows, balconies, and roofs were crammed with cheering New Yorkers, and, once she arrived, "the excitement, if possible, was still more intense. The mass of people completely filled Chamber[s] Street from Broadway to Church," reports the *Message Bird*. "The cheers, as she stepped from the carriage . . . were literally deafening. . . . It would be useless to attempt to describe the enthusiasm when Mademoiselle Lind appeared at the balcony of her window in response to the ceaseless clamor outside."

The crowd, if anything, increased in size and enthusiasm throughout the afternoon and evening, breaking into cheers every time a shadow flitted across her windows. Upon the stroke of midnight the day's festivities were gloriously crowned with a "serenade of 200 performers," which, in the words of Philip Hone (no music lover), "'blew a blast so loud and dread,' as soon as the clock of the City Hall announced the departure of the Sabbath,[60] that the marble columns of Stewart's dry-goods palace (opposite the bird-cage) could scarcely maintain their upright positions" (Hone, MS Diary, September 3, 1850).

"It was deemed proper," the *Message Bird* explained, "that the proposed serenade, or welcome, from the musical profession, should be given by the Musical Fund Society, which includes musicians of every rank and nation. Consequently, between twelve and one o'clock [A.M.], about 200 members of the Society, escorted by [Dodworth's] Band [carrying music stands], some 150 firemen in uniform [bearing torches], to preserve space and order," marched up Broadway and "assembled beneath her windows, [set up their music stands] and, under the direction of Mr. George Loder, executed the prepared program in a manner highly creditable, under the circumstances, to the Society. As this intended compliment had been no secret, the reader can easily conceive the accession of numbers which the double attraction drew to the spot. Broadway presented a literal sea of human heads in every direction.[61]

"By way of making this testimonial a national one, the airs of 'Hail Columbia' and 'Yankee Doodle' (and [testily] we do not know why the grander air of 'The Star Spangled Banner' was omitted on this occasion) introduced the serenade. The object of these honors soon appeared at the window and then arose a shout such as New-York has seldom echoed."

[59] A similar mob scene had been enacted some two weeks earlier at the Liverpool pier, as Jenny Lind departed for the United States.

[60] The *Mirror* caustically commented on the "non-church-going multitude" that chose to welcome Lind on the Sabbath instead of devoting the day to godly pursuits.

[61] It was estimated that at least 20,000 people were milling around Broadway and Chambers Street at that unusual hour.

New-York Historical Society

The Swedish Nightingale.

Lind, who had perseveringly appreciated everything she had encountered throughout the day, although unfamiliar with these tunes, nonetheless politely exclaimed, "How beautiful!" But: "On being informed that they were our national airs, she clapped her hands, begged that they might be repeated, and both laughed and wept" on their repetition. Following with a "National Pot-Pourri," some twenty minutes in duration, by one Peter Streck, and concluding their program, for some arcane reason, with "God Save the Queen,"[62] the chief dignitaries of the Musical Fund Society—George Loder, John A. Kyle,♪ Allen Dodworth,♪ John C. Scherpf,♪ and Henry C. Watson—then "proceeded to the apartments of Miss Lind, and in a 'brief' speech read by Watson [an "incorrigibly lengthy infliction," Rosenberg called it] tendered her, in behalf of the musical profession of New-York, a cordial welcome. . . .

"During this ceremony," infatuatedly continues the *Message Bird,* "Jenny Lind's demeanor exhibited the meekness of a child. Her face nearly concealed in her bosom—and shyly apologizing for her limited English—she expressed her great appreciation of their kindness, and modestly hoped to merit their approbation. 'The sight there tonight,' she said, as she pointed to the window, 'was the most beautiful I ever saw.' "[63]

This was only the beginning. Day after day the hysteria persisted—indeed, intensified. As the *Mirror* editorialized, on September 3: "The arrival of Jenny Lind has produced a mania in the public mind, the like of which it would be hard to find among all the records of mankind. Both high and low are going it blind,[64] rich and poor, coarse and refined. From noon to eve, Broadway is lined with people talking of Jenny Lind. From the inner core to the outer rind of our society nothing is heard but Lind, Lind, Lind."

Like every other New Yorker, George Templeton Strong was astounded at the Lind phenomenon, but in his own particular fashion.

September 2. . . . Jenny Lind has arrived and was received with such a spontaneous outbreak of rushing and crowding, and hurrahing, and serenading as this city has never seen before. The streets round the Irving House blocked up with a mob night and day; horses hardly permitted to carry her through the streets, so vehemently did the mob thirst for the honor of drawing her carriage, and so on. Really, it's very strange—Miss Jenny is a young lady of very great musical taste, and possessed of a larynx so delicately organized that she can go up to A in *alt* with a brilliancy and precision, and sing with more effect than any other living performer. Furthermore, she is a good, amiable, benevolent woman, fully equal, I dare say, to the average of our New York girls; and having in her vocal apparatus a fortune of millions, she devotes a liberal share of it to works of charity. But if the greatest man that has lived for the last ten centuries were here in her place, the uproar and excitement could not be much greater and would probably be much less.

[62] ". . . why an American band should play 'God Save the Queen,' in welcoming a Swede to their country, I find rather hard to divine," wrote the English critic Charles G. Rosenberg in his account of the Lind tour (p. 12).

[63] Lind, in fact, was no stranger to such serenades, having been enthusiastically serenaded throughout Europe since 1843. Nor was she unfamiliar with torchlight processions in her honor.

[64] "Going it blind" is the rough equivalent of "kicking over the traces."

Philip Hone, too, commented wryly on the progress of the Nightingale hysteria. On September 3 he wrote in his diary: "'Sing a song of sixpence' at the rate of $1000 a night. Our good city is in a new excitement. So much has been said, and the trumpet of fame sounded so loud in honor of this new importation from the shores of Europe, that nothing else is heard in our streets, nothing seen in the papers, but the advent of the 'Swedish Nightingale' . . . thousands of silly bird-fanciers [followed] the 'nightingale' to . . . her perch. . . . Five hundred ladies assembled to be introduced to her; her exits and entrances were obstructed in the streets; and her apartment offered no retreat. Presents are showered, choice flowers exhale their fragrance, and luscious fruits court the embrace of her lips. Milliners, dressmakers, and costumers contend for the honor of furnishing gratuitously her wardrobe."

Jenny Lind Hall not having been completed in time, the day after their arrival Barnum escorted Lind, her cousin and traveling companion Miss Josephine Amahnsson, and her colleagues, Benedict and Belletti, on a shopping tour of the larger halls in the city—Niblo's Garden, the Broadway Tabernacle, and Castle Garden. They decided on Castle Garden, with its huge capacity—it would purportedly hold up to 10,000 people—as the most likely place, after suitable alterations, in which to hold Lind's six forthcoming concerts in New York.

The following day, September 3, Barnum signed a lease for the rental of Castle Garden at an exorbitant $500 a week; he agreed additionally to furnish the lessors, Messrs. French and Heiser,♪ with thirty free admissions to each concert for the use of their respective families. Barnum would be permitted to make such structural alterations to the hall as he might wish, but was required to restore it to its original state after the Lind engagement was completed. He further agreed to permit the Castle Garden waiters and bartenders free access to the hall "while attending to their duties."[65] The lessors, in turn, agreed to supply all the lighting and "all the seats we possess at no additional charge"; to allow Barnum to use the premises as needed for rehearsals; and to hold ticket auctions any day but Sunday.[66]

Although admissions to the Lind concerts were—purportedly at Lind's request—announced for as little as $3, on September 7 (the last day of the Havana company's engagement) some three to four thousand intrepid New Yorkers, many of them prospective ticket speculators, braved a heavy rainfall and indignantly paid the admission fee of one shilling (12½ cents) demanded by the Castle Garden people to attend Barnum's first ticket auction. The auctioning of tickets was new to New York but an old custom in Boston,[67] and indeed nothing new to Jenny Lind, for whose performances tickets had been auctioned in Sweden, and undoubtedly elsewhere as well (Holland and Rockstro, p. 317).

Creating a nationwide sensation, the hotly contested first ticket was bought for

[65] At Lind's fourth and fifth concerts, on September 19 and 21, the Castle Garden day book regretfully reports that the house was "too full for business."

[66] The lease can be seen at the New-York Historical Society.

[67] In his early barnstorming days Barnum had witnessed a ticket auction for a Fanny Elssler performance in New Orleans; most likely he had seen, or been aware of, ticket auctions in Boston, as well.

Phineas Taylor Barnum, the supreme wizard of humbug.

$225, to the accompaniment of three lusty cheers, by John N. Genin, a canny, publicity-conscious hatter with a shop on Broadway, just next door to Barnum's American Museum.[68]

Inevitable ensuing rumors of Barnum/Genin collusion were pooh-poohed by the *Mirror* and later denied by Barnum, but Philip Hone, in whose past lurked faint echoes of the auction business, called Genin's purchase of the first ticket "a most transparent piece of 'peterfunking'" (after "Peter Funk," legendary arch-perpetrator of shady dealings at an auction). The *Albion* (September 14, 1850, p. 440) snobbishly called the bidding for the first ticket "a spirited contest between a hatter, three quack medicine-vendors, and a hotel-keeper"; Strong characterized the furious competition between Genin and the capitalistic pill-makers—Benjamin Brandreth, William B. Moffat, and A. B. Tripler—as "a rare conjunction of asses."

A second installment of the auction took place two days later without paid admission, but on September 12, at the auction for the second concert, the 12½-cent entrance price was reinstated (despite Barnum's alleged protest). The auctions were then discontinued, supposedly at Lind's request,[69] and thereafter tickets were available at

[68] Genin was no run-of-the-mill hat merchant. Not only had he written a "charming" history of the hat in 1848, but upon the recent opening of his new premises, at 214 Broadway, he had given a kind of preview reception for the gentlemen of the press, treating them to a lavish supper and choice entertainment. Even before he purchased immortality for $225, Genin had sent Lind a riding cap, together with "appropriate gloves" and a riding crop, which gifts she had reportedly "courteously acknowledged" (*Evening Post,* March 29; *Times and Messenger,* September 9, 1850).

[69] Despite Lind's purported disapproval, Barnum held ticket auctions throughout her subsequent tour.

Barnum's American Museum, where they were advertised at 25 percent below auction prices: $8 seats might be bought for $6, and so on down to $3; so-called "promenade" tickets for the outside terraces, where fragments of the music might occasionally float out from the distant stage, were priced at one dollar, but apparently were sold for three and even five. For the holders of promenade tickets, portable "walking stick chairs," capable of holding 200 pounds of weight, were advertised by the resourceful firm of John J. Browne and Company, 103 Fulton Street.

At advanced prices, tickets were available at the usual hotels and music stores; at outrageous prices—as high as $15 apiece—they were available from great numbers of enterprising private speculators who had bought up all the tickets they could procure at the auctions, and whose advertisements filled page-long columns in the newspapers. At Lind's first concert, although all the tickets had been sold, the Castle Garden day book discloses that some three to four hundred seats had remained unoccupied, the tickets having been "left on the speculators' hands." As Barnum explained it, however, many overenthusiastic bidders had suffered a change of heart and failed to call for their tickets when paying-up time arrived.

New-York Historical Society

At the right of Barnum's American Museum is Genin's hat emporium, where, in 1850, the featured item was the Jenny Lind Riding Hat.

With the public response far exceeding Barnum's fondest expectations, only two days after Lind's arrival, as he tells it, Barnum decided to scrap their original agreement in favor of an even more generous contract that not only guaranteed Lind her $1000 for each of her 150 concerts but, much to her alleged delight, gave her an equal share of the net proceeds after Barnum's expenses (set at $5500 a concert) had been deducted (*Life of Barnum,* p. 313). But although Barnum claimed the full credit for this awesome act of generosity, it was Lind—according to Maunsell B. Field, acting as Lind's attorney during the absence in Europe of his partner (and Barnum's detractor) John Jay—who demanded the revision of their original agreement and Barnum who acquiesced.

Summoned to the Lind presence the day after her arrival, Field tells how he was accosted in the lobby of her hotel by Barnum, who introduced himself and fervently announced, on the way up to her apartment: "I am going to introduce you to an angel, sir—to an angel!" Observing that Lind, wearing "a summer dress, cut low in the neck and with short sleeves . . . looked . . . wonderfully substantial for an angel," Field reports that she immediately got down to business. She had come to America, she informed him, with only a "very vague memorandum" signed in Europe by Barnum's agent, not a formal contract with Barnum himself. "She desired me to prepare a proper agreement, and we three sat down together and settled its terms."

The next day the apparently satisfactory new contract was duly delivered and signed, but soon, writes Field: "Miss Lind became dissatisfied with her contract and I was sent for to revise it." Indeed: "Again and again, Miss Lind desired changes made in the contract to her advantage, and every time, Mr. Barnum yielded." Field assessed Lind as "a calm, sensible, conscientious woman of high principles, [but] rather calculating than emotional." Barnum he characterized as "obliging and complaisant," and displaying at the time "good nature and liberality . . . in his business relations with Miss Lind" (Field, pp. 216–20).

Field credits Barnum with the tremendous idea—"a master stroke of policy," he calls it—that Lind "volunteer" to donate $10,000 to various New York charities from her share of the first concert's proceeds.[70] This news of Lind's prodigal generosity was announced by Barnum, supposedly against Lind's wishes, at the close of her first concert. It was, however, not disclosed until much later that—despite varying current reports of astronomical box-office receipts—Lind's share of the first concert—and indeed the second—had fallen short of the pledged sum. To avoid mutual embarrassment and negative publicity, Barnum is supposed to have suggested that they divide into equal shares the combined proceeds of the first two concerts—$17,864.05 for the first and $14,203.03 for the second (Barnum's figures)—and that they reckon the third concert as the first to come under their formal agreement (Field, pp. 218–19; *Life of Barnum,* p. 318).

Even so chronic a skeptic as Philip Hone was to a certain extent taken in. On September 17, after Lind's second concert, he wrote in his diary: "This Syren, the tenth muse, the *Angel,* as Barnum calls her, the *Nightingale,* by which she is designated

[70] The playwright/dentist/newspaper editor William K. Northall♪ claimed that Barnum conceived the idea of Lind's monster one-time donation as a strategy to prevent his charity-obsessed Nightingale from diluting her drawing power by appearing at too many charity concerts in New York (Northall, p. 168).

by the would-be *dilettanti,* has secured the affection, as well as the admiration, of the mass of the people by an act of munificence, as well as good policy. Her contract with Mr. Barnum has been changed; instead of $1000 a night, she gets one-half of the net proceeds; her share of which for the first night, after deducting the large expenses of a first performance, amounting to the enormous sum of $12,600, all of which, with unprecedented liberality, she distributed among the charitable and benevolent institutions of the city. The list is headed by the Fire Department Fund, to which she gives $3000, to the Musical Fund $2000, and the balance is divided in sums of $500 each to all the other charities.[71]

"The noble gratuity to the firemen is a great stroke of policy," added Hone. "It binds to her the support and affection of the red-shirt gentlemen, who will worship the Nightingale and fight for her to the death, if occasion should require. New York is conquered; a hostile army or fleet could not effect a conquest so complete."

Indeed, so complete was Lind's conquest at the outset of her American tour that she appears to have vanquished even the habitually fractious critical fraternity. After her first rehearsal, held on September 9, the handpicked group of gentlemen of the press, who, together with representative local dignitaries, had been invited, vied with each other in their untrammeled transports over Lind's vocal perfections. "We have just returned from Jenny Lind's first grand rehearsal," rhapsodized a regrettably unidentified "friend of the *Tribune*" (probably George William Curtis),♪ whose musical experience, the editor attested, entitled "his opinions to respect." "We went there by no means prejudiced in her favor," wrote this musical expert. "We have returned another man." Lind's superhuman performance had caused this critic to feel almost as if he had "entered another world." Although he had heard "nearly all the great vocalists of our age, [he] hardly believed that human voice could accomplish what the Swedish vocalist made palpable to our ear."

And it was all so effortless—so "natural": "The Nightingale, to which she had been justly compared, does not pour out its melody with more ease; its notes do not gush forth with more freedom and correctness, according to nature's pitch and scale, than do Jenny Lind's, according to art's strictest rules." In her *Trio concertant* with two flutes, a showpiece in Meyerbeer's opera *Ein Feldlager in Schlesien* (*A Camp in Silesia*) (Berlin 1844), composed especially for Lind,[72] she so astonished the orchestra with her vocal pyrotechnics that they "came to a dead stop," standing there "with their mouths open until Mr. Benedict told them they 'must not listen if they wanted to play their parts.'" Not only was Lind's voice undistinguishable from the flute sound, but it "absolutely was an improvement on it, and of the three Nightingales supposed to be heard then, she was unquestionably the best."

But for sheer, unbuttoned verbal extravagance, this reviewer was eclipsed by *Gemotice* (James F. Otis), who wrote: "As a bird just alighted upon a spray begins to sing,

[71] The ten recipients of the $500 donations were the Home for the Friendless, the Home for the Relief of Indigent Females, the Dramatic Fund Association, the Home for Colored and Aged Persons, the Colored and Orphan Asylum, the Lying-in Hospital for Destitute Females, the New-York Orphan Asylum, the Protestant Half Orphan Asylum, the Roman Catholic Half Orphan Asylum, and the Old Ladies' Asylum.

[72] In 1854, Meyerbeer revised *Feldlager* (also known as *Vielka*) and renamed it *L'Étoile du nord,* in which version it would be heard in New York in 1856.

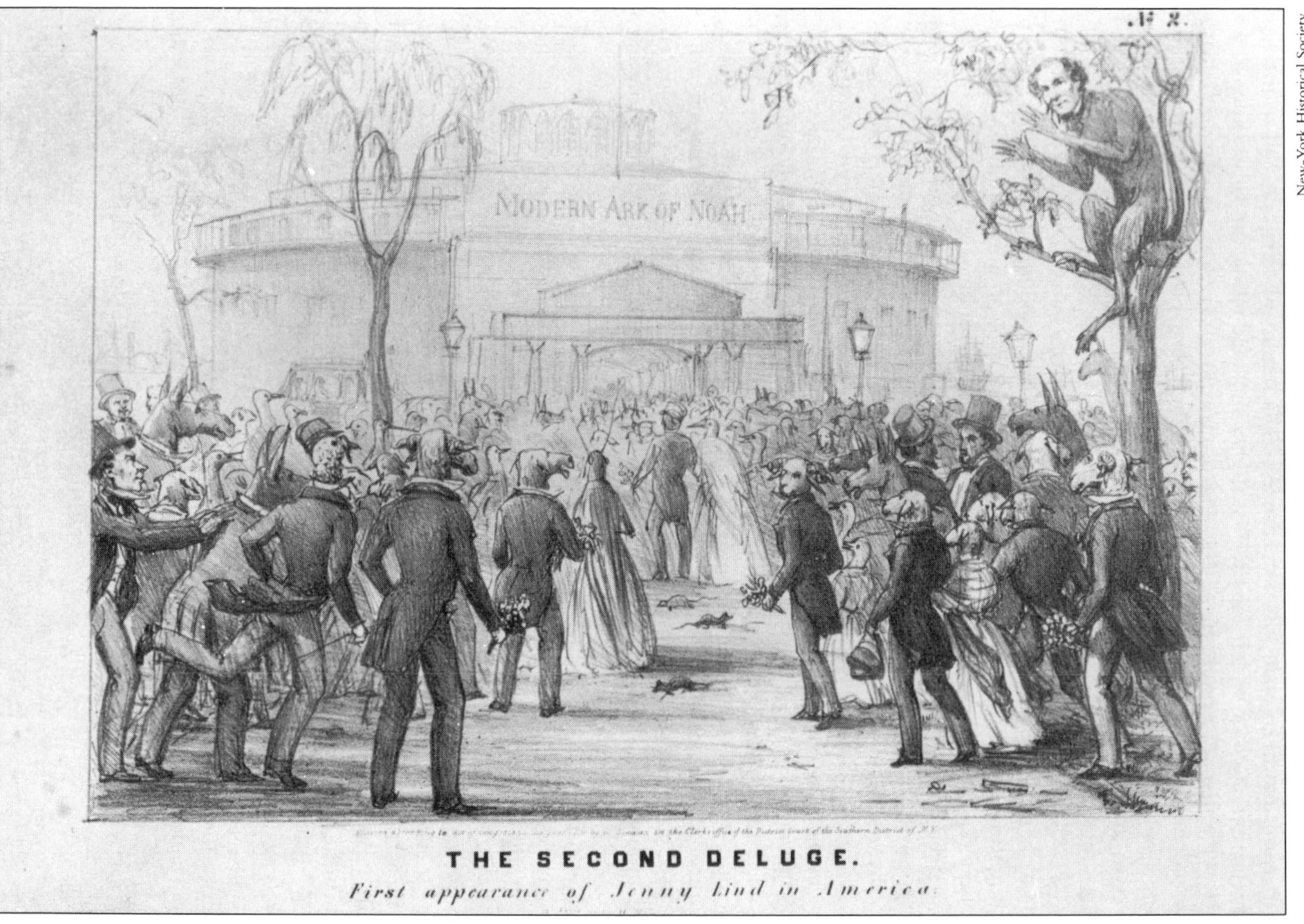

New-York Historical Society

Castle Garden is represented as a modern Noah's Ark and Barnum as a mischievous satyr sitting in a tree, thumbing his nose at the hordes of spellbound animals as they swarm to hear Jenny Lind's first concert.

he knows not why, and pours forth the increasing volume of his voice from an instinct implanted within him by the Power which made him vocal—as flowers unfold their petals to the air, as zephyrs breathe, as rivulets leave their founts, as thoughts flow, as affections rise, as feelings develop—so this wondrous creature sang. . . . So sing the birds . . . so, to the extent of their faith, sing the angels" (*Express,* reprinted in the *Spirit of the Times,* September 14, 1850, p. 360).

Apart from purely musical considerations, the press unanimously lauded Barnum for his masterly organization of Lind's first concert. The expected dense mass of humanity that swarmed over the Battery on September 11 was ably controlled by a sufficient force of police, and there was no disorder as, from five o'clock on, some 5000 ticket holders (Barnum's estimate) serenely crossed the narrow footbridge that provided the only access to Castle Garden. From the Battery gate, it was reported, the footbridge, which in honor of the event had been brilliantly illuminated and covered with an immense awning, looked like a "triumphal avenue."

The huge interior of a transformed Castle Garden had been divided into separate sections, each set apart by lamps and hangings of a different color. A corps of 100 ushers wearing correspondingly colored rosettes and carrying wands decorated with matching ribbons, efficiently guided the members of the audience by means of their color-coded, numbered tickets, to their color-coded, numbered seats.

Among Barnum's structural changes, reported the *Mirror* (September 12, 1850), the Castle Garden stage had been extended forward some ten feet into the body of the auditorium, and the drop curtain had been replaced by a wooden partition (probably for acoustical reasons), on which the intertwined Swedish and American flags had been "painted in great taste" above a base of "arabesque ornaments of white and gold"; "Very elegant chandeliers" had been suspended from the ceiling, and two gas burners affixed to each of the hall's innumerable columns. There was, nonetheless, "scarcely enough light upon the stage to enable those at a distance to distinguish the features of the performers."[73]

The only evidence of bad taste, it was generally felt, was "an inscription over one portion of the balcony—'Welcome, sweet warbler'—which was surrounded by a poor imitation of a floral border . . . rather Museumish [the *Mirror's* uppity reference to Barnum's plebeian American Museum] and decidedly out of character."

Encouraged by the success of his first auction, Barnum had caused several additional rows of seats to be installed. They were evidently too closely spaced for comfort, for ticket-holders were cautioned to buy their "concert books" (program booklets) at "the entrance to the Castle, as it is impossible for persons to get between the seats to sell the same after the audience are seated" (*Tribune,* September 14, 1850).

The handsomely gotten-up concert book displayed engraved likenesses of Lind, Belletti, Benedict, and Barnum on its cover and included in its pages biographical sketches of all four (yes, of Barnum, too). A listing of the sixty members of the orchestra reads like a who's who of the contemporary New York music community, with the two Philharmonic conductors Theodore Eisfeld and George Loder respectively leading the violin and contrabass sections. Among the prominent musicians listed in

[73] The *Mirror* suggested a row of footlights to remedy this shortcoming.

New-York Historical Society

Images of Lind and (clockwise) Benedict, Barnum, and Belletti decorated the Concert Book for Jenny Lind's first appearance in America.

the ranks were the violinists George Frederick Bristow, Joseph Noll, and Edward Richard Hansen;♪ the flutists John A. Kyle and Julius Siede♪ (Lind's collaborators in the *Trio concertant*); and many other members of the Philharmonic, among them John C. Scherpf, the secretary of the Musical Fund Society, who officiated at the bass drum. The booklet also contained, in addition to the program of the evening, the texts of all the vocal offerings, both in their original languages and in English translations.

Lind's first American audience, as all the newspapers noted, consisted mostly of men. Only an eighth of those present were ladies, reported the *Tribune* (September 12, 1850), a staunch advocate of women's rights, and pithily added: "They must stay home, it seems, when the tickets are high, but the gentlemen go, nevertheless." The other papers attributed the ladies' absence to their timidity at being caught in the expected crush.

Not only were few ladies to be seen at this historic event but also, according to N. P. Willis, an expert in such matters, few "fashionables." Leaving his "rural retreat" to attend Lind's first concert, Willis, who had not yet adopted his role of gallant courtier to the Angel/Nightingale, pointedly observed that as he rode downtown toward Castle Garden (in a plebeian omnibus!) he saw "indications of a counter-current (private carriages starting for their evening drives out of town, and several dandies of the hour strolling up, with an air of leisure which was perfectly expressive of no part in the excitement of the evening) and then I first comprehended that here might possibly be a small class of *dissenters*." In trying to determine how many fashionables had attended the concert, Willis, with the aid of his opera glass, counted "but *eleven*." He generously professed the wish to see Lind "as much 'the fashion' as the 'popular rage' [obviously mutually exclusive commodities] in our republican metropolis" (*Home Journal,* September 21, 1850).

Unhappily, the festive atmosphere was to a certain extent marred by "a noisy crowd of boys in boats who gathered around the outer walls of the Castle, and being by their position secure from the police, [they] tried to disturb those within by a hideous clamor of shouts and yells, accompanied by a discordant din of drums and fifes. There must have been more than two hundred boats and a thousand persons on the water. . . . By ten o'clock they had either become tired, or ashamed, of the contemptible outrage they were attempting, and dispersed" (*Tribune,* September 12, 1850).[74]

The audience in the hall, in the last unbearable throes of pent-up suspense, somehow managed to endure the preliminary performances of the Overture to Benedict's opera *The Crusaders* (London 1846),[75] conducted by the composer, and an aria from Rossini's *Maometto secondo* (Naples 1820), sung by Belletti. But when a virginally white-clad Lind was at last led onstage by Benedict, they exploded into a veritable hurricane of released emotion. Springing to their feet, the audience abandoned themselves to an orgy of clapping, stamping, shouting, screaming, and roaring—of waving hats, handkerchiefs, walking-sticks, and umbrellas—and of flooding the stage with "thousands of bouquets." This untrammeled demonstration so unnerved the Nightin-

[74] Not so, contradicted the *Evening Post* (September 12, 1850), which reported that the occupants of the boats, adults and children, had been "quiet as mice," attentively listening to every note of the concert, as clearly audible as if they had been in the hall.

[75] According to the reviews, the announced order of the two overtures had been reversed: Benedict's overture opened the program; Weber's Overture to *Oberon* opened part two.

Copies of the prize song were soon found on home piano racks throughout the land.

gale that she faltered as she began her first aria, the *Casta diva* from *Norma.*[76] But no matter; she soon recovered herself, and before she had finished the aria every musical pause and orchestral interlude was punctuated with wild cheering and applause.

Despite a few faint, reflexive quibbles from certain critics with overpersistent memories—Noah and Willis, for instance, professed to be disappointed with Lind's *Casta diva,* claiming in the past to have heard divas of greater musical, if not personal, chastity—the critics were unanimously and unprecedentedly overwhelmed. Notably, the ponderous Boston critic John Sullivan Dwight,♪ who had been imported from the Athens of America by the *Tribune* to review Lind's first six concerts, was swept off his

[76] As will be seen, Lind's concert repertory consisted chiefly of the very music she refused to perform on the wicked opera stage.

feet. "Jenny Lind's first concert is over," he wrote (September 12, 1850), "and all doubts are at an end. She is the greatest singer we have ever heard, and her success is all that was anticipated from her genius and her fame." From the moment—after the audience had recovered some semblance of self-possession—when "the divine songstress—with that perfect musical bearing, that air of all dignity and sweetness, blending with the beautiful confidence of Genius and serene wisdom of Art—addressed herself to Song," Dwight was vanquished.

Momentarily returning to earth, Dwight continued: "Here is a genuine soprano, reaching the extra high notes with that ease and certainty which make each highest note a triumph of expression purely, and not a physical marvel. The gradual growth and *sostenuto* of her tones, the light and shade, the rhythmic undulation and balance of her passages, the bird-like ecstasy of her trill, the faultless precision and fluency of such volume of voice as to crown each protracted climax with glory . . . and indeed all the points one looks for in a mistress of the vocal art, were eminently hers in 'Casta Diva.'"

But it was the "real and yet truly ideal humanity of her singing" that had "won the world [and Dwight] to Jenny Lind." Endowing the singer with the ideal characteristics of Transcendentalism, Dwight, the archetypal Brook Farmer, wrote: "There is plainly no vanity in her, no mere aim to effect; it is all frank and harmoniously earnest." And, above all, at one with Nature.

After a marvelously rendered duet with Belletti, *Per piacer alla signora* from Ros-

FIRST APPEARANCE OF JENNY LIND IN AMERICA.
At Castle Garden Sept.r 11th 1850.
Total Receipts $ 26238.

New-York Historical Society

sini's *Il Turco in Italia,* Lind even more overwhelmingly affirmed her "active intimacy with nature," as Dwight poetically chose to refer to the vocal gymnastics with which she shamed the flutes in the *Trio concertant* from *A Camp in Silesia.* Dwight admittedly was as dazzled as the merest musical illiterate among her hearers by her "Herdsman's Song," credited to the Swedish composer Olof Åhlström (1756–1838), with its spectacular echo effects. "Singularly wild, quaint, and innocent," he described it, with its "odd musical interval (a sharp seventh) of the repeated call of the cows, the joyful laugh, and the echo, as if her singing had brought the very mountains there." "The Herdsman's Song," Lind's indestructible warhorse, was rapturously cheered and duly repeated, The "Greeting to America" then brought the concert to a tumultuous close,[77] and the hysterical audience yet again "broke out in a tempest of cheers, only less vehement than those which welcomed her in 'Casta Diva.'"

The cheers now became mingled with shouts of "Where's Barnum?" whereupon that demure impresario appeared and, with the air of a shrinking violet, disingenuously announced that henceforth "Barnum is nowhere." He then informed the audience of Lind's munificent "bequest" to a dozen New York charities. A bombshell!

"This announcement was the signal for another storm," continues the *Tribune.* "We did not count the number of cheers given, but we never witnessed such a pitch of enthusiasm."

In the meantime, Lind had quietly departed, "and the excited crowd, after a few more cheers, reluctantly took the cue and slowly sauntered out of the Castle door and down the canopied bridge in a glow of good humor and admiration. A few disorderly vagrants collected on the bridge leading to the Bath Houses [at the Battery] hooted at the throng as it passed out, but everybody went home quietly, with a new joy at his heart and a new thought in his brain."

But not everyone went home. As the *Tribune* relates: "The members of the Musical Fund Society, on hearing of Mlle. Lind's magnificent gift to them, immediately repaired to the New-York Hotel [where Lind had moved to escape the mob scenes at the Irving House],[78] accompanied by Dodworth's Band. The occasion was not so much a serenade as a renewal of the ovation at the Garden. The band played animated airs; the thousands assembled roused the midnight with their incessant cheers; and at last Mlle. Lind was obliged to appear on the balcony and acknowledge their jubilant salutation. . . . The members of the Society expressed their heartfelt thanks on the occasion, and at last the great crowd dispersed. So ends the night of Jenny Lind's first concert in America—truly the greatest triumph of her life."[79]

[77] Rounding out the program, Belletti sang the *Largo al factotum* from Rossini's *Il barbiere di Siviglia* and Benedict and Richard Hoffman played a Thalberg Fantasie on themes from *Norma* for two pianos (all but inaudible in that vast hall). Of the "Greeting to America," Dwight tactfully reported that Benedict had set Taylor's poem to "a vigorous and familiar style of music, well harmonizing with the words," but the less subtle Saroni wrote: ". . . the author of the words seems not to have the shadow of an idea of what a song should be, and we are not astonished that Benedict has made but poor work of it" (*Musical Times,* September 14, 1850, p. 603). Nonetheless, the song could not have been more enthusiastically received, had it been the masterpiece of the ages.

[78] The choice of the New-York Hotel for Lind's relocation was rumored to have enriched Barnum by $1000.

[79] "It was one o'clock when the fine horns of Dodworth's Band died away upon our sleeping ear," reported the *Evening Post* (September 12, 1850). The following evening Lind was serenaded by the German *Liederkranz.*♪

Yet, to finish with, Dwight, an ardent Germanophile to the core, was compelled to add, even in this first rapturous hymn of praise: "We are now sure of Jenny Lind, the Singer and the Artist. . . . But we have yet to hear her in the kind of music which seems to us most to need and to deserve such a singer—in the Agatha of *Der Freyschütz,* and in Mozart and the deep music of the great modern German operas" (*Tribune,* September 12, 1850). It was a theme on which he would expand as Lind's triumphant first season in New York progressed.

Amid the overwhelming journalistic ecstasy over the Nightingale, it was notably Richard Grant White, now returned to the *Courier and Enquirer* after a two-year absence, who, if anything, exceeded Dwight's outpourings, not only in emotional intensity but also in prodigal expenditure of verbiage. Protesting that he was utterly at a loss to find words adequate to express his reactions to Lind's miraculous flawlessness, White filled vast columns of his outsized newspaper with outsized lauds in tiny print. Lind's voice he particularly described as "neither sharp nor cold, but full, luscious, and vibrating; one of those rare voices—a sympathetic soprano." It was an injustice to call her a Nightingale, he said. True, she could "warble" like a nightingale, but her voice was "too full of human emotion to be likened to anything which ever came from the throat of a bird."

Everything she sang was the perfection of perfection, but in the "Herdsman's Song," in which she accompanied herself at the piano, she created the illusion of an echo with "a skill which is past all belief, save that obtained by actual hearing."[80]

Strong seems to have remained impervious to the prevailing mania, except to be amused by it.

September 17. . . . Strolled the Battery for an hour after sunset very pleasantly, and watched the shoals of people pouring into Castle Garden to hear Jenny. She is like the good little girl in the fairy story who spat pearls and diamonds out of her mouth whenever she opened it to speak, only Jane's [*sic*] expectorations are five-dollar bills, each syllable—a variation that suits the more prosaic imagery of the nineteenth century. The house at her first concert holding $36,000 worth [by Barnum's reckoning it was $17,864.05], how much did each semi-quaver realize to the parties interested?

~

The critical rapture over Lind did not remain unanimous for long. By her third concert,[81] Richard Grant White had undergone a total about-face and, as his journalis-

[80] *Figaro!* (September 14, 1850, p. 22) reported that the members of the orchestra gathered around her when she performed "The Echo Song," as "The Herdsman's Song" was popularly called, and that they were as incredulous at this astounding *tour de force* as was the audience.

[81] Lind's second concert, on September 13, duplicated the program of the first. Her following programs at Castle Garden were similarly repeated in pairs. Thus, at her third and fourth concerts (September 17 and 19) she sang, in Italian, the Queen of the Night aria from the first act of *The Magic Flute, Qui la voce* from Bellini's *I puritani, Quand je quittai la Normandie* from Meyerbeer's *Robert le diable,* and *Ah! non giunge* from *La sonnambula;* in English, "Take this Lute," a ballad by Benedict; and, of course, in Swedish, "The Herdsman's Song." Belletti sang the *Vi ravviso* from *La sonnambula, Non più andrai* from *Le nozze di Figaro,* and Rossini's *La tarantella.* Benedict conducted the orchestra in the overtures to Rossini's *William Tell* and Auber's *La Muette de Portici;* with one Weyner, a Belgian violinist, he played a piano and violin duet on themes from Bellini (at the fourth concert Weyner was supplanted by the German violinist Joseph Noll). Richard Hoffman played an unspecified piano solo by Leopold de Meyer.♪

tic colleagues gleefully kept score, was trading blows with Dwight over their now opposing assessments of Lind's emotional capacities or shortcomings. Headed "Funny Musical Criticism," the *Herald* (no supporter of Barnum and his projects)[82] on September 24 noted: "We find the critics of the *Tribune* and of the *Courier and Enquirer* lost in a labyrinth of words and fancies about Jenny Lind's concerts." Erroneously identifying the *Tribune* critic as "Mr. Bigelow of Boston," and facetiously referring to the six-foot-two White as "the greatest musical critic, in inches, at least, known to the metropolis," and therefore able to judge the quality of a "high note quicker than any man gifted with less elevated ears," the *Herald* presented its readers with a side-by-side sampling of the conflicting opinions of the two experts.

In this the *Herald* was imitating a recent piece in the *Spirit of the Times* (September 21, 1850, p. 372) that had ridiculed the pretentious antics of the two reviewers and examined the nature of their disagreement on the respective merits of "Mediterranean" versus "Northern" music, and of Lind's capacity, or lack of it, as a child of the North, ideally to perform the more impassioned Italian opera repertory to which she inconsistently adhered. Until after her third concert, the *Spirit* observed, "criticism was very general and consisted of the most lavish praise ever bestowed upon mortal." Now, because two of our "city critics" had come to be "very diversely wrought upon by the singing of the newcomer," the *Spirit* reprinted some samples of their conflicting comments, as compiled by *Gemotice* in the *Express.*

"The critic of the *Tribune* affects the German school, and potently believes 'that it is not in the genius of the Italian school to produce, or hardly appreciate, such a new revelation of song as this human nightingale, or canary, of Sweden'; while the critic of the *Courier* says that 'the passionful utterance which he finds among the Italians he does not look for among the countrymen of Beethoven and Mozart.' The critic of the *Tribune* 'from her singing drinks a new life, after long satiety of such passion-sweets as have become habits rather than fresh inspirations in the delightful—we may almost say, perfected, but yet confined—music of the Italians'; while the critic of the *Courier* is of the opinion that 'though she must impart delight and win admiration from all, the majority of American amateurs [music lovers] bear within their breasts a void her voice never can fill. . . . Vocal expression appears to be a direct communication of individual emotion, from which the reserved Northerner instinctively shrinks.'

"The critic of the *Tribune,* noticing Jenny Lind's performance of Mozart's 'Magico Flauto' music [writes]: 'She warmed to that music.' The critic of the *Courier* says it came from her lips with a 'cold, untouching, icy purity of tone and style.'"

Going beyond the mere question of the relative hotness or coldness of Southern versus Northern music, and how ideally to perform the one or the other, this writer, after more comparative citations, quotes White's statement that Lind's "style of delivering her voice is 'not the best,' and strongly intimates its being the result of mechani-

[82] On September 7 the *Mirror* waspishly wondered how it came about that the *Herald,* or was it "Mrs. Herald?" had devoted so little space, comparatively speaking, to the Nightingale. Barnum was cautioned to "pay some attention to Mrs. Herald (an unkind reference to Mrs. James Gordon Bennett,♪ who contributed music and drama criticism to her husband's newspaper), "or you won't hear from the Thunderer" (Bennett). In fact, at the outset the *Herald* had outdone its fellow-journals in its untrammeled transports over Lind, but had soon returned to its accustomed needling of Barnum, toward whom Bennett cherished an eternal enmity.

cal skill. The *Tribune* critic says, plumply, 'she is never mechanical, whatever you may say about want of passion.'"

The *Spirit* (or *Gemotice*) now ventured into deeper waters, speculating on the many-faceted nature of criticism, its doubtful capacity for objectivity, its wider implications, the presence or absence of an underlying critical integrity, and the critic's uses, if any, in the world of reality: "Here, certainly, be wide differences between our two critics. Whether of the twain shall we believe? Who is to settle for us the question which is the critic here and which the heretic? Is there no daysman [arbitrator] to stand between us, the public, and these differing teachers of the True and the Good? . . . The *Courier* critic not only differs, *toto caelo,* with the critic of the *Tribune,* but is somewhat at variance, as it strikes us, with himself. In the commencement of his *critique* he describes Jenny Lind's voice as . . . 'a rich, clear, powerful organ of the first class, lusciously sweet, strong, vibrating, and in itself sympathetic and possessing musical quality to such a degree that it is a marvel.' In the same review he denies to the singer all power to 'thrill,' all 'pathos,' and [attributes to her] 'entire inability to touch any heart which can be moved by sorrow.' . . . Her voice he, in one part of his article, describes as 'sympathetic,' and her tone and style, in another, as 'cold and untouching.'

"Now, while we admit the convenience, perhaps, or the necessity of *criticism* as a guide to show the unlearned the way in which we should go in forming a sound musical opinion, we confess we hold it expedient that our teacher gives a good proof of his competency to teach before we can follow him with any implicitness. Consistency with himself in his teaching is just the jewel which the proverb makes it, and if we see any flaw therein, we are very apt to cast it away as worthless. What said the great teacher of certain Pharisees of his time? 'Let them alone. They be teachers of the blind.' And if the blind lead the blind, both shall fall into the ditch."

The *Spirit,* therefore, advised the public to pay no heed to the critics and their superimposed opinions, and to rely on "that test which is the truest and the best"—their own instincts: "Go to Castle Garden and listen. You will hear and see the answer, given in a way that can leave no doubt upon your mind as to whether Jenny Lind has any 'power over the emotions of her hearers,' and whether they find 'the very craving unsatisfied which they went there to have allayed.'"

There was no equivocation, however, in Henry C. Watson's pronouncements on Jenny Lind. Although she was called the Nightingale, to him she was "the Sphinx." "Why, being so great, was she not greater?" he demanded. Stressing her "coldness," Watson catalogued a great number of faults and shortcomings and, dutifully, some aspects of her technical mastery. "In the highest department of the vocal art, we cannot place her in the front rank," he declared, and grudgingly added: "The public, by its vociferous plaudits and tumultuous encores, have pronounced her great—nay, greatest—and with our conscientious protest against the latter, we record its verdict. With the public she is omnipotent; thousands flock to see and hear her; she has thrown a spell over them by the marvels of her execution and the glories of her charities" (*Albion,* September 21, pp. 451–52).

The reviewer for the *Mirror* (obviously not Watson) shared the public's bewitchment. After her fourth concert he wrote: "Jenny is a perfect bird, and all that carping about the 'icy purity' of her tone never will dispel the charm which her warbling creates. She is without a parallel in the history of the world, and whether it be science, or genius, or all these combined, she has no equal as an effective vocalist, never has had, and we doubt if she ever will have, this side of Paradise; and even there she seems fitted to lead the heavenly choirs" (*Mirror,* September 20, 1850).

After her supremely triumphant sixth concert on September 24, at which some 10,000 hysterical adorers literally squeezed into every available inch of space at Castle Garden and spilled over into boats in the surrounding bay,[83] Watson stiffened his earlier assessment of Jenny Lind, claiming that he had formerly been too lenient. He professed to be "shocked at the outrages she committed upon common sense and good taste . . . her preposterous flights of misplaced and indifferently executed ornaments . . . were like decorating solid gold with sham diamonds." Any less famous singer guilty of such transgressions would have been "ridiculed as a charlatan." She had no sympathy or aptitude for the Italian school [a school that Watson had never defended until now] and "what she does not feel she cannot make others feel. . . . Coldness and hardness are the groundwork of a brilliant superstructure, which dazzles but warms not—flashes but bears no animating fire. It is the Aurora in the Frozen Sea, bewildering in its brilliancy, but leaving no other associations but death-like coldness."

True, Watson continued, Lind had no superior in the "music of the North, which requires rude energy and startling effects," but for some reason she perversely underplayed what she did best and focused her efforts on the music she did least well. Watson also criticized Lind for transposing everything up—more than a third up—"far into the unsympathetic regions of the voice." But, he obscurely concluded, it was not charitable to "pluck the borrowed feathers of this *rara avis*" (*Albion,* September 28, 1850, p. 464).

At least one-third of the audience at Lind's final concert at Castle Garden were ladies, the *Tribune* approvingly noted. The crowd was tremendous: "All the standing room in the balcony and parquette were soon filled, the aisles blocked up, the stairways covered, and about 500 stood on the outside balcony, looking in through the doors and windows. The hall was one solid mass of human beings"; but despite the "frightful heat," they were remarkably orderly. "There was real sublimity in the scene," wrote Dwight, "when Jenny Lind's voice, after one of her brilliant soarings into the highest heaven of melody, floated away into silence, and a hush, as complete as that of death, fell upon the house. . . . These Castle Garden concerts [had been] unequalled in moral grandeur," he wrote. Dwight doubted whether they had ever been surpassed for "brilliancy and magnitude," even in Europe.

At this last concert Lind looked radiant, was more inspired than ever, and more vociferously acclaimed.[84] Nearly everything was encored, and flowers by the bushelful

[83] A boat, filled with people who had paid 50 cents apiece, was floating nearby, and the surrounding waters were "black with small craft, at two shillings [25 cents] a seat" (*Herald,* September 29, 1850).

[84] At her fifth and sixth concerts Lind sang the *Prendi per me* from Donizetti's *L'elisir d'amore;* with Belletti a comic duet from Fioravanti's *Il fanatico per la musica;* the air "By the Sad Sea Waves," from Benedict's opera *The Brides of Venice* (London 1844); again the trio with two flutes from *A Camp in Silesia;* the *Ah! non giunge* from Bellini's *Sonnambula;* and the "Herdsman's Song." Belletti sang a cavatina from Donizetti's *Gemma di Vergy* and the popular *Barcarola* from Federico Ricci's opera *La prigione d'Edimburgo* (Trieste 1838); Richard Hoffman played a Fantasia (op. 27) by Thalberg, consisting of variations on "God Save the Queen" and "Rule Britannia" (and also, according to the advertisements, "Hail Columbia" and "Yankee Doodle"); and Benedict conducted the March from his opera *The Crusaders* and the overtures to Weber's *Der Freischütz* and Hérold's *Zampa.*

were flung at her feet. At the end, after the inevitable "Herdsman's Song," Barnum made his inevitable appearance and assured the audience that in October, after a short interruption for appearances in Boston and Philadelphia, Lind's "seventh concert" would take place at the opening of Jenny Lind Hall (*Tribune,* September 25, 1850).

In a final summing-up and analysis of the Lind experience, appearing in the *Tribune* on September 27, Dwight tirelessly rhapsodized upon Lind's boundless vocal virtues—her voice, execution, style, and her thousand-and-one other divine attributes. Not for her, he proclaimed, with her "Northern strength" and "depth of intellect," was the perpetual preoccupation with "sexual love" that constituted the entire basis of Italian opera. Although she "respected the senses, it was *Nature* that Lind translated with rapture in her song." She was not cold, but possessed the "soul of passion," rather than the "temperament of passion" (a nice distinction).

Those who accused her of coldness were those who swore by Donizetti and Bellini, and who considered "(to speak *à la* Carlyle) that the 'rose-pink' sentiment of their operas is infinitely more indicative of soul and genius than the grandest symphony of Beethoven, or the finest overture or song of Mendelssohn."

Dwight's only complaint was that Lind did not perform enough serious German music: "Give her the great German music, whether in the opera or the oratorio, or the songs of Schubert and of Mendelssohn, and they who know the feeling of that music will not miss [drama] in her singing thereof." Not that the music she had been singing was worthless: "If much of it was light, it was not without character."

Then the quintessential Dwightism: "The crowds whom she has delighted have at the same time caught something from her of the spirit of Art, which is the very spirit that must save our Republic and make earth a Heaven, if that ever is to be."

The spirit of Brook Farm was not dead.

On October 5, with the newspapers full of Lind's sensational exploits in Boston, George Templeton Strong—after noting in his journal that his wife Ellen had begun "a new course of musical education" under Claudio Bonzanini,♪ an Italian musician who had arrived in 1847 with the first Astor Place Opera Company—wrote: "Lindomania unabated; instead of an epidemic *lycanthropy* like that of the Middle Ages, it's a prevalent morbid passion for assuming the form of an ass and paying $600, and so on, for the privilege of drinking in her most sweet voice through the preternaturally prolonged ears of the deluded victims of this new terrible disorder."

And on the same day Philip Hone, who, too, had been following Lind's progress in Boston (as who had not?), wrote in his diary: "The Jenny Lind excitement continues without abatement. . . . A Boston music-seller [Ossian Dodge]♪ gave for the first seat $625, and this is not all; she sang in Providence two or three nights afterwards, and there a still greater fool was found, whose extravagance for the first seat reached $650. . . . She will be here in a few days and give her concerts in the new hall, called Tripler Hall, which had recently been erected opposite to my house."

It was not that simple. No sooner had Lind completed her Castle Garden series and departed on her tour than a hot, behind-the-scenes struggle for first possession of the new concert hall burst into the open, with the dauntless team of Madame Anna Bishop and Robert N. C. Bochsa♪ surprisingly emerging victorious over P. T. Barnum.

A puzzled *Tribune,* attempting to unravel this startling development, announced on September 26: "The new musical hall in Mercer Street is to be named after its pro-

Music Division, The New York Public Library

Barnum is depicted introducing Jenny Lind to Ossian Dodge, the publicity-conscious first purchaser, for $625, of a ticket for the Swedish Nightingale's first concert in Boston.

prietor—Tripler Hall—instead of Jenny Lind Hall, as has been talked about." The *Tribune* thought it unlikely, however, that Madame Bishop would open the new hall, although it was even less likely that Jenny Lind and Madame Bishop would "sing in the same hall at the same time." And it was least likely of all that Madame Bishop would consent to perform in a hall bearing the name of Jenny Lind.

Refusing to accept this unpalatable defeat, Barnum persisted in advertising the resumption of Jenny Lind's New York concerts at the gala opening of "Jenny Lind Hall." Up to October 14, three days before Madame Bishop actually opened Tripler Hall, contradictory advertisements in the papers for Bishop and Lind continued to follow each other.

Earlier, in July, preceded by inflated reports of their vast monetary and artistic triumphs in Latin America, and heralded by flourishes of the Watsonian trumpet, Madame Bishop and her obese Svengali[85] had returned from their long tour. In the *Mirror* (July 6, 1850), Watson sang Madame Bishop's praises: with her iron will she had triumphed over the antagonisms and jealousies that so unjustly had prevented her, despite her great artistry, from being engaged for the Astor Place opera. Nonetheless, her tours throughout North and South America, magnificently managed by Bochsa, had netted her great dividends in pearls, diamonds, stocks, and fame. On her recent tour of Mexico alone, she had cleared some $23,000.

Bochsa, too, received lengthy biographical treatment in the *Mirror* (August 20, 1850), stressing his great career as a composer, conductor, and supreme harp virtuoso in the courts of Napoleon Bonaparte and George IV, and omitting both his quick getaway from France, where he had been convicted for embezzlement, and his scandalous elopement from England with Mrs. Bishop, the wife of the illustrious composer Henry Rowley Bishop.♪ Despite these formidable distractions, Bochsa had yet managed, according to Watson, to compose "innumerable ballets, several operas, symphonies, overtures, sacred works . . . besides nearly 2000 pieces for the harp."

Determined once and for all to dominate all aspects of the New York music scene—opera, concert, oratorio, the music theatre, popular music, everything—in defiance of the current excitement over the Havana opera company at Castle Garden and of the mounting hysteria over Jenny Lind's impending arrival, on August 20 Bishop/Bochsa, with mighty fanfare, brought out a spectacular "new" opera, *Judith,* written and "composed" by Bochsa for Madame Bishop. Ballyhooed as a "Grand and Magnificent Opera Spectacle in five tableaux," it was presented at the Astor Place Opera House, where a summer season of theatre was currently in progress under the management of the well-known Shakespearean actor Charles Bass.

Bochsa's libretto for *Judith,* a biblical extravaganza, was translated from the original Spanish by Henry C. Watson (apparently *Judith* had been concocted for the Latin American tour). The score consisted of some eighteen excerpts lifted from various Verdi operas—*Nabucco, Ernani, Macbeth, I Lombardi, I masnadieri,* and *Giovanna d'Arco*—and altered by Bochsa to provide Madame Bishop with a virtually non-stop showcase.[86] "The whole thing is nothing but a solo of two hours length for Madame Anna Bishop, with occasional *obbligato* accompaniment of a bass voice [Pietro Novelli's] and with *refrains* by the chorus," wrote the *Musical Times* (August 31, 1850, p. 578).

The elaborate production, stage-directed by the renowned actor/manager Francis C. Wemyss, offered, according to the advertisements, "new and costly scenery, costumes, decorations, a grand incidental ballet" led by the well-known *danseuse* Madame Augusta, a "powerful chorus, and an onstage military band, wearing "dramatic costumes." (It was funny, wrote Saroni, to see "old Wiese, of oboe celebrity, in Oriental dress showing off on the stage.") The subsidiary characters were sung by Mrs. Boulard♪ and Messrs. Müller and Beutler.

[85] It was later believed that George du Maurier's celebrated novel *Trilby* (1894) was modeled on the Bishop/Bochsa liaison.♪

[86] Saroni mentions a cavatina from *Ernani,* "from which, with the admirable foresight of Mr. Bochsa, all the disagreeable notes (too high or too low for her voice) had been abducted." Yet, "much averse as we are to clap-trap . . . and particularly so in an artist like Madame Bishop, we cannot but acknowledge that she is an artist of the first rank. Her voice, if not powerful, is fresh; her compass, if not extensive, comprises the most beautiful and even notes, and her school is FAULTLESS" (*Musical Times,* August 21, 1850, p. 589).

Girvice Archer, Jr.

Music Division, The New York Public Library

Madame Anna Bishop and Robert N. C. Bochsa, her perennial Svengali.

Following the opera, an appropriate Eastern Divertimento—*The Beautiful Captive*—was danced by Madame Augusta and her *corps de ballet*. Then, as a special treat, Madame Bishop appeared in less appropriate Mexican costume and sang "in Castillano" a Mexican song, *La Pasadita*. At her few succeeding performances at Astor Place, Madame Bishop varied her solos, presenting in costume her renowned *scena*s from Donizetti's *Linda di Chamounix* and Rossini's *Tancredi*.

To Saroni the libretto and music of *Judith* were "but one succession of incongruities, and if anything more was wanting to make the whole performance ridiculous it was the introduction of a ballet in a plot like this" *(ibid.)*. But the *Albion* (sounding most unsuitably like Watson) was lost in praise of the entire production. "Several who heard *[Judith]* said they had no idea that Verdi's music was so good." It had been transformed by Bochsa's masterly reorchestrations: ". . . instead of those outrages upon good taste with which Verdi's instrumentation abounds, that storm of *piccoli,* trumpets, drums, trombones, etc., etc., we have intelligent accompaniments full of meaning and sentiment, and supporting most effectively some really lovely melodies, whose beauties have been hitherto obscured by gross and unmeaning over-instrumenting." In short, Bochsa was a genius. As for Madame Bishop, she was, if possible, even more wonderful than before. Her voice had the ravishing effect of an Aeolian harp (*Albion,* August 24, 1850, p. 404).

The *Mirror* (again sounding suspiciously like Watson) similarly lauded Bochsa: such miracles as he achieved with his orchestra had never been heard in this city. Bochsa was one of the most accomplished conductors alive. And Madame Bishop! "Her singing is the very perfection of nature embellishing art, but every vocal effort is executed with such perfect ease that nature alone is seen."

But despite general predictions of a long run, *Judith* was abruptly withdrawn after four performances to disastrously meager houses, and mutually vengeful recriminations and accusations were forthwith traded in the press by Bochsa and Charles Bass, the latter apparently having lost his shirt on the extravagant production. In a more modest version, on September 2, *Judith* was put on at the Broadway Theatre, where, embellished by several of Madame Bishop's *scena*s in costume—among them a "grand American Allegorical Finale," in which she sang "Hail Columbia"—it ran for two weeks, then disappeared.

In the meantime, the indefatigably manipulative Bochsa had been exerting his Machiavellian wiles upon A. B. Tripler, the lessee of the new concert hall, and by some unknown means had managed to outfox Barnum, who serenely continued to believe that the franchise for the opening and succeeding use of the new auditorium rested securely with him. Rumors that Bishop/Bochsa had paid Tripler $1000 for "*the opening night only*" were hotly denied in the pro-Bishop *Mirror* (October 5, 1850).

"It has been freely stated," later reported the pro-Barnum *Tribune* (October 21, 1850), "that Mr. Barnum was headed off by Mr. Bochsa in the engagement of Tripler Hall, and was obliged to surrender the use of it for Madame Bishop's concerts without his consent." Not so, asserted the *Tribune,* and to disprove this unlikely contention, quoted a "document" to "show that the great *entrepreneur* was not out-generaled, but had voluntarily resigned his claim to the hall in favor of Madame Bishop until the present date." The *Tribune* also cited a purported letter of agreement with Tripler, in which Barnum "voluntarily waived his rights to the possession of the Hall until October 23, 1850," the new date set for Jenny Lind's first concert there.

But N. P. Willis slyly referred to the "dis-baptising of Jenny Lind Hall" as "The Tripler War" and roguishly punned on the hall's "consecration by the Bishop of Bochsa." Willis regarded the Bishop/Bochsa takeover of the hall as "but the opening hostilities of a campaign against the angelic Jenny . . . the war is to be one of classes—Bochsa and Fashion against Jenny and the People" (*Home Journal,* October 12, 1850).[87]

Once their grand coup was accomplished, Bishop/Bochsa proceeded to out-Barnum Barnum in the grandiloquence of the advertisements for their projected concerts. They would open Tripler Hall with not one, but "three First Grand Concerts" on consecutive evenings: programs of secular music on October 17, 18, and 19, at one dollar a ticket (for each concert); and on October 20, a Sunday, Madame Bishop (of course, with Bochsa's assistance) would present the first in a series of weekly sacred concerts at fifty cents. Their strategy was obvious. As Philip Hone observed in his diary on October 21: "Our sight-seeing, novelty-hunting population were treated last evening to a new entertainment at the Tripler Hall, a grand sacred concert under the direction of Mrs. Anna Bishop and Mr. Bochsa. . . . The price of admission is only fifty cents; we may go twenty times to hear Madame Bishop's Sunday evenings at the cost of one of the Nightingale's exhibitions, and get more for our money, with the exception of not seeing how 'the Jenny' looks."

The Bishop/Bochsa offensive was waged on all promotional fronts. "This Hall," stated their introductory blast, appearing in all the newspapers, "unquestionably the most magnificent Musical Edifice, not only in this country, but IN THE WHOLE WORLD, unequalled in the grandeur of its design, the gorgeousness of its embellishments, and the arrangements for the luxurious accommodation of its guests, *seating comfortably* 5000 persons, has been constructed *with special reference to the perfection of acoustic effect.*

[87] Later, after Willis had mounted the Lind bandwagon and driven off at a furious gallop, he wrote that Tripler Hall, "filled with the presence of Jenny Lind . . . was a fairer place to look on than when the most conspicuous object in its midst was the projecting stomach of Signor Bochsa" (*Home Journal,* November 2, 1850).

New-York Historical Society

"Tripler's" (Tripler) Hall, the object of the great Lind/Bishop rivalry.

"In the course of these splendid entertainments, prepared [and subsidized] by Madame Anna Bishop, choice selections of the classical and Magnificent works of the GREAT Masters and also of Deservingly Popular Music, will be given on the plan of the celebrated musical performances at THE CONSERVATOIRE IN PARIS, the LONDON PHILHARMONIC, and the Great Music Festivals in England and Academies of Germany and Italy.

"The magnitude and perfection of the Vocal and Instrumental arrangements for the occasion, both in respect to number and talent, have never before been attempted in the United States.

"INSTRUMENTAL DEPARTMENT. The Violins will number no less than 50 performers; the Violas, the Violoncellos, and Double Basses being in full proportion, The Wind Instruments will be QUADRUPLED, being DOUBLE THE NUMBER GENERALLY USED.

"Choral Department under the superintendence of Mr. William A. King,♪ Organist of Grace Church, will number two hundred voices. The whole under the direction of MR. BOCHSA." And not surprisingly: "Assistant Director of Musical Department, Henry C. Watson."

There can be little doubt that the Assistant Director of the Musical Department was the author of the foregoing, and also of a press release published by the *Message Bird* (October 15, 1850, p. 495) that not only reiterated the gaudy claims of the advertisement, but announced future plans of even more dazzling grandeur.

Madame Bishop and Bochsa (and behind the scenes, Watson) intended to preempt the field in ways undreamed of by Barnum: "As this series of grand concerts progresses," the prospectus stated, "the foundation of an extensive Musical Library will be laid, where all the Operatic, Symphonic, Oratorial, and other Scores, together with the finest practical and theoretical works in all languages, will be found for the use of all who need them. A Conservatory of Musical Education in the higher branches will also be established; and last though not least, a Vocal Society, on the scale of that at Exeter Hall, London, will be begun and carried into active operation. To Mr. Bochsa the credit of this novel scheme is due."[88] But glorious as all this was, the *Message Bird* was compelled to voice a single misgiving: "Thus far in its progress, we perceive no place for the erection of an Organ, so essential in the performance of oratorial music. How is this?"

Built under the supervision of John M. Trimble, the architect of the Broadway Theatre,♪ the new hall—the first to be built in New York specifically for the performance of music—was indeed expected to be unsurpassed in the United States. According to preliminary descriptions in the press, it would occupy 150 feet on Mercer Street to a depth of 100 feet, and would possess a "magnificent dome" 90 feet up from street level; half of its forty-eight windows in the Grecian style would face on Mercer Street and half on an opposite court; eight vomitories[89] would provide rapid exit for as many as 5000 people within five minutes in case of fire. Two entrances on Broadway (the rear of the building) would approach the hall by white marble staircases; four other staircases, fifteen feet wide, would give onto Mercer Street.

The gorgeous interior would comprise a gallery around three sides of the hall at an elevation of twenty-five feet, supported by iron columns with gilt flutings and capitals in the Italian style. Occupants of the boxes would repose on rosewood sofas cushioned in crimson velvet; the parquette seats would provide uninterrupted sight-lines to all parts of the stage. Light would be dispensed by magnificent chandeliers of Bohemian glass, each having twenty-five gas burners; three rows of burners attached to the walls would illuminate the stage; and no less than 700 burners would light the "audience part." Decorations would consist chiefly of murals and medallions painted on the walls and ceiling, and of mirrors. A kitchen in the basement would provide for banquets and other functions held in the second-floor dining and reception areas (*Spirit*, August 17, 1850, p. 312).

Although these plans were radically altered, the *Albion*'s reviewer of the opening

[88] The "novel scheme" had first been proposed in 1846 by the late critic and editor A. D. Paterson,♪ and most recently in the *Evening Post*, which on March 1, 1850, had outlined an elaborate plan for an "immense building" that would comprise "a lodging house, a musical hall, rooms, restaurants, stores, and a public garden." The *Post* credited Edward P. Fry, the failed former manager of the Astor Place Opera, with the concept.

[89] Delicately misquoted as "dormitories" in Ware and Lockhard (p. 13).

New-York Historical Society

The elegant interior of Tripler Hall.

concert (ostensibly Watson) pronounced the hall not only to be unmatched for magnificence "on this continent," but to possess acoustics—"that most incomprehensible science"—preferable to any he had heard, even in Europe.

Philip Hone, however, who had unreservedly admired the new hall at a preview for invited guests on October 14,[90] on returning there noted that the huge auditorium, for all its beauty, possessed only "one door of entrance and exit, a serious fault in the construction of the building and calculated to alarm timid people, for if the interior would be on fire, there would be no means of escape, and," Hone wickedly punned, "the immense mass of respectable men and well-dressed women would get up an awful performance of a new 'Der Fry-schutz'" (Hone, MS Diary, October 24, 1850).[91]

[90] When Dodworth's Band had been present to "test the acoustics."

[91] Hone's complaint was widely shared. In answer to the general observation that the hall, with its narrow winding stairs and inadequate single exit, was a firetrap, Frederick A. Peterson, the hall's

Bad weather marred the opening, and the *Albion* reported that the audience of 2000 to 3000 (*Figaro!* estimated 1000 to 1200)—many of whom were merely curious to see the new hall—looked insignificant in that huge space. Inauspiciously, the start of the concert, announced for eight o'clock, was delayed nearly an hour, due to some unfortunate mixup in the distribution of the orchestra parts. But it was worth waiting for: once the first bars of Beethoven's Fifth Symphony were heard, it became obvious that the true grandeur of Beethoven was being perceived for the first time in this country. Never before had the work been so totally realized. For once, there were sufficient strings to balance the usually overloud brasses, "that plague of our modern orchestras." Besides, what a pleasure to witness the simultaneous movement of those fifty bow arms!

And Madame Bishop! Again, never before had her voice been so beautiful, so dazzling, so earnest, so passionate! Her Mozart aria (*Dove sono* from *Le nozze di Figaro*) was a heavenly delight; the listeners were enchanted. "Who says the taste for good music is not increasing?" the reviewer crowed. Madame Bishop was as superb in the cavatina *Ah, quando in regio* from Donizetti's opera *Ugo, conte di Parigi* (Milan 1832) as she was in the tear-provoking Scottish ballad "Auld Robin Gray" and its encore "John Anderson, my Jo." True, Novelli, her assisting artist, labored through a Mercadante aria, and the chorus, although comprising admirable vocal material, were less than good in the first known performance in America of Beethoven's *Meeresstille und glückliche Fahrt,* op. 112 (1815), and in the Hallelujah Chorus from Handel's *Messiah.* But all the same, Bochsa deserved the highest praise for his masterly conducting and his splendid choice of program.

The critics were mostly in enthusiastic agreement. But the *Evening Post* (October 18, 1850), although conceding that Madame Bishop was beautifully dressed and sang exquisitely, nonetheless thought the event, with its rows of empty seats, unworthy of the momentous occasion. Had Jenny Lind opened the hall, the event would have been properly festive; Tripler was to be blamed for having made the wrong decision, whatever the inducements.

George Templeton Strong, his musical appetite perhaps reawakened by a delightful extempore musical visit from the Maurans on October 14, broke his prolonged abstinence from concerts and attended the opening.

October 18. . . . Last night with Ellie to Mrs. Bishop's concert.[92] Opening of Tripler Hall. Room ornate and spacious, well suited for its purposes, and its decorations, on the whole, tasteful. Concert rather a failure—orchestra a multitudinous, undisciplined mob, with Bochsa to lead it; chorus little better. The C-minor Symphony badly played, of course (except the Andante), but human bungling can't much interfere with its splendors. Chorus [sang] *Meeresstille,* called Beethoven's—never heard it—or of it—before, and it was as dead and flat as its subject. Overture to [Weber's] *Euryanthe,* air

original architect, absolved himself in a letter to the editor of the *Tribune,* published December 6, 1850. Peterson claimed that his original plans for wide, straight staircases had been disapproved by Tripler, and that litigation over Tripler's apparent breach of contract was now pending.

[92] In a confusion of errata, this entry, as transcribed in Strong's published *Diary* (II, 23), has the Strongs attending "Mr. Bishop's concert," led by one "Bochs," and sung by "Mrs. Bochsa."

Madame Anna Bishop.

from *The Marriage of Figaro,* deliciously sung by Mrs. Bishop, and for finale the "Hallelujah Chorus," which they triumphed over completely and killed dead by singing it to the time of a dead march. But for the Symphony and Overture, the performance would have been a bore. But two bars of either, intelligibly rendered, can leaven and redeem two hours of trash.

The idea of people being worried and anxious about a little more or less of income, when there are such things to make one happy on earth!

~

This program was repeated the following evening. On October 19, Bochsa conducted Mozart's "Jupiter" Symphony and Rossini's Overture to *La gazza ladra,* and Madame Bishop as usual excelled herself in a cavatina from Meyerbeer's opera *Il crociato in Egitto,* a *buffo* duet from *L'elisir d'amore* with Novelli, and "The Last Rose of Summer," which she again encored with "John Anderson, my Jo." Apparently unable to relinquish the stage even for an instant—a characteristic for which she was mightily praised—Madame Bishop joined with the chorus in a madrigal, Constanzo Festa's "Down in a Flow'ry Vale," and in the finale of Beethoven's *Mount of Olives.* The veteran English tenor Charles Manvers expertly performed an air from Weber's *Oberon,* and the *Symphonie concertante* for four violins and orchestra, by Ludwig Maurer, was played by Mott, Groeschel, Herwig, and Wiegers, evidently members of the giant orchestra.[93]

On Sunday, October 20, Madame Bishop launched her weekly series of popular-priced Grand Sacred Concerts. Assisted by Edward Seguin, Charles Manvers, and Miss Emmeline De Luce, and with Bochsa conducting and Frederick Lyster the chorus master (not W. A. King, as previously announced), her program embraced excerpts from Handel's *Messiah* and *Samson* and Rossini's *Stabat Mater.* The audience of 3000, again reportedly looking small in that vast auditorium, were treated to a taste of "the divine grandeur of the great composers [of whose sublimity] we have so long been left in ignorance," noted the *Mirror* (October 21, 1850) in a pointed reference to the absence of a singing society in New York for the past two years.

Philip Hone, who attended the concert, reported that "the ground floor and first gallery of the spacious, splendid hall were filled with a respectable, attentive audience who seemed to be seriously impressed with the grandeur and sublimity of the performance, and no doubt many of them thought (and so did I) that they were 'worshipping the Lord in the beauty of holiness.' What will some of the Mrs. Grundys say to this?" Hone was evidently questioning the Mrs. Grundys' unconditional acceptance of this notoriously adulterous couple as dispensers of sanctity. "As for my part," he liberally added, "I see *no* offense to religion or good taste in it" (Hone, MS Diary, October 21, 1850).

Indeed, *Figaro!* saw the concerts as a forceful gesture toward moral uplift: For "thousands of young men at loose ends on a Sunday, such concerts will prove a stronger attraction than the Broadway side walk, the bar room, the [oyster] cellar, and the saloon. . . . Nor will the good end here: the glorious sacred harmonies they hear will tend to cultivate their tastes, the society of female relatives and friends who will gladly accompany them will chasten their thoughts, improve the tone of their conversation, and draw them imperceptibly from the society of the base and vicious to that of home and all its happier associations" (*Figaro!,* October 26, 1850, p. 111).

To Mordecai M. Noah, more hospitable to Bishop/Bochsa than to Barnum/Lind, the effort represented as well an inspiring act of personal moral courage on the part of Madame Bishop: "If this experiment does not result in any profit to Madame Bishop—and amidst other and greater musical excitements we did not anticipate much—it nevertheless exhibits an energy and a determination not to be overshadowed by transitory meteors" (*Times and Messenger,* October 13, 1850).

[93] The four-violin concerto, heard at the Philharmonic earlier in the year (April 20), was evidently a substitution for a piano quartet (not identified), announced to be played by "four eminent professors" on Pirsson's Mammoth Double Grand Pianoforte (discussed below). This novel item unfortunately had to be canceled because, as the papers explained, none of the locally available piano professors was willing to play a "second part."

On Thursday, October 24, between Madame Bishop's first and second sacred concerts, the "transitory meteor" in question (Jenny Lind) at last appeared at Tripler Hall—"the Grand Opening of Tripler Hall," the *Post* stubbornly insisted. Announced for October 23, her concert was delayed by a day to allow the stage to be enlarged so that the orchestra and chorus might occupy the same floor level as the soloist. At first announced for Mondays, Wednesdays, and Fridays, Lind's concert nights were changed to Tuesdays, Thursdays, and Fridays, to avoid conflict with Maretzek's opera at Astor Place (whose opening, on October 21, the Nightingale had reportedly attended).

On October 7, in advance of Lind's return, the *Herald* launched a virulent campaign against Barnum, accusing him of exploiting the press, the public, and angelic Jenny Lind for his own dire purposes;[94] on October 12 it scathingly debunked the Prize Song episode; and on October 23, just before Lind's first concert at Tripler Hall, it accused Barnum of profiteering with his exorbitant ticket prices and of being in league with the speculators, who were reaping a golden harvest. People were willing to pay the already too high price of three dollars for a ticket, claimed the *Herald,* but with six, eight, or even ten dollars being demanded by those who had "monopolized the best seats," the public had become unwilling to be made "dupes of such a system." The *Herald* pointed out that with all 5500 seats in Tripler Hall occupied at $3 each, and after all expenses were deducted, Barnum and Lind would still net $6000 each per concert, or $18,000 a week, or $270,000 a year. Each. "Quite a pretty sum to make out of public curiosity and the talents of one individual." At this rate Barnum would soon be able to "buy a German principality, with all the crown jewels and royal blood in the bargain. We must therefore teach him to be contented with what the public are willing to give him—THREE DOLLARS, AND NO MORE."[95]

The next day the *Herald* continued the attack, but also published Barnum's elaborate self-justification, broadcast to all the papers, stating that apart from the tickets set aside for the press, the number of seats at Tripler Hall was 3240, not 5500, as inflatedly reported; that the ticket prices were three, four, and five dollars according to location (they were, in fact, advertised up to $8); and that the speculators received no more than a five per-cent discount and were pledged, on their sacred honors, to charge no more than the printed price. Tickets were purportedly available at the music stores at no advanced prices.

Barnum took this opportunity to lash out at the newspapers that had attacked him—the *Herald* was not alone. Their enmity, he claimed, had been instigated by a hostile editor who "does not get free tickets to the concerts" (James Gordon Bennett?) and abetted by "a noted musical individual who considers me in his way," and who had paid for the abusive articles (Bochsa?).

Perhaps Barnum realized at this point that he had pushed public malleability too far, for on October 25 he made known through the press a purported exchange of letters with Lind, wherein she had urged him to withhold tickets from the speculators and to limit prices of admission to a three- to five-dollar range, and he had assented because the hall was large enough to warrant such a reduction of the top prices. "Now," triumphantly crowed the *Herald* (October 25, 1850), "the million will rush to

[94] For the full text of the *Herald*'s indictment of Barnum, see APPENDIX 2.

[95] Commenting on this controversy, the *Evening Post* (October 23, 1850) contended that people would willingly pay anything to hear Lind.

her concerts, pay their money for three-dollar tickets, and be gratified. Nor will any sting be left behind."

The attacks on Barnum nonetheless continued, and it was obvious that his manipulation of the New York press and public—at least insofar as Jenny Lind was concerned—was a thing of the past. The original public frenzy, too, seems to have been spent. With the move to Tripler Hall, the very atmosphere of Lind's concerts appears to have undergone a transformation. At her first concert there, a capacity audience—but a decorative, orderly, and discriminating one—accorded her a warm, not a hysterical, welcome.[96] As George William Curtis, who had succeeded his friend and mentor John Sullivan Dwight (now back in Boston) as Lind's official adorer on the *Tribune,* wrote after the concert (October 25, 1850): "The first fierce excitement has passed, and, as she is promised to us for as long as we choose to hear her, there was an evident settling down to a long enjoyment in the manner of the audience."[97] Saroni remarked that for the first time it was possible to listen to Lind without "being interrupted by deafening cheers and wild outbursts of delight"[98] (*Musical Times,* October 26, 1850, p. 50).

Lind, too, seems to have gained a new poise and musical seriousness. Even Watson expressed bafflement at her great "improvement" since Castle Garden, where she had "seemed to run wild, singing without care, reveling in unbridled excess of vocal facility, regardless of propriety or common sense. Now, at Tripler Hall, how great the change! Careful, quiet, and correct, she leaves Mozart and Weber ungarnished, unornamented, keeping her voluble and brilliant *fioriture* for its appropriate vehicle, the shallow Italian framework" (*Albion,* November 2, 1850, p. 524).

The Weber works that earned Watson's approval (and undoubtedly Dwight's, even *in absentia*) were the *Leise, leise, fromme Weise* from *Der Freischütz,* which Lind sang in German at her first two concerts (October 24 and 25), and from the same opera, again in German, *Und ob die Wolke* at the third and fourth concerts (October 29 and 31). Of Mozart, she sang the *Non mi dir* from *Don Giovanni* (October 29), the *Dove sono* (November 9) and *Deh vieni* (November 19) from *The Marriage of Figaro,* and the *Non paventar (O zittre nicht, mein lieber Sohn)* from *The Magic Flute* (November 9).

In the staggering fifteen concerts that Jenny Lind gave at Tripler Hall within the scant period of a month (October 23 to November 22), her programs copiously relied as well on the maligned "shallow Italian framework." Alone she sang arias from *La sonnambula, I puritani, Lucia di Lammermoor, Norma* (again the *Casta diva*), and *Il Turco in Italia.* In various combinations with Belletti, the tenor Natale Perelli (1816–1866) (im-

[96] Despite the popular legend that Lind was the darling of "the million" rather than the "upper ten," the *Herald* (October 25, 1850) reported that Broadway after the concert was a solid mass of private carriages for several blocks on either side of Tripler Hall, and it was not until an hour later that the last of them drove away.

[97] "The mania for these concerts, although less noisy than in an earlier day, is on the increase, and having taken a sober character, may prevail for a considerable period," wrote the *Herald* on November 1, after Lind's fourth concert, and further predicted: "Those who had been unwilling to attend when the flood of excitement knew no bounds, will now avail themselves of every opportunity to hear the melodious Nightingale of Sweden."

[98] Philip Hone "gave four dollars" to attend Lind's first Tripler Hall concert, and "got a good seat in the gallery. . . . It was a beautiful performance," he wrote. "There is a magic in her voice, a sort of bird-like sweetness, which is peculiar to her and constitutes her charm" (Hone, MS Diary, October 24, 1850).

ported from Philadelphia), and a shadowy Miss Pintard (a contralto also from Philadelphia), she performed (in Italian) ensembles from *Robert le diable, La figlia del reggimento, L'elisir d'amore,* and *Il Turco in Italia.* With Kyle and Siede she frequently repeated the *Trio concertant* from *A Camp in Silesia;* with Miss Pintard she sang *La Mère grande* [*sic*], the idiosyncratic title accorded Meyerbeer's duet *Die Grossmutter (La Grandmère),* described by Curtis as "one of the most melodious popularities of unmelodious Meyerbeer" (*Tribune,* November 6, 1850).

Perhaps to take the wind out of Madame Bishop's sails (and at the same time to reaffirm her own angelic persona), at various times during her sojourn Lind performed sacred works: the *Inflammatus* from Rossini's *Stabat Mater,* which she sang with a chorus assembled and trained by George Loder; "On mighty pens" from Haydn's *The Creation;* and, after her presentation on November 1 of Handel's *Messiah,* "I know that my Redeemer liveth."

Lind's performance of *Messiah,* assisted by Emmeline De Luce, Marcus Colburn, Belletti, and the Harmonic Society, elicited a storm of mixed reactions from the wayward press. To Richard Storrs Willis, replacing his older brother N. P. Willis, who disqualified himself as a critic of sacred music, she was "Sweet Jenny Lind, the divinely-sent, [who] preached us the most faithful sermon . . . which we ever yet heard" (*Home Journal,* November 2, 1850). To an apparently regenerate Richard Grant White, her performance was "as purely beautiful as can be looked for from mortal lips" (*Courier and Enquirer,* November 2, 1850). To Saroni, now completely gone over to Bishop/Bochsa, Lind's Handel singing was "cold, correctly cold; the voice was there, but *heart* there was none"—he advised her not to repeat the experiment (*Musical Times,* November 9, 1850, p. 68). To Watson, Lind's sacred singing was a huge disappointment; not only was it colder than usual, but now she "exhibited a vulgarity in method which is altogether unpardonable—taking nearly all her intervals by *anticipation.* We could hardly believe our ears, but it was so"[99] (*Albion,* November 9, 1850, p. 536).

Everyone agreed, however, that the Harmonic Society performed magnificently, and that Belletti was the surprise of the evening, exhibiting a chaste Handelian style and enunciating the English text far more clearly than did the two natives, Miss De Luce and Marcus Colburn. It was generally conceded that Colburn, with his nasal twang, had outlived his usefulness as an oratorio singer.

Despite all the high-flown art-talk bandied about by the cognoscenti, the songs with which Lind most potently and enduringly "electrified" her audiences (the cognoscenti included) were "The Herdsman's Song," now universally referred to as "The Echo Song," and "The Bird Song" (*Ich muss nun einmal singen*), which she performed in English at her first Tripler Hall concert. Written for her by Wilhelm Taubert (1811–1891), it was a magnificent *tour de force* that paralleled "The Echo Song" in its power

[99] The *Message Bird* (November 15, 1850, p. 528) was outraged, not by the performance, but because an inferior chamber organ had been installed for the occasion—not the grand Jardine instrument that had been promised, but an insulting excuse for an organ that sat on some sort of roughly constructed high platform, "like a Yankee clock on a mantel." To reach this inappropriate instrument, Henry C. Timm, the presiding organist, had been forced to climb up a "rough board ladder of some ten or twelve feet in height . . . on all fours and in full view of the audience." It was then discovered that the organ was more than a semitone lower than the orchestra oboe, and it had to be abandoned.

to drive audiences mad. To George W. Curtis it was "a bird's warble of delight—a melodious sweep and shower of sparkling sound—the lark's love lyric to the sun as she soars to meet him." The "scenery" Lind created for this song, and for the "Echo Song," as well, rhapsodized Curtis, was perfect. "We saw the bird wheeling and tumbling in the air—we rose with him [her?] in the sun-ecstasy, and for the time it was only a bird warbling in the blue, of which we were conscious" (*Tribune,* October 28, 1850). Even Watson had to admit that in this music Lind had no equal—there seemed to be "a whole aviary of mocking-birds in her throat," all struggling to be heard (*Albion,* October 26, 1850, p. 512).

By "this music," Watson meant not only "The Bird Song" and "The Echo Song," but the entire genre of lighter songs, predominantly Swedish—"The Mountaineer's

New-York Historical Society

Barnum, as the bird-catcher Papageno, with his prize capture, a Jenny-Lind bird, perched on his finger, is seen luring his prey into Castle Garden, now renamed "Jenny Lind & Co." *Previously snared birds are seen complacently strolling on the Castle terrace, and in the foreground a small bird/urchin is hawking the evening's concert book.*

Song," the Dalecarlian dance song "Invitation to the Dance," and a "Gypsey Song" [*sic*], called by Curtis "a bright bubble from *A Camp in Silesia,*" in whose performance the Nightingale revealed the essential Lind hidden behind the fancy opera arias. Despite the artistry she displayed in some of her opera repertory, wrote the *Mirror* (November 1, 1850), it was in the Swedish songs that she showed her true self: "In these she perfectly revels in fun, and brims over with originality. Nothing can be more rude, hard, and unmelodious than these same 'Melodies,' but the fire, the quaintness, the truthfulness of her rendering make them to us, and to all, perfectly irresistible, fascinating. Jenny Lind in these is the true Swedish girl; she throws into them her whole heart and soul, and no one can resist their influence. But for very shame, we believe she would have been encored half a dozen times both in the Dalecarlian melody and the 'Echo Song.'" Indeed, it was announced that for the remainder of her stay, she would sing both "The Echo Song" and "The Bird Song" at every concert.

Assailed by the incessant repetition of some, or all, of these popular favorites at every concert, with their inevitable encores, Curtis permitted himself a tiny lapse into mild heresy. With many an elaborate apology he asked: "May we not plead a slight satiety of sparkling sweet, and long for another strain?" If Madame Bishop could elicit from a New York audience an encore of Schubert's *Ave Maria,* why couldn't Lind give us something of this caliber, so that we could hear music "of more splendid and profound passionate sweep than the whole range of Italian opera" (*Tribune* November 6, 1850).

But aside from an occasional sacred work, Lind emulated Madame Bishop only in adopting "Home, Sweet Home" into her repertory, singing it at her three last appearances at Tripler Hall on November 19, 21, and 22. Although it was not the Schubert or Beethoven *Lieder* for which Curtis pined, he was nonetheless captivated by her joyous performance of this usually mournful ballad; it was "a gust of happy, as well as sad, remembrance—a thrill of yearning joy. She showered out the [words] 'birds singing gaily' in melodious shakes, so strongly suggesting, as she certainly does more than any artist . . . the scenery of the song. Jenny Lind's little songs are not less pictures than poems" (*Tribune,* November 22, 1850).

On November 13, Lind gave an afternoon concert—an innovation—to allow those who did not go out at night (older people and children) to hear her, and on November 18 she gave another matinée, whose proceeds, $5,073.20, she donated to various New York charities. Philip Hone, who was present at the latter event, was delighted with her performance: ". . . she sang, in a most enchanting manner, all her best pieces, Casta Diva, the Bird Song, the Song of the Mountaineers, and the Echo Song, which she has never omitted since she first warbled to a New York audience, for the reason that they would not dispense with it" (Hone, MS Diary, November 18, 1850).

Each of Lind's concerts was successively reported to have attracted the largest audience yet seen at Tripler Hall and, despite some critic's cavils, to have been the greatest concert ever heard in the United States (the same was concurrently reported of each of Madame Bishop's concerts).[100] On November 14 the *Mirror* announced that

[100] Depending on the orientation of the newspaper in question, the Lind and Bishop reviews might have been interchangeable. Furthermore, as Noah noted, concerts that were coolly received were often represented in the press as gigantic ovations (*Times and Messenger,* November 3, 1850).

to satisfy the increasing demand for seats, Barnum had installed an unspecified number of additional settees in the hall at $2 a ticket. Not even standing room was available at Lind's last two concerts.

After her departure, Saroni pointed out that Benedict, not Lind, had been the real hero of the mammoth enterprise: "No series of concerts have brought us the amount of novelty which Jules [*sic*] Benedict has understood to embody in these concerts. Jules Benedict, then, deserves the credit for the only benefit thus far resulting from the unusual amount of music performed at Jenny Lind's concerts."

Thus, to give Benedict his due, it should be recorded that, aside from devising and rehearsing the fifteen-odd programs performed during the few crowded weeks at Tripler Hall, Benedict had conducted the orchestra in the overtures to Beethoven's *Egmont* and *Prometheus,* to Mendelssohn's *Midsummer Night's Dream,* Weber's "Jubilee" and "Ruler of the Spirits," Auber's *Gustavus III,* Rossini's *La gazza ladra,* Reissiger's *Die Felsenmühle,* Cherubini's *Les Deux journées,* Benedict's own March from *The Crusaders,* and his "Festival" Overture; also, for the first time in America a Beethoven *Leonore* Overture (probably the misnumbered posthumous *Leonore* No. 1, op. 138); the first movement of Schumann's "Spring" Symphony, op. 38 (Leipzig 1841); and the March from Mendelssohn's incidental music to Racine's *Athalie,* op. 74 (1843). Benedict also presented "first" performances of overtures by three American composers: on November 5, William Henry Fry's♪ Overture to *Cristiani e pagani,* an unfinished opera dating from about 1838; on November 13, a Concert Overture by George Frederick Bristow (most probably his op. 3, performed by the Philharmonic in 1847);♪ and on November 19, a Concert Overture by Theodore Eisfeld, an impermanent American.

Of the three "native" overtures, only a single review of Fry's work has (to my knowledge) so far surfaced. Fry's piece, wrote *Figaro!* (November 9, 1850, pp. 138–39), was "an ambitiously written composition, [which] at times approaches a grand effect but, to our ear, fell short ere it attained one. It is more brilliant than melodious, and the harmonies, although sometimes very skillfully worked up, lack solidity and grandeur. It is, however, a creditable production, and was well played."

Bristow's overture was merely mentioned, not reviewed, by Saroni, who thought it "not unworthy of the *Opéra-Comique*—it was melodious and in Auber's manner" (*Musical Times,* November 16, 1850, p. 78). Eisfeld's overture appears to have been ignored.

Aside from his formidable conducting and accompanying labors, Benedict, an excellent pianist, joined with assisting artists in ensemble works of various kinds. These included performances with the pianists Henry C. Timm, Otto Dresel, and Richard Hoffman (all evidently willing to play second parts) in an unidentified quartet by Moscheles (October 24) and an arrangement for eight hands of themes from Meyerbeer's *Les Huguenots* (October 29). Both were played on James Pirsson's sensational new Mammoth Grand Pianoforte, an unusual instrument equipped with two facing keyboards, that had lately captured the public fancy.[101] Benedict also performed a solo piano piece of his own composition, an "Idyllo and Galop."

[101] The four pianists played "a something fugal—it might have been something by the great Sebastian Bach, although some sections were too free to have been his," reported Richard Grant White, who had apparently failed to consult the printed program (*Courier and Enquirer,* November 1, 1850).

Music Division, The New York Public Library

Robert Tuggle

Lind's satellites: Julius Benedict (above), and Giovanni Belletti

Belletti, too, did yeoman's service with his performances of a huge repertory of arias and ensemble works from numberless operas by Verdi, Rossini, Donizetti, and one by Benedict, *La zingara,* probably an Italianization of *The Gipsy's Warning;* also a variety of Italian songs. A great favorite with New York audiences, Belletti most particularly delighted his listeners with his surprisingly excellent performances in accented, but comprehensible, English of sacred music by Haydn (*The Creation*) and, as we know, Handel's *Messiah.*

Richard Hoffman, regularly the assisting artist at Lind's concerts, was highly commended for his performances of an apparently endless array of blockbuster piano fantasies on opera themes by Thalberg and by de Meyer. Also assisting at Tripler Hall was Hoffman's friend, the violinist Joseph Burke, who received an ovation for his brilliant performance of *Le Tremolo* by his former teacher de Bériot. From time to time the singing group chosen and trained by George Loder supplied choral support in excerpts from Rossini's *Stabat Mater,* sung by Lind and Belletti. And on November 9 the German *Liederkranz* appeared, singing the Prisoner's Chorus from *Fidelio,* the Hunting Chorus from *Der Freischütz,* and their old standby, the *Kriegslied* by Joseph Panny.

Following Lind's departure from New York ("*Eheu! Posthume! Posthume!*" wailed Curtis), oceans of conflicting verbiage, reflecting all conceivable shades of opinion of the Nightingale, flooded the newspapers. Saroni, in the *Musical Times* (November 23, 1850, p. 87), spoke in excessively harsh terms: "We had hoped much from Miss Lind . . . but we must confess, we were disappointed. It is true she sang some classical music, some simple music, and some new music, but she always wound up with those pieces in which she enters into competition with the ventriloquist, the equilibrist, with the magician, and with the circus-riders. In short, she ended every concert [at Barnum's suggestion?] with an exhibition of difficult feats, and debased the very art which she had elevated in the first part of her performance." Saroni accused Lind of being "too susceptible to the admiration of the multitude, and when she found that they would not come up to her, she stooped to them. 'The Echo Song,' the 'Mountaineer's Song,' 'Home, Sweet Home,' the 'Greeting,' 'Dalecarlian Invitation to the Dance,' all these are the proofs of what we state here."

Not the least dire consequence, Saroni mischievously observed, was that scores of local "young ladies, who were formerly satisfied with slaughtering an Italian *aria di bravura,* turn now ventriloquist and sing the 'Echo Song.' Others who had an excellent voice now insist upon the *fa in alto,* and scream to make one's ears ring."

Saroni claimed, with refutable logic: "The diffusion of musical taste, which we so fondly expected, was checked by the exorbitant [ticket] charges imposed upon the Public 'by its humble servant' [Barnum], and when she, 'the incomparable Jenny,' has left us, we shall have the memory of nothing but the wonderful feats which we admired, in common with the rest of her audience, but which probably will be expelled from our mind by the next more wonderful execution of some other artist."

Instead of choosing to rule the public by forcing them to accept Saroni's idea of great music, she had become their slave. In predicting that Lind would be forgotten with the appearance of the next sensational singer, Saroni, in the long run, was proved to be mistaken. Lind's name, more than a century later, is still a byword for the ultimate in vocal achievement (a testimony to Barnum's genius).

Conversely, Noah, who had frequently found fault with Lind, now that she had departed, sought impartially to evaluate her phenomenal appeal to the great American public. "The last notes of the dying swan," he somewhat tactlessly began, "could never have been more sweet and touching than those of the departing Nightingale. The whole period from the landing of Jenny Lind to the final note of her last concert on Friday evening has been an uninterrupted scene of triumph, of conquest, and of popularity. She has given no less than 33 concerts in this country. We will not stop to count their profits, but they have been attended by crowded audiences."

"High prices," Noah questionably contended, had not been paid "to satisfy an ardent curiosity to hear her once only, but to hear her again and again, without reference to expense, and sometimes even at a cost which many could not afford." In Jenny Lind they saw an artist who embraced "immense power, immense execution, and immense skill." While Lind did not (of course) possess the ineffable purity of Malibran, she shared with her the capacity of "pleasing, delighting, astonishing, and gratifying, by turns, audiences of a varying character. The educated and accomplished, the professional critic and the amateur, the honest farmer's daughter, the hardy mechanic, and the industrious sewing-girl—every taste and every fancy were alike entranced with many, if not all, of Jenny Lind's songs. Even the rugged Mormon," Noah added for heightened effect, "with his matted and heavy beard, unused to such scenes, we have seen spellbound"[102] (*Times and Messenger,* November 24, 1850).

With only one more concert to go before embarking on her legendary tour, on November 22, the very day of her last concert in New York, Jenny Lind was unwillingly haled into court by a second subpoena—she had airily disregarded the first and was consequently being charged with contempt of court. She had been summoned in the first place (as had Benedict) to give evidence in a lawsuit brought against George Loder by certain female chorus singers who accused Loder, as Barnum's agent, of having engaged them to appear at Tripler Hall and then, finding them incompetent, of refusing to pay them. One of the plaintiffs was awarded damages of $20; another, being married and supported by her husband, received nothing. Once arrived at court, Lind was treated with the worshipful deference due a celebrity of her stature (*Evening Post,* November 27; *Saroni's Musical Times,* November 30, 1850, p. 99).

The *Herald* (November 23, 1850) did not allow its jubilation over this valedictory embarrassment to Barnum to prevent a handsome farewell tribute to Lind: "Last night closed [Jenny Lind's] campaign in this city, and such a series of triumphs were never witnessed on this continent. [Her] success is without parallel. She is acknowledged the Queen of Song, reigning without a rival in the concert room, and reigning, too, in the hearts of the people." It was noticed, however, that the blinding radiance of Barnum's habitual euphoria seemed at this point somewhat to have dimmed. At the end of Lind's last concert, after the last echo of the last encore of the last performance of "The Echo Song" had receded, and after the audience had clamored in vain for a parting word from the Nightingale, they called for Barnum. "But that modesty, which by the aid of circumstances he has been able occasionally to overcome, was last night too much for him, and the audience was obliged to leave without one word of farewell from anyone" (*Evening Post,* November 23, 1850).

Lind's actual departure from New York was tersely reported: "The great songster [*sic*] and her company left the city yesterday at twelve o'clock in the Camden and Amboy railway line for Philadelphia. She will remain two weeks in that city, then go to Baltimore, Washington, and Charleston, thence sail for the Havanas, and return to New York by way of New Orleans, St. Louis, Cincinnati, Buffalo, etc. It is supposed that about twenty concerts of her engagement with Mr. Barnum will remain unfulfilled when she reaches this city again" (*Evening Post,* November 27, 1850).

Evidently, Barnum was more concerned with entrances than with exits.

[102] Tourists journeyed from far and near to hear the Nightingale. The *Evening Post* (October 25, 1850) reported that an excursion from Burlington, Vermont, had reserved the entire second tier of

On November 14, George Templeton Strong jocularly remarked in his journal: "Jenny Lind's greatest triumph came off yesterday: my father and mother of their own free will went to hear her!!! Amphion never achieved anything more marvelous. I must hear her myself." But, dedicated music lover though he was, Strong remained unaccountably adamant in his refusal to hear Lind.

Nor did he attend any of Madame Bishop's extravagantly ballyhooed, deliriously reviewed, sacred concerts. By the time Jenny Lind departed, Madame Bishop had performed the fifth in her series to a redundant succession of "largest audiences ever seen at Tripler Hall." Similarly, according to her private chorus of worshipers—Watson, Noah, the unnamed reviewer for the *Herald,* and now, surprisingly, Saroni, who in his transports might have passed for Watson—time after time, Madame Bishop disclosed startling vocal perfections that invariably surpassed last week's startling perfections, perfect though they had been.

Ostensibly masterminded by Bochsa, Barnum's musical soul-brother, and evidently funded by Madame Bishop, the sacred concerts, with their giant orchestra and army of chorus singers and prominent assisting artists—among others, Miss De Luce, Seguin, Manvers, Novelli, Philip Mayer, and the Italian opera tenor Francesco Bailini—were, of course, presented on a scale of grandeur never before attempted in the United States.[103]

In addition to the standard oratorios, given complete or in part—*Messiah, Samson, The Creation, The Seasons,* Rossini's *Stabat Mater* and *Moses in Egypt* (performed as an oratorio), Mozart's *Requiem,* Beethoven's *The Mount of Olives*—Bochsa presented first performances in America, on November 24, of Mendelssohn's posthumous cantata *Lauda Sion,* op. 73 (1846), and Rossini's *The Faith (La Foi),* part of a set—*La Foi, L'Espérance,* and *La Charité* (Paris 1844)[104]—and on December 22, at the ninth sacred concert, of Donizetti's *Miserere.*

Beyond her marvelous and inspiring performances of the various oratorios, Madame Bishop's most lauded and frequently repeated solos were the *Gratias agimus* by Pietro Carlo Guglielmi (1763–1817), "Sweet Bird" by Handel (by some coincidence programed as "The Bird Song"), and Schubert's *Ave Maria,* for all of which Bochsa had orchestrated the accompaniments.

Of her *Gratias agimus* a mysteriously tamed Saroni wrote that it was "the most brilliant vocal feat yet accomplished by Madame Bishop, [who] in facility and brilliance of execution [had] few equals and no superior. . . . She was frequently interrupted by loud applause, and by murmurs of admiration, but in her long and elaborately beautiful closing Cadenza with the clarionette, in which she seems to exhaust the resources of ornament, showering down the most brilliant *fioriture,* and throwing off, with provoking ease, the most dazzling *tours de force*—this closing Cadenza fairly made the

---

Tripler Hall—600 seats—for Lind's second concert. Tickets for the junket, including transportation, cost $7.

[103] Henry C. Watson took full credit for the undertaking: "For years now we had been urging just such a project, but although the parties were enthusiastic, there was no place in which to hold such a series. It was *we* who had suggested the scheme to the parties now running it, and the result has exceeded even our sanguine expectations" (*Mirror,* October 31, 1850).

[104] On hearing *La Foi,* Berlioz is supposed to have quipped: "This Faith will never move mountains" (cited in Toye, p. 164).

people beside themselves—[and] called forth such a thundering encore as was never heard in Tripler Hall, and will probably never be heard again until she repeats the same song."

"This piece was undoubtedly a great physical exertion," continues Saroni, "but so unbounded was the enthusiasm of the audience that its repetition was demanded and enforced, to the great discomfort of the lady." The intrepid, if exhausted, Madame Bishop valiantly attacked it again "with her usual spirit, for she does not give up to trifles, but it was tasking nature too much" (*Musical Times,* November 2, 1850, p. 59).

In the course of the series, Bochsa, now referred to by Saroni as "a master spirit of Music," masterfully conducted works both sacred and sacred by association: the overtures to Mendelssohn's *St. Paul* and *Athalie,* and to Méhul's♪ *Joseph;* the Coronation March from Meyerbeer's *Le Prophète;* the Dead March from Handel's *Saul;* and the March from his *Judas Maccabaeus.* The assisting artists offered vast numbers of solos and ensembles. Everything continued to be performed more magnificently than ever before. Bishop/Bochsa were creating a new dimension in the musical receptivity of the great American public.[105]

But all this edifying activity evidently left Bochsa still unfulfilled, for on November 16, as Jenny Lind's sojourn in New York was drawing to a close and Tripler Hall was becoming more available, Bochsa, that benign and self-effacing philosopher and guardian of the public musical taste, announced an additional series: "American Promenades," in imitation of the brilliantly successful Musard and Jullien promenade concerts in London,♪ intended to "do for light and deservedly popular music for weekday amusements the same as has already been endeavored to be accomplished for sacred music, and the loftier works of the great masters at MADAM ANNA BISHOP'S SUNDAY SACRED CONCERTS." As usual, the promenades were conceived on a scale "hitherto unknown in this country."

Probably ghostwritten by Watson, the announcement, appearing in all the papers, goes on: "To him who looks with proper interest upon the amusements of a people as being the only true index of their advancement in civilization, and of the general happiness of their condition, a desire is unavoidable to rescue the popular musical recreations of the American nation from the triviality and insignificance to which it has too often hitherto been limited, and to offer something more worthy of it, and more in correspondence with the achievements of its people in every other department of human interest.

"Anxious to deserve Public Patronage, and confident in his resource, being already at the head of the most immense and perfect permanent orchestra in the world—the Manager of Tripler Hall [Bochsa] begs to add that, in carrying out his plan, every effort will be made to render the selection of artists wholly free from all partiality to country or individual. The greatest excellence will be the only passport to an engagement at these concerts." Bochsa had already offered "arrangements" to Mu-

[105] All the same, as the series progressed, some critics noted that the concerts were less carefully prepared than they might have been. "Rehearse, rehearse, rehearse!" admonished *Figaro!* after reporting that the *Lauda Sion* premiere had been rather carelessly performed (November 30, 1850, p. 191).

sard and Jullien to come to New York and participate, and Balfe had been asked for some of his "original writings" to be performed. And on and on.

Despite this ostentatious buildup, Bochsa's first promenade concert attracted a meager audience. (It rained on November 28, extenuated the papers.) Still, Saroni was mystified: "Excellent music—a magnificent Hall—brilliant illumination—a splendid orchestra—an experienced leader—but no audience!

"Alas for the musical taste of New York!" he lamented. "The very persons who grumble at the heaviness of the Sunday concerts fail to attend these feasts of sparkling musical humor. Lanner, Strauss, and Labitzky, who set one half of Europe in motion, failed to draw one couple from the secured seats in the first circle" (*Musical Times,* November 30, 1850, p. 108). Against Watson's judgment (also Saroni's), dancing, a Bochsian embellishment, had been added to the Promenades' features. Although fully in favor of these "Monster Promenade Concerts," Watson had counseled Bochsa "not to make Tripler Hall a Casino for public dancing if he [expected] the support of the more refined portion of the community" (*Albion,* November 23, 1850, p. 560).[106]

To instruct New Yorkers who had not been privileged to travel abroad in "how to enjoy this novel entertainment [the Promenade concert]," Saroni reprinted an article from the *Herald* (*Musical Times,* December 14, 1850, p. 119), describing this "transatlantic and most sociable entertainment." The Promenades were a kind of "musical merrymaking," an unfettered happening, at which "fashionables, as well as the million, enjoy themselves just as they please, and . . . as the spirit moves them—some being attracted by the charms of inspiring music, some by the delightful prospect of a dance to the arousing strains of a fine band, while others are there to see and to be seen, or to kill time, and members of the *haut ton,* after a stroll or two through the mazy crowd, retire to choice seats in the upper circles and [level] their *lorgnettes* upon the promenaders and dancers below. . . .

"The promenader's etiquette is to begin to move about the rooms (a most delightful maneuver in Tripler Hall), from the moment of his entrance, talking to everybody he knows, and admiring every belle he pleases. Silence is not necessary during the performance of any piece, except as a mark of respect to a singer, or instrumental solo."

At Bochsa's first Promenade, when the "stupendous" orchestra struck up the Overture to *La gazza ladra,* reported the *Herald* (November 29, 1850), "it was evident, quite, that 120 performers had been schooled to some purpose." The quadrilles and waltzes were warmly applauded, if not danced to, by the sparse audience, and "Musard's *Les Gamins de Paris,* well known to every sojourner in Paris, was a delicious treat."

Beethoven's Septet, in the *Herald*'s opinion, was "not quite the thing" for the occasion, but Cherubini's *Anacreon* Overture was "magnetic," and a flute quartet, played by Felice Eben and colleagues, was admirable. By far the best, however, was Andreas Romberg's "Children's" ("Toy") Symphony, "which is a beautiful composition made grotesque by drums, whistles, triangles, rattles, and other paraphernalia of the toy

[106] Not only dancing and "liquid refreshments," but suppers would soon be offered at the Promenades, went the rumor.

shops." In conducting this work, Bochsa continued to edify the American public by using a baton with a doll attached to its tip (a metaphor for Madame Bishop?).

On December 2 (another rainy night) the same program was repeated to an equally dismal attendance, whereupon Madame Bishop came to the rescue. Although she was only now (on December 8) resuming her Sunday sacred concerts, having (despite her iron determination) suffered a sudden indisposition in mid-performance on November 24 and consequently been forced to cancel her following concert, she appeared on December 12 at the third Promenade, a festive celebration of Thanksgiving. In "homage to the United States" she sang some of her English ballads: "On the Banks of Guadalquivir" and "Home, Sweet Home," and, as a grand finale to Bochsa's Americanization of Beethoven's "Battle's [*sic*] Sinfonia" *(Wellingtons Sieg)*—complete with "cries of the wounded"—and "Yankee Doodle," Madame Bishop sang "Hail Columbia."

Her participation in the Promenade was a tremendous success. Her presence apparently encouraged the audience to overcome its shy reluctance to dance. Noah reported that a promenading audience of 4700 left little room for those who were determined to dance. Despite the abundance of holiday spirit, however, they displayed perfect decorum: every time Madame Bishop came forward to sing, they stopped their chatter and the gentlemen removed their hats! "In return for this laudable mark of admiration, she sang in her most bewitching style, and in all her songs was encored with peals of the heartiest approbation."

Noah mentions, too, that Shelton's Band, who doubtless played the dance music—waltzes, polkas, quadrilles, and galops—added greatly to the occasion. Whatever would Bochsa think of next! It was sure to be something "*savoure* and wonderful. The *Maestro* has a long head and knows how to get on" (*Times and Messenger,* December 15, 1850). Reporting this event, Saroni somewhat outrageously informed his readers: "People little know how much Bochsa is doing to diffuse a love and taste for music. Let these concerts be attended by the middle classes, and soon they will be able to appreciate the music of the best masters, while their brethren of the Upper Ten will still be satisfied with Verdi and Donizetti" (*Musical Times,* December 14, 1850, p. 121).

No such contrived interpretation of Bochsa's contribution was expressed by the new music critic of the *Albion,* for indeed, with no prior warning and no explanation—after seven years of predominantly destructive, rarely unbiased, highly lauded musical pronouncements—the reign of Henry C. Watson had come to an end (at least, at the *Albion*). In the issue for December 21, 1850 (p. 608), John R. Young, the *Albion*'s editor, naming no names, announced that the music department would henceforth be in other hands, and he trusted that the new contributor (it was Richard Storrs Willis) would be "found competent to succeed our long and favourably-known critic, of whose judgment and thorough acquaintance with his art our readers are well aware."

Treading irreverently in hitherto hallowed precincts, Willis proceeded to demolish the Bishop/Bochsa myth, so long and lovingly nurtured by Watson. In his review of the fourth Grand American Promenade, a particularly untrammeled Bochsian hodgepodge presented on December 19 (and repeated on December 25), he dared to place Bochsa's Promenades in a more realistic perspective. Since the sole object of these productions was enjoyment, he stated, it would be absurd to review them as serious events. Promenade concerts, he explained (again revealing his unmistakably Germanic orientation), were descended from the *Kursaal* evenings at the German spas, from which Musard and Jullien had borrowed the idea; Bochsa's object in giving them here could only be to "cater for the public entertainment, to kill time for such as desire it, and, in short (according to one of the illustrious Micawber's bursts of confidence), to make money."[107]

As for improving the great American musical taste: "The difference . . . between such an enterprise and the object of an institution like the Philharmonic Society, or its counterpart (in the sacred style) the New-York Harmonic Society (to whose classic and superior concerts we propose hereafter to give an honourable place in these columns), is one, of course, well understood and admitted by those engaged in them. We presume, also, that in the public, generally, there is little danger of confounding the one with the other. And we are, moreover, far from being so illiberal a spirit as not to believe that both classes of performance may have their peculiar spheres and legitimate uses in Society at large. The one is to refine, to educate, to elevate—the other innocently to divert and entertain."

Bochsa's Promenade had begun with Berlioz's Overture to *Les Francs-Juges,*♪ a title windily explained in Bochsa's advertisements and amusedly quoted by the reviewer as "A Free Tribunal of the *Moyen Age,* a Grandioze [*sic*] and eccentric overture to an imaginary tragic drama, by Hector Berlioz: called by that celebrated Poet-musician (the musical Byron of his age) the 'Francs-Juges': with the following author's preface. 'Horrible Clamors/Threats; Supplications/Words of Death; Noble Feelings/Tears; Blood/Fire.' ([from an] Unknown drama.)" Eight trombonists, it was announced, had been engaged "to give due effect to that extraordinary composition."

"The rant and fustian of this introduction," wrote Willis, asserting an authority gained from his six years' sojourn among the musical elite of Germany (but at the same time revealing an underlying kinship with Watson) "sufficiently indicate the character of the composer, who is a very decided musical lunatic. Hector Berlioz's musical extravagances, particularly his supposed extraordinary discoveries in instrumentation and orchestral effect, have afforded a most superlative importance to very sharp *dynamical* effects, insisting in all *forte* passages, upon an accumulation of *ffff*'s, *ad infinitum,* and of corresponding *pppp*'s."

The previously unassailable Madame Bishop, too, was none too chivalrously treated. Singing a languorous song from Félicien David's *Le Désert,*♪ "O night, O lovely night" ("The Evening's Reverie") a song about which a "delicious dreaminess and poetic haze" hovered, "Madame Anna Bishop did not appreciate the spirit of it, as much as we could have wished it (it being a rainy night and not at all a 'lovely night'—perhaps). Indeed, it is a better song for 'dreamy seventeen' than for any less fanciful age."

No mention was made of Madame Bishop's other contributions: "The Last Rose of Summer," a duet from Mozart's *The Marriage of Figaro* sung with Miss De Luce, and—a particularly exotic offering—a vocalization of the first flute part of something

[107] A timely reference to the perennial optimist in Charles Dickens's best-selling new novel *David Copperfield.*

called "The National Mourning Chaunt of the Albinos," billed as a quartet for four flutes and two clarinets.

The program included as well the remainder of Part Two of *Le Désert;* Jullien's "Postillion Quadrilles," with "obbligato accompaniments of Whips, Sleighbells, etc."; Labitzky's "Scottish Waltzes," with bagpipes; Strauss's "Spanish Polka," with obbligato accompaniment of twenty castanets; Musard's "Christmas Quadrille" (without sleighbells); a *Fantasie* for violin on the Prayer from Rossini's *Mosè,* played by Signorina Lavinia Bandini, a twelve-year-old debutante; a ballad by Henry C. Watson sung by Miss De Luce; and Arditi's *Cuba incend e contra dance* [*sic*], this last "being a description of an alarm fire at Havana, which was accompanied by the shouting of the performers and the din of a firebell under the stage.[108] This produced a strong sensation in the audience," continued Willis, "one or two young men, in their enthusiasm, actually rushing across the floor of the Hall, as though tugging at an engine rope. A repetition was strongly insisted on."

But Bochsa's funmaking had hardly begun: "We were as little prepared as most of the audience, probably, for the last performance, which was really a droll affair. The orchestra came filing in, masked and in carnival costume, the figures of the Harlequin and Punch being conspicuous. But last of all, the unbounded proportions of Signor Bochsa presented themselves arrayed in a white dressing gown of characteristic adornment: upon either side of his chest swelled two enormous fiddles, upon his back a large French horn, while a black fringe of music notes bounded the entire circumference of the figure. . . . The maskers carried out their parts bravely while performing 'The Carnival of Venice,' and in the orchestra arrangement [Josef Gungl's Burlesque Variations], in which some of the instruments were concealed in distant corners of the house, startling the audience with music from unexpected quarters."

Then, to wind up the evening, the orchestra, in juvenile dress, repeated Romberg's "Children's" Symphony, which they "heroically played upon penny trumpets, nightingales, drums, rattles, etc." (*Albion,* December 28, 1850, p. 620).

On December 22, Madame Bishop gave her ninth Grand Sacred Concert, presenting a medley of repeats from earlier programs in the series. On December 25, Bishop/Bochsa celebrated Christmas by giving two shows, a matinée at one-thirty in the afternoon, largely repeating the repeat program of December 22, and a repeat of the last Monster Promenade Concert in the evening.

This was the unannounced grand finale of the Bishop/Bochsa adventure at Tripler Hall, for, abruptly, with no advance warning, they canceled all future appearances, sacred and popular, and vanished from New York. Noah explained in the *Times and Messenger* (December 29, 1850), that the cancellation had been necessitated by the bad weather and, besides, Madame Bishop had an engagement in Boston.

Persistently maintaining his musical aloofness in this year of unprecedented musical riches, George Templeton Strong attended only one more concert in 1850. On December 11 he went to hear the fledgling Harmonic Society, conducted by George Loder and assisted by the oratorio singers Mrs. Bostwick, Mrs. L. A. Jones, Stephen

[108] A modest precursor of Jullien's sensational "Fireman's Quadrille," performed with elaborate aural and visual effects at the New York Crystal Palace in 1854 (see GTS: 1854).

Leach, Robert Andrews,♪ and the tenor George Holman,♪ an alumnus of the popular stage and the minstrel shows.

December 12. . . . Heard *The Creation* last night at the Tabernacle with Ellie, her mother, and Jem [Ruggles]. Choruses admirably well done; solo parts middling or tolerable, all but a tenor with a scrannel pipe of a larynx.

Victor Prevost's archetypal photograph of the Tripler Hall interior.

New-York Historical Society

OBBLIGATO: 1850

No sooner does one musical excitement subside, in a measure, than another springs into existence. They look upon us as following, without stay or rest, the almighty dollar, and little think that we run musically mad a dozen times a year.

New York Herald
October 16, 1850

DESPITE ALL PUBLICITY TO THE CONTRARY, it was more than persistently poor audiences that drove Bishop/Bochsa to release their stranglehold on Tripler Hall and depart in search of greener fields. Having managed to outlast Jenny Lind, in December they found themselves faced with a new threat to the undisputed vocal sovereignty that Madame Bishop so passionately coveted. Max Maretzek, who could hardly have been expected passively to accept the year's successive menaces to the security of his Astor Place Opera, had produced a trump card, and one so potent as to dislodge the tenacious occupants of Tripler Hall.

But first things first. Still reeling from the enormous adverse impact, earlier in the year, of the opera company from Havana, Maretzek, with his own second opera season due to begin in mid-October, had found himself facing professional annihilation upon Jenny Lind's arrival in September. In his own poignant words, "with a [second-rate] company of Truffis and Beneventanos on his hands and the lease of the Astor Place Opera House upon his shoulders, with Jenny Lind and Barnum, real genius and undoubted 'humbug' in a strange co-partnership, staring ominously in his face," what was a "luckless impresario" to do?

Maretzek decided to "enter upon a contest with the 'Prince of Humbugs,' using Barnum's own weapons." Scraping together funds probably derived from booking miscellaneous pre-season attractions—opera, theatre, and ballet—into Astor Place,[1] and from his opera subscribership, such as it was, Maretzek imported a new attraction for his approaching season, Teresa Parodi (1827–?). An acclaimed young *prima donna assoluta* at Her Majesty's Theatre in London, the scene of Lind's great operatic triumphs, Parodi was known to be Giuditta Pasta's favorite pupil and protégée.

[1] During this brief season the long-absent comedian Joe Cowell returned for a few performances of past hits; the dancers Celestine and Victorine Franck and Leon Espinosa, "from the Paris Opera," presented various ballets; and on October 8, Rosa de Vries, a "French" *prima donna* from New Orleans, valiantly presented the first of two performances in French-cum-Italian of *Norma* in a pick-up

". . . I went to work in the same manner I had seen practiced by Barnum," writes Maretzek. "Foreign letters, puffs, portraits, biographies were manufactured under my supervision, and distributed by means of journals and the music stores throughout New York. All was of no use. Public attention was absorbed in Jenny Lind. Whatever I did was against the pyramidal puffing of Barnum. It was no more than the murmuring of a garden streamlet as compared with the roar and thunder of Niagara" (*Crotchets,* p. 124).

In desperation, Maretzek conceived the idea of having a third person "secretly" leak a sensational story to the papers: that the venerable Duke of Devonshire was hopelessly in love with Parodi and had offered to make her his duchess, just to keep her in England, and that she had accepted. As planned, the story spread like wildfire, and the "biographies, portraits, and anecdotes about [Parodi], which had dropped stillborn from the press, were now republished, admired, and listened to" (*ibid.,* p. 126).

To the ensuing storm of rumors Maretzek remained impervious. Maintaining the hoax, he removed Parodi's name from his roster of artists for the coming season, all the while impatiently awaiting her arrival. At last, on October 10 the *Herald,* which at first had swallowed the fiction, good-naturedly announced that the story had been "humbug"; the marriage of Parodi and the Duke would after all not take place, and the singer was expected on the next arrival of the steamship *Pacific,* as originally announced.

In the meantime Maretzek had opened his opera season on October 21 with an ill-advised production of *Il franco arciero* (*Der Freischütz* in Italian)[2] to general critical disapproval. Watson, wistfully evoking "somewhat olden times," when as a child he had heard the "immortal composer" conduct *Der Freischütz,* observed that Italians could not be expected fully to enter into the glorious and wild Northern Spirit of the music (*Mirror,* October 22; *Albion,* October 26, 1850, p. 512). (It was the Lind argument in reverse.)

The critical consensus had it that Bertucca (now Bertucca-Maretzek), the Agathe, was correct but cold; Lorini, the Max, was partly good; Amalia Patti, the Aennchen, had improved (yet again); and Beneventano as Caspar was either perfect or unrestrained, according to whether one read the *Albion (loc. cit.)* or the *Message Bird* (November 1, 1850, p. 515). Noah reminisced over great past performances of *Der Freischütz,* especially those in English at the Park Theatre with Charles E. Horn♪ and Mrs. Austin,♪ back in the '20s (*Times and Messenger,* October 27, 1850).

Watson magnanimously called the production a bold beginning to the season; the *Tribune* called it a perfect choice; but *Figaro!* (October 26, 1850, p. 110) remarked that

---

production with a makeshift cast of supporting singers (a frightened Madame Casini♪ as Adalgisa, Novelli as Oroveso, and de Vries's vocally inadequate husband as Pollione). Despite all the drawbacks of a shoddy production, Madame de Vries was unanimously acclaimed an artist of high quality. On October 14 she appeared for the third time in a mixed bill consisting of a condensed version of *Norma,* a scene from Verdi's *I Lombardi,* and the fourth act of *La Favorite,* presumably all in French. Madame de Vries would return.

[2] In 1841, Berlioz had supplied orchestral accompaniments to the recitatives for a Paris Opéra production of *Der Freischütz.* In 1850 the recitatives were supposed to have been performed in an Italian version, *Il franco arciero,* produced at Covent Garden, but they apparently were not used. I have found nothing to suggest that Maretzek used them in his New York production in 1851.

Music Division, The New York Public Library

Teresa Parodi, Maretzek's retort to Jenny Lind.

"in Italian 'Der Freischütz' was no more like Weber . . . than a Dutch cheese is like a diamond." *Figaro!* predicted that it would not often be heard in Italian. Indeed: "Never, if we can avoid it, by us." Richard Grant White agreed that *Der Freischütz* in Italian was a "terrible anachronism": the singers all had a "fish-out-of-water" air about them. "We might just as well call it 'Francis Archer,'" he clumsily punned.

Maretzek marked time until Parodi's arrival with two more performances of *Il franco arciero;* on October 28 he presented *Lucia* with Bertucca-Maretzek in the title role, and on October 10, *Ernani,* with Teresa Truffi (at last Truffi-Benedetti) as Elvira. People wanted "Italian music and nothing else," stated R. G. White after hearing the *Lucia* performance. "They desire the voice-displaying melodies of the modern dramatic school and have little regard for the German composers." Maretzek did well, in White's opinion, to replace Weber with Donizetti (*Courier and Enquirer,* October 29, 1850).

But all interest (or, at least all the interest that could be spared from the competing Lind and Bishop/Bochsa shows currently in full fling at Tripler Hall) was focused on Parodi, who on her arrival, on October 27, was greeted with a demonstration that in microcosm resembled Lind's welcome. As reported the following day in the *Herald,* a crowd of "thousands" gathered in front of her hotel (the Union) and demanded a glimpse of her. "She is a tall, elegantly formed young lady, with beautiful blue eyes and black hair, and admirably fitted to fill the roles made celebrated by Pasta." The *Message Bird* reported that the cheering crowd, whom she addressed in Italian from her balcony, had consisted mostly of her compatriots.

According to the *Herald,* "Maretzek and herself are equally desirous that no undue enthusiasm be indulged in till her merits have been tested by a public ordeal." A proposed welcoming serenade by the Astor Place orchestra was not forbidden by Maretzek, but neither was it approved—it was deferred. But the evening following her arrival, Parodi was serenaded by a group of her enthusiastic countrymen. She was also welcomed by Jenny Lind, who a few days later "gave her a dinner at the New-York Hotel, to which the American actress Charlotte Cushman♪ was invited" (*Message Bird,* November 15, 1850, p. 529).

Maretzek continued to emulate Barnum's methods: "From the day of [Parodi's] arrival," he writes, "I announced that I should accept of no more subscriptions for the season and raised the prices of admission exactly one hundred percent.[3] This last fact dispelled all doubts of her superiority, as it was supposed that I could not have dared to do this, with such a rival attraction as Jenny Lind in the market, if I had not been morally certain of her success" (*Crotchets,* p. 127).[4]

Parodi made her debut on November 4 in *Norma,*[5] an opera in which she had reputedly inherited Pasta's mantle of greatness. George William Curtis, who heard the dress rehearsal the day before—although he conceded that it was not the critic's place to pass judgment before a performance—reported that everyone present had agreed that she was the greatest thing since Malibran. Parodi was about twenty-five years old, he thought; she had a voice of three octaves and "in appearance, voice, and style was about as different from Jenny Lind as it is possible for two vocalists to be." There could be no fairness, stated Curtis, a Lind man, "in judging her by the same standard." Indeed, Curtis found it unfair to judge any artist on a first appearance (*Tribune,* November 4, 1850).

The house, he wrote, was crowded with a fashionable audience: "Top's Alley [a variant of N. P. Willis's "Fop's Terrace"]♪ was thronged, and all the entrances and steps were occupied by those who were only too glad, at such inconvenience, to see and hear the Queen of the evening. She is a lady of fine presence upon the stage, and of large, expressive features, admirably adapted for dramatic effect. Her hair is raven black, and [it] fell forward in two long locks before her shoulders as she advanced somewhat stiffly toward the front and inclined, clinging to her sickle, and not very gracefully, to the continued applause." After a vaguely negative preamble, Curtis openly confessed that he did not like her *Casta diva,* but he would wait for a subsequent hearing to render further judgment. After the first act Parodi was accorded a huge ovation: a shower of poems descended from the rafters, also a deluge of bouquets, and "a gentleman in the terrace on the right of the parquette [released] a white dove into the air, according to the custom of Italian ovations.[6] The bird, however, frightened by the glare and the bravos of the house, did not fly to Parodi's hand as it should have, but fluttered across the house and took refuge in the second tier. Another shower of sonnets fell from the amphitheatre" before the excitement subsided (*Tribune,* November 5, 1850).

[3] The prices were $2 for parquette and box tickets, $2.50 for "secured" seats, and 50 cents for the amphitheatre.

[4] The complaints over the raised prices for Parodi reminded Noah of similar complaints in the '20s, when prices had been raised for the Garcias.

[5] With Amalia Patti as Adalgisa, Lorini as Pollione, and Novelli as Oroveso.

[6] In the *Mirror's* version of the ovation: "Doves with handsome gold bracelets on their necks were thrown from the amphitheatre, and showers of verses, highly laudatory to the lady, fell upon the audience and the stage" (November 5, 1850).

Although Parodi had her defects, asserted the *Mirror* (November 5, 1850), she was "by far the greatest dramatic vocalist that we ever heard in this country. Indeed [warming to the subject], we might venture a little further and admit that since the days of Pasta we have not witnessed so grand and effective a representation of *Norma*." The writer attributed any minor faults to understandable first-night nerves, "but they were very trifling" compared with her grandeur, which electrified the audience.

In his second review of the "peerless Parodi," again as Norma, the *Mirror* critic cast aside all reservations: "Parodi is immense. In tragic power we have never seen her equal in this country." Her acting was as thrilling as her singing. This writer had no qualms in pointing out the difference between her and Lind: "The one exalts, the other simply thrills us. . . . Mere criticism in both cases strikes us as ridiculous, and we are not ambitious to be classed with those who are looking for flaws in diamonds, or spots on the sun" (*Mirror,* November 8, 1850).

In the *Albion* (November 16, 1850, p. 548), Watson went even further: "Never, save in the case of Malibran, have we remarked so much power over the features as

New-York Historical Society

SIGNORA PARODI IN THE CHARACTER OF NORMA.

Parodi exhibits. . . . As a vocalist Parodi appears to us almost faultless. . . . Her voice is pure and sympathetic, it has great range—over two octaves—and it has been so carefully cultivated that she exercises over it the most perfect control, so much so that it seems as if she could stop short on any note at all, even in the most rapid ascending and descending passages. . . . Her vocalizing is perfect."

But Richard Grant White found her voice to be unsympathetic and her method "by no means unimpeachable," with its defective breathing and "lack of power to sustain her notes, or to diminish them with a nice gradation." She had a "tea-kettle shake" that was not equal on the two notes. Then the typical Whitean switch: "Her remarkable voice enables her to attempt effects in *Norma* beyond any we have heard here through the years." With her equally remarkable powers as an actress, her style was impetuous and passionate, but delicacy and tenderness were foreign to her concept of the role of Norma. Her performance did not impress White, he claimed, whereupon he pronounced her to be by far the best Norma ever seen at the opera house. White was especially repelled by the one greatest fault of this compelling actress: "She smiles all the time—it begins to seem like a set grin" (*Courier and Enquirer,* November 5, 1850).

Curtis—in a huge, redundant meander that rivaled White at his most prolix and perverse—although he admitted that Parodi was an extraordinary actress, reproved her for "sometimes forgetting her voice in her acting, which confuses the mind of the spectator, to whom the singer should always be more prominent than the actor." Then, too, in her *Casta diva* she was not always in perfect accord with the orchestra's pitch, a fault commonly found in famous singers. However, Parodi did have a full and even voice, possessing a force that was very attractive. Then, a few discursive miles later—after an endless lecture on Bellini's myriad faults, and after admitting that he was "overrunning all limits," and after criticizing his brother-critics—Curtis magnanimously concluded: "Parodi is without doubt a singer and actor of fine capabilities and would be marked on any stage, and has given us *Norma* in a manner superior probably to any representation hitherto in New-York. Yet, she is not a first-rate artiste, If she were, London could not have spared her" (*Tribune,* November 8, 1850).

In short, the critics reacted to Parodi according to tradition—taking sides and trading insults. Her first performance of *Lucrezia Borgia,* on November 11 (after three of *Norma*), must have convinced the "carping critics not only of her greatness," wrote the *Mirror* (November 12, 1850), "but of their injustice in denying to this *artiste* the possession of transcendent powers." On November 14, after her second *Lucrezia,* the same writer dubbed her the "Siddons of the lyric stage." For this performance, every inch of standing room had been filled and people were turned away. "We have not the patience to controvert the detraction of critics whose musical experience is limited to Astor Place and Castle Garden,[7] nor space to dwell upon the greatness of Parodi's performance. With an intelligent audience who have ears to hear and eyes to see, she has nothing to fear."

The *Herald* (November 13, 1850), which exuberantly proclaimed Parodi to be the "the greatest artist of all time," not excluding Malibran and far exceeding Lind, loudly

[7] The critic was pointing the finger at Richard Grant White, who habitually compared performers to famous European artists he had never heard, having never crossed the Atlantic.

Both: Music Division, The New York Public Library

Parodi's Norma, a Victorian Druidess, as depicted on contemporary sheet music covers.

and lengthily denounced the critics of the *Courier and Enquirer* and the *Tribune* for their "inane stupidities against Parodi."

N. P. Willis capitulated only after witnessing her *Lucrezia;* she had made such a "false extravaganza of *Norma*" that he had given up all hope of ever being pleased with her. If only he had heard *Lucrezia* first he would have reacted differently. However, Parodi had a serious physical shortcoming: "Her upper lip is too short for uses in depicting tragedy. Too bad nature had denied her a moustache," he wrote. Apart from this flaw, however, her Lucrezia undeniably entitled her to wear the mantle of Pasta (*Home Journal,* November 23, 1850).

To Noah, who pronounced Parodi's Lucrezia the greatest ever seen in America, her face was "like Macbeth's—a book in which all the struggling passions for mastery may be read—full of expression, of woe, and of despair" (*Times and Messenger,* November 17, 1850).

On November 15 the *Tribune* reluctantly congratulated Maretzek on his great success and reported that at Parodi's last performance it was necessary to install extra seats, "which filled the passageways of the second tier, so great was the demand."[8]

After her third triumphant performance of *Lucrezia Borgia,* although suffering from a cold, Parodi disregarded her doctor's orders and on November 18 appeared as Elvira in *Ernani;* despite her obvious indisposition, her acting was again overwhelming. And on November 30 she again triumphed in Donizetti's problematical opera *Gemma di Vergy.*♪

The *Albion* (December 7, 1850, p. 584) described *Gemma* as a work whose good score was unhappily wedded to an unspeakable plot.[9] "The subject of the opera is somewhat revolting, being a combination of perjured vows, assassinations, and suicides. The hearers sup so full of horrors that the mind sickens, and even the charms of music lose their wonted power. The authors of Italian libretti seem to think that there is nothing interesting in life but infidelity and murder."

More nature and less bombast would enhance our music experience no end, proclaimed Watson. But Parodi was magnificent and, despite a disappointingly small audience, she inspired her colleagues as well. Especially Novelli, who would have been a great artist, were it not for his perpetual shaking, an affectation that was "positively disgusting to the audience": "He trembles all over as though in bodily fear or in a fit of violent ague."

In the meantime, on November 22, the night of Lind's farewell concert at Tripler Hall, Maretzek presented for the first time in the United States Donizetti's *Parisina* (Florence 1833), whose libretto by Felice Romani is based on a poem by Byron. The *prima donna* was the recently married Teresa Truffi-Benedetti, N. P. Willis's longtime protégée, now relegated to second place in the Astor Place firmament. Not only was

[8]Continuing his feud with Maretzek, N. P. Willis insisted that Parodi was singing to empty houses at Astor Place, due to Maretzek's mismanagement. The tickets were too expensive for the Many, he claimed, and Maretzek's opera had fallen out of favor with the Few. And again, at last conceding that Parodi was a "great creature" destined for future glory in the opera houses of Europe, Willis wished she could be "rescued from the unlucky star she now sings under, and be heard by 'the people,' at reasonable prices" (*Home Journal,* December 7, 14, 1850).

[9]The first American performance of *Gemma di Vergy* was given at Niblo's on October 2, 1843, not at Palmo's Opera House, as Watson misremembered.

Nathalie Fitzjames, the "amphibious" ballerina-*cum*-prima donna, *in her terpsichorean persona.*

the timing of this premiere unfortunate, but the work itself was not liked. Truffi, too, was a disappointment, even to Willis, who suggested that her newfound marital bliss might have impaired her capacity for operatic tragedy: "There are closed fountains of tears that must be broken up, and place left for the deeper and angrier passions, before she can become possessed entirely by the spirit of tragedy," he explained, and suggested a remedy: "Would not looser dresses and a glass of champagne before coming on the stage give this superb bud of genius the impulse to unfold?" (*Home Journal,* December 7, 1850).

On November 23, Maretzek added another imported attraction to his roster. Following Parodi's performance of *Lucrezia Borgia,* the renowned French ballerina Nathalie Fitzjames from the Paris Opéra made her American debut, assisted by Giuseppe Carese (or Carrese), in *Paquita,* advertised as a Grand Ballet expressly composed for her by Adolphe Adam,[10] composer of *Giselle* (*Saroni's Musical Times,* November 30, 1850, p. 97). With her arrival the New York public at last accepted the mingling of ballet with opera that it had until now resisted, and Fitzjames and her ballets were a favored feature at the Astor Place Opera House throughout the season.

On December 5, Maretzek suffered an acute embarrassment when Geremia Bet-

[10] The score of *Paquita,* first produced in Paris in 1846, was in fact jointly composed by Léon Minkus (1827–1890) and Éduard Deldevez (1817–1897). I have found no record of a *Paquita* by Adam.

tini (1823–1865), the celebrated tenor from the Paris Opéra, whom he had engaged for two mightily ballyhooed appearances during Bettini's brief stopover on the way to Havana, was overcome by hoarseness during the first act of *Lucia di Lammermoor* and was unable to continue. But worse was to come. Two nights later, with a large and expectant audience assembled to hear him in the same opera, as part of an all-star "Grand Gala Night" that also featured Parodi in the second act of *Lucrezia Borgia* and Fitzjames in a *Grand Ballet Divertissement,* Bettini, without advance warning, defaulted at the last moment. With Parodi fortunately present, Maretzek was able to offer the audience their choice of a refund or Parodi in a performance of the complete *Lucrezia.*[11] Only one person was reported to have accepted the refund.

On this thrilling occasion Parodi was rewarded with "a furor of excitement such as we never remember witnessing before," at least in New York; it reminded the *Albion* critic (by now presumably Richard Storrs Willis) of a European triumph (*Albion,* December 14, 1850, p. 596).

Reporting this episode, Noah, in a fit of patriotic paranoia, lashed out at the perfidious tenor: "We believe he never intended to sing, and has insulted our audience by paltry tricks. He intends to sail on Tuesday (December 10) for Havana, in hopes of carrying the news that he helped to break down the opera in New-York. The fact is, Maretzek is surrounded by a bevy of treacherous fellows, pretending friendship, but in fact trying to ruin him.[12] . . . Maretzek is a German [Bohemian] and not popular with the Italians. He must, however, take a stand against such paltry evasions of duty and contracts." But Parodi was great, and who cared for Bettini anyhow? (*Times and Messenger,* December 8, 1850).

For the remainder of December, with Parodi in Philadelphia, where the boundlessly energetic Maretzek was presenting an ancillary opera season, revivals of various productions were given at Astor Place: *Don Giovanni* with the earlier cast, *La sonnambula* with Bertucca, and *Il giuramento* and *La favorita* with Truffi, but regrettably without Benedetti, who had been promised, but who was indisposed.

Scarcely had Bishop/Bochsa begun to savor their undisputed possession of Tripler Hall after Lind's departure, when Maretzek invaded their domain on December 14 with a monster concert announced as "most positively Parodi's first and only appearance in any Concert in America." The program, combining opera, concert, and popular music, was clearly designed to dim the Bishop/Bochsa luster with a single blow. The participants, besides Parodi, were the opera singers Domenico Lorini and Pietro Novelli, the acclaimed new German violinist Ferdinand Griebel, the ten-year-old piano prodigy Master William Saar (1840–1864),[13] the Astor Place Opera orchestra, and, notably, Maretzek's young pupil, the young American singer Virginia Whiting, making her debut on this occasion.

[11] For some reason, Forti, who was present, refused to sing the Gennaro, and Lorini nobly came to the rescue.

[12] *Figaro!* too, referred to the dastardly clique who owned the Astor Place Opera House. They had double-crossed the former manager, Edward P. Fry, letting him "fall to the ground," and replaced him with Maretzek, who, at least, was more sophisticated and knew his way around.

[13] The son and pupil of Donat Saar, a Central European musician, little Master Saar, belying his tender years, had performed admirably at the recent first concert of the Musical Fund Society.♪

Treading upon sacred Bishop territory, Parodi sang the *Di tanti palpiti* from Rossini's *Tancredi;* also a *romanza* from Verdi's *Giovanna d'Arco;* a concert rondo, popularly known as "Ricci's Waltz," in reality an aria from Luigi Ricci's opera *Il colonnello* (Naples 1835); the Drinking Song from Halévy's new opera *La tempesta* (London 1850), especially composed for Parodi; the Masker's Trio from *Don Giovanni,* with Lorini and Virginia Whiting; and the "favorite duett" from *Norma,* with Whiting as Adalgisa.

The remainder of the program was largely devoted to popular items that might have been heard—and indeed were—at Bochsa's concurrent Promenade concerts. Maretzek scooped Bochsa's "Carnival of Venice" extravaganza with his own "virtuoso orchestral arrangement of the tune," consisting of variations in the form of "burlesque solos" for violin, double bass, clarinet, oboe, and flute, played by well-known, albeit conventionally garbed, practitioners of these instruments; he gave the first performance of his "Chit-Chat Polka," composed for, and dedicated to, Mademoiselle Parodi, and also his celebrated "Tip-Top Polka." Little Saar played a *Fantaisie de concert* on themes from Donizetti's *Belisario*♪ by the French composer/pianist Alexandre-Édouard Goria (1823–1860), and Griebel played Artôt's Fantasy on melodies from Bellini's *Il pirata*♪ and Vieuxtemps's Burlesque Variations on "Yankee Doodle." (There seems to have been a mania for musical burlesques that year.)

Providing people who for religious reasons avoided the opera with an opportunity to hear Parodi, the concert attracted an audience of "more than 4000," consisting largely of "clergymen of all denominations, and of lawyers, authors, in fact, all the intelligence of the metropolis, [who] reveled in the extraordinary entertainment," reported the *Herald* (December 18, 1850). Parodi was "supreme in her brilliancy and purity of style—confessedly the great lyrical vocalist of the age."

The concert was an unqualified success. As the *Mirror* critic confessed (December 16, 1850), all his encomiums had been exhausted in his previous reviews of Parodi—indeed, there was nothing left to say. He therefore focused his attention on Virginia Whiting, who "made a very favorable impression" at her first appearance and "gave promise of becoming an *artiste* of a high order." Seventeen years old, "of a medium figure, rather pretty, possessing a voice of great flexibility and sweetness, and a method that showed the skillful and careful training of Maretzek,"[14] she was "a well-educated musician, accomplished in the French and Italian languages, and rarely qualified for the sphere she [had] chosen."[15] Master Saar, too, was admired, not only by the *Mirror* but by Maurice Strakosch,♪ who was seen enthusiastically applauding him. And Herr Griebel performed with more feeling than had been heard since Ole Bull♪ (the *Courier and Enquirer* said not since Vieuxtemps).♪ The orchestra was splendid, as always under Maretzek, and his "'Tip-Top Polka' set the younger members of the audience wild."

So successful was this concert that Maretzek immediately announced another for December 17—this time "POSITIVELY" Parodi's last appearance before leaving for Phil-

[14]Saroni, who described Virginia Whiting's voice as a high soprano (the *Courier and Enquirer* said a mezzo-soprano), wrote that although she could not be compared with Parodi, her debut was "the most auspicious ever made by an American" (*Musical Times,* December 21, 1850, p. 129).

[15]Virginia Whiting was the daughter of D. Whiting, a comedian from Boston, currently a member of the Broadway Theatre stock company.

adelphia. Richard Storrs Willis, making his official debut at the *Albion* on this latter occasion, adopted a relaxed, affable style far removed from the supercilious pedantry of his predecessor Watson, but no less faithfully reflecting contemporary musical prejudices. First remarking that the hall was crowded from floor to ceiling, Willis plunged into the regulation attack on Verdi. A duet from *Attila* had been spiritedly sung by Beneventano and Novelli, but the critic was impelled, he confessed, to protest against Verdi's "noisy instrumentation, and likewise others of the same school, who so often mar the vocal effect with their habit of overlaying the richest of all instruments, the human voice, with a unique accompaniment of some orchestral instrument, the instrument droning along, note for note, with the voice." Parodi, who repeated the *Di tanti palpiti* "with incomparable brilliancy and grace, [was] a totally charming singer," except that she was "successively flat at the end of the aria and also flatted one of her longer trills," thus giving the impression of a modulation to another key. But these were mere trifles and served as favorable contrasts to her otherwise faultless singing.

Maurice Strakosch, just back from his long tour,[16] "did wonders at the piano, but he rode over the rhythmical sensibilities and injured the flow of the music by chopping up the time too much. . . . The 'Prayer for the Left Hand,' as it somewhat drolly read upon the programme, seemed to us uncommonly well done, even with a knowledge of the left-hand marvels performed by Dreyschock of Prague, the king of that kind of miracle, who makes the left hand his peculiar study."

It was unfair to Virginia Whiting to make her sing an unmusical, difficult, and ungrateful *Romanza* (unidentified); but she made good the second time around on her encore, when she no longer flatted, "and her fresh voice nestled in the memories, no doubt, of many leaving the hall." Bertucca was so stimulated by the general enthusiasm that she sang the *Polacca* from Verdi's *I Lombardi* "with emulative musical abandonment, which bore all hearts with her."

In the second half of the concert—act two of *Lucrezia Borgia* performed in full costume by Bertucca, Amalia Patti, Lorini, Beneventano, Novelli, and Virginia Whiting—Parodi showed her "preeminent and absorbing" dramatic gifts. "Her tragic genius is certainly extraordinary, and the more surprising from its being a decided contradiction to the shape of her head," wrote Willis, who evidently inclined to phrenology. "One does not expect from the conical outline—starting from that schoolgirl rounding and fullness of the lower part of the face and extending upward, the strength and grasp of intellectual conception which she shows. She completely possessed the audience with this phase of her genius, and we are confident that in all afterthought on this very brilliant concert, the dramatic action of Parodi will be the most admired feature of the performance" (*Albion,* December 21, 1850, p. 608).

Maretzek had "struck a gold mine" with his concerts at Tripler Hall, commented Noah. And not a single member of the audience—not a single clergyman—left the hall when the *Lucrezia* part of the program came on (*Times and Messenger,* December 22, 1850). A triumph!

It was perhaps understandable that at this point Bishop/Bochsa decided that the time had come to cut their losses and move on.

[16]During his tour of Latin America, Strakosch had served as foreign correspondent for the *Message Bird.*

About the beginning of 1850, Éduard Reményi (*né* Hoffman) (1830–1898), a young violin virtuoso and political exile from Hungary, arrived in New York with a group of his compatriots seeking asylum from the hostilities at home. In 1848, at the outset of a brilliantly promising musical career, Reményi, a fiery patriot, had become militarily embroiled in the ill-fated revolution that was consuming his native land. Closely associated with Artúr Görgey, the problematical commander of the Hungarian forces, young Reményi was forced to flee for his life when Görgey, on being appointed to succeed Lajos Kossuth as leader of the insurrection, abruptly surrendered to the enemy.

Once in New York, Reményi proceeded to resume his interrupted musical career, appearing first on January 9, 1850, at an introductory private *soirée* at the Astor House. Saroni, who had expected a grizzled, "grim warrior," was surprised when the artist turned out to be a spectacularly gotten-up youth who looked about eighteen. "He was dressed in regimentals, scarlet coat, white vest, and grey pantaloons; on his breast was a large *medaillon* with the likeness of his illustrious countryman Kossuth, and upon his watch-chain were depending amulets and trinkets of various kinds, amongst which there were some presented to him by Görgey before he turned traitor."

Despite these gaudy trappings, it was instantly apparent to Saroni that Reményi was "no ordinary artist": "His manner, his execution, and his every gesture show him to be widely different from the mercenary players who lately have sought our shores. He and his instrument appeared to be one; a strange fire flashed from his eyes, and as he stood behind the screen, trying a few passages on his violin, we could not help comparing him to a fiery steed eager for battle, and we have no doubt that if he displayed the same energy and impetuosity when at the side of Görgey, whose aide-de-camp he was, the Austrian host must have rued his prowess. . . . With the first step on the platform he won the sympathy of his audience, and when, with sparkling eyes and caring neither for audience nor accompanist [Richard Hoffman], he drew the first tone from his instrument, his listeners were convinced that they had before them a talent of no ordinary degree."

If the *Élégie,* op. 10, by Heinrich Ernst was not his forte, Reményi swept all before him when he played his unaccompanied Hungarian National Airs: "He displayed a vigor of bowing, a promptness and decision, together with a volume of tone truly astonishing." Richard Hoffman, probably ignited by Reményi's fire, played Thalberg's Fantasy on *La sonnambula* better than ever before (*Saroni's Musical Times,* January 12, 1850, p. 181).

The huge crowd that attended Reményi's public debut, which followed on January 19 at Niblo's Concert Saloon, was attributed in the *Mirror* (January 22, 1850) to the popular current interest in the Hungarian refugees. The response to Reményi, however, was not "due alone to their sympathy for this cause" but to the extraordinary quality of the young performer. As all the critics observed, his program was far above the usual standard of violin virtuosos, comprising complete concertos by Vieuxtemps and Wilhelm Bernhard Molique (1802–1869) (a German composer new to America) and, with Henry C. Timm, a duo by Osborne and de Bériot on themes from *La sonnambula.* Besides Timm, Reményi's assisting artists were William Scharfenberg and the Hungarian soprano Annette Stephani, a fellow refugee and "an artist of extraordinary talent and capacity"; she had earlier been heard at Saroni's chamber music concert on January 10 (discussed below). Theodore Eisfeld conducted the overtures to Rossini's *Otello* and Reissiger's *Die Felsenmühle.*

First commending Reményi on the brevity of his program—only five pieces in each half (albeit two of them concertos)—then commending Eisfeld as a "rapidly rising rival of George Loder and Max Maretzek," without the "iron inflexibility of the first [or] the dashing air of the second, [but] a clear-headed, self-possessed man, a good musician, and an excellent score-reader," the *Mirror* critic at last turned to the star of the evening.

Reményi, at the age of twenty, "displayed a very pure and melodious tone, a neat and sometimes vigorous use of the bow, and a more than ordinary command of the resources of the finger board. His performance is full of life, though not marked by great power; he plays delicately and distinctly, and his passages of detached notes being peculiarly neat and well articulated. His cantabile playing is graceful and flowing, but not marked with much sentiment; he seems unused to the melting mood, and at times flourishes his bow as if he grasped a saber." But if spirit, rather than pathos, was his characteristic, he was still very young and might yet "develop powers in the pathetic which he does not show at present."

However: "We regret that so unexceptionable a program should be marred by such a piece as the last, called 'Hungarian Native Melodies.' They, or it—for we could detect but one—might have been Hungarian—we do not mean to say they were not—but it might also have been French, Finnish, Choctaw, or Chinese, for any character it had. To it was attached such a *coda* of string-snapping, finger-racing flourishes as any amateur of ordinary cleverness can accomplish if he will take the trouble, but which he will play only as a bit of fun, for they are meaningless and have no merit, save that of being rather droll. To perform this piece, Mr. Reményi put on a red coat. We say nothing, but he is too good an artist for such puerile humbug."

Madame Stephani again revealed herself to be an extraordinary singer possessing a "soprano voice remarkable for its compass, clearness, and truth of intonation." In the aria of the "Fairy Queen" [*sic*] in *Die Zauberflöte* she was infallibly on pitch and effortlessly hit a high F right on the mark. She was equally fine in an aria from Hérold's *Le Pré aux clercs,*[♪] with Reményi playing the *obbligato,* and in the big *scena* from *Der Freischütz.* Scharfenberg excelled himself in Mendelssohn's *Capriccio brillant* for piano and orchestra. Altogether, it was one of the most satisfactory concerts the critic had ever attended.

Saroni, although still generally enthusiastic about Reményi, on second hearing discovered several points about which to quibble, but especially he disapproved of the red coat, which he sincerely trusted would not destroy Reményi's art (*Musical Times,* January 26, 1850, p. 206). And the *Courier and Enquirer* (January 23, 1850), too, in a lengthy, highly commendatory review, complained of the Hungarian pieces and their sartorial accompaniment: "We hope that Mr. Reményi's musical friends will suggest the omission of these or similar ones, and also of his red coat at future concerts."

Following a short tour that included Philadelphia and Baltimore, Reményi returned to New York for a second concert, on February 25 at the Tabernacle. This time he played a *Souvenir de la Hongrie* by Molique (presumably in conventional attire) and an *Andante spianato* by Ernst, both with orchestra; also, with Timm at the piano, a *Grande Fantaisie concertante* by Osborne and de Bériot on themes from *William*

Tell and "The Carnival of Venice," with the Ernst introduction. Reményi was assisted by Eufrasia Borghese, who sang an aria from *La Favorite* and a *Rondo brillant* by Donizetti. The orchestra was conducted by Signor La Manna of Niblo's; tickets were fifty cents.

Still at the *Albion,* on March 2, 1850 (p. 104) Henry C. Watson, apparently hearing Reményi for the first time, rancorously reviewed his concert. Watson was put off by the gaudy publicity lavished on Reményi, especially in the *Herald* (February 25, 1850), where a highly inflated account of the young hero's past adventures with Görgey had been topped off with a tasteless anecdote about how a woman had died after hearing Paganini and how Reményi possessed the same power.

Perhaps as a result of this dubious publicity, wrote Watson, Reményi's second concert attracted only a small audience—not more than 800, deadheads included. Had Watson swallowed all the inordinate advance puffing, he too would have gone to the concert loaded with expectations. But "the promises, *à la* Ole Bull, were altogether too transparent for even the most credulous to believe. We shall not even attempt to calculate to what extent this nauseous puffing injured [Reményi's] prospects . . . but we are sure that it was calculated to keep hundreds away."

Nevertheless, Watson conceded, but with reservations, that considering his youth, Reményi had achieved a certain proficiency on the violin: "His execution is rapid and brilliant, if not always clear and certain. He plays with much emphasis and with considerable passion, but the excellence of his performance is marred by one fault—he plays with too stiff a bow. His tone is neither pure nor liquid, but is produced by mere force. . . . This same stiffness mars the delicacy of his execution and destroys the flow of his *portamento*."

Watson warmed to his task: "Mr. Reményi is too full of gesticulation; he is continually swaying from side to side, and this exaggeration is also prominent in his playing. He digs out sentiment with the heel of his bow, as though he would tear out its heart from the quivering strings. He falls also into that error common to talented young men, the impression that strong eccentricities will be taken, or mistaken, for evidence of genius. . . . If Mr. Reményi would pay more attention to his bow arm, would abjure all affectation, and would beg his friends not to place him upon an eminence which it is hardly possible he can ever reach, he would, standing upon his real merits, be an artist of some distinction."

On May 13, the young American violinist James W. Perkins made his debut at the Apollo. Still in his teens, Perkins had been heard from time to time since 1848—most recently on April 20 at the Philharmonic, as one of the soloists in Maurer's *Concertante* for four violins and orchestra—but this was his formal debut. Possessing "an uncommon degree of musical talent . . . his playing," wrote Saroni, "is characterized by great precision, perfect tune, and good expression, and his manners are exactly as they should be—plain, modest, and unassuming"; their appealing simplicity had won him the immediate friendship of his audience.

Perkins was a worthy pupil of his master, the highly esteemed violinist and conductor Michele Rapetti, and "we can well imagine the gratification of the two, when the one for his perseverance in studying and the other for his patience in teaching were now rewarded by the smiles of the beautiful and the appreciation of the connoisseurs. The performance was a triumph for all concerned; it was a triumph for the true cause of music, too, for not many days ago, the name of Paganini and every great violinist that ever lived was abused by ushering before the New-York public a man who had nothing to sustain him in his assumed position but the few lines which a corrupted press wasted upon him."[17] How great the contrast with Perkins, who relied only on "*his own* talent" to build himself a reputation.

Perkins was heard in a somewhat dated Air and Variations by Joseph Mayseder; in Osborne and de Bériot's popular *Duo concertant* on themes from *La sonnambula,* with Scharfenberg at the piano; in a duo by Spohr for violin and viola, with Rapetti admirably playing the viola; and as a closing number, in an Andante and *Rondo russe* by de Bériot. Perkins most probably also played second violin to his teacher's first in the concert's opening piece, Spohr's Piano Quintet in C Minor, op. 53 (the version with strings of the Quintet, op. 52, for winds and piano)—so well performed, with Scharfenberg at the piano, that Saroni wished it had been repeated.

Also present were Timm and Scharfenberg, who played a *Duo concertant* for two pianos—Variations on the March from Weber's *Preciosa,* jointly composed in 1833 by Mendelssohn and Moscheles—and the American soprano Julia L. Northall,♪ who sang William Vincent Wallace's♪ ballad "Why do I weep for thee" and an aria from *I puritani,* the latter receiving a "rapturous encore" (*Musical Times,* May 18, 1850, pp. 399–400).

Native musicians to be heard in that Lind year were few and far between. The singer David Griswold♪ made his second bid as a public singer on April 4 at the Apollo, with an all-American cast of assisting artists: Mrs. L. A. Jones, Allen Dodworth, George Henry (not George William) Curtis,♪ and George Frederick Bristow. Griswold was reported in the *Message Bird* (April 15, 1850, p. 298) to have improved greatly since his unpromising debut the previous November. But Bristow, with Curtis at the piano, playing violin and piano duos by Herz and Lafont, and by Osborne and de Bériot, had apparently been neglecting his violin playing and had regressed, while Curtis's piano playing had improved. Seated at "his favorite instrument" the piano, however, Bristow "made ample amends" for his slipshod violin playing, giving splendid performances of a *Grande Nocturne* and a *Polka de concert* by Herz. Dodworth, who apparently didn't need to improve, played cornet solos on themes from operas by Donizetti and Verdi with such mastery that the mere recollection of his performance of the *Ernani involami* caused this reviewer to shiver. Mrs. Jones and Griswold sang various light ballads and duets in English, one of them being Bristow's song "I wish I were a favorite flower" (published in the December 1, 1849, issue of the *Message Bird*), which Griswold was required to sing twice.

Apparently, Griswold continued to make remarkable progress: at his next concert, on October 22 at the Chinese Rooms, Saroni reported a "large and fashionable" audience, despite the Lind and Bishop/Bochsa competition currently in full blast at Tripler Hall (*Musical Times,* October 26, 1850, p. 48).

Hélène Stoepel, a young pianist of German origin, who had recently been performing in England and France, made her local debut at a Grand Concert presented

[17] Saroni was referring to one Paul Roultz, a violinist who had been outrageously puffed by Watson, only to fail miserably at his concert at the Tabernacle on April 25.

by the Havana opera company at the Tabernacle on June 15 (badly attended, despite their great successes at the Astor Place Opera House). Miss Stoepel, although supposedly a naturalized American, was interchangeably referred to as "Fräulein" and "Mademoiselle." She had recently returned from abroad together with her fiancé, William Vincent Wallace, who had been absent from the United States for the past five years;[18] also in the party was Wallace's sister Eliza Wallace-Bouchelle, a singer.

In England, where the *Message Bird*'s English critic had frequently heard "Mademoiselle" Stoepel, she was regarded as the best female pianist after Madame Louisa Dulcken (1811–1850) and Kate Loder (1825–1904). "To her charms as a pianist," he gallantly wrote (July 1, 1850, p. 378), "may be added those of her person, as she possesses a fine and expressive countenance, which may, without exaggeration, be called beautiful." At her debut, Miss Stoepel played Thalberg's Fantasy on Rossini's *Mosè in Egitto* and Leopold de Meyer's Variations on themes from *Lucrezia Borgia* not only with decision and energy, but also with feeling in the more tender passages.

Also among the American performers was the youngest of the current crop of youthful prodigies, little Master Sebastian Emile Cook, an eight-year-old pianistic "genius." A pupil of Herr Henry Charles Becht "from the banks of the Rhine," little Cook was puffed in the *Herald* as the greatest keyboard wizard since Leopold de Meyer. Not so, wrote Henry C. Watson in his stern review of Cook's first concert, on March 25 at the Tabernacle. After delivering his usual diatribe against the evils of overinflated puffing, Watson observed that while little Cook had a good right hand, his left was woefully uneducated. Besides, he played a lot of trash—"milk-and-water trash"—ghastly, pernicious trash—all composed by his teacher.

Little Cook needed to be taught to appreciate the finer and better things in music: "A boy of such tender years may astonish us by simple and exquisite taste and expression," humorlessly preached Watson, "but in gymnastic exhibitions he cannot hope to raise a wonder where De Meyer has been, and Hoffman yet remains." Cook's assisting artists were Julia Northall, Henry Timm, John Kyle, and the culpable Mr. Becht (*Albion,* March 30, 1850, p. 152).

"To raise funds for his future education" Cook gave a second concert at the Tabernacle on April 18, assisted by Madame Stephani and the violinist Leopold Meyer, formerly of the Astor Place orchestra and an incipient member of various minstrel troupes, including Christy's.♪ In puffing this event, Noah went sadly astray in referring to the little keyboard wizard as a great wonder who may "easily become another Paganini." Little Cook, an all but instantaneous has-been, immediately joined a company of presumably juvenile ballad singers (Odell, V, 598).

For obvious reasons, locally generated concerts were comparatively few in 1850, and for the most part badly attended. Beyond the well-established standbys—the Philharmonic, the Euterpean Society♪ (who announced their fifty-first annual concert and ball for March 7 at the Apollo), and Bradbury and Nash's annual monster juvenile exhibitions at the Tabernacle♪ (on April 13 and 17), now reportedly 1000 youngsters

[18] Wallace, who still had an undivorced wife in England, had decided to ignore his former marriage, and on October 17, 1850, he and Miss Stoepel were married in Boston. In 1850, too, Wallace applied for American citizenship, winning it in 1854.

strong—fresher musical concepts were advanced in the earlier part of the year by Hermann Saroni with his innovative chamber music series for *Musical Times* subscribers, and, to a lesser degree, by the recently formed Musical Fund Society.

With their unpromising debut to live down, the Musical Fund Society gave the second in their initial series of four monthly concerts for a "large and well-dressed audience" at the Astor Place Opera House on January 26. The soloists were the Astor Place singers Teresa Truffi, Amalia Patti, Emilio Rossi Corsi, and Giuseppe Guidi, also the American concert artists Julia Northall and Joseph Burke. Eisfeld conducted the overtures to *Der Freischütz* and Lindpaintner's *Jocko,* a Potpourri "for fifty wind instruments" by Peter Streck, and Mendelssohn's Violin Concerto played by Burke. Maretzek conducted for the singers, mostly in duets from various operas sung by variously paired vocalists.

Burke's superb performance of the Mendelssohn Concerto was by far the "gem of the evening."[19] To the reviewer for the *Mirror* (Richard Grant White?) Burke revealed himself to be "among the greatest violinists of the age, and were he in any civilized country where the English language was not the mother tongue, he would receive that homage and those substantial marks of consideration which we only award to those who own a foreign birth and speak a foreign tongue."

Julia Northall was charming in a duet with Rossi Corsi, Truffi and Guidi gave a "lachrymose" performance of a spirited love duet from *Linda di Chamounix,* and Signorina Patti again displayed her faults and excellences in a duet with Guidi. The final number, the Lindpaintner *Jocko* Overture, was lost in the hubbub and "confusion of shawling and coating" of the audience making their customary premature departure.

The review ended on a discord: "We understand that there is a combination to prevent Mr. Maretzek from conducting any important pieces at these concerts. Whoever forms this evil combination disgrace themselves and dishonor the art, and the sooner they overcome their petty jealousies and disband their paltry cliques, the better it will be for the cause they are all striving to serve" (*Mirror,* January 28, 1850).

The Musical Fund Society's third concert took place on February 23 at the Astor Place Opera House, with Bertucca, Perrini, Beneventano, and Guidi singing Italian opera repertory and Richard Hoffman brilliantly playing de Meyer opera fantasies; George Loder and Maretzek conducted. At the fourth and final event of the series, and the most brilliant, on March 21, as we know, Fanny Kemble recited Shakespeare to the Mendelssohn *Midsummer Night's Dream* music. It was suggested that this last concert be repeated at Niblo's Saloon, to satisfy the public's "extraordinary desire to enjoy the exquisite blending of oratory and music" (*Mirror,* March 22, 1850).[20]

"One year has elapsed since this admirable society was established for the benefit of musicians and their widows and orphans," wrote Saroni on April 20 (*Musical Times,* p. 352), "and the first annual report of the Secretary [of the Musical Fund Society] has

[19] Burke had given the first American performance of the Mendelssohn Concerto at the Philharmonic on November 24, 1849.♪

[20] Indeed, on April 4 at Niblo's (just before the arrival of the opera company from Havana), Fanny Kemble did give another reading of Shakespeare with incidental music, this time of *The Tempest,* for the benefit of the Theatre Fund Society. She was assisted by Miss Emmeline De Luce as Ariel, with a chorus of professionals and amateurs, and an orchestra under the direction of George Loder. The musical score, probably arranged by Loder, was not identified.

convinced us that we may safely predict [their] complete success." Notwithstanding the heavy expenses involved in establishing a new organization, the Society's treasury already contained some $2000, and the membership was steadily growing. Perhaps Saroni was being overoptimistic. At this rate, the widows and orphans would have to wait ten years before receiving help, for according to the Society's Constitution, no funds could be disbursed to needy beneficiaries until the treasury held $20,000.[21]

As for Saroni's chamber music series (begun on December 1, 1849),♪ at his second concert, on January 10 at Hope Chapel (Broadway, opposite the New-York Hotel), the excellent artists were Madame Stephani (making her New York debut), the splendid harpist Madame Jenny Lazare,♪ Scharfenberg, and a string quartet consisting of Eisfeld and Noll (violins), Schmidt (viola), and Eichhorn (cello). As an added attraction, Saroni played a transcription of his own on a piano that he was promoting—an instrument equipped with the "Aeolian Attachment," another of the endless succession of pianos doctored to produce unpianolike sounds.

Struggling with a cold, Madame Stephani sang a concert aria by Otto Nicolai (1810–1849) and the Queen of the Night aria from the *Zauberflöte;* with Scharfenberg at the piano, Madame Lazare played a Fantasy by Labarre, and with Saroni at the Aeolian piano, an unidentified duet. The string players performed quartets by Mozart and by one of the Fescas—either Friedrich (1789–1826) or, more probably, his son Alexander (1820–1849), both of whom composed chamber music for strings.

At his third concert, on April 24, again at Hope Chapel, Saroni once more performed on the Aeolian piano; Eisfeld, Noll, Schmidt, and Eichhorn played quartets by Haydn and Mozart; and a Herr Brandt rendered songs accompanied by the Aeolian piano.

Among the few resident artists who ventured to give concerts in 1850 was the formidable singer/teacher Elisa Valentini,♪ who appeared at Niblo's Saloon early in the year, on February 9 and March 11. The start of the first concert was delayed because the key to the piano had been inadvertently mislaid, a fact that Valentini communicated to the audience in distraught French. After the key was at last found, Valentini, still unhinged by the incident, stressfully gave her *scena* from *Norma,* but she apparently recovered in time for her finale, a performance of *La Colasa* in full Spanish costume.

A close friend of the Patti family, then residing in New York,[22] Valentini was assisted at her first concert by Amalia Patti, and at her second by Caterina Barili-Patti. Also appearing on February 9 were Sanquirico, Beneventano, Beneventano's pupil Madiani, Woloski, a pianist unknown to me, and the chorus master Émile Millet, who accompanied the singers (*Herald,* February 9, 10, 1850).

Reviewing Valentini's second concert in the *Albion* (March 16, 1850, p. 128), Watson, after noting that there were only about two to three hundred in the audi-

[21] Virtually the same officers were elected for the second year: Henry A. Coit, president; George Loder, vice-president; Anthony Reiff, second vice-president; Ogden Haggerty, John H. Austen, and Julius Metz, directors; William Scharfenberg, treasurer; John C. Scherpf, secretary; and Henry C. Timm, John A. Kyle, C. Pazzaglia, Theodore Eisfeld, Charles Jacoby, Harvey B. Dodworth, Ambrose Schmitz, George Schneider, Daniel Walker, George De Luce, J. Windmüller, and James L. Ensign, trustees.

[22] Valentini gave singing lessons to little Adelina Patti, now seven years old.

ence,[23] unkindly wrote: "Signora [*sic*] Valentini is fair, fat, and past forty, despite which she retains considerable freshness of voice, and sings with some brilliancy." She should not, however, have attempted "On the banks of Guadalquivir," for it invited comparison with Madame Bishop, "and with the exception of [Rosine] Laborde, no one can compare with La Bishop in the *mécanique* of her art."

As always, Madame Barili-Patti, despite her worn voice, made one wish she were ten years younger, that one might have heard her in her prime. Also appearing at this concert were Madame Lazare, "the best harpist after Bochsa"; a Mr. Emiliano Ollmak, who played the violin well, but not well enough to be a soloist; Madiani, who sang well, but seldom in tune; and Herr van der Weyde, a novice accompanist and performer on the Aeolian piano, who should "practice in private before again attempting a public exhibition."

Madame Lazare gave a concert of her own on March 19 at the Chinese Rooms, assisted by Signorina Valentini, a Mademoiselle Perrichou, Timm, Scharfenberg, the violinist Leopold Meyer, and van der Weyde, who, one hopes, had been diligently practicing in the meantime.

The flute virtuoso Julius Siede announced a farewell concert at the Apollo on March 23, before departing for London. Of his assisting artists, Mesdames Stephani and Laura Jones defaulted, but Timm and Scharfenberg and Siede's fellow flutists Eben, Busch, and Kyle were present. Siede's "flute *soirée* was, alas, performed to an empty house," wrote Watson. Preeminent in his field, Siede would be missed, but he would, no doubt, be better appreciated in London (*Albion,* March 30, 1850, p. 152). Whether or not Siede actually went to London, he would soon be locally appreciated to his heart's content for his brilliant collaboration with Jenny Lind and Kyle in the Nightingale's sensational *Trio concertant* from Meyerbeer's *A Camp in Silesia.*

Madiani, Beneventano's pupil, assisted by Signora Barili-Patti, Emilio Rossi Corsi, and W. A. King, made his formal debut at the Apollo on April 1 to an empty house. And the departing Astor Place star Giuseppe Guidi bade farewell to rows of empty seats at the Apollo on May 15, despite his large and imposing cast of assisting artists—Amalia Patti, Giuseppe Forti, Madiani, Kyle, Drescher (clarinetist), Richard Hoffman, W. A. King, F. N. Crouch (who sang several of his Irish ballads), and an orchestra successively conducted by Maretzek and Loder.

Having officially welcomed the Hungarian military heroes, announced Noah in the *Times and Messenger* (January 13), we were "now about to enjoy their talented performers," and he named a Mr. Krausz, who sang in twenty-nine languages and who was about to give a concert, waiting only for the arrival of a Madame Schödl, heralded as "a splendid looking woman." His troupe once assembled, Krausz planned to take them to Washington.[24]

Indeed, for a brief spell, the Hungarian emigrants—at first officially and unoffi-

[23] A feature of Signorina Valentini's advertisements for this concert was her announcement that she had personally sold $500 worth of tickets.

[24] At about this time a company of Hungarian Minstrels, reported to be excellent artists, appeared at Barnum's American Museum. Most likely they were true Hungarians, rather than an exotically named blackface company, as Odell suggests (*Annals,* V, 588).

cially welcomed with balls, receptions, benefits, and other manifestations of enthusiastic hospitality—were all the rage. Among the most admired of the musical newcomers, aside from Reményi, was Madame Stephani, who on March 25 gave a concert at the Apollo for the benefit of her needy countrymen. Among her assisting artists two pianists were announced—Carl (or Karl, or Charles) Wels♪ from Prague and Emanuel Brandeis from Vienna—but only Wels seems to have appeared. He was praised for his charming solo on the physharmonica, described as a "sweet-sounding" ancestor of the harmonium, and for his performance on the piano of a "'Grand Hungarian Storm March' from Liszt" (1843) (Searle 232), for which Brandeis had been announced. The violinist Joseph Noll, the flutist Julius Siede, the clarinetist Xavier Kiefer, and the cellist H. Braun played an assortment of chamber music, some by Beethoven, some with Wels. Madame Stephani, who particularly excelled in the Grand Concert Aria composed for her by Nicolai, received glowing praise, not only for her superb artistry but also for the quality of her concert and its noble cause, both of which "deserved a much larger audience" (*Herald,* March 27; *Musical Times,* March 30, 1850, p. 316). Apparently the rage for Hungarians was of short duration.

Other concert-givers from abroad included a Canadian Indian family, a brother and two sisters of the Mohawk Nation, who, wearing native dress and singing in Mohawk and English, gave three uneventful "Grand Concerts" of "sacred music and sentimental songs" at the Tabernacle on April 15 and 19, and at Hope Chapel on May 7.[25]

A Monsieur and Madame Hillyer from Paris advertised a program of "selections from the most popular operas of the day, assisted by a first-rate orchestra," at the Tabernacle on October 3 (*Herald,* September 28, 1850). The *Musical Times* (October 12, 1850, p. 30) reported an attendance of fifty to sixty and found it hard to say which were more lost in that vast cavern—the audience or the orchestra. Of the performance, "the less said, the better."

Frederick and Louisa Doctor, a husband-and-wife piano duo from Vienna, also encountered difficulties in establishing themselves in New York. Despite extravagant advance publicity, their efforts to rent a hall were repeatedly frustrated. After several false starts, they finally made their delayed debut at Tripler Hall on November 30. The *Message Bird* (December 16, 1850, p. 562) praised the Doctors for their fine performance on two pianos of Herz's Duo on themes from Rossini's *La donna del lago,*♪ and lavished particularly extravagant verbiage upon Herr Doctor for his solo playing, which disclosed "a surprising strength of wrist and finger, particularly of the left hand, in which he surpasses every pianist who has visited us, not even excepting De Meyer, whom, though he may not reach in some of his manual incredibilities, he at least excels in the legitimate use of the pedal." But, exquisitely quibbled the writer, "the unusual digital strength of Herr Doctor seems peculiarly to demand more of *sleight* in the centre divisions of the keyboard, in order to justify the expectations of a marvel-craving community." (Critical double-talk apparently did not originate in the twentieth century.)

A youthful Signorina Gandolfi, a vocal pupil of Millet, made her uneventful debut at the Apollo on December 28. Her assisting artists were the infrequently heard opera tenor Francesco Bailini, the actor/singer Ferdinand Meyer, the Philharmonic bassoonist Anthony Reiff,♪ and G. F. Bristow.

[25] In English they sang a Hutchinson Family song, "The Blue Juniata."

There was no scarcity of interested auditors at the "exhibition concert" at the Apollo on May 22 of the "American Mammoth, or Grand Double Pianoforte," the novel instrument built by the double bassist and piano maker James Pirsson. The ultimate superpiano, the huge contraption with its two facing keyboards, one at either end, was to all intents and purposes two large pianos sharing a single frame. The Mammoth had great advantages, however, over two separate pianos, wrote Watson (*Albion,* May 25, 1850, p. 248): not only did it more elegantly occupy less space, but it had greater capacity and power, due to the sharing of a single sounding board. With a range of seven octaves, from A to A, its tone quality was remarkably even. It would ornament the drawing room of any large mansion.

The *Message Bird* (June 1, 1850, p. 345) commended the Mammoth for its full, even, and brilliant tone, its light and facile touch, and its highly finished workmanship. It would undoubtedly be "a valuable acquisition to any concert room." Saroni (*Musical Times,* May 25, 1850, p. 412), who had previously inspected the Mammoth, was "more than ever pleased with the hugeness of its bass and the brilliancy of its treble." Able to substitute for a small orchestra, wrote Saroni, such an instrument would be of inestimable value to musical associations for their rehearsals: "even if but one performer plays upon it, he can draw out such massive tones that one imagines to hear anything but a pianoforte."

Demonstrated by the topnotch keyboard performers Richard Hoffman, William Scharfenberg, H. C. Timm, and William A. King, the program included eight-hand arrangements of the overtures to Spohr's *Jessonda*♪ and Auber's *Le Cheval de bronze,*♪ and, with flute and strings, the overtures to Beethoven's *Prometheus*♪ and *Egmont.*♪ The accompanying instrumentalists were Joseph Burke, Richard Pell, and Samuel Johnson (violins), John A. Kyle (flute), Alfred Boucher♪ (cello), and James Pirsson himself, playing the double bass. Additionally, Kyle and Scharfenberg played a flute and piano duet on themes from *Jessonda;* Timm and King played an unidentified duo for two pianos; Burke played a violin fantasie on themes from Donizetti's *La favorita;* and Hoffman a piece for solo piano that was identified in the *Message Bird* as a Fantasia by Émile Prudent (1817–1863), but in both the *Albion* and *Saroni's Musical Times* as Liszt's Reminiscences of *Lucia di Lammermoor* (composed 1835–36) (Searle 397). Enthusiastically received, Hoffman played de Meyer's Fantasia on Rossini's *Semiramide* as an encore.

With this performance, wrote Watson, Hoffman surpassed all praise. Indeed, praise was superfluous, for no amount of praise could make him greater than he already was. The *Message Bird* reported that Hoffman played like de Meyer with the greatest of ease, and if he did not get "tripped up by vanity," he would eventually equal Thalberg, nay, even Listz [*sic*].

But Saroni thought Hoffman should have omitted the "unmeaning prelude" to the Liszt and some of the "less meaning" variations in the de Meyer. He disapproved of Hoffman's habitual "improvised prelude of three chords. This preluding has become a habit with the gentleman," he peevishly wrote. "If he knew how it mars the effect of the succeeding composition, he would probably not do it." The program was triumphantly repeated on May 29.

Less novel was the organ builder Henry Erben's exhibition on July 22 at his establishment at 168 Centre Street,♪ of a recently completed organ for a church in Richmond, Virginia. As usual on these occasions, Erben's star exhibitor was W. A. King, who this time played his arrangements of the overtures to Weber's *Oberon* and Auber's

Masaniello and a Grand Concert Overture by the German/Danish composer Friedrich Kuhlau (1786–1832). King played excellently, as usual, except for some "dirty footwork," due to what the *Message Bird* (August 1, 1850, p. 410) called his "constitutional nervousness" (possibly a polite euphemism for King's regrettable alcoholism). King's sister-in-law Mrs. Edward J. Loder, who sang two arias, "sustained her reputation," despite occasional wanderings from her usually faultless intonation. Admission to Erben's exhibition was fifty cents.

Apart from the two *Messiahs* and *The Creation* performed by the infant Harmonic Society, and excepting Madame Bishop's sacred spectaculars at Tripler Hall, the 1850 crop of sacred concerts was exceedingly sparse and almost painfully modest. On January 29 the music committee and choir of Dr. Ferris's church (Market and Henry Streets) tendered a complimentary concert to their organist, William Richard Bristow♪ (G. F. Bristow's father). On February 27, Mr. Sweetser,♪ the music director of the Church of the Puritans (Union Square), presented a Grand Sacred Festival with Miss Anna Stone (of Boston), Mrs. L. A. Jones, the opera basso Signor Rosi, and the brothers G. F. and E. T. Root in a program of music by Handel, Rossini, Verdi, Cherubini, and others.

On May 27, at the Church of the Messiah (728 Broadway) appeared the vocalists Mrs. C. E. Horn,♪ Misses Northall, De Luce, Maria Leach,♪ a Miss Jenkins, the Messrs. Henry C. Watson, B. F. Robinson, W. H. Demarest, H. W. Greatorex,♪ and S. L. Leach, and the organists Timm, Scharfenberg, and W. A. King (who took turns at the organ) in a concert of sacred music by Crotch, Handel, Haydn, Mozart, Mendelssohn, William Horsley, Cherubini, Spohr, Novello, Marcello, and C. E. Horn. (Mrs. Horn's recitative and air from her late husband's last oratorio *Daniel's Prediction: The Vision of Belshazzar* (London 1848) was considered one of the most interesting features of the concert.) The *Message Bird* (June 15, 1850, p. 360), although approving the content of the varied program, found the performances to have been marred by a lack of sympathy among the vocalists—whether toward each other or the music, or because of insufficient rehearsing, the writer was not prepared to say. Or perhaps it was because the organ was sadly out of tune. And at a fifty-cent concert, too!

Also in May, as a feature of the Second Annual Church Convention, held at Dr. Krebs's Rutgers Street Church, *Absalom,* a pastiche oratorio, received a few performances. Pieced together by the organist and music director of the Rutgers Street Church, Isaac Baker Woodbury,♪ from works by Handel, Haydn, Beethoven, Félicien David, and an unspecified Romberg, among others, *Absalom* was rehearsed under Woodbury's direction and conducted by one George Wallace; George Frederick Bristow presided at the organ. Inordinately puffed and persistently advertised in the *American Musical Review, and Choir Singers' Companion,* a new sacred-music-oriented monthly edited by Woodbury, first issued January 1, 1850, *Absalom* was included in *The Dulcimer, or New-York Collection of Sacred Music,* an anthology compiled by Woodbury, which contained nearly 1000 compositions by some 200 composers, published by Huntington and Savage, as was the *American Musical Review.*

On October 27, W. A. King, having peremptorily been dropped as Bishop/Bochsa's chorus master, offered modest competition to one of their Sunday sacred concerts at Tripler Hall with a sacred event of distinctly Italian flavor at the Church of the Nativity (Second Avenue). Signora Angiolina Morra, Signor Morra, and Francesco

Bailini, all alumni of the first Italian opera company at Astor Place in 1847, and a Miss Agnes Dressler sang works by Pietro Generali, Rossini, Mercadante, and others.

On November 25, at the Mercer Street Church (near Ninth Street), George Frederick Root♪ made a final appearance before embarking for Europe, where he planned to "prosecute his professional studies."[26] With Mrs. L. A. Jones and a group of "the best amateurs," and with Sigismund Lasar♪ at the organ, the program included excerpts from Neukomm's *David*♪ and Rossini's *Stabat Mater,* lots of Handel, some Haydn, "etc." (*Tribune,* November 25, 1850).

And on December 18 at the Hammond Street Congregational Church, Mrs. L. A. Jones. Mrs. C. E. Horn, Robert Andrews, and Messrs. Lincoln and Bell sang works by Handel, Mendelssohn, and Vincent Novello; Timm and Lasar played organ duets by Mozart, Beethoven, and Mendelssohn.

Tickets for these events, as for all sacred concerts, were fifty cents, except for the Grand Sabbath Concerts at Castle Garden. There one might enjoy the summer breezes every Sunday evening from May through the better part of August for 12½ cents, while listening to George Loder conduct excerpts from favorite oratorios, presumably in instrumental versions, for no singers were listed. Loder presented excerpts from Rossini's *Stabat Mater,* Félicien David's *Le Désert,* unidentified works by Beethoven and Pergolesi, and—permitting himself a bit of leeway—less sacred fare, such as a "Grand Military Solo" for violin by de Bériot and a violin concerto by Ferdinand David, both played by Joseph Noll. Additionally, solos for the flute were played by Felice Eben, a fantasie on the *cornetto di basso* by Drescher, and a solo on an unnamed instrument "producing the effect of a full orchestra" by its inventor, one Carl Brossius. Frequently repeating this program, Loder would combine on a single bill—as, for instance, on July 28—bits of Handel's *Messiah,* Ferdinand David's violin concerto, a flute solo, and various "overtures, solos, duos, and favorite waltzes" played by the orchestra.

On August 25, Dodworth's Cornet Band♪ replaced Loder and his orchestra at the Grand Sabbath Concerts, where "the most popular operas and oratorios" continued to be advertised, still at 12½ cents.

Except for spectacular gala events combining stars of the theatre and music worlds, the general run of benefit concerts offered little novelty, and thus attracted predominantly meager audiences. On January 5, the Ladies' Hebrew Benevolent Society, for instance, held a decidedly second-string Grand Vocal and Instrumental Concert at the Apollo, performed by the piano prodigy Josephine Bramson,♪ the singers Madiani and Jules Hecht, the violinist Leopold Meyer, the flutist Felice Eben, and the actress/singer Mrs. George Holman.

A so-called Grand Concert and Military Festival given at the Tabernacle on

26 "This gentleman, who is known to a vast number of our citizens as the Vocal Professor of the Rutgers and Spingler Institutes, important and educational institutions, leaves this city for Paris this week," wrote Saroni. "He proposes to prosecute his vocal studies there for a year or longer, and to enquire into all that is new or valuable in vocal instruction for single and class study. He leaves, as his *locum tenens* at these large institutions, an excellent musician and popular gentleman, Mr. Richard [Storrs] Willis. Mr. Root will, no doubt, glean much valuable information during his sojourn, of which his pupils will reap the benefit on his return. The urbane and gentlemanly manners of Mr. Root have rendered him generally popular and beloved, and the warmest and kindest wishes accompany him on his voyage, and await his return" (*Musical Times,* November 30, 1850, p. 109).

February 2 for the benefit of the New-York Volunteers, as the local veterans of the Mexican War were called, attracted only a so-so audience. The announced participants, a heterogeneous crew, included the singer Madame Antoinette Otto,♪ just back from another of her frequent junkets to Europe; a Madame Catherine Boernstein-Routh (or Ruth), newly from Paris and making her American debut on this occasion; and Julia Northall. Also Herr Brandt, Stephen Leach, Joseph Burke, and three military bands—Dodworth's Cornet Band, Shelton's American Brass Band, and Richard Willis's♪ (not Richard Storrs Willis) Brass Band—who were heard separately in various popular marches and collectively in a grand medley of American national airs.[27] The conductors were George Loder and Richard Willis.

As an added attraction, it was announced that the heroine Mademoiselle Apollonia Jagello, newly arrived from the Hungarian battlefields, would attend this concert in full military regalia, to meet "her fellow soldiers, the New-York Volunteers." As it turned out, Mademoiselle Jagello (later pleading illness) did not appear (nor did Julia Northall). The veterans, nothing daunted, marched through the house, waving their tattered battle flags and eliciting "three times three cheers" from the medium-sized audience (*Herald,* February 3, 1850).

On a different level, Maretzek generously donated his services to all manners of causes. On January 15, to raise funds to complete the Church of St. Vincent de Paul, then being built on Canal Street, Maretzek appeared with his Astor Place stars, chorus, and orchestra at the Tabernacle. In various combinations they were heard in arias and ensembles derived from works having a more or less religious flavor—Verdi's *Nabucco,* Rossini's *Stabat Mater,* Donizetti's *Les Martyrs* (a reworking of *Poliuto*), and Meyerbeer's *Le Prophète.* Maretzek conducted, too, the more worldly overtures to Rossini's *William Tell* and Auber's *Les Diamants de la couronne,* and Bertucca was encored for her performance of the *Brindisi* from Verdi's *Macbeth.* For this event the Tabernacle was reportedly jammed with members of the French community.

The music and theatre communities rallied warmly to the aid of survivors of the dreadful Hague Street explosion and fire that on February 4 killed sixty-three people and rendered many more injured and homeless. The first of many events organized to help the sufferers of this disaster was a concert at the Tabernacle on February 13 by the German *Liederkranz,* now numbering 150 male choristers, under the direction of Charles Weisheit. The performers were Madame Boernstein-Routh, Timm, Scharfenberg, Siede, and other German musicians. Only a small attendance was reported at this event, and a similarly sparse audience attended the performance of *Lucia di Lammermoor,* donated to the same cause by Maretzek and his company at the Astor Place Opera House on February 19. But on February 28 the opera artists, appearing at a heavily promoted super-gala at the Tabernacle for the joint benefit of the Hebrew and German Benevolent Societies, drew a huge audience.

On March 14 at Niblo's Saloon, Mrs. Charles E. Horn was tendered a complimentary benefit (alas, poorly attended), featuring the first performance of "The Seven Ages of Man," a vocal/choral work by her late husband, derived from Shakespeare's *As You Like It.* As Watson reported (*Albion,* March 16, 1850, p. 128), each section was "unsympathetically introduced" by the actor Charles M. Walcot; "Infancy" and

[27] Among other patriotic marches, Shelton's Band played "The New-York Volunteers Quick Step" by the Italian-born bandmaster Claudio S. Grafulla.♪

"Childhood" were "sweetly" sung, respectively, by the Misses Northall and De Luce; the two succeeding stages were sung by an unidentified gentleman amateur who took on the task at very short notice; Henry Wellington Greatorex, the vocally gifted organist of St. Paul's Church, "acquitted himself most admirably," displaying "fine taste and great feeling" in the "Justice with fat capon lined" [*sic*] and the "Lean and slippered pantaloon" sections; and members of the Harmonic Society assisted in the choral parts. The work was obviously put on in a hurry, wrote Watson, and for that reason he was unwilling to pass judgment on the evidence of this first hearing, but all the same, it was not Horn at his best.

The performers in the miscellaneous second part of this concert were Timm (who probably presided over the first part as well), Hoffman, Scharfenberg, and Reményi. Commenting on the meager attendance, the *Tribune* (March 15, 1850) bluntly remarked: "The truth is that after a four months' opera season, the fashionable world gets tired of music."

Perhaps things did seem a bit crowded. On March 14, the night of Mrs. Horn's benefit, the German Ladies Benevolent Association held their annual concert at the Chinese Rooms, with Eisfeld again conducting his great success of the year before, Andreas Romberg's *The Song of the Bell.*♪ The all-German cast of singers consisted of Mesdames Minna Müller, Valeska Klietz, and Madame van Gulpen (the former Mathilde Korsinsky,♪ soon to depart for San Francisco), Messrs. Brandt and Wanderer (or Wander), and Henry C. Timm, who presided at the piano. Saroni reported that the Romberg work had been insufficiently rehearsed, that after the intermission Otto Dresel♪ and William Scharfenberg had creditably performed Herz's two-piano Variations on a theme from *William Tell,* and that Siede had played an unidentified capriccio for flute and played it well enough, but his performance of "The Pesther Waltz" by Lanner was most definitely out of place (*Musical Times,* March 23, 1850, p. 303).

Adam Fecher's annual benefit♪ at the Apollo on May 25 was a different story. In Saroni's jovial words: "We owe it to our country subscribers to give a short account of who and what the above celebrated personage [Fecher] is. He has reared music from its very infancy in this city, i.e., he has carried the music and the instruments to the different concerts which have taken place here ever since we can remember.

"By birth a German, he was formerly a trumpet player in a German cavalry regiment, and in his military, as well as musical, capacity he has won himself a host of friends. On Saturday last he had his annual benefit, at which he performed, *in propria persona,* a solo on the trumpet. We understand that he insisted upon having a company of soldiers firing a volley during the course of his performance, but the President of the Philharmonic [Henry C. Timm] pleaded for the nerves of the ladies, and that part of the performance was fortunately omitted. However, he [Fecher] evidently acquitted himself to his own satisfaction and to the satisfaction of the large audience."

With Eisfeld conducting the Philharmonic, the concert opened with the Overture to *Der Freischütz;* Noll played a German air with variations, evidently composed by himself, displaying "a mass of tone . . . which would have satisfied a Sivori or a Vieuxtemps"; the *Liederkranz* sang two "German glees," the second being "rapturously encored"; Timm and Scharfenberg repeated their two-piano piece by Moscheles and Mendelssohn; and the concert wound up with Maurer's Concerto for Four Violins and Orchestra, played by Noll, Bristow, Pfort, and Perkins, followed by a waltz by Eisfeld.

"On returning from the concert," convivially concludes Saroni, "we were agreeably surprised by a subterranean serenade at the corner of Anthony (now Worth) Street and Broadway. The German *Liederkranz,* rather partial to German lager beer, had descended into a [beer] cellar at the above location, and there discussed German song and German beer. The effect was a good one" (*Musical Times,* June 1, 1850, p. 423).[28]

On a vastly different scale were the spectacular benefits that combined the resources of the theatre and music worlds, such as the monster second annual benefit of the Dramatic Fund Society, given at the Astor Place Opera House on January 8. In addition to *As You Like It,* performed by an all-star cast headed by the great American actress Charlotte Cushman as Rosalind, and with incidental music conducted by George Loder, the Astor Place singers Borghese, Guidi, Emilio Rossi Corsi, and Sanquirico performed the second act of Donizetti's *L'elisir d'amore* under Maretzek's direction.

On January 22, Maretzek, with Borghese and Forti, appeared at a similarly elaborate, hugely attended benefit given by the Young Men's Hebrew Benevolent Association at the Broadway Theatre (the appearance attacked by N. P. Willis), the proceeds to be used to distribute fuel to the needy. Between *The School for Scandal* and *The Lady of the Lake,* performed by members of the Broadway Theatre company, Borghese sang the *Romanza* from *Le Prophète,* and Forti a cavatina from Rossini's *Otello;* Maretzek, by request, conducted his "Tip-Top Polka."

Wisely withholding further super-galas until after Jenny Lind's departure, Maretzek presented a monster performance on December 3 at the Astor Place Opera House, again for the Young Men's Hebrew Association, again to raise funds for the same cause. The huge program comprised a full performance of *La sonnambula* with Bertucca-Maretzek, the third act of *Ernani* with Truffi-Benedetti, and the ballet *Paquita* with Nathalie Fitzjames.

On December 10, swarms of theatre and music folk appeared at Tripler Hall for the benefit of the Patriarch of Blackface, Thomas Dartmouth Rice,♪ who, although still professionally active, was reported to have fallen on thin times. The participants included Madame Bishop (accompanied by Bochsa), Mrs. C. E. Horn, Mary Taylor,♪ Caroline Hiffert,♪ little Miss Emma Kilmiste,♪ Edward Seguin, Philip Mayer, T. Hillyer, and Stephen Leach. Timm, W. A. King, George Loder, and a Polish (or Bohemian) pianist Jan Pychowski (1818–1900) performed on Pirsson's Mammoth piano, and Dodworth's and Shelton's bands played marches and quicksteps. Also, fittingly, the blackface troupe, White's Serenaders,♪ gave their opera burlesques and supported Rice in his renditions "in character" of some of his old favorites, such as "Come, all you Virginia gals" and (appropriately) "Smile, my fortune." At the request of the benefit committee, a poetical address was composed and delivered by the versatile playwright/actor/manager John Brougham.

And finally, an even larger cast appeared at Niblo's Garden on December 21 for the third annual Dramatic Fund benefit. In addition to pantomime by the Ravels and

[28] In January the *Liederkranz* had serenaded Anthony Philip Heinrich in anticipation of their performance of his oratorio *The Jubilee of American Freedom,* presumably a version of his variously titled work, first presented as *The Pilgrims of America*♪ on June 16, 1842 (*Message Bird,* February 1, 1850, p. 218).

ballet by Celestine and Victorine Franck, Leon Espinosa, and their dance company from Paris, J. B. Buckstone's popular one-act farce *The Rough Diamond* (London 1847) was performed by stars from the Broadway Theatre; Madame Bishop sang "Home, Sweet Home," with Bochsa at the piano; Virginia Whiting sang *O luce di quest' anima* from *Linda di Chamounix;* and Maretzek presented his Astor Place cast in the first act of *Don Giovanni.*

A foolproof device to lure reluctant audiences to concerts of less than superstellar attraction was stumbled upon by the fertile-brained theatre and concert manager (and erstwhile accordionist, instrument inventor, and opera singer) Louis Martini.♪ Adding the seductive element of gambling to otherwise prosaic concert-going, Martini's "Donation Concerts," a combined music-and-raffle event originally intended to assist unemployed Italian musicians, soon evolved into the "tombola," or "gift concert," that would flourish far into the future. The idea was not entirely new. Martini probably remembered the successful concert given by the hornist Aupick♪ in 1841, when he had raffled off his painting collection at a good profit. The lottery/concert tickets had then cost $5; Martini charged a modest fifty cents, and to whet the public appetite, he put on exhibition at Mr. Goldoni's music store his mouth-watering prizes—some 430 "donations" amounting in value to $1000, among them a "splendid traveling clock with an alarm bell, a china clock, several velvet embroidered bags, beautiful fans, etc." A chance to win one of these items and at the same time hear Julia Northall, Amalia Patti, Giuseppe Guidi, Pietro Novelli, the pianist Charles Wels, and an orchestra conducted by George Loder, all for the same fifty cents! No wonder the donation concert on February 7 at the Tabernacle was a stampede. Indeed, so violently did the audience storm the stage at the end of the concert that it became virtually impossible to distribute the prizes (*Herald,* February 8, 1850).

The fad quickly caught on. F. A. Artault, the enterprising proprietor of the Lafayette Bazaar, announced a "Grand Tombola Concert" at the Chinese Rooms on April 1, at which 250 prizes from his establishment would be distributed, amounting in value to $4000. Artault's secondary attractions were Elisa Valentini, Herr van der Weyde, little Fanny Deane, a seven-year-old pianist from Ireland, her nine-year-old brother Charles,[29] and a fifteen-minute intermission to permit ice cream and other tempting refreshments to be "carried round the room." The event was repeated on April 3 (*Tribune,* April 3, 1850).[30] This was only the beginning.

Evidently, no such blandishments were needed by the Hutchinson Family♪—Judson, John, Asa, and Abby—the "New Hampshire Nightingales," as Noah dubbed them, who returned in March after an absence of two years. Delivering their battle cry "We're with you once again, kind friends," they were off on another of their mara-

[29] The newly arrived Deane (or Dean) family, consisting of a mother and five offspring, announced their first appearance at the Coliseum for January 11 in a program that would contain "several Irish melodies."

[30] The raffle craze seems to have seized the city. A rosewood piano in a "serpentine case," worth $400, the handiwork of Tunis Smith, a piano builder of 223 Twelfth Street, would be raffled off at the New-York Hotel as soon as the list was filled. Tickets were $5.

thons, appearing first at Niblo's Saloon on March 22 and 25, then throughout the month of April at the Tabernacle (concurrently with the Havana opera company at Niblo's Garden).[31]

On May 1, having given thirteen concerts at the Tabernacle, the Hutchinsons announced their "farewell," only to pop up again on May 6, 7, and 9 at the Apollo, having in the meantime darted back and forth to perform in Brooklyn and nearby New Jersey places. By May 16 they were back at the Tabernacle, singing their temperance ditties at a complimentary concert for the "temperance advocate" F. W. Kellogg, at which Horace Greeley, P. T. Barnum, and the beneficiary lectured on the evils of alcohol. On May 17 they invaded the Eighteenth Street Methodist Episcopal Church in Chelsea, and on and on.

Shortly after their reappearance in New York, the *Mirror* (March 29, 1850) once again reassessed (repuffed) the Hutchinson phenomenon: "There is a peculiarity in the songs and in the style of singing them by the Hutchinson Family that charms the million, who do not appreciate, and therefore cannot enjoy, vocalization of a more elaborate style. It is, in fact, the extreme simplicity of their style that renders it so pleasing, and has won for this family their extraordinary popularity."[32]

The appealing Hutchinson repertory of homely songs, always listed in their concert advertisements, at this time comprised, among others: "The Good Old Days of Yore, a Song of Home," "The Bride's Departure," "The Main Truck, or Leap for Life (describing the perilous leap of a little boy from the main mast to the sea)," "The Gold of California," "The Horticultural Wife," "Once on a Time (a reminiscence of revolutionary days)," "The Bridge of Sighs," "We've Roamed over the Mountains," "Lovers of Rum," "The Real Wax Work, or, The Palateless Yankee," "Uncle Ben's Farm," "Nobody and Somebody," "The Yankee Lover's First Introduction," and on and on.

In September, soon after Jenny Lind arrived, she was visited by the Hutchinsons. As the *Tribune* (September 23, 1850) tells it, she asked them to sing, "whereupon the brothers and sister drew together in the group so familiar to all, and sang 'The Cot where we were born.' After this, they sang an original 'Welcome to Jenny Lind,' the words of which were written by Jesse Hutchinson, Jr. It was a simple and genial expression of feeling, and sung with touching and appropriate expression. Mdlle. Lind, who sat with downcast eyes during the song, at the close expressed her acknowledgement of the graceful compliment, and the Family withdrew, evidently highly gratified with her frank, cordial bearing, as simple and unaffected as their own."[33]

Downcast eyes?

Among other popular performers who resurfaced in 1850 was William R. Dempster, the perennial Scottish ballad singer, who returned to the Tabernacle on Septem-

[31] Early in April they were joined by sister Rhoda, tactlessly described in the *Mirror* (April 3, 1850) as "Abby herself, improved in voice, face, figure, and expression."

[32] It was just this American tendency toward musical simplicity for which Saroni had no tolerance. In a plea for the establishment of a National Conservatory of Music he wrote: "The United States alone are indifferent to this branch of musical culture, and as a natural consequence, we have Negro Minstrels, Hutchinsons, Woodburys, and other similar nuisances" (*Musical Times,* September 7, 1850, p. 590).

[33] Lind was also visited by a "Quartette Club," accompanied at the piano by George Henry Curtis. They entertained her with glees and, notably, with a "Welcome to Miss Lind," with words by

ber 6 from his most recent "retirement" to Scotland. A marathon-runner no less stalwart than the Hutchinsons, Dempster took up residence at the Tabernacle for the month of September, valiantly appearing opposite Jenny Lind at Castle Garden. Not unmindful of the Lind phenomenon, however, Dempster lost no time in climbing onto the Nightingale bandwagon, setting to music Epes Sargent's "Salutation to America," the runner-up poem in the recent Lind prize-song competition.[34] So clamorously had this song been received, claimed Dempster, that he was forced to extend his run at the Tabernacle, reappearing on October 2 and 4 (and subsequently as well) to satisfy the "public demand" for its repetition (*Tribune,* September 27, 1850).

Dempster's song precipitated yet another controversy. Maurice Strakosch, too, had set Sargent's poem to music, and Strakosch's publisher William Hall, claiming the copyright, threatened Dempster with dire reprisals if he persisted in performing his own version (*Tribune,* October 17, 18, 1850).[35]

During the course of the year, Dempster's compatriot, the popular ballad singer Jeanie Reynoldson,♪ appeared in widely contrasting environments, from Bowery resorts—such as Lynch's Concert Hall and Military Hall—to the Tabernacle, where, toward year's end, she gave three "farewell concerts" before purportedly returning to her native land. With Austin Phillips at the piano, she was assisted by various lesser vocal lights. On December 28 at the Tabernacle, Miss Reynoldson delivered herself of her supposed swan song, then proceeded, as did Dempster, to remain immovably fixed in the local popular music firmament for years to come.

On May 15 the Lancashire Bell Ringers♪—a group of five men, each of whom handled five bells—opened at the Chinese Museum, now owned by P. T. Barnum.[36] At first announced as splendid exponents of Handel, Mozart, Beethoven, Verdi, and other such esoteric composers, after becoming "Barnumized" the group rapidly shifted their repertory to "Marches, Quadrilles, Polkas, National Airs, Ethiopian Melodies, and select pieces from the most celebrated operas" (*Courier and Enquirer,* May 4; *Herald,* May 15, 1850).

William C. Richards, editor of the *Southern Literary Gazette,* and music by Curtis. As always, at this early stage of her sojourn in the United States, she said all the right things to the singers and everyone else present. Reporting the incident, the *Tribune* (September 24, 1850) promised soon to print Richards's beautiful poem.

[34]Land of the beautiful, land of the free,
Often my heart has turned longing to thee!
Often had mountain, lake, torrent and stream
Gleam'd on my waking thought, crowded my dream!
Now thou receivest me from the broad sea,
Land of the beautiful, land of the free!
Now thou receivest me from the broad sea,
Land of the beautiful, land of the free!

[35]At his concert of "ballads and choice arias" at the Rutgers Institute on October 15, Isaac Baker Woodbury, assisted by Pieter Hendrik van der Weyde at the Aeolian piano, performed—besides "The Gambler's Wife, the *Largo al factotum,* and "Be Kind to the Loved Ones"—both the Taylor and Sargent prize songs, but which Sargent version, Dempster's or Strakosch's, was not stated (*Herald,* October 15, 1850).

[36]In April, with his American Museum in the throes of reconstruction, Barnum purchased the Chinese Museum complete with its collections and attractions, which included the musically accomplished Miss Pwan-Yakoo, a Chinese lady of distinction, with tiny feet (2½ inches long) and a large company of compatriots.

It had been given out (undoubtedly by Barnum) that these Lancashire Bell Ringers had been the teachers of the highly successful original "Swiss" Bell Ringers[♪] he had brought over in 1844—if the truth be known, not from Switzerland, but also from Lancashire. Thus, there was a flurry of competitive bellringer publicity in September, when it was announced that the first Swiss Bell Ringers were returning from Europe, that they had increased their stock of bells to 150, and that they had added the eminent campanero J. H. Hamnet to their company (*Herald,* September 23, 1850). On October 7, billed as "the Original Swiss Bell Ringers," they commenced an extended stay at the Apollo, assisted by Miss Julia Gould, a "celebrated vocalist and pianist from the Theatres Royal—Drury Lane, Princess, and English Opera House" (*Tribune,* October 4; *Herald,* October 7, 1850).

At Castle Garden, for the month of June, Loder conducted nightly Summer Fêtes between his Grand Sabbath Concerts. Consisting, as in the past, of a Grand Promenade Concert and Ball, the admission was twenty-five cents. For the ball, promised the advertisements: "The whole of the powerful orchestra will perform a variety of the latest and most fashionable Cotillions, Waltzes, Polkas, etc. . . . Ice Creams and other refreshments of superior quality will be provided in the Saloon and served by civil and obliging attendants throughout the whole evening, as well as during the intermission; the Cosmorama, newly arranged and brilliantly lighted, will afford amusement to the promenaders; omnibusses run from every point in the upper part of the city to the gates leading to Castle Garden, and will be in readiness to receive passengers at the end of the performance. No postponement on account of the weather" (*Herald* June 10, 1850). These entertainments continued until July, when the opera company from Havana took possession of Castle Garden.

Of the other summer gardens, with the exception of Niblo's, where a full-fledged theatre season was in progress, only Atlantic Garden advertised music—Dodworth's Cornet Band three times weekly during August.

New-York Historical Society

A band of campanologians.

That the enormously active theatre scene in 1850 included great numbers of musical offerings is self-evident, but it is virtually impossible to glean from the advertisements, puffs, or reviews which of the new productions contained music, whose music it was, or who performed it. Works designated as burlettas were musically unattributed, as were various new extravaganzas that occupied the various New York stages. Without surviving scores, any attempted report of music theatre productions in 1850 must seem as sparse to the reader as it is frustrating to the chronicler.

Then, too, the New York music theatre suffered an irreparable loss in 1850 with the retirement of William Mitchell♪ and the end of the miniature theatrical and musical miracles he had wrought at the tiny Olympic Theatre since 1839. Attempting, despite his worsening health, to continue at the Olympic, early in 1850 Mitchell presented, among his innumerable classic comedic treasures, an elaborate new musical extravaganza *The Magic Horn,* loosely based on *Oberon* (to Weber's music?), and a burletta *Delicate Ground, or Paris in 1793* with unspecified music. He revived the burletta *Twelve Months;* the Arabian Nights extravaganza *Camaralzaman and Badoura, or The Peri Who Loved the Prince; Olympic Revels;* and *The Pet of the Petticoats.* He also presented a travesty on *The Revolt of the Harem,* called *The Revolt of the Poor House.* Among countless other attractions, musical and nonmusical, his star Mary Taylor acted and sang in the old favorites, the extravaganza *The Invisible Prince* and the popular farce *Jenny Lind.*

On March 9, Mitchell came to the end of his road. The *Mirror* (March 11, 1850) sadly records his departure: "On Saturday night, the season of the Olympic closed, and the curtain fell upon the last scene of Mr. Manager Mitchell's theatrical life. For some time past, his health has been declining, and his strength being unequal to the capable performance of his managerial duties, he very wisely determined to withdraw, ere the honors he so laboriously strove for, and won, should be tarnished by circumstances over which he could have no control. He takes with him an enviable reputation for energy, talent, liberality, and enterprise, for honor and uprightness in all his business relations, and retires with the esteem and regard of all with whom he has been either professionally or otherwise connected, and with their best wishes for restored health and the enjoyment of many years of happiness." At the conclusion of the performance, a benefit for Mary Taylor, Mitchell addressed his last audience. He felt, he movingly said, as if he were a mourner at his own funeral.

Soon after, on March 18, the *Tribune* announced that the new Olympic lessee, the actor/manager William E. Burton,♪ had already begun radical alterations: "The pit is to be done away with, and the lower boxes and parquette are to be on the same plan as [Burton's] Theatre in Chambers Street." Believing that Burton planned a summer season at the Olympic, the *Tribune* testily added: "The place is altogether too small for a summer theatre." In fact, the Olympic soon (in April) would become the home of a long-running minstrel troupe.

Among the old and new theatre productions of 1850 most likely to have contained music were, at the National Theatre, revivals of *Rob Roy* (with Bishop's music?), *Valentine and Orson,* the old Mitchell travesty on Auber's *La Bayadère (Buy It Dear, 'Tis Made of Cashmere), The Naiad Queen, The Swiss Cottage,* and an apparently new production *The Magic Well.* Chanfrau,♪ after a long tour, reappeared in several incarnations of his Mose character: *The Mysteries and Miseries of New York, Three Years After, New York As It Is, Mose in California,* and *Mose in China.* A confusing array of like-sounding, but apparently different, Oriental extravaganzas presented at the National Theatre (and elsewhere) included *The Female Guard, or A-Lad-in-a Wonderful Lamp* (with sixty young ladies), *The Female Forty Thieves,* and *Open Sesame. Rob Roy* and *The Female Guard* were presented at the Bowery Theatre, as was *Clari, or The Maid of Milan,* a vehicle for the rising young star Catherine Wemyss.

At Niblo's Garden on May 13, following the Havana company's departure for Boston, a season of theatrical presentations of all varieties—some of them musical—was mounted under the joint direction of John Brougham and William Chippendale. Anticipating the opening, on May 7 the theatre and music communities combined in large numbers to honor Brougham with a complimentary musical/dramatic gala. Among the musicians were Joseph Burke, Richard Hoffman, Mary Taylor, Stephen Leach, and Max Maretzek, who presumably conducted the orchestra.

Billed as an "operatical drama," on May 13, Brougham's *Home* opened the season at Niblo's, but no clue was given as to its "operatical" content. Its opening-night performance was preceded by a rousing rendition of "The Star-Spangled Banner" by the whole company and followed by Planché's vaudeville (or comedietta) *Follies of a Night,* played by Brougham and Mary Taylor.

The greatest success of Niblo's summer season was his gorgeous production of a fairy extravaganza by Planché,♪ *The Island of Jewels,* brought out on June 26. In the *Albion*'s opinion, Niblo had "hit it" with this genre of entertainment; its "whimsicality, scenic effects, [musical] parodies, and rich costumes meet the demand" (July 6, 1850, p. 320). The *Spirit of the Times* (July 6, 1850, p. 240) described *The Island of Jewels* as a "magnificent, operatic, pantomimic, spectacular, choreographical, allegorical entertainment." But of what its operatic component consisted, not a word.

On May 11, between plays at the Astor Place Opera House, Dodworth's Band performed the Quintet from *La sonnambula* and Maretzek's "Tip-Top Polka"; Dodworth (presumably Allen) repeated his virtuoso solo version on the cornet of Maretzek's Rondo, written (probably in 1849) to display the coloratura pyrotechnics of the now departed Madame Laborde as Linda di Chamounix; Mrs. George Loder, a singing actress, provided contrast with "I Love the Merry Sunshine."

Not only were the hit shows frequently duplicated in competing productions at competing theatres—in 1850, Burton's prodigiously successful vehicle *The Serious Family* (London 1849) and Barnum's smash hit *The Drunkard* (New York 1844) received multiple presentations at the various houses—but current events offered invaluable topical grist to the insatiable theatrical mill. Thus, the arrival of the Hungarian exiles in January inspired *The Siege of Comorn,* a play with music, dealing with a dramatic episode in the Hungarian uprising, written and composed by John St. Luke,♪ the music director of the Bowery Theatre, where it was produced; and Burton successfully mounted a farce *Mysterious Knockings,* satirizing the spiritualistic goings-on of the Fox sisters of Rochester, the current sensation.[37]

[37] The country was currently agog over the miraculous table-rapping phenomena, known as the "Rochester Rappings," or "Knockings," activated by the teen-aged Fox sisters, Margaret and Kate, residents of upper New York State. In the summer of 1850 they came to New York to give a lucrative series of seances, then went on a continuingly profitable tour of the United States. Later con-

Above all, the advent of Jenny Lind inspired the local satirists to their most extravagant efforts. In addition to the well-established farce *Jenny Lind,* satires on the Lind phenomenon proliferated after her arrival: two by Burton, *Jennyphobia* at Burton's Olympic and "a grand essay on Lindmania," *She's Come!* at Burton's Theatre, and at the Bowery, *Jenny Lind in America.*

The Jenny Lind obsession invaded the orchestra pit as well. In October, between plays at Burton's, a "Jenny Lind Potpourri" was performed by the orchestra; and at the loudly heralded opening, on December 23, of Brougham's new Lyceum Theatre (Broadway, near Broome Street), George Loder, the music director of the new establishment, conducted a "full orchestra" in "Echoes of the Nightingale," an "Intermezzo" of his own devising, comprising Lind's most popular hits: "'The Gypsie's [*sic*] Song,' *'La Normandie,'* 'Flute Trio,' 'Home, Sweet Home,' 'Dalecarlian Melody,' 'Bird Song,' 'Mountaineer's Song,' 'Echo, or Herdsman's Song,' and the 'Greeting to America'" (*Herald,* December 23, 1850).

At Brougham's Lyceum—besides its superb acting company, consisting of Mary Taylor, Kate Horn (not to be confused with Mrs. Charles E. Horn), Mrs. Vernon, Stephen Leach, Mrs. George Loder, and other thespian favorites, and of course Brougham himself—the elaborate supporting forces comprised an in-house chorus directed by Frederick Lyster and a ballet corps led in the opening weeks by Mademoiselle Ducy-Barre, of the Paris Opéra. Wardle Corbyn, no longer the editor of *Figaro!,* presided over the Lyceum box office, where tickets were fifty cents for the dress circle and parquet, twenty-five cents for the family circle, one dollar for "orchestra stall seats" (evidently not the same as the parquet), and five dollars for private boxes.

But it was the omnipresent Thomas Dartmouth Rice who uniquely permeated the theatrical year. In a continuous circuit, he traveled back and forth from theatre to theatre, tirelessly performing his by now worn-out Ethiopian operas—*Jumbo Jum, The Virginia Mummy,* and *Otello*—and regularly garnering the benefit performances accruing to featured actors after three evenings at a given theatre. Thus, in 1850, Rice appeared time after time at Barnum's Lecture Room (as the full-fledged theatre in the American Museum was euphemistically named),[38] at the Bowery Theatre, at Chanfrau's National Theatre,[39] and, during Bass's tenancy, at the Astor Place Opera House; Rice appeared at White's Melodeon as well.

After one of his innumerable benefits, on February 3, 1850, Rice's contribution to world culture was assessed in the *Herald* in clear-sighted, if less than charitable,

---

fessed to be a childish prank, the Rochester Rappings initiated a chain of spiritualistic activities throughout the nation (see *DAB,* III, pt. 2, pp. 570–71).

[38] In June, Barnum announced the reopening of his remodeled American Museum, closed nine weeks for enlargement and refurbishing at the cost of $50,000. The gorgeous new "Lecture Room," referred to as a "Temple of Moral Entertainment," was musically presided over by Edward Woolf, "late of the Olympic Theatre." Master Benjamin Woolf (1836–1901) a future composer and music critic of consequence, presided, in turn, over the new Chickering, "made expressly for this Museum, price $1000" (*Herald,* June 17, 1850).

[39] In addition to his interminably repeated chestnuts, Rice appeared at Barnum's in something called *Pompey Smash,* and at the National in *Rochester Knockings,* a blackface travesty of Burton's *Mysterious Knockings.*

RICE'S CROW.

Thomas Dartmouth Rice as a wistful crow in whiteface.

terms: "Last evening, Mr. T. D. Rice, the original Jim Crow—he who first set in vogue the negro rage and mania which seized upon all the world in both its hemispheres like the infection of the cholera, so that everybody for a time was jumping Jim Crow and chanting 'Clare de Kitchen' [and] 'Ole Virginny Never Tire'—Mr. T. D. Rice, the famous originator of the quasi-revolution in dramatics, for the time, which has, however, since become as flat, stale, and unprofitable as the French Revolution—he, the veritable original impersonator of the old and genuine Jim Crow—took his benefit last night at the National."

If Rice had become passé, his Frankenstein's Monster certainly continued to flourish more and more vigorously. For the fourth year, Christy's Minstrels gave their concerts (as the minstrels called their entertainments, to appease the consciences of non-theatregoers) at Mechanics' Hall (472 Broadway), known as Christy's Opera House, with a brief stopover at the Apollo while Mechanics' Hall was being refurbished. Among their featured performers were the guitarist N. Gould, the tambourine virtuoso E. H. Pierce ("Pompey"), and the falsetto singer Max (sometimes called Mac) Zorer (the selfsame Maximilian Zohrer[♪] who had emigrated from Europe with the Moravian Singers in 1848), who gave imitations in blackface of the "most eminent prima donnas," including Jenny Lind.

In April, E. H. Pierce defected from Christy's and formed Pierce's Minstrels, taking over Burton's Olympic Theatre only a few weeks after Mitchell had relinquished it. Pierce's company of ten performers included alumni of several well-known minstrel troupes: from Christy's, his fellow defector Zorer; from Dumbolton's Ethiopian Serenaders, Stanwood, White, and Bryant; from the "original" Virginia Serenaders, Farrell, J. Sanford, White, J. R. Myers, and Eph Horn. They succeeded hugely at the Olympic, getting off to a lively start with a blackface burlesque of the Shaking Quakers. By September, however, they had a new leader, J. B. Fellows, and a new name, Fellows's Ethiopian Opera Troupe. Now increased to thirteen performers, they continued to prosper, appearing at the New York Society Library during Burton's temporary occupancy of the Olympic; then, upon his abdication, briefly returning to the Olympic; and then in November moving into their own theatre, Minstrel Hall, formerly the Hall of Lyrics, next door to the Olympic. "Fitted up in a most gorgeous style," announced Fellows, Minstrel Hall was equipped with cushioned seats, was carpeted and beautifully lighted, and there "the greatest talents, as regards Ethiopian Minstrelsy in America," would present "chaste entertainment" for twenty-five cents a ticket (*Tribune,* November 3, 26, 1850).

The turnover in the world of blackface minstrelsy was apparently ceaseless, for in September Zorer announced a "musical campaign" of his own at Bleecker Hall (Bleecker and Morton streets), renaming it the "Ethiopian Opera-Comique" (*Herald,* September 9, 1850). Charles White's Serenaders continued to perform at White's Melodeon on the Bowery. At his "Mammoth" benefit, on March 18, the imposing cast included "the Juvenile Wonders, known as the Infant Vestris and the Infant Elssler . . . Mons. Rossiter, famed tightrope and wire performer; Ben Yates, fancy dancer, formerly of the Olympic"; also "Mr. Flavin,[♪] comic singer . . . W. D. Corrister, guitar, banjo, etc.; T. Wadee, vocalist, violinist, and Tyrolean solo player; J. Smith, unrivalled bones player; B. Beil, tamborinist [*sic*] and wag of the band; Master Marks, the great favorite negro dancer; W. Kohler, musical director; C. White, accordionist and negro delineator" (the beneficiary); and, most notably, "Old Dan Emmit," the original banjo player composer." White advertised that at twenty-five cents a ticket, his Melodeon was "the cheapest place of entertainment in the world" (*Herald,* March 18, 1850).

But cheaper still was Knickerbocker Hall, where a "young Miss, not eight years of age," presided at the piano for "the unequalled band of Harmonist Minstrels and the great Italian, Moro, with his most wonderful Mechanical Dancing Figures, which have received rounds of applause at this large and splendid Hall." All for 12½ cents (*Spirit,* November 23, 1850, p. 480). Cheapest of all, however, was Lynch's Concert Hall, where the customary ticket price was 6½ cents.

A group calling themselves the Virginia Minstrels (obviously not the original troupe) appeared briefly at the St. Luke's Building, Lynch's Concert Hall, and other fringe places. Other peripheral minstrel attractions were Thorpe's Minstrels at Bleecker Hall, and the four Albino Minstrels, or White Negroes, who appeared at the Minerva

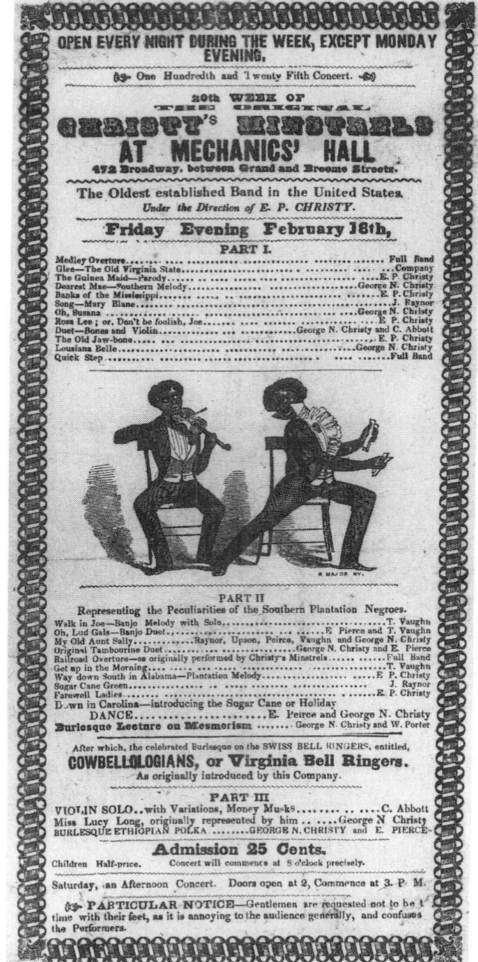

The "Particular Notice" at the foot of this elegant handbill requests gentlemen attending Christy's Minstrel Show "not to beat time with their feet, as it is annoying to the audience generally, and confusing to the performers."

New-York Historical Society

Rooms. These "singular beings," ran the advertisements, "these talented brothers, having milk-white complexions, pink eyes, and hair of a very fine, silky texture," were the children of black parents (*Herald,* February 25, 1850).

The usual troupes of "Female Minstrels" (usually male), "Female Arab Girls," and "Model Artistes"♪ held forth at such questionable places as the Walhalla (Canal Street) and the former Franklin Theatre, now the Franklin Museum (Chatham Square).

More edifyingly, musical literacy on easy terms was dispensed by various pedagogues: by the singing teacher W. D. Comes♪ at his Musical Institute, now at 187 Laurens Street (his piano department was "under the entire charge" of a "Señor" Harbardt); by C. L. Barnes,♪ who gave singing lessons at the Thirteenth Street Church Lecture Room; by J. F. Warner,♪ who lectured on music and conducted classes at 413 Broadway; and by Professor Ernst von Heeringen (1810–1855), who opened a Musical Conservatory at 220 Third Avenue. Calling it a "free school" for instruction in piano, guitar, harp, violin, and singing, von Heeringen offered lessons employing either his own copyrighted system of notation, which dispensed with accidentals, or any more conventional method, "at the pleasure of the pupil." For class lessons he charged only a dollar monthly (for the use of the instruments); private lessons, however, were $25 for twenty-four lessons at the Conservatory, or $30 at the pupil's residence.

But principally it was the indefatigable William B. Bradbury, assisted by Francis H. Nash, who was most visible in the local world of music pedagogy. In addition to his massive juvenile concerts Bradbury lectured, and throughout the year he announced a succession of music classes for various levels of students. In January he conducted a lecture/demonstration of his method (probably at his New-York Conservatory of Music, 411 Broadway), of which the *Tribune* (January 21, 1850) reported: "In a lesson of one hour, a promiscuous audience were made to sing by note several pieces of music."

In October, Bradbury announced the formation of an "Upper Music Class, or Song and Glee Union," to meet on Fridays at the Conservatory. It would be conducted "in a manner similar to the large choral classes and 'Song Unions' of Europe . . . for Ladies and Gentlemen to study Style, Musical Intonation, Expression, etc." (*Herald,* October 24, 1850). In November, Bradbury expanded this effort, advertising a free "singing meeting" at the Tabernacle, where he would explain and illustrate his method for learning to sing in classes. Several glees and part-songs would be performed by the Tabernacle choir. "Come one, come all."

In addition, Bradbury contributed an article on "Vocal Instruction in Germany" to the *Message Bird* (February 15, 1850, pp. 233–34), and in October he brought out a huge anthology *The Alpine Glee Singer,* reviewed in the *Tribune* (October 23, 1850) as a collection full of "healthy songs," fitting for the American public: "Patriotic, buoyant, elevated, pure, and lightly playful withal."

Henry C. Watson's sister Mrs. Bailey, the former theatrical singing star and siren Charlotte Watson,♪ now fallen on more sedate days, advertised her availability as a singing teacher, at 194 Fourth Street, on the west side of Washington Square, and as a choir singer for an Episcopal church (*Herald,* October 25, 1850). Antonio Bagioli,♪ a veteran of the Da Ponte/Montresor opera company of 1832, continued to conduct his highly successful singing classes at his new address, 92 Prince Street.

And the unquenchable Elisa Valentini at year's end announced "cheap singing classes," given twice a week, for only $6 a quarter. Morning classes for ladies and integrated evening classes for ladies and gentlemen would be held at Constitution Hall (650 Broadway). Valentini's elaborate teaching scenario called for twenty-eight singers to a class, each class to last two hours, subdivided into four half-hour segments of seven singers each. She promised instruction in "solfeggio, scales, and English, Spanish, French [and] Jenny Lind songs, church psalms, etc." Private lessons at the student's home were $2, at Constitution Hall $1.50. Valentini added a little vivid persuasion: "The art of singing, like the art of painting, wants, above all, incitation. Signorina Valentini executes every song she teaches; from that arises the great improvement of her pupils, while the private [students'] concerts already have been so brilliant as to place Signorina Valentini [as] the first Professor of her wonderful art in the United States."

Allen Dodworth widely advertised his classes in social dancing at his academy at 448 Broome Street. "Dodworth and dancing," rhapsodized the *Mirror* (October 4, 1850), "are as synonymous as Dodworth and music. He has visited the capitals of Europe for improvement—has had the advantage of not only seeing the best dancing, but of studying with the most accomplished professors of London and Paris. He now invents new dances, composes his own music, and may in all respects be ranked among the best teachers in the city."

The Dodworths' involvement with social dancing was twofold. In variously named combinations, determined by the addition or subtraction of certain categories of instruments, Dodworth's Band supplied dance music for many of the balls that dominated the social scene: for the Grand Masonic Ball at the Chinese Rooms, the combined Cornet and Cotillion bands; for the Grand Military and Civic Ball at Niblo's Ballroom to honor the Hungarian Exiles, the Military and Cotillion bands, with extra musicians. No inconsiderable social presence in New York, in 1850 the members of Dodworth's Band "resolved" to give a ball for the benefit of the New-York Volunteers.[40] The Cornet Band gave their own annual ball at the Apollo, as did Shelton's American Brass Band. Dingle's Band played for a great ball at the Chinese Rooms to honor Henry Clay, "the Star of the West," exhuming for the occasion (perhaps tactlessly) "Here's to You, Henry Clay," the principal campaign song of his unsuccessful bid for the presidency in 1844; Richard Willis's popular Quadrille Band played for numbers of balls and other social events.

The American Musical Fund Society held their first ball at the Chinese Rooms, charging a more modest $2 admission for two ladies and a gentleman than the "crack regiment of New York's citizen soldiery," the City Guards, who "had the courage" to charge a snobbish $10 admission for their great ball at Niblo's (*Herald,* January 19; February 18, 1850).[41]

[40]Dodworth's Band accepted out-of-town engagements, traveling as far as Dartmouth College to play at the commencement ceremonies. For this event they unveiled a resplendent new uniform: a white coat with blue facings and collar embroidered with gold lace, trousers with a white stripe, and a small, bell-crowned cap, bearing a "rich musical trophy" in front and sporting a black and red plume (*Message Bird,* June 15, 1850, p. 361).

[41]Snobbery, too, motivated the Astor Place Opera Ball, or "Wall Street Ball," accused James Gordon Bennett, still deep in litigation with Edward P. Fry and the Astor Place proprietors. It was an event, fumed the *Herald* (January 19, 1850), "given for and by the financial aristocracy, embracing

The bands played, too, at more somber celebrations. At the local obsequies for President Zachary Taylor, who died on July 9, the bands of the city combined forces, and it was reported that their "mournful strains circulated universally" (*Tribune,* July 23, 1850).[42]

During this extraordinary musical year a larger than usual number of embattled musicians took their disagreements to the law courts. Giuseppina and Emilio Rossi Corsi sued Max Maretzek for refusing to pay $100 due them for the last two weeks of their engagement at Astor Place. In an article captioned "Nightingales at Law," the *Mirror* (July 1, 1850) reported that "payment was resisted [by Maretzek] on the ground that the Signor had rendered himself liable to a fine for failing to sing at a concert on the 23rd February [the Musical Fund Society's third concert], and it was contended that if prevented by sickness, he was bound to send notice to that effect before one P.M. on the day of the concert, and, further, that a certificate was necessary from the physician appointed by the defendant. It appeared that a notice had been posted in the Opera House that Dr. Quin♪ [the erstwhile president of the Euterpean Society] had been selected by Mr. Maretzek, and the rule established was as follows: 'Sickness must be proved by plaintiff's physician that he was prevented from singing by a severe affection of the throat,' but the above rule had not been complied with." The court, however, found for the plaintiffs.

In February, George Loder sued Norman A. Freeman, a jeweler, for slander. Having previously testified against Freeman at a trial, Loder had been accosted in Chickering's piano store by the vengeful jeweler, who publicly accused him of perjury and threatened to send him to Sing Sing. The jury awarded Loder $100 (*Times and Messenger,* February 10, 1850). He would be less fortunate in the later suit brought against him by the Jenny Lind chorus singers.

In February, too, the Edward Fry versus James Gordon Bennett libel suit♪ came up for trial in the Supreme Court, but was postponed. In reporting this development, the anti-Bennett *Mirror* (February 22, 1850) observed: "It is difficult to bring great rogues to trial, it is still harder to convict them, and hardest of all, to punish them when convicted." Bennett eventually lost the case.

An altercation that stopped barely short of litigation was carried on by an aggrieved Richard Hoffman against P. T. Barnum, who, for some unknown reason, at the last minute had canceled Hoffman's engagement to go on tour with the Jenny Lind party. Reporting the affair in an article captioned "Trouble in the Barnum Camp," *Saroni's Musical Times* (November 30, 1850, p. 99) perhaps unjustly credited Barnum's unprofessional behavior to stinginess: "It was probably to save travelling expenses, for the great contractor, while realizing tens of thousands of dollars, trembles over the expenditure of cents." But on December 7, Hoffman published a card in the *Herald* to

---

all those, and their connections, who have risen from nothing to something by successful speculations in codfish and consols."

[42] At another solemn event, a memorial to the former Vice President Richard Mentor Johnson, held at Tammany Hall by the Columbian Order on December 7, a choir of professional vocalists performed a requiem composed for the occasion by George Loder to words by George Pope Morris (*Herald,* December 7, 1850).

inform his friends that "the difficulty heretofore existing between himself and Mr. Barnum having been satisfactorily adjusted, by the gentlemanly instrumentality of Mr. Jules [*sic*] Benedict, and Mr. Barnum having written to Mr. Hoffman, stating that his original agreement will be honorably complied with, and that his services may be required in New Orleans about the 8th of February, he [Hoffman] will be happy to receive professional engagements during his stay in New-York, and until he is notified to proceed South, to assist as heretofore in the remaining concerts of Mdlle. Lind in America."

Not a subject of litigation, but serious and far-reaching in its consequences, a controversy broke out in May and June that in a sense officially established the Philharmonic's long-term pattern of denying performances to American composers, an exclusion that contributed immeasurably to their struggle for recognition in their native land. In this early instance, the snubbed composer was one of the Philharmonic's most lustrous members, George Frederick Bristow. The issue was at first clearly and fairly set forth in *Saroni's Musical Times* (May 25, 1850, pp. 410–11): "The Philharmonic Society . . . has in its by-laws a certain clause, stating that whenever a resident composer should present to the government of said Society a score of an overture or symphony, said government shall cause this score to be examined, and if found worthy of performance, the society shall perform it at one of their annual concerts. . . . It is clear that the founders of this society had it in view not only to cultivate the musical taste of the community, but to arouse and stimulate the latent creative powers of native or resident musicians by placing in their hands the means to have their works performed.

"During the first few years of this society's existence, this by-law was fulfilled to the very letter. We recollect an overture by Mr. Loder, another by Mr. Bristow, and a third one performed at the rehearsal only by Mr. [Edward R.] Hansen. But from some cause or other, a crotchet came into the head[s] of the government, in the form of a strange misgiving. They thought that since their duty was to cultivate the taste of the community, they could not permit anything but the compositions of great masters to be performed at their concerts, and forgetting that occasionally they gave us such overtures as *La Gazza Ladra,* 'Joco [*sic*], the Brazilian Ape,' and any amount of factory-ware from the prolific pen of Kalliwoda, etc., etc., they refused to perform any domestic compositions at their concerts, nay, refused to play them even for the instruction of the composers at their rehearsals.

"It is needless to comment upon the narrow-mindedness of such proceedings. Enough that by this time they have thought better of it, and have arranged what we call a 'non-committal affair,' in the shape of a public rehearsal [on May 25, 1850], neither fish nor fowl. The program for the occasion consists of a Symphony by Bristow [in E-flat, op. 10][43] and an Overture by Eisfeld, and we hope that these gentlemen will be satisfied with the encomiums of their brethren in misfortune, and with the applause of the non-paying audience."

But this advance objectivity was as far as Saroni would go. After hearing the work

[43] Composed in 1848, probably at the time Bristow was studying with George Macfarren,[44] who was then in New York. The manuscript is found at the Music Division of the New York Public Library at Lincoln Center.

[44] Among Bristow's known teachers, besides Macfarren, were his father William Richard Bristow, and Henry C. Timm.

he patronizingly referred to Bristow as "the Child of the Regiment," who had "pursued his musical studies under very peculiar circumstances"; he had been "willing to learn of everybody, and everybody was willing to teach him."[44] Saroni now remembered that the principal fault of Bristow's [Concert] Overture, played at a Philharmonic concert in 1847, had been its "lack of originality, and we are sorry to say that this symphony is little better in this respect. It might be compared to a musical chessboard, with a field for each composer from the time of Haydn to Mendelssohn-Bartholdy." But worse, "There is the utter want of connection between the different ideas. Almost every sixteen bars, the composer seems to have come to a dead halt. He begins a new melody, and goes again over the same ground, suddenly drops the theme and begins a new one, which has not the remotest connection with the former. . . . And not alone that the ideas are reminiscences of 'old familiar themes,' but the instrumentation, too, is generally in close imitation of the original."

Moreover, the work, in four movements, was "too long by half, and . . . all in *major,* thus shedding a monotony over the whole composition which is anything but pleasant." Saroni advised Bristow to "be content with compositions of less extent. If former masters have began [*sic*] their career by writing symphonies, they did so at a time when that form was not developed by the master hand of a Mozart, Beethoven, etc., etc." (*Musical Times,* June 1, 1850, p. 422). Small wonder that Bristow, upon reading this review, furiously canceled his subscription to the *Musical Times.*[45]

In rebuttal of Saroni's scathing criticism, the *Message Bird,* in a highly laudatory two-part essay on Bristow's symphony, attempted to put in perspective the native composer's dilemma: "Having heard that [Bristow's symphony] had received the favorable opinion of such eminent authorities as Mr. [George] Alexander Macfarren of London, Mr. Henri Herz, and other competent judges, we were at a loss to account for the tardiness of the Society in bringing it forward, being unwilling to believe that any sectional prejudices could influence the action of [their] Government in this matter."

And continued: "This being an achievement withal so respectable, and of so much higher grade, we believe, than anything heretofore attempted in this country, something more than a passing notice is justly due both the author and the work. When the lack of facilities under which a musical student labors in this country, especially if he is poor, is duly considered—the rarity of suitable books and models, the want of sympathy and appreciation which surrounds him, and the necessity which confined him to the minor drudgeries of the art for subsistence—the attainment of sufficient knowledge and skill to construct a *Grand Symphony* under such circumstances really becomes a matter of wonder and surprise. The very attempt would naturally be considered presumptuous.

"Mr. Bristow, however, has grown up, as it were, in an orchestra. He has been in a position to hear and to study many of the best models of instrumental composition. And he has contrived during his short term of life (for he is yet young)[46] to become no mean proficient upon the violin, pianoforte, and we believe also several wind instru-

[45] As published in the *Musical Times* (June 8, 1850, p. 436), Bristow's apparently undated note, addressed to Saroni, read: "Sir, As your paper in my opinion is anything but interesting, I wish to discontinue it, therefore, you will oblige me infinitely by not sending it any more. Yours, Geo. F. Bristow. P.S. I have a bill receipted for a year's subscription, the remaining papers you may appropriate to any you may think fit."

[46] Bristow was then twenty-five years old.

ments. He may be considered, therefore, tolerably versed in the capacity and treatment of orchestral accompaniment.

"Meanwhile, his theoretical acquirements have been by no means limited or superficial, as not only this symphony, but also the various minor forms of composition, which from time to time he has given to the public, satisfactorily testify. Possessed at least of these mechanical advantages—which, by the way, have been acquired amidst the demands upon his time that *teaching* and the discharge of other professional duties have constantly made—who will dispute his right to enter an arena where less knowledge would inevitably ensure defeat and bring fresh disgrace upon the name of American musical art? Who would, under these circumstances, clip the wings of a laudable ambition that has thus, through years of patient and laborious discipline, been gathering energy for something more than a barnyard flight?"

This preliminary part of the *Message Bird*'s review appeared on June 15 (p. 362); the following part, in the next issue (July 1, 1850, p. 377), examined the work itself. Although the reviewer could not express "unqualified admiration" of Bristow's choice of an Andante to introduce his symphony (it should have been the second movement), it nonetheless was "conceived and worked up in a style deliciously *legato*." Its dreamy and languorous mood "more happily [illustrated Bristow's] unreserved and innate conceptions and peculiar temperament than any other portion of the symphony." Yet, the critic "more unhesitatingly" approved the following movements—Allegro, Andante, Minuet, and Allegro vivace—being in particular not "insensible to the vigorous effort made in the Allegro vivace, the last movement. Parts of this are in strictest contrapuntal style; and it needs no wiseacre in musical matters to perceive that the young composer has devoted many an hour of severe thought and labor to this portion of his effort. . . . On the whole, we cannot but congratulate Mr. Bristow upon this successful development of rare and enviable power. Though this field of musical endeavor offers but little pecuniary reward in this country, at present, and though it may expose a young composer to the illiberal and unmanly censure of jealous contemporaries, yet we say to him, and to others of like ability and aspirations, look beyond such petty annoyances *to the future*."

And in conclusion: "We cannot but hope that the government of this, the first instrumental society in this country, will seek in future to extend the sphere of its usefulness by a more direct and positive encouragement of the resident talent among us, and thereby lay the foundation for a school of music which shall in time compare favorably with older and time-honored European models."

A visionary hope.

2

GTS: 1851

Is music in this country a taste or only a fashion?
Home Journal
September 11, 1851

Although it was becoming increasingly "the thing" to drop in at the opera house for a single act or an aria—and despite Ellen Strong's inclination, both social and musical, to opera-going—the Strongs seem for some reason not to have attended the opera during the winter and spring season of 1851.

For the earlier part of the season, from early January through mid-February, Maretzek's star of stars Teresa Parodi, back from her triumphs in Philadelphia, totally dominated the opera scene. On January 6, with ticket prices reduced to $1.50 for the parquette and boxes and fifty cents for the amphitheatre, she appeared in the first New York performance of the mightily ballyhooed new opera *Giovanna di Napoli* by Maurice Strakosch.[1] Commissioned for the Astor Place Opera House, specifically for Parodi and her colleagues Lorini, Novelli, and Beneventano, the work had incongruously received its first performance in Philadelphia. There, as in Boston and Baltimore, Maretzek maintained concurrent opera seasons, dexterously juggling members of his company from place to place—stars, former stars, second-stringers, even chorus singers and orchestra musicians—greatly to the detriment of his New York operation, and to increasing protest in the New York press.[2]

Heralded as the "first Italian opera composed in America" (albeit by a non-Italian),[3] *Giovanna di Napoli,* despite the critics' cordial congratulations to Strakosch, was at the same time judged to be derivative from start to finish: it was more like Donizetti than Verdi, declared *Figaro!* (January 11, 1851, p. 29); more like Auber than the Italians, observed the *Tribune* (January 8, 1851). Still worse, other critics maintained that the music, although consistently melodious, bore little or no relationship to the

[1] It was apparently not generally known that Strakosch and Maretzek were cousins.

[2] ". . . without Parodi and Benedetti, and missing Maretzek in the orchestra, the thing drags" (*Parker's Journal,* January 4, 1851, p. 30).

[3] The libretto, of unattributed authorship, was "translated into English" by Henry C. Watson, temporarily relegated to behind-the-scenes employment. Watson might have derived or adapted it from the apparently unperformed play *Giovanna of Naples* (1839) by Walter Savage Landor (see Nicholl, IV, 199, 341).

Music Division, The New York Public Library

Parodi is caricatured as a ferocious Norma standing on a bag of gold dollars, with an apprehensive Maretzek in the orchestra pit urging moderation.

action. It might just as appropriately have served for "any other play," commented the urbane and musically informed (but persistently anonymous) critic of the provocative new weekly *Parker's Journal* (January 11, 1851, p. 42).[4]

Parodi, a superlative and apparently inexhaustible singing actress, wielded her compelling vocal and dramatic powers as Giovanna on January 6, 8, 10, and 17, as Norma on January 13 and 20,[5] as Lucrezia Borgia (January 15 and February 10), as Leonora in *La favorita* (January 22 and February 7), and on January 28—sporting tights

[4] *Parker's Journal, a Weekly Gazette of Literature, Fashion, Art, and Science,* co-edited by William R. Parker and Spencer Wallace Cone, first appeared on December 21, 1850.

[5] The first of these *Norma* performances was fraught with extra histrionics. On January 11, with Maretzek unexpectedly and unavoidably called to Philadelphia, Parodi had refused to sing with a German substitute conductor (presumably Kreutzer) at her widely advertised gala concert at Tripler Hall, thereby disappointing some two or three thousand people and incurring the wrath of the pre-

and (to N. P. Willis's intense satisfaction) a luxuriant, curly moustache—as Romeo, to Virginia Whiting's Juliet, in a revival of Bellini's *I Capuleti ed i Montecchi.*[6]

"Of all the sugar and milk compositions of the Italian School," caviled Saroni in the *Musical Times* (February 1, 1851, p. 192), "this is one of the worst." Only its good plot redeemed it from utter damnation. *Parker's Journal* (February 8, 1851, p. 90), on the other hand, lauded Bellini's music but found the libretto to be inferior. At any rate, Parodi, in this critic's estimation "the Rachel of the lyric stage," was great in everything, and in this role she was "a great man."

Indeed, Parodi's convincing masculinity as Romeo astounded the critics. In the *Tribune* (January 29, 1851), George William Curtis, not Parodi's greatest admirer, somewhat tactlessly declared: "Our Prima Donna makes a much better man than a woman."

Richard Grant White, an eminent Shakespeare scholar, vehemently rejected the impersonation of Romeo by a woman: ". . . the writing of Romeo's part for a female voice is a radical defect in the construction of the opera, which must ever prevent its great success, at least with an English or an American audience. . . . The absence of the manly element in its composition is . . . a fatal defect. The whole interest of the story of *Romeo and Juliet* is built upon the love of a man for a woman and a woman for a man. Take away that keystone of the arch and the whole dramatic structure falls down at once. Manliness is not made by a doublet and hose, a sword and a moustache, and when Romeo sings or speaks in a woman's voice the heart refuses to acknowledge a sympathy with his many woes, because it laughs at the absurdity of the love from which they are supposed to spring. . . . We are certain that, however excellent the artist, a soprano Romeo can never enlist the sympathies of an audience whose hearts have been touched with the manly passions and the manly grief of Shakespeare's hero" (*Courier and Enquirer,* January 31, 1851).

But N. P. Willis, flourishing his most extravagant verbiage, stated that Parodi not only made love like a man, but that the absence of petticoats caused no embarrassment to what he was pleased to call her "locomotive unconsciousness." Only in bending over, as she gathered up the final-curtain bouquets and, apparently still in character, gallantly presented them to Virginia Whiting, did she inadvertently reveal her sex: "Her knee-joints bent womanesquely inward, instead of mannishly outwards."[7]

---

dominantly German personnel of the Astor Place orchestra. Appearing two days later as Norma, Parodi found herself singing the *Casta diva* to the accompaniment of strange and uncouth dissonances. Stepping out of character, the tempestuous *prima donna* advanced to the footlights, and in "emphatic Italian" proceeded to berate the orchestra. Not understanding Italian, the audience rapturously applauded what they took to be a part of the action. The following day Parodi published a face-saving quasi apology in the newspapers, but it was generally felt that she had behaved insultingly toward her audience. The embarrassing incident was glossed over and soon forgotten.

[6] The work was apparently given with the customary substitution of the last act of *Giulietta e Romeo* (Milan 1825) by Nicola Vaccai (1790–1848).

[7] Rarely missing a chance to taunt "our Cato of the Press," *Figaro!* (March 15, 1851, p. 186) satirized N. P. Willis's stylistic affectations in a pretended prospective review of the transvestite troupe of "Female" Minstrels currently performing at the Franklin Museum: "*Figaro!* means to go in a day or two merely to satisfy himself, by ocular demonstration, touching the womanesque, or bending in, of female means of getting over the ground, and the turning-out, or *bowism* of masculine locomotive unconsciousness."

Happily noting how becomingly Parodi's moustache adorned her "short upper lip," Willis addressed himself to more musical matters: "She played admirably and sang—with that luscious satisfyingness to the ear which a ripe apricot gives to the throat in a summer noon." Her low notes "found their proper place under the hat and feathers of Romeo, and drew a murmur of delight from the audience whenever they ploughed up the mellow cadences of adolescence for the ear of the blushing Juliet" (*Home Journal,* February 8, 1851).

As a budding American *prima donna,* Virginia Whiting, making her opera debut as Juliet, elicited benign comment in the press. The kindly critics agreed that she possessed a pure, light, true soprano voice; that she had been well schooled (by her colleagues Lorini and Novelli, to say nothing of Maretzek); that once she overcame her initial fright, she revealed herself to be an actress and singer of great promise. And, although *Parker's Journal* observed that she was not likely to be "rocked by passion" (a serious lack in a Juliet), the writer allowed that she might loosen up with experience, but doubted that she would ever regain the complete use of her arms (*Parker's,* February 8, 1851, p. 90).

Following the fourth performance of *I Capuleti,* Parodi, until now regarded as the very personification of the tragic muse, to everyone's surprise revealed unsuspected comedic gifts as Rosina in *The Barber of Seville,*♪ given for Sanquirico's benefit on February 3. It was a welcome relief, reported Curtis (*Tribune,* February 4, 1851) to emerge from "many murky caves into the sunlight, and upon green meads, for we have fairly supped full of horrors with the amiable poisonings, stabbings, and other dreadful deaths upon which the curtain is too much accustomed to fall." If Parodi's voice lacked the requisite richness for *Una voce poco fa,* she undeniably disclosed a flair for comedy.

For Max Maretzek's hugely advertised monster benefit on February 12 (tickets $2), not only did Parodi appear in a revival of Rossini's *Semiramide,* but, interpolated between acts one and two of the opera, a "Grand Vocal and Instrumental Concert" was performed by Maurice Strakosch, the tenor Domenico Lorini, the recently arrived Hungarian violinist Miska (Michael) Hauser (1822–1887),[8] and fifteen pianists of assorted ages, sizes, and shapes, all accompanied, of course, by the Astor Place orchestra, conducted by the beneficiary.

Opening with the Overture to Maretzek's opera *Rizzio,* the concert, complained Richard Storrs Willis, "considerably lengthened the performances of the evening," causing most of an important scene of the opera to be omitted. "The curtain rose, between the first and second acts [of *Semiramide*], upon eight pianos, one of which soon began to sing merrily under the fingers of Strakosch" playing his new *Grande Fantaisie* on *La Fille du régiment.* Wandering off on a wordy soliloquy concerning the superiority of Strakosch's "light and fleet style" of piano playing over the currently popular "massive and startlingly *forcible*" sledgehammer approach, Willis at last returned to his original subject matter. "Lorini sang *Spirito gentil* acceptably as ever. . . . A repetition of this aria was called for while Lorini was still straggling round among the eight pianos, trying to get out, and with some one of which instruments we had serious fears he might become confounded."

[8]Hauser, who had arrived from Europe in December 1850, was being managed by Maretzek, who had now extended his managerial activities beyond the opera house.

Lorini finally having managed to extricate himself from the maze of pianos and off the stage, Hauser played his *Grande Fantaisie dramatique* on themes from *Lucia di Lammermoor.* Apparently a violinist of the flashy school, he "descended to the audience" with his encore, "The Carnival of Venice," which caused a "moral reflector" at Willis's elbow memorably to observe: "With what trinkets of art is that child, the public, after all, best pleased with, to be sure."

The Grand Festival Concert somewhat ingloriously concluded with Strakosch's *Grande Fantaisie* on the Coronation March from Meyerbeer's *Le Prophète,* arranged for sixteen pianists at eight pianos, accompanied by the orchestra. In those sections "when the pianos played alone, the effect was very like that of a multitude of guitars," wrote Willis. "Strakosch was surrounded by a musical family of some thirteen [*sic*] players of both sexes and all ages, from piccolo pianists to performers of sedater years." In Willis's opinion, the experiment was not a success (*Albion,* February 15, 1851, p. 80).

Curtis, too, thought the superimposition of an extraneous concert upon a performance of *Semiramide* to be superfluous: ". . . the opera is, at best, something long and tedious, and to sit attentive in a warm house for more than four hours is a thing 'tolerable and not to be endured.'" Besides, wrote Curtis, asserting his expertise in matters pertaining to the Middle East,[9] the score of *Semiramide* is "no more Assyrian or Egyptian than it is Patagonian." However, "Parodi was never so well dressed, and she sang with a heartiness and fullness that won the warmest applause." Of course, there was "nothing very striking in the music of her role, although her delicious duet with the splendid Arsace [Amalia Patti], *Giorno d'amore* [a typesetter's Freudian embellishment upon *Giorno d'orrore*] . . . was given with greater precision and grace than anything in the opera." But, demanded Curtis, "Will some friend of the Muse explain the significance of the North-American Indian with high-towering plumes, who appeared at intervals upon the scene?" (*Tribune,* February 14, 1851). (The English tenor A. Arthurson,♪ in the role of Idreno—described in the libretto as "an Indian prince"—wore an American Indian costume referred to in the *Mirror* [February 15, 1851] as an "exuberance of feathers [which] might have caused him to be mistaken for a gigantic dusting brush, wrong end upwards.")

This same bill, with the further addition of the German violinist Ferdinand Griebel to the between-the-acts concert, was repeated two evenings later for Parodi's benefit, her farewell appearance at Astor Place. The occasion was not devoid of off-stage drama. At about seven P.M., reported the *Herald* (February 15, 1851), the basso Pietro Novelli announced that he would not sing unless he received an advance payment against his own approaching benefit.[10] Maretzek informed the assembled audience that

[9] George William Curtis's travel book, *Nile Notes of a Howadji,* had recently been published by Harper Brothers. Although it was mightily praised in the press, particularly in the Boston/Transcendentalist-oriented *Tribune,* George Templeton Strong pronounced it to be "a very disreputable and indecent book," laden with "passages, occurring with remarkable frequency, [of] a kind of euphuistic obscenity of puppy-lewdness"—a preoccupation with sex more appropriate to boys of fourteen than of men of more responsible years (Private Journal, March 7, 1851). Despite these and other harsh criticisms of the book, Strong continued over the years to be on the friendliest terms with the socially elevated Curtis and his brother (James) Burrill.

[10] Apparently the singers were driving a brisk trade in benefits. According to Saroni (*Musical Times,* March 1, 1851, p. 232): "The spirit of Wall Street has been exhibited in and about Astor Place

his basso has demanded "that to which he was not entitled." Augusto Giubilei, however, "with great promptitude supplied the place of Novelli, and thus the unhandsome conduct of this latter singer failed to have any effect, except against himself."

Parodi received a tremendous farewell ovation, continued the *Herald*. At the end of the first act she "appeared amid a shower of Italian and English poems thrown from the amphitheatre, some of which were printed upon satin and ornamented with the Italian tricolors. . . . Bouquets fell fast and thick also, and in the second act the vocalist reappeared wearing a magnificent bracelet of diamonds and pearls (costing $500), which in the interim [during the between-the-acts concert] had been presented to her by a number of her admirers. For this and the many other gifts she received she expressed her sincere thanks and stated that she hoped to return to the city which has been the first one to encourage her to hope for success in the United States."

After the opera, the orchestra (Germans and Italians alike, as the *Herald* pointedly observed) serenaded Parodi at her hotel. The following day she took the New Haven Railroad to Boston, where, supported by principal members of the Astor Place company, and with Maretzek at the helm, she was scheduled to open an opera season on November 17 with *Lucrezia Borgia*.

In New York, on the same evening, with Cesare Lietti conducting, and at still further reduced prices—back to one dollar for the parquette and boxes, even for "secured" seats, and twenty-five cents for the amphitheatre—the slightly tarnished diva Teresa Truffi-Benedetti, back from yet another tour of the South, was heard in *Ernani*. Richard Storrs Willis reported in the *Albion* (February 22, 1851, p. 92) that the audience was discouragingly small until rather late, when a few of the subscribers began to drop in, after "earlier and graver attractions offered in the shape of historical and artistical lectures."[11] "We find it is become a custom with many persons," he explained, "to take a familiar opera, thus, just at its most interesting stage of progress, and hear it out, as a closing dream-inspirer."

Richard Storrs Willis complained of Truffi's lack of intensity. Her singing was always correct and on pitch, but she was "too natural and gently dignified," too deficient in "a certain high coloring of tone and action, which either our perverted taste in theatrical representation or the intrinsic necessities of the case have rendered necessary. It is, perhaps, not to be denied that one must be unnatural to be *natural* upon the stage," commented Willis with a perversity not unworthy of his older brother.

Astor Place was left to stumble through the remainder of the season as best it could. After the subscription season of fifty performances had been completed, Truffi appeared in *La favorita* on February 24 (Forti's benefit), and in two performances of *Il giuramento*—on February 26 for her own benefit and the following evening for Nathalie Fitzjames's. A passing flurry of mild interest flitted across the torpid opera horizon just as the season was fizzling out: on both February 26 and 27, the first of two unusual debutantes, Madame Giulietta Bozzi, a contralto, appeared with Truffi in *Il giuramento*

the last week, and speculations in benefits have become quite the rage. Forti sold out his prospects to Benedetti for $150; Benedetti sold again to Maretzek senior for $175, and the latter sold to Grow [Grau?] for $225, who held the house when the benefit came off, losing thereby $128. This is a lively account, and shows that Forti's 'benefit' [*La favorita*], all told, [netted] exactly $97."

[11] In 1851, lectures on history and other scholarly subjects were frequently given by the elder Henry James, and on art by George William Curtis.

(as she had recently done during a Maretzek season in Baltimore). Madame Bozzi's true identity was an open and well-advertised secret: she was Madame Julie de Marguerittes, purportedly a high-caste Italian of distinguished literary repute. Dispossessed of her ancestral wealth by the political chaos in Italy, so the story went, Madame Marguerittes/Bozzi, said to be an accomplished singer, was bravely attempting to forge a new career for herself in the New World.

Receiving from N. P. Willis in the *Home Journal* (February 15, 1851) an advance send-off of an ornateness befitting her social rank,[12] Madame Bozzi as opera singer elicited disappointingly cool reactions in the general press. She was variously reported to have been musically well schooled, handsome enough, graceful enough, the possessor of an agreeable enough voice, or, as the case may be, of a disagreeable voice or an inaudible one. At any rate, her prospects in opera, commented the *Tribune* (February 29, 1851), offered small compensation for the social sacrifices they entailed.[13]

Nathalie Fitzjames's unconventional benefit the following evening awakened somewhat livelier interest. Combining her farewell as *prima ballerina* of Astor Place with her debut as a singer of operatic music, the "amphibious" Fitzjames, as she was called, astonished everyone with her expert handling of arias from *Robert le diable* and *I Lombardi*. Some critics went so far as to pronounce her a better singer than a dancer: "We are rather surprised," wrote Richard Storrs Willis, in his increasingly circuitous style, "that she has kept this little accomplishment of hers so long in reserve, which none but a European, by the way, would have done, presuming, generally speaking, to shine in but one thing. It is only on this side of the water that 'double-barreled' developments of a genius increased even to the accumulated capacity of the receiver—as a clever contemporary suggests—are thought of, or half-demanded, by the increasing intensity and progress of the age" (*Albion,* March 1, 1851, p. 104).

But *Parker's* (March 8, 1851, pp. 141–42), mischievously pretended to be undecided over "which had the worst of it, [Fitzjames's] throat or legs. . . . Who ever heard of a dancer, a *French* dancer, making any other use of her lips (in public) except to conceal by a smile the painful effort of standing on one toe?"

Saroni, however, refused to be diverted by such superficial distractions. Since Maretzek's cavalier departure for Boston, the level of the performances at Astor House had severely deteriorated, and deservedly they had been badly attended, he wrote. "All

[12] It was unfortunate, wrote Saroni (*Musical Times,* March 1, 1851, pp. 232–33), for Madame Bozzi to have been introduced to the public by N. P. Willis, who with his "profligate pen . . . serves up a lady as he would a horse, and enlarges upon her points with the freedom and unction and coarseness of a jockey."

[13] Soon after, on May 29, *The Home Book of Beauty,* a drawing-room comedy by the versatile Madame de Marguerittes, was successfully produced at Brougham's Lyceum. In September 1851 she became co-editor (for fashion) with George G. Foster (for politics) and Charles Gayler (for news) of a new, short-lived periodical *The Verdict;* she had reputedly contributed to Foster's "shabby little sheet" *The New-York Day Book* (*Evening Post,* September 18, 1851). But by December 9, the *Herald* announced that Madame de Marguerittes was starting a new paper, described as a "transformation" of the recently deceased *Evening New Yorker.* Now sporting a completely revised biography, she was described as an "English lady of remarkable brilliancy and talent," the daughter of a Dr. Granville, "a physician of high rank in Piccadilly, London." Some years before, she had married a Count de Marguerittes, a French gentleman of some distinction (present whereabouts not revealed). She had recently come to this country with letters of introduction to the "fashionable circles in New York, who patronized her for a short time, as they generally do all fashionable celebrities."

has been careless and slipshod. Everything wore the spirit of neglect; it seemed as if the spirit of the artists and management had fallen in proportion to the patronage of the public." Saroni was convinced that "this decline of excellence [would] seriously injure the prospects of the Italian Opera in the future."

"Mr. Maretzek's absence from his doubly important post as Manager and Director has thrown everything into confusion," Saroni complained. However compelling his reasons for being elsewhere, Maretzek's first duty was to his Astor Place constituents: "The place for Mr. Maretzek is New York. If it is absolutely necessary that some portion of his Company should perform in Boston or Philadelphia, let them go under the direction of his Maestro [Kreutzer]; or if Maretzek's presence is absolutely necessary at these places, let him arrange his New York season in such a way, either by shortening or dividing it, that it may not suffer by the absence of himself and the most efficient portion of his company" (*Saroni's Musical Times,* March 1, 1851, p. 232).

Since December 1850, and increasingly during this period of operatic malaise, Edward P. Fry, Maretzek's defeated predecessor at Astor Place, had been attempting a professional resurrection through a scheme to build a supergrandiose new opera house "about four or five times" the size of the Astor Place Theatre. With powerful backing, Fry was rumored to have acquired a large tract of land, known as the Stuyvesant Lot, bounded on its four sides by Third and Fourth Avenues, Astor Place, and Ninth Street (a space previously occupied by visiting menageries and circuses). Intended to seat four to five thousand people and costing an estimated 250,000 to 300,000 dollars, the "New-York Opera House" would provide all "commensurate amenities," not least, a visionary system of air conditioning, both winter and summer. Complicated architectural plans and an elaborate series of proposals for financing the new house, including several grades of subscriptions, were offered in an imposing prospectus and—in frequently amended form—in the press, which over a period of several months accorded both space and credence to Fry's scheme. Only the *Message Bird* ventured to inquire, after a second lengthy article devoted to Fry's project (April 15, 1851, p. 420), what Mr. Fry intended to offer in the way of productions.

It was also rumored at this time that Maretzek was planning a similar enterprise, and that he had already acquired a plot of land at Broadway and Houston Street. Both projects came to naught.

As for Strong, except for a single approving nod to an isolated music service at church, "unusually good for Trinity, where the old English school reigns uncontrolled in austere prosiness," the music he heard during this period seems to have originated exclusively in his own music room at home. Ellen Strong, an able and devoted amateur musician, together with music-loving friends, spent many melodious hours at the parlor piano exploring the works of the masters, from operas to masses. "Goliath," as Strong had nicknamed the massive pipe organ he had acquired with great emotional travail in 1840,♪ was occasionally called into service as well.

February 11. . . . [I] hear Ellie singing downstairs, and now there goes the *Hochzeitsmarsch* [the Wedding March from Mendelssohn's music to *A Midsummer Night's Dream*]. . . .

February 21. . . . Am writing this to the sound of the "Trio of the Masks" (in *Don Giovanni*), which comes up from the music room, where Ellie and the two Miss

Maurans♪ [Josephine and Teresa] are singing together. They came here today for a visit, and we have just been getting up *Kyrie*s and *Benedictus*es on the organ. When I say "we," I mean that I did not sing the bass or any other part, but blew [pumped] the bellows. They [the Maurans] are marvelous musicians. . . .

No man can hear Beethoven's music without perceiving the significance of the etymology of the word *Incantation*—a musical strain and a formula for producing supernatural effects. If . . . the disciples of the Rochester ghosts were people of sense, they'd follow out *that* path toward the invisible world as the most promising within the reach of Man at present. Some passages of Beethoven's music, played under a concurrence of favorable circumstances, would be more likely to raise the Devil, or bring about some sort of supernatural manifestation than anything I know.

February 24. . . . [after partially subduing one of his recurrent sick headaches, Strong joined the musical party downstairs consisting of] Charley and Eleanor Strong, George and Burrill Curtis, and one Kuhn of Philadelphia, a friend of the Maurans. Then Timm came up and put himself at the organ,[14] and I presided at the bellows, and "we" sang through most of Haydn's [Mass] No. 3[15] and a good deal of Mozart's No. 12,♪ and parts of [Mozart's] *Requiem*.♪ It was very delightful, in spite of the lingering headache. The loveliest bit of church music I know is the *Et incarnatus* of Haydn's No. 3.

February 27. [managing briefly to stop off at home on an "awfully energetic day," Strong reluctantly departed] leaving William and Edmund Schermerhorn [music-loving merchant princes], Bonzanini [Ellie's singing teacher], Ellie, and the Miss Maurans in full blast over the *Kyrie* of Mozart's No. 12.

The quality of music-making at the Strongs—its style and content—were not so uncommon as one might think. To people of their privileged caste and cultivation, at least a modicum of musical capability was more or less a required social attribute. Ellen Strong and the Maurans might have been more accomplished and dedicated performers than the general run of their social peers, but there seems to have been no lack of available and enthusiastic partners capable of taking part in their music-making. Not only were such informal musical meetings an enjoyable minor social ritual, but to those who loved music, the joys of participation offered a special intimacy with great musical works, not to be gained in the concert hall or the opera house.

Nor was the inclusion of such elevated fare as Haydn's and Mozart's masses altogether unusual at these musical parties, as we learn indirectly from John Sullivan Dwight. In an article devoted to what he called a "descriptive analysis" of the work universally misrepresented in the nineteenth century as "Mozart's Twelfth Mass"[16] (Dwight magisterially pronounced it to be the greatest of Mozart's masses), he at-

[14] Not a member of the Strongs' set, Timm was engaged, rather than invited, to play the organ at the Strongs' party.

[15] Strong's numberings doubtless conform with the Novello numbering of Haydn's Masses; No. 3, the "Lord Nelson," or "Imperial," Mass (1798) is listed in the Hoboken catalogue as number XXII: 11. A listing of the Haydn Masses referred to by Strong, with their catalogue numbers and popular designations, is found in the Index to this volume.

[16] Believed by the editors of Köchel's catalog of Mozart's works (sixth edition, 1964) to have been composed by Carl Zulehner (1770–1841) a German music teacher, composer, and music publisher in Mainz.

tempted to liberate the entire genre from the toils of the Catholic Church. Willfully or unconsciously unresponsive to the profoundly religious significance of the Mass, Dwight—for a period a practicing Unitarian minister, forever a Transcendentalist—wrote: "The Catholic Mass, once a very solemn and severe musical service limited to great plainness, was in its essential form something so germinal and organic as to be very attractive to the great modern composers; and in the hands of Haydn, Mozart, Beethoven, Hummel, Cherubini, and the like, it has become expanded (some would say *secularized*) into the most perfect, in many respects, of all the forms of extended vocal and instrumental compositions." Too beautiful a body of music to be monopolized by any one church, wrote Dwight, the great composers' masses belonged to all humanity, and as music, they were to be embraced by people of all faiths.

"The depth and beauty of the Masses grow upon the hearer with every repetition, and little musical groups who study them together, singing such portions as they can, by way of practice, or holding social 'readings' of them for the edification of themselves and listening friends, soon become partial to them, before all other vocal music" (*Graham's Magazine,* January 1851, pp. 1–5). Thus, it was in the music room at Gramercy Park that Strong's lifelong passion for the masses of Haydn took root and assumed in his musical consciousness an importance equal to that of Mozart's treasured "Number 12."

His native love of music evidently reawakened by all the music-making at home, Strong at last resumed his long-neglected concert-going, and again he confided his reactions to what he heard in his private journal.

March 1. . . . Went to hear [Mendelssohn's] *St. Paul* with Ellie and the Miss Maurans [performed by the Harmonic Society] at the Tabernacle [on February 28]. Excellent performance; choruses quite perfect. It may have been a pair of overtight boots, but I did not enjoy the music very intensely, or discover much force and freshness in any of it, except the grand and glorious "Sleepers awake," the "O be gracious, ye immortals," and one or two things besides. The air "Jerusalem, Jerusalem" is a lovely composition, but it smells of "Comfort ye, my people." Indeed, a great deal of the music seems a straining after Handel, and half the choruses might have been written by Handel dyspeptic or grown senile and stupid. Except, however, "How lovely are the messengers," which is a genuine and original affair.

Mendelssohn mistook his vocation when he wrote oratorios. He is the Shelley of composers, not to be matched in exuberance of delicate fancies, and spiritual and exquisite in his conceptions to the utmost limit of intelligibleness to mortal ears, but cramped by heroics and incapable of any approach to sublimity. The *Midsummer Night's Dream* music—the Overture especially—is his characteristic production. There the peculiarity of his mind shows itself unmistakably. Where he is writing for the full orchestra he is clumsy, exaggerated, and noisy; but in the ineffable opening and finale of the Overture, and wherever he is dealing with his finer fancies and giving an intenser reality to a fairy world by translating it into his own fairy music, no mortal comes near him. Weber's *Oberon* may be better or worse, but it's utterly different. If Herrick had tried to write a Christmas hymn like Milton's, he would have put his foot in it, as Mendelssohn did when he set about *St. Paul.*

In retrograde inversion of Strong's assessment of Mendelssohn as oratorio composer, the review of *St. Paul* in the April issue (p. 168) of *The Choral Advocate and Singing Class Journal,* Mason and Law's[17] newish monthly magazine, stated that it would be "idle" to compare Mendelssohn with Handel or Haydn—they dwelt in different musical worlds. Except that in his use of the orchestra Mendelssohn was definitely "superior."

It had been predicted, wrote the critic, possibly the magazine's first editor, Darius E. Jones, that so esoteric a work would be heard "with indifference, if not disgust." Not so. Discriminating members of the audience were observed listening to *St. Paul* with "unequivocal expressions of delight."

The few other critics who reviewed the concert agreed that the choruses were splendidly performed by the Harmonic Society, under Theodore Eisfeld's expert training and direction. Indeed, they had been so well prepared, wrote Richard Storrs Willis, as to create what he called "the usual discrepancy" between the chorus and the soloists—Mrs. Laura A. Jones soprano, Miss Maria Leach mezzo-soprano, A. Arthurson tenor, and Henry Wellington Greatorex bass.

Possessing a clear, strong voice, Mrs. Jones, now the foremost oratorio soprano in New York, excelled in the "recitative and *narrative* parts," wrote Willis, although her "straining after volume" tended to produce "a certain hard, sometimes wiry, quality of tone." Miss Leach, on the contrary, "sang with great feeling and expression, producing, generally, a sensible [*sic*] effect upon the audience." Mr. Arthurson "did many things exceedingly well; if he had succeeded equally in all, he would have [had] great reason to congratulate himself." However: "We observed a slight defect in his delivery of the words. . . . We refer to the superfluous syllable *er,* which was added to certain words in the text." Willis supplied several examples of words to which the incongruous suffix had been appended. This, however, was the only defect in Arthurson's otherwise uncommonly good articulation. Greatorex, who was suffering from a cold, was happily exempted from Willis's eagle scrutiny.

Felicitating the Harmonic Society on their excellence, Willis hoped they would soon be placed on the same footing of "pecuniary security" as the Philharmonic enjoyed (a fond Willisian delusion). Although the "getting up" of an oratorio cost at least $800, he did not "despair of seeing it eventually accomplished" by the Harmonic Society. Willis's review appeared in the *Albion* (March 8, 1851, p. 116) and reappeared in the *Message Bird* (March 15, 1851, p. 661).

In an article intended to promote the Harmonic Society, Saroni claimed that their membership, both performing and auditory, was increasing. To entice prospective stockholders, he announced that the distribution of free tickets to stockholders would henceforth be doubled to two tickets for each concert. The shares were $20 each, payable in installments of $2. And—the supreme lure—Eisfeld was now preparing Mendelssohn's *Elijah,* to be performed, it was hoped, "in connection with Jenny Lind," for whom Mendelssohn had composed the soprano part, and who was expected back from her tour in May (*Saroni's Musical Times,* March 8, 1851, p. 243).

[17] The publishing firm of Mason and Law, active since June 1850, consisted of Lowell Mason, Jr. (1823–1885), his brother Daniel Gregory Mason (1820–1869), and Henry W. Law, a resident of Brooklyn.

But neither Jenny Lind nor George Templeton Strong materialized at the Harmonic Society's *Elijah* performance at Tripler Hall on June 25. In Lind's stead, Madame Eliza Wallace-Bouchelle, William Vincent Wallace's sister, appeared, together with Maria Leach, her brother Stephen, and again Arthurson. Once again Richard Willis pronounced the chorus almost perfect, except for one spot when Eisfeld mistakenly beat in four instead of in two, as rehearsed, thereby throwing everybody off.

Madame Wallace-Bouchelle sang correctly enough and undoubtedly pleased her audience, but Willis preferred Miss Leach, with her appealing alto voice—rich, sympathetic, full of feeling, and pathos backed up by an *Intelligence*—which gave point to what she sang. Arthurson betrayed a lack of self-confidence by his bad intonation and defective style (no mention of *er,* this time). Stephen Leach, when free of embarrassment, did as well as the capabilities of his voice allowed.

Then followed a disquisition on how characters in oratorio were meant to be *represented,* rather than *impersonated,* as in opera. Willis confessed, too, that it "came over" him "oddly" when Leach looked up from his music and perhaps too directly addressed Madame Bouchelle with the line, "Give me thy son."

But, all things considered, there was little to censure and much to praise in the performance. Therefore, congratulations were due the Society and its conductor. Willis could not forbear, however, to condemn the libretto booklet, whose text was accompanied by a running critical commentary. "Without reference to the ability which the gentleman who undertook the task may or—in one or two instances—may not have displayed, we should much prefer to any forestalling of the public judgment or decision, to have with the next oratorio a clear program, and liberty granted to the public of hearing and freely judging for themselves "(*Albion,* June 28, 1851, p. 308).

Willis's comments on oratorio versus opera might have been triggered by remarks in the *Tribune* review (June 26, 1851) of the *Elijah* performance, most probably by George William Curtis: "There is something essentially antiquated and traditional in the form of the oratorio. It lacks dramatic development and action, and consists of a series of scenes, or is descriptive either of events or of emotion, and so loses the connected and human charms of opera, which is the perfected form which the oratorio implies." Mendelssohn's genius, Curtis mystifyingly contended, was harmonic rather than melodic, and for that reason he was best fitted, among all contemporary composers, to write oratorios. Possessing rich contemporary orchestral resources denied to the older masters (meaning Handel), Mendelssohn was able to create "a certain musical atmosphere . . . sometimes even satisfactorily supplying the place of melody. . . . The *Elijah* is his last great work, and among the greatest for the reasons indicated; it would please a popular audience more generally than Handel's *Messiah,* with whose colossal grandeur, however, neither the *St. Paul* or the *Elijah* cope."

But Saroni the dissenter, shunning his colleagues' posturings, realistically exposed the dismal current status of oratorio in New York. Local oratorio audiences, he wrote, were endemically small because fewer New Yorkers were attracted to oratorios than to the more entertaining miscellaneous concerts. If it were not for the "religious feeling, so frequently appealed to for the support of a society of this kind, the oratorio would soon cease from among us. Even with this aid," he continued, "failure to pay expenses is the rule. . . . The various societies which have undertaken at various times to perform this class of music have each consumed their funds and sunk, burdened with debt, to give place to another with a different name but the same members." The Harmonic Society's audiences, too, were recognizably the same as those that had attended the defunct Sacred Music Society's concerts years before. "The oratorio does not grow in public favor in this city, and that which will draw admiring audiences in London and Germany meets with slight favor here" (*Saroni's Musical Times,* June 28, 1851, p. 145).

Willis neglected to comment on the libretto booklet prepared for the Harmonic Society's more modest following concert (the last of the year), so deeply did he become enmeshed in a dense preachment on the respective merits of Handel and Haydn. On December 11 at Metropolitan Hall, as Tripler Hall was by then renamed (see following OBBLIGATO), the Society presented Haydn's *The Seasons,* sung by Mrs. L. A. Jones and Messrs. James A. Johnson and Robert Andrews, with a somewhat reduced chorus. George Frederick Bristow had by now supplanted Eisfeld as the Society's conductor.

It would not be fair, loftily patronized Willis, to judge these less-than-professional soloists by professional standards. He therefore generously pronounced Mrs. Jones's "freshness of feeling and simple, unaffected good taste" to be "most charming." "Her voice is a sweet one," he wrote, "and she uses it with a warm heartiness not common to many American singers." One little flaw, if he might point it out, however, was her "too frequent use of the *portamento.* Though very effective at times, this grace is a dangerous one and becomes intolerable when constantly used. It is worthy of note that Jenny Lind rarely employs it" (*Albion,* December 13, 1851, p. 596).

The *Musical Times,* no longer *Saroni's Musical Times* since November,[18] expressed gratitude to both the Harmonic Society and "its instrumental elder sister, the Philharmonic," for "constituting that musical salt which preserves us from entire contamination from the negro melodies, traveling family music, etc., with which we are overrun. These societies," the writer added, "deserve the cordial support of every lover of truth in the art, of everyone who would honor and elevate music, instead of degrading and debasing her."

If the Harmonic Society "did not attain their usual success" in their performance of *The Seasons,* it was due mostly to "the really *frigid* temperature of the hall. Singers who are shivering cannot be expected to accomplish much, nor are an orchestra with numb fingers in a state to do their best" (*Musical Times,* December 20, 1851, pp. 101–2).

Despite his love for *The Seasons,* George Templeton Strong was not present. Nor—to go back to the beginning of 1851—had he been one of the "intelligent and appreciative audience" who on January 11 had heard the Harmonic Society's "elder sister" give the first performance in America of Schubert's Symphony No. 9 in C

[18]On November 1, *Saroni's Musical Times* (p. 63) announced various physical and editorial changes. The *Musical Times,* as it would henceforth be known, would continue under the editorial supervision of Hermann Saroni, but he would now be assisted by D. M. Cole and J. S. Black, the latter formerly associated with the *Message Bird.* As things turned out, Saroni departed by November 15, and in February 1852, Richard Storrs Willis took over as editor-in-chief. These changes and the subsequent evolutions of the *Musical Times* are recorded in Weichlein (p. 71).

(*c.* 1828) (D. 944). Conducted by Eisfeld, the symphony, according to Richard Willis (in both the *Albion* and the *Message Bird*),[19] possessed a first movement of exceeding freshness and had been "most effectively played," except for the Philharmonic's inability to produce a true *piano.* The program had included as well two opera overtures: *La Vestale* (Paris 1807), by Gasparo Spontini (1776–1851), and the more familiar *Les Deux journées,* by Luigi Cherubini, which Willis nostalgically discovered to be identical with *Der Wasserträger,* an old friend from his days in Germany. The soloists on this occasion had been Joseph Noll, who played the Second Concerto for violin by Ferdinand David (of Leipzig, as Willis pointed out), and the German *Liederkranz,* who sang a setting by the German violinist and composer Karl Ludwig Fischer (b. 1816) of Goethe's *Meeresstille und glückliche Fahrt.* It was well sung, but Willis, who was not pleased with the work, wished they had sung instead Fischer's setting for men's chorus of Theodore Körner's "Prayer before Battle" (*Albion,* January 18, 1851, p. 32; *Message Bird,* February 15, pp. 629–30).

Reacting to the intensified musical atmosphere that permeated the Strong household during a "Miss Maurans'" visit, Strong, for the first time in a year, went to hear the Philharmonic's following concert.

March 1. . . . Tonight to the Philharmonic with Ellie and the Miss Maurans. . . . Beethoven's Symphony [No. 2] in D (1802) and [the Adagio and Rondo from] a piano concerto of Hummel's [in A-flat, op. 113 (1827), played by George Frederick Bristow] made Part One. The concerto rather ponderous. Second part: Haydn's Symphony in B Flat [possibly No. 102]; Scherzo [Minuet and Trio] from Mozart's E-minor [in fact, his G-minor Symphony, K. 550 (1788]; and a selection from the *Midsummer Night's Dream* music, winding up with the *Hochzeitsmarsch,* all perfectly played.

Haven't heard the D-Symphony since the first season—in '43. It is very delicious—the second movement especially—and nobody could have written it but the man who did write it, but it doesn't seem to me very Beethovenish. Haydn took us all by surprise—every movement a gem—the whole composition a crepusculum, or a morning star, of the full light and freedom of Beethoven. I never supposed that Haydn had the boldness to write so spirited and dashing a piece of work for the orchestra. The Scherzo [*sic*] from Mozart was lovely—full of grace and tenderness beyond the power of articulate language. I'm beginning to appreciate his music. On the whole, a most satisfactory concert.

~

To Saroni the Haydn and Mozart symphonies, coming after Beethoven, "sounded—we are not afraid to say it, tame, insipid." But, too, the Beethoven symphony, badly conducted by Eisfeld, was "one of the most indifferent performances of the Society." Indeed, the entire concert was "by no means the best the Society could do."

Saroni was discontented, besides, with the sameness of the Philharmonic's programs: "We are sorry to say that in spite of Overtures and Symphonies, of *Concerti* and *Capriccii,* by the best masters, a tone of languor and *ennui,* of monotony and tedium,

[19] Many of Willis's current reviews appeared in the *Choral Advocate* as well.

prevails over the audiences of these concerts, which is particularly perceptible in the intermission of the concert. In other concerts there is all life during this interval; in these there is the silence of almost death. Gaping here, gaping there, primness and forced merriment meet the observer in every direction" (*Saroni's Musical Times,* March 8, 1851, p. 249).

Reporting the same concert in the *Albion* of the same date, Willis was euphoric over the exciting spirit manifested by the large audience that crowded the Apollo and could easily have filled a larger auditorium. "The Philharmonic Society is slowly but steadily advancing to marked success and eminence," he exulted. "There seems to be organizing a select parish of Philharmonics. The Society has been long enough now in existence to have made a strong musical impression here, and to have formed the taste of a large number of the younger musical natures just mingling with society; serving thus, in fact, as an *education* institution. This taste is so distinct, so decidedly *philharmonic* in its character as impossible to be mistaken for anything else."

Willis pronounced the orchestra's playing at this concert to have been flawless, although Bristow's performance of the movements from the Hummel concerto was "not quite of the Philharmonic stamp." Surely, among the audience, he playfully suggested, there were some "fair [amateur] fingers . . . that would have done more brilliant service than was rendered in the 'concerto.'" Like his review of the Harmonic Society's *Elijah* performance, this one appeared first in the *Albion* (March 8, 1851, p. 116), then in the *Message Bird* (March 15, 1851, p. 661).

Willis and Saroni offered differing suggestions as well for an improved choice of soloists. Saroni (like Henry C. Watson during the '40s) longed for more vocalists; Willis for more celebrities chosen from among "eminent visitor artists" instead of the ceaselessly reiterated appearances of Timm and Scharfenberg, able though they were. Why had Otto Dresel, now in Boston, not been invited to appear with the Philharmonic? While Saroni agitated for more and cheaper concerts as a means of filling the Society's "empty coffers," Willis rejoiced over the proliferation of "very young persons with a decided preference for a very classical style of music."

April 24. . . . Richard [Storrs] Willis here last night with the Curtises, Charley and Eleanor [Strong], Mr. Ruggles, etc. Then the Maurans happened in with [the future eminent chemist] Wolcott Gibbs [1822–1908] and that indomitable [Charles] Kuhn, so we had some pretty good music. Willis sings charmingly—ballads and simple things, but in good taste—with a sympathetic voice and an offhand, expressive kind of accompaniment. Some of Heine's and Uhland's songs he makes very telling.[20]

April 26. . . . Philharmonic with Ellie this evening. Beethoven's Symphony [No. 5] in C minor the great feature of the concert. Perfectly played, only the Andante rather slow. It is music that I should think an orchestra of angels such as one sees in old pictures before Raphael might love to play. No mortal instruments can do justice to the Andante and Finale. Some poetry can't be thoroughly felt when it's read out of a book, far less when it's listened to; it must be recited mentally. And these two movements—the second so magically sweet, so full of fire and majesty and many-voiced

[20]Strong was referring to the poets Heinrich Heine (1797–1856) and Ludwig Uhland (1787–1862), whose verses supplied texts for Willis's repertory of German songs.

triumph—both when best played fall far below the adequate expression of the ideas they embody. They must be thought about to be understood. The rest of the concert commonplace. It ended with an overture called "Robespierre," by one [Henry] Litolff [1818–1891].[21] Very rampant and vociferous music—seemingly elaborate and careful,. but of which I understood nothing but a highly decorated, aggravated, and flagrant reproduction of the *Marseillaise,* much enforced by cymbals and triangles, and quite dashing and agreeable.

~

Apparently heeding Saroni too literally, the Philharmonic elders had assembled for this concert, the last of the 1850–51 season, a topheavy plethora of soloists, among them Madame Wallace-Bouchelle, who sang a "Grand Aria" from Mozart's *Don Giovanni* (an unfortunate choice, wrote Richard Willis, because Lind had sung it before her) and a ballad by her brother William Vincent, "Go, thou restless wind." The song was exquisitely accompanied on the piano by Scharfenberg, who on his own part contributed the best effort of the evening, Mendelssohn's *Capriccio brillant* for piano and orchestra. "Scharfenberg is a most pure and polished player," wrote Willis, "and gave, as usual, universal satisfaction. But in this piece, again the orchestra accompaniment showed a little want of rehearsal."

The other soloists were the flutist/violinist Franz Rietzel, who played a Fantasy and Variations for flute by the German flute virtuoso Christian Heinemeyer (1796–1872), and Joseph Noll and Henry Reyer, who collaborated in a *Duo concertante* for two violins by the French violin virtuoso Jean Charles Dancla (1818–1907). The latter, wrote Willis, "would have pleased us more, could we have rid ourselves of the impression that the instruments were not in perfect tune."

But Willis confessed to having been swept away, along with the rest of the audience, by Litolff's exciting, if noisy, overture, with its "great energy and fine management of the subject [the *Marseillaise*], the counterpoint passage (or *Gegensatz*) to which was very spirited and successful." (Willis was showing an increasing tendency to interlard his prose with learned-sounding German locutions.)

Strong did not attend the final Philharmonic concert of the year, the first of the orchestra's tenth season, given on November 22. On this occasion the Society, needing larger quarters, abandoned the Apollo Rooms and appeared for the first time at Niblo's Concert Saloon, where they would perform through their eleventh season. Under Eisfeld's direction, they gave the first performance in the United States of Mendelssohn's Fourth Symphony (the "Italian"), op. 90 (1833). The three soloists of the evening were the basso Philip Mayer, who sang the air "It is enough," from Mendelssohn's *Elijah;* J. E. Drescher, who played Weber's Concertino for Clarinet and Orchestra, op. 26 (1811); and the recently arrived young Dutch violinist Henry (or Henri) Appy, who played de Bériot's Sixth Concerto, op. 70. The orchestra opened part two of the program with the Overture to *Joseph* by Méhul, and closed it with Lindpaintner's *Faust* Overture. The concert was only perfunctorily noticed in the press, except for *Parker's Journal,* whose perceptive critic was enchanted with both the program and its perfor-

[21] The English-born French composer Litolff incorrectly appears in the published *Diary* (II, 44) as "Litorff."

mance. He was particularly taken with the opening of the last movement of Mendelssohn's Symphony, whose *saltarello,* to paraphrase the "graphic poetry of the Bible," caused the heart to "leap for joy." "Of the way in which the glorious orchestra of the Society did their work, we can speak in terms of unqualified praise. It is an orchestra of which every New Yorker has reason to be proud." Indeed, this critic had never heard them play so well (*Parker's,* November 22, 1851, p. 585).

On April 30, 1851, a huge advertisement signed by "the public's obedient servant," P. T. Barnum, appeared in the various newspapers, announcing Jenny Lind's return from her tour of the South and West and her impending series of farewell concerts in New York, "prior to her visits to Western New York, Niagara Falls, the Lakes, Canada, and her final departure to Europe." Bigger and better than before, Lind's supporting company, besides the baritone Giovanni Belletti, now included the sensational tenor Lorenzo Salvi (wooed away from the Havana Italian opera company with the rumored inducement of $1000 a week and expenses), and a full complement of instrumental soloists—Burke, Hoffman, Griebel, Drescher (clarinet), Schmitz (French horn), and, of course, Kyle and Siede. Julius Benedict would conduct a Grand Orchestra of "nearly 100," comprising the best New York musicians combined with the Germania Society."[22] The concerts, to begin May 7, would be given three or four times a week "until closed," meaning apparently for as long as the demand continued.

For Lind's return, the entire interior of Castle Garden was being newly redecorated and "furnished with Sofas and Settees, made and cushioned expressly for these concerts." One hundred "attentive ushers" would "preserve the order which has distinguished these concerts throughout her tour." As before, the bridge to Castle Garden would be covered in case of rain; seats would be "numbered and secured, to prevent gouging and confusion, etc.," and although they were priced at one, two, and three dollars each, tickets would be sold at auction on the days before the concerts.

To forestall criticism of this procedure, Barnum defensively advertised: "Experience has proved this is the best and only course that can be adopted to secure justice and satisfaction to the public." All tickets not sold at auction would be made available on the day of the concert at Jollie's music store (300 Broadway), and after six P.M. at Castle Garden.

According to the relentlessly anti-Barnum *Herald* (May 8, 1851), the auction for the first concert was a "cold and dull" affair, attracting only about 100 to 150 people, in contrast to the earlier crowds of 3000 to 4000 hysterical sensation-seekers. The music dealers, formerly the most aggressive of the ticket speculators, were present but apa-

[22] The orchestra included the foremost members of the New York Philharmonic and the entire Germania (which had been touring with Parodi). Burke was the concertmaster, with Eisfeld, Griebel, and Noll "standing by him" (orchestras still played standing). Also among the first violins were Bristow, Reyer, Hansen, A. Reiff, Jr., St. Luke, Perkins, and others; among the second violins were U. C. Hill (back from England), De Luce, Windmüller, and Knaebel. The violas included A. Poppenberg, S. Johnson, and Thomas Goodwin; the cellos, Braun, Eichhorn, Zerrahn, Groeneveldt. The double basses, conspicuously omitting Loder, included Ayliffe; the flutes were Kyle, Siede, and Felice Eben. Equally distinguished musicians made up the remainder of the woodwinds, brasses, and percussion. A complete listing of the orchestra personnel is found in the *Herald* of May 11, 1851.

thetic, and, according to the *Herald,* scarcely more than one-quarter of the tickets were sold at a meager premium of twenty-five cents each.[23]

In answer to the criticizers of his ticket auctions, Barnum, whose habitually sunny countenance now reportedly "presented rather a haggard and careworn appearance" (the ravages of his five-month tour with his Nightingale?), opened the proceedings with an uncharacteristically testy speech obviously intended for his chief tormentor, James Gordon Bennett: "Whatever editors may think or say," declared Barnum, "I and those associated with me are persuaded that we are the best judges of our own business, and that we know better what suits ourselves and the public in relation thereto than any editor. We may not be the best editors, or the best tailors, or the best shoemakers in the world, but we are conscious that we understand our own business, and know what is best for the interests of the public and ourselves. If the public in this city cannot get it beat into their heads that the auction system is the most advantageous for them, we will adopt another system, and they will see by contrast who was right" (*Herald,* May 7, 1851).

The cooled interest in the ticket auctions signified the generally altered public response to Lind's comparatively unballyhooed return to New York. True, throughout the tour, Barnum's publicity machine had supplied the press with gossipy tidbits reporting her triumphs en route. But only a modest proliferation of these items immediately preceded her return, not the prodigious fanfares of yesteryear. Absent were the daily columns of Lindiana, the gaudy proclamations of her latest saintly deeds, the serenades, the armies of importunate tradespeople, the frenzied multitudes.

Twisting the knife, James Gordon Bennett—not an unbiased observer—asserted that Barnum's attempts to revive the earlier hysteria had been rebuffed by the press. In another of his blistering attacks on "the public's obedient servant" in the *Herald* (May 30, 1851), Bennett claimed that there had been "no lack of zeal on the part of Barnum and his literary bureau," as the *Herald* habitually referred to Barnum's press corps, "to renew the laughable excitement of last year."[24] But to no avail. "In fact," as Bennett stated, "it will be twenty-five or thirty years and another generation before we can have a second edition of the original Lind enthusiasm. Coronation festivals do not come very often, even in musical matters. Barnum and Jenny Lind can never gain another musical excitement like the one of last year, though one is the Napoleon of Showmen and the other the Queen of Song."

Yet, contrary to Bennett's claims that Lind's audiences had drastically diminished in size and enthusiasm, the general press reported capacity houses throughout the series of fourteen concerts that she gave between May 7 and June 6. At her first appearance, according to *Parker's Journal* (May 10, 1851, p. 246), Castle Garden had been jammed to the rafters by a well-behaved audience that manifested a sober, unhysterical

[23] Ticket speculators' advertisements, indeed sparse at first, steadily increased as the Lind season progressed.

[24] "The whole population laughs at the demonstrations of last year," jeered Bennett. "The Mayor of the city laughs—the city authorities laugh—the clergy laugh—editors laugh—everybody laughs at the fuss and antics which marked everybody's conduct on the advent of Jenny. We have now grown wiser, and judge musical entertainments on the temperance principles inculcated by Barnum himself" (*Herald,* May 6, 1851). But the last laugh was had by Barnum, who reported his share of the gross to be about half a million dollars.

appreciation of Lind. Indeed, wrote *Parker's,* Lind had by now achieved the status of a "national hero" and was accorded appropriate "hero worship," albeit "taking the form, and wearing the robes, of Art."

Again, on May 17 (p. 262) the *Parker's* critic commented on the enthusiastic (but well-behaved) thousands who continued to flock to Castle Garden to hear Lind—some traveling from great distances: "That men, American men, should come from Wisconsin to our town to hear a woman sing required an enlarged credulity," he wrote, but even more remarkable, "that New Yorkers could more than once pay an unusual sum for a concert ticket has entirely destroyed our notion of economic things."

There was really nothing left to say about Lind's singing: "Like Shakespeare, she has exhausted the vocabulary of panegyric." And again, on May 24 (*Parker's,* p. 274): "In the name of wonder, where do all the people come from who crowd Castle Garden on [Lind's] nights. We speak the simple truth when we say that we sat on Monday evening in a space six inches wide, paradised between two angelic creatures—whom we should undoubtedly have considered heavenly if they had not been quite so warm during the whole concert—and esteemed ourselves happy in the privilege of sitting at all."

George William Curtis, Lind's unfailing adorer, estimated that no less than 7500 enchanted people had crowded into Castle Garden on May 7 to welcome her back. Dressed in a "magnificent brocade" (the "robes of Art"?) and wearing "jeweled bracelets upon her arm," as he reported in the *Tribune* (May 9, 1851), Lind had "bounded forward" on the stage[25] and, although thinner and worn-looking after her strenuous tour, she had belied her haggard appearance with her glorious rendition of an aria from *La sonnambula (Come per me sereno).* Indeed, Burke's violin solo (a concerto by de Bériot), which followed, could hardly be heard through the "prolonged murmurs of delight" (civilized murmurs, mind you, not vulgar shouts).

Although Curtis would have liked to review the concert in minutest detail, space would not permit. He felt it his duty, however, to single out Lind's performance of "The Last Rose of Summer," for he had never heard it so magnificently sung. In it she permitted herself only one ornament, a "long, lingering thrill [*sic*] upon 'world,' whose dying fall was like that of audibly thrilling rose leaves trembling to the ground." (If Lind had not lost the touch, neither had Curtis.)

On May 22 in the *Tribune,* Curtis outdid himself: "To hear Jenny Lind, we need not regret too much that the Sistine Chapel is beyond the sea. For it is the hope and inspiration of all highest art to express precisely what Jenny Lind as a woman and an artist expresses."

Not all of Curtis's fellow critics shared his uncompromising worship of Lind. Even R. Storrs Willis, who pronounced her return concert to be the greatest ever heard in New York (as did the *Mirror*), confessed nonetheless that he did not "*altogether* like Jenny Lind's singing of 'The Last Rose of Summer.' Despite the many moist eyes, [he] could not quite assent to the *taste* of the performance." Willis disapproved, too,

[25] The violinist Henri Appy later recalled that Lind virtually danced sideways on and off the stage. At first, he thought she might have been lamed as the result of an accident. Unlike those who thought her cold, Appy referred to Lind's "fiery temperament," which he claimed "destroyed her" (unattributed article found in the Leonidas Westervelt Collection, New-York Historical Society).

of the inevitable trio with two flutes from *A Camp in Silesia,* disliking the combination of soprano and flutes, which seemed "all *superstructure* and no foundation." As can be seen, Lind's repertory had remained unchanged since her previous visit, except, perhaps, for some added popular ballads in English (to please the general public), such as "Comin' thro' the rye" and "John Anderson, my Jo."[26]

Like most of his colleagues, Willis commented on Lind's "newly care-worn and weary look," so different from the air of fresh joyousness that she had manifested on her first arrival. Barnum's killing schedule of performances had obviously taken its toll: "The new and strange experiences of life on this side of the Atlantic," Willis wrote, "have not been made without leaving their evident traces" (*Albion,* May 10, 1851, p. 224).

Gemotice, who vied with Curtis and surpassed Willis in his untrammeled transports over Lind, trusted that a few months in New York spent in "comparative quiet and leisure without the fatigues of traveling, would restore her to her wonted health" (*Spirit,* May 10, p. 144). A reformed Richard Grant White, after his earlier tergiversations, now maintained an unshakable adulation of the Nightingale, tirelessly filling vast columns with his prolix superlatives after each of her fourteen concerts.[27]

But there were dissenting voices as well. John R. Young, the editor of the *Albion,* took public issue with his own music critic Richard Willis on the subject of Willis's uninhibited paeans to Lind. On May 24, Young wrote in the *Albion* (p. 248): "There is [such] a wide difference between the critical notices of Jenny Lind which we now publish and those that were written for this journal [by Henry C. Watson, now temporarily *hors de combat*] on her first appearance here, that we think it necessary to remind our readers that the critical pen was changed in December last, as then announced. We exercise no control in the matter, but take this opportunity of reiterating our conviction that Jenny Lind, for the masses of the public, is a very unimpressive concert-room singer—notwithstanding the crowds which throng her performances, and in the teeth of critics, our own included. We could name twenty vocalists heard within as many years at oratorios, in Concert-rooms, and on the Stage, who have given us far more real enjoyment. But without dwelling on personal feeling, we might inquire of the writer below [Willis]—who says that 'the most *delicate* musical organizations best appreciate Jenny Lind'—whether the *public* is gifted with *any* musical organization? Certainly not; and the public, which therefore pays so freely, claps so loudly, and professes itself *through the press,* to be so hugely delighted, does not in truth appreciate her at all."[28]

[26] Blaming Barnum for what he characterized as Lind's most unfitting inclusion of popular English ballads in her repertory, Bennett (or Mrs. Bennett) fulminated: "Barnum has now succeeded in bringing down Jenny Lind to that point which ruined Catalani as an interpreter of classical music. He has gone on, step by step, to force her into songs for which her voice and style are unsuited, and, as a climax, has given a concert comprising only English songs," on the afternoon of May 29, at Castle Garden (*Herald,* May 30, 1851).

[27] White disapproved, however, of Benedict's practice of reducing the orchestra for the vocal accompaniments.

[28] "We have failed to discover the secret of this popular frenzy, without precedent or parallel for a concert singer," corroborated *Parker's* (May 31, 1851, p. 285). "We can't believe that 5000 people who [can] hear Salvi sing a beautiful melody of Rossini or Mercadante, without exhibiting any symp-

In answer, Willis, who imperturbably continued to churn out his wordy extravaganzas after each Lind concert, found it incomprehensible that seemingly sensitive people (naming no names) could remain unresponsive to "the soul's harp, as touched by the divine fingers of Jenny Lind." He could only regret their insensibility and give thanks that he was "not as they" (*Albion,* May 31, 1851, p. 260).

As might be expected, George Templeton Strong was among the dissenters. Capitulating at last, on May 14 he went to hear Lind's fourth concert, given at Tripler Hall, where—to accommodate uptown New Yorkers—she alternated her appearances with those at Castle Garden.[29]

May 16. . . . Heard Jenny Lind Wednesday night with Ellen. As much pleased as I expected to be, and no more. All that I heard her sing was overloaded with *fioriture* and foolery, marvelously executed; but I always find that sort of thing a bore.[30]

The low and middle notes of her voice are superb, and the high notes as good as such notes can be; but she runs too much on music written for the altitudes. No doubt, she does it with perfect ease, but that doesn't make it the pleasanter to hear. A man who could walk on his head as comfortably as on his feet would be a fatiguing person to look at if he abused his faculty of locomotion and was habitually upside down. The lady's personal appearance took me much by surprise. None of her portraits do her any justice, She is not pretty nor handsome nor exactly fine looking, but there's an air about her of dignity, self-possession, and goodness that is extremely attractive.

~

On June 2, Lind gave the twelfth concert of her present series at Tripler Hall for the benefit of Barnum's company manager and right-hand man, Le Grand Smith, and on this occasion appeared for the first time Otto Goldschmidt (1829–1907), a pupil of Mendelssohn whom Lind had met in Germany, with whom she had musically collab-

toms of gratified musical taste, but who burst into universal rapture when Jenny sings 'Gin a body kiss a body, need a body cry,' can be fairly said to be actuated by any very high notions, or possessed of any thorough appreciation of true art. Certainly, such an audience, so satisfactorily proving its inability to estimate *good* music, are moved by something else than Jenny's vocal attainments, to the nightly disbursement of three dollars, and the endurance of the torture of Castle Garden benches [so much for Barnum's cushioned settees]. Where lies the secret, then? What is the attraction? Answer satisfactorily, we cannot."

[29] "From Castle Garden to Tripler Hall, from Tripler Hall to Castle Garden, Jenny oscillates, and with each oscillation, like the weight fixed to the end of the pendulum, swings with her her audience of five thousand" (*Parker's,* May 31, 1851, p. 285).

[30] Virtually repeating her opening Castle Garden program of May 7, Lind sang the cavatina *Come per me sereno* from *La sonnambula,* "The Gypsey's Song" from *A Camp in Silesia,* a Rhenish ballad by Mendelssohn, translated as "Though many pretty maidens," and "Home, Sweet Home"; with Belletti she sang Benedict's "Tyrolean Duet," and with Belletti and Salvi the trio *Zitti, zitti* from *Il barbiere di Siviglia.* Belletti sang an aria from *I Lombardi,* Salvi an aria from *La favorita,* and together they sang a duet from *L'elisir d'amore.* The "fillings in," as *Gemotice* called the instrumental solos, consisted of a Fantasia on Favorite Themes from *Lucia di Lammermoor* for clarinet, played by Enrico Belletti, billed as first clarinetist of Her Majesty's Theatre, London, and the *Élégie* for violin, op. 10, by Ernst, played by Joseph Burke. Benedict conducted the *Faust* Overture by Lindpaintner, the Overture to *Semiramide,* and the Coronation March from *Le Prophète.*

orated in England in 1849, and whom she would marry in 1852. A pianist, Goldschmidt—replacing Richard Hoffman—performed in both parts of the program, a privilege not accorded any of Lind's other assisting instrumentalists.

The Nightingale had summoned Goldschmidt from Europe to replace Benedict, who was returning to England. She might all along have cherished romantic feelings toward the young German, and perhaps she had been waiting for an opportunity to bring him to the United States. Once arrived, Goldschmidt, with his apparently dry, Germanic style of piano playing and his "severe" choice of repertory, did not please his American listeners,[31] and Lind reportedly made an embarrassing public spectacle of herself in her efforts to force unwilling audiences to applaud him.[32]

The reviews of Goldschmidt's debut were eclipsed, however, by Barnum's shocking announcement, appearing in all the papers on June 3, that he and Lind had agreed to come to a parting of the ways. In dispassionate terms he stated: "The public are respectfully informed that the engagement between Mlle. Jenny Lind and myself for 150 concerts, having contained certain conditions on which the same might be terminated either at the end of sixty or of one hundred concerts, it has been determined to limit them to the latter number, and, as 91 concerts (besides those given for charity) have already taken place, there are only nine remaining, of which positively [only] one will be given in New York, viz., on Friday night, June 6, at Castle Garden. It has been determined to give the eight last concerts in Philadelphia and Boston. The concert to be given for the benefit of the orchestra on Wednesday night, June 4, is, of course, not included in the above. [Signed], The public's obedient servant, P. T. Barnum." Barnum neglected to mention that under the terms of their contract, Lind was required to forfeit the sum of $25,000 upon the completion of the hundredth concert.

On June 4, Lind's secretary (and cousin) Max Hjortsberg issued a counterstatement on her behalf, refuting the legend—promptly propagated by the *Tribune* and later perpetuated by Barnum—that he (Barnum) and Lind were parting in the greatest of mutual amity. Barnum's announcement, Hjortsberg claimed, was "calculated in some degree to mislead the public with regard to [Lind's] future intentions. Miss Lind has never authorized the statement that these concerts are to be her last in America; the

[31] Perpetuating a howler in the *Mirror* (June 4, 1851), Odell (VI, 96) reports that Goldschmidt played a (nonexistent) piano concerto in G minor by Bellini. The *Mirror* "thought him unfortunate in the selection of his pieces . . . they were too abstruse and elaborate for popular appreciation, but they were admirably performed, and to such as understood them, afforded a rare treat." In the *Tribune* (June 3, 1851), Curtis commented on Goldschmidt's "heroism" in attacking a classical work (it was in fact the Mendelssohn Concerto in G minor, op. 25)♪ at least a half-hour long. Perhaps it was Goldschmidt's performance that was forbidding; neither abstruse, elaborate, heroic, or even unfamiliar, the Mendelssohn G-minor Concerto had been played in New York as far back as 1846 and frequently repeated since then. In the second part of the program Goldschmidt played Thalberg's *Étude* in A Minor, op. 45.

[32] George William Curtis later recalled that at Goldschmidt's very first concert in America, just as he was about to begin his first number, the Mendelssohn Concerto, "the door opened quietly at the back of the stage, and Jenny Lind stood in full view of the audience tranquilly to listen. At a happy point in the performance she clapped heartily, and the whole house, following its lovely leader, burst into a storm of applause" (Curtis, *Easy Chair,* 1st series, p. 152). Although Curtis claimed that this "secured the success of Mr. Otto Goldschmidt," the young pianist was persistently rejected by American audiences.

only publication she has consented to is that of the close of the engagement with Mr. Barnum after one hundred nights. . . . The fatigue and exertion incidental to such continuous efforts," Hjortsberg explained, "make it necessary for her to enjoy, for some time, repose and relaxation. After that, she may, if her strength permits, make a short tour in Western New York and Canada, in order not to disappoint those who, from expecting to hear her at home, have refrained from visiting the Atlantic cities."

The papers agreed that without Hjortsberg's elucidation they might have been misled into believing that Lind was terminating her American tour after the hundredth concert. Indeed, on June 3, upon Barnum's announcement, the *Mirror* had prematurely lamented: "After two concerts more the voice of Jenny Lind will, in all probability, be hushed to many of us forever. Those who have listened to her delicious warblings, however, will cherish the memory of that pleasure for many years, and hereafter it will be a source of gratification to some of them, no doubt, when tottering down the hill of life, to relate to their grandchildren the wonder of the Swedish Nightingale."

On June 3 the *Tribune,* too, published a lengthy valedictory tribute to Lind (most probably written by G. W. Curtis), wherein its readers were assured that Lind and Barnum were parting on the friendliest terms. Her visit, wrote the *Tribune,* was "certainly one of the most brilliant and striking phenomena with which the history of art has ever been marked. Such a triumphal march as hers through the country was never before heard of." Much of it was "due to her great European reputation; much to the popular admiration of her personal character, her generosity, her contempt for social conventionalities; much to the admirable tact, the lavishness of expenditure, and the care for the public accommodation and comfort with which the Concerts have been managed; much, too, to the musical science and judgment which have presided on their arrangement and execution. But when all these causes are reckoned at their fullest value, the effect is not half accounted for."

In a stupefying torrent of words, the writer attempted to assess the Nightingale's universal appeal. Compounded of the good, the beautiful, the tangible, and the ineffable, she just as potently affected the knowledgeable and the ignorant, the rich and the poor.

True to its liberal principles, the *Tribune* particularly rejoiced in Lind's phenomenal triumph because it had happened in a Democracy and to a Woman: "Very few are the spheres of action which Society now opens equally to the two sexes. Fewer still are those in which a Woman can assert and maintain a superiority. The Stage [until comparatively recently taboo to the *Tribune*] and its kindred art of vocal music are almost the only pursuits in which Woman has frequently carried off the palm from Man. What man," the writer asked, "could hope for such success as this of the Swedish songstress?" And exultantly answered, "Not one."[33]

Lind's ovations surely presaged a better age to come, "when Society will no

[33] Saroni persisted in thinking otherwise. Criticizing Lind for capitulating to Barnum's commercialism, he wrote: "We were always under the impression that a true artist should live but for his art, and that a certain dignity is requisite to uphold the man as artist. With ladies this may be different. We know that a man would not have suffered another to exhibit him as a wild beast or a *lusus naturae* [freak of nature]" (*Saroni's Musical Times,* May 28, 1851, p. 82).

longer need, nor seek, to be wiser than Nature, and when those spheres of action for which the impulses and powers of soul have been adapted by its Divine Author will be freely opened to every being."

But in the meantime, "*Eheu, Posthume, Posthume*!" With heavy heart, Curtis had earlier begun to lament the prospect of Lind's eventual departure, writing in the *Tribune* on May 23: "How to lose her at last is a catastrophe which we cannot realize."

Castle Garden was packed to suffocation for Lind's two remaining New York concerts. At the ticket auction for the last one, the *Tribune* (June 6, 1851) reported that Le Grand Smith, who acted as auctioneer, had been offered certified checks by two different speculators for every seat in the house at box-office prices. Barnum, of course, refused the offers, giving as his reason that he wanted to make the memorable experience available to everybody. And indeed, the seats were snapped up at large premiums accruing to Barnum.[34] The *Tribune* predicted that by noon (of June 6) tickets would be selling for as much as fifteen, or even twenty, dollars. One holder of a seventy-five-cent ticket (for out-of-doors standing room) reportedly sold it for $11.75.

At her last concert Lind sang the arias *Prendi per me (L'elisir d'amore), Casta diva (Norma),* and *Non paventar (The Magic Flute);* she concluded the concert with "The Last Rose of Summer" and "Comin' thro' the Rye." For a final time the critics flogged their exhausted superlatives, and at the dreaded moment of parting: "As the last gush [of "Comin' thro' the rye"] showered us with its sparkling spray of joy, the muffled roar of clapping and murmurous delight [still muffled and murmurous] closed upon its cadence, and bowing low, while the bouquets fell at her feet, there was a momentary disappearance, then, coming forward between Benedict and Belletti [but no Barnum], one more bow, one more surge of applause, and Jenny Lind was gone" (*Tribune,* June 7, 1851).

The finale of the Lind/Barnum drama followed with startling swiftness. Startling, that is, to the public, but not to the protagonists—particularly not to Barnum, whose habitually unflappable air of euphoria had apparently masked great and continuous anxieties throughout the Lind adventure. As early as October 23, 1850, amid the prodigious first eruptions of Lindomania, Barnum had momentarily revealed an unsuspected vulnerability in a poignant letter—more a cry for help—addressed to Joshua Bates of the London banking firm of Baring Brothers, with whom Barnum had deposited his vast advance security payment of $187,500. "Dear Sir," he wrote:

"I take the liberty to write to you a few lines, merely to say that we are getting along as well as could reasonably be expected. In this country you are aware that the rapid accumulation of wealth always creates much envy, and envy soon augments to malice. Such are the elements at work to a limited degree against myself, and although Miss Lind, Benedict, and myself have never, as yet, had the slightest feelings between us, to my knowledge, except those of friendship, yet I cannot well see how this can long continue in the face of the fact that, nearly every day, they allow persons (some moving in the first classes of society) to approach them and spend hours in traducing me. Even her attorney, Mr. John Jay, has been so blind to her interests as to aid in

[34] Promptly on June 6, the day of the last concert, the papers (Barnum?) advertised for sale the Érard piano made especially for Lind's use; the price, a hefty $1200.

poisoning her mind against me by pouring into her ears the most silly twaddle, all of which amounts to nothing and less than nothing—such as the regret than I was a 'showman,' exhibitor of Tom Thumb, etc.[35]

"Without the elements which I possess for business, as well as my knowledge of human nature acquired in catering for the public, the results of her concerts here would not have been pecuniarily one half as much as at present, and such men as the Hon. Edward Everett, G. G. Howland,[36] and others will tell you that there is no charlatanism or lack of dignity in my management of these concerts. I know as well as any person that the merits of Jenny Lind are the best capital to depend upon to secure public favor,[37] and I have thus far acted on this knowledge. Everything which money and attention can procure for [the company's] comfort they have, and I am glad to know they are satisfied on this score. All I fear is that these continued backbitings, if listened to by her, will by and by produce a feeling of distrust or regret which will lead to unpleasant results.

"The fact is, her mind ought to be as free as air, and she herself as free as a bird, and, being satisfied with my probity and ability, she should turn a deaf ear to all envious and malevolent attacks on me. I have hoped that by thus briefly stating to you the facts in the case, you might be induced, for her interest as well as mine, to drop a line of advice to Mr. Benedict and another to Mr. Jay on this subject. If I am asking or expecting too much, I pray you not to give it a thought, for I feel myself fully able to carry through my rights alone, although I should deplore nothing so much as to do so in a feeling of unfriendliness. I have risked much money on the issue of this speculation—it has proved successful. I am full of perplexity and anxiety, and labor continually for success, and I cannot allow ignorance or envy to rob me of the result of my enterprise. Sincerely and gratefully yours, P. T. Barnum" (quoted in *Struggles and Triumphs,* 1869, pp. 304–5).

Now, some eight months later, Barnum's worst apprehensions had been realized. Lind—apparently physically and emotionally frazzled by the rigors of her crushing schedule, influenced by the cumulative goading of her friends,[38] and probably no longer able to tolerate the sight of Barnum—had obviously reached the breaking point by the time she arrived in Philadelphia. Barnum, too, despite his prodigious earnings, had by now doubtless had his fill of polishing the public halo of his uncomfortable

[35] Saroni, for example, deplored Lind's loss of dignity. If only she had "confined herself to strictly good music—if she had striven to elevate the taste of the people instead of catering for their unrefined or illegitimate taste. . . . If she had protested against the clap-trap of her managers—if she had vetoed the auctioneering system—if she had been less mercenary and more the true artist—she would have carried with her the love and esteem of everyone whose love and esteem was worth having" (*Saroni's Musical Times,* May 17, 1851, p. 82).

[36] The statesman Edward Everett (1794–1851) was an outstanding orator of his time; Gardner Greene Howland (1787–1851) was a merchant prince of fabled wealth.

[37] In 1890, after Lind's death, Barnum is supposed to have said to a reporter: "It is a mistake to say the fame of Jenny Lind rests solely upon her ability to sing. She was a woman who would have been adored if she had the voice of a crow" (quoted in Werner, p. 189).

[38] For instance, the journalist who conjectured that Lind might have come to realize the affront to her dignity as an artist in being merchandised "like Tom Thumb or [Barnum's loudly ballyhooed] nine new elephants" (*Albion,* June 7, 1851, p. 271).

angel, and of the abuse he received for his pains. The final blowup occurred on June 9, when, according to dispatches from Philadelphia appearing in the New York papers on June 11, with seven concerts still to go, Lind irrevocably broke with Barnum.

Conflicting versions were given in the press, the most sensational, of course, appearing in the *Herald,* whose Philadelphia correspondent wrote: ". . . all sorts of stories are afloat as to the provoking cause of this rupture. Common rumor attributes it to [Lind's] dissatisfaction at being forced to sing in a building [the National Theatre on Chestnut Street] generally used as a circus, and upon a platform which only half covered the ring. The effluvia from the deserted stables of the establishment," the *Herald*'s correspondent delicately added, "was [*sic*] so nauseating that chloride of lime had to be used in abundance. All present at the concert . . . noticed that Mademoiselle Lind never appeared to so poor advantage, both as to looks and voice; her face expressed the scorn of the position she occupied, and her annoyance was evidenced by the frequency with which her perfumed handkerchief was applied to her face." Lind did not resume her customary angelic persona until the end of the concert, "when her face beamed with the satisfaction she felt at being able, in future, to choose the place in which she is to sing."

As the story went, Lind had confronted Barnum with an irate refusal to appear a second time in these loathsome surroundings, reportedly declaring that she was "not a horse." Whereupon Barnum offered to release her from the remaining seven appearances upon the further forfeit of $7000–$10,000 for each canceled concert. In a stiffly correct note Lind promptly accepted.

Only in one important detail did Barnum's story differ from this version. Admittedly, he wrote, the National Theatre had formerly been used for gaudy spectacles and equestrian entertainments, but it had been "thoroughly cleansed and fitted up" for Maretzek's previous opera presentations in Philadelphia.[39] It was only because of the intrigues and plottings of "envious intermeddlers [who] recommended that she repudiate her contract . . . at all hazards, and take the enterprise into her own hands—possibly to put it in theirs" that Lind had refused to sing there. Indeed, on the day of the concert (June 8), Barnum, who "saw the influences which were at work, and not caring enough for the profits of the remaining seven concerts to continue the engagement at the risk of disturbing the friendly feelings which had hitherto uninterruptedly existed between that lady and myself," wrote her a courteous letter stating that he would be willing to release her from the last seven concerts if she would pay the forfeit of $1000 each. He was "most happy to learn from her lips" that Lind agreed.[40]

As Barnum tells it, during the intermission at the fateful concert at the National Theatre, Lind wavered. Finding the place to be not so unendurable as she had been led to believe, she declared her willingness after all to finish her Philadelphia engage-

[39] This Maretzek flatly denied, "inasmuch as the aforesaid Max Maretzek never played there at all until some three months after Jenny Lind had inaugurated it for musical entertainments" (*Crotchets,* p. 131).

[40] "Allow me to inquire how or why he was 'most happy' to learn this from her lips?" asks Maretzek, who proceeds disingenuously to ask if perhaps the concerts might have been less profitable than Barnum "would have the American public believe, or is it that Jenny herself was not *au fond* that 'angel' which he had in his first moment of enthusiastic certainty dubbed her? Was she capricious, self-willed, or difficult to manage, like any other *prima donna*?" (*Crotchets,* p. 129).

ment there. Only the intensified outcry of her scheming hangers-on at last persuaded her to go through with the divorcement. And so, according to Barnum, they parted on the politest and friendliest terms (*Struggles and Triumphs,* 1869, pp. 349–52).[41] For Lind it proved a disastrous decision.

Notwithstanding her purported exhaustion, the Nightingale ignored this opportunity to escape to the "repose and relaxation" she so desperately needed; instead she continued her tour, apparently following the itinerary plotted by Barnum. With Benedict, Belletti, Salvi, Burke, and, of course, Goldschmidt, and under the dubious management of her former ticket-taker C. S. Seton (or Seyton, or Seaton), Lind toured New England and upper New York State until August, when Benedict and Giovanni Belletti, after some 16,000 miles of touring with the Nightingale within the short space of nine months, returned to England. Lind remained in the lucrative United States, and after permitting herself an interval of rest, in mid-October announced another farewell tour. Her assisting artists were Goldschmidt (who continued to bore his audiences), Salvi, Burke, and the clarinetist Enrico Belletti. Despite her enormous earnings with Barnum, netting her some $176,675 (Barnum's figures) and her reputedly uncompromising musical standards, the thrifty Nightingale, under her own management, dispensed with the costly services of an orchestra.

Without Barnum to maintain its brilliance, Lind's blinding radiance quickly dimmed. As the *Herald* gleefully explained: Barnum's "famous literary bureau, since the flight of the Nightingale from his cage, are beginning to come down from the clouds, and to talk in an earthly and sober fashion about the object of their long-continued idolatry. Indeed, some of the journals which have been elevated by the bureau to the seventh, and even the seventeenth, heaven are beginning to admit, for the first time, that Jenny Lind—'that angel'—'that divinity'—is a woman—nothing more or less—a woman 'with flesh, blood, and temper.'" The novelty-seeking American public, evidently sated by now with the miraculous Angel/Nightingale image, had made the same discovery.

Encountering unsuspected problems in self-management, an undertaking for which she was totally unfitted, Lind only rarely evinced her former spectacular joyousness. Reporting the second of her three farewell concerts in Boston, the correspondent of the *Musical Times* (December 6, 1851, p. 75) wrote: "The countenance of Miss Lind, which had appeared so dejected at the previous concert, shone with a radiant expression which called to mind her first appearance before a Boston audience; she was then so cheerful and happy in her movements that it seemed *impossible* for her to be otherwise; but the fatigue which has attended her tour thus far in America seems to have taken strong hold upon her and rendered her naturally animated countenance a scene of mental uneasiness."

[41] A mutually agreeable parting according to Barnum, perhaps, but not to Lind. Visited some years later by a musical young American, the former Angel fiercely vented her detestations: "She hated Verdi and all he had made; she hated Rossini and all he had made; she hated the French; she hated the Americans; she abhorred the very name of Barnum, who, she said, 'exhibited me just as he did the big giant or any other of his monstrosities.' 'But,' said I, 'you must not forget how you were idolized and worshiped in America. Even as a child I can remember how they worshiped Jenny Lind.' 'Worshiped or not,' she answered sharply, 'I was nothing more than a show in a showman's hands; I can never forget that'" (Hegermann-Lindencrone, p. 86).

Lind's increasingly uninhibited black looks were less generously interpreted in Philadelphia, where she returned for final farewell appearances: "Jenny Lind has resolved to give no more concerts in Philadelphia; few persons will regret her determination, unless she should be better able to suppress the evidences of ill temper and vexation than she did on Tuesday evening last. She looked as sting-y as a hive of wasps, and as black as a thunder-cloud, all because the house was not crowded. The fact is that Jenny Lind's attractions were not strong enough to counteract the dullness of Goldschmidt's piano playing, or the merely mediocre quality of Burke upon the violin. The absence, too, of an orchestra was a disgusting exhibition of parsimony and a determination to make the most money she possibly could. Miss Lind has never succeeded since she left the guardianship of Mr. Barnum, and then she has poor advisors and has been in ill humor when even the homage paid to her talent was not manifested with the greatest enthusiasm. The Nightingale has feathered her nest well in our country, and she can go back to her Swedish home, where we wish her long health, a better disposition, and a good husband to cheer her declining years" (quoted in Werner, p. 192, from an unattributed Philadelphia newspaper).

After her unfortunate farewell to Philadelphia, Lind went on to New York, where her final concerts in America were scheduled to begin at Metropolitan (formerly Tripler) Hall on December 30 and to end on January 12, 1852. Her company still consisted of Goldschmidt, Salvi, Burke, and Enrico Belletti; perhaps heeding her Philadelphia antagonist, she had engaged an orchestra and Eisfeld to conduct it. On the day of her scheduled first concert, Lind belatedly received news of her mother's death some months earlier in Sweden. Canceling her concerts,[42] she fled the city and went into retirement in Northhampton, Massachusetts, for a period of some months. In May 1852, as Madame Otto Goldschmidt, she would return to New York for a final time.

Although the formerly controversial topic of Jenny Lind's coldness had become an obsolete issue after its great vogue in 1850 was played out, in 1851, Walt Whitman,♪ memorably recording his responses to music in his second "Letter from Paumanok,"[43] appearing in the *Evening Post* on August 14, wrote: "The Swedish Swan, with all her blandishments, never touched my heart in the least. I wondered at so much vocal dexterity; and indeed, they were all very pretty, those leaps and double somersets. But even in the greatest religious airs, genuine masterpieces as they are, of the German composers, executed by this strangely overpraised woman in perfect scientific style, let critics say what they like, it was a failure; for there was a vacuum in the head of the performance. Beauty pervaded it, no doubt, and that of a high order. It was the beauty of Adam before God breathed into his nostrils."

At the beginning of June, overlapping Lind's concerts at Tripler Hall and Castle Garden, Max Maretzek brought his magnificent new opera company back from Boston, where they had just completed a triumphal season. Having succeeded in acquiring the great Havana company at the close of their engagement with Martí (at who knows what cost?) Maretzek now commanded a mammoth company that, besides his Astor

[42] Ticket refunds were issued at Chickering's piano warerooms.

[43] An editor's note appended to the first "Letter from Paumanok" (*Evening Post,* June 27, 1851), explained that *Paumanok* was the old Indian name for Long Island.

Girvice Archer, Jr.

Angiolina Bosio as Lucia di Lammermoor.

Place contingent, included all the superb artists who had so thrilled New Yorkers the year before—all, that is, except Tedesco, who had gone to Europe to reap spectacular triumphs of her own. With Salvi away traveling with Lind, the leading tenor roles were filled by the indisposition-prone *primo tenore* Geremia Bettini;[44] Arditi, sans Bottesini, would share conducting duties with Maretzek.

While waiting for Jenny Lind to vacate Castle Garden, where Maretzek dreamed his "golden dream," as he calls it, of replicating the Havana company's smashing successes of the previous summer, he mounted (on nights alternating with Lind's concluding concerts) an introductory two-week opera season at Astor Place, opening on June 3 with the newcomer Geremia Bettini and the exquisite Angiolina Bosio in *Lucia di Lammermoor.*[45]

[44] Referring to Bettini as "that very spoiled child of his mamma," the *Albion* (June 14, 1851, p. 284) told of a recent incident wherein the tenor had refused to sing because his doctor had purportedly diagnosed a boil on his arm. Despite this infirmity, he was ordered to appear by "Dr. Maretzek," whose potent therapy consisted of circulating 100 printed handbills on the day of the performance, announcing not only Bettini's refusal to sing, but the termination of his contract. "This so far reduced the inflammation of the aforesaid pimple," reported the *Albion,* "as to give [Bettini's] voice the freest scope to do itself justice." But not without protest. During the performance the aggrieved tenor made a point of repeatedly calling the audience's attention to his ailing arm.

[45] After all his ecstatic outpourings over Lind's concerts, the *Parker's* critic (June 7, 1851, p. 297) heaved a fickle sigh of relief at being able, once again, to hear an evening of "homogenized music, not the rude, disconnected bits and pieces offered at a concert."

Bettini's voice, reported the *Mirror* (June 5, 1851), possessed the "sweetness of Salvi" combined with the "strength of Benedetti." *Parker's* (June 14, 1851, pp. 308–9) found it to be "full, round, and mellow, of sufficient power and most delightful quality of tone," suffering only from a single fault: his upper voice "lacked one note" (not identified); this would prove to be a detriment in satisfying the typically American demand for encores of the most exhausting scenes in any given work. Bettini was a superb actor, however, "the best we have seen here," even if he lacked staying power. The *Tribune* (June 6, 1851) thought Bettini's voice, although good, to be neither full nor ringing, and his style boisterous, if effective. His "personal advantages," and his well-conceived "poses," however, added up to "a very striking Edgardo." Bosio, the Lucia, was universally acclaimed as a supreme artist.

The other operas presented during the short preludial season at Astor Place—*Ernani, Don Giovanni, Lucrezia Borgia,* and *La favorita*—featured (besides Bosio) Truffi-Benedetti, Virginia Whiting, Marini, and Lorini. They received standard reviews, according to the personal tastes and foibles of the respective critics. A fair attendance was reported, but the general interest was primarily focused on the imminent summer season, to open on June 16 at Castle Garden, and on whether it would prove the widely held theory, shared by Maretzek and the general press, that opera, to flourish in New York, needed only to be rescued from the clutches of the elite and made accessible to the great public. This had apparently worked well enough the year before: "The success of Martí's experiment last summer," wrote the *Tribune* (June 13, 1851), "proves that this spacious and breezy location, with a democratic rate of admission, is in the end far more profitable for a Summer Opera than any of the more elegant buildings. . . . The moonlight view of the bay, as seen from the outer balcony, is always worth the trouble of walking to the Battery and the expense of the entrance ticket"—fifty cents.

Apparently, George Templeton Strong, for all his social bias, agreed. With the opening of six-nights-a-week opera at Castle Garden,[46] he became, surprisingly, a faithful—one might almost say avid—operagoer. Perhaps Strong had availed himself of the bargain-priced $15 season tickets issued by Maretzek in his endeavors to out-Martí Martí in establishing the total operatic democracy.

June 20. Opera has commenced at Castle Garden [with *Lucia*], and I've given three evenings this week to it. Very pleasant hearing the Havana company (first among the second-rates, if not entitled to rank among the first)[47] in a room so big that it can't be crowded, with that lovely outside gallery to walk on when one's tired of listening, and without the baneful necessity of any preliminary toilette. Tuesday was [Donizetti's] *Marino Faliero,* a threadbare reproduction of Donizetti's commonplaces—the same shabby old subjects worked over again for the fiftieth time—but well sung. Wednesday was *Lucrezia Borgia,* which is a trumpery affair enough, but its intelligible plot, its abundant dramatic situations, and its scraps of lively melody make it pleasant to hear, when rendered by a good company. Tonight [Friday] we had *Don Giovanni.*

[46] On Sunday evenings at Castle Garden, Maretzek conducted popular concerts that no longer pretended to be sacred.

[47] On what basis of comparison did Strong form this judgment?

Bosio was perfect as Zerlina—her *Batti, batti* and *Vedrai, carino* were sung as they deserve to be, without fault or failure, according to the letter of Mozart, and with full expression of their feeling. Donna Anna (Truffi), Donna Elvira (Virginia Whiting), and Don Ottavio (Forti) were satisfactory, and Marini [the Leporello] and Beneventano [the Don Giovanni] . . . sang their music with as much appreciation of their respective characters as a brace of baboons in *Romeo and Juliet.* But the music is celestial. I can't commence criticizing so transcendent a subject at a quarter-past-twelve.

Donizetti's *Marino Faliero* (Paris 1835)—based on Byron's poem (1821)—receiving its first production in the United States on June 17, 1851, elicited generally negative reactions from the critics. The *Albion* (sounding unmistakably like N. P. Willis, who might have been substituting for his vacationing younger brother), found the music unattractive and mostly uninteresting. Truffi gave the best performance of the evening—not the "singing Truffi," but the "personal Truffi." She looked even more superb than usual, although her manner was unvaryingly imperturbable, and she possessed only "one gesture and a half." But that gesture—a wave of her neatly gloved, "plumptitudinous" hand—succeeded in conveying whatever it was she wanted to convey. If Truffi seemed not to know her part, it was "almost to be expected in a new opera with so very deliberate a divinity." Marini was excellent as the Doge, but in his duet with Beneventano they "performed a tug of war to see who could be louder. Beneventano convulsed each tone out of his very boots,[48] and showed Marini that [even] if he [Marini] were an inch or two taller, it was the stout and not the long pipes which produced the biggest noise." Beneventano reminded the writer of Henry Russell,♪ "who so maltreats the third of the scale . . . until the ear is on the verge of insanity, that you wish it were extinguished altogether, and the gamut possessed it no more." Nonetheless, the critic hoped they would repeat *Faliero* occasionally—it was at least new and a relief from the incessant *Borgias* and *Lammermoors*. And much as he admired Bosio, he would love to hear Parodi as Lucrezia once again (*Albion,* June 21, 1851, p. 284).

Saroni held that, except for Ignazio Marini, *Faliero* had been very imperfectly performed, although admittedly it was not fair to criticize a first performance too harshly. But hadn't we had enough Donizetti for a while? True, he was an improvement over Verdi, but what about doing some Meyerbeer, or Bellini, or Rossini? (*Saroni's Musical Times,* June 21, 1851, p. 135.)

Parker's, on the contrary, observed that, what with *Lucia, Lucrezia, La favorita, Marino Faliero,* and *Don Giovanni* having been given in rapid succession, the "variety-mongers" must surely have been satisfied. Defending Italian opera as a valid musical genre against an attack by George W. Curtis, who had dismissed *Faliero* as "a poor opera, well sung" (*Tribune,* June 20, 1851), *Parker's* granted that "compared with the great symphonies of Mozart and Beethoven, of von Weber and Spohr, as mere musical compositions, the works of the modern Italian stage are immeasurably inferior. But,"

[48] Beneventano "begins to be really an operatic infliction. . . . The extraordinary tricks he plays with his eyes are such as to induce serious fears he will some day turn them inside out, thus losing the use of them altogether" (*Albion,* June 14, 1851, p. 284).

he argued, "whilst *Fidelio, Preciosa,* and *Der Freischütz* may be as satisfactorily expressed by a good orchestra as by the best dramatic singers, *Norma, Lucrezia,* and *Lucia* require the powers of a Malibran or a Grisi to convey their meaning to the listener, and [the operas] afford ample room and scope for the exercise of the highest dramatic ability. It is, therefore, very superficial and unfair criticism to say that the music of most Italian Operas is light and thin, compared with the works of the German masters. For, light and thin as [an opera] may be considered as a mere classical composition, in the best works of the Italian school it always tells the story and expresses the passions in the most appropriate musical language, and that, too, in the mouths of the persons of the drama."

If *Faliero* seemed to fall short, the *Parker's* critic continued, "either the subject of the drama was too grand and imposing for our range of emotional sympathy, or the terrific screaming-match between Beneventano and Lorini stopped up the avenue to our heart—or else Donizetti utterly failed in seizing the inspiration of his theme." In this production the work "failed entirely in awakening interest in us. . . . We should be very unwilling to say that, having heard it but once." Admittedly, it would require a far different production for it to be judged "by the side of *Lucia* and *Favorita* of the same master."

Parker's deplored, too, the discouragingly poor attendance at Castle Garden. The thermometer had conspired against Maretzek, "having been very hot at Astor Place and very cold at Castle Garden" (*Parker's,* June 28, 1851, p. 333).

June 25. . . . At Castle Garden tonight with Ellie—*Ernani.* Bettini far the best Ernani I've seen. The music is vile, and no living or possible company of performers can make it other than vile. But it's pleasant to listen to it; it brings back so keenly the Spring of '48—those well-remembered unisons in the finale of the third act that used to keep ringing in my ears as I walked downtown, half-delirious, from Astor Place. The fragrance of that time [of courtship] comes again whenever I think of them—so with Truffi's aria in the first act. The very extravagance and slangwhanging absurdity of the music gives it character and identifies the memory with which it is associated.

June 28. Opera still patronized by Ellie and me. Last night *Don Giovanni,* tonight Donizetti's *La favorita,* both well sung and rather listlessly performed [acted].

June 29. [a hot Sunday] Mrs. Ruggles dined here. After dinner I bathed—dozed—and bathed again—and thought of the miraculous beauty of the *Don Giovanni* music, which haunts me day and night, and of the bills I've got to pay next month, and the probability of my "busting" before the summer is gone—a very harmonious concatenation of ideas.

July 2. . . . Meant to have gone to the opera [*Anna Bolena*] last night . . . but it clouded up and threatened to shower, and the prospect scared us off.

~

On July 3 the Strongs departed for West Point, where Ellen, who was again pregnant, would remain for some weeks in the care (at Strong's insistence) of her "invaluable" Ruggles grandmother. Dividing his time between "the Point" and New York during the month of July, Strong missed the revivals not only of *Anna Bolena* but of *Il giuramento* (July 11) and Donizetti's *Roberto Devereux* (July 17), which were interspersed among the standard *Lucias*, *Lucrezias*, *Ernanis*, *Favoritas*, and so forth. During this period the public favorite Cesare Badiali returned to the company, and the audiences increased considerably; Badiali was saluted by *Parker's* (July 19, 1851, pp. 368–69) as "the best barytone we have ever had."[49]

With the arrival of warmer weather the audiences at Castle Garden further increased, still, however, leaving much to be desired. Bettini and Badiali attracted comparatively larger audiences than the others, but it was only with the return of Lorenzo Salvi, temporarily released from his engagement with Jenny Lind during her short vacation following Benedict and Belletti's departure, that Castle Garden was once again jammed from top to bottom. Salvi's reappearance on July 23 as Elvino in *La sonnambula,* with Bosio as Amina and Marini as the Count, recalled a "Jenny Lind Rush"[50] (*Albion,* July 26, 1851, p. 356). Indeed, the extra benches that were "dredged up from the deeps" of the Castle were not adequate to accommodate the crowd. Not even Lind, in her electrifying early days in New York, could have filled the hall any fuller, wrote Saroni, who inflatedly estimated the audience at 8000, or even 10,000 (*Saroni's Musical Times,* July 26, 1851, p. 194).

"The motives which drew together the immense crowd of six or seven thousand human beings who crushed through the iron gates of the Castle on that sweltering night," more conservatively reported the *Parker's* critic (August 2, 1851, p. 393), "were first, the desire to hear Salvi, probably the most popular Italian tenor who ever sang in New York, and second, to hear the *Sonnambula* of Bellini, which for many reasons was the opera most likely to draw together a large audience in a place where there is room for the people."

But, as he had written a week earlier, it was not a basic love of music that drew growing numbers of people to Castle Garden as the summer heat intensified. Rather, "like the cattle in midsummer, [they] obeyed their instincts and fled from flies and heat to the cool enclosure and fresh river side" (*Parker's,* July 26, 1851, p. 381).

Nor was it purely the love of *La sonnambula* that drew Strong to a following performance of this latest opera hit.

July 29. Heard one act of *Sonnambula* at Castle Garden tonight, and the first chorus of the second. Immense crowd. The Opera has created quite a furor. Everybody goes, and nob and snob, Fifth Avenue and Chatham Street, sit side by side fraternally on the hard benches. Perhaps there is hardly so attractive a summer theatre in the world as Castle Garden when so good a company is performing as we have there now. Cool sea-breeze on the balcony, where one can sit and smoke and listen and look out on the bay studded with the lights of anchored vessels, and white sails gleaming shadowy past, and moonlight or starlight, as the case may be. I don't wonder that the people are *Sonnambula*-mad. The plot of the opera is pretty—for an opera plot; the music is pretty and shallow and taking, and is sung by Bosio and Salvi. It's not very reasonable, to be sure, to prefer *Ah! non giunge* to *Vedrai, carino,* but that delusion is less debasing than the superstitious belief in Donizetti and Verdi that prevails so lamentably.

[49] With Badiali's return, *Parker's* gave a critic's thanks for something new to write about: ". . . what a blessing a new theme, and one on which you can be honestly enthusiastic, is, no one knows as well as he who has, weekly, to write about the same thing."

[50] The term originated in London when Lind was at the peak of her opera triumphs (Lumley, p. 191).

August 13. [Ellen, driven by a toothache, had unexpectedly returned to town] . . . We took an omnibus to the Battery tonight and, after loitering there awhile, gravitated involuntarily into Castle Garden and heard an act of *Don Pasquale,* with Salvi, Bosio, and Marini. Nice, lively music—pity Donizetti ever mistook his vocation and wrote serious operas.

August 15. . . . went with Ellie to *Don Pasquale.* . . . Good house and enthusiastic. Opera performed twice as well as it deserves, though there's much in it that's lively and piquant—for Donizetti.

~

Contrary to Strong—trapped in his compulsive ambivalence toward Italian opera and seemingly incapable of maintaining a consistent attitude toward any one work, except, perhaps, a fashionable disdain (in this instance toward *Don Pasquale*)—the critics were unreservedly enthusiastic over the revival. As Norina, Bosio "took the house by storm," especially enchanting her listeners with her singing of a brilliant rondo composed for her by Arditi, who conducted the performance (Maretzek sat in the orchestra playing the tambourine); Salvi, Badiali, and Marini were correspondingly splendid in their respective roles. Saroni's only cavil was addressed to the "gentlemen of the orchestra" for their reprehensible habit of carrying on an animated conversation during the performance: "Private conversation during such good singing as we now have at Castle Garden is intolerable," he wrote. "Moreover, it is setting a bad example to the audience," notorious chatterers that they were (*Saroni's Musical Times,* August 16, 1851, p. 222).

August 18. . . . took Ellie [who had decided not to return to West Point] and her grandmamma down to Castle Garden. *La sonnambula.* Bosio very perfect, Salvi's voice not quite equal to his part, which is a trying one [even] for tenors in their prime. He acts tamely and dresses absurdly—looks like a green and russet toad; Marini as the Count is wooden and inert. Still, it's not often that there's a concurrence of three better artistes in that opera, and their performance of it is comfortable to hear, of a summer evening.

Isn't it rather absurd to call an Italian singer of Donizetti and Bellini and Verdi an "artist?" The distinction between Artist and Artiste is parallel to that between a philosopher and a philosophe.

August 24. [after attending part of the Sabbath service at Trinity] . . . made my way to St. Peter's, Barclay Street,♪ where I heard what is much more edifying than most sermons, part of a mass of Mozart's, I think, but I did not know the music. Heard the *Credo, Sanctus, Benedictus,* and *Agnus Dei.* Tolerably sung, and then railroaded uptown. . . .

Heard the *Barber* at Castle Garden, Friday night [August 22]. Badiali [as] Figaro, Salvi Almaviva, Bertucca Rosina,[51] and Marini Don Basilio. Singing and action were both as near perfection as a sinful mortal may expect to hear on earth, and the delicious, fluent, sparkling music was rendered as it deserves to be. I've no great reverence

[51] Apollonia Bertucca-Maretzek, who had been on leave from the company, was returning after having presented Maretzek with a daughter.

for Rossini—and the mission of his art is to produce higher works than buffo recitative and to illustrate loftier themes than the loves of Lindoro and the devices of his Achates, the Barber. But, for all that, it's a delicious opera to hear, of a summer night—so brilliant, so full of exquisite melody, so finished and perfect, and so extemporaneous withal, that it seems to have been written off without revision or retouching, in the exuberant inspiration of a fit of fun and a bottle of champagne.

Last night we were at Castle Garden again. Sat on the terrace and inhaled the sea-breeze, listening only at distant intervals to the hot and heavy music of *Ernani*[52] and looking out on the bay and the stars above and the stars below—for the night was dark and nothing was to be seen a hundred yards off except the multitudinous lights great and small, near and distant, scattered over the surface of the bay, like another series of constellations below us. Now and then the white sail of a sloop drifting along glimmered faintly through the night and then dissolved out of sight again in a ghostly manner, but at other times one seemed to be at the edge of the world—the jumping off place—looking up and down at the stars of both hemispheres.

August 28. [in their opera-going the Strongs were not as a rule deterred by weather, but on August 25 they were defeated by a heat wave which forced them] to leave Castle Garden in the midst of the *Barbiere,* so oppressive was even that coolest of all summer theatres. . . . We heard *Lucia* [August 26] . . . and sad stuff it is. Badiali, the Ashton (the Figaro of the night before), is certainly a great actor—far the best I have seen in opera.

~

With fifty performances completed and the benefit season about to begin, on September 1, Rosa (now Rose) de Vries, the *prima donna* from New Orleans, made her spectacular reappearance, again in *Norma,* this time presumably in Italian. Although she had been highly praised at the time of her three obscure appearances the previous October, she was now, for entrepreneurial reasons, heralded—and accepted—as a debutante. The *Mirror* (September 2, 1851) again discovered her to be the possessor of "a tall, elegant, graceful, and flexible form, the most immediately affecting features of which are her arms, that seem to have a life and an instinct of grace peculiarly their own . . . they seem to scatter melody through the atmosphere, as a waving bough scatters the sparking dewdrops." Apart from her melodious arms, de Vries "moved through the pathetic and high-wrought story of the unhappy Druidess with a stately solemnity that awed, while it enchanted, the beholder." Yet, her singing, although it was "absolutely perfect and everything it should have been," was "not sympathetic." It was "art in the concrete" (whatever that meant). She seemed to feel what she was doing, but did not succeed in imparting it to her listeners: "There is no magnetic link that connects the hearer's heart with her as she sings . . . our pity for the Norma is less than our admiration of the de Vries and her wonderful skill." Still and all: "When she commences one of the chain-lightening roulades of hers, she attacks the note from which she starts with a precision and accuracy that are truly marvelous." Correctly identifying de Vries as a Dutch (not French) *prima donna,* Richard Willis, now back from his vacation, had nothing but praise for her wonderful natural voice with its effortless high D. But alas, her natural resources were greater than her skill,

[52] Incorrectly transcribed in the published *Diary* (II, 62) as "the not heavy music of *Ernani.*"

for her vocalization lacked "the refining finish of the true Italian school," such as we had been accustomed to hear at Castle Garden all summer. Both Bosio and Truffi-Benedetti sang better scales than did de Vries, although de Vries's voice excelled either of theirs. Willis regretted that de Vries had no *maestro* to guide her in the paths of vocal righteousness—to teach her how to sing a scale, for instance (*Albion,* September 6, 1851, p. 428).

September 1. Have just heard two acts of *Norma* at Castle Garden with one Rose de Vries as the heroine. Plenty of voice and little music; lots of action and no go, as sporting people say. The house was crowded and enthusiastic. The louder this lady screamed, the more uproariously they applauded, and her solitary windpipe was a fair match for the vociferous bravos of her 5000 admirers. In the grand explosion scene of the second act, where that unhappy man Pollione has to be bullied and repudiated by the two ladies together, Norma holloed [*sic*] so, and fell foul of her recreant lover in such desperate earnest, and so made the fur fly, that the exaltation of the audience knew no bounds, and the triumph of the Signora became a fixed fact.

~

The Strongs were not among the four to five thousand people who purportedly attended Maretzek's monster benefit "Festival" on September 4. Modestly patterned after the recent, supergigantic Jubilee tendered the manager of the Broadway Theatre, E. A. Marshall, which had been performed without interruption from ten A.M. until midnight, Maretzek's benefit was scheduled to last only from three in the afternoon until eleven at night. Two complete grand operas would be performed by four *prima donnas*, four first tenors, and four first baritones and basses. A vocally recovered Benedetti, not heard for three years, would make his eagerly awaited reappearance, joined by his wife, in the second act of *Lucrezia Borgia* (as it turned out, Benedetti defaulted); Rose de Vries would appear in the complete *Norma*[53] and Bosio in the entire *I puritani.* A Grand Ballet by the delectable Rousset sisters was announced, as were performances of the farce *My Friend Jack* by Brougham, Lynne, and other thespian stars; the fourth act of *Gli Ugonotti;* a Miscellaneous Dramatic Concert in costume; and various instrumental solos, among them one by Arditi on the violin, completed the program. Tickets were one dollar.

As if all this were not enough, an extraneous entertainment was improvised during the *Puritani* part of the program by the notoriously bellicose actor Edwin Forrest, who exchanged blows with one Robert Sinclair, a former tavernkeeper: "It seems," reported the *Mirror* (September 5, 1851), "that antecedently to the [first] blow, there had been some conversation of a not very kind character between the parties, and some unsavory expletives used." The combatants were at last separated by the police.

September 9. . . . Sultry, to the disgrace of this month of September. . . . Tonight I went down with Ellie to the Battery and [we] hung round Castle Garden awhile,

[53] At the conclusion of this, de Vries's fourth and final performance of *Norma,* every time she walked onstage she was showered with bouquets. On her presenting a particularly beautiful nosegay to Arditi, who "modestly accepted it," members of the audience were heard to murmur: "Wasn't that truly Frenchy?" (*Mirror,* September 5, 1851.)

deliberating whether we should hear an act or so of *I puritani*. But Bosio's benefit had called in a crowded house, and the evening was oppressively hot. There was no sea-breeze, the flags hung motionless, and the moonlight lay on the water with a glare as if the bay were on fire. So we gave it up and omnibused up again, stopping at Thompson's [confectionery at 359 Broadway] for some ice cream on the way.

~

On September 18, with the benefits concluded, the indomitable Maretzek closed his summer season at Castle Garden and, dividing his huge company, he sent part of it on a (disastrous) tour of the South and took the remainder to Philadelphia, where he opened at the National Theatre (the infamous former "horse circus") with Rose de Vries in *Norma*. The diverse journalistic summings-up of his memorable Castle Garden undertaking agreed on at least one point—that Maretzek had lost a great deal of money on the venture, by his own admission $22,000, an astronomical sum. (There is an ironic parallel to be drawn between Maretzek's losses and Barnum's huge profits, both accrued in the name of "good music.")[54]

It was generally doubted whether Maretzek would be able to present another opera season, at least not with this expensive company and continued low prices—and not unless he could perform in a larger winter opera house (*Herald,* August 7, 1851).[55]

As *Parker's* (September 27, 1851, p. 486) noted of the just-ended season, in the short space of three months Maretzek had presented a formidable repertory of some dozen operas performed by the best artists ever to have appeared in the United States. Yet, despite all these splendid attractions—especially Bettini, "the very best tenor, take him all in all, that ever sang in this city, [and] Badiali, the finest barytone and most accomplished artist we ever listened to—there has very seldom been a large audience inside the Garden, and on many a night, money enough was not taken at the door to pay for the gas lights." Maretzek corroborates: "Very frequently did we play before an audience varying in number from 100 to 150 persons, scarcely enough to pay the printing bills of the evening" (*Crotchets,* p. 171).

It was a paradox, continued *Parker's,* that while crowds were "suffocating at Burton's, Niblo's, and Christy's, Castle Garden, where thousands could be cooler and more comfortable than in their own houses, presented nightly a beggarly account of empty benches. And now talk of New York taste for Italian opera!" he bitterly exclaimed, "New York, fiddlesticks!"

Disastrous to the manager, the season had, however, abounded in romantic alliances among his singers: "Like their feathered rivals, they have chosen their mates and paired off, probably to build their nests in warmer climes and more sympathetic regions. Marini and Miss Maretzek [Max's sister Rose]; the silver-voiced Lorini and Miss

[54] For all his disdain of Barnum, Maretzek was not above adopting some of his promotional methods. The opening of the opera season at Castle Garden, for instance, had been advertised by a greatly admired "procession of announce bills" on Broadway (*Courier and Enquirer,* June 16, 1851).

[55] It was later rumored that Maretzek was negotiating for the construction of not one, but two, opera houses—one in New York at Ninth Street and the Bowery (the Stuyvesant Lot that Fry had attempted to acquire) and one in Baltimore (*Mirror,* October 28, 1851). The *Herald* (October 30) reported that Maretzek was already in possession of the New York property; the only thing he lacked was capital—about $250,000. Alas, no backers were forthcoming (*Herald,* November 26, 1851).

25TH EDITION.

TO

Mrs George W. Ford

THE OPERA SCHOTTISCH

ENTERED ACCORDING TO ACT OF CONGRESS IN THE YEAR 1858 BY FIRTH, POND & Co IN THE CLERKS OFFICE OF THE DISTRICT COURT OF THE SOUTHn DISTRICT OF N.Y.

(THE ITALIAN OPERA AT CASTLE GARDEN)

COMPOSED BY

H. Kleber.

LITH. OF SARONY, MAJOR & KNAPP 449 BROADWAY, N.Y.

2½

NEW YORK.

PUBLISHED BY FIRTH, POND & Co 547 BROADWAY

PITTSBURGH. H. KLEBER & BRO. | NEW ORLEANS. P. P. WERLEIN. | St LOUIS. H. PILCHER & SONS.

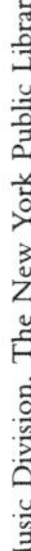

Whiting; Herr Hardmouth (we hope the name is not to be taken in the equestrian sense) [the name was, in fact, Hardtmuth] and Miss Bourgeois (*dite* Borghese) have been joined in the bands of matrimony."

Maretzek remembered his amorous songbirds less benignly. "Just as difficult as it would have been to find again such a number of admirable artists collected under one management, would it have been to bring together such a capricious, troublesome, egotistical, rapacious, intriguing, cheating, troublesome, mischievous, and malicious set of vocalists." It would be impossible to detail all their "quarrels, jealousies, and intrigues amongst themselves, or their tricks, plots, and conspiracies against their Manager," he wrote. Whereupon Maretzek proceeded to list some of the excruciating tortures he had suffered at their hands: the personal jealousies; the pronenesses to fits and convulsions and to less exotic, but equally debilitating, sudden indispositions when crossed; the dissipations;[56] the sexual peccadilloes; the officious and meddling *prima donna*s' husbands; the meddling and officious *prima donna*s' fathers; the monstrously inflated egos, and on and on. And this applied not only to the stars but to the inferior secondary singers. Yet, "in spite of their restless duplicity, their ungracious treatment of myself," unwillingly concedes Maretzek, "I am obliged to say . . . that this Company was, in every respect, the very best which has ever been got together upon this side of the Atlantic. . . . [It] presented, in all its details, the nearest approach to perfection which has ever visited this hemisphere" (*Crotchets,* pp. 158–70, *passim*).

At least one of these musically impeccable, morally fallible beings called forth in Walt Whitman all the vehement exaltation of his tempestuous soul. After hearing a performance of *La favorita* at Castle Garden, he wrote: "Have you not . . . while listening to the well-played music of some band like Maretzek's, felt an overwhelming desire for measureless sound—a sublime orchestra of myriad orchestras—a colossal harmony, in which the thunder might roll in its proper place; and above it the vast, pure Tenor—identity of the creative power itself—rising through the universe until the boundless and unspeakable capacities of that mystery, the human soul, should be filled to the uttermost and the problem of human cravingness be satisfied and destroyed?"

The "vast, pure Tenor" appears to have been a Whitmanesque elevation of Bettini, whose voice had often moved the infatuated poet to tears: "Its clear, firm, wonderful, exalting notes filling and expanding away, dwelling like a poised lark up in heaven, have made my very soul tremble. Critics talk of others who are merely artistical—yes, as the well-shaped warble is artistical. But the singing of this man has breathing blood within it, the living soul of which the lower stage they call art is but the shell and sham.

"After traveling through the fifteen years' display in this city of musical celebrities," continues Whitman, "from Mrs. Austin♪ to Jenny Lind, from Ole Bull to con-

[56] Maretzek tells of hiring "two watchmen" as a kind of "secret police" to shadow Bettini, who had "a peculiar relish for amusing himself with *petite soupées* [*sic*] *à la Régence*," at which he would "drown his brains in a Champagne-flask and afterwards lose his money at the gambling-table during whole nights." Upon Bettini's inevitable following "indispositions," Maretzek would confront him with complete documentation of his misdeeds, supplied by the secret agents (*Crotchets,* p. 167).

Geremia Bettini, whose "vast pure tenor" lifted Walt Whitman to the utmost heights of ecstasy.

ductor Benedict, with much fair enjoyment of the talent of all, none have [*sic*] satisfied, overwhelmed me but this man. Never before did I realize what an indescribable volume of delight the recesses of the soul can bear from the sound of the honeyed perfection of the human voice. The manly voice it must be, too. The feminine organ, no matter how curious and high, is but as the pleasant moonlight." (The poet then went on to give his harsh assessment of Jenny Lind, quoted above).

But Bettini! "Listen, pure and vast, that voice now rises, as on clouds, to the heaven where it pleases the audience. Now, firm and unbroken, it spreads like an ocean around us. Ah, welcome that I know not the mere language of the earthly words in which the melody is embodied; as all words are mean before the language of true music.

"Thanks, great artist. For one, at least, it is no extravagance to say, you have justified his ideal of the loftiest of the arts. Thanks, limner of the spirit of life and hope and peace, of the red fire of passion, the cavernous vacancy of despair, and the black pall of the grave."

Descending from the heights, Whitman defensively justified his extravagance: "I write as I feel, and I feel that there are not a few who will pronounce a Yes to my own confessions" ("Letter from Paumanok," *Evening Post,* August 14, 1851).

With the summer opera season ended and Ellen approaching her confinement, for the time being Strong's music-listening was restricted to what he heard in church. At a church convention at St. John's Chapel, on September 26, he reported that before the "proceedings opened with the prayer for the Church Militant . . . the Convention was invited to unite in the *Te Deum,* which was thereupon sung *con spirito* by enough of its members fairly to balance the full power of St. John's big organ." Although it was not the most effective chant that could have been chosen—"being one of the dreary, old-fashioned, country-church compositions that everybody has winced under, of hot Sunday mornings, for the last thirty years, at least—the great body of voices made it a very stirring performance."

On October 29, Ellen gave birth to a son, John Ruggles Strong, and—apart from a single reference on December 1 to "the slowest and woodenest of all *Te Deums*" at Trinity, to which Strong attributed another of his "cantankerous headaches"—for a period his only references to vocalization concerned his son's "persistent nocturnal ululations."

It was not until late December that the Strongs again went to the opera, although a season of twenty nights had been initiated by Maretzek on November 3 at the Astor Place Opera House.

Advertising that "in no country, either on this or the other side of the Atlantic, has such a variety of operatic entertainments been offered for one season," Maretzek announced a prodigious repertory of fifteen operas to be performed by Steffanone (who had been absent throughout the Castle Garden season), Bosio, Bertucca-Maretzek, Rosina Pico-Vietti, Bettini, Adelindo Vietti, Benedetti, Badiali, Marini, and Coletti. A different opera would be given every night (meaning every opera night): *Norma, Roberto Devereux, La favorita, Otello, Don Pasquale, Maria di Rohan* (a major hit with Steffanone, Pico, Bettini, and Badiali), *Lucrezia Borgia, Lucia di Lammermoor, La sonnambula, Anna Bolena, Ernani, Semiramide, I puritani, Il barbiere di Siviglia,* and *Don Giovanni.* Secured seats were, as of old, \$1.50, parquette and boxes \$1, the amphitheatre fifty cents.

Although the repertory, with some additions, was essentially the same as that given at Castle Garden, and the performing company basically the same, the season at Astor Place, for some reason, drew unusually large audiences, and the performances garnered a great deal of critical praise. Yet, as the *Herald* regretfully observed (December 4, 1851), Maretzek was still struggling, not only financially, but with his recalcitrant artists, "for the most part imprudent, quarrelsome, good-looking fellows, who think quite enough of themselves and the performances." "Some of them," added the *Herald,* were "very great humbugs."

On December 8, record crowds swarmed into the Astor Place Opera House, less for the performance of *I puritani* than to gape at New York's latest public idol: the Hungarian revolutionary hero Lajos Kossuth (1802–1894) was expected to attend that performance. Seeking official American support for his revolution, Kossuth, who had arrived from Europe only a few days earlier, was being treated to a welcome that eclipsed even the most frenetic Lind demonstrations of the year before.[57]

[57] "Kossuth's Kum," flippantly reported the *Herald* on December 6, quoting the title of a new topical show at Brougham's Lyceum, and a serenade was being planned by the German Glee Club

Although Kossuth failed to make his expected appearance at the opera on December 8, the audience nonetheless received a fair serving of patriotic fervor, obviously devised for the hero's benefit. When the curtain went up on the second act of this seventeenth-century drama, the American and Hungarian flags were anachronistically displayed at either side of the stage, eliciting from the audience a "mighty roar," echoed only by Badiali and Marini's roaring forth of the word *libertà* in what was henceforth rechristened the "Liberty Duet" (otherwise known as *Suoni la tromba*). "This cataract of vocal patriotism was vociferously encored, when the flags were again seized, crossed, and flourished lovingly together, to the intense delight of the people in general and the Interventionists in particular" (*Mirror,* December 9, 1851).

On December 10, *I puritani* was repeated with the crossed flags, but again no Kossuth. At still another "special performance" on December 13—with a visibly discouraged audience filling only two-thirds of the house—the three central boxes in the first circle, draped in the flags of both nations, were again set aside for Kossuth and his party, and several boxes in the second circle were reserved for various City Fathers. In the middle of the first act, Madame Kossuth arrived with Mrs. Kingsland, the Mayor's wife, and the performance was disrupted by wild cheering and applause. When it was discovered that it was only Kossuth's wife, "the cheering quickly died away amidst murmurs of disappointment, and Bosio resumed her part, but the chorus and orchestra were more attentive to the Magyars than to the fair Prima Donna." When Kossuth, in mid-second act, finally arrived with the Mayor, a veritable "pandemonium and whirlwind of enthusiastic cheering" was unleashed. "The whole house rose and shouted, the ladies waved their handkerchiefs, while the great Hungarian crossed his hands upon his breast and bowed and smiled his acknowledgments. . . . Some half a dozen of noisy fellows were continually calling for more cheers and making themselves particularly conspicuous—by shouting 'nine cheers for Hungary'—'twenty cheers for Kossuth'—and by other overdone demonstrations of 'patriotism.'" One young lady was reported to have been so carried away by the "entuzzy-muzzy"[58] as nearly to have lost her "center of gravity," but her venerable papa somehow managed to "hold it in." During the performance with the flags of the *Suoni la tromba,* Kossuth repeatedly had to rise and bow as the audience went blissfully mad. It was reported that Bosio addressed her efforts exclusively to the Kossuth box, which during the intermission was besieged by the all-but-hysterical members of the audience. "We shall congratulate the national guest when he escapes from the empty-headed, brassy-faced impertinents who press upon him here," sourly observed the *Mirror* (December 15, 1851).

As the opera season drew to a close, on December 25 the *Herald* editorialized that it had been successful in everything but a return to Maretzek on his investment in "labor, turmoil, and anxiety, consequent upon his relation to the public, on one hand, and to his purse and a quarrelsome, discontented, grasping set of artists, on the other." Although he deserved far greater success than had his predecessors, Maretzek had not succeeded in "putting money in his purse. In fact," wrote the *Herald,* "he is out of

(most probably the *Liederkranz*). Presumably attempted at the conclusion of the huge torchlight parade in Kossuth's honor, it is not clear whether the serenade did indeed come off, although a performance in German of "Hail Columbia" was rumored to have taken place.

[58] Partridge (p. 297), spells it *enthuzzymuzzy* and defines it simply as "enthusiasm."

Cheering multitudes welcoming Lajos Kossuth on his arrival, with military escort, at City Hall to be officially greeted by the Mayor.

Both: New-York Historical Society

Kossuth at the Astor Place Opera House acknowledging the wild ovation set off by the flag-waving performance of "Suoni la tromba" *in* I puritani. *On the stage Badiali and Marini are seen flourishing the flags.*

pocket as a result of all his meritorious exertions. He will therefore be compelled to abandon the enterprise, or make better arrangements with his artists." Asking the age-old question: How could the opera have failed financially when the season had been so successful? the *Herald* blamed the inadequate size of the opera house, with its resultingly high ticket prices, the lack of support from the "salt-fish aristocracy," and the artists, who were "bleeding Maretzek dry with their financial demands. . . . [It] would be a sad retrograde for one of the most delightful of the fine arts [to fail] in New York, while every other art is going ahead, *pari passu* with the increase of our population, the progress of our commerce, and the increasing enlightened spirit of the age."

On December 17, Maretzek, beset as he was with tribulations, unveiled his supreme effort for survival, a production of Meyerbeer's rarely heard *Robert le diable,* with Bosio as Isabella and Steffanone as Alice (arch-rivals though they were), and with Bettini as Robert, Marini as Bertram, Vietti as Raimbaut, and the American dancer Celeste (Williams) as the spectral abbess. The first performance, reported the *Albion* (December 20, 1851, p. 608), was seriously marred by a failure in the heating system that left everyone blue with cold: "The ladies, who came in expecting the usual summer atmosphere, were saluted on the rising of the curtain with a chilling blast that made their teeth chatter. A general cloaking, muffling, and hooding ensued." The performance consequently suffered. But despite the discomfort, the *Musical Times* (December 20, 1851, p. 107) found the production admirable: "Give us another presentation in a well-warmed house, and we promise an enthusiastic audience." The opera was indeed repeated on December 19, one hopes in a better climate.

December 20. . . . At the opera with Ellie last night. *Robert le diable* (in Italian) very fairly sung. Know but little of Meyerbeer's music, and I can't form an opinion of his style from hearing this very elaborate work but once. It seems a mixture of French, Italian, and German, the first and last predominant. Not very rich in melody, but copious in "effects"—complex, finished, ingenious, and brilliant. Bosio sang *Grâce* superbly; Marini as the D——l was admirable; Robert [Bettini] a mere stick. The *ballet,* a regular short-dress-and-long-leg transaction, wholly spoiled the third act; [it] wore off all the effect of the slow rising of the still, white figures that preceded it, and which by itself would have been quite ghostly and impressive.

~

The season closed on December 23 with Maretzek's benefit, a third performance of *Robert le diable.* It was the last time this magnificent company would appear together.

OBBLIGATO: 1851

Moreover, the musical concerts, *upon which the multitude are more and more prone to feast, are far better for the heavy-hearted hypochondriac than snake-root or lobelia.*

Joel H. Ross, M.D.
What I Saw in New York (1851)

IN THE *MUSICAL TIMES* OF DECEMBER 28, 1850, Hermann Saroni devoted a full page (p. 138) to enthusiastic promotion of the forthcoming Grand New Year's Gift Concert, to take place at Tripler Hall. In Saroni's opinion, the admirable plan for this event, unlike previous give-away concerts that had gulled hopeful ticket-buyers, closely resembled the reputable proceedings of the American Art-Union, at whose annual exhibition works of art were awarded to holders of winning tickets.

Saroni fervently advocated the formation of a "Musical Art-Union," similar to the Art-Union but without the lottery. If only one-quarter of the nearly 1000 musicians living in New York would join and pay weekly dues of only six cents, he reasoned, it would be possible to cover expenses and perhaps publish compositions by members of the organization, as well (*Saroni's Musical Times,* January 4, 1851, p. 150).[1]

For the New Year's Gift Concert, an event Saroni found irresistibly attractive, 500 numbered tickets at $2 each were put on sale at Jollie's music store. The holders of the first thirty numbers to be called would receive dazzling prizes, the first being an Érard piano valued at $1200, imported at the time of Jenny Lind's arrival and played on and commended by Strakosch, Benedict, Hoffman, King, and Timm. The other prizes included various lesser pianos, guitars, flutes, and accordions. Winners or not, all ticket-holders were entitled to a dollar's worth of sheet music, to be picked up at Jollie's, the originators or backers of the scheme. "As we go to press," wrote Saroni only one day after the event had been announced, "over 500 tickets have been sold, and more could have been disposed of, had it been possible to register and number the tickets fast enough."

By January 3, the day of the concert, the *Herald* reported that all the tickets had been snapped up. In the advertisements the participating artists—Mrs. Edward Loder, Miss Emmeline De Luce, Mrs. L. A. Jones, Philip Mayer, Richard Hoffman, George

[1]"Our friend and neighbor of the *Musical Times,*" commented the *Choral Advocate* (February 1851, p. 138), "is making an effort to establish what he terms a 'Musical Art Union.' He thinks [it] would make a good basis for a National Conservatory of Music."

F. Bristow, a Mr. J. F. Underner (from Albany), a Henry Tissington, W. A. King, and George Loder—took sorry second place to the mouth-watering descriptions of the prizes.

The day after the concert the names of the thirty prizewinners (among then a Mr. G. Curtis) were published in the *Herald*. "It is but reasonable to suppose," went the accompanying puff, "that the second Gift Concert will be just as brilliant and successful. There will be, doubtless, many hundreds again disappointed, for it is impossible to extend the advertised number of tickets, and there is no mention of [a third] Gift Concert." So hurry, hurry, hurry, for Messrs. Jollie can not hold tickets for anyone!

For the second Gift Concert, on January 8, with the same cast, it was advertised that Richard Hoffman would play a de Meyer fantasy on the "prize piano," Mrs. Jones would sing "Ashtore Machree," a song by Henry C. Watson, and an anonymous someone would conduct an anonymous military band.

The razzle-dazzle gift-concert idea caught on like wildfire with entrepreneurs and public alike. By January 10 the wide-awake firm of Firth, Pond—recognizing a bonanza to instrument dealers—was advertising an extravagant list of prizes: ten pianos, a harp, five melodions, twenty-five richly bound musical annuals valued at $5 each (doubtless Firth, Pond publications), and the indispensable consolation prize of a dollar's worth of sheet music—all to be distributed at a gift concert performed by undesignated artists at some undesignated time and location, after 5000 tickets had been sold at $2 each. Out-of-town ticket orders might be placed with the (apparently newly formed) firm of Jocelyn, Watson, and Cholwell (*Herald,* January 10, 1851). (The Watson was, of course, the ubiquitous Henry C. Watson.)

Nonmusical entrepreneurs invaded the field as well. Adjoining the Firth, Pond advertisement in the *Herald* was the announcement of a Grand Gift Concert at Tripler Hall, whose spectacular first prize consisted, not of a piano, but a "handsome set of mahogany furniture, comprising a wardrobe, marble-top bureau and [looking] glass, marble-top washing stand, marble-top dressing table, six spring seat chairs, carved Gothic bedstead, easy chair, sewing rocker, and towel rack, of the value of $250." It could be seen at C. C. Williams's furniture store at 137 Fulton Street. The secondary prizes were enumerated, as well, but not the performers.

On January 11 the high-minded *Tribune* delivered a serious blow to the gift-concert craze. Calling it by its rightful name, the *Tribune* proclaimed: "We have declined the advertisements of several 'Gift Concerts' and other new-fashioned Lotteries, which we find are becoming of almost nightly occurrence. These forms of modified or diversified Gambling are wrong and must be stopped; but we are not setting up our own dictum as a standard of morality for others." The *Tribune* had investigated the law forbidding this sort of activity and trusted that "our friends [the rejected advertisers], whom we have felt constrained to disoblige, will accept this as an ample explanation of our course." A copy of the ordinance followed.

On that same day the *Albion* joined the attack. Having held its fire until after the first two "mediocre" gift concerts, which were "nothing more than lotteries for the disposal of musical instruments and music," the *Albion* (January 11, 1851, p. 20) now denounced them "in the strongest terms, as degrading to the musical art and injurious to the public taste." And added: "No real lover of music will aid or countenance such innovations."

As might be expected, Saroni differed: "The *Tribune*," he wrote, "after having taken the cream off the advertising, denounces the Gift Concerts as illegal." Denying any personal interest in either the continuation or cessation of the gift concerts, he nonetheless wished to ask: (1) Why were they any more illegal than the "distribution of prizes" by the Art Union, always warmly supported in the *Tribune*? (2) Why were they branded lotteries when each ticket-holder received full value for his money and in addition a chance to win a valuable prize? (3) Were they "any more of a lottery than the summoning of a panel of jurors?" And (4), going even farther afield: Were they "any more illegal than the running a ticket for Alderman, Member of Congress, or Senator?" (*Saroni's Musical Times,* January 18, 1851, p. 171).

At this juncture, the music dealers William Hall and Son reconsidered and withdrew their sponsorship of a projected gift concert, to have featured such highly reputable artists as William Vincent Wallace, his wife Hélène Stoepel, his sister Madame Eliza Wallace-Bouchelle, Mrs. L. A. Jones, Dodworth's Cornet Band, and 100 prizes ranging from an Érard piano, chosen by Wallace, and a Boehm flute with silver keys, tips, and embouchure, valued at $120, to various lesser flutes and guitars and the customary dollar's worth of sheet music, this time "from the catalogue of Messrs. Hall and Son, the largest and most valuable in the United States."

In the papers, the Halls absolved themselves from possible culpability, at the same time providing a valuable clue to the way the gift concerts were organized. After at first having refused "their name and the use of their establishment to the various parties proposing 'Gift Concerts,'"[2] they explained, they were at last "induced" to participate in one such event, to be conducted on apparently unobjectionable terms that provided every ticket-buyer with "full value" for his money, independent of the prizes. On looking further into the matter, however, they had discovered that "all such plans are contrary to the intent and spirit of the State against private lotteries." Accordingly, they were canceling the announced concert; ticket-holders would be refunded their money at the Halls' music store (*Herald,* January 15, 1851).[3]

"We are exceedingly gratified to observe," applauded the *Albion* (January 18, 1851, p. 32), "that one of our oldest and most respectable musical publishing houses in this city have [*sic*] publicly withdrawn from a [gift concert], which they had somewhat inconsiderately engaged in, their 'sober second thoughts' condemning these enterprises *in toto.* The advertisement of a *Furniture* Gift Concert, just published, is proof of the tendency of such speculations and the unworthy purposes which the purest of arts may be made to serve."

The furniture gift concert nonetheless came off on January 24 at Tripler Hall, with a cast that included Mrs. Eastcott (later Escott) (c. 1828–1895), a vocalist claiming to have appeared with Ole Bull, Madame Stephani, Philip Mayer, Joseph Noll, the *Herren* Lacroix (trumpet), Kiefer (clarinet), Eichhorn (cello), and the Shakespeare Musical Society, comprising members of Jenny Lind's 1850 orchestra, directed by Noll. Mr. Eastcott presided at the piano, and tickets were one dollar. As to the mahogany

[2] Such as the firm of Jocelyn, Watson, and Cholwell?

[3] Firth, Pond, too, after opening an extra box office especially to accommodate the hot demand for Gift Concert tickets, abruptly made it known, on January 22 in the *Herald,* that they were no longer "in any way connected [with], or interested in, Gift Concerts of any kind."

bedroom furniture, on January 22 the *Herald* carried a mysterious notice informing a Mr. S. S. S., who had bought a ticket for the Grand Furniture Gift Concert, that he would hear something to his advantage by calling at the C. C. Williams Furniture Emporium. After the concert the *Herald* (January 27, 1851) reported that 125 unspecified prizes had been awarded, but made no mention of the mahogany bedroom furniture.

In mid-February the fad came to an inglorious end (or, at least, a pause) when a gift concert advertised for Tripler Hall culminated instead in a kind of public brawl. As the *Tribune* (February 13, 1851) noted, with evident satisfaction: ". . . when the guests were assembled, the feast was not prepared. An announcement was made that the money would be refunded at the ticket office, but that establishment had closed its door some time previously. . . . Looking around for someone on whom to take vengeance, the multitude could discover no one but a poor doorkeeper, who stood but a small chance of ever again mounting guard at Tripler Hall had not the police interfered and tendered him an escort home, which he very gladly accepted." The *Tribune* added piously: "The poor dupes who had paid their money to those swindlers who had projected the Concert came off minus the gains that they had each hoped to realize by this species of gambling. We have but a small grain of pity to bestow upon them. If the lesson made them 'wiser and better men,' they have paid very cheap for it."

On February 11 the *Herald* announced what appears to have been the last Grand Gift Concert. The participants were Mrs. L. A. Jones, Madame Stephani, Edward Sheppard, the English pianist William Dressler (1826–1914), and the Shakespeare Concert Society, as it was now called. The 101 promised prizes included the usual assortment of musical instruments. Scheduled to take place at Tripler Hall, tickets for this apparently cooperative venture, at a lowly fifty cents, were available at Geib and Jackson's, Millet's, Vanderbeek's, and other music stores.[4]

To compensate for the loss of the gift concerts, in whose behind-the-scenes operations they appear to have been involved, the hitherto shadowy firm of Jocelyn, Watson, and Purcell (Cholwell apparently having been supplanted) came out with a kind of combination lottery-*cum*-installment-plan scheme. First advertising in *Saroni's Musical Times* (May 24, 1851), they announced the formation of the American Piano-Forte Company, an ethical sounding, ostensibly beneficial, organization. "The vast amount of good accomplished by the 'Building Association,'" they explained, "has induced the above company to extend these principles to another branch of public interest. Object: 1st, Association for mutual benefit. 2nd, To procure a good piano by paying small monthly installments. 3rd, To save persons from paying three times the worth of a piano in the shape of Hire. 4th, Association of 100 persons upon the system of self-government and equality of interest." Those interested in joining were invited to visit the company's office at 289 Broadway in the Lafarge Buildings, where subscriptions might be purchased between the hours of nine A.M. and six P.M.

[4]The craze spread to other fields. At a Grand Gift Ball at Tripler Hall on February 3, more than 2000 "presents" were promised, to be awarded "without lottery, ill-luck, or favor." Civil, military, or fancy dress were acceptable, and Dodworth's Full Band would furnish the music (*Tribune,* February 1, 1851).

A month later (June 23, 1851) a puff, disguised as a progress report of the firm's expanding operations, but evidently inserted by the principals, appeared in the "Business Notices" column of the *Tribune*. Now apparently combined with Saroni's pet project, the Musical-Union, "the Association of the American Piano-Forte Company, founded upon the principles of the Building and Accumulating Fund Associations, and extending their benefits for the distribution of Piano-Fortes and Melodions" announced that they were that day opening books for their second Piano Company and their first Melodion Company, each to consist of 100 subscribers.

It is difficult, if not impossible, to follow the convoluted scheme, even with a further "explanation" (apparently again supplied by the entrepreneurs) in the *Tribune* on July 9. Each of the hundred subscribers forming a "company" paid $3 a month to establish a fund "for the purpose of supplying each member with a piano worth $300." Monthly meetings were held, and purchases were made whenever there were "sufficient funds to purchase one or more instruments." The redemption of each share was decided by auctions held at the monthly meetings, the monthly premium not to exceed $7. Then followed a deluge of Watsonian prose lauding the scheme's humanitarianism and its contribution to the enlargement of culture.

On July 26 it was reported in the *Tribune* that two shares had been redeemed and an undisclosed number of instruments awarded to an undisclosed number of unidentified members. Moreover, "hundreds of pianos will now be distributed to those who have not the means to purchase one outright." All persons interested in the "popular movement" were invited to call at the Jocelyn and Watson offices and subscribe. (Purcell seems to have been tacitly dropped.)

But the "popular movement" seems soon to have expired. After September 6 their advertisements ceased, as apparently did the American Piano-Forte Company. Watson, who might have masterminded the venture—and who, since leaving the *Albion* in late 1850, had so far remained unattached to any local journal—turned again to his freelance odd jobs, chiefly devoted to the creation and dissemination of seductive copy to promote visiting musical Britons.

In the spring of 1851, Watson exerted his powers of persuasion on behalf of the spectacular Irish composer/pianist/violinist/world adventurer William Vincent Wallace. Despite his earlier triumphs in 1843–44, Wallace had not publicly performed in New York since his return to the United States in 1850. As Watson wrote in an initialed, high-voltage pseudo-editorial appearing in the *Mirror* (March 8, 1851), Wallace had regrettably been "playing the hermit to perfection. . . . We admire modesty," wrote modest Watson, "being ourselves retiring to a fault, but there is such a thing as hiding 'one's light too long under a bushel.'" Besides, it was an "almost unpardonable folly" on Wallace's part to ignore the thousands of dollars waiting to be picked up. "Come out of thy shell, O snail! and gather the golden harvest awaiting thee," playfully coaxed Watson, thereby demonstrating that he could be frolicsome as well as shy.

Not only was Wallace remembered in New York for his thrilling virtuosity as a pianist and violinist, wrote Watson, but, since his previous visit, his operas—performed throughout England and Europe, to say nothing of the United States—had brought him even greater fame. "In short, he is one of the great men of his time, and

Music Division, The New York Public Library

Mathew Brady's portrait of William Vincent Wallace.

his sojourn among us is a credit to our city. . . . We urge him to . . . give a concert, and to afford the public an opportunity of welcoming an old and distinguished favorite."

Predictably, Wallace yielded to Watson's urging and presented a virtually all-Wallace program at Tripler Hall on April 22, assisted by his sister Madame Wallace-Bouchelle, making her New York debut on this occasion. His other assisting artists were H. W. Greatorex (substituting for an ailing A. Arthurson); Richard Hoffman, with whom Wallace played his brilliant Grand Duo for two pianos on a *Romance* by Halévy; and the string players Griebel, Bristow, and Herwig (violins), Schuberth and Tyte (violas), and Boucher and Hegelund (cellos), with whom Wallace played an unspecified Spohr double quartet. On the violin Wallace performed his Grand Fantasia on airs from *La sonnambula* and his Brilliant Variations on "The Last Rose of Summer," the latter transcription especially composed for this occasion; on the piano he played two of his newest compositions, "Music Murmuring in the Trees" and "Night Winds," also his audience-pleasing *Polka de concert*. George Loder conducted Wallace's Overture to *Maritana*♪ and his own Overture to *Marmion*.♪

According to Watson's (again initialed) ecstatic full-page review of the concert in *Saroni's Musical Times* (May 3, 1851, p. 62), Wallace was just about perfect in all he did. As a composer he belonged "among the leading spirits of the Musical World." As a pianist he had few equals in dexterity and delicacy; if he was deficient in the *force*—the vulgar loudness—that was so much demanded in our community, it was a virtue. As a violinist Wallace had few equals and "hardly one superior." Enumerating the marvels of Wallace's interpretation and technique (the latter only occasionally betraying his lack of practice), Watson stated that not even Vieuxtemps or Sivori♪ had ever excelled his double stops; indeed, his double shakes in octaves or thirds had never been equaled by anyone.

Reviewing the same concert, Richard Storrs Willis conceded that Wallace was a good enough performer, but not as good as reputed, probably due to his lack of practice. Ponderously, Willis hoped that Wallace would "always be true to himself and never suffer any desire to please the *oi polloi* to lead him away from the truthful expression of what is in him, and his own personal ideal in art" (*Albion,* April 26, 1851, p. 200).

On June 10, after Jenny Lind's departure, Madame Wallace-Bouchelle, undaunted by the less-than-glowing reviews of her debut performance, gave a concert of her own at the Chinese Rooms, newly "made beautiful by substituting Christian decorations for Chinese hobgoblins." A crowd of about 1000 people of a "most fashionable and substantial class" turned out to hear her in a program largely devoted to compositions by her brother, who assisted at this event. Described as a young and good-looking Irish woman who shared much of her brother's versatility and talent, Madame Bouchelle, whose voice had previously been judged as harsh, was this time found to be the possessor of a "particularly rich and reedy voice, especially in its lower tones; in her ballads she captivated all hearts by her sympathetic intonations." Especially her rendition of Wallace's "'Cradle Song' . . . was one of the sweetest things we have ever listened to. It touched the maternal bosom in a tender place, and made many a mother's eye glisten with emotion." Wallace played his two-piano piece on themes from Halévy's *L'Éclair* with Scharfenberg, who directed the concert; the other participants were the opera tenor Bailini and the German basso Philip Mayer (*Mirror,* June 11, 1851). As previously noted, Madame Bouchelle subsequently appeared with both the Harmonic and the Philharmonic societies.

Early in 1851, despite the public obsession with gift concerts, Max Maretzek, who was expanding his entrepreneurial activities, attracted large audiences with his outsized Grand Musical Festivals at Tripler Hall. As we know, an estimated two or three thousand frustrated people had been turned away on January 11 when Teresa Parodi refused to sing with a German conductor (the *Herald* had gallantly attributed her defection to a sore throat). On January 14, the night following her embattled *Norma* performance at Astor Place, the postponed concert took place at Tripler Hall with Maretzek in command and a cast that included Maurice Strakosch and the "far-famed" Hungarian violinist and composer Miska Hauser making his American debut on this occasion. "Max Maretzek flatters himself," read the impresario's Barnumesque advertisement, "that his efforts to combine on the same evening such an unequaled attraction of THREE GREAT MUSICAL CELEBRITIES will be duly appreciated by his patrons, and [he] has determined to put the price of admission (as on former occasions) at one dollar." Three musical celebrities for the price of one! A bargain!

Assisting these stars were the Astor Place singers, Whiting, Amalia Patti, Lorini, Beneventano, Novelli, and Sanquirico, who in various combinations sang arias and duets from *Linda di Chamounix, Don Pasquale,* and *Roberto Devereux.* With the Astor Place orchestra, Maretzek rounded out the proceedings with such unrelated works as an unspecified *Leonore* Overture by Beethoven,[5] Strakosch's Overture to *Giovanna di Napoli,* and his own "Chit-Chat Polka."

The critics unanimously praised Parodi for her dramatically illuminating performances of excerpts from *Semiramide* (a preview of that opera's impending revival at Astor Place on February 12) and of a *scena* from *La gazza ladra.* Whiting was generally commended, although she was chided by Willis for gasping audibly with every breath she took. Strakosch, too—despite his brilliant performance of his new *Fantaisie romantique, La Sylphide*—was reproached by Willis for his many "false octaves": "How is this, Monsieur Strakosch? We are unaccustomed to such things in you" (*Albion,* January 18, 1851, p. 32).

Hauser, the new violin virtuoso, played three of his own compositions, all acrobatic crowd-pleasers: a concert rondo *La Sicilienne,* a set of Brilliant Variations on an air from Donizetti's opera *Ugo, conte di Parigi,* and a chirping piece of descriptive music "The Bird in the Tree," subtitled "a fable, written for children."[6]

Hauser impressed Richard Willis as a "very sound violinist with just enough mastery of artistic tricks to appeal to the *oi polloi* in every audience, who are only reached in this way." Willis had no doubt that Hauser was capable of playing "a better style of music than he offered us on this occasion." The other critics expressed their conflicting judgments of Hauser, the most vivid, as usual, coming from Saroni. Hauser's well-written compositions, he observed (*Musical Times,* January 18, 1851, p. 171), revealed him to be a solid musician who knew how best to compose for his own style of performance, a style that was "not that of Ole Bull, because devoid of his trickery and his vigor; nor that of Vieuxtemps, because devoid of his brilliance; nor that of Hohnstock,♪ because devoid of his eccentricity—and yet, in spite of the absence of these essential characteristics of a public performance, M. Hauser is a Violinist who has few equals." Saroni was enchanted, too, with Hauser's compositions, although he had regrettably been obliged to forgo "The Bird in the Tree."

Strakosch, on the other hand, received a slap on the wrist. As an encore to *La Sylphide,* "for some reason best known to himself," he had played a "trifling Polka." Worse, as an encore to his *Fantaisie de concert,* he played "Yankee Doodle" with variations of "rather inferior quality." Furthermore, it seemed to Saroni as if Strakosch, "since he has composed an Opera, does not pay attention to the Piano, which he ought, if he cares at all to keep his reputation as a pianist." Saroni disapproved, too, of Beethoven's unfamiliar "'Overture to Leonora,' the one rejected by the Great Master himself, and we cannot see the advantage of introducing it to a New York audience, unless it is to show off the superiority of other compositions from inferior composers."

On January 18, Maretzek, with virtually the same cast, produced another of his spectacular opera concerts at Tripler Hall, this time a benefit for Strakosch. In honor of the beneficiary, portions (probably staged) of *Giovanna di Napoli* were performed. Strakosch additionally unveiled his latest piano fantasy, this time on themes from *La Fille du régiment;* he also played Weber's *Concertstück* with the orchestra, and the concert

[5] Probably the same *Leonore* Overture that Benedict had introduced in 1850.

[6] "The Bird in the Tree," Saroni explained, depicted "the sensations of a bird which, after having escaped from its cage, flies into the free forest and repeats the melodies it has been taught by its mistress" (*Saroni's Musical Times,* January 18, 1851, p. 171).

concluded with the first performance of Strakosch's new "Flirtation Polka." The assisting artists at this event were Parodi, Whiting, Lorini, and again Hauser.

Hearing Hauser a second time, the *Tribune* (evidently Curtis), who only a few days before had lauded him for the "individual style," "exquisite fancy," and "delicious character" of his playing, now produced a number of persnickety cavils: "His instrument has not shed the prose of the fiddle and become the poetic violin." Although Hauser played accurately and admirably, it was not electrical—it lacked sympathy: "We could just as soon glow with delight at the perfect play of a steam-engine" (*Tribune,* January 20, 1851).

On January 21, Maretzek presided over another elaborate concert, nominally sponsored by Parodi for the benefit of needy Italian political refugees. Virtually a carbon copy of Maretzek's earlier Festival Concerts, the event presented the same cast of Astor Place singers, assisted by the same adjunct Astor Place artists Strakosch and Hauser, and was accompanied by the Astor Place chorus and orchestra. Only in one respect did this occasion differ: as an added attraction, the "Grand Band" of the American frigate-of-war *Constitution* was heard, under the direction of its leader Signor G. Conterno. As a finale, in addition to the usual opera excerpts and the usual instrumental show pieces, the entire company united with the band in mighty ensemble to perform the Italian Hymn of Liberty, *Del prim'anno già l'alba premiera* (*Herald,* January 21, 1851).[7] Despite the excellent performances, reported the *Herald* (January 22, 1851), the event attracted a disappointingly small audience.

Nor did Madame Bertucca-Maretzek fare better at her so-called concert debut as a harpist at Tripler Hall on March 11, heralded not only as "The Greatest Musical Event of the Season," but as her "first and only Grand Concert on the Harp in America." To bestow an air of novelty upon yet another repetition of the by-now overworked advertising formula, Bertucca's honorary memberships in the Philharmonic Societies of Venice, Florence, Bologna, and Bergamo were newly listed, as if she had just arrived. Assisting Bertucca were her scarcely unfamiliar Astor Place colleagues Truffi-Benedetti, Whiting, Forti, Benedetti, Beneventano, Rosi, and Fitzjames (in her vocal persona). Griebel performed a violin work with the Astor Place orchestra under Maretzek, who had returned briefly from Boston to conduct and manage the event, and who, for once, to Saroni's delight, omitted the "Tip-Top Polka." "Because the hall was so large," the tickets were advertised at "only one dollar" (*Herald,* March 11, 1851). Richard Willis, however, thought it a mistake to charge a whole dollar for a concert so late in the season.

Bertucca, who played two harp solos by unidentified composers—a splendid Grand Fantasy with Brilliant Variations on *Robert le diable* and a *Nocturne espagnole*—was saluted by the critics as a harp virtuoso of the first rank, comparable to such transatlantic masters as Elias Parish-Alvars (1808–1849) and John Chatterton (1805–1871). The remainder of the program offered no surprises except, perhaps, for its regrettably abrupt termination when a lady in the audience was stricken with a fit (*Herald,* March 12; *Saroni's Musical Times,* March 15, 1851, p. 254).

[7] It was remarked in the papers that for this event, Parodi and Amalia Patti had decorated their persons with the Italian republican colors—Parodi wearing them as a belt, Patti as a headdress.

Perhaps the novelty-hungry New York public had become bored with the ceaseless reiteration of unintelligible entertainment performed by a redundant group of alien performers. Nor could concertgoers be blamed, after savoring the excitement of a super-attraction such as Jenny Lind—to say nothing of the extramusical thrills of the gift concerts—for failing to flock to repetitive, run-of-the mill concerts offered by overfamiliar, run-of-the-mill performers. To lure audiences, in the absence of more compelling attractions, increasingly elaborate concert extravaganzas were devised, particularly for benefits and testimonial events.

Doubtless inspired by the monster annual benefits of the Dramatic Fund Society and following in the footsteps of Maretzek, a pioneer in the realm of mixed-media audience-pleasers, a program in four parts was presented on January 23 at Niblo's Garden to honor the veteran Irish actor/singer William F. Brough.♪ First came "English Opera" (the first act of Auber's *Fra Diavolo*);[8] then a miscellaneous concert of eleven numbers performed by Brough's early contemporaries, the singers Antoinette Otto and Mrs. Bailey, Edward Seguin and Philip Mayer; they were assisted by Ferdinand Griebel, Richard Hoffman, and Dodworth's Concert Band; then the last scene of *Anna Bolena,* with Bertucca, Giulietta Perrini, Beneventano, Novelli, Giubilei, and the Astor Place chorus and orchestra, conducted by Maretzek; and finally John Maddison Morton's popular "comic drama" *Poor Pillicoddy* (London 1848), performed by the peerless comedian William E. Burton, with Mary Taylor, Caroline Hiffert, and John Dunn. Tickets were one dollar (*Herald,* January 23, 1851).

The critics did not take kindly to this trend toward gigantism in benefits and testimonials. Upon the announcement of a mammoth testimonial to honor George Loder on March 4 at Tripler Hall, for instance, the *Courier and Enquirer* (March 3, 1851) irritably observed that if a beneficiary were sufficiently famous, everybody in creation volunteered to perform, thus creating an interminable program impossible to review in the detail so dear to the contemporary critical heart. Twenty-four numbers had been scheduled for the Loder event—with encores they would easily exceed thirty. What an affliction! Especially for those who were forced to sit through endless, tiresome performances while waiting for the particular artist or artists they had come to hear.[9]

The overdue tribute to Loder—one of the few he received in all the years of his significant (alas forgotten) service to music in New York[10]—seems to have come about largely through the efforts of his kinsman-by-marriage Henry C. Watson. At a

[8]Brough had appeared in *Fra Diavolo,* probably in Rophino Lacy's English version, at the Park Theatre when he first came to the United States with the Woods♪ in 1835.

[9]On the same topic, a correspondent to the *Mirror* (January 16, 1851) complained that the overladen Maretzek Grand Festival Concert of January 14 had been a "weary" experience: "The sacrifice of being compelled to listen to a dozen instrumental pieces is too great to make up for three songs from the glorious Parodi. Mr. Maretzek greatly mistakes the public taste if he thinks the crowd go to hear the fiddlers, however good they may be; four out of five go to hear Parodi, and nothing else. . . . Let him try one concert with six songs by Parodi . . . and only two instrumental concertos and two overtures, and the result will prove not only satisfactory to the audience, but to Mr. Maretzek himself."

[10]Early in 1852, Loder would transplant to San Francisco and there renew old ties with his former ally Henry Meiggs♪ and establish the San Francisco Philharmonic Society, the first choral group to be formed on the West Coast (Lawrence, *19th Century Music,* Summer 1985, pp. 37–38).

meeting on February 13, a committee of prominent members of the music community adopted Watson's motion and resolved that Loder, as an "active and prominent member of the New-York Philharmonic Society, as the founder of the New York Vocal Society [1844], as the conductor of the 'American Musical Institute' [1845–48], as a valuable and efficient officer of the 'American Musical Fund Society,' and in every other position in which his musical abilities have been called into action, whether for charitable or other purposes, has deserved well of the public; and that therefore a testimonial, by which the public approbation of his valuable labors may be made manifest, is just due to him" (*Herald,* February 15, 1851).

"It was to be expected," later wrote Saroni in his review of the concert (*Saroni's Musical Times,* March 8, 1851, p. 243), "that all the professional talent in the City would unhesitatingly and joyfully press their services upon the Committee for the occasion." Indeed, so great had been the stampede of performers wishing to honor Loder that many had to be turned away.

Saroni sheds valuable light on the behind-the-scenes workings of testimonial concerts and the tribulations of their organizers: "Complimentary concerts are truly funny [strange] affairs. No matter how popular, or [how great] the merit of the individual 'up,' the difficulties in the way of working up a bill [program] can hardly be conceived by the uninitiated." The "poor Committee"—for this concert consisting of the music publishers James Lang Hewitt, S. C. Jollie, James Hall, and James E. Gould, and the music journalists James F. Otis and Henry C. Watson—were "responsible for everything, even to the furnishing of a piano stool of a requisite height. All the singers—all the players—wish to occupy the best positions [on the program] . . . and as it is impossible to please everybody, the concentrated wrath of the volunteer corps falls upon the heads of the unfortunate 'Committee.'" This was but the beginning of their woes, and Saroni proceeded lovingly to enumerate them.

Not least among their torments were the performers who volunteered without intending to appear, purely to reap the free newspaper publicity. In this instance the principal culprit was a Madame Schlesinger, purportedly a "*prima donna* of the Theatres of Germany,"[11] who defaulted after having been awarded—through some extraordinary feat of managerial dexterity—top billing over the huge cast of more familiar artists that included the singers Mesdames Bozzi, E. Loder, Bostwick, Otto, Jones, and Eastcott, Messrs. H. W. Greatorex, Frederick Lyster, and A. Arthurson (who also defaulted, as did Philip Mayer—the latter, according to Saroni, probably suffering from a "pain in his voice"); the pianists Maurice Strakosch, W. A. King, Richard Hoffman, and Henry Timm; the violinists Ferdinand Griebel and Miska Hauser; the flutist Felice Eben; and a Miss Wyatt (a debutante harpist who performed during the first intermission). Also appearing were the massed choral forces of the Harmonic Society and the *Liederkranz,* three military bands—Dodworth's, Shelton's, and Adkins's—and a "Grand Monster Orchestra, composed of all the Instrumental Societies, Theatres, etc. in the city, comprising the finest musical talent in the country." And added to all these, the

[11] Madame Schlesinger, whose agent claimed she was the greatest singer in the world, had not yet been heard in New York. "Mysterious hints have been thrown out," tattled Saroni, "that the great maestro B—— had paid her an immense sum not to appear while a certain delightful singer Madame B—— was singing in New York" (*Saroni's Musical Times,* March 8, 1851, p. 243).

singing thespians Mary Taylor, Mrs. George Loder, and Stephen Leach, who gave the singing lesson scene from Loder's adaptation of Auber's *The Ambassadress,* the current hit at Brougham's Lyceum. The first part of the program was conducted by William Vincent Wallace, the second and third parts by Loder, who also presided over the Grand Finale, a formidable medley of national airs performed by everybody.[12]

Following this vogue, a supergigantic testimonial was tendered to the veteran actor/manager Thomas S. Hamblin at Castle Garden on June 24. It comprised a fully staged production of John Tobin's comedy *The Honey Moon* (London 1805), performed by a galaxy of stars headed by the beneficiary and Charlotte Cushman; a "Grand Musical Interlude" of unspecified content, employing Maretzek's entire Castle Garden opera company; and additionally the third act of *Lucia* with Truffi, Bettini, Beneventano, and Marini. Expecting a large attendance (which failed to materialize because of the exorbitant ticket prices of two and three dollars), the peripatetic Wardle Corbyn, in charge of the business end of the affair, borrowed Barnum's "admirable plan of disposing the theatre," that is, color-coding the seats and tickets (*Mirror,* June 24, 1851).

This event, elaborate as it was, was eclipsed by the fourteen-hour-long festival given at Castle Garden on August 12 in honor of E. A. Marshall, the manager of the Broadway Theatre. Among its bewildering variety of offerings were complete plays in English, French, and German performed by respective ethnic troupes; various ballets, magic acts, acrobats, and every conceivable kind of other stage entertainment except blackface minstrelsy. In addition, separate acts of four operas were performed by Maretzek's complete company conducted by Luigi Arditi: the first act of *Ernani,* the third act of *"Romeo e Giulietta" (I Capuleti ed i Montecchi),* the fourth of *La favorita,* and the second of *Lucrezia Borgia.* For the final hour of the orgy—eleven P.M. until midnight—such members of the audience as might have survived were treated to a spectacular display of fireworks (Ireland, II, 591).

After Maretzek's comparatively modest eight-hour benefit on September 4, the magnitude of the benefits began to dwindle. For instance, at the benefit for Niblo's longtime orchestra leader Signor La Manna, given at Niblo's Garden on October 25, only one play, "apropos of Kossuth" (written in French especially for the occasion by the French actor/playwright/entrepreneur Robert York) was presented; the "wonderful Ravels" performed their breathtaking feats, and to round out the program, the veteran *prima donna* Caterina Barili-Patti and the former Astor Place tenor Giuseppe Forti were heard in an *Intermezzo musicale.* The evening concluded with a stirring performance of the *Marseillaise,* in which everybody joined (*Mirror,* October 25, 1851).

Probably purely in self-defense, concert-givers now began to adopt extravaganza-like features (of course, on a necessarily smaller scale), and military bands became a common, if incongruous, feature of many concerts. At a rather modest benefit for the Hungarian exiles, given on February 13 by Madame Stephani, the assisting artists were Mrs. Eastcott, a debutant American tenor Mr. Squires (1825–1907), a small group of instrumentalists, and a military band.

[12] Mercifully avoiding a detailed review of the Loder testimonial—in any case impossible with a program of such length—Richard Storrs Willis nonetheless felt impelled to take the German *Liederkranz* to task for having chosen to sing a potpourri from *La Fille du régiment.* Germans should not attempt to sing Italian music, he wrote: their strong, manly voices demand solely "the hearty music of the *Vaterland*" (*Albion,* March 8, 1851, p. 116).

On March 10 at Tripler Hall, at a purported "repetition by special request" of the furniture gift concert (but sans furniture), Adkins's Military Band was added to an already overladen program. Directed by Maximilian Zorer (the blackface falsettist "Mac" Zorer temporarily reverting to his original identity), the cast included Madame Stephani, Mrs. L. A. Jones, the thirteen-year-old violinist Lavinia Bandini, Philip Mayer, the cellist L. Eichhorn, the trombonist Knittel, the pianist William Dressler, and Joseph Noll with his Shakespeare Society chamber orchestra; their program traversed the gamut from Mozart to Schubert to Auber to James G. Maeder.♪ To this assortment, Adkins contributed military quicksteps, including Zorer's own "Grand National Quick Step," composed for the occasion and conducted by the composer, and, emulating the Dodworths, Adkins wound up the program with his own arrangement for band of the *Grand terzetto* from *Ernani*. (At fifty cents a ticket, even if the hall were filled, one wonders how, with such crowds of performers, they could clear expenses, much less remunerate the participants.)

On February 8, again at Tripler Hall, the multilingual Hungarian vocalist Krausz, now phoneticized as Krauss, presented a different kind of extravaganza, called a "Grand Pot-Pourri Musical Festival." In the miscellaneous first part of the program Krauss performed a vocal solo spanning an astonishing range from "double D in the bass to C in the soprano"; the entire second part was devoted to an epical medley of his own devising titled "The Confusion of Babel." Forgetting Bochsa's even more ethnically comprehensive *Voyage musicale,*♪ performed in 1848 and 1849, the *Herald* (January 30, 1851) puffed Krauss's "Confusion" as "the greatest novelty ever introduced in this city." With occasional vocal assistance from colleagues, Krauss would sing, in their appropriate languages: the "Rákóczy March," an English hornpipe, a Styrian quartet, a Russian hymn, a Russian mazurka, Sicilian song, Jerusalem melody *(Sholom Alachim)* [*sic*], French romance, Greek hymn, Irish melody, *Cracovienne,* Polish glee, German patriotic song, Wallachian song, Hungarian serenade, Bavarian glee, Maltese song, Neapolitan duet, Hebrew psalm, Swiss song, "Yankee Doodle," "Lucy Neale," Scotch song—then, waxing programmatic—"The Confusion in Europe and the Battle of Comorn," "Triumph of Liberty and Freedom," "The Star-Spangled Banner," and would wind up, for some reason, with "The Grand Triumphal March of Mexico."

Far more ambitious was a "Grand National Concert" at Castle Garden on April 14, celebrating the 75th anniversary of the Battle of Bunker Hill[13] with the first performance of a "descriptive symphony" *The Battle of Bunker Hill* by Simon Knaebel, a Philharmonic violinist/cellist/hornist. In two parts, the work consisted of a setting for male voices and brasses of the poem "The Battle on Bunker's Hill" by the American poetess Lydia Sigourney,♪ sung by the German *Liederkranz* under their leader Herr Agricol Paur, followed by a musical depiction in twenty sections of the battle, performed, not by a military band but by two separate "Powerful Orchestras"[14] representing the

[13] The Bunker Hill anniversary was officially commemorated at the Tabernacle on June 17 with orations and "appropriate exercises," instrumental music by Dodworth's Band, choral music by a "select choir under the direction of Brother Abram C. Hyatt," and by request, a favorite song was performed by Mrs. B. H. Bohannan♪ (*Tribune,* June 17, 1851).

[14] "Most all the resident talent is engaged for the occasion," puffed *Saroni's Musical Times* (April 5, 1851, p. 19), "and we sincerely wish a crowded house may reward the efforts of Mr. Knaebel."

American and British armies. Each of the twenty subdivisions bore a programmatic title, sometimes musically explained, as in section 2, "Digging Fortifications"; or section 16, "'The Fall of General Warren,' a *Marcia funerale* preceded by a choral of four Trombones"; or section 18, "Charlestown on Fire." It all ended with a bellicose "March and Combat, between both Orchestras, on the National Airs."

The first part of the concert, the whole of which was conducted by Theodore Eisfeld, consisted of vocal solos by Mrs. L. A. Jones, Philip Mayer, and Paul K. Weitzel; a chorus by the *Liederkranz;* and, notably, "General Taylor's Funeral March" by Anthony Philip Heinrich, a piece for brass instruments, whose performance precipitated yet another Heinrichian explosion.

Reviewing the two "domestic works," as he called them, Saroni found Knaebel's piece to be generally praiseworthy, but although expertly orchestrated, it would have benefited by judicious pruning and more rehearsals. But Heinrich's piece: "Though exceedingly well arranged . . . is not so good a composition as we expected from Mr. Heinrich. It had little melody, an indefinite rhythm, and the harmonic combinations were so original that no one else would have written them. With all our veneration for the aged composer, we must call it a complete failure" (*Saroni's Musical Times,* May 24, 1851, p. 92, reprinted from the *Message Bird,* April 19, 1851, p. 19).

Incensed at this criticism—mild for Saroni but intolerable to the composer—Heinrich addressed a caustic letter to the offending critic, but sent it, not to the *Musical Times* but to the *Journal of the Fine Arts,* the new name of the *Message Bird,*[15] where it was promptly published. The letter was just as promptly republished in the *Musical Times* on May 10 (p. 73) with appropriately acrimonious comments by Saroni.

"*Carissimo amico Saroni,*" wrote Heinrich with pen dipped in vitriol: "*General Taylor's Funeral March,* performed at Knaebel's concert, was not a 'complete failure,' as you report in your paper, but a decided triumph, well known to the public and many gentlemen of the press. Your remarks would, in my frank opinion, on the scale of able and impartial criticism, not even outweigh a tobacco seed."[16]

To refute Saroni (and at the same time garner a little useful publicity), the irascible composer enclosed a translation of a letter from the noted German composer Heinrich Marschner,♪ written in 1849, hailing A. P. Heinrich's compositions as "a splendid testimonial of German talent in the West."

Saroni, who thrived on controversy—especially multiple controversy—immediately dredged up his recent altercations with various other disgruntled musicians. He referred to Bristow and Arthurson, neither of whom, he claimed, could bear to be criticized adversely.[17] And lately he had received a letter "full of abuse" from another enraged composer, John Hill Hewitt,♪ now a prominent journalist in Baltimore. Still

[15] In May the *Message Bird* underwent the first of its innumerable transformations, becoming *The Journal of the Fine Arts;* a month later it was renamed *The Journal of the Fine Arts and the Musical World.* For these and its various subsequent mutations, see Weichlein, p. 44.

[16] The tobacco seed was apparently Heinrich's favorite metaphor of abuse: he had used it similarly against Henry C. Watson during their public bicker in 1841.♪

[17] Saroni had been conducting a serial feud, too, with *Parker's Journal* over Saroni's unkindly comments on Signor La Manna and La Manna's orchestra at Niblo's. In Saroni's estimation it was the worst orchestra in New York (*Saroni's Musical Times,* March 15, p. 254; March 29, p. 7; April 12, pp. 29–30; *Parker's,* March 22, p. 164; April 5, 1851, p. 190.)

rankling over the dismal failure in 1846 of his oratorio *Jephtha,*♪ Hewitt had read dire meanings into Saroni's reference to that work in a recent review of Hewitt's newly published "Union Quick Step." "If we are not mistaken," Saroni had written, "we have the composer of *Jephtha* before us, and in that case we are really astonished that the principal theme of the Quick Step, 'O Would I Were a Boy Again,' should be introduced with the *Quart-sext* [six-four] chord, to say nothing of the consecutive Fifths and Octaves so plentifully employed throughout" (*Musical Times,* April 19, 1851, p. 42).

Apparently the mere mention of *Jephtha* reopened painful wounds, as Hewitt's furious response—reviving all the old accusations—clearly disclosed. The affair quickly degenerated into an ugly exchange of personal insults. For example:

> Hewitt: If you cannot conduct your journal with a spirit of friendly feeling toward your composers, the quicker you throw aside your pen, the better.
>
> Saroni: We simply believe Mr. Hewitt does not know the very A.B.C. of music (as all his compositions prove), and that his time would be far better employed in learning some honest trade, like shoemaking, tailoring, etc., than in compiling notes without meaning. (*Musical Times,* May 17, 1851, p. 82)

Finding himself at the apex of a triangular controversy, with Heinrich and Hewitt joining forces against him, Saroni, in a series of articles captioned "Offended Dignity," zestfully flourished his convoluted invective. Marschner, he wrote, on perusing Heinrich's scores, might indeed have found them praiseworthy, but then, it was *we* who were "doomed to *listen* to some of them" (*Saroni's Musical Times,* May 10, 1851, p. 73).

The antagonists continued to heap abuse upon one another, faithfully reported in successive issues of the *Musical Times,* until the affair finally trailed off in a miasma of unsavory mutual vilification.

Notwithstanding John Hill Hewitt's obsessive belief that his oratorio had been critically massacred only because he was an American, native members of the New York music community were beginning more frequently to be heard and more generally to be accepted. As the *Journal of the Fine Arts* observed (November 1, 1851, p. 101): "We have native talent enough, if we will only look for it and give it a fair chance when it is found." Among the native talent was Mrs. Laura A. Jones, regularly heard with the Harmonic Society, who gave a concert of her own "before a very crowded audience" at the Chinese Rooms on April 10. She was assisted in a predominantly sacred program by a predominantly American cast: Mrs. Emma Gillingham Bostwick, Miss Julia Wheelock (Mrs. Jones's niece), a Miss Mary Hawley, Philip Mayer, J. B. Beutler (a new German tenor), the oratorio singer Robert Andrews, Dodworth's Quartette Band (an all-Dodworth brass quartet), members of the Harmonic Society, and the choir of St. Bartholomew's Church. Scharfenberg presided at the piano, replacing Timm, who was unable to appear (*Saroni's Musical Times,* April 19, 1851, p. 43).

Mrs. Jones participated in the revival, on April 25 at the Apollo, of George Henry Curtis's Grand Cantata, *Eleutheria*♪—not too enthusiastically received when it was first heard in 1849. Besides Mrs. Jones, who had sung at the work's first performances, the soloists were Julia Wheelock, J. A. Johnson, and F. H. Nash. The composer presided at the piano, and Bristow, who had orchestrated the score, again conducted. The *Tribune* (April 26, 1851) praised Curtis for his skill and patience in having fitted music to Horatio Stone's unsingable text.[18]

The American musicians tended to band together. At David Griswold's concert at the Apollo on December 13, Mrs. Jones assisted, as did G. F. Bristow, G. H. Curtis, a guitarist named Bradford, and the former violin prodigy Giovanni Sconcia,♪ now a full-fledged, naturalized, adult virtuoso.

By far the most visible American musician to appear in 1851 was the veteran singer Emma Gillingham Bostwick,♪ who in the late afternoon of her life dauntlessly pursued a renewal of her long-dormant concert career—and succeeded.[19] First giving a concert on a smallish scale at Niblo's Concert Room on January 20,[20] Mrs. Bostwick, encouraged by her many (apparently prosperous) well-wishers, announced an ambitious subscription series of six closely spaced "*soirées musicales,*" again at Niblo's Saloon, to begin on October 28. Subscriptions to the series were $5 for two tickets; single tickets for each concert were fifty cents.

Reviewing her first *soirée,* the *Mirror* (October 30, 1851) noted that her large audience represented the commercial wealth of the city: "Rarely have we seen so large a congregation of the 'heavy' down-town merchants." Mrs. Bostwick was cordially received, but "the applause was not quite equal to those occasions when *free* tickets are plentiful, and enthusiastic friends are judiciously distributed over the room."[21]

And although her Swedish song inevitably evoked memories of Lind, it was presumptuous (or foolhardy) of any singer to attempt anything reminiscent of the Nightingale's sacrosanct repertory. Nonetheless, Mrs. Bostwick's singing had improved, a remarkable achievement for a vocalist of her mature years.

The *Journal of the Fine Arts* (November 1, 1851, p. 101), on the other hand, unhesitatingly placed Mrs. Bostwick among the world's greatest singers: "Her execution is not easily equalled, her trill is exceedingly good. She sings ballads beautifully, and her not least charming trait is the quiet manner with which she executes the most difficult passages, apparently without any effort."

The newly reorganized *Musical Times* (November 1, 1851, p. 64) lauded Mrs. Bostwick for the consistently high quality of her vocalism, equally splendid in Italian opera arias and simple ballads. Her assisting artists too—the violinist Griebel, the cellist Braun, the infrequently heard Italian tenor Bailini, Timm, who presided at the piano, and Bristow, who conducted an orchestra —were warmly praised; but of the orchestra, "the less said, the better."[22]

[18] "How it smacks of Abolitionism," approved Saroni, terming *Eleutheria* "a cantata in praise of civil and religious freedom" (*Musical Times,* April 19, 1851, p. 43).

[19] Mrs. Bostwick had devoted herself during the interim chiefly to church music; she was currently the Director of Music at the Church of the Ascension, then, as now, at Fifth Avenue and Tenth Street.

[20] Assisted by Richard Hoffman, Joseph Noll, a harpist named Williams, and Timm, who presided at the piano, Mrs. Bostwick presented a mixed program that featured "Sacred songs by Haydn" (*Tribune; Herald,* January 20, 1851).

[21] The paying subscribers, doubtless chiefly members of the well-to-do Church of the Ascension congregation, were evidently less conversant with concert deportment than the lowly "dead heads."

[22] Performing the overtures to Hérold's one-act opera *La Médicine sans médicin* (Paris 1832) and Auber's *Le Cheval de bronze,* the orchestra, probably Signor La Manna's much-maligned house or-

At her five following *soirées* (November 4, 11, 18, 25, and December 4) Mrs. Bostwick and her colleagues presented copious quantities of solo and ensemble music, vocal and instrumental, to virtually unanimous critical approval. Replacing the orchestra, a flexible ensemble of first-rate string players that included Bristow, Noll, U. C. Hill, Sconcia, Braun, Hegelund, and Pirsson, with Timm presiding at the keyboard, played arrangements of opera overtures and dismembered movements of chamber works, among them Beethoven's overtures to *The Men of Prometheus* [*sic*] and *Egmont,* arranged for string septet. Pirsson's Grand Mammoth Double Pianoforte, too, was heard in eight-hand arrangements of the overtures to Hérold's *Zampa, Der Freischütz,* and *Die Zauberflöte,* played by Timm, Bristow, Maeder, and an unknown, named Beer. Of the string players, Noll, Braun, and Sconcia doubled as soloists; the other assisting artists included the singers Bailini and Philip Mayer, the Philharmonic hornist Henry Schmitz, the flutist Kyle, and the pianists Master Will Saar, Charles Wels, and a T. Augustus (or Auguste) Hogan, making his debut in America. Mrs. Bostwick sang an all-inclusive repertory of solo and ensemble music that ranged from Handel and Mozart to Bellini, Verdi, and Donizetti, to German *Lieder,* Scottish and English folk ballads, and contemporary songs by Joseph P. Knight,♪ William Vincent Wallace, and George Frederick Bristow.

So great was her success that on December 26 the remarkable Mrs. Bostwick launched a second series of six *soirées musicales,*[23] assisted on this occasion by the opera diva Rosina Pico-Vietti, making her first local concert appearance in five years. Richard Hoffman, G. F. Bristow, U. C. Hill, Noll, Hegelund, Pirsson, and Timm again filled out the cast.[24]

Other native efforts included an English Madrigal and Glee *Soirée* presented at Hope Chapel on November 20 by the oratorio singer J. A. Johnson. Evidently pleasing to an "intelligent and *patient* audience," considering the lengthy program of twenty-four pieces, the anonymous post-Saroni critic of the *Musical Times* (November 29, 1851, p. 60) found this kind of music, beautiful though it undoubtedly was, too lacking in "clap-trap" to be suitable for public performance. More than any other music, the madrigals and glees expressed the "simple and innocent delight of a happy home," and thus should be cultivated there as a welcome alternative to the reprehensible musical tendencies of the "thousands who spend their time at the Ethiopian Opera, or in cultivating the sickly sentimentalism which pervades most of the songs and piano music of the present day."

---

chestra at Niblo's, played only at the first *soirée.* Mrs. Bostwick, who bore the weight of the program, sang the aria *Robert, toi que j'aime* from Meyerbeer's *Robert le diable;* with Griebel, Artôt's variations for voice and violin on the aria *Sommo cielo* from Pacini's *La schiava di Bagdad* (Turin 1820), the Swedish dance song "Pretty, Pretty Girls" by Olof Åhlström, and two ballads in English: "Down the Burn, Davy Love" and "The Watchman's Cry." Griebel and Braun each played an opera fantasy, and Bailini sang an aria from *Don Giovanni.*

[23] The newly established *New-York Daily Times* (December 26, 1851) admiringly referred to Mrs. Bostwick as "a bird of our musical forest, and not the less to be overlooked on this score, even if her intrinsic merits, admirably adapted as they are to the concert room, could be forgotten."

[24] In addition to her solos—an aria from *I puritani,* "Let me wander not unseen" by Handel, and the old Scottish folk song "O Nanny, wilt thou gang with me"—Mrs. Bostwick collaborated with Pico-Vietti in duets from *Semiramide* and *La gazza ladra;* Pico sang Schubert's *Ave Maria;* Richard Hoffman played Thalberg's Grand Fantasy on *L'elisir d'amore* and Wallace's "Music Murmuring in the Trees"; and the string ensemble played movements from sextets by Bertini and Fesca.

Among the other American musicians giving concerts in 1851 were the recent violin prodigies Miss Marion Derwort, heard at Hope Chapel on November 21 under the patronage of the Ladies of Chelsea, and James W. Perkins, whose concert at the Tabernacle on December 1 was not noticed in the *Musical Times* (December 6, 1851, p. 77) because "no free tickets, no review."

Although 1851 yielded a full complement of prodigies, all previously known juvenile musical marvels paled beside little Master William Henry Marsh, the "Infant Drummer," who for a time created a sensation second only to Jenny Lind or the gift concerts. Less than three years old and not yet able to speak intelligibly, little Marsh wielded his diminutive drumsticks like an adult, having, according to the papers, displayed a miraculous perception of various rhythms since before he was a year old. The *Tribune* (February 5, 1851) classed him with such historic musical prodigies as Mozart, Boieldieu, and Mendelssohn, pointing out that the Infant Drummer's head was shaped exactly like Mendelssohn's. The writer solicitously hoped he would not be exploited.

But exploited he was, and by no lesser pillars of the music community than George Loder, who took the Infant Drummer under his musical wing, and William Hall, who assumed business management of the little wonder. Summoning all the trappings of musical legitimacy—a cast of reputable assisting artists that included Mrs. L. A. Jones, Mrs. Eastcott, Philip Mayer, Joseph Noll, Noll's "Jenny Lind" Orchestra, and the seasoned prodigy Master Will Saar (by now a mature eleven years old)—Loder presented the Infant Drummer in a Tripler Hall debut on February 22. To spur ticket sales, William Hall offered with every pair of tickets purchased at his music store[25] an engraved portrait of the tiny phenomenon—probably the likeness that adorned his concert advertisements showing little Marsh decked out in the miniature military uniform with outsized shako presented to him by the Lafayette Fusiliers, who had evidently adopted him as their mascot. In this uniform, promised the advertisements, the Infant Drummer would beat his little drum and march to the tunes of "The Jenny Lind Polka" and the Overture to *The Daughter of the Regiment.*

"Even the most experienced musicians—men who are *blasé* to these prodigies—were astonished at the performance," gushed *Figaro!* (March 29, 1851, p. 203), "and for once, criticism became enthusiasm." The city was agog. But the more conscientious *Tribune,* reported that the child, on being led onto the stage, was at first startled by the applause, but on hearing a familiar tune, the little automaton went into his drumming and marching routine, to the unrestrained delight of the audience. Returning for his third "solo," however, he abruptly "marched off the stage in the midst of the air and could not be made to return."

Before his next concert, on March 6 at Tripler Hall—shifted from the afternoon to the evening to accommodate the expected crowd—an anxious Loder published a plea to the prospective audience to "refrain from any demonstration of applause during the performance of this Infant Prodigy, as the loud and continued cheering made while performing at his last Concert caused him to play some childish freaks, which, although exceedingly amusing to the audience, were not set down in the program" (*Mirror,* February 27, 1851).

[25] For children under twelve, tickets were half price—12½ cents.

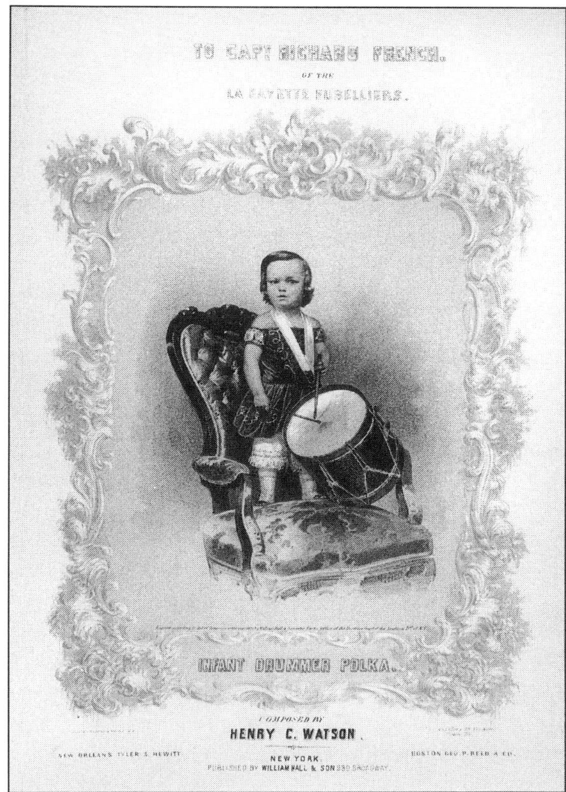

Music Division, The New York Public Library

The Infant Drummer, in civilian attire and in full military regalia.

GRAND CONCERT AT TRIPLER HALL.

FIRST APPEARANCE OF THE

Infant Drummer.

Not yet THREE YEARS old!

Assisted by

MRS. EASTCOTT,
MRS. LAURA JONES,
MR. PHILIP MAYER,
HERR NOLL,
MASTER WM. SAAR,
GEORGE LODER, and
THE JENNY LIND ORCHESTRA

This most attractive Concert will take place at TRIPLER HALL on the Evening of WASHINGTON'S BIRTHDAY, 22d inst.

Tickets 50 Cents—only a limited number will be issued, which, together with the programme, which is rich and varied, can be procured at the principal Hotels and Music Stores. Doors open at half past 6—Concert to commence at 8.

feb18 eod3dp

New-York Historical Society

Whether or not the Infant Drummer subsequently traveled to Boston or to the British World's Fair to play for Queen Victoria, as announced, in August he was again locally in evidence at Washington Hall (598 Broadway), appearing every evening (except Sundays) and on Saturday afternoons, drumming and marching to the accordion accompaniment of a Master Mallatratt (or Malletratt), age unknown. In October the little drummer progressed to Castle Garden, where he astounded out-of-town visitors to the great Industrial Fair of the American Institute (*Herald,* March 5, August 15; *Mirror,* October 2, 1851).[26]

By that time, however, Master Marsh had been superseded by an even younger, and reportedly an even more startling, Infant Drummer, who was also an Infant Whistler. From the age of nine months, little Benson A. English from Macon, Georgia, now two years and four months old, had been able, after a single hearing, to whistle a tune accurately and accompany himself on his tiny drum (*Mirror,* June 27; *Tribune,* July 9, 1851). He first displayed his astonishing gifts to New Yorkers at a Grand Instrumental and Vocal Concert at the Tabernacle on June 27, together with 1000 young ladies (allegedly representing the combined classes of the teachers Lewis A. Benjamin and

[26] Later in the year the Infant Drummer went on tour with the Alleghanians.♪

Ernst von Heeringen) who sang singly and in duets and choruses, and played single and double duets on as many as three pianos.[27]

New York suffered no dearth of monster juvenile spectaculars that year. Perhaps inspired by Bradbury and Nash, who continued to present their 1000 "appropriately dressed" little warblers in such varied fare as "The German Fatherland" and, most improbably, "Jenny Lind's Bird Song" (*Tribune,* March 1, 1851),[28] L. A. Benjamin brought out his juvenile oratorio "The American Revolution" at the Tabernacle on April 9 and 23, with a cast of 1200 little singers accompanied by an orchestra of 200 small boys.

Von Heeringen, at his concert at Tripler Hall on May 27, demonstrated his heavily promoted, revolutionary system of musical notation. His assisting artists were Adolph Zunn, "Solo Violin at the Opera of Bordeaux," and a Mr. G. F. K. Lawrence, pianist, both appearing in New York for the first time; also the local instrumentalists Noll, Drescher, Eichhorn, Rietzel, and Eltz, the popular vocalists Caroline Hiffert and Stephen Leach, an orchestra, and a chorus of 200 young ladies. On May 29, at Knickerbocker Hall, one Charles W. Syres repeated his comparatively modest "May Festival," previously presented on May 14, consisting of an opera, *The Altars of Nature,* performed by only "twelve misses." Those who had witnessed the "Coronation of the May Queen" at his earlier presentation had to agree that even if the production was lacking in numbers, it was nonetheless "the most magnificent spectacle ever witnessed [performed] by juveniles" (*Tribune,* May 27, 29, 1851).

Less spectacularly, a sixteen-year-old violinist, Master Theodore Thomas (1835–1905),[29] assisted at the otherwise unmemorable debut, at the Apollo on September 5, of a Madame Luigia Busatti, veteran *prima donna assoluta* of various European opera houses. The appearance, late in 1851, of another prodigious child, eight-year-old Adelina Patti (1843–1919) will be discussed later in this chapter.

Little Patti's teacher, the tireless Signorina Valentini, whose instructional techniques, as we know, leaned heavily on self-display, announced in February that she had taken the Tabernacle for a series of concerts featuring herself and her pupils. During the ensuing summer season, a lean time for teachers, the resourceful Valentini took over the management of a patriotic spectacle exhibited at Washington Hall, a "great National Moving Panorama" called "The Mirror of Our Country." Valentini embellished this presentation with nightly "Grand Concerts," featuring, with questionable congruity, her performances of "Italian Cavatinas and Jenny Lind's favorite Bird Song and Echo song." Tickets were twenty-five cents (*Tribune,* July 29, 1851).

[27] Benjamin conducted a music school on Allen Street, purportedly attended by some 400 students.

[28] "A thousand little seraphs singing in most perfect time and tune their happy songs, with their countenances beaming with gladness, is a sight which sends a thrill of joy though every heart. To all our readers we say go, see, and hear—and you will return with the heart softened and better prepared to meet the rough-and-tumble of human life" (*Evening Post,* March 25, 1851).

[29] In 1845, ten-year-old Theodore (*né* Christian Friedrich Theodor) Thomas, emigrated with his siblings to the United States, where their father hoped better to provide for his numerous family than his meager pay as *Stadtpfeiffer* (Town Musician) in the little town of Esens, Germany, had permitted. In New York, however, it became necessary for Theodore, as the oldest child, to pull his share of the load. Thus, from an early age Theodore Thomas worked at all sorts of musical odd jobs—playing his violin at weddings, dances, funerals, in theatre pits, and in the less reputable places of the city.

Instruction in singing "by the best Italian methods" was announced by Mr. and Mrs. Leati,♪ who claimed to have studied in Europe with the younger Garcia and Domenico Ronconi (1772–1839). The *Evening Post* (October 22, 1851) treated the Leatis as new arrivals, although they had been heard in New York—to tepid reactions—as long before as 1848, when they first arrived from Europe.

On April 8 the music class of the Spingler Institute gave a concert under the direction of Richard Storrs Willis, who, as we know, had taken over the music directorship of the Spingler and Rutgers Institutes while their regular director, George F. Root, was away studying in Europe (*Message Bird,* January 1, 1851). Graduates of the New York Institution for the Blind, calling themselves the "Memnonic Vocalists,"[30] gave a modest concert on December 11 at the Bleecker Building (Bleecker Street, between Morton and Commerce streets). On a more exalted level, on January 8 and 22 at the Lecture Room of the Tabernacle, the elder Lowell Mason,♪ referred to as "the father of church music in this country," presided over two sessions of sacred choir singing (called "rehearsals in psalmody"), at which choirs of several local and neighboring churches assisted (*Tribune,* January 14; *Evening Post,* January 22, 1851).[31]

Sacred concerts in 1851, apart from those given by the Harmonic Society, tended to be infrequent and of doubtful sanctity. Transparently circumventing the ban on Sunday shows, programs pretending to be sacred were often given in auditoriums devoted to mundane entertainment during the week and normally closed on the Sabbath. For instance, on Sunday evening, January 12, Frederick and Louisa Doctor, undaunted by their recent poor reviews, began a short-lived weekly series of "sacred" concerts at Fellows's Opera House, dedicated on weeknights to blackface minstrelsy. With the participation of the failed opera singer Giulietta Perrini, the violinists Leopold Meyer and little Emma Gandolfi, and with the former Astor Place chorus master Émile Millet as accompanist, they gave mixed programs. Tickets were twenty-five cents, the standard price for most sacred concerts.

On June 22 a series of so-called sacred concerts was launched at National Concert Hall, a new auditorium "decorated with frescoes" at 31 Canal Street "just a few steps from Broadway." Under the direction of the "Lind flutist" Julius Siede, a Signor Pagnoncelli [*sic*] made his debut playing a sensational new instrument never before heard in America, capable of imitating the human voice—in this instance a "beautiful soprano." The twenty-five-cent admission entitled the holder to a "refreshment ticket" for superior ice cream and other delicacies (*Herald,* June 21, 22, 1851).

For the benefit of the Dutch Reformed Church (107–113 Franklin Street), an ostensibly sacred concert was given on March 8 under the direction of the church's organist Pieter Hendrik van der Weyde, now sporting an "Honorary Membership in the Society of Musical Science, Rotterdam and Amsterdam." Performed by pupils of Elisa

[30] Apparently named after a colossal ancient statue of Memnon in Egypt, known as the "singing" Memnon because, upon being touched by the first rays of the rising sun, it emitted a high-pitched musical sound like the twanging of a harp string.

[31] In 1851, Lowell Mason resigned as Director of Music at the Winter Street Church in Boston and moved to New York, and in December of that year he sailed for Europe to collect new musical material for his forthcoming collections and to visit his two sons William and Henry, then studying in Germany (*Choral Advocate,* August, 1851, p. 41; *Musical Times,* December 20, 1851, p. 109).

Valentini and enhanced by the Alleghanians—the effort was so well liked that van der Weyde gave another, still less sacred, concert on April 29 at the same church, with substantially the same cast, except for the Alleghanians, and adding Kiefer (clarinet) and Eichhorn (cello), with whom he played a Mozart Trio "for piano, clarinet, and cello" (probably K. 498 in E-flat (1786), for piano, clarinet, and viola).

On December 13, in the thick of the Kossuth frenzy, Vanderweyde [*sic*] presented a concert at the Tabernacle for the benefit of the Hungarian refugees. "Neither pretentious in announcement, excellent in performance, nor large in result," wrote the *Musical Times* (December 29, 1851, p. 102), it nonetheless deserved to be noticed, if only "for the fact that Professor Vanderweyde bore all the expenses himself and handed to the Hungarian Committee the whole of the amount produced by the tickets." The performers were a Madame Florentine Szpaczek, the wife of Kossuth's physician, an amateur pianist who joined van der Weyde at Pirsson's double piano in "one or two concerted pieces," and a Madame Pettigrew, reportedly a "pupil of Meyerbeer (he must have been an awfully bad teacher, for she had neither voice nor style)." Also appearing at this inauspicious event were a Signor Antonio Paravalli, Messrs. Kiefer and Eichhorn, "a choir, which was very weak and very much out of tune," and Mrs. Laura A. Jones, who redeemed the occasion with her sweet rendition of "Liszt's beautiful song, 'The Exile,'" which was encored.[32]

Recalling the Bishop/Bochsa days, a Grand Sacred Concert "on a scale of magnificence never before attempted in this city" was given on April 27 at Tripler Hall, with the long-absent opera soprano Eufrasia Borghese and a mixed cast consisting of Mesdames Otto and Schlesinger, Fabiano Culzardo, a debutant basso from the Theatre Royal in Madrid, a Signor Debrogli (Dubreuil?), Stephen Leach, John Dunn, and others. Millet presided at the piano and Loder conducted a large orchestra.

And on December 21, to help stave off the bankruptcy that threatened St. Peter's in Barclay Street, George Loder conducted a sacred concert with the unequal assistance of the idolized opera star Angiolina Bosio, Mrs. Edward Loder (billed as the "principal cantatrice of the St. Peter's choir"), Maria Leach, Frederick Lyster, Starck (clarinetist), and W. A. King, who presided at the organ. For this good cause, tickets were fifty cents.

At Castle Garden, beginning May 4, Maretzek's Sunday evening concerts, utilizing the bulk of the opera orchestra, were sacred in name only. Nor did the competing concerts at the Apollo Rooms adhere to sacred repertory. At the first of these, on May 11, the virtually all-German cast included Wilhelm Müller, a recently arrived baritone from the Vienna Opera, the cellist Braun, the bassoonist Eltz, the oboist Hellrich, the flutist Sulzner, and Dodworth's Cornet Band. Admission was twenty-five cents.

In the field of sacred-music publishing the firm of Mason and Law, publishers of the *Choral Advocate,* brought out *Temple Melodies,* a collection of some 200 well-known tunes, adapted to "nearly Five Hundred favorite Hymns," selected by the *Advocate*'s first editor Darius E. Jones. *The Psalmista,* a collection of church music, compiled and edited by Thomas Hastings and William B. Bradbury and published by Mark H. Newman, aimed to lead away from the prevalent "sickly, unsteady [musical] appetite . . .

[32] To my knowledge, no Liszt song of that title has been found.

[and] lead onward toward sound improvement" (*Tribune,* April 16; *Musical Times,* September 6, 1851, p. 258). And Richard Storrs Willis, whose *Church Chorals and Choir Studies* was published by Clark, Austin, and Smith, was especially praised for his prose style, which in his fourteen-page introduction revealed "poetic touches" (*Message Bird,* February 1, 1851, p. 604).

Secular music publishing acquired an important new addition with the opening in June of a New York branch (at 257 Broadway) of Julius Schuberth's foreign publishing business, in existence in Germany for the past twenty-five years. On his arrival in the United States with Ole Bull in 1843, Schuberth (1804–1875) had been represented as Bull's secretary/manager, not his publisher, which in fact he was. Their relationship came to an acrimonious end when Schuberth had Bull arrested and put in jail for nonpayment of back wages.♪

In addition to publishing light music by local and foreign composers, Schuberth advertised imported editions of the more enduring classics: Beethoven's piano sonatas and songs by Schubert, Schumann, and Mendelssohn (*Musical Times,* November 22, 1851, unnumbered page).

In 1851, chamber music made a huge forward stride in New York with the introduction of Theodore Eisfeld's pathbreaking series of chamber-music *soirées,* directly evolved from Saroni's promotional chamber concerts of the year before. Eisfeld's string quartet consisted of the Philharmonic musicians Noll and Reyer (violins), Eisfeld (now playing the viola), and Eichhorn (cello). At their first concert, at Hope Chapel on February 15, they were assisted by Mrs. L. A. Jones, who performed songs by Mendelssohn and Schubert, with Eisfeld accompanying at the piano. The pianist Otto Dresel, with Noll and Eichhorn, played Mendelssohn's Trio No. 1, op. 49, in D minor (1839)—according to Saroni, "as no one else in the country can," albeit Dresel needed to gain "a little more calmness and expression before he [could] claim the title of 'performer of chamber music.'" Mrs. Jones "served her purpose" by giving variety to the proceedings, but it was in the string quartets—Haydn, op. 76, no. 4 (the "Sunrise"), and Beethoven in F major (otherwise unidentified)—that the group excelled (*Saroni's Musical Times,* February 22, 1851, p. 222). Both Saroni and the *Parker's* critic pronounced the Haydn to have been perfect. *Parker's* (February 15, 1851, p. 102) enthusiastically added: "We pity those who have not the taste to enjoy, or the opportunity to hear, classical music so well translated."

A larger, if not capacity, audience attended Eisfeld's second *soirée,* on March 15, again at Hope Chapel. This time the program offered an unspecified string quartet by Mozart in E-flat, most probably K. 428, no. 3 of the Haydn set (1783), one by Beethoven, op. 18, no. 4, in C minor (*c.* 1800), and, with William Scharfenberg at the piano, the Schumann Quintet, op. 44, in E-flat (1842), performed for the first time in New York. The *Parker's* critic (March 22, 1851, p. 164) thought Schumann's unfamiliar piece "so excessively elaborated as to be brought to a very respectable degree of dryness." He liked the third movement well enough, but in the others "the melodies were so incessantly repeated, worked over, and covered up, in every imaginable shape and form of harmonization, that, to us, all the beauty seemed evaporated and nothing but dry art left." It exposed Schumann's shortcomings to have placed him between Mozart and Beethoven.

But Richard Storrs Willis, steeped as he was in contemporary German culture, thought the Schumann Quintet the high point of the concert: "This is one of the most remarkable productions of one of the most remarkable composers of our age," he perceptively wrote. "It is characterized by loftiness of conception, richness of effect—in short, everything that gives a truly classical stamp to a composition." Scharfenberg, through whose good offices the work had been presented, had "the rare artistic merit of being able to sink his own individuality, when the occasion demanded it, for the sake of the general musical effect, and consequently there is an unusual and singularly beautiful *blending* of tone whenever his skillful hand is engaged in a concerted piece." Willis regretted that limited time did not permit the instruments to be placed behind the piano, as they should have been (!).

He was less satisfied, however, with the Mozart quartet, whose Minuetto was played at a mad pace more suited to a *scherzo*. He advised Eisfeld to pay more attention to the *values* of notes and to a steady and even tempo because his "*accelerando*s and *ritardando*s found little favor with his listeners." Philip Mayer, who sang Schubert's song "The Wanderer" (1816) in his native German, was treated as well to hairsplitting instructions on the correct stress to be given to each syllable of each word (*Albion,* March 29, p. 152, reprinted in *Journal of the Fine Arts,* April 1, 1851, p. 19).

Eisfeld's third and final *soirée* of the series, at the Apollo on April 5 (the Alleghanians having by now preempted Hope Chapel), was reviewed in *Saroni's Musical Times* (April 12, 1851, p. 31) by an obliging friend, in Saroni's apparent absence. The quartets of the evening were Haydn and Mozart, the Mozart in G major. Philip Mayer, who sang an air from Mendelssohn's *St. Paul,* "made no impression" with it, but his duet with the tenor J. B. Beutler—a barcarole by the German composer Friedrich Wilhelm Kücken (1810–1882)—was better performed, and it "achieved a well-merited encore." Henry C. Timm, who had been scheduled to take part in a quintet by Spohr, was ill, and Scharfenberg, replacing him, played instead Mendelssohn's *Rondo brillant,* accompanied by the quartet, and (too slowly) an unnamed set of piano variations by Beethoven.

So cordially had Eisfeld's chamber music concerts been received that on November 29 he began a second series, this time of six *soirées,* at the Apollo Rooms. "Whoever wishes to go to bed tonight a better man will go to the Apollo and be introduced by Mr. Eisfeld into the society of Mozart, Beethoven, Spohr, and Haydn," exuberantly wrote the chamber-music-loving critic of *Parker's Journal* (November 29, 1851, p. 895, a misprint for 595). "If his sleep be not refreshing after such intercourse," he continued, "if he do not wake up in the morning with a better heart and clearer mind than usual, it will be because he stopped somewhere between the Apollo and his bedchamber."

Of the two string quartets played at this well-attended concert—Haydn, op. 77 in G major, and Beethoven, op. 18 in B-flat—the *Parker's* writer was forced to admit (December 6, 1851, p. 606) that he preferred the Haydn: "One likes venison, the other roast beef," he explained. But the ensemble playing was superb throughout, although he wished Reyer's violin had a less harsh tone. Timm joined the group for his postponed performance of Spohr's Quintet in C minor, op. 53, and a veritable piano concerto it was. And the way Timm played it! It was doubtful that another living pianist could equal his performance. Diving into a whirlpool of editorial plurals and purple prose, the critic continued: "We esteem it one of the great privileges of our positions as journalists to pay a passing tribute to the worth of so well-tried a favorite.

"Oh! most excellent of Germans! and most accomplished of pianists! how has thy steady and unobtrusive merit outlived the many magnificent humbugs who have flared athwart the musical horizons in the gory capitals of perambulating bill-posters, or in the golden paragraphs of the Hessians of the press, whose praise is bought by the yard. We think we see thee now, unlike some others who rush upon the instrument with fists and elbows, as though it were a wild beast to be beaten into submission. Thou, with timid, almost shy, demeanor, approachest the piano like a distrustful lover stealing up to a wayward mistress, and coaxest it into perfect submission to thy will. Long life to thee, thou man of gentle heart and true artist's soul. May thy fingers never forget their cunning whilst we have ears to listen—or the inspirations of genius have need of an interpreter."

During the intermissions the tenor Beutler sang Beethoven's "Adelaide" and an anonymously composed *Tyrolienne*. His "Adelaide," reported the *Musical Times* (December 6, 1851, p. 70), "was no more like Beethoven's than was Ole Bull's *Niagara* like the mighty cataract itself." But Eisfeld deserved the greatest success, for he was "doing much for the progress of musical taste."

Eisfeld's last *soirée* of the year, again assisted by Philip Mayer, took place on December 27 at the Apollo. "The existence of such a musical entertainment in our midst," exulted the *Musical Times* (January 3, 1852, p. 134), "and the numerous attendance thereat, are among the most unerring and gratifying proofs of a correct and growing musical taste." Chamber music, the critic pointed out, required a far higher degree of musical discrimination than did opera, enjoyable as that might be to the musically uninformed.

Unleashing floods of musical terminology, the critic lauded the group's performance of a Mozart quartet in D minor, probably K. 421, Haydn set, no. 2 (1783), especially the *pianos* and *tempos*, although the *fortes*, *crescendos*, *diminuendos*, and *sforzandos*, too, were admirable. It was a mistake of Eisfeld, however, to have placed Mendelssohn's *Quartette concertante,* a work "deficient" in melody, after Mozart and Beethoven's "grand *Rodolph* ["Archduke"] Trio" in B-flat, op. 97 (1811), wonderfully played, with Scharfenberg at the piano. "Mozart alone can come after Beethoven, and Beethoven alone can bear to follow Mozart."

Philip Mayer had given chaste and tasteful performances of two unidentified songs, but Noll was chided for his total lack of pathos in his too-correct rendering of eight bars of melting melody in the Andante of the Mozart quartet, occurring a few bars after the second double bar, "where the harmony progresses from C minor to A-flat major." And too, in the Beethoven trio, although Scharfenberg accurately observed the *pianos* and *fortes*, and distinctly "enunciated" all the runs and passages, the total effect was unsatisfactory. Scharfenberg was a better interpreter of Mozart than of Beethoven, and—"Must we say it, we missed the crisp, sharp touch of Mr. Timm." And although the audience demanded a repetition of the *Canzonette* of the Mendelssohn quartet, the movement, "although very beautiful, smacks terribly of the similar movement in the *Midsummer Night's Dream.*"

Evicting Eisfeld from Hope Chapel, the Alleghanians, back from their tour, opened there on March 31, then dug in for a long and successful run of nightly performances (except Sundays). Their popular, true-blue American repertory consisted of such items as "Give, oh! give me back my Mountain Home," "Meet me by Moonlight," "The Old-fashioned Bible," "The Farmer's Elegy," "Strike the Harp Gently," "Where shall the Soul find Rest?" "My Mary Dear" (sung by the soprano Miss Miriam G. Goodenow, the sole female member of the group),[33] and "Oh! I am a merry sailor lad" (*Tribune,* April 18, 1851).

The Alleghanians even outlasted the Hutchinsons, who had followed closely on their heels with a series of "Concerts for the People," beginning on April 8 at the Tabernacle. The group now consisted of the six Hutchinson brothers—Judson, John, Asa, Caleb, Joshua, and Jesse. Abby, who in the meantime had married, wanted it known, according to the *Message Bird* (April 1, 1851, p. 19), that she was no longer professionally associated with the Family.

During this season, beyond mere musical entertainment, the Hutchinsons interspersed their "new songs and old favorites" with "Anecdotes, Declamations, General Remarks upon Health, Diet, Causes of Insanity, Its Cure, etc. etc.[34] The whole to conclude with the New Song entitled 'The Good Time coming right along.' Prices within the reach of all, and as they should be, viz., Men, 25 cents, Women, 12½ cents only (in accordance with their relative wages)" (*Herald,* April 2, 1851). Bereft of Abby, the Hutchinson brothers nonetheless maintained their staunch support of women's rights. On April 18, surrendering the field to the Alleghanians, they gave a farewell concert at the Tabernacle; they appeared the following evening at the Eleventh Presbyterian Church (Fourth Street and Avenue C), then departed.

On April 29, Ossian Dodge—the flamboyant Boston music dealer, former temperance singer, and purchaser of the first Jenny Lind ticket in Boston for $625—"yielded to the urgent solicitations [of] his editorial friends to give one of his chaste, unique, and fashionable entertainments in this city."[35] On his way to London to attend the World's Fair, Dodge was stopping off to perform at the "magnificent and world-renowned Tripler Hall." Although some 2500 tickets had been reserved for "delegations from Portland, Me., Portsmouth, N.H., Boston and Lowell, Mass., and Providence, R.I.," some fifty-cent tickets were still available at the usual music stores and at the hat store of Dodge's brother under the skin, John N. Genin, the purchaser of the first Jenny Lind ticket in New York, albeit for a paltry $225.

Between the first and tenth of October an American ballad singer named Turner ill-advisedly gave a series of five solo concerts at Tripler Hall. Assisted only by James

[33] Miss Goodenow's fellow-Alleghanians were Richard Dunning tenor, M. Boulard bass, and W. H. Oakley, who sang alto.

[34] Their "remarks" on insanity were unfortunately based on first-hand knowledge. As recently as January 1 the *Message Bird* had reported (p. 571): "We regret to learn that Judson Hutchinson has not yet recovered from his derangement, and that his brother Jesse partially shares in the unfortunate hallucination which, in a measure, has broken up this interesting family. Of the remaining members, Asa and John are still singing through New England, and Abby is residing with her husband in this city."

[35] Dodge's "chaste and fashionable" entertainments consisted partly of imitations of wind instruments and of "cattle, sheep, birds, and guinea hens" (*Spirit,* April 26, 1851, p. 120).

Maeder at the piano for the first four events, and with the addition of Dodworth's Band at the fifth, these ballad concerts, as Turner called them, presented great quantities of popular lighter fare ranging from such hallowed chestnuts as Russell's "The Old Arm Chair" and Dempster's "The Grave of Napoleon" to airs from Balfe's opera *The Maid of Honor* (London 1847) and William Vincent Wallace's *Maritana* (*Mirror,* October 1, 3, 6, 8, 10, 1851). Apparently the experiment was a failure, for on October 21 a group of compassionate compatriots and second-string performers organized a so-called "Grand Complimentary Musical and Dramatic Festival" at Niblo's Garden to help compensate Turner for some of his losses (*Saroni's Musical Times,* October 25, 1851, p. 65).

To complete the diversity of native musical talent heard in 1851, the Boston-born opera soprano Elise (*née* Eliza) Biscaccianti,♪ last heard in New York in 1849, returned in October after a prolonged stay in England, where she had reportedly reaped triumphs, "side-by-side with the greatest artists—Sontag, Grisi, Cruvelli, Alboni, etc." (*Home Journal,* November 9, 1851). In contrast to its former hostility—not least because Biscaccianti was an American attempting to be a *prima donna*—the New York press now seemed to have reversed its attitude: a general agreement to praise Biscaccianti for that very reason suddenly seems to have prevailed among the critical fraternity.

"She will be most welcome," announced the *Mirror* (October 17, 1851), "for among all these Swedish Nightingales, Irish Swans [a reference to Catherine Hayes, see below], Italian and French *rossignols,* English larks, and Scotch mavises, it is delightful to think that there is at least one American mocking-bird who need not be afraid to open her mouth with the best of them." (Biscaccianti, in fact, came to be known as the "American Thrush.")[36]

To woo the problematical gentlemen of the press, on October 28, just before her return concert at Tripler Hall, Madame Biscaccianti invited them to a *recherché soirée musicale* at the Astor House. As the chatty *Home Journal* (November 8, 1851) reported the occasion: "It was a formidable audience—the personification of the entire press of New York. Every eye gleamed criticism, and every hand which applauded had a pen to wield." After presenting a sampling of her forthcoming program,[37] "the amiable hostess led her audience, *nothing loath,* into a room where three supper tables invited to more substantial food than that on which the ears only had hitherto been feasting. The champagne corks flew in every direction."[38] Biscaccianti's success was assured,

[36] According with the current practice of bestowing ornithological nicknames upon singers, Emma Bostwick was dubbed "our native Bobolink." And later, after her arrival, the "dancer" Lola Montez was facetiously called "the Duck of Bavaria."

[37] Biscaccianti's program included a cavatina from *Linda di Chamounix,* an aria from *Beatrice di Tenda,* the rondo *Ah! non giunge* from *La sonnambula,* and "The Skylark," an English song by J. L. Hatton, with flute obbligato played by Felice Eben.

[38] The evening wound up with a "beautiful serenade . . . by Dodworth's celebrated Brass Band . . . first outside and then inside the Astor House. . . . Their concluding piece, *Giorno d'orrore* [played by Harvey and Allen Dodworth], was indeed almost a perfect performance. Mr. Harvey Dodworth played with remarkable delicacy, brilliancy, and feeling. The whole serenade was worthy the high reputation of the band and of its fair subject, who listened to the last, and thanked the gentlemen gratefully and gracefully for the honor done her" (*Musical Times,* November 1, 1851, p. 63).

wrote this reporter, not only because she deserved it, but because "it ought also to be a subject of national pride, and all Americans ought to show that (unlike the English, who exclusively patronize foreign talent) they are ready and happy to recognize and applaud a talent which belongs to their soil."

Parker's Journal (November 1, 1851, p. 546) echoed these patriotic sentiments. Although it was unfair to render an opinion on Biscaccianti's singing "in a room better suited to eating than to music," the writer was prepared to regard her with the greatest indulgence: "We have gilded, and very handsomely, too, the wings of Swedish Nightingales, Irish Swans, and English Larks . . . all sorts of foreign birds of passage [have] feathered their nests very nicely out of our downy ones. Now we have a native-born songster of undoubted talent, closely allied by relationship to a family who for generations have been engaged in the cause of music, and who were among the first to aid and extend its cultivation in our own city[39]—and it would be strange, indeed, if, after the patronage liberally bestowed upon foreign merit, we should be found cold or lukewarm to the claims of a fellow countrywoman whose accident of birth is the least of her titles to the good will of the American public."

Most startling was the glowing review of Biscaccianti's concert in the *Courier and Enquirer* (November 4, 1851), presumably by Richard Grant White, her most ruthless tormenter in the past.♪ Either Biscaccianti or White had undergone a severe metamorphosis since 1849, for instead of the critic's former cruel ridicule, even of her personal appearance, he now wrote: "When she stepped upon the stage, saffron-robed and trailing clouds of ambrosial curls upon her shoulders, her dark eyes gleaming with excitement, she made a decided impression upon the audience, and the hearty greeting given her was both a welcome and a tribute." And hardly had she begun to sing when it became obvious to all that she had greatly profited by study or observation while in Europe. She had tamed, for the most part, her former tendency to exaggerate and had become a restrained and tasteful performer, and while there was no fundamental change in her voice, it now appeared to far greater advantage, by reason of her "vastly improved use of it." The critic dwelt on the many felicities of Biscaccianti's performances, passing over "the little she did ill for the sake of the much she did well" and gladly welcomed an American *prima donna* "who has other and greater claim upon us than her American birth."

Although it was hoped that Biscaccianti would give a second concert before going to Boston, where her townspeople eagerly awaited her return (*Mirror,* November 2, 1851), she was not heard again in New York until November 29, when she appeared, together with several colleagues, at a concert for the joint benefit of the St. George's and the British Emigrant Protective societies at Tripler Hall.[40] The *Musical Times* (De-

[39] Biscaccianti's illustrious maternal grandfather James Hewitt,♪ was a musical early settler who had emigrated from England in 1792; her mother, Sophia Hewitt Ostinelli,♪ was an eminent pianist and organist in Boston; her father, Louis Ostinelli,♪ was a violinist of the first rank in that city; her uncle John Hill Hewitt was a prominent composer and journalist currently residing in Baltimore; and another uncle James Lang Hewitt was an important music publisher in New York. There were yet other musically gifted Hewitts, then and later.

[40] Among the Britishers appearing at this event were the English/French comic opera star Anna Thillon, currently drawing crowds at Niblo's Garden, her co-star the actor/singer James Hudson, Madame Wallace-Bouchelle. and the concertina virtuoso "Professor" Alfred Sedgwick. The opera

cember 6, 1851, p. 70) singled out her splendid rendition on that occasion of "the almost worn out ballad of 'Home, Sweet Home,' which seemed to revive under the influence of Biscaccianti's charming voice and [to acquire] a renewed existence of life and beauty."

This appears to have been Biscaccianti's final farewell to New York. Lured, like many musicians and stage folk, by the dazzling reports of untold treasure awaiting all kinds of performers in gold-crazed, entertainment-hungry San Francisco,[41] Madame Biscaccianti abruptly departed, "under the pilotage of New York's favorite conductor, Mr. George Loder," reported the *Musical Times* (January 24, 1852, p. 173), adding that she would probably be "the first of our celebrities [to] visit the modern Ophir." She was.

Loder would be missed, continued the *Musical Times:* "There are others here of equal skill, but Mr. Loder has been so identified with music and every movement tending to advance it in years past that he has almost become a necessary of New York musical life. But if he will go, may success attend him." And go he did, like Biscaccianti, never to return.[42]

Eliza Biscaccianti's return to New York had been unpropitiously timed. National pride notwithstanding, such public interest as she might have aroused was eclipsed by a greater, more titillating excitement. It had been disclosed that the massively ballyhooed Irish soprano Catherine Hayes (1825–1861), currently engaged in a neo-Lindian concert marathon at Tripler Hall, had all along been shockingly exploited by her American managers. A group of rapacious, would-be Barnums,[43] they had devised an infamous scheme, by mimicking the Master's inspired techniques, to make a Jenny Lind killing at the expense of a facsimile Jenny Lind. Choosing Catherine Hayes, an artist of high merit and impeccable reputation, as their dupe, they had dispatched an emissary to England to engage, or rather, to sublease, the "Swan of Erin," as she was inevitably nicknamed, from her English managers, Cramer and Beale (themselves no paragons of honesty, as it turned out).

For months before Hayes arrived from England the daily and periodical New York press had fairly overflowed with rose-colored, Swan-of-Erin puffery—flowery

---

world was represented by Badiali and Bettini, and the concert world by Miska Hauser, Mrs. Bostwick, and the recently arrived Austrian pianist Alfred Jaëll; George Loder conducted.

[41] "There can be no doubt," stated the *Herald* (January 25, 1852), "that there is a fine field [in California] for singers and other artists. The applications for artists from managers in California to managers . . . here are numerous."

[42] Information on the subsequent careers of Biscaccianti and Loder, and of many other familiar musicians who braved the arduous trip to the land of gold, is found in the copious San Francisco press of the period and in the twentieth-century WPA Project *History of Music in San Francisco,* volumes I, IV, and VII, *passim.* An entry on Biscaccianti, based on the WPA *History,* is found in the *Enciclopedia dello spettacolo* (Rome 1954, vol. 2, p. 544); also see my article "Henry Meiggs, Maverick Entrepreneur," *19th Century Music,* Summer 1985, pp. 27–41.

[43] "The very call-boys in the theatres were ambitious of becoming Barnums," wrote Maretzek (*Crotchets,* p. 184). "Not a hungry teacher of the piano, nor a theatrical check-taker, but had a longing to try his hand at the great game of sowing nothing and reaping dollars. . . . Many really talented artists were induced, by the stories told them by embryo speculators of this stamp, to visit America, and necessarily fell into the trap laid for their attractions."

biographies, glowing critiques, flattering likenesses, apocryphal anecdotes. Whether or not Henry C. Watson was the architect of this colossal buildup, he was unmistakably the author, after Hayes's arrival, of a succession of hard-sell promotional articles (occasionally initialed), followed (most unsuitably) by rapturous reviews of her concerts, usually appearing in *Saroni's Musical Times* and the *Mirror.*

Thus, on September 12, the day before Hayes's expected arrival, Watson (in the *Mirror*) predicted that her presence would "create a considerable sensation, for thousands of her countrymen—and indeed of all classes—are eager to welcome one so good and so famous. We hear that salutes will be fired at various points of the Bay, and bands of music will greet her as she passes the several islands, to say nothing of a grand serenade from the musical societies on the night of her arrival."

When, due to bad weather Hayes's ship arrived a day late (September 14)—unfortunately a rainy Sunday—and the predicted "thousands" had failed to greet her at the pier, Watson depicted her rather dismal dockside reception as a triumph of triumphs, climaxed by "three times three [cheers] shouted from good, sturdy [indubitably Hibernian] lungs"[44] (*Saroni's Musical Times,* September 20, 1851, pp. 278–79).

Because Hayes had arrived on the Sabbath the welcoming serenade planned by the Musical Fund Society was postponed until the following evening, purportedly at the pious Swan's request. Indeed, in matters of virtue and piety, as in all else, the Swan's public persona was closely patterned after the Nightingale's. In Maretzek's opinion, Hayes's unimaginative managers had "most indiscreetly followed with [too] scrupulous exactitude" in Barnum's footsteps, unaware that the "Prince of Humbugs" had worn out the virtues of virtue: "One of their greatest errors was their attempt to [proclaim] the 'holy immaculacy' of their *prima donna.*" What had worked for Jenny Lind had worked because of its "rich and unexampled novelty," but by now the public had become sated with purity—a homely commodity which, after all, was to be expected in "almost every private family." Besides, people had begun to separate vocal excellence from virtue, to recognize that "private goodness is not a quality that demands adulation," that it was rather nothing more than a "mere duty" (*Crotchets,* pp. 185–86).

The mob scene that had failed to materialize at the pier was, however, satisfactorily enacted outside the Astor House at serenade time the following evening. Closely following the model of the now-historic Lind serenade, the members of the Musical Fund Society, again accompanied by red-shirted firemen bearing torches, took their places beneath Hayes's window (after a certain amount of confusion over which window it was) and delivered themselves of a stirring program of national airs—American tunes and Irish folk tunes, the latter, according to Watson, "exceedingly cleverly arranged" by George Loder (who was then still present). In obedience to the clamorous multitude of either 5000 *(Evening Post)* or 10,000 *(Spirit of the Times),* Catherine Hayes appeared at her window,[45] flanked by her assisting artists—according to Maretzek a

[44]The local Irish constituency was evidently on call for every occasion requiring a vociferous demonstration for Hayes.

[45]The newspapers differed over Hayes's qualifications to be called a Beauty, but Watson ecstatically described her as "the very personification of all that is graceful and elegant in woman: her eyes [were] dark blue, her teeth dazzling white, her finely formed lips slightly parted as though always anxious to speak some kind thing; her hair neither golden nor auburn, but of that changeful color which sparkles in the folds. Her face is highly expressive . . . of kindness—goodness of heart" (*Saroni's Musical Times,* September 20, 1851, p. 279).

Music Division, The New York Public Library

Catherine Hayes, the "Swan of Erin."

New-York Historical Society

The first appearance of Catherine Hayes at Tripler Hall

lackluster crew—consisting of Herr Joseph Mengis, a failed tenor-turned-baritone of Swiss origin; Augustus Braham, John Braham's son, a minor tenor trading on his illustrious "patronymic," and Louis Lavenu (1818–1859), a London musician-*cum*-music publisher-*cum*-impresario "with small claims [as a conductor] for anything save quadrille-music." Perhaps for this reason, it was announced that Lavenu would share conducting duties with George Loder at the Hayes concerts. Also very much in evidence was Charles H. Wardwell, an "inexperienced and inoffensive" small-time entrepreneur, the ostensibly innocent front-man for the unseen schemers (*Crotchets,* p. 187).[46]

Faithful to the Lind scenario, the gentlemen of the press were invited to the dress rehearsal for Hayes's debut, but only Watson seems to have reviewed it. Although it was admittedly inappropriate to render a judgment prior to an official debut (to take place that very evening), Watson was nonetheless impelled to laud her magnificent voice and her capacity for great "passion and feeling." "If it is art," he wrote, executing a pirouette on his perpetual *Leitmotiv,* "it is the perfection of art; if it is nature, it is the very essence of musical inspiration" (*Mirror,* September 23, 1851).

After the concert Watson reported that Tripler Hall had been filled to overflowing, with every seat taken and 1000 standing-room tickets sold, and with further thousands of dollars refused at the door for lack of space. The other papers noted, however, that the seats were mostly filled with Hayes's noisy compatriots, apparently making their own concert debut, courtesy of the management.

The Swan was greeted with a great shout—according to Watson, a series of great shouts—that not only "reverberated like thunder through the building and made the windows fairly tremble . . . but was caught up by the thousands outside, who thronged Mercer Street in the hope of catching some stray notes of the Swan of Erin" (more Lind scenario).

Although Hayes (like Lind) seemed greatly agitated at the beginning of her first aria, *Ah, mon fils* from Meyerbeer's *Le Prophète,* she soon regained her composure and finished "gloriously." Watson had never been "so moved by any single song in our lives, and the audience seemed affected in like manner, for it was demanded again by one of those outbursts of imperative approbation which admits of no denial."[47]

But Hayes exceeded excellence in her Irish ballads. In Thomas Moore's "The Harp that once thro' Tara's halls" and Frederick Nicholls Crouch's "Kathleen Mavourneen" she seemed to "revel with a perfect gush of natural and strong emotion." If mere words were adequate to express Watson's own emotions they would "burn into the paper. Two-thirds of the house were weeping, and the rest were wordless under the spell of the enchantress. At the conclusion of each [ballad] a sort of wild hurrah arose from the whole body of the audience,[48] waving of hats and handkerchiefs attested the triumph, and a dense shower of bouquets was the graceful reward." And, Watson tri-

[46] Wardwell was a piano dealer and a kind of general factotum in the New York music community; it was he who had been dispatched to England to engage Catherine Hayes.

[47] In this aria, wrote Watson in *Saroni's Musical Times* (September 20, 1851, p. 278), Hayes surpassed Viardot, Alboni, and even Lind.

[48] The sound was alternately characterized by the eloquent *Parker's* critic as a "hurroop" and an "*ululatio hiberniensis.*" By any name, however, it threatened "the utter destruction of our auriculars" (*Parker's,* November 8, 1851, p. 558).

umphantly concluded: "She had art enough for the critic and nature [enough] for the audience" (*Mirror,* September 24, 1851).

Richard Storrs Willis found her voice, despite its extensive range, to be "rather *pyramidal,* with a broad base at the bottom and tapering toward the top." She was a moving singer, rather than a dramatic or an exciting one, but ballad singing was definitely not her forte. Willis then embarked on a learned treatise on ballad singing, an art form, he maintained, that, unlike opera, required the music always to be subordinated to the words. Apparently he found Hayes's English diction to be unsatisfactory, declaring that he had enjoyed her performances of her Irish songs, "Savourneen Deelish" and "The Harp that once thro' Tara's halls," musically, but not textually.[49]

Not to be outdone, *Parker's,* in a parallel essay, contended that the music was negligible in English, Irish, and Scottish ballads; they were essentially recitations delivered over a background of repetitive music that would become tiresome were it not for the "*eloquent* declamation of the words." And since the emphasis "must be rhetorical and not musical . . . all ornaments, fioriture, chromatic scales, and the like . . . are sadly out of place in a ballad. Thus: "The long trill with which Miss Hayes closed 'Savourneen Deelish' [was] as improperly introduced, and as utterly at variance with the true character of the piece as it would be in the closing phrase of a *German Hymn.*"

But despite scattered cavils and several pro-or-con comparisons with Lind, the critics generally agreed—especially after Hayes was heard in Handel's *Messiah* at her fifth concert, on October 2, assisted by the Harmonic Society and members of the Philharmonic—that she was truly a splendid artist. Indeed, the *Parker's* critic (October 11, 1851, p. 513), much as he had disapproved of the ornaments and curlicues with which she had strewn her folk ballads, heretically proclaimed her the greatest oratorio singer he had ever heard, with few, if any, equals in the world, Lind included.[50]

With the exception of Bertucca-Maretzek, who in her harp-playing persona regularly assisted at the Hayes concerts, the supporting cast fared less well in the press. At first politely, even cordially, received by the critics, by the second concert, on September 25 (Hayes maintained a killing, Lindish schedule of three concerts a week), Mengis, Braham, and Lavenu had outlived their welcome. It was unfair, observed the *Mirror* on September 29, to expect Catherine Hayes to carry the burden of her strenuous concert schedule with only Bertucca-Maretzek to furnish adequate assistance. Of what value were such "hardly mediocre achievements as Herr Mengis's yodelings, Mr. Braham's Balfe-isms, and their joint attempts to give effect to the operatic *morceaux* which such singers as Salvi and Belletti used so exquisitely to execute at the concerts of Jenny Lind?"

In fact, Hayes's managers had already struck a deal with Maretzek for some of his

[49] Willis disapproved, too, of the alternating conductorships of Lavenu and Loder, causing, as they did, a breakdown in orchestra discipline. During the performance, when the violinists were not actually playing they were engaged in animated conversation; and an irrepressible flutist, in full view of the audience, had removed a paper cone from one of the bouquets strewn upon the stage and placed it on the head of a fellow flutist.

[50] "In truth, this magnificent music never, to our ears, found such an interpreter, and if she possesses no other claim upon the music-loving public than her wonderful mastery . . . as exhibited by her rendering of the music of the *Messiah,* that alone would entitle her to take rank among the foremost singers of the day" (*Parker's,* October 11, 1851, p. 513).

opera stars to assist at her concerts, in the hope of stimulating the sagging box office:[51] with tickets at $2 for reserved seats and $1 for chance seating, and with the discontinuance of their non-paying Irish claque, the attendance had noticeably shrunk. Thus, it came about that Virginia Whiting and Domenico Lorini were added to the Hayes cast on September 29, Marini on October 7 (the seventh concert), and Badiali on September 9. For providing these services, Maretzek was to receive $5000 a month, from which sum he would remunerate his artists and pay their traveling expenses to Boston, where they accompanied Hayes after her ninth Tripler Hall concert, on October 11.[52]

Returning to New York at the beginning of November, Hayes was unwisely scheduled for three consecutive evenings at Tripler Hall, November 4, 5, and 6, the second concert to be a farewell benefit for the famed Irish "Apostle of Temperance," Father Theobald Mathew, who was returning home after two years of proselytizing in the United States. It was the egregious failure of this event that triggered the disclosures which sent the city into an excitement that lasted until a bigger and better excitement took over in early December with Kossuth's arrival (to say nothing of the subsidiary, yet potent, excitement over the simultaneous arrival of Lola Montez).

The Father Mathew fiasco, reported the *Herald* (November 4, 1851), had been entirely due to mismanagement on the part of the committee entrusted with the benefit arrangements. Despite considerable preliminary "lip-interest," only about two thousand dollars had been taken in at the box office, instead of the expected five or six thousand. Later, the *Herald* (December 7, 1851) named names, openly accusing the music critics Charles Burkhardt♪ and James Otis, the publishers Samuel Jollie and James Melksham Bourne, and, least credibly, George Loder, of "nicely feathering their nests" while offering Father Mathew the insulting pittance of $168.50.[53] This, to his credit, he indignantly refused.

In the meantime, Maretzek, beset by his usual financial and entrepreneurial woes, and preoccupied with the opening on November 3 of his Astor Place season, had brought suit against Wardwell and, it was rumored, against Catherine Hayes as well, for non-payment of the $5000 owed him—some $3800 of which he had disbursed in advance, borrowing on the collateral of his contract. On presenting his bill, he writes, he was "paid with abuse" and accused of having maliciously intrigued, for his own profit, to undermine Hayes's reputation in this country.[54]

Suddenly the city was ablaze in a firestorm of scandalous revelations, refutations,

[51] Notwithstanding his later condemnation of Hayes's managers and their tactics, it is not unlikely that Maretzek might all along have been secretly connected with the Hayes enterprise, as witness Bertucca-Maretzek's early participation in the Hayes concerts (see *Mirror,* September 19, 1851).

[52] The *Choral Advocate* for December (p. 103) reported that Catherine Hayes had been less successful than expected in Boston, not surprising, considering the outrageous puffery from the penny-a-liners, which had excited "unwarranted expectations." Doubtless, Hayes was "an excellent singer, especially in ballads, but we have had a number of others among us who are quite her equals, and one, at least, greatly her superior."

[53] Loder had reportedly extorted an exorbitant $195 for the services of the orchestra; Tripler Hall, briefly under Wardwell's so-called management, had cost $150. Outrageous!

[54] Maretzek denies having sued Hayes, explaining that, under the circumstances, it would have been foolhardy to have "attempted to injure her chance of filling her [managers'] treasury." The affair dragged on: "After years of lawsuits and their constant costs," Maretzek dolefully relates, he at last received a settlement "in full" of $600 (*Crotchets,* p. 188).

accusations, counter-accusations, denials, lawsuits, and counter-lawsuits. Sued by Maretzek, Wardwell sued a sheriff who, by order of Maretzek's lawyer, had attempted to impound the box-office receipts for Hayes's November 9 concert. Hayes, by now aware of having been mercilessly gulled, sued her "swindling" English managers Cramer and Beale, as did Wardwell, who claimed they had duped him, too. And on and on.

Chief among the many writers of self-exonerating letters to the press was Dr. John Joy, the Cramer and Beale's representative who had accompanied the Hayes company to the United States and who had reportedly been cutting a dashing figure in the gaudier nocturnal haunts of Broadway. In what the *Herald* sardonically termed a "real philosophical letter," Dr. Joy coolly denied accusations that he had squandered the Hayes box-office receipts on oysters and champagne for the "midnight critics" (or "oyster-house critics," as the *Herald* felicitously dubbed the hungrier members of the journalistic fraternity).[55] Dr. Joy's letter was "as full of generalities as Aristotle's, and as plentifully sprinkled with inductions as Bacon," wrote the *Herald,* but for all his fancy grammar, Joy was woefully shy on figures: "How much did it cost Dr. Joy to manage all the newspapers of New York?" disingenuously asked the *Herald,* reveling in the scandal. Estimating that Hayes had so far given about twenty-five concerts in the United States, netting her managers and the various free-drink cadgers at the oyster houses about $30,000, she had received no more than $4000 for her labors. Where had the money gone? To hungry wolves on both sides of the Atlantic: "Catherine Hayes has been made the victim of musical jobbers and managing speculators. . . . Under a series of contracts, lettings, and sub-lettings, sales and resales, Catherine Hayes has been the victim of troops of organized speculators in musical popularity almost without a parallel in the musical affairs of this continent" (*Herald,* November 13, November 16, 1851).

Now, in a supreme act of self-assertion, Hayes freed herself of all her managers and their hangers-on, retaining (temporarily) only the notoriously inept Wardwell, who somehow had managed to emerge from the fray comparatively unsullied. Taking over the reins, Hayes announced three final concerts in New York, assisted by her original company, at Metropolitan (formerly Tripler) Hall, for December 23, 25, and 27, before leaving on a tour of the South. During this valedictory season she sang "The Last Rose of Summer" and, for the first time, "Annie Laurie," sending Watson into ever more delirious raptures.[56]

On December 29, Hayes and her company appeared at the Musical Fund Society concert, an appearance that Watson, as chairman of the program committee, might have maneuvered.

[55] The *Herald* (November 14, 1851) identified the "oyster house critics" as members of the claque who were paid to applaud bad artists. But Shelley's Oyster House (Broadway and Anthony Street), in an advertisement, facetiously interpreted the term as the way "some flippant writers connected with the press (whose abilities do not procure cash enough to indulge in the classic bivalve) sneeringly denominate those brilliant wits whose sparkling critiques receive their truthfulness and brilliancy from the regal oyster" at Shelley's (*Herald,* November 18, 1851).

[56] In a pre-concert puff signed H.C.W., Watson caroled: "Verily, the Swan is the sweetest Nightingale we ever heard, and growing ever more wonderful, if that were possible (*Mirror,* December 26, 1851).

An earlier Musical Fund Society concert, announced for some time in February, seems not to have taken place. Another, for which Maretzek had offered the Astor Place Opera House and its total musical forces, was announced for December 20, then put off to December 22; it then evaporated in a cloud of conflicting engagements and operatic "indispositions." On December 23, Watson published a card in the newspapers explaining that although the Musical Fund Society appreciated Maretzek's generosity, what with the indispositions of Bosio and Bettini and various "half promises and broken pledges," Watson and his committee were declining Maretzek's offer. Instead, on December 29 at Metropolitan Hall, the Society would present Hayes and her group—Braham, Mengis, Lavenu, and Loder—joined by William Vincent Wallace, Timm, Eisfeld, and his "Classical Quartette Party," Theodore Ahrend, a new solo cellist, the flutist Kyle, and the Philharmonic trumpeter Herr C. F. W. Haase. Members of the Astor Place opera orchestra, led by Kreutzer, would augment the "superb orchestra" of the Musical Fund Society.

On December 31, at the invitation of the Board of Education, Hayes gave an afternoon concert for school children, *à la* Lind; then—with Mengis, Braham, and Lavenu—Catherine Hayes, amid Watson's loud lamentations, went forth to conquer the United States, beginning with Philadelphia. Anticlimactically, she returned a week later for yet another leave-taking.[57]

Besides Bertucca-Maretzek, the local instrumentalists who had assisted Hayes during her stormy New York sojourn were the violinists Hauser, Perkins, and Griebel, and the flutist Kyle. Additionally, three new arrivals from abroad had been heard for the first time: "Professor" Alfred Sedgwick, an English concertina virtuoso; Eduard Boulanger, a French pianist said to be a pupil of Chopin; and Henry (*né* Henri) Appy, a young Dutch violinist of French extraction.[58] Sedgwick was instantly snapped up by Barnum for his American Museum; Boulanger, despite favorable reviews, seems immediately to have departed from New York; but Appy, who was warmly received, remained and promptly gave two concerts (playing virtually the same program at both) at the Chinese Rooms, on October 23 and 29; on November 22, as mentioned earlier, he appeared as soloist with the Philharmonic.

To a public numbed by the unrelieved hard sell, Appy, whose approach was unobtrusive, was like a breath of fresh air. As the *Courier and Enquirer* (October 30, 1851) commented: ". . . he stepped so quietly among us. . . . He came over here without having sent his autobiography and his portrait before him, and he walked quietly to his hotel without making arrangements to be mobbed on his way." Appy was admired, as well, for his excellent violin playing—"brilliant, delicate, tender, and bold," and always in good taste.

But Richard Hoffman, who assisted at Appy's first concert (together with Truffi-

[57] After interminable local wanderings, Hayes's path led her at last to Barnum, who sent her to California in charge of two deputy managers (one of whom, George W. Bushnell, she later married) (Saxon, p. 378, n. 7). In San Francisco, where she became affectionately known as Kate Hayes, she achieved the enormous success denied her in the East. Then on to further triumphs in Australia.

[58] From his father, a political refugee from France and a violinist, Appy had inherited a Guarneri violin, a fact that figured largely in the young man's publicity.

Benedetti, Scharfenberg, and U. C. Hill), in the opinion of Richard Storrs Willis, had by now traveled far on the road to musical perdition, as exemplified by his "usual display of an extraordinary and admirable execution combined with a perverted and unnatural taste. We think this young and most capable player [is] *rhythmically* in a diseased musical state. He has lost all appreciation of that sound fundamental principle in music—*time.* Such chopping up of the measure in playing makes all musical thought perfectly chaotic and unintelligible, besides doing painful violence to the inborn necessity for a measured and regular *ictus,* common to us all." What a contrast to Scharfenberg, who was everything that Hoffman was not, at least, not yet (*Albion,* October 25, 1851, p. 512).

On November 15, 1851, the young Austrian pianist Alfred Jaëll (1832–1882) made his American debut, under Maretzek's management, at a typically Maretzekian opera/concert extravaganza; assisting were Maretzek's far-from-unfamiliar attractions—the opera singers Steffanone, Costini, Pico, Benedetti, Bettini, Badiali, and Coletti, and the violinist Miska Hauser. With Maretzek conducting, the program consisted of the usual opera arias and duets; Hauser, besides his indispensable "Bird in the Tree" with its laugh-provoking ornithological imitations, contributed two of his newest compositions, a Grand Fantasy on *Lucrezia Borgia* for violin, and a timely "Kossuth March" for orchestra.

Jaëll played Thalberg's Grand Caprice on *La sonnambula,* op. 46, two of his own compositions—a "'Gipsey' Polka" and *La Danse des fées*—also *La Source* by the German composer/pianist Jacob Blumenthal (1829–1908), and, neglecting to name the composer, a first performance in the United States of *Le Bananier,* "a Negro Song," by the young American virtuoso Louis Moreau Gottschalk. Described as a "small, unpretending, pale-faced man," the nineteen-year-old Jaëll was instantly acclaimed the greatest pianist ever heard in the United States. "Such execution was never witnessed in this city," rhapsodized the *Herald* (November 16, 1851). "We did not believe that so much could be done with that instrument.[59] The performer did all but make it speak." Jaëll "put his audience in ecstasies" with an air played by the left hand, "while he executed the most brilliant shakes, runs, and other embellishments with his right." Additionally, "he played several airs with variations in the most masterly manner and with tremendous applause, concluding with his 'Gipsey Polka,' which was encored. Instead of repeating this, he played 'The Gondolier' [part of somebody's "Carnival of Venice"] . . . not on the program, which was received with one universal and enthusiastic shout of applause. It was encored. He performed it again amidst uproarious plaudits. This little gentleman produced quite a *furore* with his fingers." Then the anticlimax: "He was completely successful with his concert, except in drawing dollars" (*Herald,* November 16, 1851).

The *Mirror* (November 17, 1851), too, mentioned that the hall was only half-full for this, the "greatest concert ever presented in New York since Parodi's departure." Not only did Jaëll show "what a master of the instrument he undoubtedly is, [he] stamped himself indelibly the best of them all." The writer hoped that he and Maretzek would not be discouraged by the poor attendance and that they would try again.

[59] In this case a sadly out-of-tune Érard, according to the *Mirror* (November 17, 1851). At his second concert Jaëll played a Chickering.

Music Division, The New York Public Library

Adelina Patti, the baby prima donna.

This hope was echoed in the new *New-York Daily Times* (November 17, 1851), whose anonymous critic found Jaëll to be "a pianist of the very highest rank." "We have never heard Thalberg or Listz [*sic*]," he refreshingly confessed, "but in rating Mr. Jaëll in a much more elevated category than De Meyer or Herz, we have no hesitation whatever. His command of the instrument is complete. His execution is brilliant and forcible, without being violent. The labored effects and startling descents upon the keys which grated the sensitive ear of the listener to De Meyer are [as] much avoided as the tameness and torpidity of Henri Herz."[60] The reviewer predicted that a second Jaëll concert would "crowd Tripler Hall to the roof."

The attendance was indeed improved when Jaëll returned to Tripler Hall on November 22 with the same supporting cast, joined by an extraordinary added attraction: "Mr. Jaëll will have the honor," read the advertisement, "to introduce before the American public a Musical Wonder, Adeline [*sic*] Patti, only seven years of age [she was eight] . . . the little sister of everybody's favorite, Amalia . . . said to be a worthy scion of this melodious family." Little Patti, rumored to be "a child rich in promise," would sing Jenny Lind's "Echo Song," no less, and *Je suis la Bayadère* (*Mirror,* November 19, 1851).

Under the heading "LA PETITE PRIMA DONNA ADELINA PATTI," the (*Mirror* November 24, 1851) wrote of this historic event: "The surpassing feature of the Jaëll Concert . . . was the debut of Adelina Patti, daughter of The Patti [Caterina], a child of seven [*sic*] years, yet a perfect miniature Lind or Malibran. This sweet little prodigy completely astonished the audience by her ease, self-possession, and power, singing the

[60] The *Choral Advocate* (December, p. 103), while lauding Jaëll's playing, nonetheless rated him second to de Meyer.

'Echo Song' and *La Bayadère* with remarkable perfectness and effect. It must have been a proud moment for her teacher, Madame Valentini, who was present and led her protégée before the audience,[61] when the repeated plaudits of the house were showered upon this 'newest star.'"

In the *Musical Times* (November 29, 1851), at the conclusion of a ponderous report of the concert, a long-winded replacement for the departed Saroni prophetically wrote: "Adeline Patti may justly be considered a 'musical prodigy,' and her acquirements reflect the highest credit on the skill, judgment, and perseverance of her teacher. In the simplicity of childhood, divested of all physical delineation, she executed some very difficult passages in the songs she gave, with a precision and beauty truly astonishing. Her voice possesses uncommon sweetness and flexibility for one so young, and the ease and grace with which she ascended and descended the scale would have conferred celebrity on the acquirements of older artists. We venture the prediction that she will yet merit the honorable appellation of the 'great cantatrice of the western world.'"

The fledgling *Daily Times* (November 25, 1851) focused its excitement on Jaëll: "The piano forte is a new instrument under his finished touch"—and tersely added: "Nor should the other musical wonder, the child Adeline Patti, be forgotten. A very successful imitation of the Echo Song of Jenny Lind was vehemently encored."

On December 2, at the Astor Place Opera House, between acts one and two of a benefit performance of *Maria di Rohan,* the baby Patti again sang the "Echo Song." And the following night, with Signor La Manna conducting, she joined Steffanone, Borghese, Vietti, and Forti in a "musical interlude" at the Dramatic Fund Society Benefit at Niblo's Garden. On this occasion, as Adelina Patti later recalled, accurately or inaccurately, she sang the *Ah! non giunge* with her doll tightly clasped in her arms (Haswell, p. 476).[62]

On November 25, Tripler Hall, under foreclosure for non-payment of rent by Tripler, was sold at auction—according to the *Mirror* for $47,500, according to the *Evening Post* for $44,000. The purchaser was the real estate magnate John Lafarge, on whose land the hall had been built in 1850 by Tripler, who had held a lease on it for twenty-one years at an annual rental of $14,000 and taxes, amounting annually to $1400. Now, immediately after the sale, work was begun to "complete and improve" the building, promptly renamed Metropolitan Hall. The new lessee, a Walter E. Harding, announced plans to add a dining room to accommodate 1000 people (an originally promised amenity that had not come into being) with an experienced caterer to run it. More important, he was installing improved heating and ventilating systems, an enlarged stage, a lowered floor, and, most important of all, he promised several large exits opening on Mercer Street, to allow an audience to vacate the hall "almost *en masse*" in an emergency. "This building, containing the finest concert room in the country, was to our mind a complete failure," commented *Parker's Journal* (December 6, 1851, p. 697). "Its means of egress, so badly arranged and so restricted that it re-

[61] The resourceful Valentini promptly capitalized on her little pupil's triumph by composing an "Adelina Polka," and marketing it exclusively at Vanderbeek's music store.

[62] In his book *The Reign of Patti* (p. 28) Hermann Klein tells how little Patti on her earliest tours sometimes refused to sing unless she was allowed to carry her doll onstage.

quires nearly three-quarters of an hour to empty it of its audience, must always have been open to the most serious objections. Nothing but a constant continuance of good fortune and the absence of any unusual degree of hurry could prevent the most frightful catastrophes." In its prospective new guise the hall would be capable of "any theatrical use whatever, whether concert room, opera house, theatre, or circus."

The first "Grand Concert" to be given at the refurbished hall was the greatly publicized debut on December 18 of one Octavia de Lille, a beautiful, twenty-two-year-old "*prima donna*" from the Paris Opéra-Comique.[63] De Lille's managers Wardle Corbyn and John Buckland, new to the concert game, were said to have engaged Metropolitan Hall for thirteen de Lille appearances, the intention being that she would perform on the "off nights" between the Nightingale and the Swan. As we know, the originally announced concert plans of both these songbirds underwent radical changes. And so apparently did de Lille's, for despite her extravagant advance publicity and the distinction of her assisting artists—the opera stars Marini and Bettini, the violinist Griebel, and William Vincent Wallace, who conducted the orchestra—the debut of Octavia de Lille, unornithologically dubbed the "Pet of the Parisians," was her "only and last" appearance in New York.

Among the societies—apart from the Philharmonic, the Harmonic, and the various benevolent associations—the Euterpean Society observed their 52nd anniversary, giving their annual concert and ball at the Chinese Rooms on January 30. At the Printers' Annual Banquet and Ball, on January 17 at Tripler Hall, the vocal entertainment was directed by W. B. Bradbury, George H. Curtis, and F. H. Nash and the dance music supplied by Dodworth's Quadrille Band of twenty musicians.

On April 11, at the Chinese Rooms, the German *Liederkranz* gave their annual concert and ball, later to become a major festivity of the New York year. The orchestra, conducted by Noll, played the overtures to *William Tell* and Weber's *Oberon,* inspiring the carping critic for *Saroni's Musical Times* (April 19, 1851, p. 43) to wish for another *William Tell* Overture to be composed, if only to "give a chance of doing away . . . with the one of Rossini, which . . . has become so hackneyed that every child knows it by heart, and every musician can play it *senza vista*." Furthermore, it, as well as the Overture to *Oberon,* needed a larger orchestra and better preparation than Noll had provided.

The *Liederkranz,* on the other hand, had steadily improved and by now gave promise of becoming "the best vocal society of the Union." And the most venturesome, for on December 9 the society memorably exceeded their purely choral function and once and for all established German opera in New York with a splendid, full-fledged production at the Astor Place Opera House of *Zar und Zimmermann (Czar and Carpenter)* (Leipzig 1837) by Albert Lortzing (1801–1851).[64] The city's large, music-

[63] An institution pooh-poohed in the *Herald* as "a sort of half-price theatre in Paris."

[64] To pave the way, a season of German plays had been successfully presented earlier in the year at the Olympic Theatre, temporarily rechristened the German National Theatre. Four nights a week were devoted to staged works, and Sunday evenings to "sacred" concerts. Reporting an "utter jam" at their opening, the *Evening Post* (February 17, 1851) observed that despite "squeezings and disappointments," the rosy cheeks of the Fräuleins disclosed no turbulence.

loving German population responded heartily, buying out the house in advance, despite ticket prices that soared to a stratospheric $1.50.

Richard Storrs Willis, self-appointed spokesman for all things German, termed the event a great innovation. In the *Albion* (December 13, 1851, p. 596) he approvingly described the capacity audience of "rosy, buxom damsels and their families and friends" as being totally German and utterly different from the customary Astor Place audience: "It was the most characteristically unAmerican and unique audience ever seen this side of the Atlantic." Willis hoped for more such efforts, to begin with a repetition of this amusing and entertaining opera. It was given again on December 18.

Following the second performance of *Zar und Zimmermann,* dubbed a "sour-krout and Dutch Opera" by a denigrating journalist, a critic for the *Musical Times* (possibly Willis) maintained that he not only "came away with a decided liking for these two things," but also for "an orchestra much better and much less noisy than that of the Italian opera . . . a chorus such as Italian Opera never saw in this city, good music, and an audience who could appreciate it," albeit an audience sparse in numbers. For this the writer blamed the intense cold, both outdoors and within, at Astor Place, "for we know not how else to account for the very small . . . audience. It cannot be that the Germans are unable, or unwilling, to support *two* performances of opera" (*Musical Times,* December 27, 1851, p. 122).

Another innovation had created a stir earlier in the year. Taking timely advantage of the current controversy over the unconventional costume devised by Amelia Jenks Bloomer (1818–1894) to assert Women's Rights,[65] a topically clad "Bloomer Troupe," comprising six singing-and-dancing young ladies and headed, oddly enough, by Nathalie Fitzjames and Giuseppe Carese, the former dance stars of Maretzek's opera company, announced a series of four Grand Concerts—more precisely, entertainments combining elements of concert, ballet, and fashion show—to begin on September 1 at the Chinese Rooms.

Purportedly from abroad, the young ladies, since their recent arrival, had "adopted the new Bloomer Costume," consisting of Turkish-looking trousers, or pantaloons (facetiously called "pettiloons") modestly gathered in at the ankle, a knee-length overdress, or tunic, and a "Bloomer Hat," described as a kind of sombrero. Attired in the "richest and most recherché styles of that beautiful dress, each lady in a different costume," they would perform "Gems from the Operas, English, Irish, Scotch, and French songs, ballads, duetts, and quartettes," some arranged by George Loder; also several of the fashionable "new Bloomer waltzes, polkas, etc." Fitzjames, dressed in "beautiful [Bloomer?] costumes, made expressly for these concerts"—besides singing the Mad Scene from *Lucia* and a *Salut à la France* (in a "Daughter of the Regiment costume")—would perform items from her ballet repertory with Carese, the only male performer in the company, except for Giovanni Sconcia, who conducted the (apparently male) orchestra (*Herald,* September 1; *Mirror,* September 1, 1851).

Despite untoward gossip that some members of the capacity audience at the Bloomer Troupe's debut had "burst out laughing," the *Mirror* (September 3, 1851)

[65] The sensational Bloomer costume was an all-pervasive issue of the day, dominating the news in the general press, particularly the columns of Horace Greeley's progressive *Tribune.*

thought "the young ladies displayed their Bloomer costumes to great advantage and sang with considerable taste; Mlle. Fitzjames acquitted herself well," both as a vocalist and a danseuse, and each performer received at least one bouquet.

The ethnic ballad singers in 1851 included, besides the Scottish perennials William Dempster and Jeanie Reynaldson (the current version of her name), a new Scottish group, the Fraser Family, and a Miss Worrall from England.

Miss Worrall, a singer and pianist, was heard at the New York Society Library on March 11 and 20. Her one-woman show included flashy opera transcriptions on the piano and self-accompanied English ballads by Edward Loder, Julius Benedict, Michael Balfe, Henry R. Bishop, George Linley (1798–1865), and others. "By request" she sang "God Save the Queen," and for a grand finale "The Star-Spangled Banner," with the audience joining in the "chorus" (*Herald,* March 24, 1851).

The Fraser Family, consisting of a father, two daughters, and two sons, all of

Music Division, The New York Public Library

The politically controversial Bloomer costume found its way to sheet music covers.

whom sang and played various instruments, settled into the Society Library on December 22 for an extended stay. They caught on famously with the New York public, whose capacity for Scottish folk tunes seems to have been inexhaustible.

To welcome back the evergreen Scottish troubadour William Dempster, who returned to the Tabernacle for a brief season in September, the *Mirror* (September 15, 1851) admonished the public: "Among all these swans, and larks, and linnets, and thrushes, we must not forget our Scottish warbler."

And Jeanie Reynaldson, despite the lamentable loss of her longtime partner Austin Phillips—fatally stricken with apoplexy on April 8 "as he was proceeding home through Wooster Street"[66] (*Figaro!,* April 12, 1851, p. 249)—continued to perform in a succession of places, from raucous Bowery music halls to the now somewhat disused Tabernacle and back again. At her Tabernacle concert on October 5, Reynaldson was accompanied by James G. Maeder and vocally assisted by the American popular singer and song writer W. F. Brown.

Austin Phillips's death was the second in a quartet of bereavements that in 1851 impoverished the New York music community both directly and indirectly. On March 22, Mordecai Manuel Noah, too, succumbed to a stroke. A piquant and knowledgeable social and musical observer and critic, Noah, a Renaissance man, in the course of his sixty-six years had potently functioned as a journalist, lawyer, diplomat, judge, political functionary, playwright, cultural arbiter, and, an ardent Jew, as an inextinguishable champion of Jewish causes (*Times and Messenger,* March 23; *Tribune,* March 24, 1851; *Daily Times,* January 1, 1852).

And on May 5, as George Templeton Strong informed his private journal, Philip Hone died after "a short illness, but he had been very sadly broken down for some months." Hone, in his seventy-first year, had never recovered from the after-effects of the cholera he had suffered some two years earlier (*Tribune,* May 6, 1851). On April 30 he made his final entry in the magnificent diary he had faithfully kept since 1828. With only four pages remaining to complete the twenty-eighth volume, and with a blank twenty-ninth lying ready on his desk, an enfeebled Hone had inscribed a premonitory epitaph in verse[67] and had mused: "Shall this journal be resumed? Shall it go on? Has the time come?"

To complete this somber catalogue, on December 6, midway through Maretzek's opera season at Astor Place, the basso Augusto Giubilei died of "consumption." A stranger in a foreign land, he was laid to rest by three unnamed Americans who paid the expenses of his lonely funeral (*Mirror,* December 10, 1851). It was noted that not one of his compatriots and colleagues of the opera company had been present.

[66] During his twelve-year residence in the United States, Phillips had filled a versatile range of musical functions, from church organist to blackface entrepreneur.

[67] The weary traveler on earth's dull road,
The pilgrim fainting underneath life's load.
The stout heart struggling 'gainst the adverse wave,
And sinking, with no mortal arm to save,
Finds hope and consolation in the blest decree,
Pronounced by angels's lips—"there's rest in heaven for thee."

In 1851, as we learn from the papers, New Yorkers more than ever flocked to the minstrel shows. At "Christy's Opera House" (Mechanics' Hall), Christy's Minstrels still maintained their supremacy. At Fellows's Opera House, as Minstrel Hall was now renamed, the Fellows troupe continued nightly and on two afternoons a week to present their "Burlesque Opera Scenas, Burlesque Concerts, and Ballets [among them new takeoffs of *La Dame blanche* and a "Concert a la Bochsa"] in a style equal to the originals produced at the Italian Opera of this city." At White's Melodeon bigger and better benefits for Charles White continued interminably to be given.[68]

The continuous interchange of featured blackface performers, from troupe to troupe and back again, appears to have been indigenous to the craft. On March 2, Fellows gave a benefit at his opera house for his featured performer Eph Horn, billed as "that Prince of Darkies"; by March 26 the *Herald* announced that Horn had formed a team with Charles White, with whom he had leased Constitution Hall at 450 Broadway, just a few doors from Fellows's Opera House at number 444; they had renamed it Horn and White's Ethiopian Opera House, and would be open for business on April 2.[69] On April 17 and 18, prior to their departure for the World's Fair in England, a so-called "real band of Sable Harmonists" appeared at Military Hall, located at Vanderbilt's Landing on Staten Island. According to the *Tribune* (April 17, 1851), the troupe astoundingly consisted of "nine real negroes of talent, both vocal and instrumental, whose concerts have been full and fashionably attended in all the principal cities of the West and South, consisting of Airs and Songs, Refrains, Quartettes, Parodies from the Operas, Burlesques, Solos, Dances, together with a truthful delineation of the lights and shades of the Ethiopian race, in which they are not excelled by any band of minstrels" (*Tribune,* April 17, 18, 1851).

And the Charleston Minstrels, also known as the Charleston Serenaders, or the Charleston Operatic Troupe, before appearing at Bleecker Hall on May 12 made it known to the more discriminating members of the public that they forbore "puffing themselves up by the common, vulgar system of 'gag-puffing' [and relied] entirely on their own merits, feeling assured that to be heard [was] to be duly appreciated"—at twenty-five cents a ticket (*Mirror,* May 12, 1851). Also at Bleecker Hall, on March 17 a benefit concert was given for "the original E. R. Harper, the American Negro Extravaganza Singer, who acquired so much celebrity at the Theatres Royal of Great Britain" (*Herald,* March 17, 1851). In the interval between Great Britain and benefit, Harper had been appearing in various minstrel shows at Barnum's American Museum, as had Donaldson's Serenaders and T. D. Rice. Rice was seen, as well, at the National Theatre as *Jumbo Jum, Jim Crow in London,* and *Otello.*

On March 31 the "original New Orleans Opera Troupe," or "New Orleans Sere-

[68] Charles White's benefits reached a grand climax on December 4 with a monster testimonial concert at Tripler Hall, scathingly reviewed in the *Musical Times* (December 6, 1851, p. 70), a periodical hostile to minstrel shows and popular music in general. The cast of this "gigantic spasm of public enjoyment" included two military bands, Shelton's and Adkins's; four accordionists; the popular singer Caroline Hiffert; the rock-crushing, "hard-handed Hercules, Mons. Gregoire; several masculine and feminine dancers"; and, surprisingly, George Loder. White was presented by his friends with a gold medal and by his colleague E. P. Christy with a silver pitcher (*Herald,* December 4, 1851).

[69] Evidently a transient arrangement. By mid-July, White and his Serenaders temporarily appeared at Knickerbocker Hall while the Melodeon was being refurbished.

CHARLES WHITE, THE MINSTREL.

New-York Historical Society

naders," naming among their company G. B. Swaine (Buckley), noted practitioner of the banjo, bones, and kitchen bellows, M. Sulzner flutist, J. H. Collins falsettist, J. C. Rainer vocalist, R. B. Buckley vocalist, and Frederick Buckley (alias "Master Ole Bull"), made their appearance at Tripler Hall after an "absence of five years" (it was, in fact, more like three). On April 4, for their "positively last appearance," they advertised that as a novelty they would begin their program with glees and ballads performed "in white faces," to be followed by interludes of burnt-cork fare, and to conclude with an elaborate burlesque on the Havana Opera Company. Departing for a two-week engagement in Philadelphia, they returned on April 22 "permanently" to settle in at the Stuyvesant Institute (*Mirror,* March 31, 1851).

On April 23 the *Herald* confusingly announced that they were impostors and that the true New Orleans Burlesque Opera Company and Ballet Troupe (in fact, partly composed of breakaway members of the so-called "original" New Orleans Serenaders) were currently performing in Baltimore and would momentarily be arriving in New York. On May 1 the remnants of the other "original" New Orleans Serenaders joined with Fellows's Minstrels, to form, according to Fellows's advertisements, "the greatest [and most confusing] combination of talent ever concentrated in the Ethiopian business in the world" (*Mirror,* May 1, 1851).

In August, Fellows hit on a nice promotional scheme to stimulate business. Offering a stake of $1000, he challenged Christy to a contest between his (Fellows's) spectacular seventeen-year-old violinist Frederick Buckley (the former "Master Ole Bull" of the New Orleans Serenaders) and Christy's (formerly Fellows's) showy violinists Leopold Meyer and young John B. Donniker. Fellows proposed that a jury of twelve "able musicians" be chosen, six by either side, to hand down the decision (*Mirror,* August 15, 1851).[70]

Charles White promptly capitalized on this ready-made publicity. In a tongue-in-cheek imitation of the challenge, he advertised that *his* violinist (unnamed) could "see-saw just as hard and break as many sixpenny strings as any other fiddler engaged in Ethiopian representations." Besides, he observed, it was against the law in this state to make such bets (*Herald,* August 24, 1851).

At the Franklin Museum, George Lea's Female Ethiopian Troupe, numbering fifteen performers, shared a program with Model Artistes and Arab Girls. They gave two performances daily, at 3 and 7:30 P.M.; seats on the stage were 37½ cents; box seats 25 cents, parquet 12½ cents. And, to celebrate the holiday season, at the new Cupid Lyceum, 36 Canal Street, the site of that former den of iniquity, the Walhalla, "crowded houses and roars of applause by fashionable audiences [greeted] the performances of . . . four beautiful young ladies, together with the [Female] Minstrels, Mr. Nichols, the India Rubber Man, and the Female Acrobats." Admission 12½ cents, stage seats 25 cents (*Herald,* December 23, 1851).

In the sphere of light opera, or operetta, Brougham's recently opened Lyceum, under the skillful musical guidance of George Loder, quickly rose to preeminence.[71] In January the musical items at Brougham's—usually afterpieces with unattributed music, often prefaced by Loder's "Echoes of the Nightingale" potpourri—included *Esmeralda,* billed as an "operatic, terpsichorean, pantomimical burlesque"; the durable farce *Jenny Lind,* in which Mary Taylor interpolated Samuel Lover's♪ song "The Low-Backed Car" and the "celebrated 'Sweep Song'" (probably "Buy a Broom," set to the tune of *Ach, du lieber Augustin*); also a burletta, *The King's Gardener* (London 1839), wherein "our Mary" sang James G. Maeder's "Song of Home," purportedly composed for Lind. A less successful "new opera," *The Andalusian, or, The Young Guard,* with a score composed or arranged by Loder, was withdrawn after a single performance, showing, applauded *Figaro!* (January 25, 1851, p. 58) the "good taste of Manager Brougham, for the sooner a failure is forgotten, the better." But in all justice, *Figaro!* had to admit that *The Andalusian* contained some "pretty music and a pair of handsome legs" (the latter unidentified); and great credit was due to "our friend George for his graceful composition."

By far the high point of Brougham's first season was his adaptation, together with Loder, of Auber's comic opera *The Ambassadress, or, A Manager's Miseries,* opening on January 27. It had not been heard in New York since 1845, when it was a major hit of the French opera company from New Orleans, with the delicious Julie Calvé♪ as Henriette. This was its first presentation in English. Calling the work a "small oper-

[70] In a subsidiary challenge, Fellows offered to "stake another $500 that Mr. G. Swaine Buckley will beat Mr. G. N. Christy, or any person, as a musician in . . . sentimental or comic singing, banjo playing, and playing on a pair of Kitchen Bellows, and [as a] general delineator of the Ethiopian character."

[71] The new theatre offered a number of physical amenities as well: "Brougham's Lyceum is crowded nightly, despite rain or muddy streets," wrote the *Evening Post* (January 11, 1851), "for the doors open directly on Broadway, and there are no dark and dirty bye streets [*sic*] to travel to reach it. Ladies step at once from a carriage or omnibus into a warm and comfortable hall, and thence pass to their seats without soiling even a satin slipper."

etta," the *Albion* (February 1, 1851, p. 56) pointed out that the Lyceum singers were hardly on a level with the current Italian opera stars; in fact, Mary Taylor, the only "singer" in the troupe, was, in the writer's opinion, "rather a screamy nightingale." But, all the same, the music was "so pretty and vivacious and tripping that it was a pleasure to listen to it." Mrs. George Loder, a principal member of the company, looked particularly pretty as the Countess, and Brougham, the Fortunatus, was splendid, as usual, although admittedly he had been frightened at having to sing for the first time in his life, and in front of Loder, too. Others appearing in the piece were Stephen Leach, John Dunn, and Julia Gould.

As the season progressed, Brougham produced *The World's Fair,* a topical entertainment unlike the burletta of the same name soon to open at Burton's Theatre. He presented, too, a spoof of the superspectacular *Faustus, or, The Demon of Drachenfels,* a sellout hit at the Broadway Theatre. Calling his travesty *Ye Deville and Dr. Faustus* (with a charmingly costumed Mary Taylor as ye Deville), Brougham advertised it with tongue in cheek as a "new romantic, neo-romantic, gyromatic, operatic, hippodromatic, and heterogeneous burlesque spectacle." And with the current fad for elaborately staged, melodramatic extravaganzas, another Brougham/Loder collaboration, *The Spirit of the Air,* adapted from the French, boasted scenic arrangements "got up," according to Saroni (*Musical Times,* April 12, 1851, p. 31), "with a splendor and taste surpassing anything of its kind ever seen." Too, it was another triumph for Mary Taylor, who played Asteria, the Spirit of the Air, "and certainly," quipped *Figaro!* (April 12, 1851, p. 247), in this role "'our Mary' looked the most substantial aerial we have ever seen."

In a follow-up article on *The Spirit of the Air,* Saroni apologized for his too moderate previous assessment of Loder's extraordinary achievements at Brougham's. With a histrionically able, if vocally indifferent, cast, a small but well-drilled chorus, and a really remarkable orchestra, "sixteen in number, but every one a master of his instrument," Loder had accomplished musical miracles: "We do believe that none but Geo. Loder could produce such results. His solos are adapted so completely to the powers of the respective singer that you do not discover an imperfection in the execution. His concerted pieces are so well arranged that they afford you the most unalloyed pleasure. His choruses make up in melody and harmonization for the loss of strength in execution. The orchestra is just subdued enough to keep pace with the numerical strength of the troupe. As for the purely instrumental parts of the opera, they are so well arranged that one might almost imagine an orchestra of fifty or sixty performers. To be sure, such results are owing also to the individual merits, zeal, and energy of the members, and to the good will with which they carry out the leader's and composer's intentions. Yet, to George Loder belongs the chief credit. And," pointedly added Saroni, "to those jealous and envious musicians who see in this article a puff, we would say: if so, there never was one more deserved" (*Saroni's Musical Times,* April 19, 1851, p. 43).[72]

[72] Loder was a musician's musician. In June, during the benefit season at Brougham's, Loder's evening offered, between performances of Madame de Marguerittes's recently produced play *The Home Book of Beauty* and *The Beggar's Opera,* a concert by the Germania, who played their popular "Musical Panorama of Broadway,"♪ and Dodworth's Band, who were heard in "several pieces" (*Mirror,* June 3, 1851).

The musical productions at Brougham's further included revivals of *The Child of the Regiment* and *Don Giovanni in London,* both featuring Mary Taylor, and Auber's opera-ballet *The Bayadère,* with the sensational young French dancer Caroline Rousset as Zoloe,[73] a Mr. Alleyne, possessing a small but sweet voice, making his debut in the role of the Unknown, Stephen Leach as Olifour, and Julia Bennett as the singing Bayadère. With the veteran star Mrs. James G. Maeder, who joined the company in August, a production was mounted whose intriguing title aptly expressed the ever-present dilemma of the contemporary repertory-theatre manager: *What shall We Do for Something New?*. Subtitled "A new operatic Colloquiality," the work made "indistinct" references to *La sonnambula* and other previously performed works in the Lyceum repertory. *Guy Mannering,* with Charlotte Cushman in her renowned role of Meg Merrilies, earned praise for its outstanding treatment of the incidental music (possibly the 1816 score by Henry R. Bishop and colleagues). And on June 25, Brougham, always attuned to events of the moment, produced "a new, local, unmentionable peculiarity" that might have contained music, called *The Bloomers*.[74]

Although three spectacular productions with music were presented in 1851 at the Broadway Theatre, bastion of mammoth extravaganzas, their success was apparently due to their sensational staging rather than their musical content. Two of these were revivals of past melodramatic blockbusters, the first being George Soane's melodrama *Faustus, or, The Demon of Drachenfels* (London 1825), with music adapted from the original collaborative score by Henry R. Bishop, Charles E. Horn, and Thomas Cooke; on January 13 it began an unprecedented six-week run.[75] A gorgeous spectacle, *Faustus* offered magical stage effects, elaborate ballet sequences, a large chorus, and a scary Mad Song performed by Madame Elizabeth Ponisi, a lustrous newcomer from England to the Broadway's acting company.

On April 7, after an interlude of less compelling repertory, another dazzling production, *The Vision of the Sun* (London 1823), was brought out at the Broadway. Billed as "a grand romantic fairy operatic spectacle," it was a greatly magnified version of a melodrama that had captivated New York audiences at the Park Theatre in 1825; its musical content, however, remains shrouded in mystery. In May, *Faustus* was revived, and on June 2 yet another lavish production was unveiled at the Broadway, *Azael, the Prodigal,* an English adaptation of Auber's new opera *L'Enfant prodigue* (Paris 1850).[76] Announced as a "grand romantic and operatic spectacle," it had an exotic Egyptian locale, had cost some $2000 to produce, and had kept "a very efficient orchestra" hard at work for several weeks rehearsing Auber's difficult score (*Evening Post,* May 31, 1851). But again, the focus of the production lay in its stagecraft, not its score.

As the *Spirit of the Times* observed (May 3, 1851, p. 132), huge theatrical spectacles

[73] Caroline Rousset and her siblings Adelaide, Theresine, and Clementine, together with their father, the French dancing-master Jean Rousset, captivated New York in 1851. First seen at Niblo's Garden, they appeared successfully at the Broadway Theatre, Brougham's, and again at Niblo's.

[74] The Broadway Theatre, too, brought out two productions of timely interest: *Women's Rights* and *Model Modern Masaniello, or, Female Flights for Female Rights.*

[75] *Faustus* had been a huge success in New York when it was first performed at the Park Theatre on October 11, 1827.

[76] Julius Benedict had introduced the Overture to *L'Enfant prodigue* at a Jenny Lind concert at Castle Garden on May 23, 1851.

Music Division, The New York Public Library

Anna Thillon in her piquant youth.

had become the "rage of the moment" and the New York theatres strove to outdo one another in the extravagance of their presentations. Without secure copyright restrictions, many of these were unblushingly lifted from current successes at rival houses.[77] Thus, in July the Bowery Theatre mounted a competitive production of *Azael, the Prodigal,* pronounced to be in some respects even more spectacular than the original at the Broadway. The Bowery, too, revived *The Count of Monte Cristo,* a huge hit at the Broadway in 1849, when it had been presented with a score arranged by Richard Hoffman and Joseph Burke. The music used in the Bowery's revival was not identified.

Among the most elaborate spectacles offered at the National Theatre was a revival of the melodrama *Thalaba the Destroyer, or, The Burning Sword* (London 1823),[78] with a homemade score composed, or arranged, by W. T. Peterschen,♪ the theatre's music director. Other spectaculars at the National were *The Lady of the Lake,* "with all its original music," *The Frolic of the Fairies,* and *Aladdin.*

But despite the multiplicity of theatrical presentations at these theatres, and at Burton's, Barnum's, and Niblo's—not only spectacular melodramas, but tragedies, comedies, farces, pantomimes, minstrel shows, and a profusion of dog dramas (a fad for canine thespians had sprung up in 1851)—the event of the greatest significance to the local music theatre that year was the arrival in September of Anna Thillon (1819–1883), the famous English-born, French-educated star of the comic-opera stage in both countries. On September 18, after a delay of two days beyond the announced

[77] For example, no fewer than three different dramatizations of Dickens's *David Copperfield* (1850) were concurrently played in 1851—at the Bowery, Burton's, and Brougham's theatres.

[78] *Thalaba the Destroyer* was first given in New York at the Bowery Theatre on May 13, 1833.

date of her debut (to permit needful additional rehearsals), Madame Thillon appeared at Niblo's Garden in Auber's *The Crown Diamonds,* a work written for her in 1841 by Auber and Scribe.[79]

The *Mirror* reviewer (ostensibly Watson) admiringly wrote, on September 19, 1851, of the strong impression she had made with "the beauty of her face, the symmetry of her person, and the easy playfulness of her manner as she received the plaudits that welcomed her before an American audience." The tones of her charming voice, he found, were "sweet, pure, and delicious. She has evidently been taught in a good school" (Thillon had studied in France with such masters as Bordogni, Tadolini, and her future husband Claude Thomas Thillon, conductor of the Philharmonic Orchestra of Le Havre). She was an artist of undoubted accomplishment: "Her execution is marvelously sparkling and brilliant, accurate, facile, and neat. Her voice is a soprano of good compass, and her style is faultless. She has power enough for operas of the comic French school, though if we felt called on to be rigidly critical [being Watson], we should probably be obliged to confess that we could spare some of that high, artistical [French] finish which characterizes her singing, if by such sacrifice, we could gain some of that free and effective power which, to our apprehension, she seems to lack. But there is no doubt of her success, we think, judging from the favor with which she was received last evening."

Saroni had no such reservations. "We have just returned," he wrote, "from one of her charming performances [of *The Crown Diamonds*], and have been so delighted that we feel like congratulating everybody—those who have heard her for the pleasure they have had—those who have not for the pleasure that is in store for them" (*Saroni's Musical Times,* October 4, 1851, p. 21).

She was no less ravishing in *The Daughter of the Regiment,* which opened on October 7. N. P. Willis, who pronounced her a phenomenon, deplored the lack of fanfare with which she had appeared in our midst: "How Madame Thillon has chanced to come to America, we know not. It was probably upon a sudden caprice, or she would have been advised to send the trumpets before her—as stars are wont. Here she is, however, one of the very choicest idolatries of Paris." To Willis, one of her greatest charms was "the way she embroidered the beauties of each language [French and English] upon the other—her conversational English, upon the stage, being the most exquisite perfection of utterance and pronunciation that we ever listened to."

Madame Thillon's supporting cast included the popular Irish actor/singer James Hudson and the local performers Mr. and Mrs. Holman, Mary Taylor, and Ferdinand Meyer.

On a different level of interest was the debut of the notorious Irish adventuress Lola Montez, *née* Marie Dolores Eliza Gilbert (1818–1861). Representing herself as a dancer, a career for which she was ill-equipped, Montez had scandalized Europe with her spectacular sexual escapades, particularly her infamous liaison with Ludwig I of Bavaria, which in 1848 had cost him his throne.[80]

[79] *The Crown Diamonds (Les Diamants de la couronne)* had first been performed in New York in French in 1843 by the French opera company from New Orleans, with the captivating Julie Calvé in the Thillon role. This was its first local performance in English.

[80] Among Lola Montez's more distinguished past conquests had been Franz Liszt.

The international enchantress, Lola Montez.

Arriving from Europe on the same ship that had brought Kossuth, Montez's entry into the New World had been somewhat overshadowed by the enormous welcome accorded the hero. After a journalistic bicker over whether Barnum had imported her—a rumor he flatly denied—and after a ticket auction at Jollie's music store, Lola Montez appeared on December 29 at the Broadway Theatre in a ballet titled *Betly, the Tyrolean*. As the *Mirror* reported the event (December 30, 1851): "Some three thousand 'men about town' were crammed between the walls of the theatre . . . while not more than a dozen feminines, except in the 'colored row,' relieved the dark mass of humanity, packed like figs from pit to dome."

Lola Montes [*sic*] was undoubtedly a beautiful woman, granted the *Mirror,* "but dancing is evidently not her vocation. . . . In person she is rather slight, with very slender arms and very symmetrical 'determinations downwards' [shades of N. P. Willis!]. Her feet are about the size of full-grown mice and her ankles about as large as a baby's wrist." Waxing poetic, the writer continued: "Her hair is like the raven's plumage, her lips like rosebuds, her teeth like ivory, and Oh! my stars, what eyes—large, dark, liquid, and veiled by lashes, which like mist before the sun, prevent them from dazzling one entirely."

As might be expected, the enchantress was seductively clad: "She wore a white muslin boddice [*sic*], almost as transparent as the gauzy veil sometimes worn by the Queen of the Night, only the more fully revealing what it fains to conceal, and a skirt of rainbow hue. On her head was set a jaunty, saucy-looking bonnet, a sort of compromise between a Prince Charles and a modern Hungarian hat. . . .

"Her movements are graceful," the ravished reviewer went on, "her time perfect, her smile bewitching, but she was never made for a dancing girl." And here the writer abruptly flung the remaining remnants of journalistic decorum to the winds: "She is a lost Peri, a stray Angel, a Star unsphered, a Cleopatra without a throne, another Herodias's daughter, who by her witcheries can compel kings to give her half their kingdoms, or bring her the heads of her enemies in a basket."

Nonetheless, although "as a notoriety, a beauty, a feminine phenomenon," she was undoubtedly worth seeing, Barnum's Museum would have offered "quite as appropriate a place for the exhibition as the boards of the Ballet. And probably private entertainments, or public banquets given by Lola at five to ten dollars admission would prove far more profitable than any theatrical engagement she can make in America."

It was only fair to add a postscript to reassure the timid: "Lola's style of dancing is rigidly modest—her greatest angles not exceeding 45 degrees—and although nothing in the shape of narrow, 'obsolete ideas' [pantaloons?] covered the upward continuations of her ankles [the nineteenth century was apparently incapable of enunciating the word *legs*], yet lots of lawny, cloudy muslin somewhat mystified her motions and gave a confusing indefiniteness to her figurations."[81] To say nothing of the writer's prose.

[81] According to Maretzek, a concession to American standards of strategic female concealment (*Crotchets,* p. 192).

3

GTS: 1852

Few can be sufficiently aware of the huge labor which is necessary to redeem our land from the ignoble position of provincialism in Art—to make it a creator and not a borrower.

William Henry Fry
Second Lecture, December 7, 1852

January 13, 1852. . . . Went to the Philharmonic Concert [January 10] with Ellie. . . . The first part was the "Eroica," played with much fire and accuracy. The first three [movements] gained on me, the fourth did not. Nobody but Beethoven could have written it, but it's hardly worthy to be the finale to such a work. Then came an overture of [William Sterndale] Bennett's,♪ *Die Waldnymphe* [op. 20], a charming production, full of feeling and abounding in fine effects. Mendelssohn copied from, though, almost larcenously; then Mendelssohn's lovely Piano Concerto in G minor [played by Otto Goldschmidt]; then a trumpery quintette for stringed instruments [the Andante and Finale of Antonin Reicha's Quintet No. 2, for wind instruments]; and finally Weber's *Oberon* [Overture], magnificently rendered. So the concert was very filling at the price.[1]

~

Curiously, not only George Templeton Strong but the reviewers, as well, neglected to mention that this splendid concert had been conducted by George Loder in what turned out to be his last appearance with the Philharmonic.[2] But Goldschmidt—basking in the reflected glory of Jenny Lind—was hailed by Richard Storrs Willis as "a pianist of the first water, of the Leipzig school. . . . If we mistake not, he was in Leipzig while Mendelssohn was connected with the *Conservatoire,* and grew up somewhat under the shadow of that great man" (*Albion,* January 17, 1852, p. 32). The *Musical Times* (January 17, 1852, p. 166) lauded Goldschmidt for being able to see beyond

[1] Incorrectly transcribed in the published *Diary* (II, 83) as "very fitting at the price."

[2] After Loder's departure, at a meeting on March 6, the Philharmonic officers voted on who would conduct the approaching concert. Bristow received three *yea*s and three *nay*s, whereupon Eisfeld was appointed (Philharmonic Archives). He would henceforth be the sole Philharmonic conductor until March 1854; then again in 1856–57; then intermittently until 1865.

the notes in a composition, causing his execution to be "not merely *great,* [but] also *good.*"

Without naming Loder, the *Tribune* (January 12, 1851) praised the "precision and skill" with which the "full and effective" orchestra, on this occasion numbering "nearly seventy instruments" (in fact, sixty-six), had been handled. All the finest effects of the different compositions were masterfully brought out, particularly in the "majestic *Eroica.*" Although "no novelty to Philharmonic audiences," it was doubtful "whether the most veteran dilettante present ever heard it with more satisfaction." The writer rejoiced that the "Pastorale" Symphony was scheduled for the next concert. "We have no doubt that the Society consults the wishes of its subscribers as well as the highest interests of the art, in making the productions of the great Master the staple of its performances. . . . The true lover of the art turns to Beethoven with a feeling as natural as that with which the Christian seeks in his Scriptures the fullest record of his faith."

But the press was chiefly occupied with the sensational turn of events in the world of opera. Early in the New Year several key members of Maretzek's fractious opera company, enraged at having been stranded in Savannah through the inefficient maneuverings of Maretzek's tour manager,[3] defected and set up a competitive opera season at Niblo's Garden, declaring all-out war on Maretzek. In his bitter account of the episode, Maretzek blames not only his inept deputy and the perfidious singers for the disaster but also the malevolent plottings against him of Don Francisco Martí and of William Niblo (*Crotchets,* pp. 196–200).

The wayward press welcomed the schism and gleefully predicted an operatic Utopia in New York. "It appears that we are to have two Operatic Companies in operation in the city very shortly," announced the *Mirror* on January 5, "and as competition always benefits the public, we anticipate a great deal of musical enjoyment from these rival songsters. The [breakaway] company has already been organized and is, so far as we understand it, a sort of commonwealth, with Signor Bosio [*sic*] as director and manager."[4] The principal deserters were Angiolina Bosio, Rose de Vries, Virginia Whiting, Geremia Bettini, Cesare Badiali, Domenico Coletti, Domenico Lorini, and the conductor Luigi Arditi.

Calling themselves the "Artists' Union Italian Opera Company," they opened on January 12 with *Lucia di Lammermoor,* sung by the powerful trio of Bosio, Bettini, and Badiali. Tickets for all parts of Niblo's Theatre were one dollar, and secured seats were available at no extra charge. "With such a company and such pieces and such an establishment, there can be no doubt of the success of this enterprise," euphorically wrote the *Mirror.* "The other company is to be under the direction of Max Maretzek, and will continue at the Astor Place Opera House. The magnificent Steffanone will be the

[3]Maretzek does not identify this deputy, but later infers in *Crotchets and Quavers* that he might have been the diminutive impresario Bernard Ullmann (?–1885).♪

[4]Bosio's husband, in fact, was named Panayotis di Xindavelonis. Maretzek refers to him scornfully, as he does to the general breed of managers who so "plentifully cropped out of the manure Barnum had spread upon the soil of American humanity" (*Crotchets,* pp. 160–62, 198).

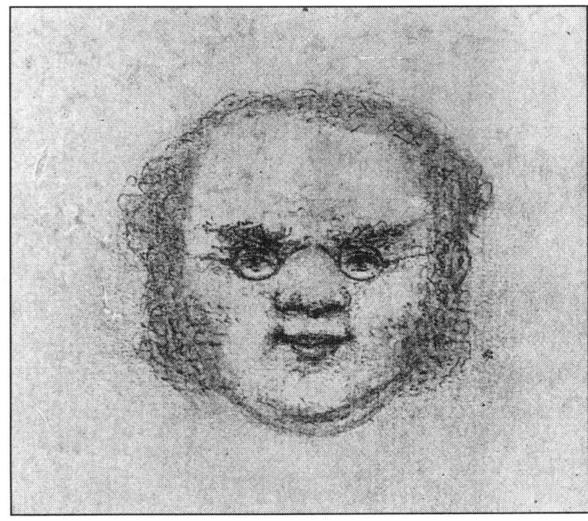
New-York Historical Society

An informal sketch of William Niblo, said to be a good likeness.

prima donna, and will be sustained by Salvi, Marini, and probably Mme. Pico-Vietti." Maretzek had personally traveled to the Midwest to fetch Teresa Parodi and Amalia Patti back from their joint opera tour (managed by Strakosch, trying his impresarial wings); Bertucca, Costini, Beneventano, Rosi, Pietro Candi, and various lesser singers filled out the company.

"The rivalry, therefore, will be very great," continued the *Mirror,* "for each company possesses sufficient talent to draw the town. The contest will be interesting, and the public will doubtless divide their patronage between the competitors. . . . There are a sufficient number of music-lovers in the city to afford each [company] large audiences nightly."[5]

The *Musical Times,* too, rejoiced: "It will give a healthy agitation to musical criticism, now some time stagnant; will give us Italian opera in greater perfection than ever before, for each company will strive to outdo the other; and, if the rumors be true, [will] materially modify managerial enterprise and artists' 'extortion.'[6] If 'republican principles' can be introduced into so thoroughly aristocratic an institution as Italian

[5] Both companies appeared on the same evenings—Mondays, Wednesdays, Fridays, and Saturdays—and on at least one occasion, on January 23, both performed the same opera—*Lucrezia Borgia*—at Astor Place with Steffanone, Amalia Patti, Salvi, and Marini; at Niblo's with Bosio, Whiting, Bettini, and Badiali. An embarrassment of riches!

[6] Together with the stranglehold exerted by the "Upper Ten," the exorbitant fees paid the stars were blamed for the repeated failure of opera in New York. The *Herald* (January 1, 1852) indignantly wrote of the inflated demands—once they came to the United States—of singers who had been accustomed to barely subsistence pay in Italy (where they did not catch colds!). For example, Bosio had been paid $300 a month in Italy, $700 in Havana, and at first $1000, then more recently $1300 by Maretzek. The singers received extra fees for benefit performances and extra pay for touring; all travel expenses were paid by the manager. And into the bargain, the artistes habitually became suddenly indisposed when they wanted to revenge themselves on the manager.

Opera, we shall not be the last to shout, *'Success to the Italian Artists' Union'*" (January 10, 1852, p. 155).[7]

Reviewing their debut, the *Musical Times* (January 17, 1852, p. 166) credited the Artists' Union's extraordinarily spirited performance of *Lucia* to the "universal" power of "selfishness." Richard Storrs Willis agreed: "The difference between singing on hire, and for themselves alone, was perhaps evinced in the unusual animation and painstaking of the entire troupe" *Albion,* January 17, 1852, p. 32).

But Richard Grant White, although sympathetic to "any movement which tends to diffuse a taste for the best music and to gratify that taste which is already developed," took a more realistic view of two Italian Opera Companies competing for supremacy in New York. "Max Maretzek, the most capable, energetic, and successful manager we have had, is barely able to stagger under the burden of his labors and responsibilities, and we cannot but think that another company will only harm him, without benefitting itself or the cause of music" (*Courier and Enquirer,* January 12, 1852).

After a week of highly lauded, if sparsely attended, performances of *Lucia, Norma, Don Pasquale,* and *Lucrezia Borgia* by the Artists' Union at Niblo's, Maretzek, with murder in his heart, opened his rival season at the Astor Place Opera House on January 19 with Steffanone, Salvi, and Beneventano in *La favorita.*[8]

Curiously, George Templeton Strong, who was present, did not refer to the prevailing operatic hostilities but had much to say about Italian opera as an art form.

January 20. . . . Heard *Favorita* last night, well sung. Richard Grant White sat near us—a person it's agreeable to hear talk. . . . *Favorita* is sad trash, except one or two melodies that are agreeable when excellently well sung. As to the finale—except the *Ange si pur—Spirito gentil*—it is execrable in feeling, composition, scenic effect, and *tout ensemble* generally. I have come to the conclusion that opera *per se* is imbecile foolery. Great music may make a performance worth hearing, but the dramatic element, as displayed in all the operas I've yet heard, is a dead drawback on whatever there was of true greatness in them. And in all the modern Italian operas the costumes and acting, etc., are a mere preposterous, paltry, idiotic show, meant to draw off attention from the flimsiness of the music.

My ideas are not clear tonight, but the difficulty seems to be that scarcely any music is adequate to express or accompany the intense situations of the libretto. Murders, treasons, suicides, and rapes are indispensable to supply the excitement which the barren brains of Donizetti and Verdi cannot generate by any musical effort of their own, or even by systematic theft of the ideas of better men. Horrors are cheap, and the plot must be fruitful of them, or the opera will fall flat. And therefore Lucrezia Borgia must poison her own son by mistake, and he must die before her eyes; Ernani must magnanimously stab himself on his wedding night before the eyes of his wife; Fernando must learn, five minutes after his marriage, that the bride he has sought so

[7] The autocratic control of the opera house, and consequently of opera, by the "Upper Ten" (or "Codfish Aristocracy") was condemned by the press as downright "Un-American"; it was treated as a social issue of some concern.

[8] With the notable exceptions of *Don Giovanni* and *Robert le diable,* both companies duplicated the repertory they had sung together in 1850 and 1851.

long is the cast-off mistress of the king; Edgardo must cut his own throat over the grave of Lucia; and every "grand" opera must abound in incident worthy of the "Mysterious Mother,"[9] and which would not be tolerated by any audience but the pit of the Bowery [Theatre].[10]

It must all be strong and stimulating, as gin is strong and stimulating. And this necessity, by the by, is the reason that the modern Italians write comparatively so few light, comic operas—a line for which they're so much better qualified than for "serious" work. Now if a lyric drama includes such features as these, no living composer is able to write its music; few men ever lived who could produce anything that would not be absolutely inadequate.

The action of the piece presents—or implies—all the agony and passion that the heart of man can suffer, brought forward naked and tangible: death and madness, at least—often with some exaggeration of horror, or some superhuman extravagance of ferocity, or heroism, that common sense revolts at—but always distinct and prominent, with no decent obscurity thrown over them, but glaring out often behind the footlights. Now (whether all this be or be not a beastly and barbaric violation of the dignity and quietness of Art), what ought to be the power and feeling and depth of the music that illustrates such positions and embodies their feeling? I don't believe that Handel and Beethoven together could do much more than distantly approximate to the musical Force that is needed for half the stories on which Donizetti and Co. have exerted their twopenny talents. No genius could make such subjects otherwise than hideous—perhaps genius would never attempt them. But when they are undertaken by indolent mediocrity feebly imitating bad models, the result is half shocking, half ridiculous, like a Massacre of the Innocents by a vile painter.

The same necessity that demands a raw-head-and-bloody-bones plot calls for "fine acting," or at least for the kind of imitative acting that is proper in the theatre; in the opera house it is a nuisance. It is an attempt to unite the imitation of nature with something wholly symbolic and conventional. If opera have any rational foundation, and be not merely the incoherent device of pleasure-seeking dilettanti, its aim is to present human action and passion idealized to the maximum. A drama in verse is the comparative, opera the superlative, degree of idealism on the stage. It must be acted ideally, therefore. The vivid mimicry which is effective in *The Stranger*[11] is a blemish in *Norma,* just as flesh tints and glass eyes would deface a statue, though they would certainly make it twice as natural. Thus, in the really fine closing scene of the *Giuramento,* Truffi, being stabbed (according to precedent) by the man she's in love with, gives up the ghost with several bars of effective melody interrupted at due intervals by the chokings, gaspings, singults, and convulsive twitchings that might be expected from a woman actually expiring from internal hemorrhage caused by an incised

[9] *The Mysterious Mother* (1768) is a tragedy dealing with incest, by the father of the Gothic chiller, Horace Walpole (1717–1797).

[10] Known for its raucous, sensation-seeking audiences. For an unexcelled portrait of the Bowery audience in its heyday, see Haswell, pp. 360–64.

[11] *The Stranger,* as the English version of the play *Menschenhass und Reue* (*Misanthropy and Repentance*) by August von Kotzebue (1761–1819) was titled, was first presented in New York at the Park Theatre in 1798 in a translation by William Dunlap (1766–1839). A hardy perennial, Strong probably saw it performed at the Broadway Theatre, where it was currently in the repertory.

wound in the region of the subclavian, or any other, artery, till with one wild cry she falls back and is dead. It was a great point in the piece and a fine piece of acting, but it always struck me as false in principle—the more glaringly wrong the more truly it was acted. If it was right and proper for her to express her dying adieux by a minor air in F and not in spoken words, it was wrong and ridiculous for her to accompany them by the bodily symptoms of diminished circulation and failing life. It was absurd to seek to increase the effect of something wholly conventional and ideal by blending with it features of imitated reality.

~

"The two rival Operas are making a much greater stir in conversation than in the newspapers," twittered N. P. Willis in the *Home Journal* (January 24, 1852). "The predominance of initial letters in the names of the two sets of performers—*B*osio, *B*adiali, and *B*ettini at one house, and *P*arodi, *P*atti, and *P*ico at the other—has divided the town into 'The *B*'s' and 'The *P*'s,' and people declare for either letter, at meeting, like the Montagues and the Capulets.

"Maretzek's two prima donnas," he continued, "are a very rare combination. Between Steffanone, a volcano suppressed, and Parodi, a volcano in action, the imaginative and unimaginative can choose a performance to their respective liking. Rose de Vries, at the other house, is very attractive to the eye, and Bosio to the artistic taste. . . . The two men at the two houses—Salvi and Marini at Astor Place, and Badiali and Bettini at Niblo's—are superb 'teams' to be in rivalry anywhere. Four such male singers are together in no metropolis of the world.

"The choice, as to music, is between luxuries, either of which would suffice; and it remains to be seen . . . whether the white-glove Opera at Astor Place or the colored-glove Opera at Niblo's . . . is more likely to 'draw.' To one you may go in an omnibus—to the other you must go in a carriage. For one you must engage seats and make a careful toilette—for the other you can propose a party at a minute's warning and 'with what you have on.' The *B*'s are cheap and comfortable; the *P*'s are expensive and ostentatious."

In his ornate way, Willis was referring to the Artists' Union's reduced ticket price—fifty cents to all parts of the house—intended both to lure reluctant audiences and to deal a death-blow to the hard-pressed Maretzek. That harassed impresario countered not only by reducing his tickets to fifty cents for the parquette and boxes and twenty-five cents for the amphitheatre, but by throwing in the free use of a pair of opera-glasses with each pair of tickets. A battle to the death!

"What will be the ultimate effect of this competition upon the two establishments it is difficult to conjecture," soberly speculated the *Evening Post* (February 7, 1852). "Its effect upon the future prospects of the Opera is still more problematical. If it should demonstrate the practicability of a cheap opera, we should rejoice in the recent rupture. If it will prostrate the opera altogether, for it is very difficult to raise the prices of any public entertainment after once being reduced, it would be a public calamity." But the myopic general press—as hostilities escalated—basked in the false euphoria of a counterfeit golden age of unlimited opera, accessible to the "whole people" at "American" bargain prices.

Strong, who impartially attended both operas, continued to disregard the issue, hot though it was.

February 2. . . . Ellie and I are going off extemporaneously to Niblo's to hear *Don Giovanni* (not my baby—we can hear him enough at home,[12] but Mozart's). Badiali is the Don—a different creature from Beneventano.[13]

. . . [later] Heard *Don Giovanni* accordingly. House crowded but cold, and interested in nothing, unless perhaps by some of Zerlina's irresistible music [sung by Bosio]. It would be strange if a miscellaneous mob of operatic New Yorkers should appreciate Mozart. They have taken it for granted that Verdi's screaming unisons and Donizetti's stilted commonplaces of languid sentiment are good, and *Don Giovanni* must therefore be to them something far from good. I should as soon expect people whose reading has been chiefly in Eugene Sue to become excited over *The Vicar of Wakefield.*[14]

~

But George William Curtis, although eminently capable of appreciating *The Vicar of Wakefield,* had strong misgivings about the Artists' Union's production of *Don Giovanni.* Reviewing the just-elapsed New York music season in the first issue of his friend John Sullivan Dwight's new Boston weekly, *Dwight's Journal of Music* (April 19, 1852, pp. 2–3), Curtis, the periodical's vivacious New York correspondent, writing under the exotic pseudonym of *Hafiz* (doubtless a reference to his new book *The Howadji in Syria*),[15] reported that Arditi's orchestra had been "inefficient"—a disaster in an opera that depended as greatly upon the orchestra as did *Don Giovanni.* The whole thing had been taken too fast—so much so that during one performance an exasperated Ole Bull (recently returned to the United States) had stormed behind the scenes "to protest against such murder of Mozart."

Strong's newly awakened recognition of Mozart owed much to the edifying influence of the Maurans' frequent visits.

February 13. . . . Miss Josephine Mauran staying here—great times in the evenings with Mozart's symphonies, four-handed. I appreciate Mozart now, which I did not of old. I can see that he stands on the same plateau as Beethoven and possibly above him. I don't know and don't care to decide. One appreciates Mozart later than Beethoven. . . . [Went] to the opera [at Astor Place] with the ladies to hear *Robert le diable* [with Steffanone, Salvi, and Marini] and had the privilege of hearing *Norma* instead [with Steffanone and Marini but no Salvi];[16] very well done, but I've used

[12] "Don Giovanni" was one of many pet names bestowed upon little John Ruggles Strong by his fond parents.

[13] Different, perhaps, but in the *Tribune*'s opinion "not a success." Not only was Badiali deficient in the "*abandon* essential to the character" of Don Juan, but he took unpardonable liberties with Mozart's musical text, a presumption as inadmissable as altering Shakespeare.

[14] The sensational novels of the French author Eugène Sue (1804–1857) appealed to the masses; *The Vicar of Wakefield,* by the English poet/novelist Oliver Goldsmith (1730–1774), on the other hand, attracted people of more exalted tastes.

[15] Or possibly a reference to Hafiz, the principal male character in Goethe's widely read *West-östlicher Divan* (1819).

[16] Like Strong, the *Herald* missed the announcement in the evening papers of February 11 that the program had been changed, due to Salvi's illness. Thus, as the *Mirror* (February 12, 1852) happily pointed out, the *Herald* "with its usual accuracy (?)" had reported a tremendous reception for *Robert le diable* and for Steffanone as Alice. But things were even worse at Niblo's that night, for their perfor-

up that opera[17]—after about the twelfth performance it is utterly threadbare and shabby.

~

On February 13, just after Strong heard the wrong opera at Astor Place, the by-now financially exhausted Artists' Union gave up the struggle. After a splendid final performance of Donizetti's *Maria di Rohan,* they suddenly cut short their season and departed for Boston, leaving the undisputed field to Maretzek, a sadly battered victor. Hardly an unbiased chronicler, Maretzek writes: "Two weeks after the first performance of 'Robert' [Maretzek's ultimate weapon] they retired to Boston, and in two weeks more, the 'Artists' Union Italian Opera Company' dispersed, amidst quarrels, blows, and mutual vituperations, having lost not only their time, but all the loose cash they had embarked in their untoward speculation. . . . The enemy had been beaten well and thoroughly, but the defeat had ruined the victor."

Despite the opera house "crammed to suffocation" for every one of his performances, what with the limited capacity of the Astor Place Theatre and the reduced prices, Maretzek's "'successful (!)' production of 'Roberto il diavolo'[18] was a dead loss. On every evening that the curtain was raised to a packed audience . . . it fell upon a loss of four hundred dollars." Only two weeks after the enemy had "ingloriously fled from New York," Maretzek—"bled to the last drop in my veins [and with "means and credit utterly exhausted"]—was obliged to succumb, [and in early March] the doors of the Astor Place Opera House were closed upon the public" (*Crotchets,* pp. 205, 213).[19]

Strong, apparently oblivious of all this off-stage high drama, attended the last benefit for Maretzek (at restored prices) at Astor Place.

February 24. . . . At the opera last night. . . . Opera was *La gazza ladra*—very well done. It's a nice opera—one of Rossini's best, so far as I can judge—next after the *Barber,* perhaps—very rich in fresh, offhand melody, delightfully helped on by the orchestra. Rossini can hardly be beat in accompaniments for the voice, but the frame sometimes kills the picture, and one would listen to the brilliant, luscious instrumentation sometimes with more pleasure if it were not interfered with by the singing. After all, his best music is sensuous, if not sensual. But I notice in this opera the dawn of the style that Verdi has developed and carried out so far that it's to be hoped that it can be carried out no further—crashing instrumentation, tearing unisons—(perhaps) angularity and abruptness in melody—all just faintly perceptible as gaucheries or

---

mance had to be canceled at the last moment when "Mdme. De Vries found herself to be too much indisposed to undertake the part of Lucrezia Borgia."

[17] Mystifyingly transcribed in the published *Diary* (II, 85) as "I've read up that opera."

[18] Probably for dramatic effect, Maretzek claims to have brought out *Robert le diable* for the first time during this desperate season, disregarding its three successful performances in December 1851.

[19] They were soon reopened by William Niblo, who for a second time leased the Opera House, this time to install an animal act—Donetti's troupe of trained dogs, monkeys, and goats—a gesture regarded by Maretzek (perhaps rightly) as the ultimate act of personal malice. Despite efforts by the Astor Place proprietors to evict the animal entertainers, culminating in litigation, the Donetti "troupe" retained their grip on Astor Place until June, when they moved to Burton's Theatre. Having "lost all *prestige* in the eyes of the community," particularly of its Upper Ten subscribers, the Astor Place Theatre was sold to the Clinton Hall Association, who in 1853 installed within its walls the Mercantile Library (1820–1989).

Pl. 16.

The Napoleon of Managers' last Charge on his used up Upperten Subscribers!

ASTOR PLACE OPERA HOUSE

Grrreat Acrobatic, Equilibrious, Lyric, Vocal & Instrumental **MAMMOTH ARIA**, sung by 5 Prime Donne:
*1, La gigantesca **Parodi**; 2, La piccolissima **Bertucca**; 3, La balladina **Catarina** (Hayes of course!) 4, La sweetissima **Jenny Linda** (not di Chamouni) & 5, La genteelissima **Thillone**; with accompaniment of the new **Steam Orchestre** of Upperten 1000 horses power, & probably concluding with a brillant Gold Eagle Firework for the **Benefit of the Manager!***

A pungent cartoon depicts Max Maretzek, the Napoleon of Opera Conductors, and now of Organ-Grinders, precariously balancing five major prima donnas *on his barrel organ, substituting for the defunct Astor Place Opera House.*

brusqueries one doesn't expect in the mellifluous and smooth-spoken author of the *Barber.* Now I must go dress for a musical party.

February 25. . . . Party last night lamentably slow—the musical people didn't come. . . .

Strange as it may seem, no sooner had this latest opera debacle transpired and the mutually vanquished belligerents gone their various ways[20] than plans were unveiled to build a bigger and better opera house. With the former five-year subscribers disdaining the now declassé Astor Place Opera House, and with the newspapers' ceaseless insistence that the New York public yearned for Italian opera and that the solution of the perennial opera dilemma lay in a non-subscription opera house accessible to everyone and large enough to sustain itself with a fifty-cent admission price, decisive action was taken to construct the often projected new building.[21]

On April 10 a charter was granted to James Phelan, John Paine [William H. Paine?], Cortlandt Palmer, and other well-to-do luminaries of Upper-Tendom to incorporate "under the title of 'The New York Academy of Music.'" The capital stock, divided into 200 shares of $1000 each, was fixed at $200,000, with the option of increasing it to $300,000.[22] The site, some 25,000 square feet on the corner of Fourteenth Street and Irving Place, had already been purchased for $60,000. The house, it was planned, would comfortably hold "from 4000 to 5000 persons" (*Herald,* May 23, 1852). The Academy of Music would at last materialize in 1854.

February 28. . . . An evening so sloppy and squashy that it has absolutely kept me at home, though the Philharmonic Orchestra is in the midst of Beethoven's "Pastorale," while I sit here listening to nothing but the quick dripping from the housetops, the splash of the unhappy people who pass through the street below in outer darkness (for this is "Corporation Moonlight"—the street lamps are not lit and it is as dark as Erebus) and an occasional patter of rain on the window. Also, Giovanni [Strong's, not Mozart's] . . . has been audible at intervals fortissimo. . . .

Those hardy souls who did brave the weather were subjected to a mammoth program that included—besides the "Pastorale" Symphony—Mozart's *Zauberflöte* Overture, Weber's "Jubilee" Overture, the Mendelssohn Violin Concerto played by Joseph

[20] "We shall probably have no opera next summer," lamented the *Musical Times* (April 3, 1852, p. 341), and added: "There are those who rail at the Italian Artists' Union as having, more than any body else, produced a consummation so devoutly to be execrated. . . . Maretzek, with a few faithful friends, has gone to Mexico, Parodi to Havana, Marini to London, and the Artists' Union is broken up. Some of this company have gone to South America, some remain unengaged here." Bosio, in particular, became a great star in England, and especially in Russia, where in 1859, while on her third triumphant visit, she died at the age of twenty-nine.

[21] It was widely believed that William Niblo would establish and manage the new opera house. Indeed, he was rumored to have gone to Europe to engage new singers.

[22] The *Daily Times* (June 12, 1852) observed that the prospectus for the Academy of Music hardly did away with the former "tone of exclusiveness. . . . It starts out with the presumption that Opera must be *patronized* to be successful; that the $1000 subscribers must lift it into respectability and fashion, and build for it a magnificent house in which it may revel, or fall through. . . . If an Academy of Music, for popular use at moderate charges, cannot be established *for the sake of music,* then it cannot, and ought not, in this republican country, to be established at all."

Burke, the *scena* from *Oberon,* "Ocean! thou mighty Monster," sung by Madame Wallace-Bouchelle; Max's aria from *Der Freischütz,* "Through the Forests" *(Durch die Wälder),* sung by Herr Emanuel Klein (a German-sounding Hungarian tenor, recently heard for the first time at a Mrs. Bostwick *soirée*); Kalkbrenner's *rondeau* for piano *La Gage d'amitié,* played by Master William Saar; and two Schubert songs, with piano accompaniment, "Thine is my heart" *(Ungeduld),* from the song cycle *Die schöne Müllerin,* op. 25 (Madame Bouchelle), and *Die Post,* from *Die Winterreise,* op. 89 (Herr Klein).

The *Musical Times* (March 6, 1852, p. 276) thought Madame Bouchelle somewhat nervous in her rendition of that "most trying and difficult *aria* of Weber's, 'Thro' the Forests'" (an inadvertent error for which the editor duly apologized in the following issue); he praised everything else except "the arrangements of the Society with respect to *weather* [and] their arrangement of the program," meaning that the concert had been far too long and that the audience was visibly exhausted: "The very best of music begins to pall upon the musical sense, if too long prolonged."

Eisfeld's overgenerous program was reviewed in the *Albion* (March 6, 1852, p. 116) by the unidentified successor to R. Storrs Willis (as he now called himself),[23] who had resigned in order to take over "sole editorial charge of the *Musical Times*" (*Albion,* February 28, 1852, p. 101). Willis's successor, apparently a Briton and a stranger to the Philharmonic (and apparently to music journalism as well) lost no time in establishing his mastery of musical terminology: "We were struck with the evidence of sympathy between the [Philharmonic] performers, found in the perfect uniformity of *crescendo* and *diminuendo;* and also with the rare advantage of hearing the fundamental harmonies distinct and triumphant in the most *fortissimo* passages, wherein too often all is crash, din, and confusion, from which the ear is gladly delivered, scarcely appeased by a return to the *piano.*" True, "a bassoon appeared rather faulty . . . when its tones frequently alternated as *tonic* and *dominant;* and the upper notes of a flute seemed to us at times to be slightly unmanageable; but taken as a whole, we assure our readers, they could not obtain more perfect satisfaction in orchestral effect, not even under the leading of Jullien himself, that prince of modern conductors."[24]

On April 3, Strong attended the fifth "Classical Quartette Soirée" of Eisfeld's second series and heard Beethoven's Quartet, op. 74 in E-flat (the "Harp"; 1809), Spohr's[25] Quintet, op. 130, with Timm at the piano, and Haydn's Quartet "No. 63 in D"; he found them to be "exquisite compositions rendered with spotless accuracy." Also on the program were Mendelssohn's duet "I would that my love" *(Ich wollt' meine Lieb'),* op. 63 (1836), charmingly sung by Mrs. Laura A. Jones and her "raven-haired" niece Miss Julia Wheelock,[26] and a trio from Spohr's opera *Zemire und Azor* (Frankfort 1819) sung by Mrs. Jones, Miss Wheelock, and Miss Maria Leach.

[23] At about the same time N. P. Willis took to calling himself N. Parker Willis.

[24] The flamboyant French conductor Louis Antoine Jullien (1812–1860), felicitously described by a contemporary as "a Barnum set to music," was nonetheless a splendid musician and a great star in London; he would make a sensational visit to the United States in 1853–54.

[25] Transcribed as *Spolia* in the published *Diary* (II, 89).

[26] Mendelssohn's duet "easily elicited" an encore, "despite the almost imperceptible sneer of complacent toleration which curled the lips of some, who doubtless fancy that all good music comes from the eyes and the fingers, instead of its true source—the heart" (*Musical World and Journal of the Fine Arts,* April 15, 1852, p. 246).

Oliver Dyer (1824–1907),[27] a versatile journalist and master hyperbolist—since March the publisher and most probably the editor of the *Musical World and Journal of the Fine Arts* (hereinafter cited as the *Musical World*), the latest incarnation of the *Message Bird*—reviewed the concert in prose whose grandeur verged on the positively biblical: "Inexplicable Beethoven! Dim and mysterious even to thyself, how shall any mortal dare to interpret thee? Yet feedest thou hope with thy very indefiniteness and playest with chaos in a manner godlike. . . . Whatever thy teaching, Seer, we thank thee! We half suspect thou'rt breaking our faith in man—but then, thou bringest us nearer to God."

Of Timm's masterful performance in Spohr's Quintet, he chanted: "Dext'rous delver in ivory! Impart the secret of that distinct, yet mellow, effect which thy touch so quietly produces; be content with an American reputation second to none who have visited these shores; and live long, with untired fingers and beautiful conception" (April 15, 1852, p. 246).[28] Eisfeld's two preceding *soirées,* not heard by Strong, had been given at the Apollo on January 31 and March 6. The January program—besides string quartets by Mozart and Haydn and Henselt's unfamiliar *Trio concertant,* op. 24, in A minor, for piano, violin, and cello, played by Richard Hoffman, Noll, and Eichhorn—had included two un-Eisfeld-like songs—a bolero, "Love's Messengers," by Alexander Fesca, and a romance, "Many Years Ago," by Henry C. Watson, sung from manuscript by his wife, a new singer.[29] "Mrs. Watson made a very successful *debut,*" wrote the *Musical Times* (February 7, 1852, p. 214), who found her tone to be pure and full, her method excellent, and her style showing "evidence of the most careful practice" (doubtless under Watson's tutelage).

Eisfeld's March program had comprised string quartets by Mozart and Beethoven; the Quartet in E-flat for piano and strings by Ferdinand Ries, splendidly played by Hermann A. Wollenhaupt, Noll, Eisfeld, and Eichhorn; and songs by Beethoven, Schubert, and Lindpaintner, less splendidly performed by Herr Klein.[30]

April 13. . . . Heard a novelty at Trinity Church this afternoon—an experimental service at which the Church Choral Society assisted. The whole service was *intoned.* Effect infinitely better than expected, though the performance was rough and faulty.

〰

The experiment, which had drawn an unexpectedly large attendance due to unwanted publicity in the papers, enlisted the efforts of three ministers, who intoned the service, and the Church Choral Society, a boys' choir, originated and trained by the Trinity music director, Dr. Edward Hodges,♪ who chanted the responses. The members of the Society were seated in the front pews, with three reliable boys strategically placed among them as leaders. But what with the too-great distance between them

[27] In the course of his long and vivid career, Dyer was a journalist, lawyer, concert manager, biographer, phonographer (stenographer), Swedenborgian minister, and publisher.

[28] Dyer's style so closely resembles that of Parker's unidentified critic as to suggest that he might have written the lively music reviews in *Parker's.*

[29] In 1844, according to Watson's obituary in *Watson's Art Journal* (December 11, 1875, p. 77), he had married Miss Francesca Lutti, a mezzo-soprano "of Italian origin."

[30] Herr Klein was an exponent of the German style of singing, inferior to the Italian because it did not "develop the full force of the voice," stated the *Tribune* (March 7, 1852). There was evidently "a good deal of Mr. Klein's voice concealed in his cravat."

and Hodges at the organ, and the unsolicited interference of an unknown busybody who ordered them to "sing alto," the result was understandably less than ideal (Messiter, pp. 54–55). Nonetheless, Hodges pronounced the music to have been "good and cathedral-like," and Strong, a vestryman at Trinity since 1847, evidently agreed.

April 15. . . . Special vestry meeting at Trinity Church last night. Tried to get some encouragement for the Church Choral Society and could have carried my resolution, but [William Ellsworth] Dunscomb [a timid fellow-vestryman] was so frightened at the bare prospect of a no-popery excitement that I did not press it.

April 16. . . . Miss Josephine Mauran arrived to spend a day or two and has been at work at Mozart, four-handed, this evening, with Ellie. I have learned to appreciate Mozart but recently. There is nothing in Beethoven or Haydn or elsewhere, to my knowledge, that is like the exquisite delicacy and tenderness that one finds in Mozart, This simple little Trio in G [not otherwise identified], for instance, is enough to break one's heart with a feeling of sadness that lies veiled under its smile.

Well for him to whom the forebodings and the sorrow that are hidden under all prosperity and happiness come in so beautiful a form, and not in the dreariness and grimness they are apt to take in real life.

April 28. . . . Philharmonic last night—its great feature Spohr's *Die Weihe der Töne.*♪ The rest of the programme poor. After the first part I took Ellie home, the temperature being beyond her capacity of endurance, and then returned for Miss Josephine and Miss Teresa Mauran.

~

The Maurans' musical perseverance was apparently limitless, for they willingly endured a program that, in addition to Spohr's gigantic symphony, contained "The Naiads" Overture, op. 15, by William Sterndale Bennett and the "Festival Overture and *Marche triomphale,*" op. 172, by Ferdinand Ries; Mrs. Bostwick sang the aria *Qui la voce* from Bellini's *I puritani* and William Vincent Wallace's song "The Happy Birdling," with flute obbligato by Felice Eben; Scharfenberg played Mendelssohn's D-minor Piano Concerto; the Philharmonic trumpet virtuoso C. Haase played his variations on "The Carnival of Venice"; and Timm and Scharfenberg played Moscheles and Mendelssohn's Grand Duo on "The Bohemian March" from Weber's *Preciosa,* arranged for two pianos and orchestra.

R. Storrs Willis (by now the chief editor of the *Musical Times*), who reviewed this final concert of the Philharmonic's tenth season, applauded the Philharmonic hierarchy for the "*esprit de corps*" they showed (probably in celebration of the anniversary) in playing the percussion instruments in the Spohr work: "the President, Mr. Timm, presiding over no less an instrument than the *Grosse Caisse*—the Vice-President, Mr. Scharfenberg, clashing the *cymbals,* and the Secretary, Mr. Ensign, gingling [*sic*] the *triangle*" (*Musical Times,* April 24, 1852, p. 390).

In obedience to Spohr's wish that the poem by Carl Pfeiffer, on which he had based the scenario for *Die Weihe der Töne (The Consecration of Sounds),* be read before hearing the symphony, the printed program included the text both in the original German and in English.[31] *Hafiz,* in *Dwight's* (May 1, 1852, pp. 28–29) thought this "a fatal

[31] The descriptively titled movements of the Spohr symphony are: 1. The Gloomy Silence of Nature before the Creation of Sounds—Busy Life After—Sounds of Nature—The Elements; 2. The

desire" on Spohr's part, because to be valid, a work of art should be sufficient unto itself: "If you are compelled for intelligibility to write under a pictured tree—'This is a tree'—it is not a proper picture." The usual program notes for Beethoven's "Pastoral" Symphony were not only superfluous, wrote *Hafiz,* but an insult to the composer, to say nothing of the audience.

Willis thought that Mrs. Bostwick—despite a "slight acidity about her tone, occasionally, which [was] not so pleasing"—sang better at this concert than on any occasion he could remember. But "The Happy Birdling," after Jenny Lind's "Bird Song," seemed to Willis "a musical profanation—our sympathies do not chime in with it." *Hafiz,* too, for the same reason wondered why Mrs. Bostwick had sung "The Bird Song," and why the Philharmonic had condoned it.[32]

May 9. . . . At Eisfeld's [chamber music] concert last night. Beethoven's *Septuor*[33] its great feature—a most magnificent composition. It was played at the third Philharmonic [concert] of the first season,♪ and I then thought it a very abstruse and rather tedious piece of profundity. Glad to find that my faculty for the highest kind of music has improved since then. I could follow and enjoy the whole of it, except parts of the finale, last night. Considering the scant material to which Beethoven has limited himself, it may stand by the side of any of his orchestral music.

~

Besides Beethoven's Septet, in which Eisfeld's group had been joined by their Philharmonic colleagues—Jacoby (or Jacobi) (doublebass), Kiefer (clarinet), Schmitz (horn), and Eltz (bassoon)—the program included Mendelssohn's Trio in C minor, op. 66 (1845), for piano, violin, and cello, with Scharfenberg at the piano; a set of variations for string quartet on the Russian National Hymn by the Bohemian composer Wenzel Veit (1806–1864); and Haydn's String Quartet, no. 57, in G major. Mrs. Watson was again the soloist, singing another of the countless bird songs of the period, this one by Spohr—"A Bird Sat on an Alder Bough"—with violin obbligato played by Noll—and again an unidentified "Romance" from manuscript (probably the one by her husband).

In mid-Mendelssohn-Trio, Eichhorn snapped a string, and while he was replacing it, Mrs. Watson filled the void with a song. Willis, who peevishly recorded the incident, found Mendelssohn's trio, although "erudite and elaborate," to be "chaotic and unclear." If it was intended to represent "a *mind in difficulties*" it certainly succeeded. Willis again commended Mrs. Watson for some of her "round, full tones," but found her to be too objective in her singing—especially when compared with Jenny Lind, who was always magnificently *subjective* (*Musical Times,* May 15, 1852, pp. 15–16).

Oliver Dyer, who outdid himself in his latest paroxysm over Beethoven ("Breathe, immortal spirit, breathe upon our famished hearts!"), had been unable to

---

Cradle Song—The Dance—Serenade; 3. Martial Music—Departure for the Battlefield—Feeling of Those Left behind—Return of the Conquerors—*Te Deum;* 4. Funeral Music—Consolation amidst Tears—Invocation of Sound.

[32] Mrs. Bostwick's voice had "a certain domestic sweetness," wrote *Hafiz,* "but the total want of freshness and the constant sense of effort, although careful and successful, make the whole impression rather mournful, like the sweetness of faded flowers" (*Dwight's,* May 1, pp. 28–29).

[33] Beethoven's Septet was commonly designated *Septuor,* a word transcribed in the published *Diary* (II, 93) as *Leonore.*

"become entirely lost" in the Mendelssohn Trio, yet found himself "most thoroughly entangled with its amazing elaborateness of execution."[34]

Dyer commented, too, on the intolerance of the predominantly German chamber-music audience toward the "genteel burlesque" of introducing "second- or third-rate vocalism at 'classical' instrumental concerts." The practice amounted to no more than "filling up the interstices of a social evening party with elastic sponge cake and elegantly diluted lemonade," he wrote. But "no possible amount of amiability of disposition, sweetness of voice, taste in the selection, conception of the sentiment, or truthfulness in the manner of rendering [could] redeem an unfortunate singer" in their eyes. If she were not the equal of a Jenny Lind or a Grisi, neither were her brother-instrumentalists equal to Ernst, Vieuxtemps, or Sivori. Such singers deserved to succeed, "and would—if [their] judges were more charitable." This unfair attitude, he explained, accounted for "the equivocal success which attended Mrs. Watson's singing." But Dyer came away from this concert, the last of the second series, "instructed [and] made happier and better." Like his colleagues, but more vivaciously, he saluted Eisfeld for his superb contribution to the music life of the city with these concerts: "Delightful *Soirées,* for the present, adieu! But come again, with the return of the long, cool evenings—in the meantime, health and redoubled energy to you, LEADING SPIRIT" (*Musical World,* May 15, 1852, p. 287).

In May, Jenny Lind, now Madame Otto Goldschmidt, returned with her husband to New York to round out her American adventure with three final concerts before returning to Europe—on May 18 and 21 at Metropolitan Hall and May 24 at Castle Garden. The news of her marriage, on February 5 in Boston, had elicited a remarkably cool reaction from the New York press. Even the *Tribune,* that Lindian supershrine, devoted only a single paragraph to the event, and that mostly devoted to Goldschmidt, about whom a goodly amount of curiosity had been awakened:[35] "Jenny Lind was married by the Protestant Episcopal rite. She is thirty-one years old and her husband twenty-four. He is a gentleman and a man of genius—of Hebrew origin, we believe. We well remember his performances on the pianoforte, too good for the popular appreciation, and never deviating from the severity of art to draw out the public plaudits by tricks of clap-trap, which he had dexterity enough to do, if he had chosen. On these occasions, Jenny, who was not on the stage at the moment, used often to stand forward in her private box and clap her hands vigorously in sight of the audience, who by no means seemed to share her admiration for the pianist" (*Tribune,* February 9, 1852). And the *Mirror* the following day: "Goldschmidt, the lucky husband" (the more acerbic *Herald* called him "the too happy Otto Goldschmidt") "renounced his Jewish

[34] *Hafiz*/Curtis always approached a new work of Mendelssohn's wondering "not if it will be good, but will it be irresistible" (*Dwight's,* May 22, 1852, p. 52).

[35] And rumors to fly—among them that Goldschmidt was the son of an immensely wealthy silk merchant in Hamburg who had supported the young Lind in her early days of adversity, and that he had loved her since he was a little lad; or that he was "a little insignificant-looking, pale-faced," impecunious piano teacher in New Jersey who had barely subsisted by giving dollar music lessons until Lind chose him over several importunate "lords and gentlemen of high degree and proud estate," thus making him a celebrity (*Musical World and Journal of the Fine Arts,* June 15, p. 319; *Musical Times,* June 12, 1852, p. 63).

faith some months ago, and was baptized by Dr. [Jonathan] Wainwright into the Episcopal Church." Then, rather ungallantly: "Leap year has opened with a marked event."

Times had indeed changed. As the *Herald* reported on March 15 (losing no opportunity to snipe at Barnum): "It seems that Jenny Lind—or rather, Mme. Goldschmidt—has been for some days in Brooklyn [where she reportedly owned a house], without attracting the least attention. She is now allowed to pass as quietly through the world as any other woman. When she was an 'angel' she could not move in any direction without Barnum, the great trumpeter of her fame, sounding a blast loud and long, which was re-echoed by all the penny trumpets in the land."

True—despite the unbuttoned outpourings of Lind's three fanatical adherents, John Sullivan Dwight (now with a journal of his own in which to sing her praises to his heart's content),[36] his disciple George William Curtis in the *Tribune,* and his former antagonist (now his ally) Richard Grant White in the *Courier and Enquirer*—without Barnum, the New York papers devoted merely token space to the Nightingale's impending return. Characteristically, it was not long before a name-calling squabble erupted between the *Daily Times* on the one side, and the *Tribune* and *Courier and Enquirer* on the other, over what repertory each desired Lind to sing at her farewell concerts: the *Times* opted for at least one program of popular ballads in English; the others for a program of the severe classics, preferably non-operatic, and omitting "that musical harlequinism which displays itself in cow songs, imitations of birds, flutes, and all that class of vocal funambulism which makes the vulgar stare, but the judicious grieve"[37] (*Courier and Enquirer,* April 24, 1852).

More significant, the press now pounced on Goldschmidt, who, lacking Barnum's master touch, aroused great public resentment with his bungling management of his wife's concerts. He had announced beforehand that tickets, at one to three dollars, would be put on sale four days before the first concert, exclusively at Chickering's Piano Forte Rooms at 205 Broadway, and that positively no tickets would be available to speculators. Yet, on May 19, the day after the first concert, the *Evening Post* reported: "Chickering's well-known establishment on Broadway was the scene of considerable excitement. This morning, between 8 and 9 o'clock, 100 persons or more assembled in front of the building, endeavoring to get admission to purchase tickets for Mme. Otto Goldschmidt's next concert, but for some reason best known to the proprietor, no one was allowed to enter. The door was barred against everyone, and even the window shutters were put up to prevent inquisitive eyes from seeing the operations that were going on inside among those initiated in the mysteries.

"At length, when the patience of the outsiders was exhausted by the delay of an hour or more, the doors were opened, and a man rushed out bearing in his hands 200

[36] The first page of the first issue of *Dwight's Journal of Music* featured an article, "Jenny Lind's Devotion to her Art," by Julius Benedict, extolling Lind for making "A CONSCIENCE OF HER ART."

[37] "Richard Grant White and I have both suggested *one* concert of the true stamp," wrote George William Curtis to his friend John Sullivan Dwight on April 28, 1852, "and the *[Daily] Times* came out against us, and we pitched back again into the *Times;* and the *Herald* and other journals have called attention to the warfare, and insist that humbug, Barnumania, and high prices shall be put down. I am going to write an article upon Jenny Lind's right to ask $3 if she thinks fit, on the principle that Dickens, [the French painter] Horace Vernet [1789–1863], and every molasses merchant acts and properly acts" (Curtis, *Early Letters,* p. 283).

All: New-York Historical Society

John Sullivan Dwight, George William Curtis, and (below) Richard Grant White, Jenny Lind's three champions.

concert tickets which he offered for sale at $6 each, $3 over the price of reserved seats. Twelve, we understand, were sold at that price. The large number [of frustrated ticket buyers] were so disgusted by the miserable trick that they refused to purchase any. We hope some means will be taken to prevent a similar deception upon the public." Goldschmidt, of course, was believed to have been in league with the speculators.

And the *Mirror* (May 19, 1852), reviewing Lind's first concert, complained of "the indifferent arrangements for seating the audience, and the prevalence of speculators who, having bought up the dollar tickets, were driving such dollar-and-a-half and two-dollar bargains as they could make."

Public indignation over the continuing ticket bottleneck intensified, and by the morning of the final concert it culminated in a near-riot when a crowd, estimated at 800 to 1000, attempted to storm Chickering's, only to find the doorway narrowed to a mere slit that barely permitted one person at a time to squeeze through with difficulty. In the violent pushing and shoving that ensued, a mob of "rowdies, bullies, loafers, and boys" took over, and although the police forcibly cleared the sidewalk once or twice, they managed only temporarily to check the tumult "without improving the chances of those who wished to buy tickets." Inside, with Goldschmidt in charge, no more than ten tickets were permitted to a single buyer, but nine out of ten of those who had pushed their way in and purchased tickets were "decidedly loafers" (apparently a synonym for speculators), for by noon when the ticket sale within was concluded, "an active traffic immediately commenced in the street—some mounting boxes and selling tickets at auction, others disposing of them by private arrangement, etc. etc., and this was continued until late afternoon" (*Daily Times,* May 24, 1852).

It was generally felt that endless confusion and dissatisfaction might have been avoided, and the speculators foiled, had tickets been sold at a number of legitimate locations.[38] But Oliver Dyer (presumably) in the *Musical World* (June 1, 1852, p. 297), bluntly asserted that it was "nobody's business how or where Mr. Goldschmidt, or anyone else, [sold] his tickets. Giving concerts," he wrote, "is simply a matter of business, just as selling bricks, lime, silks, tomatoes, boots, butter, blackberries, books, music, rum, whiskey, newspapers, or anything under heaven, including concert tickets, is; and the person giving concerts has a right to manage the business in his own way. . . . And if anyone chooses to buy up all, or a portion, of the tickets to a concert, and run the risk of selling them again, he has a right to do it." Equally, those of the "sovereign people" who could not afford his high prices had a right to "fret and chafe and grumble." It was a perfectly equitable arrangement. It would have been better, however, to have sold the tickets at auction—in Dyer's opinion by far the best and fairest system—and if Goldschmidt did not want to pocket the extra profits, he could have donated them to charity.

Speculators or not, Lind's first concert more than filled Metropolitan Hall (as did her second). Accompanied by Eisfeld and eighty musicians, mostly from the Philharmonic, Lind was assisted by Cesare Badiali (taking the place of the departed Belletti), Joseph Burke, who doubled as concertmaster and soloist, and, of course, Otto Goldschmidt.

[38] In fact, a few speculators openly advertised tickets for the Lind concerts.

As usual, the press registered widely differing reactions to the event. Dwight, who had made the holy pilgrimage to New York to assist at the final rites, ecstatically saw in Lind (as did Curtis) a renewed vitality, renewed roses in her cheeks, and a renewed joyousness, as she "bounded forward in white bridal attire, her head dressed with loose sprays of vivid green. . . . A healthy, hearty, steady joy beamed in her countenance, and she seemed the happy artist-wife, with soul now doubly wedded, knowing rest no more in the ideal only" (*Dwight's,* May 22, 1852, p. 53).

To an unidentified reporter for the *Mirror* (May 19, 1852), too: "She looked as of old, only more *spirituelle*—an Otto-rose,[39] plucked from its virgin stem, but neither drooping nor faded."

But to R. Storrs Willis, whose former worshipful attitude toward Lind had somewhat moderated: "She appeared pale, interesting, and more than usually agitated"; moreover, she was not helped by the choice of her opening aria, *Leise, leise, fromme Weise* from *Der Freischütz,* a work that did not lie within the "upper and easier register" of her voice.

Goldschmidt, too, was "painfully agitated and deadly pale," and Willis was glad for his sake that Scharfenberg was at his side to lend support as his "obliging leaf-turner" for Weber's *Concertstück,* Goldschmidt's only contribution to the program. Although his playing was that of a master pianist, he was too agitated to cope with the difficulties of the piece. And anyway, he might have chosen a livelier vehicle for his solo.

Indeed, from its very opening with Beethoven's *Egmont* Overture, the program had been largely doleful when it should have been joyous.[40] Had Willis planned it, the concert would have opened with music of "a more jubilant, *nuptial* quality"—Weber's "Jubilee" Overture, for instance. Then, according to Willis's scenario, Goldschmidt would have led his "song-bride" onto the stage and straight off accompanied her in "'The Bird Song' instead of resigning the first escort-duty to the conductor." Not only would this have set a properly festive tone, but it would have restored to "The Bird Song" some of its lost freshness; it would also have spared Goldschmidt the ordeal of having later to walk on alone—"the one embarrassing point of all the opera glasses and eyes in the house"[41] (*Musical Times,* May 22, 1852, p. 28).

But for all his caviling, Willis had to agree with his more euphoric colleagues that Lind's performance of the cavatina *Ma la sola* from Bellini's *Beatrice di Tenda* was nothing short of phenomenal. In its cadenza (a showpiece written for Lind by Benedict): "The semi-tonic descent by successive chords . . . was almost an incredible thing in point of difficulty and accuracy of execution. When the original key had been entirely

[39] An aptly punning synonym for *attar rose.*

[40] Badiali sang two arias by Donizetti; Burke played Ferdinand David's Variations on a Theme of Schubert *(Lob der Tränen);* Eisfeld conducted the first performance of his Concert Polonaise for Orchestra; and Lind, in addition to the *Freischütz scena* and a duet with Badiali from *Gli Ugonotti,* sang a spectacular cavatina from *Beatrice di Tenda,* and closed the program with "The Bird Song," the hit of the evening, as the *Daily Times* (May 19, 1852) triumphantly pointed out; but the *Albion* (May 22, 1852, p. 248) condemned it as "a composition altogether ranging beneath the dignity of such an artiste."

[41] Although this was Goldschmidt's first concert appearance in New York as Jenny Lind's husband, he was by no means being seen or heard for the first time.

eradicated and lost to every other ear, the singer emerged from the labyrinth of tones to the starting point, as surely and successfully as if the violin (which announced her safe return) had been accompanying her all the time."[42] This astounding feat of transcendent musicianship was apparently wasted on George Templeton Strong.

May 21. . . . At Jenny Lind's concert Tuesday night [May 18]. She sings marvelously, but I would rather hear the Overture to *Egmont* played by the orchestra Eisfeld leads than even the *scena* from *Freischütz* and the lovely air from the *Nozze di Figaro [Deh vieni non tardar]* sung by any possible woman. Weber's *Concertstück* I was rather disappointed in.

Strong did not attend either of Lind's two remaining concerts.[43] The critics, each according to his individual bias, lauded her for different reasons—some for her superhuman musical gifts, some for her angelic godliness, some for her epoch-making triumphs in the United States, some for her prodigious box-office receipts. Dwight, in his *Journal* (May 22, pp. 53–54; May 29, 1852, pp. 61–62), surpassed everyone with his all but orgasmic reviews of her last three concerts, of a prolixity to stupefy the most dauntless of chroniclers. His transports were nearly equaled by G. W. Curtis and R. G. White, whose respective capacities for reiteration were apparently unlimited.

But a strangely restrained *Herald* (May 25, 1852), the day after Lind's last concert, reported merely that it had grossed some five or six thousand dollars—the three concerts a total of some ten thousand—and that the speculators had profited by some two or three thousand, although "some had got stuck."

The *Daily Times* (May 25) reported that Castle Garden had been jammed to its "utmost capacity" with thousands crowding its passageways and the covered bridge leading to the Castle and, despite the rain, the walks on the Battery and the surrounding streets. The *Mirror* (May 25), however, in the most lucid review of the lot, reported a large attendance, "but not so large, and far from as enthusiastic, as her first concert in that place. A large number of tickets, running into thousands [of dollars], were dead in the speculators' hands at 5 o'clock yesterday, and the prices after that hour ranged downwards like a thermometer in June caught by a sudden frost. In the end, the tickets were sold, here and there, as low as fifty cents, an evidence of which the audience at the Garden had in the squads that continued to enter long after the

[42] Thomas Ryan corroborates: "The cadenza was sung without accompaniment; it covered two pages of music paper, and was written in a style suited to an instrumental concerto. Towards the end there was a sequence of ascending and descending arpeggios of diminished sevenths which flowed into a scale of trills from the low note to one of her highest; then dwelling very long on that note and trilling it, she gradually, tranquilly returned to the theme of the cavatina, when it was perceived that her wonderfully fine musical ear had unerringly guided her through the mazes of the long cadenza and brought her to the tonic note of the piece with surprising correctness of intonation" (Ryan, pp. 138–39).

[43] For the "thronging thousands" at her second concert Lind sang an air from Mendelssohn's *Elijah,* "Hear Ye, Israel"; *Batti, batti,* from *Don Giovanni; Ah! non giunge,* from *La sonnambula;* and "The Gypsey's Song," from *A Camp in Silesia;* also "Home, Sweet Home" and "The Echo Song." Goldschmidt played his new concerto, composed for the occasion, a sterling, but dull, piece, according to the critics. Henry Appy played an unidentified violin fantasy, and Eisfeld conducted Spontini's Overture to *La vestale.*

concert was in progress. The tickets were, no doubt, all sold from Mr. Goldschmidt's hands—his money was sure—but the poor speculators were terribly stuck, and Jenny closed her great career in this country with far less praise and satisfaction from the public than she was entitled to as an artiste, and might easily have won by following good advice. Madame Goldschmidt sang, as usual, divinely," concluded the *Mirror.* "She holds the palm above all competitors, and is unquestionably, in the quality and variety of her power, without a rival."

Willis, who declared Lind's two previous concerts to have been of a "singularly *triste* and mournful character . . . inferior to most others which she has given in this country," nonetheless found her farewell effort to have been "all that was brilliant and bewildering"; he had "never heard a more glorious and surpassing performance" (*Musical Times,* May 29, 1852, p. 45).

Lind's last program in the United States virtually duplicated her first, albeit with an altered cast[44] and with Barnum spectacularly absent. Absent from the spotlight, that is, but by his own account in evidence backstage after the concert, to play out a touching finale with his former Nightingale, for the benefit of posterity. As Barnum tells it, Lind unfailingly sent him complimentary tickets whenever she gave concerts in New York, a Barnumesque embellishment, for until now there had been no Lind concerts in New York since their break-up in 1851.

Backstage, after mutual protestations of unfading regard, Lind informed Barnum that she would "never sing much, if any more, in public, but I reminded her that a good Providence had endowed her with a voice which enabled her to contribute to an eminent degree to the enjoyment of her fellow beings, and [automatically invoking the Angel] if she no longer needed the large sums of money which they were willing to pay for this educating and delightful entertainment, she knew by experience what a genuine pleasure she would receive by devoting the money to the alleviation of the wants and sorrows of those who need it. 'Mr. Barnum,' she replied, 'that is very true, and it would be ungrateful in me to not continue to use for the benefit of the poor and lowly that gift which our Kind Heavenly Father has so graciously bestowed upon me. Yes, I will continue to sing so long as my voice lasts, but it will be mostly for charitable objects, for I am thankful to say I have all the money which I shall ever need'"[45] (*Struggles and Triumphs,* pp. 351–52). Thus dripping with unction did the Swedish Nightingale and the Prince of Humbugs part forever.[46]

[44] And not an improved one: Badiali fell far short of Belletti in brilliance and effectiveness, wrote Willis; and Goldschmidt, for all his sterling qualities, lacked "strong point," a polite way of saying that he was a tedious performer (*Musical Times,* May 29, 1852, p. 45).

[45] On September 9 the *New-York Times* labeled as "Arabian Nights fiction" a report in the *Musical World and New York Musical Times* that the net proceeds of the Barnum/Lind partnership had been $610,000, of which Barnum had received "$3,000 more than half." But Barnum, in a note denying that he had ever supplied such figures to the *Musical Times* or anyone else, claimed that his share of the profits had in fact exceeded the sum reported ($308,000) by "much more than one $50,000, and perhaps by several." In the ensuing flurry in the press the *Mirror* (September 25, 1852) pointed out that the astronomical sum Barnum had suggested was mathematically impossible: "We should rejoice that Barnum, or any other deserving man, made millions; but our sober estimate of the Lind business, and it is great, at that, would give Barnum about $250,000 and Lind $200,000. This strikes us as a reasonable figure."

[46] To Barnum's credit, he never spoke ill of Lind; unfortunately, Lind was less courteous in her remembrances of Barnum.

Lind's farewell program, in addition to the *Casta diva,* the duet from Rossini's *Il Turco in Italia,* the Flute Trio, and "The Echo Song," included "Comin' thro' the rye" and closed with "Farewell to America," a companion piece to the prize song of yesteryear, with music composed by Goldschmidt to a text by the American poet Christopher P. Cranch (1813–1892). The *Mirror* (May 25, 1852) thought Goldschmidt's music "tame and commonplace," and the words merely illustrative of "the sentiments they were meant to express."[47]

Hardly demonstrating these fond sentiments, Lind did not see fit to acknowledge the serenade performed beneath her window at Delmonico's Hotel in a misty drizzle during the small hours of May 29, the day of her departure. "For half an hour before the musicians arrived, knots of citizens gathered around the vicinity, and when the music commenced, somewhat two or three thousand were present, including three hundred firemen in uniform and bearing torches." Despite the heavy mist, which affected the string instruments, the music was "most exquisitely performed" by an unnamed orchestra, together with Dodworth's Band and purportedly the Germania.[48] "The crowd at intervals cheered for Mme. Goldschmidt, and at the conclusion called vehemently for her and her husband, but neither of them made their appearance" (*Courier and Enquirer,* May 29, 1852).

The *Mirror* (May 31, 1852), in its account of Lind's departure, dealt with the incident less blandly. First attacking Goldschmidt, the *Mirror* accused him of "abusing the public beyond all example" in his shady dealings with the ticket speculators. "We stigmatized the ticket sale as a farce," wrote the *Mirror,* "and for this and some well-meant (however received) advice, Mr. Goldschmidt flew into a rage," accusing the *Mirror* of vengefulness because he had refused to provide great blocks of free tickets. This charge, declared the *Mirror,* was as false as Goldschmidt's management was bad. To say nothing of his manners.

"We cannot think Madame Goldschmidt suggested his course of conduct, although her treatment of the musical profession of this city, and some 150 representatives of the Fire Department,[49] on Saturday night, would indicate that she had become

[47]The last of its three trite stanzas went:

> Farewell—when parted from thy shore,
> Long absent scenes return once more
> Where'er the wanderer's home may be,
> Still, still will memory turn to thee!
> Bright Freedom's clime—I feel thy spell,
> But I must say farewell—farewell!

[48]Protesting the erroneous inclusion of the Germania in reports of the serenade, John Scherpf, the secretary of the Musical Fund Society, wrote to the papers to inform the public that the event had been organized solely by the Musical Fund Society; that the orchestra had been the Philharmonic; that Dodworth's Band, who had volunteered their services, had played a duet *(Giorno d'orrore)* from *Semiramide* and "Home, Sweet Home"; and that the orchestra had played a combined arrangement of "Yankee Doodle" and "Hail Columbia," the *Notturno* from *Midsummer Night's Dream,* Weber's "Jubilee" Overture, and appropriately had concluded with the Wedding March from *Midsummer Night's Dream.* Scherpf reported that about 200 firemen were present; like the Musical Fund Society, they were deeply grateful to Jenny Lind for her earlier generosity. He did not refer to her failure to acknowledge the tribute.

[49]There seems to have been a wide diversity of opinion over the number of firemen attending the farewell serenade.

either careless of the feelings and good-will of her friends, or was so absorbed in her 'little man' as to be deaf and blind to the courtesy, at least, due them.

"The Musical Fund Society and other leading musicians, numbering about eighty—each a master in his line—among them Burke, Eisfeld, Scharfenberg, Bouchelle, Timm, etc., accompanied by the firemen aforesaid, paid Jenny Lind the compliment of a magnificent serenade at Delmonico's, tooting under her windows from 2 till a quarter past 3 o'clock A.M., until their locks were wet with the drops of the morning, but no Jenny Lind appeared, in person, or by any message or sign, to acknowledge the tribute—the high tribute—paid her, notwithstanding she had been notified of the event by personal friends.

"And this was the Musical Fund Society who serenaded Jenny on her arrival in this country—whose good opinion she was then glad to court—and to whom she, or rather Mr. Barnum, gave $2500; these were also a part of that Fire Department which she so eulogized, and to whom Barnum—*not Jenny Lind*—gave $5000. We rather guess, from all we have heard, the musical fraternity of New York, on her advent here again, will sleep and snore, rather than spend their wind under Jenny's casement.

Library of Congress

Mathew Brady's portrait of Jenny Lind.

"Jenny is gone, heaven bless her, and we subtract nothing from the praise we have ever given her as *the* singer of the age. But we do not feel bound to give the bad management of Goldschmidt the go-by on account of his wife's excellence. By his side, Barnum towers a Colossus of talent, courtesy, and every other good quality. Barnum sought by every means to strengthen the public belief that Jenny was an 'angel,' and to this end gave nine-tenths of the money credited to Jenny's charity."

A crowd, purportedly of "thousands," assembled on the pier to bid Lind farewell, reported the *Courier and Enquirer* (May 31, 1852). "She arrived on the pier about half-past eleven, and was received warmly by the crowd through which she drove. Soon after . . . she appeared with Captain West[50] and Mr. Goldschmidt upon the paddle-box, and again received an enthusiastic recognition." Lind smiled and waved and blew kisses to acquaintances spotted in the crowd, but as departure time approached, "her face lost its power to smile; she still beckoned and kissed adieus, but she did it with streaming eyes. In her hand was a wreath, and around her [were] flowers which had been sent as tokens of regard. . . . As the vessel parted from its moorings and the fervent feelings of the large assembly broke forth in hearty cheers, she bowed her head between her hands and, leaning upon the rail, sobbed like a child. . . . "[51] Soon her tear-stained face faded to a blur, and all that could be seen of Jenny Lind was the receding flicker of her white handkerchief—and soon that too disappeared.

May 23. . . . Went this morning to the new Roman Catholic Church [of St. Francis Xavier] in [West] Sixteenth Street, where I was told good music was to be heard. Result of the experiment not satisfactory. The [unidentified] Mass was well enough sung and was a very ambitious and elaborate composition, but the *Gloria* was very like the gambling chorus in *Robert le diable,* and I'm sure I heard a crescendo at the end of the *Credo* in the *Gazza ladra.* The composer, whoever he was, had overstepped the old traditional forms one meets in Haydn and Mozart, and in some cases with curious effect; and in the *Credo,* the word *credo* was brought in at intervals from the opening to the *Vitam venturi saeculi* always by the chorus and always on the same musical phrase. The effect was that of an interjectional fortissimo sneeze set to music. The *Kyrie* was not bad; the rest of the Mass seemed great trash. "In order to promote the sale of the pews" the moderate charge of 12½ cents is made to strangers for seats in the body of the church (or parquette); 6¼ cents for seats in the gallery.

~

For some reason, during the remainder of that musically abundant year Strong attended no more concerts—at least, he recorded none. On May 27 he went to Niblo's Garden with Ellen and saw "some of the idiotic foolery called *ballet,*" in this instance *La Bayadère,* performed by the Rousset sisters; the sung parts, he complained, were badly done. On July 2, "dinnerless and disconsolate," due to a prolonged headache, Strong consoled himself by "spelling over some of Haydn's Mass No. 2,[52] which," he wrote, "'do please me.'"

[50] Lind returned to Europe on the *Atlantic,* the same ship that had brought her to America nearly two years earlier.

[51] Was she shedding tears of sentiment—remorse—frustration—chagrin?

[52] Novello no. 2, Hoboken XXII:9, known as the *Paukenmesse,* or *Missa in tempore belli* (1796).

Thus, Strong did not attend the opening *soirées* of Eisfeld's third chamber music series, now moved to Niblo's Saloon. The first was given on October 30, a stormy and dismal evening that did not, however, discourage the audience, "attracted, not by European reputations, not by portentous announcements or dexterous puffery, but simply by the desire to hear classical music accurately performed." At Niblo's, according to the *Home Journal* (November 6, 1852), "the auditors were arranged in semicircles round the stage, like a family party listening to the inspiring and animated conversation of four dear, newly-arrived friends." The program included string quartets by Mozart and Beethoven, the Schumann Piano Quintet, again with Scharfenberg at the piano, and duets and songs by the Tourny sisters, Louisa and Mina, recent arrivals from Germany who were making their American debut on this occasion. Together they performed duets by Mendelssohn and Franz Abt (1819–1885), and Miss Mina, a "rather coarse" mezzo-soprano or contralto, sang two solos—Lindblad's "Birdling" and "Margery," a love song by Kücken.

Puffing Eisfeld's second *soirée,* given on November 20, the *Musical World and New York Musical Times,* as the recently merged *Musical World and Journal of the Fine Arts* with the *Musical Times* was called[53] (hereinafter cited as the *Musical World and Times*), enthusiastically urged its readers to attend: "These musical *Soirées* . . . are decidedly superior to anything of the kind ever given in this city; and aside from their intrinsic merits and the pleasure derived from attending them, their *educational* character—the salutary influence they exert upon the tastes of those brought within the magic circle of their charms—peculiarly entitle them to the most liberal support of all who are interested in musical culture—or who have a *'living interest'* in the rising generation" (November 20, 1852, p. 179).[54]

Nor did Strong hear the remaining Philharmonic concert of the year, the first of their eleventh season, given at Niblo's Saloon on November 13. Again an overlong program, it included Beethoven's Eighth Symphony, the first performance in New York of Niels Gade's concert overture "Echoes of Ossian" (1840), the first movement of Hummel's Piano Concerto in B minor, op. 89 (1816), played by Timm, a set of Variations for string trio by Maurer on Méhul's *Joseph,* played by Noll, Reyer, and Eichhorn, a repeat performance of Litolff's "Robespierre" Overture, vocal duets by Mendelssohn, sung by the Tournys, and the aria *Luce di quest'anima* from *Linda di Chamounix,* sung by Miss Mina.

The *Tribune* waxed lyrical over Gade's "new" overture. In a maze of garbled chronology, the critic[55] rejoiced that Gade had at last found his own distinctively Nordic

[53] The two periodicals had been merged in July and now appeared under the joint editorship of Oliver Dyer and R. Storrs Willis.

[54] In his review of the *soirée*—the program consisted of quartets by Beethoven and Haydn; the Grand Trio, op. 46, for piano, violin, and cello, by Alexander Fesca, with a new pianist, Charles Mueller; and two songs, Haydn's "Spirit's Song" [op. 38] and, by request, Fesca's "Love's Messengers," sung by Mrs. Watson—the critic for the *Musical World and Times* (November 27, 1852, p. 195) observed that "the unquestioned substantiality of Mrs. Watson's presence was in strange contrast to the 'spirit' of the [Spirit] song," in any case a choice "inappropriate to the occasion." But he was willing to forgive all her infelicities of intonation and declamation "in consideration of the pleasure of looking at those irreproachable arms."

[55] Possibly the journalist and future Beethoven biographer Alexander Wheelock Thayer (1817–

voice and outgrown the influence, however beneficent, of his teacher Mendelssohn—an influence apparent in Gade's First Symphony, op. 5 (1841). "Ossian" had, in fact, preceded the symphony by a year.

For the performance of this splendid, wild, and romantic work, "His Excellency, President Timm," had to play the harp part on the piano, because no sufficiently capable harpist could be found, and although the substitution was unimpeachably accurate, the "resonant twang of the harp strings" was missed.

Timm's performance of the Hummel concerto was, as always, a model of excellence; the Tournys' singing was "very German and pleasing" in Mendelssohn's duet "The May Bells and the Flowers" *(Maiglöckchen und die Blümelein)* (1844), but Miss Mina's rather rough contralto, although effective when blended with her sister's soprano, was "rather crude to be heard alone"; and besides, in the aria from *Linda,* transposed down to suit her range, she lacked the "perfect style of Italian elaboration" required to make it "at all tolerable."

Litolff's "Robespierre" Overture, enthusiastically reviewed after its first performance in 1851, was now pronounced to be "a good specimen of thunder-and-lightning clap-trap, with the *Marseilles Hymn,* groans of the dying, portentous silence of the Reign of Terror, funeral marches, guns, trumpets, and trombones unsparingly mingled into an *olla podrida* of unmeaning noise. Weber's 'Jubilee' Overture is precisely what Litolff's 'Robespierre' is *not*—but what it desperately aims to be" (*Tribune,* November 15, 1852).

In mid-November the brilliant but erratic journalist/composer William Henry Fry returned from Europe to join the *Tribune*'s editorial staff in New York as a writer and music critic. During his absence of some six years, largely spent in Paris as the *Tribune*'s foreign correspondent,[56] Fry had gained impressive journalistic stature with his splendid reporting of political, social, and cultural aspects of the transatlantic scene.

Never one for self-effacing understatement, Fry, evidently driven by an insatiable hunger to be acclaimed the Messiah of American Music, made a far-from-unheralded re-entry into his native land. As early as the preceding April his devoted brother Edward, the failed manager of the Astor Place Opera in 1849 (now, according to the City Directory a merchant at 39 Wall Street), had launched a quasi-Barnumesque buildup for a series of ten supercolossal lectures, or rather, lecture/concerts, to be undertaken by William Henry Fry immediately upon his return. Having amassed a prodigious store of historical/musical esoterica while abroad, and taking as his model the path-breaking lecture/concerts given in Paris in 1832–33 by the Belgian musicologist François-Joseph Fétis (1784–1871), William Henry Fry proposed in his series—with musical illustrations supplied by a large orchestra, chorus, band, and an assortment of

1897), who joined the *Tribune*'s editorial staff in 1852 upon his return from two years in Europe. Thayer, the New York "Diarist" for *Dwight's,* might have supplied music criticism for the *Tribune* during the interval between George William Curtis's departure and the advent of William Henry Fry in December, although Dwight later (in 1856) denied it.

[56] Fry's primary reason for going to Europe in 1846 had been his consuming desire—doomed to failure—to have his problematical opera *Leonora*♪ produced at the *Académie Royale* (the Paris Opéra). (See William Treat Upton, *Fry,* p. 51.)

William Henry Fry.

[ADVERTISEMENT.]

SUBSCRIPTION LISTS

FOR

WILLIAM HENRY FRY'S

COURSE OF

TEN LECTURES ON MUSIC,

TO BE DELIVERED AT

METROPOLITAN HALL,

Commencing in November, 1852,

Are now open at the principal Music and Book Stores, where Prospectuses may be obtained.

The aim of these Lectures will be to present in a condensed but clear form, an illustrated history of the rise, progress and present state of all departments of instrumental and vocal music: whether sacred, dramatic, symphonic, classic, romantic or national, or of those various kinds which it would be difficult to class specifically. The manner in which the subject will be treated, will enable the hearer to understand the structure of various musical compositions, to form more correct opinions of the performance of vocal and instrumental artists, and to comprehend more clearly the proper terms of musical criticism. In short, the effort of the lecturer will be to give, as minutely and thoroughly as such a course of musical lectures can, a view of the literature, an analysis of the philosophy, and an explanation of the technicalities of music both as a science and an art.

Single Tickets for the Course, - - - - - Price, $5.

Payment to be made on delivery of the Tickets, in October next.

Several hundred Subscribers have already signed the lists and numerous additional names are daily received.

The Lectures will not take place unless Two Thousand Tickets are subscribed for. After these are obtained the price of the remaining Tickets will be

RAISED TO TEN DOLLARS.

THE MUSICAL ILLUSTRATIONS WILL BE GIVEN BY

240 PERFORMERS,

INCLUDING A CORPS OF PRINCIPAL

OPERATIC AND CONCERT SINGERS,

OF THE HIGHEST GRADE,

AN ORCHESTRA OF 80,

AND A

CHORUS OF ONE HUNDRED, &c., &c.

Both: New-York Historical Society

vocal soloists—to encompass nothing less than the entire realm of music: its history, aesthetics, scientific properties, and even, for the benefit of his predominantly uninformed audiences, some rudimentary music lessons. His visionary purpose in attempting this huge undertaking was to dazzle and educate his musically "primitive" compatriots and to compel them to listen to, and accept, American music (specifically his own).

Subscriptions, at five dollars for the series, to take place on consecutive Tuesday evenings at Metropolitan Hall beginning November 30, were put on sale in May at the principal music and book stores. "The lectures will not take place unless Two Thousand Tickets are subscribed for," forewarned Edward Fry's elaborate brochure, and "after these are obtained, the price of the remaining Tickets will be raised to ten dollars"; tickets to single lectures were priced at eighty-five cents. By the third lecture, however, to coax attendance, the schedule of prices would be changed, with single tickets reduced to fifty cents and the quota for the $5 subscriptions lowered to 1000; it was later again extended to 2000.

Concurrent with the first wave of advertisements in May, the press enthusiastically puffed Fry as an inspired composer, a profound music scholar, a skilled journalist, and a forceful thinker; some papers dropped seductive hints that several "queens of fashion and society in this metropolis" had already purchased their subscriptions, to say nothing of leading merchants and professional men. And with no opera season in the offing, Fry's lectures would undoubtedly be "*the* feature of taste, enjoyment, and fashion next season; therefore, our fair friends had better secure their right to join in this instructive and melodious festival at once" (*Home Journal,* May 22, 1852).

It was, however, the pedagogical aspects of Fry's vast undertaking that were particularly stressed: his innovative project presented an ideal means for painlessly educating not only the general public but also, as it was pointedly suggested, the critics: "Mr. Fry is not only a *fanatico per la musica,*" editorialized the *Daily Times* on November 23, before the first lecture, "but a judicious musical critic eminently qualified for the office of musical instructor . . . and eminently needed in our musical world. Justly or unjustly, an idea is abroad that the musical ideas of the American press are not, to use the gentlest phrase, what they should be."[57] Might not the critics benefit by a little authoritative guidance? After all, Fry had been absorbing the real thing in Europe all these years; it was only fair that he now share it with his brethren. "Very happy results, we conceive, will flow from a lucid and popular statement of a few musical principles. They will save a vast deal of transcendentalism and extravagance among gentlemen who feel impelled to say much where they know little." Taking a further jab at its journalistic colleagues, the *Times* disingenuously suggested that Fry organize "a special class of musical editors, with reference to the correction of vulgar taste." New York audiences, in the *Times*'s opinion, needed especially to "learn the art of judicious sibilation."[58]

R. Storrs Willis disagreed. "Mr. Fry," he wrote after the first lecture, "is a manly,

[57] The editorial might have been written by Charles Bailey Seymour (1829–1869). An emigrant from England in 1849, Seymour served as music and drama critic for the *Times* from "nearly the beginning of its publication" until shortly before his death (*New-York Times* obituary, May 3, 1869).

[58] They apparently learned it by Fry's third lecture, when he was hissed during his exposition of Biblical music for calling King Solomon a "dirty debauchee" (*Musical Review and Choral Advocate,* January 1853, pp. 10–11).

vigorous, and forceful writer.[59] His manner and address corresponds [*sic*] with this, and his personal impress is that of a superior, though—we could not but think—irregular and undisciplined intellect." In this respect, noted Willis, Fry was a not unrepresentative type of American, having a mind like an eagle, which seemed to "soar, untrammeled, but wayward and uncertain."

But Fry, in Willis's opinion, was first and foremost a writer—"a musical philosopher of the Tone-realm"—not a teacher. He erred in attempting to instruct his audience in the ABCs of music, which, if plain to him and "tediously plain" to those who knew them, were totally incomprehensible to those who did not. It was a waste of Fry's gifts to dabble in the "repulsive *do-re-mi* and the *fa-sol-la* of things in music"; he should have confined himself to saying beautiful things about music and letting his large and good orchestra and chorus render such "'examples' of ancient and grotesque music as the Chinese Chant, performed on the first occasion . . . without the educational features introduced" (*Musical World and Times,* December 4, 1852, pp. 210–11). But to Fry anything short of everything was inadmissible, as the giant advertisement for his extraordinary undertaking reveals (see APPENDIX 3).

Except for "The Star-Spangled Banner," which was played to demonstrate the major triad, the better part of the "illustrative music" for Fry's first lecture was of his own composition. (Oddly enough, this transparent device for uninhibited self-display[60] escaped the comment of the normally sharp-toothed critics.) To illustrate the minor mode and the chromatic scale, according to the lengthy *Tribune* report (December 1, 1852), Fry used a "pathetic" work for chorus and orchestra "representing a Roman who had embraced the Christian faith [being] led to execution amid the imprecations of the Roman mob" (extracted from his unfinished early opera *Cristiani e pagani*); his orchestra piece *The Breaking Heart* (apparently another pathetic work) was played to illustrate "the varieties of musical quantity and expression"; two other Fry compositions were performed to exemplify compound and common meter: *The Day in the Country,* for orchestra,[61] and from another apparently uncompleted opera *The Borderers,*[62] the "Moss-Troopers' Chorus," for male voices, blithely titled "Each Merry Moss Trooper Mounted His Steed."

[59] Despite the extensive and informative coverage of Fry's series of lectures in the contemporary press, John Dizikes, in his *Opera in America, A Cultural History* (p. 104), laments: ". . . as Fry had spoken spontaneously and didn't subsequently transcribe his thoughts to paper, we have no record of what he said. It was a great loss."

[60] In the past, Fry's well-to-do family had always subsidized performances of his works in Philadelphia. And since the Philharmonic's notorious unwillingness to perform native compositions offered Fry little hope of a volunteer performance by that organization—and since he possessed the financial resources—he quite naturally assumed the expenses of having his works performed.

[61] During the famous knock-down-drag-out battle that later ensued between Fry and Willis, Fry, in a defensive, staggeringly verbose open letter to Willis, claimed that "*The Breaking Heart* and *The Day in the Country* [later *A Day in the Country*] were both written in the same week previous to the Lectures which I delivered at Metropolitan Hall last winter" (*Musical World and Times,* January 21, 1854, pp. 29–31, 34; reprinted in *Dwight's,* February 4, 1854, pp. 138–40). Fry's curious compulsion to boast about the speed with which he composed had apparently not abated in the years since his curtain speech after the first performance of *Leonora* in Philadelphia in 1845,♪ when he bragged of having dashed it off in spare moments, over a period of a few months.

[62] And unremembered. *The Borderers* is not mentioned in William Treat Upton's catalogue of Fry's works (*Fry,* Appendix 1, p. 305). But "Each Merry Moss-Trooper" is listed (p. 322) as an earlier

Although the anonymous reviewer (A. W. Thayer?) found *The Day in the Country* to be "full of fresh and natural beauty," he would have preferred an excerpt from Beethoven's "Pastoral" Symphony. He thought, too, that *The Breaking Heart* was somewhat too long (as was the lecture). The second part of the program was devoted to specimens of Chinese music, followed by the Overture to *Der Freischütz,* to illustrate "the advance of Christian upon Pagan civilization."

Despite his loudly proclaimed, fervent championship of the neglected American Musician, Fry, a master of the incongruous, chose his cast of solo singers (none of whom appeared at the opening lecture) from among the unemployed members of the defunct Italian opera companies—Rose de Vries, Rosina Pico-Vietti, her husband Adelindo Vietti, and Domenico Coletti; also announced were two members of Madame Henriette Sontag's company, the basso buffo Luigi Rocco and the tenor Gasparo Pozzolini (discussed in the following OBBLIGATO). Fry's "colossal" orchestra and chorus of more than 200 performers (comprising members of both the Philharmonic and Harmonic Societies)[63] were, however, respectively conducted and led by the native sons George Frederick Bristow and Ureli C. Hill, a fact that Fry proudly flaunted in the compulsive flood of words with which, in introducing his second lecture, he blasted the criticizers of his first.[64]

"The marvel to us," wrote Willis, who proclaimed Fry to be "decidedly the boldest lecturer of our day" and "the most *free-thoughted* man we ever heard address an audience," was the way he could "introduce so much foreign and extraneous matter into a musical lecture" (*Musical World and Times,* December 18, 1852, p. 242).[65] But the critics, apparently apprehensive of exposing their ignorance of Fry's arcane subject matter, and probably intimidated by his belligerence, generally maintained a safe, head-nodding approval of his lectures. If there were dissenters, they were silent, at least at the outset. Except, that is, for George Templeton Strong.

December 9. . . . Fry's second lecture [December 7] (of a course of ten) on *Music.* Didn't suppose it possible a sane man could be found willing to make such a jackass of

work "introduced" by Fry in his opera *Notre Dame de Paris* (performed in Philadelphia in 1864), and retitled "Chorus of the Royal Scotch Archers." (Moss-troopers were seventeenth-century marauders who operated chiefly in the mossy bogs along the English/Scottish border.)

[63] It was estimated in the papers that the overblown extravaganza cost Fry no less than $10,000 to mount; he was later reported to have lost some $4000 on the undertaking.

[64] In furious rebuttal of the *Tribune*'s comments on the excessive length of *The Breaking Heart*—and obviously hungry for praise—Fry defensively "suggested" to the audience that "it may be erroneous to apply the qualifying words, *too long*" to a piece that had received the rare honor of being applauded at rehearsals by "the scientific and artistic members of the orchestra. Neither do I see why I should have selected the great Beethoven to illustrate the first lecture." Besides (after digressing to the War of 1812, American Courage, and the Infinitude of Music): "No author [Beethoven not excepted] would have illustrated my meanings as I wished to convey them, except the pieces presented." Fry boasted, too, that nearly three thousand pages of his music had been copied for that evening alone (*Musical World and Times,* December 18, 1852, p. 242).

[65] "What [Fry] said upon the art itself," wrote Richard Grant White, after the third lecture, "was justly thought and highly interesting. . . . But with his remarks upon music he mingled so many of his own peculiar views upon religious, social, and political questions that a great number of his hearers felt that they had been beguiled into listening to a harangue in favor of Socialism under the guise of a lecture upon Art" (*Courier and Enquirer,* December 16, 1852).

himself. He had nothing of any value to say, and he said it very vilely. Whatever was not so frivolous and insignificant as to make it not worthwhile to consider whether it was true or false—whatever approached the subject itself and was not babble about Chinese instruments and the names of musical notes in Siamese—was utterly false and shallow. As to his illustrations of ancient music, I don't know where he found the copies of same, nor where he got the value of the musical notes. If he *had* settled those matters, he must have been an idiot to suppose that the unequal melody, *harmonized* by himself, and produced with florid instrumentation, could be anything like itself. It's a hopeful sign that the people of New York have sufficient sense of decency to pronounce his "lectures" a humbug.[66]

One might as well lecture on Shakespeare and commence by scraps of philology about pronouns and articles and specimens of barbarism in the lingua franca of a Manilla trader or an Anglo Dutch or a Cape boor [*sic*] or the gabble of a Georgia plantation, as to preface a lecture on Music—on the glory of Haydn and Beethoven and Mozart (which every *real* lecture on Music must be)—by all this fribble-frabble about Chinese melody and Hindoo orchestras.[67]

If his specimens of Egyptian compositions were genuine, cramp in the stomach and nervous fits must have been epidemic along the Nile; the Exodus of the Israelites was an act of self-preservation, and Pharaoh's last words as the water covered him must have been: "I shall hear marches played by my military bands no more."

But the second part of his Concert, Rossini's *Stabat Mater,* was worth hearing. That composition has never been so rendered in New York before. I never saw its real substance so distinctly.[68] It is beautiful; but it is what I suppose a Flemish specimen of religious art in the seventeenth century must be—beautiful she-saints and angels with loose-flowing tresses and full bosoms, a good deal undressed, bright red lips, big blue eyes, and tears as large as first-class achromatic lenses. It's too luscious and sensual to belong to the highest school of Art.[69]

In addition to the offending Egyptian, Chinese, Siamese, Hindoo, and Persian items, Fry's second lecture included analyses, blackboard "diagrams," an Ode of Horace (to what music?), a "Lament for Charlemagne" ("barbarous and monotonous in the extreme" to Richard Grant White), and a spirited "War Song of Roland." To leaven all this abstrusity, in the second part, aside from the sections of the *Stabat Mater,* which closed the program, the tenor Pozzolini sang a Romance from Donizetti's *Linda di Chamounix* and Madame de Vries gave a brilliant performance of the *Rondo* from Verdi's *I Lombardi* (*Courier and Enquirer,* December 8, 1852).

[66] Not according to the papers, which reported an increasingly large attendance at each successive lecture.

[67] Contrary to Strong, the *Tribune* (December 8, 1852) reported of this lecture that "the matter of [Fry's] discourse indicated the profoundest acquaintance with the history of music and a degree of curious learning in the music of China, Siam, India, and Europe of the Middle Ages, which was as novel as it was instructive to his hearers."

[68] Strong had heard the first performances in America of Rossini's *Stabat Mater* in 1842.♪

[69] Richard Grant White took issue with Fry for referring to Rossini's *Stabat Mater* as a sacred composition: "Rossini never possessed a musical idea which could be made to express a religious sentiment," wrote White. "Comic he is, noble he is; but his thoughts never rise heavenward" (*Courier and Enquirer,* December 16, 1852).

Needless to say, Strong did not attend the remaining lectures. At the third, on December 14, Fry tackled the "Laws of Sound" (acoustics); he examined the "History of Music in Ancient Egypt and among the Jews, with critical remarks upon the artistic portions of the Bible," the most critical being aimed at King Solomon;[70] he discussed as well the "Ancient Greek System of Music and its connection with Poetry." Additionally, Fry included "several Oriental melodies harmonized [by himself] for the Grand Chorus, two original Greek Hymns set to Greek Words, with a particular comment of how they were discovered and interpreted; various specimens of Medieval Music from 600 to 1000 years old"; and in the second section, contemporary music that included choral and vocal works by Beethoven, Rossini, Verdi, and Michael Balfe.

At his fourth lecture (December 21) and from then on, Fry, a fanatical worshiper of opera, particularly Italian opera, shifted the focus of his lectures to serve his major musical preoccupations, opera and the voice. Following a few "brief" presentations of "ancient Greek and Roman music," this lecture consisted largely of voluminous excerpts from his much-mooted opera *Leonora,* remembered by some critics as a great failure, by others as a great triumph (an enduring topic of impassioned defensiveness on Fry's part). After this performance R. Storrs Willis, temporarily swayed by Fry's fervor, wrote (in Fry's own words): "*Leonora* is an *American* opera. Why cannot we have it produced in this city? Mr. Fry, as an American, deserves it" (*Musical World and Times,* December 25, 1852, p. 258).

For his fifth lecture (December 28) Fry dispensed with the orchestra but not the chorus, the subject being exclusively: "The Voice, its physical structure and artistic capabilities; the philosophy of composing for it dramatically and otherwise; old and new forms of writing for it; the peculiarities of ancient and modern vocal composers: Palestrina, Jommelli, Purcell, Handel, Mozart, Haydn, Rossini, Bellini, and others. Besides this, each piece of music on the program [was] preceded by critical, explanatory, and biographical remarks" (*Daily Times,* December 28, 1852).

"Not the least interesting part of the lecture," wrote Richard Grant White, "were the remarks which [Fry] made sitting at the piano forte, explaining his music . . . and illustrating his words [to his audience's surprise, in song].[71] What he said was . . . interesting information, conveyed in a manner which made crooked paths straight and rough places plain. Mr. Fry would do well to remember this in future lectures" (*Courier and Enquirer,* December 29, 1852).[72]

But the straightening of crooked paths and smoothing of rough places would not be the mission of William Henry Fry. An embattled visionary, it was his uncomfortable destiny to sow controversy and reap frustration.

[70] Fry's overzealous characterization of King Solomon as a "dirty debauchee" seemed to Chauncey M. Cady (1824–1889), the straitlaced new editor of the *Musical Review and Choral Advocate,* an objectionable utterance that could "very consistently come from an infidel or atheist. . . . He would do well to remember that he is not now in the skeptical atmosphere of Paris" (January 1853, p. 10–11).

[71] Few remembered that Fry had made his New York debut as a singer at a concert given in 1843 by the opera diva Anaïde Castellan.♪

[72] The remainder of Fry's lectures are discussed in OBBLIGATO: 1853.

OBBLIGATO: 1852

. . . let us have all styles in the universal realm of sound.
The Musical World and New York Musical Times
November 6, 1852

WITH CHARACTERISTIC PANACHE, the extrovert Norwegian violin virtuoso Ole Bull♪ timed his return to New York, after a seven-year absence,[1] to coincide with Jenny Lind's trio of farewell appearances. Although his sole stated purpose in coming back to the United States had been to purchase land for the establishment of a Utopian colony for Norwegian emigrants,[2] it was not long before Bull "yielded" to the urgings of his countless friends and admirers, and he was soon triumphantly giving concerts, a pursuit as natural (and necessary) to him as breathing. With the assistance of the superlative young pianist Alfred Jaëll and the Germania orchestra, conducted by Carl Bergmann, Bull, after brilliant successes in Washington, Baltimore—where he settled "a long-standing dispute" (with William Burton? with Julius Schuberth?)—and Philadelphia, returned to New York for two concerts at Metropolitan Hall, the first on May 22, 1852, the night after Jenny Lind's penultimate appearance.

"We are embarrassed with musical wealth," exulted Richard Grant White in the *Courier and Enquirer* on May 24. "To hear such a celebrity as Madame Goldschmidt on one evening and such another as Ole Bull on the next is a concurrence of opportunity not often attainable even in a European metropolis."

That Bull was able to attract a large audience while Lind was still in "such possession of the public ear" clearly indicates that his former visit had left deep and enduring impressions upon the public. But then, Bull's "traits being of so peculiar a character, it would not have been surprising if his memory had been cherished even were his talents less."[3]

Bull's unique position, White maintained, was secure, because there was no one

[1] This time Bull remained in the United States for five years.

[2] In September it was reported that Bull had purchased some 120,000 acres of land in Potter County, Pennsylvania, for his New Norway, and that some thirty hardy-looking Norwegians had already arrived to begin clearing the land for its first settlement, Oleona.

[3] ". . . he throws so much of his own genial and humorous self into his playing, that there exists between him and his audiences a kind of friendly understanding, which manifests itself in applause of a peculiar emphasis" (*Home Journal,* May 29, 1852).

The charismatic Ole Bull.

"sufficiently like him to be brought into comparison with him." To be sure, he was the direct musical antithesis of Jenny Lind: "She is classical, severe, ideal; he romantic, irregular, and individual. She presents a musical conception stripped of every idea or association but that which is intrinsic; he, on the contrary, seeks in music a means of impressing himself, his own individual character and passing mood of mind upon his hearers." White permitted himself a rare witticism: "He gives us a Bull's-eye view of all the emotions he would portray."

Bull was certainly no classicist. "No practiced musician," declared the *Daily Times* (May 28, 1852) after his second concert (on May 27), "expects to find that perfect accuracy and classic art in Ole Bull which characterize those other masters of the bow, Sivori and Vieux Temps [*sic*]. His music is of the Romantic school, passionate and at times almost rapt and inspired when it might be coldly tasteful and judicious. His heart runs away with his ear. He forgets and disregards the accompaniment. It requires the perfect drill and ready action of the Germania to keep with him at all. Not one orchestra in a hundred but would throw up the effort in despair. . . . The double wonder was how the band continued to keep in as good countenance as it did, and to what delightful flights the performer was carried away. After all, Ole Bull is deficient in artistic accuracy, but the deficit is filled with a degree of genius that few mortals possess."

To R. Storrs Willis "the unmistakable *genius* of Bull" had never been so evident as at this concert. "This genius may be rough-hewn—unpolished—uneducated (so to speak)[4] . . . but the power is *there;* there is no mistaking it. . . . Yes, Ole Bull does *com-*

[4] With the exception of some violin lessons in his early youth, Bull was said to be virtually self-taught.

pel you and bend you to himself and his inspirations. And this power—whether it be the force of personal magnetism (with which he is so marvelously endowed) or his musical gift alone—the world has, and ever must, render homage to" (*Musical Times,* June 5, 1852, p. 51).

Serving his musical idiosyncrasies as no one else's music possibly could, Bull's own compositions dominated his repertory. In them, wrote White (*Courier and Enquirer,* May 24, 1852), "passages of pathos, power, sweetness, and brilliance follow each other with the most fantastic irregularity. They seem to be where they are without design or order of succession, and only as assertions that thus feels—thus thinks—Mr. Bull at the moment. In the *Cantabile* [*doloroso*] and *Rondo* [*giocoso*] at the end of the first part of the concert, he has a long cadenza, a wonderful thing and an admirable; but there is no earthly reason why it should be where it is, except that he chooses it should be there. This playing," added White, "is himself made audible."

Throughout his long career Bull continued tirelessly to repeat his old standbys, and his audiences as tirelessly to delight in them: his Grand Concerto in A major and the *Polacca guerriera,* "The Mother's Prayer,"[5] and "To the Memory of Washington"[6] (with its rousing interpolations of "Yankee Doodle" and "Hail Columbia"). These and the more recent *Cantabile doloroso and Rondo giocoso* (with the wayward cadenza), the bravura variations on the aria *L'amo, ah! l'amo* from Bellini's *I Capuleti ed i Montecchi,* and *La Verbena de San Juan*—a "descriptive fantasia" on the Spanish celebration of Midsummer Night, composed during his tour of Spain in 1846-47—together with his own version of the indispensable Burlesque Variations on "The Carnival of Venice," were heard at his two New York concerts.

The press displayed a rare unanimity in their reactions to Bull—both to his mastery and his eccentricities. After his second concert a reviewer for the *Home Journal*[7] (May 29, 1852) wrote: "We know not how to describe either the manner or music of Ole Bull. . . . His mode of playing has a dash of the grotesque in it. Sometimes he hugs and fondles his instrument, and seems to coax and wheedle from it its tender tones. Sometimes, as in a sudden rage, he *snatches* music from its strings, and then, as if appeased, he skips and plays over the gamut joyously. Sometimes, however, he rises into a higher and swelling strain, and his body sways to and fro like a Norwegian pine, his hair flying about like foliage in the breeze."

The reviewer was entranced, too, by Alfred Jaëll, whom he pronounced unequaled among the pianists so far heard in the United States: "His playing is as correct

[5]". . . and a prayer it was," rhapsodized the *Mirror* (May 28, 1852), "low, deep, tender, impassioned, and holy; drawn, as it were, from the chords of a great mortal heart. It breathed of the altar, the cloister, and of all sacred places where the soul unbends from its pride, and yearns for the counsel and consolation beyond the power of earth. The audience grew hushed under it, and only when the last note quivered like a sigh, long-drawn, melting upward in the silence, did the thousands of hearts again beat freely, and the thousands of hands make a tempest of applause."

[6]Referring to the work as an "eccentricity," the *Home Journal* (May 29, 1852) commented that it had "little of the dirge-like character which its tombstone title suggests"; it was, on the contrary, "vivacious in the extreme."

[7]Replacing the ailing N. P. Willis, who had departed in early March for a rest cure in Bermuda, the writer was probably the future eminent biographer James Parton (1822–1892), then assistant editor of the *Home Journal.*

and tasteful as it is wonderful, and not more wonderful than pleasing." And, giving an insight into an early encroachment of technology upon art: "His execution is as rapid as that of the best musical boxes, and infinitely more liquid and sweet. This rapidity of execution is the more surprising from the fact that the fingers of Herr Jaëll are unusually short." While nature had prodigally endowed Bull and other "executive musicians" with "elongated digits," Jaëll's "little, stumpy fingers—the tips half hardened into bone by incessant contact with ivory"—were compensated by a "locomotive energy and magnetic life, to a degree that barely escapes being miraculous."[8]

The Germania were as superb in the overtures to *A Midsummer Night's Dream,* the operas *Martha* (Vienna 1847) by Friedrich von Flotow (1812–1883) and Verdi's *Nabucco,*♪ and a concert overture, "Napoleon's Last Days," by Carl Bergmann, their conductor, as they were agile in following Bull's wildest flights.

After his second concert about 100 of Bull's worshipful countrymen gathered outside his hotel to serenade him with "songs of the Fatherland," to which he responded with an eloquent speech, then departed for Boston,[9] leaving the New York press doubly disconsolate at the twofold loss of Ole Bull and Jenny Lind.

Bull's loss was in no way offset by the appearance of the Italian violinist Charles Bassini, excellent though he was.[10] Following on Bull's heels with a sparsely attended concert at Metropolitan Hall on June 7, Bassini was judged to be an "exquisite" miniaturist of great refinement, with a "pure, sweet, and delicate tone [that] betrayed the heart and soul of a devotee and master" (*Mirror,* June 8, 1852); but he could never hope to measure up to the charismatic Norwegian, who swept audiences off their feet.

Bassini played a *Grand Fantasia* by Vieuxtemps and his own capriccio "Grief and Joy," of which Willis, who approved the "Grief" part, would have liked a better way of expressing "Joy" than by a waltz (*Musical Times,* June 12, 1852, p. 63). Bassini also collaborated with Luigi Arditi, the conductor of the concert, in Arditi's duet "Silver Bells," composed especially for the occasion. A self-promoting composer of apparently boundless stamina, Arditi contributed also, "especially for this concert," a vocal duet "A Night of Love," excellently sung by the unemployed opera divas Rose de Vries and Carolina Vietti,[11] and—a premonition of *musique concrète,* so to speak—"The Great

[8] At the Bull concerts Jaëll played Mendelssohn's Concerto in G minor, Heinrich Rudolph Willmers's *Un Jour d'eté en Norvège,* Blumenthal's *La Source,* his own Bohemian Polka, his "Illustration" of *Rigoletto* (Verdi's new opera, first performed in Venice in 1851) and his burlesque variations on "The Carnival of Venice."

[9] Reviewing his two concerts in Boston, John Sullivan Dwight reluctantly admitted that Bull was not a *humbug* but a genius (of sorts), although deplorably delinquent in the quality of his repertory—comments to which Bull did not respond placidly. From Boston he continued northward, but abruptly broke off his tour in Montreal. Leaving his colleagues in the lurch, he departed for points south to pursue his negotiations for acquiring land for New Norway (*Dwight's,* June 5, 1852, pp. 69–70; June 12, p. 77; July 3, p. 102; Smith, p. 100).

[10] In 1839, Bassini had appeared in New York as a violinist and conductor.

[11] De Vries and Vietti were separately splendid, too, in arias by one of the Riccis and Verdi. The other announced soloist of the evening, a Monsieur Miguel, a new cellist, was prevented by illness from appearing, but his composition, an "Indian March" for orchestra was performed and highly praised by some of the critics.

Russ Polka," a tuneful tribute to Horace P. Russ, a prominent contractor who at the time was in charge of repaving Broadway with large sandstone blocks.[12]

What would Handel, who had composed "'The Harmonious Blacksmith' (which will outlive all the polkas ever composed) have said," indignantly demanded the self-styled *"criticus incognitus"* of the *Albion,* "of 3 or 4 men powdering into dust with heavy hammers veritable blocks of stone—unmusical sandstone, too—as a *musical* accompaniment? We have had polkas of eclipse, of peacocks, of diamonds . . . and for all we know, of the sun, the moon, the stars. We have heard of pistols being fired to add excitement to the whirl of the waltz; but a polka to a paving stone, with an illustration beaten into us after such a fashion, was a something which our powers of calculation did not anticipate." Surely a more suitable occasion might have been chosen for the "pavement demonstration" (*Albion,* June 12, 1852, p. 284).

If Bassini did not succeed in replacing Ole Bull, Jenny Lind was almost instantly supplanted in the wayward affections of the New York public—and most improbably, not by one, but by two world-renowned nightingales: first the phenomenal Italian contralto Marietta Alboni (1822–1894),[13] then a little later the legendary German soprano Henriette (or Henrietta) Sontag (1806–1854).

On June 7, barely a week after Lind's departure, Alboni arrived in New York. Through the comparatively modest, but nonetheless effective, advance publicity expertly wielded by the theatre veteran W. F. Brough, who managed the opening months of her American tour,[14] by the time she arrived it was widely known that Alboni had been a pupil and protégée of Rossini in Bologna, that she had made her triumphant debut at La Scala when she was sixteen, or thereabouts, and that she had enjoyed sensational triumphs in the opera houses of Vienna, St. Petersburg, Brussels, Paris, and London, where in 1847 she had been engaged for Covent Garden as an antidote for the then raging Jenny Lind fever.

Alboni's physical appearance, tending to extreme obesity, aroused a wide range of contradictory comments in the press.[15] The *Daily Times* (June 8, 1852) righteously observed that although not the handsomest of women, she more than compensated for her plainness with her "untainted reputation and a character for many virtues"; the

[12] As "The Russ Pavement Polka," a piano version of the piece was published in 1852 by Geib and Jackson.

[13] *Grove's* and a number of other authorities give the date of Alboni's birth as 1826, *Baker's* as 1823, but the lady herself, according to the manifest of the steamship *Hermann,* which brought her to the United States, gave her age as thirty.

[14] Alboni is thought to have been brought to the United States by Le Grand Smith, Barnum's deputy in the Lind days, but ample documentation proves that Brough actually managed the first (concert-giving) phase of her tour. And ably, too, for on June 9, two days after her arrival, Alboni was serenaded under her window at the New-York Hotel by the Philharmonic, conducted by Arditi, in the overtures to *Zampa* and *La gazza ladra* and an unidentified galop (probably by Arditi) (*Mirror,* June 11, 1852). For trenchant comments on serenades and serenade-giving, and on music managers in general, see Maretzek, *Crotchets,* pp. 179–84.

[15] Henry Pleasants describes Alboni as "an amiable woman whose youthful beauty survived her subsequent obesity"; he reminds us that Rossini called her "the elephant that swallowed the nightingale" (Pleasants, pp. 219, 223–24).

Girvice Archer, Jr.

Marietta Alboni, "the elephant who swallowed the nightingale."

more ebullient *Herald* (June 9, 1852) declared, however: "In person and looks, Madame Alboni is the most magnificent looking *artiste* we have ever seen"; the *Herald* later (June 18, 1852) referred to her as "the fine, fat, handsome, magnificent, renowned Italian *artiste* who recently arrived in this city." "Her face," reported the *Mirror* (June 14, 1852), "is as round and fair as an apple, and her large laughing eye expresses an infinity of good nature. She wears her hair short, without comb, ribbon, or ornament, but it is full, lustrous, and wavy, and harmonizes well with her contralto parts."[16]

[16] This remark precipitated an acrimonious comment from the *Express,* which demanded to know what the *Mirror* meant by "contralto parts."

Both: Music Division, The New York Public Library

Augustino Rovere (left) and Antonio Sangiovanni, Alboni's assisting artists.

On one point the press agreed, Alboni uniquely and overwhelmingly radiated an air of boundless good humor and well-being.

Traveling with Alboni were her husband (or husband-to-be), at first identified in the papers as "Signor Alboni,"[17] her sister, her secretary, and her two assisting artists, Augustino Rovere, a bass/baritone buffo, and Antonio Sangiovanni, a tenor.

It was at first announced (probably to whet the public's appetite) that Alboni would not be heard until autumn, after she had completed a pleasure tour of America's scenic wonders; but despite the heat of the season, she allowed herself to be persuaded to give a concert at Metropolitan Hall on June 23. As Richard Grant White resignedly wrote in advance in the *Courier and Enquirer* (June 19, 1852): "In the present limp state of linen, a cooler prospect than a two hours' seething with four thousand mortal men and women in a huge cauldron of brick and mortar would be welcome; but if we must choose between boiling with Alboni and not boiling without Alboni, by all means, let us boil."[18]

Once he heard her sing, however, White became oblivious to the temperature.

[17] "Signor Alboni," described in the *Mirror* (June 28, 1852) "for the benefit of the ladies" as a handsome and accomplished Italian gentleman of high character "only four months married," was the Count Achille Pepoli, a Bolognese nobleman, whom Alboni is elsewhere reported, perhaps erroneously, to have married in 1853, after returning to Europe.

[18] More than the heat of the season concerned White. Together with his fellow-journalists, he violently condemned the inadequate facilities for evacuating Metropolitan Hall in case of fire. Despite frequent complaints and as frequent promises to correct this dangerous fault, only one staircase, not more than eight feet wide, continued to serve as the sole exit for as many as four thousand people.

On her first entrance,[19] White's "first thought was that she had been unjustly and ungallantly treated in the matter of her personal attractions. Although her *embonpoint* exceeds even the most accommodating standard of symmetry," as he elegantly phrased it, "her features are unquestionably fine, and her face needs only a little attenuating to be decidedly handsome." But her voice! "Rich, clear, deep, and full beyond all contraltos ever heard. . . . Madame Alboni's voice caresses the ear at once with its sumptuous quality. . . . Its supremacy was as completely asserted at the close of the recitative of the first air [the cavatina *Eccomi, alfine, in Babilonia* from Rossini's *Semiramide*] as at the end of the concert." Throughout the evening the first impression was only confirmed, wrote White, for it could not have been deepened.[20] The great charm of her voice lay in its quality, caliber, and copiousness:[21] "It comes bubbling, gurgling, gushing from that full throat and those gently parted lips and reminds us of draughts of which poets have sung, but of which bacchantes have only dreamed." Alboni's voice brought "visions of seas of amber jelly floating before [one's] enamored mental vision, so materially rich, honeyed, and pellucid [was] it." White was astounded, as was everyone else, at the simplicity and ease with which Alboni poured out her delicious miracles of sound: "She seems to give no thought to what she does, but merely to let the flood of her song pour itself forth" (*Courier and Enquirer,* June 24, 1852).

"It would be slander to call her singing an effort," wrote the *Evening Post* (June 24, 1852). "It is rather a spontaneous gush, or bubble, of sound. . . . Even in the most difficult passages, which to others would be jaw-breaking, face-distorting, neck-wringing *tours de force,* she utters her voice as a fountain sends forth its waters, itself unmoved amid a thousand gurgling jets, or it would be more in keeping, doubtless, to say . . . that it was a fountain of rich, ambrosial wine."

Her closing number, the *Non più mesta* from Rossini's *Cenerentola,* for which she was universally celebrated, continued the *Post,* showed Alboni "in all her magnificence. It was a perfect pyrotechnic display of vocalization; it was—yet more—varied, brilliant, deep, swelling, ecstatic, and seemed to throw the audience into a fury of delight. Their plaudits were tumultuous, and long before the singer closed the first stanza, they rose upon their feet, and quite overwhelmed her with clappings and cheers. She received it all in a smiling, graceful, almost nonchalant way, and began the second verse. The platform was then literally covered with bouquets, and the applause became more obstreperous than ever.

"Alboni is so different in every respect from Jenny Lind that we shall not attempt to compare the two. They are unlike in quality of voice, style, and manner, and the sympathies to which they appeal. Yet both walk in the highest realms of art—Jenny,

[19] "Madame Alboni, in a flounced white silk dress, low-necked and short-sleeved . . . with a single diamond bracelet upon her right arm, her short black hair unadorned, and holding a fan, handkerchief, and a sheet of music, was led forward by Signor Arditi," her conductor (*Tribune,* June 24, 1852).

[20] Pleasants (pp. 223–24) contends that with her sumptuous voice and flawless technique, Alboni was too perfect and consequently boringly predictable after a few hearings.

[21] Alboni's range was variously reported to have extended from low G to high C and even higher. According to Pleasants (p. 224), when she attempted soprano roles, they were transposed down, but the American singer Clara Louise Kellogg (1842-1916) vouched for the authenticity of Alboni's high C.

indeed, in her pure religious purity sings like an angel, while Alboni, of a far more earthly make, should be satisfied to be the cordial, sensuous, noble woman she is."

R. Storrs Willis, who had been led to expect a somewhat "masculine" or "brusque" contralto, was amazed at Alboni's exquisite refinement: "Even her lowest chest tones are so smooth, of so delicate a texture, so *tender* . . . with all their fullness and volume, that one never loses the impression of a refined and lady-like nature. She came before the audience," wrote Willis, "with the most thoroughly good-hearted and good-natured air. Everybody fancied her at once, and would not for the world have had her shadow a whit less voluminous than it is. She is—personally—one of those comfortable, nonchalant, delightful creatures, whom it puts one in a perfect good humor with himself and the world occasionally to see" (*Musical Times,* June 26, 1852, p. 86).

If the audience broke into cheers during and after the aria from *Semiramide,* their rapture knew no bounds when she sang the *Brindisi* from *Lucrezia Borgia.* "Delivered without ornament save a single superb shake, she brought down a tumultuous applause," reported the *Mirror* (June 24, 1852).[22] This and her duet from Donizetti's *Don Pasquale* with Sangiovanni had to be encored.[23] But it was in the *Non più mesta* that Alboni surpassed herself, if that were possible. "She poured out her voice with a prodigality of skill and a perfection of vocalization absolutely wonderful. . . . The singing of Alboni is like the flowing of an exhaustless stream. It requires no apparent effort. She scarcely moves, and, standing like a mellow, smiling statue, music leaps from her throat like a fountain-jet, like a brook, like a bounding river! Every note is under the master's rein, yet free as the melody of a sky-soaring bird. . . . In person Alboni inspires the sense of a joyous, generous, frank, artless nature."

In response to the frenzied shouts and applause at the end of the concert, the waving of hats and handkerchiefs, and the deluge of bouquets (one of which she deftly caught in mid-flight, greatly to the delight of the audience), Alboni "laughed all the time as if she were enjoying a very good joke" (*Herald,* June 24, 1852).

Despite a few faint cavils that her upper register tended to be thin—or that she was placid to the exclusion of all passion—no singer since Malibran had evoked such unanimity from the customarily divided New York press. Lind notwithstanding, it was the general consensus that Alboni was by far the greatest singer ever to have been heard, not only in the United States, but anywhere.

Alboni gave a second concert on June 28, a torrid evening on which, according to the *Musical Times* (July 3, 1852, p. 98) "kid gloves and fans [did] double duty in

[22] Oliver Dyer (presumably), although he was enthralled by Alboni's "simplicity of manner," "purity of tone," "perfect, flute-like trill," and "final cadence . . . in tones plump and good enough to eat" (in the *Brindisi*), objected to the aria itself (a drinking song) for its "corrupting influence upon its listeners' morals." Small wonder that "our honest, earnest contemporary, Horace Greeley, [a dedicated teetotaler] should deliberately get up and walk out, just in the middle of the concert" (*Musical World and Journal of the Fine Arts,* July 1, 1852, p. 357).

[23] Sangiovanni, mildly commended for his "sweet" or "pretty" tenor voice, sang a cavatina from *L'Italiana in Algeri,* with Alboni and Rovere, a trio from *La figlia del reggimento,* and with Rovere, an overstated buffo, a duet from *L'elisir d'amore.* Arditi conducted an orchestra of seventy players (with Bristow as leader) in a spirited, "slashing" performance of the Overture to *La gazza ladra;* he played his own too-long fantasia for violin, *Souvenir d'Italia,* ostentatiously applauded by Ole Bull but sharply criticized by Dyer, who called Arditi an "inexorable bore who wouldn't stop his violin!" *(ibid.)*

applause and ventilation, and men dissolved in rapture and perspiration simultaneously." On this occasion she sang a grand aria composed by de Bériot for Malibran; a so-called variation, *Carina senti un poco,* by "Stummel" (Hummel);[24] with Sangiovanni, Arditi's duet *Una notte d'amore;* and by overwhelming request she repeated her "marvelous" *Non più mesta.*

Alboni's second appearance left the critics at a loss for new superlatives. "It is extremely difficult to criticize such an artiste," wrote the anonymous critic for the *Mirror* (June 29, 1852). "She at once exhausts the superlative, and all after-praise seems only a repetition—a sugaring of sugar. . . . One thing is certain, she is destined to take a deeper, stronger, and more general hold upon the musical public than any singer who has preceded her."

After this concert Alboni and her entourage departed, to return in early September, by which time Henriette Sontag had arrived with her convoy—her husband Count Rossi, her conductor Carl Eckert (1820–1879) of the Italian Opera in Paris, and the tenor Gasparo Pozzolini (1824–1854) "of the St. Petersburg Opera."

Sontag, who was nearly twenty years Alboni's senior and who, like Lind, had grown up in the theatre, had been a supreme diva in the opera houses of Europe and England when she was scarcely more than a child. With her flawlessly pure soprano voice, exquisite vocalism, irresistible charm, and delicate blonde beauty, she was idolized in Vienna, Berlin, Paris, and London—not least by Beethoven, Weber, Berlioz, Chopin, Rossini, Mendelssohn, Cherubini, Boieldieu, Moscheles, and Auber.[25]

But chiefly Sontag had captivated the Count Carlo Rossi, a young Sardinian diplomat whom she married in 1827—secretly, because the marriage of a nobleman to a commoner (worse, an actress) was strictly taboo according to the ironbound tenets of the Sardinian court. When the sympathetic King of Prussia elevated Sontag to the rank of countess, the court of Turin relented and recognized the marriage, but only if she retired from the stage.

During the twenty years of her subsequent professional retirement, spent in the various capitals of Europe where her husband served, Sontag sang only occasionally for charitable causes, and, while Rossi was stationed at St. Petersburg, by command of Czar Nicholas I she appeared at the Court Opera in *La sonnambula* and *Lucia,* thereby precipitating mutual Russo/Sardinian truculence.

When, during the political upheavals of 1848, Rossi was stripped of both diplomatic status and wealth, Sontag, who had commanded enormous fees in her professional past, returned to the stage to restore the family fortunes. This was doubtless a most congenial "sacrifice" on her part, for with her reappearance, in 1849 at Her Majesty's Theatre in London in *Linda di Chamounix,* she was newly acclaimed for her miraculously unimpaired voice, her unexcelled artistry, her untarnished beauty.

Sontag's decision to come to the United States in 1852 was most assuredly motivated by the tempting example of Lind's financial killing—but Sontag came without

[24] Doubtless Hummel's Tyrolian Air and Variations, op. 118, written for Malibran.

[25] In 1824, when she was eighteen years old, Sontag was chosen by Beethoven to sing in the first performances of his Ninth Symphony and his *Missa solemnis;* Weber chose her to appear in the premiere of *Euryanthe.*

a Barnum. In an early announcement of her intended visit, the *Herald* (May 23, 1852) stated: "She has made no engagement with any manager in this country or in Europe, but she comes across the ocean on her own account." By the time she arrived, however, Sontag had acquired a manager, Bernard Ullmann.

In a later bitter denunciation of Ullmann, Maretzek tells how, upon the rumor of Sontag's impending visit, Ullmann, who was currently not thriving, had "implored a letter of introduction and recommendation to her from the Editor of the *Herald*.[26] Mr. Bennett, in pure commiseration of Ullmann's then somewhat precarious situation, had furnished him with one." In the mistaken belief that by hiring Ullmann she would oblige the powerful James Gordon Bennett, Sontag engaged him as her manager, much to her detriment, as it turned out (*Crotchets*, pp. 308–9).

Sontag did not arrive unheralded. On August 5 the *Mirror* reported that "a magnificent Piano Forte from Messrs. Hall and Son's establishment [was being] placed on board the *Arctic* . . . for use of Mdme. Sontag, who will be a passenger on its return voyage." On August 14 the *Daily Times* informed its readers that rooms had been booked for Sontag and her party at the Union Hotel (also called the "Union Place" and the "Union Square"), and that Metropolitan Hall had been engaged for a number of Sontag evenings around the beginning of October. On August 7 the *Times* briefly summarized Sontag's eventful past; on August 20 the *Mirror* quoted Berlioz's tribute to her artistry; and in successive issues, *Dwight's Journal* published acres of "Sontagiana."

Before she arrived, too, great plans were hatching at the Musical Fund Society to welcome her with a serenade to end all serenades—this despite Sontag's request that any welcoming rites be confined to the "strictly artistic." The *Mirror* (August 31, 1852) agreed, stating that Madame Sontag would do far better to "trust to her merits solely, after the successful example of Mdme. Alboni, than to consent to any second edition of the Lind display."

But the Serenade Committee—Henry C. Watson, Theodore Eisfeld, and John A. Kyle, doubtless in collusion with Ullmann (henceforth modulated to *Ullman*)—went to unreasonable lengths in their efforts to eclipse any previous serenade, Lind's included. They invited all of the predominantly German music societies in which the city abounded to join them in a monster tribute to Sontag, and more than 1500 musicians—orchestras, bands, singing societies, and solo performers—purportedly accepted, among them the Harmonic Society, the *Liederkranz*, the *Sängerbund*, the *Schillerbund*, the Orpheus Vocal Society, the *Teutonia Männerchor*, the *Social Reform Gesangverein*, the *Lorelei Männerchor*, Dodworth's Cornet Band, and Noll's Seventh Regiment Band. The serenade was fixed for midnight of September 10 (*Tribune*, September 10, 1852).

[26] While touring with Parodi, whom he briefly managed, Ullmann had spent some time (or been stranded) in Havana, where, as we learn from Maretzek (*Crotchets*, pp. 309–18), he published a book denouncing the United States as a cultural desert. Ullmann had been in hot water while in Havana, reported the *Daily Times* (March 8, 1852): he had been arrested by the Cuban government on suspicion of being implicated in "a plot," on the sole evidence of "a letter written in the Magyar language" found in his possession. "Mr. U.," sardonically commented the *Times*, "is well known in this city, where the notion of his being a political emissary will be considered amusing." All the same, Ullmann had reportedly been sent on a mission to Budapest and Vienna by Kossuth (*Herald*, February 6, 1852).

The beautiful Henriette Sontag.

But the Musical Fund Society's monster extravaganza was unceremoniously scooped. In the early hours of September 10 the Musical Mutual Protection Association,[27] with a band numbering about seventy, and with a minimum of fuss, killed two birds with one stone, first serenading Sontag at the Union Hotel, then Alboni at the

[27]Signor D. La Manna, president of the Musical Mutual Protection Association, had called a special meeting to plan a welcoming serenade to Madame Sontag, who had been unanimously elected an Honorary Member of the Association, A committee consisting of Edward Woolf, Claudio

New-York Hotel.[28] Nothing if not eclectic, their program ranged from the *Brindisi* from *Lucrezia Borgia* to "Hail Columbia." The divas reportedly appeared at their respective windows and waved their handkerchiefs in gracious acknowledgment of the honor (*Mirror,* September 10, 1852).

On learning of this treachery, the Musical Fund Society—"not deeming it courtesy or kindness in consequence of the Serenade of last night to disturb the rest of Madame Sontag on two consecutive evenings"—postponed their serenade to September 13, to begin at eleven P.M. (*Tribune,* September 11, 1852). That night at about half-past eleven George Templeton Strong, who had spent the evening at home playing chess with his friend George Anthon, went out "to look after the serenade to Sontag, who's at the Union Place Hotel. All Union Square dense with a miscellaneous assortment of loafers—foreign and native—including Short Boys [an organized gang of hoodlums]. Great hallooing, laughing, whooping, and miscellaneous row and confusion," he wrote.

Strong "lounged about for an hour and a half—waiting for the *Liederkranz* and the rest of the Serenaders to appear—chilled through and much disgusted. At last they came, and the rumpus and racket increased indefinitely, and after more delay the music began, with an accompaniment of all sorts of unearthly noises. Music didn't seem to be so good that the noises be regretted, and I left early, sensible of a bad headache and that I was unequivocally old. The performances terminated, it seems, in a general shindy" (Strong, Private Journal, September 14, 1852).

Strong was wise to depart when he did. "As it usually happens in this city when any public demonstration is to be made," reported the *Evening Post* (September 14, 1852), "the serenade to Sontag last night was an opportunity for the rowdies." Intermingled with the respectable people in the huge crowd, who, like Strong, had come out at that late hour to hear the music, were "a number of low fellows who soon began to show what they were, by hootings, catcalls, and coarse laughter." At about half-past eleven, when the musicians began to arrive, "noisy squads got possession of the passageways and prevented their approach. With the assistance of two fire companies, who escorted the orchestras, a place was made for them near the building, but the pressure was so great, and the shouting and whistling so incessant, that it was quite impossible for them to keep their position, or if they had been able to do so, to manage their instruments. Several sorties were made by the firemen upon the blackguards, with a view to pressing them back, but without effect, except that they led to some pretty severe encounters and increased the confusion.

"Meantime, a body of Short Boys near the entrance attempted to enter the hotel and were kept out only by main force when others went to their support, and the proprietor was obliged to barricade his doors and windows. Madame Sontag, who was in an upper room, was greatly frightened by these evidences of violence, and, not understanding the object of them, nearly fainted. But, summoning her energies, she went

---

S. Grafulla, and Joseph Noll was appointed to take charge of arrangements for the serenade, and Noll was chosen to conduct it (*Herald,* September 7, 1852).

[28] It was Alboni's second serenade that week. On September 7, after her triumphant return concert, she had been escorted to her hotel by a torchlight procession, and at about one A.M. was serenaded by "a large number of artistes" (*Mirror,* September 8, 1852).

out on the balcony with her husband, when the ruffians shouted, 'a song, a song,' at the tops of their voices, and without waiting to see whether their request would be granted, began a version of 'Old Folks at Home'[29] on their own hook." Whereupon Sontag fled to her room but came out again when one or two of the music societies, who had somehow managed to gain a distant foothold, valiantly attempted to perform something or other.

"But at this point the Short Boys began their favorite sport of smashing the white hats,[30] which led to a scene of indescribable uproar. In the melée, the musicians were beset and beaten, their instruments broken, their music books torn up, and a regular rush made upon the house. A more wanton and disgraceful row was never got up, even in this city famous for 'primary elections' and firemen's fights. It was found necessary to shut the hotel at once and to extinguish all the lights, when, with the aid of the police, who then came upon the scene in some force, the disputers were dispersed."

"This serenade," concluded the *Post,* echoing the sentiments of the press in general, "was badly managed from the outset: too much publicity was given to it, and no pains were taken to have a suitable guard of officers." It was both tasteless and pointless to attempt to re-enact the Barnum/Lind excesses of yesteryear.

Partly in reaction to the serenade and partly to "the cabals of rival managers and critics," Sontag became ill and was forced to postpone her debut, announced for September 20, to September 27 (*Dwight's,* September 25, 1852, pp. 198–99). In the meantime, on September 7, the radiant Alboni, back from her invigorating summer travels,[31] had zestfully resumed her triumphant concert-giving at Metropolitan Hall—again with the assistance of Sangiovanni, Rovere, Arditi, and additionally the defunct Astor Place Opera chorus. By the time Sontag recovered from her unnerving serenade experience, Alboni had given five deliriously received concerts at Metropolitan Hall, with another four to come.

During this second series—besides repeating the Hummel Variations, the *Brindisi* from *Lucrezia Borgia,* the various opera duets and trios with her colleagues, and the insatiably demanded rondo from *La cenerentola,* of which each succeeding performance "eclipsed anything that had ever been experienced before"—Alboni was heard for the first time in *Una voce poco fa* (from *Il barbiere*), *Batti, batti* (from *Don Giovanni*), *Di piacer mi balza il cor* (from *La gazza ladra*), *Come per me sereno* (from *La sonnambula*), an aria from Donizetti's *Betly,* the vocalized Variations for violin by the French violin vir-

[29] Stephen Foster's great hit (popularly known as "Way Down upon the Swanee River") was published by Firth, Pond early in 1851. For the sum of $15, Foster had agreed to have it appear as a composition of E. P. Christy. In 1852, Foster changed his mind and wanted to buy back the rights, but Christy refused. Although the song's authorship was soon an open secret, Foster's name did not appear on the sheet music until after the copyright expired in 1879, fifteen years after his death. In June 1852 the tune was issued by Firth, Pond in a dance arrangement as "The Home Schottish."

[30] Condemning serenades as a Barnumesque abomination, the *Mirror* (September 15, 1852) explained the attack on the white hats: In the heat of the brawl "some ardent friend of Barnum's 'Angel' called for three cheers for Jenny Lind. 'Who is that?' shouted a rowdy in the crowd. 'The fellow in the white hat,' was the reply, but every unlucky gentleman who wore one was in danger of getting his tile [hat] crushed."

[31] Her sightseeing itinerary had taken her to fashionable Saratoga Springs, where she gave two spectacularly successful concerts.

tuoso and composer Pierre Rode (1774–1839),[32] "Musical Difficulties Solved" (an ineptly titled showpiece composed for her by Arditi), an aria from *La figlia del reggimento,* William Vincent Wallace's "Sweet and Low," sung in English,[33] with the composer at the piano, and, most successful among her newer repertory, the *Ah! non credea* and *Ah! non giunge* from *La sonnambula* and the *Casta diva,* the last so breathtakingly rendered as to drive both critics and audiences into unprecedented frenzies of delight.[34]

After her second concert, the flagrantly pro-Alboni *Mirror* (September 11, 1852)[35] mingled its usual aqueous imagery—"gushing fountains," "laughing waters," and "celestial reservoirs of melody"—with the more down-to-earth information that the net proceeds, to date, of Alboni's four concerts in New York and two in Saratoga Springs had been about $12,000, and added: "Her career in America bids fair to be quite as profitable as Jenny Lind's, without resorting to the high-pressure system of management, so successfully used by Jenny's great showman." The *Mirror* warmly and repeatedly praised Alboni for her stated determination to "no make de humbug."

All the same, Alboni followed Lind's example by giving a concert (on September 21) for the benefit of the Widow and Orphan Fund of the New York Fire Department. For this gala event the elaborate floral decorations from the just-ended Horticultural Society show at Metropolitan Hall were held over. The display was, in a sense, coals to Newcastle, for, as the *Home Journal* commented (September 18, 1852), Alboni's concerts were "remarkable for the unprecedented number of bouquets that were thrown upon the stage." At her return concert there had been "not fewer than one hundred, besides one immense, two-storied floral structure, which was borne by a strong man down the long aisle and placed reverently at her feet." Apparently Alboni was responsible for a glut in the flower trade: "Not to mislead our readers," quantified the reporter (probably James Parton), "we must remind them that bouquets which formerly cost four or five shillings are now offered freely in the street for one shilling. Competition has cut down the price by certainly two-thirds. Therefore, a hundred bouquets do not now represent a greater amount of enthusiasm than was formerly initiated by thirty-three and a third."

Notwithstanding the current slump in the price of floral tributes, Alboni's phenomenal popularity continued undiminished, even after Sontag began her long-awaited, three-times-a-week concert marathon. Indeed, during this epoch of extraordinary musical plenty, New York music lovers impartially swarmed to the concerts

[32] Rode's Variations, first vocalized by the Italian opera diva Angelica Catalani (1780–1849), had been scheduled for Sontag's debut, now delayed until after Alboni had performed them "for the first time in America." "They are miracles of execution," wrote the *Evening Post* (September 18, 1852), "and yet she [Alboni] touched the highest as well as the lowest notes with such perfect ease and precision that it seemed as if no difficulties had been overcome, no triumphs achieved." (For some reason *Rode* was consistently misspelled *Rhode* in the New York papers.)

[33] Far more intelligible English than Lind's, commented the *Home Journal* (September 18, 1852).

[34] Sontag, who reportedly attended Alboni's concert on October 12, was seen to applaud her performance of the *Casta diva.*

[35] The papers vied with one another in their raptures over Alboni, but the fiercely pro-Alboni, viciously anti-Ullman, *Mirror* outdid them all, strongly suggesting that some special affiliation, or arrangement, existed between its editor, Hiram Fuller, and W. F. Brough, Alboni's manager.

(and later the opera performances) of both divas, just as they had swarmed to the performances of the rival Italian opera companies early in the year.

On September 25, Sontag, under Ullman's management, enlarged upon the Barnum/Lind precedent by prefacing her debut (September 27) with a public rehearsal at Metropolitan Hall. Her audience of 1000 invited guests[36] showed "the bad taste to applaud the performances vociferously throughout," complained Richard Grant White, "almost uniformly marring the most exquisite passages by their ill-judged plaudits. Such conduct at a concert is bad enough, but at a rehearsal is inexcusable" (*Courier and Enquirer,* September 27, 1852). Quite properly, White saved his critical comments for his review of the forthcoming concert.

The *Evening Post* (September 25, 1852), however, showed no hesitation in dulling the edge of the impending debut with a full-fledged review of the rehearsal, reasoning that with an audience of "musicians, ladies, editors, amateurs, and gentlemen in white neck-cloths" (clergymen) filling virtually half the auditorium, the occasion "quite hurried the affair into a regular concert."

The *Post* welcomed Carl Eckert, who forcefully and decisively opened the program with the Overture to *Der Freischütz,* as a "valuable acquisition to the musical talent of the country"—not least because he had successfully tamed the usually "obstreperous" brass instruments into "subordination and harmony."

Brushing aside Sontag's assisting artists—the unfortunately ailing tenor Gasparo Pozzolini, the pianist Alfred Jaëll, and the phenomenal, eleven-year-old French violinist Paul Julien (1841–1860?)[37] (for after all, the public's attention was focused on Sontag)—the review surprisingly described not a glamorous diva, but a "motherly-looking" woman with an expressive face, dressed in a pink mantle with white trimmings and a pink hat. The gossipy *Home Journal* (September 25, 1852), however, in minutest detail—down to the straw-colored gloves that "concealed the sparkle of her rings"—portrayed a bewitching beauty who, although decked in modish flounces and ostrich feathers,[38] nonetheless furnished an inspiring example of heroism to "Ye pie-eating, cake-making, tea-drinking maids and matrons of America."

The *Post* described Sontag's voice as "delicious," of extensive range (reportedly from "B-flat below the staff to C above"), wonderfully flexible, and sweeter than Jenny Lind's, although not as powerful. Only her lower register revealed the passage of time, but so slightly that only the most discerning ear might discover it.[39]

[36] In Sontag's case, such attention-getting ploys were superfluous, caviled the anti-Ullman *Mirror* (September 25, 1852): "The desire to hear her is general; and would be if there were no humbugging, clap-trap agents in existence."

[37] Little Julien, who had arrived in the United States in June, fresh from triumphs in Paris and London, had created a sensation with his first concert in New York, on July 2 (discussed later in this chapter).

[38] Richard Grant White, himself no mean dandy, disparaged the exaggerated attention paid to performers' (particularly Sontag's) costumes: "We know no more pitiful employment of time, types [*sic*], and paper, than the description of robes, petticoats, skirts, flounces, trains, corsages, berthas, lace, and jewels worn by ladies of more or less distinction" (*Courier and Enquirer,* September 29, 1852).

[39] But according to the *Tribune* (September 28, 1852), it was the lower register that had been "least impaired by time . . . the upper notes, although clear in tone and perfect in intonation, have lost somewhat of their original power and sweetness, and have to be taken with perceptible caution."

Sounding more like Dyer than Willis, the *Musical World and Times* (October 2, 1852, p. 75) evocatively sets the scene for Sontag's American debut: "We strolled through the moonlight on Tuesday [Monday] evening last to the great audience chamber of Henriette Sontag, the German 'Queen of Song.' The beauty of the night seemed befitting the Queen's first musical 'reception.' On passing casually through Union Square we saw the brightly illuminated hotel where she is accommodated, and fancied the poor lady—after the serenade-outrage and her succeeding illness—just tremblingly preparing to meet the formidable Goths of Gotham.

"Floating along with the dense mass down Broadway, the gleam of an occasional white glove betokened, at last, our proximity to the Hall. Around the entrance stood throngs of people, among whom the ticket speculators were busily passing, disposing of their *wares*.[40] Alas! poor Sontag!—we thought—that you and your divine art should be put to such mercenary uses."

Making his way through the crowd, the writer "snatched one of the programmes which bestrewed the stairway, and disdaining the libretti- and bouquet-boys (what has an editor to do with such extravagant luxuries?), we took our seat as one of the vexatious 'dead heads,' and found ourselves packed . . . into one conglomerate mass of humanity."

At last, the "tumult, and dust, and noise of preparation gradually subsided, the air cleared, the gas [lights] flashed up, and silken rustle and confused murmur died softly away. The choristers [again veterans of the former Italian Opera], male and female, filed in and took their places in front of the dense orchestra: an imposing array of musicians, altogether, to start with. Carl Eckert came in: a pale, Polish-looking young man with an ample forehead (like a German Shakespeare) and a student's stoop in the shoulders. The wand was raised, and Weber's weird overture of *Der Freischütz* boomed out upon us in majestic style. The [predominantly German] orchestra was very numerous [seventy musicians]: Eisfeld led off the violins, supported by Noll, who is a tower of strength in himself (producing a volume of tone equal to about two instruments). The horns were smooth, and the execution of the entire orchestra was square, vigorous, and uncommonly effective.

"Hereupon the new tenor Pozzolini came forward. The poor fellow had been so hoarse all day as scarcely to be able to speak, but he did his best; which of course was *not* his best, nor very good. . . . He evinced good school and skill, however, but as a tenor he is evidently inferior to what we have had already.[41]

"A few moments more, and the celebrated Sontag [led out by Eckert] stood be-

[40] "The managers of Madame Sontag's concerts, we hear, have taken every precaution to prevent speculation in tickets by selling the $1 and $2 admissions on different days. Two hundred standee tickets are reserved for sale at the door. . . . The managers . . . appeal to the public not to purchase tickets from speculators at an advanced rate, as Madame Sontag will give three concerts a week until further notice" (*Courier and Enquirer,* September 25, 1852). But the speculators reportedly continued to drive their usual brisk trade.

[41] The *Tribune* (September 28, 1852) thought Pozzolini's voice, "although of limited power and compass," possessed "rare sweetness and flexibility"; but the *Mirror* (September 28, 1852) brutally pronounced his aria from *Don Pasquale* an "utter failure. . . . He sang out of tune and out of time; and nothing but the tenderness of the auditory towards one who had been reported in ill health suppressed a general hiss." The other papers, considerate of his illness, received Pozzolini more compassionately.

Both: Music Division, The New York Public Library

Luigi Rocco and Gasparo Pozzolini, Madame Sontag's assisting artists.

fore us. How difficult it is," wrote the critic, "to reconcile a *real* with an *ideal* celebrity."[42] He described her as a typical North German, with "lovely, warm blue eyes, a fair complexion, [and] slight *embonpoint* . . . [she] carries in her very face a true, pure, and good nature. Her air is simple, retiring, and slightly *deprecatory.* She has decidedly more *ladylikeness* in her general bearing than any singer we have yet had among us[43]—creating upon you an impression of *home* quiet, seclusion, privacy, and tranquillity."[44]

Sontag's voice, continued the reviewer, was not very powerful, but this was "atoned for by the *purity* of her tone," which made it seem "almost as *pervading* as if it

[42] The *Mirror* (September 28, 1852) portrayed Sontag as a "plump, matronly looking woman—handsomely enough dressed, with rather too great a proportion of diamonds and 'head-gear,'" and unchivalrously asked: "But where is that ravishing beauty of which we have heard so much, and of which so many Kings and Princes, to say nothing of coarser mortals, have been the victims? Is it faded and gone? In our humble and honest opinion, the transcendental and ineffable beauty which the critics have ascribed to Sontag *was not there.* The charm was in her voice—in her soul, if you will; and not in her face or person."

[43] The writer was apparently unmindful of Maria Caradori Allan,♪ who had been similarly admired for her "ladylikeness" when she visited the United States in 1837–39.

[44] This image of a subdued, domesticated Sontag hardly agrees with the sophisticated woman of fashion portrayed in the *Home Journal* (October 9, 1852), who was "rather showily dressed, in a white satin skirt, over which . . . was a skirt of white lace . . . embroidered with variously-colored silks, of which pink was the prevailing color. The boddice was also white satin trimmed with lace. Upon her left arm she wore a heavy gold link bracelet, and from her diamond necklace hung an ornament blazing with gems. Her beautiful brown hair was arranged plainly over her ears, and the head-dress was composed of red and white flowers and dark velvet streamers. White kid gloves and white satin slippers completed her attire, and the general effect was superb, though, as we observed, a little more striking than we are accustomed to in the concert room." According to the *Herald,* which gave its own flamboyant version of Sontag's costume, her "magnificent" gown had been made in New York and had cost $1500.

were a very strong one. Her peculiar excellence," he continued, "lies in the consummate management of her voice—the incredible rapidity and fluency of her execution—and more than all, the *never-forgotten feeling and emotion* which she pours into her tone, *even in her most difficult embellishments,*" something that he had never heard from any other singer.[45]

The "incognito" critic for the *Albion,* who had never heard Sontag before, was surprised to discover that her "elaborateness of ornament, finish of style, and consummate art in the management of voice" were more Italian than any Italian he had ever heard.[46] "Within the compass of her voice," he wrote, "there does not seem to be any passage—chromatic, harmonic, or diatonic—which it is beyond her skill to reach. In rich and profuse store of embellishment, which she uses very lavishly, though with great judgment, we should say that she is second to no other singer; but that which struck us as most to be admired as evidence of her great skill and long experience is the art with which she reserves her voice so as to extend it with perfect ease over the longest flourishes of ornament, without break or blemish" (*Albion,* October 2, 1852, p. 476).

Unlike the unequivocal praise of Alboni, Sontag's first reviews bristled with contradictory quibbles. The *Tribune*'s ambivalent critic[47] tactlessly harped on Sontag's advancing age (she was then all of forty-six): "Alas, that time should lay its ruthless touch, ever so lightly, upon one so nobly gifted," he sighed, although, to be sure, her shake was still "preserved in exquisite perfection, and in point of flexibility, there can nothing more wonderful to be desired. . . . We are not sure but the predominant feeling last night was amazement at the infallible dexterity with which vocal difficulties were annihilated." Sontag's style tended to "extraordinary execution and profuse embellishment," he wrote. "She revels in those *fioriture* passages which display the utmost limit of vocal proficiency; every phrase is elaborated to its highest finish." Yet, this vacillating critic thought the composer's intention was sometimes "obscured by the improvised cadences of the *cantatrice.*" However, he abruptly concluded: "A more magnificent entertainment never took place in this country. Magnificent in attraction, magnificent in audience,[48] and magnificent in enthusiasm" (*Tribune,* September 28, 1852).

Richard Grant White, like the rest of Sontag's large and dressy audience, was conquered "ere she uttered a note to show what she is as an artist; the presence and manner of the woman, the gentlewoman, has carried their hearts all captive," he wrote.

[45] Appended to this review was a commendation from overseas by the *Musical World*'s Paris correspondent "the able and elegant writer, Mr. Fry" (at that time about to return to his native land). First comparing Sontag's voice to "rose leaves on velvet," Fry then yielded to his everlasting compulsion to flaunt his knowledge, with a didactic, technical definition of the chromatic scale, in whose execution Sontag excelled (*Musical World and Times,* October 2, 1852, p. 75).

[46] The *Tribune* (September 28, 1852), on the contrary, maintained that—unlike Alboni, the quintessential Italian—Sontag, like Lind, was "of the North" in both temperament and vocal style.

[47] In the journalistic controversy that followed Sontag's conflicting first reviews, the *Mirror* (October 5, 1852) scornfully alluded to "the novice who criticizes Sontag in the *Tribune.*"

[48] "Our showy ladies who have been butterflying at the Springs during the summer appear all to have returned to town," chattily reported the *Evening Post* (September 28, 1852), "and if the pick of them were not at Metropolitan Hall last night, then we are no judges, or our lorgnette must have been bewitched."

White filled an interminable column of his overlarge newspaper with lauds of Sontag's unrivaled "delicacy and grace"—her "*arpeggio* passages of such ravishing loveliness as to bewilder her hearers with delight"—her "unfading youth and loveliness." Yet, he perceived "a want, at times, of exact justness of intonation," probably attributable to her recent illness.

At this first concert—although, as the critics endlessly stressed, Sontag's voice in no way resembled Alboni's—she was heard in some of Alboni's recent repertory: the *Come per me sereno* and the Rode Variations; additionally she sang the *Luce di quest'anima* from *Linda di Chamounix,* Eckert's spectacular "Swiss Song" accompanied by *a cappella* chorus (a work resembling, but surpassing, Jenny Lind's "Echo Song"),[49] and "Home, Sweet Home" (performed with great sentiment, in contrast to Lind's rollicksome interpretation).

In addition to the indisposed Pozzolini, who bravely struggled through his Bellini and Donizetti arias, Alfred Jaëll brilliantly played Leopold de Meyer's showy Fantasia on *Lucrezia Borgia,* and little Paul Julien astounded everyone with his prodigious performance of a Fantasia on themes from *La Fille du régiment*[50] composed by Delphin Alard (1815–1888), his distinguished teacher at the Paris *Conservatoire.* Eckert, besides the *Freischütz* Overture, authoritatively conducted Mendelssohn's Overture to *A Midsummer Night's Dream.*

Exasperated by the incongruities in Sontag's first reviews, extreme even for the congenitally contentious New York critics, the *Daily Times* (September 30, 1852), sweeping aside the essentially subjective nature of criticism, demanded that a binding code of absolute artistic standards once and for all be imposed on the critics, to govern their waywardness and to guide their bewildered readers.

The reviews of Sontag's debut offered a case in point: "She is or she is not the transcendent genius of song which tradition describes her to be. Her voice is or is not possessed of the usual conditions of superiority. The concert was or was not a 'triumph.'. . . Let us pray," urged the *Times* editorial, "for a strong-hearted man to criticize the critics! These musical times have produced villainous discord. We need a dictator of taste who will bring the cacophonous crew of critics into something like harmony."[51]

"Is it at all the fair thing," the writer (Seymour? Raymond?) argued, "to identify the alleged failings of subordinates [Ullman?] with the mistress of song herself? If not, decant your ill humor against the agent who located your press seats unfavorably . . . into some other vessel than that into which the pure artistic quality of the artiste

[49] With its echo-like effects, Eckert's "Swiss Song," composed for Sontag, allowed her to display ventriloquial abilities as impressive as Lind's. In its parallel piece, a "Styrian Song," also by Eckert, Sontag exhibited, as well, her ability to yodel.

[50] Next to Sontag, Julien was the hit of the evening: "His violin is exquisitely handled," reported the *Evening Post* (September 28, 1852), "and there is a force and maturity in his style quite prodigious. . . . The unconsciousness of etiquette with which the little performer stuck his bow between his legs, during one round of applause, to screw up his strings, which had got a little flat, was a charming bit of simplicity, and perhaps added to the next round of cheers, during which, and before the orchestra had completed the stave [*sic*], he ran off the stage."

[51] It will be remembered that at this time the *Times* thought William Henry Fry might be the ideal man for the job.

should alone be held up for the public to look into and through. Sadly have we noticed that the ears of our most transcendental critics have been put out of tune by discontent with Mr. X, the manager.

"It is quite as unfair to measure our two Countesses against the immortal Swede. True, her portrait stares one impertinently in the face from above the stage at the Metropolitan Hall. But it has no business being there in the first place; and if it had, and the five thousand listeners to the Countesses cannot help making the comparison so perpetually suggested, that will hardly excuse the musical critic.[52] It is for him to compare the artiste of the day, not with the artists of other days, but with some abstract standard of musical taste."

Singers should be judged on their own merits, the writer maintained, and besides, there was room at the top for more than one diva: "It may be necessary to admit that in passionate art, the Italian [Alboni]—and in absolute culture, the German [Sontag]—wholly outstrip the be-Barnumed Nightingale of the North."

Furthermore: "In discussing the admirable Sontag, we do heartily deprecate comparisons with what she may have been a score of years ago. None of our critics, by all reasonable likelihood, enjoyed opportunities of testing her merits at that remote era. . . . Without he has actually heard it, he knows nothing in Henriette Sontag's voice which does not subsist with equal perfection in that of the Contessa Rossi. All such criticism is, therefore, spurious, and should carry no weight."

All of which unleashed a new storm of mutual journalistic recriminations, and intensified the general criticisms of "Mr. Tom Thumb Barnum Ullman" (inescapably derided for his lilliputian stature), whose rather vulgar handling of Sontag's concerts had aroused considerable disapproval.

On September 28, the night between Sontag's first and second concerts, Alboni was prevented at the last moment from giving the scheduled sixth and "final" concert of her current series by a gas failure that plunged Metropolitan Hall and a large part of the city into darkness. The problem was corrected by the following evening, when again a fashionable, if smaller, audience assembled to hear Sontag—"the curiosity of a first appearance having given way to a more legitimate desire to re-hear this great singer" (*Mirror,* September 30, 1852).

Carl Eckert, who was promptly labeled the best conductor ever to have appeared in this country,[53] gave masterly performances of the overtures to Spontini's *Fernand Cortez* (Paris 1809) and Rossini's *William Tell,* an encore of the latter being demanded. Pozzolini—depending on which paper one consulted—was either still incapacitated, as his sorry performance of the Barcarolle from *Masaniello* revealed, or was recovered and superb in his duet with Sontag from *Linda di Chamounix.*

[52] Although the critics virtuously expressed horror at the mere thought of comparing Sontag, Alboni, and Lind, they all happily engaged in the pernicious practice.

[53] But not for long. Eckert was soon accused of "gross blunders" in his conducting of Italian music, particularly in racing ahead of singers. In one instance Madame Sontag "triumphantly vindicated her rights as to *time* and expression . . . when, turning half indignantly around, she finished, emphatically, her musical period, compelling Mr. Eckert and the orchestra to fall in with her" (*Musical World and Times,* December 11, 1852, p. 225).

Sontag's first offering of the evening, Thomas Arne's "The Soldier Tir'd of War's Alarms," delighted the *Mirror* but was damned by Richard Grant White, who called it "nothing but a tie-wig-ish vocal exercise in triplets, from beginning to end." He hoped never to encounter "The Soldier Tir'd" on a concert program again—or, for that matter, "Within a mile of Edinboro' Town," a cute Scottish ballad coyly delivered by Sontag, that "delighted the good folks" but curdled White (*Courier and Enquirer,* October 1, 1852).[54] This time, however (despite her regrettable tendency to play to the gallery with foolproof audience-pleasers),[55] the critics unanimously hailed Sontag as the supreme virtuoso she was, never mind her advancing years.

Better to compete with Alboni, whose company possessed both a tenor and a basso, the greatly admired (currently unemployed) baritone Cesare Badiali was added to Sontag's company at her third concert, on October 1. A felicitous choice. Too, Sontag now added German works to her programs—*Wie nahte mir der Schlummer* from *Der Freischütz;* Haydn's "With verdure clad," and the *Deh vieni non tardar* from *The Marriage of Figaro*—also an aria from Otto Nicolai's opera *Il templario* (Vienna 1841), a Theme and Variations composed for her by Kücken, and a German *Lied* with cello obbligato by Lachner. She sang, too, a "Spanish Bolero" by an unspecified Besozzi (like Lachner, a member of a large musical tribe); and, of course, she frequently repeated her more spectacular earlier offerings, particularly Eckert's "Swiss Song" (greatly in demand and better liked than his "Styrian Song").

Alfred Jaëll continued to please with his spectacular opera fantasies, but it was little Paul Julien who invariably "brought down a *furore* of delight." With his wonderful tone, stopping, and bowing, and with his charming person, he was a perfect little wonder; some thought him better than Ole Bull. "But he is greater than a wonder," wrote Richard Grant White, "he is a genius, and one whom it will not spoil to tell him what he is" (*Courier and Enquirer,* September 30; *Herald,* October 6, 1852).

During the memorable short period between Sontag's debut (September 27) and the *final* "final" concert[56] of Alboni's second series (October 15), New Yorkers were privileged to hear two of the supreme singers of the nineteenth century in eleven alternating performances (often given on consecutive evenings)—seven by Sontag and four by Alboni (to say nothing of Alboni's six preceding concerts earlier in September).[57] When at last, to an *obbligato* of valedictory lamentations in the press, the two divas went their separate, but parallel, ways, each to perform in Philadelphia, Boston, and neighboring places (including, in Sontag's case, Brooklyn), their absence was of short

[54] In a letter to the editor of the *Courier and Enquirer* (October 1, 1852), a disgruntled correspondent complained of the "very common and worn-out music" performed at Sontag's concerts, naming, among other compositions, "The Soldier Tir'd," "Within a Mile of Edinboro' Town," and "Home, Sweet Home." "It seems to me the constant repetitions of these old affairs are almost insulting to the taste of our people," he wrote, and signed himself "not music mad, but mad at such music."

[55] Probably at the urging of Ullman, who attempted in all things to follow closely in Barnum's gaudy footsteps.

[56] According to inviolate custom, both Alboni and Sontag were "persuaded" to give several extra concerts beyond their originally scheduled final appearances.

[57] To the best of my reckoning, Alboni appeared on September 7, 10, 14, 17, 21, 24, October 5 (postponed from September 28), 9, 12, and 15. Sontag sang on September 27, 29, October 1, 4, 6, 8, and 11.

Both: Girvice Archer, Jr.

The rival divas in daytime dress.

duration, for by November 9, Alboni was back at Metropolitan Hall, again sending her New York worshipers, the critics included, into raptures, with Sontag following on November 29.

Alboni appeared only twice before again departing on tour: at the first concert she sang a rondo from Rossini's *L'Italiana in Algeri;* with Sangiovanni a duet from *Il barbiere di Siviglia;* and again the Rode Variations and the *Casta diva.* On November 12 she was heard for the first time in arias from Rossini's *La donna del lago* and Meyerbeer's *Le Prophète* (probably the *Ah, mon fils*).

Of the latter, Richard Grant White, reverting to his old-time ferocity, ranted: "The aria from *Le Prophète* is not worthy to come from the lips of such a singer; the ideas are the dry and stunted productions of a barren soil, stimulated into a meager and monstrous fruitfulness by the application of some far-fetched fertilizer. Meyerbeer has always written, with visible and painful labor, music whose every phrase is filled with an expression of artificiality, but which at the same time shows learning, taste, and talent; yet among all his compositions we know not one which exhibits at once the sterility of his mind and the inflexibility of his will in such a degree as this. . . . We trust that hereafter Madame Alboni will find for us metal more attractive" (*Courier and Enquirer,* November 13, 1852).

Still assisted by Sangiovanni, Rovere, and Arditi, Alboni—or her manager—cognizant of the phenomenal success of little Julien at the Sontag concerts, acquired not one, but two juvenile marvels for this short season. Appearing at Alboni's November 9 concert were the local twelve-year-old pianist Will Saar and the recently arrived Italian/French violin prodigy Camilla (or Camille) Urso (1842–1902), according to R. Storrs Willis, "rather a counterpart of Sontag's *Paul Julien*" (*Musical World and Times,* November 13, 1852, p. 162).

Saar disappointed Willis with his careless performance of William Vincent Wallace's Second Concert Polka: "his '*misgriffe,*' or mis-*hits,* in striking the dispersed, doubly diminished chords, were somewhat agonizing, particularly as they were repeated so often." (Saar did not appear at the following concert.)

But little ten-year-old Camilla Urso, like Julien a prize-winner at the Paris *Conservatoire,* was a full-fledged artist with a poise and total command of her instrument that had completely bewitched her hearers (among them Alboni) at her earlier performances in September (discussed later in this chapter). On the present occasion she earned cheers and bouquets with her wonderful performance of someone's fantasia on *La sonnambula.* Willis, calling her "a child violinist of considerable cleverness," wrote: "She plays tenderly, delicately, and well." Yet, he could not forbear to add: "She has not the scope of young Julien, the volume of tone, or the depth and strength of sentiment [because] she is a girl and Paul a precocious boy—such a disparity therefore is, of course, to be expected." (Apparently only opera divas were permitted to enjoy equal rights in the nineteenth-century world of music.)

To counter Alboni's sweeping success, Sontag's second series of concerts, clumsily attempting to imitate the conductor Jullien's triumphantly successful monster concerts in London, both in size and substance, was planned on so stupendous a scale as to dwarf anything that had ever been known in the New World; even William Henry Fry's concurrent lecture extravaganzas paled by comparison. Ullman's grandiloquent prospectus for the series, taking the public into his confidence and explaining the necessity for instructing them in the unusual construction of the coming programs, proceeded to lay out their fine points: "The programme of a Concert, like a musical composition or a picture, should possess the essential elements of light and shade. Monotony, especially, should be avoided. In place, therefore, of devoting an entire Concert to either classical music, selections from sacred works, complete oratorios, morceaux from Italian Operas, and what is commonly termed Concert Music, it has been thought preferable to introduce a specimen of all these at each Concert." In other words, something for every taste.

To achieve this monumental hodgepodge, Sontag—surprisingly acquiescent to the meretricious scheme—together with Badiali, Pozzolini, Luigi Rocco (a newly arrived basso buffo from La Scala), and Paul Julien (but not Alfred Jaëll), and with the assistance of Alfred Toulmin, a new harpist from London, and the organist John Zundel, would be supported by a "vocal and instrumental corps of nearly Six Hundred Performers;[58] and it is confidently believed," went the announcement, "that the array

[58] "We have an extraordinary number of resident musicians in New York, as any one may know who considers that, with the lighting of each night's gas, about thirty orchestras assemble at the vari-

of talent, both in quantity and quality, will impart to these Festival Concerts that character of grandeur and completeness in every department for which the Musical Festivals of England and Germany are so justly famed."[59] The 600 performers included the now reorganized Harmonic Society (150 male and female performers directed by George Frederick Bristow);[60] the (German) Song Union *(Sängerbund)* (300 male voices directed by Agricol Paur); selected members of various church choirs (50 ladies directed by Henry C. Watson); the Italian Opera Chorus (50 males and females[61] directed by Schüllinger, a Philharmonic violist); and "Madame Sontag's Grand Orchestra of 70 performers." Everyone was under the supreme command of Carl Eckert, "under whose direction the principal German festivals have been organized."

To accommodate this gigantic cast, the stage of Metropolitan Hall was being rebuilt "on the plan of Exeter Hall, London,[62] forming a spacious amphitheatre, occupying one-third of [the] Hall and materially facilitating the acoustic effects of the music," but drastically impinging upon the listening area.

Upon publication of his flashy announcement, the heavily biased *Mirror* declared open warfare on Ullman, virtuously attacking him for victimizing a great artist and a great lady with his blatant charlatanism, an attribute in no small way ascribed by the *Mirror* to his being "a little German Jew" (shades of N. P. Willis).

To strengthen its attack, on November 20 the *Mirror* quoted from the *Sunday Dispatch,* a minor weekly newspaper: "Madame Sontag, or rather her foolish, intriguing, and lying agent (we really pity the talented and victimized lady) publishes a Prospectus for a series of Concerts, which for impudent, ridiculous humbug throws all quack medicine advertisements completely in the shade. . . . Truly, it is too bad that such really great and deserving artists . . . should be sacrificed by the barefaced humbug, impudent misstatements, and lying assumptions of such an intriguing little rascal as Mr. Bernard Ullman." For good measure, the *Mirror* damned the *Sunday Dispatch* writer as well: "We believe the gentleman [Charles Burkhardt] who writes the musical criticisms of that *widely circulated* paper is not only a countryman of Ullman's, but a 'brother in the faith,' also."

The other papers were less hostile. When, on the morning of November 27, two

---

ous theatres and concert-rooms, and that, notwithstanding this, an orchestra of eighty or a hundred can always be procured for a Tripler [Metropolitan] Hall concert at a day's notice. The weekly salary of the members of theatrical orchestras ranges from seven to ten dollars; that of the leaders from fifteen to twenty-five. At the grand concerts, five dollars each is the pay of the orchestra, and no regard is paid to the different degrees of skill possessed by the members. The conductor of a grand concert usually receives fifty dollars. The members of the military bands receive an average of three dollars a day" (*Home Journal,* November 29, 1852).

[59] The reference to European Musical Festivals strongly suggests the involvement in the scheme of Henry C. Watson, who had long yearned for an American Birmingham.

[60] Currently appearing in Fry's concert/lectures.

[61] The chorus, soon referred to as "that mighty, but useless, musical force," was unevenly remunerated: the Italian members were "paid for their services. The services of the Americans were gratuitous, except that the female singers received one free ticket each. On nights when the chorus did not perform (like the concluding concert of this series) each male singer received one free ticket, and each female two" (*Musical World and Times.* December 11, 1852, p. 225). (What did the German singers receive?)

[62] Presumably at Madame Sontag's expense.

days before the first concert, a public "dress rehearsal" was held at Metropolitan Hall, the *Tribune* (November 29, 1852) vouched for its respectability: "This prelude to the monster concerts, with which Madame Sontag is about to lay siege to New-York, showed, by the abundance of white cravats and serious dignified faces, that the reverend clergy had liberally availed themselves of her invitation to be present.[63] And they and the others who were there had good reason to be thankful for the genius which could design and carry out such a grand and perfect musical entertainment."

The *Daily Times* (November 29, 1852), calling the rehearsal a "morning concert" (matinée), accorded it a full-scale review congratulating Madame Sontag on a program which "brings out in beautiful relief the varied elements of both vocal and instrumental talents enlisted for these concerts."

The vast program included the first movement of Beethoven's Fourth Symphony; the first American performance of Meyerbeer's overture to his brother's play *Struensee* (Berlin 1846); the *Romanza* from Donizetti's opera *Maria di Rudenz* (Venice 1838), sung by Badiali; a *Romanza* from *Il giuramento,* sung by a fully recovered Pozzolini (who spectacularly redeemed himself with all the critics); the *Papataci* trio from *L'Italiana in Algeri,* sung by Badiali, Pozzolini, and Rocco; and *Ma Celine,* a Fantasia on Auber's *La Muette de Portici* by the Dutch composer/violinist Theodor Haumann (1808–1878), and de Bériot's *Le Tremolo,* played by little Julien. The 300 male members of the ten (or was it eight?) music societies of the local Song Union performed a Grand Chorus by Lachner; Madame Sontag sang Adolphe Adam's ornate Grand Variations on the French nursery tune *Ah, vous dirai-je, Maman,* with flute *obbligato* played by John A. Kyle, and Eckert's "Swiss Song"; with Rocco she sang "The Music Lesson" by Fioravanti; with Badiali, Pozzolini, and Rocco the quartet from *I puritani;* with the 600 singers "Luther's Chorale"; and with everybody, as a grand finale, the Prayer from Rossini's *Mosè in Egitto.*

The *Evening Post* (November 30, 1852) reported the hugely attended first concert to be "most successful in every respect, with the single exception that there was too much of it, and many people got fatigued [and left] before the close. . . . Ten [*sic*] elaborate performances in the course of one sitting were more than the most instructed musical ear cares to listen to, and half the number would give greater pleasure."

The *Post* agreed with the *Tribune,* whose critic, in that morning's paper, wished that Madame Sontag, now that she had "successfully introduced a great novelty in New York concert-giving," would go further and invent a concert program "with no last piece. . . . Now, as soon as only one piece remains to be performed, a great part of the people begin to move out in couples, platoons, and all degrees of straggling, to the great disturbance and disgust of those who want to hear the remaining piece in quietness." The critic offered a whimsical solution: "If there were no such piece, all would go out together, and nobody need commit the sin of secretly objurgating his neighbors." The *Post* thought perhaps a "timely hiss" might not be amiss.

Richard Grant White lavishly praised Madame Sontag and her assisting artists, but condemned the program for its lack of cohesiveness: "We passed at one step from a strictly written, thoughtful symphony by Beethoven to a feverish, declamatory ro-

[63] ". . . to invite all the Clergy of the City with an indefinite number of children and nurses, expecting 'large returns' in the way of patronage for such *liberality,* does not take with this practical, common-sense, *sorely* humbugged community," thundered the *Mirror* (December 4, 1852).

mance by Donizetti, from a love song steeped in sentiment to Martin Luther's stern, solemn old *Chorale.* This is variety with a vengeance, and quite as much vengeance as variety." A musical circus!

But worse, the concert was "tedious." Where Sontag's (and Alboni's) previous concerts had been delightfully "short and sweet," this ponderous event "seemed something like a return to those weary musical sessions which used to be held, beginning at early candle light,[64] in that dreary old tub, the Tabernacle." White agreed with the *Post* that the concert was twice as long as was tolerable. And with all deference to the participating choral groups, he could not see that "their stentorian labors added anything to such concerts as Madame Sontag gave us on her previous visit." Besides: "We had too little of Madame Sontag last evening. . . . The strongest impressions left by the evening's performances were made by trumpets and trombones, male shouting, and female screaming. And then why all those conductors' protruding batons from a sea of heads like policemen in a mob? They were worse than useless."

"Truly," concluded White, "many of these new arrangements smack egregiously of humbug. Needless humbug; annoying humbug; for when humbug is unobtrusive and necessary, we suffer it with unmurmuring endurance. Madame Sontag's agent has hitherto shown himself, without question, one of the two most capable and energetic managers . . . in the country[65] [the other presumably being Barnum]; but his present campaign seems to us badly planned" (*Courier and Enquirer,* November 30, 1852).

To R. Storrs Willis, too, the "'combined chorus' did not quite come up to our expectation." Moreover: "The trombones were terrific; the very heavens seemed brass unto us." And Sontag's extraneous trill in the solo part of Luther's Hymn was not in good taste. "The fact is, a solemn, religious performance in the midst of so much display is not attainable" (*Musical World and Times,* December 4, 1852, p. 211).

The program was repeated on December 1, and the following day the press came out unanimously against the chorus: the *Tribune* "would have thought it a good bargain to exchange the singing of that mighty chorus of 600 for the sound of [Sontag's] single, exquisitely cultivated voice"; the *Herald* objected even to "the arrangements made for the accommodation of the monster chorus—a very appropriate name—[they were] by no means an improvement to the general appearance of the Hall; and those who had not been at the last concert stared with astonishment at the unsightly [structure] and wondered why such an array of women, men, and boys should be perched up in that huge box."[66] Sontag and her assisting artists were splendid, but the *Herald* was "not very favorably struck with the new and grand feature in these concerts, and . . . would be content to dispense with the choral department," and enjoy the undiluted pleasure of listening to Sontag and her admirable assisting artists.[67]

Bowing to critical opinion, the chorus was dropped after the third concert, on

[64] Owing to the inordinate length of the program, Sontag's Festival Concert had started at seven o'clock.

[65] Was White pretending to have forgotten his bitter feud with Ullman in 1846–47 over White's scandalous persecution of the violinist Camillo Sivori,♪ who had been managed by Ullman?

[66] "All the arrangements of the stage Madame Sontag [had] kindly permitted to remain for Mr. Fry's [first] lecture," which took place on November 30, between the first and second concerts of her series (*Evening Post,* November 29, 1852).

[67] "Aside from the choral performances, which every one has voted to be a bore," summarized the *Home Journal* on December 11, Sontag's concerts had been all that could be desired.

December 3, when they were heard only in the closing work, the Prayer from *Mosè*. ("Six hundred strong as before," grumbled the *Tribune* (December 4, 1852), "while six hundred or thereabouts [took] advantage of its performance to disturb all the others in the audience".)

The *Mirror* (December 4, 1852) reported a far-from-large audience at this concert: "The crowd of wealthy and fashionable Concert-goers who attended Thackeray's Lecture probably kept some hundreds from the concert.[68] But the main reason of the falling off we take to be the very general disgust at the humbugging management of Madame's agent."

At last, on December 7, following Sontag's fourth concert, Richard Grant White noted in the *Courier and Enquirer* that "Metropolitan Hall appeared last evening re-extended to its full dimensions by the removal of the *extra* staging upon which the chorus was placed at the last three concerts." Due to Badiali's illness the chief attraction of the evening, a potpourri of the *Semiramide* music enlisting all the singers in the company and the former Astor Place chorus, had to be omitted. Although White approved of the substitutions, "with some exceptions," Rocco, *buffo* though he was, "groped his way" through *La calunnia (Barber of Seville),* "and at the close got along so slowly that being behind Carl Eckert's baton a beat or two, or more, he was obliged to take a flying leap to be in at the death." Too, the trio from *I Lombardi,* with the violin *obbligato* played by Paul Julien, was unsuccessful "partly because it is unfitted for the concert room and partly because it is unsuited to the powers of Madame Sontag. In the art of singing she has no living superior," loyally wrote White, but in the "screaming dramatic music" of Verdi's "stupendous vocal parts," Sontag had "little skill."

On December 8, at the fifth and last concert of this problematical series: "Metropolitan Hall was crowded to its extreme capacity. Even the second circle was occupied in every available place" (*Courier and Enquirer,* December 9, 1852). Again the *Semiramide* excerpts had to be omitted because of Badiali's continued illness; among the works that were performed was Berlioz's 1841 instrumentation of Weber's "Invitation to the Dance"; with Julien, Sontag performed a duet for voice and violin composed for them by Eckert, but she especially excelled in the *Deh vieni non tardar.* It was sad to see her depart, but she would be back soon—early in January—and in Opera!

The pangs of separation were quickly assuaged with Alboni's early return—in opera, for which New Yorkers had purportedly thirsted since the joint collapse of the rival opera companies in March. On December 27, Alboni made her American opera debut in Rossini's *Cenerentola* at the capacious Broadway Theatre, where, under the able management of E. A. Marshall, a successful season of French comic opera had earlier been given (discussed later in this chapter). Supporting Alboni were Sangiovanni as Don Ramiro, Rovere as Don Magnifico, Domenico Coletti as Dandini, and the old-timers Mesdames Albertazzi and Avogadro as the two ugly sisters. Also in the cast was a new member of the Barili/Patti clan, Nicolò Barili (1826–1896), introduced as

[68] Among them George Templeton Strong, who seems not to have heard any of Alboni's or Sontag's concerts, but who enthusiastically attended the full series of six lectures on the "English Humourists," begun on November 19, by the celebrated English author William Makepeace Thackeray (1811–1863).

a "primo basso from the principal theatres in Italy," making his first appearance in America as Alidoro; Arditi presided over the "double orchestra" and the former Italian Opera Chorus.

Although the "great undertaking" had involved Marshall in "heavier nightly expenses than have yet been incurred in the United States," he advertised that he had "regulated the prices of admission to please . . . all classes of the community." Thus, box and parquette seats were $1, reserved seats were $1.50, seats in the family circle fifty cents, and in the upper circle twenty-five cents. *Cenerentola* was scheduled for four performances, on Monday, Tuesday, Thursday, and Friday of the week beginning December 27.

Alboni in opera stirred the critics to new heights of ecstasy. "Her singing, dressing, acting, were as near perfection as anything human we expect to be blessed with this side of heaven," rhapsodized the pro-Alboni *Mirror* (December 28, 1852). To Richard Grant White she "not only sang gloriously but gave us a very naive and charming impersonation of the heroine of the old fairy tale. She has been wronged by those who represented her as impassable [*sic*] and frigid upon the [opera] stage," continued White. "Extravagant and demonstrative she certainly is not; but her acting has meaning and force, her expression is quite arch and captivating, and her smile has an unaffected simplicity which makes its beaming longed for." And in the *Non più mesta,* which, after all, "was what we all went there to hear," she again "electrified her hearers" (*Courier and Enquirer,* December 28, 1852).

Alboni's supporting cast, too, was warmly praised: Rovere revealed unsuspected comedic gifts in his superb impersonation of Don Magnifico; Coletti displayed greater ability than he had heretofore shown; even Sangiovanni sounded better than ever before, probably because the acoustics of the Broadway Theatre suited his voice better than those of Metropolitan Hall.

Alboni's opera debut signaled another significant debut—that of William Henry Fry as music critic of the *Tribune.* In a pretentious ramble that occupied more than a full column of fine print in the *Tribune* on December 28, Fry (eternally tormented by his frustration over the rejection of his opera *Leonora*) began his review with an aggrieved discussion, with many digressions, of the dependence of music—particularly dramatic music—on the whims and caprices of interpreters and critics: "The best works have rotted, do rot, and will rot on musty, dusty shelves for the want of . . . interpretation. . . . All musical history is a link of artistic sorrows; of poor Mozarts, of starving Schuberts, of swaggering critics who cannot read manuscripts, of saucy singers, and stupid publics." And on and on, through a succession of remote references to James Fenimore Cooper, Milton, Beethoven's dusty garret, the cast of characters in Dickens's *Pickwick Papers,* and America's failure to support the arts: "While six thousand taverns distill damnation, no altar to the muses—to teach us taste, amenity, and render art sacred—burns with a steady flame."

It was necessary to bear all this in mind, wrote Fry, in discussing last night's production of *Cenerentola,* a production easy enough to criticize, but useless to point out its shortcomings, or to indicate how it might be improved, until it was determined if there was a public—given "theatres of the present size and under the present system"—willing to pay for anything better.

After further wanderings, Fry approached the subject of the review, but briefly: Alboni was a great artist; her triumph in opera was as complete as it had been on the concert stage. After the final curtain had been rung down, it was necessary to raise it again so that she might repeat the *Non più mesta.* "In the contralto region of her voice, Madame Alboni fills up the ear's craving," but (eternally compelled to flaunt his erudition) it lacked the "fibrous energy which tradition assigns to Pisaroni."[69]

Fry then took off on a lengthy dissertation on the contrasting styles of Rossini and Meyerbeer in writing for the contralto voice. Which led, in turn, to an exhaustive analysis of Alboni's vocal range, not only its overall range, but separate analyses of its separate registers: "The first register commences at *Fa,* the lowest note, and extends to *Sol* on the second line—and the second register begins on *Sol,* and reaches *Fa,* and then, to this we may add the four extra notes. The lower notes are superb; the notes of transition of the registers, *Sol, La, Si, Do,* are not particularly full. The extra additional notes—the *La,* etc., are not taken with apparent ease, and do not compare with the lower."

Fry disapproved of the Rossinian *Cinderella.* "We are old-fashioned, hang-up-our-stockingish enough to like the genuine Cinderella: pumpkins, mice, rats, and Pedro's jokes.[70] Execrably bad as is English poetry for the lyric stage," wrote this fervent apostle of opera in English, "Rophino Lacy's [pastiche] version of the chimney-corner Lady forms an exception." Surprisingly, Fry preferred Lacy's incongruous interpolations, plucked from the scores of *William Tell* and several other Rossini operas, to the unadulterated original. "We would really advise some Italian librettist to take Lacy's version and translate the interpolations" (into Italian). And on and on.

On December 31 the *Daily Times* reported the "fullest" attendance yet at the third performance of *La cenerentola* and predicted a still fuller one at the fourth and final performance that evening. "Were it not that the season is to be a short one, the management might run it two weeks, instead of one, and with certain success." (The remainder of Alboni's triumphant season at the Broadway Theatre, continuing through the month of January, is discussed in the following chapter, as are her following opera performances in New York.)

New York's predilection for juvenile musical prodigies was plentifully indulged in 1852. On May 5 at Metropolitan Hall little Adelina Patti, now billed as "the wonder of the age," assisted (as did her mother) at a "Grand Vocal and Instrumental Festival" given by a newly arrived Spanish musician and instrument maker Jose Gallegos to introduce and exhibit his prize-winning invention the Guitarpa, or Plus-Harp Guitar. Also assisting were Elisa Valentini, a Signor Nicolao,[71] and Giovanni Sconcia, who

[69] Benedetta Rosamunda Pisaroni (1793–1872), at first a soprano, later a contralto, was as famed for her homeliness (the result of smallpox) as she was for her superb vocalism.

[70] Pedro is a comic character in the Lacyized *Cinderella.*

[71] Signor Giuseppe Nicolao had composed an opera *Pocahontas,* of which the Italian Artists' Union had purchased the copyright and which they had planned to perform. "Seriously," wrote the *Musical Times* (February 7, 1852, p. 214), "we have little faith in the success of an Italian opera on an American subject *in America;* anywhere else, its chances would be better." To my knowledge, the opera was not performed.

Little Adelina Patti, fondly known as La Petite Lind.

conducted both a Grand Orchestra[72] and "the remains of the Astor Place chorus singers," as the *Mirror* called Maretzek's recently dispossessed opera chorus.

The *Mirror* (May 6, 1852) described the Plus-Harp Guitar as "a sort of mongrel guitar, resembling a banjo quite as much as a harp, and looking more like a *monstrosity* than any of the 'crooked things' in the orchestra." Its tones were "very sparkling and clear," but of a slender sonority better adapted to the parlor than the concert hall,

[72]Between the first and second parts of the concert the orchestra played Sconcia's *La Belle Americaine mazourka,* a work so lively that "it was hard work to sit still under such dance-provoking music" (*Mirror,* May 6, 1852).

where half its tinkling sounds were lost.[73] On the Plus-Harp Guitar, Señor Gallegos played a program of exclusively Spanish music, consisting of fantasies and sets of variations on various malaguenas, jotas, and fandangos, all composed by himself.

"Little Patti, or *La Petite Lind*," as the *Mirror* fondly called her, "gave the Nightingale's 'Echo Song' with wonderful effect, and the tiny *prima donna* was the star of the evening. She was encored with a *furore* that we have seldom witnessed at a concert. Gathering up, and getting behind, the bouquets which were thrown upon the stage, and which half-hid her from view, the little bird repeated her song with still greater force and finish of execution. In the second part she gave the difficult Rondo, 'Ah! non giunge,' in a style inferior only in volume of voice to the most accomplished artistes. It was truly a wonderful performance.[74] For the encore the little Signorina sang the 'Charming Bayadère' very charmingly."

The *Mirror* continued: "Signora Patti, the mother of *La Petite* and of several full-grown *prima donnas,* sang a cavatina from *Gemma di Vergy* with exquisite taste, and with a freshness of voice that gave no evidence of decay. It is to be regretted that we do not more frequently hear this accomplished artiste on the stage or in the concert-room. Signora Patti and *'La Petite Lind'* are, in themselves, attraction enough to fill the largest Concert Hall in America."

The following week—May 12 through 15 (receiving a benefit on the 15)—little Patti was engaged to sing between plays at the Lyceum Theatre (since April under the management of Corbyn and Buckland), drawing crowds, as the *Mirror* reported (May 13, 1852), to "witness her debut on the theatrical stage." *Hafiz* took a pessimistic view of this engagement: "It is a pity she is to sing in a theatre," he wrote. "She will be stung by the frenzied desire of applause, which will do much to ruin her as an artist" (*Dwight's,* May 22, 1852, p. 53).

Adelina Patti's debut as a full-fledged concert-giver was announced for September 22, possibly at the instigation of her enterprising new brother-in-law Maurice Strakosch,[75] but the concert seems to have fallen by the wayside, probably due to the rampant Alboni/Sontag frenzy. By October, however, Strakosch was offering a prize of $200 for a song for Adelina Patti, with whom, together with his wife, and with the assistance of Miska Hauser, he announced a tour (*Musical World and Times,* October 30, 1852, p. 137). By the end of the year, after highly successful multiple performances in Philadelphia, Baltimore, and other nearby places, Strakosch announced that he had

[73] A technical description of the Plus-Harp Guitar, appearing in the *Musical Times* (May 15, 1852, p. 15), praised Gallegos as an ingenious mechanic rather than a musician. His instrument, "a perfect triumph of mechanical skill," although inferior in sonority to the conventional harp, ranged in price from $100 to an unthinkable $6000.

[74] "The interest of this concert was . . . sustained by the . . . wonderful child Signorina Adelina Patti, whose extraordinary execution evoked more than one shower of bouquets and furore of applause. . . . If the exquisite ear which she shows . . . and the facility with which she masters some of the chief difficulties of the Italian style be sustained during some ten or twelve years of study, great things must be expected of Signorina Patti" (*Albion,* May 8, 1852, p. 224).

[75] In April, following the great opera debacle in New York, Strakosch had successfully managed an opera and concert company in New Orleans starring Parodi, Amalia Patti, and Miska Hauser. At its conclusion, on May 2—May 8, according to the *Musical World and Journal of the Fine Arts* (May 15, 1852, p. 288)—he and Amalia Patti were married. Returning to New York, in September, Strakosch opened a piano store, the Metropolitan Piano Emporium at 629 Broadway, with a branch at Springfield, Massachusetts.

"engaged" the nine-year-old Patti for an extensive tour covering thirty-four cities; he listed an itinerary stretching from New York to New Orleans to Chicago to St. Louis to Montreal and back again (*ibid.,* December 25, 1852, p. 268). On this latter tour they were joined by Ole Bull.

As we know, Adelina Patti was not the only amazing child to perform in prodigy-prone New York in 1852. A plethora of gifted children suddenly appeared from abroad, their elders doubtless lured by reports of the fabulous American concert bonanza. The first to arrive was the appropriately named Hermine Petit, an astounding eleven-year-old German pianist and purported "protégée of the Royal Family of Holland." Hearing this "diminutive phenomenon" at a pre-debut "private *soirée* uptown," the *Musical World and Journal of the Fine Arts* (June 15, 1852, p. 320) enchantedly reported: "She sits down to the piano with all the *aplomb* of a full grown artist, and her little fingers sweep over the keys with a skill and precision that seem like magic. Her style is brilliant, rapid, thorough, clean, and correct; and we predict for her a success beyond that of any little artist we have had in this country." She was an object lesson to the local "'fathers' prides and mothers' joys' [in showing] what a child may arrive at, at 11 years." The writer suggested that a kind of international juvenile event be presented, combining the talents of Hermine Petit (representing Germany), Adelina Patti (Italy), and the barely four-year-old Infant Drummer, William Henry Marsh (the United States).[76] This event indeed came to pass on June 17, causing the *Courier and Enquirer* jubilantly to comment: "We have usually to be content . . . with one infant phenomenon, but on this evening we are to have three!"

On July 2 at Niblo's Saloon, Paul Julien, whose extraordinary career in Europe had been well publicized in advance, conquered his first American audience, a regrettably small one because of the intense heat. His success was nonetheless "most decided," wrote the *Home Journal* (July 10, 1852): "There were such firmness, certainty, and power in his touch and so much sweetness and harmony in his tones, such ease and self-possession in his manner, and such variety and charm in his performance, that every one present was filled with astonishment and delight." And not only by his playing: Julien, "a little fellow, about eleven years of age, with black hair and fair, plump, and very kissable cheeks . . . was dressed in a boy's velvet coat, or frock, with a belt around the waist, a frilled shirt peeping from his bosom, a black ribbon around his neck, and his only ornament a gold chain reaching from pocket to button hole. He came tripping into the room in the most *nonchalant* manner imaginable, and placing his violin between his legs to hold it fast, began to tune it, with comical composure. The contrast between the length of his bow and the shortness of the arm that was about to wield it was ludicrous. But at the first stroke of that long bow all other feelings were lost in astonishment, until wonder itself was forgotten in the pleasure of hearing his exquisite music."[77]

Richard Grant White, too, was enthralled: "There have been violinists here of mature years, and more than mature pretensions, to whom this modest boy could afford to lend a goodly portion of the rich volume which he has at his command, and

[76] Little Marsh had been most recently heard at a concert at Metropolitan Hall on April 21 for the Ladies Fair of the Free Church of St. Jude, at which he had performed "in 2/4 and 6/8 time," accompanied by a Mr. W. Curtis on the fife, and in a Grand Medley, with Mr. Curtis at the piano.

[77] In the *Herald*'s opinion (July 3, 1852) little Julien was another Paganini.

Paul Julien in frilly shirt and velvet jacket.

even then he would be their superior. . . . Passages of brilliant difficulty flow from his bow with an easy exactness hardly inferior to Madame Alboni's vocalization. His little hand, which seems hardly able to command the stops of his instrument, takes the remotest intervals with unerring certainty, and grips the string with the firmness of a vine." If Julien tended sometimes to oversentimentalize, it was probably due to "pernicious influences" from which he would soon free himself. Playing a fantasia on themes from *Norma,* Julien performed the *Casta diva* and Finale with "a grandeur, fervor, and grace which were in the highest vocal style." But White disapproved his use of a mute in an unascribed, unaccompanied Lullaby, something White had never before seen used in solo playing; in his opinion it added nothing to the general effect.

Julien's assisting artists were "the brilliant and De Meyer-like" Richard Hoffman, the fine bass singer Philip Meyer [*sic*], and the master-accompanist Henry C. Timm. "No insignificant portion of the enjoyment of the evening was due to Mr. Timm, whose accompaniments may divide the honors with any virtuoso, however eminent, who is wise enough to secure his services," wrote White. "That Mr. Timm's reputation as an accompanist rivals that which he has acquired as a concerto player does not surprise us. Except his exquisitely pure and liquid touch, his acquirements in the latter capacity are perhaps not unattainable by severe study, but his ability to sustain and enrich the performances of a singer or a solo player is altogether intuitive, and his dexterity in keeping with them, however they may wander, is truly marvelous" (*Courier and Enquirer,* July 3, 1852).

In late September, as we know, Julien joined Madame Sontag's company. "In his becoming costume, his dreamy little face and beautiful little head . . . he was certainly a poetic object—a veritable little *maestro*," rhapsodized the *Musical World and Times* (October 2, 1852, p. 75).

In September too, Camilla Urso arrived in rather more elaborate style than had Julien. She brought her own company of assisting artists: her father Salvator Urso, a flutist, appearing under the alias of Signor Salvator; Oscar Comettant (1819–1898), a French composer/pianist and future noted critic; Comettant's wife, a singer; and Hermann Feitlinger, "tenor to His Majesty, King of Holland." The details of Urso's brief past—her debut at the age of six, her studies at the Paris *Conservatoire* with Lambert Massart (1811–1892),[78] and her European triumphs—were published in the *Evening Post* (September 27, 1852), together, by way of a puff, with a report of a *soirée* at the "residence of one of our popular French merchants, where a very large and fashionable company were gathered to welcome [Urso] to this country and to marvel at her musical gifts. "She handles the violin," wrote the *Post,* "with as much freedom and ease as a Spanish lady does her fan."

Present at this *soirée* was the *Mirror* critic, who declared (September 27, 1852) that "the old soul of Paganini looks out of her eyes and vibrates from her violin. In everything but eyes and music," he wrote, "she is an ordinary child of ordinary manners and appearance; we should also except her fingers, which are very long and very large, especially those of the left hand, being unduly developed by extraordinary straining upon the fingerboard." Urso played the most difficult and passionate music "as if she had already run through the whole gamut of human experiences." She truly overwhelmed her listeners, among them the veteran violinist Michele Rapetti, who "bent over the child with a look of mingled rapture and surprise."

At Urso's debut on September 30, Metropolitan Hall was well filled (at $1 a ticket), but not crowded. "Her appearance was singularly prepossessing," reported the *Mirror* (October 1, 1852), "her *pose* firm, correct, yet easy, and her little arm guided the bow with grace and precision. She breathed into the instrument a mellowness, an expression, a purity of sound truly remarkable. Even in the *fortissimo* parts she appeared to have the requisite strength, and the richness and fullness of her notes contrasted strangely with the delicate diminutiveness of this little mistress of the violin."[79]

With an orchestra led by Eisfeld, Urso played Viotti's 24th Concerto, an *Air varié* by de Bériot, and Artôt's *Souvenirs de Bellini.* It was interesting, commented the *Mirror,* "to notice the glistening of Paul Julien's eyes while his little sister-artiste played the 'Souvenirs of Bellini' with all the plaintive wailing of that exquisite composition."[80]

In the same issue the *Mirror* chided its journalistic colleagues, particularly the *Times* (which had just delivered its indictment of the local critics) for having neglected

[78] Massart was later the teacher of the legendary violin virtuosi Henri Wieniawski (1835–1880) and, purportedly, of Pablo Sarasate (1844–1908).

[79] Although the *Home Journal* (October 9, 1852), granted that Urso played effectively and that she was well received, it maintained that she was in no way the equal of Julien. She did not merit her expensive buildup: the elaborate private *soirée* uptown, the orchestra conducted by Eisfeld, the assisting artists, the profusely distributed free tickets, and the "large number of bouquets and other enthusiasms."

[80] Eisfeld conducted the overtures to Beethoven's *Egmont* and Rossini's *Otello;* the others contributed various inconsequentia.

to review Urso's debut: "The *Times* was right yesterday in saying that the critics need looking after. It is truly their vocation to honestly and faithfully inform the public. How do the musical critics of the *Times* come up to this rule when they have not a word to say this morning of the marvelous violin performance of Camilla Urso last night? . . . But the *Times* is not alone in leaving the inspired Camilla to take care of herself—the *Tribune* and *Courier* [*and Enquirer*] are its companions. Come, Messieurs Critics, let us have no more such neglect; it argues ill for the critical function, to say nothing of the musical taste of our critics."

But the *Mirror* was in turn reproved by the *Express* for failing to mention Urso's assisting artists—Madame Comettant and Monsieur Feitlinger—in its review of the concert. Accordingly, on October 2 the *Mirror* made good its "inadvertent" omission: "Mad. C. has a fair, sweet voice, of no considerable power, however. M. Feitlinger is of the species of singers we might imagine as potent in the glee clubs of lager beer houses in Germany." Of Oscar Comettant and Signor Salvator, not a word.

Although it had been announced beforehand that Urso and her company would give a series of concerts in New York, they departed for Boston immediately after her debut;[81] she seems not to have performed again in New York until November 8, when she and her company gave a concert for the benefit of the Roman Catholic Orphan Asylum. Her two appearances with Alboni immediately followed (November 9 and 12); she assisted at the St. George's concert on November 23, then gave her "farewell concert" at Niblo's Saloon on November 25, before departing on a tour of the South. Appearing with her were a new cast of assisting artists: Mrs. Georgiana Stuart, a leading soprano member of the Harmonic Society, who sang various opera arias and a "favorite English ballad"; a debutant Mr. Robert Heller, "solo pianist of the Royal Academy of Music, London,"[82] who played his own piano fantasy on airs from *Maritana* and something billed as Mendelssohn's "Capriccioso in E Minor"; and a chamber ensemble of Philharmonic musicians—the flutist J. A. Kyle; the violinists U. C. Hill, J. Noll, C. Pazzaglia, and one of the Reyers; the cellists A. Boucher and L. Eichhorn; and the double bassist C. Preusser, conducted by G. F. Bristow—who played Beethoven's Overture to *Prometheus* and a septet by Bertini. Tickets were fifty cents.

In a brief review, the *Daily Times* (November 27, 1852), disregarding her assisting artists, declared Urso to be no "mere youthful prodigy . . . whose only claim to attention [was] that which curiosity lends because of her tender age. . . . She is, essentially, an *artiste* of high order—comparing most favorably with the best adult Violinists of the day." Her performances of Artôt's Fantasia on *La sonnambula* and of "The Carnival of Venice" (to say nothing of de Bériot's Sixth *Air varié*) were "surpassingly fine." After her concluding piece, reported the *Times,* in the midst of the thunderous applause, "little Paul Julien stepped forward from the audience and crowned his juvenile sister

[81] In Boston she gave two concerts, "attended by an intelligent, nay, an exacting, audience, delighted almost to tears—and yet, not money enough in the house to pay expenses!" (*Dwight's,* October 16, 1852, p. 15).

[82] He was the same Robert Heller who on December 20—calling himself "The Prince of Wizards"—opened his "Saloon of Wonders" at 539 Broadway, advertised as a "Palace of Enchantment . . . as bewildering to the eye as his performances are to the understanding." Heller's true identity was William Henry Palmer (1830–1875); he would enjoy a long and successful career in the United States, more as a magician than a musician.

in Art with a wreath of white roses. This unexpected and exceedingly pretty 'afterpiece' drew out another storm of applause, which continued for several minutes."

Nor was the native juvenile scene neglected. As usual, it was dominated by William B. Bradbury, who this year, with the assistance of his brother Edward, instead of Francis H. Nash, presented three performances of the perennial "Flora's Festival"♪ at the Broadway Tabernacle on February 11, 12, and 24. In a lengthy, laudatory, and informative editorial-cum-biography-cum-review devoted to W. B. Bradbury—his mission, his teaching methodology, and his achievements in juvenile music education—the *Musical World and Journal of the Fine Arts* (March 1, 1852, pp. 173–74) described the February 12 performance as a "decided improvement upon previous representations [of the work]. The singers, again numbering some 1000 small boys and girls were tastefully arrayed in appropriate costume: the girls being all dressed in white and profusely decked with flowers. The portion of the Tabernacle occupied by the children too was dressed with flowers and evergreens, so interwoven and arrayed as to represent fairy bowers, and the girls looked so much like fairies that the illusion was complete."

No less than five thousand people were packed into the Tabernacle for this concert, reported the *Musical Times* (February 14, 1852, p. 235), "every seat and every standing place was full—the capacity of the building was tested to the utmost." The writer credited the Bradburys, who played the accompaniments on two pianos, with admirable taste in their management of the giant affair, both musically and aesthetically. "It was a very pleasing concert, not only to Messrs. Bradbury, but to the children, the 2000 parents, and the 2000 who had no capital invested in that stock. The Festival met with the same success on [the following] evening." On April 14 and 21 the Bradburys again presented a "Juvenile Entertainment" at the Tabernacle, this time a selection of miscellaneous music performed by a choir of about 1000 young singers in "uniform dresses."[83]

But Bradbury's work with very young children had adversely influenced his handling of adult choruses, wrote the *Albion* critic (March 27, 1852, p. 152), evidently a rigid disciple of the purest English choral traditions. Reviewing the second Annual Festival of Glees, Choruses, and Ballads, given on March 17 by the Broadway Tabernacle Choir (of which Bradbury was the director) assisted by the Alleghanians, the concertina virtuoso Alfred Sedgwick, and, as a special attraction, a five-year-old comic singer, the critic wrote: "As Mr. Bradbury is constantly compelled to adapt his pieces to the capacity of beginners, his performances claim our indulgence; but we must say that the quartette, in which he assisted . . . gave a poor criterion by which to judge of his powers as a *maestro di coro*. So badly sustained were the leading notes, that it was sometimes a question whether the chord was intended major or minor."

Besides: "At this concert we had one of those spectacles of an infant of 5 years of age being brought before the magnetism of a thousand adult eyes. . . . Suitable as such a display may be for the tenderness of the domestic circle, and gratifying as it may be to a fond parent's heart, we cannot believe but that there is something morally wrong

[83] Attempting to outdo Bradbury, on May 26, Messrs. Benjamin and Mather mounted a Grand Concert and May Queen Festival at the Tabernacle with 1200 young singers, assisted by a juvenile band of 100 young musicians from their musical academy.

in it, before a large and undiscriminating mass. These exhibitions should not be encouraged."

Due to fiscal problems the New-York Harmonic Society's choral concerts were comparatively few in 1852. On February 23 the Society gave a mixed program of no great consequence. By June 16, however, with all debts paid,[84] the about-to-be reorganized Society, under Bristow's direction, courageously brought out a new oratorio, *The Waldenses,*[85] by Asahel Abbott (or Abbot) (1805–1888), a prolific but virtually unknown native composer. With tongue in cheek (for he was only an American), *Dwight's* (June 26, 1852, p. 95) described Abbott as "a phenomenon." "He is a sturdy, self-made New Englander who has for some years taught music in New York; but, what is more, can boast himself the composer of an incredible number of oratorios [eleven in all, ten of them unknown] and other scores in great forms. Not only that; he has instructed several of his pupils to be likewise composers of great oratorios.[86] To hear him talk, you would think that great oratorios grew on bushes."

The Waldenses, continued *Dwight's,* was the first in a series of oratorios that Abbott planned to compose in "honor of the different races that have struggled for liberty throughout the last 1000 years." How far he may have succeeded in this ambitious undertaking is not known. Perhaps some of his ten other oratorios were part of the project.

In the opinion of R. Storrs Willis, who heard only the latter half of *The Waldenses,* the work possessed "a correct and facile arrangement of harmony—occasional good points and felicities of accompaniment, an absence of any attempt at display or claptrap effect—and an independent thinking-out (after a fashion) of the subject by the composer himself." Its faults were its "extremely fragmentary character—its psalm-tune brevity and psalm-tune quality—its repeated use of the same key in different movements creating a frequently dull, monotonous effect, a lack of fresh melody and [of] an animated, vigorous treatment of the subject—and a far too ponderous and grave quality of music altogether."

Willis admired the Society's patience in striving to do justice to the composer in the oppressively hot Tabernacle. Mrs. Georgiana Stuart (who seems to have replaced Mrs. Laura A. Jones as New York's oratorio star) was singled out for her excellent performance, as was Maria Leach;[87] and Bristow did "all that one could expect of any conductor. Patient, attentive, and persevering as ever was this valuable ally in all our musical undertakings."

[84]Through the combined efforts of a committee consisting of Bristow, Root, Camp, and Hoffman, the Harmonic Society was now "prepared to start with new hopes, *provided* a new regime were organized" (*Musical World and Journal of the Fine Arts,* July 1, 1852, p. 358.

[85]Originating in twelfth-century France, the Waldenses, named for their founder Peter Waldo, were a long-lived religious sect preaching a simple, unadorned Christianity. Through the centuries they settled throughout Europe; by the late 1840s they had emigrated to Uruguay, then to the United States. Current Waldensian activity was reported in the *Courier and Enquirer* (June 21, 1853).

[86]Among them George Frederick Root and George Henry Curtis (advertisement, *Message Bird,* February 1, 1849, p. 223).

[87]According to the *Musical World,* the other solo performers were Mrs. Brinkerhoff (the former Clara Rolph)♪ and Messrs. Lincoln and Augustine.

After hearing *The Waldenses,* Willis left the Tabernacle wondering what the eccentric "movements and demonstrations" on the part of the composer (apparently seated in the audience) throughout the performance, might have signified (*Musical Times,* June 19, 1852, p. 74).

According to the *Albion* critic (June 19, 1852, p. 296), the performance had been given to raise funds to build a church in Turin for descendants of the original Waldenses. The oratorio's text was a collection of "scenes and sentiments" drawn from the history of the sect, mingled with selections from the Scriptures. The effort was a credit to the Harmonic Society, particularly because "much of the music must be a heavy drag upon the patience and endurance of a chorus." The work was far too long, and of a dreary sameness. And—not that the writer wished to undervalue Mr. Abbott's "zeal and ability"—familiarity with Handel, Purcell, and Boyce did not an original oratorio make; indeed, it too often resulted in borrowing, consciously or unconsciously. The opening of Abbott's tenor solo, "Mid these deep solitudes," for instance, was identical with a phrase in Purcell's cantata "From silent shades." The *Musical World* (July 1, 1852, p. 357–58) reported that the insistence on many encores by a large and interested audience had made it necessary, due to the lateness of the hour, to omit the final parts of the work. In this critic's opinion *The Waldenses* was a "second-rank" work, comparable to Handel's "*Theodosius*" *(Theodora?)* or Loewe's *The Seven Sleepers.* But it had the practical advantage of being equally performable with orchestra or, as on this occasion, with organ, at which Abbott's sometime pupil George Henry Curtis ably presided.

Although great things were reportedly now in store for the reorganized Harmonic Society, their only other appearances in 1852, in addition to Fry's lectures, seem to have been those at Madame Sontag's ill-conceived monster concerts, and at a benefit concert in December for the Five Points Mission School (discussed below).

The sparseness of locally originated choral concerts was to some extent mitigated by the huge choral festival given by the *Sängerbund,* a national association of German singing societies who had chosen to celebrate their Third Annual Jubilee in New York. Some 1200 jolly Germans arrived on June 19 from such far-flung places as Washington, Baltimore, Philadelphia, Newark, Boston, Hartford, Albany, Patterson, Poughkeepsie, Kingston, Milwaukie *(sic)*, and others.[88]

Never before had New York witnessed anything like it. On reaching the city, the first group were greeted by a 100-gun salute from the Battery, and all that day the booming of cannon continued to announce the various clubs as they arrived. In the evening they congregated at City Hall Park, where some seven or eight thousand persons (mostly Germans) had assembled to greet them. There, holding lighted torches, they sang the German Welcome Song, led by Agricol Paur, the director of the Jubilee, "as Germans only know how to sing it." Then, after three cheers, they formed in ranks and marched off in torchlit procession, each society accompanied by a band, to the Jersey City Ferry slip to meet their brethren arriving from the South.

[88] Of the thirty-one participating societies, those native to New York were the *Harmonia, Lorelei Männerchor, Sängerrunde, Liederkranz, Orpheus, Schillerbund, Social Reform Gesangverein, Grütli-Verein, Teutonia Männerchor,* and the *Liedertafel.*

After further parading they assembled at their headquarters, the Apollo Rooms, which had been lavishly decorated for the occasion with evergreens and bunting, the walls inscribed with the names of great German composers, each embellished with an appropriate motto in German and encircled by a wreath of evergreen. Presiding over the whole was a "fine picture of the Goddess of Song"[89] (*Evening Post,* June 21, 1852; *Musical World and Times,* July 1, 1852, p. 358).

There, after appropriate welcoming ceremonies, the assembled societies partook of a fine supper, "and until a late hour they were enjoying themselves by a judicious commingling of eating, drinking, speaking, and singing" (*Daily Times,* June 21, 1852). Indeed, as the *Home Journal* observed (July 5, 1852), conviviality was the keynote of this lusty festival.

Before the commencement of their "sacred" concert at Metropolitan Hall on June 20, a Sunday:[90] "The large apartment of the first story was provided with tables extending all its length, at which were seated the twelve hundred members, wearing their badges and all engaged in noisy and hilarious conversation. . . . At the end of this room a temporary bar was erected, behind which as many bar-keepers as could stand were distractedly, but vainly, trying to keep pace with the demand for those mild fluids which the good Germans love—Lager-bier, lemonade, claret, and the wine of Rhine."[91]

The thirsty "good Germans" in the audience were served as well by waiters who throughout the evening "perambulated the hall with large trays of tumblers filled with various cooling drinks and saucers of ice-cream." As the *Home Journal* commented, everything was planned for the "full enjoyment of the multitude."

Adding to the festive atmosphere, Kossuth arrived, graciously acknowledged the "simultaneous rising and cordial cheering of the people," and departed after the first part of the concert, being cheered, as he left, "from his seat to his carriage."

The concert, in fact a singing contest, opened with Weber's Overture to *Oberon,* played by an orchestra of 100 musicians under the direction of Paur. Then, in turn, each of the clubs, standing in a tight semicircle, sang one piece, unaccompanied. At the close of each offering the singers were pelted with "showers of bouquets," plentiful enough in some instances to supply a bouquet to each singer.

Attending the final Grand Concert given the following evening,[92] R. Storrs Willis

[89] ". . . very considerable expense has been incurred in preparations for the festival, such as advertising, manufacture of badges, hire of the Apollo Rooms and Metropolitan Hall, payment of orchestra, etc., amounting . . . to no less than $7000." To R. Storrs Willis, such an expenditure was almost too vast to contemplate (*Musical Times,* June 26, 1852, p. 85).

[90] For once, Willis moderated his Germanophilia. This "so-called *sacred* concert" on Sunday evening was an old trick, he complained, a kind of insulting humbug perpetrated upon the American public, in which a program of secular music was printed in German but headed, in English, "Sacred Concert." If the Germans disagreed with the American way of keeping the Sabbath, why did they not come out with it honestly, instead of indulging in this burlesque?

[91] Taking exception to the *Musical World*'s remark that the members of the German *Sängerbund* were "too much under the influence of *hops* and *malt* in their concert of Sunday evening," the *Albion* (July 3, 1852, p. 320) more charitably ascribed their out-of-tune performances to an overabundance of "fatigue, exposure to the heat, and sightseeing."

[92] Tickets for this concert, at $1 and $2, were double the price of those for the "sacred concert" the night before.

wrote: "The performances of the festival, under Paur's direction, were both bad and good—insufferably bad, indeed, in some instances, and inexpressibly grand and glorious in others." Willis was seized with "cold chills" at their sublime ensemble performance of Beethoven's majestic song *Die Ehre Gottes aus der Natur,* op. 48, no. 4 (1803); he praised their singing of choruses from Mendelssohn's *Antigone,*♪ of Weber's *Jägerchor* (from *Der Freischütz*), and an unidentified setting of Goethe's *Wandrers Nachtlied.* But the remainder of the program was inferior and not worthy of notice.

To wind up the festivities, a "pic-nic" was held on June 22 at Elm Park, a former country estate, now a "boarding establishment," about four miles out of town at East 88th Street. Some 10,000 people (Willis's estimate), attended, including ladies and children. Tables were set for about 1000 singers; the trees were decked in German and American flags and banners; and after a performance of "Hail Columbia" by the assembled multitude they broke up into groups, some to dance, some to play games (not excluding kissing games with the "buxom and laughing Wilhelminas"), some—"between games and foaming glasses of *Lager*—to strike up a quartette."

"About four o'clock a squadron of German dragoons and American rifles dashed into the grove, waving and clashing their sabres and escorting in their midst the Mayor and Chief of Police. They were received with cheers and waving of handkerchiefs, and after caracoling picturesquely among the trees for a little time, they came to a stand, while the Hartford Club sang to the Mayor, in beautiful style, a very effective quartette."

At about seven o'clock, wrote Willis, "the throng dispersed quietly and happily to their homes, after a day of unalloyed enjoyment." After a good deal of comparative weighing of German and American values, he concluded that Americans had much to learn from Germans in the art of living life to the full, without dissipation.[93] "We wish the Germans and their festivals all success—*Die Deutschen sollen hoch leben*!" (*Musical Times,* June 26, 1852, pp. 85–86).

From January through May, local German musicians appeared, albeit more sedately than their visiting brethren, at their so-called "sacred" concerts on Sunday evenings. Only spasmodically advertised in the English-language press, these events, given at the Apollo Rooms, at National Hall (29–31 Canal Street), at the Chinese Rooms, and wherever else, were primarily intended for German audiences. As the *Musical Times* commented (January 17, 1852, p. 171): "How many of these [concerts] take place in different parts of the city we do not know. . . . The Germans muster in this city in sufficient numbers to render these concerts profitable [at twenty-five cents a ticket], and as the evening of the day of rest has always been deemed in the fatherland a fit time for recreation, they are not shocked by what seems to Americans so incongruous," meaning that these Sunday evening programs made no effort to be sacred in content as well as name. At one of these concerts, on January 11 at the Apollo Rooms, the program had included such profane music as the "Champagne Song" from *Don Giovanni,* scarcely fitting fare for the Sabbath.

The artists on this occasion had been Madame Elise Siedenburg, a former "Prima Soprano at the Opera of the Grand Duke of Mecklenburg Schwerin," who had report-

[93] Despite their consumption of "rivers of *Lager-bier* and light German wine," the Germans remained, in Willis's fond opinion, exhilarated but not intoxicated.

edly toured with Ole Bull in Europe (*Dwight's,* November 20, 1852, p. 55), the tenor Beutler, the baritone (or bass) Oehrlein, and the bass William Müller; also the Philharmonic cellist Frederick Bergner; and Agricol Paur, who both sang and presided at the piano, opening the concert with a solo piano version of Beethoven's *Egmont* Overture. Madame Siedenberg, probably appearing for the first time in New York, was heard in an aria from Weber's *Euryanthe,* in a trio from *The Creation* with Beutler and Oehrlein, a duet from *Die Zauberflöte* with Müller, and a song by Kücken. The other singers performed solo and ensemble works by Beethoven, Mozart, Mendelssohn, and Lachner; Bergner played a set of cello variations by the Belgian cellist and composer François Servais (1807–1866); and the concert wound up with a rousing hunting song for male quartet by Julius Otto (1804–1877).

"The performances generally were good," reported the *Musical Times,* "but gave evidence of insufficient rehearsal. The Apollo rooms were about half filled by a very well-dressed, very quiet audience. There were but few ladies, and most of the gentlemen kept their hats on—perhaps because the room was cold. The concert was in all respects better than the low price of admission would have warranted us in expecting."

Sacred concerts assumed many guises in 1852. Max Maretzek, during his uncomfortable final season at Astor Place, presented a "sacred concert" at Metropolitan Hall on February 8, at which the "Entire Strength of the Company" were heard in Rossini's *Stabat Mater* and "Gems from *Le Prophète*." Tickets were twenty-five and fifty cents.

At the Norfolk Street Methodist Episcopal Church, on January 19, an exotic sacred concert was given by "four Indians of the Oneida Tribe, two Gentlemen and two Ladies," the Ladies in native costume. Their voices, stated their advertisement, were like "so many well-tuned instruments of music." Tickets were twenty-five cents, half price for children, and the proceeds would be applied to the building of a mission church at Oneida Village. For the same cause, the Indian Family, assisted by the Alleghanians, again performed on February 3 at the Forsythe Street Methodist Episcopal Church.

On January 20, for the benefit of the Spring Street Church, a "Grand Concert of Sacred and Miscellaneous Music" was performed by the Hutchinson Family, assisted by G. F. Bristow (piano), U. C. Hill and Joseph Noll (violins), Hegelund (viola), Bergner (cello), Pirsson (double bass), and the church choir; F. H. Nash conducted. Tickets were fifty cents.

At the Bleecker Street Presbyterian Church, on January 21 an all-German cast, consisting of the singers Rosa Jaques (or Jacques), Philip Mayer, John Beutler, and William Müller, with Hermann Wollenhaupt as presiding pianist and organist, appeared in a program of sacred music by Handel, Haydn, Mendelssohn, Rossini, and Spohr.

And on October 14, for the benefit of the Church of the Epiphany (Stanton Street between Essex and Norfolk), "choice selections" from *Messiah, The Creation, St. Paul,* and *The Seasons* were "sustained by the best amateur and professional talent in the city"—the Misses Brainerd, Thomas, and Wray, and Mr. Zander—assisted by the church choir, accompanied by Messrs. Nash and Bell at two pianos, and conducted by G. F. Bristow.

Two secular concerts in sacred surroundings were given on March 16—at the Church of the Messiah (728 Broadway) by Stephen Leach, assisted by Mesdames Wallace-Bouchelle, H. C. Watson, and Georgiana Stuart, Miss Maria Leach, and Messrs. Augustus Braham and H. W. Greatorex, with Timm and Scharfenberg at the piano(s); and at the Dutch Reformed Church, with an even more secular cast that included the Union Singing Association, the Alleghanians, Jeanie Reynoldson, the Misses Wardell and Drummond (the latter an American singer), and Professor Sedgwick, the concertina player. Tickets for each event were fifty cents.

Mrs. Laura A. Jones announced (but seems to have canceled) an ambitious concert of sacred and "miscellaneous" music on April 19 at the Chinese Rooms, with a voluminous cast including Mrs. Bostwick, the Misses Wheelock and Hawley, Messrs. Timm, Beutler, Philip Meyer (Mayer?), and Robert Andrews, Dodworth's Quartette Band, the St. Bartholomew's Church Choir, and members of the Harmonic Society.

As in the past, Dodworth's Band performed semi-sacred Sabbath programs at Castle Garden on Sunday nights.

Among the more notable complimentary and benefit concerts of 1852 was a massive event at Niblo's Garden on April 29 to assist the once celebrated, now sadly depleted, double bassist and occasional opera singer, Cesare Casolani.♪ The voluminous cast included Mesdames Thillon, Caterina Barili-Patti, Vietti (presumably Pico-Vietti), Wallace-Bouchelle, Watson, Siedenburg, and E. Loder, Messrs. Coletti, Sanquirico, Rapetti, Bassini, Sedgwick, and Master Saar; also Dodworth's Cornet Band, and an orchestra of fifty performers conducted by Arditi. Timm and Signor Nicolao were listed as "Maestros."

The net proceeds of this concert, reported an obvious novice in the *Musical World and Journal of the Fine Arts* (May 15, 1852, p. 287) had "run up to a handsome figure"; but the "only performances worth mentioning were those of the Dodworths, Rapetti and Timm [apparently playing a duet], and Mr. Braham. . . . A person named Sanquirico and a stout lady called Signora Vietti attempted a duo from *Il fanatico*. Mr. Sanquirico's voice reminded us of the criticism of an Indian singer, namely, that 'it sounded as if it had been placed between two shingles and sat upon.'" (Thus fleeting, alas, is fame.)

Appearing at a less publicized benefit for one John McKibbin at Niblo's Saloon on April 1 were Madame Kazia Lovarney Stoepel,♪ seventeen-year-old Master Theodore Thomas, Felice Eben, and Xavier Kiefer; Timm presided at the piano and an orchestra composed of Philharmonic members was conducted by Alexander Tyte, a Philharmonic violinist.

Emma Gillingham Bostwick,[94] who since concluding her second series of *soirées* in February had been touring with Richard Hoffman and Felice Eben, was honored with an elaborate complimentary concert at Metropolitan Hall on October 26. Appearing with Mrs. Bostwick on this occasion were Adelindo Vietti, Henry Appy, Julius Siede, a Herr Thilow (billed as the "Pianist to his Royal Highness, the Duke of Co-

[94] Highly lauded in a biographical article appearing in the *Musical World and Journal of the Fine Arts* (March 15, 1852, pp. 197–98).

burg Gotha"), Miss Annie Oliver, a ten-year-old concertina prodigy,[95] and an orchestra of seventy players conducted by Arditi and led by Bristow.

On November 23 the St. George's Society and the British Protective Emigrant Society gave their annual joint benefit concert at Metropolitan Hall. The participating artists were Madame Bishop and members of her company currently appearing in English opera at Niblo's Garden (see below)—Rosa Jaques, Stephen Leach, Giuseppe Guidi, and Augustus Braham (singing his father's warhorse "The Death of Nelson"); also present were the concertinist Sedgwick, the harpist Alfred Toulmin, Wallace's Empire Brass Band, Camilla Urso, and a Grand Orchestra conducted by Bochsa. The predominantly British program, consisting of works by Handel, Sir Henry Bishop (a tasteless choice, considering the tangled interrelationships), John Braham, and Balfe, began with a "National American Overture" (probably composed by Bochsa) and ended, of course, with the British National Anthem sung by Madame Bishop supported by Braham and Leach.

Two benefit concerts of unusual significance were given at Metropolitan Hall in December by opposing factions but both ostensibly having the same goal—to raise funds for a building, or buildings, to replace the recently demolished "Old Brewery," for decades a foul nest of degradation, poverty, vice, and crime that had dominated the infamous slum at the Five Points.[96]

The first event, a two-part "Grand Festival Concert and Oration," given on the afternoon and evening of December 17, was sponsored by the Five Points' Mission of the Ladies' Missionary Society, who advocated the construction of "Missionary Buildings" of purely religious purpose on the site of the Old Brewery. Assisting were Rosina Pico-Vietti, Mrs. Georgiana Stuart, Adelindo Vietti, Domenico Coletti, John Kyle, Robert Heller (in his piano-playing persona), and G. F. Bristow, who conducted. Between the afternoon and evening sessions the Children of the Mission School, conducted by the editor and future music publisher Chauncey M. Cady, sang a hymn especially composed for the occasion. They appeared as well at the evening session, as did the temperance leader John B. Gough, who delivered an oration. One could attend both sessions for fifty cents; reserved seats were $1.

The opposite event—enjoying greater support in the press—was sponsored by the Society of the Iron Man, a benevolent organization advocating the continuation of the humanitarian and educational program established by the Reverend Dr. Lewis Morris Pease (1818–1897) at his Five Points House of Industry. In 1850, Pease and his wife had valiantly taken up residence in the heart of the notorious slum and dedicated themselves to rescuing "from their physical and moral degradation the children and other denizens of this polluted section of the city" (*Daily Times,* December 20, 1852). In addition to supplying these unfortunates with food and clothing, Pease's program of regeneration offered rudimentary education to prepare them for honest, self-

[95] Daughter of a bandmaster in Montreal, little Miss Oliver was billed as *La petite fille du régiment.* Her performance on the concertina, commented the *Albion* (October 30, 1852, p. 524), "was *almost* as wonderful as anything we have heard, or seen, in the prodigy way, even in this season of prodigies." In her serious approach to her art, she was no less remarkable than Julien.

[96] Situated at the convergence of Cross (now Park), Anthony (now Worth), Little Water (now vanished), Orange (now Baxter), and Mulberry streets.

supporting labor. His curriculum included, as well, humanizing music instruction for the children,[97] generously donated by George Henry Curtis.

At the December 20 concert for Pease's House of Industry, the first part of George H. Curtis's cantata *Eleutheria*[98] was performed by Mrs. Georgiana Stuart, Maria Scoville Brainerd, Anna Griswold, Marcus Colburn, the New York Sacred Harmonic Society (as the Harmonic Society was renamed),[99] F. H. Nash and Noah C. Curtis's Madrigal Association,[100] and an orchestra of predominantly Philharmonic musicians conducted by an apparently nonpartisan Bristow. Miss Brainerd followed with an enthusiastically received song by "Father Heinrich," who accompanied her on the piano. Then came an original poem "The Mission of Intellect," read by Augustine Duganne;[101] then some seventy "remarkably well-behaved . . . rescued little ones," directed by their "Friend and Teacher," Reverend Pease, and accompanied by Heinrich, zestily sang the hymn "There is a happy Land" and, much to the audience's delight, "The Old Folks at Home." Then a "long, but interesting" report was read by a careworn-looking Dr. Pease, describing the "origin, growth, and present condition of the Five Points House of Industry" and vindicating it vis-à-vis the conflicting goals of the Ladies' Home Missionary Society. Then followed an eloquent appeal for contributions by one C. C. Burr, during which "hats were carried round" and a collection taken up totaling some $286. Only then was the second part of *Eleutheria*—faring "rather badly after the long intermezzo"—at last performed. Although regrettable, the "musical sacrifice" was justified in light of the noble cause, for "what was said and done in the intermezzo [brought] in more 'material aid' than the music could possibly have done" (*Daily Times,* December 21; *Musical World and Times,* December 25, 1852, p. 258). (A sad admission.)

The vogue for more and more stupendous benefits came to glorious fruition with the "Grand Military Musical Festival," a multiple-band extravaganza in two parts, given for the benefit of the Musical Fund Society[102] at Castle Garden on the afternoon and evening of September 4. Eleven bands in full regalia participated: Dodworth's Cornet Band, Shelton's American Brass Band, Adkins's Washington Brass Band, Wallace's Empire Brass Band, Wannemacher's New York Brass Band, Schiebel's National

[97] A visitor to Pease's Five Points Mission House, writing in the *Musical World and Times* (December 4, 1852, p. 210), tells how Pease, a gentle man, summoned his barefoot, ragged little singers "to give us a parting song before going to bed. . . . Mr. Pease, in an easy, genial way, took his seat before them in a rocking chair, and then, with one foot on his knee, began swaying backward and forward and started a familiar little hymn. A dozen prattling voices immediately joined in."

[98] *Eleutheria: A Hymn to Liberty* was originally subtitled "Festival of Freedom" when it was first performed in 1849.♪ In 1852 it was published by William Hall and Son, and extensively reviewed in the *Musical World and Journal of the Fine Arts* (April 15, 1852, p. 246).

[99] Ostensibly after the famous Sacred Harmonic Society of London.

[100] Formed in October, Nash and N. Curtis's Madrigal and Choral Class had been launched at their rooms at 413 Broadway with a reading of Handel's *Acis and Galatea,* at which members of the Harmonic Society were invited to participate.

[101] In the opinion of the *Musical World and Times* (December 25, 1852, p. 258) Duganne's poem, despite its few strong points, was, "on the whole, tiresome and inappropriate."

[102] With only six to seven thousand dollars to show for their three years of existence, the Musical Fund Society had made scant progress toward reaching the base sum of $20,000 mandated in their charter.

AMERICAN MUSICAL FUND SOCIETY

GRAND

MILITARY MUSICAL FESTIVAL

AT

CASTLE GARDEN,

SATURDAY, SEPT. 4, 1852

AFTERNOON AND EVENING.

On which occasion the following extraordinary combination of Musical talent will appear

DODWORTH'S CORNET BAND,
SHELTON'S AMERICAN BRASS BAND,
ADKINS'S WASHINGTON BRASS BAND,
WALLACE'S EMPIRE BRASS BAND,
WANNEMACHER'S NEW YORK BRASS BAND,
SCHIEBEL'S NATIONAL BRASS BAND,
FISCHER'S BRASS BAND, and
NOLL'S 7th REGIMENT BAND,
THE BROOKLYN CORNET BAND,
THE TROY BRASS BAND,
THE BOSTON BRIGADE BRASS BAND

The following eminent Artists have also kindly volunteered their valuable services.

HERR MENGIS, Barritone,
M. EDOUARD BOULANGER, Pianist,
PAUL JULIEN, The Celebrated Violinist.

CONDUCTORS, GEO. F. BRISTOW & THEODORE EISFELD

AFTERNOON PERFORMANCE.

DOORS OPEN AT 2, P. M. . . . CONCERT COMMENCE AT 3½.

PROGRAMME.

PART I.

1. Overture—Fra Diavolo, ... AUBER. BY THE UNITED BRASS BANDS.
2. Grand Operatic Pot Pourri, ... WEBER. BY THE NEW YORK BRASS BAND—WANNEMACHER, Leader.
3. Gandler, ... POPP. TROY BRASS BAND—E. P. JONES, Leader.
4. Duo, for Two Cornets, ... GRAFULLA. AMERICAN BRASS BAND—JAS. SHELTON, Leader.
5. Sextette, Lucia di Lammermoor, ... DONIZETTI. WASHINGTON BRASS BAND—THOS. G. ADKINS, Leader.
6. Phœnix Guard Quickstep, ... SCHIEBEL. NATIONAL BRASS BAND—JOHN L. SCHIEBEL, Leader.
7. Rondo Finale, ... MARETZEK. DODWORTH'S CORNET BAND—A. DODWORTH, Conductor—H. B. DODWORTH, Leader.

PART II.

8. Overture—Robert Le Diable, ... MEYERBEER. SEVENTH REGIMENT BAND—JOSEPH NOLL, Conductor.
9. Wedding March, ... MENDELSSOHN. BOSTON BRIGADE BAND—BARTLETT, Leader.
10. Duo, ... RENDINI. FISCHER'S BRASS BAND—C. FISCHER, Leader.
11. Erina Quickstep, ... DOWNING. BROOKLYN CORNET BAND—R. STEWART, Leader.
12. Die Kosenden Waltz, ... GANNER. BY THE UNITED BRASS BANDS.

INTERMISSION.

NO CHECKS GIVEN.

EVENING CONCERT.

PERFORMANCE TO COMMENCE AT 7½.

PART I.

1. Musical Fund Quickstep, ... ARDITI. BY THE UNITED BANDS.
2. Ernani Involami, ... VERDI. BOSTON BRIGADE BAND.
3. Rataplan,—Accompanied by all the Side Drums of the Combined Bands, ... MALIBRAN. HERR MENGIS.
4. Grand Fantasia for the Violin, on Airs from Norma, ... ALLARD. EXECUTED BY PAUL JULIEN.
5. Loreley's Rhein Klange Waltz, ... STRAUSS. NEW YORK BRASS BAND.
6. Concertante, ... KALLIWEDA. TROY BRASS BAND.
7. Finale, 2d Act Lucia di Lammermoor, ... DONIZETTI. SEVENTH REGIMENT BAND.
8. Amelie Waltzes, ... LUMBYE. FISCHER'S BRASS BAND.
9. March, Le Prophet, ... MEYERBEER. BY THE UNITED BANDS.

PART II.

10. March from Athalia, ... MENDELSSOHN. BY THE UNITED BANDS.
11. Pot Pourri from Ernani, ... VERDI. AMERICAN BRASS BAND.
12. { Grande Etude in A Flat, ... E. BOULANGER. Finale de Concert on Elisire d'Amore, ... S. THALBERG. } EXECUTED ON THE PIANO, BY E. BOULANGER.
13. Aria, Buffa,—Lorsque mon Maitre, ... BOULCHIN. HERR MENGIS.
14. Fantasia for the Violin, on Airs from I Lombardi, ... VERDI. EXECUTED BY PAUL JULIEN.
15. Giorno d'orore, from Semiramide, ... ROSSINI. DODWORTH'S CORNET BAND.
16. Scena ed Aria, from Lucrezia Borgia, ... DONIZETTI. BROOKLYN CORNET BAND.
17. American Rifles' March, ... SCHIEBEL. NATIONAL BRASS BAND.
18. Pot Pourri, from La Fille du Regiment, ... DONIZETTI. WASHINGTON BRASS BAND.
19. Grand Quickstep, Finale, ... DODWORTH. BY THE UNITED BRASS BANDS.

Tickets for the Afternoon and Evening,

50 CENTS.

☞ NO CHECKS GIVEN.

Tickets can be obtained at the Music Stores, the Hotels, and at the door of the Castle Garden during the afternoon and evening.

Baker, Godwin & Co., Printers, Tribune Buildings, N. Y.

Handbill for the Great Band Gala at Castle Garden.

Brass Band, Fischer's Brass Band, and Noll's Seventh Regiment Band, all local organizations,[103] joined by the Brooklyn Brass band, the Troy Brass Band, and the Boston Brigade Brass Band.

At each of the sessions—at 3:30 in the afternoon and 7:30 in the evening—each band played a different "solo piece," and finally, uniting in mighty ensemble some 200 strong, with Bristow and Eisfeld dividing the conducting duties, they performed Auber's Overture to *Fra Diavolo,* Lanner's "*Die Kosenden* Waltz," Arditi's "The Musical Fund Quickstep" (doubtless whipped up for the occasion), the March from *Athalie* (Mendelssohn), the Grand March from *Le Prophète* (Meyerbeer), and, for finale, a "Grand Quickstep" by one of the Dodworths (probably Harvey). Added to all this, solos were performed by Paul Julien, Catherine Hayes's baritone Joseph Mengis, and the pianist Eduard Boulanger. Tickets were fifty cents, and because no re-entry checks were issued to ticket-holders wishing to leave the hall between sessions—and with crowds waiting to grab their places—it was a choice between missing the evening concert or hanging on, dinnerless, until exhaustion set in.

Although the event provided a gorgeous spectacle, the Castle Garden acoustics, in the opinion of the *Musical World and Times* (September 11, 1852, p. 27–28), were unfavorable for such massive musical purposes: the drums and cymbals were overpowering. Besides, the program was banal; the bands played better separately than collectively, and so on. Joseph Noll's Seventh Regiment Band, with its uncommon combination of reed and brass instruments, received the greatest share of the applause and deservedly so. Little Julien, "the star of the evening," although "clever," was not equal to the great spaces of Castle Garden or the sonorities of orchestral accompaniment. Mengis and Boulanger merely showed "evidences of talent."

The *Albion* (September 11, 1852, p. 440), too, commended Noll's Seventh Regiment Band for their woodwinds and praised their performance of the Overture to *Robert le diable,* which was encored. But the critic nonetheless awarded the palm to Dodworth's Cornet Band for their "high finish and full competence to execute the most elaborate pieces." Besides, the writer was unabashedly partial to the cornet: with its capacity for producing "a stream of melodious sound," he considered it to be "one of the improvements of the age."

Band concerts had begun to occupy an increasingly important place in the local music scene. On February 20, Dodworth's annual "Musical Festival," an event enlisting the Full Band of fifty performers (including the Cornet Band), was given under Harvey Dodworth's direction at Metropolitan Hall. The program, in addition to the requisite quicksteps and virtuosic Italian opera transcriptions played singly and together by Allen and Harvey Dodworth—on this occasion Allen played an arrangement for cornet of the aria *Ernani involami* and, with Harvey, the duet *Giorno d'orrore* from *Semiramide*—included a Grand Military Overture by Mendelssohn, played by the Full

[103] In an illuminating editorial devoted to local military bands, the *Musical Times* (March 20, 1852, p. 307) lists, in addition, among the American bands, Wheeler's Empire Band, Whitworth's City Band, and Willis's Cornet Band; among the German, Wanmaker's [*sic*] Jefferson Band, Fish's Hungarian Band, Manahan's Band, and Kobel's Band. Besides these, the article states, other bands were called upon for special occasions: the Navy Yard Band, the Governor's Island Band, and the Band of any frigate that may be in port. The bands normally consisted of fifteen to twenty-five musicians; they were paid from $2.50 a day for firemen's parades to $4 for military balls (the fee for "society balls" was $3.50).

Band; the "Bandit Quickstep" from *Ernani,* arranged for the Cornet Band by D. L. Downing, one of its members; a Grand Polka, *Bouquet de concert,* composed especially for the occasion by Thomas Coates; and a so-called "Favorite Piece" and the "Urielle Quick Step," both presumably arranged by Harvey Dodworth.[104]

The program was otherwise of special historical interest, having included what appears the first public performance of an excerpt—the air "Nay, do not Weep"—from George Frederick Bristow's opera *Rip Van Winkle* (op. 22), then in the earlier stages of its composition. It was sung by the new American tenor from Albany, Henry Squires, presumably with Bristow at the piano. Ignoring the Bristow excerpt, the *Mirror* (February 21, 1852) mentioned merely that Squires sang several songs during the evening, with good taste.

The other assisting artists were more enthusiastically received: "Master [Theodore] Thomas astonished and delighted us with his violin solo [the Fantasy on airs from Rossini's *Otello,* op. 11, by Heinrich Ernst]. Although a youth, he appears to be a perfect master of the instrument, and executes the most difficult passages with the greatest ease. He produces an exceedingly rich tone, and plays with remarkable brilliancy."

The clarinetist Xavier Kiefer, too, "with exquisite taste and fine execution" played an unidentified solo on the "Cornet Bassetto" (bassett horn), an instrument described as a "blending of the clarionet and bassoon" possessing a "peculiarly rich tone." Alfred Sedgwick played an unidentified piece on the concertina; Mrs. Laura A. Jones, who had been scheduled to sing another Bristow song, "The Dawn is Breaking o'er Us," did not appear.

On June 29, under the heading "Music for the Million," the *Daily Times* announced that Noll's Seventh Regiment Band would play "some of their best music" in Madison Park (Madison Square) that evening, explaining: "Some wealthy residents of that vicinity have made arrangements with this Band to give performances in the Park on every Tuesday and Friday evening during the summer."[105]

Probably encouraged by the public response to their summer concerts, on October 21 the Seventh Regiment Band proposed a series of six monthly concerts at Metropolitan Hall, commencing in November. "The Band is composed of some of the first musicians in the City, many of whom are members of the Philharmonic Society and were the principal performers in the celebrated orchestras of Mesdames Jenny Lind, Sontag, and Alboni," announced their prospectus. "The programmes will consist of Instrumental Solos, Overtures, Operatic Selections, Polkas, Waltzes, Marches, Quicksteps, etc., in addition to which the most available Vocal Talent will be engaged." William Hall would be in charge of the subscriptions, costing five dollars for

[104] The band arrangements were generally made "by some competent person hired for the purpose," but in most cases Harvey Dodworth arranged the music played by his bands (*Musical Times,* March 20, 1852, p. 307).

[105] Again under the heading, "Music for the Million," the *Times* (July 13, 1852) reported that at a Board of Aldermen's meeting, Alderman (William Marcy) Tweed (1823–1878) had advanced a resolution that "a committee of three be appointed to procure a band of music to perform in our public parks one evening a week . . . and appropriating $1000 to defray the expenses of same." The resolution was voted down. "Of course," disgustedly commented the *Times,* "for why should the people receive any favors from the Board of Aldermen?" Apparently the private sector, then as now, came to the rescue.

two tickets for the series, and fifty cents for single tickets to single concerts. The prospectus was signed by the Philharmonic musicians, Joseph Noll, the band's conductor, and Franz Rietzel, their leader.

At their first concert, on November 6, the first half of the program comprised music for orchestra; the second for full military band of forty-five players.[106] The soloist was a debutante Miss E. Beverly, who, "accompanied by full orchestra," sang "Kathleen Mavourneen" and a Neapolitan air; Kiefer played a solo on the *corno di bassetto;* Noll and one of the Reyers performed a *duo concertant* for two violins; and the orchestra played the Overture to *Zampa* and the "Lichtenstein Waltzes," presumably derived from Lindpaintner's opera *Lichtenstein* (Stuttgart 1846). In the second part they played band arrangements of predominantly orchestral and operatic repertory: Weber's Overture to *Euryanthe,* Jenny Lind's "Gipsey Song" (with Kiefer performing the voice part on the clarinet); the Finale from *Lucia di Lammermoor;* the Grand March from *Le Prophète;* and Rietzel's "Aurelian Polka."

Following the same orchestra/band format at their second concert, on December 4, their program was even more varied: in addition to the usual opera overtures, quicksteps and dance-tunes, they gave the first performance in America of Schumann's "*Quartetto concertando*" (*Concertstück*) for four horns and orchestra, op. 86 (1849). Philip Meyer (Mayer?) sang Italian opera arias, and, by request, Kiefer repeated his clarinet transcription of Jenny Lind's "Gypsey Song."

Rising to the challenge, Harvey Dodworth immediately announced a competitive series of six concerts, to begin at Metropolitan Hall on December 18. At the opening concert various redistributions of his personnel appeared as Dodworth's Military Band of forty-five players, his Cornet Band, and a grand orchestra of fifty performers. Allen Dodworth played his sensational cornet version of Maretzek's *Rondo finale* (presumably the one written for Madame Laborde's *Linda di Chamounix*), and a piano-playing Mr. G. Knoepfel performed something announced as Mendelssohn's "*Concertant*" (*Concertstück?*) for piano and orchestra. The Full Band played the Overture to Spohr's *Jessonda,* Harvey Dodworth's Military Quickstep and, by request, "St. Paul," a dirge that he had composed for the recent Daniel Webster obsequies. The Military Band played Weber's *Jubel* Overture (a "first performance" in America in this instrumentation); the Cornet Band played the *Terzetto* from Donizetti's *Belisario;* and members of the group played a sextet arrangement of Gungl's "Sounds from Home."

To a lesser degree, these concerts were imitated at the Tabernacle on December 15 by the Messrs. J. J. Daly and S. A. Westcott, who presented Bloomfield's U.S. Navy Band from Governor's Island, assisted by the popular vocalist Caroline Hiffert. Among their heterogeneous offerings were an arrangement of the Overture to Bellini's *Norma* for solo piano; a guitar trio; William Vincent Wallace's song "Star of Love," transcribed for two "flutinas";[107] and a band arrangement of Madame Sontag's "celebrated Polka Song." Miss Hiffert sang popular ballads. Tickets were twenty-five cents.

[106] Evidently the same players: ". . . the members of all these bands play both wind and stringed instruments, almost any band of wind instruments being able to transform itself into a *stringed* band (or orchestra) at any moment" (*Musical Times,* March 29, 1852, p. 307).

[107] Despite its evocative name, the flutina, patented in Paris in 1842, was a small accordion with a keyboard at each end.

On January 28 the long-lived Euterpean Society gave their fifty-third annual concert and ball at the City Assembly Rooms (446 Broadway), advertising only that the dance music would be supplied by Noll's Quadrille Band.

On the more legitimate concert scene, on January 8, Catherine Hayes, with her original cast—Augustus Braham and Herr Mengis, and with Lavenu and Loder sharing conducting duties—returned to Metropolitan Hall for her final concert in New York. It was hinted in the *Herald* (January 9, 1852) that she was being wooed by Domenico Coletti and Charles Burkhardt, "the musical critic of the House of the Capulets," to join the schismatic Artists' Union Italian Opera Company as a "trump card to play off against the Montagues of Astor Place." The courtship came to naught.

With Hayes and Augustus Braham coming to a parting of the ways, Braham, hardly a newcomer by now, announced his "first concert" in America,[108] to take place on March 1 at the Tabernacle. Assisted by Madame Wallace-Bouchelle, Maria Leach, Mrs. Henry C. Watson, Henry Wellington Greatorex, Mr. Busch, a flutist, and with Bristow "conducting" (accompanying at the piano), Braham was announced to sing Italian opera arias and popular ballads. Reviewing the concert, the *Herald* (March 2, 1852) advised Braham to avoid Italian arias in the future and "stick to the English ballads." To which the *Mirror* (March 2, 1852) waspishly responded: "The *Herald* critic, who applauds Mr. Braham's ballads, but condemns his trial of Italian operatic music, evidently was not at the concert, as he criticizes a programme that was finally changed for the evening."

The *Albion* critic (March 6, 1852, p. 116), although he could detect in Braham's voice a faint resemblance to his father's—and "despite a thousand imitations" of the elder Braham's style—remarked that: "The [John] Braham school has had its day and can never be revived again, even though it professes to represent the genuine and imperishable original music of the Anglo-Saxon."

Nothing daunted, on March 8, Augustus Braham gave a "second" concert in America, again at the Tabernacle, and with virtually the same cast. The first part consisted of sacred and "miscellaneous" music, the second of selections from the works of Thomas Moore and Robert Burns.

Among the lesser alien concert-givers were the pianist W. G. Dietrich (heard earlier at a Mrs. Bostwick *soirée*), who gave a Grand Farewell Concert on February 23 at the Broadway Casino (as the Chinese Assembly Rooms were temporarily renamed), assisted by an orchestra of fifty; the Misses Mina and Louisa Tourny (earlier heard at the Philharmonic) appeared at Niblo's Saloon on November 27, assisted by an all-German cast—Philip Mayer, Beutler, Eisfeld, Noll, Reyer, Eichhorn, Scharfenberg, and Timm; and a versatile Monsieur L. Poznanski from London, performed on the violin, viola, and guitar, sang a duet with Mrs. Georgiana Stuart, and delivered verbal program notes at his "Vocal and Instrumental Entertainment" on December 20 at the Stuyvesant Institute. Besides Mrs. Stuart, Poznanski was assisted by the Philharmonic cellist Bergner, and by Timm and Scharfenberg, who played an arrangement for two pianos of *Les Soirées musicales de Rossini* by Wolff, possibly the Polish composer Éduard

[108] Meaning his first essay as a concert-giver. "First performances" and debuts seem to have been as capable of flexible interpretation as were farewells.

Wolff (1816–1880). Alfred Sedgwick gave a concert at Hope Chapel on March 9, assisted by Richard Hoffman.

Of necessity, most of the local performing musicians supplemented their incomes with separate, but related, activities. Of course, just about everybody gave lessons. As we know, Allen Dodworth—when he was not playing cornet solos with the Dodworth Bands, or composing or arranging—was giving classes in ballroom dancing at his handsome new Dancing Academy at 806 Broadway, near Grace Church, an indispensable meeting-place and charm school for the offspring of Upper Tendom.[109] Harvey Dodworth, with one Charles L. Lazarus, opened a music store, at 493 Broadway, where not only foreign and domestic sheet music of all kinds was available but also band instruments and fixings of various sorts. The pianist Charles Wels, who had studied composition and theory with the celebrated Johann Thomaschek (Václav Jaromir Tomašek) (1774–1850) in Prague, advertised a course of 24 two-hour classes in thorough bass for ladies and gentlemen, four students to a class, at $20 for the course. Edward G. Bradbury, having curtailed his teaching efforts because of poor health, advertised the opening of his pianoforte warerooms at 423 Broadway. Francis H. Nash added to his busy teaching schedule with an extra series of elementary singing classes in October at the Spring Street Church on Wednesday evenings, and, as we know, with Noah C. Curtis, his madrigal class on Tuesday evenings at 413 Broadway, all the while selling and renting pianos on the side. In March, Nash engaged U. C. Hill to give a beginners' violin course at Nash's "music rooms" at 649 Broadway; terms, only $5 per quarter. Strakosch opened his piano store and plunged into peripatetic concert management. Joseph Burke gave lessons, not only on the violin, but the piano forte, singing, and "*leçons d'accompagnement.*" Eliza Valentini, with undiminished gusto, advertised her unique capacity, "having yet all her vocal powers," for being able to provide a vocal model for her pupils to imitate—and in four languages! And Leopold Meyer, between nightly feats of violinistic virtuosity in blackface, gave orthodox violin instruction every day from nine A.M. to two P.M. at his residence on Howard Street. He later enlarged his pedagogical scope to encompass piano and singing lessons.

At almost any time throughout the year New Yorkers with more down-to-earth musical tastes enjoyed concerts by their favorite ballad- and folk-singers: the Alleghanians (now under the management of the renegade Jesse Hutchinson, Jr.), the remaining Hutchinsons, persistently calling themselves the "Original Hutchinson Family," and, among the Scottish contingent, the Frasers, Jeanie Reynoldson,[110] William Demp-

[109] Among Dodworth's teaching innovations at his new academy, sessions were held on Saturday afternoons and evenings, when all the dances that had been learned during the week were practiced to unfamiliar music played by a band of music—"thus affording the pupils an opportunity of becoming accustomed to dance and *keep time* to the various styles of music in use" (*Home Journal,* November 13, 1852).

[110] For the sake of variety, Miss Reynoldson announced that at her "Scottish Concert" at the Tabernacle on February 25, "in order to suit the different tastes of the people," the program would include not only Scotch but Italian and English music. To achieve ethnic authenticity, she had engaged Eliza Valentini, Miss Drummond, and the tenors Paravalli and William Brown to participate;

ster,[111] and the newly arrived Scotch/Irish MacIntyres, a "middle-aged, sensible-looking," husband-and-wife team who interspersed their vocalized ethnic chestnuts with accordion solos by McIntyre. A master of the instrument, he did an astonishing imitation of the bagpipes that, according to the *Evening Post* (March 9, 1852) sounded better than the real thing. Mrs. McIntyre presided at the piano. The MacIntyres appeared three times in March at the New York Society Library, were accorded a com-

---

also appearing were a blind pianist Edward Kanski, and Van Der Weyde, who would preside at the piano.

[111] At Dempster's concert on March 29, reported the *Post* on March 30, 1852, "he had his audience half the time in tears, and half the time convulsed with laughter." But the *Musical World and Journal of the Fine Arts* (April 15, 1852, p. 247), albeit reluctantly, pronounced him to be "about the poorest singer we ever heard."

Music Division, The New York Public Library

Allen Dodworth's new dancing academy at 806 Broadway, with the spires of Grace Church in the background.

plimentary concert advertised as "The Meeting of the Clans" at Metropolitan Hall on April 21, then went their way.

In March, after a deluge of frenetically ballyhooed farewell concerts, the Alleghanians, accompanied by their new manager, sailed on the steamship *Daniel Webster* for an engagement in San Francisco, the new Mecca of American show business. Enacting a kind of preview of Lind's departure-to-come, a great crowd of the Alleghanians' well-wishers congregated at the dock, "determined," as the *Evening Post* put it (March 22, 1852), "to give them an enthusiastic farewell. They [the Alleghanians] appeared on the promenade deck, and their friends and admirers gave them nine hearty cheers. Previous to the steamer's leaving, Miss Goodenow sang her farewell song [set to the tune of "Home, Sweet Home"], in which the company joined, and the utmost silence prevailed. As soon as she had concluded, however, the cheering again commenced. The steamer then moved out of the dock and proceeded on her course, the Alleghanians in the meantime having begun another song, which they continued to sing until out of hearing of the crowd on the wharf."

Other vocal groups appearing that year were the blind "Memnonic" Vocalists and the New York Vocalists, comprising Kazia Lovarny-Stoepel, Lucy Burr, John Beutler, John R. Thomas, and Franz Stoepel.♪

The persistent blackface-minstrelsy phenomenon received a considerable amount of pro-and-con editorial scrutiny in 1852. In the first of two articles on the topic (February 28, p. 259, and March 6, 1852, p. 275), the *Musical Times,* observing, in a rare moment of tolerance, that even the humblest of musics had its place in the scheme of things and therefore deserved unbiased critical investigation, quoted from an article in the *Democratic Review.* Supporting the general belief that the locally concocted burnt-cork caricatures seen at the minstrel shows authentically represented the black culture of the South, the misinformed anonymous author wrote—revealing the still unsatisfied American hunger for an indigenous music: "The Negro Melodists are the only species of National Amusement that we can boast of. They sing the songs of the Plantation Slaves of the South, dance their Plantation Jigs, and imitate the language of the real Virginia Negro. These Melodists are the first indications that have been given of the possibility of a Native Drama."

But another article in the *Musical Times* (March 6, 1852, p. 277), denounced the "vile [ballad] imitations of the miserable charlatans and mountebanks of the *black school*": the "ruin these Ethiopian *ravens* have wrought in musical circles" was a "curse to a growing musical community."

Throughout 1852, Christy's Minstrels continued to dominate the field. Fellows, at the end of February, ended his long run at Fellows's Opera House and took his minstrels on tour, all the while keeping his New York following apprised of his current whereabouts in a running series of newspaper advertisements. On their departure, Fellows's Minstrels were immediately supplanted by Henry Wood's Minstrels, who very successfully took over Fellows's Opera House, renaming it Wood's Minstrel Hall. The company included, among others, the blackface star Eph Horn, the violinist Leopold Meyer, the erstwhile concert cellist Theodore Ahrend, and the spectacular dancer R. H. Sliter. Their merry goings-on notably included a "Negroized" version of *Macbeth,* titled "Macbeth, King of the Darkies."

Samuel S. Sanford's (or Sandford's) New Orleans Opera and Ballet Troupe (not Buckley's New Orleans Serenaders)[112] settled into the New York Society Library on April 5 for twelve performances of their genteel "Drawing Room Entertainment," then adjourned to the Astor Place Opera House, where, alternating with Donetti's Troupe of Acting Monkeys, Dogs, and Goats, they performed the favorite burlesque opera *Shin-de-Heela (Cinderella).* White's Ethiopian Serenaders,[113] having appeared early in the year at White's Melodeon (53 Bowery), turned over that establishment to George Lea (of the disreputable Franklin Museum).[114] On July 5, a Monday, White's troupe celebrated the Fourth with afternoon and evening performances at the newly refurbished Vauxhall Gardens. During July and August they were intermittently seen at Barnum's American Museum, where T. D. Rice had appeared in April.

On September 13, White opened his new Theatre of Varieties at 17–19 Bowery, near Chatham Square, giving mixed programs of plays, farces, and blackface entertainments and, as a special feature, Shakespeare readings by Lora Gordon Boon, a "five-year-old diseuse." Soon changing management, the theatre was renamed the St. Charles.

Captioned "Theatrical Exhibitions—Classical and Unclassical, Decent and Indecent," an editorial in the *Herald* (May 4, 1852) supplied some interesting statistics on the vastly diversified New York theatre scene in the early 1850s: "The play-going public of this city are provided with numerous places of resort, according to their tastes, inclinations, and finances. New York has now some eighteen or twenty theatres of all shades of character, from the chaste and classical drama down to exhibitions of an immodest and prurient kind. These theatres," continued the *Herald,* "are attended [nightly] by some twenty thousand persons, yielding from twelve to fourteen thousand dollars to the proprietors, and offering employment to several thousand persons in the shape of managers, box keepers, actors, actresses, scene shifters, lamp lighters, etc."

With George Loder gone and Brougham having given up the Lyceum Theatre[115]—two perhaps not totally unrelated facts—and with the retirement of Mary Taylor in May, the impoverished New York musical stage in 1852 depended chiefly on the French *opéra-comique* productions given in English and French at Niblo's Garden, the Broadway Theatre, and to a lesser extent at Castle Garden.

But first, Mary Taylor's retirement. On May 3 at Burton's Theatre, "Our Mary," adored by New York theatre-goers since 1838, when as an enchanting child of twelve she made her debut, bade farewell to the stage, "having determined to retire," as the

[112] Now reportedly reaping a golden harvest in entertainment-hungry San Francisco.

[113] In December, *White's Ethiopian Song Book,* "a collection of all the new and most popular Songs, Glees, Choruses, Parodies, Duets, Trios, Burlesque Lectures, Jokes, Conundrums, etc.," was published by H. Long and Brother. The price, 12½ cents (*Tribune,* December 9, 1852).

[114] First renaming the hall "Lea's Melodeon," then "The Palace of Beauty," Lea presented his ladies in a show featuring songs and "also the latest Bloomer waltzes, polkas, etc., each lady garbed in a different dazzling costume with unimaginable effect" (were they the old Bloomer Troupe sunken to this sorry level?); also "living marble statuary, impersonating some of the greatest pictures of ancient statuary."

[115] Brougham precipitately closed his theatre in March after a single disastrous performance of *The Maid and the Magpie* (*La gazza ladra*) featuring the boundlessly versatile Madame de Marguerittes (the sometime Giulietta Bozzi) as Ninetta.

New-York Historical Society

Mary Taylor, a plump nightingale, as Mrs. Page in The Merry Wives of Windsor.

Mirror (May 3, 1852) poetically put it, "with her well-earned laurels—may they ever be fresh as Spring violets under a dewy baptism—into the calm, quiet walks of domestic life." In November 1851, Mary Taylor had become Mrs. W. Ogilvie Ewen. "Nor can we half utter our regret," continued the *Mirror,* "at losing from the stage one who has lightened and charmed so many hours by her talent, her graces, and her modest virtues. Still in the very bloom of youth [she was then about twenty-six years old], yet we can look back over some twelve years [*sic*] since she began those gentle witcheries which, without bringing one stain or reproach upon her fair name and fame, are now more enchanting than ever. . . . Her career has been an uninterrupted success."

Mary Taylor took her regretted leave of the stage with a program that displayed her remarkable range of versatility—histrionic and musical—appearing in three contrasting spoken plays and the second act of *The Child of the Regiment.*[116]

From March 15 through June 9, Madame Anna Thillon, with a company that included Julia Daly and Messrs. James Hudson, Andrew Andrews, and Stephen Leach, and with an orchestra under Signor La Manna, appeared at Niblo's Garden three times weekly in *The Crown Diamonds, The Black Domino,* and *The Daughter of the Regiment.* But this time around, Thillon elicited some surprisingly perverse criticisms: "She is very pretty [but] narrowly escapes being beautiful," accused Richard Grant White (*Courier and Enquirer,* March 18, 1852). "She has a very pleasing voice, which comes

[116] Mary Taylor never returned to the stage; she died suddenly in 1866 (Ireland, II, 243n).

very near being a fine one; her style and method of singing are almost as good as those of the best singers; and her acting is very skillful, and falls so little short of being very effective that it is only because her skill is so apparent—her determination to be bewilderingly bewitching so very obvious—that she fails in completely attaining the effects for which she strives. But, criticism apart," he conceded, "there are few pleasanter modes of spending an evening than in watching her through one of Auber's delightful operas."

The *Tribune* critic (George William Curtis?) was seized with the same ambivalence. To witness Madame Thillon's delicious performances of Auber was to be transported to Paris, he wrote (March 17, 1852). But although the possessor of "great and very effective beauty, it is like the music she sings and her style of singing it . . . too sweet, too elaborate, too careful." Nonetheless, her voice, though "somewhat worn and thin, has the sparkle and flexibility which the music requires, and her vocalization is extremely elaborate and beautiful." After further cavils that her manner of speaking and her acting were "somewhat overdone," the critic, "having relieved our critical conscience," pronounced her performance "fascinating."[117] More succinctly, the *Daily Times* (March 23, 1852) wrote: "The prima donna has a bewitching eye and fascinating manner. Her acting is agreeable, her beauty above praise, and her voice not quite so superlative." The critics notwithstanding, New York audiences adored her.[118]

On May 10, alternating at Niblo's with evenings of ballet by the Rousset sisters, Madame Thillon added another Auber work, *The Devil's Share (La Part du diable)* (Paris 1843) to her predominantly Auberian repertory,[119] and on May 31, just before completing her engagement, Balfe's *The Enchantress.*

On August 30, in *The Enchantress,* Madame Thillon—with Hudson, Ferdinand Meyer, "a very fair male chorus, and a really awful female ditto"—opened the short-lived New York Theatre, as the last theatrical gasp of the Astor Place Opera House was fleetingly named. "The orchestra played nervously and unsteadily," wrote the *Spirit of the Times* (September 4, 1852, p. 348), "and Mr. Thillon, who conducted, was altogether too vehement and energetic in his directions and movements." Ticket prices ranged from seventy-five cents downwards.

In September, Madame Thillon returned to Niblo's, repeating her former repertory,[120] and on December 17 she presented the first American performance of Balfe's comic opera, given in London in 1852 as *The Devil's In It,* now renamed for American consumption *The Basket-Maker's Wife.* Despite the excellent efforts of a large cast that included, besides Thillon and Hudson, Mrs. Maeder and Messrs. Alleyne, Beutler, and Lyster, the work, having a book by the prolific English librettist/impresario Alfred

[117] In his *Hafiz* persona, Curtis wrote in *Dwight's Journal* (May 1, 1852, p. 28) that Madame Thillon's prettiness was "Frenchy," in the style of "rosy-face wax dolls with golden ringlets. . . . Everybody consents that it is sadly artificial—but she has crowded Niblo's on her three evenings in the week for two months, with only three operas, and her audience is enchanted."

[118] "Madame Thillon, at Niblo's, is the personification of Grace, Beauty, and Elegance, and so are the gaiters, slippers, etc., at MILLER's [shoe store] in Canal Street. One draws crowds at Niblo's, the other draws crowds at MILLER's. . . . Performances over, all come away delighted, determined to go to Niblo's and J. B. MILLER'S, 134 Canal Street" (advertisement, *Mirror,* March 27, 1852).

[119] The *Mirror* (May 13, 1852) recalled that in 1845 a spoken version of *The Devil's Share* had been given at the Olympic Theatre under the title of *Asmodeus, or, The Little Devil's Share.*

[120] Seen at her performance of *The Daughter of the Regiment* on September 13 were, "in one of the stage boxes Madame Sontag, and in the other Madame Alboni" (*Tribune,* September 15, 1852).

Music Division, The New York Public Library

Anna Thillon in her American heyday.

Bunn (1796?–1860),[121] was harshly criticized: "The music has scarcely one redeeming feature. . . . There is not an air or melody throughout the piece that fixes itself upon the memory. . . . The 'Basket-Maker's Wife' will not, we think, add to the fame of the composer; nor do much to enrich the treasury of any theatre." Nor of its players.

In keeping with the curious dualism that marked the 1852 musical year—two Italian opera companies, two great European divas, two French violin prodigies—New Yorkers were treated as well to a second *prima donna* of French *opéra-comique,* and not an unfamiliar one: Madame Fleury Jolly,♪ who arrived in June with a splendid French singing-and-acting company from New Orleans (the first since 1845), had appeared in concerts in New York in 1847.

Immediately following Madame Thillon's earlier departure, the New Orleans company opened at Niblo's on June 21 for a short introductory season of operas and vaudevilles, beginning with Ambroise Thomas's locally unknown "Shakepearean" opera *Le Songe d'une nuit d'été* (*Midsummer Night's Dream;*) (Paris 1850). The cast included Mesdames Fleury Jolly and Pillot, the tenor Debrinay (or Dubrinay), the baritone Gaart, and the actor/singer Menehand.

Thomas's opera did not please the *Spirit of the Times* (June 26, 1852, p. 228): ". . .

[121] In the course of his long career, Bunn, who had unsuccessfully managed both the Drury Lane and Covent Garden theatres in London, wrote librettos and adaptations for countless English operas, many by Balfe—among them *The Maid of Artois, The Bohemian Girl,* and *The Enchantress.* Bunn was also the librettist for Julius Benedict's *The Brides of Venice* and *The Crusaders,* and for William Vincent Wallace's *Matilda of Hungary.* He was currently in the United States, vainly trying to retrieve his fallen fortunes with a one-man "Entertainment" consisting of theatrical anecdotes and reminiscences, "somewhat more familiar here, we suspect, than he is aware," wrote the *Daily Times* (October 12, 1852). A "short, fat, heavy man, decidedly John Bullish in appearance and manners," Bunn was tersely described as "an English edition of Brigadier Gen'l Geo. P. Morris, with a few marginal notes picked up in the green room" (*Mirror,* October 23, 1852).

Queen Elizabeth, Falstaff, and Shakespeare are introduced under most ridiculous circumstances, and in absurd relations to each other. We could forgive our Gallic friends for scandalizing Queen Bess and rendering fat Jack ridiculous, but to profane the memory of the sweet Swan of Avon by introducing his name into such balderdash is at once an insult to all who reverence him and an evidence that the French are wholly ignorant of his glorious works. Poor fellows!"[122]

But the *Daily Times* (July 5, 1852), reviewing the company's second offering, *Le Caïd* (Paris 1849), also by Thomas, was enchanted with their talented and sprightly performances, their exquisite costumes and scenery, their superb characterizations, and their general air of being "in every way at home on the stage." Madame Fleury Jolly, with her artistically managed high soprano, did "admirable justice" to her part; the baritone Gaart was irresistibly funny as a French drum-major. Too bad the work was being laid aside: "Our amusement-loving people must know M. Gaart better." In fact, Gaart appeared the very next evening as Sergeant Sulpice in *La Fille du régiment.*

Amusement-loving New Yorkers had ample opportunity to enjoy Gaart and his gifted colleagues throughout the summer and until October. Closing at Niblo's on July 9, the French company, without missing a beat, opened at the Broadway Theatre on July 12 with *Le Caïd,* and for the remainder of July they gave a large and varied repertory of French operas and vaudevilles. In addition to the operas mentioned above, they were heard in Paer's *Le Maître de Chapelle* and Adam's *Le Châlet* (both previously performed by earlier visitors from New Orleans), and on July 21 they introduced an unfamiliar work, *Ne Touchez pas à la reine* (Paris 1847), inelegantly translated as *Hands Off the Queen,* by the French composer Xavier Boisselot (1811–1893).

At the close of their season at the Broadway, the New Orleans company promptly resurfaced on August 2 at Castle Garden, in the Roussets' possession since June.[123] Opening with *Les Diamants de la couronne,* they garnered a fresh crop of highly favorable reviews. On August 26 they added Hérold's *Zampa* to their large repertory and the following night closed their engagement at Castle Garden with the second acts of *Les Diamants de la couronne* and *La Fille du régiment,* Fleury Jolly singing the leading roles in both. Briefly returning to Niblo's between Madame Thillon's departure and Madame Bishop's arrival, they gave a single performance of *Zampa* on September 29 and one of *Ne Touchez pas à la reine* on October 1, then departed.

After two years of persistently publicized triumphs throughout their extended travels, Madame Bishop and Bochsa returned for a month-long, three-times-weekly (and as it turned out, final) joint season of "English opera" in New York. Despite advance rejoicing in the press that at last authentic English opera would be restored to the New York stage, their first offering proved in fact to be a polyglot affair. With a cast consisting of Fräulein Rosa Jaques, the Signori Giuseppe Guidi and Severo Strini,

[122] What would the *Spirit* have said of the aberrant opera productions in vogue in the late twentieth century?

[123] Again the delights of Castle Garden were sung in the press: "The music of the opera is heard to great advantage in that cool and spacious place, and the south wind brings over the water the [military] tattoo from Bedloe's [now Liberty] Island to mingle with the softer strains of the orchestra. Smokers sit on the outer balcony, in the doorways, with their chairs canted backward, listening to the opera with one ear and the tattoo with the other" (*Home Journal,* August 28, 1852).

a Monsieur Rudolph (or Rodolphe), the Britishers Augustus Braham and Stephen Leach, and a probably local Mrs. Barton Hill (believed to be a pupil of Madame Bishop), they opened their season at Niblo's on November 1 with a German work "specially translated" for Madame Bishop, Friedrich von Flotow's *Martha, or the Richmond Market,* immensely popular in Germany since its first performance in Vienna in 1847, but not yet performed in New York (nor, evidently, in London). Not surprisingly, the "indefatigable" Bochsa, the supreme dictator of the project, was "determined" to present it "in a style and manner hitherto unattempted in this country" (*Spirit,* October 16, 1852, p. 420).

For all their advance puffery, the Bishop/Bochsa *Martha* received a mixed press. The *Mirror,* which had delivered an all but full-scale review in an advance puff, managed to be enthusiastic again—in both a short review on November 2 and a veritable hymn of praise the following day:[124] "So carried away were we by the beauty of the music [a blessed relief after all the Rossini, Bellini, and Donizetti] and the brilliancy of the whole affair, that we can scarcely trust ourselves, even now, to comment upon the performance, lest our feelings should betray us into extravagance of language." *Martha* was a great masterpiece and Flotow at least another Weber. Madame Bishop was more divine than ever; the spirited Rosa Jaques was a great hit, even if "not a word of her part could be understood," and Forti, a hopelessly Italianate relic of the early Maretzek days, although he grossly overacted, sang "sweetly and with exquisite feeling."

But the *Tribune* (November 2, 1852) bluntly pronounced *Martha,* although it abounded in "slight and agreeable melodies," to be a "poor" work, and the performance as well: "Madame Anna Bishop, Miss Rosa Jaques, Signor Guidi, and Mr. Leach cannot sing well enough for a leading metropolitan theatre, and still less can they lay the foundation for a regular English opera." Nonetheless, they "reaped a liberal harvest of applause from a house more full than critical."

Richard Grant White found *Martha,* although pretty enough, to "possess a taint of vulgarity." And Madame Bishop, despite "the charming coquetry of her acting and the elegance and appropriateness of her toilette," was, most regrettably, "poorly endowed in voice": with all her captivating and bewitching ways, she "spoiled her own triumph by singing so much, and so often out of tune." However, Bochsa, "the prince of operatic conductors," exhibited a "control over his orchestra [that seemed] truly magical" (*Courier and Enquirer,* November 2, 1852).

The *Musical World and Times* (November 6, 1852, p. 150), however, reported that in the first act a backstage chorus sang "just a 'beat' or two in advance of the music going on in front; and in the last act, Madame Bishop became enmeshed in a certain labyrinth of modulations, by which she lost the key entirely, and was in the clouds for several oblivious measures." Rosa Jaques was "very indefatigable," and Forti, with his overdone Italian-opera histrionics, supplied a "singular and somewhat violent contrast

[124] In its November 2 review the *Mirror* discredited the *Herald* for erroneously stating that Bochsa had repeatedly interpolated "The Last Rose of Summer," the traditional Irish tune of unknown authorship used by Flotow throughout the opera as a kind of *Leitmotiv.* Duplicating the *Herald*'s error, the *Albion* (November 6, 1851, p. 536) chided Bochsa for his too insistent and tedious "interpolations" of the tune, only to be exposed by the *Sunday Dispatch* and forced shamefacedly to retract in the next week's *Albion* (November 13, 1852, p. 548).

to the English element and style of singing in the opera."[125] "English is a desperate language for music," especially for foreigners, wrote the critic, "and English skill is *angular* in matters of vocalization; but let us have all *styles* in the universal realm of sound."

On November 18, after seven performances of *Martha,* Bishop/Bochsa brought out, "in broken English," *Lucy of Lammermoor,* of which the volatile *Mirror* (November 19, 1852), in a complete about-face, wrote: "Madame Anna, although looking somewhat too substantial to be 'crazed in love,' sang portions of her part very charmingly; but either our ears are a little too obtuse, or her upper notes are a little too acute. In other words, she sings *sharp*." However: "The lady was dressed, as she always is, like a picture."

The *Mirror* was disappointed, too, with Augustus Braham in opera: "He was uneasy in his 'new clothes' and made us feel uneasy, too." Besides: "The English words of the opera, so far as we heard them—and Braham was grotesquely distinct—only served to mar the effect of the music. The dying scene of *Edgardo* was rendered ludicrous by the twattle of the *libretto*." (Apparently opera in unintelligible Italian has its compensations.)

[125] "We wish Signor Forti could be persuaded to take rather a more healthy view of the passion of *love*. He is so weeping-willow-y in his style that it is painful to contemplate him: his arms droop, his shoulders droop, his head hangs on the side, and his voice is impregnated with the very quintessence of despair" (*Musical World and Times,* November 13, 1852, p. 162).

Girvice Archer, Jr.

Dauntless Madame Bishop "looking somewhat too substantial to be 'crazed in love.'"

The *Times* (November 20, 1852) had words of censure for Bochsa as well. The attempt to perform *Lucia* in English "was not creditable to Mr. Bochsa. His orchestra was like a volunteer army without a skillful leader, each playing or running on his own hook; the leader himself, mounted on the director's chair, learning his own lesson, book in hand, and beating time with his right foot with an energy only equaled by the fierceness of the big drum. Mr. Bochsa should rehearse at mid-day, not before an audience brought together to hear the opera complete."

Briefly reviewing their following production—*La sonnambula,* given on November 22—the *Mirror* (November 23, 1852) commented that the performance betrayed "the undue haste with which it has been brought out, many points not being in harmonious working order." With a further performance of *Martha* and one of *Linda di Chamounix,* Bishop/Bochsa concluded their inglorious New York season and departed.

Other musical productions of this theatrical year included Auber's *La Bayadère* and *Masaniello (La Muette de Portici)* presented respectively on June 9 and June 15 at the Broadway Theatre, as part of the "farewell" season[126] of the superb French actress/dancer/mime Celeste, who had been captivating New York audiences since 1827. Dancing and miming admirably in both these works, Celeste was supported vocally by Thomas Bishop and the Seguins, now members of the Broadway company. Also at the Broadway Theatre on December 13 and continuing nightly throughout the ensuing week, the fairy-tale opera, *The Peri: or The Enchanted Fountain,* composed by James G. Maeder in the 1830s, was at long last brought out.[127] Originally planned for production in 1839 at James William Wallack's National Theatre (originally the Italian Opera House at Church and Leonard streets), *The Peri* had apparently been a casualty of the fire that destroyed the National in 1839.[128]

With an American origin and locale—its fanciful libretto (dealing with Ponce de Leon) was adapted by S. J. Burr from an Indian legend in Washington Irving's *History of the Life and Voyages of Christopher Columbus* (published in London, 1828)—*The Peri* had preceded by six years the Fry brothers' *Leonora,* a work perhaps less eligible to be regarded as the first American "grand opera."

Grand opera or not, Maeder's score, comprising "thirty prominent pieces of music,"[129] received a generally favorable, if somewhat equivocal, press. Not of a "class to produce a *furore,*" wrote the *Mirror* (December 14, 1852), the score contained no "wild beating of cymbals and thumping of big drums *à la* Verdi"; it offered instead a "continuous strain of soft, harmonious sounds that charm with their sweetness, though

[126] In fact, Celeste would return to fresh triumphs on the New York stage in 1865.

[127] "At the cost of several thousand dollars," the Broadway Theatre production of *The Peri* had been in preparation for more than a year, announced E. A. Marshall in a gaudy advertisement that listed its myriad wonders: an extra orchestra, corps of auxiliary dancers, double chorus, scenery covering many thousand feet of canvass [*sic*], resplendent costumes, properties and decorations, and startling mechanical effects. A separate "synopsis" enumerated twelve "principle scenes," that included a "Splendid Choral Bower and Fairy Revels."

[128] At that time Wallack had been mightily lauded for not rejecting *The Peri* just "because it was an American opera" (*Knickerbocker,* November 1839, p. 467).

[129] Many of them published by William Hall and Son.

they might slightly weary you by the monotony." To the *Mirror,* "the sameness of the music" was the score's "one great fault; that and its lack of originality." Yet, Maeder was to be congratulated "upon the production of a very pleasing and entertaining opera and upon the success it [had] achieved, which, if not triumphant, [was], at all events, sufficient to stamp the talent of the composition." At the end of the performance, the cast—Caroline Richings, making her New York debut; her adoptive father Peter Richings,♪ the early Park Theatre idol; Madame Ponisi, T. Bishop, and W. P. Davidge, together with the composer—received an ovation; and Maeder was obliged to make a brief speech.

With their appearances at the Broadway Theatre the Seguins' lustrous joint career came to an end. Upon James W. Wallack's succession to the Lyceum Theatre in September, after its brief regime under Corbyn and Buckland, an ailing Edward Seguin, resolutely attempting to cling to the shreds of his great career, although no longer able to sing, joined Wallack's company as an actor. Three months later, on December 13, Seguin died. His disease, reported the *Tribune* (December 15, 1852) was an "affection of the heart"; Ireland (II, 277) says he died of a "hasty consumption."[130]

Throughout the year the usual number of routine stock revivals of old musical chestnuts—*Cherry and Fair Star, No Song, No Supper,* and others of like vintage—were dished up at the various other theatres. More important was the production on August 23 at Purdy's National Theatre of a dramatization in three acts by the actor/playwright C. W. Taylor of *Uncle Tom's Cabin, or Life Among the Lowly,* the world-kindling novel by Harriet Beecher Stowe (1811–1896). Serially published (June 1851–April 1852) in the Abolitionist magazine the *National Era, Uncle Tom* was a runaway best-seller when it was issued in book form in March 1852. Taylor's distorted dramatization, one of innumerable adaptations that would swamp the theatre (and various other media) for decades to come, for some reason (according to Odell, VI, 229–30), omitted the central characters of St. Clair, Topsy, and Little Eva, and renamed the surviving characters. Uncle Tom, who was spared, was played by Taylor. That this production included music is indicated in a frustratingly elusive playbill of unspecified provenance, cited in Odell (VI. 231–32). Among the titles listed are "Nigga in de Cornfield," "Come Then to the Feast," "We Darkies Hoe de Corn," a "Kentucky Breakdown Dance," and a chorus and "Grand Finale."[131] A moderate success (the phenomenally successful version by the actor/dramatist George L. Aiken (1830–1876) would follow eleven months later), the Taylor adaptation was played nightly for two weeks, then intermittently; it received some twenty performances in all.

Whether or not the music heard in this earlier dramatization of *Uncle Tom's Cabin* was published—and I have discovered no trace of it—a phenomenal deluge of Uncle Tom songs now began to descend upon the land.

[130] Despite the "handsome competence" Seguin left to his widow and four children, Anne Seguin, who had permanently left the stage, announced ambitious plans for opening an academy of music.

[131] Between-the-acts entertainment at this production consisted of Jim Crow Rice's blackface "delineations" and, less congruously, Herr Cline's tightrope dancing. "Although not so effective as he was some years since," wrote the *Mirror* (August 27, 1852), Rice was "still the best darky on the stage."

4

GTS: 1853

The attraction of the Opera is not so much the music, as the singers who are engaged to sing it. If a great vocalist arrives, it becomes a necessity of our fashionable existence that we patronize the celebrity. But for this prestige, we doubt much if the Opera would be patronized at all.

New-York Daily Times
April 15, 1853

IT WAS NOT UNTIL THE END OF JANUARY, a month musically monopolized by the hot Alboni/Sontag rivalry transposed to the opera stage, that George Templeton Strong at last heard one of the divas. Attending Sontag's third performance as Maria in Donizetti's *La figlia del reggimento,* the role in which she had made her local opera debut at Niblo's Garden on January 10, Strong commented in his journal (awarding her three gratuitous years) that she was "marvelously preserved for a woman of fifty, in face and figure and the power of putting on girlish buoyancy and spirit. . . . Like the lady much," he wrote. But apparently not enough to hear her again, although there would be no lack of opportunity, for Sontag would be heard in opera at Niblo's for the following three months and again at Castle Garden throughout July and August.

Doubtless more by design than by accident, Alboni, following her four triumphant performances of *La cenerentola* at the end of December, scooped Sontag's grand opening in *La figlia* with her own electrifying portrayal of the same role[1] at the Broadway Theatre a week earlier, on January 4.[2] "It is not easy to imagine a success more complete than that of Madame Alboni in *La figlia del reggimento* last evening," wrote Richard Grant White (*Courier and Enquirer,* January 5, 1853), echoing the universal chorus of praise. "[She] goes on surprising and delighting us by her powers as a dramatic singer, and throughout this whole opera she exhibited delicate traits of character and expression with a truthfulness and effect worthy of a professed comedian. She was irresistibly droll at times . . . and her drumming capped the climax of comicality."

Not the least surprising feature of Alboni's *vivandière* was her expert performance

[1] Assisted by Rovere as Sulpizio and Sangiovanni as Tonio.

[2] "The great mistake that opera managers are too apt to make," complained the *Musical World and Times* (January 1, 1853, p. 2), "is to *change* one new opera for another, just as the public are getting familiar with [it] and begin to like it." The general usage during the present season was to present an opera twice—at most, three times—before moving on to the next production.

"upon a real full-grown drum, like a drum-major"; indeed, "the roll of the drum [was] a hit in feminine hands; and Madame Alboni, being a good timist, showed off that little novelty well" (*Mirror,* January 5; *Tribune,* January 7, 1853).

The *Home Journal* (January 15, 1853), cherishing fond memories of Anna Thillon's vivacious *vivandière,* had wondered beforehand how Alboni would "acquit herself in a part apparently so little adapted to her voice and person—how the grand church organ would play this lively war-waltz. A melodious gurgle behind the scenes" announced Alboni's first entrance, wrote the critic: "She came, dressed in the usual red skirt with black stripes around it, a dark blue jacket with round buttons, an open vest, her hair behind her ears, and a black, low-crowned hat fluttering with red ribbons. It was a dress which, without being very becoming to her person, partially concealed its most conspicuous misfortune [her huge size]. She . . . advanced with a step as much like 'tripping' as could be expected." To this dubious reviewer, the "odd contrast between the rich solemnity of her melodious tones and the energy of her gesticulation was as though Dr. Hodges should play a waltz upon the organ of Trinity." But after her rather "heavy" start, Alboni took complete possession of her audience with the kettledrum scene: "She drummed in a style that would pass muster in a French barracks; the lively scene was warmly encored," and from then on, all incongruities were forgotten. In the emotional parting from her comrades: "With her handkerchief pressed upon her streaming eyes. . . . she poured forth a flood of melting lamentation that can never be forgotten by any that heard it. All the resources of her wonderful voice were displayed; and her acting was worthy of her voice. The effect cannot be described." In the music lesson scene Alboni surpassed even herself, "filling the vast and crowded theatre with the most magnificent and stirring music that ever flowed from the throat of woman—rising triumphantly above the crash of the orchestra, and only lost in the thunder of acclamation which burst from every part of the theatre."

During the scant two weeks that Alboni solely possessed the opera scene an unaccustomed unanimity reigned among the critics, but with Sontag's arrival they gleefully reverted to their normal disputatiousness. With two of the supreme *prima donna*s of the age competing on the same evenings (Mondays, Wednesdays, and Fridays) and virtually wresting the same repertory from each other's clutches, comparisons and taking of sides were inevitable. Piously condemning comparisons, the reviewers nonetheless deluged their readers with contradictory views on the relative excellences and shortcomings of the two divas.

As the pro-Sontag *Evening Post* peevishly complained on January 18, 1853: "A competition is to be expected, and not unpleasant to the public, but it seems strange to us that Alboni should go so much out of her way to sing high soprano parts.[3] . . . We notice, too, that she always advertises the same piece as Mme. Sontag.[4] We are sorry to see this. It seems to us that such a proceeding is somewhat wanting in the courtesy which should reign between artists so distinguished."

On January 10, 1853, the day of Sontag's opening in *La figlia,* the ferociously pro-Alboni, anti-Ullman *Mirror* proclaimed Alboni's *figlia* to be "all that could be desired

[3]Almost invariably transposed down, it was reported, to suit her voice, if not the design of the composer.

[4]It was a question of the chicken or the egg.

and more than could be imagined." And venomously continued: "It is true that there are attractions at the other house, where the setting sun of a great artist still lingers and plays upon the horizon, reluctant to leave the heaven of her former glory; and tonight a comparison of the two great luminaries will be forced upon us. With Alboni it is morning—Springtime. The dew is on the grass, the flowers are fragrant and fresh, and the birds fill the grove with the melody of their loving music. With Sontag it is, at least, late in the afternoon, a sort of Indian Summer, golden, glorious, and beautiful. But there is no dew on the gorgeous flowers of Autumn, the roses are pale and scentless, and the notes of the birds lack the gushing fullness and tenderness of the Spring."

All this ruthless poesy was merely the prologue to another savage attack on Ullman: "That these artists should be forced into immediate competition for popular applause is entirely owing to the contemptible conduct of Madame Sontag's manager, who after signing a contract in Baltimore for Niblo's Garden, came to New York and entered into a bogus negotiation with Marshall for the Broadway Theatre, in order to prevent Madame Alboni from appearing in opera."[5]

On the other hand, in the first issue of *Putnam's Monthly Magazine* (January 1853, pp. 117–18), George William Curtis, the new publication's associate editor and music critic, surprisingly praised Ullman's management of Sontag, although he agreed with the *Mirror* about the two singers' relative vocal merits. Apparently limited by an early deadline, and thus writing (in December) in advance of Alboni's impending opera debut at the Broadway Theatre, Curtis, in a quirky, rather revisionist summary of the musical highlights of 1852, stated that Sontag's concert career in America had surpassed Alboni's due to Ullman's superb, Barnum-like management.[6] Despite Alboni's vocal superiority, her youth, and her charisma, Curtis perversely claimed that it was Sontag—despite a voice that was "long past its prime," "hard and wiry and weak," "its bloom and richness gone"—who had "carried the city."

"The genius of advertising and of other means of catching the public eye," wrote Curtis, "has been lavished upon one, but it has been only carelessly and lightly employed by the other."[7] Sontag, moreover, enjoyed the advantage of superior assisting artists, a superior orchestra, and a superior conductor. But her artistry amounted merely to a "trick of study," he claimed: "Whatever the impression of her singing may once have been, it [was] now that of an elaborate and artificial elegance." Curtis equated Sontag's appeal with her exalted social status: it was "the Countess Rossi singing as countesses should sing[8] . . . unexceptionably lady-like," that had captivated her predominantly Upper Ten following. "To hear Sontag sing is to be in good society,"

[5] On January 6 the *Mirror* had "trusted" that Sontag's "contemptible manager [would] have the honesty to pay up his old advertising bills before commencing a new campaign. . . . It is the marvel of the town that Madame Sontag will retain in her employ one who is daily, publicly and privately, branded as a liar and a blackguard. But the letter of recommendation from 'the only musical critic of the *Herald*' [Mrs. James Gordon Bennett?] is a wonderful shield for humbug."

[6] Like his mentor Dwight, a lifelong adorer of Lind, Curtis shamelessly admired everything and everybody with whom the Nightingale had been associated, even unto Phineas T. Barnum.

[7] Upon Alboni's switch to opera, Le Grand Smith had taken over from Brough as her manager.

[8] Harping on Sontag's title, Curtis, for some reason, chose to ignore Alboni's equal status as the Countess Pepoli (present or future).

he wrote (recalling his light social satire, *The Potiphar Papers,* published in 1853). "White kids are *de rigeur.* She must be heard *en grand tenue,* in full dress; nothing less satisfies the sense of propriety."[9]

In the February issue of *Putnam's* (pp. 237–39), Curtis clumsily attempted with honeyed words to gloss over his embarrassing gaffe in having neglected to comment on Alboni's opera debut. With her "sudden" opening at the Broadway in *La cenerentola,* he wrote, she had at last assumed "that position which she has always occupied in Europe, and which she had not yet attained in America." Then, getting in deeper: "Not only has she charmed with her wonderful organ, her large manner and exquisite method, as she did in the concert room, but she has developed a dramatic talent hitherto entirely latent" (Curtis later claimed that she had first learned to act in America). How fortunate for everybody that she had not given in to the "dazzling prestige of her worthy rival" and departed the scene! "Both the artists and ourselves are the gainers in this tournament of music."

Attempting to be all things to all divas, Curtis contended that Alboni's opera triumphs had only "piqued curiosity for Sontag at Niblo's," particularly with Sontag having chosen to make her debut in *La figlia.* Her success in this role, he somewhat lamely stated, was "also unequivocal." Admittedly, the first act was not brilliant, the drumming was omitted, and the music lay largely out of her range; but the music lesson scene was "as fine a piece of lyrical acting" as Curtis could remember. The incongruous interpolation of her spectacular concert hit, Alary's "singing polka," as a finale to the opera, was, however, ill-advised. After some flittering about on the subtleties and sophistications of Sontag's performance, Curtis startlingly blurted out: "It is better to hear Alboni sing one good song than Sontag through an opera," a statement upon which the Alboni-fanciers happily pounced.[10]

To William Henry Fry,[11] with his European indoctrination and his predilection for the lyric stage, Sontag's appearance in opera signified "a historical point in our art."[12] "Whatever may be said of the attractions of concert singing," he wrote, "it must necessarily be inferior to that of the [opera] stage." In his densely wordy review of Sontag's opera debut (*Tribune,* January 11, 1853), Fry elaborated on this theme: "The scenery, dress, and decorations—the movements, looks, climaxes, ecstasies—the laughter—the desolation and death of the scene, are all wanting on the prosaic platform of the concert. Its glory is instrumental music, where the flesh is cast off, and the spirit revels in the infinite, undogged by words, millinery, paint, or proper-

[9] Curtis quasi-satirically envisioned Sontag's approaching opera season as a kind of super fashion show: "We shall all be elegantly dressed in the boxes; our flowers and jewels will flash and thrill responsive to hers. We shall be a brilliant circle, and as clever in the *entr'actes* as we can manage. We shall indulge freely in our foreign musical reminiscences [something Curtis in fact frequently did, in common with his colleagues, particularly Fry] and allow generously that, on the whole, this is not so bad. . . . It will be an epoch. We shall date from the Sontag opera" (*Putnam's,* January 1853, p. 118).

[10] One of the most ardent being opera-loving Walt Whitman, who in his later years remembered that he had heard every one of Alboni's performances in "New York and vicinity" (Whitman, p. 14).

[11] Although deeply immersed in his lecture-giving at the time, Fry managed simultaneously to turn out overflowing columns of music criticism.

[12] Sontag was no stranger to Fry: he had frequently heard her in Europe and enthusiastically puffed her in dispatches to the *Tribune,* especially upon learning that she intended to visit the United States.

ties.[13] Hence, beautiful as is Madame Sontag in the lady-like requisites of appearance and action in Metropolitan Hall, she needs the arena of an opera to give vent to her artistic qualities."

Fry thought Niblo's Garden, with its three tiers of boxes and its open spaces, better suited to opera than the more confined *Académie Royale* in Paris;[14] he noted the elegant audience of some 2000 that crowded the house,[15] commended Sontag's supporting artists,[16] the chorus, the admirable staging,[17] and Carl Eckert's orchestra of forty-eight musicians (although "more care in warming one or two of the brass instruments beforehand would have secured a better tone, but let that pass"). Fry commented on Sontag's "singular elegance," her "step, light and elastic," "her well-made gestures," and her "lively abandon of manner." Of her singing he wrote: "The remarkably fine-drawn tenuity which the cantatrice can give to the climaxes of an adagio movement were particularly evidenced." (But it raised a question in Fry's mind of how many times a slow movement could be repeated without a change of key or some variation in the accompaniment, a fault he had frequently noted in Italian composers.) In the music lesson scene, Sontag had unleashed a "rich spray of fioriture that would have made old Porpora[18] rub his hands with glee," but she shouldn't have concluded the opera with Alary's singing-polka; it was anticlimactic and unworthy of her.[19]

To Richard Grant White, the Sontag production of *La figlia* "hardly fell short of being actually perfect." Sontag was "the most bewitching of Maries—capricious, kind-hearted, willful, simple-minded, coquettish, prettily outrageous and charmingly uncontrollable. . . . We all knew that it was inevitable that she should present us with the daintiest possible conception of the character, but few could have been prepared for the exquisite humor and naturalness of her performance."

But it was unavoidable, continued White, "not to place her Marie and that of Madame Alboni mentally side by side; not for the pitiful purpose of a comparison in

[13] ". . . the concert room is a dull substitute for the Opera house," agreed Richard Grant White, "and we hope to see the time when Concerts—save those of the Philharmonic Societies, Quartette Clubs, and Choral Societies—will no longer vex our souls" (*Courier and Enquirer,* January 20, 1853).

[14] Richard Grant White, on the contrary, found the acoustics at Niblo's inadequate for the performance of music.

[15] According to the advertisements for Sontag's "second series" of operas, Niblo's contained 1700 secured seats, besides sufficient standing room for 1000 persons, divided into sixteen sections.

[16] Cesare Badiali was universally lauded for his Sulpizio; Gasparo Pozzolini, the Tonio, received a mixed, but generally favorable, press. The remainder of the cast was ignored in both advertisements and reviews.

[17] The stage director was Federico Badiali, the chorus master Angelo Torriani. Tickets were sold for single performances only—no subscriptions—at $2 for secured seats and $1 for unsecured. Confusingly, both categories carried a certificate entitling the holder to "a secured seat, good for the whole evening," a system that defeated itself on opening night, when Eckert's "admirable execution of the overture was lost on an audience which was divided into two hostile camps—the one seeking the number corresponding to certain green tickets ostentatiously held up to the usher, and the other angrily demanding that peace be restored, at whatever cost" (*Herald,* January 11, 1853).

[18] More of Fry's erudition. Nicola Antonio Porpora (1686–1768), the prolific Italian opera and oratorio composer and singing teacher, in the course of his long career had been a collaborator of Domenico Scarlatti, a rival of Handel, and a teacher of Haydn.

[19] Alboni, too, reported Fry, had added an inappropriate finale to *La figlia,* an unidentified waltz by Balfe.

Girvice Archer, Jr.

Alboni's "fine lady's fine ladyism."

favor of one and against the other, but to discriminate between their differing features." And differences there certainly were.[20] Sontag was always the fine lady, even when engaging in the boisterous antics of her "rude playfellows." Alboni's "fine lady's fine ladyism," on the contrary, consisted only in the fine clothes she wore in the second act. An incorrigible tomboy, she plunged into the regimental chorus and march in act two with a "keenness and zest, a riotous and almost savage enjoyment, like that of a young tigress breaking loose." Not that Sontag did not deliver the passage with gusto; her singing, of course, was always impeccable, and, despite the poor acoustics, she was heard in every part of the house (*Courier and Enquirer,* January 11, 1853).

On January 10, at the same time that Madame Sontag was making her bow at Niblo's Garden in *The Daughter of the Regiment,* Alboni was thrilling a large audience at the Broadway with her first performance of *La sonnambula.* As Amina she achieved a "royal success," wrote the *Mirror* (January 11, 1853), but it was "attributable to herself alone," for "with the exception of [Nicolò] Barili [the Count Rodolfo], who made a hit, we can only say that Pellegrini [a new tenor who sang Elvino] made a fiasco."[21]

[20] In weighing the differences, the *Musical World and Times* (January 15, 1853, pp. 33–34) concluded that Sontag's Maria would make a more amusing companion at a lively party, but Alboni's would make a better wife.

[21] Both "Pellegrini and Barili had better be kept out of sight—or, at all events, out of *hearing,*" threatened the *Musical World and Times* (January 15, 1853, p. 33). And indeed, Pellegrini was "wisely

Richard Grant White, who had missed Alboni's first two performances of *Sonnambula,* soared to new altitudes in lauding the third, given on January 20: "We sweep them all away with a dash of the pen," he imperiously proclaimed. "All the other Aminas who have sung on these shores have sung but to be forgotten. They have been but the degrees by which we have mounted to this Amina; and now we kick away the ladder by which we have risen. This is ungrateful, but," he grandly added, "it is as inevitable as it is ungrateful."

Belying all advance reports that in opera she was "a heavy human pendulum, vibrating sluggishly between joviality and phlegm," Alboni, as Amina, revealed a profundity of emotion—an intensity of dramatic power—that was nothing less than heroic; Alboni was heroic in both grief and joy. Her *Ah! non credea* had been an overwhelming vocal experience in the concert room, but it was only on the opera stage, with her magnificent acting, that she realized it to the full. She was "not only different in degree, but in kind, from that of the most eminent of all those who have won our admiration upon the lyric stage" (*Courier and Enquirer,* January 21, 1853).

White was seconded by the newly installed *Albion* critic Charles Burkhardt, a rabid Alboni-worshiper, who proclaimed this performance to be "positively one of the greatest triumphs we ever witnessed upon the lyric stage" (*Albion,* January 22, 1853, p. 44).[22] In the meantime, on January 17, both divas had simultaneously presented their opposite, "but equally attractive," versions of Rosina in *Il barbiere.* Alboni's Rosina,[23] wrote Burkhardt *(ibid.),* was "almost an entirely original conception of the part." She resorted to less coquetry and "that peculiar style of intrigue which belongs especially to 'singing chambermaids' in English Comedies and Vaudevilles" than any Rosina he had ever seen. Burkhardt praised her "jolly, merry, almost broad humor, mischief, mingled wit, most naively-expressed touches of true sentiment, and honest, maidenly love."[24]

Sontag's Rosina, on the other hand, was an "elegant, coquettish lady, delightful to see, peculiarly artistic, full of intrigue and smartness, symmetrical and studied."[25] But "as to her singing of the part," wrote Burkhardt, "we are determined, without passion, to have our plain say about it." As an artist "acknowledged by all civilized society, and for nearly a quarter of a century past, as [being] of the first—the very first—rank in the world of song," Sontag was not to be judged by everyday standards. To Burkhardt's professed regret, she fell far short: "Not once nor twice, but again and again

withdrawn" after the first performance and replaced by Adelindo Vietti; Barili, who received a mixed press, was retained. A frightened Madame Siedenburg, making her local opera debut as Lisa, was moderately liked.

[22] Burkhardt highly praised Vietti, the Elvino, but he chided Arditi for his failure to supply "a few modulatory chords in the orchestra when Madame Alboni sings a particular aria or scena in a transposed key."

[23] Assisted by Coletti as Figaro, Barili as Don Basilio, Sangiovanni as Almaviva, and Rovere as a screamingly funny Dr. Bartolo.

[24] Richard Grant White agreed: Alboni's Rosina was "distinguished dramatically by its exuberance of humor and good nature," he wrote, and added: "It may be that humor and good nature are the individual traits of the great contralto's character (*Courier and Enquirer,* January 18, 1853).

[25] As Rosina, wrote R. G. White, Sontag was "the daintiest of *comediennes* [and] the most finished gentlewoman among prima donnas." But, he gratuitously added: "Madame Sontag will certainly not impress any one with the idea that she is, or ever was, or ever can have been, a great tragedian" (*Courier and Enquirer,* January 20, 1853).

Madame Sontag sang painfully, nay disagreeably, sharp." Besides, she interpolated her own *fioriture* in her arias—"rapidly and clearly executed," to be sure, and "telling upon the ear of the Million," but nonetheless "meretricious, not meritorious," and, above all, not Rossini's. "This may seem harsh criticism," wrote Burkhardt, "but no one knows its truth better than the great artiste herself, whom years ago we heard render this role in quite a different manner, when remarks like our present ones would have been almost sacrilegious."

The performance as a whole lacked the spirit and style, the soul, vital to Italian opera, owing to Eckert's hard and angular, if unyieldingly correct, Germanic conducting,[26] complained Burkhardt (himself a German). Cesare Badiali was a flawless Figaro;[27] Pozzolini, the Almaviva, was fair. The other members of the cast—Rocco as Don Bartolo; Alessandro Gasparoni, a veteran of earlier opera days, as Don Basilio; and Angiolina Mora (or Morra) another veteran, as Berta—were, in Burkhardt's opinion, not worthy of mention.

An unannounced assisting artist appeared in Sontag's *Barbiere,* reported the *Evening Post* (January 20, 1853): "When the Abbé 'Don Alonzo' [Almaviva] came to give the music lesson to the fair Rosina, and had driven Doctor Bartolo almost crazy by his prolonged *gioia e pace,* he asked permission of the jealous tutor to produce a trio, composed by the renowned Maestro, Signore Carl Eckert, for the voice, the piano, and the violin. Don Bartolo having consented, the false Alonzo introduced a little Abbé in black, by the name of Paul Julien, who proceeded to accompany Rosina in a manner which drew the applause of the whole house. The trio was vehemently encored. Even Don Bartolo seemed to yield to the charm of the music, for he presented this little Abbé, when he took his leave, with a large red apple." In a subsequent performance of the *Barber,* Eckert was announced to sing his "Swiss Song," Sontag an English ballad, and little Julien to play the "Witch's Dance *à la* Paganini" (Herald, February 2, 1853).

On January 21, Sontag presented Donizetti's *Lucrezia Borgia.*[28] "It is altogether the most unpleasant part of the critic's duty to be compelled to censure, where he fain would praise," sanctimoniously wrote Burkhardt, "but the honest one must not shrink from it." With no discernible reluctance, then, Burkhardt proceeded to inform his readers that Sontag had once before attempted this unsuitable role in Berlin, and he wondered "that she should have attempted it again"; indeed, "she would have been wiser had she never undertaken it" (*Albion,* January 29, 1853, p. 56).

R. Storrs Willis, who described the *Lucrezia* opening as a triumph, in equal parts, of brilliant fashion and superb vocalism, observed that Sontag's "very modified

[26] Attesting to Eckert's Germanic thoroughness, the *Home Journal* (January 22, 1853) reported a mathematical impossibility: that each of Sontag's three-times-a-week operas was rehearsed five times "before the public performance, which is exactly four times more than was the custom under the sway of Maretzek." Also, that the audiences at Niblo's were very large, but "the *toilettes* not remarkable. Two-thirds of the ladies wear bonnets, and the house does not present that dazzling splendor which we were wont to be astonished at in Astor Place."

[27] But C. M. Cady, in the *Musical Review and Choral Advocate* (February 1853, p. 26), caviled at the "unjustified liberties" taken by Badiali in "strutting to the front of the stage, as he too often does, leaving Madame Sontag and the others behind his back to take care of themselves as best they may." For some reason, the published Strong *Diary* (II, 115n) states that Sontag was the *prima donna* of *Badiali's* Opera Company.

[28] With Badiali as the Duke, Pozzolini as Gennaro, and Rosina Pico-Vietti as Maffio Orsini.

Lucrezia" in the "celebrated poisoning scene . . . was a very lady-like case of tragic violence."[29]

On January 27 and 28, as the extraordinary Alboni/Sontag opera duel drew to a close, Alboni—as a parting shot before departing to fill an opera engagement in Boston—appeared for the first time anywhere in *Norma,* her crowning triumph.[30]

"It seemed but yesterday that she could produce no new impression with her voice; that she must have exhausted the variety of her powers," wrote Richard Grant White (*Courier and Enquirer,* January 28, 1853), "but last evening she exhibited in its highest perfection just that style which, judging by the reputation she brought with her, we should least have expected from her—that of fierce impetuosity." She sang and acted with overwhelming passion, strength, and dignity, and in some scenes with overflowing agony and reproachful tenderness. "It was not enough for Madame Alboni to make us forget all the Aminas, she must be the only Norma whose performance as a whole can live in our memories.[31] . . . What a wonderful woman is this Alboni, who triumphs not only in spite of hindrances proper to herself [her tremendous size?],[32] but floats on the topmost waves of popular favor, with such millstones as her assistants around her neck."[33]

The *Mirror* (January 29, 1853), after its valedictory raptures over Alboni's performance, estimated that the box-office receipts for her two performances of *Norma* had amounted to "no less than Eight Thousand Dollars." Indeed, every inch of standing room had been exhausted and many disappointed, would-be standees had to be turned away.

Madame Sontag began her "second series" of operas[34] on January 26 with *La figlia del reggimento* (probably the performance heard by Strong). On the 28th, the night of

[29] "There was a kind of dainty diabolism" in her Lucrezia, "like a devil in lemon kids [gloves], that was altogether too amusing," daintily wrote Curtis, who tended increasingly to assume the preciosity of N. P. Willis. "The truth is that only very sinewy feet can fill and properly propel the seven-league boots of high lyrical tragedy; and a singer may have a beautiful voice, exquisitely cultivated, without being able to impersonate Lucrezia or Norma" (*Putnam's,* March 1853, p. 349).

[30] Luigi Arditi, Alboni's conductor, relates that E. A. Marshall had promised him a jeweled baton if he would persuade Alboni to appear in *Norma.* Marshall kept his promise (Arditi, pp. 17–19).

[31] "The enthusiasm for Alboni is very great. In the street, in omnibuses, on ferry boats—everywhere—her magnificent performances furnish themes of conversation in which all seem anxious to take a part; persons who are total strangers to each other grow quite friendly and confidential in discussing a subject which gives such keen and general pleasure" (*Musical World and Times,* January 29, 1853, p. 67).

[32] As Norma, she seemed to Burkhardt "several inches taller than usual, and not a bit too corpulent" (*Albion,* January 29, 1853, p. 56).

[33] In *Norma,* Alboni's "millstones" were Vietti as Pollione, Coletti as Oroveso, and Madame Siedenburg as Adalgisa. "The first (upper) part, that of Norma, having been transposed for Madame Alboni, brought Adalgisa's part rather too low for that lady's compass," wrote Burkhardt, "and her singing became almost inaudible in some of the passages" *(ibid.).*

[34] The original scale of prices for tickets would be retained, explained a lengthy announcement, but a limited number of subscriptions for six operas would now be available for the convenience of those wishing to attend several performances. The announcement implored would-be opera-goers not to purchase their tickets from speculators, a pernicious breed that brazenly hawked $1 tickets for $2 right in front of Niblo's.

Alboni's farewell performance of *Norma,* Sontag appeared for the first time as Amina in *La sonnambula.* With most of the critics evidently at the Broadway Theatre bidding their sad adieus to Alboni, Sontag's *Sonnambula* was not reviewed until its second performance, on February 1, by which time Alboni was safely gone.[35]

Sontag's Amina was enthusiastically received, except, of course, by Burkhardt, who brutally accused her of having "no soul, no warmth, no heart," and thus no capacity for moving an audience.[36] Where Alboni's *Come per me sereno* had engulfed her hearers in a "flood of melody that inundated every heart," Sontag delivered it "with scrupulous correctness," like a schoolgirl at a singing lesson, overloading it with "unmeaning ornaments." With her inexhaustible supply of "*fioriture, roulades, tours de force,* etc." and her admittedly flawless technique for delivering them, Sontag indiscriminately lavished ornaments on everything, however incongruous. Too, her always-shaky intonation was not helped by her "crawling about the stage" in the chamber scene, wherein the "melodramatic violence of her gesticulation so distorted her voice . . . that the curtain fell almost in dead silence"[37] *(Albion,* February 5, 1853, p. 68).

To the *Home Journal* (February 12, 1853), her chamber scene was "one of the most powerful representations of agony and despair that we have ever beheld," causing the viewer to "sympathize painfully with the anguish which is too truthfully depicted. She performs the latter part of the scene upon her knees . . . clinging to her lover when he endeavors to tear himself away, and still clings, though in his effort to escape he drags her along the floor."[38]

The sole possessor of the opera scene for the following two months, Sontag interspersed her Aminas and Rosinas with four new operas by Donizetti: *Don Pasquale* on February 7, *Lucia di Lammermoor* on February 14, *Linda di Chamounix* on February 25, and *Maria di Rohan* on March 9. Her Norina in *Don Pasquale,* a light, effervescent role that fitted her like a glove, was received with all the customary Sontag compliments: she was delicately coquettish, magnificently gowned (the opera was given in modern dress), and many thought it to be her best role.

Her Lucia, on the contrary, provoked a squabble between her too-ardent admirer *Gemotice* in the *Express* and the less infatuated Richard Grant White in the *Courier and Enquirer,* chiefly on the subject of Sontag's ability, or lack of ability, to portray tragic

[35] It should be noted that during this period each of the divas gave a concert: Alboni, assisted by her opera colleagues presenting Rossini's *Stabat Mater* and *Moïse* at a sacred concert on January 15 at Metropolitan Hall, and Sontag in an ultra-fashionable charity event at Niblo's Saloon on January 19, assisted by Mesdames Wallace-Bouchelle, Pico-Vietti, and Wallace, and Messrs. Rocco, Frazer, Eben, and William Vincent Wallace, who conducted.

[36] George William Curtis likened Sontag's Amina to Marie Antoinette pretending to be a dairymaid at the Petite Trianon: "She is just such a peasant girl as a genuine princess royal would be at a masquerade" (*Putnam's,* March 1853, p. 349).

[37] Not according to R. G. White, who reported "great demonstrations of delight" on the part of a huge audience that crammed every inch of Niblo's Garden. Many thought Sontag's Amina her finest operatic achievement yet. Although scheduled for only two performances, a third was demanded and given on February 4.

[38] The sharp-tongued critic of the *Daily Times,* presumably Charles Bailey Seymour, at first highly praised Sontag's Amina, but after a few performances wrote (March 15, 1853): "We should have been better pleased if Madame had omitted the operation on her knees in the second act; it is a mere physical appeal to the audience, clumsily executed."

roles.[39] Everyone agreed (even Burkhardt!) that in the first two acts, at least, wherein she had curbed her usual excess of ornamentation, she was superb.[40]

Her Linda, however, precipitated a grand controversy when, on Ullman's orders (at Madame Sontag's behest? at her husband's?),[41] Burkhardt was barred at the box office from buying a ticket for its first performance. Indignantly reporting the scandalous incident in the *Albion* (March 5, 1853 p. 116), its editor, John R. Young, announced that legal proceedings had already been initiated against Ullman "for the purpose of vindicating at once a citizen's right and a proper independence in criticism." In the meantime, Young added, "we shall abstain from troubling our readers with further remarks about Madame Sontag's performances. Enough has been said in these columns already on the subject; nor is it probable that anything will be seen or heard likely to change the opinions hitherto recorded."[42]

The *Mirror,* which as a matter of policy had chosen not to review Sontag's opera performances until now, explained (February 26, 1853), in reply to a reader's complaint, that it had purposely done so to get even with Ullman, who, it claimed, had taken offense at the paper's untrammeled praise of Alboni and "falsely accused one of our critics of being bribed to puff her" (a not unreasonable accusation). On being proved "a traitor to the truth," Ullman had retaliated by refusing to pay his advertising bill. Thus, no reviews of Sontag.

This had nothing to do, of course, with the *Mirror*'s professed admiration for Madame Sontag: "Her personation of Linda last night was a beautiful, chaste, charming performance," even if she did overdo the ornamentation in spots. And although the house was crowded with the "'beauty and fashion of the city,' [and] although Madame was repeatedly called before the curtain, there was very little enthusiasm in the applause."

As indignation spread in response to Ullman's "outrage upon the liberty of the press," the *Mirror* gleefully reprinted denunciatory editorials from the other papers.[43] And in a furious article, presumably by Oliver Dyer (probably written in collaboration with his co-editor, R. Storrs Willis), the *Musical World and Times* (March 12, 1853,

[39] White, who took the negative view, also ungallantly pointed out that Madame Sontag's over-eager friends did much to mar her *Lucia* performance with their "premature explosions" of applause in inappropriate places (*Courier and Enquirer,* February 15, 1853).

[40] Understanding of the opera was assisted by Sheridan Corbyn's new "Opera Books," which many members of the *Lucia* audience were seen consulting. A great improvement over old-fashioned opera libretti, they supplied the Italian and English texts of the opera and the music of its principal airs, and cost only 25 cents. Richard Grant White informed Corbyn, however, that a knowledge of Italian was obviously not one of his proofreader's strong points *(ibid.)*.

[41] It was no secret that Count Rossi played a dictatorial role in the management of his wife's career.

[42] Young mentioned further that Sontag's manager had reprinted Burkhardt's derogatory review of her *Sonnambula,* with derisive comments, on the playbills for that opera, "by way of showing the incompetency of our critic!" The incident had then seemed too ludicrous to be noticed, he wrote, but considering the present turn of events, he wanted to put it on record.

[43] On March 8 the *Mirror,* once Burkhardt's foe, sympathetically published his lengthy, self-justifying "card," reviewing his honorable life and his career in America, and bemoaning the personal loss of income to which Ullman's action had subjected him (no more reviews of Madame Sontag in the *Albion*).

p. 163) implicated Sontag's husband as well: "Count Rossi and his agent (for we presume, of course, they act in concert), seem to deal with the press in this country very much as the former would deal with his petty dependents at home, had he still control over them." His autocratic behavior was "ill return for the courtesy which Madame Sontag received at the hands of the Americans; a courtesy not proportioned to Madame's artistic deserts, but proportioned to the warm-heartedness of the American people and that prompt and warm sympathy which spontaneously springs at the family misfortunes of a once great singer, a once exquisite and magic voice, a once inspired and youthful artiste. Americans appreciate well the difference between what was Sontag and what is Sontag no more, although the Count and his agent may not think so; and the lenient criticism and forbearance of the public press may have served to confirm them in their mistake."[44] Probably to prove its objectivity, the *Musical World and Times* (March 5, 1853, p. 147) reported Sontag's performance of *Linda di Chamounix* to have been "the most agreeable opera of the season": in "dress and acting," Madame Sontag was "more charming . . . than in any opera yet given." But Seymour, in the *Daily Times* (February 26, 1853), stated flatly that, despite having "created a sensation" with the audience, Sontag lacked dramatic force as Linda: where "alternate bursts of wildest agony and dreamy snatches of tender memory" were required, she confined herself to the "latter phase." The critic made caustic observations about other members of the cast as well: Badiali sang and acted excellently, but his performance caused the writer to wonder why "human nature on the Italian stage [was always] so subject to palsy"; "Pozzolini punished the audience with his hackneyed mannerisms and sang out of tune most exquisitely in the quartette"; and "of Mr. Eckert, we are too charitable to say half of what we feel."

George William Curtis, fastidiously avoiding the Ullman/Burkhardt controversy, executed elaborate verbal pirouettes in praising the felicities of Sontag's exquisite opera presentations, of which the most recent was always the best. In the latest, he wrote, the spectator's "agony for the woes of Linda blend with admiration of her delicious toilette; with one eye we cry for the unhappy peasant girl, ill-suited in a palace, and with the other smile upon that superb brocade, that powdered wig, that ravishing ensemble. . . . We all go moist-eyed into embroidered handkerchiefs, while she goes mad in flowered silk and diamonds. She comes out of it dexterously as she went in, and singing a brilliant rondo, goes off happy. We come out of it with eyes not very red, and go off home." *Linda* was the great success of the season, wrote Curtis, as he had infallibly written of each of Sontag's previous offerings. "As a study of characteristic costume, it is worth while to assist at these soirées. Such color, such elegance, such tournure, such genuineness are rare, indeed, upon the boards. They only prove what you feel every moment, that you are watching a *lady*—a lady to whom we all owe the most delightful evenings." Sontag's following new opera, *Maria di Rohan,* was "equally successful with the rest," Curtis hastily added, having apparently run out of space (*Putnam's,* April 1853, pp. 469–70).[45]

[44] Richard Grant White blithely dismissed the whole incident as just another "contrivance of Madame Sontag's most adroit and indefatigable business man to get up a profitable excitement" (*Courier and Enquirer,* March 8, 1853).

[45] In *Maria di Rohan,* wrote the *Spirit of the Times* (March 12, 1853, p. 48), Sontag for once gave the audience a chance to hear her voice, "devoid of the interlardations she generally bestows in the

Richard Grant White thought Sontag's Maria de Rohan "one of the most finished among [her] many carefully elaborated impersonations" (*Courier and Enquirer,* March 18, 1853), but Seymour in the *Daily Times* (March 10, 1853) declared the character to have lost much of its dramatic interest in Sontag's hands: "All the resources of art are brought into active operation; there is a great amount of optical execution, and of gesticulation, and promenading. . . . Still, it is but art, apparent and unpleasant." Furthermore, in the higher passages of her role "Madame [was] very apt to be out of tune." Seymour vented his abundant acerbity on his *bête noir,* Pozzolini, who, as Ricardo, seemed "somewhat worse than usual." "In according him this praise," wrote the critic, "we are fully sensible of his great ability to be bad on all occasions. We think, however, he certainly achieved the superlative degree last evening—at least, we hope so."

Sontag closed her opera marathon on March 21 with *La sonnambula*—her thirtieth opera performance within a period of about ten weeks; then—apparently indestructible—she immediately took off for opera performances in Philadelphia and Boston before returning to New York for a summer season at Castle Garden.

Timed to coincide with the end of Sontag's sojourn at Niblo's, the *Musical World and Times* (March 19, pp. 177–78; March 26, 1853, pp. 193–94), published a translation of a scathing criticism that had appeared in the *Neue Zeitschrift für Musik* of February 13, 1852, upon the completion of Sontag's 1852 opera season in Weimar. Willis, who had translated the article, titled "The Opinion of the Minority," mistakenly attributed its authorship to Liszt; it was in fact written by Liszt's acid-tongued young pupil Hans von Bülow (1830–1894) (see *Dwight's* comments on the false attribution, March 26, 1853, pp. 198–99). Calling Sontag the "Thalberg of song" (obviously not intended as a compliment), the criticism mirrored in advance the adverse comments in the New York press about her faded voice, her excessive ornamentation, her overelaborate wardrobe, her artificial acting.[46]

In a clumsy epilogue, Willis piously justified publishing this attack on Sontag, partly because it was "a fine piece of legitimate criticism" (although admittedly a bit "mischievous" for his taste) and partly because "in this day, when journals seem nothing more than a record of the 'triumphs' of every artist that comes among us, it is refreshing to hear veritable *opinions* in Art." But particularly it was an example of how criticism was done in the old country, "when writers take hold who are in earnest."

Despite the article's unmitigated harshness, Willis was for some reason "happily confident" that his publication of this painful criticism would be "of as little moment to Sontag in this country as it was in Germany" (where it had in fact aroused great controversy). "A clear-sighted artiste like this lady," he fatuously explained, "must regard with perfect contempt the wholesale flatteries of such scribblers who assert her to be that which she *once* was . . . knowing perfectly well that she is it no more"—in other words, Willis expected Sontag gratefully to embrace the label of "has-been."

---

execution of all her music; and, with the exception of false intonations at times, her vocalization was admirable."

[46] Times had indeed changed. In 1826 another German critic, Ludwig Rellstab (1799–1860), had served a three-month prison sentence for having written a pamphlet titled *Henriette, oder die schöne Sängerin,* satirizing Sontag and her highly placed diplomatic connections.

He was happy for her sake that, as a woman, she had accomplished her noble aim in providing for "her home, her husband, and her children," an aim, however, quite separate from "the revived character, accomplishments, and career of the artiste. And just because we are honest in our warm sympathy for the one," he righteously added, "we must be just as honest in the opinion we express and publish of the other."

From a far different vantage point, William Henry Fry, in what he called an "aesthetical article on the opera," devoted a full, digressive column in the *Tribune* (March 24, 1853) to a summing-up of Sontag's season and its effect on the development of opera in New York. He approved of the enterprise as "a well-devised scheme to present good works to the community in a becoming manner," and—having come to appreciate the scarcity of outstanding actor/singers, even in Europe—it was one with which the public "ought to be well satisfied."

Fry examined the musical attributes of Sontag's company: the orchestra was good, but it needed ten more string instruments for proper balance; the chorus was well trained but not full enough and at a disadvantage from "the necessity of putting on a new Opera on the stage every two nights" (and why?); and the conductor—whereupon Fry wandered off on a long, circuitous detour involving Sir George Smart, Napoleon, the "filthy barbarisms of our present society," the diplomatic skills demanded of an opera conductor, and the disparity between what the advertisements ballyhooed as a full orchestra and the real thing—something New York had never yet heard, as it had never yet heard a truly full chorus.

Fry did not agree with the general complaints of Sontag's overornate style of singing. Her vocalization was beautiful and uncommonly neat, he wrote. Besides, he had no wish to become embroiled in the "philosophy of elaborate cadenzas," for that would lead to a series of new considerations, including that of "making vocal music the medium of dramatic expression at all. . . . The most that can be said for it [opera or ornamentation?] is that it is Art, and because it is Art," incontrovertibly declared Fry, sounding like Watson, "it is not Nature." Ornamentation had its reputable antecedents—in Mozart, "The Queen of Night's Song" in *The Magic Flute*—and in Beethoven, the "Vauxhall flourishes" in *The Mount of Olives*.

In any case, wrote Fry, all criticisms of singers should be merely comparative until we had a Conservatory of Music of our own in which to train American singers to sing American operas in a language that people could understand, and an Opera House in which to sing them. In his untrammeled fashion, Fry called in the Greeks and the Egyptians to illustrate this point, as he had earlier cited the "Feejee" Islanders to explain another.

More pragmatically, the *Courier and Enquirer* (March 22, 1853) summed up Sontag's season as "probably the most successful series of opera performances ever known in America, and one by which she cannot have failed to realize, above all expenses, quite fifteen thousand dollars."

Throughout this period of operatic surfeit, Strong seems to have been too preoccupied with his busy professional and social life to listen to music other than what he heard at enjoyable evening musicales at Richard Storrs Willis's and from his own occasional explorations of Haydn's masses at the organ at home. The idea of forming a private singing group to perform the Haydn masses he loved best was evidently beginning to take shape in his mind.

March 10. . . . Dawdled at the organ over Haydn's Sixteenth Mass a while. . . . That Sixteenth Mass, as a whole, is Haydn's finest, I think, though it hasn't the purity and religious feeling that run through No. 1, nor the dash and fire of the "Imperial" Mass [No. 3], and perhaps there's nothing in it quite equal to the superb Finale of No. 2.[47] Wonder whether it wasn't written just before *The Seasons.* The *Sanctus* and *Benedictus* contain the germ of the beautiful duo and chorus ["God of Light"] with which "Spring" winds up.

March 16. . . . an appointment with Richard Willis fell through—to meet the Roots and Miss Belcher and the Masons,[48] and take further steps toward our long-desired organization of a private Mozart and Haydn Society.

March 29. [contemptuously] . . . Hodges told me this morning that he'd been looking through Haydn's and Mozart's Masses to see if there was anything he could adapt!!!

April 10. [after a sick headache] . . . This evening an hour at the organ, but even Haydn's No. 2 came all wrong and Beethoven [Mass] in C [op. 86 (1807)] was impracticable.

~

In April the Strongs heard the Grand Combination Opera Company, as the recently merged Alboni and Maretzek forces were named, in residence at Niblo's Garden since Sontag's departure. The merger was another in the ongoing series of last-gasp self-rescues contrived by the ever-fertile Maretzek, who, together with the remnants of his former Astor Place company (Steffanone, Bertucca-Maretzek, Salvi, Marini, Beneventano), had found himself immobilized in Havana early in 1853 after the completion of their wildly adventuresome Mexican tour (see *Crotchets,* pp. 229–301).

With antennae always attuned to the far-off vibrations of opera in New York, Maretzek, upon hearing of the Alboni and Sontag activities, lost no time in bringing his company back (in early March) and—despite his disastrous previous experience with the combined Havana and Astor Place Opera companies—in forming another joint opera enterprise with Alboni's opera manager, Le Grand Smith, of hallowed Barnum/Jenny Lind memory.[49]

As Maretzek tells it (*Sharps and Flats,* pp. 8–9), to prevent the deadly competition of three rival opera companies performing simultaneously—a no-win situation for everyone—he had decided before his return to make the best of all possible worlds by effecting separate connections with both the Alboni and Sontag companies, but in sequence. Knowing, he wrote, that Alboni wished to return to London for the sum-

[47] Novello no. 16, Hoboken XXII:12, is known as the *Theresienmesse* (1799); Novello no.1, Hoboken XXII:10, is the *Heiligmesse* (1796). As we know, No. 2 is the *Missa in tempore belli,* or *Paukenmesse.*

[48] The Roots doubtless were George Frederick Root's vocal Quartette Party, consisting of Root, his wife, his sister, and his brother; they had been heard at Eisfeld's quartette *soirée* on February 19 and at the Philharmonic on March 5. Miss Belcher was a talented amateur singer whom Strong had heard and admired at Willis's; the Masons might have been any of a number of Masons, social or musical.

[49] But with Smith, as manager of the company (or was it Alboni?), apparently to assume the expenses and Maretzek to act as artistic director and co-conductor with Arditi. Maretzek did not, however, conduct an opera until the final performance of the season, on May 6.

mer and that Sontag intended to remain in America indefinitely, he "closed at once with Alboni" for a short spring season at Niblo's, and leased Castle Garden for the summer months, "thus preventing Mr. Ullman [whom Maretzek loathed] from playing an opposition during the spring . . . and forcing him [Ullman] to accept either an arrangement with [Maretzek] for the summer at Castle Garden, or to remain idle with Madame Sontag, as at that time Castle Garden was the only available place for a summer season of opera." (This may or may not have been the way it really happened.)

"There is no question," exuberantly proclaimed the *Mirror* (March 22, 1853), paraphrasing the overblown advertisements of the Combination Opera Company, "but we shall have the best opera company in the world,[50] and we do not hesitate to predict crowded houses for a hundred successive nights."[51]

But all did not progress serenely within the precincts of the Combination Opera Company, due, it would seem, to the nefarious plottings and machinations of their trouble-making *primo tenore assoluto* Lorenzo Salvi. Opening on March 28 with *Don Pasquale*[52] (an unspectacular vehicle for a grand opening), the second presentation *La favorita,* scheduled for April 1, had to be postponed because the indispensable Salvi was stricken with one of his nicely timed indispositions. As the *Albion* gossiped (April 9, 1853, p. 176): "Salvi caught cold by going to Staten Island [where he lived]—for, be it known that the great Tenor is engaged there in the laudable business of making candles (!) and money."[53]

During Salvi's week-long dereliction, one opera night had to be canceled, and two emergency substitutions presented—*La figlia* on April 2 and *Il barbiere* on April 4, in both of which Alboni appeared[54]—as she did in every other opera of this turbulent, if vocally superb, season.

Although she sang as gloriously as ever, it was perceived by some that Alboni no

[50] Not for nothing had Le Grand Smith learned his craft at Barnum's knee: "The manager begs to assure the musical public," he advertised, "that no labor or expense shall be spared to give the great metropolis of the United States an Opera which shall not only vie with, but surpass (with the solitary exception of St. Petersburg), the Grand Operas of Europe of the present season." Such advertising "quackery," recalling the degrading "Jenny Lind heralding business," indignantly wrote R. Storrs Willis, would not again be tolerated (*Musical World and Times,* April 2, 1853, p. 210).

[51] Tickets were $1 and $2. Replying to a letter from a "Two-penny Clerk," arguing for a 50-cent opera admission, Fry, in the *Tribune* (March 16, 1853), reminded his readers that the plan had failed at Castle Garden; that 50-cent tickets would not pay half the expenses of the new company; that if people wanted opera, the most expensive of all entertainments, they must expect to pay for it, even up to $3 a ticket! "There has been more talk than sense about this impracticable idea of a cheap opera. Italian Opera for the masses! Fudge! The masses don't want it."

[52] With Alboni as Norina, Salvi as Ernesto, Beneventano as Dr. Malatesta, and Marini as Don Pasquale, Arditi conducted an orchestra of thirty-eight well-known musicians, many from the Philharmonic, among them La Manna and Kreutzer violins, Boucher viola, Belletti clarinet, and Daga trombone (*Spirit,* April 2, 1853, p. 84).

[53] Salvi had acquired the candle factory from the exiled Italian hero Giuseppe Garibaldi (1807–1882), who had operated it in 1850–51, when he was "living quietly" on Staten Island. Maretzek (*Sharps and Flats,* p. 10) reports that Garibaldi was Salvi's partner in the enterprise in 1853, but, according to the *Tribune* (February 10, 1851), the hero had left for Nicaragua in 1851 (en route to Peru).

[54] Also appearing in *La figlia* were Rovere, Sangiovanni, and a Signor Zanini; in *Il barbiere,* Rovere, Sangiovanni, Beneventano, and Marini.

longer communicated the joyous spirit of her earlier performances. Curtis, a wayward observer, declared that she "had lost the trick" (*Putnam's,* May 1853, p. 590). Even Seymour, Alboni's great admirer, was at a loss to account for the "indifference," the "regardlessness for the spirit of the piece," that she had displayed in both the *Barbiere* and the *Figlia* (*Daily Times,* April 5, 1853).

La favorita, finally given on April 8 and repeated on April 11, was a spectacular hit. Drawing huge, and—more important—*paying* audiences,[55] it was reported by the not always reliable *Mirror* (April 9, 1853) to have brought in at least five thousand needed dollars to the box office.

"Alboni is never other than Alboni," inscrutably wrote the *Musical World and Times* (April 16, 1853, pp. 241–42), although "Salvi is not always Salvi, nor Marini Marini." At the first performance of *La favorita,* Salvi's voice had been "slightly under a cloud and the true pitch, due to his recent illness,[56] [but] Marini and Beneventano [the latter sounding magnificent, as everyone agreed, but, as always, holding his high notes to unbearable lengths][57] were in high feather and sang true tones . . . while Alboni melted upon the susceptibilities like a generous snowflake."

This triumph was followed by another, *La sonnambula,* on April 15 and 18, with Alboni, Salvi, and Settimio Rosi (again sometimes spelled Rossi) in the leading roles. It eclipsed "any other operatic performance heard in this city for twenty-five years," declared Richard Grant White (*Courier and Enquirer,* April 16, 1853); the *Mirror,* going even further, proclaimed it the grandest operatic performance ever witnessed in New York. At its close the performance was accorded something the *Mirror* (April 16, 1853) elegantly referred to as a "*grand fracas de claque.*"

Strong regarded it more coolly.

April 21. . . . Took Ellen to hear Alboni in the *Sonnambula* Monday night [April 18th]. She makes a robust Amina. It certainly is a pretty and captivating opera, very respectable of its kind. Bellini is no great light in the musical firmament, but when the bills announce one of his operas, and I go, I prefer hearing his music to hearing Mrs. Marietta Alboni's. So Wednesday night I cut the *Gazza ladra* [the following presentation],[58] turned over my ticket to Mr. Ruggles, and George Anthon spent the evening

[55] ". . . it is no longer possible to know whether a full house implies a full purse, or not," wrote Curtis (*Putnam's,* June 1853, p. 698).

[56] Not according to Seymour, who had never heard Salvi sing better: "Not the slightest remain of the Staten Island 'influenza' [was] perceptible" (*Daily Times,* April 11, 1853).

[57] The formerly abused Beneventano was now credited with having "so much life, and vigor, and animal spirits, and such tremendous resources of voice that when he does get upon a tone he likes, he so luxuriates in it, so revels in and dotes upon it, so dreams himself away upon it, that he positively forgets to stop. . . . The first effect upon an audience is 'What a magnificent tone'; then 'How long he sustains it' (our hands meanwhile impatient to applaud); then 'Why the mischief doesn't he stop' (enthusiasm subsiding); soon, 'Will he never have done?' (enthusiasm quenched); at last, 'What a bore'" (*Musical World and Times,* April 16, 1853, pp. 241–42).

[58] Besides Alboni, the cast for the single performance of *La gazza ladra* included Carolina Vietti-Vertiprach and the Signori Rosi, Beneventano, Sangiovanni, and Marini. For once, Richard Grant White conceded that the overall musical quality of the ensembles suffered from being transposed to suit Alboni's vocal range; but "For every passage that lost by the pitch of her voice, there were ten

here. Last night at the Willis's—small party—some nice music—one Gockel, an athlete of a pianist who plays like a young Titan. The piano quaked and trembled under his blows, and I feared its legs would come off in the *fortissimo* passages.[59] . . . Great respect for Richard Willis. His only drawback [is] his brother N. P. Willis, author of the Blidgims story[60] and (according to common report) of other things, only not quite so flagitious. Wish he would go to Australia.[61]

La gazza ladra, although enthusiastically acclaimed, was immediately withdrawn in favor of a lavish new production of *Lucrezia Borgia.* Rose de Vries, apparently forgiven for her defection to the Artists' Union Italian Opera Company, was restored to the Maretzek fold as the Lucrezia; Alboni, a rare sight in "tunic, feathered hat, and white stockings," was the Maffio Orsini,[62] Salvi the Gennaro. The other roles, even the minor ones, were filled by luminaries of the company; thus, the choruses were given with unprecedented splendor. "At last we have an Opera!" rejoiced the *Spirit of the Times* (April 30, 1853, p. 132) (repeating many such premature rejoicings), "one to be proud of, and one to be patronized"; this company completely "out-Heroded the efforts of past impresarios" and established a lofty standard for those to come.

But this lustrous opera venture was doomed to go the way of its predecessors. Although it was no secret that Le Grand Smith was having difficulties with his principal tenor, the death-blow fell with unexpected suddenness. On April 30 a performance of *Norma* with de Vries and Salvi was suddenly canceled, owing to "some domestic dissention." "We hope the 'enemy' will be brought to terms," wrote the *Mirror* (April 30, 1853), "so that we shall have 'Don Giovanni,'" scheduled for May 2.

Don Giovanni was not performed, however, until May 6, after an interim of suspenseful waiting. Not surprisingly, the *Mirror* (May 2, 1853) named Ullman as the villain responsible for the fiasco: his latest "dirty trick is an offer to pay Salvi three hundred dollars more than he contracted to sing for with Mr. Le Grand Smith, and hence all the difficulty in the 'Grand Combination Opera Company.'"

Despite rumors that three "new" operas were in preparation, "the season closed rather abruptly and inharmoniously" with the postponed *Don Giovanni* given as a complimentary benefit for the beleaguered Smith. The *Spirit of the Times* (May 7, 1853,

---

that gained by its incomparable richness and the inexpressible grace and brilliance of her style" (*Courier and Enquirer,* April 22, 1853).

59 August (or Augustus) Gockel (1831–1861), advertised as an "*élève* of Mendelssohn," had recently arrived from Germany. On March 23 he gave an introductory private concert at the Apollo Rooms for an audience of 300 invited guests, and the following day the *Daily Times* reported that he was familiar enough with all the "'moves' on the keyboard" but too apt to "thump out a volume of sound," something Seymour attributed to the young man's insecurity. (See conflicting criticisms of Gockel in the *Musical World and Times,* April 2, 1853, pp. 210–11.) Gockel made his public debut at Niblo's Garden on April 19.

60 "Those Ungrateful Blidgimses," a short story in N. P. Willis's collection *Dashes at Life with a Free Pencil* (1845).

61 Australia was the currently popular next stop after California for gold-seekers and entertainers.

62 Alboni's Maffio Orsini was "simply folly," wrote Curtis. "Even when she rushes for the knife in the banquet scene and throws herself upon the spy, it [is] done so archly and with such a magnetic smile, that even censorious critics like ourselves would have gladly been so assaulted" (*Putnam's,* June 1853, p. 698). Alboni had created her first great sensation as Orsini, the role in which she made her debut at La Scala in 1841.

Girvice Archer, Jr.

Lorenzo Salvi, Max Maretzek's nemesis.

p. 144) openly blamed Salvi for the collapse: "Salvi was engaged at a very large salary to sing thirteen times. Up to that period he had sung but seven, and with his salary in his pocket in advance—for the management were foolish enough so to act—he bred a complete mutiny in the establishment—a strike operatic—by demanding that the salaries of the residue of the company should be paid in advance, and at higher rates. Taking them all under his wing, he flung down the gauntlet, and by so doing completely disorganized the plans and prospects of the management, who justly felt that they must [shut down] in order to avoid gross imposition. . . . The problem of a successful and harmonious opera troupe is still unsolved. Who will be the next to essay the task?"[63]

George Templeton Strong attended the final performance of this memorable company. Seemingly unmindful of the opera crisis, he made his usual obeisances to Mozart's celestial score but now, like many of his contemporaries, disparaged Da Ponte's "vulgar and stupid" libretto.[64]

May 7. . . . picked up George C. Anthon and marched him down to Niblo's to hear *Don Giovanni,* his first introduction thereto. Alboni was Zerlina and did so

[63]Before the corpse was cold—indeed, even before the company's demise—widely divergent rumors named Maretzek, Niblo, E. A. Marshall, Le Grand Smith, and even Salvi as possible managers of an ensuing opera venture or ventures.

[64]In an article on *Don Giovanni, Dwight's* (May 14, 1853, p. 46) refers to "moral critics of the libretto, who reject the *subject* [of Don Juan] beforehand, without considering in what spirit it is treated."

unsuitable a part better than one had a right to expect.[65] I'd rather hear Bosio in it, however.[66] It was a satisfactory performance; no part but was decently filled except Elvira's, which was given to a poor, nice-looking Siedenburg girl, who was frightened and ashamed of herself for undertaking such a thing. How glorious that music is—surely not among the least of the things we should be thankful for. That heartbreaking first quartette, for instance, that Elvira begins *(Non ti fidar)*—the "Trio of the Masks"—and above all, the celestial sweetness and purity of *Vedrai, carino*. Shame that such music—that would do honor to the noblest verse ever penned by mortal—should be debased by association with the vulgarity and stupidity of such a plot. I dubitated a little about going, and went at last in a sort of conscientious sense of one's duty not to omit an opportunity of storing one's memory with those exquisite phrases of melody unless for good reason, which did not exist last night, for I was too imbecile with headache either to work or to be entertaining at home.

Of all the critics, William Henry Fry alone probed and protested the practices that had brought about this latest in New York's lamentable succession of opera calamities. It was deplorable, he wrote, that Le Grand Smith, whose "unusual liberality" had provided the city with the best opera yet heard in the United States, should suffer a loss of thousands of dollars, due to the insatiable greed of his star singers.[67] To Fry, an uncompromising idealist, it bordered on the "morally hideous and religiously atheistic that artists can be found whose sense of salary so far outweighs their sense of justice that they will see any worthy gentleman deliberately pay out more than they can draw into the house.

"As much as we desire to see lyrical art flourish in this country," he passionately declared, "we would sooner a thousand times see it blasted from existence and consigned to oblivion than to find it habitually connected with avarice, jealousies, quarrelings, and the bankruptcies of the high-minded and liberal."

If the public could ever extricate itself from the "maelstrom of trade" sufficiently to develop an ethical perspective, wrote Fry, they would recognize the need for "setting the seal of terrible reprobation upon all grasping cupidity [so that] the quackery and pharisaic parade of a Jenny Lind would never be repeated."

[65] Even Curtis, Alboni's most problematical critic, pronounced her Zerlina "exquisite"—the best he had ever heard, by far. It was better than Bosio's, he wrote, because Bosio was too much the fine lady, like Sontag as Amina. But Alboni, "a blithe Bacchus in ample skirts," whose most tragic expression was to "look sorry," was incomparable in this purely rustic part (*Putnam's*, June 1853, p. 698).

[66] The *Evening Post* (May 7, 1853) concurred. The remainder of the cast—de Vries as Donna Anna, Beneventano Don Giovanni, Rovere Leporello, Zanini Masetto, Rosi the *Commendatore*—were splendid, except for Salvi, the Don Ottavio, who was "greeted with a discouraging salute of hisses." Maretzek, who along with the cast contributed his services, conducted for the only time that season.

[67] Richard Grant White ascribed the failure to the overblown size of the company, unwieldy and "more imposing than profitable." He recommended, too, a future repertory "more to the taste of the public," for instance: *Ernani, Lucrezia,* and *Semiramide*. But by all means "let *La favorita* be avoided," for although it contained some of Donizetti's best music, it was, as a whole, heavy and uninteresting (*Courier and Enquirer,* May 3, 1853).

Fry attributed the recurrent failure of opera in the United States to the absence of a "combination among capitalists to set it in regular motion" and a lack of "religious feeling among artists to save it from habitual wreck. The profanity of paying four, five, or six hundred, or more, dollars a night for a single voice [was] submitted to by the public, who, if dignity were as pervasive as folly, would . . . see [to it] that a right division of rewards was determined. They would even find out," wrote Fry—his unfulfilled composer's ego coming to the fore—"that at least one half of the success of an opera depends upon the composer, and would not let singers prey upon his works without giving him the rights of authorship under an international law of Copyright."

"We can never have any art in this country," argued Fry, "so long as crazy cupidity fires every artist, based on the Jenny Lind auctioneering, charity-giving, angelic charlatanism."[68]

A compulsive iconoclast, Fry then addressed himself to the score of *Don Giovanni* from the vantage-point of a would-be, and not too approving, composer of a more advanced period: "We deem the opinion so often expressed that *Don Giovanni* is unapproachable [to be] utterly baseless," wrote Fry. Nowadays, we heard "more modern instrumentation, which is much more varied and interesting." Too, the treatment of accentuation and of writing for the voice had radically changed since Mozart's day; the pitch of the tenor voice had risen by some two whole tones since then, and the latter-day developments that permitted the "splendid resonance, the declamatory vigor, the tragic sorrow which make Salvi so eminent, are thus wanting." Fry decried the "monotony" of Mozart's "stringed orchestra [!] in unbroken continuity for three hours," as he did "the elaborate ingenuity of the orchestra [that] hardly ever leaves the voice any prominence."[69]

It was also an error, claimed Fry, to regard parts of the *Don Giovanni* score as "comic." Mozart wrote "pensively and sublimely, like a man who was doomed to die early"; such an air as *Madamina mia* [*sic*] was distinctly not comic (*Tribune,* May 9, 1853).

Not until late September does Strong's journal again refer to music, and even then, it omits any mention of the unceasing opera activity, henceforth solely under Maretzek's direction, that recommenced in July and persisted in various forms to the end of the year.

Following the breakdown of the Combination Opera Company, vague and contradictory rumors of an imminent new opera season were rife in the newspapers. Most specifically, on May 27 the *Mirror* reported that Maretzek had at last managed to reunite the key members of the dispersed Combination Company (except for Alboni), and that under Niblo's management[70] he would begin an opera season the following week (at Niblo's) with *I puritani.* Steffanone (who had been conspicuously absent dur-

[68] It might well have been these attacks on the Lind legend that inspired John Sullivan Dwight's later hostility to Fry.

[69] Because *Don Giovanni* lacked spectacular vocal show-pieces, corroborated George William Curtis, it was not a favorite with singers, and thus "quite sure to drag a little and seem tedious" (*Putnam's,* June 1853, p. 698).

[70] Niblo was universally believed to be the only manager capable of successfully taming the wild beast of opera, but he wisely avoided it.

ing the Alboni era) would be the *prima donna;* the other members were Beneventano, Marini, and, unbelievably, Salvi.

"We have no hope for the speculation," wrote Seymour in the *Daily Times* (May 27, 1853). "The principal tenor has proved himself to be utterly unreliable and completely unworthy. It was he who broke up the last opera company; it was he who compelled [the now departed] Madame Alboni to leave our shores; it was he who inflicted a serious loss on our last operatic manager; it was he who *consented* to disappoint the public, and it is he who must be taught a stern lesson ere we can have anything like decent behavior on the lyric stage."[71] Seymour sincerely hoped the public would treat Salvi with the hostility he deserved—especially after his insolent behavior at the last opera performance.[72]

The new opera venture did not come to pass. According to *Dwight's* (June 11, 1853, p. 76), three days before its planned opening with *Roberto il diavolo* (not *I puritani*): "Signor Salvi found something in the arrangements that did not suit him, and *again* [he] had the pleasure of disappointing his manager." It was only because of Niblo's "forethought and good judgment" that an announcement of the performance had been withheld, thus denying Salvi the opportunity of giving the public "another specimen of his amiability and high-toned sense of humor!"

In the meantime, on June 1, Alboni had sailed for Europe, after completing her triumphant and financially profitable year in the United States with a farewell concert at Metropolitan Hall on May 26 for Arditi's benefit.[73] For the last time she was heard in her great *Casta diva* and her *Ah! non giunge,* and for the first time in the *Di tanti palpiti* (from Rossini's *Tancredi*), and the third-act finale aria of Don Carlos in *Ernani,* a male role she had performed in Europe. Despite a few inevitable quibbles, the critics vied with one another in the fervor of their parting eulogies. It was generally felt that Alboni was leaving a void that would never be filled: "We have heard the last delicious strains of the best and most fascinating singer of the age," lamented Seymour. "The chain of enchantment is broken, and we may go home to our pianos and play dismal requiems" (*Daily Times,* May 26, 1853).[74]

On July 11, after a month of "anxious expectation and at least half a dozen false starts,"[75] Maretzek, the unquenchable, at last succeeded in launching the second phase of his grand plan: a summer opera season at Castle Garden with another combined

[71]But Salvi had his supporters as well: ". . . some few are endeavoring to whitewash [Salvi] by attributing to Alboni the cause of the defection of the Le Grand Smith ranks," reported the *Spirit of the Times* (June 4, 1853, p. 192).

[72]But in vain. The public had an apparently boundless tolerance for Salvi's derelictions, as, perforce, did Maretzek: he was the only opera tenor of his caliber in the United States.

[73]Assisting at this testimonial to Arditi were Rose de Vries, Sangiovanni, Rovere, Coletti, Forti, and Maurice Strakosch, who played some of his latest piano compositions.

[74]But Fry perversely contended that Alboni's concerts had never been crowded; that although she was a great singer, she was not a great actress; that she lacked that quality of magnetism which inspires popular ovations. Nonetheless, she had "no reason to be dissatisfied with the [financial] results of her career in this country," for (unlike Sontag's), her concerts had been economically managed (*Tribune,* May 23, 1853).

[75]During this anxious period, it was reported that the city was "full of 'artists' out of employment and many of them out at elbows. They may be seen and heard, chattering Italian or French at the barrooms, the cheap restaurants, and the music stores at almost any hour of the day. . . . The

company—his own and Sontag's—to coincide with the great influx of entertainment-hungry visitors to the Crystal Palace Exhibition of Industry of All Nations.

Housing the first world's fair to be held in the United States, the Crystal Palace was a smaller version of the London Crystal Palace of 1851. A spectacular, octagon-shaped, glass and iron structure occupying some 250,000 square feet, it had been erected in Reservoir Square (now Bryant Park) with funds raised by Horace Greeley and other public-spirited New Yorkers, and was expected to attract great numbers of tourists.[76]

To what extent the opera's ultimate business arrangements had involved the detested Ullman is not clear. According to Maretzek: "I, as manager, took the first $1100 of the nightly receipts when Sontag appeared, for a part payment of artists and house, and the remainder was divided equally between Mme. Sontag and myself. Therefore, if the receipts should not reach $1100 (which, however, never happened), Mme. Sontag would have had to sing for nothing"[77] (*Sharps and Flats,* p. 9).

The Sontag component of the company included—besides the diva—Badiali, Rocco, and later, a miraculously transformed Pozzolini;[78] the Maretzek contingent consisted of Steffanone (receiving distinctly second billing), Bertucca-Maretzek, Amalia Patti-Strakosch (billed as "*Prima Donna Contralto*"), Salvi (yes, Salvi!),[79] Adelindo Vietti, Marini, Rosi, and Rovere. The orchestra and chorus, numbering some seventy persons, were chosen from among the best of the two preceding opera companies, and an "efficient ballet troupe," headed by Ducy-Barre, was engaged. With Eckert gone from the Sontag ranks,[80] Maretzek was the sole music director and conductor of the enterprise.

During the ensuing season of twenty-four performances, Sontag, the supreme *prima donna* of the company, was heard in *Lucia di Lammermoor, Robert le diable, La sonnambula, Il barbiere di Siviglia, L'elisir d'amore, Don Giovanni, The Daughter of the Regi-*

---

opening of Castle Garden by Sontag . . . [is] the chief [prospect] on which their present hopes are founded" (quoted in *Dwight's,* July 2, 1853. pp. 103–4).

[76] At the elaborate opening ceremonies on July 14, 1853, anthems were sung by the Sacred Harmonic Society conducted by Bristow, with Henry C. Timm, music director of the event, presiding at a powerful organ specially constructed for the Crystal Palace by Albert Gemunder and Brothers of Springfield, Massachusetts; patriotic music was played by Bloomfield's United States Band; and background music, while the guests were "occupied in viewing the exhibition," was alternately supplied by Noll's National Guard Band and Dodworth's Band (*Courier and Enquirer,* July 15; *Mirror,* July 26, 1853). Tickets were 50 cents, children's tickets 25 cents, and season tickets $10.

[77] Maretzek extols Sontag's uncompromisingly high artistic standards and her great nobility of character (*Crotchets,* pp. 305–6; *Sharps and Flats,* pp. 9–10).

[78] Pozzolini, who had been touring with the Arditi/de Vries opera company formed after Alboni's departure, rejoined the Sontag troupe in August. Of his transformation, Seymour, formerly his severest critic, wrote: "Signor Pozzolini created quite a sensation as Ernani. . . . He has greatly improved since the up-town campaign. He possesses considerable power, with much sweetness, and if he is ambitious, may yet occupy a foremost place among the tenors of the lyric stage" (*Daily Times,* August 16, 1853).

[79] It was reported that Salvi was enthusiastically hissed on opening night.

[80] Maretzek tells an ugly tale of blackmail practiced by the despicable Ullman: on being told (by Count Rossi) that Madame Sontag no longer required his services, Ullman threatened, if he were let go, to publish a malignant falsehood, scandalously linking her with both Eckert and Pozzolini. As a further condition for his silence Ullman demanded that both Eckert and Pozzolini be dismissed forthwith. An unhappy Sontag apparently submitted (see *Crotchets,* pp. 322–25).

ment (titled in English but sung in Italian), and *I puritani*.[81] Steffanone appeared in *Norma, Robert le diable, Don Giovanni, La favorita, Lucrezia Borgia,* and *Ernani*.

Doubtless remembering his former bitter experience with fifty-cent tickets at Castle Garden, Maretzek set the admission price to all parts of the house at a uniform dollar. To assist post-performance transportation, more than 100 omnibuses were stationed at the Battery gate, extra cars were added on the "city railroads," and Staten Island residents (among them Sontag, Salvi, and Maretzek) were served by a late ferry leaving Whitehall Street at 11:30 P.M.[82]

For a wonder (an evidence of Maretzek's genius for diplomacy), the Castle Garden season progressed comparatively serenely and—an even greater wonder—profitably. As expected, out-of-town visitors to the Crystal Palace exhibition supplied a large part of the attendance.[83] A special excitement was generated by the loudly heralded visit to the opera on July 15 of President Franklin Pierce, in New York to attend the opening of the exhibition. To do honor to the illustrious guest (who arrived late,[84] accompanied by the Mayor, the members of the Common Council, and several visiting foreign dignitaries), both Sontag and Steffanone appeared in a truncated version of *Robert le diable*—Steffanone as Alice, and Sontag democratically assuming the subsidiary role of Isabelle (much against the wishes of the caste-conscious Count Rossi) (*Sharps and Flats,* p. 9).

Exceptional among the prevailingly stereotypical reviews of this opera season were William Henry Fry's repeated attacks on Mozart's *Don Giovanni,* a work he regarded as musically archaic, incompatible with the tastes of contemporary audiences, and inapplicable to the capabilities of present-day singers—particularly tenors. In Fry's estimation, such composers as Meyerbeer and Donizetti had advanced far beyond Mozart in their masterly writing for voice and orchestra: "The opera of *Robert le diable* is especially marked for its magnificent treatment of the tenor voice," he wrote. "That great, manly ingredient of the lyrical drama had no prominent place in the operas of Mozart" (*Tribune,* July 21, 1853).

Following the first of three performances of *Don Giovanni,* featuring all the stars of the combined companies (except Salvi),[85] Fry claimed that only the simple airs of Zerlina (Sontag) appealed to the public; the ensembles were *caviare* to the general listener, and a number of the auditors "began to quit before the piece was over."

[81] With the *Suoni la tromba* again embellished by the anachronistic flag-waving, this time with the American and Italian colors.

[82] "The public is well satisfied with the price of admission," wrote Fry (*Tribune,* July 12, 1853). "The scores of omnibuses in waiting are a great convenience and 'annihilate the distance.' The police arrangements within and without the building are good—a consideration worth mentioning where there is a crowd of people and a rush of coaches."

[83] But an unruly one. In his overlong, overfussy review of the opening performance, R. Storrs Willis complained of "a succession of nuisances, in the way of running about, loud talking, getting up and down, and compelling others to get up and down, altogether intolerable" (*Musical World and Times,* July 23, 1853, p. 178).

[84] The President had the good taste to arrive during an intermission, wrote Fry, and thus did not interrupt the performance. "He was most enthusiastically welcomed, the entire audience rising and cheering vociferously, while the orchestra played 'Hail Columbia'" (*Tribune,* July 16, 1853).

[85] "Salvi is accustomed to sing modern music at the pitch and in the style such as is now written," explained Fry, and thus his Ottavio had been less than successful; nor was his replacement, Vietti, any better. Obviously, the fault lay with Mozart (*Tribune,* July 23, 1853).

TO THEODORE SEDGWICK, ESQ

THE

CRYSTAL SCHOTTISCH,

COMPOSED BY

W^{m}. BYERLY.

NEW YORK.

PUBLISHED BY FIRTH, POND, & Co 1 FRANKLIN SQ.

38 C^{ts} Nett

Music Division, The New York Public Library

The Crystal Palace.

Too, the part of Donna Anna (Steffanone) was no favorite with *prima donnas* because, explained Fry, "they can get very little applause in it." In general, Mozart's women's parts were "written very high and [were] not distinguished by striking contrasts of grave and acute notes. The ingenious accompaniments, so full of dramatic meaning," only distracted listeners from the singers, from whom they expected a "greater dominance than such combinations allow."

The interpolation of unidentified, anachronistic ballet music for Ducy-Barre and Monsieur Maugin's *pas de deux* in the ballroom scene apparently did not, however, offend Fry;[86] it only emphasized the strides made in music for dance since Mozart wrote his dated minuets for "the early hearts and gentle hands of our grandmothers." To Fry, only Mozart's "working up of the last scene [of *Don Giovanni*] is, under favor, good enough to keep everyone in his seat, which fact was overlooked last night."

Again Fry took occasion to renew his assault on his *bête noir* in his "summing-up" of the Castle Garden opera season, which closed on August 23 with a "Grand Operatic Festival" for Maretzek's benefit, consisting of two Donizetti operas—*Lucrezia Borgia* (with Steffanone) at four in the afternoon, and *Lucia di Lammermoor* (with Sontag) at eight in the evening.[87] Filling the greater part of a page-long column in the *Tribune* (August 25, 1853) with his idiosyncratic pronouncements, Fry wrote: "When we speak of operas we must mean Italian operas, because the contributions of the other nations are so secondary that they form an exception and not a rule." Even *Robert le diable* bore unmistakable traces of Meyerbeer's early adherence to Rossini, and *Don Giovanni,* in its "melodic phraseology, harmonic combinations, and orchestral treatment," was closely modeled on the general run of its Italian contemporaries. "We do not join in the opinion expressed by many that *Don Giovanni* [most recently performed on August 22] is a matchless work," reiterated Fry. Among its many shortcomings, "no very great prominence is given to any instrument, for [eighteenth-century] solo players were vastly inferior to the same class now, as were their instruments equally inferior." It was utter nonsense to expect a present-day composer (like himself) to write in Mozart's limited style, tailored to a period when theatres were small, orchestral players few and of limited capability, and voices undeveloped (especially tenors).

Mozart's failure to write spectacular solos for his orchestra musicians was another of his glaring defects, wrote Fry: "We think it a duty which the composer owes to the virtuosi in his orchestra to give them, from time to time, solo performances to show the public what they can do. . . . For example, the clarinet solo in *Lucia,* wide-arching and brilliant as a rainbow, was played in exquisite style [the night before] to the delectation of some two or three thousand people. . . . Is this not a legitimate effect in opera music?" demanded Fry. And if not, why not? If the singers, orchestra, and public liked it, "why should the deadheads grumble?" Because *Don Giovanni* lacked such effects, "with the public here it never enjoys [anything] beyond a *succès d'estime.*" And on and on.

Fry concluded his lengthy essay with a cursory nod to each of the stars of the

[86] But the *Albion* (July 30, 1853, p. 368) made an "earnest and solemn protest against the introduction of the vile, trashy music in the ball room scene. . . . It is a profanation of the sublime strains of Mozart's 'Don Giovanni' to have them interrupted by such abominable [but unidentified] dancing-music."

[87] A bargain at a dollar for both operas.

Castle Garden season and a pat on the head to Maretzek, who had been presented by his appreciative "co-laborers" with yet another splendid silver vase to add to his collection.

Again punctuating the conclusion of a Sontag season with a damaging article, the *Musical World and Times* (August 27, 1853, pp. 257–58) published a purported exposure of the unsavory tactics by which Sontag's career in the United States had been advanced. Titled "The New York Press Bribed," its "anonymous" author (Oliver Dyer) accused Sontag's management (Ullman) of buying good reviews from all of the local papers (and probably those in Boston and Philadelphia as well) at the expenditure of some $15,000. Dyer named the *New-York Daily Times, Courier and Enquirer, Journal of Commerce, Commercial Advertiser, Express, Herald, Tribune,* and *Evening Post* as the culprits who, for a price, had furnished "material aid and comfort to Madame Sontag."

Neglecting to cite a source for his statements, Dyer, showing no mean flair for yellow journalism, nimbly oscillated between outright accusation and virtuous disbelief that such honorable gentlemen as "Fry of the *Tribune,* White of the *Courier and Enquirer,* Callicott of the *Commercial Advertiser,* Parton of the *Home Journal,* Briggs of the *Sunday Courier,* etc., could be influenced by such means." Nor, in his jumble of contradictions, could he believe that any reputable newspaper would "tolerate such practices in anyone connected with its editorial department." Yet, the charges had been "made openly . . . whispered about by Sontag's *attachés,* [and] discussed in restaurants, Lager-Bier saloons, offices, and parlors." Dyer challenged each newspaper, naming them one by one, to "speak out."

Sontag, the innocent victim in this elaborate scheme of extortion, wrote Dyer, had received very little of the great sums of money accrued from her concert and opera performances, and when she had asked her manager for an accounting, she was "presented with enormous bills of expenses," chiefly owed to the press. "'Oh, the newspapers cost so much!'" she is reported to have wailed, "elevating her hands and eyes toward heaven, 'it is impossible to make anything.'"

Dyer's article aroused a mighty storm of protest from the accused papers, as well as prompt and indignant denials from Sontag and Ullman. Categorically stating that no money had been spent for any such purposes, Sontag accused the (supposedly anonymous) author of the defamatory article of falsely quoting her: "I am at a loss to conceive the motive that may have guided the Editor . . . in making me falsely utter words equally repugnant to my feelings and the *amour propre* an artist ought to possess." His object, she stated, was obviously to insult her and the press and to discredit "the gentlemen who have the direction of my affairs" (*Daily Times, et al.,* August 30, 1853).

In answer to Sontag's denials and Ullman's counter-accusations, Dyer, in a signed letter to the *Times,* dated September 6 (reprinted in the *Musical World and Times* on September 10, pp. 9–10), hotly denied Ullman's counter-charge that it was in fact Dyer who had offered to write 2000 "complimentary letters to the out-of-town newspapers for the sum of $2000," and that following Ullman's virtuous rejection of the infamous proposal, the *Musical World and Times* had vengefully attacked Madame Sontag and himself.

In answer to the outcry from the maligned newspapers that he identify their accuser, Dyer—in his letter to the *Times*—named as his indirect informant F. B. Helmsmüller (?–1865), a disgruntled former minor member of Ullman's management team[88] who had "voluntarily" tattled his information to Richard Willis; Willis had then passed it on to his associate Dyer. Finding himself at the center of a firestorm of his own making, Dyer attempted to absolve himself by reminding his readers that in his original bribery story he had "expressly avowed his disbelief" of the malfeasance of all those honorable journalists. And it now appeared that not $15,000, but possibly a mere $2000—certainly not more than $3000—"had been paid *directly* to the musical critics and editorial *attachés* of the New York papers." Instead, they had taken it out in "loans" which were not expected to be repaid[89] (see *Musical World and Times,* September 3, 1853, pp. 1–2; *Dwight's,* September 3, pp. 171–73, September 10, 1853, pp. 181–82).

But, for all his disclaimers—and much as he disliked to contradict a lady—Dyer refused to budge from his assertions concerning Sontag. In her "card," he wrote, she had attempted to "make the public believe that she and Mr. Ullman are the best of friends—that she is perfectly satisfied with his conduct as her agent—and that what has been said in regard to her not having made anything, or but very little, during her sojourn in this country, is a sheer fabrication on the part of the *Musical World and Times,* the object of which must have been either to bring Mr. Ullman into discredit or to insult the Press and herself."

Lady or no lady, "neither justice nor courtesy demands that we should permit these assertions to pass uncontradicted," asserted Dyer. "We think, however, that *Madame* acted under *advice* (not to use a stronger term) when she permitted [her statements] to be published and that she did not understand (from her perhaps imperfect knowledge of English) the full import of them." Dyer offered to hold off further disclosures until Sontag would publicly deny that she had "for some time been dissatisfied with her agent, Mr. Ullman, and *that she herself so declared,* and that she had said that she has 'made very little (much less than the amount recently published)[90] during her professional career in this country.'"

But Sontag made no such denials. And with the sudden cessation of Sontag news items following the bribery scandal, the extent and circumstances of her continuing

[88] Helmsmüller, formerly the manager of the Germania Society, had settled in Providence in 1852 to devote himself to teaching and composing (*Dwight's,* September 4, 1852, p. 174). After Sontag's arrival, he claimed, he had been engaged by Ullman as an assistant manager. But according to Ullman, Helmsmüller had been employed only as a "runner," whose lowly duties included "attending to the press, handing in advertisements, carrying the customary complimentary tickets to the newspapers, etc." Perhaps Helmsmüller's scandalous disclosures were made in revenge for Ullman's alleged refusal to pay his salary (*Courier and Enquirer,* September 9; *Mirror,* September 12, 1853).

[89] In a cosier time, Ullman had allegedly confided to Dyer that his break with Burkhardt had resulted from Burkhardt's inordinate demands for money (thus Burkhardt's cruel reviews of Sontag). The same applied to the *Mirror,* who "had tried to borrow money of him [Ullman], but failed" (*Musical World and Times,* September 10, 1853, p. 10).

[90] From October 1852 to May 1853, reported the *Daily Times* (August 3, 1853), Sontag's performances had realized a net profit of $41,801. Advertising expenses had added up to $6701.32 (Sontag's figures); commissions to the manager were $3900. "There were other expenses incurred in the lost time during which the salaries ran on—namely, the September election week, Holy Week, and three weeks between concert and opera campaigns." Inexplicably, the *Times* added: "In addition to the above, the first management in New-York realized nineteen thousand dollars." First management?

Henriette Sontag.

relationship with Ullman become increasingly obscure. That she remained tied to him for a period after this painful episode is indicated in the *Mirror,* which on September 17, two days before the opening of Maretzek's new opera season at Niblo's Garden, "regretted" that "the obstacle of her agent" had prevented Madame Sontag from continuing to appear with his (Maretzek's) company.[91] Perhaps her "first New York concert of the season," on October 11 at Niblo's Saloon, was intended as a public declaration that she had broken with Ullman: not only was the event managed by Helmsmüller,[92] but it was given for the joint benefit of Eckert, apparently reinstated as the "Conductor and Director of Madame Sontag's Concerts and Operas," and Pozzolini, again featured as the "primo tenore" of her "Concert and Opera Co.," both of whom appeared.[93] Eckert conducted again the following evening, when the concert was repeated in Brooklyn, and on October 13, when Sontag and Rocco assisted at the concert of her favorite young colleague Paul Julien.

But these were unavailing efforts to inject life into a career that had obviously run its course—in New York, at least. Despite repeated announcements of a future autumn series of "farewell concerts," Sontag was heard only twice more—at two somewhat unprepossessing benefits: on October 20 at Niblo's Saloon, for the Italian Benevolent Society, and on October 27 at Metropolitan Hall, to aid the Home for the Destitute Children of Seamen. Eckert, who was to have conducted the latter event,

[91] The *Spirit of the Times* (September 17, 1853, p. 372) more tactfully explained that Sontag's touring schedule prevented her from remaining with the Maretzek company longer than one month, and that Max had "felt himself compelled to decline this, as her departure so early in the season would be likely to have the effect of lessening its attractiveness."

[92] "The concert was intrusted by Madame Sontag to Mr. Helmsmüller, a most trustworthy, capable, and energetic agent, who always carries his point, and is a favorite with the public," pointedly commented the *Musical World and Times* (October 15, 1853, p. 50).

[93] The other assisting artists were Badiali, Rocco, Gasparoni, and Paul Julien.

suddenly departed for Europe on October 22 to accept an appointment as conductor at the Royal Opera in Munich (*Herald,* October 24, 1853). As George William Curtis observed in *Putnam's* (November 1853, pp. 561–62), the announcements of Sontag's farewell series "gradually fell out of the newspapers. There could hardly have been a very active response," he wrote. "We have heard her a great deal and with great pleasure. But in the constant stress of novelty presented in New-York, a singer must be very eminent and in the prime of voice and frame to succeed in permanently retaining the public interest." Apparently the charm of vicariously hobnobbing with a real countess had worn thin. Madame Sontag made her final departure from New York with no farewell fanfare.

Seven months later, on June 17, 1854, Sontag, who had been touring with Rocco and Pozzolini after leaving New York, perished of cholera in Mexico, where she was giving an opera season free at last from Ullman's clutches. According to Maretzek, she had given Ullman a large sum of money and sent him to Europe, ostensibly to engage a hypothetical new company to sing in a hypothetical future season of English opera (*Crotchets,* p. 325).

At the close of the summer opera season, with Castle Garden no longer practicable and Astor Place a fast-fading memory,[94] Maretzek, the quintessential pragmatist, lost no time in leasing Niblo's Garden from his longtime adversary (Niblo) for a season of opera, to begin on September 19. His company again included Steffanone, Patti-Strakosch, Bertucca-Maretzek, Salvi, Vietti, Marini, Beneventano, Rosi, Gasparoni, Rovere, and Luigi Quinto, a utility tenor.[95] Despite having announced several new productions—Verdi's *Louisa Müller* [*sic*] (Naples 1849) and *Rigoletta* [*sic*] (Venice 1851), Rossini's *William Tell,* and a mysterious "entirely new work by an [unidentified] American composer"—Maretzek reverted to his too-familiar repertory: *I puritani, Norma, Ernani, Lucia* (introducing a physically beautiful, but vocally uneventful, new Italian soprano Costanza Manzini), *La favorita, Il barbiere, L'elisir d'amore, Don Giovanni,* and *Robert le diable* (with Bertucca on one occasion bravely singing both her own role, Alice, and, substituting for an indisposed Steffanone, Isabelle).

Yielding at last to persistent criticism of his stale repertory (and persuaded by the sparsity of his audiences), on October 17, Maretzek at last brought forth an ill-chosen "novelty"—a revival of Verdi's *I Lombardi,* no better liked than when he had presented it at the Astor Place Opera House in 1848 in the turbulent days of Edward P. Fry.[96] "Despite the large doses of Verdi we have had from time to time given to us," complained the *Albion* (October 22, 1853, p. 512), "he has not made headway in the affections of the Opera-goers." The critic, who admittedly had "heard or seen but little of . . . the composer's latest Operas, such as 'Louisa Müller' and 'Rigoletta,'" had been told they were "more melodious, less brassy, and better instrumented. . . . But we speak of 'Lombardi,' 'Ernani,' 'Nabucco,' 'Macbeth,' and others when we say that

[94] On July 9 the *Home Journal* noted the final passing of the Astor Place Opera House: "It is now little more than the shell of an opera house, and it stands there, in Astor Place, empty, windowless, and surrounded with a wooden railing, the wreck of an ill-considered enterprise."

[95] Equally utilitarian in Italian opera as Signor Luigi Quinto and in German opera as Herr Ludwig Quint.

[96] *I Lombardi,* the first Verdi opera to be heard in the United States, had been a failure in its initial production at Palmo's Opera House in 1847.

such productions are enough to ruin all singers and to depopulate the musical world of rising vocalists. No young Soprano can possibly, without unnatural and constant straining of the voice, hang through four acts at the skirt of the Piccolo Flute and overtop the noises of all the brass and reed that are brought to bear against her. And if she be lucky and strong enough to accomplish it . . . it is almost certain that her middle and *natural* voice is either gone or has become weak, false, or uncertain." Verdi was equally destructive of tenors, baritones, and basses, but apparently not contraltos (only because he had so far neglected to write contralto arias).

More perceptively, Charles Bailey Seymour in the *Daily Times* (October 18, 1853) referred to Verdi as "the best abused composer of the day." He was "one of those unfortunate men of genius who fail to excite the sympathy of a general audience." Verdi's "excessive use of brass instruments and repetition of hurried passages chopped up into staccato notes for a chorus," wrote Seymour, were "some of the peculiarities to which a new audience [had] to accustom themselves. We say peculiarities," he added, "because if we look on them as faults, we shall fail to detect any originality in Verdi's compositions."

In any case, the poorly attended opera season, scheduled to close at the end of October, received an unexpected, last-minute reprieve with the triumphant production on October 27 of Auber's *Masaniello (La Muette de Portici),* sung in Italian for the first time in New York.[97] Pronouncing it to be Maretzek's greatest achievement, the critics unanimously praised the work (not least because it brought blessed surcease from Donizetti). The cast, too, was acclaimed—particularly Salvi, who triumphed as Masaniello, but also Beneventano as Pietro, Steffanone as Elvira, and the dancer Mlle. Leontine Pougaud (later replaced by the equally admirable Mlle. Christine Leeder) as the dumb girl Fenella. Despite scattered cavils over the physical shortcomings of the production, obviously a shoestring affair, the great Market Scene, with the stars Marini, Beneventano, Vietti, Rosi, and Rovere gamely joining in its mighty choruses, was pronounced magnificent.[98] That audiences, regardless of bad weather, flocked to hear *Masaniello,* crowed the critics, went to prove that only novelty was needed for opera to succeed in New York,[99] that is, novelty sung in Italian. "Go hear and see it," urged an euphoric William Henry Fry in the *Tribune* (October 31, 1853), and apparently that is what New Yorkers enthusiastically and repeatedly did until November 18, when *Masaniello* was given for the last time (except for Salvi's benefit on December 13, when it drew a surprisingly small audience).

This new infusion of life (and presumably funds) spurred the indomitable Maretzek to bigger and better efforts. "The immense success of *Masaniello,* unprecedented in the history of the Lyric Drama in this country," he modestly announced in the pa-

[97] *Masaniello* had been a favorite in New York since 1831, when it was first produced in English at the Park Theatre; in its original French it was successfully presented by the great New Orleans Opera Company that visited New York in 1845.♪

[98] On one occasion Rovere extemporaneously joined Mademoiselle Pougaud in dancing the Tarantella, a spectacular hit that had to be encored (*Herald,* November 3, 1853).

[99] On the opening night of *Masaniello,* reported the *Home Journal* (November 5, 1853): "The rain fell steadily and fast. The streets were as forbidding as the fireside was agreeable. Yet on that evening Niblo's was crowded literally to the ceiling, and the adjacent streets were one prodigious turmoil of omnibuses and carriages—so irrepressible is the desire of New Yorkers to be in at the birth of a novelty." After it opened, people were "glad to obtain standing room in the passages" (*Herald,* October 31, 1853).

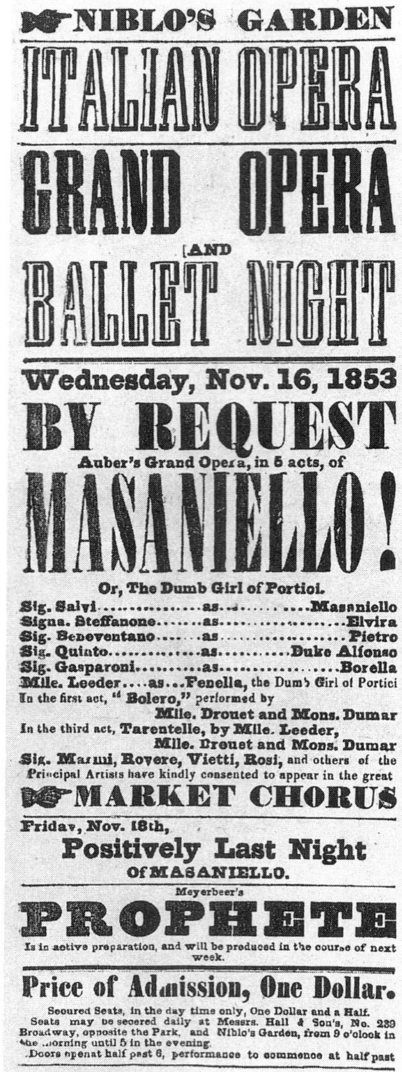

New-York Historical Society

pers on November 3, "has determined the manager, always grateful for the appreciation and patronage of the public, to continue the Opera Season for a limited time." During this "renewed season" he would "positively" present Mozart's *Nozze di Figaro*[100] (he didn't) and, for the first time in the United States, "that most wonderful

[100] In Sir Henry Bishop's pastiche English version (London 1819), *The Marriage of Figaro* was first heard at the Park Theatre on May 19, 1824; it was performed in a French adaptation by a visiting company from New Orleans in 1831. Despite Maretzek's optimistic announcement, it was not given in a purportedly authentic Italian version until November 23, 1858, at the first Academy of Music.

musical creation of the age," Meyerbeer's *Le Prophète* (Paris 1849), now "in active preparation."

At last performed on November 25, the long-awaited *Le Prophète* was unanimously proclaimed a supreme musical and dramatic masterpiece[101] and its sumptuous production Maretzek's crowning triumph. Not, agreed the critics, that it could rival the splendors of its Paris and London productions, where the scenery had been "an attraction in itself." But Maretzek had spared no expense in copying scenery, costumes, and machinery from European models and drawings, and his production boasted, besides a singing cast equal to any in Europe,[102] a *corps de ballet,* military bands, and 200 auxiliaries in the coronation scene.[103]

The critics agreed, too, that *Le Prophète*—for all its splendor, a somber work with "fewer lights than shadows"—required several hearings to be understood. Besides, as Seymour commented: "Probably there has not been a single auditor at Niblo's Garden who will be content with a single performance" (*Daily Times,* December 1, 1853). Thus, after eight crowded, rapturously received performances of *Le Prophète,* Maretzek extended his season to allow for two more, on December 14 and 16, and then, on December 19, for his closing benefit, to follow a gala performance of *Masaniello* with the fourth act of *Le Prophète.*

In announcing this schedule, however, Maretzek did not reckon with his pernicious *primo tenore,* who appears to have been misleadingly quiescent since the stormy debacle of the Combination Opera Company the previous spring. On December 23 the *Mirror* furiously reported: "The large audience attracted by the operatic programme for the benefit of Maretzek at Niblo's, last night, were taken aback and made not a little indignant at finding a placard posted on the theatre doors announcing Signor Salvi's indisposition, and the postponement of the Opera and benefit until further notice." True, the tickets had been refunded at the box office, "but who, we should like to know, will refund the carriage hire, gloves, bouquets, and other incidental expenses attending an outfit for the Opera? The public have stood about enough of these outrages and would be pleased to know the nature of the *indisposition* which subjected them to such annoyance and expense—if not insult. Was it . . . simply an *indisposition* to sing? . . . It is pretty near time professional gentlemen and ladies who depend upon the public for subsistence were taught that the public can be indisposed

[101] But by none so discursively as William Henry Fry, who dispensed oceans of passionate verbiage on a drop-by-drop analysis and dissection of the composer, his life, his *oeuvre,* this opera, its Paris rehearsals and production as contrasted with those in New York, opera's link with ancient Greece, and the modern composer's obligation to use all available new instruments and techniques—to name only a fraction of the vast content of his review (*Tribune,* November 26, 1853).

[102] With Salvi as John of Leyden, Steffanone as Fides, Bertucca as Bertha, Beneventano as the Count Oberthal, and Marini, Vietti, and Rosi as the three Anabaptists.

[103] Also a spectacular optical effect representing the setting sun, contributed by the "celebrated" local optician Professor Scott Franks (*Mirror,* December 2, 1853). Maretzek avers that both electric lights and roller skates were introduced to America in this production; and that Niblo, after witnessing the opera, had advised him to "dispense with all the artists, orchestra, and choruses, etc., etc., and to lay simply a floor over the parquet, and to give only the *roller-skating scene* lighted by the *electric apparatus;* to charge admission of fifty cents; and furnish skates to any gentleman or lady who would like to try the new amusement of roller-skating" (*Sharps and Flats,* p. 13). Thus did William Niblo invent the public skating rink nearly a decade before it materialized.

as well as *artistes,* and that they [the public] are indisposed longer to tolerate this kind of outrage."

In all the papers Maretzek informed the public that he had received a note from Salvi at noon on the 19th, coolly stating that unless he received his share of the benefit proceeds ($500) within the hour, he would "go out of town" and not appear that evening. Maretzek had not acceded.

Of all his twenty-three benefits since coming to the United States, declared Maretzek with some passion, only once had he kept the proceeds for himself; all the others had been divided among the members of his company or used to pay off outstanding bills. As on the twenty-two previous occasions, Maretzek had planned again to distribute the proceeds of his benefit among the members of the company.

The press was irate. Reflecting the prevailing climate of resentment, Seymour wrote: "So far as the public is concerned, it remains for Mr. Salvi to explain his extraordinary conduct. It is the more necessary, as this is not the first occasion of such impertinence. It will, we think, be the last, unless Mr. Salvi can disprove the withering allegations of Mr. Maretzek" (*Daily Times,* December 21, 1853).

Salvi, in a letter addressed to the papers, blamed "Max" for everything: it was, in the first place, Max's published announcement of the company's imminent departure for Havana and Mexico that had brought down the deluge of unpaid bills (amounting to $2200) that had forced him to ask for his share of the benefit money in advance.[104] (The papers assessed the enormous sums Salvi had received from Maretzek during the period of their uneasy professional relationship at something like thirty to forty thousand dollars.)

A master of Mephistophelian guile, Salvi craftily sowed the seeds of revolt among Maretzek's company, from the stars to the extras to the orchestra, and even to the treasurer. Again proclaiming himself their champion and protector against the arch-fiend Max, Salvi avowed his everlasting willingness to perform for their benefit, but for Maretzek—never! In the end Salvi triumphed. Giving no further performances, in late December this memorable company departed for Mexico and Havana, leaving a defeated Maretzek to shift for himself in New York.

More than Maretzek's hackneyed repertory had been to blame for his disappointing showing at the Niblo's box office. During the greater part of his sojourn at Niblo's, New York audiences had flocked nightly to the spectacular promenade concerts of Louis Antoine Jullien (1812–1860),[105] the most extraordinary musical presence ever to have invaded these shores, Lind included.

An improbable blend of Pied Piper, consummate showman, dream merchant, re-

[104] Not the least intriguing in the published list of Salvi's debts was the druggist Delluc's bill for $253 for eighty gallons of cod liver oil shipped to Italy, and $55 for three wicks, ostensibly to be used in Salvi's candle manufactory.

[105] Jullien, the son of a bandmaster, had supposedly received 36 given names from his 36 godfathers, representing the membership of the Philharmonic Society (a society rather overendowed with Thomases) in the French mountain village of Sisteron, where he was born. He was purportedly christened Louis George Maurice Adolphe Roch Albert Abel Antonio Alexander Noé Jean Lucien Daniel Eugène Joseph-le-brun Joseph-Barême Thomas Thomas Thomas-Thomas Pierre Arbon Pierre-Maurel Barthelemi Artus Alphonse Bertrand Dieudonné Emanuel Josué Vincent Luc Michel Jules-de-la-plane Jules-Bazin Julio César Jullien, no less (*Musical Review and Choral Advocate,* September 1853, p. 137).

Music Division, The New York Public Library

Jullien the Resplendent.

splendent dandy,[106] superlative orchestra conductor, and dedicated music missionary, Jullien was idolized in England, where he was credited with having induced—by techniques of subliminal persuasion—an unwitting tolerance of the classics among the musically uninformed pedestrian masses who swarmed to his spectacular promenade con-

[106] Offstage as well. The English journalist F. A. Sala, encountering him on a train journey, describes the entrance into his compartment of "a magnificent incarnation, all ringleted, oiled, scented, dress-coated, and watered-silk-faced, braided, frogged, ringed, jeweled, patent-leathered, amber-headed-sticked, and straw-coloured-kid-gloved. . . . His gloves and boots fitted so tightly that you felt inclined to think that he had varnished his hands straw-coloured and his feet black. There was not a crease in his fine linen, a speck of dust on his superfine Saxony sables, his waxed mustachios, and glossy ringlets" (Sala, p. 16).

certs.[107] This he had accomplished by unobtrusively slipping into his programs of popular polkas, potpourris, waltzes, galops, and quadrilles a movement of a symphony by Beethoven or Mozart or Mendelssohn, an opera aria or a concert overture.[108] Gradually, two movements of a symphony would be unprotestingly endured by the promenaders, then a whole symphony, and eventually half a program would be dedicated to the works of a single master.

As *Punch* felicitously described the process (December 1852, p. 260, quoted in the *Musical Review and Choral Advocate,* August, 1853, p. 118):

> . . . With ophicleides, cymbals, and gongs
> At first thou didst wisely begin,
> And bang the dull ears of the popular throngs,
> As though 'twere to beat music in.
>
> . . . Then leading them on, by degrees,
> To a feeling of Genius and Art,
> Thou made'st them to feel that Beethoven could please,
> And that all was not "slow" in Mozart.

This painless musical indoctrination was dispensed amid surroundings of lavish splendor[109] at the minimal price of a shilling for promenaders and proportionately more for various types of seating accommodations.[110]

Jullien's programs in America adhered to his established pattern: each included an overture and two movements of a symphony by one of the great masters, an opera aria, sung or instrumentally arranged, spectacular solos by two of Jullien's transcendent instrumental virtuosos, and popular items chosen from his vast repertory of dance music, predominantly of his own composition. Several concerts were set aside (meaning half the program) as "Festivals in honor of Mozart, Beethoven, and Mendelssohn." Each program featured, as well, one or two of Jullien's famous National Quadrilles: English, Irish, Scotch, French, Russian, Chinese, East Indian, Hungarian, Polish, and particularly his new "American Quadrille," purportedly composed after his arrival in the United States and featuring twenty solos with variations for twenty of his twenty-five top-notch star performers.

Jullien's immensely popular quadrilles, evolved from the five-part danced quadrilles of the earlier nineteenth century, were showily orchestrated medleys of familiar music, each having a specific subject or scenario, national or derived from a myriad other sources—operatic, comic, topical, and so forth.[111] He frequently flavored his

[107] Although not the originator of the promenades, Jullien vastly elaborated on the earlier efforts of Jean-Baptiste Tolbeque (1797–1869) and Philippe Musard (1793–1859).

[108] In this regard, too, Jullien had followed in Musard's footsteps, but with incomparably greater success, doubtless due to his overpowering charisma, a quality the grim-visaged, austerely dressed, Musard appears to have lacked.

[109] Jullien seduced his audiences in a dream-world contrived of plashing fountains, glistening mirrors, fragrant flowers, and opulent draperies.

[110] Tickets at Castle Garden were fifty cents for "standing or walking space" and $1 for seats in the balcony.

[111] As, for example, the "Great Exhibition Quadrille," written to celebrate London's World's Fair in 1851. One of Jullien's more elaborate efforts, it was performed, in addition to his large orchestra, by four English military bands and a corps of drummers of the *Garde Nationale* of Paris, the latter

quadrilles with extra-musical show elements—visual devices, such as simulated flames and elaborate lighting effects—and sound effects, such as the firing of guns or cannon, the pealing or jingling of bells, and other evocative sounds. Often his musicians contributed vocal effects—chanting or cheering—as in the "American Quadrille." Jullien was said to have improved Beethoven's storm in the "Pastoral" Symphony by adding the sound of falling hailstones, simulated by the rattling of dried peas in a tin container—something the Master had overlooked.

In a period abounding in brilliant orchestra musicians, Jullien surrounded himself with the foremost instrumentalists of the time, and—a wizard orchestral arranger—he highlighted his quadrilles with breathtaking solos designed to display each star's particular brand of virtuosity. These solos, a special favorite of the promenades audiences, called forth spontaneous outbursts of applause and cheers in mid-performance, much as spectacular jazz riffs do in the twentieth century.

Not all of the twenty-five handpicked orchestra virtuosos who accompanied Jullien to the United States ("a constellation of which the single stars are planets," wrote George William Curtis) were unknown to New York audiences. Among them were the prodigious double-bassist Giovanni Bottesini, whose tireless shuttlings across the Atlantic since 1847 had made him as familiar a figure in New York as he was in Europe, and the diminutive master of the flageolet Collinet, who had visited New York briefly in 1846.♪ Soon to become local household words were such phenomenal performers as the cornetist Adolph Koenig, the flutist Mathieu-André Reichert (b. 1830), the oboist Antoine-Joseph Lavigne (1816–1886), the clarinetist Wuille, and the brothers Mollenhauer—Friedrich (1818–1885) and Éduard (1827–1914)—violinists who "played together as one." Each was successively acclaimed the greatest living exponent of his particular instrument, as were their colleagues.[112]

Jullien brought only a single vocal soloist, the German soprano Anna Zerr (1829–1881), reputedly able to sing three notes higher than Jenny Lind.[113] According to Jullien's biographer Adam Carse, he brought over some eleven tons of luggage, containing elaborate props for transforming ordinary concert halls to fantasy-palaces and—among other famous Jullien indispensables—his sculptured, gilt music stand, his scarlet and gilt armchair, his jeweled baton, and his famous monster instruments: the huge ophicleide, the gigantic drum (built for him by Henry Distin),♪ the colossal trombone some ten feet in length and "nearly as large as the smoke pipe of a steamer" (*Mirror,*

being simultaneously conducted by Jullien and their own leader. Bristling with multinational tunes and anthems, this quadrille introduced several exotic new instruments, among them the *Corna Musa* (saxophone), the octo-bass (a monster double bass), a monster ophicleide, a bombardon (tuba), and castanets (Carse, *Life of Jullien,* p. 67).

[112]Jullien's musicians, most of whom did double duty as soloists and orchestra players, were Thomas Baker (leader), Henry Weist Hill, and the Mollenhauer brothers, first violins; Louis Barque, second violin; Schreuss, viola and viola d'amour; Lütgen and Engelke, cellos; A. Winterbottom and White, double basses; Collinet, flageolet; Reichert, flute; Lavigne and de Prins, oboes; Wuille and Sonnenberg, clarinets; Hardy, bassoon; Stenebrugger and Hughes, horns; Duhême (or Duhem) and Holt, trumpet and cornet; W. Winterbottom, trombone; S. Hughes, ophicleide; and F. Hughes, drums.

[113]Unfortunately falling ill immediately after her first appearance, Zerr was replaced by the mezzo-soprano Henriette Behrend, a beautiful, seventeen-year-old New Yorker of German extraction, who remained a regular member of the company after Zerr's recovery.

Jullien the Ambidextrous.

Music Division, The New York Public Library

August 12, 1853), the monster triangle, and Jullien's piccolo, only six inches long, on which he occasionally played a solo, as he did on the violin, the clavicor (a valved brass instrument), and the bagpipes, sans bag.

The Jullien tour in America, originally planned to open in July at Castle Garden synchronously with the Crystal Palace Exhibition, was for some reason delayed. The project was undertaken, according to the *Musical World and Times* (September 3, 1853, p. 1) by "three or four gentlemen (English, we believe) [in fact, the durable music-publishing/concert-managing firm of Chappell & Co.] at their own risk, and with a capital of 40,000 pounds sterling ($200,000)." Jullien was to receive $15,000 for six months; Bottesini $1000 a month, three months of which were already paid in advance.

Jullien arrived in advance of his company on August 7, accompanied by his wife and collaborator,[114] and by "our old friend" Dr. John Joy, his godson and manager (the boon companion of the "oyster house critics" in 1851). They were conveyed in style from the pier to the Clarendon Hotel in a "new and beautiful carriage, drawn by four magnificent bays." Despite the surprising absence of a dockside reception, Jullien's arrival was hardly unanticipated: immediately after midnight (he had arrived on a Sunday, apparently the inevitable day of arrival for transatlantic musicians) he was serenaded by Adkins's Cornet Band, under the direction of Thomas Coates (*Spirit,* August 13, 1853, p. 312).[115]

No waster of time, on the evening after his arrival Jullien inspected Castle Garden

[114] Madame Jullien, an Englishwoman and a former florist, was the uncommonly gifted designer of the bewitching environments that were a requisite part of the Jullien magic.

[115] Two nights later "Dodworth's incomparable Cornet Band, the pride of the city, paid the great Maestro the compliment of a serenade, with which he could not have been otherwise than de-

(where the Maretzek/Sontag summer opera was still in residence) to assess the Garden's possibilities, both acoustical and architectural, for the transformations that were an essential part of his show. And scarcely had Maretzek given the closing downbeat of his season (on August 23) when Jullien's workmen moved in. "The public may expect something dazzling," promised the *Mirror.* "Manager Joy and his valiant aide Brough have already got their carpenters astir, and the Garden is to be transformed into a second Aladdin's palace" (*Mirror,* August 9; August 12, 1853).[116] And indeed, in the scant five days between Maretzek's departure and Jullien's debut "the interior of Castle Garden was metamorphosed, hung with banners, decorated with a glistening star [outlined in flaming gaslight], wreathed with the national flag,[117] and provided with a commodious orchestra [an ambiguous synonym for platform] for the hundred musicians of Jullien" (*Home Journal,* September 10, 1853).

But Joy and Brough (acting under the direction of Arthur Chappell, in whose charge Jullien's musicians arrived a few days later) had been busy with far more than the physical transformation of the Garden, as we learn from Richard Grant White's column-long critique in the *Courier and Enquirer* on August 30, the day after Jullien's sensational debut at Castle Garden. So vivid is White's account of the event that to read it is the next best thing to having been there. It is therefore quoted at some length.

"Monsieur Jullien, having blazoned himself and his principal artists in infernal scarlet and black [posters] all over the town for some months[118]—having issued an infinite series of portraits of himself, and ruined the prospects of the Art Union by establishing several free galleries of portraits of his colleagues—having occupied (and handsomely paid for) a large portion of valuable space in our columns and those of our principal contemporaries by informing people of what they knew perfectly well before, or did not want to know at all—having brought over from England forty and odd [*sic*] orchestral performers, when we could hardly support those who were already here, and created a dearth in the musical market by recklessly buying up the services of sixty more[119]—having had six advertisements daily in every journal to announce

lighted" (*Spirit,* August 13, 1854, p. 312). (Allen Dodworth, returning from a European trip, had been a fellow-passenger of Jullien's on the *Baltic,* and together they had given the inevitable shipboard concert for the benefit of the crew.)

116 With W. F. Brough acting as Dr. Joy's assistant, the conspicuously pro-Brough *Mirror* provided a continuous *obbligato* of colorful Jullien gossip and chitchat.

117 "The magic transformations and adornments of the Garden alone are worth one evening's visit," reported the *Musical World and Times* (September 3, 1853, p. 1).

118 ". . . every wall, brick pile, omnibus, car, pavement, and barroom in New York has been red with the bills of Jullien," reported the *Home Journal* (September 10, 1853). "The outside of Castle Garden blazes with the name of Jullien, to catch the eye of the passing steamboat passengers. A Drummond light, at the entrance of the Battery, sends its blinding rays far up into Broadway, reminding everyone of Jullien. . . . In the entrance to the old fort stands a packing-case with one end open just far enough to let the passing public catch a glimpse of the greatest drum in the world, the drum that was made expressly for Jullien."

119 As in England, Jullien filled out his orchestral ranks with the best available local musicians, carefully chosen from the Philharmonic and other likely sources. In New York his total orchestra added up to just under 100 musicians; on tour about 60, according to *Dwight's* (October 29, 1853, p. 29). The Philharmonic luminaries in Jullien's orchestra included G. F. Bristow, U. C. Hill, Theodore Thomas, Thomas Goodwin, and Julius Siede, to name only a handful.

what could just as well have been told us in one—having withdrawn a rather middle-aged-looking portrait of *Madame* Anna Zerr to substitute a younger and prettier (but not too young and pretty) portrait of *Mademoiselle* Anna Zerr—having announced that the well-beloved Castle Garden of the New Yorkers could be formed into 'the most perfect *salle de concert* in the world,' and that he had built '*an entirely new orchestra* on the most approved acoustic principles'[120] for their especial delectation—having done all this, he sends us a vast and ponderous card of admission printed in scarlet and gold, in the folio form, upon brilliantly enameled board, and bound in crimson morocco, the meaning of all this being that if the New York public, ourselves included, would go to Castle Garden on last evening we would hear some very fine orchestral music. And this was humbug," contended White, "although Monsieur gave us all he promised us, and more."

But all this extravagant advance ballyhoo had been the merest foretaste of things to come: "If this were humbug before we got into 'the most perfect *salle de concert* in the world,'" wrote White, "what shall we say of the performance after we entered into that *seventh* musical heaven?[121] We mean the performances of Monsieur Jullien. Exactly in the middle of the vast orchestra[122] was a crimson platform edged with gold, and upon this was a music stand formed by a fantastic gilt figure supporting a desk, and behind the stand a carved armchair decorated in white and gold and tapestried with crimson velvet, a sort of throne for the musical monarch.

"He steps forward, and we see those ambrosial whiskers and moustaches which *Punch* has immortalized; we gaze upon that immaculate waistcoat, that transcendent shirt front, and that unutterable cravat, which will be 'read about' hereafter.[123] The monarch graciously and gracefully accepts the tumultuous homage of the assembled thousands, grasps his sceptre, and the violins wail forth the first broken phrase of the Overture to *Der Freischütz*."

But Jullien was more than a showman. "The overture is splendidly performed. The vast body of strings, the perfectly pure quality of tone, and the absolute execution of the wind band, the marvelous drilling of the entire body, and the conductor's unex-

[120] "In order to obviate the only defect of this concert room, viz., the repercussion of sound inseparable from all circular buildings, ornamental draperies have been so arranged as to entirely remove this objection; and while preventing all reverberation, will add materially to the splendor of the general *coup d'oeil*" (advertisement, *Tribune, et al.,* August 24, 1853).

[121] The audience was transported into a dream-world: "Wreaths of roses, and garlands, and vases, and baskets, and festoons of all the most brilliant flowers . . . and flags and banners are displayed from every 'coigne of vantage' [*sic*], entwining every column and giving to the greatly enlarged stage the appearance of a floral temple. The multitude of minstrels [orchestra musicians] stand in and out of trellised summer-houses, and discourse their delicious music from leafy bowers, and the great maestro sits in the midst of all this bravery, the monarch of all he surveys, with his potent ministers spell-led and spell-governed around him, and five or six thousand willing subjects standing mute and breathless before him. And now he rises from his red plush armchair and raises his magic wand high in air. A moment more and the secret is out. One can see now wherein consists the great genius of Jullien—whereon his imperishable fame is founded" (*Gemotice,* in the *Spirit of the Times,* September 10, 1853, p. 349).

[122] Jullien conducted surrounded by his players and presumably facing the audience.

[123] In *Dwight's,* for example: "Yes! There stands Jullien, in faultless coat—irreproachable shirt-bosom—immaculate wrist-bands—unexceptionable trowsers [*sic*], and glistening little boots" (John Ross Dix, *Dwight's,* November 5, 1863, p. 36).

ceptionable construction of the score make this hearing of *Der Freischütz* an event to be remembered."[124]

Jullien's baton possessed a hypnotic virtuosity of its own: "Other conductors use their batons to direct their orchestra. Not so with Monsieur Jullien. His orchestra is so well drilled at rehearsal that it conducts itself at performances.[125] He does everything with that unhappy bit of wood but put it to its legitimate purpose of beating time. It is continually in motion, but to judge from its position, whether it is moving in the first, the middle, or the last part of a measure would be a puzzling matter. Its use in Monsieur Jullien's hands is to seem to draw out the music from one instrument and another as if it were an enchanter's wand. Now Monsieur Jullien lets it float lazily over the heads of the violins as they bow off a graceful *legato,* now he brings it chickering down through the air as he stretches himself and it toward a flute which is executing a descending *staccato;* and it chickers up again as the oboe responds in an ascending reply. Suddenly he wheels bolt around with his back to the audience and brings it down with vigorous blows and ponderous manner over trumpets, horns, trombones, and ophicleides, and the very Castle rocks with the tremendous peal which it seems to startle from their brazen throats. An undulating murmur runs through the string band; it follows, or is followed by, the inevitable baton which is swept slowly round the orchestra with an ineffable and weary grace. The movement quickens and the baton accelerates its inspiring pulsations. It seems to lift the performers with it as it is jerked convulsively into the air above their heads.

"To the uninitiated, that baton seems to compel them to come one by one into the crush and conflict of sound; its vivid energy becomes terrific as the climax approaches, and as it culminates in a crash which sounds like the wreck of matter and the crush of worlds made musical, Monsieur Jullien is seen standing with both hands raised in phrenzy [*sic*] as if he expected to be borne aloft by the explosion—the baton gleaming above his head.

"The last idea to be allowed to enter the minds of the auditors is that the composer or the musicians have any agency in producing these fine effects. It must be Monsieur Jullien who not only rides the whirlwind and controls the storm, but who furnishes the tempest, the thunder, and the lightning."

[124]The remainder of the program consisted of Jullien's quadrille on Lindpaintner's song "The Standard Bearer"; the Allegro and "Storm Movement" from Beethoven's "Pastoral" Symphony (presumably complete with hailstones); Mozart's "Queen of the Night" aria, sung by Anna Zerr; Jullien's waltz *La prima donna,* played by the orchestra; a Fantasy on themes from *La sonnambula,* magnificently played by Bottesini; Jullien's "English Quadrille"; then—following the intermission—a Jullien arrangement of themes from *Les Huguenots;* his polka *Les Échos de Mont Blanc,* astonishingly played on the cornet by Koenig; the Scherzo from Mendelssohn's "Scotch" Symphony; Charles Haas's Alpine medley "Forget Me Not," sung by Zerr; an unidentified flute solo, gloriously played by Reichert; and for finale, another of Jullien's National Quadrilles, "The Irish."

[125]"The first rehearsal at Castle Garden established a perfect understanding between the conductor and his orchestra," wrote Henry C. Watson, who was privileged to be present. Jullien "wished perfection; they were willing to work up to that point; and the consequence was a community of feeling such as we have rarely known in orchestral bodies in this city. . . . The Scherzo from the 'Pastoral' Symphony was tried back a dozen or fifteen times until the fiddles went together as one instrument and the wind instruments breathed in the place of blasting" (*Musical Review and Choral Advocate,* December 1853, p. 182).

Between numbers, too, Jullien commanded total attention: "The music is magnificent and so is the humbug, as Monsieur Jullien caps its climax by subsiding into his crimson gilded throne, overwhelmed by his exertions, a used-up man."

The discipline of the orchestra, wrote White, was "marvelous." Nothing like it had ever been heard before. Jullien "obtains from fifty strings a *pianissimo* which is scarcely audible, and he makes one hundred instruments stop in the midst of a *fortissimo* which seems to lift the roof, as if a hundred men dropped dead at the movement of his hand."[126]

"Orchestral effects finer than those produced by Monsieur Jullien's colossal band could hardly be, and we do not wonder at the enthusiasm which they awakened in the enormous audience which listened to them."[127]

And his musicians! "He gave us Koenig, whose cornet utters a tone so pure, so vocal, so human, and whose execution leaves praise without words to utter itself; Bottesini, the Paganini of the *contra basso* . . . and Anna Zerr, with a voice which seems to start in its ascent where other voices stop, and an execution which puts to shame instrumental precision."

All this having been said, why then, asked White, did he call Jullien a humbug? Defining his use of the term, White wrote: "Humbug does not necessarily imply a cheat on one side and a dupe on the other. It is the art of drawing attention and attaining success by a bold but delicate adaptation of one's course to the taste, whim, and prejudice of an individual or community, which generally results in allowing people to deceive themselves. Thousands thought they were delighted last evening with Jullien's music; and so very many of them were. But if Jullien would dress in a Quaker coat, stand at a conductor's desk of pine wood, and make no use of his baton except to *direct* his performers," that is to say, eliminate the humbug, "he might play to empty benches."

Be that as it may, the Castle Garden benches (and standing and walking spaces) were thenceforward far from empty, and only words of incredulous wonder were uttered by the overwhelmed critics (except perhaps words condemning Richard Grant White for calling Jullien a humbug). White, for his part, insisted that humbug, as wielded by Jullien to promote great art, was "not only justifiable, but laudable; it takes its place among the cardinal virtues; its successful practicer deserves canonization, and St. Cecilia may justly look for a rival in St. Jullien" (*Courier and Enquirer,* August 31, 1853).

To meet the voracious programing demands of nightly concert-giving,[128] Jullien—for all his famous repertory of 1200 compositions accrued in the course of some

[126] "A *forte* in Jullien's orchestra," wrote Watson, "is not a loud noise made by a vast rude power, in which the strongest lungs stand out most prominently, but it is a vast body of sound harmoniously and beautifully blended, and rich from perfect unity. To Jullien is due the distinguished honor of having been the first [in America] to achieve a perfect *pianissimo*" *(ibid.).*

[127] The vast range of dynamics and the perfect precision of Jullien's orchestra were a source of universal astonishment among the musical cognoscenti, John Sullivan Dwight included. Like his colleagues, Dwight excitedly acclaimed it the greatest orchestra in the world.

[128] On Sundays, Jullien presented "sacred and miscellaneous" concerts—the vocal or choral sacred works being performed in arrangements for orchestra.

3000 purported concert performances—primarily adhered to a basic revolving repertory, frequently repeating his most successful pieces, both symphonic and popular, and artfully, but systematically, introducing new works (and new soloists) in various combinations to keep the box office continuously stimulated. Although the *Daily Times* critic Seymour, after the first week of Jullien's concerts complained of "too many repetitions," they nonetheless allowed audiences to hear frequent replays of their favorite overtures, symphonies and popular pieces, an unprecedented luxury in those dark days before the advent of sound recording.

Nothing, however, rivaled the staggering number of replays given the "American Quadrille," by far Jullien's greatest triumph in America. Introduced on September 5 at his seventh concert, the work aroused so overwhelming a demand that by late December it had received 88 consecutive performances,[129] with an 89th played "by particular desire," at Jullien's "American Night," given near the end of his third concert series in New York.

Each of the work's five sections was based on an American "national" tune, the first two, according to *Gemotice,* being "Hail Columbia" and "The Star-Spangled Banner,"[130] then "The Old Folks at Home" (regarded by some as a questionable choice because of its low "Ethiopian" associations, but all the same magnificent, as played by Koenig on the cornopean), then "Hail to the Chief," and, for its overwhelming finale, "Yankee Doodle."

With a "running succession of solos on the flageolet, flute, oboe, ophicleide, bassoon, trumpets, and trombones, [played] by Collinet, Reichert, Lavigne, Hughes, Hardy, Duhem, and Winterbottom," wrote *Gemotice* in the *Spirit of the Times* (September 17, 1853, p. 372), "the great feature, which brings into play all the instrumental forces of Jullien's amplitude of orchestra is 'Yankee Doodle,' so arranged as to afford a perfect flood of solos, duets, trios, and quartettes, rapidly following each other in bewildering succession, the intertwining and commingling of the various tunes rendering the effect most miraculous; the whole concluding with a grand march and battle piece, in which, amid the roar of artillery, the rattling of musketry, the tramp of horse and foot, the shrill clarion's cry, the call and recall of bodies of troops, and the booming of heavy ordinance, the theme is still preserved and at times soars above the musical din; and when the actual *finale* arrives, the huzzas of the orchestra work in most admirably in consonance with the music and are caught up by the audience, while cheer on cheer awakes the echoes of the Castle. Of course, this grand piece of work comes off nightly, and the *finale* is always warmly and successfully encored."

The excitement over the "American Quadrille" was not confined to the musically uninformed. C. M. Cady, the somewhat austere, if not downright stuffy, editor of the *Musical Review and Choral Advocate,* wrote (October 1853, p. 154) that after "working up 'Yankee Doodle' in all sorts of variations, [the work] closes with a grand battle

[129] The number obviously includes performances in Boston and Philadelphia, where Jullien appeared in late October and throughout November before returning to New York for the month of December.

[130] In the piano arrangement of the "American Quadrille," published in 1853 by S. C. Jollie, the five parts comprise "Our Flag is There," "The Old Folks at Home," "Land of Washington," "Hail to the Chief," and "Yankee Doodle."

Jullien's Concerts.

FIRST NIGHT OF THE GRAND ILLUSTRATED PROGRAMME.

QUADRILLE NAPOLITAIN.
Pianissimo ! *!* *!*—JULLIEN

SOLO, CORNET-A-PISTON.
L'Adieu Maritime.—HERR KONIG

SOLO, CONTRA-BASSO.
On Themes from La Sonnambula.—SIGNOR BOTTESINI.

SOLO, CONTRA-BASSO (*Encore*).
Carnival de Venise.—SIGNOR BOTTESINI.

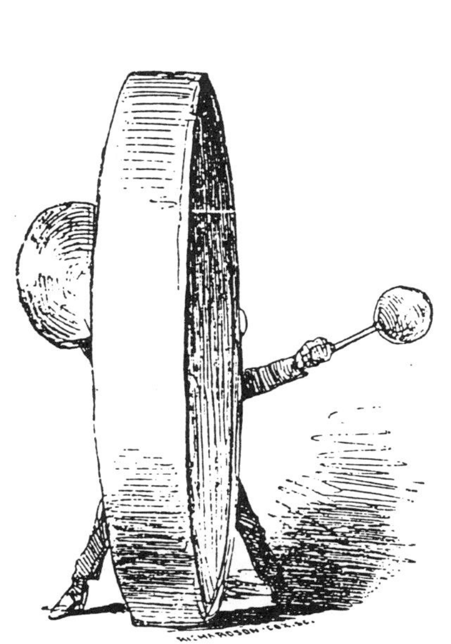

GALOPPE, AMAZON AND TIGER.
Descriptive of Hunting in South Africa.

THE GREAT EXHIBITION.
God Save the Queen!!

FINALE.

New-York Historical Society

scene, in which you hear the tramp of the soldiery, the blast of the war clarion, the booming of distant guns, and the rattling of the musketry. Snatches of 'Yankee Doodle' are heard in different sections of the American Army as the combat thickens, till, in the height of the fray, all the forces take it up in double-quick time, and rush on to a desperate encounter. Jullien, with arms tossed aloft, urges them on to the utmost in their power, till, amid the shouts of the victors and a grand orchestral crash, the day is won by American valor and 'Yankee Doodle.'

"A scene of the wildest enthusiasm follows. The ladies in the audience wave their handkerchiefs and the gentlemen swing their hats and shout and stamp till it is repeated. We were ourselves just as much excited, the last time we heard it, as the first. It will never wear out!"

And, miracle of miracles, even the supreme musical pontiff John Sullivan Dwight succumbed to the Jullien sorcery, citing such "happy touches" as his "simply isolating the first note of the strain all the time by a strong accent [making] almost a new thing of the 'Yankee Doodle'; then the manner in which it is first boyishly whistled in the flageolet and the flute, then grotesquely tooted on the bassoon, then droned out, bagpipe-like, by two oboes, etc.; and finally, and chiefly, to the crescendo progress in the entire arrangement, 'Yankee Doodle' at last coming in fortissimo by all the instruments, in swifter and swifter *tempo,* and then the battle and drum cannonading, and 'Yankee Doodle' stronger still in sign of triumph, and the shout of voices, too, thrown in; the inevitable uproarious applause of the many; the pre-concerted rising of the musicians, as Jullien turns with air of solemn invitation to the audience, who involuntarily rise also, as 'Hail Columbia' peals forth in large chords!"[131] (*Dwight's,* October 29, 1853, pp. 29–30.)

Charles Bailey Seymour unequivocally declared: "Every man, woman, and child should hear the 'American Quadrille' if they wish to appreciate the national airs of their country." And Richard Grant White emotionally maintained that in giving us the "American Quadrille" as a "national keepsake," Jullien had "persuaded us to respect our national airs, and at the same time respect ourselves, as citizens of the country which owns them. How can we repay Jullien all we owe him?" (*Daily Times,* September 6; *Courier and Enquirer,* September 22, 1853.)

Most indebted to Jullien were the performance-starved American composers William Henry Fry and George Frederick Bristow, whose orchestral works Jullien had welcomed with open arms, adopting them into his repertory and performing them repeatedly in New York and on tour. He presented the first of these, Fry's one-movement work *A* (formerly *The*) *Day in the Country,* now designated a "Grand Descriptive Symphony," at Castle Garden on September 20. Although previously performed—at Fry's first lecture on November 30, 1852, and again at the eleventh (and last) on February 8, 1853, when it received at least one fairly exhaustive critique (see

[131] A victory for the *Herald,* which on September 14 had chided Jullien's audiences for "failing to rise for 'Hail Columbia.' . . . When the national airs of England or France are played, the public of those countries evince their respect by standing. . . . Why should we grudge a similar mark of honor to our national air?" In fact, the United States did not acquire its official national anthem until 1931.

New-York Historical Society

The American Quadrille at full blast.

following OBBLIGATO)—it was advertised as a "new work" and was generally accepted as such by a conveniently forgetful press, who lauded it anew.

R. Storrs Willis, resolutely objective despite having in the meantime crossed swords with Fry, conscientiously examined the work in the *Musical World and Times* (October 1, 1853, p. 34). It was a three-movement piece consolidated into one, he wrote, consisting of an *Andante amoroso* ("The Disappointed Swain"); an *Allegro* ("Village Music and Village Dance"); and a *Finale stretto* ("A Recruiting Party, Boisterous Mirth, Revelry").[132] "This symphony is novel in form as regards the disposition of the movements. Symphonies have usually four distinct and musically disconnected movements, so that each one of them can be given as a separate piece, which is often done. This symphony, however, is so composed that the different movements are all connected, making an unbroken musical discourse.[133]

"We think," wrote Willis, "that Fry, who possesses more remarkable versatility of talent than any one other man that we know—in a political article, a chapter on national abuses, or an essay on Art equally brilliant, striking, and original—combines also all the elements of a composer lacking only a chance to *hear his own works* and to profit by that hearing.[134] Here is a striking instance [echoing Fry's words] where a National School of Art is needed; an arena where a man of genius like Fry may try his powers and hear himself talk, musically, in order to see whether he talk correctly and effectively. Fry, without an occasional orchestra at his command, is like a gifted, but unpracticed, orator without an audience. Musical composition is not only a matter of genius, but of practice as well."

The *Albion* (September 24, 1853, p. 464), whose progressive critic (Burkhardt) did recall the earlier performances of *A Day in the Country,* declared that apart from its "merits or demerits as a composition, we look upon it in an aesthetic point of view as a cheering sign, indicative of progress in the right direction, of an attempt to throw off the shackles of time-honored conservatism and scientific legitimacy which have sat brooding, like ill-omened birds, over every attempt to develop, by the extended resources of art, the new ideas of the age." Here was further fuel for the smoldering conflagration—Fry (later Fry/Bristow) versus Willis/Dwight—that would erupt in full force after Jullien introduced Fry's "Santa Claus" Symphony in December.

But first: on September 23, George Templeton Strong, who until now had remained aloof from the Jullien madness, at last succumbed. Upon the announcement that Jullien would depart after his month at Castle Garden, Strong attended his penultimate concert there. "Much clap-trap," he informed his journal the following

[132] More elaborately, according to Fry's program note: "The Symphony opens with an Adagio Movement descriptive of a summer morning, hymn of nature, the rising sun, 'the cocks' shrill clarion and the echoing horn.' The next is an Allegro, musically painting the festivities of the villagers, the lads and lasses in their best array are about to join the dance. An Andante Amoroso describes the jealous pangs of a disappointed swain. Then comes the rustic dance, the rude and grotesque steps of the peasants to the music of Oboes and Guitars, pictured in an Allegro. The sun is setting as a recruiting party arrive; the soldiers join the dance, and more rude and boisterous becomes the mirth as the Symphony concludes with a grand Finale Stretto."

[133] Dwight, the arch-conservative, took a dubious view of Fry's radical departure from the established "so-called symphonic or sonata form" (*Dwight's,* November 5, 1853, p. 38).

[134] Even to Dwight, reviewing its first performance in Boston, *A Day in the Country* "seemed very clearly and skillfully instrumented"; but, of course, it did not "translate the sense of summer and the fields into unmistakable music," as did Beethoven's "Pastorale" *(ibid.)*

day, "perfect of its kind, and some real music, most effectively played. Especially his Overture to *Fidelio* and the Scherzo [Allegretto] of Beethoven's F-Symphony" (the Eighth).[135] Realizing what he had been missing, upon the last-minute announcement that Jullien would give a month-long second series of concerts at Metropolitan Hall,[136] Strong was there again within the week for the "Beethoven Night."

September 30 . . . . Last night at Jullien's. Tripler [Metropolitan] Hall. Overture to *Leonora* [No. 1][137] long, labored, peculiar, and not clear on a first hearing; Scherzo from F-Symphony, most lovely and Haydenish; the C-minor Symphony played through with some mutilation of the third and fourth movements. Lights and shadows come out grandly in so massive an orchestra. That noblest of compositions was never so played in this city before. Ellie was cured of a cold by it.[138]

October 13. To Jullien's with Ellie [Mendelssohn Night]. . . . Mendelssohn's ["Scotch"] Symphony in A,[139] the *Midsummer Night's Dream* music, and the usual amount of "Yankee Doodle" and other clap-trap.[140] The [*Midsummer Night's Dream*] Overture was better played than I've ever heard it before. The Symphony also well done, but parts of it were heavy, perhaps because I'm not familiar with it. Finest things in it the Scherzo and a wild, martial finale. The *Hochzeitsmarsch* [*Midsummer Night's Dream*] was rather over-peppered with cymbals, and so on.

. . . Mendelssohn's conception of the musical accompaniment to that exquisite,

[135] If Strong stayed through the concert, he heard, as well, orchestral excerpts from Jullien's opera *Pietro il grande,* unsuccessful in London in 1852; his waltz *La prima donna;* the "Queen of the Night" aria, sung by Anna Zerr; *Trab, Trab,* a song by Kücken, performed by Henriette Behrend; Lindpaintner's song "The Standard Bearer," played on the giant ophicleide by S. Hughes; an Air with Brilliant Variations for flute, played by Reichert; a Tarantella, composed and played by Bottesini; and by the orchestra, "The Atlantic Galop," the "Irish Quadrille," and the inevitable "American Quadrille" (its 17th performance).

[136] "Our readers ought to know," over-optimistically wrote Richard Grant White, "that the means of egress from [Metropolitan] Hall have been increased fourfold, a measure very necessary and one which we have again and again demanded on the part of the public. Each floor has now two vomitories, through which the Hall, if filled, as it is nightly sure to be during Mr. Jullien's stay, can be emptied in three minutes. We are glad to be able to assure our readers that at last they may enjoy music in this beautiful room with perfect safety" (*Courier and Enquirer,* September 17, 1853). (Metropolitan Hall would burn down in 1854.)

[137] Advertised as the one with "the distant Solo on the trumpet played by M. Duhem."

[138] Additionally, in the Beethoven half of the program Henriette Behrend sang *Kennst du das Land* and the orchestra played a gaudy set of five variations on the waltz dubbed *Le Désir* (Schubert's *Trauerwalzer,* op. 9). At first attributed to Beethoven, it was now credited to a work called *Homage to Beethoven* by Roch Albert, a pseudonym for Jullien, compounded from two of his thirty-six names. The "clap-trap" after the intermission consisted of Anna Zerr's performance of the Proch Variations, a violin duo faultlessly played by the Mollenhauers, a flute solo by Reichert, Jullien's popular waltz *La prima donna,* the Tarantelle from his ballet *Belphegor* (also credited to Roch Albert), and, of course, the "American Quadrille" (22nd time).

[139] A work whose Scotchness was largely plagiarized from Boieldieu's opera *The White Lady,* claimed W. H. Fry (*Tribune,* October 14, 1853).

[140] The Mendelssohn half of the program comprised, in addition, the song *Das erste Veilchen* and the air "Hear ye, Israel," from *Elijah,* sung by Anna Zerr (both of which, wrote Fry, "fell quite dead on the audience for want of salient melody"), and the "well-constructed" Violin Concerto, "exquisitely" played by Henry Weist Hill. The second part of the program consisted of Jullien's "The Katydid Polka" (a fond reminiscence of Castle Garden and a huge hit); "The Exhibition Galop" by Comettant; solos performed by Koenig and Lavigne; and the "American Quadrille" (34th time).

KATYDID POLKA,

OR

SOUVENIRS OF CASTLE GARDENS

BY

JULLIEN.

PRICE
SOLO 3/

fanciful, half-lyric drama is perfectly true, though I used to think not. I missed in it, at first, the deep feeling there is in, for example, the fairy part of the *Oberon* Overture. But that would be out of place in an illustration of Shakespeare's fairy world. Nothing can be truer than the feeling of that overture.

Instead of symphonies, etc., designated as in [the key of] A or B, I would have such compositions written more frequently on particular and well-known works and entitled accordingly, such as *The Tempest, Macbeth, Romeo and Juliet, Tristram, Undine,* Schiller's *Wallenstein* and *The Robbers,* and so on. For each I can conceive most characteristic music. Opera has interfered with the adoption of that obvious plan, and so, as in other and weightier matters, done harm to musical art.[141]

October 22. . . . went to Jullien's [Mozart Night] Thursday night [October 20]. Heard the "Jupiter" Symphony and an admirable arrangement from *Don Giovanni* which did fuller justice to parts of the opera (for example, the finale of the first act) and expressed Mozart's ideas more clearly than any performance on the stage within my experience.[142]

~

But, as Henry C. Watson tellingly observed in the *Musical Review and Choral Advocate* (December, p. 182), it was not upon the "few" who, like Strong, crowded Metropolitan Hall on Jullien's classical nights that the wizard worked his greatest sorcery, but upon the many, "whom Jullien has enticed into his magic circle until he has charmed into them a musical soul."

Jullien completed his second series on October 21 with his forty-ninth concert in New York in less than two months, then departed for Boston and Philadelphia (with a stopover between cities on November 8 for a quick single concert in New York, attended by a wildly enthusiastic audience of more than 3000). He would return to Metropolitan Hall in early December, remaining there until the New Year, a period during which Strong, distraught over his mother's mortal illness, attended no concerts.

Having in the meantime given numerous performances of *A Day in the Country,* on October 12 Jullien presented the Minuet movement of Bristow's "new" Symphony in E-flat, op. 10 (the symphony spurned by the Philharmonic in 1850). Like Fry's piece, it was billed as a first performance, although Benedict had performed a movement of it in 1851, and its last movement had been played under Bristow's direction at Fry's explosive eleventh lecture, on February 8, 1853 (see following OBBLIGATO).

Making common cause with Bristow, Fry, the perpetually angry young man, pounced on this opportunity to needle the Philharmonic: "We trust to be able to hear the whole of [Bristow's] work," he unseemly wrote, having himself presented only its

[141] It should be remembered that in those days, committed as they were to programmatic music, the distinguished critic A. D. Paterson had bemoaned the lack of a plot for Beethoven's Ninth Symphony, and had obligingly supplied one.♪

[142] Dwight disagreed. True, in "the sublime and freezing harmonies of the ghost scene . . . those ponderous marble tones of Hughes's ophicleide spoke grandly for the statue." But rather than following the opera sequentially, Jullien's arrangement jumped about, its various unrelated sections being joined together by "Donizetti-ish transitions"—in Dwight's estimation a form of blasphemy (*Dwight's,* November 5, 1853, p. 38).

last movement. It was "quite as well written as the last German Symphonies played by the Philharmonic Society and should be fitly performed by the members of that Association, as their main object should be to encourage Art on the spot." Then, lashing out at the public: "When an Artist has qualified himself to write a Symphony, he has a right to be heard, and the public should insist on hearing him, instead of, like low provincials, taking works exclusively at second hand. Shocking and disgraceful is the want of pride in such subjects in this city. Is not New York as large as Vienna and larger? Then why defer to any German town?" (*Tribune,* October 14, 1853.)

Upon resuming his New York concerts at Metropolitan Hall on December 5,[143] for the remainder of the month Jullien repeatedly performed the Fry and Bristow works already heard, and on December 10 he presented the Adagio from Fry's "dramatic symphony" *The Breaking Heart,* a work that he (Jullien) had frequently performed on tour, together with *A Day in the Country.* Despite its "sentimental name and program," Dwight, who heard it in Boston, thought *The Breaking Heart* the superior of the two works: "It seemed to have more to say, and said it in a manner that commanded consideration, with more unity of development and some fine management of accompaniment" (*Dwight's,* November 5, 1853, p. 38).

Appropriately, on December 24, Jullien introduced Fry's new Christmas Symphony, "Santa Claus," as part of an otherwise incongruous "Irish Night," chiefly featuring works redolent of Ireland by William Vincent Wallace and others.[144] Fry's Christmas piece, especially written for Jullien's orchestra and ostensibly inspired by, if not directly modeled after, Jullien's compositions, was designed to exploit the special abilities of his marvelous soloists; too, like Jullien's programmatic pieces, it contained a variety of evocative sound effects.[145] Its tortuously detailed scenario appeared not only in Jullien's concert book and advertisements, but, in various versions, in the *Tribune,* where, in unseemly self-promotion, it was even tucked into Fry's review of Jullien's later *Messiah* performance.[146]

According to the advertisements, the "Santa Claus" Symphony consisted (in one massive movement) of an "Introduction, Slow Movement, Christmas Merrymakings, Juvenile Dances and Songs, Separation of the Merrymakers as midnight approaches, Prayers of the Children, Lullaby, Stillness (all being hushed in slumber), A Snow Storm and Episode of a Perishing Traveler, The Church Bell tolls midnight, Santa Claus

[143]Jullien inaugurated this apparently less-than-sold-out new series (see the *Musical Review and Choral Advocate,* January 5, 1854, p. 12), with a benefit concert for the St. George's and British Protective Emigrant Societies. On December 17 he donated a concert to the Widows and Orphans Fund of the New York Fire Department, and on December 26 he conducted the Harmonic Society in a grandiose performance of Handel's *Messiah;* the announced soloists—an odd mix—were Anna Zerr, Maria Scoville Brainerd, Rosina Pico-Vietti, a Miss A. Honeywell, Cesare Badiali, and Marcus Colburn. According to Dwight's New York Diarist (Thayer), Fry had supplied Italian words for Badiali's solos and recitatives (*Dwight's,* December 31, 1853, p. 100).

[144]In addition to the Overture to Wallace's *Maritana,* the first part of the program included Jullien's "Irish" and "Hibernian" quadrilles; Anna Zerr sang "The Last Rose of Summer"; and Koenig played Wallace's Recitative and Variations for cornet. The remainder of the program comprised, in addition to Fry's "Santa Claus" Symphony, Bottesini's prodigious variations on themes from *William Tell;* the *Ah! non giunge,* sung by Zerr; a new duet by the Mollenhauers; and the "Échos de Mont Blanc Polka," the "Atlantic Galop," and the "Great Exhibition Quadrille," by Jullien.

[145]A whip, sleighbells, and toy instruments—trumpets, whistles, drums, rattles, and so forth.

[146]It appears, as well, in Upton (*Fry,* Appendix III, p. 335).

comes in his sleigh and distributes Christmas Gifts, Visions of happy sleep, Angels chaunting the glad tidings, Sunrise, Joy of Children on discovering their toys, Christmas Hymn, *Adeste fidelis*—'Hither, ye Faithful'—and Grand Finale—Hallelujah Chorus!"

The critics agreed that Fry's "Santa Claus" was a most entertaining Christmas piece, but too flimsy in substance to justify the half-hour it consumed.[147] Subjecting the work to careful, apparently unbiased, scrutiny, Burkhardt wrote in the *Albion* (December 31, 1853, p. 632): "It is a capital musical Christmas piece, written expressly for M. Jullien's orchestra and for the present occasion. We presume that the composer claims for it no higher rank than that of a *pièce d'occasion,* and as such it is exceedingly clever, rising occasionally above the standard of a mere time-serving production.[148] Its principal fault is its great length. Many effective points are spoiled by 'too much cherishing' on the part of Mr. Fry. This is the case with the Lullaby, which is well enough of itself, but is clung to with a pertinacity that makes the auditor wearied of it. The same remark may apply to the night-scene, with the snow storm and the gliding of string-semitones. The effect[s] produced by the violins, *con sordini,* and throughout the snow-storm scene are excellent, though perhaps not quite legitimate . . . with all due deference, we deny their entire originality. We do not for a moment wish to insinuate that the composer is willfully guilty of the slightest plagiarism, but several of M. Jullien's recent performances must have made a peculiarly strong impression on his mind.

"The introductory slow movement is, we opine, the best portion of the Symphony, as far as good writing and scoring are concerned. This movement, the Scotch dance movement, and the *Adeste fidelis,* when it is taken up by the whole orchestra, are the points which pleased us the most, and which we consider the most meritorious in the composition.

"But we regret to have to state that there is not enough material in the Symphony to occupy the space of half an hour in its performance. Its style and formation are not of the high school of art. They are of a modern Italian or French pattern, devoid of the severe, but effective, simplicity of Mozart or Beethoven. The solo, duo, or trio parts for instruments appear like Donizetti-ish vocal parts, and hence, we suppose the critic of the *Tribune* [Fry] speaks of the Symphony as 'requiring Paganinis for the violins, Bottesinis for the double bass, Wuilles for the clarionet, Lavignes for the hautboy, and Reicherts for the flute' [a reference to Fry's wordy program note for the work, reportedly requested by Jullien and reprinted in the *Tribune* on December 29]. "But is a work like this to live?" asked the critic. "Are Paganinis, Bottesinis, Wuilles, and Lavignes to be found in every orchestra? . . . What is to become of this Symphony when there is no Wuille with his saxophone, no Koenig with his cornet, no Bottesini with his wondrous double bass? The *Tribune* critic himself seems to imply that an effective performance, under such circumstances, would seem impossible."[149]

[147] Defensively, Fry retorted that, far from being too long, an encore of the entire work had been demanded by the enthralled audience and obligingly granted by Jullien (*Tribune,* December 27, 1853).

[148] "It is a most ingenious, original, effective, entertaining production," wrote Dwight, or an assistant (January 14, 1854, p. 118), after its first performance in Boston. "Marvelous effects of instrumentation are produced, and the imitative and description parts of it are often very admirable."

[149] Howard Shanet, conducting the Columbia University Orchestra, revived the work—or a version of it—on December 6, 1958.

Burkhardt conceded that these "crude remarks" were perhaps unfair after only one hearing of the work. Besides, the production "demands our attention for more reasons than one. It is American; it is home-made and therefore entitled to fair hearing and to lenient judgment . . . and although it cannot be called a first-class work, yet its merits are great enough to command our respect and attention."

The critic's patience was, however, exhausted by Fry's excruciatingly verbose program note: "A long, printed Synopsis of Mr. Fry's Symphony has been furnished the audiences, detailing not only the plot, but all the minutiae of the work." True, such wordy scenarios had recently become fashionable, their principal exponent being Jullien, whose bills and advertisements carried a full and elaborate description of each work performed. "This practice may do for puffing purposes," wrote Burkhardt, "but we hold it as derogatory to the cause of art. It seems like an inscription underneath a painting informing the beholder 'this is a horse.' If a Symphony be a music-picture, pray let the listener's intelligence furnish him with the description. If he cannot discern it, the picture is defective."[150]

But Fry furiously rejected any suggestion, however well meant, that his "Santa Claus" Symphony (or anything he composed) might be anything less than a towering masterpiece of sublime art. In a "third-person" defense of the work, appearing in the *Tribune* on January 2, 1854 (reprinted in *Dwight's* on January 7, 1854, p. 108), Fry passionately protested: "We have seen it stated that the composer of 'Santa Claus' intended it for an occasional piece—a sketch, etc. This is not so. He intended it—in regard to instrumentation—as the means of exposing the highest qualities in execution and expression of the greatest players in the world. As to spirit, he designed it, in the introductory movement, to represent the declamatory style in which he conceives oratorios ought to be written. Next, the verisimilitude which should mark music adapted to festivities from its rollicking traits and abandon. Then he designed to show all the sexual [*sic*] peculiarities of the orchestra *dramatically* treated. Likewise the accents of English speech as related to music. He wished also to prove, as he believes, that the *Lullaby,* poetically handled, is as sublime as the *Madonna and Child* if looked at artistically, and connected with it may be four separate counterpoints, all distinct and all painting different ideas and facts.

"Next, he wished to connect the music of nature with the tragedy of human life—the latter played by Monsieur Bottesini, an artist who exhausts wonder and dumb-founders [*sic*] praise; and the composer essayed, too, to paint the sublimest music in the world—that of the deity singing the monody of the passing world in the winter's wind. Next, he wished to individualize in music our only remaining fairy—the character being grotesque, yet withal gentle and melodious, and with the sweetest mission that ever fairy performed. Next, he desired to paint the songs of the stars—the fluttering ecstasies of hovering angels—on the purest harmonies of the violins, only to be achieved by artists who have given a life of labor and love and lyrical devotion to extract the transcendental element in their instruments. Next, he designed to paint the change from starlight to sunlight by poetical analogies and mathematical facts. Then he sought to imitate the mother's cry to her little ones by rousing them on Christmas

[150] As we know, the almost identical words had been uttered by *Hafiz* in his review of Spohr's *Die Weihe der Töne* in *Dwight's* (May 1, 1852, pp. 28–29).

morning, and by the playing [of] Bo-peep, which as a little love story, admits of dramatic harmonies.

"The introduction of toys into the orchestra at this point may be considered by the thoughtless as a burlesque, but not so did the composer consider it. The divine words, 'Suffer little children to come unto me, for of such is the kingdom of Heaven,' make the artistic painting of children and their toys as much a mission of art as the writing of a hallelujah chorus. The finale, too, of this symphony, where an orchestra of drums is introduced to represent the rolling of the spheres, is among the composer's ideas of the necessity of towering sonority to crown a long work designed to be of a religious and romantic character."

Jullien repeated the "Santa Claus" Symphony not only on December 27, but at a "Grand American Night,"[151] on December 29, when he also performed two works by Bristow: the first movement, Allegro moderato, of Bristow's newly composed Symphony in D minor, op. 24 (the "Jullien" Symphony, played by the Philharmonic in 1856), and the by-now familiar Minuet from his Symphony in E-flat—and two by Fry: *A Day in the Country* and the Adagio from *The Breaking Heart.* The American section of the program was topped off with the inevitable "American Quadrille."[152]

Bristow's symphony, approvingly wrote Willis in the *Musical World and Times* (January 7, 1854, pp. 5–6), was a "good specimen of [his] musical abilities. . . . He writes easily, his thought is clear, translating itself in round forms and phrases, and moving always at an expeditious pace. The main idea, at first entrusted to the violoncelli, is well conceived and skillfully developed, and the connecting episodes come in naturally and are well adapted to the subject." The work, composed for the occasion, exhibited a notable "modification in the style of the author"—a distinct advance over the Menuetto of his first symphony. "A clever thing is this composition," wrote Willis, "reflecting much credit upon Mr. Bristow."

Fry, too, was generously praised. Because Willis had given a "detailed analysis" of *A Day in the Country* after hearing it at Castle Garden in September, he noted only that its orchestration had since been revised, or rather recast, "to adapt it [*à la* Jullien] to the style in vogue at Metropolitan Hall."[153] Apparently forgetting, or unaware, that along with *A Day in the Country, The Breaking Heart* had been performed in 1852 at Fry's first lecture, Willis mistook it to be of later composition, and thus "an unquestionable improvement upon the *Day in the Country,* even after the changes introduced into the latter by the author. The parts move more freely; the melodies are of a broader style, and the various departments of the orchestra are more dexterously called into

[151] For the final events of his New York season, Jullien presented, in addition to his Irish Night, a Shakespearean Night, at which he played Matthew Locke's *Macbeth* music, Mendelssohn's *Midsummer Night's Dream,* and Berlioz's Overture to *King Lear;*[a] and now an American Night. What next?

[152] The remainder of the program consisted of an aria from *La sonnambula,* sung by Anna Zerr, a cello solo by Lütgen, a clarinet solo by Wuille, and the Jullien favorites: "The Katydid Polka," "The Eclipse Polka," "The Paul and Virginie Waltz," and the superspectacular "Great Exhibition Quadrille."

[153] A statement, or rather, misstatement, that invoked thunderbolts of angry rebuttal from Fry (see his letter to Willis, *Musical World and Times,* January 21, 1854, pp. 29–31, 34; also see OBBLIGATO: 1854).

use."[154] Waxing enthusiastic, Willis wrote: "We like much this symphony. There is warm feeling in it, and the theme expresses emotions which music is perhaps better able to express than poetry. Mr. Fry has produced in it a veritable elegy. We will not enquire [gently unsheathing his dagger] whether in this, as in the other works of our brilliant friend, there be unity, musically speaking. He rejects such unity as something antiquated and worn out, quite opposed to the expression of an idea."[155]

Then the lethal thrust: "Mr. Fry's 'Santa Claus' we consider a good Christmas piece, but hardly a composition to be gravely criticized like an earnest work of Art. It is a kind of *extravaganza* which moves the audience to laughter, entertaining them seasonably with imitated snow storms, trotting horses, sleigh bells, cracking whips, etc. Moreover, in the production of these things there is no little ingenuity displayed. The discordant winds are most discordantly well given; and among the graver features of the piece, our Lord's Prayer (as given in musical recitative) is marked and impressive." Mortally injured, Fry responded savagely, and thus began the musical battle of the century.

At Jullien's purportedly final New York concert on December 31 (he would, in fact, squeeze in two more, on January 2 and 3), he repeated the "Santa Claus" Symphony and the movement of Bristow's new symphony.[156] Then to Boston for two weeks of concerts; he was due back in New York on January 18 to give the *bal paré,* or "Grand Full Dress Ball," with which it was his famous custom to close a major concert series.

During this period Strong, grief-stricken over his mother's hopeless illness, became morbidly obsessed with Beethoven's Seventh Symphony, ascribing to it strange powers as a harbinger of evil.

November 16. . . . The music of that Seventh Symphony (the A-major) has been running in my head for a fortnight, carefully kept out of my thoughts for four years as uncanny and perilous. That looks absurd, I daresay, but few facts are more real to me than the deadliness of that composition. I've scrupulously tried to forget it since the time of Ellen's illness, then it kept ringing in my ears. Always, when I've thought of it, sorrow and sickness of heart—a dread of coming evil—have been with me and have grown darker under its shadow.[157] It cannot be a mere vagary of my own; that unwholesome, unearthly mark is stamped on it from opening to finale. It depicts despair, and its atmosphere is darkness—the vivid memory and realization of its melodies an omen of ill. It is not more keen, intense and overpowering than the C-minor—it

[154] Not so, stormed Fry in his letter to Willis *(ibid.).* Not a single note had been changed since the work was composed (with miraculous speed, together with *A Day in the Country*) during the week before his first lecture in 1852.

[155] The wrangle over which form of symphony possessed "unity," and which did not, represented a major issue in the great controversy to follow.

[156] Also the Overture to *Fra Diavolo,* the Andante from Beethoven's Fifth Symphony, arias from *Lucia di Lammermoor* and *Robert le diable* sung by Zerr, solos by Bottesini, Lavigne, and one of the Winterbottoms, and Jullien's "Napoleon Quadrille, his "Great Exhibition Quadrille," "The Baltimore Clipper Waltz," and "The Amazon and the Tiger Galop."

[157] Hardly "always." In the past, Strong had repeatedly lavished words of adoration upon the symphony.

is not, therefore, any special temperament of my own that gives it its power over me. But the bride in her wedding robe and the corpse in its grave-clothes are not objects more diverse and irreconcilable than these two compositions. And it has come to me of late irresistibly. I could not but think of it and follow out its chilling images. And its fearful second movement is always half audible to me from morning to night.

Most fine and grave music—most *real* music, that is—one can adapt mentally to—*Kyrie,* or *Gloria,* or *Agnus Dei,* or *Benedictus.* Not so with this. It can be conceived—such adaptation can—only of the part of the third movement that's written in D, and to what would that be fitting in any liturgy? "*Exaudi orationem meum—ad Te omnis caro veniat*" [Psalm 65]—some such passage might find its embodiment there. Even that, hardly. The music expresses all the grave, but nothing of the prayer and the hope beyond the grave.

The fourth [movement] is frenzy—the first, the excitement of nascent madness growing up out of deep, silent sorrow; the dividing line of the two stages found in the unisons (E), out of which the music bursts into the seemingly commonplace, but most keen and pungent, melody that is characteristic of that movement and gives it its special tone and color. The second [movement] might do for a Deadmarch. It is far worse and deeper and darker than the *Marcia funebre* in the "Eroica," or that in one of the early [piano] sonatas [op. 26 in A-flat]. Rather than a *marcia funebre,* it is the march of the half-waking, half-conscious spirit downward into Hades.

~

No less strangely, Strong, for all his disdain of popular "clap-trap," was so taken with a catchy, anonymous minstrel tune—a vulgar form of music that he categorically rejected—that he wondered if it might not merit a place in the highest rank of the musical hierarchy.

December 10. . . . I've just been making chords on the organ, and I avow that I know nothing equal to the wail of that nigger melody known as "Rosa Lee" [anonymous, 1847]. A single, simple musical thought may have worth—and the highest worth—though allied to trashy words. If the "Rosa Lee" music occurred in a symphony or sonata of Beethoven's, I should appeal to it as evidence of his supremacy.

~

When I lib'd in Tennessee,
U-li-a-li o-la-ee,
I went courtin' Rosa Lee,
U-li-a-li o-la-ee.
Eyes as dark as winter night,
Lips as red as berry bright,
When first I did her wooing go,
She said, now don't be foolish Joe!
Chorus: U-li-a-li o-la-ee,
Courtin' down in Tennessee,
U-li-a-li o-la-ee,
'Neath de wild banana tree.

OBBLIGATO: 1853

Our Composers, we are persuaded, will strike out a field for themselves, in which they will surmount all visionary and real difficulties. They will be governed by the popular taste (a taste which remembers the Opera merely for the melodies it contains) and portray the man of the Western sphere in a distinctive and characteristic music of his own.

New-York Daily Times
April 15, 1853

BACK AT THE BEGINNING OF 1853, on January 4—amid the excitement over the Alboni/Sontag rivalry—William Henry Fry delivered the sixth in his series of monster lecture/concerts at Metropolitan Hall. Having established his preoccupation with opera and the voice, in this lecture Fry dealt exhaustively with "the culture of the singing voice; method and style in vocalization; different qualities and capacities of the masculine and feminine voice; sources of vocal expression in the Madrigal, the Glee, and in Church and Dramatic compositions; the philosophy of lyrical criticism; nature and progress of musical ideas; similarities in the melodic and harmonic phraseology of different composers, how far referable to the nature of the Art." His illustrative music (not specified) was supplied by Rose de Vries, the Viettis, and the chorus, conducted by Bristow.

Fry took this occasion to condemn the general run of "Method-Books for the voice as not written by persons either understanding the voice or capable of composing for it," reported the *Tribune* (January 7, 1853); he dwelt chiefly on "the Voice in its musical relations and its appropriate culture"; he asserted that "the time devoted to vocal culture may be greatly shortened, and that under the proper treatment, most of the voices now spoiled or undermined may be turned to good account."

Opera-loving Fry declared, too, that "dramatic music for the voice is the parent of all expressive music"; he "entered at length on the requirements of that branch of the art." Musical textbooks, Fry maintained, only obscured, rather than explained, the difficulties of "the philosophy and mechanism" of harmony, and he accompanied this section of his remarks with "a close résumé of the harmonic system [illustrating it on a blackboard] and elucidating it on the piano forte. The matter set forth," continued the apparently benumbed reviewer, "was so technical and bound up with practical illustrations that a report of it is hardly possible for our columns."

Less abstrusely, Fry abruptly declared that Democracy was requisite to the growth of High Art: "He said he has spent much time in Europe, and his profession as a writer made it his business to examine particularly into the influences of political institutions on the aesthetic development of the people, and that under our own institutions as much progress was made broadly and popularly in Art in ten years as any other country could show in fifty or a hundred" (an apparently spur-of-the-moment reversal of his customary censure of the low state of art in the United States).

At his seventh lecture (January 11) Fry examined in minute detail another of his dearest obsessions: "The English language for lyrical uses considered and contrasted with other languages; Idiomatic structure of English verse and susceptibilities of imitative varieties; Accent, Rhyme, Euphonic Characteristics; Dependence of melodic phraseology on verbal phraseology; Adaptation of music to words; and Sources of satisfaction and pleasure in Vocal Music."[1]

Fry's eighth lecture (January 18) was devoted to a complicated multinational history of opera from the earliest times and its general influence on music in general, especially religious music. A feature of the musical illustrations, performed on this occasion by American soloists—Mrs. Brinkerhoff, John A. Kyle, and G. F. Bristow, together with the Grand Chorus and Orchestra—was "Mozart's Twelfth Mass."[2]

The ninth lecture (January 25), again devoted to Fry's *idée fixe,* the Lyric Drama, presented, for the first time in America (although Fry considered Mozart an outmoded composer of opera) three choruses with solos from Mozart's opera *Idomeneo* (1781, K. 366).[3] Sung by Madame Annette Stephani, Miss Maria Scoville Brainerd, and the chorus, the Mozart excerpts were interspersed with arias from Meyerbeer's *Robert le diable* and *Le Prophète* and Donizetti's *Les Martyrs,* sung by Madame de Vries, and from Pacini's *Gli Arabi nelle Gallie* (Milan 1827) and Mozart's *Die Zauberflöte* (the Queen of the Night aria) by Madame Stephani. A transcription of "Farinelli's celebrated old bravura"[4] was played on the flute by Kyle, and a violin and piano duet by de Bériot and Benedict was performed by young Theodore Thomas, with Bristow at the piano.

With a sudden shift in the opera schedule at Niblo's, due to Sontag's indisposition, the greater part of Fry's orchestra was preempted on February 1, the evening scheduled for his grand finale. Thus, he was forced at the last minute to improvise a replacement lecture, desperately "writing against time," and consequently, as the *Tribune* reviewer too bluntly observed (February 3, 1853), suffering "the drawbacks of haste."

The bewildering number of subjects Fry discussed at this hastily-gotten-up substitute lecture (nonetheless consuming some two-and-a-half hours), comprised, according to the revised advertisements (February 1), "the forms of Musical Pieces—Oratorio and Opera Solos, Duets, Trios, Finales, etc.; the Fugue, Sonata, Quartet, [and]

[1] So taken was R. Storrs Willis with this lecture that he printed a goodly part of it, with musical and textual examples, in the *Musical World and Times* (January 19, 1853, pp. 69–70), as Fry would remind him in the opening salvo of their later conflict (see OBBLIGATO: 1854).

[2] Like George Templeton Strong and John Sullivan Dwight, Fry was apparently not aware that the work was counterfeit Mozart.

[3] Preceding by nearly a century the unstaged performance at Tanglewood on August 4, 1947, generally believed to have been its first hearing in America.

[4] Which bravura sung by the legendary *castrato* Farinelli (1705–1782) was not named—it might have been his formidable *tour de force* known in its day as a "concerto for larynx" (Pleasants, p. 77).

Sinfonia in Instrumental Music; Musical Plagiarisms; Improvisations, Vocal and Instrumental, with practical Illustrations; History, Biography, and Criticism connected with the Opera and Oratorio." At the piano Fry "developed at length . . . various forms of musical pieces; entered upon the doctrine of permutations; treated of plagiarisms;[5] and indicated the art of improvisation" (*Tribune,* February 3, reprinted in *Dwight's,* February 12, 1853, pp. 147–48).

Reverting yet again to opera and its multifarious evolutions through the ages in the various countries of Europe, Fry harped on the need for "nationalizing" opera in America through the use of the English language, something he claimed the English composers and librettists had neglected to do in England.[6] Despite his repeatedly declared advocacy (and imitation) of Italian opera, he perversely chose on this occasion to state that he had "no belief in the permanency of Italian opera in this country," and incongruously cited as an ideal example of opera in English, Rophino Lacy's *Cinderella,* a hashed-together hodgepodge of several Rossini operas, first produced in London in 1830. Fry lovingly recalled its production at the old Park Theatre in 1831, in "good old intelligible English [with an English cast]—a success which ran up to seventy nights, some three times a week . . . it shows how the popular heart beats," he wrote. "Verily," in a blaze of misdirected passion, "the Grecian Muse spoke Greek, according to the Greek poets. Shall our American Muse chant in a foreign tongue? Forbid it, national sense, pride, ambition!"

The musical illustrations for Fry's substitute lecture, performed by Madame de Vries, Miss Brainerd, a quartet (presumably vocal), and the chorus of two hundred, included an unidentified double vocal quartet by Bristow. Introduced by Fry as "an elegant and classical production," it was reportedly warmly received by some 2000 auditors.

"Determined to give everything promised in the prospectus" (a brave and generous determination hardly uninfluenced by the fact that the musical "illustrations" intended for his final lecture had consisted mainly of his own compositions), Fry announced an eleventh lecture for the following Tuesday evening, February 8, when the postponed program would be presented gratis to his subscribers and at the usual admission price of fifty cents to the general public.[7]

At his delayed Grand Finale, Fry fully indulged his compulsion for self-display, reveling in a virtually all-Fry program performed "on the grandest scale" by a huge cast headed by Madame de Vries, an orchestra of fifty, a military band of fifty, and a chorus of two hundred. His subject matter comprised an "Analysis of the Orchestra Instruments, severally and in combination, as accompaniments and principals; Remarks on Military Music [illustrated by his new "Metropolitan March" for band]; Illustrations

[5] A sensitive topic: in 1845 several critics had accused Fry of wholesale plagiarisms in his score for *Leonora.*

[6] Fry had clung to this whimsical notion since 1845, when he proclaimed his Italianate opera *Leonora,* derived from Bulwer-Lytton's English play *The Lady of Lyons*—its locale for some reason transposed from France to sixteenth-century Spain—to be not only the first American grand opera to be performed, but the first authentic grand opera ever to have been written in English.

[7] "We regret that he has felt it to be proper that he should do so," commiserated Richard Grant White, "for so very expensive a course can have afforded him but little profit, but we are not surprised at such generous dealing from him" (*Courier and Enquirer,* February 1, 1853). The extra lecture indeed added an extra $1200 to Fry's already substantial loss on the series.

of [the band's] uses in the field"; and remarks on the "state of American music" and the "Art, in general."

The *Tribune*'s detailed report (February 11) of Fry's final lecture vividly evokes him in his disparate guises: erudite, egoistic, eccentric, reckless, unfocused, hot-tempered, idealistic, impassioned, belligerent, misdirected, inexhaustibly eloquent, and more. Too, the reporter, albeit obviously mimicking Fry's technical terminology, offers invaluable—perhaps unique—insights into the characteristics, if not the actual content, of the Fry compositions that were performed that evening, now, alas, mostly vanished.

The "earnestly expected" event, he writes, "came off with full force. There were some three hundred performers, and certainly not less than three thousand auditors filling the house to the second gallery and the ceiling. At the appointed time [7:30 P.M.], troops of young ladies dressed in white, forming the chorus, took their places at the front sides of the platform, followed by their harmonious partners of the tenors and basses, and the great orchestra. The lecturer then spoke for about one hour and a half,[8] illustrating the compass, powers, and combinations of each and every instrument in the orchestra, accompanied by practical illustrations in a symphony composed by him, entitled 'Day in the Country,'[9] which represented the religious and material aspects of Nature, the traits of rural life as suggested by instruments calling up country associations. Its last movement[10] was an Allegro representing a village dance, enormously difficult of execution. This was suddenly intercepted by a slow movement, chiefly by the Violincellos [*sic*] with rapid violin passages extending in every bar over three octaves, and this continued till the wailing cantabile, expressing the woes of an unsuccessful lover, died away. Then succeeded the dance; a ponderous air upon the keyed brass instruments gave the rude steps (so explained), and various imitations, figured passages, changes of key, enharmonic transitions, concluded by the air fortissimo and furious, concluded the work. "It was loudly applauded, and understood," the writer continues, "because portions of it were first played in bits and detail, and then analyzed, and afterward engrossed [*sic*]. We must not omit to mention the magnificent execution of a horn quartet, representing the Hymen [Hymn?] of nature, in the earlier movement of this symphony."

"The lecturer explained the limits of descriptive music," continues the reviewer. Always a committed proponent of program music, on this occasion Fry waywardly "denied the value of music as a descriptive agent, except it called up locality by a horn, a pipe, a trumpet, drum, etc., or some air connected with memory. He said a 'cave' could no more be described in music than a greatcoat or a round of beef. (Laughter.)

"The second piece was a Waltz and Chorus, given superbly by the choristers and orchestra. This was from Mr. Fry's opera of *Leonora*[11] and was explained to be music

[8] With the young ladies in white, to say nothing of their harmonious partners, standing idly by?

[9] It should be borne in mind that this performance of *A Day in the Country,* its second, preceded Jullien's numerous performances of the work by seven months. This applies as well to the last movement of Bristow's symphony.

[10] The term "movement" is to be construed as "section." Fry, as we know, was an ardent exponent of the free-wheeling, one-movement symphony, in his opinion an ultra-modern advance over the archaic, four-movement form.

[11] The piano/vocal score of its earlier version had been published in 1846 by E. Ferrett & Co. of New York and Philadelphia.

of the Southern voluptuous type. It was received with a storm of applause from parquet and galleries, and was encored and resung with equal excellence. Next followed the Finale to Act 1 of the same opera, sung by Madame de Vries and the chorus, being a continuation of the ball scene (so pointed out) of the previous chorus. This piece is a bravura of unsurpassed difficulty in 3/4 time, unaccompanied, and its coda is distinguished by a series of rhythmic chromatic passages of two octaves, in which the most startling enharmonic transitions are introduced by a rasping trait on the violins. The chorus, too, has most difficult changes of key, which they executed with splendid precision. Notwithstanding the length of the piece, it was called for until Madame de Vries had to return and give it again, which she did with brilliancy and accuracy. If the object of a composer be to secure the plaudits of thousands, it was gained fully on this occasion."[12]

Next came a work by a fellow American, the last movement of Bristow's E-flat Symphony, op. 10. Despite Fry's personal rejection of the antiquated four-movement form, he "explained briefly the nature of a symphony, and stated that [Bristow's] symphony was as good as the earliest symphony of any composer—that it had received the approval of men of the caliber of Mr. Benedict and others of equal note, and it was the duty of Americans to support such works—to insist on hearing them and thus evoke them."[13]

"The symphony was well played," reports the writer. "It is admirably written. The traits are symphonic—the treatment elaborate—the instrumentation clear—and the applause as great as that bestowed upon any one symphony. Mr. Bristow has shown himself a skillful instrumental composer, and we hope to hear more of his works."[14]

Another American fragment followed: "Stormy Oceans," from George Henry Curtis's cantata *Eleutheria,*[15] sung by Misses Brainerd and Honeywell and Messrs. W. B. Smith and Ball. Apparently a last-minute addition to the program, "it showed the want of rehearsal, and this was explained by the lecturer, who stated the impossibility of getting together the orchestra sufficiently often to secure good rehearsals.[16] Mr. Fry, never having heard this quartet before, could not analyze it [!].[17] He stated that several pieces

[12] Heavenly sustenance to the chronically applause-famished heart of William Henry Fry.

[13] Considering Fry's ceaseless reiteration of this demand, one wonders that he saw fit to program only a single movement of Bristow's deserving symphony.

[14] The German/American music publisher Julius Schuberth was so taken with the movement of Bristow's symphony that he volunteered to assist, if necessary, in its very expensive publication. In Schuberth's opinion, the symphony deserved not only to be repeated but to be heard in all the great cities of Europe (*Tribune,* February 12, 1853, translated from Schuberth's review of the lecture in the *Staats-Zeitung*). The work was in fact not published by Schuberth, nor by anyone else. Its MS score is found at the New York Public Library at Lincoln Center.

[15] The reviewer's apparent unfamiliarity with Curtis's frequently performed cantata intriguingly suggests that he might after all have been A. W. Thayer, who had taken up residence in New York only a little before Fry.

[16] An "impossibility" chiefly attributable to the fact that, while chorus singers were willing to contribute unlimited rehearsal time, orchestra musicians had to be paid. (The Philharmonic, for instance, paid supplementary musicians $5 for a concert and two rehearsals, and for extra rehearsals $1 each.)

[17] This hardly accords with Fry's derision of the New York critics for failing to write analytical reviews because they were unable to read (much less write) musical scores (*Musical World and Times,* March 26, 1853, p. 196).

were not rehearsed with the orchestra, this among the number." The reporter permitted himself a cavil: "This is a perilous undertaking, to give pieces without rehearsing."

Also unrehearsed was "The Metropolitan March,"[18] Fry's new piece for military band, a work he boasted of having written in a hurry, "at the instance of Mr. Harding, the proprietor of Metropolitan Hall." That it went fairly well, considering it was played without rehearsal, was "not a little due to the elaborate side-drumming of a part peculiarly accented for this instrument." Too, "the trio of the March has very curious passages for all the clarionets, which would put the best solo player on his mettle, as they spread out through three octaves. This large looming of instruments is a peculiarity of the writer," added the critic, but (disapprovingly) "he should have rehearsals, and plenty of them." Fry might have been referring to these "curious passages" when, in describing "the requisites of a march, throughout he insisted on the adaptation of means to ends in music, without pedantic 'organ-loft criticism,' as he described it." Fry's "Moss-Troopers' Chorus" which followed, "was very badly sung, not having been rehearsed with the orchestra. It had better been omitted than botched," chided the reviewer.

A chorus from Fry's newly anglicized opera *The Christians and Pagans* was, however, well rehearsed. Portraying "the impending martyrdom of a Christian patrician at Rome, [it] brought out all the strength of the orchestra, the brass instruments, and the chorus. The chorus is divided into two parties, the excoriating pagans and the wailing and despairing Christians. While the sopranos and tenors sob their mournful *minore,* the basses roar up and down with furious energy. In one or two passages there are minor unisons [!], in which every voice and instrument—wood, string, and brass—rush up and down some two octaves.[19] In other parts, all the instruments cease, and the cry of the Christians alone to the Savior is heard."

The reviewer found the piece "too serious to be appreciated at a first hearing,[20] besides being evidently of tremendous difficulty, having involved changes of key, syncopations, running passages, and so forth."

The event did not end serenely. Before closing the musical part of the program with the Grand March from *Le Prophète,* Fry unleashed a vitriolic valedictory blast at his compatriots, his colleagues, and his native land for their woeful failure to live up to his standards—artistically, politically, and socially. As the *Tribune* reporter blandly described it: "Mr. Fry took the platform and spoke for half an hour on artistic duties and relations, on the interests of society in art, and the shortcomings of the American mind in that regard. This was the most exciting time of the evening among the audience. The lecturer had been speaking of American prowess in various things, and that all we wanted now was self-reliance to place us as high in the fine arts as in Literature."

For once—for the sake of argument—Fry conceded some literary excellence among his benighted compatriots. Approvingly referring to Washington Irving and

[18] Listed in Upton (*Fry,* p. 321) as "The Metropolitan Hall March."

[19] Fry apparently had a predilection for rangy passages, as did the critic for referring to leaps of octaves.

[20] Faulty memories seem to have been an occupational characteristic among New York music critics. Like *A Day in the Country,* this work had been performed at Fry's first lecture, only two months before.

James Fenimore Cooper, he added (diving heedlessly into turbulent political waters): "'At this moment, a book, more read in Europe than any since the Bible was first printed, was written by an American lady' [a reference to Harriet Beecher Stowe's controversial novel *Uncle Tom's Cabin*]. A storm of applause followed, attended by vehement hissing. 'I like to hear hissing,' said the lecturer. 'No speaker or artiste is good for anything until he is soundly hissed.' (Laughter and continued hissing.)"

Then, abruptly furious: "I tell this audience that I ask no favors of them. I was a freeman before I was an artist. (Tremendous cheers, and hissing continued, but quiet having been restored.)" Then, backing down somewhat: "'Yes, I ask nothing of this audience but the liberty of speech; and now having settled that matter, let me say to my friends who have hissed me, whom I do not like to lose for so doing, that I did not allude to the book in question in any political sense whatever, but simply as a mention of American literary art.' (Marks of approval.)"

The music critic for the *Daily Times* (February 10, 1853), presumably Charles Bailey Seymour, a comparatively recent American, reacted less passively to Fry's display of belligerence. "In the concluding remarks of Mr. Fry, *apropos* to the subject of American Music," wrote Seymour, "reference was made to the want of independence manifested by artists and the public, and severe strictures were passed upon the coldness with which really good home music is so often received. When we in this country shall have produced a great work of Musical Art," he pointedly added, "we have little fear that the public will pass it slightingly, or refuse to hear and praise it."

Understandably, Fry's relentless disparagement of America's cultural inadequacies, particularly in the area of music, was by now beginning to wear on his colleagues' tolerance. In a comprehensive summing-up of the lectures in the *Musical World and Times* (February 19, 1853, pp. 114–16), Richard Storrs Willis undertook objectively to examine Fry in all his kaleidoscopic complexity. The lectures, wrote Willis, had been "in many respects . . . the most original, interesting, audacious, and exciting literary and musical entertainments ever given in this country." But although Fry was undeniably a genius ("had he gone no further than the publication of his syllabus alone,[21] his claims to rare genius would not have been disputed")—and although he was "a literary and artistic tomahawk," and "although as a critic he [had] few equals"—he was nonetheless fatally disorganized and undisciplined. Fry lacked "synthesis, continuity, method," and these lacks accounted in great measure for the financial failure of his colossal undertaking.[22]

Apart from his lack of business acumen, wrote Willis, mixing honey with gall: "Mr. Fry is one of the most manly and independent of lecturers, his command of cutting, stinging words is remarkable. He is much given to sarcasm, and is also humorous and witty. In short, we know of no more brilliant and interesting speaker than Mr. Fry; but he is inconsistent and contradictory, and sometimes gets on both sides of a question in the same paragraph. When he becomes excited and absorbed in his subject, he

[21] Fry's elaborate lecture-syllabus had been reprinted in *Dwight's* (July 24, 1852, p. 126).

[22] Willis attributed Fry's failure to make expenses, in part, to "unprecedented attractions elsewhere: Alboni and Sontag and a host of distinguished lecturers (Thackeray among them) having been Mr. Fry's competition. . . . It is worthy of remark," he added, "that the only *paying* lectures of the season were Thackeray's."

R. Storrs Willis, William Henry Fry's adversary in the musical battle of the century.

is truly eloquent and says most happy things, but his feelings often carry him away, and his desire or tendency to say biting things causes him to contradict himself most openly."

Yet: "Mr. Fry has said more bold, manly, searching, audacious, and *American* things concerning Art than have ever before been said in America. He is intensely patriotic and intensely artistic in feeling; consequently he longs to see this country take high rank in Art. He evidently thinks we are now in a sad way, artistically considered—that there is no Art in the country—that there is no sympathy for artists here—and that there is little probability of there being any very soon."

Then, in a numbered list, Willis cited thirty-one statements, or rather, accusations allegedly made by Fry at his eleventh lecture—some contradictory, some redundant, some ludicrous, and some still keenly relevant after the passage of more than a century. The list includes many variants of Fry's perpetual themes: unremitting condemnation of the deplorable cultural, social, and political conditions in America[23] and bitter censure of Americans' provincial attitudes—their willful ignorance of art and their indifference to it, their snobbery,[24] their disregard of American artists, their slavish worship of Handel, Mozart, Beethoven, and European artists in general.

[23] "Who ever heard Art or any eminent artist toasted, or complimented, or in any manner referred to, at Fourth of July celebrations, or at any public occasions?" indignantly demanded Fry.

[24] "There is a vast deal of snobbishness in this country in matters of Art," raged Fry. "An ignorant and pretentious and self-elected aristocracy, whose only tests of distinction and passports in society are fashionable apparel and a greater or less degree of vulgar ostentation in the display of wealth, assume to criticize the immortal productions of genius and to pass judgment on works of Art, which neither nature nor education has fitted them to comprehend."

Not until American artists declared a cultural Declaration of Independence from all foreign models and influences, Fry had proclaimed, would they be free to "discard their foreign liveries, and found an American School in Painting, Sculpture, and Music."[25] He demanded that American audiences be required to listen to, and encourage, any and all compositions of American origin;[26] he demanded that "our musical societies" (meaning the Philharmonic) should devote rehearsal time to reading American works; that American symphonies, operas, and cantatas—great numbers of which existed, he claimed[27]—deserved the same attention that in earlier days had been bestowed upon the earlier works of Handel, Beethoven, and Mozart.

Eternally bemoaning his own professional frustrations,[28] Fry, the martyr, contended that an American composer could not get his works performed in America unless he could afford to subsidize their performance; that in Europe, even if he were able to pay, he not only could not get his works performed but was "spit upon," into the bargain. And on and on, ad infinitum.[29]

Willis responded with all the proper denials. He named a goodly number of American writers, painters, and even musicians (among them Fry) who were honored in their own country, and in Europe as well. "Celebrity, especially in art, is too dear and precious a boon to be lightly won," he loftily proclaimed. "The Muses will not descend from Olympus to crown every aspirant for that honor—not, at least, at his first awkward, and perhaps impertinent, summons" *(ibid.)*.

Under the heading "Mr. Fry's 'American Ideas' about Music," self-righteous John Sullivan Dwight, in his *Journal* (March 12, 1853, pp. 180–82), systematically took up Willis's thirty-one points, point by point.[30] Beginning on an elevated level of kindly benevolence, Dwight politely regretted that Fry's keenly expected lectures would, after all, not be heard in Boston—due, he explained, to the overwhelming number of opposing attractions (due, in fact, to the unsatisfactory response from prospective Bostonian subscribers,[31] a new source of bitter frustration to Fry).

[25] American writers, painters, and sculptors, if not composers, had in fact long since established their place in the world of arts and letters.

[26] Excepting, apparently, compositions by such authentic Americans as Stephen Collins Foster—never, to my knowledge, recognized by Fry.

[27] A claim until now unsubstantiated through scholarly research.

[28] "Owing probably to disappointments in his career," acutely observed C. M. Cady in the *Musical Review and Choral Advocate* (February 1853, p. 26), "Mr. Fry has exhibited, we are sorry to say, an acerbity of temper in his later lectures which is, to say the least, in bad taste. . . . It may or may not be true that the American people lack 'public spirit,' 'education,' 'sympathy,' and all that, but it is not very modest in Mr. Fry to *assume* all this because people don't want to hear his opera."

[29] At his final lecture, wrote Cady, Fry held his unusually large audience to a late hour "by a witty, cutting, yet *regular scold,* interspersed, by way of contrast, with the most *harmonious* [musical] illustrations. Such a tirade against the American public, foreign artists, in short, everybody, we have not heard for a long time" (*ibid.,* March 1853, pp. 42–43).

[30] C. M. Cady *(ibid.)* boiled down Willis's thirty-one points to three of his own:

> 1st. I, William H. Fry, am a very great man.
> 2d. The American people don't appreciate me.
> Ergo (an aggravated case of non sequitur)
> 3d. The American people don't know much.

[31] Attributed by Upton (*Fry,* p. 131) to local resentment of his "dirty debauchee" remark about King Solomon.

Dwight, who had not heard Fry lecture, found some items on Willis's list to be true, some false, some a mixture of the two, and the whole redundant and overlong. Fry, wrote Dwight, had "evidently stirred up some feeling in New York by the novelty and boldness of his positions, and especially by their 'Americanism,' as if it were part of the 'manifest destiny'[32] and duty of this republic to accept the teachings of the old world quite as little in Art and Music as in political and social life."

At least, Dwight was happy to report, Fry's accusation of American indifference to good music could not be leveled at Boston, where Beethoven, Mozart, Handel, and the best of the lesser masters were properly revered and listened to more than anywhere in the Union.

However: "It seems [citing Fry] 'the American public are too fond of quoting Handel, Mozart, and Beethoven.' How does this tally with [Fry's] first charge of 'no taste or love for true art?'" It was, regrettably, the other way around. Rather than Beethoven or Handel, in Dwight's estimation, Americans were too fond of the "remarkable creations of the psalm-book makers and the sentimental song-writers"—the Lowell Masons and the Isaac Baker Woodburys—who were esteemed the greatest composers in the world by thousands and thousands of deluded Americans!

As for the "'snob aristocracy,' what great partiality has *it* ever shown for Beethoven and Handel?" demanded Dwight. "Has it not pronounced them antiquated, obsolete, dry, learned, and unfashionable, and set up the pure, yellow-kid exclusivism of the most modern Italian and French opera as the only music worthy of 'our best society'?"

Yet the portents were encouraging. Art was slowly making headway in America; in time it would blossom into a force for universal peace and love. "If we believe that human society is ever fully to emerge from barbarism," preached Dwight, as deluded a visionary in his way as was Fry, "there will be comparatively less need of politicians and of merchants—we trust, no need of military heroes—their functions will shrink and the artists will occupy the foreground of humanity, as leaders in the work of making life on earth entirely harmonious and beautiful."

Contrary to Fry, Dwight maintained that only through the cultivation and love of such masters as Beethoven and Mozart would we outgrow our "provincialism in Art. . . . The greater our appreciation of them, the greater our chances of becoming composers and creators in our turn." To seal our ears against such supreme masters was "a poor way of 'scaring up' originality among ourselves."

By now indignant, Dwight concluded: "If it be necessary to lessen our admiration of Beethoven [unthinkable!] in order that we may appreciate the symphonies, operas, cantatas, *bananiers,*[33] etc., of our native aspirants, we think the worthy public shows its prudent common sense in cleaving to the former and letting the latter abide their time, as genius of all kinds has had to do in all times and places."

Inevitably, the combination of Dwight's and Willis's comments set off fresh eruptions of outrage in Fry's tempestuous soul. Killing two birds with one stone, he addressed to Willis and his co-editor Dyer a violent rebuttal of astounding length (even for Fry). "I did not intend, Messrs. Editors, to trouble you at all," he wrote, "leaving

[32] The phrase, popular lingo in the 1840s and '50s, had been coined to express the overwhelming American drive toward territorial expansion.

[33] A waspish reference to Louis Moreau Gottschalk's delicious piano piece *Le Bananier,* made familiar to Boston audiences by Alfred Jaëll.

what was said [at the lectures] to speak for itself in New York, but I find an eminent musical journal in Boston quotes your summary with fresh annotations, in which I am made to sin in the way of iteration and reiteration, and to want logic and synthesis." Therefore, Fry demanded that, "as a matter of justice," his vast document be published—"I mean the letter in full"—in their journal and also in *Dwight's*. Fry's letter appeared, presumably in full and without editorial comment, on March 25 in the *Musical World and Times* (pp. 195–98) and, with deletions but no comment, on April 2 in *Dwight's Journal of Music* (pp. 200–201).

Fry's formidable statement bristled with boasts ("the orchestra, eighty-four in number, which played at my lectures, [was] the largest and most splendid ever heard in America"); complaints ("no analytical criticism was written of the original pieces they played,[34] involving the latest development of orchestra power and combinations"); self-glorification ("it was impossible for any compositions to be better received or more strenuously encored by the public than were those of mine, well sung at the Eleventh Lecture in presence of three thousand people"); and denials ("I did not say that we will pay nothing to hear a sublime work of Art performed because we do not know enough to appreciate it").

Fry denied having said that Americans were "too fond of quoting Handel, Mozart, Beethoven, and other European artists and decrying whatever is not modeled after their rules"; or that the American public "decry native compositions and sneer at native artists." He denied having said that American artists were spat upon in Europe, delicately qualifying: "I said [that] when there I tried to have an opera [*Leonora*] produced, and I was spit upon because I was an American. . . . I took the best possible introductions and offered to pay the expenses of a rehearsal, according to my invariable custom to expect nothing as a favor.[35] I wished the music to be heard simply: given, book in hand, without dress or decoration, and so pronounced upon—a frightful hazard, but one which I was willing to abide by, in the same way that I had my works performed at my lectures in New York, without the necessary aids of the Opera House.[36] . . . When I asked for this simple rehearsal—so easily accorded and fairly required—the director of the Opera in Paris said to me: 'In Europe we look upon America as an industrial country—excellent for electric telegraphs and railroads, but not for Art.[37] . . . They would think me crazy to produce an opera by an American.' . . . He would not even look at the work, but rejected it solely on the ground of its being American, not knowing whether it was good, bad, or indifferent."[38]

[34] For all his professed chauvinism, Fry was indignant that there were no American equivalents of such European critics as Berlioz, Fétis, Reicha, Scudo, and others who were capable of analytical criticism, being able—like Fry—to read and write a musical score.

[35] A face-saving (self-deluding?) declaration frequently resorted to by Fry to justify the numerous "vanity" productions of his music.

[36] This was obviously not what Fry, obsessed as he was with opera, wanted. It was common knowledge that his chief purpose in going to Europe had been to vindicate his opera *Leonora,* after its humiliating failure to be produced in New York in 1848,♪ by having it mounted with full pomp and splendor at the Paris Opéra (see Upton, *Fry,* p. 51). That the work might be considered musically unworthy was inadmissable to Fry (or to Upton).

[37] Yet, young Gottschalk was being wildly acclaimed in Europe during Fry's sojourn there—not only for his playing but for his compositions.

[38] Can it be that Fry's relentless abuse of his fellow Americans was his way of punishing them for the French impresario's rejection of *Leonora*?

Telling the story of his rejection in Paris was intended, Fry wrote, to disprove Willis's statement that some American artists had been successful in Europe. Anyway, it was a different and simpler matter for an American painter or sculptor or writer to be recognized abroad than for an opera composer who depended for public presentation upon "the intervention or immediate interpretation of two or three hundred people, and [Fry spitefully added] the fiat of an irresponsible director who, nine times out of ten, cannot read a note of music and has no artistic sympathies."

Without missing a beat—indeed without even beginning a new sentence—Fry was back to condemning America for her lack of a national institution for a native lyric stage, and excoriating the American public for tolerating the "comings and goings of [foreign] singers, all furiously bent on making from fifty to five hundred thousand dollars in a given number of months . . . even [going] into an epilepsy of asininery as did New York with Jenny Lind." (It was a particularly sore point with Fry that singers were sometimes labeled geniuses, when it was obviously the composers, whose works they sang, who deserved the glory.)

Even George Washington did not escape Fry's rancor. Raging against the importance assigned by Americans to politics and politicians (as opposed to their disregard of art and artists, who "ranked as inferiors in society"), Fry wrote: "The [American] world is bullied by names: one man Washington absorbs like a maelstrom the sweat, agony, glory, and immortality of the Revolution; and the public rear an unequalled monument to him, instead of to THE PEOPLE OF SEVENTY-SIX, each one of whom contributed his might and his mite."[39]

As to Fry's everlasting obsession with the English language as a medium for grand opera: "It has been assumed as a theory, and laid down as a practice in England," he claimed, "that the English language is unfit for the grand opera or the high class of opera which properly rejects all spoken language and carries out the monologues and dialogues entirely in music accompanied by the orchestra." Thus, maintained Fry, "as England denies the possibility of having a grand opera written originally in our tongue, it was the business of America to prove the possibility; and I did so."

Fry followed this modest claim with yet another retelling of how, at the expense of thousands of dollars, he had brought out his *Leonora* in Philadelphia in 1845 in a sumptuous production—fifty in the orchestra and seventy in the chorus, being double the number ever engaged in performing opera in New York.[40] "In this American 'grand opera,'" he wrote, "the wretched and vulgar plan of speaking and singing by turns was rejected, and all the scenes, even the longest dialogues, [were] carried on in singing recitative. The poetry was written [by Fry's brother Joseph] after no English model, for the best of reasons, there was none."

Leonora had proved to "an audience of acumen that it was not only possible to render the English language the medium for the grand serious or tragic opera, but,"

[39] Fry was contemptuous, too, of the inflated denizens of Capitol Hill: "'the Great Virginian,' 'the Great South Carolinian,' the great this, that, and the other, means a speaker in Congress who has spoken for or against (no matter which) a few material, or so-called national, interests, such as Banks and Roads, that are passed by small majorities one session, to be rescinded at the next session—the prismatic hues of a soap bubble not being more transient or trivial." (Banks and roads were apparently of less importance to Fry than opera—particularly opera in English.)

[40] After exposure to the spectacular *concerts monstres* in Europe, Fry was incurably prone to equate the excellence of a performance with the size of the forces involved.

Fry outrageously asserted, "that any other form of opera was unworthy of lyrical treatment. So the first successful grand opera in the English language was produced in this country."

"There may be other American operas not known, and I trust there are," magnanimously stated Fry. As an example, he cited Bristow's as yet unperformed *Rip Van Winkle,* which "if it be like his symphonies, which there is no reason to doubt, its success must be assured."

There was too, claimed Fry, a composer "who has always lived and studied here, who writes quite as well for an orchestra as Young Germany or France." Fry offered to compare this composer's scores against those of any European with "any person who can read them, of which class there are, alas, but few, though 'critics' abound," he wickedly added. Tantalizingly, Fry gave no hint of who this mysterious composer might have been.[41]

Fry had his devoted adherents as well.[42] George William (not George Henry) Curtis, temporarily shedding his professional frothiness and carefully avoiding any reference to Fry's bellicosity, was astounded by the tremendous scope of the lectures and by their "good intention," which, he wrote in *Putnam's,* (January 1853, p. 119), had insured their unequivocal success. "To present an historical, aesthetical, scientific, and critical review of music in the compass of ten lectures, and so distribute this huge material as to leave some marked and permanent impression upon the public, is certainly an imperial prospectus." Fry's lectures had shown him to be "thoroughly competent to write such a history of Music as has not yet been attempted. How gladly would we rank among the many imposing proofs that America is not callous to the deepest persuasions of art a comprehensive history of Music written by one of the most American of Americans."

In the March issue of *Putnam's* (pp. 350–51), Curtis referred to Fry's controversial pronouncements at his final lecture as "humorous, pointed, brilliant, vehement, sensible, and enthusiastic," leading to what the critic (regaining some of his frothiness) was pleased to call "some amusing demonstrations of a difference of opinion, all of which Mr. Fry met in the most manly and generous way." It did not surprise Curtis that Fry had lost money on the endeavor; and although it was doubtless cold comfort to Fry that he had achieved merely a "*succès d'estime,*" his lectures had made their mark not only upon the musical season in New York "but upon the musical history of the country." Curtis consoled Fry in suitably nationalistic terms: "Were it only for the display of the radiant energy and ability which characterize the American, we hope he will not consider the undertaking altogether a loss. Not every man can afford to fail so finely." (Cold comfort, indeed.)

Proving that Fry enjoyed a faithful following in New York, a committee appointed by the Sacred Harmonic Society—consisting of George Frederick Bristow,

[41] In the light of later developments, the composer might have been Charles Hommann, a native of Philadelphia then living in Brooklyn, whose compositions were at last played in 1856 (see OBBLIGATO: 1856).

[42] And even in the twentieth century, especially among the more credulous readers of William Treat Upton's over-infatuated, under-documented, and generally misled and misleading biography of Fry, published in 1954 and unfortunately not yet supplanted.

Walter E. Harding, John A. Kyle, Clarence W. Beames♪ (now Dr. Beames), Francis H. Nash, James F. Otis, Antonio Bagioli, and other local luminaries, musical and otherwise—signified their appreciation of Fry by presenting him with a complimentary concert at Metropolitan Hall on March 1.

Besides the nearly 300 grateful members of his chorus and orchestra, the volunteer performers included Mesdames de Vries, Stephani, and Otto, Sontag's basso Luigi Rocco, the youthful violinist Theodore Thomas, the Seguins' Scottish tenor of old, John Frazer,♪ recently returned to the United States after an absence of some five years, and seven young debutants—six of them vocal pupils of Bagioli. The concert was jointly conducted by Bristow and Maretzek, the latter just back from Mexico and Havana. Walter Harding handsomely contributed the use of Metropolitan Hall.

Despite "the shocking state of the weather" on March 1, reported the *Musical World and Times* (March 5, 1853, p. 147), "Mr. Fry had reason to congratulate himself on the attendance, which was still quite respectable, for no ordinary attraction would induce anyone to venture out on so inclement an evening." The program, consisting of works by Bellini, Mercadante, Rossini, Donizetti, Mozart, Balfe, and others, included Bristow's Concert Overture, op. 3,[43] and choruses from Fry's *Leonora* and *The Christians and Pagans.*

"During the second part," continued the reviewer, "Mr. Fry was loudly called for. After some hesitation, that gentleman bowed his acknowledgments from the first circle; but the audience would not permit him to escape so easily; they insisted on a speech, and Mr. Fry complied. His remarks were characteristic, and consequently pointed, brilliant, and telling. He said, among other things, that he was confident we should yet have a National Lyric Stage, a consummation for which all doubtless earnestly wish."

Then the lethal blow! "We hope Mr. Fry will yet favor us with a course of lectures on music without the cumbrous accessories which weighed down his first series. The public would rather hear him talk half an hour than listen to any orchestra or chorus he could bring together."

Hardly less devastating was Cady, who, according to his curmudgeonly custom, declared Fry's complimentary concert to be merely a "*salvo*" to make up for the general "lack of 'appreciation'" of his lectures. "The people care much more for music—simple, downright *music,*" he wrote, "than for Mr. Fry's rambling talk *about* it" (*Musical Review and Choral Advocate,* February 1853, p. 26; March, pp. 42–43).

A wry choice of codas to crown a Grand Messianic Supers Extravaganza.

As if in answer to Fry's anguished cries in the wilderness, in January 1853 the dream-prince of American virtuosos materialized in the elegant person of Louis Moreau Gottschalk (1829–1869). To be sure, Gottschalk's homecoming, for such it was, had nothing to do with Fry, nor was it unexpected. Indeed, the young pianist/composer was far from unknown to his compatriots: over a period of years, reports of Gottschalk's phenomenal European triumphs—both as a performing virtuoso and

[43] Bristow's overture, a bone of contention in the future Fry/Bristow quarrel with the Philharmonic, enjoyed the distinction of being the only work by an American composer to have been played by the Society in the eleven years of their existence.

composer—had been proudly heralded in the local press, and in recent months the public had been subjected to a systematic, cumulative conditioning toward his impending return to his native land. "We Americans have been for years indebted to Europe for our artists," wrote the *Home Journal* on October 16, 1852, and "now we are to welcome to our shores one of our own countrymen—one of us—a young man named Moreau Gottschalk,[44] a native of Louisiana." Then followed a description of Gottschalk's artistic and social conquests in "the highest circles of Europe," where, despite his youth, he had "already made himself a reputation for original talent equal to that of Listz [*sic*], Thalberg, and Jaëll."

If this seemed like routine puffery, it was nonetheless true. At the comparatively tender age of twenty-three, Gottschalk was returning home a full-fledged international celebrity. By January 10, when he arrived in New York, the salient facts of his short, already legendary, life had become established lore:[45] his birth in exotic New Orleans to Aimée de Bruslé, a beautiful and aristocratic French/Creole Catholic and Edward Gottschalk, an English-born, German-educated Jew;[46] his astounding musical gifts, overwhelmingly evident since babyhood; his subsequent years of study with eminent masters in Paris, where he had been sent to complete his musical education when he was only twelve;[47] his private debut before a distinguished Parisian audience at the Salle Pleyel in 1845, when Chopin, whose E-minor Concerto he had played, publicly acclaimed him, and he was crowned with a wreath of oak leaves;[48] his intoxicating subsequent triumphs, both professional and personal, in the most aristocratic salons and important concert halls of Paris; his meteoric tours of France, Switzerland, and particularly of Spain, where he was idolized no less ardently by members of the royal family than by a hotly impassioned populace.[49] Hector Berlioz's glowing praises of Gottschalk in the *Journal des Débats* were endlessly quoted in the various New York

[44] Gottschalk, the oldest of eight children, was named after his mother's uncle Louis Moreau de l'Islet (or Lislet), a prominent jurist.

[45] Later attributed, in Vernon Loggins's largely fictitious Gottschalk biography (*Where the Word Ends,* pp. 121–23), to William Vincent Wallace's inspired advance efforts as "manager" of Gottschalk's first two concerts in New York. No such management is suggested in the contemporary New York press, where so extraordinary a collaboration would hardly have been ignored. Nor has a source been located for Loggins's contention (p. 44) that Wallace, who had purportedly arrived in New Orleans from South America in May 1842, had formed a close friendship with little Moreau, who, according to the most trustworthy Gottschalk authorities—his bibliographer John G. Doyle and his biographer S. Frederick Starr—had departed for Europe a year earlier, presumably in May 1841.

[46] Moreau Gottschalk was reared in his mother's faith.

[47] After a peremptory rejection sans audition by the Paris *Conservatoire* (because he was a foreigner), young Gottschalk had piano lessons briefly with Charles Hallé (1819–1895), then more enduringly with Camille Stamaty (1811–1870); he studied composition with Pierre Maleden (1806–?). In varying degrees of intensity, Gottschalk was instructed as well in the graceful and elegant accomplishments befitting a contemporary man of the world, according to Loggins (p. 45), riding, fencing, modern languages, some mathematics, some Greek and Latin, and moral philosophy.

[48] All recounted in the timely biographical essay, "L. M. Gottschalk," by Henry Didimus (a pseudonym for Edward Henry Durell), appearing in *Graham's Magazine* (January 1853, pp. 61–69) and reprinted as a pamphlet (Philadelphia 1853).

[49] Gottschalk especially ignited his Spanish audiences with his Grand Symphony for Ten Pianos, *El Sitio de Zaragoza* ("The Siege of Saragossa"), based on popular Spanish tunes and including the national hymn *La Marcha real.* See Doyle, *Bibliography,* D-79–79/B, MS-29; also see V. B. Lawrence, ed., *The Piano Works of Louis Moreau Gottschalk* (hereinafter referred to as *Piano Works*), V, 265.

papers,[50] as were alluring descriptions of his beguiling, innovative piano pieces, based on Creole and Negro melodies, a great sensation in Europe.

Indeed, upon his return, no attention-getting device was neglected,[51] nor was any time lost in giving his pre-debut *soirée d'artiste* for the gentlemen of the press. On January 18, only a week after Gottschalk's arrival, the *Mirror* scooped the other papers with what seems to be his first New York review: "We yesterday had the pleasure—and a very great one it was—of hearing this young American pianist and composer at his rooms at the Irving House. M. Gottschalk[52] is scarcely recovered from an illness commencing in Spain some time prior to his departure for this country, and which was heightened by the sea voyage. Nevertheless, no signs of illness were discernible in his manipulations of the splendid 'Pleyel' piano [which he had brought from Paris], on which he both delighted and surprised us.[53]

"M. Gottschalk is one of the most effective pianists we have heard," continued the *Mirror.* "His style is largely original, being characterized by great distinctness and purity of theme, boldness and freedom of ornament, and brilliancy and delicacy of execution. M. Gottschalk is decidedly American in manner, sympathy, and enthusiasm—though he has been abroad eleven years—and he gave us a magnificent apostrophe to our national airs, which he informed us was the outline of a grand composition he has long contemplated, to be called 'Bunker Hill,' and calculated for ten pianos." It was, in fact, "The Siege of Saragossa" metamorphosed into Americana, its Spanish tunes being replaced by "Yankee Doodle" and "Hail Columbia," with sometimes an up-to-date dash of "Oh! Susanna" or "The Old Folks at Home."[54]

The *Mirror* declared itself "satisfied, from a first hearing of young Gottschalk, that he is destined to great success in his native land, both as a pianist and a composer. He is entirely free from affectation—is slender, but fine looking;[55] and seems fully aware

[50] And grudgingly by Dwight (*Dwight's,* February 5, 1853, p. 143), who added his own petulant disapproval-in-advance of Gottschalk, "his *Bananiers* and his *Bamboulas.*"

[51] "Promenaders in Broadway have, doubtless, observed, from [Gottschalk's] portraits in the music-store windows, that he is depicted as a very handsome young fellow," gossiped the *Home Journal* (January 22, 1853), and, corroborated the reporter: "We are happy to state, from personal observation made in the office of the *Home Journal,* that the artist has done him no more than justice—he *is* a handsome young fellow."

[52] *M.* for *Monsieur,* not *Moreau.* Probably because this American pianist—whose first language was French and who spoke English with a foreign accent—was essentially a Frenchman, the *Mirror,* even while stressing his Americanness, persistently referred to him as *M.,* not *Mr.,* Gottschalk.

[53] Gottschalk remained faithful to the Pleyel until 1855, when he transferred his allegiance to the Chickering.

[54] Doubtless, at this stage of his career, box-office considerations rather than patriotic inspiration prompted this nationalistic display. According to Offergeld (*Catalogue,* entry 31), Gottschalk frequently performed this piece on tour in 1853–54, giving it in several versions—solo and ensemble—and under various titles, among them "National Glory," "American Reminiscences," and "The Battle of Bunker Hill." Although no version of the work is known to have been published, nor a relevant manuscript found, "Union," op. 48, a descendant of the piece—popular (in the North) during the Civil War—was published in 1863 (listed in Doyle as D-156–156/C; *Piano Works,* V, 265).

[55] There was a good deal of disagreement over whether Gottschalk was handsome or not handsome. He was, in fact, a romantic figure, slight and delicate of build, with a poetically sensitive face and dreamy, far-off gaze veiled by heavily drooping eyelids that would, throughout his career, send hordes of feminine adorers into unladylike transports. His downward-slanting, Charlie-Chaplinesque moustache was acquired after his return to the United States.

of the competition and censorship challenged by his entrée in the musical field. He will give a first concert about the last of the present month."[56]

In expectation of his debut, announced for February 4 but postponed to February 11 because of his persistent illness, the *Herald* editorialized, even as it puffed (February 4): "A native of this country—a young American . . . endorsed by the greatest critics of Europe as a pianist of the highest order of genius—the only one that has been ranked with Listz [*sic*] and Thalberg—comes among us and makes his first appearance . . . at Niblo's Saloon, when the connoisseurs, the critics, the dilettanti, and the public

[56] Present at this, or a similar, *soirée* at the Irving House, the *Musical Review and Choral Advocate* (February 1853, p. 25) reports that Gottschalk played his "Carnival of Venice" Variations (1850) (Doyle D-27; *Piano Works,* I, 221), Liszt's Reminiscences of *Lucia di Lammermoor* (1840), and Wallace's Second Concert Polka. The reporter, all aglow over Gottschalk's artistry, his handsomeness, his cordiality, refinement, and modesty, warned "the ladies" to "watch their hearts."

Music Division, The New York Public Library

Young Louis Moreau Gottschalk, encircled by his early hits.

at large will have an opportunity of judging whether his merits have been exaggerated, or whether he is destined to rank with a Powers, a West, or a Trumbull."[57]

Accurately putting its pragmatic finger on Gottschalk's principal motivation for returning to his native land at this stage of his career, the *Herald* continued: "Great musical artists have found that they are better remunerated in the United States than in any other part of the world.[58] The people of no other country can afford to pay so well."[59]

The impact of Gottschalk's debut at Niblo's Saloon, on February 11, was somewhat dulled by Sontag's performance on the same evening of *La sonnambula* (for the third time) at Niblo's larger auditorium.[60] Gottschalk was assisted by Madame de Vries, who sang her well-worn arias from Verdi's *I due Foscari* and *I Lombardi* and Meyerbeer's *Le Prophète;* the tenor John Frazer, who sang Scottish ballads; Kyle and Bristow, who, in lieu of an orchestra, opened the program with an unidentified "Concertante" for flute and piano;[61] and by Richard Hoffman,[62] who, with Gottschalk, performed two of Gottschalk's works for two pianos: his *Grande Fantaisie triomphale* on Verdi's *Jérusalem* (the revised version of *I Lombardi*), op. 84 (*c.* 1850–51),[63] and a "Waltz di Bravura" (1852).[64] Alone, Gottschalk played a section of Liszt's Reminiscences of *Lucia di Lammermoor,* the Sextet (persistently referred to in the papers as Septet), to which he had reportedly appended a brilliant finale of his own; his solo version of *La Chasse du jeune Henri,* op. 10 (*c.* 1850), adapted from his transcription for two pianos (1849)[65] of the Overture to Méhul's opera *Le Jeune Henri* (Paris 1797); and—under the collective heading "Poetic Caprices"—*La Moissoneuse,* op. 8 (*c.* 1848–49) (a mazurka dedicated to Alfred Jaëll); *Danse ossianique,* op. 12 (*c.* 1850); and *Le Bananier,* op. 5 (*c.* 1846–48).[66]

[57] The foremost American culture-symbols enjoying worldwide recognition were the painters John Trumbull (1756–1843) and Benjamin West (1738–1820) and the sculptor Hiram Powers (1805–1873).

[58] Throughout his life the obligation to earn money purportedly weighed heavily on Gottschalk, who from childhood had been reared in the concept—civic as well as familial—that he, as the oldest son, inherited the responsibility for the support and well-being of his voluminous family.

[59] Looking back a decade later (February 15, 1862), a somewhat disenchanted Gottschalk wrote in his journal (*Notes of a Pianist,* Behrend edition, p. 48, hereinafter cited as *Notes*) that "America was at this time [1853] the El Dorado, the dream of artists, especially [with] the exaggerated accounts of the money that Jenny Lind had made." Posthumously translated into English by his brother-in-law Robert E. Peterson, and edited (and doubtless censored) by his sister Clara Gottschalk Peterson, Gottschalk's journal was first published in 1881.

[60] A poor example of W. V. Wallace's managerial judgment, if indeed he was responsible. It is not implausible, however, that Gottschalk's father, who had journeyed from New Orleans to New York to welcome him back—and who, despite a lack of professional experience, took a dictatorial hand in his son's career—might have been responsible for the inept timing of the debut.

[61] The absence of an orchestra (ostensibly to save money) is a further evidence of the inauspicious handling of Gottschalk's American debut.

[62] Through the years Gottschalk would retain the highest regard for Hoffman, "the admirable and conscientious pianist, whom at all times I have found ever ready to oblige me" (*Notes,* September 15, 1862, p. 46; see also his eulogy of Hoffman, *ibid.,* p. 44).

[63] Doyle, D-77–77/A; the solo version of *Jérusalem* —Gottschalk's op. 13, published in the United States in 1855 by William Hall and Son—is found in *Piano Works,* III, 195.

[64] *Valse di bravura,* now vanished, is listed as an unpublished work in Arpin, p. 64.

[65] *La Chasse de jeune Henri:* Doyle, D-32–32/B; *Piano Works,* II, 21.

[66] *La Moissoneuse:* Doyle, D-98; *Piano Works,* IV, 67; *Danse ossianique:* Doyle, D-39; *Piano Works,* II, 119; *Le Bananier:* Doyle, D-14, 14/C; *Piano Works,* I, 103.

Gottschalk closed the program with his breathtaking Grand Caprice and Variations on "The Carnival of Venice." Tickets were one and two dollars, but it is likely that the large audience was mostly invited,[67] for Gottschalk in later years ruefully recalled that his debut in America had been a financial fiasco.[68]

The critics, if not universally ecstatic, were approving—but in varying degrees and with conflicting quibbles. Richard Grant White, who opened his review in the *Courier and Enquirer* (February 12; reprinted in *Dwight's,* February 19, 1853, pp. 154–55) with a heavy-handed satire on the shortcomings of the piano, currently in great disfavor as a solo instrument,[69] wrote: "To be able to concentrate the attention of an audience upon a piano-forte once during a concert is evidence of extraordinary ability, and nothing less than genius will serve to make it the chief part of a satisfactory evening's entertainment. The truth is, that we—we, the public—have begun to regard the piano-forte in a concert-room as an intolerable bore." It was thus no small tribute to Gottschalk that "he was able to break down the frigid barrier which has of late arisen between pianists and their audiences, though [a pointed reference to Gottschalk's flamboyant publicity] we are well aware that the favorite of the most distinguished circles may regard with indifference such apparently negative praise.

"Mr. Gottschalk's style is full of dash and glitter and quaint conceits. He piles the Pelion upon the Ossa of difficulty, but his Titanic labors do not enable him to mount heavenward. His command of the mechanism of the instrument is so vast, so unerring, that it seems as if it must have been born with him; as if it were impossible that mere practice and mere will could enable a man to do all that he does with his fingers. In this respect he has few rivals, perhaps no superior, in the world. He annihilates difficulties; they fall around him, heaps upon heaps. . . . He is ambidexter and, reversing the old saying, his thumbs are fingers."

But despite Gottschalk's startling virtuosity, the ambivalent critic "failed to discover any remarkable purity of tone, or any indications of a chaste *cantabile* style in either of his performances . . . and we must confess," he added, "that his dexterity, his power, his sparkle, his dainty, quaint conceits did not compensate us for the want of those higher qualities of the artist, especially since he seemed to avoid instinctively all attempts at pathetic, or even tender, expression, as foreign to his nature."

Gottschalk's compositions, wrote White, "show that he is a musician if not a genius, and geniuses are very rare. The introduction to the 'Jérusalem Fantasy' was striking, bold, almost grand, and worked out with a coherence of thought which we did not find evident in the rest of his music. On the other hand, we continually longed for the melodies which we felt sure must soon come, but which did not come. Striking progressions of harmony there were often enough; we thought them more startling than beautiful; but perhaps . . . his compositions only need frequent hearing for the perception in them of beauties of a high order."

[67] Among its more luminous members, it was widely noted, were the former President of the United States, Martin Van Buren, and his son John.

[68] "My first concert in New York was a success, but the receipts did not amount to half of the expenses" (*Notes,* p. 46).

[69] "The Pianoforte has become too hackneyed for the Concert-room. Most people have been subjected to so much thrumming of the instrument at home, that they become nervous when they see an artist preparing to attack them with it in public" (*Mirror,* September 28, 1852).

Yet, White was reluctant to believe this: "As an executant, [Gottschalk] is certainly a phenomenon and a prodigy. We could not but regret that so much stupendous and wonderful labor produced so little music; and [superciliously] we could not but smile at seeing the enthusiasm of his audience always rise in direct proportion to the manual exertion which his performance required."

To George William Curtis, however, even greater than Gottschalk's "colossal style that surprised us . . . was the profound sense of a musical enthusiasm and devotion which pervaded all the performance and removed it from the merely 'astonishing' and 'sublime,' and all the other proper terms of star-playing, into a realm of pure music and the highest art" (*Putnam's,* March 1853, p. 350).

Although Charles Bailey Seymour, too, disparaged the piano as a solo instrument "in inadequate hands" (*Daily Times,* February 12, 1853), "under the touch of a thorough artist—and such M. Gottschalk proves himself to be—its melody is delightful." Seymour was particularly taken with "The Carnival of Venice" and *Le Bananier.* It was hardly necessary to add, he wrote, that Gottschalk, despite his extreme youth (the reviewer took him to be "not twenty years of age"), was "a finished master of his instrument." Although "in some difficult passages [he] may seem to lack strength . . . his taste is exquisite, his execution elegant, and the general effect of his playing every way pleasant." Having earlier written (in the *Times* on January 25, 1853) that Gottschalk's style was similar to de Meyer's, the critic now modified this statement: "In power he has De Meyer's idea, but hardly his execution, while in the softer and more delicate touch of the keyboard he is not surpassed by the great artists who have previously drawn forth the hearty commendations of our musical public. He will become a general favorite," predicted Seymour.

R. Storrs Willis, too, was struck by Gottschalk's youthful appearance. In the *Musical World and Times* (February 19, 1853, p. 116) he wrote: "Gottschalk is a youth of twenty or twenty-two (we should say) with an easy, winning, southern manner . . . dresses neatly and in good taste, is not handsome, but 'decidedly genteel,' wears a decoration in his buttonhole (a Spanish reminiscence),[70] and [sardonically?] is a fine young American gentleman.

"In playing, he does all the impossible things which a rampant Art accomplishes nowadays. His fingers are like a row of disconnected and perfectly independent little hammers, which play up and down upon the keys with inconceivable rapidity and nervous energy, while in swift and inevitable leaps they make the action upon the extremities of the instrument and the central keys almost simultaneous, binding together the entire piano range into one common center, under the complete and immediate control of one pair of hands."

Gottschalk apparently did not scruple to play down to his audiences: "A very little trade-trickery is observable in Mr. Gottschalk's execution," wrote Willis, "such as the play of hands in the air, etc., by which curious *aerial* effects are produced in the eye of the audience, although a corresponding increase of musical effect is not observable. A child-public," Willis patronizingly added, "*will* have such a droll little innocent by-play, and what shall the poor artist do? Nobody will believe that he is accomplishing a difficult thing unless he hoists signals of some kind to that effect. Indeed, when he

[70] A decoration from the Queen of Spain in recognition of "The Siege of Saragossa."

is *really* doing the difficult thing, he has no time to hoist them; therefore he must do something of this kind between whiles." But such posturing was hardly necessary: "Mr. Gottschalk, moreover, has so much real merit behind all this demonstration that a severe taste is content, while the free play of hands gives a certain easy *nonchalance* in a young player."

Willis was particularly pleased with "The Chase [Hunt] of Young Henry,"[71] with its many descriptive effects, but the audience, he reported, were more taken with the "Poetic Caprices," especially the *Bananier.* "Everyone went away satisfied that America has produced an artist every way worthy to compare with the noblest of the old world in his department." Willis somewhat inappropriately concluded that "the new yacht 'America' [the first winner, in 1851, of the America's Cup and a proud symbol for Young America] is in more senses and more courses than one, a very 'fast' and reliable craft."

The *Mirror* (February 12, 1853) found Gottschalk "far superior to, all things considered, any pianist who has preceded him here, and we doubt if even Thalberg or Liszt would be able to pluck away his laurels." In time, predicted the *Mirror* (perhaps in answer to Richard Grant White's carping remark about Gottschalk's "Titanic labors"), he might even "merge the master with the Titan. . . .

"What we regard as the capsheaf of Gottschalk's triumph," continued the *Mirror,* "was the fact that he produced the greatest impression with his own compositions. They were as brilliant as his performance of them—especially the first part of 'Jérusalem,' full of tenderness and pathos, his 'Bananier,' and his 'Carnival of Venice.'"

The *Mirror* hoped soon to hear Gottschalk at Metropolitan Hall in a performance by ten pianos of "The Siege of Saragossa." "He has raised an appetite for more of his delectable food, and should give us a full feast. It cannot be long ere a portion of his compositions—the compositions of our first great American pianist—will be demanded by the public."

Curiously, William Henry Fry, the loudly self-proclaimed champion of native music and the native musician, instead of jubilation at the presence of an authentic American virtuoso/composer of high rank, expressed his reactions (in the *Tribune,* February 12, 1853) largely in evasions, ambiguities, and abstractions. He devoted a lengthy preamble to an elaborate discussion of metaphoric mountain peaks, and how a relatively small hill might seem like a majestic mountain in an otherwise level landscape, explaining that—lacking such grandiose pianistic peaks as Liszt, Thalberg, and de Meyer—Gottschalk seemed, comparatively, a mountain in the flat musical topography of the United States: "He is a little above the plain of pianoforte playing, and yet [in America] that little is the Alps." It was, after all, relative. Dealt with as an American, Gottschalk was "a superlatively great artist. . . . In a national point of view, he stands alone. Who compares with him? No one."

After this rather deflating opening Fry hailed Gottschalk as a new type—for an American: "You would never take him for a Bull or a Bear," or for a "Leatherstocking," or a "Franklin," or a "Davy Crockett." Disdainful of the dearest American stereotypes, Fry designated Gottschalk as that rarest of all beings, an American who was

[71] Puzzlingly, the *Mirror* referred to *La Chasse du jeune Henri* as a beautiful duet played with Hoffman, perhaps an error on the reviewer's part. Gottschalk had indeed composed a four-hand version of the work, but he appears to have played the solo version at his New York debut.

made for his art and his art for him. He would not pass muster, however, with the old-fogy critics whose horizons were restricted to such outmoded composers as Beethoven, Mozart, or Haydn, and the outmoded style of performance demanded by their outmoded sonatas.[72] Dredging up analogies of older old-fogy unwillingness to embrace The New, Fry caustically cited the musically bigoted, fifteenth-century "execration of such innovations as Bo-Peep" and the acrid comments by the eighteenth-century English music historian Sir John Hawkins (1719–1789) on the introduction of "such profanities as Haydn's now innocent piano-forte sonatas." Fry climaxed his argument with a harangue on the inexorable laws of evolution that rendered yesterday obsolete, in all its aspects, to advanced members of the present, forward-looking generation: "The world is divided into two classes, those who swear by the past in religion, politics, socialism, and art, and those who wish to widen the dominion."

Gottschalk obviously belonged to the second classification. "We had anticipated a different style of performance in young Gottschalk," wrote Fry.[73] "We looked for pearly trills, dazzling rapidity, but we did not expect such a massive left hand, such a facility for hurling chords of a separate octave in one [hand?], and thus *orchestrating* the piano."

Fry shared the prevailing antipathy toward the piano, but for his own reasons: "The instrument is deficient: unlike the violin, it has neither continuity nor gradation of tone. . . . If evanescence is the quintessence of sorrow," he wrote, "its sounds are all jeremiads, for they are no sooner struck than they are gone." But the piano excelled the violin in its ability to mimic the orchestra, and on this characteristic rested Fry's philosophy of modern piano-playing. According to his arcane reasoning, it was "based on the deficiency of the instrument and not the mere desire of display—even assuming that word to have a fixed, and not a relative, meaning.

"We deem these somewhat abstract remarks more important in introducing Mr. Gottschalk to our readers, than special tributes to his pieces [an opinion that Gottschalk can hardly have appreciated]. His apparition is a matter of history. It may not touch tangible interests, vulgarly viewed," wrote Fry, growing more and more obscure, "but still it is potential. It shows a young American, seconded by the ordinary advantages of competence and social position, who has gone out of the dry stereotypism of law, medicine, theology, trade, or politics, and entered into lyrical Art—into Piano-Forte playing—and public Piano-Forte playing—for the love and veneration which he bears the Eternal Spirit of the Beautiful.

"We trust we are not transcendental," hedged Fry. "We simply mean to be matter-of-fact. We wish to hold up Mr. Gottschalk as a splendid artistic model of originality, enthusiasm, devotion, triumph." Yet, Fry—caught in the classic dilemma of the critic/composer required impartially to discuss a rival's music—seemed unable to summon the needed objectivity: "As for the catalogue of the pieces which he played," wrote Fry, "that is of small account. He has rendered his rank indisputably great in the opinion of everyone who heard him, and in the lyrical history of the country he is one of the medals placed in the corner stone."

[72] These statements incited Dwight to an outraged defense of Beethoven, with furious daggers aimed at Fry and at Gottschalk, whom he had not yet heard (*Dwight's*, February 19, 1853, p. 158).

[73] Surprisingly, Fry seems not to have heard Gottschalk during their long concurrent sojourns in Paris.

Then, at last: "If we must signalize any one of [Gottschalk's] pieces, his Creole melodies are admirably beautiful. The ["Jérusalem"] duet (so ably seconded by Mr. Richard Hoffman) was excessively brilliant and loudly redemanded."[74]

But the *Home Journal,* sweeping aside all critical cavils, focused its report (February 19, 1853)—testily refuted in *Dwight's* of the same date (p. 158)—on Gottschalk's extraordinary impact on his first American audience: "To say that his success was of the most unequivocal description can convey to the reader's mind no idea of the *frenzy* of enthusiasm which his playing excited. His playing is precisely of the kind which most palpably hits the popular taste. His efforts are strong and powerful. He dashes at the instrument as Murat charged the enemy,[75] and has a command of its most latent possibilities. His playing has the effect of an orchestra and the modulation of a single instrument. He is the only pianist we have yet heard who can electrify and inflame an assembly. He produces the same sort, and the same degree, of effort as that which oratory sometimes has, in times of public commotion.[76] This is not an exaggeration, as everyone will bear witness who has heard him perform, but a simple statement of facts. A sober judgment of his powers, as compared with other eminent pianists, we are not prepared to give, since it was impossible not to be carried away with the enthusiasm of the occasion. But we hope to hear him again, at an early day, and to consider his performances more coolly."

By now the critics had been able to make a further appraisal, for on Thursday, February 17, Gottschalk appeared for the second and last time before departing for the hero's welcome that awaited him in New Orleans, pausing en route for triumphs in Philadelphia and apparently in numerous other places as well. He had acquired the needful assistance of a professional manager, W. F. Brough,[77] and thus his second New York concert avoided the unprofessional blunders of his first.[78] Taking place at Niblo's larger auditorium (on an opera off-night), Gottschalk was supported this time by an orchestra of forty "of our best instrumentalists" conducted by William Vincent Wallace[79] in a performance of the March and Finale of Weber's *Concertstück*[80] (apparently

[74] Fry noted, too, the reappearance in New York of "our quondam English [Scottish] tenor Frazer," a participant in the 1845 production of his *Leonora.*

[75] The dauntless Napoleonic Marshall Joachim Murat (1767–1815).

[76] "We think we have heard some pianists who could not be set down as mere rhetoricians," starchily responded Dwight (February 26, 1853, p. 166).

[77] "Madame Alboni's opera engagements having given our friend W. F. Brough a release for a time from the management of her affairs, he has taken the young American pianist, M. Gottschalk, in hand for a tour to the South. Mr. Brough leaves for Philadelphia today, where Gottschalk is announced to appear on Tuesday next [March 1]. Mr. G. could not have selected a more capable or popular manager" (*Mirror,* February 25, 1853). As we know, Brough would be back in New York by midsummer to engage in the vast Jullien extravaganza.

[78] But not the financial hazards: Gottschalk sorrowfully records in his journal (September 15, 1862) that he lost $2400 on his first two concerts in New York (*Notes,* p. 46).

[79] "The excellent Wallace," wrote Gottschalk in his journal (September 15, 1862), "had offered me, with that good-natured kindness which was so natural to him, to conduct the orchestra" (*Notes,* p. 46). Gottschalk does not, however, refer to a previous friendship with Wallace in New Orleans.

[80] ". . . Rather a strange choice," writes Richard Hoffman, "as it was physically impossible for him to execute the octave glissando passages as marked, from a habit of biting his nails to such an extent that his fingers were almost devoid of them, and a glissando under these circumstances was

to lay to rest any doubts of his ability to play traditional music). Curiously, Gottschalk, known to be the possessor of an extensive repertory and a phenomenal memory, chose to repeat most of the works he had played at his first concert only a week before: his "Jérusalem" Triumphal Fantasy with Hoffman,[81] his "Carnival of Venice" Variations, and, in a group again headed "Poetic Caprices," *Le Bananier,* to which he added his sensational European successes *Le Bamboula,* op. 2 (*c.* 1847) and *La Savane,* op. 5 (*c.* 1848–49).[82] He was again assisted by Madame de Vries, who sang the *Casta diva* and the *Grâce* from *Robert le diable,* and by Luigi Rocco, who sang Mozart's *Non più andrai* and an unnamed "Grand Duo" with de Vries; Wallace conducted the overtures to *Masaniello* and *Oberon.*

As an encore to "The Carnival of Venice," Gottschalk "very sensibly substituted another piece," wrote Willis in the *Musical World and Times* (February 26, 1853, p. 131), "a no less national one than *Yankee Doodle,* which was blended with *Hail Columbia,* the right hand giving the former and the left the latter, each striving for the mastery, until *Hail Columbia* subdued *Yankee Doodle,* compelling him into subservience and a union at the close with the more dignified *Columbia* melody." (A contrapuntal foretaste not only of Jullien-soon-to-come, and William Mason, but of Gottschalk's popular Civil War piece "Union.")

"The house was a very large one, and we congratulate Mr. Gottschalk on his very decided success in New York, albeit," wrote Willis, "a pianoforte is a desperate instrument to draw a house *with,* or appeal to an audience—be it never so well played."

In the *Daily Times* (February 20, 1853), Seymour, however, adversely revised his earlier estimate of Gottschalk: "It is not every pianist of ability that can fill Niblo's Theatre on a second appearance," he began, amiably enough. "There is no doubt that Gottschalk's command of the mechanical difficulties of the piano is little less than wonderful. . . . He plunges as fearlessly at a bunch of notes as a child would at a bunch of grapes, with this difference—that he never destroys or damages any in his grasp."

But Seymour was no longer willing to equate Gottschalk with Thalberg, or even with de Meyer: "There is something wanting; we listen and are astonished, not delighted." Reversing his earlier opinion, Seymour split hairs: "Mr. Gottschalk has sentiment, but it is more the sentiment of strict science than of imagination. The light and shade are that of a consummate musician rather than of a passionate genius. We are reminded unpleasantly of the letter of the composer rather than the spirit."

Seymour confessed, too, that he "did not particularly admire the '*Bamboula.*' It was neither brilliant, imaginative, or even difficult."[83] He conceived Gottschalk to be

---

out of the question." Gottschalk substituted a brilliant flourish in interlocking octaves, effective, but not the composer's intended effect (Hoffman, p. 133).

[81] For which "the two grand pianos were placed upon a staging built out onto the orchestra (to bring the instruments into the center of the room and assist the acoustical effect), while the orchestra were formed on the stage in the rear" (*Musical World and Times,* February 26, 1853, p. 131).

[82] *Le Bamboula* and *La Savane* are listed, respectively, in Doyle, D-13–13/A and D-135; *Piano Works,* respectively, I, 87, and V, 51.

[83] Richard Grant White, too, found little to commend in the *Bamboula,* which, he wrote: "has a quaint, pretty rhythm, is irregular, capricious, fanciful, but in which we are unfortunate enough not to find music sufficient to excuse so much irregularity and caprice. The fault," he added as usual, "perhaps is entirely ours" (*Courier and Enquirer,* February 19, 1853).

"a dexterous, devoted pianist, loving his instrument for all it can do, rather than for the capabilities it possesses in enunciating ideas clearly, voluptuously, and pathetically. There is an unbroken excellence in his right-hand execution that is truly wonderful. With his left, it is rather different. He needs strength—and, we almost venture to say—dexterity."

Then the ultimate insult: "Mr. Gottschalk is a young man, and will have to submit to criticism. We doubt not he will eventually reach the highest point of excellence. In the meantime, he will have to continue his studies and rest content with a less exalted position than that of the masters we have named."

But the euphoric futurist at the *Albion* (presumably Burkhardt) regarded Gottschalk as the true man of tomorrow. Reviewing both concerts, he wrote (February 19, 1853, p. 92) that in this essentially utilitarian age, "Gottschalk's talent and his genius will be more beneficial and useful to musical art than any of his friends now dream of. His fame we deem no passing effulgence, his dazzling reputation no mere meteoric glare; he will make his mark on the age in which he lives. We believe his compositions and playing—pure, national, and classical—will have a happy effect on the rising generation and be the foundation of a school at once legitimate and characteristic. His 'Bamboula,' 'Bananier,' etc., are truly original specimens of a new and delightful, a truly American, or, if you please, Southern Creole, school—the Gottschalk school, as it may yet be called. The warmth, the feeling, the poetry of the compositions we have named are Mr. Gottschalk's own, are legitimate, national and classical, and will hereafter be identified with his name."[84]

Evidently a man of the Fry ilk, if more tolerant, the critic wrote: "With great good judgment, and as if anticipating the doubts of captious cavilers and sticklers for legitimacy, who believe that classical music began and ended with Mozart, Beethoven, Spohr, and Weber, Gottschalk played, at his second concert, the finale to the *Concertstück* of the last named author, which has now become almost an *experimentum crucis* for every new aspirant to the honours of the Piano. Of this performance we do not hesitate to say that it was by far the most masterly of any we have ever heard, for rapidity, neatness, precision of execution, and justness of conception. . . . If we were called upon to state the most marked characteristic of his playing, we would say *finish*. When we take into consideration the extent and variety of his performances, embracing transcriptions, bravura, ballad, characteristic and eccentric pieces, and classical music [on the basis of a single fragment of the Weber *Concertstück*?] and reflect that equally exquisite finish pervades them all, we shall not be accused of extravagance in assigning him so high a position."

To confirm his objectivity, the writer cited a few negligible faults in an otherwise flawless paragon: "There are some slight mannerisms which mar the general effect of his playing, and which critics may chose to harp upon, such as unnecessarily preluding,[85] sometimes too, in a remote key, and an apparent *ad captandum* [crowd-pleasing]

[84] Yet, recalling these statements, Burkhardt still returned "with pleasure, to Strakosch," as a pianist and composer, albeit his piano piece "The Banjo" was "redolent with 'The Bamboula,' and 'Bananier'" (*Albion*, May 28, 1853, p. 260). In fact, Strakosch's "Banjo" preceded Gottschalk's tremendously popular piano piece of the same name.

[85] In the most approved early nineteenth-century European tradition, Gottschalk appeared onstage wearing white kid gloves, and, wrote Richard Hoffman (pp. 133–34), "his manner of taking

excessive motion of the arms. We mention these, rather, to show that we have observed them, than for any purpose of fault-finding; they are entirely too trivial to merit any serious reprobation."

It was after this second concert that Barnum, who knew a good thing when he saw one, offered Gottschalk $20,000 and all expenses paid for a year's engagement. But Gottschalk *père,* who apparently disapproved of Barnum (or probably dreamed of a greater golden harvest), said no, and Gottschalk *fils*—obviously still under his father's domination, despite his years of independence abroad—obeyed, to his abiding regret.[86]

Gottschalk's ensuing activities were periodically reported in the local press. On July 9 the *Musical World and Times* (pp. 149–50) described his all-but-frenzied reception in New Orleans—an untrammeled carnival of concerts, ovations, honors, receptions, celebrations, tributes, awarding of honors, of jewels, and, from the collective citizens of New Orleans, of a massive medal of "California gold," bearing his likeness, "weighing sixteen ounces, and costing five hundred dollars."

Returning to the North, Gottschalk was reported throughout the summer to be giving concerts at the various fashionable resorts, among them Newport, Saratoga, and Cape May, and frequently playing to aid the victims of the yellow fever epidemic then raging in New Orleans.

On October 13 he returned to Niblo's Saloon for his third concert in New York. Seemingly disregardful of his New York audience, to say nothing of the critics—he coolly offered the very same pieces he had played at his first two concerts:[87] again the *Jérusalem* Fantasy, this time with Jan Pychowsky [*sic*] replacing Richard Hoffman at the second piano; again *La Savane* and *Le Bananier* and Liszt's *Lucia* Sextet transcription with his own finale. His only change in the program—a small one—was the addition of his "American Reminiscences," probably a version of the "Yankee Doodle" piece he had played as an encore at his preceding New York concert.

Gottschalk's assisting artists, aside from Pychowski, were Henriette Behrend, who sang a cavatina from *La gazza ladra* and German songs by Franz Abt and one of the Fescas, and the newly arrived Welsh harpist Aptommas (*né* Thomas Thomas) (1829–1913),[88] who opened the program with a Fantasy on *Semiramide* by Parish-Alvars; later in the program he played a *Danse des fées* by the same composer, and, as an encore, his own arrangement of "Yankee Doodle" (two "Yankee Doodles" on the same program!).[89]

---

them off, after seating himself at the piano, was often a very amusing episode. . . . His deliberation, his perfect indifference to the waiting audience was perfectly manifest, as he slowly drew them off, one finger at a time, bowing and smiling to the familiar faces in the front rows. Finally disposing of them, he would manipulate his hands until they were quite limber, then preludize until his mood prompted him to begin his selection on the programme."

[86] "My father had his prejudices (unjust) against Barnum, in whom he obstinately insisted on seeing only a showman of learned beasts," wrote Gottschalk in his journal (*Notes,* p. 46).

[87] He seems to have repeated this program throughout his travels in 1853.

[88] Not to be confused with his older brother, the renowned harp virtuoso John Thomas (1826–1913), also known as Aptommas (Welsh for "son of Thomas").

[89] The dual "Yankee Doodles" were apparently repeated in Boston, much to John Sullivan Dwight's disgust (*Dwight's,* October 22, 1853, p. 22).

Because, by some mischance, no printed programs were available at the concert, the critic for the *Musical World and Times* (October 22, 1853, p. 60), apparently hearing Gottschalk for the first time, was unable to name anything else on the program. He singled out "a duo for two pianos" *(Jérusalem)* as the best and most effective of Gottschalk's compositions.

But Gottschalk's playing! The great popularity he had achieved in the short time since his arrival was more than deserved, "for his talent places him in the very first rank of modern pianists." His style was "light and sparkling, yet pure and correct." He possessed the quintessential quality of being able to establish a rapport with his audience, without which no artist could succeed: "His soul is warm and electrifies every soul around him."

On this last point George William Curtis slightly differed, writing in *Putnam's* (November 1853, p. 572): "He is a performer of the highest class, distinguished by marvelous power and facility rather than by an especially sentimental style. It is brilliant, gorgeous, amazing playing—betraying an exuberance of youth and strength, which is of itself electrical. But we are not sure that the permanent impression will not be rather of the performer and the performance than of the music. Yet it is something nobody can afford to miss. And let us hope that greatness in his way will not be denied to him because he may not chance to make the hearer cry."

Immediately following his third New York concert, a triumphant Gottschalk, with the same assisting artists, departed on a tour of New England.[90] Starting in Boston on October 18, he again presented the same program, this time to taste bitter defeat at the hands of a wrathful John Sullivan Dwight, who seems to have been lying in wait for this opportunity to annihilate him.

Granting him full credit as a master of pianistic virtuosity, albeit mostly of the cheap, razzle-dazzle variety, Dwight, stalwart defender of the classics, systematically demolished Gottschalk with the cosmic vindictiveness of an avenging angel—calling him, in effect, a non-composer, a musical vulgarian, a perverter of art, and—with his vile repertory—an insulter and corrupter of audiences.

But despite Gottschalk's unspeakable musical iniquities, Dwight was willing to grant him absolution—to "forgive and forget all hitherto—if, with his splendid execution," Gottschalk would, at his following concert (on October 21), keep his promise to perform classical compositions by Beethoven and Onslow. Gottschalk kept his promise,[91] but the two men remained dedicated adversaries forever after.

The circumstances surrounding Gottschalk's even more unfortunate second concert in Boston are cloaked in apocrypha. According to Loggins (who gives no corroborating source for his story),[92] a pretendedly penitent Gottschalk had planned a prank to trick Dwight into denouncing a composition by his god Beethoven: Gottschalk would secretly substitute one of Beethoven's little-known Bagatelles for "one of his own Ossianic ballades" listed on the program (Loggins, pp. 137–38).

[90] Managed by F. B. Helmsmüller, Gottschalk and his company were booked for New Bedford, Providence, Hartford, Springfield, and other New England towns.

[91] With F. Suck, a local violinist (and conductor), Gottschalk played movements from Beethoven's "Kreutzer" Sonata, and with Pychowski a sonata for piano, four hands, by George Onslow.

[92] Most probably derived from W. S. B. Mathews's article "L. M. Gottschalk, the Most Popular of American Composers," in *The Musician* (October 1908, p. 440).

If indeed such a hoax had been intended, it was probably abandoned,[93] for on the day of the concert Gottschalk received word from New Orleans that his father was dangerously ill with yellow fever. Unwilling to cancel the concert,[94] a purportedly frantic Gottschalk is supposed immediately afterwards to have hastened to New Orleans by rail and ship (a journey of some "eight or ten days" that Loggins describes in minute detail), to be at his father's bedside, only to arrive too late.[95]

Yet, well into November—at the very time that Loggins places a bereaved Gottschalk in New Orleans, sadly installed in the family house on Robertson Street (*ibid.*, p. 140)—he was still in the North, having been seen in New York after completing his tour of New England. "Mr. Gottschalk, the pianist, has just returned to our City after an Eastern journey," reported the New-York *Tribune* on November 18, continuing: "Upon his return, he received the sad particulars of the death (on October 23) of his father."

The *Mirror* noted Gottschalk's presence at Niblo's Saloon on November 17, at the debut of his townswoman, the pianist Gabrielle de la Motte (discussed later in this chapter), and the *Albion* (November 19, 1853, p. 560), in its review of La Motte's concert, tells how "at the eleventh hour, her generous brother-artiste and compatriot" Gottschalk had come to her rescue by lending her his piano for the occasion. Indeed, Gottschalk himself, later recalling this painful period, tells in his journal, (with a regrettable disregard for chronological clarity) how, evidently after the Boston fiasco: "Throughout all New England (where, I am eager to say, some years later I found the most sympathetic reception), there was but a succession of losses. . . . I lost sixteen hundred dollars in a few months" (*Notes,* p. 48).

In any case, in December, when Gottschalk eventually did reach New Orleans, he found himself burdened with heavy new responsibilities. He did not return to New York until 1855, by which time he had made his first memorable trip to Cuba.

In mid-March, close on the heels of Gottschalk's New York première, came the announcement of an even more sensational debut: a Grand Concert at Metropolitan Hall to be given by an artist who was not only American, but black!

The singer Elizabeth Taylor Greenfield (?–1876),[96] according to current usage dubbed "the Black Swan,"[97] was born in slavery in Natchez, Mississippi. Through some unclear circumstance, she was freed and adopted in infancy by a Mrs. Elizabeth H. Greenfield, an enlightened Quaker of Philadelphia, who brought her up in that de-

[93] At any rate, neither Dwight nor his critical colleagues were reported to have noticed any substitution.

[94] As Gottschalk revealingly describes his desolation: "I might have put off the concert, but the expenses had been incurred; the least delay would have augmented my loss. . . . I drove back my despair and played" (*Notes,* p. 47).

[95] Again Loggins (pp. 138–40) neglects to document this story. It might have been derived from Clara Peterson's edition of *Notes* (p. 60), not an infallible source; see also Doyle, p. 10.

[96] Her year of birth is uncertain, with such widely differing dates as 1809, 1817, 1819, and 1824 being given by various authorities. The year 1809 seems unlikely, considering the New York critics' observations on her youthful appearance.

[97] As Richard Grant White pointed out, doubtless with tongue in cheek: "That we have heard the Swedish Nightingale and the Irish Swan is the very reason we should hear this Black Swan" (*Courier and Enquirer,* March 18, 1853).

vout community as her own daughter. On discovering that young Elizabeth possessed a prodigious singing voice (covering a range of more than three octaves from bass/baritone to high soprano), her benefactor, despite the Friends' censure of such frivolities as music, allowed the gifted young woman to pursue what was essentially a homemade study of voice, guitar, and piano. In 1851 the mostly self-taught Elizabeth Taylor Greenfield, a woman of indomitable courage, made her successful concert debut in Buffalo, New York, a hospitable community, where—shorn of her inheritance—she had made her way after Mrs. Greenfield's death in 1845. Nebulous rumors of her subsequent concert appearances throughout the free states and Canada[98] had occasionally trickled into the New York papers. And now here she was in person, astoundingly announcing a full-fledged, formal concert at Metropolitan Hall on March 31, just prior to her departure for Europe, where she planned to further both her music studies and her concert career. Unheard of!

On March 18 in the *Courier and Enquirer,* Richard Grant White, misquoting Juvenal, semi-facetiously referred to the phenomenon: ". . . rare as black swans were in Juvenal's day,[99] and equally rare as they are now," he wrote, "we have one in the city whom there is no little curiosity to see and hear." White explained: "The *Black Swan*—for the African prima donna is known to us by no other name—proves to be no myth but a most substantial entity of ebony flesh and blood, possessing a voice which those who have heard her pronounce to be both remarkable and beautiful.[100] She is, we hear, truly an American artist, being the daughter of a Negro father and an Indian mother.[101] We hear," added White, "that she might not be well received if she announced a concert here. No fear could be more unfounded: her *soirées* would be thronged by good-humored thousands."

White could not have been more mistaken. It was no secret that "there was some apprehension of a riot," as Charles Bailey Seymour informed his readers in the *Times* on April 1, the day after the concert. "Several letters were sent to the [local] manager [Sheridan Corbyn, Jr.], threatening dire disasters to the building if the dark lady were permitted to sing. Consequently there was a great parade of the Police force in the lobbies and in the body of the house."[102]

[98] Arthur La Brew reports numerous concert appearances between 1851 and 1853, under the management of a Colonel J. H. Wood of Cincinnati: in upper New York State (including Rochester and Albany); Massachusetts (including Boston); Rhode Island; Vermont; Ohio (including Cleveland, Cincinnati, and Columbus); Michigan (including Detroit); Illinois (including Chicago); Wisconsin (including Milwaukee); and Canada (including Toronto). Some of these concerts might have taken place after Greenfield's return from England in 1854, such as her concert in Boston (see *Dwight's,* September 39, 1854, p. 206, 207 (advertisement); October 7, p. 6).

[99] "*Rara avis in terris nigroque simillima cygne,*" wrote the first-century Roman satirist Juvenal of an earlier black swan.

[100] "The 'Black Swan' has been giving private rehearsals among the amateurs," noted the *Mirror* on March 28. Among them was the critic of the *Spirit of the Times,* who reported (March 26, 1853, p. 72): "We have heard Miss Greenfield; she possesses a most remarkable organ; in fact, *two voices,* a *mezzo-soprano* of excellent quality, full and forcible, and a fair *basso baritone,* clear, round, and flexible, one that many a man would glory in. Her voice is of three and three-quarters octaves, running from F-sharp to A-flat." The *Spirit* added: "She possesses in a very remarkable degree her nation's inherent taste for music."

[101] Elizabeth Taylor Greenfield's parentage is unclear (see La Brew, pp. 9–10).

[102] A force of 60 uniformed police and 100 plainclothes men successfully "suppressed any thought of a disturbance," reported the *Mirror* (April 1, 1853).

The police, in fact, served a double function: not only to prevent the threatened violence, but also to enforce the odious prohibition appearing in both the concert advertisements and the handbills: "No colored persons admitted, as there is no part of the house appropriated for them."[103]

Ironically, therefore, the only "colored person" allowed within the pristine precincts of Metropolitan Hall was the star of the evening. Her cast of assisting artists consisted of a debutante pianist, Miss Ida l'Ecluse, a "pupil of the Royal *Conservatoire* in Brussels," who played a Weber Concerto accompanied by an orchestra of "over thirty" musicians led by G. F. Bristow, and the popular singer Stephen Leach, who sang songs by Cooke, Balfe, and, with cello obbligato, by one of the Lachners. "The Swan," as Greenfield was billed, sang two songs by Sir Henry Bishop—"Sweetly o'er my Senses Stealing" and "Like the Gloom of Night Retiring"—the *Brindisi* (in English) from *Lucrezia Borgia,* wherein she startled her audience by precipitately plunging to a deep bass note at the bottom of her phenomenal low register; also a sacred song by Hummel, "Sound the Trumpet," and a ballad by Balfe, "Then You'll Remember Me." In addition to overtures by Reissiger and Adam, Bristow conducted a work of his own, *La Sérenade;*[104] Mueller presided at the piano.

Needless to say, critics and audience had eyes and ears only for the Swan. "Metropolitan Hall was filled as if Sontag or Alboni had been the attraction," wrote Richard Grant White (*Courier and Enquirer,* April 1, 1853).[105] A huge American flag, probably intended to subdue potential troublemakers, dominated the stage; and, perhaps for the same reason, "the footlights were not lit, and duskiness prevailed over the platform." White embroidered upon this tasteless pun: "At times during the evening the gloom here was undeniably quite Egyptian, for at intervals there came upon the stage a darkness that might be felt."

When an apparently (and quite justifiably) uneasy Greenfield was led out by the hand by an unidentified white man, "coming forward very modestly, almost timidly, she was received," according to White, "with hearty and prolonged applause, which did not quite overpower" what he was pleased to call "a sound of gentle, good-natured laughter which ran through the room."[106]

White described Greenfield as a "fine-looking Negress" of about thirty years of age (the *Evening Post* thought her about twenty-five). "Her voice," he wrote, "is a very deep contralto of unusual compass. So low is its range, in fact, that in ordinary music she uses only its middle and highest registers, which," he added, "show in excess that attenuation of tone always found in the upper part of contralto voices, and which may be noticed in a degree even in the singing of the peerless contralto [Alboni] now performing at Niblo's. The Black Swan's voice is agreeable in quality, and many of its in-

[103] Frederick Douglass (1817–1895), following Greenfield's progress in his Rochester, New York newspapers, *The North Star* (April 8, 1853), execrated this prohibition as "mean, bitter, and malevolent" (quoted in La Brew, p. 80).

[104] Probably his unpublished "Serenade Waltz," composed for the Columbia College Commencement of 1849; its autographed manuscript score is found at the Music Division of the New York Public Library at Lincoln Center.

[105] Tickets were 50 cents; $1 for secured seats. According to Seymour (*Times,* April 1, 1853), the concert was profitable, for "the free list was entirely suspended."

[106] Mincing no words, the *Mirror* (April 1, 1853) more bluntly reported: "Her appearance created a good deal of merriment and boisterous applause."

flections indicate a certain feeling on the part of the singer. She is, however, even far less cultivated than we expected to find her; she having yet to learn to deliver her voice, and her scale passages being given without the slightest articulation of successive notes, but with a continuous sound, such as is produced by running the finger up a violin string.

"The Swan was heartily applauded after each performance and was recalled after having retired from the stage. She was not left without floral honors." White continued: "We understand that it is her intention to prosecute her vocal studies in Europe under the best masters; they will find her voice to be of rare occurrence. She will first give some concerts in England, where the effect of Mrs. Stowe's book cannot fail to prove a very valuable auxiliary to her pecuniary success."[107]

The *Mirror* described the Swan as "a dark mulatto of low stature, quite stout, with a broad, round face, and genuine Ethiopian features. She was dressed very simply in a low-necked, blue brocade dress, with short sleeves and a deep lace cape. Her wooly hair was done in the Jenny Lind style; her only ornament was a bunch of white flowers, which graced the 'place where the wool ought to grow.'[108] Her gloves were of the purest white."

Like Richard Grant White, the *Mirror* critic commented on Greenfield's clearly evident uneasiness; she seemed, he wrote, "very much worried by the excessive attentions of her (white) usher," a circumstance that might quite reasonably have caused her embarrassment and anxiety. Rather than indignation, however, the bizarre situation seemed to rouse the audience to uncontrollable hilarity.

Of Greenfield's vocal performance the *Mirror* reported that "she sang Bishop's 'Sweetly o'er my Senses Stealing' very gracefully and correctly. But her rendering of the famous 'Brindisi' was certainly something new to musical ears. The compass of her voice is perfectly unparalleled. It has considerable sweetness and purity, but without the least cultivation." As an encore to the Balfe ballad she sang "Sweet Home" (Bishop's? Maeder's?) with "simplicity and considerable taste. With proper cultivation and discipline," conceded the critic, "she will yet become a powerful and favorite singer. But," he quickly backtracked, "she is at present in a fair way of ruining what voice she professes by her extraordinary method of running the gamut."

The other critics more or less agreed. "Her voice consists of a few good, strong, and clear upper, or Soprano, notes and about the same number of Baritone notes of very fine quality," wrote the *Albion* (April 2, 1853, p. 164). But its middle register was "poor and not so pleasant. With some good instructions earlier in life she might have become a fine singer—she may do so yet, as we learn that she goes to Europe immediately, to place herself under a good teacher." Like White, the *Albion* casually referred to the audience's derision as "good-humored amusement."

The abolitionist *Evening Post* (April 1, 1853), however, was less ready to condone what it called "ill-mannered laughter from certain individuals who were more nice [discriminating] in matters of color than [in] those of tone. Escorted on the stage by a

[107] Harriet Beecher Stowe had just departed (or was about to depart) for England, where her *Uncle Tom's Cabin* was then at the height of its universal popularity.

[108] An insulting, frequently used locution, appearing in the text of Stephen Foster's minstrel song "Old Uncle Ned" (1848).

Music Division, The New York Public Library

Elizabeth Taylor Greenfield, the courageous "Black Swan."

young white gentleman, the Swan, who is a stout, good-looking colored woman of about twenty-five years of age, received her bouquets and frequent encores with a propriety of demeanor that operated decidedly in her favor.

"About her musical achievements we cannot say so much," regretfully continued the *Post.* "At present, her voice, though of extraordinary compass, lacks cultivation; but we should not be surprised if her intended three years' study abroad[109] should put her on a level with the most celebrated *prime donne* of a different complexion. She seems much more at home in her upper than her lower notes. We noticed this in the Drinking Song from *Lucrezia Borgia,* where her voice made a descent at once so deep and so sudden that her audience laughed out with surprise and amazement."

To the less tolerant Seymour: "It would be perfectly ridiculous to attempt a criticism of 'the Swan's' singing. She has some notes in her voice that are musical, and which might possibly be improved by cultivation, but at present there is not the faintest approach to the latter qualification." That she had attracted a large audience, he wrote, was due to "the novelty of the exhibition rather than the talent which might be exhibited in the singing" (*Daily Times,* April 1, 1853).

[109] She would remain abroad only a little more than a year.

But a rarely compassionate William Henry Fry, writing in the staunchly abolitionist *Tribune* (April 2, 1853), "could not sympathize with the rollicking gaiety of a considerable portion of the audience in seeing her led forward on the platform. Her behavior was strictly in good taste, and gentlemen should not have laughed at her.[110] Had her auditory been the English House of Lords," continued Fry, "they would have received her with marked respect."[111]

Fry alone among the critics empathized with Greenfield as a member of "a poor, peeled, defrauded, abused, despised race. A race that in Africa enslaves itself, and has infernal gods that demand human sacrifices. A race that in this country is either manacled or repulsed. To witness this humble creature seeking to be an artist—to enter the arena of a Sontag or Alboni—has its interest."[112]

Despite his humanitarian sentiments, Fry, in common with his critical brethren, "did not expect to find an artist on this occasion. She has a fine voice but does not know how to use it. Her merit is purity and fullness, but not loudness of tone. Her notes are badly formed in the throat, but her intonation is excellent. She sings, in a word, like a child. The extent of her voice is great. She takes easily the lowest chalumeau note of the clarinet, and when it is taken it is worth nothing."

If Fry harbored no racial prejudice, neither had he tolerance for women who in any way exceeded the conventional format. Greenfield's astounding lower register offended him: "The idea of a woman's voice is a feminine tone; anything below that is disgusting," he asserted. "It is as bad as a bride with a beard on her chin and an oath in her mouth." The single startling low note in the *Brindisi* would pass, he wrote, but "the infliction of a whole ballad lying in the baritone region between E and E was quite unendurable. We hear a great deal about Woman's sphere, and," in Fry's opinion, "it is the soprano region of the voice."

What Elizabeth Greenfield might gain—if anything—from vocal culture at this stage remained to be seen, wrote Fry, but hers was "certainly a voice that ought to be cultivated in Europe, and ought to stay there. The bills of the Concert stated that no colored persons would be admitted, and a strong police was there in anticipation of riot, which did not happen. Under these circumstances," wrote Fry, "we advise Elizabeth Greenfield to go to Europe and there remain. . . . That she has succeeded to the extent shown is evidence of intellect which merits development. She has had everything to contend against—an education neglected—a spurned thing in social life; but her ambition has thus far triumphed, and we hope to hear a good account of her studies in a country where [the elder] Alexandre Dumas [the son of a black mother] has learned how to read and write." A nice point.

The *Herald* (April 1, 1853), not noted for its starry-eyed generosity of spirit, mischievously portrayed the event as a triumph for Greenfield: "The Black Swan took her

[110] And apparently a goodly number of ladies, of which "a very large portion of the throng consisted" (*Courier and Enquirer,* April 1, 1853).

[111] As a protégée of Harriet Beecher Stowe, Elizabeth Greenfield was indeed soon accepted by the highest English society (*Mirror,* June 10, 1853): in May she sang at a command performance for Queen Victoria.

[112] It was reported that both Lind and Alboni, for whom Greenfield had sung, had "expressed themselves astonished with her remarkable powers, and it is owing to the former's kind encouragement that she is at present the vocalist she is" (*Spirit,* March 26, 1853, p. 72).

first public flight in the city last evening. . . . The occasion was a novel and interesting one, and as novelty is the one thing needed to draw a crowd here, the consequence was that the hall was densely thronged." If the audience was lacking in sartorial elegance, it was strong in numbers, "and it was easy to see from the good humor depicted on the countenances of all that the matter was looked upon as decidedly the best joke of the season."[113]

Giving its own version of Greenfield's entrance and the merriment it aroused, the *Herald* reported: "She was timidly led forward to the front of the stage by a little white representative of the *genus homo,* who seemed afraid to touch her with even the tips of his white kids, and kept the 'Swan' at a respectful distance, as if she were a sort of biped hippopotamus. The audience laughed at the attitude of the gentleman usher and still applauded with all their might." When quiet was at last restored and Greenfield had begun her first ballad, "her natural sweetness of voice at first astonished and captivated her hearers, but as she progressed, the defects of her execution, partly caused, we think" the *Herald* added, with surprising perspicacity, "by want of confidence, became apparent. Yet, still, she concluded amid universal applause." When an encore was demanded, Greenfield, "with much condescension, came out, took her seat at the piano, and [accompanying herself] sang, in an exquisite bass voice, the ballad 'When the stars shine in the gentle sky.'"

She was, according to the *Herald,* "a fine looking woman, of low stature but most magnificent roundabout proportions." Describing her costume, the writer noted that "the ladies, as usual, criticized her appearance and her performances very minutely"; he was particularly "struck by the appositeness of one lady's remark, who said she admired the Swan most because she had 'so much pluck, and was, in fact, such a sassy nigger.'"

Attached to this review, with no comment, appeared two letters. The first, dated March 30, the day before her concert, was addressed to Greenfield and signed by five black clergymen of the city, pastors respectively of the Prince Street Presbyterian Church, the Bethesda Congregational Church on Wooster Street, the A.M.C. Church on Second Street, the Immanuel Presbyterian Church on Cottage Place, and the Zion Methodist Episcopal Church.

"The undersigned," they wrote, "profoundly regret that themselves and their numerous colored friends in the city are denied the privilege of attending your concert at Metropolitan Hall tomorrow evening. That they may not be left with the present painful impression, they hereby respectfully request, if consistent with your engagement, you will be so kind as to repeat your concert on Monday evening, the 4th of April, at the Broadway Tabernacle. Should you decline further benefit for yourself, we would suggest that the proceeds, after paying expenses, be divided between the home for Aged Colored Persons and the Colored Orphan Asylum."[114]

Following the five signatures was a meaningful postscript: "We enter into this arrangement with the distinct understanding that the concert, if repeated, will be public, and that no one shall be excluded who complies with the terms" (fifty cents a ticket).

[113] Evidently the audience was determined to treat the occasion as a kind of super minstrel show.

[114] Citing this proposal, the *Mirror* (April 1, 1853) caustically commented: "Now there is a triumph of liberal feeling."

Greenfield's reply, dated March 31, suggests that it might have been dictated by her manager (Colonel Wood or Sheridan Corbyn?):[115] "Gentlemen: I received your kind letter inviting me to sing at a concert previous to my visit to Europe, at which the colored people of this city might have an opportunity of hearing me sing. I regret that you have been debarred from attending the concert to be given at the Metropolitan Hall this evening, but it was expressly stated in the agreement for the use of the hall that such should be the case.[116] I will with pleasure sing for the benefit of any charity that will elevate the condition of my colored brethren, as soon as the necessary arrangements shall be completed for the same, which must necessarily be arranged for an early day, as I shall take my departure for Europe on the 6th proximo."

The second concert seems not to have taken place.

Despite the general disfavor into which the piano had fallen, three more new pianists (in addition to Gottschalk)—each flashing similarly dazzling "credentials"—arrived from abroad: in April, the athletic August Gockel, who, as we know, claimed to be a pupil of Mendelssohn;[117] in July, Julie de Berg, who claimed to be not only a pupil (or protégée) of Liszt, Thalberg, de Meyer, and Henselt, but a Viennese Baroness; and in November, Gabrielle de la Motte, like Gottschalk a native of New Orleans, who had been studying in Europe, according to her publicity, with Liszt, Mendelssohn, Prudent, and Thalberg.

It was a new trend in humbug, declared Dwight in an introductory note to an article debunking this pernicious practice (in *Dwight's,* November 26, 1853, p. 61): "Formerly the virtuosos who came over from Europe to astonish us and conjure the dollars out of our pockets and the souls out of our bodies as we sat listening with open mouths, announced themselves with courtly titles: 'Pianist to the Emperor of All the Russias,' 'First Violinist to Her Royal Highness, the Princess So-and-So,' 'Flutist to the Grand Duke of Weiss-nicht-wo,' etc., etc. That was the style of the flaming placards by which the magicians had it all their own way with us before we knew such from artists." But times had changed, as had the fashion in humbug; "Nowadays they try the virtue of artistic titles and call themselves pupils of such and such great masters."

The claims of "pupil-ship" made by these newly arrived pianists were palpably impossible, wrote Dwight's unidentified correspondent, who was evidently familiar with the inner workings of the *Gewandhaus* in Leipzig in Mendelssohn's day. "Neither Mendelssohn or Liszt ever gave private lessons on the piano," being concerned with

[115] In an appendix, La Brew gives the text of a "Contractual Agreement" for concerts in New York and overseas, signed in Buffalo on February 16, 1853, by Greenfield and witnesses but not by the prospective manager, whose identity remains unknown.

[116] No such stipulation appears in the draft of Greenfield's "Contractual Agreement," angrily responded *Frederick Douglass' Paper,* bitterly castigating Greenfield for putting her personal ambition above this humiliating dishonor to her race (La Brew, p. 80).

[117] "Mr. Gockel is by no means as finished an artist as Mr. Gottschalk or Mr. (Heller) Palmer," commented the *Spirit of the Times* (April 23, 1853, p. 120) after Gockel's debut on April 19 at Niblo's Garden. Contrary to all other reports of his ferocious assaults on the piano, the *Spirit* thought "his touch delicate, at times too much so, if it is not indeed genuine slurring"; he needed more force and originality to join the first rank of "gentleman pianists." At his debut Gockel was assisted by Timm, Bristow, and Rosa Jaques, who might have had her admirers, but who, in the *Spirit*'s opinion, marred her singing by the "violent contortions of her face."

greater and more momentous musical matters than correcting wrong notes and bad fingering. Anyone who had attended Mendelssohn's large "upper classes" at Leipzig, claiming to be his pupil, was just plain fibbing.

Thus, Gockel, a promising pianist now grown noisily exhibitionistic, had been a pupil of the Leipzig Conservatory, not of Mendelssohn. Indeed, the writer seriously doubted "whether such a manner as Mr. Gockel [now] exhibited at the instrument would have gained the approbation of his teachers at Leipzig, whoever they were. Striking chords from a distance of several feet from the keyboard and whipping the air by the most audacious evolutions of the hands are some of the astonishing tricks of Leopold de Meyer and of Gottschalk; and to cramp the hands in the most affected manner (representing sentiment or gracefulness) when lifting them, is a practice which a 'pupil of Mendelssohn' never witnessed in his master."

As to those who claimed to be pupils of Liszt, a few, at most, might have played one or two pieces in the presence of the master at one of his musical gatherings at home; others had merely been present and had never even spoken to Liszt. "Yet, as soon as they reach the American shore they become 'pupils of Liszt.'" A particularly flagrant example was the young lady pianiste (evidently Gabrielle de la Motte), whose extravagant claims in this regard "beat all previous self-recommendation of the kind."

But La Motte's outrageous pretensions (she was billed as "the only artist who can number among her teachers those distinguished and illustrious maestros, Mendelssohn, Listz [*sic*], Prudent, and Thalberg") alas brought her no success in New York—nor had she been helped by the glamorous attendance at her inauspicious debut (November 17) of the renowned pianists Gottschalk, Hoffman, Wallace, and Rakemann♪ (*Mirror,* November 18, 1853). Indeed, the very elements had been against her: "The heavens and the earth were unpropitious . . . rain above and mud below rendered concert-going last evening a self-sacrificing process."

Perhaps it was La Motte's overblown advance publicity that elicited an extra degree of harshness from the critics—more probably it was her sex. "The young lady is petite and pretty," wrote the *Mirror,* "but evidently a novice in the concert room, and it [would have] required the nerves of a veteran to resist the inverted inspiration of empty benches."

Not only the elements but "Fate, or perhaps accident, added its due share to spoil [La Motte's] success in another way," commented the *Albion* (November 19, 1853, p. 560). "The Grand Piano on which she performed—kindly loaned to her at the eleventh hour by her generous brother-artiste and compatriot Gottschalk . . . was somewhat out of order, a portion of the support of the pedals being wanting, which incommoded her so much as to materially interfere with her performance." Considering these calamities, the critic, who had heard her a week earlier at a private *soirée,* thought it more fair to evaluate her talents on the basis of her earlier performance: "Mlle. de Lamotte [*sic*] is very young, very pretty, and very *spirituelle.* She possesses no small degree of proper and honorable ambition, and her present performances fully entitle her to a place in the first rank of Pianistes of her own sex."

Gabrielle de la Motte had been assisted by a Miss Emma Esmonde, a young and pretty vocal debutante who fared just as miserably, having been stricken with a hoarseness that prevented her from speaking, much less doing justice to an aria from *La sonnambula,* an English ballad, and a duet from *Linda de Chamounix* with the multinational opera tenor Luigi Quinto (or Ludwig Quint). Alone Quinto sang arias from *Le Prophète* and *Der Freischütz.* The other assisting artists were the violinist Joseph Burke, who played a Fantasy on *La favorita,* and the cellist Alfred Boucher, with both of whom La Motte joined in trios by Mendelssohn (op. 49) and Beethoven (op. 97);[118] Henry C. Timm accompanied the singers.

Alone, La Motte played Émile Prudent's Fantasy on *Lucia di Lammermoor,* op. 8, and Liszt's virtuosic transcription of *Les Patineurs,* part two of his "Illustrations" of *Le Prophète* (1849–50) (Searle 414), and it was her performance of the latter that aroused the dire condemnation of William Henry Fry. Overcoming his unwillingness to discourage American musical aspiration, he unleashed the full force of his sexist prejudice against La Motte for presuming to play such an essentially masculine composition: "We do not regret that we cannot fully praise Miss de la Motte's performance of the 'Prophète' arrangement by Litzst" [*sic*], he fulminated. "We have never heard a woman who could play the music of that master, and, what is more, we never wish to hear one." Piano music attempting to emulate the orchestra, he wrote, required "nothing less than the masculine grip of the author, or a Gottschalk, to execute it; and if, by any monstrosity, a woman could do it, it would be too much of a manly effort to illustrate the lyrical gentleness of the sex, and hence would be a triumph in the wrong direction. [A can't-win situation for females.] Let Miss de la Motte stick to what her sex entitles her,[119] and she will fully succeed with the culture which ripe age (for she is very young) alone can give." In time, condescended Fry, she would doubtless prove "a brilliant acquisition to the culture of New Orleans," where she was rumored to be returning, and where she evidently belonged (*Tribune,* November 18, 1853).[120]

Gabrielle de la Motte was by no means the only female pianistic casualty of the year. Preceding her by a few months, the Baroness Julie de Berg, sporting similarly Olympian musical references, had fared no better. Modestly headed "The Female Liszt," an overflowing "card" (in effect, a paid advertisement) appeared in the *Herald* on July 1, announcing de Berg's arrival from Europe and apprising the public that she was a member of "the highest classes of society in Vienna, Germany," that she had been declared by "all the greatest artists and connoisseurs to be the greatest living pianiste," that she knew how to "enchant in the highest degree all her hearers by her genial and *spirituelle* performance," and that "we only wish she would give us an opportunity to admire her in New York."

The following day the *Herald* continued the attack. Not only was Madame de Berg rated "the greatest female pianist by Liszt, Thalberg, and de Meyer," but her compositions had created a sensation in Vienna, where they were acclaimed "the best ever made by a lady." And in consequence of her "frequent practice with Mr. Liszt,

[118] Well enough at a Philharmonic concert or a chamber music *soirée,* wrote Burkhardt, but a deadly bore at a miscellaneous concert (*Albion,* November 19, 1853, p. 560).

[119] Better embodied in the Beethoven trio. But then, Fry strongly disapproved of piano/violin/cello trios in general: "The sounds [of those three instruments] do not coalesce, and the one interferes with the other." Such trios should be banned from the concert-room, he wrote.

[120] In fact, Miss de la Motte found her niche in Boston, where she apparently succeeded very well, both as a teacher and performer, and where she remained until a ripe old age. During the month of January (1854) she gave a series of four evidently successful *soirées* at the Chickering Rooms (see *Dwight's,* January 14, 1854, p. 118).

who is quite an enthusiast for her great talents, her execution on the piano received so high a degree of finish that she has been called the 'Lady Liszt' in Vienna."

After these introductory salvos, Madame de Berg's debut was duly announced for August 27, and as it approached, the name-dropping intensified: not only did she bear testimonial letters from Liszt, but also from Thalberg, de Meyer, and Berlioz. And although she belonged to one of the "first families of the Austrian Court," she had "undertaken the professional life from a love of the art, against the wishes and regrets of all of her relatives."

The *Musical World and Times* on August 27, 1853 (p. 257), on the contrary, harking back to earlier Sontag/Countess Rossi lore, replaced the glamorous darling of the Viennese Court with the courageous little woman bravely facing adversity—an admirable example to "every lady of refinement, whose fate it may also yet be to be thrown, like this lady, upon her own resources and compelled to struggle with the rough world."

Yet, despite these varied allurements, and despite her splendid cast of assisting artists—Amalia Patti-Strakosch, Paul Julien, and Henry C. Timm—and despite her novel program, a concerto by Pixis (accompanied by a small orchestra conducted by Timm), Moscheles's *Hommage à Handel,* op. 92 (with Timm at the second piano), and a group of unhackneyed solos by the contemporary Bohemian pianist/composer Julius Schulhoff (1825–1898)—a *Chant du pêcheur,* a Polka, and, as a finale, Schulhoff's version of the perennially favorite "Carnival of Venice"—she attracted only a "thin" audience and generally negative reviews.

As Seymour observed in the *Daily Times* (August 29, 1853): "There appears to be a fatality in the ambition of lady instrumentalists. It was but the other day we had to record the failure of a fair pianist,[121] and it is, we regret to say, our duty to report a similar mishap." The day was past, he wrote, when New York audiences could be satisfied with mere drawing-room accomplishments. Moreover, it was now "no longer sufficient that the performer be a pupil of Thalberg or Leopold de Meyer, or any other celebrity." In Seymour's opinion, Madame de Berg was "nothing more than an ordinary drawing-room pianist. . . . The concert-room is certainly not her proper sphere."

Nothing daunted, on September 15 Madame de Berg tried again, this time on a grand scale at Metropolitan Hall with the assistance of Maretzek's opera stars Lorenzo Salvi and Ignazio Marini, again the incandescent Paul Julien, and "a full grand orchestra" conducted by Maretzek.[122] On this occasion "Madame, the Baroness de Berg," as she was now ceremonially billed, performed Henselt's Fantasy on *Robert le diable,* op. 11, for piano and orchestra, and contemporary solo pieces: de Meyer's *Souvenir d'Italie,* Liszt's transcription of Schubert's song *Die Post* (1839) (Searle 561), a Mazurka by Schulhoff, and Thalberg's Fantasy on Hungarian Melodies (presumably his *Souvenir de Pesth,* op. 65a).

[121] Seymour was referring to Aurelia Ferenczy, a refugee Hungarian pianist and vocalist who had fared badly at his hands in the *Times* of June 1: "Her piano-forte playing and singing are creditable—for a lady—but not up to the high standard of artistic polish to which we have been accustomed." Ferenczy had been assisted at her debut, on May 28 at Niblo's Saloon, by Theodore Eisfeld and Paul Julien, no less.

[122] Maretzek's participation and the presence of artists from his opera company suggests that he might indeed have had a hand in managing de Berg's American career.

"Madame de Berg played chastely and well," reported the *Musical World and Times* (September 24, 1853, p. 26). There was a surprisingly good turnout, considering the disastrous last-minute announcement, "by one of those mysterious accidents of concert management," of Ole Bull's concert on the same evening at Niblo's Garden, postponed from September 13. "Droll coincidence, this—very," meaningfully added the writer, probably Willis.

But C. M. Cady (apparently a reader of the *Daily Times*) thought de Berg's assisting artists far superior to the Baroness, in whom he found "little to commend beyond scores of drawing-room performers that are to be met with in all our large cities" (*Musical Review and Choral Advocate,* October 1853, p. 154).

For the Philharmonic, 1853 was a year of unprecedented fulfillment. On January 15, at the second concert of this their second decade, Niblo's Saloon had been so overcrowded that many were obliged to stand. "We hope these concerts may be given in a larger place," wrote Cady. "They are of such a character that everybody with any appreciation of the beautiful in music ought to hear them." Indeed, Cady commiserated with "anyone so unfortunate as to be away" from the concerts. "Metropolitan Hall ought to be quite small enough to accommodate the lovers of these classical and rare entertainments,"[123] he propagandized (*Musical Review and Choral Advocate,* February 1853, p. 26). After a decade of struggle the Philharmonic had at last come into its own.

With Eisfeld conducting, the soloists were Madame Siedenburg, who sang German songs by Ferdinand Gumbert (1818–1896) and Alexander Fesca; and Paul Julien, whose exquisite performance of Paganini's "Witches' Dance" so delighted the audience that he was forced to play an encore, the unaccompanied "Lullaby" he had played at his debut.

Eisfeld's reading of Schubert's great Symphony in C was highly praised by Cady, as it was by Willis in the *Musical World and Times* (January 19, 1853, pp. 66–67), but Willis had his reservations about Mendelssohn's "Fingal's Cave" Overture, op. 26 (1830, 1832), an intentionally vague work, he wrote, fraught with metaphysical implications. Although it was faultlessly played by the Philharmonic, the overture lacked "warmth of melody." The program closed in jolly fashion, however, with the descriptive overture *Die Reiselust,* op. 26, a kind of musical travelogue by the German composer/editor Johann Christian Lobe (1797–1881).

At the following Philharmonic concert, on March 5, Niblo's Saloon was again so crowded that "scarcely a spot for standing could be found." The soloists were Joseph Burke, playing the first movement of de Bériot's Third Violin Concerto, op. 44; John Kyle and Theodore Groeneveldt, who exhumed Bochsa's *Dialogo brillant* for flute and clarinet (an inferior piece not heard since 1845); and George Frederick Root's Quartette Party, who were heard in Mendelssohn's "Hunting Song" and a Serenade by the young American pianist/composer William Mason,[124] still in Europe pursuing his

[123] This would come to pass on November 25, 1853, with the first Philharmonic concert of their twelfth season.

[124] Was this choice of an American composition, presented by American performers, perhaps intended to placate Fry?

studies and launching his performing career. Eisfeld conducted Spohr's Overture to *Jessonda,* Gade's "Scotch" Overture, "In the Highlands," op. 7 (1844), and, principally, Beethoven's Fifth Symphony.

"The Symphony was never more finely done," wrote George William Curtis (*Putnam's,* April 1853, pp. 468–69). "The Andante was unanimously encored, and the triumphal march of the Finale inspired the audience as no other music can—at least," Curtis qualified, "as no other music can inspire *that* audience." Curtis then traced the Philharmonic's evolution through their first decade, from their earliest struggles in 1842 at the Apollo Rooms♪ and related how the original fashionable membership had soon been replaced by subscribers more truly attuned to German music, being themselves perhaps "two-thirds German." To say nothing of the orchestra, which was, "with a few exceptions, foreign."

Burke's performance of the de Bériot concerto, a great success with the audience, was "clear, polished, exact, and effective," and Root's Quartette Party sang so "simply and pleasantly," and so admirably in Mason's piece—"a sweet strain of summer moonlight, delicately conceived"—that an encore was demanded.

Like Curtis, Willis, in the *Musical World and Times* (March 12, 1853, pp. 161–62), recalled the Philharmonic's stormy beginnings. He commended the Society's principal founder U. C. Hill for having the vision and perseverance to overcome all obstacles in bringing the Philharmonic into being.[125] "At the first start," wrote Willis, "the Philharmonic was advocated by many of the fashionable amateurs of New York," but the "somewhat changeful and uncertain enthusiasm of this class of patrons . . . soon subsided." Undaunted, the Society rose above all obstacles and "*actually* educated in this city an audience for itself—gradually forming a taste for classic instrumental music in the community, which had never existed." By now the Philharmonic was solidly established as a great force for good. (Not that Willis agreed with Eisfeld's tempi in Beethoven's Fifth, a disagreement that he flaunted in four musical examples taking up a full column of his lengthy review.)

But although the present Philharmonic audience was "unquestionably more discriminating than any other among us," except, perhaps, the audience for Eisfeld's *soirées* (essentially the same audience), many "would-be connoisseurs" were nowadays seen posturing around at the Philharmonic's concerts, to say nothing of out-of-town ignoramuses who kept up a steady flow of loud and idiotic conversation during the performances.

The *Albion* review (March 12, 1853, p. 128), too, referred to the Philharmonic's early trials, their shifting audiences, and their edifying effect on the public musical taste. Like Curtis and Willis, but with his own embellishments, Burkhardt recalled the "ultra-fashionable people" who had attended the Philharmonic's first season only to drop out because the concerts offered less opportunity for personal display than did the opera house. He remembered how bravely the Philharmonic had coped with adversity, and how they had brought their audiences to the present high level, representing "an

[125] And the enthusiasm: Willis recounts that Hill, on his return from his studies with Spohr in Germany (1835–37), was so obsessed with music that "he used to get up early winter mornings (the only time he could snatch from his teaching) and, in company with two or three friends, play the trios and quartettes of the great masters, by candlelight."

array of intellect and refinement not to be found at any other public entertainment." He had more to say on the subject, threatened Burkhardt, but in the future.

After their following concert, the last of their eleventh season, given on April 23 at Niblo's Saloon, Burkhardt sourly made good his promise in the *Albion* of April 30 (p. 212). But first, he verbosely and disapprovingly dissected Schumann's First ("Spring") Symphony, op. 38 (1841), heard for the first time in New York. It was a pretentious work, he wrote, skillfully enough orchestrated and showing acquaintance with the great masters, but although in no way imitative, it was not new enough to be called original. Its most glaring fault was its "poverty of melody and its incongruous and incoherent character"—it was fragmentary and tedious, frustrating and discursive, formless and undisciplined; it lacked Unity and Intention. "The writer seems to have sat down to write without having any fixed idea to evolve and elucidate," accused Burkhardt. In endless analytical detail he compared Schumann's First Symphony with Beethoven's peerless C-minor Symphony, much to Schumann's detriment. Not only was Schumann inferior to Beethoven, he wrote, but to such lesser masters as Mendelssohn, Spohr, Gade, and so on.

With Eisfeld conducting, "one of Beethoven's greatest works"—his first *Leonore* Overture in C (1805)—was badly played; Weber's *Euryanthe* Overture perhaps less badly. The soloists Rosa Jaques and Philip Mayer sang their duet from *The Marriage of Figaro* well enough, but the work was unsuited to the concert-room; Mayer's aria from *Jessonda* was more satisfactory. Jaques, although frightened, sang charmingly and correctly, but she might have found something better to sing than the inadequate *Jeanne d'Arc à Rouen* aria by Louis Bordes, an obscure composer who had Italianized his name to Luigi Bordese "to make his vocal compositions go down." And down is where they should go, vengefully added Burkhardt.

The extrovert pianist August Gockel, playing Weber's *Concertstück* and his own "Polichinelle" for solo piano, also mightily displeased Burkhardt: Gockel's execution, concededly of unparalleled rapidity and distinctness, was "only equaled by a steam engine [a favorite Burkhardtian simile], to which he is inferior in point of feeling or expression." Gockel possessed no light and shade, and Burkhardt "abominated such antitheses"; he advised Gockel by no means to attempt the career of a "first-class virtuoso."

But Burkhardt reserved his most lethal barbs for the Philharmonic itself. Now that it had completed its eleventh season, it was time for a reassessment of what the Society had achieved—what year-by-year strides it had accomplished. In Burkhardt's opinion the orchestra had sadly deteriorated in the past three years. "Why is this?" he demanded (sharpening his knife for Eisfeld).

Although only a few years earlier the Society's musical ills had been commonly attributed to their constant turnover of conductors, Burkhardt now blamed their "deterioration" on "the continuance of the same conductor, while the Society possesses several members equally capable of filling that important post and even more ambitious [than Eisfeld] of raising the standard of the performances." (Echoes of early Watson.)[♪] Besides, the Philharmonic had an obligation to educate conductors: "We do not wish to be dependent upon any *one* conductor; we wish competition, in short, the Democratic principle—rotation in office."

Too, Burkhardt deplored the insufficient size of the Philharmonic (sixty-seven players), comparing it unfavorably with the great transatlantic orchestras. Quantity produced quality, he maintained: "Fifty violins playing *piano* may produce a sound no louder than that of one, but then the quality of the tone produced by the fifty is what gives *the effect*." Besides: "In an orchestra it is necessary that every man be able to play, and play well, the part allotted to him. If he cannot, he only mars the general effect and had better be left out. . . . We are induced to believe that some of the members of the Philharmonic do not add to its effective powers, although they may to its numbers. In view of this, we boldly assert that no such thing as a *Pianissimo* is ever produced by this Society [the eternal cry]. Those who have heard the wonderful effect of a *Pianissimo* as contrasted with a subsequent or previous *Forte* or double *Forte* will appreciate how great a defect this is in the Philharmonic performance."

It was only the purest motives that prompted these remarks, protested Burkhardt, all the while—for reasons of his own—aiming directly at Eisfeld's heart.

A nonetheless euphoric Philharmonic, in its self-congratulatory eleventh annual report, published in the *Musical World and Times* (October 8, 1853), pridefully pointed to the "favorable position it now [held] as a Musical Society, and the improved condition of its prospects for an adequate support" from an increasingly well-disposed public. Beginning the eleventh season with a deficit of "about $130," they had finished it with a surplus of $42.54. "All of which," exulted their treasurer, William Scharfenberg, "proves the Society, in a financial point of view, at least, to have passed through a season of unprecedented success, and to be at this moment in a most flourishing condition.

"It is our particular pride that this Society shall stand second to few or none in the world," exuberantly continued the report. As an idealistic "association of artists, having uppermost in our minds the true interests of our Art," the Society planned to make their concerts still more interesting "by bringing out many works that we have not yet produced, and by repeating in better style many that we have already performed."

Greater efforts would be made, too, to attract a larger attendance to the already large "day and afternoon" audiences at the public rehearsals (held at the Apollo Rooms), "a new thing and quite popular" among the Society's non-professional associate membership now grown to "nearly 500" (largely composed of women).[126] "They will undoubtedly run up to nearly or quite double that number during the coming season," was the optimistic forecast.

"The number of Subscribing Members (eligible to attend only the concerts) is also larger, and the new style of members, called Professional, has made a very good beginning, and for the advantage of their acquaintance and assistance, we feel desirous that their number should be very large, embracing the most, if not all, of the professional musicians in the city." This new category of membership admitted professional

[126] And talkative women. *Dwight's* "Diarist" (Thayer), after attending a Philharmonic public rehearsal in December complained (*Dwight's,* December 31, 1853, p. 100) that, "of all Babels, the Apollo Rooms, considering the occasion, rank nearly with the worst." It was a mystery how "poor Eisfeld" could get on with his work "amid the noise, chattering, talking, laughing, coming in and going out, beau-ing and belle-ing, and so on, through the whole catalogue of anti-music." Perhaps it was for this reason that the board of directors voted to hold one private rehearsal for each concert (Philharmonic Archives).

musicians of all classes, including teachers, to both the concerts and rehearsals for the minuscule fee of $3.[127]

And to facilitate the management of their fiscal affairs, the Society had at last been granted an Act of Incorporation, something they had persistently sought since 1844. "Thus it will be seen that one thing has been added to another to place us on a more permanent footing for genuine usefulness in the city as one of its Institutions. But [symbolically touching wood] let us not be actuated too much by a mercenary spirit in the matter, but rather let our thoughts be directed to the elevation of the Society to its proper position, by the greatest excellence in our future performances."

For the first concert of their twelfth season, on November 26, the Philharmonic Society—to accommodate the increased subscribership—performed at Metropolitan Hall,[128] available because Jullien was currently absent on tour.[129] The soloists were Mrs. Bostwick, who sang the *Non mi dir* from *Don Giovanni* and Alexander Fesca's song "The Wanderer"; the harpist Aptommas (engaged in lieu of Gottschalk, by now departed for New Orleans), who played a Grand Fantasia by Parish-Alvars on combined themes from *I Capuleti ed i Montecchi* and *Semiramide,* and a Fantasy of his own composition on *Lucia di Lammermoor;* and a debutant violinist Mr. C. Hahn, playing Vieuxtemps's *Fantaisie caprice* for Violin and Orchestra, op. 11. Eisfeld conducted an orchestra increased to eighty-one players[130] in the first American performance of Spohr's "exceedingly descriptive" Symphony No. 9 ("The Seasons"), op. 143, and in Berlioz's *King Lear* Overture, and Marschner's Overture to *Der Vampyr,* op. 42.

On December 3, 1853, R. Storrs Willis (in the *Musical World and Times,* p. 106) and Charles Burkhardt (in the *Albion,* p. 584) each devoted the greater part of his review to Spohr's splendid musical depiction of the passage of the seasons. For the rest, while Willis had "never heard Mrs. Bostwick sing so well," Burkhardt had often "heard her sing in better voice and more effectively";[131] and while Willis found Mr. Hahn's light and graceful style to be nothing less than virtuosic, Burkhardt thought him a respectable utility violinist but hardly in the "first rank of the *virtuosi* we have now and have recently had among us." Surprisingly, Willis and Burkhardt agreed that Berlioz's *King Lear* Overture was a magnificent work.[132]

Willis could not understand, however, why the orchestra still clung to the anti-

[127] Fifty-nine professional members were admitted to the Society in 1853. As before, subscribing members paid $10 for three tickets to each of the four concerts; associate members paid $5 for admission to rehearsals, but not to concerts. All members could purchase extra tickets for $1; nonmembers for $1.50.

[128] Engaged at the huge rental of $150 per concert (Philharmonic Archives).

[129] At a meeting of the Philharmonic officers on November 21 it was resolved to send a letter of thanks to Jullien's manager, Arthur Chappell, for allowing the Society to use Jullien's orchestra (platform) and music stands, left in storage at Metropolitan Hall during Jullien's absence on tour (Philharmonic Archives).

[130] The orchestra now consisted, according to the *Daily Times* (November 28, 1853) of 31 violins, 11 violas, 7 cellos, 9 double basses, 2 flutes, 2 oboes, 2 clarinets, 2 bassoons, 4 horns, 2 trumpets, 2 trombones, and one each of bass horn, tympani, bass drum, cymbals, and side drum.

[131] At the meeting of the Philharmonic officers on December 1, Mrs. Bostwick was vainly proposed for honorary membership in the Society (Philharmonic Archives).

[132] A far cry from Willis's earlier dictum that Berlioz was a "musical lunatic" (*Albion,* December 28, 1850, p. 628).

quated custom of standing throughout the performance: "Aside from being uncomfortable to them, this looks badly [*sic*], and impresses the spectators uncomfortably. The artists appeared like men in a hurry, refusing seats, as it were, to dispatch their task the sooner and be quicker off."[133]

Burkhardt, after congratulating the Philharmonic Society on "the prosperity which made this change to a larger Concert Hall necessary" (glad tidings announced in their Eleventh Annual Report) and felicitating them on the acquisition of additional string players,[134] resumed his attack on Eisfeld, who, he was beginning to believe, threatened to become the perpetual conductor of the Society: "With every respect and appreciation for Mr. Eisfeld's talents, it strikes us as a somewhat humiliating and silent acknowledgment on the part of the Society (one of whose aims and objects is, or should be, to create, to make *conductors*) to be unable, concert after concert, and season after season—at least, since George Loder's departure for California—to find any other capable conductor among their number."[135]

Not Eisfeld but his first violinist Joseph Noll bore the brunt of Burkhardt's dissatisfactions at Eisfeld's "Quartette *Soirées*," of which the remaining events of the third season were given at Niblo's Saloon on January 3 and 22 with the assistance of Madame Siedenburg and on February 19 with George Frederick Root's Quartette Party, and at the Apollo Rooms on March 12 with Miss Thomas. Despite his consistent harshness toward Noll's violin playing, Burkhardt, in the *Albion* of March 19, 1853 (p. 140), nonetheless summed up this third series as a rare musical treat and the source of much refined enjoyment and edification.

In these six concerts Eisfeld had presented a vast and splendid repertory: for strings, "three Quartettes and a Septette by Beethoven; two Quartettes of Haydn's; one by Mendelssohn; and two by Mozart [also Onslow's Quartet, op. 21, no. 3]. With Piano, two trios, both played by [Richard] Hoffman—one by Fesca and one by Mendelssohn [op. 66 in C minor][136]—two Quintettes—one by Spohr, [magnificently] played by Timm, and one by Robert Schumann, played by Scharfenberg; one Quartette by Lachner, played by Wollenhaupt—in all, eleven Quartettes, one Septette, and five Piano pieces—nearly three grand compositions of the classic authors for each concert!" Also at the sixth concert Eisfeld had performed three request items: the Variations on the Austrian Hymn from Haydn's Quartet, op. 76, no. 3 (Burkhardt's request);

[133] Willis disapproved as well of the erratic new placement of the instruments—the cellos scattered among the double basses, for instance.

[134] They included Herwig, Döhler, Dean, Thomas, Matzka, Zeiss, and La Manna (violins) and Poznansky [*sic*], Weyrauth, and Pauli (violas). Also engaged were Kuhlemann (second bassoon), Kiefer (first clarinet), and G. Schmitz (second clarinet). Extra or substitute musicians were still paid $5 for a concert and two rehearsals; for every additional rehearsal they received an additional dollar (Philharmonic Archives).

[135] Eisfeld nonetheless continued to be the Philharmonic's sole conductor until the third concert of their thirteenth season.

[136] If Fry considered piano trios the "worst combinations in music" because the piano was the most imperfect of instruments (*Tribune*, January 4, 1853), Burkhardt looked on the violin as an inferior instrument because its tones were "produced by friction . . . the least pleasing method in which sound is obtained" (*Albion*, January 8, 1853, p. 20). Both agreed, however, as did the other critics, that Mendelssohn's greatest fault was his lack of melody.

the Canzonette from Mendelssohn's Quartet, op. 12; and the "Andante religioso" (Adagio sostenuto) from Haydn's Quartet, op. 76, no. 1. Madame Siedenburg had sung German songs by Alexander Fesca, Ferdinand Gumbert, Friedrich Kücken, and Gustav Graben-Hoffmann (1820–1900); Root's Quartette Party had been heard in Mendelssohn's Hunting Song and a "Faeries' Glee" by Asahel Abbott; and Miss Thomas was as universally praised for the extraordinary beauty of her voice as she was censured for her unintelligible diction[137] in a Barcarole by Schubert and Mendelssohn's "Suleika" (one of his two songs of that title, either op. 34, no. 4, or op. 57, no. 3).

On November 30 the indefatigable Eisfeld launched his fourth chamber-music series at Hope Chapel, a hall much disapproved by Burkhardt.[138] The soloists were Mrs. Clara Brinkerhoff, who in a small but pure voice sang two songs by Eisfeld, one—"I go, but wheresoe'er [I] flee"—to words by Byron, and "our inimitable Timm," who played the piano part of Mendelssohn's Quartet in B minor, op. 3 (1825), as only Timm could. String quartets by Beethoven and Mozart completed the program.

The National Guard Band, its thirty-five members resplendent in full military regalia, gave the third concert of their series at Metropolitan Hall on January 8. Conducted by Noll and assisted by Rietzel, Wollenhaupt, and the singer Klein, they devoted half of their program, as before, to symphonic literature, half to military band music. At their following concert (February 5), they were assisted by Madame Otto[139] and the clarinetist Kiefer; on March 19 by Eltz (bassoon), Ohlemann (oboe and clarinet), Rietzel (flute) and Kiefer and La Croix (cornets à pistons); and at their grand finale, on May 31 at Castle Garden, the band's assisting artists were Kiefer, the Philharmonic horn virtuoso Henry Schmitz, and the opera basso Alessandro Gasparoni. The National Guard Band announced a further "short series" of promenade concerts at Castle Garden, to commence on June 15.[140]

The Dodworth Band, too, continued their series at Metropolitan Hall on January 22, with solos by Charles R. Dodworth, Harvey B. Dodworth, the clarinetist Edward Boehm, and Theodore Thomas and G. F. Bristow, who played a piano and violin duo by Benedict and de Bériot. On February 26, their soloist was Harvey Dodworth; on April 9, Jefferson Dodworth, C. R. Dodworth, and M. K. Batsford; on April 28, Harvey, Allen, and Charles Dodworth and the oboist Henry Gortelmeyer; on May 14, Allen Dodworth, W. Bushman, and Professor Robert Heller. The following night (May

137 Fry had difficulty in telling if she was singing in "English, German, or Italian" (*Tribune,* March 14, 1853).

138 "Hope Chapel is a small, ill-constructed, and ill-sounding room," wrote Burkhardt, "well enough for the exhibition of Panoramas or for lectures, but acoustically unfit for musical purposes, especially for chamber music" (*Albion,* December 10, 1853, p. 596).

139 "Madame Otto . . . it is plain to see, will not sing as well at fifty as she did at thirty," uncharitably observed the reviewer (probably Oliver Dyer) for the *Musical World and Times* (February 12, 1853, p. 97). Apparently Madame Otto, who had a cold, was out of sorts and in mortal conflict with "poor Noll," to say nothing of the audience. Noll's exhibitionistic conducting, too, according to the reviewer, required "pruning": "We cannot see the necessity of employing two arms and two legs to indicate the movements of a piece." Yet, these National Guard concerts were "among the very best concerts given in the city."

140 They were soon succeeded by Dodworth's Band, who performed on Sunday evenings at Castle Garden until Jullien's arrival at the end of August.

15) they scooped the National Guard Band by a month with their first Grand Promenade Concert at Castle Garden.

True to their custom of performing music by American composers, at their February 26 concert Dodworth's Military Band played William Henry Fry's "Metropolitan March," and on April 9 a medley of three selections from his "American Opera of *Leonora*" was heard, arranged respectively for Military Band, *Ebor Corno,*[141] and the Cornet Band. The soloists were Charles and Harvey Dodworth.

What with the enormous and varied music activity throughout the year, miscellaneous concerts by resident musicians were comparatively few in 1853. The doughty veteran Emma Gillingham Bostwick, returning from another of her tours, announced a Grand Concert at Niblo's Saloon on May 30, with the assistance of the secondary opera basso Severo Strini, the flutist Julius Siede, the hornist Henry Schmitz, the pianist Jan Pychowski (as accompanist and composer of a song dedicated to Bostwick), and a small orchestra led by Joseph Noll.

During November, Mrs. Bostwick gave her annual series, this time consisting of only four "*soirées musicales,*" performed within the span of one month. At the first, on November 1, her assisting artists were the pianist Augustus Gockel and the young violinist Theodore Thomas.[142] The formidable Gockel played two of his own compositions, "The Naiad Queen" and a *Souvenir de Russie,* quite well, but on an instrument unequal "to his powers." The reviewer for the *Musical World and Times* (November 5, 1853, p. 73) thought Gockel's remarks to the audience, "explanatory of the inferiority of the instrument," unfitting and unfair to the manager, who was in no way to blame. Theodore Thomas "played very badly," wrote the critic. "He should have an extinguisher put on him at present, and not appear in public again until he can play at least half as well as so young a boy as Paul Julien."

Earlier, on February 22 (Washington's Birthday),[143] phenomenal little Paul Julien, who purportedly was returning to Europe to fill engagements there, had given a brilliant "farewell" concert at Metropolitan Hall, assisted by his friend Henriette Sontag[144] and her satellites Cesare Badiali, Luigi Rocco, and Carl Eckert. Reviewing this event, Burkhardt, in the *Albion* (February 26, 1853, p. 104), vainly exhausted his repertory of superlatives in attempting to describe the perfections of this wonderful boy, "whose career and genius [seemed] to have no parallel except in those of the youthful Mozart."

Immediately following this leave-taking, on March 3 Julien's father announced in the papers that before returning to Europe his son would visit the principal cities of the United States, giving only one concert in each, in response to "the flattering

[141] A tenor horn developed by the Dodworths and much used by them for solos.

[142] Among Mrs. Bostwick's other assisting artists during the series were Miss Marie Beattie (a singer), Jan Pychowski and Florentine Szpaczek (pianists), Wells (singer), Seidler (violinist), Michele Rapetti (a voice from the past), who played violin *obbligatos* for some of Mrs. Bostwick's solos, Frederick Bergner (cellist), and Timm, who presided at the piano.

[143] According to a report in *Dwight's* (February 26, 1853, pp. 166–67), young Julien, in honor of the day, closed this program with "an original Fantasia in honor of the Father of our Country, introducing national airs." The *Tribune* (February 23, 1853) reported that a transparency of Washington was shown when Julien reached the "Yankee Doodle" finale of his Fantasia.

[144] To everyone's delight, Julien led Sontag out on the stage.

wishes expressed to him by the American press." The farewell turned out to be premature: as late as 1857, *Dwight's* (January 17, 1857, p. 127) commented that Julien, who was still giving farewell concerts right and left, seemed "determined *never* to leave the country."

Premature, too, was the "Grand Valedictory Concert" given with great advance fanfare by the septuagenarian Anthony Philip Heinrich, the "Log-Hut Maestro," on April 21 at Metropolitan Hall. Father Heinrich's purpose in mounting this event, explained the *Home Journal* (February 19, 1853),[145] was "to realize from this concert a sum sufficient to pay the expense of a visit to Europe, where he intends to lay his compositions before the great masters of the musical art."

To kindle public interest, the Heinrich legend was again exhumed and refurbished: his lost wealth, his heroic struggle to eke out a meager livelihood with teaching and various menial musical odd jobs,[146] his vast musical output, cramming his humble attic to overflowing with scores of "oratorios, operas, symphonies, and songs—merely composing, not publishing them—till he has accumulated several large chests full of elaborate, original musical compositions, his only wealth. A pure love of art has been the sole motive for his labors, and the joy of composing his only reward."

This reward apparently did not suffice, for: "Now, far advanced into the vale of years [he was 72 years old], the desire has sprung up in his mind to submit some of his compositions to the judgment of the world."[147] At his approaching concert, six of them were to be "for the first time, performed by the best orchestra the city can furnish." In fact, five of Heinrich's huge, multimovement works were programed (not all first performances), of which two were omitted, not unusual for a Heinrich concert.

The *Musical World and Times* (April 30, 1853, pp. 273–74) reported an audience of 1500 to 2000 at the concert, but thought the proceedings "should have been more cordially responded to. A band of seventy musicians, the best the city affords, and conducted by Mr. Heinrich himself, undertook the difficult task of giving his music a fair interpretation, after meager and unsatisfactory rehearsals." The two works the reviewer had most wanted to hear—*National Memories,* a "Grand British Symphony" in four movements, dedicated to Queen Victoria in 1851, and *The Tower of Babel, or Language Confounded,* a two-movement piece consisting of a *Sinfonia canonicale* and a *Coda fugato*[148]—had been "entirely omitted." Those that were performed (like most of Heinrich's larger works, infinitely reworked, transplanted, and retitled)[149]—*The Wild Wood Troubadour, a Musical Autobiography* in four movements; *The New England Feast of Shells*

[145] In an article attributed by William Treat Upton (*Heinrich,* p. 217) to a Mr. Harris, a member of the Society of the Iron Man.

[146] The log house in Kentucky was never overlooked by Heinrich's promoters, nor by the patriarch himself.

[147] Hardly sprung up. Throughout his long career, Heinrich had habitually sought testimonials to the excellence of his music, chiefly from well-known European composers.

[148] Like Papa Haydn's "Farewell" Symphony, Father Heinrich's *Tower of Babel* ends with a "Dispersion," calling for "a gradual cessation of melodies, and consecutive retirement of each individual performer" (Handbill, Upton, *Heinrich,* p. 219).

[149] For the daunting permutations and relocations of Heinrich's stupendous output, see Upton, *Heinrich, passim.*

in three movements; "The Adieu," a vocal quintet with a bewildering genealogy; and a "Pastorale" for orchestra, conducted by Eisfeld, replacing the missing *National Memories*—unfortunately "gave evidence of great haste in the getting up."

As always, the critics resorted to ambiguities in attempting to describe Heinrich's problematical music. Of *The Wildwood Troubadour,* the apparently bewildered reviewer for the *Musical World and Times* wrote: "Without any of the somber harmonies or sudden transitions which are peculiar to the Beethoven and Von Weber school, it gives to the impartial, unprejudiced listener a faithful picture of the forest home of the self-reliant Western man, by means of simple harmonies united to melodies highly florid. New and fantastic passages of imitation are distributed among the different instruments of the orchestra in a style entirely the composer's own. The harmony reminds one of Mozart and Haydn; but the orchestral treatment is to the last degree original."

More directly, Richard Grant White, in the *Courier and Enquirer* (April 22, 1853), credited Heinrich with "pleasing ideas, treated at times with great skill and almost always with much elaboration," but added, "a lack of coherence and purpose is too palpable throughout."

The announced soloists were Madame Otto, Madame Stephani (who did not appear), Mrs. Brinkerhoff, the Misses Brainerd, Dingley, and Brown, Messrs. Nash and Conkey (singers), the brothers Christian and Mathias Schneider (pianists), C. Haase (cornetist), Van Der Weyde (playing the Phys-Harmonica [harmonium] in the first movement of The *Wildwood Troubadour*), Timm (presiding at the piano) and Eisfeld (conducting the second part of the program). Caroline (or Cornelia) Dingley and the Schneiders were especially singled out: "Miss Dingley," singing "The Captive Greek Girl" by the English composer John William Hobbs (1799–1877), "displayed a noble mezzo-soprano voice, well worthy of the discipline which it so sadly needs," convolutedly wrote R. G. White; and the *Musical World* reviewer noted that "the Messrs. Schneider played a duet, called *Impromptu champêtre,* on the piano in a way that puzzles all attempt at recollection or explanation." The program further included vocal works by Edward Loder, W. V. Wallace, and Weber, a piano duet played by eight-year-old Ernst Perabo (1845–1920) with Vanderweide and a lovely little five-year-old girl—inevitable at a Heinrich concert—presenting the venerable maestro with the indispensable "handsome present."

After all this valedictory ritual, it was not until the end of 1856 that Heinrich eventually sailed for Europe. He would return for the last time in 1860.

A wider-than-usual range of causes elicited help in 1853. Three benefit performances in aid of sick and needy members of the New York Regiment Volunteers were given at Hope Chapel in April by the celebrated comic entertainer Dr. Valentine, assisted by Kazia Lovarny and Herr Franz Stoepel.

At Chinese Hall, where he appeared nightly, Professor Robert Heller, "The Wizard of Wizards and Great Modern Conjuror," with the assistance of Dodworth's Band, donated an evening, on April 21, to a "Grand Performance" of music and magic for the benefit of the American Musical Fund Society. As "one of the most eminent pianists and composers of the day, and highly distinguished in the musical world—a King's Scholar; Associate and Professor at the Royal Academy, London; Honorary Member of the London Philharmonic Society, etc."—Heller would, "in addition to the attraction of Second Sight [and] Exposures of Rappings,[150] the Inexhaustible Bottle, and other atrocities . . . perform a grand solo on the pianoforte, one of his earliest compositions." Tickets were twenty-five cents—fifty cents for reserved seats.

At the Musical Fund Society's more conventional benefit concert on May 16 at Metropolitan Hall, the star was little Paul Julien, who, already an honorary member of the Philharmonic, on this occasion received an honorary membership in the Musical Fund Society from its vice-president Henry C. Watson.[151] Besides Julien's two superb solos—Haumann's Fantasy on *Ma Celine* from *Masaniello* (encored) and a *Grande Aria militaire* (first time in America) by the Belgian violinist/composer François Prume (1816–1849)—the program consisted entirely of a repeat reading of Shakespeare's *Midsummer Night's Dream* to Mendelssohn's music (so memorably performed by Fanny Kemble in 1850), this time by Miss Kimberly, a lesser *diseuse*. As before, Eisfeld conducted.

To a disapproving Richard Grant White the mingling of music and drama, particularly the uneven combination of Shakespeare and Mendelssohn, was inadmissible. There could be no synthesis of the arts, maintained White; it was no more reasonable to combine music with poetry than it would be to write St. Luke's narrative across the face of Raphael's *Transfiguration,* so that viewers "may enjoy the story and the picture together. . . . Music, Painting, Sculpture, or Poetry," wrote White, "will not receive divided homage" (*Courier and Enquirer,* May 17, 1853).

On July 21, prominent members of the opera, theatre, and German-music communities united to rescue a stranded troupe of forty-two Chinese entertainers—the Tong, Hook, Tung Company—whose nightly performances at Niblo's Garden since May 20 had proven to be a fiasco. Announced to appear in their behalf at Castle Garden were Sontag, Steffanone, Anna Thillon (who was indisposed but sent a check for $50), Mrs. James G. Maeder, Stephen Leach, August Gockel, and the *Liederkranz* and *Social Reform Gesangverein* together with their respective directors. They presented a program of predominantly German music, preceded and followed by exotic entertainment by the beneficiaries.

Even more spectacularly, an extraordinary trio of benefit events took place in September 1853, when the music community, both foreign and native, rallied splendidly to a national appeal by the Howard Association of New Orleans[152] for aid to the victims of the devastating yellow fever epidemic then raging in that city.[153] On September

[150] Not only did Heller debunk the popular Spirit Rappings, but he promised in a forthcoming book to supply "diagrams of machinery, etc., employed to effect the whole business." His show included, as well, Heller's performances of his new piano composition "The Rap Polka," while "Mr. Cobble, of the Moon, kept time on the Rapping Table."

[151] Watson, at this period not recognizably connected with any specific newspaper, seems to have devoted his efforts almost entirely to teaching and composing. In 1853 he was awarded first prize ($100) for a four-part vocal piece in a contest held by the *Musical Review and Choral Advocate.* The judges were William Vincent Wallace, James Gaspard Maeder, and John Zundel.

[152] Formed in 1837, the Howard Association was an organization of benevolent New Orleans citizens dedicated to alleviating the suffering of their townspeople in times of crisis. The Association rendered magnificent service during the terrible yellow fever epidemic of 1853, soliciting and receiving help from all over the country (Duffy, pp. 31–33, 54–55).

[153] Among the victims (on August 23) was Dr. W. K. Northall,♪ the renowned Brooklyn editor/dentist/playwright and father of the singer Julia Northall, who had recently been serving as an editor of the New Orleans *Delta* (*Herald,* September 1, 1853).

1, Ole Bull and his touring companions, still "the musical phenomenon" Adelina Patti and Maurice Strakosch (in the multiple roles of solo pianist, accompanist and manager), attracted a greater-than-capacity attendance to Niblo's Saloon.[154] For the same cause, on September 5 at Niblo's Garden a gala "Grand Operatic Festival," presented by Maretzek and Niblo, offered separate acts from five operas—*Favorita, Barbiere, Figlia, Norma,* and *Linda*—performed by all the stars of Maretzek's current opera company: Sontag, Steffanone, Amalia Patti-Strakosch, Salvi, Pozzolini, Badiali, Marini, Rovere, Beneventano, Vietti, Belletti, and the opera chorus and orchestra conducted by Maretzek.[155] And at Castle Garden on September 11, a Sunday,[156] Jullien donated a Grand Sacred and Miscellaneous program, from Handel to Meyerbeer. As we know, Jullien would later perform for the benefit of the St. George's Society (December 5) and for the Widows and Orphans Fund of the New York Fire Department (December 17).

In October, Ole Bull announced a "Grand Series" of three charitable concerts—at Niblo's Saloon on October 28 and November 1 and 5, again with little Patti and Strakosch—to assist "the suffering colonists at Oleona," where his grand social experiment had collapsed.[157]

Only one other, rather vague, announcement for a single "Grand Philanthropic Concert" followed, explaining that Bull was "trying to save some fragments of the fortune he had devoted to the establishment of a colony for his countrymen, and of which they have been defrauded" and were "actually suffering for food for themselves and their families." Like his New Norway, Bull's altruistic concert seems to have come to naught.

In October the Hutchinson Family returned from their travels, and during their ensuing season at the Tabernacle, they performed at Metropolitan Hall on November 22 for the benefit of the Five Points Mission, assisted by Dodworth's Band.

Soon after, on December 21 at the Broadway Tabernacle, Dr. Pease's supporters sponsored a Grand Juvenile gala, in which one hundred of the "Little Ones attached to Pease's Five Points House of Industry" performed "Scenes from Opera at the Five

[154] So great was the crush at this concert that Fry "found it impossible to get within seeing or hearing distance of the performers" and thus was "forced" to go to Jullien's concert at Castle Garden instead (*Tribune,* September 3, 1853). The *Mirror* reporter, who managed to squeeze in, wrote (September 2): "Adelina Patti, the youthful musical wonder, was encored furiously, and sang 'Home, Sweet Home' in addition to the announced arias from *Linda de Chamounix* and *La sonnambula,* 'Comin thro' the rye,' and Jenny Lind's Echo Song. Her execution of the 'Ah! non giunge' was perfect, and the audience could not wait for the conclusion of the piece to testify their admiration." The concert reportedly netted $800, remarkable—in a time attuned to grand spectacles—for an event offering "only the trifling attraction of one violin, one piano, and a little girl," whimsically observed the *Spirit of the Times* (September 10, 1853, p. 360).

[155] With tickets at a uniform two dollars, some $1500 were reportedly collected for the Howard Association (*Spirit,* September 10, 1853, p. 360).

[156] Apparently to the great disapproval of the so-called "semi-religious" papers, the *Journal of Commerce* and *Commercial Advertiser.* Irate at their better-than-thou comments, the *Mirror* (September 12, 1853) declared that by attending the concert, it had rendered "quite as acceptable a service to the Divine Master as if we had accompanied the pious editors of those immaculate sheets to their respective churches and enjoyed the softer seats of cushions more highly bottomed on the almighty dollar."

[157] In 1853, Bull discovered that he did not own the title to the land he thought he had purchased. Enmeshed in a tangle of liens and litigations, Bull withdrew from the project. The destitute Oleona colonists eventually headed West.

Points," a cantata composed for them by "their friend and teacher" George Henry Curtis; the solos (including two "Little Katy" songs)[158] were performed by Maria Scoville Brainerd; Curtis accompanied and conducted (see *Musical World and Times,* December 31, 1853, pp. 139–40).

In December, Maretzek's opera singers, soon to depart, rallied to the rescue of Ferdinand Palmo,♪ the failed restaurateur/opera impresario of 1844, now grown old and fallen on shockingly evil days. "A benefit for Mr. Palmo, who did such great service formerly in building his pioneer opera house in Chambers Street and sustaining it, is on foot, and for the best of reasons," announced the *Tribune* on October 29. "Palmo has lost his fortune. Others have benefited by his enterprise—the public has been delighted and instructed with it—but he is old and in want of a sixpence. Now something is to be done for him."[159] A large committee of prominent citizens headed by Mayor Jacob A. Westervelt supported the cause, and with their help the event took place at Metropolitan Hall on December 3, with an all-star cast of Italian opera singers consisting of Steffanone, Vietti-Vertiprach, Salvi, Marini, Beneventano, and Rovere, and an ephemeral new pianist Signor Beretta; La Manna conducted.

Concerts of sacred music (an increasingly flexible commodity) were given for and at various churches. George Henry Curtis's uplifting, if not sacred, *Eleutheria* was performed on February 9 at the Spring Street Presbyterian Church by the Misses Brainerd and Bennett, Messrs. Colburn and Curtis, assisted by Curtis and Nash's Madrigal Class and the Church choir; Nash conducted and Curtis (organist of Central Church) presided at the piano. On March 2 a Grand Sacred Concert for the Thirteenth Street Presbyterian Church presented a large cast that included Mesdames Brinkerhoff and Pierson, Misses Thomas, Girard (or Gerard), Wray, Robjohn, and Pease, and Messrs. Nash, Bell, Conkey, and Van Der Weyde. A Grand Sacred concert on October 2 at the Church of St. Francis Xavier was performed by a polyglot cast including a Mademoiselle Bauman, Signora Colletti, Signorina Sconcia, Signor and Signora Bailini, Signor Quinto, Miss Girard, Herren Philip Mayer and William Müller, and others, all under the guidance of St. Francis Xavier's organist/composer William Berge (or Bergé). And on December 16 the Ladies Benevolent Society of the Church of St. Vincent de Paul (Canal Street near Broadway), sponsored an event, again with Signorina Sconcia, the Bailinis, Messrs. Müller and Berge, and Gabrielle de la Motte, who—together with Joseph Burke and Alfred Boucher—played movements of the Beethoven and Mendelssohn trios they had played at her recent unfortunate debut.

[158] "Little Katy, the Hot Corn Girl," was the abused, angelic child-protagonist of an immensely popular series of temperance tales portraying the appalling evils of life at the Five Points. Written by Solon Robinson (1803–1880), agricultural editor of the *Tribune* and a friend and supporter of the Reverend Pease, the stories first appeared serially in the *Tribune* in 1853. By year's end Little Katy had become the heroine of innumerable songs and the first two of a succession of dramatizations (discussed below). Published in collected form in 1854, Robinson's "Hot Corn" stories were a runaway best-seller, with some 50,000 copies reportedly having been instantly snapped up, one of them by George Templeton Strong (*Diary,* II, 148–49).

[159] The fanatically jingoistic *New-York Clipper* (December 3, 1853) urged its readers not to assist the Italian Palmo. That he had lost his money was his own business: "The American people cared not a straw whether he succeeded or not—the Italian Opera never was and never will be a popular institution in this city."

On Sunday evenings at the Apollo Rooms, from September 25 through November 13, if not longer, the New York *Sängerbund* gave "grand sacred concerts" consisting almost exclusively of vocal and instrumental German secular music from Haydn to Gungl, conducted by Julius Unger, formerly of the Germania Society and now a violist in the Philharmonic.

German opera, too, was given by a small, but able, ethnic company: Weber's *Preciosa* in April and May at 53 Bowery (Charley White's versatile Melodeon), *Der Freischütz* in early November at the St. Charles Theatre, and Conradin Kreutzer's *Das Nachtlager von Granada,* later in November, at Washington Hall at 103–07 Elizabeth Street. The *Musical World and Times* (November 12, 1853, p. 85) had the highest praise for the intelligent and able performers and their excellent productions of German opera, given "as only Germans could give them." Tickets for these superior performances were twenty-five cents.

In 1853 the reborn New-York Harmonic Society, now the New-York Sacred Harmonic Society, like the Philharmonic, joyfully issued a favorable annual report, their first. They had achieved solvency in the one short year since their reorganization—proudly boasting a balance of $30 after paying all expenses. A glowing article in the *Tribune* (September 6, 1853), written by a member of the Society, told how in the past year they had bravely maintained their weekly rehearsal schedule, regardless of weather, and how they had unanimously elected to forgo their summer vacation (an act of devotion rare in the history of such institutions!).

During the period of the Fry lectures, in which, as we know, the Society had regularly participated, the members had willingly attended as many as four weekly rehearsals: "We cannot but bear testimony to the great influence which the course of lectures . . . has exerted not only on the general public, but more particularly on our own members. Coming opportunely at about the time of our [second] commencement, they did much in awakening a greater interest in chorus singing and the cultivation of a taste for the more advanced styles of musical compositions."

Under the dedicated direction of Bristow, the Society's public performances in 1853 had included—in addition to their testimonial concert to Fry on March 1—a presentation of *The Creation*[160] at Metropolitan Hall on June 20, for the benefit of the aged and infirm members of the Methodist Episcopal Church; an appearance at the opening of the great Crystal Palace Exhibition on July 14; a repeat of *The Creation* at Poughkeepsie, New York (on their first annual musical excursion♪ on July 27); and on December 26, as we know, they had collaborated with Jullien and his orchestra in his spectacular performance of Handel's *Messiah.*

William B. Bradbury presented less elevated choral fare at his Annual Glee and Ballad Concert at the Tabernacle on March 2, performed by his Tabernacle Choir, with George F. Root as elocutionist and singer and James Ensign presiding at the

[160] With an all-American cast of soloists, as the *Tribune* noted (June 21, 1853): Maria Brainerd, Cornelia Dingley, Reuben Munson,♪ Francis H. Nash, and James W. Alden. Conducted by G. F. Bristow, with George H. Curtis at the piano, the performance was "extremely creditable to all concerned, and proved that with the advantages of fuller rehearsals with the orchestra, nothing more could be desired."

piano. The *Musical World and Times* (March 17, 1853, pp. 162–63), probably Oliver Dyer, a fervent advocate of simple, accessible American music as opposed to the too-prevalent, complicated, alien variety, congratulated Bradbury on having built up a "voluntary choir" at the Tabernacle to perform "music of this character [which] appeals directly to the sympathies and appreciation of the people. As models of the highest artistic excellence, Jenny Lind, Sontag, Alboni, etc. fill an important place and exert a most useful educational influence in the dissemination of correct taste, yet, these luminaries are on a pinnacle to which common singers can never aspire. . . . Not one in ten thousand can ever hope to be a Jenny Lind or a Sontag. But these choir concerts present music of a more practical character, and therefore serve a most useful purpose in awakening pleasant and profitable emulation."

But Bradbury pursued a loftier purpose as well, embarking, together with a hand-picked group of prominent music educators, on an innovative pedagogical project. Headed by the Boston music educator Lowell Mason, just back from Europe, on April 25 they opened the New York Normal Musical Institute, whose function—in an intensive three-month course—was to teach teachers how to teach, unlike the foreign conservatories, which were designed to turn out performers and composers. Although the *Musical World and Times* (April 30, 1853, p. 73) reported that the Normal Institute—the "most original musical institution of the day"—had "quietly sprung into existence," its concept had been developed and practiced by Mason and his disciples for some years past; furthermore, the opening of the New York Normal Institute had been prominently advertised in *Dwight's Journal of Music* since the latter part of January.

From April 25 to July 15, classes were held daily in Allen Dodworth's large and handsome Assembly Hall at his Dancing Academy: from 9 to 10 A.M. a lecture by Lowell Mason on the art of teaching; 10 to 11 A.M. (on Tuesdays and Thursdays), R. Storrs Willis on harmony and composition; 11 A.M. to noon, George F. Root on the culture of the voice; and 12 to 1 P.M., Bradbury's class in part-singing.[161] Thomas Hastings soon joined the faculty, holding forth, more elevatedly, on the "side-culture—mental and physical—of musicians" (*Dwight's,* May 14, 1863, pp. 446–47). Additional private lessons in various disciplines might be had from John Zundel (organ), (Harvey?) Dodworth (band instruments), Clarence W. Beames (voice), and Elias Howe (melodion and piano). The class of fifty students was "greater [in number] than there was any reason to expect."

Indeed, so successful was the undertaking that a continuation, with the same faculty, was announced for the following year, to begin on May 1, 1854. In the meantime, beginning September 15, a ten-week course in voice and instrumental music would be launched under the direction of Mason, Root, and Bradbury, to be followed by two successive courses (the details are found in the *Musical Review and Choral Advocate,* August 1853, pp. 118–19).

Conventional pedagogy was dispensed by the usual pedagogues. Additionally, Mrs. Seguin, "Professor of Vocal Music," advertised her availability "for a few hours each day" for the instruction of young ladies. Mr. and Mrs. Edward Barton, professors

[161] At their commencement exercises, on July 15, Bradbury's class performed the principal choruses from *Messiah* and George Frederick Root's new sacred cantata *Daniel,* included in *The Shawm,* a huge anthology of church music compiled by Bradbury and Root and recently published by the Mason Brothers (see *Musical Review and Choral Advocate,* August 1853, p. 118).

of singing, guitar, pianoforte, and "that truly wonderful instrument, the concertina," announced that they could accommodate a few more pupils.

In January, Signorina Valentini—ever a zestful practitioner of public performance as teaching tool—presented a students' concert at Hope Chapel. In February and March she took over the Chapel as its official "Prima Donna and manager," presenting nightly vocal "Concerts and Shakespearean Entertainments" by members of her class—seven young ladies, four gentlemen, Master Hill, a ten-year-old "Musical Wonder," and "those truly astonishing young tragedians" Lora Gordon Boon, eight years old, and Anna Isabella Boon, nine, "costumed in scenes from *King Lear,* Hamlet advising the players, and Brutus and Cassius in the quarrel scene from *Julius Caesar.*"[162] As the *pièce de resistance,* the Signorina (elsewhere ungallantly referred to as "the Fat Lady"), vivaciously performed *La Colasa* in full Spanish regalia, and "by request, nightly, 'The Star-Spangled Banner' in full national costume." (!) A bargain at twenty-five cents! (*Mirror,* March 8, 1853.)

The other extrovert pedagogue, Lewis A. Benjamin, in addition to prosaic violin, flute, and bass-viol lessons at his Allen Street Music Academy, at $1 a quarter, gave five performances of his latest "juvenile oratorio" *The Crystal Palace* at the Tabernacle in March. His usual cast of "1000 little singers and a full orchestra of Young Musicians" appeared as well in the afterpiece "Yankee Tea Party," a spectacle representing fourteen different nations in "full costume."

Of greater moment was *The Flower Queen,* or *The Coronation of the Rose,* George Frederick Root's highly praised school cantata (Willis called it an operetta), with a text by the blind poet Frances J. (Fanny) Crosby (1820–1915). First performed by the young ladies of the Spingler Institute on March 14, it was immediately repeated by Root's students at the Rutgers Female Institute. Willis lauded the work in the *Musical World and Times* (March 26, 1853, p. 195), and especially the singing of Miss Thomas, "a musical gem."

In July a more commercially oriented juvenile show could be seen every afternoon and evening at "Kook's Concert Hall," a newly renamed building on Sixth Avenue facing the Crystal Palace. "Kook" was none other than Sebastian Cook, the tiny piano prodigy of 1850, now a mature twelve years old and, according to his advertisement, "for the past two years under the direction of the celebrated and familiar Pianist, Mr. Timm." Assisting Kook was his nine-year-old brother Louis, a precocious vocalist, who would, "through his delivery of songs, contribute to glorify these concerts."[163] To say nothing of additional support by unspecified "great artists lately arrived from Europe" (*Tribune,* July 21. 1853).

As for the popular scene, the Hutchinson Family—now reduced to John, Judson, and Asa[164]—returned in October from another of their prolonged tours and estab-

[162] Valentini's persistent association with young children probably signified her hope of finding another little Adelina Patti to teach.

[163] In September, Sebastian Kook and his tribe (there was also a little sister Louisa) joined forces with Signorina Valentini for a tour of Albany, Troy, Rochester, and Buffalo. For a hilarious review of a "Kook Koncert" in Troy, see *Dwight's,* October 29, 1853, pp. 26–27.

[164] An ailing Jesse Hutchinson, back from his California tour with the Alleghanians, had died on May 16, 1853, at a water-cure establishment near Cincinnati (*Musical Review and Choral Advocate,* June, 1853, p. 90).

lished their usual beachhead at the Tabernacle. For the remainder of the year and beyond, the amusement columns overflowed, as of old, with "We're with you once again, kind friends" and with listings—sometimes couched in Hutchinsonian verse—of their simple, homespun, morally uplifting repertory. In tune with the times (the phenomenally successful Aiken production of *Uncle Tom's Cabin* was now in full blast at the National Theatre), their programs now included such significant sociopolitical fare as "Little Topsy's Song"[165] and "The Ghost of Uncle Tom." Probably encouraged by their successful concert to aid the Five Points Mission on November 22, the Hutchinsons reappeared on their own behalf at Metropolitan Hall on November 30—again with Dodworth's Band—then returned to the Tabernacle, where on December 22 they launched a second series of concerts.

Dempster the Eternal also returned from his travels, and for the week beginning November 11 he nightly recapitulated his ballad repertory at the Tabernacle.

The Scottish tenor John Frazer began a series of nightly solo performances at Stuyvesant Hall on May 9. Frazer's entertainment, a kind of lecture/recital, consisted of "Historical, Biographical, and Humorous Anecdotes of Artists, Musicians, and other distinguished persons, illustrated by Songs and Ballads." As the *Mirror* (May 14, 1853) approvingly commented: "His observations are characterized by great good taste and sound judgment; while some of his songs are sung with exquisite simplicity and grace." Then pointedly: "The music of our own language has some little claim upon the public ear after so long a banishment."

But Frazer's literary/vocal entertainment was no more successful than Henry Phillips's had been in 1844.♪ Despite "fair audiences and a good deal of applause," by the time he concluded his series on May 21, according to the *Musical Review and Choral Advocate* (June 1853, p. 91), Frazer had "nevertheless lost some money."

Not discouraged by Frazer's disappointing box-office showing, Alfred Sedgwick, the concertina virtuoso (and apparently a man of unlimited resourcefulness)[166] adopted Frazer's format, giving a similar entertainment intriguingly titled *Crotchets and Quavers,*[167] *or, Musical Notes on Manners and Things,* at the Stuyvesant Institute on June 13 and 15. Apparently his "lectures," as they were called, caught on, for on September 19, on a larger scale, Sedgwick presented a series of nightly "Apollonicon Concerts" at Hope Chapel, with an able supporting company of actors and musicians: Miss De Forest, the American actress/singer who had been his sole assistant in the *Crotchets and Quavers;* the seasoned actor/singers Alleyne and Rea; Kazia Lovarny; her versatile husband, Franz Stoepel; and, of course, Sedgwick, who did not confine his efforts to the concertina. His rendition, with Miss De Forest, of "You Know," a comic duet "with

[165] Composed by Asa B. Hutchinson to blazing words by Eliza Cook:

> This is Topsy's savage song;
> Topsy cute and clever;
> Hurrah! then for the white man's right!
> Slavery forever!

[166] In January, Sedgwick advertised the availability of his Quadrille Band for private parties, or for smaller gatherings the combination of concertina and piano. He gave singing lessons and later in the year supplied musical accompaniment for John Owen's exciting lecture/panorama describing his ascent of Mont Blanc; Sedgwick also composed songs for Wood's Minstrels.

[167] Later picked up by Maretzek as the title of his delightful book, published in 1855.

affecting dialogue," by John Orlando Parry,♪ was, in the *Mirror*'s opinion (September 24, 1853), alone "worth the 25 cents admission." Sedgwick's interesting program was drawn from a wide range of sources: from favorite opera arias and ensembles by Rossini and Auber and Bellini to popular ballads by Samuel Lover and Henry Phillips; it included as well a medley of "The Old Folks at Home" and "Yankee Doodle," given on the concertina "with some beautiful effects, the chorus being echoed from behind," and even a solo by Stoepel on the xylochordeon. If properly managed, optimistically wrote the *Mirror,* this entertainment was a sure success, providing, as it did, "the link that has so long been wanting between the Opera, Metropolitan Hall, and Negro Minstrelsy."

In the thriving world of blackface minstrelsy, the Christy's and the Wood's troupes continued their fierce competition for supremacy, playing to capacity audiences at their respective Opera Houses for the better part of the year. In May, G. Swaine Buckley, with due fanfare, announced the forthcoming return of his original New Orleans Serenaders "after an absence of seventeen months, during which time they performed with unparalleled success through the principal cities and mines of California." They opened with afternoon and evening performances on July Fourth at the former Chinese Buildings (539 Broadway), now rechristened Buckley's Ethiopian Opera House, then settled in for a long and successful stay.[168]

In June the partners Charley White and Dan Emmet [*sic*] announced their return to White's Melodeon with a company of "splendid" blackface performers, including the dancer John Diamond and White's "original" Serenaders.[169] The Grand Old Man of minstrelsy T. D. Rice returned to the Bowery Theatre and Niblo's Garden in his perennial repertory: *Jumbo Jum, The Virginia Mummy, Otello, and Oh! Hush!* On December 23, at the Bowery, Rice was given a benefit to celebrate the twentieth anniversary of his first benefit in New York.

Minstreldom was rocked to its very foundations in October, when E. P. Christy's star of stars, the supremely comic bones virtuoso George N. Christy (né Harrington), after an enormously successful and profitable association of some twelve years, perfidiously defected to the enemy.[170] On October 24 (and for at least a month thereafter) the papers carried Henry Wood's terse announcement that he had entered into a "copartnership with the gentleman professionally known as George Christy, late of Christy's Minstrels" and that Wood's Minstrels would henceforth be known as "George Christy and Wood's Minstrels." Harrington's succinct corroboration accompanied this statement, as did Edwin P. Christy's longer, more emotional declaration of his company's superiority over all others and their unparalleled worldwide fame, with or without Harrington. Christy denounced Harrington for continuing to use the name Christy, to which he had no claim—E. P. Christy being the "Sole Proprietor and

[168] Resuming their travesties of *Lucia, Lucrezia Borgia,* and *The Gipsey's Warning,* among others, and later introducing a burlesque of a Jullien concert (*Herald,* August 7, 1853).

[169] In July, White's Serenaders shared a bill at Barnum's with Donetti's ubiquitous Performing Monkeys, Dogs, and Goats.

[170] In the general side-taking that ensued, Harrington's desertion was widely reprehended, especially because it so closely followed upon his long and serious illness, during which E. P. Christy had solicitously looked after him.

Manager—the only individual at this time, or previous, of the name of Christy engaged as a performer in representations of Ethiopian Minstrelsy."

Despite (or because of) the continuing controversy, the Harrington/Wood partnership prospered. Although Wood's (now Christy and Wood's) Minstrel Hall had been enlarged to accommodate an audience of 1300, some 500 to 1000 were purportedly turned away every night "since the accession of 'George Christy Bones' to the troupe." According to the *Mirror* of November 22 (rubbing salt in E. P. Christy's wounds): "The two proprietors are realizing each a nightly profit of $100, equal to $30,000 a year. Henry Wood is destined to become a millionaire." To say nothing of George N. Harrington/Christy. It was the beginning of the end for Edwin Pierce Christy.

What with the vast influx of out-of-town visitors to the Crystal Palace Exhibition, the New York theatres enjoyed a banner season, as did all forms of amusements.[171] But oddly, although music was considered integral to theatrical production, no outstanding new musical shows seem to have been introduced in 1853. Apart from stock revivals of such ancient bromides as *The Pet of the Petticoats* or *The Naiad Queen,* it was chiefly Anna Thillon who more or less single-handedly sustained the legitimate music theatre with her operetta performances at Niblo's, where she opened on July 6 with *The Child of the Regiment.*[172]

It was like "'old times' at Niblo's Garden," rejoiced the *Home Journal* (July 16, 1853): "The inimitable Ravels alternate [on Tuesdays, Thursdays, and Saturdays] with that charming 'Child of the Regiment,' that enchanting 'Enchantress,' that 'Crown Diamonds,' that bewitching 'Basket-Maker's Wife,' Madame Anna Thillon. Has anybody else played the 'Child of the Regiment' forty nights in two years in the same city, and been still *certain* of a crowded house whenever she chose to announce a repetition of the performance? We believe not."

The wonderful Ravels were as wonderful as ever, continued the *Home Journal,* and "Niblo, the 'majestic manager' is always at his post, with an eye on everything and a welcome for his friends. . . . The Garden is in perfect condition. The trees increase in magnitude; the walks have not a pebble out of place; the saloon presents the same assemblage of frantic waiters and desperate table-rappers as of old. Go to Niblo's. You have been? Well, go again."

On July 20, Thillon added Balfe's *The Bohemian Girl* to her handful of roles and Frazer to her company, to play Thaddeus, a role he had performed for the first time in America with the Seguins in 1844;♪ and on August 17 she revived Michael Rooke's *Amilie,* a huge hit in 1838♪ but apparently of small appeal to the more sophisticated audiences of 1853. "There are pretty Tyrolean melodies in it," wrote the *Tribune* reviewer (ostensibly Fry) on August 18, 1853, "but, as a whole, it wants dramatic nerve

[171] Notably Franconi's Hippodrome, an equestrian quasi circus, with horse races, chariot races, tournaments, gorgeous pageants, and gladiatorial contests featuring beauteous "Amazonian drivers" in extravagantly ornate costumes. From May to November the spectacle was given twice daily (except Sundays) in a huge tent-like structure at Madison Square, built for the purpose. An apparently continuous musical accompaniment to the proceedings was supplied by J. C. Adams with his Cornet Band and an orchestra directed by Thomas Coates. For a delightful descriptive commentary on the Hippodrome entertainment, see *Dwight's,* July 2, 1853, p. 100.

[172] Her company again included Mrs. Maeder, James Hudson, and Stephen Leach.

and style. The words are badly written for music, and the singers cannot execute their task as [they would] if disposing of smooth Italian translations. . . . *Amilie* in former times—some fifteen years ago—was a great favorite in New York, and with more care in its execution, it would have a run again."

But *Amilie* was not destined to survive. On September 2, Madame Thillon took her final benefit at Niblo's, having been evicted by Maretzek and his opera company upon their own eviction from Castle Garden by Jullien. On November 15 and 17 (opera off-nights) Thillon gave final performances, respectively, of *The Daughter of the Regiment* and *The Crown Diamonds,* then joined the general exodus of showfolk to California.

In 1853 *Uncle Tom's Cabin,* in George L. Aiken's dramatization, demolished all previous theatrical records and many for a long time to come.[173] Opening at the National Theatre on July 18, the massive production—in six acts, eight tableaux, and thirty scenes—played to packed houses nightly and two afternoons a week, running for more than 300 consecutive performances. "A complete triumph," proclaimed the *Mirror* (July 19, 1853).[174] Most tellingly, Little Eva, phenomenally portrayed by angelic, five-year-old little Cordelia Howard (1848–1941), reduced her audiences (both sexes—adults and children) to floods of uncontrollable tears: a "*veritable pièce de mouchoir,*" the *Tribune* called it (August 8, 1853).

The production was in fact a family triumph: Topsy was played to perfection by little Cordelia's mother, Mrs. George C. Howard (a cousin of Aiken's), St. Clare by husband-and-father G. C. Howard, who had also composed the words and music for the play's many "beautiful songs and dances";[175] other relatives played various roles, and Greene C. Germon, the veteran blackface minstrel, played Uncle Tom.

By year's end at least one other dramatization of *Uncle Tom's Cabin* was concurrently playing in New York—at P. T. Barnum's American Museum—and a diorama consisting of twenty-five Uncle Tom tableaux was being shown at the less reputable Franklin Museum.[176]

Uncle Tom's Cabin was, however, not the only moralistic entertainment to take New York by storm in 1853. With the success of the various dramatic treatments of Mrs. Stowe's novel, it was inevitable that Solon Robinson's "Little Katy," or "Hot Corn" stories depicting the horrors of life at the Five Points—having created a sensation in the *Tribune*—be put on the stage. On December 5 the National Theatre again

[173] "Probably the most successful American play ever written," wrote Arthur Hornblow in 1919 (*History,* II, 69); as late as "the summer of 1902," he recalls, "no fewer than sixteen companies [played] the piece under canvas." Once a supreme symbol of flaming resistance to injustice, *Uncle Tom* ironically has come to assume an opposite significance in the latter part of the twentieth century.

[174] But in fact also the subject of great editorial controversy between the newspapers advocating abolition and those supporting slavery. Notable among the latter was the reactionary *New York Clipper,* which throughout the run sought to discourage clergymen from attending *Uncle Tom* performances (a much-mooted topic), by branding the National Theatre a happy hunting ground for pickpockets.

[175] Among Howard's "Uncle Tom" songs (issued by the piano builder and music publisher Horace Waters in 1853) were "Little Eva to her Papa," "St. Clare to Little Eva in Heaven," Topsy's song, "Oh! I'se so Wicked" (dedicated to Aiken), and "Uncle Tom's Religion."

[176] Odell (VI, 320) reports two performances of *Onkel Toms Hütte* by German thespians at the St. Charles Theatre on October 20 and 24.

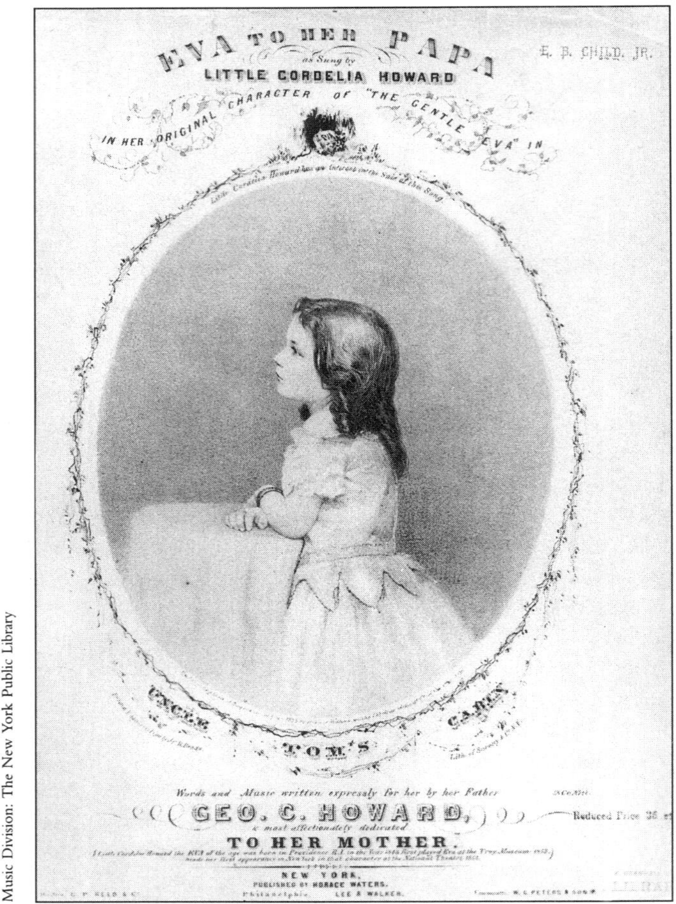

Music Division: The New York Public Library

Little Cordelia Howard, a heartwrenching Little Eva in Uncle Tom's Cabin.

scooped the field with a "Hot Corn" dramatization starring little Cordelia Howard, apparently a child of boundless stamina, as Little Katy. Wringing from her audiences supplementary torrents of tears on Monday, Tuesday, Thursday, and Friday afternoons as Little Katy, little Cordelia continued nightly, and on Monday and Saturday afternoons, to open wide the floodgates as Little Eva.

Barnum's "Hot Corn" production, opening a day after the National's, was found to be less appealing because his Little Katy was played by a full-grown actress.[177]

Boasting of what it called the "Hot Corn Epidemic," the *Tribune* proudly editorialized on December 7 that the "Hot Corn" stories had been reprinted in more papers

[177] The real Hot Corn Girls, creatures of the Five Points, were, to all intents and purposes, grown-up young women who peddled "piping hot, roasting ears [of corn] from cedar-staved buckets. . . . Dressed in spotted calico and wrapped in a plaid shawl, but barefooted, the Hot Corn Girl appeared on the streets at dusk, and throughout the night she mingled with the crowds on the sidewalks and in the dance houses, hawking her wares" (Asbury, pp. 7–8).

Songs of laughter and Tears in
Uncle Tom's Cabin

Both: Music Division, The New York Public Library

"than any other article that ever went the rounds of the press. More songs than some farmers raise bushels of corn have been written, the burden of which is 'Hot Corn.' The collection of piano music [at home] is not complete without 'Hot Corn' set to music. Minstrels have made a golden harvest out of 'Hot Corn.' Tracts for the promotion of Temperance are not *the tracts* unless they have 'Hot Corn' upon the title. We don't know how many cartloads have been printed. . . . Next comes a book of 400 pages of Hot Corn stories."[178]

And now "Hot Corn" dramas! The reporter had attended the opening performances at both the National and Barnum's and found both versions, like the dramatizations of *Uncle Tom,* to bear only a nominal resemblance to the original. "In the meantime," exulted the *Tribune,* "the epidemic rages. . . . *Viva la Hot Corn!*"

In closing, the editorial reported that Barnum had invited Mr. Pease and all the children of the Five Points House of Industry to "witness the performance of *Hot Corn* at the Museum." They would see some familiar scenes "daguerreotyped," promised the *Tribune.* A busman's holiday!

[178] The *Daily Times* furiously denounced Robinson's uplifting best-seller as an "indecent and filthy" book (February 11, 1854).

New-York Historical Society

5

GTS: 1854

Quartet playing and quartet singing have been very popular in private *life this winter in New York. A friend of ours up town who has quite a large organ in his spacious and elegant house, has been getting up the masses of the old masters; the performers being amateurs, except the organist.*

The Musical World and New York Musical Times
March 18, 1854

AT ABOUT ONE A.M. ON JANUARY 8, 1854, as George Templeton Strong sat quietly reading in his library, the early sabbath stillness was shattered by "an alarm of fire," and, as he records in his journal, "the sight of a fine, rich column of smoke lit up with a very angry red light, rolling off to the southwest seemingly not far off, sent me on a brisk trot down the Fourth Avenue and Bowery, through the frosty air and along the silent streets of a January midnight. No one was stirring but now and then a pedestrian on the same errand as mine." The fire—"very showy and splendid"—was in Metropolitan Hall and Lafarge's adjoining new hotel. "It began in Mercer Street in that much-to-be-regretted Music Hall[1] and worked east toward Broadway, destroying the whole structure. . . . When I came off at a little before four, the fire was rampant and volant throughout all the building, and this morning it appears thoroughly burnt up and burnt out."

Later in the day Strong, an avid fire-fancier, walked all the way home from church in order to "inspect the ruins of last night's fire." He assessed the losses suffered by the real estate tycoon John Lafarge and his co-investors in the newly completed hotel, an ultra-luxurious marble edifice in the Greek revival style designed by James Renwick, Jr.,[2] at half a million dollars; the *Daily Times* (January 9, 1854) put it at a million.

[1]The destruction of Metropolitan Hall, "in some respects the most splendid concert-room in the world," wrote William Henry Fry, was an irreparable blow to Art in New York, from which it would take years to recover (*Tribune*, January 9, 1854).

[2]James Renwick, Jr. (1818–1895), a classmate of Strong's at Columbia College, was the illustrious and wide-ranging architect of a variety of important New York buildings, among them Grace Church (consecrated in 1846) and later St. Patrick's Cathedral (completed in 1887). In 1846 Renwick was appointed to begin work on the design of the Smithsonian "Castle" in Washington, D.C.

Listed among the army of suppliers, tradespeople, artisans, technicians, art dealers, cabinet makers, upholsterers, silversmiths, carpet weavers, and the countless other victims of the disaster was, surprisingly, Jullien, currently in Boston for a two-week season. According to his custom, Jullien, who toured with a reduced orchestra, had left several items—some of them irreplaceable—for safekeeping at Metropolitan Hall during his absence. Valued at first at three to four thousand dollars but later reassessed at ten thousand, Jullien's losses included his famous giant drum, several double basses and other musical instruments, printed and manuscript scores and parts, ornamental props used at the Castle Garden concerts, and a variety of new decorative objects meant for Jullien's eagerly awaited *bal paré,* or full-dress ball, scheduled for January 18 at Metropolitan Hall.

Among the attractions planned for this extraordinary happening—a combined leave-taking for Jullien and official unveiling of the gorgeous new hotel—were the transformation of the "entire area" of Metropolitan Hall into the "most extensive and perfect *salle de danse* in the world," with Jullien's virtuosos to supply the dance music; "splendid Apartments" in Lafarge House to be thrown open as "Reception, Promenade, and Withdrawing Rooms"; the entrance halls, stairways, and corridors "thoroughly warmed, carpeted throughout, and decorated with Natural Flowers and Exotic Plants" (Madame's handiwork); and an elaborate supper, served in the "spacious banqueting rooms of the Lafarge House," offering "the most delicate and recherché viands, with the wines of rare vintages specially selected for the occasion."[3] For this festive event, an indispensable feature of any extended Jullien season, Jullien and his entourage were stopping off in New York before continuing on an extended tour that would take them as far south as New Orleans and as far west as Cincinnati (*Daily Times,* January 9; *Mirror,* January 10, 1854).

Probably to compensate for his inauspicious recent season,[4] during the three-day interval between his Grand Farewell Concert at Metropolitan Hall (on New Year's Eve) and his departure for Boston, Jullien had chosen, instead of his *bal paré,* to give a pair of post-farewell "New Year's Gift Concerts," or "Music for the Million Nights." Presented on January 2 and 3 at Metropolitan Hall[5] in collaboration with his resourceful New York music publisher S. C. Jollie, the gift concerts were in fact an elaborate promotional scheme to launch Jollie's newly published collection of twelve of Jullien's "most popular" pieces,[6] democratically titled *Jullien's Music for the Million* and grandly dedicated—Jullien fashion—to "the People of the United States." The "gift," a copy

[3] Tickets for a lady and gentleman (including everything but the wines) were $10; extra ladies were $5 each. Full evening dress was mandatory.

[4] Noted in the *Musical Review and Choral Advocate* (January, 5, 1854, p. 12). Perhaps New Yorkers were suffering from a surfeit of Jullien. The hostile *New-York Clipper* (January 7, 1854, p. 3) credited his unsatisfactory box-office showing to his too-high ticket prices.

[5] At the first of these concerts Jullien repeated Fry's controversial "Santa Claus" Symphony and the "American Quadrille" (91st time).

[6] In simple piano arrangements, the album, priced at $1, contained the "American," "English," "Californian," *Pietro il grande,* and "Great Exhibition" Quadrilles; the "Prima Donna" and "Paul and Virginia" Waltzes; the "Target" and "Atlantic" Galops; the "Mont Blanc Polka"; and two of Anna Zerr's best-liked songs, "Forget-me-not" by Charles Haas and "'Twas on a Sunday Morning" by Frank Mori (1820–1873).

of the album, was gallantly distributed to all the lady occupants of the reserved (more expensive) seats.

At the latter gift concert Jullien himself received a gift from the New York contingent of his orchestra (not engaged for his forthcoming tour). Led by G. F. Bristow and U. C. Hill, they "presented their maestro with a magnificent silver salver as a testimonial of their appreciation of what he has done and is doing for art" (*Daily Times; Mirror,* January 4, 1854).

On returning to New York after the disaster, a bereaved Jullien, obviously unable to conjure up a ready-made *bal paré,* announced instead "ONE GRAND CONCERT" at Niblo's Garden on January 18. The public response was overwhelming.[7] "It is scarcely possible that there ever were so many people congregated within Niblo's," reported the *Daily Times* (January 19, 1854). "The parquette, boxes, lobbies, stage, and passages were one solid mass of human beings."

As if by magic, despite the lack of time (and probably of cash), some Jullienesque transformations had nonetheless been effected at Niblo's. To provide the requisite promenading space, the parterre seats had been boarded over, bringing the floor to the level of the stage (over which a "fanciful awning" had been hung), thus permitting the promenaders to circumnavigate the orchestra to the strains of their favorite quadrilles, waltzes, and polkas, to say nothing of Beethoven. "The effect was good, particularly animated and elegant," wrote the *Times,* although the arrangement cut off the view from the first tier of boxes. Excepting a 'Sleigh Polka,'[8] there was nothing new in the program," continued the *Times.* "The polka is lively but not strikingly original. A popular negro melody—'Jordan is a Hard Road to Travel' [Dan Emmett's current song hit]—is introduced for the finale very effectively."[9] Indeed, despite the regrettable loss of the ball, the concert turned out to be a gala event. As the *Mirror* (January 19, 1854), bidding a reluctant adieu to the "prince potent of musical enchanters," wrote: "The audience were in capital spirits, the orchestra ditto, and as for the great Jullien, he was majestic, weird, exultant, satisfied! The smiles of Apollo and Adonis mingled on his lips—signs of joy and triumph. . . . The occasion was a continuous gush and glow of rare enjoyment." Ruefully the *Mirror* concluded: "Well, Jullien is gone. We are a sad set, having henceforth only a memory of the monster (delightful monster) concerts" that now were about to captivate new audiences all the way from Newark to New Orleans. And "won't the alligators wag their tails in the Bayous!"

To George Templeton Strong, observing a period of mourning for his mother, concert-going was taboo. Not that there were concerts to attend. Except for the Philharmonic concerts, Eisfeld's chamber-music *soirées,* and a limited number of sacred and benefit events, a virtual eclipse of concert-giving had followed upon the destruction

[7] This despite Fry's peevish insistence that the "culture and refinement" of New York had dismally failed to appreciate Jullien and his unequaled contribution to music in America (*Tribune,* January 4, 1854).

[8] Composed while in Boston and dedicated to the Boston City Guard.

[9] Another example of Jullien's unfailing faculty for utilizing the popular music of the day and place to the greatest advantage.

of Metropolitan Hall.[10] Doubtless it was this dearth of concerts that greatly contributed to the currently spreading vogue for music-making at home—especially at the fashionable houses that the Strongs frequented.[11]

As R. Storrs Willis, an ardent aficionado of home music, exuberantly proclaimed in the *Musical World and Times* (April 22, 1854, pp. 181–82): "The music of private life . . . is a thousand times more enjoyable than public music, because there is a certain *Weihe*—a baptism—about Art produced in the midst of our Penates, and surrounded by those we love and esteem . . . which we do not find under more public circumstances." The proper enjoyment of Art, declared Willis, demanded not only a comfortable but a sumptuous environment: "Nothing can be too elegant, or even luxurious, as a surrounding for Art." Besides, at home one avoided the distracting proximity—the foot-tapping and snuffling—of compulsory neighbors. And at home there was Supper: "Song and supper are associated by the closest, the most subtle and indissoluble laws of inevitable sequence," rhapsodized Willis.

With the scarcity of concerts leaving the critics idle, the amateur musicales received an unusual amount of attention in the press—not only chatty social gossip but even, on occasion, reviews. Willis perhaps overstepped the strictest bounds of critical objectivity in writing so expansively about his own musicale and declaring its star, the harpist Aptommas,[12] a genius. Aptommas's colleague, a new English basso named John Camoenz, was praised, too, if more moderately,[13] and Timm, who delivered his usual unimpeachable accompaniments at the piano, received his usual bouquet of superlatives. (As did, for some reason, his "twin-brother" Scharfenberg, who seems not even to have been present.)

To Strong, who, together with Willis, had for some time past been trying to form a "private Mozart and Haydn Society," such autonomous music-making at home represented the fulfillment of a long-cherished dream—one that allowed him to drench himself to his heart's content in his most treasured sacred music[14] performed by a cast of socially impeccable amateurs of his own choosing, and delivered in an agreeable atmosphere of high piety blended with high society. Nostalgically looking back on the musical evenings at home in 1851 and '52, and doubtless spurred by the growing prevalence of amateur music-making among his social peers,[15] Strong, after long planning

[10] An eclipse largely due to the absence of the great concert and opera stars of recent years.

[11] "It has become the fashion among our prominent resident artists and distinguished amateurs to have private classical Quartette parties at their residences, where the works of the immortal masters are regularly performed, and whence everything of a lighter and more trivial character is excluded," wrote Burkhardt in the *Albion* (January 7, 1854, p. 8).

[12] Affectionately known to his friends as "Ap," wrote Willis, because of his diminutive stature.

[13] Camoenz, soon to become *Camoens,* had frequently appeared with Aptommas in Boston during December (1853) and January, where he was listed (and disapproved of) in *Dwight's,* for some reason, as "Signor" Camoenz.

[14] Despite his disdain for Catholics and Catholicism, Strong highly cherished the masses of Haydn and Mozart, particularly the spurious "Twelfth Mass," attributed to Mozart.

[15] And among lesser folk as well: "A lady and gentleman are forming a small musical party," announced a want-ad in the *Daily Times* (September 19, 1854), "to meet weekly at their house, uptown, and sing glees, etc., under the charge of a professional leader. The object is only for practice and improvement in reading good music." The advertisers sought a soprano, contralto and four gentlemen, "the expense of the leader to be borne by the gentlemen"; the advertisers would supply the piano and the room.

and effort, at last succeeded in assembling a satisfactory group of musically literate, socially compatible friends, to meet fortnightly at his house to read and rehearse his beloved masses. He referred to these delectable occasions as "Mass-meetings."[16]

February 8. . . . Tonight was the beginning of our musical meetings, labored for so long. Timm at the organ[17] [with GTS operating the bellows], and Ellie, Mrs. Isaac Wright, Mrs. Gibbs, and Mrs. C. E. S., Kuhn, Cousinery, and Jem Ruggles[18] . . . as vocalists, did Haydn's Mass No. 1 all through twice, the first chorus in *The Seasons,* and part of Mozart's No. 12. It was an uncommon evening. God be praised for that which he has given us through the compositions and conceptions of men. This Mass music has an especial charm from the sense of its *reality.* It is not, like opera and oratorio, written to entertain or edify, or promote its composer's artistic reputation; it may have been in fact written with the sole object of adding dignity to the services and rites of the Church. We are at liberty to assume that it was produced for that end and none other.[19] Its words are the ritual of Christendom for 1800 years—[they] enforce and illustrate the ideas and the very language that generation after generation of good men have used and dwelt on and loved and repeated, day by day. It is the highest art allied with the highest truth. It is the only objective music—the only music that does not terminate in itself, like oratorios and symphonies.

~

For reasons of musical expediency it was sometimes necessary to engage lesser folk to fill vocal lacunae at the Mass-meetings. In his general transactions with them (as with social or ethnic inferiors in general) Strong assumed the air of delicately ironic condescension indigenous to members of his caste in dealing with servants and other people of lowly station.

February 22. . . . Found a note from Billings at the office when I got there (Billings is, or rather was, our specially retained Extra Professional (Tenor) stating that after reflection he had concluded that, being strictly a high baritone, he might suffer damage from singing a tenor part, and was therefore under the necessity, etc.—and regretted, etc. So I went straight up to Dr. Hodges—193 Hudson [Street]—to inquire about the *tenori* above *his* horizon. Received by the Dr. and Mrs. Hodges with enthusiasm: having fought the Doctor's battles in Trinity Church Vestry for two or three meetings

[16] Throughout his life Strong periodically reverted to increasingly ambitious versions of the Mass-meetings, culminating in the formation of the Church Music Association, a grand choral aggregation that in the '70s gave full-scale concerts for a socially restricted subscribership (to be discussed in a subsequent volume of this work).

[17] The ubiquitous Timm was the token professional who kept musical affairs from going astray at the Mass-meetings.

[18] Mrs. Isaac Wright was the wife of an early shipping magnate; Mrs. Gibbs was the former Josephine Mauran, recently married to the eminent scientist Wolcott Gibbs; Mrs. C. E. S. (sometimes referred to as "Mrs. Eleanor") was the wife of Strong's cousin Charley Strong; Charles Kuhn and Firman Cousinery were prominent commission merchants of Wall Street; Jem Ruggles was Ellie's brother.

[19] But as the Mass-meetings progressed, Strong tended more and more self-indulgently (and wordily) to superimpose upon each detail of each mass a musical, textual, theological, and philosophical interpretation of his own devising.

back, I'm considered, I think, his "organ" in that body, as Erben's structure is his organ in the Church. Had quite a pleasant little visit—very nice, funny little couple that could be effectively depicted in a work of fiction. Referred to three tenors, one of whom I saw and may perhaps succeed in making available.

. . . [later, after a crowded day in Wall Street], came the Mass-meeting. Performers Timm, Cousinery, Kuhn, and (by fits and starts) [Richard H.] Tucker and Jem Ruggles, Mrs. Gibbs. Mrs. Eleanor, Miss Teresa Mauran, Ellie, Mrs. Isaac Wright. I presided at the bellows. Haydn's No. 1 done as far as the *Sanctus;* Mozart's infallible 12th, *all* but the *Cum sancto spiritu* and *Agnus Dei;* and Haydn's Second from the *Sanctus* to the end. Oh, how nice it was!

In No. 1, especially the melodic parts of the *Kyrie,* the opening of the *Gloria,* and the *Et incarnatus;* in No. 12 the *Kyrie,* so simple and revealing the power that underlies its simplicity only by degrees—the grandeur of the *Gloria*—the *Qui tollis* and the lovely quartette that follows the *Et incarnatus* that it seems wrong to call *dramatic*—the majestic *Sanctus*—and that most splendid and vigorous finale to the *Credo*—the noble phrase that opens the *Et resurrexit*—and the grand lights and shadows of the *Et vitam venturi.* . . . And all Haydn's Second—the beautiful *Benedictus*—the modification of the *Hosanna* that follows it—the most Haydenish *Agnus*—and the glowing finale with its grand contrasts and the bursts of living light with which the Mass winds up.

Thank God for the beauty with which he has enabled his feeble and fallible creatures to make mankind happy—for revealing His infinite glories through the labors and conceptions of men—for the laws of melody and harmony whereby such an unfathomable abyss of Truth and Beauty is revealed.

Only one sad, sorrowful thought was always present tonight: I've long counted on getting up these evenings and have always felt it a special inducement that my mother would have so enjoyed them.

March 3. . . . [after further negotiation with Hodges's tenor] Had our proposed new tenor (for the Mass-meetings) here tonight—one [J. W.] Good—a clerk at 91 Liberty Street and one of the three *tenori* of the Trinity Church Choir. So-so, as to qualifications, but he can't attend and refers me to *Safford,* another of Dr. Hodges's nominees.

March 9. . . . Our new tenor here tonight. C. H. Safford (369 Broadway)—rather gentish, but a good musician and an acquisition to the Mass-meetings—and better than Good.

March 10. Mass-meeting came off Wednesday night [March 8]. Sore throat and influenza kept away Mrs. Gibbs, Mrs. Wright, and Tucker. Miss Lucretia Stevens[20] and the new tenor Safford (who did his work very well) were added unto us. Performances were all of Haydn's No. 2 and parts of his No. 1, and of Mozart's 12th. Very satisfactorily done. Quite an audience assembled.[21] . . . We must repress that tendency as well as we can: Kuhn and Cousinery don't like it. William and Edmund Schermerhorn, by the by, also allied themselves with us and did good service.[22]

[20] The vocally gifted daughter of the famed surgeon Alexander Hodgdon Stevens (1789–1869).

[21] Consisting of "the two Beldens, Mrs. W. H. Anthon, and Miss West, Mrs. Goddard (quondam Miss Anna Fearing), little Anderson, George C. Anthon, *et al.*"

[22] A social triumph! Strong's deceptively casual references to The Schermerhorns—supreme Knickerbocker aristocracy—cloaked his high elation at their participation in his Mass-meetings.

That music ought to be more known. It is an office worthy of that Art to illustrate such words as *Kyrie eleison, Et in terra pax hominibus, Gratias agimus tibi propter magnam gloriam tuam, Et incarnatus est [de Spiritu Sancto] ex Maria Virgine: [et homo factus est.] Crucifixus etiam pro nobis, Pleni sunt caeli et terra, Dona nobis pacem*—all the "libretto" furnishes to music the noblest themes it is called on to express or can be brought in contact with.[23] Even the dogmatic assertions of the *Credo* demand the highest exertion of the resources and language of the Art and its legitimate subjects. "Orthodox and heretical," "true and false," are terms strictly applicable to the music of a *Credo*. It is very obvious that such music may express and enforce most energetically the truths embodied in the Creed, and may point to their mutual relations in the Catholic system by suggestions in its own structure: e.g., the identity of the thought (i.e., the musical phrase) which characterizes the *Et resurrexit,* and the *Expecto resurrectionem mortuorum, Et vitam venturi saeculi*—or the binding together by repetitions, choral accompaniments of a solo, and other like devices of the *Deum de Deo, lumen de lumine*—or with the *Et incarnatus, Homo factus, Passus et sepultus est.*

It may properly be said of a deep and thoughtful Mass that it is Catholic, or Arian, or Humanitarian,[24] and so on.

March 24. . . . Mass-meeting Wednesday night [March 22] uncommonly successful. Triumphant! Present, Mrs. Gibbs and Miss Teresa [Mauran], Mrs. Wright, Mrs. Eleanor, Mrs. Ellen Ruggles Strong, Kuhn, Cousinery, Tucker, Jem Ruggles, a couple of newly caught and much intimidated *Scolls* of 23rd Street (who confessed that they were out of their depth and had never come in contact with people who could read that kind of music "that way" before), the two Schermerhorns, and Timm, of course. Music: Haydn's Third Mass to end of *Benedictus; Gloria* and *Qui tollis* of his No. 2, and finale of the same Mass from the *Sanctus* onward; and the *Gloria* of Mozart's 12th down to its final fugue, all very well done indeed. Vast improvement in execution recognized by everybody. They sang as if more used to each other, more perfectly together, and with clearer distinction between *pianos* and *fortes*. Some of the rather showy and difficult movements of the Third Mass went perfectly in the first trial, the several parts traceable in their separation and the lights and shadows well defined. No outsiders. It was found that one or two objected to an audience, however small; and a little tact conveyed that fact without offence to the Beldens and Miss West, and so on, who dropped in on former occasions.

Mrs. Boonen Graves,[25] on whom I called last Sunday, has conceived an amateur charitable [sacred] concert for the benefit of some "House and School of Industry" [a benevolent institution on West 16th Street], which she wants our Mass-meetings to further. By all means.

Strong soon had reason to regret his too-ready assent to Mrs. Graves's request. Not only did she inhabit a socially inferior stratum, but rehearsals for her project impinged upon the time he regarded as sacred to his Mass-meetings. More than a tinge

[23] Strong evidently possessed an insatiable appetite for enunciating the vocabulary of the Mass and reconciling it with his own theological-*cum*-musical interpretations.

[24] Coming from Strong, a rare ecumenical sentiment.

[25] The wife of a well-to-do, if less than socially lustrous, commission merchant of Wall Street.

of condescension and no little resentment figured in Strong's progressive disparagement of the lady and her worthy effort.

March 27. . . . to Mrs. Graves's [at University Place], where was an informal preliminary organizing for our (or rather her) proposed charitable concert—with four *soprani,* two *contralti,* one tenor, and no bass, and a piano so tuned for the occasion that six notes in its middle octave wouldn't sound at all, as elements of a rehearsal. Rehearsal wasn't brilliant, and I don't think the prospects of the concert brilliant just at this moment, but they may improve.

Philip Mayer came here last night, and I retained him for our Mass-meetings.[26] Ellie has been suddenly invoked by William Schermerhorn to assist in his contemplated performance of Mercadante's "Septem ultima verbem" [Strongese, or possibly Schermerhornese, for *Le sette parole di Nostro Signore (The Seven Last Words)* (Novara 1838)].[27] . . . Next Mass-meeting will probably have to give way to a rehearsal of divers things for Mrs. Graves's concert—Haydn's No. 6,[28] I fear, must be postponed.

March 29. . . . The [William] Schermerhorns are getting up a kind of musical party for next Monday—Mercadante's *Seven Last Words*—with eight voices and five instruments (Eisfeld's people). Mrs. Josephine Gibbs, the mainstay and pillar of the *contralti,* is laid up with a severe cold and may probably be unable to sing, so William C. Schermerhorn came to me yesterday, and Mrs. William to Ellie, to request her to be "so celestial" as to learn the part on short notice, with the proviso that if Mrs. Gibbs entirely recovered, her [Ellie's] services might perhaps not be needed. Somewhat of a request to make—but Ellie's plenitude of kindliness and good nature, her singular insensibility to all selfish considerations, and her delight in being able to do a service were conclusive. Though copies of the piece can't be had, and she had only the temporary loan of the score[29] (voice parts in some *clef* or other that she doesn't read) and manuscript copies of the contralto part, she went to work this morning resolved to conquer or die. . . . I went to the Schermerhorns' and listened to the rehearsal with fear and trembling, for Ellie was laboring against every difficulty—unused to singing with orchestral accompaniment and with no efficient help, for Miss Maggie Delprat, the other contralto, is no musician and looked to Ellie for guidance. Mrs. Ellie did nobly, made scarcely any mistakes, and covered herself with glory. . . .

[later, after dining with the Schermerhorns and attending a political meeting at the Tabernacle, Strong returned home to find] Ellie and William and Edmund [Schermerhorn] reading over Mercadante again with Bonzanini at the piano. They stayed indefinitely.[30]

. . . This production of Mercadante's wants to be heard more than once; but it

[26] Mayer frequently performed at the Schermerhorns' recherché musicales.

[27] This might have been the "beautiful mass by Mercadante" whose score the music-loving Rev. Dr. Cumming had brought back from Italy to be performed at the consecration of his new church, St. Stephen's, on East 28th Street. Alternate choirs had been engaged to perform the work, in order to "prevent fatigue" (*Musical World and Times,* March 18, 1854, pp. 123–24).

[28] Novello no. 6, Hoboken XXII:14, is the *Harmoniemesse* (1802).

[29] Probably borrowed from Dr. Cumming.

[30] "We certainly get on pleasantly in all our relations with the Schermerhorns, reserved and unpopular as they are," rejoiced Strong.

certainly has depth, more or less. There's a solo of Mayer's, with choral accompaniment, that seems to mean something, and a duo for tenor and bass. And there is traceable, throughout, the same peculiar quality or feeling or expression—or something else—that makes [Mercadante's] *Giuramento* lovely—loveliest in my memories of all modern Italian music.[31] Don't know that I can define the special quality to which I refer, though I see it so distinctly and recognize it nowhere else. It is the melancholy, *sehnsüchtig,* sensuous, dreamy yearning embodied in the first sextette of the opera, where Truffi in 1848 used to lead off with that pungent phrase of melody—so well remembered—repeated by all the solo parts together, and followed by another yet more voluptuous movement alternating with a very counterpointy chorus. I'd give $5 on the spot to hear the unison of Truffi and Benedetti and Beneventano, through which the current of song passed from the choral fugue (if it was a fugue) into the luscious melody of the solo parts once more. It is all of the earth earthy, but of the earth flooded with Sicilian moonlight—of the earth, where great masses of tropical forest growth in alternate light and shadows and festoons of pendant vines and successive terraces of verdure crowned with marble colonnade or castle are "hanging in the shadowy air" of the sultry, moonlit night—where earthly lovers are wooing and winning—and earthly maidens listening and yielding.[32]

Perhaps the same feeling may be found in Schubert's Serenade. The moonlight of Provence or Andalusia or Naples surely lights up that most intense and exquisite measure of love and hope and longing. And this "ecclesiastical" composition embodies the same feeling or somewhat like it. Most inappropriate and wrong, but very recognizable and most characteristic of the composer.

April 1. . . . Went to William Schermerhorn's tonight with Ellie for the final rehearsal of the Mercadante production. Mrs. Gibbs was there and the contralto part with three voices on it—two muffled by sore throat—was just about strong enough to hold its own against Mayer and Miss Lucretia Stevens. Without Mrs. Ellie, I think they'd fail signally, as Mrs. Gibbs's voice has given out strangely but perhaps it will rally before Monday night. I see through the music of this piece far better than I did on Wednesday, and I don't think a very great deal of it. It is not ecclesiastical, of course, it attempts only to be dramatic, and perhaps its subject may be so treated. But is it true and valuable as a dramatic treatment of that subject? I rather think not.

April 4. . . . That respectable but misguided man, my waiter Henry Colum, goes to California tomorrow. How we shall get along tomorrow night, when some forty people will be here in council *saga* and rehearsal of Mrs. Graves's charity concert, remains to be seen. Ellie has gone to the [Alexander] Stevens's tonight to rehearse something or other[33] that's to be sung Friday evening at the last of their musical evenings.

April 6. . . . Mrs. Graves's people sang here last night. We had a rather refreshing season, but I apprehend the concert will be a failure. It wants a Director or Direc-

[31] With this single exception, Strong seems to have regarded Italian music much as he did social inferiors.

[32] Strong had allowed himself—but only briefly—to transpose his musical raptures from shadowy cathedral to torrid Sicilian moonlight.

[33] Evidently a rehearsal socially superior to the one for Mrs. Graves's concert.

tress,[34] and it wants someone to exorcise people who sing as false as Miss P. M.[35] Ellie has gone to the Stevens's tonight to read some music which is to be sung there Friday evening.

. . . Barnum's transfusion of new blood into the Crystal Palace seems like to succeed and to give new vigor to that very disabled association.[36] I've always recommended its stockholders to appoint him Agent or Manager or Counsel.

April 7. . . . Ellie has gone to Mrs. A. Stevens tonight, where she is to do some music.

April 10. . . . [following a rather uneventful meeting of the Trinity Church Vestry], through the rain to Mrs. Graves's, where was a rehearsal of the concert—postponed now to the Thursday in Easter week. Trust it won't kill another of our Mass-meetings. Rehearsal better than the last preceding. Miss Lucretia did the *Inflammatus* (from Rossini's *Stabat Mater*) with the energy of ten prima donnas. The Chorale from [Mendelssohn's] *St. Paul* went decently; the *Gloria* of Haydn's No. 1 splendidly. Everybody calls the Chorale a bore. It strikes me as among the grandest things of the sort now extant, and as remarkable, moreover, for the cleanness with which it conveys the austere, but splendid, conception.

April 15. . . . Ellie went to a rehearsal of the Graves concert; has just got back. The interval between her departure and return—twelve o'clock—spent in dawdling over the organ. . . .

April 17. . . . Ellie has not been at all well, and I declined permitting her to attend the [Graves] rehearsal tonight. The Graves concert is getting on in a shiftless, reckless, Hibernian way, entirely characteristic of its originators and promoters, Mrs. Graves and X + Y Emmets.[37] If it doesn't turn out a *fiasco* total and ridiculous it will be extraordinary. Very glad Ellie doesn't take very conspicuous solo parts. She has been cultivating her contralto faculty of late—very successfully.

. . . As I expected, this concert and its rehearsals have broken up our Mass-meeting for next Wednesday night.

April 19. . . . Have been tonight to Potts's Meeting House [Dr. Potts's ivy-clad church at University Place and 16th Street], attending the last rehearsal of the Graves concert, which comes off [there] tomorrow evening. Went decently on the whole, but I think it will be a failure.

N.B. Enriched my vocabulary with a new compound: Wishing to be useful in any sphere, however humble, I offered to "spell" the man who was pumping wind for Timm. But that functionary declined my offer because he was used to it—*Organ-bellowing* was his business and never tired him.

The *Kyrie* of Haydn's No. 3 is certainly most spirited and splendid, but like all that Mass, with the possible exception of the *Et incarnatus,* it does not suit me. It seems without a trace of reverential feeling. It is an "Imperial Mass" and celebrates the coronation of the Earthly Sovereign rather than the Mystery which binds Heaven and Earth

[34] Strong, or Mrs. Strong, for instance.

[35] Surely Timm, who had volunteered as musical director of the event, was capable of such exorcism.

[36] Not only Strong, but all New York pinned their hopes on Barnum's ability to resuscitate the financially ailing Crystal Palace, closed since December 1, 1853.

[37] Probably generic Hibernian names for Mrs. Graves's associates.

together. It may be the merest delusion, but the composition seems to me different in tone from the rest of Haydn's works—as if he had been oppressed by the more secular grandeur of the solemnity in view of which he was writing and had exerted all his powers only to produce an effective contribution to its pageantry. What he produced is most vigorous and effective, but—it seems to me—far more fit for some grand secular celebration than for an Act of Worship.

I can't get rid of the notion that the magnificent, energetic phrases with which the *Kyrie* opens should accompany the rise of the curtain on some superb tableau, and are alien to the words and thoughts they profess to enforce and embody. So with the magnificent *Gloria, Hosanna,* etc.; they are all great, but the religious element is wanting. Not because they are brilliant—the *Gloria* of his No. 2 and its *Sanctus, Benedictus, Agnus Dei,* and finale are more brilliant, but they leave a different impression. So do even Mozart's Twelfth and Seventeenth, which appear at first entirely artistic and undevotional, and his First, which is certainly free from any imprint of the cloister or the chapterhouse. But Haydn's First and Sixth (and Sixteenth, and Mozart's Third and his short *Requiem,* not *the Requiem*) and Beethoven's [Mass] in C furnish the standard by which I would test a religious composition.

The *Et in terra pax* and *Et incarnatus* of the First Mass (Haydn's) would make a formidable standard for composers, were I arbiter of their merits. There seems to be in both a quiet, childlike purity and simplicity of feeling such as is not often embodied in any work of man.

April 21. . . . The Amateur [Graves] concert last night went off infinitely better than anybody expected, or had a right to expect. Even the Duo from the (Rossini) *Stabat Mater* was decent. Miss Maggie did not sing so false but that a person without any ear for music might have supposed it alright, and Lafitte [evidently the "gentish" Safford's successor] got through very fairly. Miss Lucretia's *Inflammatus* was delivered in the bravura style thereto appropriate, and with forty-prima-donna power. Mrs. Costar's ungracious solo—*Fac ut portem* (also from Rossini's *Stabat Mater)*—was better done than it deserved. The trio from [Mendelssohn's] *Elijah* fell flat, as I expected it would. In the *Kyrie* of [Haydn's] Third Mass, Mrs. Wright sang the soprano part very effectively indeed. All the choral pieces went very well, and everybody commended and admired and complimented everything. Church . . . jammed and the net result about $1500.

In his rather grudging report of the concert, evidently too great a success, Strong neglected to mention its most intriguing feature. Willis (or a deputy),[38] in an all-but-ecstatic review, reported that the performances of the socially eminent ladies [delicacy forbade positive identifications]—many of whom possessed voices of "uncommon power and richness"—indeed, some of them "thrilling" and "magnificent"—would have been still more effective if their "natural unwillingness to appear before a critical and numerous audience had not rendered an intervening curtain of silk necessary to their comfort and self-possession."

[38]Probably Émile (or "Emilius") Girac, a French musician and teacher, who seems briefly to have joined Willis's editorial staff in 1854, probably upon the departure of Oliver Dyer for the *Musical Review and Choral Advocate.*

After the concert "the hospitable and elegant mansion of Mrs. G——, closely adjoining the church, was opened to the performers and a few friends. Mrs. G——, the lady-manager *par excellence* of this charitable effort, showed herself throughout to the singers concerned a kind and hospitable hostess, providing after each preliminary rehearsal [except, presumably, the single rehearsal at Strong's] a recherché supper, with which was combined the luxury of a picture gallery and a conservatory of plants (a winter-garden), all of which beautiful luxuries her beautiful house comprises." Even Mr. G—— was praised, having shown himself to be a "courteous host" by throwing open his billiard room "for *between while* recreation" (*Musical World and Times,* April 29, 1854, pp. 193–94). It is doubtful that the Strongs attended.

Strong was relieved, after this distasteful interlude, once again to take full control of his beloved Mass-meetings.

April 27. . . . One of the not too numerous, positively delightful things of this world has just ended: to wit, a "Mass-meeting." Performers: Mrs. Wright and Mrs. Eleanor Strong, Mrs. Gibbs and Mrs. G. T. S., Cousinery, "Rich" Willis, Philip Mayer, Edmund Schermerhorn, and, in an intermitting way, Mr. Lafitte. Haydn's No. 6 sung twice through and, after some oysters, the *Sanctus* and *Benedictus* of the Second. The Sixth is very lovely; its finest points [are] the splendid *Gloria,* the *Gracias agimus, Credo* (especially *Qui propter nos homines, Et incarnatus,* the *Sanctus, Hosanna, Agnus Dei,* and *Dona* [*nobis*] *pacem*). The opening phrase of the *Hosanna* is inimitable—at least, it has an altogether peculiar charm for *me.* Another is the *Qui tollis,* where the solo parts come in with a reminiscence of the *Gratias agimus.*

But that *Benedictus* of the Second Mass combines all the refinement of Mozart, all his spirituality and shrinking delicacy of sentiment and expression, with the honest, human, genial, hearty, kindly tone characteristic of Haydn, just as the highbred gentleman and the simple country squire are fused together in Sir Roger de Coverley.[39]

. . . Eleanor took the first soprano part in the spirited *Hosanna* of the Second Mass, with fire and vigor worthy of Miriam the Prophetess, the sister of Aaron, when she sang "The horse and his rider hath He thrown into the sea" [from Handel's *Israel in Egypt*]. When Mrs. Eleanor knows her part well and likes it a good deal, she puts much life and passion into it.

April 29. . . . Edmund [Schermerhorn] is jubilant over the Mass-meetings, which he pronounces the best arrangement for producing good music ever effected within the memory of man. Indeed, all the performers enter into their work with zeal and enthusiasm. And the arrangement *is* comfortable. Not so much for the enjoyment of the single evening as for the fragrance each meeting leaves in one's memory—for the consolation each gives to many following days and nights.

May 2. . . . Edmund Schermerhorn dines here and has been looking through music with Ellie all the evening, with a view to deciding what's to be sung next after Haydn's Sixteenth Mass.

May 3. . . . tonight raining hard. Of course, for this was one of the Mass evenings, which have introduced a new element into meteorology and furnished almanac makers with new data for prophecy. Present tonight: Mrs. Eleanor and Mrs. Wright,

[39] Sir Roger de Coverley was the quintessential, eccentric English country squire, as portrayed by Joseph Addison (1672–1719) and Sir Richard Steele (1672–1729) in *The Spectator* (1711–12).

Ellie, Cousinery, Mayer, Lafitte, Edmund Schermerhorn, and Jem Ruggles. . . . Timm, of course.

Haydn's Sixteenth done through twice and parts of it three times. CRITICAL NOTICE. *Kyrie* dry and barren, except its opening and finale; *Gloria* not so good as I expected; *Gratias agimus* better—most sweet and simpleminded in its feeling; *Qui tollis* decidedly strong; the fugue that follows it satisfactory but needing to be heard again; *Credo not* effective; *Et incarnatus* strong and beautiful beyond anticipation; *Et resurrexit, etc.* very vigorous and expressive; *Et vitam venturi saeculi* would prove, I think, one of Haydn's finest fugues. Its winding up is most melodious and *drastic.* The *Sanctus, etc.* did not come up to my anticipations; the *Benedictus* far surpassed them. It's an intense expression of the sentiment peculiar to Haydn's best music and is abundantly elaborated without the least prolixity or dilution. It includes the germ of the last movement of the first part of *The Seasons. Agnus Dei* not especially noteworthy. *Dona [nobis] pacem* most masculine, well-defined, and splendid.

After some oysters they sang No. 2 (Haydn's) from the *Sanctus* to the end.

~

And, to relieve all this sanctity:

May 5. . . . Somebody is serenading the Beldens on the other side of the square. "Auld Lang Syne" is floating mournfully through the midnight stillness.

~

In mid-May, Jullien, back from charming the alligators in the bayous,[40] announced, with suitable fanfare, ten final concerts at Castle Garden before returning to Europe. Strong, long absent from public entertainments, attended the opening event on May 15, advertised as Jullien's 78th concert in New York and his 205th since arriving in the United States nine months earlier.

May 15. . . . Miss Rosalie [Ruggles] and Jem dined here, and we went to Jullien's concert (first of the final series) at Castle Garden. Overture to *Masaniello* and that delicious Allegretto from Beethoven's F-Symphony. The rest of the concert made up of "Prima Donna Waltz,"[41] "Sleigh Ride Polka," "Grand American Quadrille," and the like trash,[42] executed with power and precision worthy a better cause and subject.

~

Trash notwithstanding, Strong returned to Castle Garden on May 22 to hear Jullien conduct the Overture to *William Tell* and the "delightful third movement of [Beethoven's] D-Symphony. Pleasant evening," he wrote.[43]

But Strong was irrevocably attuned to a different music.

[40] And having covered some 8000 miles at an expenditure reported in the *Mirror* (May 22, 1854) of "at least a quarter of a million of dollars."

[41] By now elevated to a psalm sung by a Connecticut River congregation (*Dwight's,* May 20, 1854, p. 55).

[42] Consisting of Jullien's *Mélange* from *Les Huguenots,* with spectacular solo performances by S. Hughes, Schreuss, and particularly Lavigne; also "The Californian Quadrille," "The Target Galop," and familiar solos by Zerr, Koenig, Wuille, and the Brothers Mollenhauer.

[43] The remainder of the program was made up of what Strong called "the usual trumpery": cornet and trumpet solos by Koenig and Duhem; opera arias by Rossini, Bellini, and Meyerbeer; and

May 18. . . . Last evening another Mass-meeting, at which assisted Mrs. Eleanor, Mrs. Gibbs, Ellie, Cousinery, Richard Willis, Mayer, Edmund Schermerhorn, who persists in wearing out his shoulder joint by the measured brandishing of a baton (which no one looks at), and Timm, of course. . . . They sang Haydn's Sixth through, and very nicely it went. The *Gloria* onward to the end of the *Qui tollis* is certainly most vigorous and beautiful, the *Credo* and *Et incarnatus* very strong, the opening melody of the latter a special gem for any collection of Haydniana. *Sanctus* very grand—first phrase of the *Hosanna* most intense—the *Benedictus* improves on better acquaintance, and the *Agnus Dei* can't be beat, not even by that of Haydn's Second Mass. Then they attacked Mozart's No. 12, and did the *Gloria* and *Credo,* with especial view to the concerted pieces, the *Quoniam tu solus* and *Et incarnatus.* Mozart is surely the Raffaele of music—the same perfect purity of Art characterizes both. Art so clear and so perfect that it is not seen till it is looked for. How delightfully Cousinery did his tenor solo, especially that ineffable phrase that introduces the key of C major—"*ex Maria virgine.*"

Whether Mozart or Beethoven be the truer artist is a question that would carry one far down into the abysses of Art and Truth.

〰

Strong undertook to explore these "abysses."

June 1. . . . Mass-meeting last night. Mrs. Eleanor, Mrs. Wright, Mrs. Gibbs, Ellie, Cousinery, Kuhn (for a season), Mayer, and Lafitte. . . . Tried some very respectable music of Timm's first, then Beethoven [Mass] in C straight through—some movements twice—then the *Kyrie* of Weber's Mass in G [op. 76 (1818–19)].

Beethoven's Mass is grand—deep and wonderful. It doesn't come near his transcendental instrumental works, but it bears the same marks—is of the same kind but less exalted in degree. It has their variety and intense pungency of single phrases, which though so different and so sharply defined, do not destroy the breadth and unity of the movement to which they belong. And it shows the same supremacy over the laws of music—the same imperial control of its language. He steps abruptly from one chord to another in defiance of rule, but achieves in so doing what the rule helps common minds to attain.

The *Kyrie, Gloria, Qui tollis, Et incarnatus, Sanctus, and Dona [nobis] pacem* of this work are stupendous, each in its kind, each most unlike the other, as it should be; each austere and subdued into reverential reserve, but all embodying thought most intense and most true and real.

The *Credo* must not be forgotten. Beethoven gives it through its accompaniment a kind of martial tone—*suggests* the March of the Church Militant through the World to the World's End, by the simple sequence of notes with which it begins and which runs through it. (Isn't it said that in Poland, under the Jagiellons,[44] the usage was that

---

English and American popular ballads sung by Zerr and Madame Wallace-Bouchelle, who joined Jullien's company on May 22; also Jullien's "Katydid" and "Sleigh" polkas and his "Nepaulese" and "American" quadrilles, the last for the 200th and "positively last time in America." (It wasn't.) "House very full," wrote Strong. "Received gallery seats—intensely uncomfortable. I'm 'not Caliban but a crump'[?], and comatose with the dilute carbonic acid gas breathed for three hours."

[44] Followers of Jagiello, a fifteenth-century King of Poland.

all the knights and nobles in church should draw their swords when the *Credo* was chanted?) All this is far above Haydn, our special subject thus far. But there is in Haydn a certain comfortable, genial goodness and kindliness—not so profound as Beethoven—which one misses [in Beethoven].

June 14. . . . Tonight a Mass-meeting, supposed to be the last, but I've squeezed out one more (June 23). *Soprani:* Eleanor, Miss Teresa Mauran; *contralti:* Mrs. Gibbs and Ellie; tenor Cousinery; Mayer basso. . . .

First they did Timm's *Sanctus, Benedictus, and Et incarnatus.* All three very nice and compact and logical, with an occasional gleam of life and light, especially in the last. Then most of Haydn's No. 2 and a scrap of Mozart's infallible No. 12.

In the meantime, Jullien continued to draw great crowds to Castle Garden, but—except for William Henry Fry's high-voltage eulogies[45]—some new critical cavils had begun to surface after the Maestro's return.

During his absence a demon real-estate developer H. R. Conklin had succeeded the longtime lessees French and Heiser[46] as the landlord of Castle Garden. On taking over, Conklin, who planned to enlarge the Battery with landfill, had thoroughly refurbished the Castle with a fresh coat of paint, recushioned seats, great numbers of new gas lights, and an improved ventilation system that would "cut off all draughts of air." In short, as the *Mirror* reported, (May 13, 1854) the Castle was in "tip-top condition to receive Jullien," who had "democratized the enjoyment of the highest creations of music [and] given us an imperial feast at a republican price."

But Burkhardt, in the *Albion* (May 20, 1854, p. 236), complained of the dinginess that had pervaded Jullien's return concert: "The great brilliancy of the former *coup d'oeil,* all the telling effects of light, drapery, lattice work, and painting, which made the first series of his Concerts here a feast for the eyes as well as the ears, were wanting." So dim was the lighting at Castle Garden that one could distinguish Jullien from Koenig only because one held a baton and the other a cornet. Even "Jullien's *sans pareil* shirt front and stunning neck cloth were without their wonted effect—lost in obscurity."[47]

[45] "To say that M. Jullien has done more than any one in this country for music of a high order is to say very little," wrote Fry in the *Tribune* on May 26. "He has done more than all others put together." If Jullien lured audiences with his popular extravaganzas, "once in the concert room they would hear something more spiritual, [something] they would learn in no other way." Jullien's concerts, in Fry's up-to-the-minute opinion, were the musical parallel of "first-rate journalism" as compared with (old-fogy) "literature."

[46] Who before leaving had unbecomingly "proceeded to dismantle the Garden by removing all the fixtures, but an injunction was obtained, and the work of demolition arrested" (*Mirror,* May 8, 1854).

[47] The *Mirror,* on the contrary, reported that the great auditorium "was fairly ablaze under the myriad gas lights, and the spectacle of a sea of upturned faces and mouths agape, as it were, to drink in the floating, whirling, rushing, thrilling, rousing, crashing melodies of horn, viol, cornet, oboe, flute, drums, etc., was a study for a painter or a poet. . . . The great conductor never shone more in his glory. He wielded his *baton* as though he were a very Neptune, trident in hand, evoking Arion and the dolphins from the surrounding deep" (May 16, 1854).

Musically, Jullien and his virtuosos (those who remained)[48] were, of course, as wonderful as ever: they still performed with "a style and effect rarely equaled and never excelled." But to Burkhardt—although the orchestra had allegedly been restored to its former numbers by the addition of local musicians, again mostly from the Philharmonic—the performance seemed "somehow diminished."[49] For the first time at a Jullien concert Burkhardt felt "a want of more string instruments," and for the first time "certain effects sounded in that vast hall thin, instead of massive." At the same time, however, Burkhardt wished to stress that he was only comparing the present Jullien with the earlier one—and the present one still towered head and shoulders above "all orchestral competition."[50]

The *Herald* (May 16, 1854) complained of Jullien's repetitive programing: "There being but little that was new . . . our task in criticizing the performance is easy.[51] The extract from Beethoven's Symphony in F was executed in good style and was so well appreciated by the audience that we trust their musical taste will not again be impeached" [an obvious thrust at Fry]. Herr Koenig plays as well as usual; but, in truth, the 'Prima Donna Waltz,' the 'American Quadrille,' and many other pieces which were given last evening have been heard about four or five hundred times too often to be very popular at this date. We wish Miss Zerr, too, would not sing 'Home, Sweet Home' any more. . . . People were genuinely bored."[52]

But the *Evening Post* (May 16, 1854), believing that, even for Jullien's superb orchestra, "practice makes perfect," wrote: "We are not disposed to complain of repetitions of old pieces in these concerts, for in music we desire not so much novelty as finish. . . . Anyone who knows anything about orchestral music is conscious that a large band, even when marshalled by the rapid tactics of a Jullien, requires time and endless drilling to perfect its movements."

As his farewell season progressed, Jullien did in fact bring out a few new pieces, among them, on May 17 (and mercilessly at every following concert) his waltz "Farewell, or Adieu to America." And upon the inevitable "extension" of his season[53] for

[48] In January a group of Jullien's stars—Hardy (bassoon), Reichert (flute), both Winterbottoms (trombone and double bass), and White (double bass)—had returned to Europe to fill engagements purportedly made prior to the American tour (*Musical World and Times,* February 4, 1854, p. 50). Bottesini, too, had departed at about the same time to conduct opera in New Orleans and Mexico.

[49] Yet, the complete orchestra personnel, listed name-by-name in the *Tribune* (May 16, 1854), totaled ninety players.

[50] To a blindfolded listener, wrote the *Courier and Enquirer* (May 16, 1854), a single chord would have served to recognize that Jullien was in command of the orchestra: "Its quality was so grand, so imperial, the volume of tone was so large, and the different varieties of sounds . . . were so richly and skillfully blended that no musical ear which had once heard those mingled vibrations could be at a loss as to their identity."

[51] The reviewer was probably the Boston-born playwright and journalist, Edward G. P. Wilkins (?–1861), lately engaged by James Gordon Bennett to write music and drama criticism for the *Herald* (see Winter, pp. 84–89).

[52] The *Tribune* (but surely not Fry!) concurred, stating on May 22: "We would suggest that when the audience demands a repetition of 'God Save the Queen' in the 'Exhibition' fantasia [Quadrille], 'Hail Columbia' should not be given, as the change is for the worse; and that when Miss Zerr is required to repeat *Vedrai, carino,* she does not render the hackneyed 'Home, Sweet Home.'"

[53] The term "positively last night" fooled no one, wryly commented the *Musical World and Times* (July 1, 1854, p. 99); it was more likely to imply the "positively first of a new series, if an audience

a "Grand Week" of benefits[54]—he introduced two new works at his own benefit (June 1): his quadrille on themes from Spohr's opera *Faust* and the first (and possibly only) performance of Fry's latest "continuous [one-movement] symphony" *Childe Harold.*[55] Presumably inspired, or suggested, by Berlioz's *Harold in Italy* (Paris 1834), the work, dedicated to Jullien and allegedly "composed expressly for this concert," bore as an epigraph an arcane fragment from Byron's *Childe Harold's Pilgrimage* (1816; Canto III, Stanza 3), paraphrased as follows:

> In my youth's Summer, I did dream of one,
> The wandering image of his own dark mind;
> Again I seize the theme but then begun,
> And bear it with me as the rushing wind
> Bears the crowd onwards; in that tale I find
> The furrows of long thought, and dried up tears,
> Which ebbing leave a track behind,
> O'er which all heavily the journeying years
> Plod the last sands of life—where not a flower appears.

As an "emotional illustration" of this "transitory and retrospective" passage from Byron's epic poem, wrote the *Daily Times* (June 2, 1854), Fry had succeeded tolerably well in a difficult task, but "without producing a work which will bear comparison with his 'Breaking Heart' or even 'Santa Claus.' Mr. Fry has availed himself of the full capabilities of the orchestra and has written down to the lowest, and up to the highest, notes of the scales. Strong contrasts are used, without—so far as we were capable of detecting—any specific object for their introduction."

The critic, presumably Seymour, nonetheless praised the work's many fine solo passages for the various instruments, particularly its "introductory *motivo*" for the *Corna Musa* (saxophone), wonderfully played by Wuille, and a duet for two horns. But the piece suffered from "sketchiness and its apparent effort to *stretch* the orchestra." In fairness to Fry, however, it had to be added that *Childe Harold* had been very badly played despite self-contradictory claims of numerous "laborious rehearsals." Perhaps on a second hearing one might be able to appreciate it more completely and to "perceive its design." But in no way, stressed the critic, was it an improvement over the "three able works that have preceded it from the same pen."

Burkhardt, on the other hand, after some telling remarks concerning Fry's perverse insistence on calling his one-movement, descriptive pieces "symphonies," pronounced *Childe Harold* to be the best-scored and best-harmonized of all of Fry's works. Its "surprising, novel, but legitimate and artistic effects . . . deserved all the applause, and even more, that was meted out to them." Burkhardt noted, however, that for

---

of decent size appeared to bid the artist farewell." "New series," too, had come to assume a false meaning, as had the terms "benefit" and "complimentary"—the proceeds of a benefit being more apt to benefit the management than the beneficiary, and those of a complimentary concert to compliment the complimenters rather than the complimentee.

[54] The announced beneficiaries were Koenig, Zerr, Brough, Arthur Chappell, and Jullien.

[55] Fry was not neglected during this "final" season at Castle Garden: the Adagio from *The Breaking Heart* was performed on May 17, 20, and 30; and *A Day in the Country* on May 25. Bristow, too, was well represented with performances on May 24, 26, and 31 of the Andante from his Symphony in D minor, op. 24.

someone who looked on Beethoven as an "old fogy," Fry had made surprisingly free use—"without credit or quotation marks"—of the waltz *Le Désir* by Schubert (erroneously attributed to Beethoven), which indeed, in Burkhardt's opinion, was the best part of Fry's composition (*Albion,* June 3, 1854, p. 260).

No such resemblance was noted in the extravagant critique of *Childe Harold* appearing in the *Musical Review and Choral Advocate* (June 9, p. 201). Probably written by the flamboyant Oliver Dyer, who had joined the editorial and publishing staff of the *Musical Review* early in 1854,[56] the critique signified a radical departure from C. M. Cady's invariably grim pronouncements in that journal on Fry and his music.

Childe Harold was far from a simple-minded musical travelogue laden with such platitudes as "Spanish fandangoes, Swiss yodelings, or Greek plaints," wrote the critic; it was an authentic work of "towering genius and glowing imagination." Plunging headlong into the purplest of purple prose worthy of Fry himself, the writer termed the work "simply a passional and emotional illustration" of its Byronic protagonist as set forth in its motivic stanza—an amalgam of "misanthropy, sorrow, darkened sensuousness, and a persistent gloom from the first to the last, illuminated only as lurid flashes burst from the black concave upon a stormy night and hurl into apparently supernatural being hill, dale, stream, rock, and the whole expanse of external nature.

"A piece of this kind," he went on (continuing to sound like Fry), "can not, in the present state of the musical perceptions of this country, be popular": it inspired no "foot-beatings," nor did it offer such obvious audience-catchers as "trumpet calls, drum-thunders, cornet-echoes, and other things which are most easily grasped by the popular ear." Instead: "At one moment it echoes in the harmonic regions like a spirit which flits away; at another it groans in the deepest basses as an imprisoned soul." And then, after "running into a double *fortissimo,* where the utmost sonority of the orchestra, long sustained, gives the intensity of romantic sorrow and blasted passion . . . the highest notes of the violins dialogue with the deepest notes of the bassoons,[57] the whole vanishing in upper harmonics—the 'baseless [bassless?] fabric of a vision.'"

Not only was the *Childe Harold* Symphony far beyond common comprehension, but it was beyond the capabilities of the average orchestra musician—even Jullien's virtuosos had had their difficulties with its "ticklish" figures in the high regions of the violins and its "hurricane passages like clouds before a storm" for the basses, to say nothing of its "fiendish" brass figures intended to portray the "diabolic traits of the misanthropic hero."

The reviewer pronounced *Childe Harold* to be Fry's finest composition and a great and enduring masterpiece. In the fullness of time, he prophesied, it would be "classed among the classics of the art." But alas, it was not to be. As with many of Fry's works, all traces of his *Childe Harold* score seem to have vanished.[58] Perhaps Jullien took it

[56] If not before. With Dyer's accession to the staff, the *Review* modestly hoped to come closer to becoming "such a musical journal as the world has never before seen" (*Musical Review and Choral Advocate,* January 5, 1854, p. 8).

[57] A premonitory use of noun-as-verb, one of the more irritating verbal quirks of late twentieth-century jargon.

[58] Conflicting as they are, only the reviews (of which Fry's biographer Upton seems to have been unaware) offer any clue to what the *Childe Harold* Symphony might have contained.

back to England, where it might have perished in the Covent Garden fire that consumed most of his scores in 1856.

Having completed his current "farewell" season, Jullien at last gave his long-delayed "Grand Fancy and Full Dress Ball" on June 2 at Castle Garden. Although seductively ballyhooed as a replica of the great Court Balls he had devised for the Queen of England, the event was only moderately attended and the merrymakers only mildly convivial. As the *Daily Times* observed the following day, the would-be frolickers were "unaccustomed to the *abandon* necessary for such an amusement," although eventually Jullien's "admirable orchestra" succeeded in coaxing even the "heaviest" of them to "Terpsichorean effort." Perhaps by then they had drowned their inhibitions in the bubbly cascades of a "Magnificent Champagne Fountain," which—to the strains of Jullien's new "Max Sutaine Polka"—began at a few minutes after eleven to gush forth "the pure wine of Max Sutaine & Co. of Rheims." Some 4000 bottles of Sutaine's elixir were reportedly consumed by the reticent revelers.

The following evening (June 3) Jullien gave the first of two extra performances, a Grand Testimonial Concert, sponsored by the musical and social elite of the city, to honor the newly naturalized American citizen William Vincent Wallace, and on June 5, the expiration date of Jullien's contract with the Chappells, another Grand Testimonial Concert as a gesture of thanks to Arthur Chappell for his able management of Jullien's American tour.[59]

But although Jullien was purportedly about to return to England, it was persistently rumored that he and P. T. Barnum (truly a marriage made in heaven), were concocting a gigantic musical collaboration, soon to materialize at the Crystal Palace, now, as we know, under Barnum's jurisdiction. Not so, claimed Jullien in a self-contradictory letter, appearing in both the *Times* and the *Tribune* on June 2, in which he explained that until his contract with the Messrs. Chappell & Co. expired, on June 5, he was not free to so much as think of any future project. True, the possibility of holding a Musical Congress[60] at the Crystal Palace had been discussed with Barnum, but "when it came to figures, it was found the expenses would exceed $20,000. The idea was then, I believe, abandoned."[61]

To which Barnum grandly replied: "The public will bear me witness that if this is correct, it is the first time for some years that I have been deterred from consummating a great enterprise for fear of the expense, whether it was '$20,000,' or six times that amount." Once Jullien had completed his contract with the Chappells, wrote Bar-

[59]But the *Musical Review and Choral Advocate* (May 25, 1854, p. 186) reported that "so far as money-making is concerned, Jullien's visit to this country has been a failure—that the managers of the enterprise . . . lost many thousands of dollars . . . owing to the fact that [Jullien's] business agents did not understand how to manage such matters in this country."

[60]A term for the great music festivals periodically given throughout Europe. Jullien had presided over his first *Congrés musical* in Paris, at the Tuilleries Gardens in 1837 (or 1838), and later, in 1849, over two successive Musical Congresses in London—at the Surrey Gardens and at Exeter Hall (Carse, *Life of Jullien,* pp. 62–63).

[61]"The public will soon not know who or what to believe," peevishly commented the *Mirror* (June 2, 1854). "One day we are told that Jullien and Barnum have leagued to astonish the world at the Crystal Palace; next that Jullien's passage is paid to England; then that he will neither go nor stay."

num, "We shall see what we shall see" (*Tribune,* June 3, 1854). The deal was by then, of course, consummated.

In fact, since Barnum's recent assumption of the Crystal Palace presidency (on May 4), music had become an integral part of its daily attractions.[62] The mammoth reopening ceremonies (expanded under the wizard's tutelage nearly to the magnitude of a "national solemnity," it was wittily observed) commenced with a parade that left City Hall at ten A.M. and reached the Palace three hours later. There the rites began with the performance of a prize-winning Ode by the popular poet William Ross Wallace (1819–1881),[63] set to music—of all people—by William Henry Fry, who, despite his past denunciations of Barnum-*cum*-Lind, had apparently modified his conscience sufficiently to become director of music for Barnum's grand opening.[64] Thus, as might be expected, the Ode was musically a huge affair, employing a force of "nearly 400 performers"—a chorus of more than 300 members of the Harmonic Society accompanied by "Dodworth's Orchestra" (the full band of 40 supplemented by 30 orchestra musicians), all under Bristow's direction.

The ensuing speeches, delivered by several of the city's most luminous celebrities,[65] were interspersed with music performed by Dodworth's Band; W. L. Bloomfield's United States (Governor's Island) Band; Louis Drouet (1792–1873), the celebrated Dutch flute virtuoso and composer;[66], Louis Drouet, Jr., a pianist (pupil of Mendelssohn); Madame Victor Chome (or Chomé), a *prima donna* from the Brussels Opera; and the popular local actor/singer Ferdinand Meyer.

Unfortunately, the Palace's acoustics proved to be as disastrous to music as to oratory: virtually nothing of either could be heard.[67] The domed glass and iron struc-

[62] With a band "in attendance" throughout the day and a nightly concert performed by the singers Ferdinand Meyer, Luigi Quinto, and a Miss Josephine Remington of the Theatre Royal, Dublin, accompanied by a "grand orchestra" of twenty-two players conducted by the versatile F. B. Helmsmüller. The orchestra was also heard in favorite overtures and current hits such as Jullien's "The Katydid Polka" and "The Prima Donna Waltz"; Dodworth's Cornet Band was soon added to these attractions. Admission to the Palace, with its myriad allurements, was only twenty-five cents.

[63] Lo! the transitory darkness
From our palace floats away.
Lo! the glorious gems of genius
Glitter in the rising day.

Followed by six similarly inspired stanzas.

[64] Signifying his incipient marriage of convenience with Barnum, Fry had in fact recently served on a distinguished jury on Musical Instruments, currently being exhibited at the Crystal Palace. His co-jurors included, among others, G. F. Bristow, Émile Girac, Theodore Eisfeld, Alfred Boucher, Leopold Meignen of Philadelphia, Jullien, Maretzek, and R. Storrs Willis (reported in *Dwight's,* January 29, 1854, pp. 132–33).

[65] Among others, the newspaper publishers Horace Greeley, Parke Godwin, and Erastus Brooks; the eloquent Reverend Dr. Henry Ward Beecher and the so-called "learned blacksmith" Elihu Burritt.

[66] "On leave" from the Court of Saxe-Coburg Gotha, where he had served as *Hofkapellmeister* since 1836.

[67] The *Musical Review and Choral Advocate* suggested that future "orators have their speeches printed beforehand and distributed among the audience" before they spoke (May 11, 1854, p. 153). (A kind of forerunner of the supertitles in use in twentieth-century opera houses.)

ture, built in the shape of a Greek cross, with its four equal wings sprawling "in every direction," abounded in naves and alcoves and arcades fatal to the diffusion of sound. Moreover, with no seats provided for the auditors and no platform or stage for the performers, whatever sound was produced was all but swallowed up in the noisy shuffling and ceaseless chatter of the strolling multitude (*Musical World and Times,* May 13, 1854, pp. 17–18).[68]

Thus, Fry's Ode, because of its great volume of sound,[69] was judged the "most satisfactory" presentation of the evening. "The author was evidently inspired by his mental view of a vast auditory when scoring his work," wrote Willis. "His rich and fiery imagination, thus excited and roused, set forth broad, tasteful, and always well-developed melodies, sustained by a judicious and brilliant orchestration." Fry had "entrusted" Henriette Behrend with the solos, but only in isolated spots could her "brilliant and powerful" voice be heard over the "confused, oceanic noise which surrounded her."[70] The Harmonic Society fared better with their rousing performance of "the Grand Hallelujah Chorus" presumably from Handel's *Messiah* but just possibly the unidentified other composition by Fry reportedly performed on this occasion (perhaps the Hallelujah Chorus "introduced" into his opera *Notre Dame de Paris,* performed in Philadelphia in 1864).

On June 7, immediately upon the termination of Jullien's contract with the Chappells, the papers carried the first massive announcements of the superextravaganza to take place at the Crystal Palace on June 15—a Musical Congress that would enlist the efforts of 1500 instrumental and vocal performers. In the *Tribune,* Fry, who appears to have played an important role in the planning, execution, and promotion of the vast undertaking, unleashed a torrent of irrelevant verbiage glorifying the early Greeks and their Olympian Games; they represented an "evangel of beauty" whose attributes he urged Americans to emulate. Indeed, he asserted, New York's Crystal Palace Exhibition, with its displays of the futuristic, labor-saving machinery that had "taken the place of the rude strength necessary to the defenses and industries of the State in olden times," was to be regarded as the "Olympian Festival of the nineteenth century." Already outstripping the London Crystal Palace with its exhibitions of painting and sculpture, our Crystal Palace was now about to add their sister-art, Music, heretofore inadequately represented, in a manner truly worthy of the ancient Greeks.

With Jullien's "old orchestra" as a nucleus, the enormous cast of performers would include the various bands and choral societies not only of New York but of the "leading cities and towns of the United States." "In grandeur," euphorically wrote Fry, "it will of course very far exceed anything of this kind ever heard in this country, and in

[68] "Americans talk and walk and shuffle their feet while the best music is being rendered," complained the *Musical Review and Choral Advocate* (June 22, 1854, p. 217).

[69] "Not counting the doubles," the orchestra consisted of "octave flute, grand flutes, oboes, clarionets, bassoons, cornets, trumpets, horns, trombones, tubas, ophicleides, snare drums, base-drum [*sic*], cymbals, kettle-drums, violins, violas, violoncellos, and double bases [*sic*]. The choral parts are, beside a principal soprano, three sopranos, three tenors, and three bases" (*ibid.,* May 11, 1854, p. 153).

[70] For a detailed examination of Wallace's prize Ode, see the *Musical Review and Choral Advocate,* May 11, 1854, p. 153.

point of numbers will surpass any yet given in London.[71] As a means of showing forth the varied talent in the country it will be valuable, and," he mischievously added, "the generous rivalries it will set forth may prove most interesting."

Blithely disregarding the acoustical facts of life at the Palace, Fry rejoiced at the prospect of "colossal [musical] effects, attracting such a crowd as has never yet been collected within the walls of any hall in this country," and offering the public "higher ideas of the sublimity of sound than they have ever yet enjoyed, from a Niagara of music, whose roarings and rushings are still guided by eternal laws." Plunging yet deeper into the surging inscrutable, Fry added: "The amateur of musical vastness will be fully gratified in hearing an immense plunging of the sonorous elements, and be lifted to a more generous appreciation of their laws and outworkings of lyrical beauty and grandeur."

The exciting details of the epoch-making event were announced with miraculous speed. By June 10 the newspapers carried a prodigious advertisement occupying a full column and a half, partly consisting of high-flown, descriptive prose redolent of both Barnum and Fry, and partly listing the stupendous cast of performers pledged to take part in what was now referred to as a "long-projected and difficult undertaking."

Under the dome of the building[72] a vast "orchestra" (stage) was being constructed (at a cost of $2000) "with reference to acoustic effects," that would accommodate—in addition to Jullien's own group—the Germania Society of Boston, the Musical Fund Society of Philadelphia, Dodworth's Band, Bloomfield's United States Military Band, the Italian Opera Orchestra,[73] and many individual orchestral "artists and amateurs" from Boston, Philadelphia, Baltimore, Cincinnati, New Orleans, and New York, adding up to an orchestra of about 500 players.The choral societies included: from New York, the Harmonic Society, the Chorus of the Normal Institute (under Professors Lowell Mason, Bradbury, and Root), the newly formed Arion German Glee Club,[74] and (Maretzek's) Italian opera chorus; from Boston, delegations from the Musical Education Society, the Mendelssohn Society, and the Handel and Haydn Society; singing societies from Hartford and Bridgeport; numerous other singing groups and German glee clubs—seven from Philadelphia and two from Baltimore—and members of church choirs from the above cities, and from Newark, Elizabethtown, Trenton, Albany, Buffalo, Rochester, Syracuse, Providence, New Haven, and yet other places, totaling an estimated 1000 singers.

The soloists, in addition to Jullien's virtuosos, included Monsieur Drouet, Sr., Paul Julien, Madame Wallace-Bouchelle, the William Vincent Wallaces, Maria Brainerd, Henriette Behrend, Misses E. Hawley and C. Mallory (apparently of the Harmonic

[71] Seemingly obsessed with the London Crystal Palace (as he was with the Olympian Games) Fry pointedly observed that in its recent move from Hyde Park to Sydenham, the London exhibition had been reinaugurated with a concert directed by Michael Costa, employing a paltry thousand musicians (*Tribune,* June 12, 1854).

[72] Where had stood a colossal equestrian statue of George Washington; its removal to "a still darker corner was a judicious movement," in the opinion of the *Daily Times* (June 9, 1854).

[73] Assembled for Maretzek's imminent opera season, scheduled to open at Castle Garden on June 30.

[74] Comprising a splinter group of thirteen dissident members of the *Liederkranz* who had recently seceded after being served an inferior meal of red cabbage and sausages at a *Liederkranz* function.

New-York Historical Society

Under the dome of the Crystal Palace, where Washington's statue was replaced by a huge stage to accommodate some 1500 participants in the Musical Congress.

Society), Aptommas, Camoenz, a Signor Pasquale Rondinella of Philadelphia, and Allen Dodworth. The orchestra leaders were Jullien's Henry Weist Hill and Edward Mollenhauer,[75] G. F. Bristow, and Maretzek's I. Kreutzer; the conductors were Carl Bergmann of the Germania, Leopold Meignen of the Philadelphia Musical Fund Society, Harvey B. Dodworth and W. L. Bloomfield, conducting their respective bands, and William Vincent Wallace, listed as "Maestro at Piano." Everyone was, of course, under the supreme command of Jullien.

"Such a rehearsing of orchestras, bands, choirs, and glee-clubs as is going on today was never before heard in Gotham, and will not be heard again in this generation," reported the *Mirror* on June 14. "A thousand or more instruments and voices are tuning, preparatory to tomorrow's fête."

But Dwight harbored Cassandra-like misgivings concerning the colossal undertaking: vastness of numbers by no means presupposed a high quality of performance, he wrote. And despite Jullien's phenomenal prowess, with a mere day-and-a-half of musical preparation, "how much rehearsing, with such multifarious elements, can be achieved in that time? Verily, the chances of failure in an enterprise so vast, so bold, and so extempore, are great." Yet, Dwight was captured by "the aspiration" of the venture, which "if it fail for once, may lead to future triumphs." Dwight foresaw more perfect Musical Congresses to come. "May all success, therefore, attend the first great Musical Congress," he benignly concluded (*Dwight's,* June 10, 1854, pp. 77–78).

The East Nave of the Palace was completely filled by the immense, steeply banked "orchestra," which rose, amphitheatre fashion, nearly to the lofty ceiling. The semicircular front of this huge stage was charmingly decorated (by Madame Jullien?) with a "double line of flowers, green plants, and marble statuary." From a vantage point high up in the West Nave, Fry looked down with satisfaction "upon the immense throng, and over upon the musicians piled one above another in an ascending scale, upon whom the light of a thousand gas burners" (forming a "blazing pyramid suspended from the center of the noble dome," echoed by hundreds of ancillary "starlike circles" of lights hung throughout the structure) "shed a brilliancy of illumination" (and the alarming fumes of escaping gas, for the first half-hour of the five-hour event) (*Daily Times, Tribune, Evening Post,* June 16; *Dwight's,* June 24, 1854, p. 9).

For this tremendous happening, admission to the Crystal Palace was doubled to fifty cents;[76] tickets could be purchased at the music stores and hotels throughout the city and environs. "Reserved Stalls under the Dome, in the West Nave fronting the Orchestra (limited to two thousand)," were available at a dollar and a half surcharge and could be purchased only at William Hall's music store on Tuesday, June 13, from nine A.M. to six P.M.[77] All ticket-holders were provided with free transportation to and from the Crystal Palace on all omnibus lines and railroads, and "from about five to nine o'clock all the stages and cars on the routes to the Crystal Palace were overladen,

[75] Promptly on completion of the Chappell contract both Thomas Baker and Anna Zerr had left for London (*Mirror,* June 3, 1854).

[76] "Notwithstanding the immense outlay caused by the organization of the Musical Congress," lamented the advertisements, the Directors were "compelled by the terms of the charter" to limit the price of admission to fifty cents instead of the dollar they had intended to charge.

[77] The day following the concert the *Daily Times* reported an audience of 4000 in the reserved section, as Burkhardt corroborated in the *Albion* on June 17 (p. 284).

overcrowded with passengers all bound for the Congress." Barnum was mightily praised for this nicety, as he was for his vision in undertaking the whole audacious enterprise: "There is no other man in the country," applauded the *Times* (June 12, 1854) "with the boldness to stake $20,000 on the issue of an entertainment."

Surprisingly, George Templeton Strong attended the opening concert.

June 18. . . . The conjunction of Barnum and Jullien at the so-called Crystal Palace, Thursday evening [June 15], in a so-called "Musical Congress with 1500 performers" naturally produced one of the grandest humbugs on record.[78] Went with Ellie, G. C. Anthon, and Miss "Tote" [Anthon's sister Charlotte]. . . . The crowd was enormous; it is estimated at 15,000 by some and 40,000 by others.[79] I've no opinion at all as to the accuracy of either estimate, but for some time after taking our seats I was seriously exercised about the possibilities of falling galleries and panic-stricken multitudes and was tempted to evacuate the building at once.

The building is most defective acoustically: sound passes off into the dome and transepts and is not reverberated by its flimsy walls of sheet iron and glass. The solos were inaudible;[80] an occasional emphatic note or two, or a phrase from the orchestra kept one *au courant.* To those who did not know the *Messiah, etc.,* the solo pieces must have been a great mystery. Beside the unfitness of the building, there was the great mass of muslin and broadcloth behind the solo singers[81] (and the orchestra and chorus) [for acoustic purposes], which absorbed, instead of reflecting, their voices. And the incessant shuffling in and out of the vast crowd that was marching into and about the building was sufficient to drown the voice of any but Stentor or Boanerges.[82]

Four choruses from the *Messiah* including the Hallelujah, which was encored (!!), and the first chorus, "All flesh shall see it together" and [Haydn's] "The heavens are telling"[83] were reasonably audible. Distance and great mass of voice certainly gave to

[78] Rather than a humbug, it was, in Burkhardt's estimation, the beginning of a "new era" in music in America, although admittedly we had had "many 'beginnings' of these eras recently." At any rate, it was the "first truly grand Musical Festival" to be given in this country (*Albion,* June 17, 1854, p. 284). The *Musical Review and Choral Advocate,* too, called it "The Great Musical Event of the Century in this country" (June 22, 1854, p. 216).

[79] At any rate, wrote the *Evening Post* (June 16, 1854): "It was the largest audience, we presume, that was ever [seen] on this continent. . . . One vast, unbroken sea of heads . . . was stretched out before us, bounded by a grand amphitheatre of musicians of many hundreds, in the centre of which stood the Grand Maestro, the irresistible, the unapproachable Jullien. To see him last night dispensing the music of that great company . . . was worth a transatlantic voyage. . . . He sawed air enough with his two kidded hands to have supported an orchestra of ten times the size. Meanwhile his face never parted with that self-possessed and assured air, which seems to defy all the possible appearances and calamities in the great arsenal of fate."

[80] ". . . soloism was frittered away and lost, except, possibly, to those immediately around the orchestra" (*Mirror,* June 16, 1854).

[81] Madame Wallace-Bouchelle, Misses Brainerd and Hawley, and Messrs. Frazer and Camoenz.

[82] Stentor, a Greek herald in the Trojan War, was credited by Homer with possessing a voice equalling the combined voice-power of fifty men; Boanerges, the surname given to the disciples James and John by Christ, is interpreted as meaning "sons of thunder" (Mark 3:17).

[83] The overture and some ten excerpts (solos and choruses) from Handel's *Messiah* occupied the entire first part (lasting about an hour) of the giant, three-part, five-hour-long program. Jullien was censured in the *Musical World and Times* (June 24, 1854, pp. 85–86) for sitting in his easy chair during the solos, leaving the accompaniments to fend for themselves—particularly during Miss Hawley's solo "Oh! Thou that tellest glad tidings to Zion," which in consequence nearly came to grief.

them all new power and clearer expression of their meaning. That first chorus of the *Messiah,* it seems to me, may perhaps be *the* most awful [awesome] embodiment of thought extant in music, with the possible exception of the Hallelujah.[84]

The rest of the concert was mostly trash.[85] Overture to *William Tell* [played by the combined orchestras and encored] was unheard, except the sharply cut, martial finale. We watched Jullien leading its opening movement and wondering what he could be doing till a familiar squeak or two, very high up in the scale, indicated that the orchestra was at work on this overture.[86] Wagner's *Tannhäuser* Overture [Dresden 1845] was rather better audible and seems nice.[87] Of the [Beethoven] Symphony in C minor, only the third movement and part of the finale were played[88]—the former half-audibly, the latter very vilely.

As to the grand "Fireman's Quadrille," words can't express its clap-trap.[89] It's a pleasure to see humbug so consistently, extensively, and cleverly applied.[90] Military

[84] "The Hallelujah was such a Hallelujah as we never heard before and can scarcely hope to hear again," reported Dwight's enthralled New York correspondent, probably Thayer (*Dwight's,* June 24, 1854, p. 9).

[85] Thus did Strong dismiss the performances, among a multitude of other works, of the Adagio of Fry's symphony *The Breaking Heart,* played by the Musical Fund Society of Philadelphia conducted by Fry's old teacher Leopold Meignen, and the Andante of Bristow's Symphony in D, presumably conducted by Jullien. Apparently not performed was a symphony *Niagara,* composed by Fry for the Musical Congress (Upton, *Fry,* Appendix I, p. 317). *Baker's* erroneously reports a performance of this work in New York on May 4, 1854.

[86] On the other hand, the *William Tell* Overture was one of the few pieces Richard Grant White could hear sufficiently well, from where he sat, to tell whether or not they were playing the correct notes. But the greater part of the program, he wrote, was given in "inexplicable dumb show" (*Courier and Enquirer,* June 16, 1854).

[87] The *Daily Times* (June 16, 1854) thought the *Tannhäuser* Overture, heard for the first time in New York, a "masterly and quaint piece of scoring"; it was interpreted with "great delicacy" by Bergmann and the Germania, who had introduced the work in Boston as early as November 1852 (see *Dwight's,* December 4, 1852, p. 71). Burkhardt derided the Philharmonic for its "sleepiness and old-fogyism" in having neglected to present the overture in New York, while the Germania had repeatedly played it in Boston and a number of other places as well (*Albion,* June 17, 1854, p. 284).

[88] As the interminable program began to wear down their endurance, many auditors and performers departed, thus necessitating some spur-of-the-moment cuts and program alterations (see *Musical World and Times,* June 24, 1854, pp. 86–87).

[89] Although Jullien's eloquent scenario for his "Firemen's Quadrille" was included in the concert book, before it was performed Barnum cautioned the audience not to be alarmed at its "frightful effects." Written as a companion piece to the "American Quadrille" and dedicated to the New York Fire Department, the work began with a depiction in sound of the annual Firemen's Parade (cheers and marching bands); then the descent of night and the quiet of the sleeping city (serene slumber music); then the wild and fearful clangor of alarm bells (large churchbells and firebells pealing throughout the interior of the Palace) announcing the arrival of the dread "Fire-Fiend," of "evil heart and volant prowess" (contrapuntal figures "out of the depths of the double basses" mixed with "murky bits of the violas and bassoons" and a "wild flute quartet," combined with "pinking, batlike scintillations on the little flute"); then the heroic fire-laddies doing battle with the Fire-Fiend amid a mighty pandemonium of shouts, bells, yells, grinding of gears, sounds of gushing hoses and collapsing of buildings; and finally Victory, to the combined cheers of the vast multitude of performers and listeners (see *Musical Review and Choral Advocate,* June 22, 1854, pp. 216–18).

[90] "To produce the necessary effects," reported the *Daily Times* (June 16, 1854), "M. Jullien has had to invent a variety of instruments and machines to imitate the workings of the [fire] engines, the falling of the houses, the hissing of the water on the flames, etc., etc."

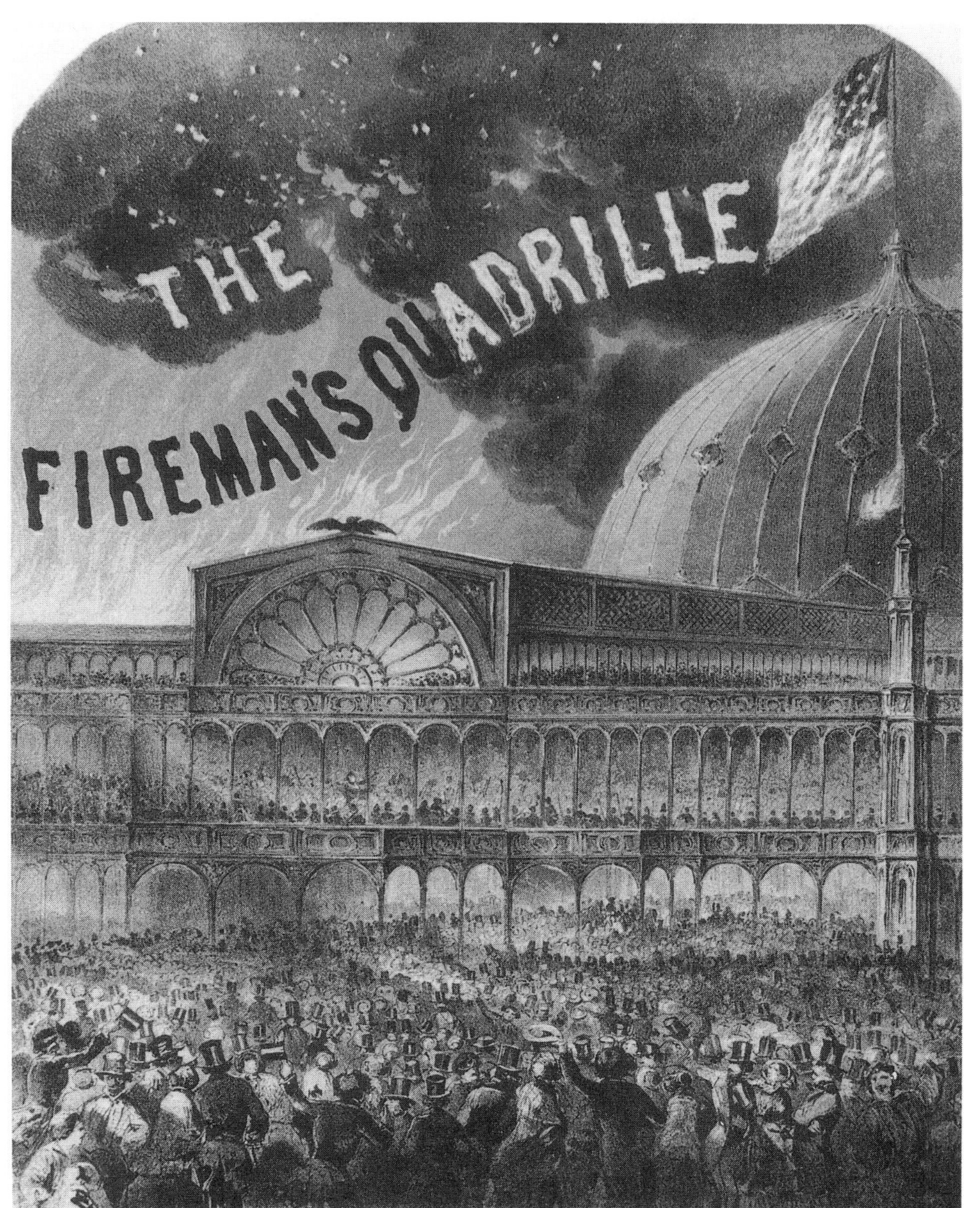

Music Division, The New York Public Library

bands [first Dodworth's, then Bloomfield's] beginning to play in the distance, drawing nearer and nearer, and finally marching into the orchestra; red and blue fire visible through the windows of the dome;[91] a clamorous chorus shouting "go it 20, play away 49, hay-hay-hay," etc.[92] The audacity of the imposition reconciled one to its grossness.[93]

But Jullien is a genius, after all, and there were taking points even in this atrocious production, e.g., a very clever appropriation of phrases from the second movement of Beethoven's *devilish* A-Symphony,[94] and some admirable pieces of instrumentation meant to imitate the thundering, quivering, shuddering crash and roar of fallen walls.[95]

Friday and Saturday nights[96] the performances have been less ambitious[97] and the audiences much smaller, though the price was reduced. I doubt the success of the speculation. I doubt whether the [Crystal Palace] stock ever struggles much above 21. I sympathize with those who bought at par and held on for a rise at 175. The building seems all but gutted. Its character has changed. It is now merely an extension of Barnum's Museum.

~

And even that, not for long. For all their unsurpassed gifts as showmen, neither Barnum nor Jullien was willing (or able) to admit that the ultimate, once attained, could not be encored.[98] Despite palpably misleading announcements that the Musical Congress, with original cast intact, would continue nightly for a "short series," including a single hotly disputed "sacred and miscellaneous" Sunday evening concert[99] (on June 18), the attendance necessarily fell off,[100] and after some ten or eleven insufficiently attended concerts—despite such attractions as Paul Julien, Aptommas, and Wil-

[91] Made realistic by the aid of what Fry called "Stronchium" (*Tribune,* June 16, 1854).

[92] Firemen's occupational jargon, mightily chanted through "speaking-trumpets" (megaphones) by the assembled choruses and orchestras, and fervently joined by the audience in what Richard Grant White described as a "tornado of *hi hi's*" (*Courier and Enquirer,* June 16, 1854).

[93] But surprisingly not Fry, for all his grateful adoration of Jullien. "The extra musical and not classical effects which M. Jullien—considering the low state of public taste—uses," he wrote, "were all that could be desired of their kind. We are not admirers of such extras, but the masses are, and they must be appealed to—up to the time that a limited class has the taste and liberality to support art pure" (*Tribune,* June 16, 1854).

[94] An "appropriation" that only Strong seemed to detect.

[95] Simulated by cannon balls rolled through a resounding wooden tunnel, or trough, placed under the stage.

[96] After speeches by Barnum and Jullien at the conclusion of the great "monster concert," Barnum (who throughout the evening had been "calm and serene as a saint on the doorstep of paradise"), took no chances with the acoustics and unfurled a "mighty banner on which was inscribed the tidings that the Congress would be continued at the reduced admission of twenty-five cents standing and $1 reserved seats" (*Mirror, Daily Times,* June 16, 1854).

[97] Necessarily so with the immediate departures of the out-of-town participants.

[98] As the *Musical Review and Choral Advocate* (July 6, 1854, p. 232) wisely commented, such an extravaganza as the first Musical Congress should not be attempted more often than once a year.

[99] Provoking great controversy and a swarm of forbiddingly moral editorials, despite the unopposed performances of pseudo-sacred Sunday concerts for years past.

[100] The *Mirror* (June 19, 1854) reported only a moderate attendance (a mere 8000) at the Sunday evening concert, made up distinctly of the "'*oi polloi.*' The choruses were rather thin, but the instrumentation was very fine. . . . The place was cool and comfortable, and candy and soda were sold in

liam Vincent Wallace, supported and embellished by the Germania and Dodworth's and Bloomfield's bands—and despite nightly performances of the "Firemen's Quadrille"—Jullien's irreversibly final *Concert d'adieu* was announced for June 26. He departed for England on June 28.

Following his departure, George Templeton Strong remarked in his journal on June 22: "The 'Musical Congress' has not done much for the Crystal Palace. Its stock is down to 17—lower than any point yet reached. I fear that Barnum will find his Waterloo here."

Jullien's farewell appearance in America, a benefit for once accruing to him,[101] attracted an attendance purportedly as large as the one at the first Musical Congress, if not larger.[102] "From six to half past seven," wrote Richard Grant White, "every omnibus on those routes which approach the Crystal Palace was full both outside and in, and the Sixth Avenue Railroad cars carried not only those that could hang on, but all that could with safety stand upon their roofs" (*Courier and Enquirer,* June 27, 1854).

For this final farewell (his 105th concert in New York), in pale imitation of the first Musical Congress, Jullien's forces were augmented only by the Germania and Dodworth's Band, and by the Harmonic Society and singing societies from Brooklyn, Williamsburgh, and Newark (comparatively modest, but all the same adding up to a combined chorus of 600 singers), conducted by Bristow. The soloists were Madame Wallace-Bouchelle, Henriette Behrend, Misses Dingley and Brainerd, and, of course, Jullien's remaining virtuosos: Koenig, Wuille, and Lavigne. The program (in two parts this time) included—besides several familiar overtures, solos, and choral pieces—three "first performances": the Andante from Jullien's symphony *The Last Judgment* (London 1846), a work whose seven major trumpet parts were performed on this occasion by Koenig, Duhem, Holt, Lacroix, Asche, and the Dodworths—Allen and Harvey; also the "'West Park Polka,' composed especially for this concert," and a group of "War Marches, Quick Steps, Songs, and Hymns of the present belligerent nations of Europe" (England, France, Russia, and Turkey), currently engulfed in the Crimean War. Jullien also gave, for the last time, his "American" and "Firemen's" quadrilles.[103]

Just after Koenig's final performance of the waltz, "Adieu to America," Fry appeared on the stage and after fervently lauding Jullien, proceeded, amid thunderous applause and cheers, to present him with a magnificent, appropriately Olympian, gold laurel wreath, together with a gold tablet, on which was inscribed: "Laureate to Jullien, From Fifteen Hundred Performers at the First Musical Congress in America, and upwards of Thirty Thousand of his warmest friends and admirers present at the Crystal Palace, New-York, June 15, 1854."

After further encomiums from Fry, Jullien, radiating Gallic charm, replied, at first

---

the body of the Palace." And as for those who objected to the concert as a "desecration of the Lord's Day . . . such music, wherever heard, and on whatever day, is like the caroling of sky-soaring birds, next of kin to religion—if not religion itself."

[101] It was now disclosed that Jullien's managers had pocketed the proceeds of his previous benefits in order to retrieve some of their losses on his tour (see footnote 53 preceding).

[102] At twenty-five cents admission and $1 for reserved seats, an audience variously estimated at 20,000 to 45,000 persons attended.

[103] As a last amiable gesture, Jullien invited the entire New York Fire Department to the concert.

rather haltingly, that he didn't deserve the honor (great protestations and cheers). Then with growing eloquence he graciously declared his reception in America to have been the crowning experience of his eventful life; even more graciously he pronounced the New York musical institutions—the Philharmonic and the Harmonic societies—to be of the very highest order of musical excellence. But most graciously of all, he pronounced Fry and Bristow to be composers with no superiors in Europe or anywhere else—Fry as a master composer of Romantic works for the orchestra and Bristow as a model of purity in compositions in the classical style, such as symphonies and quartets (see *Musical Review and Choral Advocate,* July 6, 1854, pp. 232–33).

"We are unable to do anything like justice to M. Jullien's remarks," wrote the *Daily Times* (June 27, 1854), "for the crowd, noise, and enthusiasm were constant interruptions. The speech, however, was unique and happy; metaphysical and prophetic; grateful and fatherly. In short, it was Jullienesque, slightly Barnumized."

To all this the *Musical World and Times* (July 1, 1854, p. 99) added that the climax of Jullien's speech, "a French climax, could not have been better—for, after remarking that to his dying day he should never forget this *scena,* an unutterable shrug—a shrug which expressed whole volumes, yes, libraries, of unutterable emotions, feelings, and sensations—closed the speech."

To Richard Grant White, writing in the *Courier and Enquirer* the day after the farewell concert, the tribute to Jullien signified the increased love of music that he had engendered "on a grand scale" in this country, not only among the cultivated classes but among the masses as well. "He has given us the opportunity of hearing both such masses of sound and such a union of first-rate instrumental artists as were unknown to us before his arrival on our shores." White, always a master of ambiguity, did not, however, regard Jullien's visit as "likely to do much to extend or to cultivate a taste for music among us. His merit," wrote White, was "strictly limited to a knowledge and mastery of *effect,* and the benefit of his performances, in our judgment, terminates exactly with the present pleasure which they effect."[104] Nonetheless: "As a musical director and conductor, we doubt that there has ever been his equal."[105]

After Jullien's departure, music at the Palace, now closed at night, was reduced to daily afternoon performances by the Germania (about to disband).[106] On July 11, in an article captioned "Too Much for Mr. Barnum," the *Times* announced Barnum's resignation as president of the Crystal Palace: "He has found its embarrassed finances and the uphill work of popularizing anew the great Exhibition of 1853 too much for his physical man in this hot season."[107]

Strong, with ears only for his Mass-meetings, had not attended any of Jullien's final concerts. Through his devoted persistence, with the cooperation of a few diehards, he had managed to stretch the Mass-meetings until June 23.

[104] White was refuted when Theodore Thomas, an alert member of Jullien's American orchestra, later patterned his enduringly influential, popular symphony concerts on the Jullien model.

[105] Jullien's subsequent, larger-than-life ups and downs ended in 1860 when he died, a pauper, in a Paris insane asylum.

[106] The various Germanians went their separate ways, but Bergmann, after a false start in December 1854 as conductor of the Chicago Philharmonic Society, returned to New York, where he conducted the Arion Society, and sustained himself with various musical odd jobs (Thomas, I, 35).

[107] On November 1 a bankrupt Crystal Palace closed its doors to the public.

Music Division, The New York Public Library

June 26. . . . Held our last Mass-meeting last Friday night, when Mozart's longer *Requiem* [K. 626] was achieved all through by a quartette: Ellie, Mrs. Eleanor, Cousinery, and Mayer. Understood it better than heretofore. Any surpassing majesty, depth, or beauty it may contain is still hidden from me, but although it seems as a whole to drag a little and to want freshness, I can see that it's not unworthy of Mozart, and that some single movements, e.g., the *Tuba mirum* and *Benedictus,* are very effective. My aesthetic vision penetrates no deeper. I don't doubt that the rank given the composition by the unanimous judgment of musical criticism is justly given. But I should not have found out the merits of the *Requiem* to myself.

. . . [bereft of his Mass-meetings, Strong, despite his disdain for Catholics and Catholicism, sought musical solace at the alien Jesuit Church of St. Francis Xavier on 16th Street between Fifth and Sixth Avenues] Service almost entirely choral: good organ brilliantly played [most probably by Berge], very fair voices, and elaborate music. But such music! The worst commonplaces of Verdi and Donizetti strung together in jig-time; some scrap from *Lucrezia* or the *Favorita* or *Ernani* constantly just under the horizon and on the verge of protruding in definite form and fashion. Instead of *Pange lingua* and *O salutaris hostia* and such like, one was expecting to hear *O cielo, Ah mio tesor,* or words to that effect. Some of the music was below even that degree of footlight dignity, being unmistakably *buffo* (borrowed, I think, from the *Elisir d'amore*), both in the expression of its jolly row-de-dow, devil-may-care melody and in the alternating phrases of its basso solo, which were manifestly meant for some Dr. Dulcamara.[108] They were far beneath Figaro, not to speak of Leporello.

[108] A principal character in Donizetti's *L'elisir d'amore.*

As to the organ business, it fully corresponded with the tinsel trumpery of the High Altar with its French polish, painted marbles, gilt gingerbread, and artificial flowers. Protestantism has never, to my knowledge or belief, caricatured and desecrated Religious Art more vilely than did this service in a church attended by the "best" of our Roman Catholics.

Strong reacted more tolerantly, indeed almost sentimentally, to an unusually well-planned, well-performed midnight serenade—a musical ritual of courtship apparently still extant in New York.

August 3. . . . Midnight minus a quarter of an hour. Little that's new or good, except that a Serenade has this minute sprung up for the benefit of some young woman of the neighborhood, and that instead of the routine Donizetti music, they've begun with that pretty *Scheiden tut weh* [folk] melody, very *adagio.*

. . . Serenade continues—something Verdi-esque now, I know not what, but there's no mistaking the handiwork of the Grand Maestro of the Mechanico-spasmodic school.

. . . It's *Ernani,* after all!!! From the first act. How Benedetti used to agonize over that angular aria, with his two hands on his abdomen! I've a kind of affection for that opera. Some of its phrases are associated with my dearest memories:[109] e.g., the end of the third act and the *Pietà.* Wish it were better and truer music that is so bound up with my past life, but I can't be critical about it.

There goes *Grâce* capitally played. I don't believe in the long life of Meyerbeer's fame; but that air has power and merit, I think.

Succeeded by the "Katydid Polka" (Jullien).

Go it, Serenaders! I thought you couldn't get through it without a touch of *Lucia.*

. . . This serenader, whoever he may be (I think the Beldens are his object), knows more than most of his craft. His selection has included only two scraps of *Lucia,* and he's now (or rather his band is now) at *Wie nahte mir der Schlummer: Leise, leise, fromme Weise [Der Freischütz].* Hurrah for the beautiful Allegro, which I suppose ends the performance. For that, too, I've a special affection, for the sake of the *[Freischütz]* Overture, with which it's so nearly allied, and which (heard at the Schlesinger concert in the Spring of '39)♪ introduced me to good music and taught me to *reverence* an orchestra.

In October, with his desire for music evidently whetted by the Mass-meetings, Strong resubscribed to the Philharmonic Society after a lapse of two years.[110]

[109] Memories of Strong's courtship,♪ at the Astor Place Opera House.

[110] After their single brilliant concert at Metropolitan Hall on November 26, 1853, the Society had been forced to give the remaining three concerts of their disputatious twelfth season (discussed in the following OBBLIGATO) at the gloomy old Tabernacle. They were now embarking upon their thirteenth season in a vastly improved setting: Niblo's Theatre (not the smaller Niblo's Saloon, where they now held their public rehearsals).

October 22. . . . Have subscribed to the Philharmonic; went to the first rehearsal [for the December 2 concert] at 3:30 yesterday, with Ellie, at Niblo's Saloon. Heard the "Eroica" played, most of it twice. Beethoven was undeniably "some pumpkins."

I'm still unable to hold the fourth movement of that symphony worthy of the other three.[111] The first half of it is simply *outré,* grotesque, and unmeaning—*to me.*[112] Perhaps a hint or suggestion may yet show me that it has significance and fits in with the rest. The conclusion of the movement is very delightful—includes phrases that could have come from Beethoven alone. But it seems labored, in contrast with the fresh, flowing, inspired freedom of the movements that precede it—that seem to have been improvised without conscious effort—each embodying and expressing most vividly its own distinct idea and feeling. The object and sentiment of this last are dubious. I suppose it means to set forth the mingled joy of victory and lamentation for the fallen. The second movement—the most sad, solemn, and lovely *Marcia funebre*—was more intelligible and satisfactory to me than ever before. I observe plainly that Beethoven was not thinking of a funeral pageant like Wellington's. The soldiers, whose march to their leader's grave is painted in this wonderful music, have their arms in their hands and expect to fight again tomorrow.

But the first movement is the finest and strongest. I don't yet half understand it, but its sentiment is expressed with a distinctness and intensity that can't be surpassed. The opening phrases tell the subject—speak it out more explicitly than articulate words—the two quick, short, emphatic chords that are like two cannon-shot signals of attack—and then the column is instantly moving, to that glorious war-song, of conscious strength and thirst for battle and confidence of victory, which no extant musical phrase can beat for simplicity and power.

Das hat eine wundersame,
Gewaltige Melodei.[113]

It is the characteristic phrase of the whole movement, blended and worked in with much besides that needs study and thought to ascertain its precise significance. There are contrasted with it suggestions of the failing strength and departing life of the fallen, and there are passages that seem meant to express the struggle and wrath of hand-to-hand battle—one brief emphatic phrase surely tells of the heavy strokes of sabres—perhaps rather of battle-axes and two-handed swords—so heavy and trenchant are the blows with which the orchestra in unison cuts its way downward. This sounds nonsensical, but I've long remembered the passage, and always with the same feeling of what it suggests. The whole movement embodies and expresses the Norse Spirit of War—love of battle—the *furor Normannorum*—the Berserkian orgasm of combativeness—conflict, not strategy. I think Froissart,[114] that genial and enthusiastic connois-

[111] With the resumption of his Philharmonic subscription, Strong promptly transferred his passion for exhaustively dissecting and fantasizing upon the Haydn masses to the Beethoven symphonies.

[112] On later rereading this passage, Strong added an "!" in the margin.

[113] *It has a wondrous, mighty melody.*

[114] Jean Froissart (*c.* 1333–*c.* 1400), the Flemish poet and court historian.

seur in carnage, would have liked it particularly—so would Haakon, Jarl, and Skald[115] who sang in exultation that "Wolves shall lick the bloody strand." And when

> *Der Taillefer ritt vor allem Normannenheer*[116]
> *Auf einem hohen Pferde mit Schwert und mit Speer,*
> *Er sang so herrlich, da Klang über Hastings Feld,*
> *Von Roland sang Er, und manchem frommen Held.*[117]

The Taillefer certainly sang something not very unlike the opening melody of the "Eroica."

To me, Beethoven's finest instrumental music is fearful—a subject to be thought of only with self-distrust and reverence. It seems to lead one straight to the door of the Unseen World. It brings one into contact with Invisible Powers, of Good and Evil, one hardly knows which.

November 5. . . . Rehearsal of the "Eroica" again yesterday afternoon, with Ellie. I like the latter half of the fourth movement better and better; some of its simple, melodic phrases are like shocks of a Leyden jar.[118]

November 15. . . . [last night] Ellie and Jem [Ruggles] and I went off after dinner to hear *The Seasons* at [Dr. Chapin's] Church of the Divine Unity [548 Broadway] by the Harmonic Society.[119] Creditable performance, except for the bass [John Camoens], who sang false and out of tune and out of time, with a voice of disagreeable quality.[120]

It's a most genial and glorious composition, but it can't be very popular: it falls off so after the first two parts. Except the amatory duo and the splendid Hunting Chorus there's nothing in the third [part] worthy to be sung on the same night with the delightful music of Spring and Summer. Still less in the fourth—nothing indeed but the first soprano solo and the pleasant "spinning-wheel song." Then the phrases of the recitative are monotonous throughout—its voice part intended merely to suggest the meaning of the little scraps of descriptive music, always very good in its way, that make up the accompaniment. Explanatory notes as brief and dry as possible.[121]

[115] Legendary Scandinavian bards of old.

[116] Taillefer was the warrior/minstrel who sang the Normans to victory at the Battle of Hastings in 1066.

> [117] Taillefer rode before the Norman horde
> With spear and sword, upon a tall steed,
> So noble his song, over Hastings sward,
> Of Roland he sang, and many a valiant deed.

[118] The earliest device for storing electricity, invented in 1745.

[119] No longer the Sacred Harmonic Society.

[120] The soloists—Mrs. Georgiana Stuart, Miss Maria Brainerd, Messrs. James A. Johnson, J. W. Alden, and Camoens (current spelling)—and the chorus of 300 were conducted by G. F. Bristow. The *Evening Post* (November 15, 1854) praised the performance in general but agreed with Strong that the bass Camoens was "not so good; the orchestra, however, threw a veil of harmony over his delinquencies." *The Seasons* was repeated on Thanksgiving night, November 30. (The other activities of the Harmonic Society in 1854 are discussed in the following OBBLIGATO.)

[121] Fry, never missing an opportunity to refer to his European experience, observed in his review that the program booklets containing the text supplied by the Harmonic Society—so helpful in un-

But the glorious choral movements of the first two parts can't be beat. The first Chorus of Spring, the final duo and chorus of the same movement, and the finale of Summer are the loveliest specimens of flowing, joyous, simpleminded music that I know—and nonetheless deep for their simplicity.[122]

November 26. . . . Tuesday night [November 21] with Ellie to Eisfeld's quartette *soirée,* no. 1. Schubert's Quartette in A minor (op. 29) [1824], very rich and abundant in beauties, especially the first and second movements; Quintette, Beethoven's E-flat (op. 16) [in the version for winds and piano (1796)] with Timm at the piano], most delightful throughout.[123] Not in the style of Haydn (commonly said to be that of Beethoven's earlier music), but in that of Mozart, most emphatically. The first phrase of the Andante [is] *Batti, batti* verbatim. Haydn's Quartette in D major (op. 63) [*sic*], very genial and Haydenish.

~

In renewing past musical ties, Strong had also resubscribed to Eisfeld's highly regarded chamber-music *soirées,* now entering their fifth season. Instead of Hope Chapel, they were more congenially housed at Dodworth's charming assembly room,[124] where from January through April, at roughly monthly intervals, Eisfeld presented classic chamber music by Haydn, Mozart, Beethoven, and Mendelssohn, and contemporary works by Fesca (probably Alexander) and Carl Eckert. Eisfeld's string quartet still comprised, besides himself, Noll, Reyer, and Eichhorn;[125] his soloists were the singers Madame Wallace-Bouchelle, Mrs. Henry C. Watson, Mrs. Georgiana Stuart, her sister Miss Anna Griswold, and the pianists Mrs. William Vincent Wallace, Madame Florentine Szpaczek, William A. King, Charles Wels, and, on March 31 at the penultimate concert of his fourth series, Richard Hoffman, who played two pieces by Chopin: the Nocturne, op. 32, no. 2 (1836–37), billed as *La consolazione,*[126] and the Polonaise, op. 53 (1842), both in A-flat.

The reviewer for the *Musical World and Times* (April 15, 1854, p. 177) found the title *La consolazione* to be "insignificant and, like most composers' titles, unmeaning": Chopin's piece lacked "sufficient feeling, gentle inspiration, or anything else suggestive of its being called 'The Consolation.'" The Polonaise, although without a striking motive, at least possessed a certain originality; it produced "a greater effect," largely owing to "the energetic [left] hand of the pianist, who gave some remarkable bass passages

derstanding the "sentiment" of the work—were "strangers" to European concert rooms (*Tribune,* November 15, 1854).

[122] Fry pronounced *The Seasons* to be "too old-fashioned in ideas and instrumentation, and too didactic in the sentiment, to meet the musical needs of the age." Yet, he admitted, there were moments when both poetry and music soared, expressing "great and immortal thoughts" *(ibid.).*

[123] The other soloist of the evening was Clara Brinkerhoff, who sang two unidentified works, but—despite her good voice—not to the satisfaction of the critic for the *Musical Review and Choral Advocate* (December 7, 1854, p. 419), in whose opinion she failed to open her mouth properly and thus pronounced her words badly.

[124] A favorite concert-giving place after the destruction of the vastly larger Metropolitan Hall.

[125] Following the completion of the fourth series, the cellist Eichhorn returned to his native Mannheim; he was replaced in the quartet by Frederick Bergner.

[126] One of the many catchy titles engrafted upon Chopin's works by his promotion-minded London publisher, Christian Wessel (1797–1885).

with uncommon skill and power." Clearly the writer (Girac?) was not attuned to Chopin.

Not so Willis, who was present at this concert (and had evidently heard Chopin play). In a footnote to the review, he rebuked his reporter, and Hoffman as well. It was Hoffman's too "ponderous" performance of the Nocturne, not Chopin's music, that had been at fault: "Chopin, who from his delicate health and debility always breathed, rather than played, his exquisite creations upon the piano," wrote Willis, "used to play this piece with the most extreme sensibility and delicacy. . . . According to Chopin's standard," Hoffman had played it "with twice the force" it demanded.

December 3. . . . Philharmonic concert last night. The glorious "Eroica,"[127] Gade's Reminiscences of Ossian [the harp obbligato played by Aptommas],[128] very grandiose, a little bombastic and tumefied—on the whole effective and good; some of its phrases of melody very pungent. Lindpaintner's Overture to "Abraham's Sacrifice" seemed to me commonplace and worthless.[129]

Mademoiselle Caroline Lehmann, a *prima donna* from Copenhagen [the Royal Theatre], just imported,[130] sang *Wie nahte mir der Schlummer* and *Casta diva* effectively and well; the former especially. She's a well-looking young German or Danish blonde, not pretty, but with a good face and an honest, truthful eye.[131] Also there was a Concerto [Concertino] for Clarinet and Orchestra by Eisfeld [played by Xavier Kiefer], which was very creditable. The concert was well attended.[132]

Very few compositions can stand being played immediately after one of Beethoven's greater works. Even Mozart and Haydn suffer by the comparison. Handel, I suppose, might bear it. In the *Messiah* and in what little I know of *Israel in Egypt,* and nowhere else within my experience can there be found the vigor and the intensity of life that belong to Beethoven's finest productions, such as *The Mount of Olives,* the *Septuor,* the "Eroica," the symphonies in C minor, D major, A minor, and the "Pastorale."

December 5. . . . Have been diligent in the public service for the past few days. Yesterday morning with the Building Committee [of Trinity Church], the Rector, and

[127] Whose "grandeur is as well recognized as that of Niagara or the Alps" (*Evening Post,* December 5, 1854).

[128] Who had chosen for his solo his "very pleasing, but somewhat monotonous," arrangement for harp of "Home, Sweet Home" (*Tribune,* December 4, 1854).

[129] "It was not only an Abrahamic sacrifice, but a sacrifice of the talent and time of the Philharmonic," wrote Willis in the *Musical World,* as his periodical was renamed in September (December 9, 1854, p. 178). And Fry, always gunning for the Philharmonic, declared the programing of such works as this and Gade's overture to be a mystery to anyone but the benighted, German-oriented "Music Committee" of the Philharmonic. Both works—albeit they did not violate "the rules of harmony or grammar of music"—were lacking in "passion and sentiment." Indeed, "it would be difficult to find in them any even negative recommendatory quality" (*Tribune,* December 4, 1854).

[130] That is, just imported from Boston, where she had been a great favorite since her arrival from Europe in 1852. For a review of her Boston debut, see *Dwight's,* October 10, 1852.

[131] In appearance Caroline Lehmann was "truly a noble German," wrote the Germanophile Willis. She possessed a "remarkably fine presence, a superb figure, and great *lift* and natural nobility of style, combined, also, with much womanly sweetness and modesty. She captivated the audience at once, personally, before she did so musically." She was the possessor, too, of a "very musical voice, but drawn *heart-deep,*" in contrast to the "open-mouthed tone of the Italian school" (*Musical World,* December 9, 1854, p. 178).

[132] According to Willis, Niblo's Theatre was "filled nearly to the ceiling" *(ibid.).*

Hodges, at the Chapel,[133] discussing among other things the locale for the choir, which is an important question, for on it depends practically whether we can have female voices or only men and boys—whether we must restrict ourselves to the dreary respectabilities of Gregorian chant and English Cathedral music, or may choose from a wider field and dignify the services at the Chapel by art higher than that of Boyce, and Tallis, and Jackson—Smith, Brown, Jones, or Robinson. Long jaw [palaver] and little result. I fear Dr. Hodges will consider me a recreant, but I've always given him to understand that I considered his school [to be] snobbery and infinitely below what he is pleased to describe as "operatic church music," viz., the compositions of Haydn. Mozart, Hummel, Beethoven.

December 18. . . . Philharmonic rehearsal Saturday afternoon [December 16, for its January 20, 1855, concert]. Mendelssohn's Symphony in A [the "Italian," op. 90 (1833)]. Brilliant and pretty—not much more, I think. There is some glow in the first movement, the finest of the four. The Andante has a dreary suggestion of Presbyterian psalm-singing in its principal subject that spoils it altogether. It seems to me that the germ of almost every good thing of Mendelssohn's that I've heard exists in the Overture to the *Midsummer Night's Dream*. Weber's Overture to *Preciosa* also played; don't think I've heard it before.[134] Some passages seem as if they must have been written by Rossini: they suggest the Overture to the *Gazza ladra*—not in structure or in phrase, but in sentiment, or rather, the absence of sentiment, the substitution for it of *sense,* if that be a musical possibility. But it's a very reasonable composition.

December 20. . . . Eisfeld [second] concert Tuesday evening [December 19]: Quartette [Ferdinand] Ries; ["Kreutzer"] Sonata (piano and violin) Beethoven [played by Burke and Hoffman]; and Quartette [by] Haydn. Ries was not much, except the Scherzo, and I don't think Haydn was fairly represented. But the Beethoven, especially its Andante (well-known so long), was very grand and beautiful. On the whole, inferior to the former concert.

December 29. . . . Prospect of a grand ball[135] at the Fourteenth Street Opera House [the recently opened Academy of Music, discussed in the following OBBLIGATO], "for the relief of the poor in this city,"[136] originating with [the Reverend Dr. Benjamin Isaac] Haight, to which I'm "particularly requested" to be an accessory, by note signed *Mrs. William H. Jones.*[137] It looks very dubious and questionable. To a poverty-stricken demagogue, the plan of feasting the Aristocracy on boned turkey and

[133] Trinity Chapel, a kind of suburban branch of Trinity Church, was now being constructed on West 25th Street near Broadway, and Strong, as their most musically aware vestryman (and sharply critical of Hodges's decidedly English taste in church music) concerned himself with the plans for its future musical arrangements.

[134] A memory lapse. In the not too distant past, a youthful Strong had in fact been deeply infatuated with Weber's music for P. A. Wolff's play, *Preciosa.*♪ (Berlin 1821).

[135] Misquoted as *ballet* in the published *Diary* (II, 203).

[136] "Financial distress" and unemployment were rife during this devastatingly cold winter. On August 30, Strong, whose bank account was currently "at its lowest ebb," wrote in his journal: "Everything in Wall Street looks black. Some failure or other almost daily and constant reports of others, doing nearly as much harm as the reality could do." On December 13 he referred to "hundreds, or rather thousands, of men with wives and children to be fed and kept warm, whom this cruel 'pressure' has thrown out of work." And on December 29: "*Hard times* is the general subject of talk. No sign yet of any let-up on their hardness."

[137] Of the socially omnipotent "Joneses."

paté de fois gras that the Democracy may be supplied with pork and beans—assembling the *Upper Ten* in brocade and Valenciennes [lace] that the *lower thousand* may be helped to flannel and cotton shirting—would furnish a theme most facile and fertile.

December 30. . . . To a Philharmonic rehearsal this afternoon with Ellie. Heard the Mendelssohn ["Italian"] Symphony and then came off. It seems a rather incoherent composition; there's no reason apparent on its face why its four movements are put together and called a symphony, instead of being kept apart and called four "concert overtures."[138] Considered separately they severally improve on better acquaintance, except perhaps the second, which is certainly dismal. The first is far the most vigorous. It may possess somewhat of living *inspiration*—at any rate, it has breadth, geniality, and vigor enough to give it a high rank.

But a symphony, like an epic poem, is either very great or worthless. Perhaps the same thing may be said of all orchestral compositions. Why should fifty violins, trombones, flutes, etc. waste their time in laboriously rehearsing and studying out a production that is "exceedingly clever," "remarkable for its good taste and ingenious instrumentation," "full of striking effects," and "of higher merit than anything that has been produced for twenty years," when they might be so much more profitably employed on truly great and transcendent works, of which we all know far too little because we hear them so seldom? Why should the Philharmonic Society bother itself to produce correctly this beautiful product of Mendelssohn's (which would make the fortune and reputation of any composer) when so many of the Philharmonic subscribers have but the vaguest notion of Beethoven's symphonies in C minor, A, and D, the "Eroica" and "Pastorale," Mozart's in E-flat and the "Jupiter," Weber's and Mendelssohn's great overtures, and so forth?

~

A narrow, alas persistent, point of view indigenous to symphony subscribers through the ages.

[138] A reaction, perhaps, to the recent, bitter Fry/Willis controversy (see following OBBLIGATO), of which Strong seems otherwise to have taken no notice.

OBBLIGATO: 1854

How are Americans to win their way in composition unless their compositions are played?

William Henry Fry to Richard Storrs Willis
The Musical World and New York Musical Times
February 18, 1854

You must come up to . . . high standards of art, if you, or any one else, expect to be heard.

Richard Storrs Willis to William Henry Fry
The Musical World and New York Musical Times
February 25, 1854

True to form, an outraged Fry—on January 10, 1854, immediately upon the appearance of Richard Storrs Willis's too casual, too brief, review of the "Santa Claus" Symphony—dispatched a blistering, inordinately long letter to Willis,[1] who obligingly published it in full in the *Musical World and Times* on January 21 (pp. 29–31, 34). With Willis's tit-for-tat reply, appearing in the following issue, and with their ensuing exchange of insults,[2] they provoked a free-for-all that, if nothing else, served to enliven the bleak period of musical famine that followed upon the burning of Metropolitan Hall.[3] Becoming embroiled in the rapidly spreading controversy were John Sullivan Dwight, who in his *Journal* zestfully stoked the conflagration by faithfully reprinting both sides of the disputatious correspondence as it evolved; Dwight's "Diarist" Alexander Wheelock Thayer; his pseudonymous New York correspondent "Pegan"; George Frederick Bristow; the Philharmonic Society collectively and individually; the *Musical Review and Choral Advocate* only peripherally,[4] and, from the sidelines, numerous other journalists and independent onlookers.

Although Fry's gargantuan letter has been widely hailed in the twentieth century

[1] Stretching to some forty pages of manuscript, according to Fry (second letter to Willis, *Musical World and Times,* February 18, pp. 74–76; reprinted in *Dwight's* February 25, 1854, pp. 163–64).

[2] ". . . one of the most extraordinary public correspondences in the annals of American music," writes Gilbert Chase (*America's Music,* 3rd ed., p. 313).

[3] Manna from heaven to the temporarily disenfranchised music journalists.

[4] "We presume it is a free fight, but as Senator [Stephen A.] Douglas says, we see no cause to 'mix in,'" wrote the *Musical Review and Choral Advocate* (March 16, 1854, p. 93).

as the archetypal Declaration of Rights for American Music and Musicians,[5] it was rather an uninhibited display of self-glorification intermingled with an outpouring of personal grievances, frustrations, wounded vanity, boastfulness, bitterness, abusiveness, defensiveness, offensiveness, pretentiousness, idiosyncratic pronouncements,[6] and an apparently unappeasable hunger for adulation. Leaping from topic to tangential topic and back again, Fry unfailingly reverted to his abiding refrain: how great was William Henry Fry, how unique his works, how superior to anyone else's, how unappreciated because he was an American!

Fry's vast document clearly affirms that it was avid personal ambition rather than Emersonian aspiration (with which he is frequently credited) that motivated his fierce championship of American music—specifically, American symphonic music—at that time a largely hypothetical commodity.[7] The only "chances for an American to put before the public any work of musical High Art," he asserted, "depend in this country upon the accidental presence of such a liberal-minded man and consummate musician as M. Jullien."[8] As to the Philharmonic, a despicable institution "consecrated to foreign music," Fry denounced it as "an incubus on Art, never having asked for, or performed, a single American instrumental composition."[9] Not, he wished it understood, that *he* had ever "solicited a favor from the Philharmonic."

"My dear Willis," Fry aggrievedly began, "as a well-wisher to yourself and your journal, I regret to see such a notice as you made in the *Musical World* . . . a dozen lines, all told, on my Symphony of *Santa Claus,* with a paragraph on two other symphonies of mine, containing several *egregious* and injurious misstatements. To both of these editorial paragraphs, permit me to reply at length, simply for the cause of truth and in the interests of High Art."

And reply at length he did. Beginning with a eulogy of his "Santa Claus" on the dubious basis of its great length, he claimed that it was longer than any "unique symphony" ever composed "upon a single subject with unbroken continuity" (meaning in one movement). With its "tens of thousands of notes . . . written with the most conscientious regard to the philosophy of Art, as I understand it," he wrote, it was grossly unfair of Willis to call it an "extravaganza. . . . A work of this length and seriousness" obviously demanded a comparably long and serious criticism.[10] And because Fry was

[5] An opinion largely based upon Upton's skewed testimony.

[6] Even Upton, for all his indulgence, admits that in these letters, among Fry's innumerable sublime utterances, he had "said many foolish things" (Upton, *Fry,* p. 135).

[7] Despite Fry's insistence that the country teemed with native composers of unperformed operas and major symphonic works, American works in these ambitious forms were few and far between.

[8] Of Jullien's liberal-mindedness toward American music, Irving Lowens writes: "When Jullien arrived . . . in 1853, he found that conducting music by American composers was an easy and effective way to get an audience. He also undoubtedly realized that as music critic of the influential New York *Tribune,* Fry was a good person to cultivate. He therefore performed no less than four of Fry's symphonies—*Childe Harold, A Day in the Country, The Breaking Heart,* and the *Santa Claus Symphony* (Lowens, p. 221).

[9] An inaccuracy, as it was soon pointed out in the *Musical World and Times* by an anonymous member of the Philharmonic.

[10] ". . . the length of a piece is novel ground, certainly, upon which to base its musical excellence, or its requirement for a very long criticism," was Willis's response. And anyway: "What has the length of a piece to do with its merits?" (*Musical World and Times,* January 28, 1854, p. 147).

an American, composing "for the mere dignity of musical Art, without recompense," he certainly deserved "better treatment at the hands of his countrymen, at least."

How differently did Fry fulfill his own professional obligations! Exemplary as a critic—as in all other things—he related as an object lesson how, following Maretzek's first performance of *Le Prophète,* he (Fry) had considered it his duty to sit up all night at his desk poring over the score, disregardful of sleep, in order to provide the *Tribune*'s early morning readers with "three columns of analytic criticism—historical, vocal, instrumental, and personal."

"But [and how great the contrast!], I give the public a symphony . . . corresponding in rank and magnitude with *The Prophet* . . . a symphony written in the school of Romantic and not formalistic Art—novel in design, novel in treatment, novel in effects, novel in instrumentation . . . written so as to double the resonances and sonority of the orchestra, compared with classic models, and your journal dispatches it with a dozen lines—and these, in my judgment, embody a total misapprehension of the intention and spirit of the piece."

Raging over Willis's belittlement of his "Santa Claus," a most serious work, Fry launched into one of his massive, free-form rambles: he speculated, among a profusion of wildly assorted topics, on the true meanings of "serious" and "comic" as applied to art. Shakespeare possessed a mastery of both—a mastery, however, by no means shared by Beethoven or Mozart,[11] both of whom were totally deficient in expressing mirth in music. He examined the various aspects of music: of musical forms, of which he was an unsurpassed innovator—of instruments and instrumentation, of which he was an unprecedented master—of unity and the unities (a persistent bone of contention throughout the dispute), in which his revolutionary, one-movement "symphonies" far exceeded any stereotyped, "classical," four-movement symphony extant, whether by Mozart, Haydn, Beethoven, or anyone else.

Fry berated Willis at great length and with great asperity for his errors regarding the chronology of *A Day in the Country* and *The Breaking Heart*[12] (both superb and unique works that he had composed within the space of a single week); he referred to what he called the "eroticism of Nature," quoting from *Macbeth* to illustrate a nebulous point; he debunked the widely held idea that Beethoven's "Eroica" Symphony was a great example of symphonic composition[13]—it was in fact far inferior to Weber's Overture to *Der Freischütz,* a work that in Fry's opinion eclipsed all its predecessors.

And back to the unities: Fry's unities derived from the "musico-dramatic" properties of his compositions, each having its own plot. His "Santa Claus" possessed the greatest unity of all, possessing the greatest plot of all. Beginning "in Heaven, [it] then

[11] "I have heard [Beethoven] called the Shakespeare of music a hundred times," stormed Fry, "to which I reply . . . 'Fudge!'"

[12] The latter work, he explained, realistically depicted an "educated, delicately reared, young lady" dying of love in the Cologne Cathedral. "To be sure, it begins in seven flats before it gets into four, the key, but that is to express the mysticism of the place with the uncertain wanderings of the sufferer."

[13] Beethoven's "Pastorale" Symphony fared no better, with its "dismal botch" of a storm—a winter storm, not a summer storm, as it should have been written and as Fry would have written it. But then, Haydn (in *The Seasons*) and Rossini (in *William Tell*) had done no better. They could not attain to Fry's more advanced instrumental effects, because, wrote Fry, "they did not know how."

swings down to Hell, returns to Heaven and thence to Earth to depict the family joys of a Christmas party; [it] puts the Lord's Prayer to music, not with the drawl of monks *à la* Palestrina or the frizzle of eunuchs *à la* Farinelli, but according to the colloquial accents of innocence and love." And over and over again Fry dwelt tenderly on each minute detail of his "Santa Claus" Symphony—not only its "dramatico/musical" content but the performances by each of Jullien's virtuosos for whom each passage had been lovingly fashioned.

If this communication was unduly long, wrote Fry, thousands of words later, he had been compelled to make it so "in order to define my position as a composer, or the apostle of a new lyrical faith, if anything, and not an almsman, receiving thankfully the broken meats from the tables of classic composers and rehashing them, instead of offering fresh, substantial viands." And, he declared: "I make common cause with Americans, born or naturalized, who are engaged in the world's Art struggle and against degrading deference to European dictation."

"Now, my dear Fry," urbanely replied Willis, first having listed some fourteen of Fry's more egocentric statements, "I consider any man who honestly entertains (as I really think you do) such truly pleasant opinions of himself . . . a fortunate fellow."[14] But Willis did not envy Fry his opinions of others: "I think it would qualify my own happiness were I to think, as you do, that Beethoven, Mozart, Haydn, Rossini, Palestrina, Farinelli, Corelli, and all the rest of those old blunderers had made such 'dismal botches' in Art as you attribute to them."

Willis then got down to cases. In the first place, he most emphatically did not agree with any of Fry's opinions—either of himself or of others. "Santa Claus" was by no stretch of the imagination a symphony, despite Fry's insistence that it was; it was, rather, a "Fantasia," wherein a composer might wander at will with no formal constraints ("a capital chance always for you, Fry"). Symphonies consisted of three or four movements, each being complete unto itself and each having its own unity. But "a symphony of one movement I think has never been heard of, this side of 'Santa Claus.'"

Unity, moreover, did not consist in the number of movements a work comprised, nor in its programmatic content, as Fry inflexibly maintained. Symphonic unity implied "an intelligent, consecutive, proportional work of Art, a work that has a beginning, a consequent middle, and an inevitable end"—unlike a "vague, disconnected, illogical, planless composition like a Fantasia." And, added Willis: "Santa Claus" was unquestionably a fantasia and thus had no musical unity. And rail against it as Fry might, unity was an immutable reality: it denoted musical coherence, and it was this quality of coherence—"sequence, connectedness, logical arrangement, musical coherence"—that Fry lacked. In his compositions, in his writing, and in himself. "You are all Fantasia, from beginning to end."

Willis then proceeded to discredit Fry's pronouncements on the larger meanings

[14] Of course he was egotistical, Fry proudly replied. Not only did he have "too good an opinion" of himself because of his great success with the public, if not the critics, but in defending himself and always proving himself right, he used "just as much egotism as the necessities of the case demand[ed]" (second letter to Willis, *Musical World and Times,* February 18, pp. 74–76; reprinted in *Dwight's,* February 25, 1854, pp. 163–64).

of music, on "imitative" music,[15] and on his "nonsensical" claim that *The Breaking Heart* realistically portrayed the demise of a lovelorn young lady in a cathedral.[16]

As to having called "Santa Claus" an extravaganza, Willis declared himself "convinced" by the huge bulk and intensity of Fry's arguments, if nothing else, that "every composer certainly knows best whether he was in earnest, even in the handling of children's rattles and playthings." Thus, with tongue in cheek, did Willis "grant" *Santa Claus* its "earnestness."

Unwilling to match the immensity of Fry's document—"a sure way to lose one's readers"—Willis summed up: "We differ entirely and utterly; we *unspeakably* differ in our estimate of the honored names in Art you have so recklessly tossed about in that extraordinary letter. The heart of every musician must stand still at the relative value you put upon them and—upon yourself.

"My dear Fry," he concluded, "I admire your genius, but it is genius astray. You are wrong in your views of Art, as I think you are in your views of handling what is sacred in secular discussion. You are a splendid frigate at sea without a helm" (*Musical World and Times,* January 28, pp. 37–39; reprinted in *Dwight's,* February 11, 1854, pp. 146–47).

Thus the first round. Those that followed endlessly retraced the same ground, with Fry and Willis each displaying a seemingly inexhaustible capacity for reiteration, hairsplitting, and childish wrangling over semantics. In their endless bicker over "unity," upon Willis's assertion that Fry did not know the meaning of the word, Fry defiantly offered to prove that he did by composing a four-movement symphony (presumably overflowing with unity) in the space of four to six days[17] (a task known to take other composers from four to six months, he slyly added), if the Philharmonic would agree to play it under Jullien's direction. Furthermore, Fry had no objection to their playing it "sandwiched between any two classical symphonies" they might choose (*Musical World and Times,* February 18, pp. 74–76; reprinted in *Dwight's* (February 25, 1854, pp. 163–64). As might be expected, Fry's challenge was ignored by the Philharmonic.

Neither Fry nor Willis gave an inch. If anything, they intensified their hostility, recklessly trading insults as they went along. In answer to Fry's deprecation of the Philharmonic's musical standards, Willis strongly affirmed his unqualified faith in the Society's integrity. Indeed, he taunted Fry, "you must come up to their high standard of Art if you, or anyone else, expect to be heard. The Temple of Art is an universal temple, and that you are an American is no reason that you should have free admission

[15] Fry: "All music is imitative, or it is good for nothing." Willis: "Making music imitative is . . . making a parrot of that which is a nightingale."

[16] Without an accompanying synopsis, wrote Willis, no audience could possibly have guessed at such a plot, and this applied as well, for all its sound effects, to "Santa Claus."

[17] A boast that aroused a good deal of journalistic derision, particularly from a no longer benign Dwight, who wrote: "If he be truly conscious and persuaded in his own mind . . . that he can produce these excellent things . . . at a day['s] or four days' warning, as Mr. Fry seems to be—why, what more could a man ask to make him inwardly the serenest and blissfullest of mortals? How can the world's opinion or any outward irrecognition cloud such inward sunshine? Out of the serene rapture of such an undimmed consciousness of power, who could even *see* a critic?" (*Dwight's,* March 4, 1854, pp. 173–74).

there. . . . Nothing surely could be more determined and persevering than your championship of American Art . . . simply, as it strikes me, because it *is* American Art." But this was a "one-sided view of Art."[18]

"As your sincere friend," wrote Willis, suddenly modulating to a mellower key (perhaps having had his fill of the controversy by now): "I wish with all my heart that you would retire from the angry arena of antagonism in Art-matters and, in the sequestered seclusion of your own Art-world, calmly and earnestly work—strive—woo the divine Muse *herself*"[19] (*Musical World and Times,* February 25, pp. 86–87; reprinted in *Dwight's* (March 4, 1854, pp. 171–73). This advice was hardly appreciated by Fry.

Nor did Fry's hot-tempered fellow-combatant Bristow take kindly to Willis's "advice." Ignited by Fry's flaming passion, Bristow entered the lists (on February 27) with a fiery blast of his own, aimed exclusively at the Philharmonic. Addressed to Willis and appearing in the *Musical World and Times* on March 4, 1854 (p. 100; excerpted in *Dwight's,* March 11, 1854, p. 182),[20] Bristow corroborated what he called Fry's "perfectly accurate" estimate of the Philharmonic. As one of the earliest members of the Society and a recently elected director, and as a composer, it was Bristow's not unbiased opinion that the predominantly German Philharmonic was dedicated to a "systematized effort for the extinction of American music."[21]

On the pretext of correcting Fry's misstatement that the Philharmonic had never played an American composition, Bristow caustically wrote: "As it is possible to miss a needle in a haystack, I am not surprised that Mr. Fry has missed the fact that during the eleven years the Philharmonic Society has been in operation in this city it played once, either by mistake or accident, one single American composition, an overture of mine. As one exception makes the rule stronger, so this single stray fact shows that the Philharmonic Society has been as anti-American as if it had been located in London during the Revolutionary War and composed of native-born English Tories. Your anonymous correspondent [a member of the Philharmonic], who is not worthy of notice . . . says that a symphony of mine [op. 10] also was rehearsed [in 1850] and not played in public. So Uncle Toby says—'Our army swore terribly at Flanders'—but that army didn't fight.

"It appears the Society's eleven years of promoting American Art have embraced one whole performance of one whole American overture, [and] one whole rehearsal of one whole American symphony. . . . Now, in the name of the nine Muses, what is the Philharmonic Society—or Harmony-lovers' Society—in this country? Is it to play exclusively the works of German masters, especially if they be dead, in order that our

[18] "Art soars above all narrow nationalities," wrote Dwight (*Journal,* February 4, 1854, p. 141). George William Curtis agreed: "Art is not, in any limited sense, national. . . . A devout Catholic of the western hemisphere feels [the meaning of Raphael's *Transfiguration*] and enjoys its beauty as much as the Pope" (*Putnam's,* May 1854, pp. 564–65).

[19] Upton, for some reason, doubts that Willis wrote such "unbearably condescending" words (Upton, *Fry,* p. 136).

[20] And approvingly quoted at considerable length by Fry in his review of the Philharmonic concert given on March 4.

[21] "They could not very well extinguish that which had no existence," sardonically commented Ritter (p. 287n).

critics may translate their ready-made praise from the German?[22] Or is it to stimulate original Art on the spot? Is there a Philharmonic in Germany for the encouragement solely of American music? Then why should there be a society here for the encouragement solely of German music, to the exclusion of American? Unless, as Mr. Fry says, the object is to render us a Hessian Colony, which we most incontestably are."

Referring to Willis's paternal admonition to Fry, Bristow indignantly demanded: "Who are the men who told you Americans cannot 'write up' to the standard of the New York Philharmonic Society? The same style of *illuminati* that in the London Philharmonic, after attempting to rehearse it, kicked Beethoven's C-minor Symphony under their desks and pronounced the composer a fool or madman.[23] Can any of these men who so decry American music read a score? Not one.[24] And what right, then, have they to prejudge, unread and unheard, everything American simply because it is American?

"You speak of 'writing up' to the Philharmonic Society; better say write down to it." In no way could the Philharmonic compare with Jullien's orchestra—neither with a *pianissimo* nor a *fortissimo,* wrote Bristow. "And yet [a passionate *non sequitur*], Mr. Jullien—a stranger, a traveler—finds, during a visit to this country, American instrumental compositions that he adapts [*sic*] in his symphonic repertory and will carry back for performances in Europe, although the members of the Philharmonic Society have never been able to discover any such works during eleven years; and under such fostering care as theirs, none would ever attain to existence in eleven hundred years."

And besides, added Bristow for good measure, the Philharmonic had deteriorated in the past three years. Indeed, "the best disposed persons towards the Society could not find it in their consciences to praise the last concert."[25] "It is very bad taste, to say the least," fumed Bristow, for Philharmonic members recently emigrated from Germany to "bite the hand that feeds them. If all their artistic affections are unalterably German, let them pack back to Germany and enjoy the police and bayonets and aristocratic kicks and cuffs of that land, where an artist is a serf to a nobleman, as the history of all their great composers shows. America has made the political revolution which illumines the world, while Germany is still beshrouded with a pall of feudal darkness. While America has been thus far able to do the chief things for the dignity of man, forsooth she must be denied the brains for original Art, and must stand like a beggar, deferentially, cap in hand, when she comes to compete with the ability of any dirty German village.

"Mr. Fry has taken the right ground," Bristow staunchly declared: "Against fearful odds he has, as a classical composer . . . challenged all Germany to meet him before the audiences of the Philharmonic and Mr. Jullien, and the challenge has not been accepted."

And in closing: "It seems that as about nine-tenths, to say the least, of the per-

[22] As habitually did Dwight and Willis.

[23] The story was a gross falsehood, protested Dwight's Diarist (*Dwight's,* March 25, 1854, p. 197). Throughout the controversy, the Diarist had been kept continuously busy refuting Fry's reckless misstatements concerning various European composers, each rebuttal eliciting a characteristically furious counter-rebuttal from Fry. And now Bristow!

[24] Surely an exaggeration.

[25] Given on January 14 at the Broadway Tabernacle (see below).

formers and critics are foreigners, American composers must be forced into the politics of asserting their rights to be heard in their own country unless they will submit to be denied any existence whatever, or to be trampled out of existence altogether, when they have begun the great work of building a national school of Art.[26] In this they should find sympathy, at least, from all their countrymen, as they have to learn composition under circumstances, and against obstacles, which have no parallel in the history of Art in Europe, ancient or modern. For there, every country has protected its own artists through a national school supported by the government. Here, however, the development of Art, [like] the development of political liberty, depends solely upon the courageous and long-sustained efforts of individual men. There are but few composers now, and there will be none at all if musical matters are exclusively controlled by foreigners, as at present."[27]

On March 9, Bristow's letter of resignation was read at a meeting of the Philharmonic board of directors; Louis Spier, their secretary, was directed to write to Bristow asking for a "clarification," and Scharfenberg and Ensign (treasurer and librarian, respectively) were appointed to draft a public reply to Bristow's letter. Their letter appeared in the *Musical World and Times* on March 18 (pp. 121–22) and was reprinted in *Dwight's* (March 25, 1854, p. 195).

To the astounded directors of the Philharmonic, Bristow's behavior signified nothing less than high treason committed by a trusted comrade. Bristow might more properly have faced them with his complaints, they protested, instead of publicly attacking "the spirit and action of the . . . Society in such a remarkable and unjustifiable manner"—so inaccurately and so unfairly. To Bristow's accusation that in their eleven years of existence they had performed only two American works—one at a concert and the other at a public rehearsal—the Society somewhat lamely replied that for their first four years no American work had been submitted, thus reducing their period of culpability to only seven years. And during those years they had performed numerous works "written on American soil" by locally resident composers, albeit mostly of assorted foreign origins. In this category they listed Loder (English), Wallace (Irish), Miguel (French), and Hansen, Eisfeld, and Knaebel (German), as well as Dodworth, Bristow, and William Mason (American). Additionally, works by Heinrich (German/Bohemian) had been accepted for performance but had been withdrawn by the composer.

The Philharmonic brought up (but quickly dropped) the eternally knotty question of what constitutes American music or an American composer. Admittedly, "only such a work is the production of American Art as emanates from an American mind, that is, from a native of this country" (an uncomfortable definition, uncomfortably expressed). Gingerly skating away from that slippery terrain, they obscurely claimed that their list of performances of works by resident composers proved that full justice had in any case been done to Bristow, "whose merits and talents as a musician and com-

[26] Either a wishful statement or a reference to the misleadingly named Academy of Music, then in construction, which turned out to be not an academy but exclusively a fancy opera house.

[27] Although, in his answer to Bristow, Willis loyally defended the Philharmonic, he conceded that it would be "a nobler thing" on their part "to have *one* of the four [yearly] concerts devoted to the production of *American* compositions" (*Musical World and Times,* March 4, 1854, p. 100).

poser," they were quick to add, had "never for a moment . . . been called in question by any of the members of our Society."

None of this, however, had any bearing on the universally recognized superiority of the works of "Beethoven, Mozart, Haydn, Weber, Spohr, Mendelssohn, Gade, Bennett, Schumann, Cherubini, Rossini, Spontini, Méhul, Berlioz, etc., etc., to the works of Mr. Bristow, or any other American composer now publicly known" (presumably referring to Fry, whose name, for obvious reasons, was evidently taboo at the Philharmonic). To fulfill their ethical and aesthetic obligations to promote the best Art in this country, it was the Philharmonic's duty to give preference to the works of these masters. (They did not refer to the preference they gave to works by such composers as Kalliwowda, Lindpaintner, Marschner, Reissiger, Lachner, Lobe, and Litolff, among others.)

Having answered (to their own satisfaction) each of Bristow's accusations and complaints—"which for his sake we wish he had framed in a somewhat nobler spirit"—the Philharmonic's letter closed with their reiterated regrets that he had not "honestly and frankly laid his grievances, if he had any, before the Society . . . instead of writing and publicizing a letter full of vehemence and passion,[28] condemnatory of a body of musicians of which he had been himself a member for many years . . . and in whose spirit and action he [had] always acquiesced, from the commencement of his membership up to his late extraordinary attack in your journal."

The letter—signed by the Society's president Henry C. Timm, and its board of directors: U. C. Hill vice president, Louis Spier secretary, William Scharfenberg treasurer, J. L. Ensign librarian, and Theodore Eisfeld assistant director—had reportedly been fully approved for publication, except for "only three dissentient votes," one of them cast by an anonymous voter who "preferred that no notice whatever be taken of Mr. Bristow's letter." Bristow's resignation[29] was then accepted and his successor announced—erroneously published as Mr. Beames, in fact Mr. Brannes of the cello section (*Musical World and Times,* March 18, 1854, pp. 121–22).

That all was not serene within the precincts of the Philharmonic was revealed by U. C. Hill's ensuing letter to the *Musical World and Times* (March 25, p. 133), written, he said, to make it known that the Society's reply to Bristow had *not* been handed to him (Hill) to sign, that he had thus been denied the opportunity of expressing his views, and that he did not entirely endorse either Bristow's statements or the Philharmonic's policies. "Although a director," he wrote, "I do not wish to be held responsible for the management of the association, as I am in a minority at present on most subjects."

Bristow, refusing to accept the Philharmonic's self-justifying reply to his letter, responded with a seething second indictment, appearing on April 1 in the *Musical World and Times* (pp. 148, 153). He categorically rejected the Philharmonic's claim that they had actually "performed" the works by the resident composers on their list: only

[28] Incited, wrote Scharfenberg in an earlier angry letter to the *Musical World,* by "egotistical advisors" (March 11, 1854, pp. 109–10).

[29] Following his resignation Bristow remained away from the Philharmonic Society until the opening of their fourteenth season (November 24, 1855). Significantly, at that season's third concert (March 1, 1856) they would play his "Jullien" Symphony.

one—Bristow's Concert Overture—had been performed at a concert, all the others had been played at public rehearsals. And "there could hardly be any greater insult to any composer than to rehearse his piece and not perform it."

The Dodworth, Mason, and Wallace pieces heard at concerts seemingly did not count because they were not symphonic works.[30] Since soloists appearing with the Philharmonic were usually unpaid volunteers "and as such had to choose their own pieces," the Dodworths, Harvey and Allen, had chosen (in 1846) to play a duet for two cornets, apparently by Allen; the Root Quartette Party (in 1853) to sing a beautiful serenade by William Mason; and Madame Wallace-Bouchelle (in 1851) to sing two songs by her brother, apparently now considered an American (whose fine orchestra works the Society had shunned, wrote Bristow). Thus, these smaller works had been given at concerts only because their performances "could not have been prevented." That Bristow's overture had been performed at all, he wrote, was only because of U. C. Hill's intervention.

And what, he demanded, of their treatment of Hill, the "Father of the Philharmonic?" His name—according to his own statement—had been affixed to the Philharmonic's recently published letter without his authorization, a telling comment on the quality of ethics practiced by the Society. Referring to Hill's letter, Bristow wrote: "It would have been much more to the purpose had Mr. Hill plainly detailed in his letter, as he has done in conversations with me and others . . . to have stated what he really meant, viz., that the Philharmonic Society, originally founded by himself and others, Americans or men with liberal American views," had soon been overrun, ten to one, by a German clique whose purpose it was to "crush and extinguish everything American."

Bristow announced his intention of founding an American Philharmonic Society, "which I trust will be free from all *cliques,* and whose aim will be to promote and cultivate the Divine Art, regardless of any *national* prejudices"—an announcement that inspired a full range of reactions, from approval to derision.[31]

But the hostilities soon began to taper off—perhaps because of oversatiation, more probably because their chief instigator (Fry) had turned his formidable attention to the reopening of the Crystal Palace (on May 4), for which, as Barnum's music director,[32] he was enabled to compose music for William Ross Wallace's prize-winning Ode and hear it performed under Bristow's direction. As we know, Fry subsequently devoted himself to Jullien's valedictory concerts at Castle Garden, to the composition and performance of the *Childe Harold* Symphony, and to the Musical Congress,[33] all

[30] In his letter Bristow cited an article of the Philharmonic bylaws: "If any Grand orchestral Compositions, such as Overtures or Symphonies, shall be presented to the Society, they being composed in this country, the Society shall perform one every season, provided a committee of five, appointed by the Government, shall have approved and recommended the composition." No such committee had ever been appointed, he wrote.

[31] The idea of an American orchestra (and why not Italian, French, and Chinese orchestras as well?) was first put forward in terms of so-called "good-natured banter"—much to Bristow's outrage—by Dwight's New York correspondent "Pegan" (*Dwight's,* March 11, pp. 181–82; April 22, 1854, p. 23). For Bristow's furious reply, see the *Musical World and Times,* April 22, 1854, pp. 183–84.

[32] The matchmaker for the unlikely union of Fry and Barnum might have been their mutual friend Horace Greeley.

[33] As did Bristow, who was also occupied with Harmonic Society doings.

of which, together with his editorial duties at the *Tribune*, occupied him until late June, when Jullien returned to England.

During this turbulent period the beleaguered Philharmonic—as if they did not have problems enough—attempted business as usual at the dismal old Tabernacle, apparently the only fairly sizable auditorium available to them after the destruction of Metropolitan Hall. Lovers of good music, hoped a suddenly (but temporarily) benign Burkhardt, would surely not be put off by the unfortunate change of locale.

Apparently they were not, for a large audience reportedly attended the concert on January 14, 1854, to hear Eisfeld conduct an all-German program consisting of Schumann's Second Symphony, op. 62, in C (1845–46), performed in New York for the first time, Beethoven's Second Symphony, and Mendelssohn's overture *Calm Sea and Prosperous Voyage*, op. 27 (1832). The soloists were the soprano Maria Brainerd, who sang Schubert's *Ave Maria* and Handel's "Rejoice greatly," from *Messiah*, and the bassoonist Paul Eltz, who played Weber's "Adagio and Rondo in F," presumably the second and third movements of the Bassoon Concerto, op. 75 (1811).

As usual, the critics' reactions were poles apart. Although Schumann had a good knowledge of orchestration, wrote Burkhardt, his symphony was scored in a manner that "pleases us not": in attempted imitation of Mendelssohn, the symphony's "latter portions are written in a manner that would drive an old-fashioned contrapuntist crazy from their superabundance of unisons." And because the exquisite Larghetto of Beethoven's Second Symphony had—"fatally for the reputation of the Philharmonic—been played repeatedly by Jullien's incomparable orchestra, the public had their eyes opened to the defects even of the Philharmonic."[34]

And while everyone—even Fry—praised Maria Brainerd's performances of Schubert and Handel, Burkhardt considered her unfit to be heard at the Philharmonic. A thousand times better to have no vocalist at all than one who failed to meet the high standards expected of an organization calling itself "Philharmonic" (*Albion*, January 28, 1854, p. 44).

Burkhardt's sniping at the Philharmonic was child's play, however, compared with the ferocity unleashed by William Henry Fry. Fresh from his first letter to Willis, a fire-breathing Fry wrote that the Philharmonic was "conducted on principles which, if carried out in Europe, would extinguish music there in a fortnight, and would have utterly prevented its advancement beyond the condition it must have been in . . . when Julius Caesar invaded Gaul and Britain." Fry added: "If the Philharmonic Society can only play European pieces—if it be an almighty fiat that nobody here, native or naturalized, can write a piece of music as poor as Mendelssohn's *Happy Voyage* [*sic*] or Handel's *Rejoice Greatly*—then the cause of music is hopeless in this country, and the sooner the Philharmonic Society shuts up, the better" (*Tribune*, January 16, 1854).

Mendelssohn's so-called overture, wrote Fry, was a misnomer (again semantics): its title was "nonsensical," for it introduced no opera or oratorio; it was, in fact, an overture to nothing. As descriptive music ("which we think all music should be") it

[34]But the critic for the *Musical World and Times* (January 21, 1854, p. 27), probably Girac (no Jullien partisan), thought the Larghetto "far more impressively and ably rendered by the Philharmonic" than by Jullien's orchestra.

failed utterly, depicting the opposite of what its title implied. Besides, it was a monotonous work "destitute of a single memorable idea, not having the first blush of melody about it." And besides, the Philharmonic's performance of it was comparably poor.

As for Schumann's symphony, it was not only non-descriptive, but a less melodious throwback to antiquated symphonies such as Beethoven's, except that Beethoven at least wrote better music. The air from Handel's *Messiah* was made up of "stupid old Italian roulades not having the least religious signification," and Schubert's *Ave Maria,* although concededly the work of a genius, allowed the voice to be drowned out by the accompaniment. Besides, it possessed an objectionable modulation where the dominant of C, instead of resolving to that key, "broke off suddenly" into the key of F—"the rudest license, and at the same time the most offensive one, that we know of in any great author."

By the following Philharmonic concert, given on March 4, Burkhardt complained of the "disheartening and gloomy effects of the old Tabernacle. . . . Could not the [Philharmonic] government obtain Niblo's or some other cheerful, clear, nice room, instead of compelling their friends to bury themselves for two or three hours in the 'living tomb,' the gloomy Tabernacle?"[35] (*Albion,* March 11, 1854, p. 116).

The program included a belated first performance in New York of Beethoven's Symphony No. 1 in C, op. 21 (1788–1800)—a delightfully melodious work, according to the critics; also a first performance of Niels Gade's Symphony No. 4, op. 20, in B-flat (1850);[36] the Overture to Spohr's opera *Faust* (1816) (another first for the Philharmonic); Spohr's Concertino for Violin in A Minor, op. 110, "Past and Present" *(Sonst und jetzt),* performed by Joseph Burke; and arias from Lortzing's opera *Peter the Great (Zar und Zimmermann)* and from Mendelssohn's *St. Paul,* inadequately sung by one Julius Schumann, a rank amateur. Too, the second and third movements of Chopin's E-minor Piano Concerto, erroneously announced in the *Musical World and Times* as a first New York performance, were played by Richard Hoffman, wrongly designated as a debutant with the Philharmonic (March 11, 1854, p. 115).[37] Aside from this uninformed reporter, the critics generally agreed that in this performance Hoffman had revealed a newfound profundity and sensitiveness far beyond his previous purely virtuosic style.

Particularly noteworthy is Henry C. Watson's review of this concert,[38] appearing

[35] On February 25 the Philharmonic directors had voted to retain the Tabernacle for the remainder of their 1853–54 season; they appointed Ensign (who apparently still served as the Tabernacle's organist) a "committee of one" to improve its unsatisfactory lighting arrangements (Philharmonic Archives).

[36] Only Burkhardt and "Pegan" referred to an earlier (untraceable) performance (thus offering a clue to Pegan's probable identity).

[37] Timm had given the first New York performance of the Chopin concerto (the same two movements) as long ago as 1846.♪ Hoffman had made his debut with the Philharmonic in 1847,♪ shortly after his arrival from England; he had appeared with the Society again in 1848,♪ but apparently not since.

[38] Absent from the journalistic scene as a regular reviewer since his departure from the *Albion* in 1850, Watson had in the interim continued to be visible as a teacher, composer, publicist for various artists, translator, musical and literary handyman, occasional critic, and, of course, as vice president of the Musical Fund Society.

in the first and apparently the only issue of his latest publishing venture *The Philharmonic Journal* (March 23, 1854, pp. 6, 11).[39] Effusively protesting his "deep attachment" to the Philharmonic "from the first hour of its organization"[40] (although, to be sure, he sometimes had had occasion to be avuncularly "severe with the management"), Watson extravagantly lauded the Society for their great influence for good, their "educational mission," and their public rehearsals.

Briefly lapsing into his former acerbity, he rebuked Burke for his inferior performance of the Spohr Concertino, and—referring to the singer Schumann—he outrageously suggested that if the Philharmonic were so determined to foster really bad singing, they should organize a "Philharmonic Negro Band."

But Watson piled extravagant lauds upon Hoffman, who at last had progressed from mere executant into the "Art-Sphere": his playing was now pure, elevated, dreamy, and his rubato perfect; it was indeed great and idiomatic Chopin playing. Hoffman was encored, and here he fell into Watsonian disfavor: he played "a pretty trifle, full of quips and cranks, curious twistings and turnings, rushing hither and thither, and never stopping until it ran right into a brilliant waltz, by Gottschalk.[41] Questionable taste, Mr. Hoffman! A study, a fugue, or simply a bow, rather than this fall from the sublime to the pretty."[42]

Burkhardt agreed. "Mr. Richard Hoffman truly astonished us by the progress he has made since last we heard him." Now a full-fledged artist, Hoffman fully earned all the warm applause that greeted him,[43] "but the audience deserved, and demanded, a repetition of what he had played [the Chopin concerto], not the unworthy trifle he gave them, even though that trifle was (we believe) Gottschalk's and pretty enough, *but not in this place.* We cannot too severely (as we have done before) reprove this practice of giving for encores trifling pieces different from those demanded. It is the abominable practice with some artists," stormed Burkhardt (*Albion,* March 11, 1854, p. 116).

Fry's review of the concert was mostly concerned with his all-consuming obsession—the culpability of the Philharmonic and the worthlessness of their repertory. Gade, although a Dane, was tarred with the German brush, having been a disciple of the non-melodist Mendelssohn. The inadequate instrumentation of Gade's symphony was "violinism throughout." The tendency of German music, wrote Fry, quoting (or rather, misquoting) the Boston composer and painter Charles Callahan Perkins (1823–1886), then in Europe, was toward "chaos." And dullness, added Fry. It was all form and harmonization, with no melody. Chopin's concerto, brilliantly played by Hoffman, was more Italianate than most of Chopin's works, which were predominantly nationalistic. But Fry devoted the better part of his review to substantial extracts, with support-

[39] Undertaken in editorial partnership with James Simmonds, a writer of ballads, and published by the piano builder and music publisher Horace Waters.

[40] Watson had in fact been their implacable enemy for the first four years of their existence.♪

[41] Perhaps a solo arrangement of Gottschalk's unpublished *Valse di bravura,* whose two-piano version he had played with Hoffman in 1853; it was most likely the same work, programed as "Introduction and Grand Waltz *di Bravoura,*" that Hoffman played at Paul Julien's concert on April 18, 1854.

[42] Reviewing Watson's new journal in advance, the *Daily Times* (March 15, 1854) assessed his critique of the Philharmonic concert as "discriminating, but too patronizing in its tone."

[43] According to Fry, Hoffman "brought down the house" (*Tribune,* March 7, 1854).

ing comments, from Bristow's first letter to Willis, which had appeared only a few days earlier in the *Musical World and Times* (*Tribune,* March 7, 1854).[44]

At the final concert of their eventful twelfth season, on April 22, the Philharmonic, in a huge program, gave the first performance of the Symphony No. 20 by the prodigiously prolific German composer Friedrich Schneider (1786–1853),[45] a work dedicated to the Society in appreciation of the composer's having been elected an honorary member *in absentia* in 1853. Additionally, the Society yet again repeated Spohr's "ponderous" *Die Weihe der Töne* and Beethoven's *Egmont* Overture. The soloists on this occasion included the William Vincent Wallaces, who brilliantly played Wallace's highly praised *Grand Duo concertant* for two pianos on a theme from Halévy's *L'Éclair,* and Philip Mayer, who sang an aria from Spohr's *Jessonda,* a song by Meyerbeer, accompanied at the piano by Timm, and—with Schmitz and Knaebel—an arrangement, with two French horns and orchestra, of "Araby's Daughter."[46]

R. Storrs Willis, who found the Schneider symphony to be a pleasant enough work, complained, however, of the exhausting length of the program: by the time the orchestra "sounded the retreat and curfew" with the *Egmont* Overture, "the tolerance of the audience [half of whom had already departed] was at an end."

But despite all cavils: "We heartily shake hands with the Philharmonic, complimenting them for the hard battle they have had to fight this winter, which they have fought bravely, never looking back, but always pushing forward with unflagging zeal and unfurled standard" (*Musical World and Times,* April 29, 1854, p. 201).

Burkhardt, however, after virtuously absolving himself of any rancorous feelings toward the Philharmonic, unleashed a mighty tirade of complaints and criticisms. In summing up the season he declared that the Society, "instead of advancing with the age—instead of fulfilling the objects for which it was formed—[was] retrogressing, and that the charges made against it by Mr. W. H. Fry, by Mr. Bristow, and others, are in a great measure only too true."

Burkhardt resumed his attack on Eisfeld, particularly for his long, unthreatened tenure as conductor of the Society. "At present," he wrote, "Mr. Eisfeld, a very able artist, 'tis true, seems to be *Conductor for life.* Do the directors mean to tell us that there is no other Conductor to be had?"

Prosperity had spoiled the Philharmonic, contended Burkhardt. Its "selfishness, cliqueism, and overbearing old-fogyism" were effectively driving away its "best and

[44] Back at his old tricks, "Pegan," after properly lauding Chopin and Hoffman and acidly commenting on the mass exodus of the ill-mannered Philharmonic audience before the last movement of the closing piece (the Beethoven symphony) sardonically addressed Dwight: "You will have noticed the premonitory symptoms of a musical revolution—a declaration of independence is expected soon—America is on the point of throwing off allegiance to Germany. In vocal music the victory is already achieved. Three negro minstrel bands draw nightly crowds of devotees to their temples, while a German four-part *Lied* . . . is unknown (*Dwight's,* March 11, 1854, p. 181).

[45] Schneider is said to have composed, among numberless other works, 23 symphonies, 60 sonatas, 7 operas, 6 concertos, 13 oratorios, 14 masses, 25 cantatas, 200 songs, and 400 part-songs for men's voices (*Grove's,* 5th ed, VII, 504–5).

[46] Popular in the earlier nineteenth century, as set by the English composer George Kiallmark (1781–1835) to a poem from Thomas Moore's *Lalla Rookh* (1817), the tune was later adapted to Samuel Woodworth's poem "The Bucket," and retitled "The Old Oaken Bucket" (*c.* 1833).

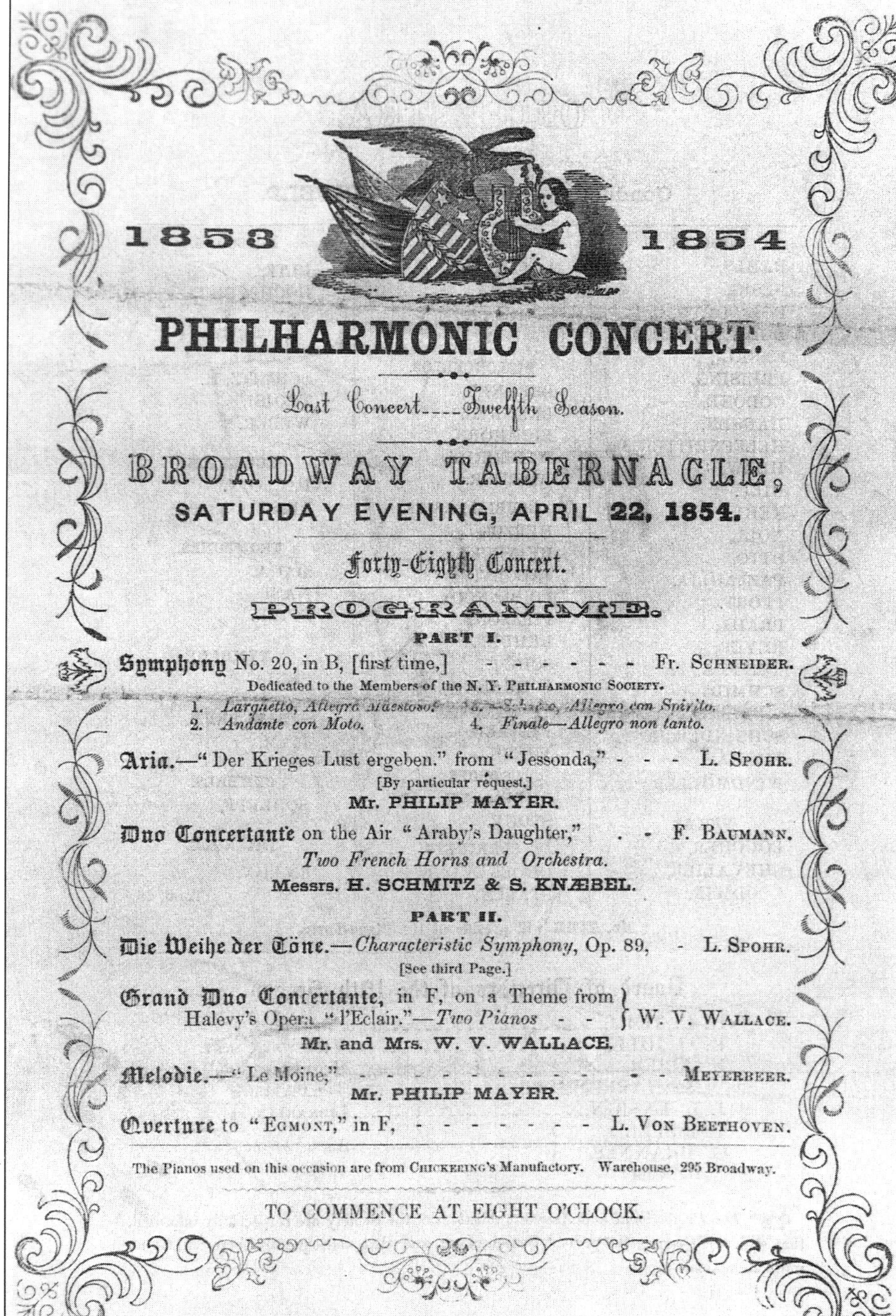

1853 1854

PHILHARMONIC CONCERT.

Last Concert.....Twelfth Season.

BROADWAY TABERNACLE,

SATURDAY EVENING, APRIL 22, 1854.

Forty-Eighth Concert.

PROGRAMME.

PART I.

Symphony No. 20, in B, [first time,] - - - - - - - Fr. SCHNEIDER.

Dedicated to the Members of the N. Y. PHILHARMONIC SOCIETY.

1. *Larghetto, Allegro Maestoso.* 3. [illegible], *Allegro con Spirito.*
2. *Andante con Moto.* 4. *Finale—Allegro non tanto.*

Aria.—"Der Krieges Lust ergeben." from "Jessonda," - - - L. SPOHR.

[By particular request.]

Mr. PHILIP MAYER.

Duo Concertante on the Air "Araby's Daughter," . - F. BAUMANN.

Two French Horns and Orchestra.

Messrs. H. SCHMITZ & S. KNÆBEL.

PART II.

Die Weihe der Töne.—*Characteristic Symphony*, Op. 89, - L. SPOHR.

[See third Page.]

Grand Duo Concertante, in F, on a Theme from Halevy's Opera "l'Eclair."—*Two Pianos* - - } W. V. WALLACE.

Mr. and Mrs. W. V. WALLACE.

Melodie.—"Le Moine," - - - - - - - - - - - - - MEYERBEER.

Mr. PHILIP MAYER.

Overture to "EGMONT," in F, - - - - - - - - L. VON BEETHOVEN.

The Pianos used on this occasion are from CHICKERING'S Manufactory. Warehouse, 295 Broadway.

TO COMMENCE AT EIGHT O'CLOCK.

most deserving members" and shutting out worthy new ones. And why? "Simply to make their own annual dividend a little larger at the end of the season; to have an entirely German supremacy; to play nothing but good, bad, and indifferent German compositions; to reject indiscriminately all American, French, or English works; and to blackball, at will, good candidates for membership who are supposed to entertain independent opinions." Originally founded on noble American aspirations, the Philharmonic had been "perverted into a German, money-making affair, solely devoted to German music and German interests."

Not, hedged Burkhardt—suddenly remembering his own German origin—that he disapproved of the Philharmonic because it was a German institution; it was the cliqueism to which he objected. "Be it German or American, Polish or French, we want no Nationalism in Art. It is time that a thorough reform took place here, or that a new or American Philharmonic Society be formed, liberal in principles, devoted to the general interests of Art, and acknowledging its universality. We are glad to hear that such a Society is about to be formed, and we earnestly wish it success.

"Still," paradoxically concluded Burkhardt, "we would much prefer a reformation in the old Philharmonic to all new Associations" (*Albion,* April 29, 1854).

During Bristow's self-imposed exile from the Philharmonic he broadened his already widespread freelance activities; he formed a lifelong association with the New York Public School System, opened a piano and melodion store (at 423 Broadway) in partnership with a Mr. Morse (*Musical World and Times,* May 20, 1854, p. 30); and faithfully as ever he devoted himself to the Sacred Harmonic Society.

Members of the Harmonic Society, more frequently heard separately than collectively, largely dominated the various "miscellaneous and sacred" benefit concerts given for and at the various churches. On January 25, for instance, "favorite amateurs of the Society" appeared, under Bristow's direction, at the Tabernacle for the benefit of the Free Episcopal Church of the Holy Martyrs, and with Bristow at the piano, on March 1 at Knickerbocker Hall to assist the North Presbyterian Church (West 30th Street). Reviewing the latter event in the *Musical World and Times* (March 11, 1854, pp. 115–16), Willis's maladroit assistant (Girac?), added his mite to the currently raging musico/chauvinistic hostilities. Commenting pointedly on the Sacred Harmonic Society's infrequent performances of complete oratorios, he wrote: "We regret to see them so inactive." Only once this season had they been seen "in full operation" and that was for the purpose of "assisting a band of foreign speculators to produce the *Messiah*" (a snide reference to the Society's gala collaboration with Jullien on December 26, 1853). Would it not have been more proper and patriotic, the critic disingenuously asked, for the Harmonic Society to have formed an association with the Philharmonic, as the Boston singing societies had done with the Germania?

"How is it that in this city . . . where only the negro song reigns triumphantly,[47] the two musical bodies, which could indemnify the public for the total absence of serious and refined music, go their ways separately and sulk with each other as if they professed a different faith?" And if the Sacred Harmonic Society had decided on "keeping

[47] A reference to the current craze for blackface shows, particularly opera travesties.

off from their sister, the Philharmonic,"[48] then they should at least provide themselves with an adequate number of orchestra musicians in order to "keep their honor safe." It was astounding that such a "skillful general" as Bristow would allow the Harmonic Society to appear with such meager accompaniment as they had at this concert.

The inevitable hot rebuttal, written by James H. Aikman, the general secretary of the Harmonic Society, promptly appeared in the *Musical World and Times* on March 25, 1854 (pp. 133–34). Far from idle, he retorted, the Society's members were meeting weekly, enthusiastically studying the great classical works of sacred music under a "competent director" (Bristow) and preparing themselves "to produce in a proper manner that music before the public"; they were self-sustaining, were amassing a library "and other necessary auxiliaries toward the permanent establishment of a great musical association," and their long-range plan was to build "a large vocal Society familiar with all the works of the great masters, prepared to illustrate them before the public, and capable of judging . . . such new [American] works as may be brought forward." Through the Society's influence, he hoped, the public taste would be encouraged to rise above Negro minstrelsy and "find out at last that music has something better to offer than the tickling of the ear or exciting to laughter—[something] ennobling the heart and purifying the soul."

As to the critic's preposterous reference to the Society's *Messiah* performance with Jullien and his orchestra as "helping a band of foreign speculators," a perusal of the Harmonic Society's contract with Messrs. Chapple [*sic*] and Joy (total gentlemen both) offered proof that the performance had been initiated by the Society, not by Jullien or his managers. Indeed, never would the Harmonic Society adopt a subservient position to anyone.

This applied to the Philharmonic as well: since the inception of the Harmonic Society, the idea had been repeatedly broached that the two societies form an alliance to perform the great oratorios, and as frequently dropped because the offers had been "of such a character as could not be entertained for a moment. We stand ready and willing to join the Philharmonic in any performance at any time," asserted Aikman, "but on no unequal terms. . . . We are willing to share the responsibility, the profit, and the glory, but not to take the leavings."

On March 31, again at the Tabernacle, the Harmonic Society (now having reverted to its original name), with the financial assistance of "ten enthusiastic members . . . willing to run the risk," revived Neukomm's long-neglected oratorio *David*[49] (beloved of George Templeton Strong in 1840).♪ In his review of the performance, Fry, deploring the Harmonic Society's chronic sparsity of concerts, wrote: "It should not be asking too much of this public, as is asked and received in London, to come several times to concerts simply to hear and study such a work." The chief obstacle to the Society's achievement of first-rate performances, he wrote, was the unfortunate necessity of limiting their rehearsals with orchestra to a single, final session, because the in-

[48] Here appears an editorial interpolation: "(Is this a fact?—Ed.)."

[49] With the Misses Brainerd and Dingley, and the Messrs. James A. Johnson, F. H. Nash, Albert Schnyder, Fred Lyster, J. W. Alden, and H. E. Halloway in the solo roles, and with Dr. Clare W. Beames presiding at the organ and Bristow conducting.

strumentalists had to be paid. "Until the public is sufficiently interested in music to endow, so to speak, our local concerts, so that they may be properly rehearsed, we must take performances with many grains of allowance, and trenchant criticism under the present state of such affairs will be quite out of place."

Opera-prone Fry suggested, however, that the soloists receive some dramatic training, "including gesticulation and action, in order to enforce the intensity of expression which marks opera singers." Such dramatic action could be restricted to rehearsals, but it would nonetheless be reflected in their performances of the oratorios.

It was gratifying, wrote Fry, that such a society existed at all "in this our busy City of money-making," whose members were willing to serve Art while "paying their own expenses." Properly managed, the Harmonic Society could become as renowned as the Exeter Hall Chorus (Sacred Harmonic Society) in London. Fry visualized a prosperous New York Harmonic Society allied with a fine orchestra (an American Philharmonic?), commanding sufficient popular support to give weekly miscellaneous concerts, and sometimes a complete oratorio, for at least six months of the year (*Tribune,* April 1, 1854).

The Harmonic Society did not appear again, however, until the two performances of *The Seasons* (on November 14 and 30).[50] As they had given only two complete oratorios in public during their 1853–54 season, the *Evening Post* (November 15, 1854) wondered how the Society could fulfill the obligation, stated in their constitution, of "diffusing among the people a knowledge of the great masters. . . . We do not see how two performances per annum can bring it about.[51] . . . If the public of this city should have the road to the oratorio made as familiar to them as that to the opera house, they would soon accustom themselves to frequent it.[52] [But] first we must have a music hall fit to sing in. When will this be done?"

The Harmonic Society in fact inaugurated their 1854–55 season on Christmas Night at the new Academy of Music with their "annual" performance of Handel's *Messiah.* The soloists were Madame Carolina Vietti-Vertiprach and Cesare Badiali, both members of the Grisi/Mario opera company (see below), and from the Harmonic Society, Mrs. Georgiana Stuart, Maria Brainerd, and Mr. J. A. Johnson.

Miscellaneous concerts with sacred overtones were few and in most cases given to assist the churches where they took place. Among the singers generally heard at these events were Georgiana Stuart, Maria Brainerd, Cornelia Dingley, Clara Brinkerhoff, Marcus Colburn, and A. B. Lincoln; among the organists were Clare Beames and Pieter Hendryk Vanderweide (who seems also to have sung on occasion). Among the

[50] Their appearances at the reopening of the Crystal Palace and the Musical Congress were apparently not regarded as official activities.

[51] Meaning performances of complete oratorios. Yet, according to their annual report, with 321 performing and non-performing members, the Harmonic Society continued to be solvent: "Free from debt, and with $190 balance in the treasury, after a large amount having been expended in the purchase of music and in the advancement of the interests of the Society" (*Musical World,* October 14, 1854, p. 77–78).

[52] The recently opened, heavily publicized Academy of Music had apparently replaced the minstrel shows in the *Evening Post*'s estimation as the chief hindrance to the public appreciation of good music.

churches benefited in early 1854 were the Thirteenth Street Presbyterian Church (between Sixth and Seventh avenues) and the Reformed Dutch Church (Seventh Avenue between 12th and 13th streets). At the Bedford Street Methodist Episcopal Church (corner of Morton Street) on April 25, a miscellaneous concert was given by the church choir assisted by "several singers of acknowledged talent," with the stern editor Chauncey M. Cady conducting and G. F. Bristow accompanying at the piano. Mrs. Bostwick was heard on May 17 at the Market Street Church (near Henry Street) in a mixed program of sacred and secular music, presumably for the benefit of the church.

Sometimes these events took place in more worldly surroundings: on January 21, Mrs. Bostwick appeared at Niblo's Saloon in a sacred and secular Grand Concert for the benefit of St. John the Evangelist's Protestant Episcopal Church (262 Bleecker Street). And even more imposing, a benefit for Dr. Cumming's new church (St. Stephen's in East 28th Street) took place on December 14 at the Academy of Music, with a cast that included Signorina Elise Donovani of the Grisi/Mario opera company, currently appearing at the new Academy of Music, Madame Giuseppina Martini d'Ormy, a veteran of Maretzek's most recent opera fiasco (both discussed below), Mesdames Wallace-Bouchelle and Caroline Lehmann, and from the Grisi/Mario company, the Signori Arnoldi, Coletti, Morra, and Badiali, and presumably the chorus and orchestra.

Benefit concerts for various non-ecclesiastical causes were correspondingly sparse. On January 28 at the Stuyvesant Institute, Mrs. Bostwick, together with Madame Wallace-Bouchelle, Signor Corradi, and Henry C. Timm, appeared in aid of a "Destitute Family." For the benefit of the Five Points House of Industry, on January 20 at Niblo's Theatre, George Henry Curtis's highly successful *Five Points Opera* was repeated, under Curtis's direction, by the Five Points children. Dr. Pease, Solon Robinson, and the Reverend Dr. Henry Ward Beecher lent their eloquence to the occasion. On April 26, at the Central Presbyterian Church (Broome Street, corner of Elm), Curtis presented the first performance of his new juvenile sacred cantata *Joseph,* sung by the (Five Points) Juvenile Choral Society, for the joint benefit of the church and the Five Points House of Industry (*Evening Post,* April 22, 1854).[53]

Root's sacred cantata *Daniel,* or *The Captivity and Restoration,* heard the year before at the Normal Institute's graduation ceremonies, was performed for an invited audience at the Mercer Street Church on March 19 by Maria Brainerd with all four Roots and a large chorus of volunteer amateurs; Clare Beames presided at the organ and Root conducted. "The performance was effective and interesting and indeed, one of the best we have had during the winter," reported the *Musical World and Times* (March 18, 1854, p. 130).

On April 10 the German *Sängerrunde* gave a Grand Vocal and Instrumental Concert at the Tabernacle for the benefit of the "Medical Fund." At the Tabernacle, on April 18, Bristow conducted a concert for the benefit of William H. Dayas, organist of St. Stephen's Episcopal Church; among those assisting were Madame Steffani [*sic*],

[53] On July 11, Lowell Mason, with several members of the Normal Musical Institute, were scheduled to travel to the "once dreaded precincts" of the Five Points to "unite" with their friends at the House of Industry in a musical exercise. The Five Points children, under the direction of their present teacher, the Reverend Mr. Van Metre (or Van Meter), would participate and sing "a number of their pretty songs" (*Courier and Enquirer,* July 11, 1854).

Mrs. Dayas, Cornelia Dingley, Marcus Colburn, and Francis H. Nash. At the Seventh Street Methodist Episcopal Church, on December 21, Mrs. Georgiana Stuart, her sister Miss Anna Griswold, P. H. Vanderweide, William H. Oakley (the Alleghanian), F. H. Nash, and others, together with an "efficient chorus," with Vanderweide at the piano, performed for the benefit of Michael Lamarr, a teacher.

More stylish complimentary concerts were hardly more plentiful.[54] On March 13 the socially elevated ladies of Grace Church honored their solo soprano Julia Northall (now Mrs. Bodstein) with an ultra-fashionable testimonial concert. "Niblo's Saloon was filled with beauty and fashion," wrote Burkhardt (*Albion,* March 18, 1854, p. 128), adding acidly: "People chatted and admired each other's toilettes, listened occasionally to the music, languidly and delicately patted their kids [gloves, not children] once in a while, by way of applause, and retired home soon after ten o'clock, satisfied with themselves for having patronized their pet and a concert which was altogether *distingué* and *comme il faut*." The distinguished assisting artists were Cesare Badiali, Antonio Barili, Joseph Burke, and William A. King; Mrs. Bodstein not only sang but presided at the piano.

Not to be outdone, on March 22, also at Niblo's Saloon, the ladies of Calvary Church (Fourth Avenue, between 21st and 22nd Streets) accorded a similarly handsome tribute to Madame Wallace-Bouchelle, Julia Northall's opposite number at Calvary. Appearing at this concert, largely a family affair, were the William Vincent Wallaces, who played a duo by Wallace (probably his *L'Éclair* Fantasy) on two Chickerings; alone he performed his Second *Grand Polka de salon;* Frank (Franz?) Stoepel, Mrs. Wallace's brother, sang a ballad composed by Madame Bouchelle; Philip Mayer (solo basso of the Calvary Choir) sang an air from Wallace's *Maritana* in German (accompanied by the composer); and Burke, Noll, and Eichhorn performed works composed by various non-Wallaces.

John C. Scherpf, percussionist, composer, arranger, secretary of the Musical Fund Society, and now the proprietor of a kind of all-purpose music agency/emporium (at 317 Broadway),[55] was honored with a testimonial concert at Niblo's Saloon on April 26, for which a sizable representation of the city's established performers and several newcomers were announced. Among the former were Madame Bouchelle, Mrs. Brinkerhoff, Mrs. Henry C. Watson, Ferdinand Meyer, Frank Stoepel, Fred Lyster, Allen Dodworth, Felice Eben (who did not appear), and G. F. Bristow. Among the latter were the Belgian *prima donna* Madame Victor Chome, making the first of her repetitive "first appearances" in the United States; Charlotte Pozzoni, a pupil of Mrs.

[54] They were sometimes instigated by the complimentees themselves, as seems to have the case with a "complimentary testimonial" to the Boon Children on February 6 at Hope Chapel, where the Boons gave their customary scenes from Shakespeare, including on this occasion the balcony scene with Mrs. Anna Boon appearing as Romeo to her little daughter Lora's Juliet. A highlight of the occasion was Signorina Valentini's rendition of *La Colasa* in English.

[55] At Scherpf's agency, wrote the *Daily Times,* September 25, 1854), "a musician may obtain everything, from an opera company—singers, orchestra, and all—down to the fife part of a dead march. They keep a list of resident musicians, instrumentalists, teachers, and theorists; they have the scores of operas, symphonies, overtures, waltzes, polkas, and every other kind of music; they can tell you what's being done musically here or in Europe; they put the scraggy notes of a composer into proper shape for the printer." In December, Alfred Sedgwick, with a partner E. Warden, announced the opening of a similar service.

Seguin, making her debut; Matilda Sallinger, a talented young pianist; an unclassified Monsieur Basquin; and the Arion Society led by a Mr. Meyerhofer. Dodworth's Cornet Band under Harvey Dodworth, and a "full orchestra," conducted by the honoree, completed the list.

"The program was composed of eighteen pieces," carped the reviewer for the *Musical World and Times* (May 6, 1854, p. 7), "four of which were with full orchestra; two with full brass band; two were grand choruses; five solos; two were operatic Duetts; one was a piano performance; one a solo for flute [played by Eben's unnamed substitute]; and one for cornet. Certainly this may be called liberality on the part of Mr. Scherpf [who appears to have chosen the program]. Why, therefore, those incessant shouts for *encore,* which arose at the close of almost every piece of music? . . . all of these injudicious repetitions . . . swelled the concert to about thirty performances. . . . The consequence was that attentive hearers grew soon wearied, and early began to make for the doors, so that the last performance was given before only fifty or sixty of the most obstinate auditors."

Probably for charity, on March 29 a band of five Indians, singing in their native language, were heard in a "Grand Concert" at the Seventh Street Methodist Episcopal Church; and on April 23 a less exotic concert of sacred music was given at St. Anne's Church (Astor Place), under the direction of W. A. King, with a singing cast consisting of Miss Anna Griswold, Signor Bailini, and Philip Mayer; Joseph Burke contributed a "sacred violin solo," and King presided at the organ.

In March the formation of a new secular singing group, the New-York Glee and Madrigal Society, was announced, and on April 20, under the splendid direction of George Washbourne (or Washbourn, or Washburn) Morgan (1823–1892), a newly arrived English organist and choral director, they held their first *soirée* at the Chinese Buildings.

In March, too, the Philharmonic violinist and co-conductor of the National Guard Band, Joseph Noll, together with his Shakespeare Concert Society, launched a Sunday series of so-called "sacred concerts," continuing through the month of May. At first given at the St. Nicholas Exhibition Room[56] (495 Broadway), a small auditorium, so named because of its proximity to the St. Nicholas Hotel (Broadway and Spring Street), the series was moved to the newly refurbished Saloon of the Shakespeare Hotel. Among Noll's soloists were the popular singer Caroline Hiffert and the juvenile vocalists Miss Palmer Smith and Miss Maria Gillespie.

Noll's series, apparently designed for German consumption, was supplanted in September at the St. Charles Theatre, now a stronghold of German drama and opera, by a more ambitious series of pseudo-sacred Sunday night entertainments performed by "opera singers" and conducted by the Philharmonic violinist F. Herwig.

Providing otherwise nonexistent Sunday entertainment, these concerts evidently began to attract a non-German audience as well, and in October a still more ambitious "sacred" series was begun at the National Theatre, of all incongruous places, where its music director W. T. Peterschen presided over an orchestra of thirty players and a motley assortment of performers, more thespian than musical: Miss Hiffert, Mr. and Mrs.

[56] Where a succession of minstrel troupes held forth during the week.

Holman, Julia Barton, the "National Quartet Club," (consisting of male vocalists recruited from the National's resident stock company), and others. Tickets for all these performances were a uniform twenty-five cents.

These concerts were followed, in turn, by a series of "Broadway Sunday Concerts," beginning on November 19 at the Great Saloon of the Chinese Buildings. The opening program, consisting in equal parts of sacred and secular music, ranging from Mozart to Jullien, featured Madame Martini d'Ormy, currently appearing in German operas at the new *Stadt-Theater,* the basso John Camoens, a Mr. Henry Phelps from Drury Lane in London, a Monsieur M. G. Le Jeune "from the Paris *Conservatoire,*" the bandmaster Thomas G. Adkins, who played a cornet solo, and an orchestra of forty, conducted by V. Guerin, who had conducted for the Roussets in 1851. Tickets were twenty-five cents; reserved seats fifty cents. After a few concerts, this series—greatly expanded—was transferred to the new Metropolitan Theatre, as the replaced Metropolitan Hall was called, but of that, more anon.

The world of the juvenile choral spectacular was greatly diminished in 1854 with the retirement of W. B. Bradbury for reasons of ill health.[57] Without Bradbury, a sadly curtailed version of "Flora's Festival" was given on May 15 at the Reformed Dutch Church in Harlem, with only "about 150 young scholars." Thus, the flamboyant L. A. Benjamin was left in uncontested possession of the juvenile chorus field. On January 14 he gave a Grand Concert at the Tabernacle with his usual 1200 young singers and instrumentalists;[58] on February 22, again at the Tabernacle, they celebrated Washington's Birthday in song;[59] on April 20 and 21 they held a "Fairy Queen Festival," concluding with something called "Alice Dale, the Village Queen"; and on May 31 Benjamin presented his annual "May Queen Festival."

At Knickerbocker Hall, on June 7 and 9, G. F. Root's cantata *The Flower Queen or, Coronation of the Rose* was sung by the Young Ladies of the Ward School, under the direction of their teacher Aaron C. Williams.

Among the sparse miscellaneous concerts was a "farewell" appearance on March 7 at Hope Chapel by August Gockel, assisted by Mrs. Bostwick, the violinist C. Hahn, and Timm and Wollenhaupt, who with Becht and one Woeltke (or Woeltge) played an overture by Spohr, arranged for two pianos, eight hands. On March 28 at the Stuyvesant Institute the long-absent guitarist Signor Bini reappeared in company with a violin-playing Signor Filippo Passaroli from Havana. Apparently a success, in April Bini advertised afternoon and evening "Family Concerts" at Stuyvesant Hall, charging fifty cents admission for gentlemen and twenty-five cents for "ladies and children." On April 21, Aptommas gave a concert at Dodworth's Saloon, assisted by Maria Brainerd, Charles Wels, Timm, and the new singer Mr. Phelps. Aptommas appeared again on May 12 with Wels, Miss Beattie, a charming vocalist, and a Dodworth (probably Allen),

[57] Bradbury was forced as well to resign his conductorship of the Tabernacle Choir. Upon his deeply regretted departure, the choir and some members of the congregation presented him with a service of silver plate, "in token of their appreciation of his most able and arduous services as Conductor of the Music in the Church" (*Tribune,* May 11, 1854).

[58] Half of the proceeds were promised to the Five Points Mission (Pease's rivals).

[59] An occasion on which the flag used at Washington's inauguration in 1789 was displayed.

who with Aptommas played a cornopean and harp duet on a theme from *Norma.*[60] Aptommas appeared again (at Dodworth's Rooms) on October 18, when he was assisted by Madame Wallace-Bouchelle, Timm, and Allen Dodworth.[61]

On April 18, 20, and 24, Paul Julien, recovered from a serious illness that had removed him from the concert scene for a period of several months, returned to reap greater triumphs than ever before. The critics agreed that he had improved, if that were possible—the *Courier and Enquirer* (April 21, 1854) stating that he had now joined the "rank of violinists, to rise from which is to attain a fame which will be posthumous" (alas, a false prophecy). Julien was assisted at these concerts, all given at Niblo's Saloon, by the singers Henriette Behrend, a debutante Miss S. Jones, Miss Beattie, Madame Oscar Comettant, and a Signor Andrea Manzini; also Richard Hoffman[62] and A. Loreau, a conductor. On May 3, Julien gave a concert at the Tabernacle for the benefit of the New York Fire Department, assisted by Mesdames Wallace-Bouchelle and Chome, Miss Behrend, Messrs. Colburn and Nash, and Bristow, who conducted a full orchestra. As we know, in May and June, Paul Julien appeared at Louis Antoine Jullien's concerts both at Castle Garden and the Crystal Palace.

Probably encouraged by the Fry/Bristow crusade, on May 12 a young American composer/pianist T. Franklin Bassford gave his first *soirée* (program unspecified), assisted by Madame Comettant and others, at L. J. Descombes's Rooms (585 Broadway). Although Bassford played well, his forte was obviously composition, wrote the *Daily Times* critic (May 13, 1854), who, apparently having also imbibed of Fry/Bristow, continued: "If the opportunity be afforded him, he [Bassford] will doubtless distinguish himself in a higher department of art than he has yet essayed. . . . The new Academy of Music *should* open a more ample field for the native artist. By its charter, it pledged to present English Opera—and [stretching a point] that definition includes of course all works in which the English language is used as the spoken [or sung] medium."

Varieties of the English, if not the American, language were both spoken and sung in a series of three lecture/concerts of Scottish lore, titled "Tales and Music of the Olden Time," delivered at the Stuyvesant Institute on May 10, 11, and 17 by a Mr. Outram of Glasgow; he was assisted by a "select quartette of ladies and gentlemen," accompanied and conducted by George Henry Curtis. Tickets for the series were one dollar, for single sessions fifty cents. And immediately following, on May 18 and 25, a parallel historical series, "The Vocal Music of England," was given at Dodworth's Rooms by Dr. Gordon Hake, a scholarly lecturer from London. Indeed, Hake's offering might have been too scholarly, for the *Daily Times* regretfully observed on June 2, 1854, after his second lecture, that the audience "was by no means what it should have been." Hake was ably assisted by a Mrs. Neill, who illustrated his remarks with songs ranging from Thomas Arne to Charles E. Horn; she was accompanied by Timm.

[60] "On the piano," enthusiastically wrote the *Tribune* (May 13, 1854), "the great lights include Listz [*sic*], Thalberg, Gottschalk, etc., and on the harp the late Parish-Alvars and the present Aptommas."

[61] At this point Aptommas announced that he had permanently settled in New York and that he and his wife were ready to receive applications for instruction in harp and piano (*Tribune,* October 13, 1854).

[62] Who brilliantly repeated Gottschalk's Introduction and *Valse di bravoura,* his adversely criticized encore at the Philharmonic.

Less scholarly, but not more successfully, a series of three "Entertainments" was presented at Hope Chapel on October 19, 20, and 21 by one H. S. May, an English pupil of Moscheles, who presented a bewildering hodgepodge, from glees to overtures, apparently assisted by a Miss Comstock.

On June 11, immediately following Jullien's "farewell" season at Castle Garden, H. R. Conklin, the new landlord, announced the opening of the Sunday concert season at the Castle with Adkins's Band of forty performers, augmented by an additional reed and string band of forty, performing "selections from the most popular Oratorios and Operas." In July (with the commencement of Maretzek's opera season) they were supplanted by Dodworth's Band, who continued their Sunday concerts until late September.[63] On October 5 they inaugurated their weekly Promenade Musicales at the Assembly Room of Dodworth's Dancing Academy, where the school term was about to begin.

To Harvey Dodworth and Bristow fell the dubious honor of giving the first "Grand All-American Concert" at the new Academy of Music, on December 9. With an unknown Miss E. K. Baxter substituting for the suddenly indisposed Mrs. Georgiana Stuart, the audience—small to begin with—diminished perceptibly as the evening progressed (*Daily Times,* December 11, 1854). Dodworth's full Military Band, augmented by his "admirable" Serenading Cornet Band, was conducted by Harvey Dodworth, and an orchestra of sixty, by Bristow. "The *baton* becomes [Bristow] better than Mr. H. B. Dodworth, probably from being more used to it," wrote the *Times* critic. And besides, the program "possessed all the objectionable characteristics of Jullien with none of his genius for musical painting." All kinds of music except classical were performed, disapprovingly wrote the *Musical Review and Choral Advocate* (December 21, 1854, p 438). Of the two primitive, pseudo-Jullienesque program pieces played—both "destitute of merit"—Lenschow's once popular "Panorama of Broadway in 1848"♪ now sounded like a mere "musical daguerreotype of Broadway," and the anonymous "Historical Sketch of New-York"—with its would-be depictions of the Indians (war dance), the arrival of the white strangers (Dutch national anthem), the English conquering New-Amsterdam ("Rule, Britannia"), "and, finally, the colonists arising in their might," breaking the yoke of dependence with "Hail Columbia" and loudly proclaiming "Freedom and Independence"—would never find a place beside the great historical writings of George Bancroft (1800–1891).

But although "by no means favorably impressed with the first Concert here," the critic hoped its successors would receive "sufficient support to justify their continuance. There is a want, a great want, of an independent orchestra to perform the works of native composers," he wrote. "Such an orchestra can be had easily enough, and there is certainly no better place for hearing it than the Academy. But the brass band," he added, "might be dispensed with; it is very good undoubtedly, but can be heard to greatest perfection in the street."

On a higher musical level—indeed in direct competition with Eisfeld's chamber-music *soirées*—the Brothers Mollenhauer (who on Jullien's departure had elected to re-

[63] On August 21 they performed at the cornerstone-laying ceremonies for the new Firemen's Hall, in Mercer Street, between Houston and Prince.

main in the United States), together with an excellent, newly arrived French pianist, Madame Cécile Peaucellier, launched an ambitious weekly series of "Public Conservatory *Soirées*" of ensemble music at Dodworth's Academy on October 10. Although open to the general public, the concerts were tied to the Conservatory of Music that the Mollenhauers and Madame Peaucellier had opened on October 2 at 141 East Ninth Street, where they gave instruction in piano, violin, cello, voice, and theory, and where fortnightly students' recitals were part of the curriculum, as were the Public Conservatory *Soirées*.

Their first program, typical of those to follow, consisted of quartets, trios, duos, and solos by Haydn, Beethoven, Mendelssohn, and contemporary composers played by the Mollenhauers and Mme. Peaucellier, with the assistance of the Philharmonic musicians George Matzka (violist), F. Allner (cellist), and Julius Siede (flutist), and a German male quartet consisting of the Herren Beutler, Adams, Urchs, and Friedeborn.

Under the heading "A New Great American Pianist," the *Tribune* (Fry) announced on October 2: "Mr. William Mason of Boston [Lowell Mason's third son], who has been six [five] years studying in Germany as a Pianist, and finally completed his labors with Listz [*sic*] . . . is now in Boston, about to give a concert. It excites—as an American event—there, in connection with music, more interest than has ever taken place, the best judges speaking of him as a first-class artist, thoroughly versed in the modern magnitudes of his instrument."[64]

Mason (1829–1908), whose European progress had been closely followed in the musical press,[65] was now, in fact, about to give not one, but two eagerly awaited concerts in Boston (October 3 and 7), both programs of which he repeated in New York at Niblo's Saloon on October 12 and 14. As in Boston, he preceded his New York concerts with an introductory private musicale, given at Niblo's Saloon on October 5 for an invited audience. An unusually dulcet William Henry Fry, who was present, wrote: "Being an American, [Mason] is entitled to extra attention, inasmuch as the first-class artists we have produced are very few, and hence there is a novelty in the idea of an apparition of one of our own nation measuring strength with the celebrities of Europe, and to every right-minded citizen an interest not to be imported."

Fry described Mason as "well-built for his profession, with abundant muscular force and power of endurance. A young man [he was then 25],[66] he has all the advantages which the impulses of youth give the artist." Reflecting his European indoctrination, Mason's short program included predominantly unfamiliar works: an unspecified

[64] Mason had been a favored native son in Boston since childhood, when he assisted his illustrious father as accompanist and general musical assistant; he was subsequently admired as a gifted soloist when, at the age of seventeen, he appeared with orchestra at the Boston Academy of Music and later at chamber-music concerts of the Harvard Musical Association at Chickering's Rooms (Howard, p. 275).

[65] Mason had studied with Ignaz Moscheles and Moritz Hauptmann (1792–1868) in Leipzig, with Alexander Dreyschock in Prague, and lastly he had been admitted into Liszt's charmed circle in Weimar. Added to his concert appearances on the Continent before returning to the United States, in 1853 he had—at the invitation of Julius Benedict—played Weber's *Concertstück* at a concert of the London Harmonic Union at Exeter Hall (*Dwight's,* September 30, 1854, pp. 203–4).

[66] Mason and Gottschalk were born in the same year.

Music Division, The New York Public Library

Young William Mason.

Rhapsody on Hungarian Airs by Liszt, the Impromptu in A-flat, op. 29 (1837) by Chopin, and a Fugue in E minor by Handel; also pieces by the contemporary composers, Willmers, Dreyschock, and the Polish composer/pianist Antoine de Kontski (1817–1899).

In all of these works, wrote Fry, Mason exhibited a command of contemporary virtuosity. "It is almost superfluous to say that Mr. Mason has overcome the present difficulties and, up to the time of Liszt, the impossibilities of the piano-forte. These melt under his fingers, so that they cease to appear wonderful. Independent of that, he plays with light and shade, making the masterly distinctions between the prominence of whatever theme and the background of its accompanying details." Mason possessed, too, a remarkably sensitive and delicate touch in quiet passages. "In a word, he is a master of the instrument in the wide signification now attached to the term."

As an encore, Mason played a piece of his own (not identified), "which shows," wrote Fry, "that he has well studied the art of piano-composition and," Fry (who did not compose for the piano) added, "he may well mix his works with those of others." With Mason's "rank being now settled," his approaching concert would surely be "crowded by his countrymen, especially ready to do him homage," suggested Fry. "It is one of the cheering prospects in art," he continued (neglecting to mention Gottschalk by name), "that within two years, two pianists of American birth have appeared and safely competed with the best of European origin." (Albeit both were products of European training and performers of European repertory.)

Despite Fry's parallel classification of Mason and Gottschalk, the contrast between them, personally and professionally, could not have been greater, nor could their New York debuts have been more radically different. Where Gottschalk's first appearance had been heralded by flamboyant puffery, Mason's was minimally advertised and thus virtually unpuffed; Gottschalk's elaborate and lengthy program had been shared by several assisting artists; Mason's consisted of nine pieces in all, four of them played by his only assisting artists, the Mollenhauers, accompanied by Timm; Gottschalk had performed, with a single exception, only his own compositions and transcriptions; Mason programed none of his own pieces. To the works he had played at his musicale, he daringly added all three movements of Beethoven's "Moonlight" Sonata, op. 27, no. 2 (1801),[67] and was thus, unlike Gottschalk, hailed as a man for the classics.

Mason's debut was most inauspiciously timed. Only the day before, the shocking news had reached the anxious city that the long-overdue transatlantic steamship *Arctic* had been sunk in a collision off Newfoundland, with the loss of many lives, among them many New Yorkers. Thus, Mason played to an auditory of small size and somber mood. He was nonetheless appreciatively received by his audience and, with one exception, by all the critics. The *Evening Post* (October 13, 1854) acclaimed him as a pioneer in the "toilsome march of American musical art" and a master of the "impossibilities of his instrument."[68] With his "firmness of outline," and "wonderful strength of wrist and finger," wrote the *Post,* "the piano thunders like a mimic orchestra," and when "delicacy of touch is wanted, he strikes the keys so lightly that it would ravish the ear of a listening fairy."

But, more than a virtuoso, Mason was a serious artist, probing far beyond mere technical dazzlement into the deepest "intention" of what he played. This he amply displayed in his performance of the Beethoven sonata, especially its first movement, which to the *Post* critic (perhaps under the pall of the *Arctic* tragedy), was the "spirit of grief embodied in musical language. The melancholy which pervades it sinks down into the very soul. It is not fitted to the concert room, demanding tears rather than applause—secret sympathy rather than any overt manifestation."

The Hungarian Rhapsody, being by Liszt, was quintessentially exotic/rhapsodic: "full of abrupt pauses, sudden transitions and singular ideas—[it was] a work of wildness, but of the wildness of genius." And because it was a work of great variety, it was ideally suited to display Mason's talents "in several different styles," and he displayed them in masterly fashion. But "could not 'Yankee Doodle' and 'Hail Columbia' (played as an encore) and that 'Carnival of Venice' [perpetrated by the Mollenhauers] *(horrisco referens)* have been spared us, at least for this once?"[69]

Richard Grant White pronounced Mason's concert to be a bold experiment in concert-giving, with its brevity and minimum of assisting artists: "It was a remarkable testimony to Mr. Mason's power to interest an audience, as well as to [his] skill." In the Liszt rhapsody, Mason had ample opportunity to display his many splendid pianistic accomplishments and indeed, the Rhapsody "produced a marked impression. But," added White, "the impression was due only to the young musician, for the composi-

[67] Probably its first complete public performance in New York.

[68] During this year the *Evening Post* seems to have acquired a knowledgeable music critic of apparently foreign origin and Romantic leanings; his identity is alas unknown to me.

[69] Had Jullien's "American Quadrille" at last cured New York audiences of their old infatuation with "Yankee Doodle"/"Hail Columbia?"

tion was very rhapsodical and, we are willing to believe, extremely Hungarian, but certainly not very melodic."[70]

But Mason's performance of the Beethoven sonata stamped him a true artist, wrote White, especially in the first movement, whose "dreamy passion-tones vibrated in the very soul of everyone present who had a soul.[71] So large and simple a style of performance is rarely heard in the concert-room in these days." White, however, disagreed with Mason's tempo in the Handel Fugue: "too fast—faster than it could possibly have been played in Handel's day, but Mr. Mason's light and even finger thridded [*sic*] the intricate mazes of this labyrinth of notes with equal celerity and certainty."[72]

In White's opinion, Dreyschock's *Zum Wintermärchen* was the "most effective" performance of the evening, and picture his dismay when, in response to the audience's demand for its repetition, Mason played instead "Yankee Doodle" coupled with "Hail Columbia." In his hands they were admittedly less vulgar than usual, "but when he wants to play 'Yankee Doodle' again we trust that he will shut himself up in a room alone and have a good time by himself. He is a man of too much merit to play such things in public" (*Courier and Enquirer,* October 13, 1854).

At Mason's second concert, his "entire change of program" embraced other (unidentified) works by Dreyschock, Willmers, Chopin, Stephen Heller, Handel, and Mason,[73] closing with Liszt's spectacular "Illustrations of *Le Prophète*."[74] "We were glad to observe a crowded attendance at Mr. William Mason's concert on Saturday evening," briefly noted the *Daily Times* (October 16, 1854). "The entertainment was very fine and merited not only the attendance, but the applause. . . . It is a little difficult to popularize entertainments that depend mainly on the piano for their attractiveness, but Mr. Mason will, we think, undoubtedly do so."

Following these two concerts, Mason, without assisting artists (*à la* Liszt), went

[70] White was apparently no more tolerant of Hungarian music in 1854 than he had been in 1850, when the fiery young violinist Reményi had introduced Hungarian airs to American audiences.

[71] Not including, it appears, the rambling, fatuous critic (Girac?) who was currently conducting a column of heavily playful criticism in the *Musical World,* titled "The Man in the Omnibus." In his numbingly wordy review (October 21, 1854, pp. 89–90) he wrote: "Mr. Mason, one must fain admit, cannot yet play classical music. [Its] feeling is far too deep, and sincere, and truthful for the spasmodic and twitching style of modern piano playing." The critic was particularly dissatisfied with Mason's handling of the eighth-note triplets in the first movement of Beethoven's "Moonlight" Sonata: "Instead of three even 8ths, we had an 8th and two 16ths . . . all the way through, jerking and twitching to the close."

[72] "He plays too fast," wrote the "Man in the Omnibus." "Mr. Mason sometimes plays faster than he can (and he *can* play fast enough for the fastest of young Americans) . . . in the [Handel] Fugue his tempo was so over-fast that a clear, transparent fugue became a jumble." After giving instructions in how to play a fugue, the critic flatly asserted that classical music was beyond Mason and suggested that he take some lessons from Timm (who had turned pages for him at the concert), or from Dr. Hodges, Scharfenberg, Wallace, or even Mrs. Wallace, all of whom had been present at his debut *(ibid.).*

[73] Probably his *Amitié pour amitié* and/or his "brilliant bravura waltz," both of which he had played in Boston (*Dwight's,* October 14, 1854, p. 13).

[74] "Compared to these," wrote the not-unbiased reviewer in the *Musical Review and Choral Advocate* (October 26, 1854, pp. 370–71) (probably Oliver Dyer, Mason's future manager), "Liszt's [Reminiscences of] *Lucia di Lammermoor,* heretofore perhaps the most difficult composition attempted in

on tour, heading first for New England—New Haven, Hartford, Springfield, Worcester, and Providence—then westward as far as Chicago. "My friend Oliver Dyer managed the tour," writes Mason in his *Memories of a Musical Life* (pp. 184–85, 187). "My brothers Daniel and Lowell were at this time booksellers and publishers in New York, under the firm name of Mason Brothers, and Mr. Dyer was connected with them in business. He was a man of action, and possessed good literary ability." As a sophisticated and resourceful newspaper man, Dyer's promotional tactics en route entertainingly reveal life on the road as it was lived in those rambunctious days. But the experience convinced Mason that, unlike the more extroverted Gottschalk, he was not destined for the touring life.

At about the same time another American returned after a long absence. The singer Isadora Clark, *née* Isadora Esprit Hansen♪ (daughter of the Philharmonic violinist and composer Edward Hansen) had last been heard in New York in 1847, when she was unkindly advised "not to give another concert." Having apparently disregarded this harsh counsel, she was returning as "a Prima Donna, late from Cuba." Appearing at Niblo's Saloon on October 24, she was assisted by a debutant Signor Giovanni Leonardi, a baritone from the Italian opera in Vienna; Henry Appy, still (or again) calling himself "Solo Violinist to the King of Holland"; Henry C. Timm, who accompanied; and the Philharmonic players Noll, Besig, Bergner, Brannes, Eltz, Boehm, and Herzog, who played Beethoven's Septet.

Madame Clark was unanimously judged to possess an uncommonly beautiful and powerful voice, miserably and idiosyncratically used. Her *Casta diva,* wrote Seymour (*Daily Times,* October 25, 1854) "was one of the funniest things we have ever heard in a concert-room. . . . Mme. Clark has not the first idea of singing Italian music, and if she would win a reputation in New York, she must avoid it." Not that she did better with "Kathleen Mavourneen," which emerged, under her treatment, as Madame Clark's song, not Crouch's. Yet, for all her faults and foibles, as the mystifying critics agreed, it was a pleasure to listen to her, especially her flawless trill.

As the long-awaited completion of the Academy of Music approached, dauntless Max Maretzek, despite the defection of his perfidious opera company at the end of the preceding year, entered into negotiations for a year's lease of the Academy, to begin in September 1854, and early in the year he departed for Europe to engage a new opera company.[75] It was not until May—after futile long-distance haggling with the high-handed Academy landlords, and after reluctantly advancing an extra payment of $6000 as security against the exorbitant year's rental of $30,000—that Maretzek received "the promise of a lease" of the Academy. But although until just about the last moment it was thought that he would open the Academy of Music, it was his rival, the noted Shakespearian-actor-turned-impresario James H. Hackett (1800–1871),[76] who inaugu-

---

public, is ease itself. But Mr. Mason's remarkable quietness of playing and absence of display make the greatest difficulties seem light to an audience."

[75] The nineteenth-century opera-impresario syndrome—veering from solvency to ruin and back again, but somehow always able to launch a new opera season—is keenly satirized, presumably by George William Curtis, in *Putnam's* (reprinted in *Dwight's,* September 23, 1854, p. 195).

[76] Particularly noted for his Falstaff.

rated the new opera house on October 2[77] with the legendary stars Grisi and Mario, whom he had brought to the United States in August, after some two years of painstaking negotiations.

This denouement was not too surprising in the light of Maretzek's disastrous 1854 summer season at Castle Garden with the indifferent company of unknown singers he had brought back from Europe in June. Upon his return, Maretzek ballyhooed his troupe of unknowns in blatantly overblown managerial terms: they had been chosen "at great expense and effort" from among the "choicest artists" in Europe—they were "the strongest company . . . entirely beyond all comparison as regards talent, that [had] ever been gathered together, either in this country or in Europe." Such a company, explained Maretzek, offered "the only effectual means of abolishing the prime cause of all operatic failures in this city—the starring system." It was his intention, he claimed, to produce opera "with a view to perfect rendition in all its parts [and] not for the gratification of the vanity or whim of any particular artist [*O despicable Salvi!*], to the sacrifice of all the other parts and the marring of the whole work. Reliance will not be placed upon a single star," asserted Maretzek, "but upon the whole company, forming, as it were, a constellation."[78] (An opera-manager's wistful dream, unrealized throughout the ages.)

Despite Maretzek's rationale for choosing an obscure cast, and despite the overlong absence of opera from New York, the opera-going public, to say nothing of the critics, reacted unfavorably to his new singers: coldly to the soprano Donna Valeria Gomez, a thin-voiced and uncharismatic *prima donna assoluta* from the *Teatro Real* in Madrid, and—despite their vocal excellence—only reservedly to the splendid baritone Francesco Graziani (1829–1901) and the tenor Pietro Neri-Baraldi (1828–1902), both from the Italian Opera in Paris.[79] Best liked among the newcomers was Giuseppina Martini d'Ormy, a tall and beautiful contralto from the Vienna Opera; Domenico Coletti and Luigi Quinto (in his Italian persona) helped to round out the meager cast.[80]

Maretzek's repertory was as unprepossessing as his company. With the exception of the often-promised American premiere of Verdi's *Luisa Miller* (or *"Louisa" Miller,* as the local papers had it) and a revival of *Maria di Rohan* (as a vehicle both for the return of Bertucca-Maretzek and the debut of Martini d'Ormy), his repertory consisted of such tired chestnuts as *Lucia di Lammermoor* (with which he opened on June 30, immediately after Jullien's departure), *La sonnambula* (July 10), *Masaniello* (July 31), *I puritani*

[77] It was reported that the lease had first been offered to Hackett, one of the Academy's original stockholders, who had declined it "not only because the rent demanded in money seemed to him more than any Opera . . . could afford," but because of his "insuperable objections to concede . . . to the stockholders for every share [some 200 in all] the *free* privilege of *an admission with a seat secured,* and the right to dispose of, and to transfer, any and all of such liberal privileges on every occasion during the whole year" (*Courier and Enquirer,* May 8, 1854). The details of the transaction, at least from Maretzek's point of view, are found in the rather bitter concluding chapter ("Postscript") of his *Crotchets and Quavers (passim)* and his *Sharps and Flats* (pp. 13–16).

[78] There were to be other innovations as well: "'Dead heads,' who have affected the profits in past seasons," announced the *Mirror* (June 16, 1854), "will find no favor now, as the rule will be inviolable to give no free admissions, save to those legitimately connected with the press."

[79] And both to attain future renown in the European opera houses.

[80] As usual, several well-known singers who were announced for the season never surfaced.

(August 11), with the flag-waving "Grand Libertà Duetto" as a special feature, and one performance of *Lucrezia Borgia* at the Maretzeks' joint benefit (August 23). The third act of Donizetti's *Torquato Tasso* (Rome 1833) received its first American hearing at Graziani's benefit (August 21).

The season was dogged by disaster. At its very outset both of the Maretzeks fell ill, and *Maria di Rohan,* scheduled for July 10, had to be replaced at the last minute by a virtually unrehearsed performance of *La sonnambula,* with the orchestra leader I. Kreutzer (incorrectly named in some papers as Keyzer) bravely standing in for Maretzek, and with Gomez, Neri-Baraldi, and Graziani struggling with the leading roles, unprepared as they were.

Maretzek was still too ill to conduct when *Maria di Rohan* was finally performed (to a small audience), on July 12. Bertucca, who had been rusticating on Staten Island for the past year, was warmly welcomed back; not only was her voice more beautiful than ever, wrote Richard Grant White, but also her arms. But critical interest centered mainly on the debut of Madame Martini d'Ormy, who appeared in the breeches role of Armando di Gondi.[81] A fine contralto of commanding presence[82] and splendid vocal and acting ability, she pleased all the critics except William Henry Fry, who was unable to review her performance objectively, having a "constitutional horror of seeing the worst of farces—that of women dressed in men's clothes—and strutting duello-like about the stage—touching sword-hilt and challenging, and so forth, all in the *harmonic* tones of the sex consecrated by nature to gentleness. Alboni, even, was a nuisance in such characters," he wrote. "In point of truth, they are not a remove above the lyrical monster of the Pope's chapel [the castrato], and could only come of a nation whose political philosophy needs regeneration." In Fry's opinion, the "feminine-man business on the stage . . . should be, if we must have them, balanced with men, bearded and bewhiskered, doing the . . . Juliets and Violas" (*Tribune,* July 13, 1854).

Bored by the "threadbare," mostly Donizettian fare that so successfully kept audiences away from Castle Garden,[83] Charles Bailey Seymour at last begged for "Verdi, Halévy, Flotow, any of the small-fry, for a change!" Now that Maretzek was back,[84] the critic hoped for a more stimulating repertory: with "the scores of several operas entirely new to the American public in his possession [Maretzek would] of course place them in rehearsal, as necessity requires." The very announcement of the first performance, on July 20, of *Luisa Miller,* albeit by Verdi, gave "the first indication of sound policy," a fresh, new direction: "Whether this opera be successful or not," wrote Seymour, "it must, and will, benefit the management" (*Daily Times,* July 18, 1854).

A doubtful prognostication. With even greater than usual disparity, the critics pronounced *Luisa Miller* to be anything from a complete failure to "the most successful opera ever produced in America." Seymour, who defended the work, referred to its

81 "A costume always disgusting on the stage, as well as off," commented the *Mirror* (July 13, 1854), apparently referring to the prevalent Bloomers; the critic nonetheless found Martini d'Ormy, with one incomparable exception (Alboni), to be "the best contralto ever heard in this country."

82 "Her inches rather dwarfed Signor Baraldi" (*Courier and Enquirer,* July 13, 1854).

83 It was a double-edged sword: "The meagerness of the attendance told upon the manner of the performance," wrote the *Evening Post,* in reviewing *La sonnambula* (July 17, 1854).

84 To everyone's delighted surprise, Maretzek unexpectedly returned to conduct the third (and last) performance of *Maria di Rohan,* on July 17.

premiere as the true beginning of the Castle Garden season—everything preceding it had been mere preparatory exercises. "*Luisa Miller,*" he wrote (*Times,* July 21, 1854), "is unlike any work by the same composer. It is the offspring of a more matured and sober judgment. The [toned down] orchestration and the choruses indicate this change more than the solos and concerted pieces—the latter retaining, notwithstanding their increased sobriety, a tone and coloring essentially Verdi-ish.[85] . . . In general, we may sum up the opera as an unqualified success."

"Verdi is welcome," wrote the not-too-satisfied *Evening Post* critic (July 21, 1854). "His fervid muse breaks pleasantly in upon the unceasing stream of Donizetti's melody," with which the musical market had been "drugged." But in his efforts to break away from the too-smooth-flowing melodies of Donizetti and Bellini, Verdi resorted to such devices as overly noisy orchestrations employing too much brass, and "remarkable and unwarranted use of the *crescendo.*" These effects, together with his "lack of melody," were the characteristics that provoked immediate censure among musicians, and in these traits *Luisa Miller* showed no improvement over Verdi's past works; in fact, an unregenerate Verdi had even added a "new trombone" to his orchestra. "Verdi is Verdi," resignedly concluded the critic, and thus "always prophetic of brass."[86]

Richard Grant White was less indulgent: "*Luisa Miller* is far from a work of genius," he wrote in the *Courier and Enquirer* (July 21, 1854).[87] "It has all Verdi's mannerisms, with little of the sensuous richness, barbaric pomp, and material strength of style which mark some of his earlier compositions. It depends for effect almost entirely upon abrupt modulation, broken rhythm, and elaborate instrumentation, which do not spring from the melodies but are painfully added to them, and of necessity, for so poor a soil could bring forth nothing. These melodies are without grace and without decided form of any kind. . . . To give them importance, the old trick of loud and pompous prolongation of the cadence into the returning melody is again resorted to, the poverty of the melody, after so much parade in its introduction, reminding the hearers of the Turkish cry: 'In the name of the Prophet—figs!'" In White's opinion: "Verdi [had] written all he had to write when he finished *Ernani* and *I Lombardi.*"

Like his colleagues, Fry did not find the melodies in *Luisa Miller* comparable with those in *Ernani.* But unlike them, Fry considered Verdi to be—since Donizetti's death—"the only man of the Italian opera who has shown originality and sustained power. It is the fashion to abuse him (as it is with certain persons to abuse everybody

[85] On the other hand, *Meerschaum,* who had replaced *Gemotice* (now on the editorial staff of the New Orleans *Picayune*) as music critic for the *Spirit of the Times,* thought the "music of the choruses very *un-Verdi-ish*" (July 29, 1854, p. 288).

[86] The *Mirror* (July 21, 1854) commiserated with the conductor of "Verdi's noisy operas, where great attention seems to be paid to the production of startling effects, oftentimes with less regard to strict musical unities and proprieties." And concluded: "While the opera of *Luisa Miller* is very pleasing, it cannot, on the whole, rank with *Ernani* or *I Lombardi.*"

[87] Directly pointing at Fry, White wrote: "We do not think, with an able and eloquent contemporary, that the mere fact that a musician or a poet has spent much time and labor in putting together thousands of words, or of notes, entitles his production to elaborate criticism. We do not measure the importance of a work by its size, or the amount of labor which has been spent upon it. We allow stupid epics to go by us by the ton, unnoticed, while we linger with loving admiration over the analysis of a song or an elegy which has touched the heart. Genius in greater and less degree alone is worthy such consideration."

who is not a century old)," Fry feelingly added. But admitting Verdi's faults, which were many, Fry found him "energetic, not diffuse—[he] seeks after new effects—and is not satisfied with mere sugar, but likes dramatic renderings, though he is called grim, for his pains."

The libretto of *Luisa Miller,*[88] however, met with Fry's intense disapproval. Adapted by Salvadore Cammarano from the famous play *Kabale und Liebe (Intrigue and Love)* (1784) by Friedrich von Schiller (1759–1805), it was, wrote Fry, an example of the inability of librettists in Italy (as well as in England) to "construct the plot of an opera or understand the necessary versification." The libretto was simply not good—not, Fry protested, that he was "finding fault." Compulsively subjective, Fry merely wished to point out the "dearth of literary genius, which to the same extent operates against the dramatic composer" (*Tribune,* July 21, 1854).

To Burkhardt, however, the libretto was a loathsome desecration of a masterpiece: "There are sins against the mighty dead," he fulminated, "outraging the feelings of the living, and which deserve more severe reproof than they ever receive." Burkhardt proceeded to correct that failing: Cammarano's libretto for *Luisa Miller,* he wrote, was a "vile, abortive mutilation of Schiller's beautiful domestic tragedy. . . . We presume it is the same unholy hand which desecrated Shakespeare's *Macbeth* and Schiller's *Robbers* to produce *I masnadieri;*[89] may a kind providence forgive him the sacrilege, we cannot. Why don't these libretto scribblers stick to 'Mother Goose Stories'. . . instead of laying sacrilegious hands upon the works of immortal genius? . . . Mozart, Weber, and Rossini wrote *Don Juan, Zauberflöte, Freischütz, Oberon,* the *Barbiere,* and other operas that will live when Verdi shall be long forgotten, upon libretti which chance, fancy, and occasion furnished them and there was no vampyrism upon the heritance of genius required by them."

Attempting to regain his composure, Burkhardt finally turned to the music, which, he wrote, was unlike anything Verdi had written in the past, with its reduction of brass instruments—something for which to be grateful, if for nothing else. But, aside from this boon, the work was "the best instrumented, the best scored, and most musician-like of his Operas. It abounds in flowing melodies, as indeed, all his Operas do, but heretofore these have been what are technically called *wide,* whilst *Luisa Miller* presents a series of *close* melodies, approximating more nearly the legitimate, classical model."

The only aspect of the production upon which the critics agreed was Maretzek's masterly grasp of the work and his brilliant conducting—authoritative, vital, and gripping. The singers were coolly received.[90] Upon the withdrawal of *Luisa Miller* after its fourth performance (played to an "array of empty benches") the *Evening Post* critic evaluated the season until now as "unfortunate: money is very tight and people are afraid of the cholera [then threatening to become a serious epidemic] and don't travel;

[88] Fry referred to a "good" English translation of the libretto by Henry C. Watson.

[89] Burkhardt's presumption was in error. Not one, but two "unholy hands" were responsible for the libretto of Verdi's *Macbeth* (Florence 1847)—Francesco Maria Piave and Andrea Maffei; it was Maffei who adapted the libretto for *I masnadieri* (London 1847) from Schiller's play *Die Räuber* (1781).

[90] With Gomez as Luisa, Martini d'Ormy as Federika, Neri-Baraldi as Rodolfo, Coletti as Count Walter, Graziani as Miller, and the German basso William Müller as Wurm, the performances were at best adjudged undistinguished.

and to depend on New Yorkers to support an opera is to lean on a broken reed.[91] There is considerable disappointment with *Luisa Miller* because it is an opera whose beauties can be found only by critical examination and study . . . it is not of a character to satisfy on one hearing and to leave an echo ringing in the ears and keep one humming as he goes home." Verdi lacked "passionate *abandon* of feeling and thrilling passion," for which he compensated by "an amount of instrumentation and fullness of orchestral accompaniment which few appreciate, but which grow upon the ear on repeated representations."

Abroad, he continued, *Luisa Miller* was fashionable, rather than popular, because its merits were "not popularly appreciable." And not acceptably familiar. Thus (despite the widespread complaints of Maretzek's hackneyed repertory), when any of the tried and true favorites—the *Sonnambula*s, the *Lucrezia*s, the *Norma*s—were produced, they were a source of easy enjoyment both to audiences and performers. "Give us what we *know,* and we will enjoy it and be glad to pay for it; but when money is two percent a month, we can't go often, and when we *do* go, we will be sure to enjoy ourselves. So much for opera as a whole." Rather, so much for critical opinion.

When Burkhardt remarked in the *Albion* (July 15, 1854, p. 331) that "the opening path of the Italian opera season of 1854 and '55 seems by no means to be a way strewn with flowers," his comment was no mere figure of speech. To add to Maretzek's woes, the city government, apparently in collaboration with the Castle Garden lessee H. R. Conklin, had chosen, as a distasteful *obbligato* to the opera season, to extend the Battery—an operation that included the annexation to the mainland of the spot of land on which Castle Garden stood.[92] As the *Evening Post* reported on June 29 (the day before the opera opened): "The river on both sides of Castle Garden is now filled in with earth and refuse matter, which send forth a most disagreeable odor at times. The entrance to Castle Garden is in a bad condition from the tearing up of the old bridge today. Tomorrow, however, we understand the passage will be entirely unobstructed to visitors to the Italian opera."

This was apparently wishful thinking, for a month later Maretzek was heavily involved in a lawsuit against the City Corporation, in consequence, according to the *Herald* (August 16, 1854), of the "stench created by the filth used to enlarge the Battery. The Corporation pleads . . . that the matter used for filling up the Battery is not filthy.[93] [But] everyone who has been to the opera can testify to the effluvia which arise from the foul matter. At times, it needs nerves of unusual strength to withstand the shock of so abominable an odor; and we are quite of the opinion that it has militated seriously against the interests of the opera."

In a masterstroke of ironic timing, by August 23 when the ill-starred season (of

[91] Besides, with the extremely hot weather, those New Yorkers most likely to attend the opera were off to the summer resorts.

[92] It was intended to raze the "old granite Castle to the ground" once the enlargement was completed (*Tribune,* September 4, 1854). Happily, after several metamorphoses, the old Castle still stands—in the mid-1990s, at least.

[93] A plea not unfamiliar in the late twentieth century.

thirty-six performances) closed with the Maretzeks' benefit,[94] it was at last proudly announced that one might walk or drive right up to the "brilliantly lighted entrance" of Castle Garden.

Only two weeks after Maretzek's inglorious departure, Castle Garden, after a hasty brush-up of its interior,[95] opened its resplendent new portal to another and far grander season of grand opera.[96] As *Meerschaum* proudly boasted in the *Spirit of the Times* (August 26, 1854, p. 336): "A few years since, anyone predicting that ere this time all the great vocal artists of Europe would submit their claims to the fiat of a New York audience would have been laughed at as a visionary enthusiast." Yet, we had already welcomed Lind—then the "quiet, but truly classic, Kate Hayes, the whole-souled and joyous Alboni . . . and the charming and highly-finished Sontag." And now we were about to receive "the greatest . . . female singer and actress, combined, of the age,[97] the world-renowned Mario to support her, and, if report speak truly . . . an orchestra, chorus, and scenery, such as we never yet have seen here. It is said the curtain will rise nightly to $3500 expenses." Indeed, after an eternity of tantalizing hints and rumors that the unrivaled opera stars Giulia Grisi (1811–1869)[98] and Mario (1810–1883) were being courted to visit the United States,[99] here they actually were, about to commence an opera season at Castle Garden on September 4 with *Lucrezia Borgia,* one of Grisi's most celebrated roles.

Meerschaum did not exaggerate. For some two decades Grisi and Mario, both pos-

[94] A Maretzekian "Grand Lyric Festival," consisting of the complete *Lucrezia Borgia* (Bertucca-Maretzek, Martini d'Ormy, Neri-Baraldi, Graziani), followed by a Grand Concert (Costanza Manzini, Bertucca-Maretzek, Martini d'Ormy), and concluding with the third act of *Luisa Miller* (Manzini, Neri-Baraldi, Graziani). After their New York season the company filled a short engagement in Philadelphia, then disbanded. Madame Martini d'Ormy remained in New York, appearing later in the year in German opera and, as we know, at the Broadway Sunday Concerts.

[95] Inadequate, according to the *Evening Post,* which complained (September 5, 1854) that after all the "promised alterations and improvements . . . the painted figures were still tripping in ceaseless round upon the painted ceiling, and the allegorical figure still blew its trumpet, while the four allegorical horses pranced upon the dingy drop scene. The scenery was the same old scenery, and the painted garden seemed to have been suffering with the long drought. Indeed, there was no perceptible change except that the corpulent and awkward pillars which group themselves so irritatingly about the front of the stage had been reduced in their dimension, and this was certainly a great improvement."

[96] "The opera in this country seems, like the fabled Hydra, to grow stronger after every fresh defeat," observed the *Evening Post (ibid.),* "and even the Hercules of poor patronage is insufficient to destroy its vitality. Mr. Maretzek has scarcely withdrawn his discomfited forces, after an ill-starred campaign, when Mr. Hackett takes the field with a stronger force."

[97] A London newspaper quoted in the *Evening Post* (June 15, 1854) saluted Grisi as "the greatest artiste, musically and vocally, that the world ever saw."

[98] Among an assortment of conflicting birth dates for Grisi, 1811 is most generally accepted.

[99] They were finally induced by Hackett's reputed payment of a staggering $95,000 for a season of sixty-three nights. As advance security, Hackett had been required to deposit $50,000 in cash with the Baring Brothers bank in London. Grisi and Mario were expected in late August on the Collins Line steamship *Baltic,* aboard which, in the best tradition, William Hall had placed a piano for their use during the voyage (*Dwight's,* July 29, 1854, p. 135). Their advent was ecstatically heralded in the press.

Robert Tuggle

Grisi and Mario, the supreme divinities of mid-nineteenth-century opera.

Music Division, The New York Public Library

sessing extraordinary physical beauty as well as matchless voices, separately and jointly reigned supreme in the European world of opera, from London to Paris to St. Petersburg. In 1831 at La Scala, a precocious twenty-year-old Grisi,[100] already well launched on her career, had sung the first Adalgisa to the first Norma of Giuditta Pasta, for whom Bellini had composed the role. (Grisi later inherited Pasta's mantle—dramatically and vocally—as the greatest Norma of her day.) A superlative actress, equally compelling in tragic and comic roles, Giulia Grisi had excelled in such diverse characters as Juliet (with her sister Giuditta as the Romeo) in Bellini's *I Capuleti ed i Montecchi;* Semiramide in Rossini's *Semiramide;* and with the other members of the legendary "quartet" consisting of the *basso* Luigi Lablache (1794–1858), the baritone, Antonio Tamburini (1800–1876), and the preeminent tenor Giovanni-Battista Rubini (1795–1854), as Elvira in *I puritani* (Paris 1835), composed for them by Bellini.[101] Later, with Mario, who replaced Rubini in the quartet in 1839, they gave the first performance of *Don Pasquale* (Paris 1843), written for them by Donizetti.

Mario (the stage name adopted by Giovanni Matteo, Cavaliere di Candia), son of an aristocratic Piedmontese general, began his career as a devastatingly handsome young army officer with an extraordinary social accomplishment—a magnificent, albeit uncultivated, tenor voice. Finding himself in dire straits as a political exile in Paris in 1836, he was persuaded by musically appreciative friends to study singing, and after some two years under the eminent tutelage of Theodore Michelot of the *Comédie Française,* Giovanni Marco Bordogni of the *Conservatoire,* and Louis-Antoine Ponchard (1787–1866) of the *Opéra-Comique*—and with an occasional extra lesson from Meyerbeer—Mario made his memorable debut at the Paris Opéra in 1838[102] in the title role of *Robert le diable* (Pearse and Hird, p. 71). During his lifetime and beyond, Mario was and is still widely regarded as the possessor of the greatest tenor voice of the nineteenth century.

The great Grisi/Mario romance seems first to have flowered in 1841, three years after Mario replaced Rubini in the quartet. It lasted the remainder of Grisi's life; Mario outlived her by fourteen years (after bravely surviving her innumerable farewells and returns to the stage).[103] Although they are reported in some sources to have been married in 1844 (or 1845), after Grisi had allegedly succeeded in freeing herself from her first husband, a rapacious Vicomte (or Monsieur) Auguste Caesar Achille Gerard de Melcy,[104] Maretzek states that because divorce was not permitted in Catholic France,

[100] Giulia Grisi was the niece of a famous singer, Josephina Grassini (1773–1850), and the sister of another, Giuditta Grisi (1805–1840); their cousin Carlotta Grisi (1819–1899) was one of the supreme ballerinas of the nineteenth century, and Carlotta's sister Ernesta was an opera singer of note.

[101] For a period they were celebrated as the "Puritani Quartet."

[102] It was then that he took the name of Mario to spare his family the disgrace of having a son on the stage.

[103] Grisi was forty-three years old when she and Mario came to the United States, following the first of her emotional "farewell forever" seasons in London. On arriving in New York, according to the *Baltic*'s manifest (August 21, 1854), she gave her age as thirty-eight; Mario gave his as forty.

[104] Grisi's marriage to de Melcy in 1836 and its lifelong consequences are omitted in Mario's biography *The Romance of a Great Singer* (London 1910), written by their daughter Cecilia Maria di Candia Pearse.

de Melcy remained her lawful husband for life. Thus he legally received a percentage of her enormous earnings and upon her death inherited her possessions, leaving Mario and their three surviving daughters virtually penniless[105] (*Sharps and Flats,* p. 16; see also Forbes, p. 31).

The Grisi/Mario arrival in New York, scheduled for Sunday, August 20, was not without incident. The Musical Fund Society, as the self-appointed official greeter of visiting musical dignitaries, probably fearful of reawakening the disastrous violence of their welcoming serenade to Sontag in 1852, decided to stick to safe ground—or rather, safe water: they would greet Grisi and Mario, as their ship approached the city, with a floating serenade performed in mid-bay, aboard a small excursion boat, the *Josephine.* From its deck the serenaders, Dodworth's Band, would appropriately "discourse in eloquent tones the exquisite airs which Grisi and Mario have rendered famous throughout the world." Only four hundred tickets were issued, "as a private and particular favor, [to] well-known musical amateurs, all the best of the musical profession, operatic ladies and gentlemen, and otherwise, the various professions—legal, literary, reportorial, and so on." The fortunate ticket-holders might board the *Josephine* at the Collins Line pier at the foot of Canal Street at 8:30 A.M. or at the Staten Island Ferry landing at the Battery at nine.[106] In the event of an unforeseen change of plan, their tickets would admit them to an alternate welcome/serenade, to take place *indoors,* it was stressed, at the St. Nicholas Hotel on Monday, August 21 (*Tribune,* August 17, 1854).

The original plan was in fact thwarted by Captain Comstock of the *Baltic,* who perversely brought in his ship ahead of schedule on Saturday afternoon,[107] sending such members of the Musical Fund Society hierarchy as could be hastily summoned scurrying to the Collins pier to extend a somewhat disheveled welcome.[108] Hackett, who had been a fellow passenger on the *Baltic,* was fortunately on hand to present them to his stars, who immediately thereafter gathered up their entourage—a secretary, a doctor, a servant, and two members of their opera company[109]—and swept off in waiting carriages to the St. Nicholas Hotel,[110] to the extempore accompaniment of cheers from some 200 to 300 chance onlookers (*Daily Times,* August 21, 1854).

The substitute welcome on Monday evening unmercifully strained the limited space of the St. Nicholas's south dining room, what with the presence of the 400 ticket-holders (representing "the *élite* and fashion of our City") together with Dod-

[105] Their union had been blessed with six daughters, of whom three had died in infancy.

[106] "Another day than Sunday would have been more appropriate for the reception," grumbled the *Mirror* (August 17, 1854).

[107] Not entirely unexpectedly: "Grisi and Mario will probably arrive today," hopefully predicted the *Courier and Enquirer* on August 19, "in good time to prevent the well-meant, though in every way objectionable, excursion to greet them in the bay tomorrow."

[108] Scherpf, Ernst, and Kyle, and among others, Brough, who might have been associated with Hackett in the Grisi/Mario enterprise.

[109] The obviously Italianized contralto (or mezzo-soprano) Elise Donovani and the basso Augustino Susini.

[110] Where Grisi and Mario occupied a palatial suite of five apartments on the first floor, fronting on Broadway and Spring Street. Its furnishings were minutely described in the *Tribune* (August 21, 1854), from its green and gold wall ornamentation to its white lace bed curtains.

worth's Full Band. After a preliminary, ear-splitting performance of Weber's "Jubilee" Overture, the guests of honor ceremonially made their appearance—Grisi, a vision of regal elegance,[111] on the arm of the flutist John Kyle, with Mario discreetly following. The awed crowd parted to permit their stately advance to the far side of the room, where, after a few "brief and suitable remarks," they were each presented with an honorary membership in the Musical Fund Society by Louis Ernst, the Society's second vice-president.[112]

"At this moment," writes Willis (*Musical World and Times,* August 26, 1854, pp. 198–99), the crowd, throwing etiquette to the winds, broke ranks and closed in "to take a fair stare at the noble lady and the very handsome man before them." "Stare," stressed Willis, was not too strong a word, for their scrutiny conveyed no warm and friendly interest that might have called forth an answering response; it was a "downright rude ogle" at crushingly close range. Willis found himself stampeded by those bent on "catching a glimpse of the noble Grisi; [and] dropped back with a painful feeling at the awkward position we saw the noble lady in." Musically, too, the welcome was an embarrassment. After the presentation of the diplomas, the Dodworth Cornet Band struck up a noisy rendition, with solos by Harvey and Allen Dodworth, of the *Giorno d'orrore*[113] from *Semiramide* (one of Grisi's most famous arias), then the full band played the "Lucrezia Borgia Quickstep" and then—perhaps a better choice—the *Casta diva,* in which Allen Dodworth particularly distinguished himself on the cornet, earning him polite compliments from Grisi.

The music, wrote Willis, intended to be performed on the deck of a steamer, "when brought into the small saloon of the St. Nicholas, made such a terrible din that the spectators experienced all the sensations of a fly imprisoned in a vigorously thumped military drum. . . . The idea of bringing a full military band, calculated to drown down the din of Broadway, into a small place . . . was, we cannot but think, in singularly bad musical taste." Had the Dodworth Band performed amid the bustle of Broadway—"surrounded with colored transparencies, the omnibuses, etc., [with] Grisi and Mario at an open window in a room of their own, the passing thousands becoming *advertised* of the fact of a serenade to Grisi and Mario, and enjoying the music—in short, a quasi-public demonstration . . . instead of a limited private one—then a good hearty cheer might have gone up (worth just $2000 worth of advertising). The music would have sounded well and been greatly enjoyed, and Grisi and Mario saved some embarrassment."

The ineptitude of this welcome set the tone for Hackett's bungling mismanagement of his great stars, earning him both public blame and the harsh criticism of the press even before his opera season opened. With an astronomical investment to make good, Hackett—disregardful of the darkening economic landscape—set his base ticket

[111] "Madame Grisi made a very neat but rich appearance. Her hair was plainly dressed, presenting no ornaments whatever. She was attired in light, straw-colored silk, with three heavily embroidered flounces of green, etc. The bodice was trimmed with embroidered frills matching the flounces. Dress, low necked, trimmed around the edge with lace. Over her shoulders hung a lace scarf. With the exception of four elegant bracelets, she wore no jewelry" (*Musical World and Times,* August 26, 1854, pp. 198–99).

[112] Where was their first vice-president, Henry C. Watson?

[113] A tactless choice of title, considering the occasion.

prices at an exorbitant $5 for center seats and $3 for those on the side. Moreover, the best tickets would be available only at auction, by which Hackett hoped to make a killing in premiums, primarily from ticket speculators.

With all due deference to the world-renowned stars, angrily protested the *Mirror* (August 30, 1854): "five-dollar tickets, in these impinging times, even for the choicest 'locality,' and to witness the greatest artistic performers the world ever saw, WILL NOT DO." In setting these prices Hackett had made a sad business mistake: "The times are hard, money is tight, and even people with plethoric purses, who are really fond of music, will look at a five-dollar note twice before exchanging it for notes of air, and especially when they know that the price *must* come down within a day or two."[114]

On September 1 about 1000 people attended the first auction at Castle Garden, mostly out of curiosity, wrote the *Mirror* (September 2, 1854). "The first ticket was knocked down to 'Coutts' for $250";[115] the adjoining pair to "Councilman Wild, the candy man" [confectioner] at a surcharge of $20 per ticket. After these exorbitant bids the premiums dropped precipitately, most of the tickets being bought up for resale, chiefly by Hall, Jollie, "Snooks," and the Metropolitan and St. Nicholas Hotels, about 2000 single seats being reportedly sold at a one-dollar premium. On opening day, September 4, Hackett, probably with tickets left on his hands, announced that a limited number of "Promenade" tickets for that evening would be available at one dollar.

With the exception of Donovani, Susini, and the tenor Carlo Fabricatore (respectively from the Italian Opera Houses of Lisbon, London and Paris, and Florence), Hackett's company was assembled from within the local colony of currently unemployed, more or less resident Italian singers: Amalia Patti-Strakosch, Signor and Signora Morra (early settlers), the tenor Luigi Perozzi,♪ the *bassi* Pietro Candi, Lorenzo Biondi,♪ Salvatore Patti♪ (formerly a tenor), and a mysteriously named "Amati Dubreuil," a basso/stage manager (apparently billed as "Amati" when he sang, "Dubreuil" when he stage-managed).[116] The chorus of thirty-six and orchestra of forty-six[117] were conducted by Luigi Arditi, just back from a prolonged opera tour with de Vries, Pico-Vietti, Coletti, Lorini, and other alumni of the Combination Opera Company of 1853.

The day after the opening, with *Lucrezia Borgia,*[118] the critics abandoned themselves to an unprecedented orgy of contradiction and perversity—disagreeing even on the size of the first-night audience: Fry reported "multitudes of people" and an enthu-

[114] As indeed it did: the day after the opera opened the ticket prices, except for the amphitheatre, were revised to a uniform $3, but still to be sold at auction.

[115] Miss "Coutts," as an English Miss Giles was known, was a familiar object of derision in Europe and now in the United States. So obsessively enamored of Mario that she haunted every one of his performances—bizarrely attired and always in a conspicuous first-row seat or a box—she followed him to the ends of the earth, from London to St. Petersburg to New York and back again (see Pearse and Hird, pp. 157–63). For this opening performance her first-row ticket was purchased by an agent who came to the auction supplied with her check for £50.

[116] Might he have been the French baritone Dubreuil♪ who had appeared with Fleury Jolly in 1849?

[117] Hackett had retained the musical agency of John Scherpf and F. Hughes to engage the chorus and orchestra, according to an advertisement in the *Daily Times* (August 1, 1854).

[118] With Grisi as Lucrezia, Mario as Gennaro, Susini as the Duke Alfonso, and Fabricatore as Rustighello—Patti-Strakosch, not Donovani, sang the Maffeo Orsini, and Amati, Candi, Perozzi, and Salvatore Patti made up the remainder of the cast.

Both: Music Division, The New York Public Library

CASTLE GARDEN

THE OPERA

FOR A SHORT SEASON ONLY,

Under the Direction of

Mr. HACKETT

FIRST APPEARANCE IN AMERICA

Of MADAME

GRISI

And SIGNOR

MARIO

The public are respectfully informed that numerous alterations and improvements are in progress by which the audience will be more comfortably seated, and have increased facilities for seeing and hearing. The seats have been newly arranged and numbered. The prices will be according to locality $5 and $3, and the choice of seats will be sold at auction.

The Company will be complete in every department. Among the members of it already engaged, are the following:

PRINCIPAL SINGERS:

SIGNORINA DONOVANI,

From the Italian Opera, Lisbon—her first appearance in America.

SIGNOR SUSINI,

Primo Basso from the Italian Opera, London and Paris—his first appearance in America.

SIGNOR FABRICATORE,

From the Italian Opera, Florence, his First Appearance in America.

Mme. PATTI-STRAKOSCH, Madame MORRA,

Signor AMATI DUBREUL, Signor CANDI,

Signor PATTI, Signor MORRA,

Sig. PAROZZI, and Sig. BIONDI

THE ORCHESTRA

Is composed of FORTY-SIX Eminent Performers.

THE CHORUS

Has been carefully selected, and numbers THIRTY-SIX WELL-TRAINED VOICES.

THE COSTUMES

New and Appropriate, have been expressly made by the Costumer of the Grand Opera, Paris.

MUSICAL DIRECTOR & CONDUCTOR.......SIGNOR ARDITI
STAGE MANAGER.......SIG. AMATI DUBREUL
PROMPTER.......MR. SALABERT
TREASURER.......MR. L. C. STUART
ASSISTANT TREASURER.......MR. W. R. DINSMORE

OPENING NIGHT

MONDAY, SEPTEMBER 4th, 1854,

Will be presented, Donizetti's Grand Tragic Opera, in Three Acts, of

LUCREZIA BORGIA

LUCREZIA.......MADAME GRISI
GENNARO.......SIGNOR MARIO
DUKE ALFONSO.......SIGNOR SUSINI
MAFFIO ORSINI.......MADAME PATTI STRAKOSCH
GUBETTA.......SIG. AMATI | RUSTIGHELLO.......SIG. FABRICATORE
PETRUCCI.......SIG. MORRA
GAZELLA.......SIG. CANDI | LIVEROTTA.......SIG. PAROZZI
VITELOZZO.......SIG. PATTI

CHORUS OF LADIES, NOBLES, MASKS AND PAGES.

Doors will be opene at half-past 6 o'clock. Performance will commence at half-past 7 o'clock.

The main walk of the Battery from Broadway has been extended and paved to the entrance of the Garden.
A carriage-way has also been made from opposite Greenwich street, in Battery place, to the Garden.
Experienced ushers will be in attendance to direct visitors to their seats.

A limited number of Promenade Tickets, not entitled to Seats, price One Dollar, will be issued on Monday, and can be had at the Music Store, 297 Broadway, and also at the Ticket Office at Castle Garden on the Evening of the Opera.

NOTICE.—The Public are respectfully cautioned against the purchase of SPURIOUS BOOKS OF THE OPERA. The only [illegible]

New-York Historical Society

siastic welcome,[119] while the *Evening Post* spoke of "several hundred unoccupied seats"[120] and diminishing enthusiasm as the evening progressed.[121] Richard Grant White, in the *Courier and Enquirer,* alluded to Grisi's voice as a mezzo-soprano of "remarkable compass and power"; Fry defined it as a "positive soprano of two octaves." White described the physical Grisi (in somewhat questionable taste) as "an eye-filling woman—a sumptuous creature who should be brought in upon a silver-gilt salver," but Wilkins more matter-of-factly reported that, due to the inescapable ravages of time, her figure had "assumed a fullness and a heaviness not quite consistent with our notions of classical grace" (although admittedly her features were still "commanding and expressive"). *Meerschaum,* who had not heard Grisi in twenty years, found her magically unchanged, still the greatest singer and actress in the world (*Spirit,* September 9, 1854, p. 360); but Willis regretted that, although "enjoying still a brilliant position" in the world of opera, she had not "found courage to withdraw in time from a career of acknowledged triumph, where she no more can shine, save by the gradually paling reflection of her most glorious past." And yet, considered "abstractly," Willis, with traditional critical ambivalence, described Grisi as still the same—"unrivaled in excellence . . . sublime, all palpitating with passion and despair (and yet as a *lady,* not as an everyday tragedy queen may give way to such emotions), she embodied the most exalted conceptions of her master Donizetti" (*Musical World,* September 9, 1854, p. 15).

There was less disagreement on the subject of Grisi's magnificent acting: "In the expression of scorn, rage, jealousy, and similar passions," wrote Dwight's anonymous new New York correspondent "she is, so far as I know, absolutely unapproachable. She can concentrate in the tip of her index finger an amount of vengeance perfectly annihilating." Her Lucrezia was "highly triumphant," dramatically speaking, but vocally she left much to be desired: "Some of her upper notes are thin, easily fatigued, and regrettingly remind us of what she has been" (*Dwight's,* September 30, 1854, p. 206).

Mario, too, was subjected to the omnipresent critical waywardness. Apparently in a state of preservation superior to Grisi's, he was pronounced by Richard Grant White (September 5) to be "in the prime of his beauty and his voice, and . . . undeniably a very pretty fellow. He gets himself up with exquisite elaboration.[122] . . . His singing is

[119] With "jocular cheers as the fair Unknown who bought the high-priced ticket was seen to enter" (*Tribune,* September 5, 1854).

[120] Unoccupied due to the auctioning of the tickets, vindictively claimed the *Mirror* (September 6, 1854): "Putting them in the hands of real or collusive speculators is unjust, and we are glad to hear that some of them got severely bitten with their first purchases—one, we hear, in the amount of $1000, and another $500."

[121] "While the plaudits with which [Grisi and Mario] were greeted on their entrance were deafening and long-continued, those which succeeded their exit were faint and hardly sufficient to call them before the curtain," claimed the *Evening Post* (September 5, 1854). But Fry reported that Grisi, with her wonderfully refined vocalism—never resorting to coarse, melodramatic exaggerations either in tone or action—established her mastery and was repeatedly and "vociferously called before the curtain and received with a storm of stamping, clapping, bravos, and waving of handkerchiefs" (*Tribune,* September 5, 1854). Richard Grant White, however, claimed that before she had sung a note, Grisi had alienated her audience by failing to remove her mask in acknowledging their applause upon her first entrance (White, *Century,* June 1882, p. 193).

[122] Mario was noted for the magnificence of his meticulously researched costumes.

of the light and graceful school. His voice, mellow and full in its lower register, is limited in the range of his upper chest tones; and he transposes, or rather, modifies, all high passages of energy; those of a graceful character he executes very prettily by use of his head voice and falsetto, over which he has obtained marvelous control. The ease with which he sings is partly due to natural advantages and partly to the excellence of his method. He gave the *Di pescatore* with a remarkable degree of grace and tenderness." Indeed, Mario was "incontestably the first singer of the world." If his voice was a shade too impassioned it was to compensate for his "inaptitude for dramatic action, which he thus replaces with a more interior emotion. . . . The more he is heard," wrote Willis, "the more he will be liked." Mario would surely win over "many of those, who have recently done him, in their hasty judgment, so much less than justice" (*Musical World,* September 9, 1854, p. 15).

Chief among these, as might be expected, was Burkhardt, who had expressed astonished disappointment upon his first hearing of Grisi and Mario. He reported Mario's voice—"beyond a few lower notes and the easy use of the falsetto"—to possess no remarkable features. "He sings well in tune, knows evidently that his fine head notes are sure to pass current and to gain him the favor of the masses, and relies, it seems, thereon alone. He enunciates the text, aye, each syllable of it, with most charming and telling distinctness. . . . And yet, in the *Di pescatore* and in the Trio, [sung mostly in half-voice] he failed to produce the favorable impression his predecessors invariably created in the same *morceaux*." Burkhardt alluded to the *Romanza* [written for Mario by Donizetti to be interpolated in this opera] as a "shilly-shally composition of the modern, *soft,* Italian school . . . by whom, we know not and care not"; it was obviously composed to show off Mario's high A (admittedly "very purely taken"), "which seemed to delight the audience and even the critics, though but a few weeks ago, the latter found great fault with Baraldi for doing precisely the same thing, and fully as well, in the *Puritani*" (*Albion,* September 9, 1854, p. 427).

Even Fry observed that Mario, although possessing a voice of superior delicacy and beauty, on this occasion was virtually inaudible. Only in Donizetti's *Romanza* did he do himself justice; otherwise he might just as well have been performing in "dumb show" (*Tribune,* September 5, 1854).

But the *Evening Post* (September 5) recognized in Mario a "tenor of a different type from those who have preceded him here. Throughout the opera he sang with a smoothness of tone and sweetness of modulation quite different from the noisy endeavors of former Gennaros; and the Lucrezia of Grisi was remarkable rather for its exquisite finish and dramatic coloring than for any noisy appeal to the audience."

New York audiences were apparently not ready for Mario's refinement: "Mario is so entirely different to every other tenor that we have ever heard that we cannot describe him by any combination of comparisons," wrote the *Home Journal* (September 23, 1854). "He neither tears his lungs to pieces, nor resorts to the many various tricks to convince his audience how hard he works. He does not make sign-posts of his arms, pound his chest, nor labor with his shoulders. His attitudes are graceful, natural, and appropriate, and the exquisite ease with which he moves across the stage contrasts curiously with the awkward strides in which most singers indulge. His voice is full, rich, fruity, and even, and possesses a sweetness of tone that enchants the senses. His *diminuendos* are often extraordinary. . . . His precision and reliability are unsurpassed; and in the tender, *piano* passages he exhibits an exquisite delicacy and sentiment we have never seen equaled."

Susini, a "splendid looking fellow," was unanimously and unconditionally acclaimed for his magnificent, sonorous bass voice, despite his tendency to sing flat. The other members of the cast, being familiar, were not commented upon. Arditi, however, was alternately stroked and slapped—as the individual critic's mood dictated.

With the critics' unexpectedly equivocal reception (especially of Grisi) and a virtually empty house at the second performance of *Lucrezia* on September 6 (despite the reduced prices), it is understandable that these great stars, accustomed to unstinting adulation at home, were ready immediately to return to Europe.[123] This was no mere rumor. After the third *Lucrezia* performance to a better house amounting purportedly to about 3000 auditors, a relieved *Tribune* dared to hope (September 9, 1854): "If the houses go on improving as they now seem to be by this last evidence, there may be no cause why Mr. Hackett should let the vocalists throw up their engagement, which they are ready to do at the end of next week if he requires it."

Citing classic show-business lore involving Barnum's mythical management of the Swedish Angel/Nightingale, the *Mirror* (September 6, 1854) none too accurately enumerated the reasons for Hackett's spectacular failure. In the first place, he should never have attempted to exceed Barnum's "democratic" ticket prices (the *Mirror*'s error, for Barnum's prices had exceeded Hackett's). With a price scale of $1 to $3, Hackett could easily have filled Castle Garden for at least a score of nights. Auctioning the tickets to speculators had only compounded the disaster.[124]

Opening night had been chaotic, continued the *Mirror:* "The passageway on the Battery was almost impassable from the rush of ticket speculators and sellers of [outrageously overpriced] opera books. . . . There was too much confusion in the seating—and many of the seats [were] miserable. Then there was such a clatter of bottles and glasses at intervals in the adjoining saloon, and shuffling of feet by attachés, that the finest passages of the opera were marred. The scene-shifting worked badly, and it was complained that not a scenic addition or improvement had been made, though much was promised." Worse, "there was the shameful nuisance of a gang of fellows (loafers, probably), with now and then a woman, [who] with vulgar stare and slang phrase, gathered between the acts around the crazy and ghostly occupant of the $250 seat.[125] If she was a pitiable object, they were disgusting."

And finally, Hackett's clumsy mishandling of the press: "We do not consider complimentary tickets a favor, by any means. They are paid for over and over again by the newspaper space [puffs] devoted to amusements. We should be glad to see the free-ticket system done away with altogether, but until it is, the tender of a free ticket to

[123] On September 6, George Templeton Strong, who did not go to hear them, noted in his private journal: "Mario and Grisi don't seem to call out any special Lindesque furor. Bad lookout for their enterprising manager."

[124] The auctions were a farce, wrote the *Musical Review and Choral Advocate* (September 14, 1854, p. 321). "We are not so foolish as to suppose that our music-dealers were simple enough to purchase thousands of dollars' worth of tickets at a premium without the privilege of returning such as should be left on their hands."

[125] Grisi and Mario habitually referred to Miss Giles, a sinister presence, as "the Skull" (Pearse and Hird, p. 158).

an editor is no compliment. . . . To send a single ticket, without seat, to an editor with a notice that he can bring a 'lady' or a 'friend' and somebody will be in waiting . . . to save him from being stopped by a perhaps rude doorkeeper is nearer an insult than a courtesy. . . . There are some ten or twelve journals in this city indispensable to amusements, and to these are attached some twenty- five or thirty persons entitled to managerial consideration."[126]

All thoughts of cutting short the opera season were abandoned with the tremendous success, both popular and critical, of Grisi's magnificent Norma, which followed on September 11. "It is not surprising," wrote Richard Grant White, "that when the Norma of Normas was to be seen and heard, Castle Garden should be thronged"; indeed, the audience (estimated at 4500)[127] far exceeded the opening-night attendance. Although White, a master of paradox, claimed that Grisi's Norma differed only in degree, not in kind, from many of the other Normas he had heard, he was nonetheless impelled to sing the praises of "her face beaming with tender joy; her breathing as gently as a child; her eyes bright with the light of youthful love," and then her spectacular metamorphosis—in a scene "as grand as wrath and scorn hurled from female lips can be—[wherein] the woman towered above her towering passion. . . . Her eye flashed [Pollione's] doom upon him; her arms waved the doom of Heaven down to him;[128] she spurned him with her voice as a man spurns with his foot a thing he loathes the most; she looked a graceful Fury." And her vocalization in this scene, wrote White, was "incomparably fine, brilliant, powerful, impetuous. . . . The notes flashed out like lightning, and when they were arrested with the same suddenness with which lightning vanishes into darkness, there was just an instant of utter silence, and then thunder shook the house. Few who saw it will forget that scene." And yet, perversely concluded White: "As a vocalist merely, we are inclined to doubt her pre-eminence even in the plenitude of her powers" (*Courier and Enquirer,* September 2; *Dwight's,* September 16, 1854, p. 187).

It was generally agreed that Susini was the best Oroveso ever heard in New York, that Donovani was a very acceptable Adalgisa,[129] but that Mario had not been in good voice, although in the *Times*'s opinion (September 12, 1854) he "displayed the power of his voice more liberally . . . than we have yet heard him."[130]

Burkhardt, true to form, announced that he had not changed his original opinion of Grisi and Mario, although Grisi was "winning upon our admiration," while Mario had "rather fallen off." He described Grisi's characterization of Norma as a magnifi-

126 Willis complained, too, about the location of his seat, which might as well have been outside on the Battery; but then, Grisi and Mario were equally out of place in the inadequate old Castle (*Musical World,* September 16, 1854, p. 27).

127 Hardly uninfluenced by the further reduction of the top ticket price to $2 and the discontinuance of the auctions. As the *Musical Review and Choral Advocate* prematurely observed (September 14, 1854, p. 321), the management seemed to have regained its reason.

128 "We do not know anything to which to liken it, except Mrs. Siddons's Lady Macbeth," rhapsodized the *Mirror* (September 16, 1854).

129 The cast was rounded out with Angiolina Morra as Clotilda and Salvatore Patti as Flavio, a tenor role.

130 Pollione was a role not congenial to Mario (probably because of Grisi's punishing ferocity); he avoided it whenever possible. But in the absence of an appropriate substitute tenor, he was performing it in New York to allow Grisi to display her most famous role.

Both: New-York Historical Society

"Who that has seen Grisi will ever forget her?" wrote the French critic, Jules Janin. "The bust, superb neck and shoulders, and the Juno-like head that sits so perfectly and proudly upon them." And her beautiful arms, "the lost arms of the Venus de Milo."

CASTLE GARDEN

THE OPERA

FOURTH APPEARANCE in AMERICA

Of MADAME

GRISI

And SIGNOR

MARIO

FIRST NIGHT OF

NORMA

Monday Evening, September 11th,

Will be presented, for the first time, Bellini's Grand Tragic Opera,

NORMA

NORMA.......MADAME GRISI
POLLIONE.......SIGNOR MARIO
Adalgisi.......Signorina Donovani
Her first appearance in America.
Oroveso.......Signor Susini
Clotilda.......Signora Morra
Flavio.......Signor Patti

Doors will be opened at half-past 6 o'clock. Performance will commence at half-past 7 o'clock.

Seats may be secured at $3 each, and a limited number of Promenade Tickets, at $1 each, may be obtained from 9 o'clock A. M., to 4 P. M., daily, at the office of the Treasurer,
Berry & Gordon's Music Store, 297 Broadway.
Also, at W. Hall & Son's Music Store, 239 Broadway; S. Jollie's 300 Broadway; H. Waters, 333 Broadway; VanOrden & King's, 45 Wall-st. Tickets can also be had at the Ticket Offices, Castle Garden, in the evening

NOTICE.

Promenade Tickets not admitted until quarter-past 7 o'clock.

cent, unforgettable, superlative achievement, but that her vocalization of the role was inferior to many Normas who had preceded her in New York. Mario had sung with increased vigor (doubtless having heeded "strictures generally made by intelligent critics" upon his rather bland earlier performances). Susini was superb. "Miss Donovan"[131] was timid and ill at ease—why had not Amalia Patti-Strakosch been cast as Adalgisa? The chorus and orchestra were only fair,[132] the scenery inferior, and "the dresses of the Druids were remarkable for unwonted and unwanted richness and utter disregard for propriety. Druidical simplicity was sacrificed for a blaze of red and gold" (*Albion,* September 16, 1854, p. 439).

The great success of *Norma,* attracting six large houses through September 22, was, if possible, surpassed by the sensational response to *I puritani,* which followed on September 25. "From first to last it was an artistic triumph such as we have never before witnessed and scarcely hope to see exceeded," reported an overwhelmed Seymour in the *Daily Times* (September 26, 1854). "It is difficult to speak of Madame Grisi's Elvira in suitable terms." Not only had she surpassed herself dramatically in this role, but "in every musical respect Madame Grisi *must* sing the music of this fine part as superbly now as when it was written for her [nineteen years earlier]. We cannot realize the possibility of her ever having been better." Even Burkhardt, after a few reflexive quibbles, was forced to concede that her singing of the *Vien, diletto,* with its "delicious" contrasts of half- and full-voice, ending with a "*trillo* on high G and then taking the C above," stamped her as "the first of living *prime donne*" (*Albion,* September 30, 1854, p. 464).

As Arturo, Mario, who until now had seemed rather "blasé," displayed a new enthusiasm, and as a consequence he sang "divinely," wrote Seymour (*Daily Times,* September 26, 1854). But Richard Grant White was disappointed, despite Mario's tenderness and delicacy in the *A te o cara,* with his "disjointed phrasing" and lack of "sustained, flowing *cantabile* and that exquisite utterance of passion and sentiment" that lived in "our mind," and that "we" had fully expected to hear from the "first tenor of the day." Then, too, the third-act "Romance," otherwise unimpeachably sung, was disfigured by a "falsetto passage which should not have been sung at all."[133] Besides, White (vying with Mario as an expert on period costume) claimed that Mario's wardrobe and hairdo in this role were anachronistic (*Courier and Enquirer,* September 26, 1854).[134]

[131] Fry referred to her as an "Irish lady, nonsensically called, Italian-fashion, Donovani, as if anybody cared a fig where she was born, if she knows her business" (*Tribune,* September 12, 1854). (Apparently, to Fry, singers' birthplaces were of less importance than composers'.) The *Musical Review and Choral Advocate* (September 14, 1854, p. 323) observed that Donovani had a good mezzo-soprano voice and sang well, but that her gaunt appearance was much against her, and suggested that "an Italian diet would have done more for her than an Italian name."

[132] Willis (in the *Musical World,* September 16, 1854, p. 27) took exception to Fry's praise of Arditi's "admirable" conducting (in the *Tribune,* September 12). "In the course of our whole experience," wrote Willis, "we never heard an orchestra worse conducted. . . . So, dear Fry, we are at loggerheads again."

[133] The *Evening Post* critic (September 26, 1854) complained, too, of "the equivocal taste which prompts Mario to the frequent use of his falsetto in the third act."

[134] And the *Evening Post* (September 26, 1854) echoed everyone's dissatisfaction with the Riccardo, a newly engaged baritone, Francesco Cuturi (recently heard in Boston), whose "sad blundering . . . succeeded in marring the effect of the 'liberty' duo."

The second performance of *I puritani* drew an audience unequaled at Castle Garden since the days of Jenny Lind, reported the *Mirror* (September 28, 1854), "and we do not hesitate to pronounce the singing and acting of Grisi and Mario the finest exhibition we have seen upon the lyric stage." As a momentarily mellowed Burkhardt explained (*Albion,* September 30, 1854, p. 464): "New York audiences have their priorities; and if this artist-pair had originally understood them, some mortifications might easily have been spared them and their management." They had mistakenly offered an overabundance of refinement and *mezza-voce:* "We want pith, bone, roundness, marrow, and power in our vocalists *first;* delicate *nuances* and artistic niceties are never appreciated here until *after* the above primary requisites have been made apparent."

With their third triumphant performance of *I puritani* (September 30), Grisi and Mario took their leave of Castle Garden. Two days later, on October 2, they opened the new Academy of Music with a performance of *Norma,* and Castle Garden's glorious opera career became history.[135]

Not that the loss of Castle Garden was mourned by the public: New York operagoers had had their fill of its discomforts, its inadequacies, and its inaccessibility;[136] it

[135] Except for a short, inglorious season of "horse opera." But plans to raze the building were abandoned, and within the year Castle Garden became an immigration depot (remaining so until 1889), where untold hordes of incipient citizens took their first steps on American soil.

[136] "The public rejoice in leaving the unsightly pillars, uncomfortable seats, faded and miserable scenery, and cheerless house" (*Mirror,* September 30, 1854).

Music Division, The New York Public Library

Castle Garden, scene of past musical glories.

had never been intended for a music auditorium in the first place. Public expectation was now focused on the Academy of Music, an imposing brick edifice occupying some 25,000 square feet on 14th Street at Irving Place (Union Square);[137] its step-by-step progress had been closely monitored in the press throughout the past year. Boastfully puffed as the largest, most magnificent, most up-to-date opera house in the world, upon its opening the building proved on the whole disappointing, both to opera-goers and the press. In the first place, the music journalists unanimously declared the name "Academy of Music" to be a transparent deception on the part of the structure's Upper Ten builders and developers, a ruse to satisfy the legislature's directive, in granting them a charter, that they build a music center with facilities for both performance and instruction. No effort had been made to fulfill the latter part of this obligation; not only had the expected school, or academy, not materialized, but it never would. To call the new opera house an "Academy of Music," was, as William Henry Fry angrily protested and as his colleagues agreed, a "misnomer and a fraud" (*Tribune,* October 2, 1854).

A parallel disregard of architectural ethic had governed the interior design of the "Academy." Although the acoustics were splendid, as everyone concurred, the resident German architect, Alexander Saeltzer, had neglected to provide a view of the stage to a great part of the audience. With some 4600 seats unmercifully squeezed "corset-like" (presumably at the landlords' behest) into an insufficient, horseshoe-shaped space, too narrow for its length and culminating in a still narrower stage, only the occupants of dead-center seats could see the performance;[138] for the others it was a purely aural experience.[139] Worse, as a display-case for magnificent sartorial confections and dazzling jewels (after all, the essential function of an opera house to its Upper Ten constituents), the Academy was a disappointing loss.[140]

In order to crowd as many seats as possible into the available space, the center aisle in the parquet had been sacrificed, causing access to seats in that part of the house to be something of a trial, especially to ladies sporting the currently fashionable, space-consuming crinolines. The first tier of boxes encircled the parquet; three additional

[137] George William Curtis thought it about a mile too far uptown, but, he wrote, "this is a fault soon remedied by New York progress" (*Putnam's,* November 1854, p. 568).

[138] "By a singular error of judgment, the sides contract toward the stage instead of projecting outward, and the consequence is that there is not a single side seat in any of the tiers from which the stage can be seen" (*Herald,* October 3, 1854).

[139] Noting rows of empty side seats at the second performance (again *Lucrezia Borgia*), the *Evening Post* (October 5, 1854) indignantly wrote: "And why not? They were never intended to be filled—if you sit in them it is a physical impossibility to see anything of the stage—it is folly to expect that the architect contrived them for any such purpose. . . . They were not, and they never will be, occupied, so long as the building continues in its present form."

[140] In his *Treatise on Acoustics in Connection with Ventilation,* published in 1872, Saeltzer recalled a far different theatre: "In the old Academy of Music," he wrote, "the galleries descended 8 feet deep from the middle, opposite the stage towards the proscenium. This mode of construction allows better sight and more seats are gained; another advantage is, the sound reaches directly in every spot without interruption, and it gives an increased perspective effect, which adds to the splendor of the building, and, in fact, transforms the theatre to a most cozy place. This arrangement should never be neglected, especially for opera houses, where most of the visitors desire to be seen in their most costly attires, as well as to see" (p. 19). For Saeltzer's further comments on the Academy of Music, see APPENDIX 4.

Both: New-York Historical Society

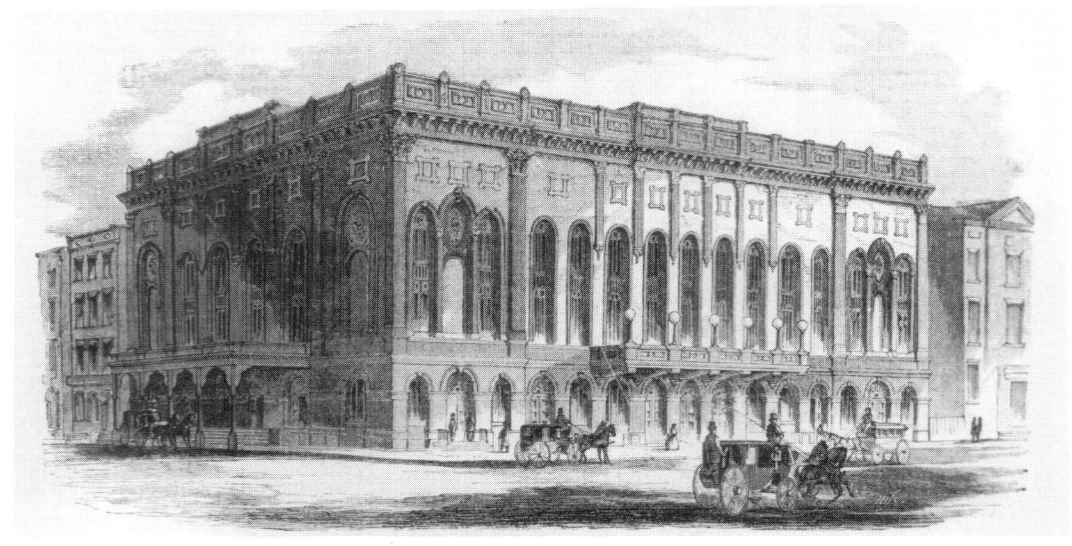

The first New York Academy of Music.

tiers rose above it, two of boxes and the topmost being the cramped amphitheatre; there were also twelve proscenium boxes.[141]

The Academy abounded in architectural innovations: the seats, upholstered in crimson plush, were equipped with a new-fangled mechanism that caused them automatically to spring upright when not occupied; an advanced air-conditioning system, with apertures for expelling exhausted air, boasted a device for circulating currents of fresh air through registers similar to those used in heating. Fire precautions included four great reservoirs of water stored on the roof, each holding 1500 to 2000 gallons, and each connected to a kind of sprinkler system consisting of perforated pipes capable of flooding (or at least spraying) the interior of the house and the stage.[142] Flashy, illumination was provided by 400 gas chandeliers, supplemented by 500 additional lights placed around the edge of the massive dome, ornately decorated by Mario Bragaldi.

The greatly admired drop curtain and sets for six operas were painted by the gifted resident Italian artist Joseph Allegri (a former pupil of Daguerre), who also designed the stage machinery.[143] The Academy's interior flaunted as well a full complement of sculptured plaster cherubs playing a variety of musical instruments and, most spectacularly, a row of massive, poorly illuminated caryatides holding up the second tier of boxes. In addition to the "absurd" caryatides, George W. Curtis acidly commented on the theatre's other decorative accouterments: its "needless brackets . . . its fluted pilasters with capitals larger than their shafts, ponderous pillars which support nothing; its dome, which has no supports; its super-gaseous brilliancy in some parts and its cavernous gloom where light and brilliancy are most needed." The flat, white-and-gold color scheme was generally found to be cold and "chalky," and it was widely thought that the judicious application of a little subdued color would be a great improvement (*Putnam's,* November 1854, pp. 567–68).[144]

With *Norma*—hardly a novelty—as its opening attraction, the Academy's first-night reviews were chiefly devoted to pro-and-con evaluations of the new house and to lamentations over the poor attendance, the latter being credited entirely to Hackett's excessive ticket prices. "Never before was an opera house opened more inauspiciously," wrote the *Evening Post* (October 5, 1854). "There were whole banks of vacant seats, and in the second tier, where there should have been six or seven hundred auditors, there were only thirty or forty. The lower circles told the same tale of vacancy, and the amphitheatre was the only portion of the house which was well filled."[145]

[141] Parquet and single box seats in the various tiers were a uniform $3; private boxes, according to location, $12 to $40 each; amphitheatre seats were 50 cents.

[142] The Academy would nonetheless burn down in 1866, to remain *hors de combat* for a year, while it was being rebuilt.

[143] As the first season progressed, Allegri's beautiful stage sets received the kind of ovations usually reserved for great singing stars.

[144] In Curtis's opinion, the Academy's interior was "the greatest glorification of gew-gaw that we have ever seen in the New World." Burkhardt, who thought the showy interior appointments magnificent, nonetheless called them "a superb hodgepodge, a splendid botch" (*Albion,* October 7, 1854, pp. 475–46).

[145] The *Herald* (October 3, 1854), on the contrary, reported an unprecedentedly dazzling representation of the "fashionable world" in the well-filled parquet and first tier of boxes; but Richard Grant White noted that the audience was "neither very large nor very brilliant" (*Courier and Enquirer,* October 3, 1854).

Scant attention was devoted to the performance itself: the Grisi/Mario *Norma* had already been exhaustively discussed, and there was little more to be said about it.

With bankruptcy staring him in the face, Hackett immediately slashed his ticket prices to a more accessible $2 for seats in the parquet and first circle of boxes, with $1 extra for reserved seats.[146] Even so, the attendance at the following performance—*Lucrezia Borgia* on October 4—was, except for the $1 seats and the amphitheatre, pitifully small.[147]

Norma was repeated on October 6; and on October 9, *I puritani* was presented with a new baritone, Oswald Bernardi—better than Cuturi, but by no means another Badiali. At this point *Meerschaum,* out of patience with the repetitive repertory, wrote: "We think Mr. Hackett will do well to produce one or two novelties, as the three operas to which the talents of the troupe have been till now confined begin to pall on the ears of all frequenters of the opera" (*Spirit,* October 14, 1854, p. 420).

The *Evening Post* (October 7), too, had grown bored with the limited repertory, arguing, after the *Norma* on October 6: "If we are to have nothing but Bellini and Donizetti, let us at least have some variety of their composition. Neither the genius of Grisi and Mario, nor the resources of the new Opera House, are confined to three operas, and we all remember the glowing accounts which came to us from England of her success in *La favorita,* an opera which has always been successful in this country."

To silence these complaints, on October 16, Hackett presented his stars in *La sonnambula,* in the critics' opinion an ill-considered and patronizing choice. As the affronted *Evening Post* (October 17, 1854) complained: "We were somewhat surprised . . . that the manager should have concluded to bring forward [an opera] so trite in the ears of the people as this" (although it had attracted a "fuller house than any previous one of the season"). It was disappointing, too, for although Mario had "but little to do in this opera . . . he left that little undone last evening through sickness. At the conclusion of the first act an apology was made, and Mario went through the remainder of his part in pantomime."

It was, besides, a most inappropriate choice of role for Grisi: "She did not look the part," wrote Wilkins (*Herald,* October 17, 1854). "For once, the beautiful Grisi, the queen of so many hearts, was positively unpleasing to behold. To say that she could not play the Amina of the first act is merely to say that she is Giulia Grisi," a superb tragedienne and not a portrayer of simple, country lasses.[148] She did not measure up to Alboni or Sontag as the naive, girlish Amina, nor did she compare favorably with Louisa Pyne, who was currently creating a sensation in the role (in English) at the Broadway Theatre (discussed below).

To compound the general disaster, Mario continued to be ill, and a humiliated

[146] Seats in the other tiers were $1; in the private and proscenium boxes, from $6 a ticket to $30 for the entire box; amphitheatre tickets were still fifty cents. In answer to complaints about Hackett's high prices, Fry reminded his readers that $2 had been paid for tickets to Garcia's operas nearly thirty years before, when "one dollar went as far as two do now" (*Tribune,* October 6, 1854).

[147] Little comment was expended on this performance, except generally adverse criticism of Donovani, the Maffio Orsini, for her painful timidity in wearing masculine attire.

[148] Grisi was "immensely great as Norma, Semiramis, and even Elvira [in *I puritani*], although at that time she had passed the period of youthful freshness," writes Maretzek, "but she was never fitted for such parts as Lucia, Amina, and Rosina" (*Sharps and Flats,* p. 16).

Both: Girvice Archer, Jr.

Grisi and Mario, still regal in later life.

Grisi was forced to sing a following *Sonnambula* (on October 18), as well as *Norma* (on October 21) with the second-rate tenor, Fabricatore.

With Mario showing no signs of immediate recovery, it became necessary to cancel the few remaining performances of the ill-starred first season at the Academy of Music.[149] After a hiatus of about a week, on October 30, Hackett inaugurated a new season of twelve performances (still lacking Mario) with a presentation of Rossini's *Semiramide,* another of Grisi's most celebrated roles.[150] The production, despite a few anachronisms,[151] was almost unanimously judged to be the most sumptuous opera

[149] During this interval several additional gas burners were installed in the Academy under the galleries, dispelling some of the gloom in which the back seats had been buried (*Daily Times,* October 31, 1854).

[150] The cast consisted additionally of Donovani as Arsace, Bernardi as Assur, Fabricatore as Idreno, and Susini as Oroe. Special features of the elaborate production were a *pas de deux* danced by Señorita Soto and the American dancer George Washington Smith (*c.* 1820–1899), and the onstage appearance of Noll's Seventh Regiment Band.

[151] Among them Allegri's nineteenth-century Italianate villa, a style of architecture, it was pointed out, not familiar to the ancient Assyrians, and "*La Sicilienne,* danced *en costume* . . . 4000 years

production ever seen in the United States.[152] Only the *Evening Post* (October 31) thought it crude. Grisi, "every inch a queen," exceeded all expectations; Donovani, again embarrassed to be seen in male attire, was either excellent or unsatisfactory; Susini, too, was variously reported to be either magnificent or out of tune.

After a second performance of *Semiramide* (November 3), on November 6, Hackett suddenly announced another suspension of the opera season, even canceling the third performance of *Semiramide,* scheduled for that very evening. He ascribed this further cancellation to Mario's continued illness, but knowing hints were dropped in the various papers that Hackett was having difficulties with his landlords (doubtless over rent money, or its lack).

By the time the opera reopened, on November 14, it was announced that a committee of the Academy's stockholders had taken over its management from Hackett. A judicious decision, editorialized the *Herald* (November 14, 1854): "It is, we presume, no longer a secret that the 'season' which closed a few nights since with *Semiramide* was in most respects a complete failure." If Mario had not been ill, some other excuse would have been found to close the operation. The *Herald* delicately forbore to discuss the reasons for Hackett's ouster—it was no secret in any case, "nor were warnings wanting to guard the manager against the consequences of the errors that were being made."

But with the shift in the Academy administration, the *Herald* (presumably Wilkins) began to harbor misgivings that New York would be ridiculed for its capricious reception of such world-renowned artists as Grisi and Mario: "It is right, therefore, that it should be known that both these eminent artists *have* been appreciated in New York. . . . The failure of the operation—as a speculation—was in spite of them." The writer heaped mountains of retrospective blame upon Hackett: "Had there been no dealing in clap-trap and humbug before their performances began; had the price of admission been more reasonable and better suited to the times; had the management been prepared with music [scores and parts], so as not to be reduced to playing one very hackneyed opera, in which Mario appeared *contre-coeur—Norma,* nine times—two others *Puritani* and *Sonnambula,* which contained no parts adapted to Madame Grisi, five or six—and a fourth, *Lucrezia,* which, with the exception of the parts of Lucrezia herself and Orsini, we had seen better played before, about as often; in fine, had the impresario displayed as much judgment as any of his predecessors, he would undoubtedly have reaped a handsome harvest.[153] Scores of people have not heard Grisi

before the Christian era," to say nothing of Noll's "musicians in green-and-gold-rimmed spectacles in the Babylonian Horse-Guard Band" (*Albion,* November 4, 1854, p. 523). (Which goes to prove that chronological dislocation is not the sole province of twentieth-century opera directors.)

152 "One only thing seemed wanting to give completeness to the opera—Miss Coutts was not there! For Mario sang not: and where Mario is not, Miss Coutts, alas, is equally not!" (*Musical World,* November 4, 1854, p. 114).

153 More sympathetic to Hackett, the *Musical Review and Choral Advocate* (November 23, 1854, p. 402) wondered if anyone realized the extent of the outrageous rent demands at the "improperly so called" Academy of Music. "Counting the actual rent and the free admissions at their market value, it will be no less than $78,000 per annum." The stockholders, receiving some 240 free admissions for each of about 100 performances in a year, would each annually receive about $200 on his $1000 investment, to say nothing of his share of the $30,000 rent. No wonder Hackett could not succeed!

because whenever they had arranged to go, they found she was playing *Norma,* which they had heard some dozens of times before.[154] Others have been once, and seeing her in a part so utterly unsuited to her as Amina, have never cared to return."

Hoping to encourage attendance, the new management engaged the great public favorite Cesare Badiali, recently returned from his tour of Mexico with the ill-fated Sontag. With Grisi, Mario, and Susini, he was announced to appear (November 14) in *I puritani,* the opening opera of their new season. But fate again intervened: at the last moment Mario discovered that he was still unable to sing, and thus, only the first two acts of *I puritani* were given, followed by the second act of *Semiramide.* A large attendance was reported, and despite Mario's absence, the evening was a great success, what with three renderings by Badiali and Susini (without the "clap-trap" flag-waving) of the *Suoni la tromba* being demanded by the audience before the performance was permitted to continue.

Mario at last returned to the cast on November 17, when *Il barbiere di Siviglia* was triumphantly presented to an audience estimated at 4000.[155] According to the now benign critical consensus, although Mario sang the role almost entirely in *mezza-voce,* it was a marvelous performance. He was the perfect Almaviva—the ideal gentleman—elegant, graceful, and urbane. Grisi astounded everybody with her deliciously droll characterization of Rosina, revealing as great a gift for light comedy as for her most searingly tragic roles.[156] Susini, too, as Dr. Bartolo, exhibited unexpected comedic gifts, and Badiali as Figaro was perfection itself. The orchestra, under Arditi, played admirably—for once it was "quite pleasant to be relieved from the clangor of the kettledrums and trombones, those satellites of the tragic muse" (*Evening Post,* November 18, 1854). Only Amati was chided for his "pointless" performance as Don Basilio.

On November 23, with Mario still enjoying good health, the complete *I puritani* was at last heard, and on November 24 at one P.M., a highly successful matinée performance of *Il barbiere,* "to accommodate ladies and children, invalids, who cannot go out in the evenings, and persons residing in the vicinity of the city." *Lucrezia Borgia,* with an unembarrassed new Maffio Orsini, Carolina Vietti-Vertiprach, followed on the evening of November 25, a Saturday, to a "thin" house.[157] On November 27 another

[154] Novelty was clearly of the essence, agreed the *Evening Post* (November 13, 1854): "The large houses which attended the production of *Semiramide,* and the small ones which gathered to the representations of *Norma,* sufficiently indicate the popular demand for novelty. The managers can hardly fail to profit by the lesson which their audiences have so plainly read to them." But they had been failing to learn that lesson ever since it was first taught them by Garcia in the 1820s.

[155] The *Albion* (December 2, 1854, p. 572) reported, however, that "the *Barbiere,* in everything but attendance, was a decided triumph."

[156] "It is a remarkable fact," wrote the *Mirror* (November 28, 1854), "that this wonderful woman, who has now appeared thirty-one nights in New York, in all sorts of weather, has not once disappointed the public, nor asked an apology on her behalf; and this, too, at times when the weight of the opera has rested upon her own fair shoulders." By the end of December, when the engagement ended, Grisi, a disciplined professional, had chalked up forty-five consecutive performances without a single break.

[157] "Saturday appears to be completely tabooed by opera-goers," extenuated the *Daily Times* (November 27, 1854). "We have no recollection of ever having seen a good attendance on that night."

composite bill was presented, again the first and second acts of *I puritani,* with Bernardi substituting for Badiali, who was ill (and with the objectionable flags reinstated in the *Suoni la tromba*), this time followed by the finale of *Lucia di Lammermoor,* unforgettably performed "in its greatest dramatic purity" by Mario.

"A monkey's body tied to a fish's tail does not form a mermaid," philosophized Fry,[158] "and the half of one opera tied to the third of another does not, on the same principle, constitute a complete musical entertainment." It was an emotional jolt, he wrote—after being immersed in "puritanic, insane, and heroic antecedents" and being denied the proper resolution of a finale—to be catapulted into "a new circle of grief—griefs at their climacteric, but without having been worked up into the proper state of sympathy."

But not entirely unprepared, for even before Mario made his woe-enshrouded entrance as the bereaved Edgardo, the audience—Fry included—were transported to a different world when the curtain rose upon Allegri's lyrical set. It was, wrote Fry, "the finest yet represented on the American stage. . . . Such a sky, moon, stars—so aerial, and bright, solemn, distant, and infinite looking; and such a mournfully beating sea; and such dark, stern, monastic architecture hurled in the foreground—as man's grand epic, when night and shadows blacken nature and art; this was the artist's triumph." Upon the rise of the curtain, there were loud and long cries for Allegri, but he did not appear. Instead Mario came on "in the plenitude of weeds and woe, and detailed his griefs in a manner more vivid than the reading Jeremiah, and wept in song in such a manner as no speaking voice can approach. . . . Having thrown his auditors into an artistic melancholy, the scene closed. But how much is also due to the composer? Poor Donizetti! If he had never written anything but this act, he would be as immortal as Homer" (*Tribune,* November 28, 1854).

With Hackett evidently in arrears for rent, a "final series" of twelve nights was announced by the Academy stockholders' committee, to begin under their management on December 1; but the opening opera, a loudly heralded superproduction of *La favorita,* encompassing the "entire strength of the company, with a magnificence of *mise-en-scène* and costume never before attempted in this city," had to be postponed to December 4 because of Badiali's continued illness. Instead, Grisi and Mario appeared in an "immensely spirited" performance of *La sonnambula,* and this time the regenerate critics pronounced Grisi's Amina to be "perfectly delicious"—indeed "among the finest displays she has yet given." Mario's Elvino, too, was imbued with "sentiment and fire," although in Fry's opinion his performance "lacked the intensity of Salvi's." Together, in the opera's finale, they created a positive "furore" (*Daily Times,* December 2; *Tribune,* December 4, 1854).

The promised extravagant production of *La favorita* came off on December 4, according to most reports, to the "largest and most brilliant audience ever gathered within the walls of a New York theatre."[159] Yet, how great the shock when, despite

[158] A caustic reference to Barnum's earlier Mermaid exploit.

[159] But, according to the *Evening Post* (December 5, 1854): "To judge from the thinness of the house last evening, there will be many . . . who will live to regret that they did not hear Grisi, Mario, Badiali, and Susini sing together in one of the finest of operas at one of the finest of opera houses."

the superlatives showered upon the production and its performers,[160] the "Committee of Management" chose this occasion to announce that the just-begun opera season would terminate after only three more performances—two repeats of *La favorita* and, for the committee's benefit, a final performance of *Semiramide* on December 11.[161]

In a maze of conflicting explanations and accusations, the papers ascribed this startling turn of events to thin houses, heedless overextravagances on the parts of the unprofessional managers,[162] the futility of attempting to meet the huge basic expenses of opera-giving,[163] even with large audiences, the repetitive repertory, but chiefly, the lack of support from both an indifferent public and a carping press.

"We have one word for our contemporaries of the press," evangelized the *Mirror* (December 9, 1854): "Gentlemen: the opera needs your support. You have not done it justice." The newspapers had often dismissed the opera with a mere line, preferring to fill their pages with "reports of 'nasty divorce cases'" and such trash. "Men and women, too," thundered the *Mirror,* "had better go to the opera and bathe their hearts in music than to go to soul- and body-suffocating parties only to gossip nonsense, guzzle champagne, and gobble oyster salads—dancing all night till broad daylight, and going home with a headache in the morning."[164] The *Mirror* caviled, too, at the misguided concept of giving a benefit performance for a group of millionaires who did not need it, but the *Tribune* (December 11, 1854) defended the committee's right to receive this tribute of appreciation for their "liberality in assuming the Opera direction."

Just as all seemed lost, Hackett suddenly rematerialized and announced a new season, or rather a continuation of the present one, to begin under his "sole direction," on December 13, with a repetition of *Semiramide*. Immediately, the whimsical press struck up a hymn of praise for "individual enterprize" in general and Hackett in particular. They urged the public to support the opera for brave Mr. Hackett's sake; it was he, after all, who had brought Grisi and Mario to America, and for this boon he deserved our undying gratitude.

160 Except by *Meerschaum,* who pronounced *La favorita* "the poorest of the popular Italian operas now having possession of the stage" (*Spirit,* December 9, 1854, p. 516).

161 With Carolina Vietti-Vertiprach (mistakenly referred to in the *Albion* (December 16, 1854, p. 595) as Rosina Pico-Vietti) replacing the unsatisfactory Donovani as Arsace, and with a gorgeously attired Mario in the minor role of Idreno.

162 They could have reduced their expenses in the *Favorita* by doing away with the four balletic Rousset sisters, who with their irrelevant, unmercifully prolonged solos and ensembles, added nothing to the occasion but boredom. What with their interminable dances, the opera's four long acts, of intrinsically feeble dramatic interest, and its three long intermissions, amounting in all to a wasted hour-and-a-half, it was midnight before the final curtain was lowered (*Daily Times,* December 5, 1854).

163 Chiefly the purported payment of nearly $4000 a week to Grisi and Mario. This sum may or may not have been included in the reported nightly expenses, now assessed at about $3000.

164 To induce attendance, other papers threatened their readers with self-reproachful old age for having heedlessly ignored this once-in-a-lifetime opportunity to hear these great artists. Although times were hard, wrote Fry (*Tribune,* December 4, 1854), with businesses and banks failing on every side and money hard to come by, people who really cared about music should remember that "a lifetime may pass before they may have an opportunity to hear again such perfect operatic representations"; Fry adjured his readers to "retrench in some other expenditure to find means to prolong to the utmost limit the stay of this company."

On December 15, however, further conflict arose when Mr. William H. Paine, a wealthy music patron and a principal member of the Academy stockholders' committee of management, surprisingly announced (in the *Tribune*) that, contrary to Hackett's claim, he (Paine) was the opera's sole manager. In the jumble of claims and counterclaims that pervaded this final season, it was believed by some that Hackett and Paine collaborated in the venture, with Paine presumably supplying the funds.[165]

As for the performances, it was business as usual: large or small audiences were reported, as were unceasing reminders that the opera would positively close on December 29 and that this was the last chance to hear these glorious artists, and how could one ever forgive oneself if one had missed them.

At the *Semiramide* performance on December 13, Fabricatore substituted for Mario, who was again suddenly indisposed; at the *Norma* performance on December 15,[166] Domenico Lorini, "four years absent from the New York stage," replaced Mario. *Il barbiere di Siviglia* followed on December 18, with Mario, and on December 20, *La favorita*. On December 22 a composite bill was presented: the first act of the newly reinstated *Norma*,[167] followed by *Lucia di Lammermoor*, entire, with Bertucca-Maretzek as Lucia and Mario as Edgardo. According to Richard Grant White, Grisi sang the *Casta diva* "unequally" and Mario sang sweetly and correctly as Edgardo, but "failed to present the character, either in his acting or by the tones of his voice"; Bertucca sang, as always, "like a musician and an artist, and was looking very well"; the small audience applauded "with more zeal than discrimination" (*Courier and Enquirer*, December 23, 1854).

On December 26 the first act of *I puritani* was followed by the second and third acts of *Lucia;* and on December 28 at last a novelty—*Don Pasquale* with Grisi as Norina, Mario as Ernesto, Badiali as Dr. Malatesta, and Luigi Rocco, a last-minute replacement for an ailing Susini, as Don Pasquale.

The charming work was perfectly performed (apparently for Paine's benefit) with a "promptitude and spirit which left nothing to be desired," reported the *Evening Post* (December 29, 1854). As for Grisi's Norina, "Humanity has no phases which are not mirrored in her representations of character. Last evening she was inspired of Momus,[168] and teased and worried, and then soothed the poor Don Pasquale with the consummate skill of a practical coquette."

Seymour described Grisi's Norina as "one of those thrilling, captivating, intoxicating exhibitions of coquetry and conscious beauty which must be seen and cannot be described. . . . Musically considered, we have not listened to anything more perfect than Madame Grisi's vocalization" (*Daily Times*, December 29, 1854).

And Richard Grant White, who carped over the insignificance of the work, dis-

[165] According to Maretzek, they shared the management of the December season at a loss of at least $4000 (undoubtedly sustained by Paine). "In spite of the invariable declarations of success and prosperity," wrote Maretzek, "the losses sustained by [the committee], who had so nobly (yet I must say, so ignorantly) rushed into management, were singularly heavy," (*Crotchets*, pp. 342, 359).

[166] After this performance the papers reported audiences clamoring for *Norma* to be repeated.

[167] During the *Norma* excerpt a fire broke out in the backstage wardrobe room, filling the auditorium with smoke; it was quickly dealt with (by Saeltzer's sprinkler system?), and the performance was allowed to proceed.

[168] Momus was the Greek god in charge of capriciousness.

dainfully calling it a "pretty opera," found Grisi's "demure coquetry . . . bewitching, and her vixenism very astonishing." Badiali was accorded his usual adulation; Rocco was thought properly comic (indeed, perhaps too much so); Mario, who was reported by White to be hoarse and by Seymour to be "in admirable voice," lacked animation (*Courier and Enquirer; Daily Times,* December 29, 1854).

A capacity audience "from pit to dome" turned out to do honor to James H. Hackett on the forty-fifth and final night of the Grisi/Mario engagement in New York, a performance of *La favorita.*[169] The unaccustomed sight of so huge and festive an audience at the Academy convinced Seymour that it was only the "hard times," not indifference to the opera, that had been responsible for the poor attendance throughout the somewhat problematical sojourn of these great artists. More realistically considered, rather than a public passion for opera, it was the massive and insistent prodding in the papers, to say nothing of the powerful social and civic sponsorship of Hackett, that was responsible for the spectacular attendance on this occasion. Only recently the object of public disfavor, Hackett was now represented as a great and brave public benefactor who, against all odds, had brought to the city the "finest opera company, beyond all comparison, which has ever visited us." It was only fitting, urged the *Evening Post* on December 29, the day of Hackett's benefit, that the public pay tribute to "the gentleman to whom we primarily owe all this." Thanks to Hackett, the formerly mythic names of Grisi and Mario had become "household words" in New York. "It was a somewhat hazardous experiment," and the fact that it had not been an altogether successful one was reason enough for "every friend of art to go to the 'Academy'. . . to ensure Mr. Hackett a more than nominal benefit."

In a curtain speech, Hackett, after the usual mix of heartfelt and humorous remarks, announced that Grisi and Mario were leaving immediately for a week's season in Philadelphia, to be followed by two weeks in Boston. They had generously offered, however, to stop off between cities to donate a benefit performance for the poor and needy of New York. This they did on January 11, 1855,[170] at a crowded Academy of Music, realizing, it was rumored, some $8000.[171]

New York opera-goers of 1854 were by no means limited to Italian opera. Indeed, during a memorable week in October the papers proudly boasted that one might hear excellently performed opera in any of three languages: Italian, English, or German; and in November at any of four theatres. In July, English opera resumed its interrupted course when Anna Thillon stopped off in New York after a vastly profitable California tour to give a farewell-forever season at Niblo's, before returning to England and retiring from the stage. Coinciding with Maretzek's unfortunate season of Italian opera at Castle Garden, she opened on July 4 with Balfe's *The Enchantress* and for the following month repeated it together with the remainder of her well-worn repertory:[172] *The Bohemian Girl, The Daughter of the Regiment,* and *The Crown Diamonds.* On

[169] With Grisi, Mario, Badiali, and Susini, and with Señorita Soto replacing the inexhaustible Roussets in a single, short, but equally anachronistic solo, *La Madrilena.*

[170] Assisted by Badiali, Susini, and Fabricatore; Donovani, who was ill, did not appear.

[171] For this event, it was reported, Miss Coutts had bid $130 for a proscenium box holding twelve seats (*Mirror,* January 10, 1855).

[172] Performed by her well-worn cast: Frazer, Lyster, Ferdinand Meyer, and Mrs. Maeder.

All: Girvice Archer, Jr.

Louisa Pyne (left), Susan Pyne, and William Harrison, foremost exponents of English opera.

August 5 she was heard as Arline in the first and second acts of *The Bohemian Girl* and Stella in the first act of *The Enchantress.* And on August 8, at her positively last appearance—a complimentary benefit tendered by her many friends and admirers—she appeared as Zerlina in the first and second acts of *Fra Diavolo,* Marie in the second act of *The Daughter of the Regiment,* and Stella in excerpts from *The Enchantress.* The following day Thillon and her husband, laden with dollars, departed for Liverpool.

A new era of English opera was initiated—concurrently with the inaugural tribulations at the Academy of Music—with the arrival at the Broadway Theatre on October 9 of the Pyne/Harrison troupe from London. "Choice Italian is well enough in its way, but it should not monopolize every sweet sound," observed Seymour in his review of the Pyne/Harrison opening (*Daily Times,* October 10, 1854).[173] Echoing a sentiment recurrent among local journalists since the days of the Garcias, he continued: "There is music in the Anglo-Saxon soul which might as well be heard now and then, *in* the Anglo-Saxon." (Bellini's anglicized *La sonnambula,* with which the new English troupe opened, seems hardly to offer the ethnic satisfaction for which Seymour's transplanted Anglo-Saxon soul thirsted.) The *Evening Post* (October 5, 1854), too, shared Seymour's longing for lyric drama presented "in all the attraction and simplicity of the language with which the majority of the people are most familiar and can best understand and appreciate."[174] It would be refreshing, too, wrote the *Post,* not to be confronted with "one star only, while the lesser lights be dim, obscure, and uninteresting."

But, as Fry (who categorically denied the very existence of English opera) wrote in the *Tribune* (October 10, 1854), it was Louisa Pyne (1832–1904), the young *prima donna* of this company, who brought the "so-called English opera in this country [to] assume a new phase and life at her hands." Though her colleagues—her co-star, the tenor William Harrison (1813–1868), her older sister Susan Pyne, who sang the contralto roles, and the bass (or baritone) Borrani—were varyingly praised, it was Louisa Pyne who took audiences and critics alike by storm.

Apart from her graceful and spirited acting, wrote Seymour, she possessed an "exquisite soprano voice. . . . It is wonderfully cultivated and seems as certain, distinct, and brilliant as a flute. Her executive powers are very great and place her in the foremost rank of artists.[175] The great and distinctive characteristic of her singing, however," he wrote, was "a certain vibratory sweetness—a trembling softness of sound, perfectly irresistible. It is like the warbling of a bird, only more tender. We have never heard anything more admirable than the way in which this perfectly artistic effect is produced by Miss L. Pyne" (*Daily Times,* October 10, 1854).

Seymour's colleagues vied with one other in their praises of Louisa Pyne. "A more

[173] "Excepting the burlesque which Madame Thillon perpetrated," unkindly continued Seymour, "we have had no attempt at English opera for several years."

[174] Despite all this intelligibility, Corbyn advertised opera books in an authentic American edition, "transcribed from the most correct prompt-books used in England . . . with full Plots of the Operas, Cast of the Characters, Descriptions of Costumes, and full Stage Directions."

[175] A member of an old musical family, Louisa Pyne had studied with Sir George Smart; she had successfully appeared with the London Philharmonic and had sung with distinction in Italian opera both in England and on the Continent.

finished and accomplished vocalist and actress it has seldom been our good fortune to hear," wrote an enchanted *Herald* (October 10, 1854), describing her voice as a soprano *sfogato* with a range of three octaves and perfect intonation; her "brilliant and florid execution reminded one strongly of Sontag.[176] . . . She deserves the more credit . . . from the fact that she has some personal disadvantages to overcome." Louisa Pyne, described as an "English blonde," was no beauty. Bearing a well-known resemblance to Queen Victoria, she was below average height, with a "well-rounded" figure; her features, "although well formed, [had] not much natural expression." But these physical deficiencies were obliterated by her gracefulness and the overwhelming sweetness of her smile.

The reviewers were more reserved in their praises of Harrison. A man of "Herculean proportions and stature," he possessed an "essentially English" tenor voice of good range and power, and of extreme sweetness. Shining particularly in ballads and airs, Harrison was particularly commended for his beautifully clear enunciation. But he regrettably tended to slip from true pitch.

"Miss Pyne" (as differentiated from "Miss Louisa Pyne") was a "clever contralto and fine actress," and Borrani's delectable bass voice (according to Burkhardt, a "true baritone") and his "artistic merit and modesty" were intermittently admired and disparaged. As a whole, the company was generally welcomed as the finest, most perfect English opera troupe ever heard in New York—superior to the fabled Woods, Bishop/Bochsa, and even the Seguins.[177]

Presented under the astute auspices of E. A. Marshall and managed by Le Grand Smith, the Pyne/Harrison company included, among its supporting members, Camoens, making his inept debut on the lyric stage, and various members of the Broadway Theatre stock company, called upon as required. The theatre orchestra, enlarged to thirty players, and the augmented chorus of thirty-six singers were excellently conducted by La Manna.

Avoiding Hackett's fatal error of saturating the public with a single attraction, they immediately brought out a new one on October 12, *The Bohemian Girl*,[178] a work in which Harrison had created the role of Thaddeus in 1843. "His performances of last night justified the [great] reputation he had achieved in it,"[179] but it was again Louisa Pyne, as Arline, who carried the evening, displaying "an energy, pathos, and intensity of feeling which . . . drew down a perfect tempest of applause" from an audience that (in contrast to the attendance at the Academy of Music) crowded the house from floor to ceiling (*Herald*, October 14, 1854).

[176] She reminded Burkhardt of Laborde.

[177] Only the reviewer for the *Evening Post*, by now competing with Burkhardt in curmudgeonliness, picked flaws, not only in the current troupe, but retrospectively in the departed Thillon troupe, whose "tenor had a poor, broken-down, squeaky voice which distressed the ear of anyone who had heard any singing above that of a chimney-sweep." The others had been equally unsatisfactory, and thus by comparison the present company were the best since the days of the Seguins.

[178] In their initial advertisements, the Pyne/Harrison company listed a repertory of thirty-two works.

[179] But the *Evening Post* compared him unfavorably with the fine Italian tenors we had known, finding him inferior even to Forti and Vietti. Camoens, as Devilshoof, a role made memorable by Arthur Seguin, was actually hissed, having by his incompetence spoiled the closing tableau of act one.

After another performance of *La sonnambula* and two more of *The Bohemian Girl,* on October 19 the Pyne/Harrison troupe presented their most ambitious effort, William Vincent Wallace's *Maritana,* not heard in New York since 1848 when the Seguins had unsuccessfully performed it at the Bowery Theatre.♪ For the current presentation, Wallace, still (or again) in New York, conducted a greatly enlarged orchestra and chorus, and Aptommas, seated in the orchestra, played the *obbligato* to "The Harp in the Air," exquisitely sung by Louisa Pyne.[180] It was "never to be forgotten," wrote the staunchly Anglophile *Albion* (October 21, 1854, pp. 499–500).

William Henry Fry, a professed admirer of Wallace (his admiration probably intensified now that Wallace was a bona fide American citizen), after erroneously announcing this performance as *Maritana*'s first hearing in New York, proceeded to attack Wallace's English librettist, the prolific playwright Edward Fitzball (1792–1843)—but then, "there is nobody in England who can construct a drama especially for his [Wallace's] musical purposes, and so he takes a variation of an acting melodrama [Dumanois and d'Ennery's popular *Don César de Bazan*], with such versification as he can get." Fry also took occasion again to disapprove of spoken dialogue in an opera, instead of accompanied recitative. And although Louisa Pyne had admirably acquitted herself as Maritana, "like most English singers, she does not pronounce her words distinctly"; Fry advised her to follow Mario's admirable example in matters of diction. Harrison, who had triumphantly created the role of Don César in London in 1845, on this occasion sang out of tune, which, wrote Fry, "forbade a judgment of his other merits" (*Tribune,* October 20, 1854). But the *Herald* (October 20, 1854) again proclaimed Louisa Pyne the most perfect of singers: "A more finished method than hers, combined with a voice as sweet, we have never heard, and can scarcely hope to hear again."

With the Pyne/Harrison company nearing the end of their three-week engagement at the Broadway Theatre—to close on October 28 with Auber's *Fra Diavolo* for Louisa Pyne's benefit—their final performances were devoted solely to repeats of their towering hit *Maritana. Fra Diavolo* was replaced at the last moment by *The Crown Diamonds,* probably because the latter work enabled her to display her phenomenal vocalization of Rode's Variations for violin (previously sung in New York by Alboni and the lamented Sontag). In flaming superlatives, Seymour wrote: "The feature of the evening was the marvelous execution of Rode's air in the finale by Miss Louisa Pyne. As an exhibition of perfect vocalism this effort has probably never been surpassed. It exhibited in a wonderful degree the remarkable cultivation of Miss Pyne's organ, embracing as it does every note of an extensive soprano range. This air, with its variations, presents every difficulty and defect an ambitious artist [might wish] to overcome. The evident facility with which Miss Louisa Pyne gave it—not a single effort being perceptible—can only be described as marvelous. The last variation, moving entirely in semitones—first in the full-, then in the half-voice—could not have been played on the flute with equal precision.

"As the curtain descended on this brilliant effort, there was a perfect hurricane of applause. The house rose *en masse* and gave repeated and prolonged cheers; handkerchiefs and hats were waved, bouquets thrown; and a *furore* produced which has never

[180] Aptommas seems to have sat in the orchestra as well for *The Bohemian Girl.*

been equaled in our remembrance. The curtain again ascended and Miss L. Pyne repeated the last variation. There was a recurrence of the preceding scene, and only after twice reappearing before the curtain was Miss Louisa Pyne permitted to retire to her dressing room."

Seymour informed his readers that the Pyne/Harrison troupe would immediately depart for engagements in Philadelphia and Boston, and concluded: "We hear it rumored that [another] English Opera will commence here in a fortnight. The Prima Donna—Mdlle. Nau."

It was more than a rumor. Niblo, who had been to Europe on one of his talent-hunting expeditions,[181] returned in late October with an English opera company headed by (Maria) Dolores Nau (1818–1891), an expatriate American *prima donna* prominent at the Paris Opéra. Dolores Nau was born in New York of Spanish parents, refugees from the political upheavals in Santo Domingo; in early youth she had been transplanted to Paris, where in the 1830s she studied at the *Conservatoire* with Madame Cinti-Damoreau,♪ became a protégée of Rossini, and was engaged for the Paris Opéra. Nau's distinguished subsequent career had taken her to London, back to Paris, and now to the United States.[182]

Her all-English supporting company consisted of newcomers to the United States: Mr. A. St. Albyn, tenor (from the Surrey Theatre, London), George Harrison (apparently not related to William Harrison), second tenor, and Allan Irving, first bass; also the old-timers Eliza Brienti,♪ second soprano, and Henry Horncastle,♪ second bass. Thomas Baker, Jullien's popular former leader, returning to settle in the United States, was the music director of the Nau company.[183]

Announcing a repertory of twelve English and Italian opera staples,[184] the Nau company opened at Niblo's on November 20[185] with a novelty, Auber and Scribe's *The Syren* (*La Sirène,* Paris 1844), a work Nau had successfully performed in London.[186] Although a large and brilliant audience reportedly attended, the impact of their debut was appreciably blunted by the sudden reappearance on the same evening at the Broadway Theatre of the Pyne/Harrison company, en route from Philadelphia to Boston, in a performance of *Maritana* for Wallace's benefit.[187]

Miss Nau and her company suffered from remarkably bad timing on Niblo's part: to appear in such close proximity to the sensationally successful Pyne/Harrison com-

[181] During his absence it had been rumored that he had engaged the great dancer Carlotta Grisi, but her American tour came to naught.

[182] *Grove's* (5th ed., VI, 32) reports a previous "triumphal progress" through the United States in the late 1840s, but I have found no contemporary reference to such a tour.

[183] More permanently, Baker had been engaged to take charge of the publishing department of the Horace Waters piano and sheet-music enterprise.

[184] *Lucy of Lammermoor, Don Pasquale, Fra Diavolo, The Bohemian Girl, Ernani, The Puritans, The Somnambulist, The Crown Diamonds, Norma, Lucrezia Borgia,* and *Der Freischütz.*

[185] At no increase in ticket prices: $1 for orchestra seats, 50 cents for others, and $5 for private boxes.

[186] Only its overture previously had been heard in New York (George Templeton Strong had attended its first performance at a concert of the Euterpean Society in 1845).♪

[187] They remained for three additional performances of *The Crown Diamonds* before pushing on to Boston.

Girvice Archer, Jr.

Dolores Nau, a victim of unfortunate timing.

pany in a period otherwise drenched in opera was hardly to their advantage. Thus, shrinking houses were reported throughout their stay at Niblo's, even though the critics—for all their crabbed ways—generally agreed that Nau was a splendid artist, with a pure, beautifully trained, agile soprano voice, even if it failed to clutch at the great critical heartstrings. Some papers judged her virtuosity to be equal (and even superior!) to Jenny Lind's; her English diction (despite her American origin she spoke with a pronounced French accent) was better than Anna Thillon's,[188] although Thillon surpassed Nau in physical attractiveness.[189]

Nau's colleagues, too, were for the most part favorably enough reviewed. St. Albyn, young and handsome, possessed a "light, pretty" tenor voice, immaculately on pitch, if rather shrill, but pleasingly so; he was "well up" in his music, if not in his dialogue. The bass Allan Irving, despite a pleasing voice, either did not know his part or had forgotten it; the same was true of George Harrison. Indeed, except for Horncastle, a seasoned professional, none of the male performers seemed to know his part; Miss Brienti was for the most part ignored. Thomas Baker conducted the orchestra, if not the chorus, admirably, although R. Storrs Willis complained that the orchestra had been too *piano* in the first-act accompaniments to Nau's backstage *solfeggio,* and that Baker, whose "excitement on this first occasion probably led him into rather a more demonstrative style of leading—coupled with a very audible stamping—than he was probably aware of," might do well to remember that such things, "which though of

[188] But it was Burkhardt's opinion that she (and her colleagues) might just as well have been singing in Choctaw (*Albion,* November 25, 1854, p. 560).

[189] As the *Mirror* had it (November 22, 1854): "Miss Nau is a bright, agreeable looking woman, with a sharp nose, sharp chin, and sharp eyes—a very pretty piece of music set in three sharps." Yet, after the first act, which she had performed entirely behind the scenes, when she appeared onstage, "radiant with smiles and pink satin, the impatient audience, which had been so tantalized with the sweet music of the invisible minstrel, warmly welcomed to their eyes the fair Syren who had so bewitched their ears and imaginations."

use sometimes in rehearsals, are better dropped in public performance" (*Musical World,* November 25, 1854, p. 154). The consensus, however, was that the Nau company was a valuable addition to the English Opera resources of the city.

On November 29 they unveiled their ill-advised production of *Lucy of Lammermoor.* Only bad managerial judgment, claimed Seymour (*Daily Times,* November 30, 1854), would have exposed this production to comparison with all the great performances of *Lucia* to which New York had been treated in the past few years, much to the detriment of this company of non-actors. The performance was beneath criticism, he wrote—a "species of musical hallucination from beginning to end." This unfortunate production was followed by an apparently undistinguished presentation of *The Somnambulist* on December 7; then, after revolving this repertory throughout December, they presented *The Bohemian Girl* on Christmas night.[190]

In the meantime, on December 18 the Pyne/Harrison company returned to the Broadway Theatre from their triumphal season in Boston, opening in a surprisingly ill-prepared performance of *Fra Diavolo* (at least, according to the *Albion,* December 23, 1854, p. 608). On December 20 they brilliantly brought out *The Beggar's Opera.* Everyone enthusiastically agreed that Louisa Pyne as Polly was a delight, and William Harrison was better as Macheath than in any of his preceding characters. On Christmas night they revived *The Crown Diamonds,* and again the critics were agog at Louisa Pyne's miraculous performance of the Rode Variations.

During this year German opera increasingly came to the fore. On February 20, during the musical famine following the destruction of Metropolitan Hall, a performance in German of Donizetti's *Mary, or, The Child of the Regiment* was given at Boettner's Theatre on Chambers Street, featuring Madame Spitzeder and Herr Adolphus Liberati, with Julius Unger conducting the orchestra of the then recently departed (Maretzek/Salvi) Italian opera company of 1853. On May 11, Flotow's *Alessandro Stradella* (Paris 1843/Hamburg 1844) was produced at the St. Charles Theatre by an unnamed cast and again conducted by Unger.[191]

German performances were most frequently reported in the English-language press by the *Evening Post,* whose critic, probably for ethnic reasons, displayed an interest in the development of German culture in New York. Thus, on September 4 the *Post* covered the opening of the *New-Yorker Stadt-Theater* at 37–39 Bowery, remodeled to hold some 2000 people. Its ambitious plans included productions of German drama, music drama, music, and (more or less German) dance, under the general directorship of its proprietors, August Siegrist and the able German actor/director Otto Hoym; Julius Unger was the musical director. At the opening, an evening devoted to the spoken drama, some excellent music had been heard as well.

On October 5 and 7, *Der Freischütz* was presented "in the original tongue—that spoken by Mozart and Haydn, Mendelssohn and Meyerbeer," as the *Post* exulted. The

[190] On December 22, for Horncastle's benefit, Miss Nau appeared, with St. Albyn and Horncastle, in the second and third acts of *The Somnambulist;* additionally Mrs. Buckland, the former Kate Horn, appeared (with Horncastle) in *The Savage and the Maiden,* excerpted from Dickens's *Nicholas Nickleby,* and G. F. Bristow played a piano solo.

[191] At the St. Charles, box seats were $1, parquet and first circle 50 cents, and gallery 25 cents.

performers (according to Odell, VI, 400) were a Fräulein Wild (Agathe), Fräulein Fuchs (Aennchen), and the Herren Turvald (Max), Schwegerle (Caspar), and Dardenne (Killian), apparently all actor/singers in the *Stadt-Theater* stock company.

On October 20, Hoym and Siegrist announced a more legitimately cast series of operas in German, to begin with the *Barbier von Sevilla,* featuring Madame Martini d'Ormy as Rosina, Quint (in his German persona) as Almaviva, Oehrlein as Bartolo, Vincke as Basilio, and Schwegerle as Figaro. "It will be seen that the proprietors of this establishment do not deem it beneath their dignity to yield to the general demand for novelty, though their expenses are thereby increased nearly threefold," somewhat obscurely puffed the *Evening Post.*[192]

The extra outlay was, alas, hardly justified—at least, not in this instance, for, according to the *Post* (October 21, 1854): "As the tardy orchestra came to their seats, they were saluted [by a large and indignant audience] by a perfect hurricane of *a-ahs,* this being the style of noise-making at that theatre. The overture commenced and was instantly detected as being that of *Martha,* and not the *Barber.* Another round of 'A-ahs!' accompanied hisses and cries of '*Tis Martha*!' The curtain rose, and the manager announced his regret that the *Barber* was 'unavoidably unready' for representation, and that a small concert would take place instead, and after it a German drama.

"D'Ormy then came forward and sang *Una voce,* and after a few moments the drinking song from *Lucrezia.* She did not appear in the best humor, nor did she equal Grisi." Undaunted, the same cast again attempted the *Barber* on October 24—more successfully, one hopes.

On November 4, *Der Freischütz* was repeated, this time with the capable actress/singer Madame Hoym as Aennchen and Quint as Max. *Masaniello* was presented on November 11, followed by several performances during November and December of *Martha,* the hit of the season, with Martini d'Ormy, Madame Siedenburg, and Quint; and on December 27, *Stradella* was again given with d'Ormy in the title role, and, presumably, with Siedenburg, Quint, and Vincke.

There remains yet another category of opera: burlesque opera in blackface, in 1854 a phenomenon whose popularity exceeded all the other operas combined. As the *Evening Post* (August 14, 1854) observed: "While the 'legitimate' opera is languishing, either because the public has been surfeited with European stars of the first magnitude, and hence refuse to go and hear inferior singing [a thrust at Maretzek's 1854 opera season then in its final throes at Castle Garden], or from some other cause, the burlesque opera is rapidly gaining in popularity, and at least one troupe in this city can boast of crowded and delighted audiences and an overflowing treasury. Of course, we allude to the Buckleys. These gentlemen are entitled to the credit of having introduced a new epoch in negro minstrelsy—the most decided improvement . . . since Tom Rice first jumped to the tune of 'Jim Crow.' Their performances are in reality burlesque operas, not mere caricatures of certain scenes or personages; their scenery is new, pretty, and appropriate, and their operatic travesties consist of an intermingling of the beautiful and the grotesque.

[192] Opera tickets at the *Stadt-Theater* were $1 for box seats, 50 cents in the dress circle, 25 cents in the pit, and 12½ cents in the gallery.

"On Saturday night we attended their performance of *The Bohemian Girl*. The house was crowded in every part, even the center aisle being filled with chairs to accommodate the late-comers. Thaddeus, the proscribed Pole metamorphosed into 'Lemuel, a runaway slave,' was enacted by G. S. Buckley; Count Arnheim, no longer a Bohemian nobleman, but still very dignified as 'Corncob, a slave overseer,' was excellently represented by W. Percival; his daughter Arline, was represented by the '*prima donna assoluta*' of the company, Miss A. Eleanor . . . and Devilshoof, most appropriately nicknamed 'Possumheel,' was in most excellent hands.

"The opera was well performed throughout, the original music being rendered with fidelity and the plot of the opera strictly adhered to. [!] The solo parts were generally well sung, and the singing of some of the concerted pieces and choruses would, to say the least, bear comparison with that of the so-called legitimate stage." The satisfied reviewer added that managers of other places of amusement might do well in this hot weather to emulate Buckley and provide a fan with each seat.

Other "operas" given at Buckley's Ethiopian Opera House during 1854 were *Lucia, Norma, La sonnambula,*[193] *Cinderella, Lucrezia Borgia* (a "diabolical burletta"),[194] and, in October, *Fra Diavolo,* a new production that did not, however, entirely measure up to the highest critical standards: "The Burlesque Opera House of the Buckleys was crowded last week, as usual," puffed the *Daily Times* (October 23, 1854), "and its customary variety—music, negro delineations, and burlesque[195]—was served up in the Buckleys' best style. The new burlesque on *Fra Diavolo* was good, but is inferior to their *Lucrezia Borgia* or *Sonnambula.* The last act, though brief, drags, owing to the want of appropriate stage business and music. The ending is decidedly 'horse operatic,' and reminded us much of the afterpiece in the ring of a country circus."

A hot fad, the opera burlesques flooded the various minstrel establishments along Broadway and the Bowery. In a sense they contributed to Edwin Pierce Christy's abrupt professional demise. Continuing to trade bitter blows with George Christy/Henry Wood in a growingly uneven competition, in March, E. P. Christy, in a gesture of reckless bravado, announced his intention of enlarging Christy's American Opera House (Mechanics' Hall) to accommodate an audience of 2500, with commensurate expansion of his stage facilities to handle the most elaborate production demands of burlesque opera. Shockingly, in mid-July, with no advance warning and no explanation, Edwin Pierce Christy, the King of Minstreldom, at the age of thirty-nine retired from the stage.[196]

Twisting the knife, George Christy and Henry Wood lost no time in acquiring

[193] With a rechristened cast of characters: Dinah (Amina), Dan Tucker (Count Rodolpho), Gumbo (Elvino), Lazy Joe (Alessio), Susannah (Lisa), Aunt Sally (Teresa), and Deacon Ducklegs (notary); the orchestra was led by Fred Buckley.

[194] Produced concurrently with Grisi's *Lucrezia Borgia,* according to the Buckleys' advertisement, "in order to keep pace with the present musical excitement."

[195] Among his burlesques, Buckley continued to present his "Mons. Jullien Concert," with R. Bishop Buckley as "the Black Jew-Lion," an entertainment introducing its own versions of the "Prima Donna Waltz" and the "American Quadrille."

[196] A man of melancholy temperament, E. P. Christy is said to have been obsessed by the specter of a penniless old age. On his retirement, the papers estimated that he had accrued a profit (from some 2792 performances over a period of twelve years) of $160,873.60 (*Mirror,* August 9, 1854). In 1862 Christy committed suicide.

the lease to Mechanics' Hall (472 Broadway), so long sacrosanct to E. P. Christy. Acquiring as well his forsaken troupe, among whose many stars were Frank Brower, W. Birch, and Dr. Valentine, the victors immediately put the hall into successful joint operation with their nearby establishment at 444 Broadway, announcing that George Christy would perform at both theatres every evening. In addition to their thousand-and-one "Ethiopian Melodies, Banjo, Guitar, and Violin Solos, Duets and Trios," their "Negro Jigs and Fancy Dances," and their presentations of "White Characters," their bills included such opera and theatre burlesques as *Lend Her De Sham Money (Linda di Chamounix), Fra Diavolo* (with George Christy in the character of Julius Crow), Charles Selby's popular 1835 burletta *Robert Macaire,* an "operatic" version of *Uncle Tom's Cabin* (with G. Christy as Topsy),[197] and *Macbeth;* also updated versions of the "Ethiopian opera" classics *The Mummy* and *The Virginny Cupids.* In December their theatre at 444 Broadway burned down, and they were, ironically, forced to compress their overextended activities into E. P. Christy's old stronghold, Mechanics' Hall.

In October, Josiah Perham, a flashy gift-ticket (lottery) operator, suddenly invaded the world of minstrelsy. At Perham's Burlesque Opera House, as he renamed Academy Hall (663 Broadway), the scene of his erstwhile gift-ticket operations, he proceeded with great fanfare to present "Pantomime, Negro Melodies, Choruses, Jigs, Fancy Dances, etc.," performed by a heterogeneous company of entertainers designated the "Star Troupe of New York." Conforming to the conventional minstrel-show format, Perham presented a two- part "concert" followed by a new burlesque production, described as "the Rabble [Ravel] Family's[198] new comic pantomime of 'Sampatchieno, or, The Perils of Love'" (later subtitled "The Red Gnome"). *Sampatchieno* was the brain-child of E. Warden, a member of Perham's company, who played the title role.

In November, at the peak of the Grisi presence in New York, Perham offered a new burlesque, *Gnaw-More,* billed as "Warden's grotesque personation of Grisi's Norma." This confection was whipped up by the protean Alfred Sedgwick. "The world is challenged," ballyhooed Perham, "to produce anything to equal the burlesque opera of *Norma,* as altered and improved from Bellini's well-known version." His other attractions included burlesques of *Jocko, or, the Brazilian Ape* and *The Black Barber.*

As the holidays approached,[199] Perham ingeniously combined his present and former vocations, offering gift tickets at $1, each to admit four persons to the minstrel show and each to carry a "certificate of share in the 100,000 valuable and costly articles donated by Mr. Perham to his patrons." Some 60,000 tickets had already been snapped up, he advertised, leaving only a paltry 40,000 still to be had.

Charley White's Serenaders appeared at the St. Nicholas Exhibition Room and many other places; Sanford's Opera Troupe settled into the Stuyvesant Institute in September; Murphy, West, and Peel's "Original Campbell's Minstrels" appeared at the St. Nicholas Exhibition Room in March; Pell's Plantation Melodists appeared at White's former Melodeon at 53 Bowery in November.

[197] In January the Bowery Theatre had presented a highly successful version of *Uncle Tom's Cabin,* with T. D. Rice as Uncle Tom.

[198] The "Wonderful Ravels" were separately and collectively satirized as "Gabriel, Jerome, Antoine, François, Marie, Celestina, and Common Rabble."

[199] Perham's Christmas offering was a burlesque of *Don Giovanni, or, the Spectre on Horseback.*

In contrast to the abundance of burnt-cork entertainment, simple, popular ballad concerts were sparse in 1854. At the Tabernacle on January 11 the Hutchinson Family—Judson, John, and Asa—completed their short concert series, begun in late 1853. On January 18 they sang for the benefit of the Daughters of Temperance, again at the Tabernacle, and on February 6 at the First Mariners' Methodist Episcopal Church (Cherry Street, between Clinton and Montgomery streets), for the benefit of that congregation; then they departed. Late in the year, on December 4, Dempster returned from his travels to give his annual "season" at the Tabernacle. It was announced that at his opening concert he would sing his heart-rending masterpiece "The May Queen" and a new ballad, titled "Some things love me."

At the theatre, apart from the Thillon, Nau, and Pyne/Harrison performances of English opera, two splendid productions of special musical interest—both of *A Midsummer Night's Dream* and both with Mendelssohn's music—originated in New York early in 1854. Of the first, mounted by William Burton at Burton's Theatre on February 3, Fry, for once approving a work of Mendelssohn's, wrote: "The celebrated music of Mendelssohn [arranged for this production by a Mr. James Locke] was given entire. . . . The overture, which we prefer to any subsequent works of the same hand, may be cited as a noble piece of dramatic painting, expressing in idea and orchestration what is needed. The mock death of Pyramus, as rendered by the music, is a most felicitous hit. The Wedding March *needs*—as indeed all the music—more resources in the orchestra than it is possible to command in a small theater." In all its attributes, however—"the grotesque, the sylvan, the grandiose—the music came alive . . . when so interlinked with scenes and characters" (*Tribune,* February 4, 1854).

Hot on the heels of Burton's triumph—on February 6 at the Broadway Theatre—came E. A. Marshall's even more spectacular, if musically inferior, production of *Midsummer Night's Dream.* A less mellow Fry, this time bristling with harsh criticism of Shakespeare for his false portrayal of the working classes in this work, had scathing words for the orchestra as well, probably for subjective reasons: "Though there were in that department perhaps as many as a dozen of the artists who perform at the Philharmonic concerts, yet the overture of Mendelssohn [led by a Mr. Roberts] was scraggily given, and there was a want of correct musical interpretation in various ways throughout the whole play. The fact is, every orchestra requires a leader to beat time and supervise—a lyrical canon of which the special authority appeared oblivious last night" (*Tribune,* February 7, 1854).

The *Mirror* (February 7), agreeing with Fry about the orchestra's poor performance, resented as well the interpolation of an unidentified duet by Sir Henry Bishop.[200] The *Times,* restraining itself with difficulty from making "a savage attack" on the musical arranger, would have preferred even an interpolation of the popular minstrel tune "The other side of Jordan" to the unremitting reiteration throughout the play of the Wedding March.

Apart from the usual stock revivals of the usual musical chestnuts, the theatres offered little further of musical interest in 1854. The Grand Opening on September 18

[200] Might it have been derived from Bishop's 1816 incidental music to *A Midsummer Night's Dream*?

of the Metropolitan Theatre and New York Opera House, as the rebuilt Metropolitan Hall[201] was renamed, was a disappointment to the music community. Contrary to all hopes and expectations, it was opened as a legitimate theatre by the theatrical speculators Henry Willard and Harry Eytinge,[202] who had leased it from Lafarge in midsummer. The theatre's huge staff was headed by Willard and Eytinge as co-managers[203] and included such pretentious exotica as a Dramatic Censor (the author and editor Cornelius Mathews (1817–1889), two "physicians in attendance," a ballet corps of forty dancers headed by the four Roussets and their father, a "Leader for Spectacle, etc." (our old friend John St. Luke), and, among many others, a "maestro" (Luigi Garbato), who, it was announced, would bring out "A Grand Italian Opera" in which the Signora Drusilla Garbato would appear as *prima donna* "for the first time in this country."[204] A resident cast of some forty-two actors was headed by Julia Dean.

Not until Sunday, December 24, did a specifically musical event take place at the Metropolitan Theatre (misleadingly referred to on this occasion as the "Metropolitan Opera House").[205] No opera was given, but a Broadway Sunday Concert, a blatantly Jullienesque *concert monstre* that featured one hundred performers: a "full and efficient chorus"; a "double orchestra" conducted by Luigi Arditi; Adkins's Cornet Band; and, as soloists, Mademoiselle (formerly Madame) Victor Chome, again "making her first appearance in America," Mrs. Henry C. Watson, and John Camoens. Jullien's latest "Grand March," just arrived from London, was featured amid a lengthy hodgepodge of sacred and secular works.

On New Year's Eve, at the following Broadway Sunday Concert at the Metropolitan, Mademoiselle Chome and Mrs. Watson were again featured, also William Doehler (or Döhler), a violinist, and a Herr Wedemeyer, "solo cellist to the King of Prussia"; the conductor was I. Kreutzer, Maretzek's leader.

As *Meerschaum* remarked to the editor of the *Spirit of the Times* (September 23, 1854, p. 384), it was no wonder that audiences were sometimes "thin," what with the multitudinous competing attractions to distract pleasure-loving New Yorkers; the marvel was, rather, "where all the people who do attend come from."

[201] Designed by the eminent theatre architect John M. Trimble, whose professional pride was reportedly "piqued . . . since the projectors of the new Opera House in Fourteenth Street would not look at him, simply because he had not been to Europe" (*Mirror,* cited in *Dwight's,* April 1, 1854, p. 204).

[202] Former lessees of the Howard Athenaeum in Boston.

[203] But not for long: on October 12 the *Tribune* reported a "flare-up" between Willard and Eytinge during rehearsal, "when some pretty hard words passed between them. The row resulted in Eytinge taking his leave, which he did last evening."

[204] Not so. The Garbatos, husband and wife, were members of an ill-fated Italian opera company who earlier were stranded in New York en route to California. Engaged by Willard and Eytinge to appear in August at the Howard Athenaeum in Boston, they found themselves locked out of the theatre after giving six performances (*Dwight's,* September 2, 1854, pp. 165, 175). By late September the Garbatos (who after all did not appear at the Metropolitan Theatre) departed for an engagement at the flourishing opera house in Lima, Peru, in company with the Domenico Lorinis, the Adelindo Viettis, Francesco Cuturi, Luigi Rocco, and one Timoleone Barattini, a secondary tenor (*Daily Times,* September 27, 1854).

[205] That enduring temple of the arts did not come into being until 1883.

6

GTS: 1855

Music is the one thing in life in which the less novelty, the better. The oftener a story is repeated, the more we tire of it. The oftener we hear a tune, on the contrary, the more we love it.

Home Journal
February 17, 1855

Regarded in his own set as a kind of musical Solon, Strong was increasingly called upon to render his expert opinion on a variety of musical matters. During a New Year's call on the Rector of Trinity Church, the Reverend William Berrian (*c.* 1787–1862), Strong was drawn into a long conversation, for instance, with "that very exuberant Miss B. [Berrian's daughter Jane?], mostly on music (in re Trinity Church). That enterprising damsel," Strong wrote in his journal (January 2, 1855), "has made a *coup d'état* in the choir of St. John's Chapel,♪ it seems, and assumed its administration into her own hands. People differ widely as to the merits of the result. The rector and the young lady beg me to come and hear it because it's so good; Hodges entreats me to do the same because it's so very vile, and would convince me that there is salvation only in the 'good old' English cathedral school. This domestic influence 'of the back stairs' it is that has so modified the Rector's views on Art, of late, and made him propose [Frederick] Rakemann as organist of Trinity Chapel,"[1] currently being built in West 25th Street.

As Trinity's most musically informed vestryman, on January 3 Strong went to the unfinished Chapel to hear and render judgment on some "choral experiments by Hodges"[2] and found them satisfactory: "The organ seems to 'come out' as it should, even in its present unfinished state; but the choir will have to be placed, I think, on the level of the chancel, behind the stalls for the clergy."[3]

[1]But, as Strong noted in his journal on February 14, Hodges's star pupil, Dr. Samuel Parkman Tuckerman (1819–1890), was appointed organist of the Chapel. "The Rector wished to nominate Rakemann," wrote Strong, "but Harison and Hodges have converted him. So the strictest school of Anglican dreariness will be represented in the music of Trinity Chapel."

[2]Because of Tuckerman's ill-timed absence abroad, Hodges himself served at the Chapel for its first two months, then was recalled to Trinity Church, where musical matters had fallen into serious disarray during his absence. The tangled facts are somewhat testily related in Messiter, pp. 63–64.

[3]Altogether a novel arrangement: the "superb" organ, built by Hall and Labagh, was "sunk in a niche over against the pulpit," causing both organ and organist to be "invisible to the congregation" (*Tribune,* April 12, 1855).

As Strong's musical preferences narrowed, so did his faculty for verbalizing them expand—sometimes to numbing lengths. Attending "a sort of musical party" at Mrs. Hills's, he remarked in his journal (January 10) that one of the amateur performers, a Miss Quincey from Boston, had delivered herself of *Il va venir,* from Halévy's *La Juive,* with "the exaggerated contrasts of *piano* and *forte*—whisper and screech—whereby second-rate amateurs commonly eke out their performances of opera music. Such pieces belong to the stage, for which they were written," he declared, "other compositions befit the drawing-room" (such as Haydn and Mozart Masses?).

Despite his disdain for opera—in or out of the drawing-room (always excepting his beloved *Freischütz* and the score, if not the libretto, of *Don Giovanni*)—Strong, on the strength of his reputed musical expertise, was invited by his influential father-in-law Samuel B. Ruggles[4] to join with a select group of critics and stockholders of the currently dormant Academy of Music[5] in passing judgment on a prospective *prima donna* in whom Ruggles was interested.

January 14. . . . to Mr. Ruggles's [January 12] in the evening, where a *petit comité* of operatic magnates, [Henry A.] Coit, [James] Phalen [president of the Academy of Music], Dan [Daniel Butler] Fearing, and Co., and of cognoscenti, as Dick [Richard Grant] White, [Firman] Cousinery, and [Régis de] Trobriand,♪ had been brought together to pass on the merits of Signorina, or Fräulein, Vestvali, a Cracovienne *prima donna* who's here in company with her brother, a whiskered Polack, and wants a professional engagement.[6] The lady sang [arias] from *Tancredi* and *I Montecchi ed i Capuletti* [*sic*]. Verdict not unfavorable. Very great voice (low contralto), fine person,[7] much declamatory power, probable deficiency in vocalization.[8] [James W.] Gerard♪ brava-a-a-ed vigorously, and the lady made a good impression. She is Mr. S. B. R.'s latest enthusiasm, and he is pushing her claims to attention very earnestly.

Mr. S. B. R.'s championship of the fascinating Pole brought Strong into unprecedented social proximity with a stranger from an alien planet: for all his ostensible musi-

[4]Ruggles, the founder of Gramercy Park and Irving Place, was interested in the general development of Union Square real estate. For business, social, and music-loving reasons he was most likely a stockholder in the Academy of Music.

[5]Although the Academy was scheduled to reopen in mid-February under a new management headed (surprisingly) by Ole Bull, with Max Maretzek as conductor/music director and Maurice Strakosch as agent/manager, the autocratic landlords of the Academy of Music were apparently not deterred from meddling in the management of the approaching opera season. For the Byzantine skulduggeries that epitomized the world of opera in 1855, see the following OBBLIGATO.

[6]The physically prepossessing candidate, Felicita Vestvali, *née* Felicja Vestvalowicz (1834?–1880), had studied in Italy with Romani and Mercadante; in 1853 she appeared at La Scala as Romeo in Bellini's *I Capuleti ed i Montecchi* and Azucena in Verdi's *Il trovatore* (Rome 1853); she was later heard in London on the concert stage (and probably the dramatic stage as well, being reputedly fluent in "nearly every language of Europe . . . including the English") (*Evening Post,* February 20, 1855). Vestvali had recently arrived, armed with a battery of introductions from the best people in London to the best people in New York, and she was aggressively seeking an engagement at the Academy of Music via the social route.

[7]Vestvali was the possessor not only of a magnificent physique but also of an irresistibly ingratiating personality.

[8]By "vocalization," Strong probably meant *fioriture,* a showy style of singing that he did not admire, and one in which Vestvali did not particularly excel.

The spectacularly prepossessing Felicita Vestvali.

cal sophistication, his personal acquaintance with professional performers had been limited almost solely to his employer/employee relations with Henry Timm and Philip Mayer in connection with private music-making. His exposure to *prime donne* had thus been restricted entirely to the drawing-room divas of his own social milieu who sang at his Mass-meetings and at his friends' amateur musicales. But an *actress!*

It was thus a titillating adventure when soon after, on January 14: "Mr. Ruggles brought up the *Vestvali* and her brother, who took tea here . . . and spent the evening very agreeably. The Vestvali is a handsome woman: young, genial, fresh, naive, enthusiastic, good-natured, intelligent, and somewhat cultivated," gushed an obviously smitten Strong. To propitiate Propriety he added: "Seems a lady,[9] and seems free from all trace of the taint her profession is apt to bring with it. Her instincts and impulses appear to be good and pure and true. She is a Lutheran—goes to St. Thomas's Church and affects sacred music. I hope she may succeed to her utmost wish, but I think she won't. Our people need to be *astonished* by an 'artist' in order to shake them out of their normal indifference to art. And I don't believe this lady will be able to excite them into a furor."[10]

January 21. . . . [more prosaically] Tuesday night [January 16] with Ellie at Eisfeld's [third *soirée* of his fifth series, at Dodworth's Academy]. Quartette No. 2 [for strings, K. 421 (1783)] in D minor, Mozart, not very pungent. Trio [No. 1 in D minor, for violin, cello, and piano], Mendelssohn, op. 49 [1839], *outré* and extravagant and not much more that I could perceive.[11] Beethoven [String] Quartette, op. 18, no. 2, in G

[9] Vestvali was reputedly of aristocratic lineage (see Kutsch and Riemens, I, 726).

[10] Perhaps as a form of touching wood, Strong persisted in predicting dire failure for Vestvali.

[11] The piano part was played by A. Woeltge, a recently arrived German pianist, apparently of the athletic school.

New-York Historical Society

A charity ball at the Academy of Music.

[composed 1878–1800], included some genial and delightful phrases of melody and was the best, by far, of the three compositions. There was also some rather dead-alive vocal music, *Dove sono* [from *The Marriage of Figaro*] substituted for something else *(Voi che sapete)* [from the same opera] on the program and sung mechanically.[12]

Wednesday night . . . the great charity ball [the "Ladies' Ball"] at the Opera House with Ellie. . . . There was a vast crowd of well-dressed and well-behaved people, far more homogeneous than I expected.[13] Seen from the back of the stage, it

[12] The singer was Miss Anna Griswold, who was laboring under a vocal indisposition. With her sister, Mrs. Georgiana Stuart, she also sang a charming duet by Eisfeld, "There sat a playful bird on a spray," the only "quite modern" work on the program, commented *Bornonis,* Dwight's current New York correspondent (*Dwight's,* January 27, 1855, p. 132).

[13] Probably to encourage the desired homogeneity, a promotional article in the *Times* on January 12 warned prospective revelers that no ladies dressed in merely "demi-toilette" or wearing bonnets would be admitted to the dance floor.

was a very splendid and brilliant spectacle.[14] All the details were well arranged and worked smoothly, except only the administration of the *cloak room,* where one had a life-and-death struggle to get his chattels *in,* and another to get them *out.* We came off at eleven, after a rather pleasant evening.[15] Saw lots of people I knew. The Vestvali was there, very radiant and handsome. . . .

Yesterday . . . went with Ellie and her mother to the Philharmonic [now at Niblo's Theatre]. Very great crowd.[16] Sat in the third gallery, where the orchestra is far more intelligently to be heard than elsewhere in the house. The very elaborate and involved instrumentation of the Mendelssohn ["Italian"] Symphony (the first and fourth movements particularly) I never heard before. This performance differed from that of the rehearsals, as a view of a landscape with no obscuring medium differs from a [narrowly focused] view through ground glass. We could see the whole anatomy of the composition and could trace the harmonious movement of its subject through all the uproar of accompaniment. Mendelssohn was clearly no melodist. Many of his phrases of melody are characterized by something that I don't want to call *grossness* or *coarseness.* But contrast them with the delicate, retiring, suggestive reserve with which Mozart introduces and quickly withdraws his melodic thoughts of spiritual beauty and purity. The Overture to *Preciosa* went nicely. Miss Lehmann sang *O mio Fernando* [from *La favorita*][17] and *Una voce* [from *Il barbiere*] very prettily.[18] We came off before Wallace's Overture to *Maritana.*[19]

[14] "The parquette was floored over . . . affording room for one or two hundred couples at once. . . . The stage was handsomely draped, festoons of flowers depended from the boxes, and the lighting of the house was exceedingly brilliant. . . . Two bands of music, consisting of eighty performers, were conducted by Mr. Monck and Mr. Noll. . . . Dancing was prolonged until the 'wee sma' hours'" (*Daily Times,* January 18, 1854).

[15] Despite malicious sabotage by the *Herald,* the "Ladies' Ball" was a huge success, both social and financial: "By 11 o'clock a dense crowd of carriages had blocked up Fourteenth Street, Irving Place, and the adjacent avenues," and it continued to increase until midnight, reported the *Times.*

[16] According to their Annual Report, the Philharmonic's thirteenth season had been the most prosperous since their inception in 1842. Not only had the Society's "professional membership" grown remarkably to 144 from last year's total of 116, and their associate membership from 555 to 747, but the various categories of members were allowed to buy tickets to rehearsals at fifty cents for their non-subscribing friends (a distressingly loquacious group, they turned out to be). With this added revenue the Society was enabled to shift the concerts to Niblo's Theatre, at a rental of $300 per concert (the rehearsals to continue at Niblo's Saloon, holding 1200 auditors); to increase the performing members' annual dividend to $65 (from the original $25 in 1842); to pay a fee to their better-known soloists; and to do various goodly works of charity for "actual members in distress."

[17] In *Dwight's* (January 27, 1855, p. 132), *Bornonis* gleefully reported the *Daily Times*'s error (January 22) in attributing the aria to *Lucrezia Borgia.* In the *Albion* (January 27, pp. 43–44) Burkhardt fulminated against performances at the Philharmonic of such hackneyed trash as Donizetti. A few years ago no one would have dreamed that such inferior music would be tolerated there. According to the Philharmonic account book, Lehmann received $40 for singing these inappropriate arias (Philharmonic Archives).

[18] The other soloists were Camilla Urso (looking quite grown-up and playing "*very* well for a woman"), who gave a Fantasy on Themes from *Lucrezia Borgia* by the French composer/violinist Prosper Sainton (1813–1890), and Louis Schreiber, a hornist from the Cologne *Conservatoire,* who played the first movement of his own Concertino for *cornet à pistons.* Although an able enough performer, he was by far no Koenig, and besides, his concerto was "balderdash" (*Dwight's,* January 27, p. 22; *Musical Review and Choral Advocate,* February 1, 1855, p. 42).

[19] Its first performance by the Philharmonic, and although one might have expected it to fare better here than at the Broadway Theatre (for the Pyne/Harrison performances), it was worse, sourly

February 11. . . . Philharmonic rehearsal Saturday (week before last) [February 3]. Mozart's delightful Symphony in B-flat [*sic*],[20] (with the unrivaled, tender, graceful Trio, one of the loveliest things in all music) and an overture (of Spontini's, I think) [to the opera *Olympia* (Berlin 1821)] that seemed to promise well.

~

Mr. Ruggles, in his tireless efforts to promote Vestvali, seems to have chosen the Strongs' house, rather than his own, as the official meeting-place for top-level negotiations with the opera magnates. Strong was not displeased.

February 18. . . . This evening an unexpected gathering at tea. John Whetten Ehninger [(1827–1889) the American painter], Miss Rosalie [Ruggles], the Vestvali, and her brother ("the lobster"—think of Ellie's excellent grandmamma's query to Mr. S. B. R.: "Samuel, is that man's name really *lobster*?"), who seems quite well bred and sensitive. Afterward, Charley [Strong], Dick Willis and his nice wife, [William P.] Talboys, Henry A. Coit, and Phalen. After talk and music, to the library. Books, microscope, polarized light [Strong's favorite interests, after music]. I should have been scared had I foreseen this assemblage, but as it turned out, it seemed as if everybody was entertained and interested and had a good time and went off wishing to stay longer. The Amazonian Vestvali certainly a very fine, frank, genial, fresh young woman, full of *life* and *Teilnehmung* [readiness to share].

She sang Arsace in *Semiramide* last night at the Metropolitan [Theatre] with brilliant success. Ellie went; I couldn't. . . . It is to be settled tomorrow whether [Vestvali] is engaged by the Fourteenth Street Academy[21] or by Hackett's opposition.

~

By "Hackett's opposition," Strong most probably meant the rival opera enterprise that Hackett was rumored to be hatching. After a triumphant month in Boston[22] he had brought Grisi and Mario back for three farewell performances at Lafarge's Metropolitan Theatre[23] before their return to Europe on February 21. So tumultuously were they now acclaimed by the wayward critics and by audiences cheering the very repertory they had only recently deprecated,[24] that in the brief week before their depar-

---

wrote Burkhardt, who put the entire blame on Eisfeld and his bad conducting. He then launched into his usual attack on the conductor and his apparent lifetime stranglehold on the Philharmonic (*Albion*, January 27, 1855, pp. 43–44).

[20] For some reason Strong still insisted on assigning the key of B-flat to Mozart's Symphony in G minor.

[21] Where preparations were now in full swing for its reopening on February 19 with the first performance in America of Verdi's *Rigoletto*.

[22] So triumphant that Hackett was now said to have profited on the Grisi/Mario American tour by some $20,000; he admitted to a more modest $12,000. For an ecstatic running account of the Grisi/Mario season in Boston, see *Dwight's*, January 20 through February 17, 1855, *passim*.

[23] It being the first time opera was performed at the Metropolitan Theatre, the *Times* took the occasion to assess its "appropriateness for the purpose": the stage was "all wrong," and besides, it was "the ugliest thing of the kind ever devised"; acoustically, too, the theatre was a great disappointment: "Such a conglomeration of chattering sounds as assailed the ear . . . has seldom been heard in a hall devoted to music. . . . In a word, the Metropolitan Theatre will not do for operatic purposes" (February 14, 1855).

[24] "Why such enthusiasm should be exhibited now, in contrast to former apathy, wiser heads than ours must decide" (*Spirit*, February 24, 1855, p. 24).

Both: Girvice Archer, Jr.

Vestvali as a doughty protagonist in the roles of Arsace and Maffio Orsini.

ture[25] Grisi and Mario appeared not three but six times—in *I puritani, Lucrezia Borgia, Semiramide* (with a manly and magnetic Vestvali replacing the pusillanimous Donovani as Arsace), *Norma, La favorita*—and, on February 20 to conclude their American adventure, again *Lucrezia* (for Hackett's benefit),[26] this time with Vestvali as an irresistibly handsome Maffio Orsini.[27]

Strong attended neither of her performances, but he evidently followed her reviews, for he noted in his journal on February 20: "The Vestvali seems to have covered herself with glory—beyond my expectations. All the newspaper critics with one consent sing her praise."

[25] "Signor Mario (Marquis di Candia), Madame Grisi, and Miss Coutts will sail in next Wednesday's steamer for Europe," wickedly announced the *Herald* (February 19, 1855); but the *Mirror* (February 20) reported, true or false, that "the remarkable Miss Coutts, who has so constantly followed Mario, is not going to Europe with him; she will remain in this country for some considerable time, at least."

[26] For this last performance, tickets were again sold at auction. The music stores where they were subsequently available at exorbitant prices included Dodworth's, who advertised tickets at $7 for orchestra box seats, $6 for balcony box seats, $5 for the parquette and parquette circle, and $3 and $4 for seats in the first circle (whatever locations those fancy denominations might have signified).

[27] Fry, who detested the "execrable" custom of women appearing in breeches parts, contemptuously remarked that Vestvali's animated rendition of the drinking song had "afforded the lovers of

Indeed the critics (to whom, thanks to Mr. Ruggles's efforts, Vestvali was no unknown debutante), strained their most extravagant superlatives in glorifying her phenomenal attributes, both vocal and physical (but predominantly physical). A hopelessly overcome Richard Grant White wrote: "Signorina Vestvali's fresh, full, and sympathetic contralto voice has the happiness to dwell in a person of such entire and stately symmetry, and to be aided by a countenance so blooming with healthful beauty, so radiant with intelligence, and so expressive of emotion, that she might with some impunity have fallen far short of the vocal and dramatic excellence which she displayed on Saturday evening." So magnificent was her appearance, he babbled on, that it would be impossible to give an unbiased judgment of her singing unless one were "smitten with blindness." With eyes open, "we were struck by her action, in which grace tempered energy and passion, and a tinge of womanly tenderness occasionally softened the haughty mien which the character required, and which so well became her. Indeed, as she moved so superbly about, her helmed head o'ertopping that of every woman on the stage, it seemed as if Britomart had stepped out of the pictured pages of the *Faerie Queene*"[28] (*Courier and Enquirer,* February 19, 1855).

Vestvali's vivid personality—Slavic rather than Italianate—was something new to New York opera-goers. Richard Storrs Willis, who with White had attended her first audition at Mr. Ruggles's, was, like White, struck by her "symmetry": "Her symmetrical womanhood, possessing a degree of nervous vitality and power," he wrote, in a confusion of sexual attributes, "admirably suited the character of the young commander. Vestvali came on the stage in as gallant and effective a manner as ever woman could . . . [Her] voice is an excellent contralto, effectively managed; it is sufficiently voluminous in tone for power, and being sustained by her unusual nervous energy and vividness of dramatic conception, it is actually far more effective than a voice of much greater natural volume." Although (as throughout this farewell season) the opera had not been rehearsed,[29] Vestvali had betrayed no first-night nerves and indeed had received an ovation, with an encore demanded for her part in the great duet with Grisi. With her dazzling gifts, wrote Willis, Vestvali's great success was a "*predestinate* thing" (*Musical World,* February 24, 1855, p. 85).

Mr. Ruggles had done his work artfully and well (as had Vestvali), for only a few days later (on February 25) Strong informed his journal, with a certain measure of pride: "The *Vestvali* engaged at the Academy of Music,[30] partly brought about by our meeting of last Sunday night. Her person and acting will make her effective with the masses, but she won't satisfy the knowing ones in vocalization."

Notwithstanding Strong's Cassandra-like forebodings, the fiery Vestvali continued

---

model-artists' performances a great treat in the delicious opportunity to survey her nether continuations," apparently models of symmetry (*Tribune,* February 21, 1855).

[28] Britomart is the chaste, pure, and fearless female knight in *The Faerie Queene* by Sir Edmund Spenser (1552–1599).

[29] "If any one ask *why* the rehearsal was omitted," wrote Willis, "it need only be remarked that a rehearsal costs no little wear-and-tear of solo voices, and—about $140." So casually were the performances prepared that when Mario complained of fatigue, Arditi ordered the orchestra, with no advance warning, to transpose down a half-tone. "There was a little floundering at first, but they soon . . . became used to the thing and played on as if there were 'nothing in it'" (*Musical World,* February 24, 1855, p. 85).

[30] Purportedly a three-month engagement at a huge monthly salary of $800.

throughout her short stay at the Academy to be as great a favorite of the cognoscenti as of the benighted. But, fascinating though his momentary brush with the glamorous, behind-the-scenes world of opera had been, it was not opera for which Strong's soul thirsted.

February 21. . . . This evening I called on Timm and arranged for an attempt at another season of Mass-meetings. Then saw Mrs. Eleanor and the two Schermerhorns and notified them; also stopped at Kuhn's and left a note. If we succeed in getting up these performances again, I trust they may be half as pleasant as those of last year, unanimously pronounced so overwhelming. But I anticipate nothing; a "second series," or continuation, generally falls off.

~

Strong's misgivings were to a certain extent justified. With the resumption of the Mass-meetings he discovered to his chagrin that he was no longer in complete possession of *all* the felicitous, soul-satisfying "points" in his beloved Masses. No longer did his post-Mass-meeting musings reflect a state of radiant self-fulfillment: Strong had fallen prey to the nagging suspicion that perhaps, after all, he had not really encompassed the full extent of the Masses' musical riches at last year's Mass-meetings. He seems to have become possessed by an almost greedy compulsion to fathom the unfathomable: once and for all to fix—in vast, rambling outpourings—the precise emotions, thoughts, intuitions, impulses, and motivations of his favorite composers—Haydn, Beethoven, and Mozart—in creating the works he most deeply treasured.

February 23. . . . Mass-meeting no. 1, second season, just terminated. Mrs. Eleanor, Mrs. Wright, and Mrs. G. T. S., William and Edmund Schermerhorn, Charles Kuhn, Cousinery, and Jem Ruggles, with Timm at the piano, went through with Haydn's No. 6—George C. Anthon and myself the audience—very successfully, most of it twice.

It is aggravating to find this composition, which I was sure I knew thoroughly and appreciated fully, revealing so much new beauty when heard once more—the *Kyrie, Et incarnatus, Qui tollis,* and *Cum sancto spiritu,* for instance, standing out this time as special *points* which would redeem any composition, though the rest were utterly flat. But (the *Et incarnatus* excepted), I had not found out before that they were on a level with the rest of the Mass. The soprano solo of the *Et incarnatus* blends celestial purity with human tenderness, the Divine and the mortal, as none but Haydn would have united them. Even Mozart could scarcely have written these beautiful phrases of melody.

But the *aggravation* of all this is the avaricious regret for the multitudinous embodiments of beauty in musical art that exist but that one will never be the wiser for. If one may hear Haydn's No. 6 half a dozen times without drinking it dry, how of all the rest that he has written, and that a hundred other composers have written, which ten human lives could not exhaust? It recalls the feeling with which one hears some specially glowing and fervent and overwhelming composition, great or small—the C-minor Symphony, e.g., or the *Erblicken so freundlich die Sterne* chorus of *Preciosa,* or the first chorus of *The Seasons*—a wish that all other music were abolished and destroyed and that one could live to the end of his days on that alone.

March 4. . . . Yesterday . . . Philharmonic rehearsal [with Timm replacing Eisfeld, who was ill]. Piano and orchestra concerto—Beethoven, I think [the "Emperor"], full of beautiful points of melody and instrumentation—on *first impression* a most lovely and valuable composition. Overture (Spontini?)—sound and fury, signifying a good deal—fine contrasts of light and shadow—great elaboration and finish of detail, with notable breadth and massiveness—a very vigorous affair indeed. Another overture (Mendelssohn? More probably Spohr) [in fact, Mendelssohn's Overture to *Ruy Blas,* op. 95 (1839)], very good but not as striking. It will be a good concert.

Having missed Eisfeld's fourth *soirée* (February 20)—given without Eisfeld, who was in the throes of a long and critical illness—Strong did not recognize the pianist, Gustav Satter (1832–1879), a recent arrival from Vienna who on that occasion had made his highly lauded American debut.[31] So superbly had Satter played Schubert's Trio in E-flat, op. 100 (1827), with Noll and Bergner, that the usually undemonstrative audience had excitedly demanded an encore (someone's "frivolous" Fantasie on *Norma*). Not since Liszt himself, wrote a swept-away *Bornonis* (in *Dwight's,* February 24, 1855, p. 166), had he heard such marvelous piano playing, such dazzling brilliance and virtuosity, such sensitivity and profundity.[32]

March 9. . . . *Mass-meeting* has just terminated. Mrs. Eleanor, Mrs. Wright, Mrs. Gibbs, Ellie, Cousinery, William Schermerhorn, Alfred Gibbs, Kuhn, Edmund Schermerhorn, and Humphreys, a new-caught basso. Also present Mrs. William Schermerhorn, as gracious as ever, Wright, Charley, George C. Anthon; Timm, of course.

They took up first Mozart's No. 17 [Mass in C] (Novello's edition).[33] Rather roughly done, but well enough to show the value of the composition. Most of it seems written in haste, without much care or thought, especially the earlier movements, which are thin and barren. The *Kyrie* is made up of repetitions of one phrase—very beautiful and valuable, but repeated verbatim, except in change of keys. The *Gloria* is neither deep nor original. Its only notable point is the graceful melody of the *Gratias agimus*. The *Credo* is more elaborate and studied, but not very effective, except, however, the very solemn and serious *Et incarnatus*. That, I think, would not be easily surpassed, *in its way.* It is most vigorous and pungent, but does it express with this vigor and pungency the meaning of its subject—the advent of Life into a world of Death—God assuming our feeble mortal humanity and all its infirmities, that He may show us the way to conquer them—infinite Truth and Love and Power taking for our sakes the form of a little child? The words that affirm all this ought to be allied to music *unlike* the opening phrases of this movement. The rest of the *Credo* showed nothing

[31] Satter might have been heard on January 20 at Paul Julien's concert for the benefit of the New York needy.

[32] Also heard was Madame Wallace-Bouchelle, who "with too many guttural notes and too many grimaces" sang *Batti, batti* (from Mozart's *Don Giovanni*) and Mendelssohn's song *Das erste Veilchen,* op. 19a; Beethoven's String Quartet in F, op. 18, no. 1 (*c.* 1800), and a "light and rather trivial" quintet for strings and flute, op. 51, by the German/Danish composer Friedrich Kuhlau.

[33] Köchel *Anhang* C.1.01, another spurious work.

very notable. The *Sanctus* [is] well enough, the *Benedictus* elaborate, finished, and pre-eminently beautiful. Nobody but Mozart could have written it. So the *Agnus Dei* with its lovely melody of supplication. The finale is very vigorous, but rather too brilliant and unecclesiastical. Then they went through again with Haydn's No. 6, which gains in favor at each repetition. On the whole, clearly his finest Mass—more uniformly good than any other. Of course, new *points* revealed themselves, which I've no time to enumerate, except only the splendid bits of *nervous,* living melody, with which the *Cum sancto spiritu* concludes.

March 13. . . . Saturday night [March 10] to Philharmonic concert. George C. Anthon and Miss Tote dined and went with us, and the former was put to sleep by the Andante of the symphony. Symphony (Mozart in B-flat [G minor]) nicely enough played, came wonderfully strong and beautiful. Third movement encored for the sake of its lovely trio,[34] whereupon a newspaper critic observes that a *Minuetto* is an old-fashioned dance and that this encore shows that a New York audience "prefers the music of the heels to that of the head."[35]

. . . Sunday night, divers people called, among them Vestvali and "the lobster." The lady stands the test of further acquaintance—seems a genial, intelligent Titaness.

. . . Forgot to mention the great feature of the Philharmonic concert, viz., Beethoven's Concerto for Piano and Orchestra No. 5 in E-flat, op. 73, the "Emperor" [1809].[36] The pianist [Satter] did his work most effectively[37]—orchestra perhaps a little slovenly. The composition is matchless of its kind. Certainly, I've never heard its equal. Like all its class, it sacrifices a good deal to the exhibition of dexterity in the principal performer; aims to set forth skillful manipulation rather than *Art;* substitutes, more or less, for true musical thoughts difficulties for a pianist to triumph over.[38] But it is wonderfully rich in musical *coloring* and instrumental effect, and its principal subjects are the clearest and loveliest melodies. Those of the first and second movements, especially, have a peculiar *Scotch* flavoring about them that carries me sadly back to a very early period in my musical reminiscences.

Fry, who found Beethoven's concerto, although "not up to the mere pianism of later authors, a noble piece of conception and detail," nonetheless disapproved (as did Strong, but for different reasons) of concertos in general: they were invariably an unequal struggle between solo instrument and orchestra, he wrote. Besides, Satter "introduced the Cadenza of Listz [*sic*],[39] wherein, compressed at the starting point of the

[34] Encored because it was the only adequately rehearsed movement of the symphony, sourly wrote the *Times* (March 12, 1855).

[35] The critic was, of course, William Henry Fry, who—after his usual disparagement of Mozart and of the *passé* four-movement symphony ("for which pattern there is no reason")—criticized the taste of the Philharmonic audience in demanding an encore of the Minuet, an obsolete dance form that "in the age of hair powder and buckram, was the polka of the day" (*Tribune,* March 12, 1855).

[36] Its first hearing in New York. The concerto had been performed in Boston in 1854 by the Germania conducted by Carl Bergmann, with the magician/pianist Robert Heller at the piano.

[37] In Fry's opinion, Satter was "certainly one of the strongest of the piano strong-men that the new school has turned up."

[38] Egregious attributes strictly taboo in Strong's rigid musical canon.

[39] A cadenza unknown to the Liszt scholars Rena Mueller and Charles Suttoni.

dominant chord, are the force-leaps of his invention—a mastery of the instrument which secured Mr. Satter an encore (which we fear the Concerto, pure and simple, would not have commanded)" (*Tribune,* March 12, 1855).

An infuriated Burkhardt raged mightily against the cadenza: whether composed by Liszt or anyone else, "it had no business there, is in bad taste, and is a sacrilege upon Beethoven." It was about as appropriate, he wrote, as "a pair of boots and spurs would be to a fine antique statue of Apollo" (*Albion,* March 17, 1855, p. 128).[40]

Fry censured the audience, who tended to applaud the soloist but to disregard the vastly more deserving orchestra, whose cultivation of "harmonious intricacies is of itself the highest and holiest of all the arts and requires a pure worship all its own." But, lamented Fry, to expect proper appreciation from our uncultivated general public was to "presuppose higher aims than the materialism of society allows us at present."

Satter's piano playing had evidently impressed Strong more greatly than he was willing to admit, for on March 19, despite his professed disdain of solo performers and performances, he attended Satter's first concert, or rather, musicale.[41] Strong was not converted.

March 21. . . . to a private-invitation piano concert by Satter (with Timm to aid) at Breusing's music store, 701 Broadway. About 150 present. Sat close to the performer and could *see* his feats of dexterity and strength—many of them better to see than to hear. His fingers were a mere misty blur, like the wings of a big, nocturnal moth over a thistle. The Overture to *Egmont* on two pianos was refreshing, and I was glad to hear the Ninth Symphony again (the "Choral") [in Liszt's 1851 transcription] for two pianos, with which the concert ended. But as to the latter, my desires are for the present satisfied. Rendered by orchestra and chorus, it's about as pleasant to listen to as Fearne on Contingent Remainders[42]—only comprehensible in scraps here and there. But arranged for the piano it is most dreary[43]—doubly so because one feels bound to listen reverently and to clutch despairingly at every floating straw of an intelligible idea.

The rest of the concert was gymnastic rather than musical: Truck—chiefly of Chopin [Ballade in G minor, op. 23 (1836), also Schumann's *Carnaval,* op. 9 (1834–36)]—unmeaning sequences of notes to show off a player's muscle and aplomb;

[40] The program consisted additionally of Mendelssohn's Overture to *Ruy Blas* and Spontini's Overture to *Olympia;* Mrs. Georgiana Stuart sang the aria *Per pietà,* from Mozart and Da Ponte's *Così fan tutte,* and "Winged Messenger," a ballad by Fesca; and Philip Mayer sang a too-familiar aria from Spohr's *Jessonda* and a "rather tedious" unfamiliar one from *Guttenberg* (Graz 1846), an opera by Ferdinand Fuchs (1811–1848), a German composer currently popular in Europe.

[41] Following the unconventional model established by Liszt, Satter dispensed with assisting artists (except for Timm at a second piano) and confined his program to compositions for piano and transcriptions for two pianos. "For a piano-forte entertainment the program was quite lengthy, occupying two hours in performance," caviled the *Daily Times* critic, presumably Charles Bailey Seymour (March 20, 1855). "A vocalist or two would have relieved the situation and brought it to bear more freshly on the ensuing efforts of Mr. Satter."

[42] Charles Fearne (1742–1794) was the lawyerly author of *An Essay on the Learning of Contingent Remainders and Executory Devises* in two forbidding volumes.

[43] To the *Times* critic it was a "cruel infliction," especially as the last piece of a long program.

puzzles for an *artist* to undo.[44] What idiocy most of our fashionable piano music is! And I believe the performers who ought to know, and must know, better, try to keep the public in its blindness, and prefer these exhibitions of legerdemain to real music. Not without reason. After hearing the latter, people would think of Mozart or Beethoven and forget the man who played it.

It's a miserable perversion of language to call the individual who executes musical compositions an *artist.* He's not necessarily or presumably any such thing. To make him a first-rate performer he should have a strong *feeling for art.* But that is very different from the creative power—the "vision and the faculty"—by virtue of which alone one is an Artist.

As well give Raphael's title to a perfect copyist of his madonnas—or to a pre-eminent engraver—promote [William] Burton to fellowship with Shakespeare because he enacted Caliban to perfection (as they say).[45]

Giving the style [name] of *artist* to the *performer* is mischievous, because the common familiar misapplication of the term fortifies people in the delusion that skilled, brilliant *execution* is somewhere nearly on a level with the power and beauty of composition, and leads half the world to tolerate and to think it enjoys productions that ought to be cast into the fire because they encumber the Earth—to find pleasure not in music, but in the ground and lofty tumbling[46] of a singer or a pianist—to discourage the simple sincerity and clearness of Art and to demand in its place some *bêtise* that enables a performer to exhibit his or her personal powers to advantage.

Even true music has to be defiled by the introduction of some impertinence—the creation of some difficulty—whereby its performer may remind the audience of his insignificant self. Witness Beethoven's concerto played by Satter at the last Philharmonic, and the interpolation of Liszt's wonderfully difficult and much lauded "cadenza." What business had it there? What did it mean? If Mr. Satter wanted to give special testimony of his power and was not satisfied with rendering clearly and forcibly what Beethoven wrote, he might have played ten or twelve bars of the composition standing on his head and balancing a music stand on his heels. But why introduce an unmeaning scrap of manual dexterity into a beautiful creation like that?[47]

[44] In obscure terms the *Times* critic (April 20) agreed: he disparaged the Chopin Ballade for too tenaciously preserving "the individuality of the composer. . . . The thin, thought-like outline of his ballad became lost in what should have been the subordinate characteristic coloring"; he dismissed the *Carnaval* as "a trashy and interminable thing by Schumann—music fit for accompanying a panorama only" (a species of cheap entertainment popular in the nineteenth century). More bearable were a Liszt transcription of *Le Rossignol,* a favorite Russian song by Alexander Alabieff (1787–1851); a Villanelle by an unidentified member of the Italian Fumagalli family of pianists and composers; and Satter's own paraphrase on themes from *Le Prophète.* But whatever Satter chose to play, his playing was invariably splendid; he was "by far the most finished and enjoyable pianist we have had." Willis, who airily dismissed the Schumann *Carnaval* as "a droll thing," pronounced Satter to be "the only real piano phenomenon which we have had among us for years" (*Musical World,* March 24, 1855, p. 134). (What of Willis's recent dithyrambs over Louis Moreau Gottschalk? William Mason?)

[45] Burton's notable achievement as Caliban, and indeed his entire production of *The Tempest* (which Strong evidently did not attend), had been widely acclaimed in 1854.

[46] Contemporary parlance for acrobatic feats.

[47] *Bornonis,* who held the work to be "Beethoven's grandest Concerto" and Satter's performance of it "masterly," approved of the much-maligned cadenza, which "might have seemed out of place,

Just as well might Romeo pause in the balcony scene to say "six slim slick saplings" three times over very fast, and demonstrate his power of articulation. Difficulty of execution is not a *merit.* It is, rather, a fault—at least a misfortune.

March 23. . . . Just at the end of another of our musical meetings. All present, and "Howadji" Curtis, George C. Anthon, and Wolcott Gibbs for audience. Humphreys came out very strong in the *Qui tollis* in Haydn's No. 2—sang the bass solo so as to redeem it from the sin that seems to lie at its door—viz., the total absence of expression suited to its subject. No. 2 and No. 6 were sung all through. There can be no doubt that the latter is the weightier composition. But the lovely quartette of No. 2 (the *Benedictus*) can't be matched in No. 6 or elsewhere.

~

With Eisfeld's illness showing no signs of abating, the Philharmonic was forced to replace him with a conductor more satisfactory than Timm, who had not covered himself with glory at the last concert. Carl Bergmann, who had been living in New York following the breakup of the Germania the year before, was chosen to conduct the final concert of the season, on April 21. As it turned out, he remained for the following two decades, alternating with an eventually recovered Eisfeld, who finally retired in 1866, leaving Bergmann an undisputed field. A gifted, forceful, and venturesome musician, Carl Bergmann introduced a new era at the Philharmonic,[48] exposing his audiences, steeped as they were in Mozart/Beethoven/Mendelssohn/Spohr, to the shocks of Wagner/Liszt/Berlioz and other revolutionary composers. For his first Philharmonic concert Bergmann programed Wagner's Overture to *Tannhäuser,* heard under his direction the year before—but barely—in the general pandemonium of Jullien's Musical Congress; it was now (and justifiably) being presented as a first performance in New York.[49] Beethoven's Seventh Symphony shared the program, and with its reappearance Strong valiantly resumed his unequal struggle with that diabolical work for possession of his immortal soul. In finally making his peace with the symphony he became submerged in impenetrable thickets of agonizing introspection on the meaning of music, doubtless influenced by the philosophy of the English aesthete and critic John Ruskin (1819–1900), whose works were being increasingly published in the 1850s.[50]

---

had it not served as a foil to the beauty of its surroundings. Toward its end, as light gradually broke, and at last, in a perfectly ethereal *pianissimo* of high notes, the theme reappeared, there was a breathless hush throughout the whole house until, with the joining in of the orchestra, there was one deep, long-drawn breath, and all gave vent to the most unqualified admiration" (*Dwight's,* March 17, 1855, p. 188).

[48] In 1892, the noted critic and first biographer of the Philharmonic, Henry E. Krehbiel (1854–1923), wrote: "Bergmann's genius for conducting (for his gifts reached the degree of genius) lifted the Society to the pinnacle of its efficiency, and his methods became a tradition" (Krehbiel, p. 73).

[49] And a splendid performance it was, eliciting an encore—"a degree of favor" it had rarely, if ever, been granted in Europe, commented Theodore Hagen (1824–1871), the recently arrived editor and critic of the Mason Brothers' *New York Musical Review and Choral Advocate* (April 26, 1855, pp. 140–41), soon to merge with their short-lived *Musical Gazette,* to become the *New-York Musical Review and Gazette.*

[50] In 1853, Strong had read Ruskin's *The Stones of Venice* (1851–53), serially issued by the New York publisher John Wiley; in 1855, Ruskin was a contibutor to *The Crayon,* a splendid new monthly "aesthetic journal," devoted to literature and the arts.

March 25. . . . Yesterday afternoon with Ellie to Philharmonic rehearsal.[51] The *Seventh Symphony* (A minor) roughly but forcibly played.[52] So many uncanny, unhealthy, bad associations and memories are connected with it in my mind that I went reluctantly, resolved to shut out the old imaginings and to see the composition from a new point of view—to put a new construction on it. To retain the old interpretation is to debar myself of the privilege of ever recalling a single phrase of this all-but-*most*-vigorous of compositions, for, except *the C-minor,* no orchestral work seems to me so full of fire and power. I succeeded in seeing it in a new light—in finding a new set of impressions in it—even in the opening of the second movement—and the A-major melody of the first—and the majestic sorrow that inspires the second subject of the third.

May some new Ruskin soon arise to discuss the aesthetics of music and to tell us how to discover what music is meant to tell us. Is it possible that the true significance of even so noble a work as this varies with each individual who hears it, and with the varying moods and nerves of each? Can it be that language so keenly expressive as that of Music *expresses nothing* and merely depends for its meaning on its hearer—merely enforcing what he happens to feel? That is impossible. The finale of the C-minor, the "Eroica"—the "Pastorale"—a thousand productions besides—have a significance and expression with which the temper of a listener has nothing to do—a meaning as *distinct* as can be conveyed by any form of words. But there are exceptions. Music may be most keen, vigorous, and pungent in *expression,* as in this Seventh Symphony, the Overture to *Egmont,* etc., and yet *what is expressed may be a problem.*

Probably it is impossible to systematize and discuss the subject because it lies outside the domain of articulate speech, because music takes up and begins to deal with thought and emotion at the point where language—the wooden mechanism of speech—becomes inadequate to express them. Yet, painting can be criticized, though a picture may express as much beyond the scope of words; and a sunny landscape or a lovely portrait may embody beauty which folios of double-columned, close print could not define.

The want of vocabulary[53] is a bar to critical discussion of music. One can speak of it only in vague phrases, describe it only by loose epithets. A movement by Mozart is "vigorous" and another by Haydn and by Beethoven no less; yet each differs in *expression* from the other by absolute dissimilarity, how, and wherein, I know of no *command of language* that would enable me to tell.

[returning to the Philharmonic rehearsal] Wagner's Overture to the *Tannhäuser* [was] also played—a composition on which I'd rather not commit myself until after a

[51] To a true music-lover the public rehearsals were a frustration: "If one could only enjoy the rehearsals more," complained *Bornonis,* "but they are getting more and more to be an occasion of rendezvous, so that there is hardly a place in which one is not disturbed by the shameless talking and flirting by which most of the audiences amuse themselves" (*Dwight's,* April 21, 1855, p. 21). For the coming season the Philharmonic board of directors ordered the officer presiding at rehearsals to "see that conversation and loud talking during performances is hereafter strictly prohibited" (Philharmonic Archives). In vain.

[52] It is noteworthy that Strong, who unfailingly listed every participant at every Mass-meeting, only rarely named performers at the Philharmonic, not even a highly regarded new conductor making his first appearance with the Society.

[53] Surely no failing of Strong's.

rehearing.[54] Novel, most elaborate, and full of talent, clearly, but not altogether pleasing, and whether truly original and genial, or merely outré and labored I can't say. . . .

Apropos of the *Tannhäuser,* the calamity of our modern music seems to be that composers have not the inclination, or the ability, to devise, or create, a distinct *theme*—subject—tangible, self-subsistent, melodic phrase as the foundation-stone of each composition.[55] Generally (there may be exceptions), a work is valuable in proportion to the truth and beauty of the subjects on which it is built, be they many or few. Instrumentation, orchestral effects, laws of harmony, counterpoint, light and shadow, bring out the value of the subject and develop its worth. But no ingenuity or boldness in their employment can make good its absence or compensate for its feebleness.

Mozart, Haydn, etc. provide for each movement of the symphony, quartette, etc. a palpable subject of its own—a musical thought that needs no orchestra to express it—a phrase that a child can express on its piano—an honest, independent melody, on which, and for the sake of which, they bring out their resources of harmony and instrumental effects. But our orchestral composers adopt a commonplace subject and rely on novelties of instrumentation, or spasms of modulation, to give it effect: the piano composer looks to the muscle of the performer doing incredible runs, and playing octaves worthy a prize at the Olympic games; the writer of opera expects dramatic power and expression in his *prima donna* to enable people to swallow his musical inanities.

So, a century ago, the composer who had mistaken his vocation relied on skillful fugues and musical learning to save his credit. Yet people go to hear *The Messiah, The Seasons, The Creation,* and say they "don't like scientific music—they want to hear something that has a melody in it that gives them something they can carry home with them." *They can't see the wood for the trees.* It is *all melody,* but without the false, adventitious accessories to which their ear is used, and so, while they listen to the noble melodic phrases of Haydn's "Spring," they hold it all scientific—rococo—antiquated—because they miss the *mere cry of passion* which Steffanone or Bosio can put into a barren air of Donizetti's, or the surprise with which they would hear a pianist or violinist execute some wonderful piece of notation by a composer who never conceived a melody.[56]

March 27. . . . Eisfeld's [fifth] concert tonight with Ellie. . . . Beethoven's Septette in E-flat [op. 20], and Trio [the "Archduke," for piano, violin, and cello], op. 97.[57] Both very nice indeed—subjects of each movement strong and beautiful—the former especially very clear and full of melody—its Scherzo very notable.[58] But I was a little

[54] But this *was* a rehearing: Strong seems to have forgotten that he had heard the *Tannhäuser* Overture the preceding summer at Jullien's Musical Congress, and had termed it "nice" (see GTS: 1854).

[55] So much for the Berliozian *idée fixe* and the approaching Wagnerian *Leitmotiv.*

[56] In a pinch, every man his own Ruskin.

[57] The Septet was played by Noll (violin), Reyer (viola), Bergner (cello), Rehder (double bass), Kiefer (clarinet), Schmitz (horn), and Hochstein (bassoon), and the Trio by William Mason, with Noll and Bergner.

[58] Only four movements of the Septet were played, but even these "proved still too long" for Seymour (*Times,* March 28, 1855). The program offered, besides, a duet from Méhul's *Joseph,* beautifully sung by Philip Mayer and less so by his recently acquired wife, Rosa Jaques; she, however, earned an encore with her vivacious solo rendering of Abt's Barcarole. In addition to the Beethoven

disappointed: was not knocked down and dragged out, as I expect to be by *something* in every work of Beethoven's. Perhaps I've "lost my taste," for the present, being fresh from the red pepper of the Seventh Symphony. One [William] Mason, *pianized* very creditably—very transparently, is the proper expression—that is, he gave Beethoven's meaning fully—transmitted it sharp and well-defined, undistorted by impressions of his own personal prowess and attainments. "Execution" is bad when it is so good as to withdraw attention from the musical thought it is meant to convey. So a perfect style is that which communicates thoughts or facts so clearly—through which ideas reach the mind of the reader so distinctly and vividly—that he has no perception at all of diction—elegance—purity, etc. *Force* and *Beauty* cannot belong to *Style,* though so often assigned it. They are attributes of *Thought*—of what comes to us through the medium of *Style.* Clearness is the one merit of language—just as defining power and achromatism (perfect transmission of an image) alone make an object glass [lens] respectable. It does not exist for its own sake, but in order to inform us of something else. So far as it is itself perceptible, it is defective and bad.

March 31. . . . Mass-meeting last night. All present but Mrs. C. E. Strong, who was inopportunely afflicted with a something—it is in the throat. Haydn's No. 6 sung through and thereafter sundry scraps from No. 3 and 4,[59] and from Mozart's 12th, to wit, the *Et incarnatus,* which aggravates one with the sense of underlying, infinite purity and beauty that one can't quite get hold of.

April 9. . . . Music on Easter Sunday (at Trinity Church) [under Hodges] rather abundant if not good, excepting always the Easter hymn "Christ the Lord is risen today," sung to that noble melody from the *Kyrie* of Haydn's First Mass. The *Te Deum, Jubilate,* and *Gloria in excelsis* (the last by Hodges, and the least bad of the three) were labored, flat, and false in construction—specimens of the very faults from which he (Hodges) claims his precious English school to be free. They included elaborate solos without thought or feeling—parade of counterpoint that helped out the expression of nothing—commonplace contrasts of light and shade—commonplace discords setting off commonplace harmonies. Far better a little true music, even though it might have suggested somewhat of good opera—reminded one of high dramatic art—or even borrowed bodily from some of the great musical expressions of deep sentiment and true thought which Hodges is content to leave in undisputed possession to the World and the Devil.

~

From time to time the Strongs assisted at fashionable amateur concerts given for various charities. Musically speaking, Strong was prone to regard them with tongue-in-cheek condescension.

April 10. . . . we backed out from a meeting at Lewis [Colford] Jones's tonight to arrange preliminaries and program for a certain amateur concert, about which Mrs.

Trio, William Mason played several piano solos, among them a Suite by Handel, a Chopin Impromptu, and *Pensées fugitives,* an impressionistic, Gade-like composition of his own. *Bornonis,* who reviewed this concert in *Dwight's* (March 31, 1855, p. 207), went to great lengths to point out the superiority of Satter's playing over Mason's.

[59] Novello no. 4, Hoboken XXII:13, is the *Schöpfungsmesse,* or "Creation Mass" (1801).

Lewis and Mrs. [Cornelius] Dubois and others are busily arranging for the benefit of The Nursery [for the Children of Poor Women], of which Ellie is a manageress, or she-Trustee. I'm to be a "manager" of the concert, I believe, but I'm profoundly ignorant of its plan and particulars. Trobriand and [Émile] Millet have been consulted about the music, so I suppose the program will be made up mostly of "sacred" compositions of Rossini, Bellini, Donizetti, and Verdi. It is said, however, that *Miss Gould* [an acquaintance at Rockaway Beach last summer] is to sing something from the *Messiah* (!!!). Query: if a hand organ might not be provided with a new barrel and made to render Handel's melody with quite as much feeling and with more precision.

April 17. . . . Trinity Chapel duly consecrated this morning, and I didn't get to Wall Street till three o'clock. The services were well conducted and impressive. Church packed full, of course. . . . Music was tolerable.[60] The multitude of voices gave much dignity to the chants, etc., in which the congregation joined. The *Te Deum* and *Benedictus* were from the old Trinity Church Consecration Service. The Anthem (20 minutes long) disappointed even my moderate expectations. One movement ("Peace be within thy Walls") was nice; certainly very far from "severe." For the rest, it was made up of the dreariest choral counterpoint interspersed with solos. Don't know whether the latter were meant to be recitative or air; probably the latter from their flourishes of musical rhetoric. Anyway, they seemed to be written to show that "as the object of language is to conceal thought," so that of musical science is to enable a composer to be elaborate without committing himself to the expression of any particular sentiment or idea whatsoever. . . .

[bypassing the final Eisfeld *soirée* of the season][61] Mrs. Ellie has gone to one of the charity concert rehearsals at Mrs. Lewis Jones's. Don't think the prospects of that undertaking brilliant, but it will doubtless procure two or three thousand dollars for the "Nursery," or baby house, which its promoters seek to benefit.

April 20. . . . Ellie has gone to another rehearsal for the future charity concert. It comes off the 26th instant, and all the program not yet decided on! I fear it will make all who assist at it slightly ridiculous, and rejoice that Ellie has thus far resisted all entreaties to sing in anything but chorus.[62]

Mrs. Gibbs and her husband were here last evening to say that the lady's mamma (Mrs. Mauran) is in a very precarious condition, and that Mrs. Gibbs can't pledge her contralto to anything from one day to another. This probably kills Ellie's projected performance of selections from Haydn and Mozart before an audience of forty or fifty people, two or three weeks hence. Sorry her troubles and anxieties over program and parts have been for naught. But for *myself,* I'm very willing that the *soirée* be abandoned and our Mass-meetings go on as of old, consisting merely in the reading of new [unfa-

[60] The music was "grand," reported the *Musical World* (April 21, 1855, pp. 181–82): with the congregation singing antiphonal responses to a double choir of twenty-five voices placed on either side of the chancel, the effect was truly exciting.

[61] And just as well. It was something of a disaster: not only was Eisfeld still absent, but the scheduled performances by Root's Quartette Party of his (unidentified) vocal quartet and Mendelssohn's Hunting Song had to be canceled, due to the illness of the contralto. The program was thus reduced to Spohr's Nonet in F, op. 31, for strings and woodwinds, and Hummel's Septet in D minor, op. 74, the piano part played by a Miss Eliza Brown, a highly regarded pupil of Timm's.

[62] Echoes of Strong's prognostications of disaster at the Mrs. Graves concert of the previous year.

miliar] music, without any attempt at an accurate performance for the entertainment of anybody.[63]

April 21. . . . Just in from the Philharmonic. Little time to write about it. At Niblo's [Theatre]; crowd excessive and most enthusiastic; concert a great success. Beethoven's Symphony No. 7 greater than ever.[64] Trio ("Lift up thine eyes") [sung by Mrs. Brinkerhoff and two "amateur ladies"] and two choruses from Mendelssohn's *Elijah.*[65] The trio beautiful, though feebly rendered; the choruses obscure, perhaps because I heard them for the first time. Wagner's *Tannhäuser* Overture; Weber's *Concertstück,* nicely done [by William Mason], and the finale of the first act of Mendelssohn's posthumous [unfinished opera] *Loreley* [op. 98 (1847)], of which neither Ellie nor I could comprehend much. Certainly the [*Tannhäuser*] Overture is a great work, as compared with the productions of the last 25 years. It's effective; it has unity and breadth, with great elaboration in detail; it is thoroughly and honestly studied and worked out, and includes no slovenly passages of noisy nonsense; and some of its phrases are novel at least—perhaps truly original and valuable. Time will tell.

What did Beethoven mean by the Seventh Symphony? Unlike the others, it gives me the impression of having been written not merely to express a sequence of emotions—harmonious contrasts of feeling—but to tell some story, so far as music may. The old Philharmonic programs used to set forth a brief printed analysis showing how the music was the biography of Orpheus,♪ and how he sang to Pluto in the Allegretto, lost [Euridice] forever on the final chord of that movement, and bewailed her in the third, and went crazy in the fourth. That interpretation won't do. Never saw till tonight the full beauty of the brief introductory movement. Its pathetic melody of sorrow and lamentation is the utterance of a breaking heart. But it is no plebeian passion. The majestic march of the orchestra speaks the mourning of a hero or a demigod and is fitting prelude to high tragedy in its ancient sense. Then the upward movement of the violins have, to me, a strange, weird expression that awakens expectation, and prepares one for the development of some fearful and supernatural creation. Passing over the intermediate movements, the finale is chaos, frenzy, anarchy, acute inflammation of the brain, with violent mania—Paris in triumphant insurrection—infinite vitriol in contact with infinite carbonate soda—Bacchus and Comus and all their train raging and roaring in some place where no constables are (the Bacchantes bilious, mad but not jolly)—the reveling crew of a sinking ship—the streets of a city just taken by storm—Hell broke loose and jubilant—or anything else that is mad, reckless, and lawless. No trace there of exalted passion or kingly sorrow. The sentiment of the beginning and the end seem unmistakable. If one could find out how they are connected, we should have a solution of the symphony, which, as a whole, I don't understand.

~

The critics agreed that Bergmann was far superior to any conductor previously heard at the Philharmonic; that his superiority was immediately apparent in the im-

[63] Was Strong's alleged preference for his friends' poor performances a kind of defensiveness of the less-than-optimum musical quality of his Mass-meetings?

[64] Apparently the reconciliation was complete (or almost complete).

[65] Sung by the Mendelssohn Union, the highly promising singing society founded in 1854 by George W. Morgan (now organist at Grace Church), with Henry C. Timm and the durable music patron Dr. Quin as co-founders.

provement shown by the orchestra (particularly their new-found ability to play *piano,* even *pianissimo*); and that the concert was the best of the season (indeed, in the opinion of the *Evening Post* (April 21, 1855), the best ever given by the Philharmonic).[66] While Bergmann's performances of everything were enthusiastically praised, it was Wagner's *Tannhäuser* Overture that aroused the greatest curiosity—the music of its controversial composer until now being an unknown quantity in New York.

The overture met with a mixed reception. The *Evening Post* critic hailed it as "a perfect work . . . a work full of the fire of genius but still consistent and rational." Burkhardt, on the other hand, was disappointed: "it bears the imprint of great, very great, talent united to but little genius," he wrote (*Albion,* April 28, 1855, p. 200). The *Daily Times* (April 23, 1855), reviewing Wagner's exploits overseas, wrote of his present appointment "for some perfectly inexplicable reason [as] director of that particularly orthodox body, the Philharmonic Society of London.[67] He has [already] directed two of their concerts with eminent success and is beyond doubt a lion of magnitude. . . . But it seems to us extremely improbable that he will excite any enthusiasm as a composer."

But to Fry the *Tannhäuser* Overture was an example of the new doctrine that "music should express something definitely beyond the general emotionalism of music." The piece had been attacked by some as being obscure, but Fry saw no obscurity in it; he approved of its clear ideas and superlative orchestration and its "extraordinary violinism," even if the thematic material was "not of the first class"; and of course he lauded Wagner for "breaking through the stereotyped form of the symphony" (*Tribune,* April 23, 1855).

As for the audience, they "vociferously" demanded an encore, but, as the *Times* reports, "a member of the Philharmonic stepped forward and asked the audience to excuse the repetition, on account of the fatigue of the performers."[68]

Although this was the last concert of the season,[69] it was announced that the Philharmonic—contrary to their Constitution—would officially, "as the Philharmonic," give an unprecedented extra concert to assist the physically and financially depleted Eisfeld. But first:

April 26. . . . Amateur sacred concert [for the Nursery] last night at Dr. Cheever's hideous joss-house [Church of the Puritans at Union Square] went off better than I anticipated. Vast crowd and general good humor. Program mediocre, performances

[66] On April 24 the directors of the newly prosperous Philharmonic voted to pay Bergmann a fee of $50 for this concert (Philharmonic Archives). Eisfeld and his predecessors had labored without compensation through all the preceding years.

[67] Currently conducting a season of eight concerts with the London Philharmonic, from March 12 to June 25, Wagner aroused a storm of conflicting responses from the English critics. At the seventh concert of his series, on June 11, he performed the *Tannhäuser* Overture, with a benignly approving Queen Victoria in the audience.

[68] All the reviewers commented on the extreme technical difficulties of the overture, especially its strenuous demands on the violins.

[69] A time of financial reckoning for the Philharmonic. Not only was Bergmann paid, but the performing members received their increased annual dividend, and Niblo was paid $365 on his bill for $381.50 for rental of the hall; the remainder would follow in due course (Philharmonic Archives).

not brilliant, especially in the choruses and concerted pieces, which needed more rehearsals. Berge (organist of the 16th Street Jesuit Church) did his work ill—tried to make a respectable organ sound like a bad orchestra—and succeeded.[70]

April 29. . . . Friday was the first *failure* of our "Mass-meetings." Both Cousinery and William Schermerhorn were missing (each with ample excuses), so we had no tenors, and the evening was spent pleasantly enough in doing little scraps of various things, from Pergolesi's *Stabat Mater* to *Don Giovanni.*

~

Strong's proliferating professional duties in Wall Street prevented him (with no great regret) from attending the opera, then in full, problematical swing at the Academy of Music, which Ellen frequently visited; nor was he able to join her at many of the socially elevated private musicales that she attended. Nothing, however, was allowed to interfere with his precious Mass-meetings.

May 2. . . . Ellie has just returned from *Il trovatore* [its first performance in the United States], with Jem [Ruggles] for escort, and pronounces the opera decent, for Verdi [discussed in following OBBLIGATO].

May 6. . . . Ellie went last night . . . to hear Eisfeld's people and had a nice time. Wished much to go myself, but tomorrow is the first Monday of May and my pet case is no. 3 on the calendar.

May 9. . . . Ellie matronized Miss Rosalie, Miss Betty Rhinelander, Jem, Charles Hoffman, and Newbold Edgar to *Il trovatore* this evening, and they came here to supper after the opera and spent a very pleasant hour or so.

May 13. . . . Mass-meeting Friday night. All present but Mrs. Eleanor. Miss Tote Anthon and Miss [Mary] McIlvaine as audience. Haydn's No. 4 done through—thereafter parts of No. 6 with organ accompaniment. Very satisfactory evening. *Kyrie* good (of No. 4), though its most vigorous phrases are rather bacchanalian than ecclesiastical. *Gloria* and *Qui tollis* very handsome, particularly the latter (some phrases, by the by, recall the latter part of the *Creation*). *Et incarnatus* good, tenor solo; *Et vitam venturi saeculi* brief but very splendid and forcible; the *Benedictus* a gem—on a level with those of the Second and Sixteenth, its concluding phrases [are] unsurpassable—Agnus Dei and *Dona pacem* [*sic*] fully up to the standard of Haydn, the finale especially masculine and emphatic. But No. 6 is surely [Haydn's] finest mass. It is inspired throughout by the purest and highest feeling. If there be such a thing as "sacred" music, it is surely to be found in the Quartette of the *Gratias agimus* in that Mass, as rendered by Ellie's full, honest contralto, [by] Mrs. Wright's soprano *(Domine Deus, Pater omnipotens, Jesu Christe)* with its clear articulation and expression of reverence and meekness, truth and purity, [and by] Cousinery's sympathetic tenor (so effective in the *Filius Patris*). I don't believe that movement has ever been much more justly rendered on Earth; I won't

[70] Not according to the *Evening Post,* which faithfully advertised, puffed, and reviewed the concert: "The church, though a large one, was filled even to the aisles. As the expenses were small and the price of admission large, it follows that the little children must have pocketed a surplus of several thousand dollars [reportedly close to $2000]. . . . The selection was altogether of a sacred character," continued the reporter (no soul-brother of Strong's), "a kind of program which it is very difficult to make altogether pleasant, the mass of good music being of a secular character."

answer for the Angels in Heaven. Very probably they sing it, and I shouldn't wonder if they sang it even better.

May 21. . . . Couldn't go with Ellie to Eisfeld's [complimentary] concert [May 19], though the C-minor Symphony was among its items.

May 26. . . . Mass-meeting: Ellie, Mrs. Wright. Mrs. Gibbs. Cousinery, William Schermerhorn, Edmund Schermerhorn, [and] Humphreys; Jem Ruggles, Mrs. d'Oremieulx, Mr. S. B. Ruggles, and George G. Anthon audience. Performance rather rough. Everybody, Timm included, uncertain and inclined to get "out." Beethoven [Mass] in C done to the end of the *Gloria.* Then most of Haydn's Sixth (into which we always tend to gravitate this season) with organ accompaniment, and scraps of *Don Giovanni* (!). Very satisfactory evening.

[repeat of] Eisfeld's concert[71] with Ellie, Mrs. Gibbs, Mrs. d'Oremieulx, and Mrs. Wright. Thin assemblage—hardly 300;[72] we're not yet ripe for "morning concerts."[73] Overture by Cherubini *(Les Deux journées)* odd and uninteresting. Air (Miss Lehmann) from *Fidelio*[74] not effective; concertos (clarinet, trumpet, and piano),[75] shallow as concertos are apt to be—and for finale, the C-minor Symphony, for the existence whereof all should be profoundly thankful who are happy enough to be impressable by music. Not because it is most transcendent as a work of art, but because it embodies, conveys, teaches a lesson of Truth and Right which no extant poem, essay, or sermon speaks out with as much clearness and vigor.

Whoever can translate into *articulate* song its glorious message of Hope and Love and Effort blossoming out from chaos, uncertainty, indolence, and coldness of heart, leaving doubt and loneliness and desolation far behind them—a joy and glory in themselves, but triumphant at last in consummate victory over all things—whoever can put this into poetry, as *truly* as Beethoven has pictured it in music, can do what this uneasy, self-conscious age wants, and will place him, the Poet, far up on the slopes of Olympus.

Twaddle, rhapsody, rigmarole, and hyper-flutinated bosh. Transcendental German gas. Artificial ecstasy over a piece of very nice music. Ridiculous pretense of something grand, gloomy, significant, profound, and mysterious in a very pleasing composition. My "criticism" of the symphony is an easy thing to criticize. To set forth what I mean—fully, accurately, and without apparent exaggeration and *real* slip-slop would

[71] Strong did not miss the C-minor Symphony, after all. To make up for the minuscule attendance (credited to a torrential rainstorm) at the complimentary concert for Eisfeld on May 19, the Philharmonic and all concerned (including Niblo) voluntarily repeated the concert the following Saturday afternoon at 3:30. As Burkhardt truly observed, "the concert was intended as a *Benefit,* not a loss" (*Albion,* May 26, 1855, pp. 247–49).

[72] Consisting, it was commented, mostly of "ladies," but on this occasion disappointingly deprived of the "Philharmonic *beaux*" who so delightfully enlivened the public rehearsals.

[73] A reference to the term "matinée": the concert began at 3 P.M.

[74] With Timm at the piano; Lehmann also sang Schubert's *Erlkönig.*

[75] Eisfeld's clarinet concerto, previously heard at the first concert of the season, was played by Xavier Kiefer, and his *Chanson d'amour,* for trumpet *à pistons* and orchestra, by Louis Schreiber. Richard Hoffman repeated the Romance and Rondo movements of Chopin's E-minor Piano Concerto and as an encore Gottschalk's popular tearjerker "The Last Hope," op. 16 (1854). Although Bergmann had handsomely offered to conduct, Eisfeld, debilitated though he was, nonetheless insisted on

require two pages of very careful writing. So subtle and intangible and evanescent a subject as the significance of a musical work can't be fairly defined or discussed, except in words the most precise and carefully chosen. Offhand scribbling about it in one's journal can't be much more than fustian or flummery. But probably the most studied and eloquent recital and argument would convey no meaning, save to one who saw with the same eyes as its writer.

Probably no two people hear the same music exactly in the same way. Beethoven (e.g.) addresses the better part of every man, but the precise meaning of his message differs with the personality of each. Each fits the music with a different story. It means one thing to *A* and another to *B*. But the true meaning—the real actual intent of the composer? Very like, he had none.

An Alpine landscape by [Joseph] Turner [1775–1851] or [Karl Friedrich] Lessing [1808–1880] would teach one lesson to Byron and another to Wordsworth, another to Keble, another to Longfellow. We can't be sure that the artist saw—contemplated—designed one rather than the other. He sought to embody *objective truth* in the forms—and through the means—of his art. The moral significance of his work varies, just as the teaching of his subject would vary, according to the moral vision of its observer. To this one, the glacier and snowy peak or mountain-torrent would suggest thoughts of victorious self-will, isolated pride, individual supremacy; to another, images of Eternal Truth, pure and everlasting, amid storm and change and decay, the "Everlasting Hills"—the "City of God." So will a glorious sunset speak to one man of joy and hope—to another by his side of bereavement and sorrow without hope—to another of trial and trouble, past or to come, through which he shall surely be upheld—of tears that shall surely be wiped away—of a glory in Heaven above all the accidents, confusions, calamities of Earth.

I suppose the works of Mozart and Beethoven, and many more, reveal to us *something* (*what,* I cannot guess) as true, real, objective as the hills and forests and running streams with which the landscape painter has to do. *Something* is seen in the symphony or the overture, in the musical work *quo cumque nomine,* as in the painted canvas—something speaks through the orchestra or the piano to each auditor. The Donizettis and Verdis and other faineants, of course, say nothing and merely ape the utterances of real music. Except, however, that every musical phrase, however commonplace, embodies and expresses somewhat of supernatural and supermundane beauty.

The difficulty is that whereas form and color, in which the painter and sculptor work, are patent to our daily observation—independently of the artist, who merely idealizes their ordinary manifestations—the world of musical sound is known to Man only in and through the composer—does not exist until the Mozart or Beethoven reveals it—does not exist, I mean, practically, for the purposes of man. So there is no standard with which the musical work can be compared—no external object whereby the *truth* can be tested.

Certainly a great musical thought is something more than the mere imagining of a composer. It could not so stir the hearts of men if it were merely the cunning collo-

doing so himself. At the repeat concert—because several Philharmonic cellists had gone to Boston with Maretzek's opera company—Bergmann agreed to play in the cello section of the orchestra (*Musical Review and Gazette,* hereinafter cited as *Review and Gazette,* June 2, 1855, p. 179).

cation of sound. That language which speaks to us so vaguely, yet with an expression so much keener and deeper than that of any other, must convey Truth and Reality, or something of the relations of Truth toward our own being.

How shall we learn its real meaning? How learn what it tells us? Would Beethoven's own commentary be reliable on one of his own works? I suppose not—unless we will admit that Turner's individual exposition of the significance and moral teaching of, e.g., the lovely landscapes in [Samuel] Rogers [1763–1855] poems would be the best guide to the meaning and right influence of Nature, and the surest help to a right understanding of her ministrations, through mountain and forest and river, to the spirit of man. His gift was the faculty of catching and embodying—ignorantly, perhaps—the essence of those forms. That of Beethoven was to do the same office for forms which exist in, and are known through, the Kingdom of Sound—the audible world. These forms were grasped by his faculty and given to us. Whether he recognized their value independently of their artistic truth is another question. Whether he understood them aught is still another.

So do three lines of bosh call sometimes for thirty more—of apology and explanation—which only carry one deeper still into a ravine of fog.[76]

The Mass-meetings took an unexpected turn.

June 2. . . . Thursday evening we had most of our Mass-mongering friends here, [with] Mrs. Gibbs at the piano, reading through *Don Giovanni*. Not a very perfect performance, but that music can bear a rough and feeble rendering, just as thoughts that are true and beautiful require no elocution to make themselves felt but are the same when spoken by the stammering voice of a child.

June 6. . . . Last evening at Mrs. Mary Wright's, where was music, mostly *Don Giovanni* by our Friday evening set.

June 11. . . . Friday night was our last Mass-meeting for this season. The "Mass" was *Don Giovanni,* with some omissions. Philip Mayer and Lafitte aided, and some dozen or so of outsiders were present.

This opera is degraded by its plot and program. Its immortal music is profaned by marriage with a story of vulgar intrigue to which Mozart *could not write down*. The two scenes of supernaturalism are an exception, though I don't *myself* see their grandeur and power. It was not possible for him to conceive anything low enough for Leporello, and most of that personage's music is consequently a contradiction of its subject and inconsistent with itself. The composition reminds one of some picture like Couture's *Decadence*[77] (or of a *petit souper, tempore* Louis XV), in which the features of the revelers and the prostitute have been blotted out and replaced by those of Raffaelle's cherubs and madonnas. The saint and angel are constantly making themselves visible where only the roué and his roguish valet and a flirtatious, salacious country girl and a very earthly Donna Anna and Donna Elvira and a very insipid Don Ottavio belong, according to

[76] Only too true.

[77] Strong was making a far-fetched comparison with a flamboyant painting, the *Romans of the Decadence,* depicting antique naughtiness in nineteenth-century terms, by the celebrated French artist Thomas Couture (1815–1879).

the terms of the libretto. Think of the celestial purity and beauty of *Non ti fidar, o misera; Vedrai, carino; Ah, taci ingiusto core,* etc., and then think of the commonplace intrigue these ineffable phrases of melody are debased to consort with![78]

~

To add to the musical barrenness of the ensuing summer months—a period of mourning for Strong, whose father had died on June 27—he suffered from a painful infestation of street musicians clustered around Gramercy Park. "Even as I write," complained Strong on July 31, "an itinerant brass band is playing a polka on the corner, while a broken-winded hand organ plays *Casta diva* under the window, very slow. I never heard so excruciating a combination of noises in my life." And on August 7 Strong was plagued by "an itinerant minstrel—a troubadour—with a guitar and green spectacles—singing [Henry Russell's] 'The Newfoundland Dog,'♪ and so forth."

On a Friday evening in September, with Ellen and Johnny still vacationing at West Point, Strong dined "sumptuously" with Anthon at Delmonico's new restaurant in Chambers Street, then, repeating an unadmirable exploit of his youth, he stopped at the Greene Street Synagogue to hear the sabbath service, but not with reverence.♪ "Israel does not make a joyful noise," he commented in his journal (September 14). "The monotone solo ululation of the reader, or rabbi [cantor], are sufficiently dismal, but the people vociferate their responses in discord unspeakable, like eager bidders at a sale of stocks. It is strange that the sentiment and expression of their worship should be unlike that of any Christian culture I ever witnessed."

It was not until mid-October, with the onset of the Philharmonic's fourteenth season[79] (under Bergmann's sole leadership)[80] and the resumption, shortly after, of Eisfeld's *soirées* (with Eisfeld, greatly restored by his summer in Europe,[81] again in charge) that Strong regained possession of his musical persona, both aural and expository.

October 14. . . . [yesterday] met Ellie at Niblo's. [First] Philharmonic rehearsal.[82] Heard Beethoven's "Pastoral" Symphony through. . . . How delicious the "Pastorale" is, especially the first and second movements. So genial, fresh, and flowing—every note is significant—the embodiment and expression of feeling, so fine and vivid—the work so full of meaning and of life. The vice of *imitative* music is avoided, though the

[78] As we know, Strong's objections to Da Ponte's libretto were symptomatic of his time. Even Mario, who sang the role of Don Ottavio so enchantingly, would not allow his young daughters to attend a performance of *Don Giovanni* ([Byrne], p. 134).

[79] "From the annual report now before us," wrote Hagen in the *Review and Gazette* (October 20, 1855, p. 349), "we are glad to learn of the prosperous condition of this excellent Society; the dividend declared to the members last season was greater, by nearly twenty percent, than in any previous year."

[80] With an increased orchestra and some "much-needed new rules with regard to rehearsals."

[81] "Having departed in an emaciated condition," wrote the *Musical World* (October 13, 1855, p. 277), Eisfeld had returned in a state "fast approximating to the desirable rotundity of German Burgomeisterhood." On October 10, he announced that he was now back and ready to resume his "professional labors in teaching singing, piano, and thorough-bass." During Bergmann's conductorship Eisfeld resumed his former place in the orchestra's viola section.

[82] To their previous schedule of two public rehearsals on Saturday afternoons, running from 3:30 to 5:30 P.M., the Philharmonic had now added a third on the morning of each concert (10 A.M. to 12 noon).

subject is of all others the most full of temptation, except just at the end of the Andante, where its effect is good.[83] The phrases of imitation harmonize perfectly with the subject of the movement—occur naturally—and are not stuck to the music like a flower glued to the locks of a marble Venus. It is introduced also into the Storm movement, and though it's much to expect of a composer that he should avoid thunder claps and whistling winds and sputtering rain in dealing with this subject, I think Beethoven might have instrumented his summer shower without them if he had tried.

October 28. . . . to Philharmonic rehearsal[84] [now moved to Niblo's Theatre to accommodate the increased demand for tickets], Ellie and George Anthon, Miss Tote and the little McIlvaine. Heard the "Pastorale" and [again] the *Tannhäuser* Overture. The latter is certainly a very noteworthy composition. As to the former, I doubt whether articulate language could express more intensely and distinctly than its opening movement the sense of joy and freedom with which one "long in populous city pent"[85] finds himself, some bright summer morning, strolling through pleasant fields on his first day of liberty, after a good breakfast and with a healthy liver.

November 4. . . . [Ellie] has commenced [sight]-reading lessons with Timm.

November 16. . . . Ellie has gone [to the Academy of Music] to hear *Puritani* with Jem.

November 17. . . . Just from Eisfeld's quartette concert [the first of the sixth series, now moved to Saturday evenings], where were Dick Willis and wife, old Schlesinger, Mrs. D. C. Murray, Timm, and Scharfenberg, *et al.* . . . Concert was not bad. Mendelssohn Quartette, op. 12 [1829], tolerably interesting; Chopin Trio, op. 8 [in G minor (1828–29)], very good, some of it a little grandiose; two of the movements decidedly earnest and significant.[86] Mozart Quintette for stringed instruments in G minor [K. 516 (1787)]—delightful exceedingly, the Adagio and Finale very memorable indeed.[87] Packing for the interspaces was furnished by Mrs. Clara Brinkerhoff, who "did" a song ["The Tear"] by one Kücken and a cavatina [*Und ob die Wolke*] from the *Freischütz*.

[83] To Theodore Hagen, however, although the symphony fulfilled its promise—with its faithful delineations of "sunshine and rain, quietness and a thunder-storm, the cuckoo's crying and the bird's singing"—the work was "much too long and too elaborated, especially in the Adagio" (*Review and Gazette,* December 1, 1855, p. 399). Heresy!

[84] Now an occasion of enforced austerity, facetiously wrote the *Albion* (October 27, 1855, p. 512): "The Directors, having apparently discovered that Youth and Love do not combine felicitously with music, [have prohibited] all flirtation! Ye Gods! No more flirtation! What say ye, fair dames and damsels? . . . For ourselves, we cannot consent to this most ruthless banishment of Cupid from the temple of Euterpe; and were we forced to choose between this pleasing, frolicsome youth and the shadowy author of *Tannhäuser,* we fear that our selection might expose us to the imputation of flippancy."

[85] "To one who has been long in city pent,
'Tis very sweet to look into the fair
And open face of heaven." (Sonnet, John Keats)

[86] Played by Richard Hoffman, Joseph Noll, and Frederick Bergner, this apparently first local performance of Chopin's Trio received a widely mixed press, as did Hoffman, who was hailed by some as a master interpreter of Chopin, and censured by others for his ironbound obliviousness to Chopin's essential qualities of waywardness and "sentimentality."

[87] Played by Joseph Burke with the restored quartet: Noll, Reyer, Eisfeld and Bergner.

. . . I value Mozart's music higher and higher every year, and am reluctantly conceding him place above Beethoven himself. Quiet strength is a nobler gift than vehement energy and restlessness. The highest art is not that which electrifies and intoxicates artist and audience alike. Self-control in the artist and repose in the work are better than "Inspiration" and dithyrambics. But if the crown were in my hands, I should pause and ponder before awarding it. Neither Mozart nor any other mortal to my knowledge or belief has ever spoken to man as Beethoven in some of his orchestral works, and Handel in his sublime choruses. Handel, Mozart, Beethoven—"these three" may abide in joint sovereignty.[88] It's unprofitable and ungracious to consider which of them shall be called supreme.

Surely music is a marvel which should teach one the worthlessness of all a priori doubts about the possibility and credibility of mystery or miracle. Given a few octaves of musical sound and a few crude shades of musical color, an erratic, half-cracked, good-for-nothing man as composer, and a score or two of foolish, fourth-rate men and women as performers, and it is required with this material to create and convey to man the unutterable things that are embodied in the music of, e.g., *Don Giovanni* and the C-minor Symphony to give him a vision—a reflected image, at least—of Eternal Truth, Purity, and Beauty, such as he may seek elsewhere in vain—to awaken longings and mysterious, vague aspirations which words cannot create and cannot describe—to address his innermost being, face to face. Let him who knows and has felt the supernatural power that resides in the material out of which our wonderful treasures of modern music are built explain, if he can, why he rejects as a traditionary superstition the teaching of the Church about *Water—Bread*—and *Wine;* why he holds it extravagant to attribute spiritual powers to inanimate matter and to vain, shallow, commonplace men.

Can music embody and express what is bad, degraded, impure, false, any more than the language of mathematics? Is there such a thing as "voluptuous" music? Someone has suggested the deadly power that must have been exerted by the elegant-profligate poetry of Paganism (Catullus, etc.),[89] when allied to music *equally flagitious*—it's somewhere in the *British Critic,*[90] I believe. One may easily conceive a combination of agencies in which music should be a most potent stimulus to evil passion, but only where its influence is perverted and overborne by the agencies of unmixed evil with which it is allied. In itself it speaks only of truth, purity, and peace. Degraded to consort with sensual ballet or trivial opera, or with the nameless profligacies of Paris or old Rome, its voice may be drowned, its power made practically evil, instead of good. But I think that the language of Music can convey no lesson of ill. The very Allegro that may have stimulated the licentious revel of the Regency had its message of good, and of good alone. Its composer may have been a very Boucher[91] of musicians in intent, but his work could no more have expressed impurity than an equation can express falsehood.

[88] Where was Strong's beloved Haydn in this pantheon?
[89] Gaius Valerius Catullus (*c.* 84–*c.* 54 B.C.), Roman lyric poet.
[90] A prestigious, early nineteenth-century English periodical.
[91] François Boucher (1703–1770), another wicked French painter.

November 23. . . . [descending from the heights] I must ascertain whether the mighty bug-destroyer Lyons has no modification of his cockroach powder that will exterminate organ-grinders. We suffer peculiarly here, for the street is very quiet, and they play all round the square before they leave it, and are more or less audible at each successive station. I have been undergoing the performances of one of the tribe for an hour and a half and have heard *Casta diva, Ah! non giunge,* the first chorus of *Ernani,* and some platitude from the *Trovatore,* languidly ground out six times each. It makes me feel homicidal. If Abel had gone about with hand-organs, I shouldn't censure Cain so very harshly. There goes the *Casta diva* for the seventh time!

Ellie is spending the evening at Mrs. [Richard] Tighe's, and I'm trying to work here and getting everything wrong, thanks to that caitiff outside.

November 24 . . . . Am smoking the pipe of meditation over the fragrant memory of the Philharmonic concert just ended.[92] . . . Vast crowd. Niblo's filled full. Seats obtainable only in the third gallery.[93] N.B., it's the best part of the house for hearing the music. Part I was the "Pastoral" Symphony; Solo (bass) [by Otto Feder, a new German singer] from [Mendelssohn's] *St. Paul* ["Lord God, have mercy!"]—very minor and very dreary. Concerto for two violins—the Mollenhauer brethren, composers and performers—trivial and tiresome. Part II: [first time in New York] Overture to Gluck's *Iphigenia in Aulis* [Paris 1774], two German songs [sung by Feder]—one by Schubert *(Morgenständchen)* ["Morning Serenade"] was very fresh and pretty.[94] A sleight-of-hand violin solo [played] by [Edward] Mollenhauer (encored),[95] and Wagner's *Tannhäuser* Overture.

Note: that one of the great aims of an accomplished "artist" in violin playing is the faculty of eliciting from his instrument a sound as nearly as possible resembling that of a squeaking door some way off—closed very *adagio.* Another is to be able to play any two-penny scrap of melody in tones like those of some minute, dipterous insect—cicada or grasshopper—so high up on the scale as to be just this side the limit of audibility. Either feat will be received with tumultuous applause.

Gluck's overture was new to me. I know very little about his music. It was archaic, rather, in its structure, but clear and vigorous. I think it will last. I don't find in it the pungency and intensity of *single phrases,* which seem to me the characteristic mark of the highest order of music; but as a whole it is impressive and splendid.

[92] With this concert, Bristow returned to his desk in the violin section of the Philharmonic.

[93] "From the parquet to the second tier, every seat was filled, and a great many ladies had to accommodate themselves on the stairs" (*Review and Gazette,* December 1, 1855, p. 399).

[94] Feder's other song was *Die Lockung* ("The Temptation"), by the Bohemian composer Josef Dessauer (1798–1876).

[95] The solo, *La Sylphide,* was probably an arrangement of Jullien's piece of the same name. *Gamma,* the ostensibly Gallic critic (Girac?) who had replaced Burkhardt at the *Albion* in September, inveighed mightily against the Philharmonic's pernicious practice of allowing mediocrities to perform at their concerts merely because they didn't have to be paid. Now that the Society had become rich enough to pay their conductor, he wrote, they might extend themselves a little more to engage suitable soloists. We were, it seemed, "perpetually condemned" to such rank amateurs as Feder or professional mountebanks as the Mollenhauer (or "Siamese") Brothers, with their trivial Polka. "Oh! Shade of Beethoven! Oh! Divine Master! Forgive us!" (*Albion,* December 1, 1855, p. 572.)

Gluck and Wagner were poles apart, wrote Hagen (*Review and Gazette,* December 1, 1855, p. 399), yet Wagner was in some senses the modern Gluck, having, like Gluck, "cleared the opera of its nonsense and unnecessary accessories."[96] But Seymour, in the *Daily Times* (November 26, 1855), lashed out at Wagner and his "pretentious" *Tannhäuser.* "The skill which Wagner displays in the filling up of this score becomes tiresome after a few repetitions," he wrote. "There is no rest for the ear, no quiet topic for the mind to dwell upon. From the double bass to the piccolo, there is a perpetual race for the victory. What is really admirable is so overlaid by what is purely mechanical that Mr. Wagner's genius, equally with Mr. Wagner's skill, becomes tiresome and annoying."

December 9. . . . Walked up [in the snow] from yesterday afternoon's Philharmonic rehearsal [for the January 12, 1856, concert] with Ellie. . . . Very crowded. As there are no programs, one has to grasp at the music played. We heard what I took to be a Symphony of Gade's [No. 1, in C minor]. It was very nice. All very clear and intelligible—some of it very pretty—the second movement (a Scherzo, I suppose) most vigorous and beautiful—the Andante rather insipid—the Finale showy but *outré,* a sort of "Hail to the Chief" melody running through it, flagrantly instrumented. Mr. Gade (if it was Gade) is rather fond of exaggerations and glaring contrast, but he is probably entitled to pretty respectable rank among the *Di minores* [*sic*].

December 18. . . . We went to Eisfeld's [second chamber music] concert Saturday night [December 15] through fog and filthy air, and without very special reward. [String] Quartette [in F major, op. 17, no. 3] by [Anton] Rubinstein [1830–1894] was a work of labor, trouble, industry, fuss, and excitement;[97] its author was vehement and erudite, but what he had to say amounted to very little.[98] Certain variations (Beethoven) [String Quartet in A, op. 18, no. 5, (1798–1800)] were unusually agreeable for variations, and a quintette by Spohr [op. 130, for piano and strings] was nice and not much more.[99] The concert was respectable but not a brilliant success.

December 20. . . . This evening went to Mrs. Wright's [to call] for Ellie, who

[96] In September, Hagen, a staunch German and a passionate Wagnerian, vainly sought, under the Masons' auspices and with Liszt's intercession, to bring Wagner to Boston to conduct the forthcoming Beethoven Festival Concert, given on March 1, 1856, to celebrate the installation in Boston Music Hall of the highly acclaimed Beethoven statue by the American sculptor Thomas Crawford (*c.* 1813–1857) (see *Wagner and Liszt, Correspondence,* II, 111–12, 114; see also *Dwight's,* March 1, pp. 164–65, 167, 173–74; March 8, 1856, pp. 181–83).

[97] According to Henry C. Watson, who had once again resumed his interrupted journalistic career, Rubinstein's quartet was uneven, strange, beautiful, eccentric, brilliant, earnest, impassioned, and obviously the work of a master hand (*Frank Leslie's Illustrated Newspaper,* December 29, 1855, p. 42).

[98] As the work of an unknown composer, wrote *Gamma,* Rubinstein's quartet, although a youthful composition of unequal quality, announced the advent of a great master (*Albion,* December 22, 1855, p. 607); to Theodore Hagen, the work offered "a superfluity of riches. . . . riches which no composer since Beethoven and Schubert has presented to the world" (*Review and Gazette,* December 29, 1855, pp. 431–32).

[99] The piano part of Spohr's Second Quintet was admirably played by Timm, who also accompanied Madame Wallace-Bouchelle in Mozart's recitative and aria *Ch'io mi scordi di te,* K. 505 (Vienna 1786), and in Eisfeld's ballad "Oh, Come to me, my darling love."

took tea there with Charles Kuhn and one or two more. Heard some refreshing scraps of *Don Giovanni* sufficiently well sung, including *Non ti fidar,* the loveliest [vocal] quartette extant.

December 22. . . . to the Philharmonic rehearsal at Niblo's. Full, in spite of the weather. Mr. S. B. R. and Mrs. d'Oremieulx sat with us. Berlioz overture [to *Les Francs-Juges*] played twice, [Weber's] Overture to *Euryanthe,* and first and second movements of the Gade Symphony. There is talent and much industry in the first, but I care little for it: its *orchestration* is most admirable, but there is only dead mechanism in the work—no freshness, no geniality that I can discover.[100]

The Gade Symphony is far *thinner,* sketchy in comparison, but these two movements are very clear, melodic, and delightful; the second (Scherzo) especially strikes me as a real inspiration. Perhaps it is shallow, but it's certainly vigorous and good, as far as it goes, and better than music that is pretentious, learned, and labored, but *agreeable* only as a problem or puzzle, the solution, or appreciation of which gratifies one's vanity.

December 23 . . . . Haunted by the second movement of the Gade symphony.

December 24. . . . I should like [Christmas Eve] to find me in some old Church, with arches that were rounded six hundred years ago—some vast Romanesque cathedral—and as the clock strikes twelve, to hear the choral outburst of Haydn's *Gloria* (No. 1) proclaim the coming of Christmas Day—or the exulting solo that begins his Sixth *Gloria.* No music is so Christmas-like as his: Mozart's is too ethereal—Beethoven's too deep. Only Haydn has blended the material and the spiritual as to embody the feeling and sentiment of the Christmas festival.

. . . Why has no one yet given us an orchestral interpretation of Christmas—a Christmas Symphony? Probably Beethoven's C-minor covers the ground, though not exactly. It might do for an expression of Milton's awful [awesome] and glorious Christmas Hymn, but not of the Christmas Carol. Its sentiment is that of a transcendentally noble Christmas sermon, not of *the Festival*—half-secular, half-sacred.

Strong had evidently remained blissfully unaware of William Henry Fry's "Santa Claus" Symphony.

[100] This was the greatest praise that Strong would ever accord a work by Berlioz.

OBBLIGATO: 1855

The history of the Italian classic opera in the United States is a history of reverses, of quarrels, of newspaper warfares, of passée prime donne, *of* blasé *tenors, and ruined managers.*[1]

New York Herald
February 13, 1855

Taken in context, the joint tenancy of the Academy of Music, early in January 1855, by the unlikely triumvirate of Ole Bull, Max Maretzek, and Maurice Strakosch, was perhaps less improbable than would appear on the surface. For some two years past—since the New Norway fiasco—Bull, with the assistance of Strakosch, Amalia Patti-Strakosch, and little Adelina Patti, had successfully been touring throughout the United States; Maretzek and his wife had joined their company in 1854 (on a share-and-share-alike basis) upon the twin disasters of Maretzek's failed opera season at Castle Garden and his inability to secure a lease for the Academy of Music.

Maretzek credits Bull with the idea of extending their tripartite collaboration to the field of opera management (*Sharps and Flats,* pp. 16–17), but he does not mention that earlier—in September 1854—with hungry eyes fixed on the Academy—he (Maretzek) had formed (or purportedly formed) a similar three-cornered copartnership with Strakosch and one John C. Jacobsohn (or Jacobson) a local entrepreneur (or "speculator"),[2] and that they had sent Bernard Ullman to Europe to engage opera singers for their venture. Immediately upon Ullman's departure Jacobsohn was dropped from the patnership in favor of Ole Bull, and Strakosch was sent to Europe to supersede Ullman.[3] The Bull/Strakosch/Maretzek copartnership was, however, of

[1]The reader must be warned at the outset of this chapter that the bizarre tangle of feuds, intrigues, betrayals, chicaneries, defamations, and venality committed in New York's world of Italian opera in 1855 baffles the most conscientious attempts at reasonable unravelment.

[2]Sardonically identified in the *Daily Times* (January 11, 1855) as an "ex-doorkeeper at Castle Garden, wealthy capitalist of Wall-street, etc.," Jacobsohn is listed in the 1854–55 City Directory as an importer, located at 233 Broadway.

[3]Ullman later denied that Strakosch had ever belonged to the initial partnership. He asserted, however, that Strakosch—with whom he claimed not to have been on speaking terms—had approached him in Paris with an offer from Maretzek that he desert Jacobsohn and join with the new partnership. Ullman claims to have indignantly refused and proudly boasts of having prevented Stra-

like brevity. As Maretzek tells it *(ibid.),* no sooner had Strakosch hastily departed for Europe than Bull "obtained from Mr. Phalen a lease of his own,[4] giving me [Maretzek] an engagement as conductor and forgetting to provide for Strakosch."[5] At this point a rival trio consisting of Ullman, Jacobsohn, and Niblo promptly materialized and announced their plan to present competitive opera at Niblo's. First Jacobsohn, then Niblo, departed for Europe to join the talent hunt.

Gossip ran rampant, and legendary names were wildly bandied about. Strakosch was rumored to have engaged Pauline Viardot-Garcia (1821–1910) for the Academy of Music—Ullman to have engaged Sophia Cruvelli (1826–1907) for Niblo's. It was even rumored that Verdi was being wooed to compose an opera especially for the Academy of Music.

On January 15, Bull, now very much the dynamic administrator-in-residence,[6] unfurled his own electrifying announcement. In conformity with his intention of "carrying out both the letter and the spirit" of the Academy's charter, he planned not only to reinstate the originally specified school of music but to "direct all his efforts toward the encouragement, the development, and the elevation of AMERICAN ART AND ARTISTS."[7] He was therefore offering a prize of $1000 for the "best Original Grand Opera composed by an *American composer,* and upon a strictly *American subject.*"

"The National History of America," continued Bull's proclamation, "is rich in themes both for the poet and the musician, and it is hoped that this offer will bring to light the musical talent now latent in our country, which only needs a favorable opportunity for its development." Contestants were required to submit a legible, unsigned full score and libretto of a three- or four-act opera by August 1, 1855—the authors' names to be secured in a separate, sealed envelope. The winners would be awarded the copyright to the opera and any earnings that might accrue; the Academy would retain the performance rights; the "second-best" opera would receive a performance, but no prize.

"This certainly opens a new era in the history of music in this country," applauded

---

kosch from engaging several desirable artists for the Academy of Music (*Courier and Enquirer,* May 19, 22, 1855).

[4]To further complicate matters, the *Mirror* learned (January 8, 1855) that "a gentleman who took a very active part in getting up the 'Academy' [ostensibly Phalen] [had] taken a lease on the premises for two years, at the rate of $14,000 a year." Thus, if this were true, Bull (and his various successors) were Phalen's subtenants.

[5]"In regard to the partnership entered into by 'Ole Bull & Co.,' we are inclined to believe it a mere sham," later asserted the *Mirror* (March 6, 1855).

[6]Years later, Maretzek scornfully recalled Bull's flamboyant posturings during his abbreviated managerial tenure: he "surrounded himself with secretaries . . . employed expressly a lawyer [L. E. Bulkeley] with an office in the Academy, to cross-examine anyone at length who dared to present a bill; [and] established a red-tape aristocratic administration, to the delight of Mr. Phalen, who, in expectation of the great things that Mr. Ole Bull would accomplish, advanced him $4000" (*Sharps and Flats,* p. 17). According to reports of the complicated ensuing litigation—Phalen versus Bull, Strakosch, and Maretzek, and vice versa—it developed that the loan had been made to all three partners (see *Mirror,* March 26, 1856).

[7]And why not? As Willis pointed out (*Musical World,* January 27, 1855, p. 39), Bull was, after all, a naturalized American citizen, something he had become in 1852 in the vain hope of gaining the land title to New Norway.

Music Division, The New York Public Library

Ole Bull, temporary autocrat of the Academy of Music.

Richard Grant White in the *Courier and Enquirer* (January 16, 1855). "Westward the star of empire has taken its way; why shall not the star of music follow? We have produced almost everything in this country, shall we not produce an opera?" But White disagreed with the limitation to American subject matter: "The subjects of Mozart's operas were not German," he argued, "and those librettos for which Rossini, Bellini, and Donizetti wrote the music were very rarely indeed Italian in subject; while of Shakespeare's twenty-seven tragedies and comedies, the scenes of only three are laid in England. What matter where a dramatist finds his story?"

The ensuing glorification of Bull as the latest and greatest hero/savior of American opera[8] was rudely interrupted by the disclosure, at a stockholders' meeting on January 18, that the Academy was in serious fiscal difficulties. To finance their mismanagement of the Academy (i.e., their repeated bailouts of Hackett), the corporation had

[8]The *Home Journal* (January 27, 1855), for example, did "not know how to express ourselves moderately in speaking of Ole Bull—for we admire him quite over the horizon of ordinary adjectives. . . . Music being the language of the next world—the alphabet of angels which we are permitted to learn on earth [echoes of GTS]—[Bull] wished to be its headmaster for America." As lessee of the Academy of Music, "the *money* he expects to make will be something, but the *moral sway* will be more. Music is the locomotive of religion, and he is the Engineer. Well," concluded the *Home Journal*, "we believe in Ole Bull."

gone into debt to the tune of some $150,000, of which $50,000 was "pressing." Despite their general unwillingness to be drawn into a second mortgage, it was hoped—should the Academy be put on sale for the payment of its debts—that some of the more concerned stockholders would unite "for the purpose of buying it in and carrying out the original intention of the friends of the project"—to assist the noble cause of art in America[9] (*Tribune*, January 19, 1855). The stockholders, however, voted to sell the Academy if, upon further solicitation, a majority refused to subscribe to a second mortgage.

General consternation! Except, of course, for the New York *Herald* (January 20, 1855), which gleefully reminded its readers that the collapse of the Academy was only to be expected, although, perhaps, not so quickly. The Astor Place Opera House had lasted until its second season before going under, and the Crystal Palace had somehow managed to survive through a season, not breaking down "until Barnum got hold of it,"[10] but the Academy of Music had succumbed after only three months! If it should become necessary to sell the Academy, the *Herald* suggested that it might be put to better use as a "lottery office, an establishment for curing codfish, or a soap factory."

More soberly, the *Herald* reverted to its old argument that it was futile to attempt to "establish Italian opera here upon the same plan as in Europe—by exclusive subscription and favoritism." It was a system that would never succeed in a democracy: "No theatrical establishment that caters to the prejudice of the aristocratic class, so called, can expect to be successful in America. The principle is directly opposed to the spirit of our institutions." Not until the presentation of opera served a democratic social concept could it hope to succeed here.

To reassure the public of the Academy's solvency, James Phalen, as its president, addressed a soothing "card" to the press, dated January 26. The corporation, he stated, had never intended their original capital of $200,000 to cover both purchase of the site and construction of the building; rather they had counted on an overall sum of at least $275,000 to $300,000. The incidental "floating debt" of $40,000 (not $50,000, as reported) represented unforeseen increases in the costs of materials and labor as the project progressed; at any rate, it had already been disposed of. In closing, Phalen recapitulated the many wonders of the Academy—its architectural beauties, its splendid accessibility, its reasonable ticket prices,[11] its noble intentions. But despite these assurances, the mischief-making *Herald* (January 29, 1855), now assuming a judicial role in the opera crisis, reiterated, and even intensified, its argument: Italian opera had no future—not in the United States nor anywhere else—and especially not at the Academy of Music.

[9] With an original investment of only $1000 each, the income from an annual rent now assessed at $24,000, and free, transferable (salable) seats to each performance, sardonically comments Maretzek, the 200-odd stockholders could have elevated the public taste for Art "in the most profitable manner possible to themselves personally" (*Crotchets*, pp. 336–37).

[10] The *Herald* (Bennett) derisively referred to Barnum's great Crystal Palace reinaugural parade as "the greatest practical joke Barnum ever made."

[11] Set for the coming season at $1 for the lower part of the house including the first tier of boxes, 50 cents for the upper tiers of boxes, and 25 cents for the amphitheatre; secured seats on the first level cost an extra 50 cents. "This seems reasonable enough," commented the *Evening Post* (January 30, 1855), "provided the opera be good."

On January 30 the *Herald* addressed itself to Ole Bull's exuberant public reply (dated January 24) to the myriad would-be contestants of foreign origin who had requested an elucidation of the eternally problematical term "American composer." "At a time when so many doubts have been raised as to what constitutes a legal identification with the soil," wrote the *Herald,* "this spirited offer of the Norwegian violinist has naturally led to numerous inquiries on the part of foreign musical aspirants who have not as yet completed their probation for citizenship."

Bull's definition lay in "the Constitution of the United States, which gives to every adopted citizen equal rights with those born upon this soil. Upon this broad ground," he declared, "I base my offer [of the opera prize], and offer it to every full and resident citizen of the United States."

Clear-cut as this definition might seem to Bull, commented the *Herald,* it failed to answer some "very embarrassing questions. . . . Indeed, it was hardly to be expected that the great violinist could solve, with a single flourish of his pen—as in a *staccato* passage with his bow—the difficulties with which his proposal is surrounded." What chances of competing had our "native-born citizens of ebony tint?"—a race abounding in "rich musical genius and invention." And what about the Indian bards with their vivid and highly individual music? What about the Americans of Irish origin, with their splendid heritage of song from the time of Turlough Carolan (1670–1738) to Thomas Moore (1779–1852)? Bull had better revise his definition of the term "American composer" if he wanted his Academy of Music to succeed. (The discussion was purely hypothetical, for in a few short weeks both Bull and his contest would vanish from the mercurial opera scene.)

For the moment, however, elaborate preparations were going forward for Bull's gala reopening of the Academy of Music on February 19, inaugurating a pre-Lenten "Carnival Season" with the long-awaited American premiere of Verdi's *Rigoletto.* As we know, the keen edge of this much-heralded event had been considerably dulled by the cunningly timed farewell season of Grisi and Mario, concurrently in progress at the Metropolitan Theatre (February 13 through 20). With Strakosch's promised European opera stars still missing, the hard-pressed Academy management filled the leading male roles with two unfamiliar Italian singers who fortuitously happened to be stopping over in New York en route to opera engagements in Latin America. Thus, Beagio Bolcioni, an unknown young tenor, was engaged for the role of the Duke of Mantua and Ettore Barili (1829–1889?), yet another gifted member of the seemingly inexhaustible Barili/Patti tribe, for the Rigoletto.[12]

A moderate, or large, first-night audience was variously reported, because of—or in spite of—the Grisi/Mario performance of *Semiramide* (Vestvali's debut) at the Metropolitan Theatre that same evening. More to the point, as Burkhardt pointed out, the

[12] The other roles were filled by long-familiar members of the local Italian opera community: Bertucca-Maretzek (as Gilda), Amalia Patti-Strakosch (Maddalena), Luigi Rocco (Sparafucile), Giovanni Leonardi (Count Ceprano), Signora Barattini (the Countess), the perennial comprimaria Signora Avogadro (Giovanna), Coletti (Monterone), Müller (Marullo), and Quinto (Borsa). An able orchestra and chorus totaling 100 performers conducted by Maretzek, beautiful new scenery by Allegri, and a new system of subscription—reserved seats for twelve nights for twelve dollars—completed the attractions of the evening.

smallish audience at the Academy signified general apprehension over the reported indecency of the *Rigoletto* libretto: "Rumors prejudicial to the morals of *Rigoletto* had been most freely circulated throughout the city," he wrote, "inducing many, who would otherwise gladly have heard the new opera, to bide their time until the press should have pronounced its dictum upon the nature of the plot" (*Albion,* February 24, 1855, pp. 91–92).[13]

The reviews were indeed so overloaded with lengthy synopses of Francesco Piave's libretto (based on Victor Hugo's 1832 play *Le Roi s'amuse*) that little space remained for critical comment. In Burkhardt's opinion, the plot was no worse—perhaps even a little better—than the plots of such popular operas as *Don Giovanni, Lucrezia Borgia, La favorita, Norma,* or *Ernani;* he objected only to the "superabundance of horrors that prevail with a sort of nightmare effect in the *dénouement.* . . . The style of the composition is Verdi's throughout," he wrote, "but for Verdi very fine." A few sentences later, however, Burkhardt complained of "an occasional poverty, baldness, and nakedness of harmony and instrumentation that is not characteristic of Verdi. The loud, blatant, and obtrusive trombones in the last-act Quartette," he wrote, "are decidedly objectionable and lead to the suspicion that a portion of the scoring is not Verdi's; if it be, it is very, very bad for him."

More than a suspicion, it was an open secret[14] that the *Rigoletto* orchestration heard at the Academy had been fabricated from a piano score by the local German opera maestro and Philharmonic violist Julius Unger.[15] Thus, Fry, although he approved in general of Verdi, was prevented from "analyzing" the score of *Rigoletto;* the music, although seemingly well-written, could be evaluated only on its dramatic and vocal merits, he wrote.[16] It was tantalizing, from time to time in various passages, to find oneself asking, "Is it by Verdi?"

The production was otherwise attractive, with an "extra blaze of musical splendor" provided by a military band in the ballroom scene, "alternating and coalescing with the well-directed orchestra led by Mr. Maretzek," wrote Fry. Of the performers, the newcomer Barili, with his carefully cultivated, if small, high baritone, almost tenor, voice (and a somewhat overactive tremolo), portrayed Rigoletto with dramatic intensity but perhaps a shade too much of vehemence. Bolcioni's "clear, muscular, and manly tenor *robusto*" impressed Fry (and his colleagues) most favorably; he could reach a high B-flat without straining, could sing *piano* as well as *forte,* and would make a valuable acquisition to the local opera scene. Among the others, Madame Bertucca sang

[13] Foresighted Burkhardt had provided the *Albion*'s readers with a synopsis of the plot on February 17 (p. 89), two days prior to the premiere.

[14] Except to the *Evening Post* (February 20), whose critic was "not so much deafened with the din of brass and the thunder of drums as he might be led to expect by Verdi's well-known predilection for noise." Indeed, the orchestration, he wrote, was "so elaborate as to indicate that [Verdi had] bestowed unusual care upon it."

[15] It is unlikely that an authentic orchestra score was not procurable. If such piracy, indigenous to contemporary shoestring opera operations, was committed to shirk payment of copyright, purchase, and/or rental fees, it raises the question of how many other opera instrumentations of the period might have been similarly falsified.

[16] Fry's uncharacteristic tolerance of the desecration of Verdi's score might be attributed to the fact that his new *Stabat Mater* had been accepted by the Academy and was scheduled to be performed at one of Maretzek's forthcoming "sacred" concerts.

Gilda with her "ordinary correctness," and Madame Patti-Strakosch was "dressed to a charm and justified the Duke's admiration of her good looks." The others were satisfactory in their respective parts; the production foretold a successful season to follow (*Tribune,* February 20, 1855).

Rigoletto, continuing to be avoided because of its "repulsive" plot, was a disappointment at the box office.[17] And although its score admittedly possessed a few "gems" (*La donna è mobile* and the Quartet being made to order for the barrel organ), the opera was found to offer little of lasting musical substance. Richard Grant White wrote that the last-act quartet was "not remarkable for its ideas, but for its attempt—in a great measure successful—to carry on simultaneously the expression of three emotions—love, gaiety, and grief."

After the second of *Rigoletto*'s four tightly compressed performances[18]—on February 19, 21, 23, and 25—the *Daily Times* (hereinafter cited as the *Times*) decided that the work improved upon acquaintance and might bear repetition, after all. But by its fourth hearing an angry Richard Grant White thundered: "Verdi's *Rigoletto* does not prove a favorite with the public,[19] and we are not surprised. Much as we clamor for novelty, mere novelty without merit will not charm us into giving our dollars or our time. *Rigoletto* should be withdrawn as soon as possible"[20] (*Courier and Enquirer,* February 24, 1855).

Rigoletto was followed on February 28 by *La favorita,* a spectacularly ill-chosen vehicle for Vestvali's debut at the Academy.[21] Inappropriately cast in the mezzo-soprano, "petticoat" role of Leonora, she received merely passable reviews—a far cry from the frenetic outpourings following her two performances with Grisi and Mario. If she was again admired for her bold and commanding stage presence, the critics now picked flaws in her singing, especially in a role that admittedly suited neither her voice nor her person. With her good, but not great, contralto (some said mezzo-soprano) voice, she struggled unequally with the hostile *tessitura* of Leonora, albeit some passages had been transposed down to her range,[22] and "not always to the improvement of the music" (*Evening Post,* March 1, 1855). As for her persona, Burkhardt spoke for most of his colleagues when he advised her in the future to stick to masculine roles such as Orsini, Arsace, Pippo, and Romeo.

Vestvali's presence at the Academy did little to calm an atmosphere laden with hostilities, jealousies, suspicions, resentments, plots, intrigues, and crises. For Maretzek, the "Napoleon of Conductors" (and of impresarios), it was doubtless galling to

[17] Moreover, deprecated Richard Grant White, the "very poor" plot of *Rigoletto* required "the setting of [certain] words to music for which music is as unfit a vehicle as it would be for a sum in long division or a genealogy in Leviticus" (*Courier and Enquirer,* February 20, 1855).

[18] Dwight's New York correspondent reported paltry audiences of about 400 to 500 at each of its two final performances "before it was wisely withdrawn" (*Dwight's,* March 10, 1855, p. 180).

[19] But the *Mirror* (February 27, 1855) reported an enthusiastic reception of the fourth performance, with the last-act quartet, "which is truly a remarkable production . . . encored, as usual."

[20] After its third performance Burkhardt had begun to get the hang of *Rigoletto;* it was, he decided, "too good an opera to be shelved so soon" (*Albion,* March 4, 1855, p. 104).

[21] An especially poor choice, agreed the critics, with Grisi's marvelous Leonora still ringing in our ears. Besides Vestvali, the Academy cast consisted of Lorini (as Fernando), Badiali (Alfonso), Coletti (Balthazar) Quinto (Don Caspar), and Signora Avogadro (Inez).

[22] In the controversy that followed, Maretzek claimed that six copyists had been employed in transposing the role down to suit Vestvali's "power of execution."

be subservient to Bull's amateurish managerial fumblings.[23] Nor can Maretzek have enjoyed the arbitrary, highly unprofessional meddling by the stockholders in engaging Vestvali over his head (and apparently against his will). Vestvali, on the other hand, with a huge opinion of herself and driven by a huge ambition, must have been infuriated at what she considered Maretzek's demeaning treatment. Nor can the stockholders have been happy about the worsening financial chaos into which Bull's mismanagement had plunged the Academy—to say nothing of the escalating Maretzek/Bull antagonism, sometimes bordering even on physical violence.[24] As for Bull, he was rapidly sinking deeper and deeper into the quicksands of disaster.

After a repetition of *La favorita* on March 2 a defiant Vestvali, with perhaps an inflated view of her influence over her Upper Ten friends on the board, ill-advisedly declared open warfare on Maretzek. As George Templeton Strong noted in his journal on March 2: "The Vestvali . . . seems to have got into some sort of shindy with Maretzek & Co." Then, on March 4, when the Strongs went with Mr. Ruggles to hear Maretzek's first sacred concert at the Academy, "where our friend the Vestvali was announced to sing something of Naumann's[25] . . . [she] did not appear at her proper place in the program, and in answer to some hissing and clamor Maretzek stated that the lady had not appeared at rehearsal, or at the concert, and that he could give no explanation. So I suppose she has concluded to break her engagement.[26] Probably Maretzek has not treated her well. His wife, little Bertucca, [Amalia] Patti, and most of the others form a kind of family party.[27] The Vestvali complains she was compelled to sing in *Favorita,* an unsuitable part, against her will[28]—that Maretzek willfully misplayed her accompaniments and tried to *put her out,* etc. Luckily one's not called on to decide who is right and who wrong."[29]

Vestvali attempted to justify her unprofessional conduct in a "card," dated Saturday night (March 3) and addressed to the *Herald,* where it appeared on the morning of March 5 (and was reprinted in various papers). In a guileful blend of feminine fragil-

[23] ". . . scarcely was the opera organized than one of the members of the new 'musical firm,' Mr. Maretzek, issued a 'card,' repudiating all 'responsibility,' and from that date he acted as though he felt neither interest nor responsibility in the result of the undertaking" (*Mirror,* March 6, 1855).

[24] An enraged Maretzek was rumored to have hurled his baton at Bull when Bull disparaged Bertucca's singing (*Dwight's,* March 10, 1855, pp. 180–81).

[25] Emil Naumann (1827–1888) was a pupil of Mendelssohn and a reputable composer of religious music. Vestvali had (most inappropriately) been announced to sing his sacred air "Christ, the Messenger of Peace."

[26] She didn't go that far.

[27] It is true that at this time the Pattis, Barilis, Strakoschs, and Maretzeks formed a closely knit group.

[28] In her letter to the press, dated March 1, Vestvali admitted that she had accepted the unsuitable role at the behest of Ole Bull (not Maretzek). "But," commented Dwight's New York correspondent, "if she had not consented to sing it, the manager would have been compelled to 'shut up shop,' for *Rigoletto* would not do, and they were not prepared to present anything else except *La favorita*" (*Dwight's,* March 10, 1855, pp. 180–81).

[29] At this concert, writes Strong: "The great house [was] scantily filled. First part included most of Rossini's luscious *Stabat Mater,* not particularly well done except Badiali's *Pro peccatis.* Second part chiefly *Le Prophète* and the Prayer from *Mosè* (not the Mose of the Bowery)," quipped Strong. Secular works by Mercadante, Auber, Bellini, and Donizetti, performed by Mesdames Bertucca-Maretzek and Patti-Strakosch, and Messrs. Bolcioni, Lorini, Barili, Coletti, Rocco, and Quinto, filled out the program.

ity and masculine valor, Vestvali wrote: "My engagement at the Academy has been from the very first unpleasant, by the obstacles thrown in my path by Mr. Maretzek, who previous to my engagement did everything to prevent it,[30] and now, when I am connected to the Academy, he and his friends do everything that can be unpleasant to an *artiste*. Mr. Maretzek . . . asked me to sing a piece at the sacred concert, which I handed to him, or the person he sent to me, in order that he should have it prepared for the orchestra. I was not able to get that piece instrumented, and was waiting the whole of Saturday for instructions from the manager, but received none. As Mr. Maretzek did not, for some cause unknown to me, prepare the said piece, or give me any information regarding it, I leave it to the public to judge if it was in my power to sing or not. Mr. Maretzek had probably prepared the speech which he delivered to the audience on Saturday evening already on Thursday, as he knew *then* perfectly well I could not sing without music.[31]

"I am happy to be in a country, where women enjoy the same rights with men, in regard to self-defence," craftily continued Vestvali, "and I have the courage to unmask my enemy and to defend myself when I am most basely and causelessly attacked. If Mr. Ole Bull, the manager, had not been indisposed,[32] I trust that this unpleasant circumstance would have been avoided."

Indisposed or not, by March 3, Bull's days of decision-making at the Academy had come to a thunderous halt. At a stormy meeting that afternoon, the board of directors (apparently consisting entirely of Phalen and Coit) unequivocally expressed their confidence in Maretzek in preference to Bull. Seized by panic, Bull precipitately ordered the Academy closed, dismissed the personnel, and vanished—purportedly in possession of the box-office receipts, such as they were, including the sparse proceeds of that evening's sacred concert.[33]

On Monday morning, March 5, the papers carried Bull's staccato proclamation: "Notice to the Public: In consequence of insuperable difficulties, the Academy of Music is closed. [Signed] Ole Bull." Furthermore, at his orders placards had been posted on the Academy doors "summarily discharging all the [unpaid] artistes"[34] and commanding Mr. Tunison, custodian of the Academy, "not to admit any person

[30] According to Henry C. Watson, writing in his current capacity of secretary to the Academy management, Maretzek had been willing to engage Vestvali for one month with the option to renew her engagement. But she had held out for three months, which had been granted by Bull at an outrageous salary of "$800 per month with security" when Vestvali had requested only $400 (Watson, letter to the *Herald,* March 15, 1855, cited in the *Musical World,* March 17, p. 123).

[31] Reprinting Vestvali's card on March 6, the none-too-sympathetic *Times* commented: "However aggravating the circumstances . . . she was under a moral obligation to the public to do what she had been announced to do—even if it involved the necessity of a thin piano accompaniment. Whenever an *artiste* forgets this responsibility and treats an audience as something beneath a manager, it is our duty to remonstrate."

[32] On February 20, Bull had suffered a "severe accident" while walking on Broadway (*Times,* March 16, 1855).

[33] "During the six performances [at the Academy], including the concert," reported the *Mirror,* "there was a large amount of money received, to say nothing of the season-ticket swindle, for which payment was received in advance. . . . What has become of all the money?" Bull later admitted that he had kept "no account of the receipts of the Opera" (*Mirror,* March 6, 9, 1855).

[34] "The summary discharge of the artists, without pay or explanation by Ole Bull, is outrageous," fumed the *Evening Mirror* (March 6, 1855). Having as recently as February 8 predicted a "brilliantly successful season for Ole Bull and Co.," the *Mirror* now stated: "We never had any faith in his suc-

whomsoever under any pretext until you receive an order written and signed by me." Additionally, Bull had ordered all doors leading to the Academy barroom from other parts of the house to be "securely fastened so that no one can pass," adding, for emphasis, "You must strictly follow these instructions" (*Times,* March 6, 1855).

In the ensuing pandemonium: "Vociferations and threats in German, Italian, French, and broken English . . . swelled up a small storm, and, as it was supposed for a time that these might lead to open demonstrations of violence, or, as we say in the vernacular, to fisticuffs, the police were called in to keep the polyglots in order" (*Evening Post,* March 5, 1855).

In their desperation the frustrated Academy employees appealed to Phalen, who magnanimously ordered the barroom to be opened to them for a council of war. An attendance of between 200 and 300 was reported,[35] "from the conductor down to the humble charwoman," and including all the stars (except, of course, Vestvali). Officers were elected: Tunison president; Allegri, Torriani, and Vint [*sic*] vice-presidents; and two secretaries, D. W. Taylor (the Academy treasurer) and Henry C. Watson (already associated with the Academy).[36]

Grievances against Bull were aired: "Even in the first week of the enterprise he had failed to pay regularly, and in the second week, on the appointed day, had not paid artists, chorus, orchestra, ballet, carpenters, tailors, property men, gas men—in fact, nobody, not even the cleaners of the house or the band on the stage." What had become of the funds nobody knew. Bull's action in closing the Academy without prior notice was pronounced illegal; numerous resolutions were passed designating Bull a rogue and an unprincipled scoundrel.[37] Maretzek, who apparently dominated the meeting, received a unanimous vote of confidence "as a man and a manager" (*Times,* March 6, 1855).[38] A counterstatement from Bull was awaited momentarily.

By March 7, with Bull still not heard from, Phalen graciously offered the one-time use of the Academy for a benefit to the dispossessed personnel. Maretzek, Bertucca, Badiali, Coletti, Quinto, and Signora Avogadro volunteered to appear, as did the newly arrived tenor Pasquale Brignoli (1824–1884);[39] and *Lucia di Lammermoor,* originally scheduled for his canceled debut on March 5, was performed on March 12.[40]

Opera crisis or not, for the critics it was business as usual. Reporting only a "tol-

---

cess. He had neither money or business talent to begin with. It is but a few weeks ago that he was under arrest for debt, and his violin, if not his person, was in limbo."

[35] By the daily papers, that is. The *Musical World* (March 10, 1855, p. 110) more conservatively put the number at some 25 or 30 ladies and 35 or 40 men.

[36] According to the *Mirror* (March 9, 1855), as Bull's secretary.

[37] Although the *Herald* maintained that Bull was more sinned against than sinning, it had to be admitted that through the years he had consistently been entangled in financial peccadillos —with Julius Schuberth, at New Norway, and now with the Academy of Music.

[38] Strong (apparently inaccurately) reported on March 5: "There is a fierce triangular duel between Maretzek, Ole Bull, and Strakosch [still absent]; and orchestra and chorus war on all three and demand arrears of salary in vain. Vestvali seems to be all right and to have been oppressively treated."

[39] Billed as a *primo tenore assoluto* from the Paris Opéra, the spectacularly handsome Brignoli was the first of Strakosch's singers to arrive. Watson stated, in an open letter to the press, dated March 6, that Bull had refused to put Brignoli on the payroll, although his debut had been announced in the Academy advertisements.

[40] On March 9 the *Mirror* reported an offer from Bull to appear as an assisting artist at this benefit performance. An insult, retorted Allegri, as spokesman for the Academy personnel.

Pasqualino Brignoli at the beginning of a distinguished career in America that would continue for three decades.

erable" attendance at the benefit,[41] the *Evening Post* (March 13, 1855), showered negatives upon the debutant. Although apparently "capable of all the refinements and embellishments of the most florid Italian music," wrote the critic, Brignoli was "deficient in strength and dramatic expression . . . and made but a slight impression upon the audience in two or three very telling scenes."

The *Times* (March 13), on the contrary, reported a large attendance (except in the stockholders' seats) and a splendid performance on Brignoli's part. He was "an agreeable alternation to the *artistes* recently imported. He does not depend on the roar for his principal effects; he may not be able to sing E-natural from his chest (and Heaven grant he may never be able!), and he may be open to objections of a similar modern Italian character, but we are disposed to think he will become popular and please the simple—which, after all, is the great desideratum."[42] Brignoli possessed a "sympa-

[41] The benefit netted the beneficiaries some $1200, reported the *Mirror* (March 13, 1855). Among the "host of talent" in the audience were Vestvali, Steffanone, and Lorini. "We don't think there is one among them," crassly added the *Mirror,* "who is worth more to the management than $500 a month—or $6000 a year."

[42] A true prediction: Brignoli became an unparalleled favorite in the United States for the remainder of his life.

thetic, sentimental sweetness" but also "power and skill": he reminded the writer of Mario. Fry, too, found Brignoli's "sweet and tender voice" appealing, except that in the final scene the "ante-penultimate note of the Allegro air . . . was not given as it ought to be" (*Tribune,* March 13, 1855).

Meanwhile—to a deafening fusillade of claims in the law courts against Bull—Phalen, "for his money advanced, seized upon the scenes and dresses, etc. of *Rigoletto, Trovatore,* and *William Tell* . . . declared his intention of personally taking over the management of the opera with Mr. Coit as partner, [Maretzek] as musical director, and Mr. [Henry] Wikoff♪ as business manager, [and] continued the season" (*Sharps and Flats,* p. 17). They opened on March 16 with *Lucrezia Borgia,* with the long-absent *prima donna* Balbina Steffanone—conveniently just in from Havana en route to Paris[43]—as Lucrezia. An apparently somewhat tamed Vestvali was the Orsini, Brignoli the Gennaro, and Badiali the Duke Alfonso.

"Since her sojourn in the indolent tropics," wrote the *Times* (March 17, 1855), "the Signora [Steffanone] has increased the ample proportions of her fair person, but she looks the same good-natured, impulsive *prima donna.* Her reception was genuine and enthusiastic—and with reason: Steffanone has always been an excellent, reliable, painstaking artist. She is one of the few worth welcoming back again." Brignoli "created quite a sensation by the really charming quality of his voice . . . and bids fair to be the most popular tenor we have yet had." As for Vestvali, the *Times* critic (presumably Seymour) admitted that he was "incapable of appreciating the excessive exaggeration of this lady's methods—vocal or dramatic—but others seemed to relish it vastly, and she was liberally applauded."

An enraged Richard Grant White, however, could scarcely remember ever hearing "so much false intonation." During Steffanone's absence, he wrote, her voice had degenerated into nothing so much as "a bewildered shriek." Brignoli was a poor imitation of Mario, and in their ensemble efforts they were "too rarely of one mind." Not to be outdone in technicalities by Fry, White chided Brignoli for dwelling, not once but twice, upon the penultimate note of a cadence while Steffanone prolonged the ante-ultimate—"his note belonging to one chord and hers to another. The effect was dire and hideous, but both artists had screamed at the tops of their lungs while one rushed about with a bottle and the other rushed about without one, and the audience therefore—for there was no other reason—sought relief for their feelings in applause" (*Courier and Enquirer,* March 17, 1855).

Coincident with the reopening of the Academy on March 16, Ole Bull at last rematerialized and issued his long-delayed "manifesto." Blaming his delay on the Academy's refusal to supply him with necessary documents, Bull delivered himself of a litany of the wrongs he had suffered at the hands of the sinister cousins, Strakosch and Maretzek. He told of how, after rescuing them when the "pecuniary affairs" of each had been in "a most embarrassing condition," they had repaid his generosity with basest

[43] After some five years of performances in Havana and the United States, Steffanone was returning to Europe. The basso Federico Beneventano, her colleague and shipmate on the *Black Warrior* from Havana, was also bound for Europe. For some undisclosed reason he was not engaged to appear at the Academy of Music.

duplicity; of how, after having equally shared with them the proceeds of their joint tours, Maretzek had rapaciously seized all power upon their occupancy of the Academy; of how Maretzek had filled all the jobs, at outrageous salaries, with his own close relatives and connections;[44] of how they had then formed a cabal against Bull and sought financially to destroy him; of how Mesdames Bertucca-Maretzek and Patti-Strakosch, instead of contributing their services as they had done during the preceding concert tours, had demanded huge annual salaries of $7000 and $4800 respectively. What with one thing and another, Bull claimed a personal loss of more than $12,000 on his opera venture.[45]

In an equally voluminous document appearing in the next day's papers, Maretzek acidly replied that his participation in Bull's concerts had in fact merited more than an equal share of receipts,[46] Bull having become by now a "worn-out attraction." As to the alleged salary demands of the two *prime donne,* Maretzek pointed out that Bull had forfeited their free assistance when he seized the Academy lease and repudiated his three-way partnership with their husbands. Anyway, Bull's references to yearly salaries were fictitious since all engagements had been made on a four-month basis, his lease for the Academy running only until June 19 instead of the originally planned period of eighteen months.

And by the way, taunted Maretzek, "the curious may inquire what has become of the $1000 prize Opera, for which competitors were to send in their works before August, which will consequently arrive about two months after the expiration of Bull's lease." In conclusion, by Maretzek's reckoning, Bull, rather than suffering a loss of $12,000, had gained a clear profit of at least $4 on his Academy venture.

As the scandal continued to rage unabated in the law courts and newspapers,[47] the resumed opera season reportedly proceeded in what was described as "remarkably efficient fashion." On March 19, *La favorita* was repeated, with Steffanone replacing Vestvali as a more appropriate Leonora; on March 21 Steffanone reappeared in *Lucrezia Borgia,* and on the 23rd she sang the title role in Donizetti's *Maria di Rohan,* with Vestvali suitably cast as Armando di Gondi,[48] Badiali as Chevreuse, and Bolcioni, now a

[44] Not only had Maretzek demanded $1000 a month for his own services, but he had engaged his brother Albert as stage manager at a monthly salary of $120; his younger brother Raffael as ticket-counter at $60 monthly; Salvatore Patti, Strakosch's father-in-law, as superintendent of the wardrobe at $120; the dancer Mrs. Leeder, wife of the Academy's bartender (a particular friend of Albert Maretzek's), as prima ballerina at $150; Mrs. Avogadro (identified by Bull as Maretzek's housekeeper) at $100; and various others, including an unspecified Barili, for unspecified duties. Taylor, the Academy's treasurer, was also a Maretzek employee, at a monthly salary of $80, claimed Bull.

[45] On a different tack, Bull accused Maretzek of conducting in a manner to "break down" any *prima donna* other than his wife. (Bull conceded that he had never personally witnessed this behavior but had been told about it. Probably by Vestvali?)

[46] Maretzek's contribution to the concerts seems to have consisted in playing piano accompaniments for his wife's solos.

[47] Even Julius Schuberth attempted once again to collect his claim against Bull, still unpaid since the 1852 judgment in Baltimore. To report the mass of litigations against Bull, the *Herald* instituted a daily column, headed "The Opera Wars." On March 19 the *Times* rejected yet another voluminous self-justification from Bull, peevishly observing: "We must cry enough—and our readers will probably second us—on this subject."

[48] As Armando, she looked "every inch a man, and truly a very handsome one, and sang with all the spirit and fire that the assumption of male attire appeared to call for," reported the *Spirit of the Times* (March 31, 1855, p. 84).

bona fide member of the company, as Chalais. These performances completed the Academy's first (albeit interrupted) subscription series of twelve performances. On April 9, immediately following Holy Week, during which all operatic and theatrical performances were suspended, a second subscription series of twelve nights was scheduled to begin with the long-awaited production of Rossini's *William Tell* in Italian.

That matters at the Academy were beginning to assume a more "steady and orderly" aspect was astoundingly attributed by a suddenly dulcet *Herald* (March 23, 1855) to the expert management of the "Chevalier" Henry Wikoff, a notorious adventurer and self-proclaimed diplomatic advisor to European royalty.[49] Since 1840, when he had managed Fanny Elssler's fabled American tour, Wikoff had been treated by the *Herald* with a loathing second only to the detestation it cherished for the Frys. Now, suddenly, in an inexplicable reversal, with not so much as a single modulatory chord, the *Herald* was lavishing tender sentiments upon the Chevalier and the formerly despised Upper Ten directors of the Academy of Music as well[50]—even going so far as to suggest that Italian opera might after all have its uses, both as an art form and a social institution.[51] Wikoff, cooed the mysteriously regenerate *Herald,* was devoting himself to his administrative duties selflessly and "*con amore,* being actuated by pure love of art . . . without pecuniary reward.[52] [He] gives to the [Academy's] committee the result of his experience in the management of artists, in which vocation he spent a dashing part of his life.[53] By his unrivaled talents in diplomacy he has succeeded in making the contracts with the artists on terms more satisfactory and much more practical than those heretofore consummated. Madame Steffanone demanded fifteen hundred dollars per month, but through the exercise of the unrivaled diplomatic talent of Chevalier Wikoff, she was induced, with perfect delight, to accept one thousand dollars a month." Vestvali had similarly been persuaded to accept $500 monthly instead of the $800 originally promised her by Bull.[54] Even Maretzek had "cut down his demands

[49] Wikoff, an American, was said (like Gottschalk) to have received his title (to which he tenaciously clung) from the Queen of Spain.

[50] The *Herald*'s suddenly seraphic attitude toward the Academy, insinuated the *Tribune,* was due to monetary persuasion on the part of the well-to-do Academy management. It was also hinted that the strange reconciliation with Wikoff had followed upon his abject apology to Bennett for past iniquities.

[51] Under the new administration, season tickets and boxes would no longer be reserved, and an extra half-dollar for reserved seats would no longer be charged; the twenty-five-cent price for seats in the amphitheatre, however, would be retained. The *Herald* was satisfied that this price schedule did away with "the old system of exclusive privileges and high charges which made the Opera so unpopular under the old regime."

[52] The *Herald*'s extravagant rhapsodies over Wikoff were later reported to have been written by Wikoff himself (see *Musical World,* June 30, 1855, p. 209).

[53] Never so dashing as during his headlong pursuit in 1851 of his unwilling "fiancée" Miss Jane C. Gamble, an American heiress. This bizarre exploit earned Wikoff a fifteen-month-long sojourn within the inhospitable walls of the Genoa prison, when Miss Gamble sued him for abducting her and forcibly detaining her in a borrowed *palazzo* in Genoa. Shamelessly describing the affair in a book, *My Courtship and Its Consequences,* Wikoff was thought to have written it in the hope of extracting blackmail from the wealthy Miss Gamble to prevent its publication (*Courier and Enquirer,* May 19, 1855). This, too, was apparently unsuccessful: the book was issued in 1855, during Wikoff's present stay in New York.

[54] In his March 6 letter to the press, Watson had included a table of the "actual" monthly salaries to which Bull had agreed: Bertucca was to receive $600 a month, Patti-Strakosch $400, Ettore Barili

to a reasonable figure [not disclosed]. The Chevalier Wikoff has managed all this, and he has also drawn up a code of stringent rules for the government of the whole troupe, whereby the utmost harmony will be secured, both behind the scenes and before the audience. . . . For the first time, under the influence of the unrivaled skill of Chevalier Wikoff, and the calm and gentlemanly co-operation of Messrs. Phalen and Coit, it appears that the opera is to be founded upon a practical basis." The *Herald* pronounced it "the first fair chance ever given Italian opera to succeed in this country."[55] But this unaccustomed tranquility was not destined to last, and this time the disturbance would be provoked by William Henry Fry.

On April 2 it was first announced in the general press that Fry's newly composed *Stabat Mater, or, The Crucifixion of Christ* would be performed at Maretzek's sacred concert at the Academy on Holy Saturday, April 7. A complicated work[56] in fourteen sections, lasting an hour and a half, although it required four solo singers its principal parts were listed in the *Tribune* (April 2, 1855) to be performed by "Mesdames Steffanone, Vestvali, [Bertucca] Maretzek, with Badiali, Brignoli, Bolcioni, etc."; it employed as well a large chorus combining the resources of the opera chorus and the Harmonic Society, and the full opera orchestra.

Unfortunately, what with the premiere of Rossini's monumental and exacting *William Tell*[57] scheduled for April 9, it was announced that the concurrent rehearsals for the two works were proving too great a burden for the overworked company. Rather than jeopardize *William Tell,* it was decided to postpone Fry's piece until April 19 and to replace it at the April 7 concert with a "sacred and miscellaneous" program consisting mainly of recently performed works[58] requiring a minimum of rehearsal time, if any.[59]

Announcing this shift in schedule, on April 5 the *Tribune,* in far from objective terms, warned James Gordon Bennett, whom Fry blamed for the postponement of his

$600, Bolcioni $400, Rocco $250, Coletti $300, Badiali $1000, and Vestvali, as we know, $800 (*Musical World,* March 17, 1855, p. 123).

[55] Fully supporting the *Herald's* democratic stance, the modish *Home Journal* (March 31, 1855) informed its readers that aside from certain sections of the Academy, "where full dress seems by common consent to be appropriate, ladies attended [the opera] in the same toilette that would be in good taste for the theatre—wearing bonnets, cloaks, shaded gloves, or anything that may be comfortable or convenient—and that most of the gentlemen have abrogated white kids and dress coats." The *Home Journal* was happy to see these "sensible modifications." With them, audiences would surely increase in size and enthusiasm, "for many will attend that would otherwise be kept away by the expense and annoyance of an elaborate toilet."

[56] Classified as an oratorio, the work was set to the text of the *Stabat Mater,* a sequence in the Roman Catholic liturgy appointed for the Friday of Passion Week and September 15.

[57] Despite announcements that this was the first performance of *William Tell* in the United States, it was, in fact, its first performance in Italian. In the original French it had been (not successfully) performed in New York in 1845 at the Park Theatre by the splendid visiting opera company from New Orleans, where it had first been heard in 1842.

[58] And one recently unperformed work: Vestvali at last sang Naumann's formerly embattled aria, presumably with orchestral accompaniment. It was anticlimactically described in the *Times* (April 9) as "an old-fashioned composition . . . quite out of place in the secular part of the program."

[59] In a waspish review of the substitute program (*Tribune,* April 9, 1855), Fry went to great lengths to belabor the concert's obvious lack of adequate rehearsing.

Brady's portrait of James Gordon Bennett, dread publisher of the New York Herald.

Stabat Mater, that the "Satanic Press," as the *Tribune* had taken to calling the *Herald,* was not to seize upon the deferral to launch another "brutal and characteristic attack upon Mr. W. H. Fry, such as appeared in the Satanic of Sunday last [April 1], in which [Bennett had] threatened and warned the [Academy] management not to produce it, in a tone the compost of the sneak and bully, and said of this yet unheard work that 'its production would disappoint and disgust' every person in the house,[60] except a box containing the composers' friends."

Referring to the ancient and ongoing Bennett/Fry vendetta,♪ the *Tribune* (ostensibly Fry) complained that "the editor of the Satanic had in this [instance] simply attempted, as usual—whenever any of Mr. W. H. Fry's works are in rehearsal—to prevent their performance and bully the management.[61] But in this case he has not succeeded. He will not pull Mr. W. H. Fry down, and let him make up his mind for that!"

[60] In almost identical terms, in 1848 Bennett had warned the public against an announced, but frustrated, New York production of Fry's *Leonora.*

[61] As early as 1841 the *Herald* had pounced on an alleged financially questionable production in Philadelphia of *Norma,* translated into English by Joseph Fry and musically adapted (or supervised) by W. H. Fry.♪

If Fry brashly declared his hatred (and revealed his fear) of Bennett, that incorrigible editor—although he wasted no undue affection upon any Fry, living or dead—had been careful to name no names in his thinly veiled condemnation-in-advance of Fry's composition. (Bennett had evidently become wary of libel suits since his recent defeat in his long-drawn-out legal dispute with Edward Fry.) According to William Henry Fry and his supporters, Bennett's sinister influence over the Academy of Music consisted chiefly in his power to refuse its advertisements, thus effectively reducing attendance by keeping his readers ignorant of any attraction he might wish to undermine.[62]

Accordingly, although advertisements for the delayed attempt to present Fry's *Stabat Mater* were resumed in the general daily press on April 10, they were discontinued in the *Herald* from April 13 on, as were its advertisements (April 16–23) for the forthcoming *William Tell* production. During this hiatus, however, on April 19, all the papers (the *Herald* included) ran the following announcement[63] (most probably ghostwritten by Wikoff): "The Committee of Management of the Italian Opera have the honor to inform the public that the *Stabat Mater* announced for Thursday evening, the 19th instant, is withdrawn in order to afford the necessary time for the rehearsals of [Verdi's] new opera of *Il trovatore.* When the Committee assented to the performance [of the *Stabat Mater*] at the Academy of Music, it was distinctly and positively asserted by its composer that 'two full orchestral rehearsals were all that would be required'; whereas it turns out that already three rehearsals have been given, and on Monday evening [April 16] a paper in the handwriting of the composer was handed to the musical director, M. Maretzek, insisting on four more full rehearsals, thus monopolizing the whole time and resources of the establishment up to the day of its final performance.

"Under these circumstances the committee, finding that the new opera is likely to be endangered for want of sufficient preparation, and the large interests they have at stake proportionately sacrificed, they have unanimously decided to make no further concessions to the unexpected and unreasonable demands of the composer of the *Stabat Mater* in question. They have consequently ordered the immediate resumption, in its stead, of the interrupted rehearsals of the forthcoming opera of *Il trovatore.*

"The committee have thought fit to trouble the public with this brief explanation touching the *Stabat Mater,* announced for Thursday evening, in order to anticipate any misrepresentation of their motives."

A note from the chorus master, Angelo Torriani, addressed to Maretzek, was added as "conclusive proof of the exactitude" of the above statement: "I beg to inform you," wrote Torriani, "that it is clearly impossible for the chorus to go on with the rehearsal of two musical compositions at once. They have been laboriously occupied for some ten days past, as you are aware, with the *Stabat Mater,* and in spite of the fatigue attending the arduous [concurrent] performances of *William Tell,* and yet the

[62] A flimsy theory. It seems unlikely that any single newspaper, however potent, could exercise such power in a city so richly endowed with newspapers—and so avid for entertainment—as New York in the mid-1850s.

[63] William Treat Upton, regarding Fry's skewed reactions as purest gospel, apparently didn't consult any of the numerous contemporary references to this incident other than those appearing in the *Tribune.* Since Upton therefore makes no reference to this informative document, it is only fair to give it here in its interesting entirety.

composer [Fry] declares he is not satisfied and must have more rehearsals, even to the extent of forty or fifty, if he thinks fit. I shall be at my post at 11 o'clock, as notified, and you will be good enough to decide which of the two compositions we are to go on with—*Il trovatore* or the *Stabat Mater.* I repeat what is self-evident, that one must give way to the other."

Fry was obviously not unprepared for this eventuality: the very next morning (April 20) his accusation—two columns of it—was carried in full in the *Tribune* and in extracts in the other papers (some of them sympathetic to Fry). In this document, Fry, citing his correspondence with Phalen and Maretzek and his contract with the Academy, aired every injury, disappointment, and betrayal he had suffered, from the signing of his contract (March 17) to this latest fiasco. Primarily, of course, Fry bewailed his intolerable persecution at the hands of "the foulest villain of this hemisphere or epoch" (Bennett).[64] But equally he accused the perfidious Academy Committee of failing to live up to the terms of their contract, specifically concerning the number of rehearsals of his work.

But Fry was his own worst accuser: by some baffling manipulation of semantics he explained that the "two rehearsals" agreed upon by both parties meant in fact a "first rehearsal," consisting of as many rehearsals as might be required to correct copyists' errors, to make desirable compositional changes,[65] and to devote to any exigencies that might occur; and finally a second, or "general," rehearsal. "The number of two rehearsals, first and last," elucidated Fry, "was merely indicated by me to fix respective periods for them, but had necessarily nothing to do with the whole number of rehearsals."

After being refused the four additional rehearsals he had demanded, wrote Fry, and after breaking off an unsuccessful attempt to struggle through a chaotic "general rehearsal"[66] without Maretzek, who was purportedly ill, Fry instructed Dubreuil, the Academy stage manager, to inform the management that he would consent to another week's delay in order to gain his additional rehearsals. But Maretzek—who despite his illness was apparently somewhere in the building, or had just departed—had left word that "no more rehearsals would be allowed by the Committee." To compound the indignity, when Fry returned to the Academy that evening, for some reason expecting to resume the morning's interrupted rehearsal, he found the building dark, its doors locked, and "crowds of members" of the Harmonic Society wandering about in the rain—some of them ladies, "even from Brooklyn and Williamsburgh."

"However averse I may be, constitutionally and by habit, to have the least difference with anyone—stranger, acquaintance, or friend," declared docile Fry, "I must protest against such treatment. I have not the slightest pecuniary interest in the pro-

[64] "For eight or ten years we have been endeavoring to teach the editorial corps of the *Tribune* to talk and write, and behave like gentlemen," sardonically editorialized Bennett in the *Herald* on April 24, "but we are afraid we will have to give up the job in despair. 'Liar,' 'scoundrel,' 'villain,'. . . 'foreign rascal,' 'Scotch caitiff,' 'foulest villain,'—these are the savory epithets [referring to Bennett] which have run through the columns of the *Tribune.*"

[65] Characteristically, Fry boasted that he had composed his orchestration, consisting of approximately "a quarter of a million of notes," in only a few weeks.

[66] With disgruntled members of the orchestra in open revolt, complaining that they had been hired to rehearse operas, not concerts, and deserting in droves (see *Tribune,* April 20, 1855).

duction of the *Stabat,* but it is a matter of principle with me, as it should be with every gentleman, that a contract should be fulfilled, and therefore, as this one is essentially vitiated by the neglect of the Academy, the only course I have to pursue is to offer to consent to the postponement of the performance of the *Stabat* for a week or two, till it can be, as the contract provides, 'carefully rehearsed.'"

Firmly locking the cage door after the bird had flown, Fry laid down his ultimatum: "I shall not consent to this postponement till it is put in writing in the shape of a new contract, naming the day of performance, the days of two general morning rehearsals and one general evening rehearsal; and that such contract shall be handed to me by 8 o'clock tonight at the Academy. Should this offer be declined," Fry faintly thundered, "I shall, however reluctantly, be compelled to protect myself by making known to the public the manner in which I have been treated by an Institution which obtained its character chiefly through its promised, genially national character."

Phalen responded to this bizarre demand in a card (April 21): "Nearly a month since, Mr. Fry applied to me, as one of the Committee, for the performance of an Opera of his [presumably *Leonora*], which, for manifold reasons, was declined. He then urged upon me the acceptance of an Oratorio, which, he said, could be played in an hour and a quarter. From a long acquaintance, I was desirous of obliging him, and consented to make his *Stabat Mater* the second part of a concert about to be given at the Academy. The rehearsals began, but soon after, the *artistes,* chorus, and orchestra generally complained of the peculiar nature of the music, and if they were compelled to go on with it they would be obliged to neglect the Opera of *William Tell,* then under rehearsal. For this stringent reason the Oratorio was postponed.

"It was then arranged that Mr. Fry should have an entire evening for his Oratorio, and Mr. Maretzek, the Musical Director, agreed to bring it out on the 19th instant. Rehearsals began once more, but whether owing to the character of the music, the impatient temper of Mr. Fry, or the extreme fatigue of the artists, the matter went on so slowly that the Committee had to decide either to jeopardize their whole establishment for Mr. Fry's Oratorio, or to lay it finally aside in order to rehearse the new Opera of *Il trovatore,* on which thousands of dollars are already spent in scenery, dresses, and music."

As proof of his good will, Phalen had offered to donate $150 toward the copying costs of the *Stabat Mater,* an offer that Fry scornfully rejected. Indeed, wrote Phalen: "There has been no want of good faith on the part of the Committee, as Mr. Fry so unfairly alleges, nor yet on the part of any individual in the establishment. When he accuses Mr. Maretzek of being absent from rehearsal on Tuesday morning, he ungenerously neglects to state (for he was aware of it) that Mr. Maretzek was too ill to conduct. The disappointment of Mr. Fry may be painful to him, but he ought to reflect that a vast establishment like the Academy of Music, entailing an expense of not far from $20,000 a month, cannot be endangered for the satisfaction of any individual, and when it was found that, after *the utmost exertion and considerable sacrifices,* his Oratorio, consisting of a 'quarter of a million of notes,' could not be conducted on the 19th instant, and Mr. Fry further declared that he would go on rehearsing till he was content, even to forty or fifty repetitions, then, it must be admitted, the Committee were justified in withdrawing his composition finally and ordering the immediate resumption of the rehearsals of *Il trovatore.*"

Phalen profoundly regretted, as did the Committee, "the additional and irksome labor imposed on the *artistes* and *employés* of the Academy, who, though worn out by eight hours daily rehearsal of *William Tell,* besides the regular performances, were called upon to study the Oratorio of Mr. Fry, to which one and all cheerfully consented."

And finally: "The attempt of Mr. Fry to drag the New-York *Herald* into the matter is really preposterous. He asserts that the *Herald* refused the advertisements of the Opera since the Oratorio was announced. If Mr. Fry will examine the files of the *Herald* of last week, he will find not only the usual Opera advertisement but his own Oratorio advertised under his name. This is a manifest misstatement on the part of Mr. Fry, and for what purpose I am at a loss to imagine, since the real causes of his disappointment have already been explained. . . . The imputation that the Committee are desirous of the support of the New-York *Herald* is entirely true,"[67] wrote Phalen, "and they are equally desirous of the support of all other journals, to which they consider they have some claim, from the fact that they are bestowing much of their time and risking large sums of money, solely for the sake of promoting art, without a chance of honor or a dream of gain."

Be that as it may, the *Herald* (April 21, 1855) loftily referred to the controversy as "a sort of tempest in a small way" and of course disclaimed all responsibility for the cancellation of Fry's *Stabat Mater.* Although Bennett had admittedly on occasion "taken an interest" in the Academy, he had certainly never communicated with any member of the Committee of Management or anyone else in authority "as to what compositions should or should not be played." His highest ambition for his paper, he virtuously stated, was "to become the correct exponent of public opinion—to make this journal the organ of the free, unfettered, common sense of the American people, upon every subject of art, music, politics, commerce, law, religion." As to the cancellation of Fry's oratorio, it indicated the increasingly discriminating tastes of cultivated audiences who demanded the best operas "by recognized composers, sung by good artists, properly put on the stage, and well done in every respect." Audiences were tired of those (still naming no names) "'small-fry' affairs, which so disastrously affected the Italian opera of former days." In a flurry of repetitive puns, the *Herald* applauded the Academy for having rid itself first of "small-fry managers" and now "kicking the small-fry compositions out of its doors."

As for Fry's *Stabat Mater,* the *Herald* (April 24, 1855) playfully suggested that it be performed, now that the *Tribune* had taken its rejection so much to heart, at the Metropolitan Theatre by "native American minstrels—black or white, as they may choose." To this end the *Herald* was ready to subscribe $100—or even $200—"if the other lovers of original American compositions will come forward and do the same, in order that this much injured and very amiable genius, Mr. William H. Fry, may have a chance of being heard in a proper way before an American audience."

Endlessly rehashing the affair, on April 23 the *Tribune* (ostensibly Fry) once again reviled the Academy's managing committee for submitting to the *Herald:* "There is something degrading in a state of society in which such servility is not only practiced, but publicly avowed, by persons claiming to be gentlemen. We should suppose that the Directors and Proprietors of the Musical Academy would sooner see the earth open

[67] As reported in the *Courier and Enquirer* (April 25, 1855), Fry's response to this disgraceful admission was: "O *tempora!* O *mores*! Shame of shames!"

and ingulph their splendid edifice than see it sustained by a sacrifice which must elicit the contempt of every honorable mind."

As an anonymous opera-goer felicitously summed up the affair:

The Opera folks have made a dreadful clatter,
  Only a *ruse de guerre,* twixt you and I—
They didn't want to get a *Stabat Mater;*
  But, 'stead of that, to get a stab at Fry.[68]

Punctuating the first installment of the Fry/Academy controversy, on April 9, Rossini's *William Tell* was triumphantly performed for an audience of "overwhelming" size—an event that, according to the press, ushered New York opera-goers into a new era of operatic opulence. The magnificent production—equal in grandeur, the critics agreed, to the best Europe had to offer—continued to draw large and enthusiastic audiences throughout an extraordinary run of nine consecutive performances. The *Times* (April 10, 1855), like the *Herald,* credited the radical change at the Academy to "the gentlemen who are managing this establishment—[their] energy, capital, and taste—requisites, all of them, for satisfying the most cormorant public's demands."[69] Not only did *William Tell* offer welcome surcease from the Donizettian glut, but, in contrast to the vicious plots that characterized Italian opera, it offered a healthy political philosophy with which true-blue, freedom-loving Americans could, for once, empathize.

"To thus awaken noble sentiments and lofty aspirations should ever be the aim of the lyric drama," loftily proclaimed the *Musical Review and Choral Advocate* (April 12, 1855, p. 123) (presumably Hagen), gratuitously adding: "It is because *Rigoletto* is revolting to every feeling of justice and Christianity that it has proved such a failure in this country. We are glad it has; we hope its failure will teach opera-givers a salutary lesson. The moral enormities that were acceptable twenty years ago to infidel, licentious Paris are not yet palatable in America, thank God! We hope they may never be."

The *Times* thought it "a little remarkable that a work so thoroughly Republican should have been shelved so long in America. The *story* of 'Tell' is naturalized with us. He is one of our heroes—a familiar figure of strength and virtue in our picture books." The writer attributed the long neglect of the work to its complex and expensive production demands: elaborate scenery, an increased chorus, processions, supernumeraries, banners, and appropriate costumes. It was assuredly no opera for the "speculators," who liked to "get all without giving anything but vocalism in return."[70]

Of the large cast,[71] the *Times* (and its journalistic colleagues) particularly singled

[68] These lines, scribbled on the flyleaf of a libretto of *Il trovatore* said to be found at the Academy of Music, were published in the *Musical World* (May 26, 1855, p. 37).

[69] The changed approach was unanimously credited by the press to the sophisticated leadership of the Chevalier Wikoff and the solvency of the board members.

[70] Seemingly a reference to Maretzek, a chronically impoverished impresario, only rarely able to command the wherewithal for such lavish productions.

[71] With Steffanone (as Matilda), Avogadro (Edwiga), Badiali (Tell), Bertucca (their son Jemmy), Bolcioni (Arnoldo), Rocco (Gessler), Coletti (Walter Fürst), Adelindo Vietti (the Fisherman), Quinto (Rodolfo), Müller (Melchtal), and Eugenio Crouza, a recently arrived baritone "from the Paris *Conservatoire*" (Leutholdo). The various choreographic sequences were performed by Mesdemoiselles Lavigne and Leeder and Signor Carrese, accompanied by a somewhat wanting, so-called *corps de ballet;* the beautiful sets were designed and painted by Allegri; and the musical direction was, of course, in the capable hands of Maretzek.

out Bolcioni, who, although suffering from hoarseness, exceeded all expectations in his treatment of the pivotal and demanding role of Arnoldo, a role in which he was destined to create "a *furore*." Badiali as Tell was, as always, vocally and histrionically admirable, especially in the apple-shooting episode. Everyone else was splendid. But *William Tell* was a work "so complete in itself" and depending "so greatly on its completeness, that it [was] useless to refer to separate *morceaux*. . . . It is a monument of descriptive, emotional genius," wrote the *Times*, "a perfect work of art, rendered in a suitable building and in a suitable manner. If *William Tell* does not attract large audiences, musical taste in New York is a sham."

In the *Musical World*'s opinion the grandiose production signified the coming-of-age of opera in New York, as it did the fulfillment, at last, of the Academy's promise and its essential purpose; with this production was "suddenly gained that dignity which appertains to this splendid institution, [which] almost for the first time seemed in its right position before the public."

Fry went completely astray in a huge, digressive essay that only toward the end of its fourth column found a little space for the previous evening's performance of *William Tell* (a magnificent work, he reminded his readers, that he had often heard in Paris). Although the overture was well played by an orchestra of about fifty (in which the winds were inferior to the bass and string instruments), the effect was lost in the

New-York Historical Society

The Apple-shooting Scene in William Tell, *as played at the Academy in Joseph Allegri's greatly admired set.*

great confusion in seating the "monster audience, which was hardly accomplished when the curtain rose and displayed Allegri's beautiful scene—a mountainous landscape, with lake and waterfall, cottages occupying the foreground." The well-trained chorus and each member of the cast were praised, especially Badiali, a perfect Tell, who "looked and declaimed like a hero." Bolcioni, too, "magnetized the audience," with his robust tenor voice; although "his style was better than his method," he had "moments of inspiration" (*Tribune,* April 10, 1855).

Given in its massive entirety, the first performance of *William Tell* lasted until nearly midnight, but the enthralled audience, variously estimated at five to six thousand,[72] remained to the very end. By the second performance, however, "judicious cuts" had been made and curtain time advanced from 8 to 7:30 P.M., allowing the opera "industriously" to end by eleven.

Following the third presentation the *Tribune* (April 14), in a short follow-up notice, reported another "enormous house,"[73] and "in every respect" an admirable performance. "All the artistes, instrumental and vocal, are well up in the music." The opera's "freshness and massiveness" and the hearers' enthusiasm justified its several repetitions. Yet, by its second presentation, the *Evening Post* (April 12, 1855) had already begun to urge the management to "get another first-class opera ready" before the novelty-hungry New Yorkers began to weary of *Tell.*

The advice was hardly necessary. Along with their nine performances in three weeks of *William Tell*—a *tour de force* in itself—the company were, as we know, strenuously rehearsing Verdi's *Il trovatore,* scheduled for its American premiere on April 30, but delayed until May 2 by Steffanone's illness (to say nothing of fending off William Henry Fry's importunate demands).

An enormous first-night audience enthusiastically received the new opera, as they did the new baritone Alessandro Amodio (1831–1861), the second of Strakosch's singers to arrive. A young singer "from the Royal Theatres of Milan and Naples," Amodio was making his American debut on this occasion as the Count di Luna.[74] *Il trovatore,* jocularly observed the *Times* (May 3, 1855), possessed the essential attributes of Italian opera: two men in love with the same woman—"one a rugged *basso* or *baritone* [Amodio], the other a tender, languishing *tenor*" (Brignoli)—and a heroine named Leonora (Steffanone). It also contained a vengeful "gypsey" (Vestvali), and lesser characters played by Avogadro, Rocco, Quinto, and Müller.

Although the *Times* found *Il trovatore* lacking in intense dramatic situations—at least, until the last act—Verdi's writing was careful and showed a new "regard for the proprieties." The last-act *Miserere,* similar to (but even gloomier than) the last act of *La favorita,* displayed a masterly command of musical resources. For once, no mention was made of Verdi's noisiness; indeed, observed Seymour, he appeared to be changing for the better: "The early peculiarities which gave this composer so many enemies, and

72 In their euphoria the reviewers forgot that the capacity of the house was 4600 seats, of which only about 2700 were supposedly "fit to occupy" (*Tribune,* May 22, 1855).

73 By now "upwards of seventeen thousand" cheering people had purportedly gone to hear *Tell;* it was indeed a "*furore*" (*Times,* April 16, 1855).

74 Amodio was destined to enjoy great success in America, where, like Brignoli, he remained for the rest of his too short life.

which are remembered with so much tenacity, are being abandoned for something of a purer . . . character."

Amodio, unfortunately as broad as he was tall,[75] nonetheless was an extraordinarily fine artist with a full, rich baritone voice of uncommon freshness and sonority ("the throat and nose forming no part of Signor Amodio's method"). Steffanone was, as always, at home in Verdi, and Vestvali, as Azucena, fully availed herself of the dramatic scope of her role. Although she took great care to render the music faithfully, wrote Seymour, there were "so many breaks in her voice, and so little skill displayed in covering them, that we must wait for more cultivation before we can thoroughly appreciate her otherwise excellent vocalism." Her makeup, however, was "perfectly admirable."

The production was superb: Allegri's sets were even more beautiful than usual, although Seymour wished he would find "some method for preventing the oscillation of the scenes that are suspended from above." Also devoutly to be wished was "the burning of all the wooden swords. No amount of genius can brandish a stick like a sword, and no force of imagination can make it look like one."

Recalling that the best works of Rossini, Donizetti, and Bellini had been written for the Paris Opéra and were thus distinctly French in character, Seymour found *Il trovatore* to be the most "Frenchy" opera Verdi had so far produced.

In the opinion of the *Evening Post* (May 3, 1855), although the plot of *Il trovatore* followed the hated Italian model,[76] being "brimful of passion, crime, intrigue, and murder; and the denouement equal in horror to anything we could reasonably hope for in modern Italian opera—which seems to have become the exponent of all that is atrocious and extravagant upon the lyric stage—these defects were quite eclipsed by the real beauty of the music and the excellent rendering it received from all the members of the company."

Like the *Times,* the *Post* critic accused Verdi of self-plagiarism—only to be expected of one so prolific—but he disagreed with a French critic who had claimed that Verdi hid his poverty of musical ideas in the "crash of the orchestra, like a man who flies into a great passion and makes a great outcry when he has nothing further to say." There certainly had been "no great din in the orchestra last night"; indeed the writer had wondered if the score of *Il trovatore,* like that of *Rigoletto,* might not have been locally "written out from some pianoforte arrangement." It sounded suspiciously so, from the unusual "mildness of the brass instruments, [commonly] Verdi's most effectual orchestral aids."

In the *Albion* (May 5, 1855, p. 212), Burkhardt hailed the production of *Il trovatore* as "a decided hit," both musically and theatrically. "Never in New York has a new work more superbly been put on the stage." Allegri had outdone himself with his exquisite sets; never before had the orchestra been so well prepared at a first performance—or the chorus. Amodio, despite his "rather short and rotund figure, created

[75] "Amodio had a great and beautiful voice," later wrote the American opera star Clara Louise Kellogg (1842–1916), "but, poor man . . . he was so fat that he was grotesque, he was absurdly short, and had absolutely no saving grace as to physique" (Kellogg, p. 14).

[76] It was, in fact, of Spanish extraction, being based by Salvadore Cammarano on a play *El trovador,* by the Spanish dramatist Antonio Garcia Gutiérrez.

a most favorable impression [with his] rich, round, full, and well-cultivated voice." Brignoli sang well, if perhaps overenergetically (probably in an effort to outshine the newcomer); he sang the last-act *romanza* beautifully. Steffanone showed remnants of her recent illness and her singing thus suffered; Vestvali "*acted* the gipsy astonishingly well." Burkhardt was "surprised at her dramatic powers and equally surprised at her false intonation, bad phrasing, and indifferent singing. She has yet to learn a great deal, and unlearn more," he wrote, "before she can assume the rank as a vocalist which her friends claim for her."

Commenting act-by-act on salient musical points in the score, Burkhardt quipped that the demand for an encore of the Anvil Chorus[77] could only have been meant to show respect for the dignity of labor. But the *Miserere,* "interrupted by Manrico's *romanza,* Leonora's sighing strains, and the tolling of the bell at intervals, was sufficient to redeem any Opera."

If some critics seemed to be growing more tolerant of Verdi, the truce was by no means universal. On May 10 an ironbound Hagen delivered himself of a ferocious blast in the *Musical Review and Choral Advocate* (pp. 153–54): "Verdi's *Il trovatore* is another step on the bloody path of modern Italian horrors; one of those plots which attempt to interest only by continued murders, suicides, and the like . . . the stake, the prison, the rope; the cloister, the castle, and the cave. We have no idea of exactly who the personages represented are; everything is confusion from commencement to end. And as to the music, this could not in any way have been more inappropriate. It is almost throughout of the lightest dance kind, relying mainly upon rhythmical (the lowest kind of) effects, or ear-tickling, frivolous bits of what Mr. Verdi, no doubt, intends shall be called melody. Nor has the music, by way of recompense for its lightness, the merit of grace or originality. At every new phrase you feel confident that you have heard it before. . . . Nor is all this well put together. . . . The chorus sing mostly in unison, and oftentimes they are joined by the violins, and even brass instruments of the orchestra. Some critics speak of the able manner in which the *Miserere* is introduced . . . while the soloists are singing something else, and a big bell, out of tune, is ringing at intervals. As though it was very remarkable to be able to bring in the word *miserere* at intervals, sung by a concealed chorus." Verdi, fumed Hagen, appealed to "the exaggerated and evanescent passions of frivolous humanity."

John Sullivan Dwight, who was visiting in New York and had attended the opening of *Il trovatore,* was baffled, too, at the spontaneous public response to so distasteful a work: "It was really a marvel to us," he remarked in his interminable review of the opera (*Dwight's,* May 12, 1855, pp. 45–46), "and discouraging, in view of any progress of sound public taste, to witness the almost insane outbursts of applause which uniformly followed every aria, scene, and effect. . . . We could not account for it."

Although the Academy seemed at last to have achieved the utmost pinnacle of success and tranquility, new trouble lurked just around the corner. As far back as February (during the brief regime of Ole Bull), Jacobsohn, the first of the speculators, had returned from Europe and announced that he had engaged the great opera stars Anna

[77] A bit of incongruous musical typecasting that aroused a good deal of merriment among the critics, for why would gypsies go in for blacksmithing as a mass vocation?

de LaGrange (1826–1905) and Marietta Brambilla (1807–1875), and that the divas would be sailing from England within the next two weeks (*Times,* February 22, 1855). Perhaps they were deterred by reports of Ole Bull's fiasco at the Academy, for no diva arrived. Then, at the beginning of April, Ullman returned to the United States (probably not coincidentally on the same ship with Strakosch), and announced that the LaGrange company—consisting, besides Madame de LaGrange, of the tenor Raffaele Mirate and the baritone Filippo Morelli—had been supposed to arrive with him, but in the meantime had been commanded by the Emperor of France to sing at the Tuileries on April 9, and *que voulez-vous*? They would, however, follow immediately, which they did, as did Teresa Parodi, whom Strakosch was bringing back to the United States, doubtless with designs on the Academy. Niblo, too, returned from Europe at about this time, but made no announcement of opera plans.

On April 19 a shower of "exceedingly pompous," not to say ungrammatical, leaflets "*à la* Barnum" announced to the city that "Madame la *Baronesse* de la Grange"[78] had arrived and would inaugurate a season of Italian Opera at Niblo's on April 30 with a performance of *The Barber of Seville.* The season would be managed, however, not by Niblo, who for reasons of his own had apparently withdrawn from the combination, but by the "expert hand" that had managed the American career of the lamented Sontag, and—a further enticement—no opera would be given more than twice. The company included—besides Madame de LaGrange, Mirate, and Morelli—the *basso profundo* Ignazio Marini and the *basso buffo* Augustino Rovere (both recently returned from Mexico), the tenor Domenico Lorini, and the conductor Luigi Arditi.

Immediately following this announcement, and with not even the pretense of an explanation to the public, the opening was postponed for a week while behind-the-scenes negotiations were held by the Academy hierarchy and the threadbare speculators who managed the LaGrange troupe.[79] The outcome was not made known until May 7, the day of the promised debut, when the Academy management, in another of their heartfelt cards to the public, announced that they had "effected a junction" with the LaGrange company—that instead of Niblo's, the company would henceforth perform at the Academy of Music, where their delayed debut (still *The Barber of Seville*) would take place on Tuesday, May 8, a regular "off night" at the opera.[80] Doubtless

[78] If the incorrect term "*Baronesse*" aroused condescending merriment among the more linguistically accomplished of the New York critics, they quickly enough recognized in Anna de LaGrange, Madame *la Baronne* de Stankovich—the French wife of a titled Russian, a protégée of Rossini and Meyerbeer, and a *prima donna* of high repute in the opera houses of Europe from Paris to Budapest—"one of the greatest *prima donna*s that ever visited the United States"; in Maretzek's opinion, she was "the only one who could replace Bosio, Alboni, and Madame Sontag" (*Sharps and Flats,* p. 18).

[79] Last-ditch negotiations for the speculators— Ullman, Jacobsohn, and their purported backer, one David Rowland. Ullman later admitted that at this point he (they) possessed no costumes, sets, or money, having relied until the last minute on mythical props in Jacobsohn's possession, long since deposited by Maretzek as collateral for various loans. Except for some musical scores, everything had proved to be unusable (*Courier and Enquirer,* May 22. 1855).

[80] Because it was an off night, the management felt free to double the ticket prices in the family circle and the amphitheatre to 50 cents, thus arousing a great outcry. Fearing the loss of the most faithful part of their audience, they immediately restored the old prices, apprising the public in another comradely card.

to avoid collision with the resident company, the LaGrange group's second presentation, *Lucia di Lammermoor,* was announced for Thursday, May 10, another off night (the superstitious tenor Mirate purportedly refusing to make his American debut on a Friday).

Radiating piety, the Academy's announcement of the merger—obviously composed by Wikoff, now universally known as "the gentleman who manages the press"—informed the public that "great risk, much trouble, and large sums of money have not prevented the accomplishment of an object equally conducive to the interests of both parties, but still more advantageous to the cause of art, which has been the sole aim of the committee from the first." Not only would "a struggle between the Academy of Music and their rivals have entailed loss to both parties, but worse still, it would have jeopardized the final establishment in this country of the loftiest form of the lyric art—the Italian Opera—and that, too, at the moment when its fortunes seemed so near the zenith." To safeguard the future of opera, the Academy had nobly "turned a ready ear to the first whisper of parley from the opposite camp."[81]

Thus, at a sacrifice, and from motives of purest idealism, the Academy had accepted the speculators' conditions: for a period of two months to "take charge of the rival company and defray all the expenses connected therewith." Any monetary loss to the Academy would be cheerfully met in the knowledge that they had supported a musical institution "whose refining influence admits of no question [and] is established on a solid basis."

The papers unanimously applauded this decision as another demonstration of the wisdom, liberality, and boundless good will of the Academy administration. The *Herald* (May 8, 1855) gave Wikoff all the credit for having conceived and accomplished this merger—a feat, wrote the *Herald,* comparable to the "coalition of Christianity and Mohammedanism under the auspices of the Holy Alliance."[82]

On May 4, midway through these negotiations, the LaGrange company were put on display at Niblo's (probably to nudge the Academy) in a so-called "private rehearsal" of *The Barber of Seville,* to which critics and members of the musical profession were invited; it was, in effect, an unstaged, but otherwise complete, performance of the work. "Let us say at once," wrote an overwhelmed Theodore Hagen in the *Musical Review and Choral Advocate* (May 10, 1855, pp. 157–58), "that Madame LaGrange is the greatest performer our present age has at command. We have heard all those celebrated vocalists of the day, who have been admired for years by the French, Russian, German, and English *dilettanti,* but not one of them can be compared with Madame LaGrange as to the finished execution of unheard-of difficulties." Her singing could best be compared to the supreme pianism of the great Sigismund Thalberg: it possessed "the same neatness, the same sureness, the same brilliancy, elegance, and grace"—rare in the most virtuosic pianists, but beyond one's wildest expectations in a singer. With a voice that exquisitely and seamlessly traversed a span of some three octaves LaGrange was

[81] According to Ullman, the Academy had rebuffed his group's first two advances, and only on the third had they agreed to discuss the possibility of taking on a second troupe (*Courier and Enquirer,* May 22, 1855).

[82] An impermanent, post-Napoleonic organization of states, formed in Paris in 1815, and backed by several of the major European powers.

Girvice Archer, Jr.

Anna de LaGrange, the Baroness de Stankovitch.

able to "preserve the bird-like color of the notes above the high C"—indeed to the F above (or even G-flat)—with miraculously unchanged beauty of tone.[83]

Not only was she a magnificent artist, corroborated the *Evening Post* (May 5, 1855), but LaGrange, who was in the "prime of her youth," also possessed a charming face and petite figure, was most tastefully dressed (in a modish Paris evening gown),

[83] William Mason, who had heard LaGrange in Leipzig in 1852, wrote: "She was one of the finest singers I ever heard. Her style was brilliant and dazzling, but never lacking in repose. Her high tones were clear and musical, without any trace of shrillness, and in the most rapid passages the tones were never slurred or confused, but distinct and in perfect rhythmic order. The rôles in which she most appealed to me were as Queen of the Night in *The Magic Flute,* by Mozart, and Rosina in *The Barber of Seville.* But she also sang both parts of Isabella and Alice in Meyerbeer's *Robert the Devil* in the most admirable manner" (Mason, pp. 157–58).

and in every movement revealed an authentically ladylike demeanor; she reminded the writer of Sontag. In the *Una voce poco fa,* LaGrange rendered her astonishing *fioriture* "with such facility and accuracy, and with such a wealth of embellishments—apparently, too, without the slightest physical exertion—that the audience instinctively held their breaths . . . jealous if the least of those fine, air-drawn warblings should escape them. . . . No instrument could give to mere bravura ornaments a tithe of the expression which Madame LaGrange infused into them."[84]

Morelli, too, was an "immense success" with his splendid, vivacious portrayal of Figaro (albeit in contemporary evening dress). But more than that, he possessed a huge baritone voice "under excellent control" and was "quite at home in all the business appertaining to the stage." (Mirate did not appear in the *Barber;* Lorini sang the Almaviva and Marini the Bartolo.)

In his review of the company's official debut at the Academy, Seymour, in the *Times* (May 9, 1855), after various ambivalent quibbles, predicted that LaGrange, "within her capabilities," would surely create a *furore* in the "three or four operas that suited her style." That style, he stated—or rather accused—belonged to the French school, with its stress on "brilliant execution and a fastidious nicety of phrasing . . . everything is finished and perfect, soft and flute-like." The lower range of LaGrange's extensive compass of some twenty-three notes was a "distinctive" mezzo-soprano and her upper voice "a pure soprano of delicate, but beautiful, quality," both perfectly blended. In the lesson scene she had swept the audience away with a florid "Hungarian Melody" by Ferenc Erkel (1810–1893),[85] the father of Hungarian opera, and with a spectacular waltz of her own composition, the latter unsuitably reprised as the finale of the opera. Morelli, with a "vocal organization of magnificent proportions," delighted the audience, and Arditi brilliantly conducted an orchestra (not Maretzek's) of fifty musicians, but the chorus, with little to do in this opera, "managed to do that little in the worst possible manner."[86]

The coalition was not welcomed by the Academy's company-in-residence. Infuriated at the arbitrary imposition of a rival company, and further enraged at the threatened withdrawal of *Il trovatore,* their greatest hit, they unleashed an uproar of such ferocity that LaGrange, fearing for her life, took refuge in an "indisposition" and did not appear in the *Lucia* scheduled for May 10. Nor was there a substitute performance that evening.

So fierce was the upheaval that the *Herald,* which only three days earlier had hailed the opera rapprochement as a landmark in the annals of American culture, now reported (May 10): "Ever since the first contract was signed . . . between Mr. Row-

[84] Despite the absence of staging, she was judged the greatest Rosina heard in New York since the legendary *Signorina* had bewitched the city in 1825–26 (*Albion,* May 12, 1855, p. 334).

[85] A souvenir of her engagement in Budapest in 1850, when (according to the *Musical World,* May 12, 1855, p. 13) Madame de LaGrange had performed Erkel's opera *Hunyadi László* (Pest 1844) in such splendidly enunciated Hungarian that she was "elected The Queen of the Hungarians." Especially composed for her, the "Hungarian Melody" became "traditionally known [in Budapest] as the LaGrange aria" (*Grove's,* 5th ed., II, 962).

[86] Perhaps Seymour was not aware that the chorus singers (not Torriani's) had been hindered from entering the Academy by a hostile stagedoor keeper (*Review and Gazette,* May 19, 1855, p. 162).

land, the capitalist of the Niblo group, and the committee of the Academy, it seems that nothing but jars, difficulties, personal recriminations, explosions, and *émeutes* of every description have resulted from the fusion, all tending to the general breakup of the whole concern. The artists, the agents, the choruses, and even the leaders of the two troupes are all parties to this effervescence. One refuses to do this *rôle,* the other to do that, a third dislikes a particular artist, and a fourth has a holy horror of a fifth, and cannot possibly think of performing in the same place with him. Even the faithful and pliant Maretzek . . . had his dander roused and had actually resigned for a period of seventeen hours and a half because his rival Arditi was to be admitted to a divided enjoyment of the sovereignty of the baton. Mirate, the unrivaled new tenor (who has not been heard as yet here), refuses to perform in the same theatre as Badiali, because the latter expressed an unfavorable opinion of him many years ago in Italy. Ullman, the agent, who has been jumping about here and there like a hungry grasshopper—sometimes on this, sometimes on the other side of the Atlantic—finding himself in water too hot for him, has vamoosed for Boston."

The *Herald* named Strakosch the "Mephistopheles" of the whole episode, "fanning into flame the smoldering, but ever active, element of artistic jealousy,"[87] while Jacobsohn anxiously eyed "the 'monish,'[88] seeking to lay his clutches upon it, even before the first representation by the new company had taken place."

As if by magic, the chaos at the Academy seems to have released the press (except the *Herald*) from Wikoff's dire domination. In an abrupt reversal, the papers suddenly filled column upon lengthy column with revelations and condemnations of the schemings and plottings and misdeeds committed by the formerly sacrosanct Academy management, as maneuvered by the villainous Chevalier. The LaGrange company, wrote the *Courier and Enquirer* (May 11, 1855), in being brought into the Academy had been "betrayed, to their ruin. The events of the past few days [had] surely taught them how unwise they were in going to the Academy while the gentlemen who lease it are under the influence [Wikoff's] to which they have subjected themselves for a few weeks past." No sooner had the LaGrange troupe arrived in America, wrote the *Review and Gazette* (May 19, 1855, p. 162) "than a series of intrigues commenced, which had for its object either the union of the two companies or the destruction of that lately arrived, we cannot say." On the night of the LaGrange troupe's debut at the Academy, when "*a diplomatic attempt* [apparently by Wikoff] *to induce Mr. Morelli not to sing having failed,*" renewed attempts "at intrigue and low deception were again at work." The *Review* denounced the insufficient distribution of posters advertising the LaGrange troupe as another effort to keep people away. Having failed in these skulduggeries, the management then "refused to fulfill the contract with Jacobsohn."

The *Times* (May 11, 1855), too, confessing that it had been premature in congratulating the Academy on its merger with the LaGrange company, now sarcastically wrote: "Notwithstanding the superhuman efforts of the 'Gentleman who manages the

[87] Strakosch, it seems, was after all a partner of Ullman and Jacobsohn in the LaGrange enterprise, as were the music publishers William Hall and Son, and David Rowland—the latter, like Jacobsohn, listed in the city directory as an importer; Rowland purportedly had the backing of a bank—at least, according to the *Herald* (May 14, 1855).

[88] *Monish* is defined by Partridge as a "jocular imitation" of Jewish pronunciation of the word *money.*

press,' there has been a hitch in the arrangements . . . and it seems more than probable that the Academy will go to the wall. Low cunning and petty intrigue have begun their work of inevitable destruction; crimination and recrimination will follow . . . and then, when everyone is disgusted with the tortuosity and duplicity of the opera management, there will be a grand 'burst up.'"

To give its readers some idea of the "anarchy now raging within the walls of the Fourteenth Street house," the *Times* compactly itemized some of the goings-on:

> Mr. Jacobsohn has a difficulty with the Management.
> Mr. Jacobsohn has a second difficulty with Mr. Ullman.
> Mr. Ullman has a difficulty with everybody on general principles of policy.
> Signor Mirate (a singer not known here) has a difficulty with Signor Badiali.
> Signor Mirate has a second difficulty with the Management.
> Signor Mirate has a third difficulty with Mr. Maretzek.
> Signor Arditi has also a difficulty with Mr. Maretzek.
> Signor Arditi's chorus has a difficulty with Mr. Maretzek's chorus.
> Signor Arditi's orchestra has a similar difficulty with Mr. Maretzek's orchestra.
> Mr. Maretzek has a difficulty with the 'gentleman who manages the press,' and generally with everyone who has the misfortune to be under the latter's influence and control.
> And last and most serious of all, Madame Anna LaGrange has a difficulty in her throat, which prevents her singing.

At the moment of going to press, mischievously added the *Times,* there seemed to be a probability that *Il trovatore* would be performed on May 11: "But in the present state of things . . . an uprising of the *tenors,* or a disaffection among the *basses* may raze the Academy to the ground, or . . . Signor Arditi and Mr. Maretzek might have a death struggle at the stage door in Fourteenth Street. In these dreadful times who can foretell the events of four-and-twenty hours."

Il trovatore was indeed performed that evening "for the last time" to a huge audience estimated at 5000 (more of Wikoff's inflated reckoning?), and the following evening the season ended with a performance of *William Tell.* The company, it was announced, would immediately depart for a season of eight or ten performances of their major hits in Boston.

During the period of these disturbances the Academy committee issued another of their disingenuous cards, informing the public that much as they had tried, they had been unsuccessful in coming to an agreement with the Jacobsohn group. The disagreement was blamed on some complicated intramural disagreement among the speculators about a contract, or contracts, and not until it was resolved could a decision be made.

Commenting on this latest announcement, the *Times* on May 14, in a full column, openly accused the Academy administrators of taking on the LaGrange troupe with the definite intention of finishing them off. Through infamous plotting, documents had been manipulated and "dissensions were suggested and fomented. . . . For duplicity, cunning and groveling intrigue," wrote the *Times* "this latest *fiasco* exceeds anything we have before experienced." What with the machinations on both sides, the

Times believed that several artists had been "immolated in the slimy slough of intrigue." Indeed, in the *Times*'s opinion, the predicted "burst-up" had already occurred.

In acres of fine print, the other papers advanced bewildering conflicting hypotheses, too convoluted for mortal brain to fathom. Wikoff was characterized by some as the basest of scheming villains and the source of all the trouble, by others as the savior of the Academy. By May 15 the Academy management turned yet "another somerset": "Instead of going to Boston they have found an excuse [to remain in New York] for two more nights," reported the *Times*. The Boston theatre manager had allegedly requested a postponement of their engagement until May 21, and thus on May 16 *Il trovatore* was again performed at the Academy. The *Times* reported, too, that the Academy management had again made a final offer for the LaGrange troupe and, if nothing came of it, Madame de LaGrange, Mirate, and Morelli would be returning to Europe immediately, and perhaps better so.

By May 18, however, it was hinted that Jacobsohn, of all people, had made a fresh bid for a lease of the Academy during the resident company's stay in Boston. A startling development, but true, for the very next day the papers carried an outsized advertisement announcing the LaGrange troupe's Grand Opening under Jacobsohn's management in *Lucia di Lammermoor* at the Academy of Music on Monday evening, May 21. Besides LaGrange, Mirate, and Morelli, the company included Signora Costini and the Signori Marini and Rovere; Arditi was the music director and the minor opera tenor Barattini the stage manager. The *Herald* chose this inappropriate moment to congratulate the public on "the success of the Chevalier Wikoff's operatic tact and tactics" in effecting this wonderful victory for the Academy.

Wikoff, in fact, had begun to recede from the New York opera scene, for upon the LaGrange company's move into the Academy, his employers, Phalen and Coit, understandably having had enough of opera management by now, announced their joint resignation, effective at the end of the present opera season.[89] Recognizing the handwriting on the wall, Wikoff, too, resigned and in June returned to Europe.[90]

Meanwhile, another wealthy Academy stockholder, William H. Paine, incurably tainted with the desire to be an opera impresario—especially since his exhilarating adventure with Hackett/Grisi/Mario the year before—lost no time in snapping up the Academy lease,[91] to run from September 1855 to May 1856, as Maretzek informs (or misinforms) us (*Sharps and Flats*, p. 17).[92] At the same time, Paine astutely acquired LaGrange's contract from Ullman (no mention of Jacobsohn or Rowland).[93]

For the present, however, under their original management, the LaGrange troupe, during their present short occupancy of the Academy, gave unsurpassed performances

[89] Having lost some $20,000 on their opera junket, and "being fully satisfied with their experiment, Phalen and Coit again offered the lease to the highest bidder" (*Sharps and Flats*, p. 17).

[90] Where his diplomatic gifts were perhaps again in demand; or perhaps he would be writing another book, while "the press would be left to 'manage' itself and a certain daily journal [the *Herald*] furnish its own editorials" (*Musical World*, June 30, 1855, p. 209).

[91] Reportedly wresting it from Ullman's hungry grasp.

[92] Although Paine relinquished management of the opera at the Academy of Music in April 1856, his lease seems to have continued until October (if not longer).

[93] Paine also engaged Brignoli, Amodio, and Morelli, but not Mirate, who apparently returned to Europe.

of *Lucia* (May 21 and 23), *Ernani* (May 25 and 28), *I puritani* (June 4 and 6), and *Norma* (June 8), and additionally a concert at the Academy (June 7).

LaGrange, previously heard only in her delicious Rosina, astounded the critics[94] with her unexpected mastery, both vocal and histrionic, of a range of roles and styles that spanned the emotional boundaries of Italian opera—from *Lucia* to *Norma*. As Richard Grant White summed it up, following her *Norma* performance (*Courier and Enquirer,* June 9, 1855): "It was reasonably supposed that one who had made herself such a consummate and really unequaled mistress of the lighter graces of vocalization would find her voice and her style unequal to the demands of dramatic and declamatory music." But her wide-ranging repertory had "afforded her opportunities for the display of the versatility of her talents. It was perilous indeed for her appearance in *Norma,*" wrote White, "with Grisi's impersonation of the Arch-Druidess so fresh in our memories. . . . Not to fail is greatly to succeed; but Madame LaGrange did far more than this. . . . Her conception of the character and her execution of the music [were] nearly faultless. Her rendering of the *Casta diva* was remarkable for its sustained flow and its serene and solemn grace. . . . In the *Allegro,* Madame LaGrange was delicate and brilliant and florid to a marvel."[95]

At her concert,[96] continues White, her execution of a *Souvenir de Varsovie,* a mazurka originally for piano by Julius Schulhoff, was "the climax of musical wonder-working . . . to its marvelousness [she] adds a melodious beauty which enchants all ears, cultivated and uncultivated. It would be impossible to give a reader not educated in music any notion of the difficulties which she overcomes. . . .

"It can be compared only to the most exquisite work of the greatest violinists, and even that is not quite as delicate or nearly as elastic.[97] She, among other feats, descends an octave and a half by a diatonic succession of *grupetti,* or 'turns,' diminishing the volume of tone by exquisitely symmetrical gradation; and upon the immediate recurrence of the passage, while executing it in the same manner, astounds the ear by giving every note with a *staccato* so sharp and clear as a point of light. But, indeed, to describe the grace and finish of this performance surpasses the power of our poor pen."

Although there were those who caviled that her slight physique was too frail to sustain the weightier roles she undertook, she was nonetheless clearly heard above the most vociferous masses of accompanying choral and orchestral sound. Both White and Fry unequivocally called her a "phenomenon."

Mirate and Morelli received generally enthusiastic, if mixed, reviews. Mirate, everyone agreed, was an uncommonly handsome man—the handsomest, wrote Richard Grant White, since Fornasari♪—but there was less agreement on the subject of his

[94] And thrilled her audiences. Among the numberless bouquets showered upon her at the first *Lucia* performance was "a hat, which one enthusiast [having no flowers] hurled upon the stage with a facility of aim rather dangerous to the recipient of such favors" (*Evening Post,* May 22, 1855).

[95] Indeed, in Hagen's opinion, she sang the *cabaletta* "with a brilliancy Jenny Lind could never have attempted, even" (*Review and Gazette,* June 16, 1855, p. 195).

[96] Miserably attended, even allowing for the bad weather. The virtually invisible audience were estimated to have numbered about five hundred.

[97] "We were well aware that Madame LaGrange had swallowed Paganini's violin, but we did not know that she had also devoured Schulhoff's piano-forte," commented the *Courrier des États Unis* (cited in the *Review and Gazette,* June 16, 1855, p. 104).

Robert Tuggle

Filippo Morelli sporting his uncurtailed facial adornment.

voice. Some, like Fry (*Tribune,* May 22), judged it to be "robust, pure, cultivated, sure, extensive, and sympathetic," while others, like Seymour (*Times,* May 22), thought it "past its prime, although still well-preserved and unusually sympathetic for a *tenore robusto*" but in his lower register lacking in sweetness. Mirate was a seasoned professional, but by far no second Mario, nor yet a second Salvi. It was noted that Mirate usually excelled in his last acts, having carefully saved his voice throughout the opera for a grand finale.

Morelli, at first acclaimed "a treasure" and the "best baritone we had ever had," was now faulted by some critics for his overabundance of energy and indiscriminately applied volume of sound.[98] To Seymour, however, Morelli's voice, in the "full freshness of its beauty, [was] rich, clear, and vibrating, entirely under his control and delivered with a purity rare among baritones and basses." But Burkhardt was disappointed by the "raw and harsh meagerness of his delivery"; he later decided that Morelli was not a "first-rate artist," nor even a "serious" one (*Albion,* May 26, 1855, pp. 247–48). Despite the divergence of opinion, it was generally agreed that the trio represented the best that was now to be heard in opera—in Europe or anywhere.

[98] His physical appearance, too, was criticized: "He is not as handsome as he might be if he would curtail his moustache a little," carped the *Musical World* (May 25, 1855, p. 37). It was so long that when he sang, "the moustache suddenly [changed] from a horizontal curve to a perpendicular arch, exceedingly *frappant* to the eye, the long imperial below intensifying the effect."

Following their triumphant performance of *Norma* on June 8, the LaGrange troupe, exchanging places with their rivals (now called the "Steffanone troupe"), headed for Boston, where on June 11 they were heard—not in opera (doubtless due to scarce funds), but in the first of three wildly acclaimed concerts (see *Dwight's,* June 16, pp. 85–87; June 23, 1855, p. 95).

Meanwhile, at the Academy the Steffanone troupe began their final week of benefits. Still under the aegis of Phalen and Coit, they opened on June 11 with *Il trovatore* for Brignoli's benefit; on June 13 for Badiali's benefit they gave *William Tell* and on June 15, for Vestvali's, a varied bill consisting of the last act of *Rigoletto,* the last act of Vaccai's *Giulietta e Romeo* (with Vestvali a splendid-looking Romeo in her black habiliments), and the second and fourth acts of *Il trovatore.*

On Saturday, June 16, the benefits were interrupted for a widely publicized and eagerly awaited special event, the New York debut[99] of Elise (or Eliza) Hensler (1836–1929), a young American *prima donna*[100] who had recently made her successful debut at La Scala in Milan. Hensler, the Swiss-born daughter of a German tailor, had been brought to the United States as a small child and had grown up in Boston. When she was only sixteen, admiring friends, solicitous for the proper schooling of her promising voice, sent her (in her father's safekeeping) to Europe, where she studied singing with Bordogni at the Paris *Conservatoire,* winning there, after only a few months, the prestigious second prize at their annual *Concours.* After about a year in Paris the Henslers moved on to Milan, and there, after being heard at a private musicale, Elise was engaged for La Scala, where in late 1854 she made her bow in Donizetti's *Linda di Chamounix.* Her beckoning career in Europe was abruptly interrupted when her father suffered a stroke and had to be brought home. On their arrival in New York, on June 6, 1855, Miss Hensler announced to the press that she had returned for personal, not professional, reasons. Yet, here she was, less than two weeks later, about to make her loudly heralded debut[101] at the Academy of Music in *Linda di Chamounix.*

In their reviews of the young American singer there was for once no disagreement among the critics. Everyone was charmed by her appealingly simple and unpretentious, yet dignified, demeanor and her charming voice. In appearance, wrote Fry (*Tribune,* June 18, 1855), she had a "sweet, frank, ingenuous, expressive face, [and] a dark, sympathetic eye. . . . Her figure is of moderate height, her age about nineteen—so she has ample time for [future] culture and improvement." Her voice, a pure and silvery soprano of modest size, "did not *command* admiration but rather *beseeched* it," wrote Seymour (*Times,* June 18, 1855). With proper practice and study, he foretold that Hensler would doubtless "take a high rank among eminent sopranos." And in the meantime, she had no bad mannerisms to unlearn: "At present, a quiet neatness of style, correct intonation, and a charmingly sweet voice [of "about two octaves plus a

[99] Originally scheduled for June 14 but delayed to permit a needed extra rehearsal.

[100] Our third *prima donna,* it was proudly pointed out, the first being Elise Biscaccianti (also from Boston), and the second Virginia Whiting, now Virginia Lorini.

[101] The *Times* (June 15, 1855) sharply criticized a proposed serenade to Miss Hensler: "Things of this kind before a *debut* are simply absurd. If they have any purpose at all, it is the miserable one of creating a fictitious excitement." But after all, caustically added the *Times,* Miss Hensler deserved a serenade, not only for her achievements, but because she was an American, and thus "entitled to little politenesses of this kind."

note or two" were the] characteristics of her singing." Although she needed to learn just about everything about stage deportment, "her debut was triumphantly successful—sufficiently so," hoped Seymour, "to secure her an engagement for next season." The *Evening Post* (June 18, 1855) reported a great ovation, with bouquets and curtain calls galore, and a curtain speech from Miss Hensler in "genuine Anglo-Saxon—a dialect not often heard on the Italian operatic stage." She was well supported by Vestvali (the Pierotto), Brignoli (Carlo), Rocco (the Prefect), and Badiali (the Marquis), all of whom were praised, especially Brignoli, who interpolated a *romanza* by Mercadante in the second act, so well liked that it had to be repeated.

On June 18, Miss Hensler even more successfully appeared, again in an act of *Linda,* at Maretzek's benefit,[102] the final event of the eventful Phalen/Coit season. A typically elaborate Maretzekian extravaganza, the program included—besides Miss Hensler's contribution—three acts of his perennial hit *Masaniello,* sung by Martini d'Ormy,[103] Bertucca, Brignoli, Badiali, and Quinto, and mimed by Mademoiselle Zoë (Wiethoff); the begging scene from *Le Prophète* sung in German by Martini d'Ormy; and an act of *Don Bucephalo,* a hilarious buffo opera composed and performed by Rocco. A merely so-so attendance was reported.

After the performance, reports Dwight's New York correspondent, the "initiated" of the Academy, in uninhibited overbubbling of high spirits, "adjourned to the operatic *Bierkneipe* in Third Avenue, [where] pretty soon the entire Teutonic portion of the troupe and their friends (including many Yankees) were assembled." Following a goodly consumption of lager beer they "proceeded to Mr. Phalen's in 14th Street, to whom the orchestra brought a fine serenade. The same was done to Miss Hensler at the Everett House [17th Street], Mr. Coit (the other manager) in 8th Street, Steffanone in Houston Street, and Max, in 4th Street." The writer left them "about to proceed again to the 'house of the muses'" (the beer palace); he thought it likely that they wouldn't go home until morning (*Dwight's,* June 23, 1855, pp. 92–93).

Following this stirring finale, Maretzek retired to his farm on Staten Island to complete his *Crotchets and Quavers.*[104] The company scattered to the far places: Steffanone and Marini to Europe, soon followed by Mirate. Signora Costini and (reportedly) Badiali were expected to leave shortly, as were the Lorinis. Vestvali, whose contract with the Academy had expired, planned to remain in America.

Scarcely had the echoes of Maretzek's finale begun to subside when the LaGrange troupe were back on the Academy stage, giving their own final week of opera. Drawing reportedly good (or sparse) houses, they opened on June 21 in *Norma,* followed on June 23 by *I puritani,* and on June 27—to a "suffocatingly" crowded house—their

[102] Maretzek's tribulations at the Academy were recalled in the *Times*'s advance notice of this event (June 18, 1855): "It seems to us that in spite of Ole Bull's silliness, Signora Vestvali's hatred, and Signor Mirate's superciliousness, Max Maretzek has a legitimate claim on the musical public of New York; more so than any fiddlers, singers, or Committee of Management who now reign, or wish to reign, omnipotently."

[103] Since her days with Maretzek at Castle Garden, Madame Martini d'Ormy had become a star of the evolving German opera scene (discussed below).

[104] First called *Music in Hesperia,* after a multitude of intervening titles Maretzek's book was finally named *Crotchets and Quavers,* a title probably lifted from Sedgwick's entertainment, which had resurfaced in 1855 (see below).

delayed major effort, Mozart's *Don Giovanni* (advertised as *Don Juan*).[105] Announced for June 25, it had been postponed because the recently arrived mezzo-soprano Catarina di Ferrari, engaged to sing Donna Elvira, was suddenly indisposed; continuing to be so, she was at last replaced by Madame Siedenburg. Madame de LaGrange sang Zerlina; Rose de Vries (back after a two-year absence), Donna Anna; Morelli, Don Giovanni; Rovere, Leporello; Mirate, Ottavio; a new (and transitory) Signor Giulio, Masetto; and Gasparoni, the Commendatore. Arditi conducted, Allegri contributed new scenery,[106] and Señorita Soto and Signor Carrese danced a minuet in the first act. The LaGrange season closed on June 29 with a repeat performance of *Don Giovanni* to another "packed house."

In varying measure, the critics pronounced the *Don Giovanni* production to be

[105] Using its German title of *Don Juan* was probably a bid to attract members of the visiting German singing societies then holding their National Festival in New York for the second time (discussed below).

[106] Beautiful but incomplete, for, as the *Evening Post* (June 29, 1855) pointed out, the last act incongruously took place—instead of in Don Giovanni's palace—in the same town square fringed by Swiss mountain scenery that had previously represented the town of Altdorf in *William Tell*. Too, at the climactic end of the opera, the Commendatore descended solo through the floor, leaving the Don casually to make his own way to Hell through a rear door. (For other incongruities perpetrated in this production, see *Dwight's*, July 21, 1855, pp. 126–27.)

Luigi Arditi, whose playful conducting antics did not suffice for Don Giovanni.

Music Division, The New York Public Library

vocally superlative—all, that is, but Burkhardt, who damned it as "from first to last . . . the *worst* performance of that greatest of all operas that was ever heard on this side of the Atlantic." Only Rose de Vries escaped his attack. The chief offender, it seems, was Arditi. Concededly, he was a clever enough conductor for the general run of Italian operas, having at his fingertips such hackneyed works as *Ernani, Norma, Nabucco, Don Pasquale,* or even *I puritani*—all operas he could conduct without a score, his eye wandering everywhere: "He gives a wink to the chorus, a nod to the clarionets, and beckons the drums; his arm—nay, both his arms—move on, whilst he may look round upon the audience, or carry on a telegraphic flirtation, and yet the opera will proceed and . . . be effectively brought out. But in *Don Giovanni* he cannot look around, he must study, and 'whilst teaching spelling, learn himself to read.'" As to having *Don Giovanni* at his fingertips, only the "end of Arditi's finger rested upon the score, while his right hand beat the time—as nearly as he can come to it—which was almost the entire evening too slow."

LaGrange's managers (ostensibly still Ullman/Jacobsohn), in their eagerness to turn every minute of their Academy tenancy to profit, scheduled an unaffiliated single performance of Donizetti's long-unheard *Belisario*♪ for June 26, an off night. The event was advertised as the debut of a Signor Antonio Rosetti, who had arrived some months since but still remained unheard, despite an earlier debut announced in March. Rosetti's supporting cast of predominantly second-string singers included Signora Manzini, Madame Siedenburg, and such veterans of past opera disasters as the Signori Taffanelli, Arnoldi, and Candi; Arditi was the conductor. On June 27 the *Times* disgustedly reported: "*Belisario* was not given last evening. Some squabble among the artistes prevented the performance, and Signor Rosetti has yet to make his debut."[107]

Concomitant with these goings-on, a sort of attempt at opera-giving was made at the Metropolitan Theatre on June 22, when the second act of *Lucrezia Borgia* and the last act of "Romeo and Giulietta" (probably Vaccai's), bisected by a Grand Concert, were presented as a complimentary benefit to Carolina Vietti-Vertiprach, who had apparently fallen on meager days. Besides the beneficiary, the participants were Bertucca, Catarina di Ferrari, Bolcioni, Badiali, Cuturi, Coletti, Adelina Patti, billed as "the Little Phenomenon," and La Manna, who conducted.

The event was thinly attended, reported the *Herald* (June 23), probably because of the rain—a pity because it was a superior effort and the tickets were only twenty-five and fifty cents. The writer particularly singled out Ferrari, making her first appearance in opera, as a "fine artist—her execution of the cavatina from [Verdi's] *Macbeth* was distinguished for its finish."

With Ullman purportedly engaged by Paine as the new director of the Academy, it was rumored that a short season of summer opera might be forthcoming before Jullien's eagerly awaited return on August 1. Both rumors came to naught.[108] Not that there was any dearth of opera that summer, or, for that matter, at any time during that year. Even before Ole Bull had initiated his memorable regime at the Academy, German opera productions were achieving small triumphs at the *Deutsches Theater* (17–

[107] Odell (VI, 396) erroneously reports that the performance took place.

[108] As did the rumor that Michael Balfe would replace Maretzek as conductor at the Academy.

19 Bowery), with an increasingly large audience reported at each succeeding performance. On January 23 the company ambitiously presented Mozart's *Zauberflöte,* no less, in its first supposedly authentic production in the United States.[109] "Allowing for the smallness of the stage and the abrupt effect by the *artistes* being nearly as tall as the houses," reported the *Times* (January 27, 1855), "the opera was placed on the stage in a highly creditable and satisfying manner." Not only did the costumes "bear comparison with any establishment in the city," but "the miniature scenery [was] appropriate and neat. Throughout, there was an air of completeness worthy of appreciation and support.

"The leading artistes, Madame Siedenburg, and Messrs. Vincke [basso], Beutler [tenor], and Müller [baritone], were sufficiently powerful for the house, and seemed sufficiently well up in the music"; the excellent conductor was Julius Unger (the future orchestrator of Verdi's *Rigoletto*). The effort deserved support, continued the *Times,* especially if the high standard of the *Zauberflöte* performance were to be sustained. On February 1 the company presented (in German) Adolphe Adam's comic opera *Der Brauer von Preston* [*Le Brasseur de Preston*], seldom heard since 1846, when the Seguins had first presented it in English.♪

The venture prospered: "While all is 'noise and confusion' among the discordant elements at the Academy, and the prospects of a long and successful season are dashed by the appearance of Mr. Ole Bull's very brief advertisement in the papers," wrote the *Evening Post* on that fateful March 7, "the musical public will be very interested to know that another project for operatic performances is under way, with a fair prospect of a successful issue. It is, moreover, something of a novelty . . . from the fact that it contemplates the production of neither the Italian or English opera, but of the German opera, in the German language, and by German singers." To promote the enterprise, several "German gentlemen of respectability and taste" joined forces to support ten nights of German opera at Niblo's "in a more perfect style than has hitherto been attempted in this city." With the Bull fiasco offering a sad example, they foresightedly "deemed it expedient . . . to procure two hundred subscribers before incurring any expenses in hiring a theatre or company." Indeed, a subscription list was already begun and could be viewed at Scharfenberg and Luis's music store. Thus (while the long-awaited Niblo/Ullman/Jacobsohn opera had languished in mysterious limbo) on March 13 the German company moved into Niblo's Garden, where they scored a success with a delightful production of Flotow's *Martha.*[110] The cast included Mesdames Elise Siedenburg (whose sweet, if small, voice charmed all who heard it), Giuseppina Martini d'Ormy (now described as a "large, handsome, Vestvali style of girl [with] a strong contralto and considerable vivacity and adroitness as an actress"), Messrs. Quint, Behringer, and Vincke (tenor, baritone, and bass), all of whom were excellent, and a large orchestra well conducted by Julius Unger (*Musical World,* March 17, 1855, p.

[109] In an English adaptation by Charles E. Horn, *The Magic Flute* had received its first American performance at the Park Theatre on April 17, 1833.

[110] The opera should have been called *The Last Rose of Summer,* contended the *Mirror* (March 14, 1855), "as the air is served up hot and cold—in solos, duets, choruses—and, in fact, is the air which chiefly makes the piece. The audience encored it—many of the good people believing it, doubtless, one of the airs of the Fatherland and the composer Flotow, instead of Ireland and by nobody in particular."

122). Non-subscribers might purchase tickets for fifty cents, except in the dress circle where an extra fifty cents was charged.

"The reproach that German Opera had never succeeded anywhere but in Germany will, it seems likely, be reversed in New York," wrote the *Times* (presumably Seymour) on March 14, in a vivacious account of the opening night. Despite dreadful weather "pleading fiercely for the fireside, Niblo's presented an auspicious appearance": Present were the best German families, as well as the "square-headed artizans [*sic*]. Blue eyes and flaxen hair flashed from the dress circle and the parquette. . . . Gentlemen with beards to their waists and an incurable habit of speaking loud! Opera books printed in agonizing [Gothic] type; playbills a yard long and ruinously extravagant in large letters! Five hundred people talking in five hundred different accents but all talking loud and enjoying themselves in a disreputably happy manner! Such [was] the appearance of the house—impressing the astounded critic with the belief that the people present actually went to enjoy themselves, and not for the mere purpose of display. . . . We should not be surprised if German Opera became a permanent thing with us!"

After *Martha* and *Der Brauer von Preston* the German company presented *Der Freischütz,* on March 22, with Caroline Lehmann (noticeably ignored by the Academy hierarchy) making her belated American opera debut as Agathe; the other major roles were filled by Siedenburg, Quint, and Vincke.

Despite his determined avoidance of opera, George Templeton Strong succumbed to irresistible temptation: "Went by myself last night to hear *Der Freischütz* at Niblo's," he wrote in his journal on March 23. "Agathe, Miss Caroline Lehmann, quite respectable; the [other] parts vilely filled; the orchestra weak and not very accurate.[111] But it takes a great deal to spoil Weber's music, and I enjoyed it. The *Spokereien* [*sic*] of the Wolf's Glen were on an extensive scale of mechanism and pyrotechnics, including an owl with fiery eyes, two bat-winged ghosts with pinwheels fizzing on their abdominal parts, several groups of moving pasteboard skeletons, crackers and blue lights behind the scenes, and a great dragon, or crocodile, that crawled about the stage with its nose on fire. But Samiel's grand final entree through a trap door was an utter failure, and that Demon and the carpenter had to exert considerable strength and activity to prevent the Bengal lights and red fire [from] communicating with the scenery."

On April 10 the German company, apparently at Lehmann's insistence, incongruously brought out Bellini's *I Capuleti ed i Montecchi,* or, as it was advertised, *Romeo and Julia,* with Caroline Lehmann as Romeo.[112] Of her performance the *Musical World*

[111] Not so the critics. Not only did Lehmann receive high praise, but so did the others—that is, all but Quint, the Max, who was suffering from a throat ailment. His replacement, a Herr Una (or Unah) from Philadelphia, was immediately replaced by an unpronouncable Herr Schraubstadter (a name that sounded like "Sharpshooter" to the *Times*) (March 28, 1855). As for the orchestra of about forty players, the *Tribune* (March 27, 1855) observed that "the wondrous weird music of *Der Freischütz* requires the skill of a German orchestra [which this apparently was] used to rendering it," and that Unger was one of the most solid musicians in the country.

[112] Apparently determined to display her prowess in a masculine role (apparently all the rage that season, what with Vestvali and Martini d'Ormy), Lehmann, it was rumored, adamantly refused to repeat *Der Freischütz* or to sing in any other German opera unless she was allowed to appear as Romeo (*Dwight's,* April 14, 1855, p. 11).

(April 21, 1855) wrote that although not an accomplished actress, Lehmann had vocally earned "golden opinions, the only complaint being made that, as Romeo, she did not know how to make love to one of her own sex."

For their ninth night (April 12) the company announced a performance of Flotow's *Alessandro Stradella* with Martini d'Ormy, Siedenburg, Quint, and Müller. Literally at the last moment Martini d'Ormy, the Stradella (a tenor role), became suddenly indisposed, and a valiant member of the chorus, identified in the *Times* (April 13, 1855) as one Liberati (presumably Adolphus Liberati, a well-known local German actor/singer), volunteered to go on instead. Despite his understandable nervousness, and despite his obvious shortcomings, he was "a better tenor than any of his predecessors," wrote the *Times,* and he certainly deserved more applause than he received (see *Dwight's,* April 21, 1855, p. 20).

The company completed their season on April 17 with a repeat performance of *Romeo and Julia.* On May 1 they gave a benefit for Unger (who, despite the foresighted subscription plan, had reportedly lost money on the enterprise). Their program included the first act of *Romeo and Julia* and the first two acts of *Der Freischütz* separated by a "concert" consisting mainly of works for male chorus sung by the *Sängerrunde,* a new German singing society (*Dwight's,* May 5, 1855, pp. 37–38). It was widely hoped that the excellent opera season would bear fruit in the permanent establishment of German opera in New York.

In June a promising, but, alas, short-lived, German opera season opened at Wallack's Theatre under Albert Maretzek's management. Employing virtually the same cast of singers—with a fine orchestra of players from the now closed Academy of Music, expertly conducted by Robert Stoepel (1821–1887), a brother of Mrs. William Vincent Wallace and former conductor at the Princess Theatre in London—they opened on June 19 with Donizetti's *Die Regimentstochter (La Fille du régiment),* featuring Martini d'Ormy as an enchanting Marie.[113] On June 22 they gave Lortzing's popular *Zar und Zimmermann,* and on July 2 *Masaniello,* with Caroline Lehmann. But their audiences were so sparse that they were forced to end their season before presenting their projected production of Beethoven's *Fidelio* (with Caroline Lehmann), already in rehearsal.[114]

A solid pillar of constancy amid the prevailing operatic convulsions was the Pyne/Harrison troupe, who throughout the better part of the year serenely and almost uninterruptedly continued to dispense their delectable performances of English opera to enthusiastic audiences. On January 1, still at the Broadway Theatre, they successfully added Sir Henry Bishop's *Guy Mannering* to their formidable repertory, and on January 15 they unveiled an elaborate and much-publicized production of Rophino Lacy's patchwork concoction fastened onto Rossini's *Cinderella.*[115] A handsome spectacle, it

[113] So enchanting, in fact, that she inspired Quint, the "Tony," to kiss her with a vehemence that left half of his moustachio reposing on her "beautifully chiseled nose" (*Times,* June 20, 1855).

[114] It had been vainly hoped that their performances would attract members of the currently visiting German singing societies.

[115] At Buckley's Opera House, a "grand burlesque" of *Cinderella* was played in blackface at this same time.

The Misses Pyne and Messrs. Harrison and Borrani.

was greatly lauded for its many beautiful effects,[116] but it was generally felt that the part of Cinderella, because of its too-low *tessitura,* just didn't suit Louisa Pyne's delicious voice. More felicitous was the "delightful and brilliant" song "The Skylark," written for her by Julius Benedict, interpolated in the third act, in which she was "tumultuously encored."

Finishing their long engagement at the Broadway Theatre in mid-February, the Pyne/Harrison company went on tour, presumably taking with them their new music director, George Frederick Bristow. In Baltimore and Philadelphia, rather than operas, they appeared in concerts (doubtless for reasons of economy) with such success that they decided to pause in New York on their way to Boston to give two such concerts at Niblo's—on April 2 and April 9 (the latter crowded despite the *William Tell* premiere at the Academy that same evening).

Accompanied at the piano by Bristow, who properly opened the proceedings on April 2 with an "overture," their program, in three parts, covered a wide musical expanse, from popular Italian and English opera arias and concerted pieces, to excerpts from Handel and Haydn oratorios, to familiar English and Scottish ballads. Best of all, wrote Seymour (*Times,* April 3, 1855), was Louisa Pyne's rendering of Haydn's "With verdure clad," offered with a "chasteness and purity of phrasing and intensity not often found in an opera singer." Her performance of Benedict's "The Skylark" produced such a storm of applause that she was forced to give not one but two Scottish ballads as encores. Susan Pyne, too, sang Scottish ballads, and together they exquisitely blended their voices in a duet from *The Crown Diamonds.* Harrison, "tolerably in tune" for once, sang a Romance by Donizetti and a ballad by John Liptrot Hatton;♪ Borrani sang an aria from *La sonnambula;* and a new (and temporary) basso J. O. Atkins "attempted" an air from *Messiah.*

Although, according to most of the reviewers, Bristow "presided at the piano in a very able manner," the avant-garde critic for the *Spirit of the Times* (April 7, 1855, p. 96) hoped the troupe would soon return to opera: "Pianoforte concerts had, we supposed, become bygones, and nothing less than an orchestral accompaniment (however small) would go down nowadays," he remarked "but we found we were mistaken."

At their second appearance a week later[117] the troupe compromised, giving an abbreviated "grand concert" followed by a short operetta, apparently both accompanied by an orchestra under Bristow's direction. The operetta, heard for the first time, was *The Marriage of Georgette,* William Harrison's English adaptation of *Les Noces de Jeannette* (Paris 1853), a light opera currently popular in Paris, by the French composer Victor Massé (1822–1884).

These appearances were merely a foretaste of things to come, for upon returning from their successful season in Boston, the Pyne/Harrison troupe settled in at Niblo's on May 23 for a hitherto unparalleled run of 125 opera performances, continuing, with

[116] Particularly the enchanting fairy coach, "a beautiful English phaeton drawn by four well-trained Shetland ponies with coachman and footman all *en miniature* and in handsome liveries" (*Albion,* January 20, 1855, p. 31).

[117] On April 5, between the two concerts, Dolores Nau gave a similar Grand Concert at Niblo's, assisted by Allan Irving, St. Albyn, Konrad Treuer, a pianist, and Thomas Baker, who accompanied. Featuring excerpts from *Elijah,* the program consisted additionally of opera arias, English ballads, and piano fantasies.

only a few small breaks,[118] through the summer and autumn until November. During this extraordinary engagement they repeated their voluminous repertory many times over, periodically adding new productions. On June 23 they presented a spectacular grand opera *The Daughter of St. Mark* (London 1844) by Michael Balfe and Alfred Bunn;[119] on July 2, *The Queen of a Day* (London 1841), an adaptation by the English playwright John Buckstone, with added music by Edward Fitzwilliam (1824–1857),[120] of Adolphe Adam and Eugène Scribe's opera *La Reine d'un jour* (Paris 1839).

To celebrate July 4 the Pyne/Harrison troupe gave a rousing performance of the *Daughter of the Regiment* (advertised as a "Military Opera"), with all the "original music restored and performed for the first time in New York." As an added attraction the "National Anthem, 'Hail Columbia'" was sung by the entire company.

On August 6 they revived *Cinderella* in a spectacular new production designed by the prominent scenic artist Henry Hillyard, and as an extra dividend—"in order to render the cast perfect"—George Holland, "the facetious," was engaged to play the comic role of Pedro. Sullying the otherwise cordial reception of this production, an angry confrontation between Bristow and the *Times* critic, in all probability Seymour, broke out in the *Times* on August 8. Infuriated at the critic's statement that a certain flute *obbligato* had been inaudible at the opening performance, Bristow, the hot-tempered, wrote an explosive letter to the *Times* editor: "Sir: An attempt at criticism appeared in your paper . . . upon the performance of 'Cinderella' on Monday evening, the writer of which must have been out of his mind, or he would never have written such twaddle. However, for the future, I would advise him to learn something of the art [of music], and then he will probably find out that the obbligato was not 'mutilated,' and not 'nearly omitted,' as every single note was played. Whether the supposed criticism, above alluded to, arises from vandalism or inefficiency, it is equally disgraceful to the *critic*."

The critic replied that if the flute *obbligato* had indeed been played, it had been difficult, if not impossible, to detect it "above the chattering of the orchestra. . . . In the general confusion it escaped our unfortunate (!) ears. . . . Great men have their foibles," he went on, dripping with venom, "and insolvency [insolence?] appears to be Mr. Bristow's. Absorbed in those massive studies of the art which now so eminently fit him for the conductor's chair, he has, we regret to say, neglected the less oppressive, but more dignified, study of politeness—unless, indeed, the above letter is an 'attempt' at what he conceives to be the article. If so, we can only say that it is more signally unsuccessful than his 'attempt' at conducting the orchestra at the theatre."

The new production of *Cinderella* was so sweeping a success that it was given

[118] Mostly to permit appearances by William Burton, who, as in the past, was a favorite summer guest at Niblo's.

[119] Seymour, who had heard the work in London, remembered a production abounding in "processions, palaces, moonlights, banners, ballet dancers, pages, maids of honor, and every other human and artificial contrivance of the advanced stage. As a spectacle at Drury Lane this opera had been superb; as a spectacle at Niblo's it [was] ridiculous" (*Times,* June 19, 1855).

[120] Buckstone, usually a writer of witty dialogue, had not exercised that faculty in this exceedingly uneventful libretto set in Cromwellian England, complained Seymour, and Fitzwilliam had overloaded Adam's score with inappropriate glees and ballads. Yet it was an agreeable little work, "worth seeing in every respect" (*Times,* July 3, 1855).

nightly for the following month. Not until September 8 was it withdrawn and some older repertory restored, in response—according to the *Spirit of the Times* (September 8, 1855, p. 360)—to the requests of "numbers of strangers now in town who have not heard *The Daughter of the Regiment, Maritana,* etc."

The following week, however, promised the *Spirit,* Bristow's long-awaited opera *Rip Van Winkle* would at last be brought out—"the advent of which will be an epoch in the history of the 'Lyric Drama' of America, it being essentially national in its subject; the original story [by Washington Irving], the libretto [by Jonathan H. Wainwright, son of the late Bishop Wainwright], and the musical composition [by Bristow] being all native, we trust its success will be commensurate with its intrinsic merit, and the sincere wishes of those who desire to establish a national school of music here." The writer failed to mention that Henry Hillyard's sets and costumes were based upon the evocative etchings by the celebrated American illustrator Felix O. C. Darley (1822–1888) for the lavish 1849 edition of *Rip Van Winkle* commissioned by the American Art-Union.[121] Nor was it pointed out that the all-American characters in this all-American creation were portrayed by an all-British cast: the Pynes, Harrison, Horncastle, and, replacing Borrani, a newly imported bass singer, Stretton, from the "Theatres Royal, Covent Garden, Drury Lane, and the [London] Philharmonic Concerts," incongruously making his American debut as Rip. Bristow, of course, conducted the orchestra.

Frustratingly, the premiere did not take place at the expected time. Indeed, it was not until after a series of disappointing postponements accompanied by a persistent tattoo of patriotic puffs[122]—and after a private dress rehearsal to which outsiders were not admitted—that *Rip Van Winkle* was at last presented to a crowded and expectant house on September 27 (just three days before the opening of the fall season at the Academy of Music).

The critics were divided between those who hailed *Rip Van Winkle* as a success purely because it was an all-American musico/dramatic creation and those who for the same reason opposed it and found it wanting; there were also a few who genuinely liked it. Belonging to the first category, the *Times* (September 28), in a short preliminary review,[123] praised its "light, pleasant, and rhythmic [score], largely pervaded by a martial spirit,[124] and of a decidedly popular character in other respects. It was loudly applauded . . . most of the principal airs being encored." In a more searching review after a rehearing, the *Times* the following day tempered these opinions, explaining that while the first and third acts were faithful to Irving's story, the second was purely the

[121] In August, James H. Hackett, now returned to the dramatic stage, had successfully presented a non-musical dramatization of *Rip Van Winkle* at the Metropolitan Theatre.

[122] For example: "So many foreign operas have been produced, and so much attention and such large means given to them, that it is more than time that an American Opera should be heard" (*Courier and Enquirer,* September 27, 1855).

[123] Necessarily short, because its columns were crowded with the tremendous news that Sebastopol had at last fallen, and the Crimean War was nearing its end.

[124] Among other new matter, Wainwright had added a military element, an army officer named Edward Gardenier (Harrison) to woo Alice Van Winkle, Rip's daughter (Louisa Pyne); other additions were a sequence of intricate, eighteenth-century military exercises in the second act and a group of fairies in the first.

National Portrait Gallery, Smithsonian Institution

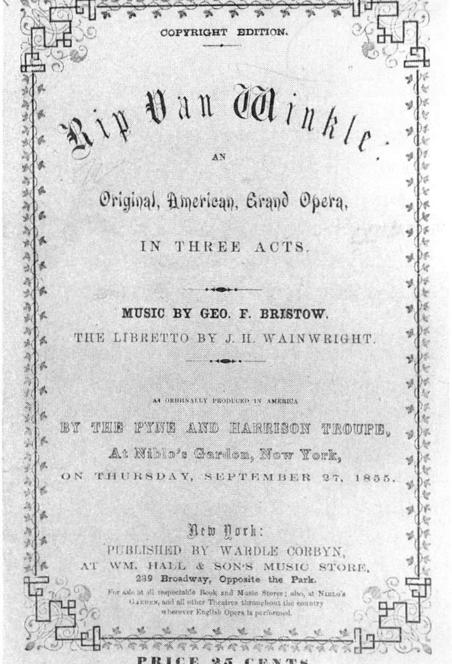

COPYRIGHT EDITION.

Rip Van Winkle:

AN

Original, American, Grand Opera,

IN THREE ACTS.

MUSIC BY GEO. F. BRISTOW.

THE LIBRETTO BY J. H. WAINWRIGHT.

AS ORIGINALLY PRODUCED IN AMERICA

BY THE PYNE AND HARRISON TROUPE,

At Niblo's Garden, New York,

ON THURSDAY, SEPTEMBER 27, 1855.

New York:

PUBLISHED BY WARDLE CORBYN,

AT WM. HALL & SON'S MUSIC STORE,

239 Broadway, Opposite the Park.

For sale at all respectable Book and Music Stores; also, at NIBLO'S GARDEN, and all other Theatres throughout the country wherever English Opera is performed.

PRICE 25 CENTS.

Music Division, The New York Public Library

Portrait of George Frederick Bristow by an unknown artist, and the title page of the Rip Van Winkle *libretto.*

creation of the librettist, supplying the events that took place at home during the years of Rip's prolonged slumber. "It would scarcely be profitable to discuss the merits of the *libretto*," wrote Seymour, "the least that is said about it the better." As to Bristow's score, it was primarily on the light side, "with a leaning at times towards the sentimental and martial school[s]." While it was pretty enough, it had not "given birth" to any original or startling musical ideas. Bristow had remained aloof from the dramatic or emotional values rightly belonging to opera. The instrumentation was deft and tasteful enough but tended to be "monotonous." The staging was magnificent and the performers able; Louisa Pyne played her exacting role as Rip's daughter "with exquisite precision and sweetness." While *Rip Van Winkle* would surely enjoy an extended run and achieve popularity, and while "one or two of the melodies will get on the street organs, when they have had their day and the Opera its career," predicted Seymour, "Mr. Bristow will do something better."

The *Courier and Enquirer* (September 28) pronounced *Rip Van Winkle* to be a "decided 'hit,'" receiving the unreserved "acclamations of a crowded audience. The music is destined to become universally popular." The *Herald* (September 28), of course, championed the work simply because it was not by Fry, and found "more real merit in it than most of the modern English operas that have held possession of our stage."

In the second category of critics was the *Evening Post* reviewer, who after hearing *Rip Van Winkle,* continued to live "in hope that the time will come when an American shall compose an opera worthy to rank with those of the great German and Italian composers. Mr. Bristow has apparently not tried to do so. His opera is light and pleasing, but without giving the hearer any impression of earnestness or moral purpose. It is far from being a great work, although it may be for a time a popular one, and while it evinces talent in the composer and a fair degree of contrapuntal learning, there is no trace of genius in all its harmonies. The overture is boisterous; indeed, Mr. Bristow has made too free use of his brass instruments throughout the opera." (At least, Bristow had that much in common with Verdi.)

The *Post* reviewer was better pleased with the libretto than the music, but he sharply condemned the employment of a visual device whereby, at a given moment, the actors would freeze into a fixed attitude resembling one of Darley's famed illustrations. All very well as tableaux, he grumbled, "but an extraordinary and unpardonable dramatic license, against all rules of art, interrupting with a sudden jerk the whole progress of the play. . . . These dramatic syncopes were best omitted" (September 28, 1855).

Basically agreeing with the *Post,* Hagen, in a massive review in the *Review and Gazette* (October 6, 1855, pp. 334–35) after two hearings of *Rip Van Winkle,* pronounced it first of all to be overlong: "The work has the length of a grand tragic opera, while it is in itself only a melodrama, with very few *ensemble* pieces and some choruses. Ballads, songs, duets, occasionally a trio, form the staple of the opera, and this for almost four hours." It was as much the fault of the librettist as the composer, he wrote, not that the libretto "was ineffective in its ingredients," but there was too much of it: "people talk and sing too much." The best thing that could be done for the work would be to shorten it by half. Hagen suggested omitting or curtailing, among other things, the *tableaux vivants,* the too-long quarreling scene between the Van Winkles, the military maneuvers,[125] and the fairy scenes, all of which stopped the dramatic action and added to the inordinate length of the piece.

And of the score: the orchestration was monotonous, sounding much more symphonic than operatic. "The brass mingles not skillfully enough with the wood and the strings, and modern orchestral effects in operas seem to be altogether avoided."

But what Hagen missed most was musical characterization. In Bristow's instrumentation "the joy and the grief have almost the same coloring, and certainly, in most instances the words are rather an objection to the estimation of the merits of the composer." The character of Rip, "that humorous old Dutchman, loses, by the music he has to sing, all his primitive character, and in a musical sense, almost nothing but Dutch phlegm remains."

The staging was admirable—the best Hagen had seen in this country. And the cast "did their best" for the work, although Stretton, who had learned the part of Rip in a great hurry, seemed to have but little command over his voice in the role.

Fry, seething with envy and unable to conceal it, outdid himself in a colossal, al-

[125] Later in his review Hagen inconsistently applauded the "evolutions of the old Continentals, [and] their march and counter-march in as perfect step as the best-trained soldiery. . . . The scene in which they appear," he wrote, "may be called the point of the opera." Indeed, they elicited the greatest applause of the evening.

New-York Historical Society

The Return of Rip Van Winkle, *one of Felix O. C. Darley's etchings that was translated into* tableaux vivants *for the first production of Bristow's opera.*

most embarrassing ramble occupying four full columns of the *Tribune* (September 29). In the first place he argued that the billing of Bristow's work as a "grand opera" was a false designation because much of the dialogue was spoken. "A grand opera," he maintained, "is one in which the words are set to music throughout, and the recitatives are accompanied by a full orchestra. Operas with spoken dialogue are termed comic to distinguish them from grand operas."[126]

Although its prosody was more adaptable to vocalization than most English opera texts (always excepting Rophino Lacy's matchless *Cinderella*), it was nonetheless fraught with shortcomings, as Fry demonstrated in a lengthy example of Wainwright's faulty versification.

About the score, Fry chose to be enigmatic: "As it is by an American who depends on the verdict of his countrymen—there being no ready-made opinion from Europe to be adopted, parrot-like—we have great pleasure in stating that Mr. Bristow's debut as a dramatic composer was equally successful with those of the established composers of Europe, if we may believe their biographies." There were some rough spots in the performance, inevitable on a first night, but "if the performers were not perfectly familiar with their parts," he added, neither were the public, and anyway the public were not—nor would they ever be—concerned with the finer points of the music.

Following a lengthy "analysis" of the score (not omitting his usual deprecation of Mozart), Fry took off on one of his interminable meanders, filling his second and third columns with innumerable unrelated grievances. Well into column four, losing sight of whose opera he was supposed to be reviewing, Fry (suddenly shifting into the third person) proceeded to proclaim the priority (and superiority) of *Leonora* "composed by Mr. W. H. Fry" over Bristow's *Rip Van Winkle*.[127] Claiming that the press had never properly reported *Leonora*'s history, he embarked on yet another reiteration of the *Leonora* saga: its momentous premiere in Philadelphia in 1845, its "perfect success," its embodiment of true "grand opera in the technical sense of the term, that is, without spoken dialogue, and [its position as] the first grand opera of the modern school by either an English or American composer."

Then, continuing in the third person, the eternal plaint: "Mr. Fry has composed several other operas which have not yet been produced. The managers of all the theatres in New York [no longer only the Academy of Music], as is well known, are in utter fear of a journal whose editor has made war on Mr. Fry and all his productions from the moment *Leonora* appeared. The public is . . . hardly aware that [this hostility] has up to this time, through the acknowledged subserviency of the managers of all the theatres, deprived Mr. Fry of a hearing in New York for any of his operas, though his symphonies, through Mr. Jullien who defied the wrath of the editor in question, have been frequently performed.[128]

[126] Thus classifying Beethoven's *Fidelio* as a comic opera, scoffed Dwight's Diarist, writing from Europe. (For the Diarist's pungent comments on Fry's review, see *Dwight's,* November 24, 1855, pp. 59–60.)

[127] Upton (Fry, p. 154) accepts this shift as the actual interposition of another writer into Fry's review.

[128] See OBBLIGATO: 1854, footnote 8, for Irving Lowens's comment on Jullien's performances of Fry's (and Bristow's) music.

"These being the facts, the following statement of the Satanic Press in relation to the opera of *Rip Van Winkle,* which is the first American opera performed in New York and the second only in America,[129] may be taken for what they [*sic*] are worth." And Fry quoted:

"'If Mr. Bristow's opera succeeds, he will have the credit of being the first American composer who has written anything that kept the stage beyond its first night. There is one American opera, so called, which has long been a bugbear to artists, as its composer never loses an opportunity to endeavor to bully them into playing it. We never heard of anyone who ever heard the whole of it. There may be survivors, but they cannot be found in the usual haunts of men. As *Rip Van Winkle* is truly an American opera on an American subject by an American composer, we hope that it will succeed.'"

Thus did William Henry Fry, vociferous champion of American music and musicians, greet a significant American musical milestone—attained, however, by the wrong American composer.

The *Musical World* (October 6, 1855), reprinting parts of Fry's review (pp. 265, 266–67), uttered the most frequently quoted (and mistakenly attributed) pronouncement on *Rip Van Winkle:* "Sebastopol has fallen, and a new American Opera has succeeded in New York." Ascribed to R. Storrs Willis, although signed G. H. C. (George Henry Curtis), the wordy critique, wandering about in thickets of murky patriotic abstractions, never rose again to the power of its resonant opening.

In its following issue the *Musical World* (October 13) ran two additional reviews of *Rip Van Winkle,* at least one of them by Willis. "Our 'George' has every cause of congratulation on his success," jovially began the first (pp. 277–78), then settled down to a series of didactic pronouncements—particularly that Bristow would learn a great deal if he surrendered his baton to some assistant, so that he might sit in the upper circle, where he could clearly hear the "blemishes" of his opera—especially his orchestral excesses—and profit in future efforts from his earlier mistakes.

The other review (pp. 278–79) subjected the work to a fine-tooth-comb analysis. True, it was in all its aspects an American effort, indeed "*pure blood*"; but was Bristow's music in his first dramatic effort really "quite American? . . . It takes a long time before a nation has adapted art to its own nature," something only to be achieved by "perseverance of effort and struggle. . . . It would be absurd to demand of one who writes for the stage for the first time a great creation or a masterpiece." Bristow's music abounded in pretty melodies, but he did not shine in the writing of stirring choruses. The critic was also disappointed in Bristow's instrumentation and his erratic and unjustified climaxes: Besides: "The orchestra of *Van Winkle* is in general inanimate and lifeless, devoid of that brilliancy which we must meet in the modern opera."

Despite all quibbles and cavils, Bristow's opera was a genuine hit, playing to reportedly packed houses—nightly for the first week, on alternate nights during the following week,[130] then nightly again until October 18. On October 23, *Rip Van Winkle*

[129] Not so: it had been preceded in 1824 by Micah Hawkins's *The Sawmill* and in 1825 by John Davies and Samuel Woodworth's *The Desert Rose* (see *Resonances,* p. 337, footnote 13).

[130] Alternating with a mixed program shared by Pyne/Harrison in *The Marriage of Georgette* and a company of sixteen Spanish dancers under the direction of one Don José Maria Llorente, who per-

was given for Bristow's benefit, and on October 29 its first two acts were repeated at a benefit for Niblo's stage manager, W. A. Moore.

Throughout its run, the papers kept up an ostinato of praise. On October 1, after the third performance, the *Herald,* with sure aim at Fry's heart, had written: "The composer, Mr. Bristow, may now claim to be the most successful writer of this style of opera in America, and in many respects this work is superior to anything that has yet come from the pen of any English composer." On October 6 the *Spirit of the Times* (p. 408), naming *Rip Van Winkle* one of the Pyne/Harrison company's major achievements, had words of praise for both Bristow and Wainwright. The story was well told, the versification smooth and flowing, and the "character of the music . . . suited to a refined, and at the same time popular, taste."

And on October 11 the *Courier and Enquirer,* in a kind of summing up, attributed the unusual success of Bristow's opera to "the patriotic sympathies to which it appeals, but to this element of interest there must be added undeniable merit in the work itself. Mr. Bristow is in the first rank of native musicians—indeed we do not know his superior among them in culture and purity of taste."

As the Pyne/Harrison troupe neared the end of their prodigious run at Niblo's they repeated their greatest successes—*The Crown Diamonds, Cinderella, The Bohemian Girl*—but also they introduced "new" works: on October 26 for William Harrison's benefit, *The Barber of Seville,*[131] with Stephen Storace's *No Song, No Supper*♪ as an afterpiece; and on November 2—the 124th and penultimate performance of their engagement—for Louisa Pyne's benefit they gave *The Love Spell (L'elisir d'amore)* for the first time. "No artist who ever appealed to a New York audience has more worthily earned a reputation than this admirable *cantatrice,*" wrote the *Times* (November 3, 1855).

In a card dated November 5, Louisa Pyne and William Harrison bade a grateful farewell to their New York public and promised to return in April after their "numerous Eastern, Western, and Southern engagements."[132]

With the Pyne/Harrison company preempting the music-theatre scene for the better part of the year, competitive productions were few and far between. On October 11, William Burton, probably inspired by the Pyne/Harrison success, presented *The Daughter of the Regiment* at his little theatre in Chambers Street, and on October 17, harking back to earlier days, *John of Paris*♪ (Bishop, London 1814, after Boieldieu, Paris 1812). In both works the *prima donna* was Miss Rosalie Durand, an admired young American actress/singer. The productions were surprisingly well-staged, wrote the *Herald* (October 12, 1855): "The scenery was new—so were the dresses, good and appropriate. 'The Regiment' never looked so well in New York, and [it was] sung in excellent time and tune." Miss Durand "charmed the musical dilettanti. . . . In short,

---

formed a "Grand Divertissement 'The Vintage of Xeres'" [Jerez]; another, "The Seashore of Malaga"; and various "Grand Tableaux, Jaleos, Boleros, Fantasias, etc."

[131] Not only did Louisa Pyne delight her audience with her charming piano playing in the lesson scene, but another Pyne sister, a Mrs. Galton, appeared for the first time as a "pianiste," receiving "almost universal applause" (*Spirit,* November 3, 1855, p. 456).

[132] Their tour was managed by W. F. Brough (*Spirit,* September 8, 1855, p. 350).

the performance created a sensation, and Miss Rosalie may be reckoned as a fixed success." In *John of Paris,* Burton excelled as Pedrigo Potts, "with all that comicality which distinguishes his presentations."

To somewhat round out the picture, an Egyptian confection, *The Enchanted Temple, or, The Spectre of the Nile,* for which the Philharmonic violinist Anthony Reiff, Jr.,[133] composed and directed the music, was given at the Bowery Theatre in June. And in late December a lavish production of Planché's fairy extravaganza, *King Charming, or, the Bluebird of Paradise* (London 1850), supplied Christmas entertainment at the Broadway Theatre. With Mrs. Henry C. Watson in the title role, a corps of forty "Amazons" demonstrated the "warlike spirit of the feminines" in tableaux, marches, and evolutions devised by Monsieur Monplaisir.

The *Review and Gazette* (December 29, 1855, p. 430) gives a rare clue to the musical content of an entertainment of this ilk: "Happy local hits [were] interspersed with music of all kinds. Now you have *La donna è mobile,* then 'Katy Darling'; now a Scotch, Irish, or English ballad, or a Negro refrain, and then the grand denunciation of the Druidess in *Norma;* airs of every kind, but all happily and appropriately brought in." The music director responsible for this tuneful hodgepodge was J. Cooke, formerly of Burton's Theatre.

But unquestionably it was Pyne/Harrison who dominated the popular music theatre in 1855.

As a prelude to the opening of the Academy of Music on October 1 under William H. Paine's aegis, it was announced that, according to the Academy's charter, a free school for instruction in singing would be opened on August 28 under the direction of Amati Dubreuil and Angelo Torriani. As an added benefaction: "such scholars as may desire will have the opportunity of being employed at the Academy." Evidently there was a good response, for a notice appeared in the papers on September 17, directing the school's first, second, and third ladies' classes to assemble at Hope Chapel at two o'clock the following day, and the gentlemen at seven in the evening.

On September 18, Paine issued a card formally announcing his directorship of the Academy. He promised a season of forty performances, to include, in addition to favorite familiar operas, productions of Meyerbeer's *Les Huguenots, Le Prophète, L'Étoile du Nord,* and other "novelties" to be performed by a company of distinguished artists, an orchestra[134] conducted by Max Maretzek,[135] an augmented chorus, and Mademoiselle Lavigne as *Première Danseuse.* Added to the usual Monday/Wednesday/Friday opera nights, matinées at reduced prices would be given on Saturday afternoons. Evening admission to the parquette and first circle was raised to $2; tickets to the second circle

[133] Reiff, according to Krehbiel, had recently been music director of the opera in Sydney, Australia, where he was succeeded by George Loder (Krehbiel, p. 54).

[134] Whose members included Theodore Thomas and Carl Bergmann.

[135] "One morning in 1855, Mr. William H. Paine . . . sent for me," writes Maretzek, "and asked me whether I would accept the position of musical director, for a salary and a percentage of the profits, if he would take the lease of the Academy and procure an entirely new and complete opera company, dispensing with all the artists now in New York, with the exception of Brignoli and Amodio [and Morelli]. I at once agreed, putting my salary a little higher and my percentage of the profits a little lower than what he had offered" (*Sharps and Flats,* p. 17).

were $1; non-transferable and unsecured single subscriptions for the full season of forty nights were $50; transferable and secured, $70; single seats in boxes, of which twenty-eight had been added in the first circle, were $2; subscriptions to boxes with four seats were $275, with six seats $400; admission to the amphitheatre was fifty cents. The public was assured of Paine's determination to "give the lyric drama a permanent foot-hold in this community."

A week later the cast of singers was announced: the sopranos were Anna de La-Grange, Elise Hensler, and—momentarily expected from Europe—the renowned diva Anaïde (Jeanne) Castellan♪;[136] the contraltos were a Signorina Zoë Aldini and Giuseppina Martini d'Ormy (apparently Paine was forced to engage some local singers, after all); the tenors were Brignoli, Quinto, Arnoldi, and a new tenor Alberto Salviani; the baritones were Morelli, Amodio, and the newcomer Giulio; the basses were Rovere, Gasparoni, Müller, and another newcomer, Vincenzo Caspani. It was reported that the new artists, of whom only Madame Castellan was accredited to an opera house, had been selected for Paine by Signor Mario.

"Everyone will be agreeably astonished at the quiet activity of Mr. Paine, who, by the way, is sole director and manager, and alone assumes all risks and responsibilities towards artists and the public," wrote the *Times* (September 24), evincing the customary pre-opera-season euphoria indigenous to contemporary journalists.

Less euphoric was Richard Grant White's lengthy editorial on opera, appearing in the *Courier and Enquirer* on September 29. In vindication of the Academy's raised admission prices, over which considerable public unhappiness had been expressed, White argued that the increase represented no profit to the director. Opera production and financial success were mutually incompatible: "There could not be more erroneous notions upon this subject than those which are generally entertained by the public, and which, we regret to see, are encouraged by a part of the Press, which knows, or ought to know, better."

To those who believed the solution lay in more seats at lower prices, White declared that "there never was a successful season at Castle Garden, at any price." Indeed (echoing the *Herald* of an earlier vintage), there had never been a financially successful opera season in New York—or anywhere else, for that matter. The last season at the Academy of Music had been "eminently unsuccessful," wrote White, despite houses purportedly "'crowded to the roof' (with deadheads). . . . Italian Opera is a luxury which 'the mass of the people' do not want to buy, and for which those who do wish to enjoy it must pay accordingly."

To correct the general belief that the principal singers' high salaries represented opera's major outlay, White appended to his article a schedule of monthly salaries based on the flimsy "judicious arrangements of the last season." The star soprano and tenor singers were listed each at $1200 a month (in fact, LaGrange and Mirate were rumored individually to have cleared $3600); first baritone $1000; basso $600; the other singers ranged from $800 to $100 a month. The forty-eight orchestra musicians received (collectively) $600 monthly; orchestra leader $100; thirty-six choristers (collectively) $400;

[136] Since leaving New York in 1844, Castellan had become a leading *prima donna* at Covent Garden and the Paris Opéra. Definitely announced for the Academy of Music season, she was awaited in vain.

chorus master $20; forty supernumeraries (collectively) $75; prompter $20; stage manager $37.50; callboy $3; nine ushers $27; stage doorkeeper $8; three doorkeepers $13.50; three policemen $13.50. Other items included gas for illumination $100; two gas men $20; three tailors $28; hairdressers $10; runner (messenger) to the press $6; treasurer and officer $60; bill posting and distributing $20; sweeper, cleaners, and firemen $21; and music, wardrobe, and scenery $250. As White pointed out, this did not include a contralto ($800), another tenor ($1000), and secondary contralto, tenor, and baritone ($200 each), to say nothing of the conductor, whose salary remains a mystery. According to White's computation, the Academy's monthly expenses, including sundry other expenditures, but exclusive of rent, interest, and insurance, came to an astronomical $16,530.

The salaries paid the leading singers were really not that unreasonable when compared with what was paid in Europe, wrote White, and besides, singers had but a short career span, being in their prime for only about ten to fifteen years.

Opening on October 1 with *Il trovatore,* Paine's opera season was by no means a success. With the same overfamiliar repertory—*Il trovatore, Linda di Chamounix, Masaniello, Norma,* and *La sonnambula*—endlessly repeated at virtually doubled prices, there was little to attract the novelty-hungry New York public, especially now that they were universally smitten with Rachel-madness. Flocking to the Metropolitan Theatre, where the legendary French (Swiss) actress Rachel, *née* Elizabeth Rachel Felix (1820–1858), wielded her magic (unfortunately for the Academy, on opera nights), the predominantly non-French-speaking New York public—in contrast to their discontent over the raised prices at the Academy—willingly paid $3 (and besides, a surcharge of twenty-five cents for reserved seats) to see Rachel.[137]

Not only were few opera-goers attracted by the repetitive proceedings at the Academy, but mutterings were beginning to be heard that LaGrange, who valiantly took on Steffanone's weighty roles, was perhaps after all—with her frail physique—not suited to every role she attempted: "The delicate beauty of her voice," wrote Seymour (*Times,* October 2, 1855), "is altogether too feeble to struggle with the masculine vocalistics of the composer of the *Trovatore.*" Thus, on opening night LaGrange had "untriumphantly" appeared as Leonora, with a "visibly terrified" debutante Signorina Zoë Aldini as Azucena;[138] Brignoli and Amodio, who sang their accustomed roles, and Gasparoni, who replaced Rocco as Fernando, reaped their accustomed praise.

Evidently the new Academy management immediately found itself in a tight squeeze, according to the first issue of *L'Entr'acte,* a gossipy little publication that was distributed gratis at the Academy on opening night and for a short period thereafter. Published and edited by the protean Ullman,[139] obviously dispossessed from the Acad-

[137] Strong, who was no admirer of the French, much less the Jewish French, wrote on October 21: "George Anthon is made captive by the Israelitish woman Rachel. . . . Mrs. Eleanor [Mrs. Charley Strong] also goes every night and experiences fevers and nervous flustrations, with ebullient and explosive hysterical tendencies."

[138] Following her debut, the Signorina Aldini, the possessor of a "pleasing voice of excellent quality," seems for a period to have vanished; subsequent performances of Azucena were assigned to Martini d'Ormy, who inspired only lukewarm reactions in the role.

[139] In collaboration with John Darcie, a peripheral publisher of concert books and opera libretti.

emy directorship, *L'Entr'acte* was pungently described by Seymour (*Times,* October 3, 1855) as "an entertaining little paper" started in connection with the Academy:[140] "It has a little telegraphic news; a little local intelligence; a little musical chit-chat; a little analysis of the performances; and a great many little puffs. It is a savage little sheet and bristling with *italics*. It is also learned and speaks many languages—a little at a time . . . it is a little curiosity, and deserves a little attention."

According to *L'Entr'acte:* "Another opera [*Le Prophète*], with new artists engaged in Europe, had been selected for the first night, but . . . the non-arrival of Madame Castellan and Signori Salviani and Caspani, who embarked only on the 29th of last month, had compelled the manager to abandon his original intention." Thus the replacement, *Il trovatore,* "had, as it were, to be almost 'extemporized,' neither Madame LaGrange nor Mlle. Aldini knowing a bar of the music five days ago." This haphazard procedure was cited as proof of the Academy's excellent resources in dealing with an emergency (quoted in the *Herald,* October 2, 1855).

Upon the continuing absence of the new singers, *Linda di Chamounix* was repeated on October 3, with LaGrange replacing Hensler as Linda, and with Martini d'Ormy instead of the now departed Vestvali as Pierotto; Brignoli, Morelli, Rovere, and the fast-improving Gasparoni repeated their former roles. As a finale to the opera, LaGrange sensationally sang "The LaGrange Polka," a spectacular, albeit incongruous, showpiece, written for her by the Russian composer Otto Dütsch (or Djutsch) (1823–1863). On October 5 a repeat of *Il trovatore* and the following afternoon a matinée performance of *Linda* completed the unpromising first week of Paine's regime.

On October 12, assisted by Brignoli and Amodio, and with Lavigne miming the Fenella, Hensler appeared as Elvira in *Masaniello,* singing it, according to the *Post* (October 13, 1855), "with scholarly ease and grace, but acting with much coldness." Seymour, however, wrote that Hensler had been frightened half out of her wits. The house was only half-full, but then, he sardonically remarked, "how could the attendance be good [when] the heavens pelted water, and Rachel offered her services at twice the prices asked here?"[141]

Next came *Norma,* with an "improved audience" on October 17, featuring LaGrange as Norma, Hensler as Adalgisa, and Morelli as Oroveso. Hensler's Adalgisa was mildly received, Morelli's Oroveso proclaimed a masterpiece, LaGrange's Norma was less arresting than in the past.

On October 20, Paine at last announced the imminent arrival of the steamship *Hermann* bearing his new singers: the tenor Alberto Salviani from Florence, the basso

[140] But soon appearing at other theatres, and in November accepted for distribution at the Philharmonic concerts, at the cost to the Society of $7 per thousand copies (Philharmonic Archives). Not only did *L'Entr'acte* serve as the official program for the evening, replacing the old-fashioned handbills previously supplied by the theatres, but it claimed to be "a complete newspaper, published at a later hour than any other evening newspaper in the city, containing the latest telegraphic dispatches up to 5 P.M., and epitome of the news of the day, New York, London, and Paris gossip; musical, dramatic, and literary intelligence; extracts from *Punch, Charivari,* etc. Only a limited number of select advertisements being taken" (advertisement in the various newspapers, October 22, 1855).

[141] By now, prices in the balcony and first circle of the Academy had been reduced to $1.50; the other locations remained unchanged.

Vincenzo Caspani from Milan, and Mesdames Eliza Derli (or Deli) Patania, a *prima donna* from Madrid and Venice, and Adelaide Ventaldi, an unaccredited contralto. No mention of Castellan. Until they arrived, the resident company continued to hold the fort with repeats of *Norma, Linda di Chamounix, Il trovatore,* and a revival of *La sonnam-*

A "LaGrange Polka" of local manufacture sported a portrait of questionable resemblance to the dedicatee.

bula (another new role for LaGrange). "The opera season at the Academy thus far has not been so brilliant as the merits of the company and the taste of the city would warrant," wrote Fry (*Tribune,* October 26, 1855),[142] "but the houses are now improving, and there is a fair chance of good ones, judging by the latest." Novelties were being rehearsed—new operas and new singers were not far off.

It was not until October 27 that the new singers finally arrived, to general rejoicing. Unexpectedly arriving with them, instead of Castellan, was the mezzo-soprano (or contralto) Constance Nantier-Didiée (1831–1867), identified in the papers as "a singer of very high rank, who succeeded Alboni at Covent Garden. . . . She has been singing the three last seasons with Mario and Grisi, and in the winter in Madrid." Nantier-Didiée was of course promptly engaged, and greatly to the Academy's advantage.

Within a week of the singers' arrival it was announced that *Le Prophète,* after "immense preparations,"—with new costumes, new decorations, new scenery, and new singers—would at last be presented on November 5. The very survival of opera in New York, chorused the critics, depended upon the public's full support of this great effort. "Cannot the musical public bestir themselves and attend the Academy?" urged Fry (ostensibly so far on good terms with the Paine regime). "It [the Academy] has been shamefully neglected—all the more shame, considering the vulgar trash that meets encouragement. . . . Mr. Paine, simply an amateur of music, has the management on his shoulders. If the people fail to support him, who will try opera again?"

Perhaps in response to these urgings, *Le Prophète* was presented "under the auspices of a good house,"[143] reported Seymour (*Times,* November 6, 1855). "After fourteen nights of indifference, the 'patrons' of the Academy roused themselves to a state of attendance, if not actually to a state of enthusiasm, last night. Perhaps by the next performance they may make up their minds to be genial and appreciative." Seymour recalled Maretzek's 1853 production of *Le Prophète* as "the most successful opera produced here up to that time," so successful, indeed, that it had staved off the impresario's failure until the end of the season. In the present production LaGrange's portrayal of Fides "proved indubitably that she [was] equal to the severest *rôles.*" She was the greatest Fides that Seymour had ever seen. Hensler, the Berthe, with her "delicious, timid sweetness," greatly appealed to the audience; the three Anabaptists were sung by Arnoldi, Morelli, and Gasparoni, and the Count Oberthal by Amodio. Despite Morelli's having good-naturedly allowed himself to be miscast in a basso role, due to the shortage of bassi, he was harshly criticized for being unequal to the demands of its range. The chorus and orchestra were superb and reflected great glory upon Maretzek. Seymour became so lost in admiration of Meyerbeer's genius, however, that he failed to mention the debut of the new tenor Salviani, the John of Leyden.

[142] And apropos the poor attendance: "Will Mr. Paine try the dollar business or not?" demanded the *Spirit of the Times* (October 27, 1855, p. 444). "We hope for the sake of all, manager and public, that he may. 'Twill pay better than the $2 experiment."

[143] A "slim, unmistakably slim" house, in contrast to the crowded houses that had attended Maretzek's superior production of *Le Prophète* at Niblo's in 1853, reported the *Spirit of the Times* (November 10, 1855, p. 468). It was all the fault of Paine's outrageous admission price, apparently still $2.

The *Evening Post* (November 6, 1855) found LaGrange's voice totally unsuitable to the role of Fides,[144] as was Morelli's to Zaccharias. "Nor have we much upon which to congratulate ourselves in the advent of Signor Salviani," although he was admittedly "a very fair singer." The chorus and the staging were unusually fine, and the orchestra excellent.[145] Whatever its shortcomings, the production was worth seeing, for it would probably be a long time before *The Prophet* would again be so well presented.

But *Gamma,* Burkhardt's rather ornate successor at the *Albion*[146]—an unidentified Frenchman apparently intimately conversant with the Paris music scene and thus inured to interminable productions at the Paris Opéra—declared his antipathy to the "ponderous, dreary undertaking" of sitting through endless hours of French grand opera[147] as customarily abused by performers who "shriek and roar in preference to singing"; it had grown to be a "positive penance" instead of entertainment.

If LaGrange was inferior to Pauline Viardot in the thankless role of Fides, wrote *Gamma,* she nonetheless displayed "infinite skill, tact, and artistic resources . . . she succeeds indeed in persuading us that she possesses what she has not in reality, and by dint of talent and force of will, she misleads, or disarms, her most exacting critic." Salviani, generally judged to be a sweet but inaudible tenor, had "more a certain excellence of method and correctness of taste than power or vigour of style," but the choruses had certainly been no better sung in Paris than here. Indeed, Gamma was "amazed at the *satisfactory results*" after but one general rehearsal of what had taken months to accomplish in Paris. It all went to show that "the Americans are decidedly in the right, and theirs is a great country" (*Albion,* November 10, 1855, pp. 535–36).

Fry, also an old Paris hand, after a generally commendatory, mercifully short, review of *Le Prophète*[148] (explaining that he had given it the full treatment only two years before and had nothing further to add in the way of musical analysis), wondered how such a work could run in Paris "for weeks, months, almost years! But here—how many nights shall we count [on] it?" It ran, in fact, for five consecutive performances; then, after a short recess to allow for LaGrange's benefit and Nantier-Didiée's debut, *Le Prophète* was resumed on November 26 and repeated on November 29 with a terrified Madame Patania, described as "short, stout, and German," making her debut as

[144] A role for which she had purportedly been chosen by Meyerbeer.

[145] Allegri's sets were magnificent, the cathedral scene earning him an excited ovation, but Dwight's New York correspondent thought he recognized the last-act prison scene from *Il trovatore.* In this production, doubtless for reasons of economy, the "skaters" were reduced to a quartet of dancers—Mesdames Lavigne and Ciocca and Messrs. Monplaisir and Wiethoff—who performed a *pas de quatre* and a *pas de patineurs;* the sunset was eliminated.

[146] Burkhardt had left the *Albion* to become the co-proprietor and editor of the New-York *Dispatch,* the Sunday weekly for which he had for some years past written music and drama criticism (*Times,* January 12, 1856).

[147] In the present production, *Le Prophète* had been "immensely" cut.

[148] Although LaGrange had "come out in strong and varied relief" as Fides, and a "military band on the stage, in addition to the orchestra, a powerful chorus, numerous accessories of soldiery, peasants, priests, singing boys, etc. completed the sumptuousness of the stage arrangements," it was Allegri who reaped the greatest admiration with his magnificent cathedral set: "Indeed," wrote Fry, "so prolonged was the cheering that it seemed nothing but the presence of the painter on the stage to receive the homage of the audience would be acceptable at the moment" (*Tribune,* November 6, 1855).

Berthe (Hensler was absent on tour). According to the *Mirror* (January 5, 1856), it was given nine times in all.

On November 16 a strangely chaotic performance of *I puritani*[149] took place at LaGrange's benefit, at which Rachel assisted.[150] Maretzek was clearly not himself, losing control of his orchestra and performers and making no effort to regain it. Perhaps he was shaken by a reported encounter (perhaps that very evening) with Ullman in a corridor of the Academy. After an exchange of mutual insults, Ullman had allegedly threatened Maretzek with a revolver, "but before he could pull trigger, the parties were separated by friends. . . . The cause of the *émeute,* which we believe is of long standing, has been aggravated by the late issue of 'Crotchets and Quavers,'" reported the *Herald* (November 21, 1855). (And small wonder.)

Hostilities broke out, too, between Brignoli and Patania's husband, Giuseppe, a gifted painter and witty caricaturist whose comic delineations of various Academy stars—Amodio, Morelli, Salviani, and Brignoli—were currently being shown at the Goupil Galleries (366 Broadway). Brignoli, mortally affronted at his likeness, traded angry words with the artist (apparently during a rehearsal at the Academy), culminating in a challenge to a duel. Small swords were agreed upon, being less noisy (and less dangerous) than pistols, but before they were wielded, apologies were exchanged and all was forgiven (*Albion,* December 8, p. 583; *Dwight's,* December 15, 1855, p. 84).

In this charged atmosphere, after another performance of *Il trovatore* on November 19, Nantier-Didiée made her highly successful debut on November 21 as Arsace in *Semiramide.* Described in the *Times* (November 22, 1855) as "young, graceful, and vivacious" (Richard Grant White thought she looked like a "bright, sensible American"), she had a beautiful contralto voice. With a style of her own, "based on the pure and solid method of the Italian school," Didiée defied Seymour's powers of description. He could only say, as did many of his colleagues, that if anyone deserved a "companion niche" to Alboni's in the Temple of Song, it was Didiée: "The quality of her voice is fresh, loving, elastic, and utterly subduing." And not only as a contralto, but also as a mezzo-soprano, and even as a soprano: "her upper notes [were] clear and thrilling."

In December, Paine capitulated to the demands of his undernourished box office and lowered his admission price to $1 "for the whole house" (except the amphitheatre), but the change did not bring the desired results, and he decided to close his season at the end of the year. The operas given in December were *Lucrezia Borgia,* with LaGrange audaciously attempting Lucrezia, to the usual blend of praise and blame (but mostly praise), and Nantier-Didiée a triumphant Orsini. Also repeated were *Semiramide, I puritani, Il trovatore* (with Didiée hailed as a superb Azucena), *Il barbiere* (in

[149] With Caspani an instantaneous failure in the role of Sir George Walton.

[150] LaGrange had recently assisted at Rachel's benefit, and Rachel was returning the courtesy. She performed the second act of Racine's *Athalie* between the second and third acts of *I puritani.* "For the first time," twittered *Gamma,* "we beheld —Oh! most amazing and thrilling sight!—we actually beheld an eager public turned away from the doors of our Italian Opera." The ovations were untrammeled; not only were both artists deluged with flowers but "one frenzied viewer gave vent to his ecstacy by launching a pair of pigeons in the air, by whose vicarious and unwilling cooing he vainly hoped to appease his excited feelings" (*Albion,* November 24, 1855, p. 560).

Constance Nantier-Didiée, considered to be the equal of Alboni.

which Salviani, as Almaviva, at last received a modicum of approval), *Linda di Chamounix* (again with LaGrange, Hensler still being away on tour), *Norma* (with Salviani relapsed into inaudibilty as Pollione), *William Tell* (with members of the Free School of the Academy joining the chorus), and *La favorita* (with Didiée less admired than usual in the vocally uncongenial role of Leonora). On December 29, advertised as the penultimate opera night, an "eleventh hour" debut uneventfully introduced the remaining newcomer Signorina Ventaldi as Orsini in *Lucrezia Borgia*. The season was announced to close on New Year's Eve with a "gala" performance of *Norma* followed by the last act of *Lucia,* featuring Brignoli, *à la* Mario. Still to follow, however, were two post-finale benefit performances—*Il trovatore* for Brignoli on January 2 and *Don Giovanni* for William Paine on January 4.[151] The company immediately departed for Philadelphia, Baltimore, Washington, and principally Boston, leaving New York's Upper Ten bereft of Italian opera until the following March, except for a single, mid-transit performance of *Don Giovanni* on January 18.

Symptomatic of the numerous summings-up of this latest chapter in the melancholy saga of opera in New York, the *Evening Post* on December 29 gloomily editorialized: "We see no fresh grounds for hope in the permanency of Italian opera in this city from the results of the present season. . . . Musical doctors of every school have endeavored to give life to this institution, but almost uniformly with complete ill success. Whatever vitality it has ever had has been galvanic in its nature, and due rather to some famous singer, or the rumored splendor of some operatic spectacle, than to any legitimate and wholesome love of music, *as music,* for its own sake."

More probing was William Henry Fry's exhaustive essay appearing in the *Tribune* on January 5. Tracing the sorry history of opera-giving in New York from the days of the Garcias on, Fry condemned the self-indulgent, elitist social structure, the extravagant limitation to only three performances a week, and the perverted fiscal setup that awarded enormous multiple returns to the Academy's profiteering landlords, mostly to the ruin of the tenants: exorbitant rents, excessive interest revenues, and the juicy prerogative-in-perpetuity of a free ticket or tickets to each shareholder for each performance at the Academy.[152] (Ironically, Fry's condemnation of the operatic institution agreed largely with Bennett's.)

No such pessimism afflicted the jolly exponents of the reverse opera—the burlesques in blackface (and increasingly in whiteface) that prospered mightily throughout the year.[153] As the *Tribune* democratically commented on October 8: "To those lovers of music for whom the Opera is too intricate, the Oratorio too dull, the Concert too scientific, and all too expensive, Ethiopian Minstrelsy is a melodious benefaction coming within reach of both their appreciation and their pockets."

The "Africanized operas" were the particular domain of Buckley's Serenaders, who continued successfully to present them (along with conventional minstrel fare) at their Ethiopian Opera House (sometimes called the American Opera House) at 539 Broadway. With their formidable repertory—*La sonnambula, Cinderella, Lucy of Lammermoor, L'elisir d'amore, The Bohemian Girl, Lucrezia Borgia, Norma* (the last "in white faces"), and more recently *Le Chalet, or, The Cottage,* and *The Daughter of the Regiment*—they continued to draw large audiences,[154] as with their "operetta" productions

[151] For which "there was a very large house, particularly upstairs," where, according to the *Times* (January 5, 1856), "the 'masses' oozed over the amphitheatre railing with extatic [*sic*] and attentive enjoyment."

[152] Copious excerpts from Fry's vast article were reprinted in *Dwight's* in three installments: January 12, p. 116, January 19, pp. 123–24, and January 26, 1856, pp. 131–32; to a lesser extent it was quoted by Watson in *Leslie's,* January 5, 1856, p. 58; also see *Review and Gazette,* January 2, 1856, pp. 3–4.

[153] "While Italian opera is sadly neglected," observed the *Spirit of the Times* (December 8, 1855, p. 516), "colored musical entertainments are at their zenith. Wood's and Buckley's are nightly crowded."

[154] In their way, wrote Dwight's New York correspondent, the Buckleys were "doing as much for the elevation of musical taste of the people as the Philharmonic [was] doing in a higher sphere" (*Dwight's,* April 21, 1855).

of *Spirit Rappings, The Two Pompeys,* and a dramatization of the "'original,' doleful, 'heart rending' tragedy of *Villikens and his Dinah.*"[155]

To stress the superiority of these productions over the pretentious proceedings "in Fourteenth Street," on October 12 the ever volatile *Herald,* greatly disparaging the "fastidious people [who] elevate their aristocratic noses at the African Opera and call it a 'perverted taste' for music,"[156] conducted its readers on a delightful guided tour down Broadway, where "a few doors above Spring Street the evening promenader will notice a profusion of gaslights and a highly ornamented corridor leading to Chinese Hall, which has been occupied by the Messrs. Buckley during the past three years as an opera house. . . . There was a short summer recess here," wrote the *Herald,* "and the place was put in first rate order for the winter, while the company was gaining laurels and dollars in Albany, Boston, and other provincial towns.[157] We find now a fine parquette and a spacious gallery thrown open to the public at the uniform charge of twenty-five cents, with the front seats reserved for ladies. Nightly one may see the prettiest women here or at Wood's. The audience [in contrast to the Academy] is purely an American one, nicely dressed, quiet, polite, and often quite fashionable. The stage is amply large enough. . . . The scenery is all new and done by the best artists at the regular theatres. The landscapes are much finer than those at Fourteenth Street. . . . There is a small but effective orchestra. The proscenium is prettily decorated, and there is a light, cheerful air about the entire place which is quite taking."

The *Herald* gave the Buckleys' current program, the first part consisting of an overture, then "The Chough and the Crow," a chorus from Bishop's opera *Guy Mannering,* sung by "seven or eight colored gentlemen in full evening costume," a bones solo by George Buckley, several characteristic ballads sung by various members of the troupe, and for finale "Buckley's Sleigh Song" by the ensemble.[158] Part two began with a minstrel entertainment offering a variety of eccentric dances and showy solos on various instruments including a one-stringed "Chinese Fiddle." Then followed the Buckleys' latest opera burlesque, *The Daughter of the Regiment,* in two acts. "Donizetti in black is really something new [well, almost], and a daring achievement, with the *souvenir* of Alboni, Sontag, and Anna Thillon fresh in the public mind," asserted the *Herald,* presumably with a straight face.[159]

[155] Perhaps a version, far removed, of F. C. Burnand's farce of that name, successfully produced in London in 1854. The song "Villikens [or Vilikens] and His Dinah," first published in London in 1853 and in New York in 1854, was quickly snatched up by the minstrels. With different words the tune was later popularly known as "Sweet Betsy from Pike."

[156] In its attempts to rescue the failing opera at the Academy, the *Tribune* (November 7, 1855) passionately urged people to go to the *Prophète* performance that evening: "Go, if anything but dirty negro minstrelsy is to triumph among us."

[157] Evidently the New York/Boston acrimony had not abated over the years.

[158] "The Italian chorus singers in Fourteenth-street should hear these singers and learn how effective a small group of voices could be when properly trained," wrote the *Herald.*

[159] The Buckleys' performances, wrote the *Spirit of the Times* (December 8, 1855, p. 516), "while delighting the lovers of fun and frolic, offer occasionally to the critical musician much satisfaction." The admirable playing of Messrs. Brandeis and Fred Buckley on the piano and violin, the "marvelous feats" of George Buckley on the bones, and the artistic performances of Mr. Stevens on the "wood and straw instruments" (shades of the Rock Harmonicon in 1846)♪ were of a degree of excellence to please the most fastidious music critic.

The writer, evidently a purist, lamented the decline of the old plantation songs, many of which had by now been "refined out of existence" by the minstrels; nowadays, everything was sentimental ballads. Nostalgically he quoted well-remembered stanzas:

Missie eat de green persimmon,
Ho! meleety, ho!
Ho! meleety, ho!
Mouf all drawed up in a pucker.
Ho! meleety, ho!
Ho! meleety, ho!
Stayed so till she went to supper,
Ho! meleety, ho!
Ho! meleety, ho!

Continuing down Broadway, the touring party was again "dazzled with a blaze of light in front of [George Christy and] Wood's new hall, and therefore [stepped] in." Built on the site of their former establishment at 444 Broadway, destroyed by fire last December,[160] the new Wood's was entered through a "spacious corridor leading from Broadway. On the right," described the *Herald* reporter, "is a ladies dressing room, furnished in most luxurious style, with toilette appliances, useful in cases of sudden illness, or fainting, to which latter disability," the writer slyly added, "the belle sex is often subject, where there is a large crowd to see them do it gracefully." The hall, with "severe packing and jamming," would hold 1600 persons. The sight lines were all good, as was the ventilation. It possessed all the features of a well-regulated theatre: spacious aisles and lobbies, an able orchestra, a profusion of mirrors and painted decorations, and additionally, two "elegant and spacious" private boxes on either side of the proscenium, "gloriously" done, like the ladies dressing room, in "rosewood, brocatel, Brussels [carpet], and lace."

"The entertainment varies somewhat from the Buckleys," continues the writer, "but resembles it in its general features." The first part of the program for that evening—like the Buckleys'—consisted of an overture, an opening chorus (from Balfe's *The Enchantress*), and a variety of songs, among them Stephen Foster's exquisite "Jeanie with the Light Brown Hair" (1854), sung by the minstrel tenor J. A. Herman, but not attributed to Foster;[161] a popular "darkie" love song "Nancy Till" (anonymous, 1851) was sung by George N. Christy, and a "Styrian Song" (doubtless with yodels galore) by the falsettist Max Zorer. Part two was devoted to novelties—virtuoso banjo performances by Thomas Vaughn; a falsetto take-off by Zorer on Louisa Pyne's "The Skylark"; a burlesque of the dancer Ciocca's *Jaleo de Jerez* by M. Lewis; also the skits "The Promenade of Miss Bloomer," "Wanted, 1,000 Milliners for Haiti," and "The Grand Railroad Explosion," featuring the irrepressibly comic George Christy.

In December "the principal members of the original and well known [E. P.]

[160] Since then they had been performing at their other establishment, Mechanics' Hall, E. P. Christy's old stronghold.

[161] "'Jeanie with the Light Brown Hair' is decidedly not a negro melody," wrote the *Herald*. "It is a delicate Romance, wherein the gentle tenor laments long for 'Jeanie with the day-dawn smile,' who seems to have been too good for this mundane sphere. . . . The music is very clever, but [unfairly] the least said about the words, the better for the poet [Foster]."

Christy's Minstrels, organized in 1842," including several dispossessed members of the Christy and Wood's troupe, announced their return to New York (from Philadelphia) for a series of twelve "Chaste and Fashionable Soirées" at Academy Hall, formerly Perham's Ethiopian Opera House at 663 Broadway. Their program, as advertised, was "replete with new musical gems, new character dances, and new burlesques: 'The Hutchinson Family' and 'Ten Minutes at the Academy of Music,' with some new, quaint, quizzical, and quiet bon mots—in fact a little of everything for everybody. For eight years the above troupe performed at 472 Broadway [Mechanics' Hall] under the direction of E. P. Christy, who is not longer connected with the corps. In fact their names are as familiar as household words." And to conclude, a disclaimer: "Particular Notice: The above troupe have (now) no connection with E. P. Christy."

Among the countless other minstrel troupes appearing in 1855 were White's Serenaders (the *Spirit of the Times* dubbed White "one of the head devils in Ethiopian matters"), holding forth, among other locations, at "Charley White's Place" now at 49 Bowery; Professor E. Ramsbottam's (or Ramsbottom's) Ethiopian Minstrels at Vocal Hall (430 Grand Street, tickets 12½ cents, reserved seats twenty-five cents); Donaldson's Minstrels, at first at Donaldson's Opera House (718 and 720 Broadway) and later at Academy Hall, and Perham's Ethiopian Opera Troupe, now "permanently located in Boston," but briefly appearing at Perham's Burlesque Opera House (intermittently known as Academy Hall), in a burlesque on Barnum's "National Baby Show."[162]

Homely American songs and popular ballads were presented at Academy Hall on the afternoons and evenings of July 11 and 18 by the Alleghanians, now back from California and managed by their basso J. M. Boulard. They soon returned for a two-a-day engagement, sharing billing with a "splendid" patriotic diorama representing "The Battle of Bunker Hill," and on Thanksgiving afternoon and evening (November 29) they gave Grand Concerts of "their old popular pieces and many new ones" at Mechanics' Hall.

The Hutchinsons—Judson, John, and Asa—returned to the Tabernacle on April 2 and 11,[163] appearing in the meantime at several neighborhood churches and perhaps a temperance meeting or two. On April 28 and 29 they sang for the inmates of the workhouse on Blackwell's Island.[164] Giving a final concert at the Tabernacle on May 23, the Hutchinsons were off on another tour of upper New York State.

Other ethnic musical entertainment, usually Scottish or Irish, this year included a concert of Styrian music performed by a group of newly arrived Styrian Vocalists in national costume. Their debut at the Tabernacle on March 8 was directed by their versatile compatriot Max Zorer; they were assisted by the actress/singer Mrs. Sarah A. Barker, George Harrison (of the Dolores Nau company), John Camoens, J. B. Don-

[162] A kind of beauty contest for babies up to five years; the winners in various age groups received cash prizes awarded by "Barnum himself, in person."

[163] Along with their more uplifting repertory they were known occasionally to perform something called "The Italian Operatic Burlesque."

[164] Appearing at both the female and male divisions of the prison, the Hutchinsons were reported to have drawn repentant tears from the prisoners with their renditions of "My Mother's Bible," "Where shall the Soul find Rest?" and, not least, their "Song for Cold Water." "Slowly but surely," editorialized the progressive *Tribune* (May 1, 1855), "advances the idea that kindness, even in the management of prisoners, is more potent than severity."

niker (formerly E. P. Christy's star violinist), and the exotically named Wugk Sabatier, former "pianist to the Duchess of Montpensier"—an unlikely assortment.

At the Stuyvesant Institute on April 19 and again at Knickerbocker Hall on May 21, Jeannie Reynoldson, dubbed the "Queen of Scottish Song," gave her perennial "Grand Ballad Entertainments." Less expectedly, in September the long-absent actress/singer Mrs. Alexander Gibbs (after two decades still billed as "the former Miss Graddon")[165] advertised a series of "Hibernian" entertainments "as performed by her [in London] upwards of 300 nights." Given at the Apollo Rooms, Mondays through Fridays and on Saturday afternoons beginning September 24, Mrs. Gibbs's apparently one-woman show, titled "The Emerald Isle and the Lakes of Killarney," consisted of "Songs, Legends, Traditions, Anecdotes, and Pictorial Illustrations of that Fairy Land."

On October 15, coincident with Mrs. Gibbs's departure from the Apollo, a more elaborate series of Irish Concerts began a week's engagement at Niblo's Saloon. Featuring the popular Irish comedian/singer John Collins, the distinguished cast comprised the harpist Aptommas, the singers Mrs. Georgiana Stuart, Maria and Stephen Leach, and George Simpson (all normally identified with the loftier musical preoccupations of the Harmonic Society); James G. Maeder presided at the piano. Collins's inimitable comic tales and "illustrations" of scenes from his large repertory of favorite Irish farces were intermingled with a heterogeneous assortment of songs—from Tom Moore and Bobby Burns to Sir Henry Bishop, Weber, and Bellini.

Held over for a second week, Collins presented a new program with a different cast consisting of Carlotta (formerly Charlotte) Pozzoni replacing Mrs. Stuart;[166] Allan Irving, formerly of the now defunct Dolores Nau company, replacing Stephen Leach; the actor/singer Francis Trevor, formerly of Wallach's Theatre; and Alfred Sedgwick, the concertinist.

Ubiquitous among the fringe performers, Sedgwick, assisted by the actress/singer Maria Duckworth, George Harrison, and a Mr. Brown, briefly revived his *Crotchets and Quavers* on June 10 at Continental Hall, located up- and across-town at Eighth Avenue and 34th Street. By June 14, Sedgwick moved *Crotchets* to the more accessible Chinese Rooms. On July 19, with the singers Carlotta Pozzoni, Kazia Lovarny, John Frazer, and Allan Irving, the pianist T. F. Bassford, and Alwyn Field, a fellow-concertinist with whom he played duets, Sedgwick participated in a "miscellaneous concert" at Dodworth's Academy for the benefit of their conductor and accompanist, one H. Craven Griffiths, a composer/pianist.

The weekly Broadway Sunday Concerts, begun at the Metropolitan Theatre in December 1854, continued through January, with Kreutzer continuing to conduct a changing cast of soloists: the singers Mlle. Victor Chome, Mrs. Henry C. Watson, George Le Jeune, Ludwig Quint, and Oswald Bernardi, the brilliant young violinist Camilla Urso, the horn virtuoso Louis Schreiber, and, incongruously, three members of the Buckley family—George Swaine, Richard Bishop, and Frederick. The final Broadway Sunday Concert seems to have taken place on February 4.

[165] Originally from London's Drury Lane Theatre, "Mrs. Gibbs, formerly Miss Graddon," had been a leading member of the local theatre scene in the 1830s and '40s.

[166] Soon to become Mrs. Stephen Leach.

A foretaste of Jullien, whose return was eagerly awaited, was attempted in a so-called "*concert monstre à la Jullien*" at the Tabernacle on June 5. With a "double orchestra conducted by Julius Unger, the heterogeneous cast of assisting artists included Martini d'Ormy, Camilla Urso, a Miss Marion McCarthy from Burton's theatre, Francis Trevor from Wallach's, the Brothers Mollenhauer, and Shelton's Band, led by a Mr. Voho [*sic*]. The program ranged from opera to pop songs to Jullien quadrilles, ending with "The Fireman's Quadrille," no less.

What with Jullien's continuing failure to return, Dodworth's Band offered the only regularly scheduled summer concerts in 1855. Castle Garden now being *hors de combat,* the band returned to Atlantic Garden,♪ their former abode at 9–11 Broadway, where throughout July and August they gave free Sunday evening "sacred" concerts, whose programs spanned the realm of lighter secular music from Mozart to Dodworth. Later, from the beginning of October through November 10, the Dodworth Band gave nightly promenade concerts at the Crystal Palace,[167] reopened for the great American Institute Fair.

There the committee on piano-fortes—consisting of the pianists William Mason, Louis Moreau Gottschalk, and Frederick Rakemann, the organist/violinist William H. Sage (a non-performing member of the Philharmonic), and the music journalists Charles Bailey Seymour and Theodore Hagen—awarded the first prize, "with warm commendations, to the instruments of Mr. Steinway, a German manufacturer in New York, of whom we have never before heard, and no wonder, as he does not advertise" (*Review and Gazette,* November 3, 1855, p. 366). The first Steinways (né Steinweg) had emigrated from Germany in 1850.

The merging of the piano dealers Ely and Munger with the music publisher Samuel C. Jollie was celebrated at their new music store (519 Broadway) on April 27 with a private musical *soirée* for about 200 invited guests. Presented by Henry C. Watson, the program included airs from *Don Giovanni, Il barbiere, Cinderella,* and *Romeo and Juliet,* sung by John Frazer, George Le Jeune, and Allan Irving, assisted by various singing actors from the various theatres. "During the evening, several distinguished pianists and other instrumental performers, among whom was Mr. Kyle, the flutist, performed many popular fantasies" (*Tribune,* April 28).

On July 10 the press and public were invited to a "Grand Vocal and Instrumental Concert" at Dodworth's Rooms by a Mr. Spencer B. Driggs of Detroit, the inventor of a newly patented piano attachment toothsomely named the *Linguine* (a term mystifyingly translated as "sweet-voiced"). To demonstrate the "power and beauty" of his invention—a six-octave piano purportedly as brilliant as one with seven octaves, and capable of being easily tuned by "any intelligent person possessing a correct ear"—Driggs had engaged the singers Mrs. Henry C. Watson, John Frazer, George Le Jeune, and Oswald Bernardi, and the keyboard performers W. A. King (now organist at St. Stephen's), Carl (Charles) Wels, one Louis Hehl, and the gifted G. Washbourn Morgan. A feature of the program was a song "descriptive of the Linguine melody," composed especially for the occasion and charmingly sung by Mrs. Watson (*Spirit,* July 14, 1855, p. 264).

[167] On November 10 they played the Quickstep from Bristow's *Rip Van Winkle.*

Music Division, The New York Public Library

A photograph (c. 1855) of the manufactury and first piano showrooms, at 82–86 Walker Street, of the rising firm of Steinway & Sons. Grouped in front of the premises are their personnel and seated in the two carriages to the left are presumably two of the brothers Steinway, perhaps Charles and Henry.

As always, benefit concerts abounded, as did volunteers to perform them. In January, to assist the destitute victims of that year's financial near-panic, performances were donated by Dolores Nau and her English opera company at Niblo's Theatre (January 3);[168] by George Andrews conducting members of several church choirs at the Taber-

[168] This was just before their departure for the South, under Corbyn's management, "in search of audiences," as the *Musical Review and Choral Advocate* (January 18, 1855, p. 20) unkindly put it.

nacle (January 10); and by Paul Julien at Niblo's Concert Saloon (January 20), with the assistance of Adelina Patti, Luigi Rocco, and August Gockel.[169]

Later in the year, to aid the victims of the yellow-fever epidemic at Norfolk and Portsmouth, Virginia, Teresa Parodi, now in triumphant mid-concert-tour (discussed below), appeared at Niblo's Saloon on August 28, assisted by her touring companions Maurice and Amalia Patti Strakosch, and additionally by Aptommas, Bernardi, Julius Siede, Allan Irving, and others. On October 6 the Pyne/Harrison troupe, with Bristow conducting and with the participation of Niblo's total onstage and backstage forces, donated a gala performance to the same cause.

The singers most frequently heard at church benefits were Georgiana Stuart, Maria Brainerd, Anna Griswold, Mrs. Jameson (or Jamieson, or Jamison), Francis H. Nash, J. Connor Smith, David Griswold, and other members of the Harmonic Society. They were most often accompanied by Bristow, sometimes by Clare Beames, rarely by Henry C. Timm, and at least once each by George Henry Curtis and the promising young American musician Charles Jerome Hopkins (1836–1898), currently organist at the Church of the Holy Evangelist (Beekman Street).[170]

Appearing at Niblo's for the Hebrew Benevolent Association on February 27 were the singers Madame Comettant and Oswald Bernardi, the veteran violinist Michele Rapetti, and the pianists Carl Wels, T. Franklin Bassford, and Harry Sanderson (1837?–1871), a pupil of Wels's. And to assist the German Benevolent Society at the Tabernacle on May 2 the volunteer performers were the *Liederkranz* Society and Caroline Lehmann (who was taken to task by the Germanophile critic of the *Evening Post* (May 4) for unsuitably singing such trashy Italian barrel-organ fodder as the *Casta diva*—and she a German, too!); also Scharfenberg and Timm, who played a Grand Duo for two pianos by Pixis, the Mollenhauer Brothers, and the National Guard Band led by Noll.

At the Academy of Music, on December 16, an ultra-fashionable benefit concert sponsored by the Benevolent Society of the Ladies of St. Vincent de Paul turned out to be something of a fiasco. With tickets at one dollar (fifty cents extra for reserved seats). it drew a disappointing house, despite a cast that included virtually the entire roster of Academy performers—LaGrange, Nantier-Didiée, Hensler, Patania, Brignoli, Morelli, Caspani, Amodio, the chorus, the orchestra, Maretzek, everybody—including a pretentious Dutch pianist M. E. Engelberts (brought over by Salviani as his ac-

[169] With every seat and standing space filled, as the *Times* reported (January 26, 1855), the concert had taken in $483.50 at the box office. To this sum young Julien generously added $50 of his own, then—in cooperation with the Relief Association—he personally superintended the distribution of the funds.

[170] Hopkins, an incipient force on the American music scene, is frequently misidentified in musical reference books as "Edward Jerome Hopkins," confusing him with his illustrious brother, Edward Augustus Hopkins. On June 5, 1855, the precocious C. Jerome Hopkins "directed" a miscellaneous concert for the benefit of his church, given at Botanic Hall (68 East Broadway), with the assistance of Maria Duckworth and Messrs. J. W. Alden (baritone), T. J. Cook (violinist), and C. J. Muller, a pianist with whom Hopkins played duets. His solo rendition of his "Impromptu Extravaganza *sur Lucrezia Borgia*," stamped Hopkins a "true genius with not a few eccentricities" wrote the *Musical World* (June 16, 1855, p. 80). As an encore, he played "three extemporaneous variations on 'The Last Rose of Summer,' in seven flats, which evinced extraordinary powers of composition."

Both: New-York Historical Society

Sheet music cover-art advertising instrument makers and music dealers and publishers.

companist), who, with his arrogant manner and pianistic incompetence, was received with hisses.

Madame Patania, too, fell into critical disfavor for performing what the outraged reviewer for the *Musical World* (possibly Girac) (December 22, 1855, p. 397) described as "an *Ave Maria* in polka time (!), with an entirely new style of accompaniment—eccentric piano on the stage [wielded by Engelberts] playing a triplet obbligato, and organ behind the scene giving forth sustained chords—both instruments at serious disagreement as to pitch." The critic blamed the whole mess on Maretzek, who, either through ignorance or indifference, very much needed "a general stirring up in musical matters."

More edifying was a farewell testimonial concert to honor Father Heinrich (whose departure for Europe still impended). Given at the Tabernacle on July 2 (tickets at twenty-five cents) by the grateful pupils of the Colored Ward School, No. 2 (Eighth Ward), the concert was directed by their teacher, one Samuel W. Waldron, Heinrich's "pupil and friend." It was in fact a repeat, by request, of a concert they had given on June 18, but this time, as a special "tribute of esteem for [Heinrich's] interest in [their] advancement in Musical Science and for his kindness to all during his long sojourn in America," they programed two compositions he had written especially for the occasion. This touching farewell tribute was, as we know, once again premature: not until the end of 1856 would Heinrich at last take his long-delayed departure, returning to the United States for a final time two years later.

At an earlier public-school concert at the Tabernacle, on May 22, Bristow, recalling the Bradbury days, conducted some 1200 of his young pupils of the Ward School at 44 North Moore Street in a program of "solos, quartets, and choruses." Tickets at twenty-five cents were available at the Tabernacle at concert time and earlier at Bristow and Morse's piano warerooms, now at 419 Broadway. "Those interested in the effort to introduce music into our schools, and lay thus the foundation for a new musical generation, will attend," prodded the *Tribune* (May 22, 1855).

Other juvenile efforts included a widely publicized concert at the Tabernacle on January 31 by a chorus of New York newsboys, painstakingly organized, trained, and conducted by W. C. Van Meter of Dr. Pease's Five Points House of Industry. Van Meter also officiated at a concert jointly given at the Tabernacle on December 21 by the Five Points Children and the newsboys. L. A. Benjamin continued at regular intervals to bring out more of his apparently inexhaustible fund of juvenile cantatas performed by vast aggregations of small singers and instrumentalists; the latest was *The Priestess and Six Queens*. In May and June, George F. Root's popular juvenile cantata *The Flower Queen* was sung "several times," under Root's direction, by the young lady students of the Spingler Institute.[171] In December the Alexander Family, a company of juvenile vocalists and bell-ringers, offered pre-Christmas entertainment for children and their parents at 472 Broadway.

In November a troupe of juveniles, the Marsh Family (apparently no kin to the

[171] On April 18, Root unveiled his new patriotic adult cantata *The Pilgrim Fathers* at the Mercer Street Church, sung by the "ladies and gentlemen of the Choir aided by some of the best amateur singers of the City." A booklet containing the words of the cantata was supplied with each 50-cent ticket.

Infant Drummer), successfully invaded the professional theatre with a charming, well-produced, and reportedly well-performed presentation at the Broadway Theatre of Planché's extravaganza *Beauty and the Beast* (London 1841). George Washington Marsh, who headed the company—all "two-feet-six-inches of him"—was pronounced a nimble and sophisticated comedian not far removed from Burton. He was assisted by several little sisters, a sizable cast of juvenile thespians, and a *corps de ballet* of thirty tiny dancers. "It seemed," wrote the *Herald* (December 11, 1855), "like looking at a very clever company through a reversed opera glass." In their afterpiece *The Wandering Minstrel,* a farce of ancient vintage now popular at both the black and white theatres, little G. W. Marsh, as Jem Baggs, triumphed with his side-splitting rendition of the "tragic" song "Vilikens and his Dinah."

The Harmonic Society, in addition to their annual *Messiah* at Christmas,[172] departed from tradition to give two concerts of secular music, masquerading as "public rehearsals," at Dodworth's Rooms on February 19 and April 2.[173] Following the second event, conducted by Timm in Bristow's absence, the *Evening Post* (April 3) found the performances "such as to demonstrate that native talent, properly cultivated, has nothing to fear from competition with the imported artiste." Miss Brainerd was particularly singled out for her "somewhat ambitious [but splendid] attempt of the 'Casta Diva.'"

With Bristow again at the helm and Carl Wels at the piano, the Society gave another miscellaneous concert at Dr. Chapin's Church on May 9, repeating the program at Dodworth's Rooms on May 21 for those who had been prevented by the bad weather from attending on the 9th. Again at Dodworth's Rooms, on October 15, accompanied at the piano by George Henry Curtis, they presented a sacred program consisting of familiar excerpts from *The Seasons* and *The Creation, Judas Maccabaeus, Messiah,* and Rossini's *Stabat Mater.*

In general, the givers of independent sacred concerts were apt to lean on members of the Harmonic Society. For instance, on February 2, at a concert of sacred music by the ladies of Calvary Baptist Church (West 23rd Street), under the direction of Marcus Colburn, the assisting artists were Mesdames Stuart and Jameson, Miss Dingley, and F. H. Nash; the choir was conducted by George Andrews; Bristow accompanied at the organ and piano. At a concert of sacred and miscellaneous music at the Rutgers Institute on March 14, Mrs. Stuart appeared, together with William H. Oakley (of the Alleghanians); Bristow conducted and accompanied.

Departing from the Harmonic Society orbit, the concert at the Reformed Dutch Church (23rd Street between Sixth and Seventh avenues) on April 4 presented a quartet consisting of Mr. and Mrs. Philip Mayer, a Miss Bennett, and a Mr. Julius E. Mayer,

[172] Given this year at Dr. Chapin's Church of the Divine Unity (brightly illuminated for the occasion) and sung by Mrs. Jameson, the Misses Brainerd and Hawley, and Messrs. Beutler, Nash, and D. B. Bell; and of course conducted by Bristow.

[173] They were doubtless attempting to broaden their constituency; in February it was reported that the Harmonic Society was applying for incorporation.

[174] On a less secular plane, at the services of the Presbyterian Church (Fifth Avenue and 19th Street), where William Mason served as organist, congregational singing was regularly presided over by Lowell Mason, the church's music director (see Ogasapian, p. 118).

who, with Van Der Weyde [current orthography] at the organ, sang solos and ensembles by Mozart, Mendelssohn, Rossini, Van Der Weyde, and others.[174]

In 1855 the hitherto unchallenged Harmonic Society faced a new problem—competition—something they had never confronted since their founding in 1849. The Mendelssohn Union, although less than a year old, was already a formidable rival, having in April performed with the Philharmonic—something the Harmonic Society had not managed to bring about in all the years of their existence. Consisting of eighty-five singing members (mostly choristers from the various New York churches), the Mendelssohn Union (like the Harmonic Society) aspired to establish in New York a "permanent, first-class, sacred music society." As a first step toward acquiring subscribing members, they gave a highly praised concert—their first—on May 22, at a new music-hall in Houston Street. Repeating excerpts from Mendelssohn's *Elijah,* and presenting a variety of sacred solos and choruses, they were superbly conducted by G. Washbourn Morgan and as superbly accompanied by Henry C. Timm. The female members of the chorus were especially lauded in the *Musical World* (May 26, 1855, p. 38), but the critic (probably Willis) found fault with the men's tight-lipped, closed-up method of singing. The *Musical World* had previously criticized this same fault in the otherwise splendid performances of Morgan's Glee and Madrigal Society, whose successful series of six *soirées* had been completed at Dodworth's Academy on March 26.[175]

Among the male German singing societies, (or "Glee Clubs," as they called themselves), on January 22 the New York *Sängerrunde,* led by J. Siedler, were heard at the Tabernacle in both the sentimental and warlike songs favored by kindred groups. In May, as we know, the *Liederkranz* appeared for the benefit of the German Benevolent Society. But the great event of the year occurred in June, when for the second time the assembled German singing societies of the northern, southern, and eastern states celebrated their *Liederfest* in New York,[176] with Carl Bergmann (replacing the absent Eisfeld) as their conductor.

Displaying a high degree of musical integrity in his handling of the great festival concert at the Metropolitan Theatre on June 25, Bergmann, shunning the popular chestnuts, conducted an orchestra of 100 players in the first American performances of two works by Wagner—the Overture to *Cola Rienzi* (Dresden 1842) and the Grand March from *Lohengrin* (Weimar 1850)[177]; he led the 1200 members of the united

[175] A glowing review of the third concert of this series is found in the *Musical Review and Choral Advocate* (February 1, 1855, pp. 42–43); informative reviews of the fourth and fifth concerts, and a brief notice of the sixth, appear in the *Musical World* (February 17, 1855, pp. 73–74; March 17, p. 123; March 31, p. 146).

[176] As aggressively convivial as ever, the German visitors again "illuminated our streets with a torchlight parade . . . visited, sang, and quaffed [oceans of] lagerbier, paraded by day under the Stars and Stripes and the 'German Revolutionary Tricolor,'" and again boisterously "pic-nicked" at Elm Park, where, despite having exhausted the local supply of beer, no one showed any signs of tipsiness (*Review and Gazette,* June 30, 1855, p. 214).

[177] The critics had surprisingly little to say about the Wagner works. The *Rienzi* Overture, wrote Hagen (*Review and Gazette,* June 29, 1855, pp. 214–15), was in no way representative of Wagner's "music of the future," having been composed some fifteen years earlier, when Wagner was under the

choruses,[178] whom he had strenuously drilled, in thrilling performances of the second-act finale of *William Tell,* the Chorus of the Priests from Mozart's *Die Zauberflöte,* and the *Kriegerscene* (Warriors' Scene), by the prominent German composer Carl Ludwig Fischer. Although separate singing societies independently performed a number of favorite hackneyed works, as the *Review and Gazette* (June 30, 1855, pp. 214–15) remarked, the program in general was far above the common level of sentimentality which the German Glee Clubs favored. The uncommonly high quality and success of the festival were indeed "owing mainly to the intelligent, energetic, and faithful conducting of Mr. Carl Bergmann," who had "taken great pains to produce something better than usual, or than was to be expected of singers who were no artists, and generally very badly trained in their private societies."

By the end of the year Bergmann, apparently a man of boundless stamina, had taken on, besides the Philharmonic and the Arion,[179] the conductorship of the New York *Sängerbund,* a chorus of 300 singers, who, accompanied by an orchestra of fifty and with Quint and Feder as soloists, were heard at the Tabernacle on December 20.[180] Bergmann had been appointed as well to conduct three proposed concerts for the long-dormant Musical Fund Society, announced U. C. Hill and Louis Ernst, their present chairman and secretary. The best soloists were promised, as were programs of the "highest order, without, however, excluding the better works occasionally composed in this country." (Alas, in vain.)

Among the few native singers brave enough to accept the risks of individual concert-giving in this inauspicious year were Georgiana Stuart (May 2); Maria Brainerd, who after myriad public appearances in the preceding few years announced her "first" New York concert (December 20);[181] and Emma Gillingham Bostwick (December 21). Their assisting artists (an interchangeable, infinitely repetitive crew) included Anna and David Griswold, John Frazer, Oswald Bernardi, Carl Wels, Madame Comettant, Alessandro Gasparoni, Aptommas, J. B. Beutler, and the Brothers Mollenhauer; the most frequent accompanists were Bristow, Timm, and, invariably for Miss Brainerd, Dr. Clare W. Beames.

The problematical American singer Isadora Clark gave two concerts at the Metro-

influence of Meyerbeer; and the fragment from *Lohengrin* was too fragmentary to be judged. But the performances of both had been splendid.

[178] One wonders how performing forces of such size could have been squeezed into the available space.

[179] In January the "Glee Club Arion," in all ways competitive with their progenitor the *Liederkranz,* advertised their first Grand Ball, to be given on January 25 at the Chinese Buildings. Joseph Noll and his Seventh Regiment National Guard Band supplied the dance music and the best caterers were engaged to provide the food and drink. Tickets, $2 for a "gentleman with ladies."

[180] A delightful occasion, except that "nearly two-thirds of the men kept their hats on during the evening, and many of them shut off from a large part of the audience all view of the stage by standing in the aisles, even when there were plenty of seats at the side," to say nothing of a constant buzz of conversation from "two or three young *Herren* with their sweethearts." Newly arrived Germans seemed to confuse the concept of American freedom with uninhibited bad manners, such as would never be tolerated at home, indignantly wrote Willis (*Musical World,* December 29, 1855, pp. 409–10).

[181] Unfortunately for Miss Brainerd, on the same night that Gottschalk returned to the New York concert stage (see below).

politan Theatre on April 16 and June 12 to thin audiences and generally poor reviews. Assisted by Camilla Urso, Oswald Bernardi, David Griswold, the flutists Siede and Eben (for the Jenny Lind Trio with two flutes), and an orchestra conducted by Carl Bergmann, her first program included a composition by William H. Fry, "Hear the right, O Lord," set to the text of Psalm 27.[182] At her second concert she was assisted by the opera singers Arnoldi and Gasparoni, the violinist Henry Appy, and again by Bergmann and Bernardi. She then departed on a tour of the South and the West.

The black American singer Elizabeth Taylor Greenfield, recently returned from England, announced two concerts at the Tabernacle on March 1 and 3. Referring to her as "Miss Greenleaf," the *Tribune* wrote (February 28): "Since her first appearance in New York she has been for twenty months studying under Sir George Smart in London, and report speaks favorably of her progress." Her recent concerts in Washington and Philadelphia had been warmly received. "Altogether," the *Tribune* admitted, "the sight of a black woman playing vocalist is strange and may pique curiosity, not to say philanthropy."

But local curiosity seemed to have been spent in the outrageous public display attending Greenfield's New York debut in 1853. Now, although after her first two appearances she announced, and presumably gave, a great many concerts at the Tabernacle, stretching through the better part of March—and again on July 5 and 6 and December 24—none of these events seems to have elicited a review in the New York press.

Still featured as "the Black Swan," Greenfield was assisted by her pupil, a young tenor billed as the "Indian Mario,"[183] by an unnamed violinist,[184] and by a Professor Ambold, who accompanied at the piano. Her programs, consisting mainly of the lighter opera arias and duets with Bowers and an occasional air from an oratorio, invariably closed with "I Am Free," advertised as a "duet" entirely sung by the Swan, consisting of "one part in Baritone, the other in Soprano Voice, written expressly for her in London by Stephen Glover [1813–1870], in which she reaches thirty-one clear notes in the scale, a greater compass of voice than any other mortal had ever reached."

At her Tabernacle concerts Elizabeth Greenfield was doubtless assisted by members of the gifted Luca Family, a vocal and instrumental quartet of brothers—Alexander Jr., Simeon, John, and Cleveland—who had made their New York debut in 1853 at an anti-slavery meeting at the Tabernacle. Under the tutelage—and with the collaboration—of their father, Alexander Luca, Sr. (1805–?), they were frequently heard at the African Methodist Episcopal Church (Bridge Street) in Brooklyn (*DANB,* pp. 406–7; Odell, VI, 422).

On June 27, sixteen-year-old Master Augustus Luca, billed as the "Ethiopian Thalberg," gave a Grand Concert at the Tabernacle, assisted by his brothers and Miss Allen, a singer. Augustus Luca was sure to have been a *nom de concert* for Cleveland, the youngest Luca sibling, who sang soprano and played piano in the family quartet. His program, according to the advertisements, included "Liszt's Concerto by Herz"

[182] Another bone of Fry/Bennett contention, according to Upton (*Fry,* p. 153).

[183] This was Thomas J. Bowers (1836–1885?) of Philadelphia, who was also billed as the "Colored Mario," sometimes the "American Mario."

[184] Most probably a member of the Luca Family.

and Wallace's *Polka de concert.* According to Dwight's New York informant, young Luca had created "some sensation by concerts in New York," but he disapproved of the critics who called the young pianist "another de Meyer, Thalberg, Jaëll, etc." Although Luca possessed "rather extraordinary talent," the correspondent found his execution "more brilliant and forceful than tasteful." Referring to "Liszt's Concerto by Herz," he advised young Luca to abandon such trumpery as the "above title indicates" and dedicate himself to the study of "genuine compositions" (*Dwight's,* June 30, 1855, p. 101). (Frustratingly, I have found no review of his concerts in the New York press.)

On October 11 a concert was given at the Tabernacle by Mr. W. H. Jones, a young black tenor, accompanied by piano, violin, and flute, most likely played by members of the Luca Family. Again no reviews.

Among the "imported artistes," Caroline Lehmann gave her one and only Grand Concert, a notable event, on March 3 at Niblo's Saloon. Lehmann sang familiar opera arias and less familiar *Lieder* by Schubert, Schumann, and Robert Franz. Her all-German cast of assisting artists included the then newly arrived pianist Gustav Satter, who with Noll, Reyer, and Bergner played Mendelssohn's Piano Quartet in B minor, op. 3 (1825); in contrast to the prevalent showy piano fantasies, Satter attested to his seriousness by choosing for his solos modest piano pieces by Mozart, Beethoven, and himself; J. B. Beutler sang solos and, assisted by a trio of German vocalists, gave a German Psalm and Mendelssohn's vocal quartet "Farewell to the Woods" *(Abschied vom Wald),* op. 59, no. 3 (1843); the flutist Edward Lehmann (a brother), played a fantasy on themes from *Masaniello;* Henry C. Timm splendidly presided at the piano. The *Times* (March 5, 1855) pronounced Lehmann's concert one of the best of the season and Lehmann, "without exception, the most accomplished and enjoyable concert singer in America."[185] Satter, who had been heard only a few days earlier at Eisfeld's *soirée,* again reaped "golden opinions."

With the Academy of Music a powerful magnet, hopeful Italian opera singers and their satellites increasingly flocked to New York from Europe and Havana. On March 8 (amid the Ole Bull opera turmoil) the soprano Drusilla Garbato, apparently back from her season in Lima, announced her debut at a "sacred concert" at Niblo's Garden, to be given jointly with the then recently arrived tenor Antonio Rosetti. The assisting artists for this event, a motley crew, were Carolina Vietti Vertiprach, Maria Brainerd, the Morras, the "Ferdinando" Meyers, and Signor Arnoldi; a "large" orchestra (probably conducted by Luigi Garbato) and "a great number" of currently dispossessed chorus singers from the Academy of Music completed the cast. The concert might or might not have taken place.

At Niblo's Saloon on April 24, Catarina di Ferrari, "from the Conservatory of Milan and *prima donna* of the Carlo Felice Opera House in Genoa,"[186] by way of Havana, combined her North American concert debut with Federico Beneventano's fare-

[185] But not for long. Apparently tired of being ignored by the powers at the Academy of Music, Caroline Lehmann departed these shores in August, and soon after appeared at the Amsterdam opera, reportedly with great success.

[186] Persistently relocated by the local press to Geneva, the Carlo Felice in Genoa, founded in 1828, was named after the reigning monarch Charles Felix (1756–1831), Duke of Savoy and King of Sardinia.

well after five years in the Western Hemisphere. Probably hoping to pick up an engagement at the Academy of Music, Beneventano had stopped off in New York on his way from Havana to London and Paris where he had engagements. The assisting artists for this beginning-and-end event included an unknown Miss Helen Deming, the guitarist/violinist Leopold de Janon,♪ the French composer/pianist and noted critic-to-be Oscar Comettant, and Jullien's former concertmaster Thomas Baker, now ballyhooed as "the great American Pianist," who most probably accompanied. The *Times* (April 25, 1855) reported a "very slim attendance" but "quite excessive applause" and no less than three bouquets for the debutante. Possessing a mezzo-soprano voice of limited range but agreeable quality, Ferrari sang with skill and taste: "The audience had more than they expected, and applauded vociferously," wrote the *Times.*[187]

Beneventano's swan song, wrote the *Times,* was accorded the kind of applause that was more than applause, conveying, as it did, a distinct flavor of "Auld Lang Syne." His voice had gained greatly in finish since last heard here, but although "he sang the *Figaro* aria from the 'Barber' with irresistible gusto," the program was "badly selected, badly written, and badly followed [attended]. Its extreme gaseousness, doubtless, kept many people away."

In July, Donna Valeria Gomez, the failed *prima donna* of Maretzek's failed 1854 season at Castle Garden, at last announced her departure, an event she commemorated on July 23 with a Grand Vocal and Instrumental Festival-*cum*-farewell-benefit. Flashing an inflated list of credits—the Madrid opera, the Fenice in Venice, the Carlo Felice in Genoa, the Royal Theatre in Brussels, and "most recently, Castle Garden, where she introduced the opera of 'Louisa Miller' with great success"—Donna Valeria announced as her assisting artists Ole Bull, Vestvali, Rocco, and Martin Lazar, a new pianist appearing for the first time in New York. It was Gomez's final fiasco in America: neither Vestvali nor Bull materialized,[188] as the *Spirit* testily reported (July 28, 1855, p. 288).

Of far greater consequence was the reappearance in August of Teresa Parodi, who, as we know, had been brought back to the United States by Strakosch in April during the no-holds-barred power struggle for control of the Academy of Music. Having failed in that endeavor, Strakosch lost no time in organizing an extensive, continuous concert tour for Parodi, in which he and his wife participated, much as they had done in their collaboration with Ole Bull and little Patti. With the New York press systematically apprised of her triumphs en route, by the time Parodi arrived for her well-publicized philanthropic concert at Niblo's Saloon on August 28, the public had been worked up to the desired state of eager anticipation. Attracting a large and fashionable audience and receiving a warm welcome in the press,[189] Parodi and her col-

[187] Di Ferrari's opera debut in June at the Academy of Music, as Donna Elvira in *Don Giovanni,* as we know, had been canceled because of her illness.

[188] Not until October was it hinted that Ole Bull, who in the meantime had been licking his wounds, was at last ready to return to the concert stage (*Herald,* October 22, 1855).

[189] In both the *Ah, mon fils* (from *Le Prophète*) and the *Casta diva,* Parodi "brought out all the sonority and mellowness of which a great and admirably cultivated voice is capable," wrote the *Times* (August 29, 1855). She shone no less in the brilliant "Ricci Waltz" and in her duets with Amalia Patti Strakosch, whose solos were of an essentially light character. Maurice Strakosch was praised, too, for his delightful compositions and for his "quiet mastery of the [piano] after the eternal thumping of the modern school."

leagues immediately reappeared at Niblo's on August 31, then again on September 5, September 11, and finally on September 18. They were most often assisted by Aptommas and Bernardi, and occasionally by the Brothers Mollenhauer.

After Parodi's departure, the *Times* (September 19, 1855), in summing up her brilliant New York season, compared her series, "in point of merit," to the superb concerts given by Henriette Sontag in 1853, a time when audiences had been more responsive to concerts. Since then, wrote the *Times,* "there has been a change in the public appetite, and concerts have failed to remunerate the artistes who assisted at them. Indeed, we were of opinion that the concert room could no longer be filled, however superior the attraction." But now, at concert after concert,[190] Niblo's Saloon had been crowded "to suffocation" by audiences eager to hear Parodi, and this despite predominantly bad weather.

Vestvali, whose Academy of Music contract had not been renewed, performed throughout the summer at Niagara Falls, Saratoga Springs, Newport, Cape May, and the other fashionable resorts frequented by her large circle of elite friends. Returning to New York, on September 12 she gave an elaborate farewell concert at Niblo's Saloon, assisted by a widely assorted cast. Vestvali sang her most successful opera arias and various duets with Bernardi and a new tenor from the Italian Opera House in Paris, variously spelled *Ceresio* and *Cerisio* in the newspapers, but in fact named Ceresa; with the cornet virtuoso Louis Schreiber supplying the *obbligato* she sang Heinrich Proch's "Wanderer's Lament" (her suggestively titled final number). Somewhat incongruously participating was William Mason, who played two of his compositions—*Toujours,* a waltz (op. 7, no. 2), and "Silver Spring," op. 6[191] (both to be published the following year by Firth, Pond and Co.—and de Kontski's *Grand Caprice héroique;* Allan Irving sang a *scena* from an unidentified opera by Julius Benedict; H. Gardner, an English tenor, sang an air by Balfe; and the English-born pianist William Dressler accompanied. On September 25, Vestvali gave another farewell concert, in Brooklyn; then, amid outpourings of journalistic adulation, she departed for Mexico,[192] where she had been engaged to form and head an opera company.[193]

Concerts by instrumental performers, a category of musical practitioner not in current public favor, were few and far between. On January 27 at Niblo's, Paul Julien, a week after his concert for the New York needy, gave another of his numberless farewells before going on an extended tour. He was again assisted by his little friend Adelina Patti, Martini d'Ormy, the opera baritone Eugenio Crouza, and the pianists Gockel and Sabatier.

The dauntless balletmaster/entrepreneur Llorente, following his abrupt dismissal from Niblo's, took the Metropolitan Theatre "for a few nights" and on October 21

[190] At her last concert Parodi sang an aria from Fry's *Leonora,* "a brilliant composition and written with much fluency, although the melody fell somewhat familiarly" on the ear (*Times,* September 19, 1855).

[191] A Lisztian work named after Lowell Mason's estate at Orange, New Jersey.

[192] George Templeton Strong, for all his earlier preoccupation with Vestvali, seemed unaware of her departure.

[193] It had been rumored that Vestvali, rather than going to Mexico, was—together with Parodi, Strakosch, and Maretzek—planning an opposition opera company, to perform at the Metropolitan Theatre.

began a series of "Grand Operatic and Instrumental Concerts and Choreographic Tableaux and Ballets by his Dancing Company, among them again the 'Vintage and Feast of Xeres' and 'The Siege of Zaragoza.'" To enhance his appeal, Llorente engaged a cast of singers: Carolina Vietti-Vertiprach, Luigi Ceresa (still typographically misrepresented), Vincenzo Morino, first baritone of the Royal Theatre at Turin, and Agostino (or Augustino) Robbio, the sensational, thirty-seven-time violin soloist at Jullien's London concerts. "Signor Robbio," stated the *Times* (October 27, 1855), "is a perfect prodigy in his way. In the marvelous effects of his instrument he surpasses all his predecessors, not even excepting the wild Norwegian Ole Bull. The age is not favorable to solo players," added the *Times,* "but once in a while a marvelous player like Signor Robbio should meet with success."[194]

On November 27 at the Metropolitan Theatre the composer/pianist Oscar Comettant gave a concert, assisted by Mesdames Wallace-Bouchelle and Vietti Vertiprach, a Mademoiselle Louise Brandeis, Messrs. Bernardi, Appy, Schreiber, and a debutant pianist, a Señor Narciso Lopez, son of a defeated Cuban general. Lopez attracted an audience composed chiefly of "fierce-looking but diminutive Spaniards," reported the *Times* (November 29, 1855); although not untalented, he was "deficient in strength and superabundant in daintiness."

The arid concert year closed in an unexpected twin blaze of musical radiance: the launching in late November of the historic Mason/Bergmann (later Mason/Thomas) chamber-music concerts (to continue for thirteen years), and a month later the return to the New York concert scene of Louis Moreau Gottschalk, who began a prodigious series of sixteen concerts that continued well into the following June.[195]

Early in November, William Mason and Carl Bergmann announced six "Classical Musical Matinées" to be given at Dodworth's Saloon at the unusual hour of 2 P.M., the first on November 27, the others to follow on the last Tuesday of each succeeding month. Besides solo and ensemble performances by the two principals, a string quartet consisting of Theodore Thomas and Joseph Mosenthal (1834–1896), violins, George Matzka (1825–1883), viola, and Bergmann, cello,[196] would play the great chamber-music works of the past and present, often assisted by Mason. A single subscription to the series was $3; $5 for two; $1 for a single ticket to a single matinée.

The novel concept of daytime concert-giving[197] was rationalized in the *Tribune* (November 14): "In consequence of the numerous evening engagements of the city, and to enable lady amateurs and students to be present without escort, it is proposed

[194] It was gossiped that on failing to be billed as a pupil of Paganini, Robbio had refused to play. As Robbio explained it, he refused because he had been incorrectly billed as a product of the Paris *Conservatoire* (*Review and Gazette,* November 3, 1855, p. 366). The matter was evidently solved, but Robbio, not the most stable of men, finally "burst the bubble [when he] uttered his moans of complaint from the stage, interrupting his solo to do so" (*Dwight's,* November 3, 1855, p. 36).

[195] John Tasker Howard in *Our American Music* (p. 206) erroneously reports eighty Gottschalk concerts given in New York that year, a mistake that is duplicated in the *DAB* and repeated in the published Strong *Diary* (II, p. 258n).

[196] The members of the quartet were chosen by Bergmann, at Mason's request (Mason, pp. 193–94).

[197] Aside from the minstrel-show and model-artiste matinées, only a rare opera performance had been known to take place in the afternoon.

to give matinées in preference to soirées.[198] This arrangement will also enable those residing in the suburbs to attend, as each performance will occupy only about an hour and a half."

But the project's most important attribute was the opportunity it offered of hearing chamber music "rarely afforded to listen to,[199] except in some very select circles of Europe—the later quartets of Beethoven, rarely heard in public, even abroad—the works of Schumann, Schubert, Frank [*sic*], Volkmann, Brahms, Rubinstein, and Berwald[200] will form the leading features of the programs." Each program was planned to include two important chamber-music works, usually one with piano, and a variety of unhackneyed solos and ensemble pieces. "In short," concluded the *Tribune,* "it is intended to arrange these matinées after the celebrated ones of Liszt at Weimar."[201]

A large audience—so large that many of the fashionably dressed ladies, of whom it principally consisted, had to stand—turned out on November 27 to hear a massive program that consisted entirely of unfamiliar works: Schubert's "Death and the Maiden" Quartet in D minor for Strings (1824); Brahms's hot-off-the-griddle Trio in B major, op. 8 (1854), for violin, cello and piano (probably its world premiere);[202] Mendelssohn's *Variations concertantes,* op. 17 (1829), played by Mason and Bergmann; Chopin's posthumous *Fantaisie impromptu* in C-sharp minor, op. 66 (composed 1834, published 1855), and two Preludes, op. 24, by Stephen Heller, played by Mason; and two vocal offerings by the basso Otto Feder—the *Romanza, O du mein holder Abendstern* ("To the Evening Star") from *Tannhäuser,* and a song *Feldwärts flog ein Vöglein* ("Toward the meadow a birdling flew") by Otto Nicolai.

Schubert's little-known quartet, wrote Hagen, blissfully basking in his native element, transcended mere music-making: it touched the deepest chords of the heart, causing the "sublimest thoughts of an elevated mind to vibrate in the listener long after the sounds have passed." The performance was superb: "The intentions of the composer were brought forward with such a noble spirit, in such an artistic manner, that the greatest attention and sympathy seemed to prevail amongst the listeners. . . . From an aesthetical point of view, the performance was faultless." If the first violin was somewhat lacking "in boldness and purity of sound," Hagen generously attributed the defi-

[198] More realistically, the idea of daytime concerts might have been suggested by the great popularity of the Philharmonic public rehearsals.

[199] "It was my purpose in organizing these concerts," wrote Mason, "to make a point of introducing chamber-work[s] which had never before been heard here, especially those of Schumann and other modern writers" (Mason, p. 195).

[200] Of the locally unknown names on this list: "Frank" was doubtless a typographically misidentified César Franck (1822–1890), Robert Volkmann (1815–1883) was an immensely popular composer in Germany, Brahms was, of course, the fledgling Johannes Brahms (1833–1897), Anton Rubinstein (1830–1894) was about to receive his first local performance at an Eisfeld *soirée,* and Franz Berwald (1796–1868) was the foremost composer in Sweden. It is not unlikely that Mason had encountered most, if not all, of these men at Liszt's home in Weimar.

[201] Except for the unconventional hour of their performance, and perhaps their more pronounced missionary intention, the general philosophy and content of the Mason/Bergmann matinées seem in fact to have differed little from Eisfeld's *soirées.*

[202] "I wished especially to introduce to the public the 'Grand Trio in B Major, Op. 8,' by Johannes Brahms, and to play other concerted works, both classical and modern," wrote Mason, "for this kind of work interested me more than mere piano-playing" (Mason, p. 193).

ciency to nervousness on the part of the "young and talented Thomas" (*Review and Gazette,* December 1, 1855, pp. 400–401).

But Henry C. Watson, at last restored to the world of journalism as the music critic and editor of the new weekly, *Frank Leslie's Illustrated Newspaper* (hereinafter cited as *Leslie's*)—after proclaiming (December 15, 1855, p. 10) that "all works are not classic which are written in classic form," and doubting that time would "accord that high term to some of the works selected for this occasion"[203]—condescendingly wrote that Schubert's quartet, although "a composition of much merit . . . does not rise above fair mediocrity. It contains nothing to call for particular remark, being rather pretty, ingenious, tedious, but certainly below the level of the classic standard."

Although Watson had admittedly approached Brahms's trio with a certain amount of preconceived prejudice—largely because Brahms was heralded in some quarters as yet another "prophet in the art"—on this, his first hearing of Brahms's music, Watson was "joyfully compelled to acknowledge that there was the ring of genuine metal in him." Brahms's ideas were fresh and originally treated, sometimes even to the point of grotesqueness. "We shall be much mistaken if we do not find in the future of Brahms that strong, clear light which shall eclipse the Wagner mining-lantern forever," wrote Watson.[204]

In the *Times* (November 29), Seymour half-mischievously assessed the social pros and cons of the afternoon-performance phenomenon, defining it as "a choice whipping together of the *créme de la créme* of public fashion and taste assembled in broad daylight." The audience of elegant women attending the first matinée demonstrated that to a certain part of the public "the half-dozen hours preceding dinner [were] a weary Sahara." The "gay display of female charms and furs" that completely crowded Dodworth's Hall had presented, he wrote, "a scene of great and novel interest."

Seymour had words of highest commendation for the quartet's performances: despite obvious nervousness they were "artistic, excellent, and faultless." Mason's solos were brilliant, although somewhat hampered by a piano with a "clipping, thin sound."

But it was the Brahms trio upon which his interest was focused. Seymour granted that it contained "many good points and much sound musicianship. It possesses also the defects of a young writer, among which may be enumerated length and solidarity. The *motivos* seldom fall on the ear freshly. They suggest something else that has been heard before, and induce a skeptical frame of mind, not altogether just, for the composer evidently has ideas of his own." The performance of this difficult work had been excellent. Mason, who was particularly lauded for his masterly playing of chamber music, had splendidly collaborated with Bergmann as well in their performance of Mendelssohn's *Variations concertantes.*

Hagen, after a lengthy, learned-sounding meander, concluded that, for all its faults—too "orchestra-like" writing for the piano, too great length, too little fluency—Brahms's trio was a remarkable creation for one so young (there was much divergence of critical opinion as to whether Brahms had composed it at the age of fif-

[203] The *Times* (November 29), on the contrary, found the choice of program "classical in the severest sense of the word." Indeed: "A slight admixture of something not German would have been a relief."

[204] The great Wagner controversy had apparently begun to cross the ocean.

teen, sixteen, or eighteen). More significantly, the trio faithfully bore aloft the eternal spirit of Beethoven.[205]

The only blemish upon this admirable occasion was Otto Feder's ponderous vocalization. Seymour found his *Tannhäuser* excerpt to be "simply heavy and unintelligible"; Hagen, however, credited Feder with "decidedly artistic feelings and a satisfactory method of singing, if [wistfully] he would only sing a little more in tune, sometimes."[206]

The second matinée, on December 18, drew another capacity house, again with "seven-eighths of the company being ladies." In fact, patronizingly wrote Watson (*Leslie's,* December 29, 1855, p. 42), "it was a pleasure to see so large an assemblage of elegantly dressed, lovely women displaying such earnest and intelligent attention to the highest class of musical composition."

The program comprised Beethoven's "Razoumovsky" Quartet in F, op. 59, no. 1 (1806)—a work that evoked much flowery introspection on the part of Theodore Hagen in the *Review and Gazette* (December 24, 1855, p. 431)—Schumann's Piano Quartet in E-flat, op. 47 (1842); Gounod's *Méditation* (1852) for piano, violin, and cello on the C-major Prelude of Bach's *Well-Tempered Clavier,*[207] played by Mason, Thomas, and Bergmann; and Chopin's Ballade in A-flat, op. 47 (1840–41), splendidly played by Mason. Summing up the performances, Seymour observed that it was almost unfair "to particularize any one artist for commendation where all labored so zealously, but we cannot help again expressing our satisfaction with Mr. Mason's admirable assistance at the piano. Classical chamber music is unquestionably this gentleman's forte, and we are inclined to think that he has no superior in America" (*Times,* December 18, 1855).

But Mason's supremacy was soon to be challenged by a far different breed of American pianist. On November 17, with elaborate Gallic fanfare, *Gamma* proclaimed in the *Albion* (pp. 547–48): "Gottschalk is in New York! We knew not where he was, and sighed for him, when we accidentally encountered him the other evening. Our delight at the encounter was great, for Gottschalk is not only in our eyes one of the

[205] But Burkhardt's musically learned stand-in, reviewing the concert for the *New-York Dispatch* (December 2, 1855) in Burkhardt's enforced absence, found Brahms's trio to be a flagrant example of the "ultra-new school" of composition and totally "beyond our powers of comprehension." And although the writer appreciated Schubert's classical form, his quartet was marred by "a visible straining after effect, giving an air of unnaturalness. . . . The dearth of melody is the greatest blemish and deficiency noticeable: this was quite apparent in the *Andante,* where, if anywhere, the composer is bound to display originality as a melodist."

[206] "The vocal pieces were inserted in deference to the prevailing idea that no musical entertainment could be enjoyed by the public without some singing," wrote Mason, but: "We quickly got over that notion, and thenceforth, with rare exceptions, our programs were [more] confined to instrumental music" (Mason, p. 195).

[207] The first public performance in the United States known to me of a work by Bach (albeit diluted and trivialized), or of one by Charles Gounod (1818–1893). Seymour (*Times,* December 18, 1855) was inclined to think lightsomely of Gounod's effort, comparing it to "the meditations of the elder Willett [?], who used to stare at a copper boiler without thinking of anything in particular. . . . By splitting up a good prelude into three parts, [Gounod] has neither improved the one nor made the others interesting," wrote Seymour. The other critics took the transcription more seriously.

most marvelous pianists of the present epoch, but he is also a composer of the first rank, a man possessing both head and heart, a poet, a genuine poet! Since Chopin, we know of no one so capable of filling his place as Gottschalk. Like his illustrious predecessor, he is really erudite in musical matters. Endowed with a memory more extraordinary even than his acquirements, it is impossible to name a piece before him that he is not able to play by heart from beginning to end. He overcomes the greatest difficulties with perfect ease; and with a fascinating Creole indolence, he drops from his fingers pearls, diamonds, and the most precious gems of sound. In hearing this incomparable pianist, we leave behind us this dull, prosaic planet and revel in a world of our illusions—listen to his *Bamboula*! What a charming Creole poem! And in his last and still more pleasant production, 'The Banjo' [op. 15 (1854–55)],[208] what a fiery, impetuous peroration! But if you would feel the tears well up from a long forgotten source, perhaps, however little you may have loved, and thereby have suffered, ask Gottschalk to play for you his Elegy ["The Last Hope"?], or one of his Ballads, and then tell us if it is not true music, ineffable poetry.

"Gottschalk is said to be American, but we do not believe it. His birthplace was the country of Poetry and Love, and his cradle the lap of the presiding Goddess of the Piano. If he were actually born in this country, his path would be strewn with flowers, from Boston to St. Louis, and would echo with acclamations of honour and triumph. But no! he is not American, not of the United States—otherwise, would he leave for Lima? And would there be no effort to retain him captive, by dint of chains of gold and garlands of flowers?"

Indeed, Gottschalk, who in utter discouragement was purportedly about to depart for South America, was rescued at the last minute by William Hall, who offered—not chains of gold or garlands of flowers, but, more welcome by far—publication of his music and backing for a concert at Dodworth's Saloon.

Things had not been going well for Gottschalk. In February he had returned to New Orleans from his first Cuban adventure in ill health and apparently without funds. In May he went to New York,[209] where he vainly tried to resume his interrupted concert career in his native land, and to find a publisher for his compositions. In his *Notes of a Pianist,* Gottschalk later recalls how, during this trying time, the music publishers Firth, Pond had bought a small, "melancholy piece" of his for $50, humiliatingly "advising me to endeavor to copy the style of the pianist Gockel, of whom a certain piece—how, I do not know—had just obtained a great run.

"At last one day," continues Gottschalk, "I played some of my compositions for Mr. Hall, the publisher. 'Why do you not give a concert to make them known?' he said to me. '*Ma foi,*' I answered him, 'it is a luxury that my means no longer permit me!' 'Bah! I will pay you one hundred dollars for a piano concert at Dodworth's Rooms,'" was Hall's reply.

[208] "The Banjo," subtitled "Grotesque Fantasie. American Sketch," op. 15 (1854–55) (D-15; *Piano Works,* I, 109). Published by Hall in 1855, its sheet music flaunts a distinctive cover resplendent with festive banjos, lithographed by J. C. Pearson. "The Banjo" is dedicated to Richard Hoffman.

[209] "We very much regret to hear that this distinguished American pianist [Gottschalk], the best our country has yet produced, is in a very precarious state of health. . . . He was lately in New York, at the house of a friend in Fourteenth Street, but has now returned South, or is about doing so" (*Musical World,* July 21, 1855, p. 134). Only a rumor.

To
Richard Hoffman.
GROTESQUE FANTASIE

Music Division, The New York Public Library

This was the crucial turning point: "Eight days later," continues Gottschalk, "I played my new pieces in this [acoustically and dimensionally ideal] small hall: 'The Banjo,' the *Marche de nuit,* the *Jota aragonesa,* and *Le Chant du soldat.*[210] My success surpassed my most brilliant expectations. During five months I continued, without interruption, a series of weekly concerts for the piano only,[211] in the same place, without being forsaken by the public favor. 'The Banjo,' *La Marche* [*de nuit*], and many other pieces bought by Hall were published [in 1855–56] and sold with a rapidity that left no doubt as to the final result of Hall's speculation, which time has only corroborated."[212] Signing Gottschalk to an exclusive publishing contract for the United States,[213] Hall bought back the "melancholy piece" from Firth, Pond—another fortunate coup, for the piece was "The Last Hope," op. 16 (1854),[214] a phenomenal bestseller of the nineteenth century. "I always kept at the bottom of my heart a sentiment of gratitude for the house of Hall, who first discovered that I was worth something," later wrote Gottschalk, lovingly enumerating the publishers he subsequently had the satisfaction of rejecting (*Notes,* pp. 48–50, entry for February 15, 1862).

Doubtless thanks to Hall's potent press-agentry, the journalistic quibblers of 1853 now unabashedly heralded Gottschalk's impending return as an event of major musical importance; thus, Dodworth's Hall was "literally jammed" at his first concert. And thanks to Henry Watson's item-by-item account,[215] we have a clue to the content of some of the unpublished, now lost, works that he performed on that occasion. With Carl (or Karl) Wels at a second piano, Gottschalk opened with his "Italian Glories," a fantasia on themes from *Norma, Lucrezia,* and *Sonnambula,* which contained "some facile and brilliant writing, and some wonders of execution by the author."[216] The following piece, "Fragments of the Fantasy on *Lucia,*" for solo piano (*c.* 1855, unpublished), consisted of variations on one or more themes from the opera, of which "the variation where the *tema* is accompanied by an unbroken scale throughout, ascending and descending, elicited unbounded admiration." Then came a group of original pieces: two ballades,[217] the *Marche de nuit,* and an unspecified mazurka. "The first ballad," wrote Watson, "was a delicious *morceau* of quiet but profound sentiment, the sec-

[210] *Marche de nuit,* op. 17 (1855); *La Jota aragonesa,* op. 14 (1855); and *Chant du soldat,* op. 23 (1855) (respectively, D-89, D-79, D-31; *Piano Works* III, 283; III, 223; II, 1). Not all of these pieces were played at the first concert.

[211] Here Gottschalk is stretching the truth: throughout his series he was invariably assisted by vocal and instrumental artists, usually pianists, to allow performances of his two-piano works.

[212] It was an ideal, mutually advantageous, self-perpetuating arrangement. No wonder Gottschalk's programs consisted almost entirely of his own compositions, disregardful of the critics who persistly censured him for neglecting the "classics."

[213] At about the same time, Gottschalk formed his equally felicitous connection with the house of Chickering.

[214] "The Last Hope" (D-80–81; *Piano Works,* III, 241). Published by Firth, Pond and Co. in 1854, and in a revised version by William Hall and Son in 1856.

[215] Watson's subsequent reviews in *Leslie's* provide an invaluable, albeit incomplete, chronicle of Gottschalk's extraordinary series as it unfolded.

[216] According to Doyle, this piece, D-76 in his splendid Gottschalk *Catalogue/Bibliography,* was derived from a work, or works, written about 1853 under Gottschalk's pseudonym "Oscar Litti." Unpublished, the manuscript has not been found.

[217] Probably "Ossian," subtitled "Two Ballades," op. 4, nos. 1 and 2 (1847–49) (D-109; *Piano Works,* IV, 177).

ond a quaint *tema* after the Spanish model—broken, half-uttered sentences, with that strangely characteristic, interrupted bass. The *Marche* was an exquisite reverie—sad, tender, and thoughtful—and the Mazurka eminently graceful and characteristic. These four pieces were performed to perfection; the thoughts literally sang themselves, and the audience listened with breathless attention, as though unwilling to lose a single sound. 'The Banjo,' which closed the first part, took the house by storm and drew forth a tumultuous encore. It is a composition so perfectly truthful that it almost becomes classic. We shall not attempt to describe it—to judge of its effect, it must be heard."

To open the second part, Gottschalk and Richard Hoffman played George Onslow's overlong Grand Sonata in E minor for one piano, four hands. "It was worth far more than the price of admission to hear these two great players together," wrote Watson. "There has never been such duet-playing in America." Then came "The Last Hope" (a sensation!), appropriately paired with Chopin's Funeral March in B-flat minor (1838).[218] With Joseph Burke, Gottschalk played a Mozart violin and piano Sonata in A, and to conclude, his own Fantasia on *La figlia del reggimento* (*c.* 1855, unpublished, manuscript lost), "a work of breath-taking brilliance."[219]

"We find in Gottschalk many characteristics in common with Chopin," wrote Watson. Although Gottschalk did not share Chopin's "high tone of classic thought," nor were his works likely to form the basis of a "school" of composition, he nonetheless possessed the "restless temperament, that same unquiet yearning, that constant reference to personal emotions . . . forming that subtle charm which few can define, but all must feel" (*Leslie's,* December 29, 1855, p. 42).

Theodore Hagen, emerging as a sort of junior Dwight, vehemently disagreed. In the *Review and Gazette* (December 29, 1855, p. 432) he wrote: "The time when pianists need only come forward with a fantasia on *Norma, Puritani, Lucia,* or similar favorite operas to raise a storm of applause and to be considered as great men is long since gone by." Nowadays it was required of a pianist, to prove his mettle, that he play the music of Liszt, Chopin, Schumann, and other moderns, and above all, of Beethoven. Not that he should entirely neglect his own compositions, but in the mere show of technical brilliance "there is no opportunity for the display of a higher order of artistic intelligence, a deeper feeling than mere outside effects require."

If Gottschalk, as it was rumored, could play "everything he chooses . . . why not, then, for his own sake and that of a better art than the one which his fantasias present, play something of the serious masters?"[220] Beethoven's later sonatas, or Chopin's ballades, or one of his "mighty polonaises, for instance, that in A-flat."[221] Hagen dismissed the non-Gottschalk works that he did play—Onslow and Mozart—as mere trifles that any ordinary pianist could have played equally well. Besides, in Gottschalk's hands—capable as they admittedly were—there was little variety of approach, be it Mozart, Onslow, or even Chopin. Despite his conceded mastery of the keyboard, Gottschalk was sadly lacking in Chopin's characteristics—both as composer and per-

[218] Incorporated by Chopin into his B-flat minor Sonata (op. 35) in 1839.

[219] For the complete programs of Gottschalk's sixteen *soirées,* as listed in the newspapers, see APPENDIX 5.

[220] For one thing, because they were not published by William Hall and Son.

[221] It was the critical hullabaloo over Jenny Lind's avoidance of the more substantial German classics all over again.

former—his tone, spirit, and harmonic treatment. Yet, all the same, Hagen was reminded of Chopin by Gottschalk's *Marche de nuit,* the only one of his compositions that exhibited "a real artistic feeling, elevation of mind, and some noble phrasing." Too, in his performance of "The Banjo," Gottschalk displayed aspects of individuality; "his nervous touch [evidently a highly admired pianistic attribute], his dashing, daring playing, his restless melodic phrasing . . . created really interesting pictures . . . of Southern life and negro enjoyments [belonging] to the soil and, at least, the traditions of its people."[222]

But to Seymour, who deplored the proliferating race of ruthless piano-thumpers whose performances had become an endurance contest between performer, piano, and audience, Gottschalk possessed not only exquisite sensibility and immense mastery of the keyboard, but an "unequivocal manifestation of genius—nonetheless genuine that it is peculiar [meaning individual]." Contrary to his earlier fault-finding, Seymour now pronounced Gottschalk's playing to be brimming over with "inner meaning and suggestiveness. All his wonderful mechanical skill and dexterity are kept in the background by the strong and impalpable force of a predominant idea," wrote Seymour. "Those flying chords; those odorous chromatic scales; those zephyr-like tremolos; those perfectly spiritual arpeggios, leaping up to Heaven like a flame from the altar; those passionate combinations struggling for mastery like man's desires: why, they all seemed as simple and wholesome, to our mind, as truth itself." Every sound that Gottschalk produced was marked by a "remarkable individuality, all his best thoughts are uttered in a language of his own." Loud or soft, one drank in the "luxury of this new quality of sound"[223] (*Times,* December 22, 1855).

Of Gottschalk's pieces heard at this first concert, Seymour, too, singled out the *Marche de nuit* as "a composition not unworthy of Chopin himself, whose style it resembles. In this work Gottschalk displayed an unequaled breadth and vastness"; he performed "'The Banjo' in a way that no one else can hope to approach." Seymour was "also delighted" with "The Last Hope," describing it as a "lamentation of decidedly Hebrew character."

Gottschalk played to an even larger and more ecstatic audience on December 27. His program was announced to open again with his "Italian Glories," with Wels at the second piano; then his *Danse des sylphes (d'après Godefroid),* op. 86;[224] the *Andante con variazioni* and Finale of Beethoven's "Kreutzer" Sonata with Joseph Burke (announced but not performed);[225] and, to complete the first part, "The Banjo." The second part included the *Jérusalem* Triumphal Fantasy, with Richard Hoffman at the second piano,

[222] *Gamma* (*Albion,* December 15, 1855, p. 595) suggested that "The Banjo" had been inspired by the banjo virtuosity of Thomas Vaughn of Christy and Wood's Minstrels. That Gottschalk made the piano sound uncannily like a banjo was reluctantly conceded by Dwight's New York correspondent, but wasn't it a desecration of a beautiful Chickering grand to put it to such use? (*Dwight's,* January 5, 1856, p. 108).

[223] "Gottschalk's *soirée* was a perfect success," reported the *Spirit of the Times* (December 29, 1855, p. 552). "He is undoubtedly one of the first executants of the age."

[224] A transcription of a piece for harp by the Belgian composer/harpist Félix Godefroid (1818–1897). Composed *c.* 1853, Gottschalk's transcription (D-40; *Piano Works,* II, 127) was posthumously published by Schott in 1877.

[225] "The one interesting piece in the programme, which could have attracted the attention of the artist, was left out," carped Hagen (*Review and Gazette,* January 12, 1856, p. 3).

three solo pieces by Gottschalk—an unspecified Ballade, the *Marche de nuit,* and the *Souvenirs d'Andalousie,* op. 22 (1851)[226] (also omitted)—and, for finale, Weber's *Concertstück* (as in 1853, he played only the second and third parts) with Hoffman supplying the orchestra accompaniment at the second piano.[227] For an encore, reported Seymour (*Times,* December 29), he played "'The Last Hope,' a composition so perfectly spiritual and admirable that it should never be withdrawn from the program" (and it rarely was); as a substitution for the missing *Souvenirs d'Andalousie,* Gottschalk repeated a portion of his Grand Fantasie on the *Daughter of the Regiment.*

The *Danse des sylphes,* wrote Seymour, "enabled Gottschalk to introduce some of his best *arpeggio* and *pianissimo* effects and to revel in that calm and graceful luxuriousness of style which he alone possesses." But the great feature of the concert was the *Concertstück,* "a composition that seems to enjoy a perfectly perennial vitality." Often played, but rarely with the "completeness of detail" (if not of text) it received from Gottschalk, "we have never heard it given with such delicate perception of meaning and masterly elaboration of effect. . . . Every remembrance of other pianists pales before the perfect pleasure we enjoyed from this performance."[228]

The critic for the *Spirit of the Times* (January 5, 1856, p. 564), too, having heard "all the great players, who, during the past fifteen years have exhibited in this city, [accorded] the palm to this gentleman. For depth of feeling, liquidity of touch, marvels of execution, easy accomplishment of great difficulties, and variety of tone, his performances are, in our estimation, unrivaled," he wrote. The *Marche de nuit,* "the gem of the program," and Gottschalk's performance of it, entitled him to "a place among the best classic music executants and authors, [as did] 'The Banjo,' the most Gottschalkish piece of the evening."

But the *Evening Post* (December 29), Hagen-like, caviled because, "with one single exception, the compositions were all from Mr. Gottschalk's pen. His ubiquity in the program was wearisome." And although he played with "the same surprising dexterity and strength of hand and wrist which have made him famous, by giving greater variety to the program, by recognizing the works of other and more celebrated masters than himself, and by calling in the aid of other instruments than the piano, Mr. Gottschalk may make these *soirées* as pleasant as any concerts in the city and might easily fill Dodworth's room once a week, at least, with the friends of Apollo."

Willis, although disappointed at the omissions and substitutions, made allowances for them because Gottschalk had reportedly risen from a sick-bed to play his second concert. "But it was hardly a sick man's playing that was offered, being "*à la* Gottschalk throughout in fire, precision, and force." Indeed his style was "*sui generis*—his own. His compositions evince decided individuality—nationality," wrote Willis. "This trait none can dispute him." And his playing! "His fluency of style is remarkable, even in

[226] *Souvenirs d'Andalousie,* published by Hall in 1855 (D-148; *Piano Works,* V, 211).

[227] Played far too fast, in Hagen's opinion, thereby lessening the "intended effect of the composer," albeit a display of "the wonderful bravoura for which [Gottschalk] is distinguished."

[228] But Dwight's New York correspondent "——t——," although he had never heard Gottschalk's equal "as far as mechanics is concerned," except perhaps Liszt, found his performance of the *Concertstück* to be far from that of a true artist, for—echoing Hagen—"though its technical execution was wonderful, it was very much wanting in fire and inspiration" (*Dwight's,* January 5, 1856, p. 108).

these days of remarkable pianoforte fluency. The instrument talks, *breathes* under his hand—and what more can an instrument be made to do? One thing more, doubtless—*interpret*. . . . That Mr. Gottschalk interprets his own compositions successfully no one will doubt. How he would succeed with other compositions, particularly with the older and more significant masters, we are not prepared to say" (*Musical World*, January 5, 1856, p. 1).

Thus did Gottschalk's admirers and detractors mingle their agreements and differences. His avoidance of the classics, despite the cavilers, by no means deterred his ardent worshipers—mostly female and fashionable—from flocking to Dodworth's Rooms week after week and month after month, as his unprecedented series progressed.[229] Louis Moreau Gottschalk, with his thrilling music, his "fascinating Creole

[229] It did not harm attendance that ladies were admitted at half price, an example of Gottschalkian gallantry at its most astute.

Louis Moreau Gottschalk

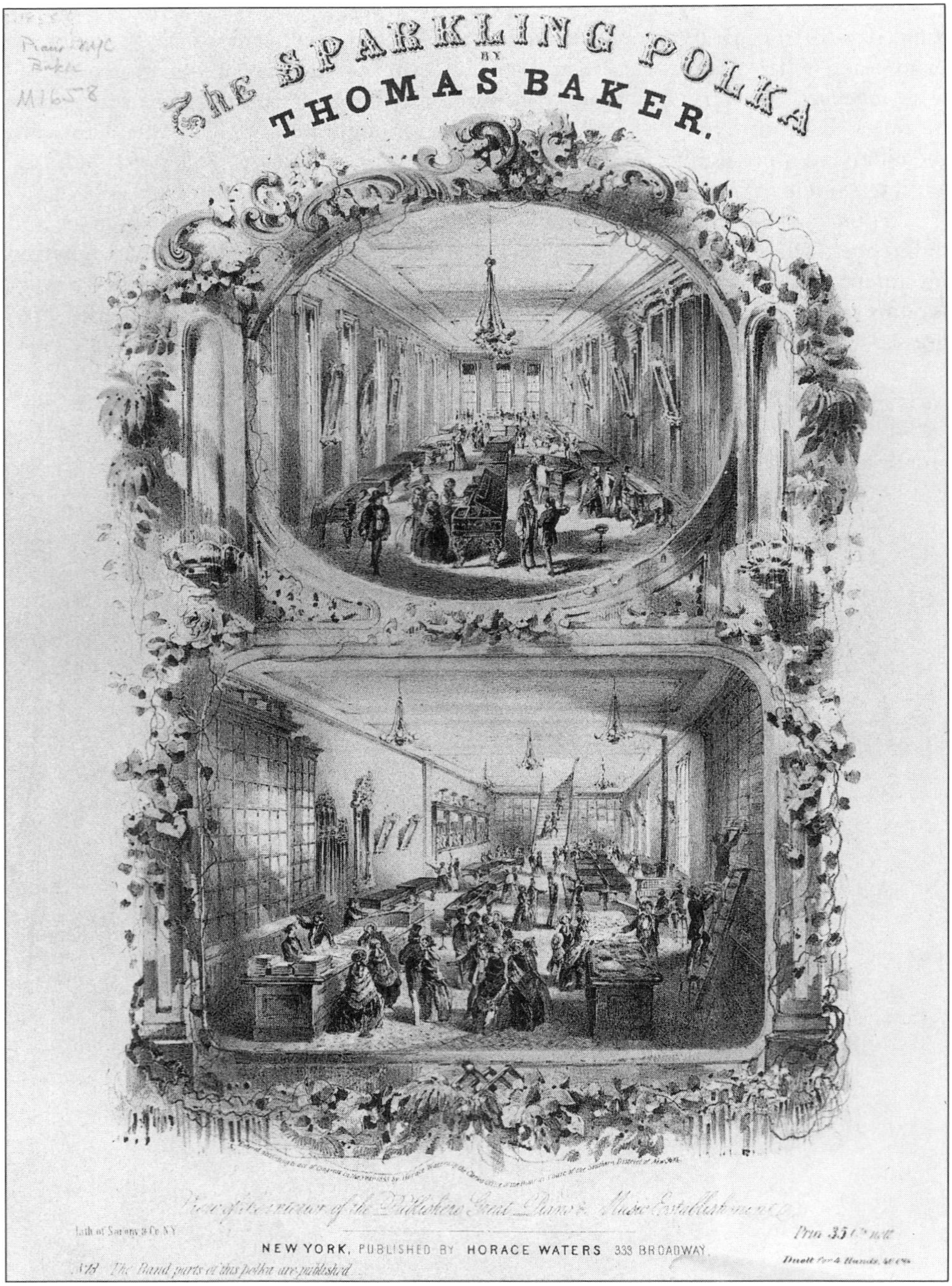

New-York Historical Society

The sheet music cover for Thomas Baker's "The Sparkling Polka" attractively depicts the interior of Horace Waters's versatile establishment, with piano showrooms above and a well-patronized music store below.

7

GTS: 1856

Italian Opera is a necessity of civilized life. Without it, refinement languishes and hides itself in solitude and commonplace. . . . Where can you see so many pretty girls, so many handsome men, so many admirable coats, so many unimpeachable neckties, as at the Italian opera? Where can you find a fashion-plate vitalized, except there? Where can you practice virtue and study morality so excellently as in the lobby of the Academy, where everyone looks down upon you? Everything that is refined, from patchouli *to* Lagerbier *can be found at our Academy.*

New-York Daily Times
March 13, 1856

With the discontinuance in 1856 of his treasured Mass-meetings, Strong depended for musical sustenance almost entirely on the rehearsals and performances of the Philharmonic Society and the Eisfeld chamber-music *soirées;* only on rare occasions did he attend an extra concert or visit the (continuingly turbulent) Fourteenth Street Opera House, as the Academy of Music was commonly called. If anything, Strong's musical tolerance had grown narrower and more rigidly fixed than before. Sometimes, in the privacy of his journal, he expressed his dislike of a work or a performer in somewhat less than elegant terms.

January 14, 1856. . . . The Philharmonic [January 12 at Niblo's Theatre] was a fair concert. Overture to *Euryanthe* good, of course, but there's very little of it—it's a flash of beautiful light—over in a minute.[1] Berlioz's *Francs-Juges* is ponderous.[2] There were a couple of solos from Mercadante and Verdi, better rendered than they deserved,

[1] And that precious minute was marred by the boisterous mass exit of the huge audience, seemingly as avid to depart as they had been to arrive. A "frenzied American crowd," wrote *Gamma* (*Albion,* January 19, 1856, pp. 31–32), had stormed Niblo's portals "a full half hour before their opening," resulting in an "inevitable demolition of hoops," the current "framework of feminine society." This situation called loudly for "atonement" in the form of a more spacious concert room. Indeed, it was the general cry; more space was needed—if not for the crinolines that were currently all the rage, then certainly for the spectacularly increased Philharmonic audiences.

[2] Although Berlioz's Overture to *Les Francs-Juges* (*Frances Tufes* in the published *Diary,* II, 251) had occasionally been performed in New York since its Philharmonic premiere in 1846, the critics mostly continued to regard it and its composer as musical monstrosities. Despite Berlioz's "marvel-

by Badiali.[3] Also a dismal, flatulent "Concertino" for the horn, by Weber [op. 45, in E minor (1806, revised 1815)], but suggestive only of the murmurings and vocal cadences of one's alimentary canal after an indigestible dinner:[4] "*Concerto pathétique:* The Colon and its Functions"; "*Andante con variazioni:* Beans!" The program should have been modified to state that "the composer in this piece for the first time attempted, and succeeded, in producing the effect of full chords on the instrument,"[5] and *also* of sub-acute colic on a double-barreled cock-rhinoceros, or a mild cathartic on the Siamese Twins. Its *binomial* character was marked: what seemed its chief feature was an uncertain, tremulous duplication (a third below, or something of that kind) of its forlorn, feeble, ventriloquial wail.

Whoso would hear Weber's Concertino for the Horn, let him stand awhile near one of Delmonico's tables where two obese Frenchmen are picking their teeth and glowering at each other in silent repletion after a special little dinner, silent but vocal—saying naught, but eloquent within. So Alp speaks unto Alp. One might modify Tennyson's "Bugle Song"[6] to suit Weber's Concertino.

I don't think any profession or art can furnish so many and so stupendous specimens of idiocy and imbecility as Music. Weber, who wrote *Der Freischütz* and *Oberon* and *Euryanthe* and *Preciosa,* actually perpetrated and published this foppery!

Gade's Symphony is sneered at by the critic of the *Evening Post* as merely "pretty."[7] Perhaps he's right. But it (at least its first half) is *very* pretty—and clear—and genial. I'd rather hear it than lots of things that Spohr and Mendelssohn have writ-

---

ous, almost *diseased,* perception of instrumental effect," wrote Seymour (*Times,* January 15, 1856), he lacked the gift of melody. The *Evening Post* (January 14, 1856) avowedly preferred Berlioz in his persona of "brilliant, discriminating, and candid musical critic of the *Journal des Débats* [to the] *composer of strange music.*" Henry C. Watson, who over the years had vainly tried to like this overture, now gave it up as "a rambling, unmeaning composition—grandly instrumented, of course—but beyond the conception for ordinary musical comprehension" (*Leslie's,* January 26, 1856, p. 106).

[3] Cesare Badiali (*Badish* in the published *Diary,* II, 251)—who had not returned to Europe, after all—was the hit of the evening with his marvelous performances of the *romanza, Ella piangea,* from Mercadante's *I Normanni a Parigi* (Turin 1832), and the cavatina *Il balen del suo sorriso,* from *Il trovatore.*

[4] Strong, who suffered from chronic dyspepsia, on occasion evoked gastro-intestinal images for his more vivid musical denunciations.

[5] As the Philharmonic program note explained, Weber's multiphonic effects require a technique of mingled blowing and humming, or singing "through the nose," according to the *Musical World* (January 19, 1856, p. 25). However, two simultaneously sounded pitches do not a triad make, and the disapproving reviewer supplied musical examples of intervals to illustrate that fact. According to *Gamma,* the work was excellently well played by the Philharmonic hornist Henry Schmitz, but "some very appalling chords [and thirds] were the result"; Seymour, who in any case disliked the French horn as a solo instrument, described the effect as "very unpleasant"; Dwight's New York correspondent dismissed it as "ludicrous" (*Dwight's,* January 19, p. 127; *Albion,* January 19, pp. pp. 31–32; *Times,* January 15, 1856).

[6] Blow, bugle, blow, set the wild echoes flying,
Blow, bugle; answer, echoes, dying, dying, dying.
Tennyson, *The Princess* (1847), Part III

[7] Finding the Gade Symphony lacking in the massiveness requisite to a proper symphony, the *Evening Post* critic (January 14, 1856) explained that its musical themes, albeit "quite pretty in themselves . . . gave an impression of delicateness, prettiness, and littleness to the whole composition—qualities which . . . are not to be sought for and admired in a symphony." Hagen concurred, referring to Gade as "a painter in miniature," but, in essence, "nothing but Mendelssohn with a Danish soul and Danish views" (*Review and Gazette,* January 26, 1856, p. 18).

ten. And I'd be willing to compare its Scherzo with a good many of Haydn's, though I suppose nobody holds Haydn in higher esteem than I.[8]

January 28. . . . Eisfeld's concert last night [third concert of the sixth series].[9] Haydn Quartette No. 57 [op. 54, no. 1, in G major (1788?)], wonderfully fresh and genial, full of various and beautiful phrases of melody, the Adagio and Finale particularly good. Mendelssohn's Trio, op. 49 (piano, violin, and violoncello, in D minor) [1839] not satisfactory or suggestive. Its rendering may have been faulty: the piano part was muffled and muddled and obscure, from a defect in Chickering's instrument or want of power in Mrs. [William Vincent] Wallace.[10] Beethoven's Quartet (E-flat, no. 10) [probably the "Harp" quartet, op. 74], much elaborated and full of originality, but I don't want to hear it again were it twenty times Beethoven's.[11]

So people pass offhand judgment against works which I know by abundant experience may be found full of beauty unutterable when heard once more and better understood. But has an *artist* the right to send out creations which do not even suggest (to one very willing to be a believer) that they can do anything but bore and puzzle?

~

Bereft of his Mass-meetings, Strong fantasized a compensatory Super-Mass—an ultimate collaboration with Haydn—to be performed at a kind of Super-Mass-Meeting, convened exclusively for the enlightenment of 75 or 100 of Strong's more musically underprivileged friends.[12]

February 5. . . . Philharmonic Society said to have bought Philip Hone's house (Broadway and Great Jones Street), and to propose the erection of a music hall. I'm exercised by the problem whether it be feasible *(if we are alive and well and prosperous)* this time next year to get up a Mass of Haydn's on those premises, with full orchestra and a chorus of 16 or 29 and an audience of 75 or 100. It would be a charity, or missionary movement, to proclaim to our music-loving friends who sit in Darkness and the shadow of Donizetti a musical revelation beyond their dreams. I would make up the Mass thus-wise: *Kyrie* [from] No. 3 ["Lord Nelson" or "Coronation" Mass]; *Gloria* and *Credo,* No. 6, [*Harmoniemesse*] except the *Et vitam venturi,* which should be substituted from No. 16 [*Theresienmesse*]; *Sanctus,* etc. No. 6; *Benedictus,* No. 4 [*Schöpfungs-*

[8] As a composer of scherzos?

[9] According to *Gamma,* a frothy spirit, the Eisfeld *soirées* "metamorphosed" Dodworth's festive Saloon "into a school of conscience, fidelity, and all the model virtues . . . and while there, one becomes sober and virtuous, in one's own despite. Consequently, the audience is composed of good husbands, accomplished women, young girls who are troubled with no frivolous inclinations, and bachelors who deserve to be Benedicks" (*Albion,* April 5, 1856, p. 164).

[10] Although Mrs. Wallace was "recognized as the *only* pianist of the gentle sex in the country," wrote Watson, a Wallace devotee, she was "evidently not in full practice; this was evidenced . . . in a comparative weakness in her right hand . . . in the first movement"; she regained her customary spirit, force, and brilliancy in the following movements, however, and it was pleasant to see Dr. Stoepel's look of pride as he turned the pages for his gifted daughter (*Leslie's,* February 9, 1856, p. 135).

[11] The program included as well two new quartets for male voices by Eisfeld: *An die Entfernte* ("To the Absent One") and *Lebewohl* ("Farewell"), sung by Beutler, P. Mayer, J. E. Meyer, and Oehrlein. "Charming compositions, badly rendered," commented Watson *(ibid.).*

[12] A concept that would eventually materialize in 1870 with Strong's founding of the ultra-exclusive Church Music Association.

messe] (or No. 16), and *Agnus Dei* and *Dona* [*nobis*] *pacem,* or (if the keys of F and C major were not an objection) of No. 2 [*Missa in tempore belli*]. That would make a magnificent Mass, and the want of unity would not be much felt.

Expecting to bask unimpededly in the radiance of Haydn and Beethoven at Eisfeld's concert, Strong was rudely exposed to the distasteful antics of Gottschalk, and duly protested.

February 24. . . . Eisfeld [fourth *soirée*] last night. Tolerable concert. Haydn Quartette No. 78 [op. 76, no. 4] in B-flat (think I've heard it before) and Beethoven's Quartette No. 9 in C major [perhaps the "Razoumovsky" Quartet, op. 59, no. 3] were the features of the concert. Both worth hearing, but neither seemed entirely characteristic of its author. The former was very satisfactory, though—especially its Andante and Finale. Herr Otto Feder did some creditable singing,[13] and Gottschalk (with an order in his buttonhole) gave an unfortunate piano fits with a hysterical scherzo of Chopin's [op. 31, in B-flat minor (1837)]. He was honored with a double encore, and played first a sledgehammer Fantasia,[14] which may have been meant to depict the bombardment of Sebastopol—and if so, was a creditable composition—and second, a composition, judiciously chosen to show off by contrast the performer's delicacy of fingering, the subject of which was manifestly this: "The Traveler having gone to sleep in the depths of a tropical forest is gradually awakened by ants and other bugs crawling over him." It was an admirable musical expression of the sensation produced by the pressure of a lively bug or bugs down one's back.[15] Perhaps music might aim at some higher result, with advantage, but I don't know. Gottschalk is universally conceded to be a prodigiously great "Artist."

And unswervingly admired by Watson, who in his report of this event in *Leslie's* (March 8, 1856, p. 199) wrote: "The inimitable Gottschalk played the *Scherzo* by *Chopin, op. 31,* in an irreproachable manner[16] and elicited an enthusiastic encore" (Liszt's Berlioz transcription). It created "quite a furor, and in obedience to the continued plaudits, Gottschalk played again, and was listened to with an almost breathless

[13] In a greatly improved performance of the air "God, have mercy," from Mendelssohn's *St. Paul;* he also sang "Doth she ever think of me," a "mawkish" German song by Proch.

[14] Liszt's 1854 transcription of the *Bénédiction et serment (Benediction and Sermon)* from Berlioz's *Benvenuto Cellini* (Paris 1838). Gottschalk had performed it "magnificently" at Dodworth's Saloon the night before (February 22) at his sixth *soirée,* wrote Watson. "Great as we knew his power to be, we were surprised on this occasion into additional wonder. He interpreted his author in a kindred spirit which would have rejoiced the many-handed Titan, Liszt himself" (*Leslie's,* March 8, 1856, p. 199). But *Gamma* thought it a waste of Gottschalk's individuality to expend himself on such "terrible" music as this of "Liszt engrafted on Berlioz. . . . Mr. Gottschalk should borrow only from himself." And *Gamma* lovingly enumerated Gottschalk's three felicitous styles of composing: his thrilling two-piano fantasies, his seductive Spanish and Creole pieces, and his dreamy elegies and ballades (*Albion,* March 1, 1856, pp. 103–4).

[15] Strong had affixed this entomological scenario to "The Last Hope."

[16] But in Hagen's severe opinion: "Mr. Gottschalk played . . . Chopin's difficult Scherzo, Op. 31, more abruptly than even Chopin's music can endure" (*Review and Gazette,* March 8, 1856, p. 70).

LMG with his medals.

attention. This triple encore was the highest compliment that could be paid to the genius of Gottschalk. It was the most flattering acknowledgment of his wonderful powers that has yet greeted his career in America, for it was not conferred by an audience specially convened to listen to him, but one accustomed for years to consider and scrutinize works of the highest character and performances of the topmost merit."[17]

As to audiences "specially convened to listen to him," there seemed to be no limit to their number or their unquenchable ardor.[18] By now Gottschalk had given the sixth in his phenomenal series of concerts—after the second he had announced that "encouraged by his reception," he would delay his purportedly imminent departure for Europe (or Lima, as the case may be) in order to satisfy the flattering demand for more.[19] The demand seemed endless.

[17] "We are curious to know," gloated Watson, "what Mr. Dwight of Boston, who publishes a journal of his own peculiar opinions upon musical matters, thinks of this particular opinion of this same Gottschalk. The unlettered Dogberry [in Shakespeare's *Much Ado About Nothing*], in the height of his indignation, wishes heartily that some one were by to write him down an ass—there are men more learned than Dogberry who do this for themselves without the aid of a second party."

[18] "He has taken New York fairly by storm; it is very long since anyone created such an enthusiasm," wrote Dwight's New York correspondent (March 1, 1856, p. 173). "All young ladies in their teens are said to be desperately in love with him." (To say nothing of his notorious, if insufficiently substantiated, affair with the flamboyant poetess/actress/journalist Ada Clare, known as the "Queen of Bohemia.")

[19] At first he had intended that "these performances shall not be only of musical interest but of instructive tendency—an exemplification, in fact, of the different styles of piano-playing. . . . The series of concerts [would] be completed in one month—two or three coming off each week. Some [would] be *matinées,* others *soirées*" (*Times,* January 11, 1856).

"Public appreciation seems finally attending to Gottschalk (it has taken a somewhat stupid while to do so)," wrote R. Storrs Willis after Gottschalk's second concert (*Musical World,* January 26, 1856, p. 37). "He is fast growing into his proper sphere—the sphere long accorded to him in the artist-world abroad—as one of the first living pianists."[20] His compositions were not like anyone else's, nor were his concerts.

Gottschalk's programs typically opened with a brilliant curtain-raiser, usually one of his own transcriptions, assisted at a second Chickering by Richard Hoffman or Karl Wels, or one of Gottschalk's younger disciples: Candido Berti, of frustratingly undisclosed origin, or the Americans, T. Franklin Bassford and Harry Sanderson. Each program contained one or two groups of Gottschalk's own characteristic and fascinating piano pieces, and each closed, of course, with a blockbuster finale, usually an opera fantasy of his own or Liszt's (or a mixture of both), or else the second and third sections of Weber's apparently inexhaustible *Concertstück* (accompanied by a second piano). Within this basic framework were interspersed short offerings by various assisting artists, among them the violinist Joseph Burke,[21] the harpist Aptommas, the violinistic Brothers Mollenhauer, and the singers Vincenzo Morino, Otto Feder, Henriette Behrend, Oswald Bernardi, Eliza Wallace-Bouchelle, Emma Gillingham Bostwick, and Anna de LaGrange.

Gottschalk had no qualms about repeating the same works, concert after concert, nor did his admirers ever tire of hearing him play them. Indeed, his audiences invariably demanded their favorite pieces, calling out their requests, a practice Gottschalk invited—usually for the *Marche de nuit,* "The Banjo," and "The Last Hope."[22]

For his fourth *soirée* (January 31), Gottschalk, for once departing from his pattern, announced an unconventional all-Hispanic program—half-Iberian and half-Caribbean—"dedicated to the Spaniards and Cubans." Except for the opening piece, a *Marcha triunfal* for two pianos composed by T. Franklin Bassford and played by Gottschalk and Berti, everything on the program was composed or arranged by Gottschalk. The novel event was even advertised in Spanish.

The capacity audience, although largely composed of foreigners—mostly Spanish and Cuban—surprisingly found this unrelieved ethnicity to possess a monotonous "sameness of character." But not for long. As Watson tells it (*Leslie's,* February 16, 1856, p. 150): "The Second Part, although it commenced in the Cubano style, very

[20] And besides, wrote Willis: "Personally, we know Gottschalk to be a man of *ideas;* and he could talk off to us a much more brilliant article on Art than we could possibly write. . . . He is the sort of man we should like to engage as a contributor. . . . What say, Gottschalk?"

[21] Burke was apparently not a placid performer: "When our esteemed Burke takes part in such music as this," wrote the *Spirit of the Times* (February 2, 1856, p. 612), after he and Gottschalk had at last played the Andante and Finale of Beethoven's "Kreutzer" Sonata at the third *soirée* (January 25), "he seems to lose sight of all else, and his movements of body would seem to indicate to those 'unknowing to his ways' that he was at great pains to accomplish the task. So far from this, it is the intensity of his pleasure which carries him away."

[22] Hall's publications of these works were soon announced in Gottschalk's concert advertisements. By February 14 (advertising the fifth concert), for instance: "A new and correct edition of the 'Last Hope' is in course of publication. It will be published exactly as played by Mr. Gottschalk, and the difficulties of execution will be much less than in the old [Firth, Pond] copy. Inquire for Hall's new and only correct edition. The 'Marche de Nuit' will also be published in a few days, and may be found at the music stores."

soon changed its character, as various requests from the audience for certain pieces were acceded to by Gottschalk. First he performed in most magnificent style Liszt's arrangement of *Lucia di Lammermoor;* then his own exquisite *Romanza* 'The Last Hope,' which is, to our mind, one of his most chaste and thoughtful compositions. He also performed his dreamy Creole ballade *La Savane,* which was very cordially received, and then dashed into his dazzling fantasie founded on themes from *La figlia del reggimento.* 'The Banjo' was, of course, given, and the tumult of applause which greeted its close proved that its popularity is as great as ever."[23]

Gottschalk, resilient showman that he was, had grandly risen to the occasion: "Never in public or in private have we seen him so entirely abandon himself to his subject as on this occasion," writes Watson. "He fairly reveled in his work, throwing into it the whole force of his mental and physical energy. He literally held his audience spellbound—so much so that we verily believe he could have chained them to their seats by the magic of his music for some hours longer. We have rarely seen an audience so fascinated and delighted."

Not so George Templeton Strong.

March 1. . . . Gottschalk's [seventh] concert Thursday night [February 28]. . . . Absurd crowd, idiotic excitement, infinite bother in getting seats for the ladies.[24] Any blacksmith excels this wretched, diminutive, Jewish-looking coxcomb in strength of muscle; many mechanics could surpass his nicety and quickness of manipulation, and there was nothing in his performance save his combination of a coalheaver's vigor with an artisan's dexterity. Music there was none. He pounded his piano and tickled his piano with wonderful energy and delicacy, and that was all. He showed that he had the mechanical capacity to execute music by performing certain tedious phrases of elaborate nonsense, which the crowd took for music and applauded accordingly, instead of rising like one man and one woman and kicking him out of the concert room as a profane puppy desecrating a noble art—doing his best to delude people into acceptance of his frivolities for Truth—and sacrificing Music, of which his profession makes him an Apostle, to the display of his own personal prowess and skill.

Last night Timm was here playing four-handed music with Ellie—Gade's Symphony, Mozart's in B-flat [G minor], and one of Haydn's—and beating me cruelly at chess afterwards. Very pleasant evening. . . . Philharmonic concert this evening. Ellie went without me. Its great feature was a Symphony of *Bristow's,* which I deliberately shirked. Tolerable music is not to be endured: a decent and creditable symphony is an abomination and an offence.

[23] "Mr. Gottschalk has given two other crowded concerts," reported Hagen's gossip column in the *Review and Gazette* on February 9 (p. 34), "one of which was very curious, as it exhibited, according to the programme, nothing but Spanish and Cuban music. Amongst the latter, we heard Liszt's Fantasia on *Lucia,* with some alterations by the concert-giver."

[24] The ladies who attended Gottschalk's concerts, a tough breed, were evidently able to shift for themselves: "Crammed, jammed, squeezed, and overheated were the devoted disciples of the Prophet Gottschalk," wrote Watson (*Leslie's,* March 8, 1856, p. 199), reviewing the sixth *soirée.* "As we ascended the stairs [to Dodworth's concert room], we had an elevated rear view of a row of ladies [in

As we know, Bristow and the Philharmonic Society had made up their differences some time since, and this performance of his "Jullien" Symphony, op. 24, was evidently something in the nature of a peace offering on the part of the Society. Although the critics more or less automatically professed to encourage performances of American music, it was at best lip-service: their actual responses to such infrequent American performances as were given were usually a mass of reservations, if not downright disdain. Thus, the critical reactions to Bristow's symphony were generally patronizing—polite on the surface (except for the growingly cantankerous, and growingly visible, Hagen) but by no means enthusiastic. Watson pontificated on the several requisites of successful symphony-writing, eventually boiling them down to two: "*Genius,* to conceive; and *Knowledge,* to carry out." And, he weightily added, "Genius is a rare gift, and consequently great symphonies are few." Undoubtedly, Bristow was a painstaking musician and an able orchestrator and all that—his work had pleasing, if not distinctive, melodies—it was a praiseworthy effort—but it possessed no individuality. And besides, knowing when to stop was a problem that Bristow had obviously "not yet solved." The overlong work was successful in parts, but it was by far not a symphony (*Leslie's,* March 15, 1856, p. 215).

Willis—taking issue with the title "Jullien" Symphony (after all, Jullien was "not very *symphonic* in his musical attitude in the artistic world" but rather a "professor of the polka and the waltz, the incendiary-and-fire-engine style"), and deploring the excess of "*talk obbligato*" in the overcrowded hall, that drowned the first movement of Bristow's symphony—at last proceeded to give a movement-by-movement rundown of the work, complete with musical examples and learned German locutions. Taken all in all, wrote Willis, "the work needs scissoring, and suffers from excess of modulation and from lack of harmonic unity" (*Musical World,* March 8, 1856, p. 110).

But Hagen the supercilious, although he recognized the "obligation to encourage the efforts of American composers," strongly resented the wanton waste of precious Philharmonic time and substance "on account of our patriotism. . . . Certainly the works of our own composers must have a chance to be heard somewhere," he conceded, "but can it not be in some other place than just where only the purest taste and the greatest finish in our art ought to prevail? If our composers can not rival the renowned masters of instrumental music, then let them be heard in our theatres between the acts, or in the promenade concerts, where they may give pleasure in the appropriate frame in which they appear."

Bristow's symphony was doubtless the laudable effort of an honest musician who was constantly trying to improve himself, condescended Hagen, but the value of what he wrote did not bear severe scrutiny: "All goes on with as little artistical effort as possible, reminding us of the so-called symphonies of Küffner and similar composers,[25] whose compositions were formerly played by some bands of amateurs, or in some garden concerts." Bristow's symphony started out well, but it degenerated from movement to movement, until at last we heard "only noise, no music." Too, Hagen depre-

crinolines], who, standing upon benches, not only barricaded the door, but prevented even a glimpse of the interior of the room. The many, who having bought tickets returned home unable to gain admission, grumbled considerably, but will probably attend Gottschalk's next *soirée*."

[25]Josef Küffner (1777–1856) was a minor German bandmaster and composer.

cated Bristow's introduction of a "polka" in the Scherzo—or rather Andantino—intended in a sense to parallel Haydn and Mozart's use of contemporary dance forms in their symphonies.[26]

Bristow was, however, not the only object of Hagen's disapproval: Mendelssohn's *Capriccio brillant,* played by Richard Hoffman, was a work of "very uninteresting character";[27] Joseph Burke "did not satisfy us" in his performance of Mendelssohn's Violin Concerto; and the audience again behaved unspeakably in their frenzy to depart, despite an intermission of five minutes provided before the final number—William Sterndale Bennett's overture *Die Waldnymphe* ("The Wood Nymphs")—so that those wishing to remain might hear it undisturbed. But the noisy exodus only continued; indeed, wrote Hagen, "there was far too much moving about during the whole concert" (*Review and Gazette,* March 8, 1856, pp. 68–69).

To William Henry Fry, however, the mere fact that the Philharmonic had programed Bristow's Symphony represented a heroic triumph, and one that, Fry-like, he claimed for himself: "Some three years since, we agitated a reform for the Philharmonic Society, that its character should be made to accord with its charter—by laws providing for the performance of original works composed in this country.[28] Mr. Bristow afterwards took up the matter in a series of letters, followed by his resignation from the Society" (discussed in OBBLIGATO: 1854).

Fry was willing to make allowances for foreign musicians who preferred to listen to the masterworks of their former compatriots, but he found it most discourteous of them not to "seize any opportunity, with exuberantly magnanimous interest, for the distinction and liberty which our glorious institutions alone guarantee to them . . . we might think that the foreign members of the Philharmonic would rush to do honor to the musical works of the country of their adoption, which has elevated them to the rank of citizens and gentlemen in their own right." But Bristow's music had been shunned by the Philharmonic Society until Jullien had "taken hold" of him and even played some of his compositions in London.

"The price of the creative faculty," wrote Fry in perpetual self-commiseration, "is the penalty of not being readily sustained where the cooperation of others is necessary." It was not that American listeners rejected native music. Such self-performing American composers as Gottschalk and Mason who, unlike Fry, needn't depend upon collaborators for the performance of their works, enjoyed the unlimited enthusiasm of local audiences. "It is simply the want of proper gentlemanlike feeling on the part of

[26] Willis detected in it a resemblance to a schottisch, probably intended, he wrote, as a reference to Jullien.

[27] It apparently pleased the audience, for Hoffman was required to play an encore, the Fantasy on *Rigoletto* by Jaëll, as unattractive as the Mendelssohn *Capriccio,* wrote Hagen.

[28] Burkhardt was quick to pounce on Fry for coolly" assuming the "sole patronage and all the credit of encouraging 'native' talent," when it was he, Burkhardt, who for years past had championed the cause of the American composer and conductor at the Philharmonic. In vain: the Society had stubbornly clung to "one man power," particularly in the case of conductors (meaning, of course, Eisfeld). Bristow's symphony was a fine effort, wrote Burkhardt, even if he persisted in squandering his thematic resources—"using up his ammunition too soon"—then needing to resort to elaborate padding "to fill up the requisite number of music pages." Yet, Burkhardt would willingly "award the palm of superiority to the American original composer over the English imitator of Mendelssohn," William Sterndale Bennett (*Dispatch,* March 9, 1856).

Academies of Music and Philharmonic Societies that there actually at this time is not a rich repertory of American works," wrote Fry.

Then an emotional outburst—an unbridled outpouring of Fry's most devouring frustrations: Genius would not forever tolerate being slighted, he defiantly asserted: "It will not brook the opposition of every fool in its attempts to reach the public. . . . It will not flatter to gain a point. Without vanity it knows its own resources, for it is the province of one man of genius to see more deeply than millions without it, and to hold the opposition of mere pretension at defiance." Only with an organized barrage of such defiance and the public's corroborative insistence would we at last, season after season, regularly hear the symphonies and operas composed by Americans.

And how did this fiery champion of American music review his colleague and countryman's symphony? In the first place: "The form of the symphony has nothing new in it. It is safely in the beaten track, with the tonic and dominant relations, the four separate movements, and so forth. . . . You can always tell what he is driving at. The first movement is in triple time, and would very well pass for an established classic." But it was in the second movement that Bristow, following a "hint we had expressed long ago for the laws of progressive esthetics in music," made his only approach to innovation with his use of a polka-like motive, in lieu of the trite and obsolete minuet of Mozart and Haydn. Indeed, with its "piquant and graceful" theme, the polka was the "best hit" of the symphony. The slow movement was "a little muddy as to its leading melody," and Fry proceeded to instruct how it could be improved so as to "please all parties." The last movement, however, was more satisfactory, being "particularly well stocked with modern effects; much violinism of wide extent as an accompaniment, sonority of climax, and greater vigor than Mr. Bristow has hitherto exhibited. The whole was well received, and constituted an era in the annals of the Society" (*Tribune,* March 3, 1856).

With John Ruskin a growing influence on contemporary thinking—volume three of his five-volume *Modern Painters* (1843–60) had just been locally issued by John Wiley—Strong, a faithful disciple, more and more tended to soar amid lofty Ruskinian immensities.

March 2. . . . Ruskin opens a query in this volume that has exercised me before now: How do you know that hillside and river and forest are entitled to awaken in you these emotions of joy and veneration? Homer and Dante, better and greater men than you, would have been unable to comprehend your raptures over a mountain gorge or a woodland clearing. Till the last seventy years the feeling was unknown—never expressed, at least; it is genuine with you. But is not its very reality a sign of sentimentalism—a badge of unfruitfulness and of incapacity to bear fruit? Does it not stamp your nature as being unable to *do works* of righteousness, and as substituting for efficient *action* the aesthetic contemplation of the Works of God?

It is a grave question. The same query may be made and must be answered about Mozart's and Beethoven's music—about the C-minor Symphony itself and [Haydn's] 6th Mass. They are beautiful, but so are the fleeting forms of radiant cloud that wait on the setting sun. Are they realities which men should study and reverence, or mere graceful forms of perishing mist?

ἀλλ οὐράνιαι Νεφέλαι, μεγάλαι θεαὶ ἀνδράσιν ἀργοῖς,
αἵπερ γνώμην καὶ διάλεξιν καὶ νοῦν ἡμῖν παρέχουσιν
καὶ τερατείαν καὶ περίλεξιν καὶ κροῦσιν καὶ κατάληψιν.[29]

March 8. . . . Yesterday we dined with Kuhn, and Ellie and Mrs. Isaac Wright. Kuhn and one Hewitt sang bosh from [presumably Verdi's] *Corsaro* [Trieste 1848] and *Masnadieri,* and [Donizetti's] *Anna Bolena.* This evening Mrs. Gibbs was here reading music with Ellie.

March 17. . . . Apropos . . . one of Edgar Allan Poe's hideous stories I've just read for the first time, "Adventures [*sic*] of Arthur Gordon Pym":[30] There are "artists in hair," *vide* newspaper advertisements, *passim,* and artists in dexterity and muscular strength, *vide* Gottschalk's concerts, so I suppose Poe may be called an artist in putrefaction (both moral and material)—in foetor and charnel house effluvia.

March 22. . . . Tonight with Ellie and Miss Rosalie to Eisfeld's [fifth] concert—tolerably good. Concerto [Sonata] (MS) piano and violin, Pychowski, composer and pianist [with Noll playing the violin], very bad.[31] Rubinstein's Quartette (op. 17) improved on acquaintance, the second and fourth movements are vigorous. Selection of movements from Haydn, *et al.,* was quite satisfactory: Allegro from Haydn's Quartette No. 63 [in C, op. 64, no. 1], and Adagio from Beethoven's ["Sixth"] Quartette [of op. 18] were delightful.[32] Noll played badly, probably a "little drunk."[33] "*Quel diable de charivari,*" said a tall Frenchman, as we came out, "they made of the Andante (Rubinstein)."

March 29. . . . Went with Ellie to the Philharmonic rehearsal, hoping to hear Beethoven's B-flat Symphony [No. 4, op. 60 (1806)], but they did not play it. Mendelssohn's "Melusina" Overture [op. 32 (1833)] and an overture of [Heinrich] Marschner's *(Hans Heiling)* [Berlin 1833] were rehearsed. Either Bergmann, the leader, was captious, or the orchestra was stolid, for never were two compositions so fussed over. The orchestra could not play ten bars without being brought up by a rap from the conductor's baton, and I got nervous, at last, and tired even of the beautiful, characteristic phrase with which the "Melusina" begins. Though not of the same order or of like

[29] "The clouds most holy, clouds in heaven, great deities for idle men—it is they that bring us fancy and opposition, wit and fairy tale, sophistry, chicanery, and challenge" (Aristophanes, *The Clouds,* vv. 315–18).

[30] First published in 1838, Poe's novella *The Narrative of Arthur Gordon Pym of Nantucket* had recently (March 1856) been reissued by Redfield as part of a collection of Poe's works.

[31] Despite Pychowski's "clever playing and two or three points of exceeding beauty" (albeit "rare as springs in the desert"), his violin and piano sonata was "incomprehensible" to Watson; it was a work devoid of all meaning. Up-to-date Watson decided to designate it as "classical," a term that in the future, he predicted, would commonly be applied to music that was "dull, tedious, form without substance—scientific but soulless" (*Leslie's,* April 5, 1856, p. 263).

[32] This potpourri additionally comprised separate movements from Mozart and Onslow quartets—admirably played, despite their "lack of oneness," wrote Watson *(ibid.).* Dwight's New York correspondent (March 29, 1856, p. 204) heartily disapproved, finding the effect disjointed and unsettling, as did Hagen for more exalted reasons. He mildly praised Maria Brainerd for her performance of Beethoven's *Ah! perfido* and a song "Our Home" by her teacher Dr. Clare Beames, with Beames at the piano (*Review and Gazette,* April 5, 1856, pp. 98–99).

[33] Drunk or sober, "Mr. Noll is an excellent Quartette player, but he does not appear favorably as a Soloist," commented Watson.

glory with the *Midsummer Night's Dream* and "Fingal's Cave" overtures, that is a very nice composition. As to the *Hans Heiling,* it struck me as a very successful attempt at imitating the style in which great composers have expressed great musical thoughts, but without any musical thought whatever. So elaborate, so carefully studied, so much in earnest is Mr. Marschner's work that one insensibly takes it for granted (unless one has heard other productions of his) that he must have something valuable to tell—but he hasn't. His learning and industry have reproduced something like the armor of Achilles, but the arm and the heart of the hero are wanting.[34]

April 8. . . . Murray Hoffman[35] dined here yesterday, and we heard *Don Giovanni* thereafter in Fourteenth Street, about which opera I could write much, were it not late and were there need for dribblings of dilettantism about Mozart's transcendent power and fertility.

With this performance of *Don Giovanni* (a benefit for LaGrange) an apparently chastened William H. Paine bade farewell to the glamorous world of opera, ostensibly waiving the final month (or months) of his lease of the Academy.[36]

[34] Had Marschner been endowed with "humor and brilliant imagination, invention and skill"—and had he composed operas based on better librettos—and had he better studied the requirements of the stage—he might have been a worthy successor to Weber, wrote Hagen in his review of the concert (*Review and Gazette,* May 3, 1856, pp. 131–32).

[35] A lawyerly colleague and friend of Strong's.

[36] "Mr. Paine had already sold one of his houses during the season to meet the losses," wrote Maretzek, "and when at the close he had to sell another one, Mrs. Paine, according to rumor, only gave her consent . . . on condition that he should give up that funny business of managing opera" (*Sharps and Flats,* p. 20). Maretzek states that Paine's lease ran out in May; it continued, in fact, until the following October (if not longer) and Maretzek's subsequent two seasons might have been effected by means of a mutually advantageous subleasing arrangement with Paine.

Adelaide Phillips, budding American prima donna.

Music Division, The New York Public Library

Having returned from their tour in early March in an unaccustomed state of solvency,[37] Paine's splendid company, with the addition of the young English-born, Boston-bred contralto and future diva Adelaide (sometimes called Ada) Phillips (or Phillipps),♪ [38] had been heard not only in the obligatory repertory—*Trovatore, Lucia,* and *Lucrezia*[39]—but, as the high point of their short, ineptly timed season,[40] had unfurled Luigi Arditi's new "American" opera *La spia.*

But first, about Adelaide Phillips: she had only recently (1855) returned from three years in Europe, where, on the advice of Jenny Lind, she had been sent by caring Boston friends, among them Jonas Chickering, for advanced vocal study with Lind's teacher Manuel Garcia. Lind herself had purportedly contributed the generous sum of $1000 and a letter of recommendation to Garcia. Young Adelaide Phillips, a former dancing and singing prodigy, had been a favored daughter of Boston since her childhood appearances at the Tremont Theatre and the Boston Museum (*Dwight's,* September 15, 1855, p. 188). Following her less-than-auspicious debut (as Signorina Fillippi) in Italy—at Brescia and Milan—and faced with scant prospects of a promising future in European opera, Phillips sensibly returned to Boston. After a return concert at Music Hall and participation in various local music events, she finally (doubtless for pecuniary reasons) joined an English-opera venture, appearing in such superannuated chestnuts as Horn and Braham's *The Devil's Bridge* (London 1812), the pastiche *The Cabinet* (London 1802), and Linley's *The Duenna* (London 1875). Maretzek probably heard Phillips while in Boston, and, about to lose his star contralto, he engaged her for the coming season in New York.

Phillips's debut at the Academy, as Azucena in the opening-night *Trovatore,* was unfortunately twice delayed. Due to her ill-timed indisposition (and Brignoli's), the opera opening was postponed from March 11 to March 13,[41] when Phillips, still unable to appear, had to be replaced by Zoë Aldini.[42] It was not until March 17 that "the Boston Lassie" finally appeared—in the third *Trovatore* of the short season.

Although Phillips received a predominantly cool critical reception, Richard Storrs Willis pronounced her Azucena (despite a wobble here and there) to be vocally and histrionically superior to both Vestvali's and Didiée's (*Musical World,* March 22, 1856, p. 135). And William Henry Fry, who described her voice as a "mezzo-soprano of excellent quality, round and sympathetic," wrote: "Her intonation is good, her method Italian, and her readings correct. Her appearance and bearing are much in her favor"

[37] Paine was rumored to have cleared some $20,000 on the season in opera-loving Boston alone.

[38] Replacing Nantier-Didiée, who upon the termination of the tour returned to Europe.

[39] With LaGrange arousing ever greater astonishment by her perfect vocal and histrionic artistry in whatever she attempted, but also with her unfailing graciousness and good humor, and her perfect, indestructible health—never missing a performance for any reason whatsoever.

[40] "The present opera engagement has opened in the midst of Lent, which has closed the doors of the fashionable world against the usual gaieties of the season, and will doubtless produce its effect, especially during the coming Holy Week, the last in Lent, upon [opera] attendance" (*Evening Post,* March 13, 1856).

[41] "It was very unwise policy to commence the Spring season of the Italian Opera with a disappointment," chided the *Mirror* (March 12, 1856). And scarcely the way to "create public interest in the opera."

[42] If Aldini was not as sensational an actress as Vestvali, she gave a more vocally correct rendition of Azucena, indeed, it was second only to Didiée's, wrote the *Mirror* (March 13, 1856).

Music Division, The New York Public Library

Luigi Arditi, composer of an overpatriotic "American" opera.

(*Tribune,* March 18, 1856). Fry congratulated the "good city of Boston" on the successful debut of its gifted daughter; he gave no hint, nor did Willis, of the excessive nervousness that, according to Seymour and Watson had—among other defects—marred her performance.

But Hagen, apparently unaware of Phillips's study with Garcia, found her to be "deficient in method, having the appearance of a self-taught vocalist." Although her debut was a success, he found her singing to be "at times heavy" and detected "a disposition to sing not exactly in tune." Yet, about-faced Hagen, Phillips possessed a "very fine, deep-colored mezzo-soprano voice, [albeit] not of great natural compass"; her conception of the role was "superb, and there is not the least doubt that she is a very gifted dramatic singer" (*Review and Gazette,* March 22, 1856, p. 84).

Immediately following Phillips's debut, performances at the Academy were discontinued for the duration of Holy Week, fortuitously allowing extra time for rehearsals of Arditi's opera *La spia.* With its Italian libretto by Filippo Manetta loosely adapted from James Fenimore Cooper's novel *The Spy* (1821), it was heavily touted as a fervently patriotic American opera. Following its successful premiere on March 24, Easter Monday, the reviews, all bulging with lengthy synopses of the plot set in Revolutionary America, praised Arditi's operatic expertise—especially his instrumentation, his choral writing, and his easy and flowing, if derivative, melodies.[43] But while the critics unanimously predicted enduring success for *La spia,* they also agreed that it lacked originality.[44] ("It is all the more charming for its want of originality," babbled *Gamma.*)

[43] So Donizettian as to provide a "real storehouse for organ-grinders and composers of potpourris and piano fantasies," wrote Hagen (*Review and Gazette,* April 5, 1856, p. 100).

[44] "It is full of reminiscences of other composers," wrote ——t——. "Weber, Mendelssohn, Spohr, Haydn, Mozart, and I know not what others seem to be playing ball with snatches of their

Most sharply criticized was the work's overpeppered patriotism, which, according to Seymour (*Times,* March 25, 1856), "insists on bursting out on every unfortunate opportunity. Everything is sacrificed to the patriotic exigencies of the moment. Consequently, the three acts are precisely similar in their passional characteristics. . . . The play begins with Dragoons and Skinners,[45] goes on with Dragoons and Skinners, and ends with Dragoons and Skinners." But despite critical disapproval, the finale, an unprepossessing treatment of "Hail, Columbia," brought a cheering audience to their feet.[46]

And why, indignantly demanded Richard Grant White in the *Courier and Enquirer* (March 25, 1856), was this work represented as an American Opera? "Because its subject is American? Then is *Don Giovanni* a Spanish opera? *Norma* a British opera? *Semiramide* a Babylonian opera?[47] . . . Written by an Italian to Italian words, in the Italian style, for Italian singers,[48] there is not even the shadow of a ground for calling *La spia* an American work. Let us not deceive ourselves. It is well for the arts to flourish here, but it is not well for us to be deluded with the idea that we have American art, when we have no such thing, but are cultivating an *exotic.*

"The time will come," predicted White, "when we will have American music, but it will *come;* we cannot bring it, or hasten its arrival. There has yet to be the first step taken towards the formation of an American school of music. All the music which has been composed here, worthy of the name, has been of necessity German or Italian, whether written by Germans or Italians or Americans, and so it will be for long years to come."

But Fry (*Tribune,* March 26, 1856), in a triumph of convoluted reasoning (extreme even for Fry)—although he pronounced *La spia* to be an Italian opera written in the Italian language by an Italian composer—perversely hailed it as an American opera be-

---

melodies, and seem to be tossing them to and fro in merry confusion" (*Dwight's,* March 8, 1856, p. 180).

[45] American guerillas active in Westchester County during the Revolutionary War—both Republican and Loyalist—were known as "Skinners."

[46] "The opera closed with 'Hail Columbia' and the reading of a letter signed George Washington, at the mention of whose name three cheers were inevitable," wrote Willis. "Such is our nationality just now, that it were not difficult to fancy an entire opera composed upon the name of George Washington" (*Musical World,* March 29, 1856, p. 145).

[47] To which an enraged Burkhardt indignantly replied: "The fact that the subject is strictly American, that it is patriotically so (which alone would make the opera American) goes for nothing with the learned critic; the facts that the libretto was written here, every word of it, that the music, every note of the whole work, was written and conceived here, and by resident producers [albeit not naturalized citizens], have all nothing to do with it, in the critic's opinion. . . . Does the critic possess a German overcoat because his New York tailor employs a German journeyman to make it, or French dickies because a French laundress attends to them?" (*Dispatch,* March 30, 1856).

[48] Not precisely so. Purportedly written especially for the Academy of Music (perhaps originally as an entry in Ole Bull's American opera competition?), *La spia* was performed by a mixed cast: LaGrange, superb as Maria, mother of the Spy; Brignoli as Harvey Birch, the Spy; Elise Hensler as Francesca Wharton, fiancée of Carlo Dunwoodie, Colonel of the Virginia Lady Washington Dragoons, portrayed by Morelli; Gasparoni as Wharton, Francesca's father; Quinto as Lawton, Captain of Dragoons; Müller as Dr. Sitgreaves; and Angiolina Morra as Betta, a *vivandière.* Arditi conducted; Allegri designed the sets and was responsible for a spectacularly realistic conflagration, which in the second act destroyed Wharton's house.

cause it had been composed in America. Indeed, he even took credit for having recommended its production at the Academy after having examined three of its pieces while still in manuscript. And here it was—a success.

"We have," wrote Fry, "in opposition to the habit hitherto pursued at the American Academy of performing exclusively European operas, held uniformly that the American public are just as ready to listen approvingly to a work of American musical art, or one composed in this country, as to a foreign one, and," he added, "it only required a manager here with a speck of brains to prove the fact. Mr. Paine happily possessed the comprehensive understanding to rely on the judgment of technical criticism."

True, confusedly (and confusingly) backtracked Fry in a mingling of logic and nonsense, *La spia* was not *really* an American opera, "the composer being an American neither by birth nor adoption, but it has been evoked in this country by the means available for musico-dramatic presentation. This shows, too, an improvement on the very mean and squalid exclusiveness heretofore exercised by musical establishments in New-York toward works composed here" (yet another reference to *Leonora,* a perpetually open wound).

And back to the old refrain: "Grand operas have been written in this country twenty years ago which never have been heard in New-York, owing to the want of liberality on the part of managers, and the want too, of a lively sense of justice on the part of the public, who should call for original works. Had there been common honorable fairness exercised toward composers in this country during that time, as many good operas as Europe has produced in the same period might have been composed here—but how can there be supply without demand?

"We hope therefore that the innovation at the Academy that Mr. Paine inaugurated . . . may lead to a systematized production at that establishment of opera composed in this country. Two or three new grand American operas should be given each year at the American Academy of Music . . . without interference to the claims of European composers of popular and standard works. Until this is done, there can be no American school of music."

La spia received five consecutive performances,[49] the fourth for Arditi's benefit.[50] Then, after closing presentations of *Il trovatore* on April 4, again with Adelaide Phillips, and the *Don Giovanni* on April 7 (attended by Strong),[51] the Italian opera again found itself, to quote Hagen, in a "tight place. Each new day brought a rumor of some new attempt to 'establish the lyric drama in America.' To go on at the old rate was not to be expected; Mr. Paine had already made unprecedented sacrifices, but was still willing to meet the artists, orchestra, and chorus halfway. Amid these negotiations, Italian op-

[49] To exemplary audiences composed of "Merchants, Lawyers, and Judges, with a sparse sprinkling of Clergymen," reported the *Mirror* (March 27, 1856).

[50] Following which Arditi returned to Italy for a brief stopover before taking up a conducting post in Constantinople. He would not return to the United States until 1878.

[51] And by a "crowded audience with a very uncomfortable proportion of standees." Resuscitated from the past, Attilio Arnoldi, the Don Ottavio, "neither knew what to say (being entirely ignorant of the part) or how to act"; and in the final scene, "the single imp who came to bear off the wicked Don . . . pitched heels over head in running after the Don, who thus doubtless made his escape, after all" (*Musical World,* April 12, 1856, p. 173).

era took a rest until Wednesday, April 16, when the indefatigable Max Maretzek[52] once more stepped into the breach[53] and [with reputed "strong backing behind the scenes"] commenced a [four-week] season of Italian and German opera[54] with Verdi's *Ernani*" (*Review and Gazette,* April 19, 1856, p. 113). As Richard Grant White commented: "With the experience of the past winter before him, [Maretzek] is brave to tempt fortune. . . . At any rate, we thank him for the opportunity of hearing *Ernani* again" (*Courier and Enquirer,* April 16, 1856).

George Templeton Strong attended the opening for sentimental, if not musical, reasons.

April 17. . . . Last night to the Opera House with Ellie and Miss Betty Rhinelander. . . . *Ernani.* We sat in the balcony—just in the locale of my Astor Place seat in '48—and at the end of the third act, when Morelli (or whoever it was)[55] was proclaiming his *"Carlo Magne—Gloria ed onor,"* and in the keen phrases of the solos in unison and the heavy chords of the chorus that follow and make up the very effective finale of that act, I felt as if I were in Astor Place again, and Miss Ellen Ruggles was over there on my left on her papa's sofa, and old Peter Schermerhorn on the sofa in front, and Mrs. Mary Jones and Miss Emily in their box just behind me. I was walking homeward down Broadway again in a kind of delirious whirl—with that music ringing in my ears—and thinking whether I should "call tomorrow night."

April 19. . . . Tonight with Ellie, her mother, and Miss Mary Bostwick to [the] last Philharmonic concert of this season, at Niblo's. Vast crowd, of course; all the little music-studying girls and all Young America, their lovers and friends.[56] We had to take

[52] Hardly had Paine relinquished the Academy, writes Maretzek, than "I was actually waited upon by Messrs. Phalen, Coit, and W. C. Wolfe, with the request to continue the present season for some time longer, and the inquiry whether I would take the lease for the next theatrical year" (*Sharps and Flats,* p. 21).

[53] As a last resort. "It is rumored that the season just inaugurated by Mr. Maretzek is to be the final experiment with the Academy," reported the *Times* (April 16, 1856). "They *do* say that in the event of its failure, the building is to be turned over to a charitable object, a hospital, we believe. . . . We wish a better fortune for Mr. Maretzek, but if the wish be fruitless and the event unhappy, we shall think the Academy condemned without a fair trial, unless the seats reserved to stockholders be abandoned, and the doors be opened to the public at the usual theatrical charge."

[54] "The old troupe is kept much as it was," wrote Hagen, "and additions are to be made: Coletti and Bolcioni are already announced, while hopes are held out of Badiali and the Signoras Vestvali and Parodi upon their return from the South." German operas would be given on Saturday evenings, with LaGrange singing the starring roles (in German). Ticket prices ranged from the usual dollar admission, with 50 cents extra for secured seats, to 25 cents for the amphitheatre.

[55] The singers were LaGrange, Morelli, Coletti, and Bolcioni, standing in for Brignoli, whose horse had fallen on the slippery Russ pavement on Broadway, thereby causing a waggish journalist to remark that "Horseness is very unfavorable to tenors."

[56] The Philharmonic had by now become the favorite hangout of the city's teenagers: "It was crammed, jammed, steaming hot, noisy, and uncomfortable," wrote Watson. "The entire youthful population of the city was present. All the ladies . . . were under eighteen years of age, and all their male accompaniments . . . twenty or twenty-one. Those are the recognized Philharmonic ages. . . . Not only were all the regular seats occupied, but the lobbies were filled by the youthful musical enthusiasts seated on chairs and arranged in groups of from four to ten, enjoying the Beethoven accompaniment to their chit-chat and tittle-tattle. . . . It had been suggested that another Society should be

the very highest seats (third gallery, or Cock-loft, in the [illegible] of a Diaboli, according to Mr. Prynne),[57] the best places in the house, however, for hearing an orchestra. Beethoven's Symphony in B-flat [No. 4], a tedious, fragmentary concerto by the inevitable and merciless "Brothers Mollenhauer,"[58] and some Verdi, sung by Badiali—and he couldn't have sung it better, had it been worth singing, which it was not in the least.[59] These made Part I. Then came Mendelssohn's "Melusina," which was refreshing, and some tolerable Mercadante by Badiali, and then we came off, without hearing the Second Revelation of Art by the Mollenhauer fiddles, or the final Marschner overture.

I don't think I ever heard this B-flat Symphony in any shape, or heard anything about it.[60] By some fatality I've missed it at all the rehearsals for this concert. It plainly belongs in *time* to Beethoven's first period for many of its phrases, and, I think, its principal subjects are in the spirit of Mozart and Haydn, only worked up with an originality and disregard of conventionalism and freedom of fancy that its first audience probably thought erratic and extravagant. Its tone and sentiment are light for Beethoven. The D-Symphony I don't know very well, that in F still less, but the former is far more earnest, even in the magnificent phrases of the first movement; and the joyousness of the "Pastorale" is the short-lived exultation with which the man of cares and sorrows forgets them all in his holiday. This composition seems without much trace of Beethoven's depth and intensity, but it is most lovely. I think one might well call it the most "brilliant" and "pleasing" of all his works I've the happiness to know—the gayest and brightest. A careless smile from Beethoven is worth something! One prizes *L'Allegro* more because Milton wrote it. . . .

[gratefully meditating on the rich bounty of natural beauty bestowed on humankind by a beneficent Creator] . . . it seems to me that in all [the] multitudinous testimony to the goodness of God, the *Existence of Music* speaks with the loudest and clearest voice. That mere inarticulate noises—grouped together and combined according to laws He has impressed on them should have the power so to speak to the inmost soul and heart of man—always with a message of infinite, ineffable beauty—always bearing gifts beyond articulate speech—always suggesting impulses toward what is good and pure and gentle and without reproach—that out of the notes of the musical scale a feeble and foolish biped can construct the music of Mozart and Beethoven—*there* is indeed a gratuitous gift to man, such as only Good Will to Man could have prompted. For the whole system, for aught we can see, could have got on as perfectly well without it. Sun and moon and tides and oxygen and carbonic acid and the

---

started, to be called the 'Old Philharmonic,' to which mamas and papas should be eligible" (*Leslie's*, May 3, 1856, p. 327).

57 Presumably William Prynne (1600–1669), the fiery, anti-theatre Puritan pamphleteer of the English Restoration.

58 Only one of the "unspeakable Mollenhauers," Edward, played the first movement of Vieuxtemps's Violin Concerto in E, op. 10. In the second part of the program they were heard together in a Grand Duo of brother Frederick's devising.

59 In the first part Badiali sang a *scena* and aria from Verdi's *Attila;* in the second, by request, he repeated the *romanza, Ella piangea,* from Mercadante's *Normanni a Parigi.*

60 It had been played by the Philharmonic in 1849, during a period when Strong had absented himself from the Society's concerts.

vegetable system and the annual system and the various parts of each and the "social machine" and all the rest of the Universe would have been as harmonious and wonderful and beneficent and effective had these marvelous properties and capacities not been given to Sound—had Music not been possible.

Further, this act of Bounty is to us alone, to men and to no other earthly thing. Elsewhere, beauty is mostly an accessory of utility. Most beautiful things have their tangible work to do and their place to fill. Their existence was necessary to the system of which they are part, and we wonder less at their beauty because they could just as easily have been made beautiful as not. The lovely landscape feeds the cattle on a thousand hills—the plants of the greenhouse and the meadows have each its special form of animal life to sustain—the splendid Brazilian butterfly plays its subordinate part in the great system of checks and balances—without it, some insectivorous bird would be unprovided for, and the disorder would spread till animal life was extinct. But Sound seems consecrated to Man alone. Only for our sake has this latent power been given us to develop—only for us has the wonderful *Extra-World* of Musical Expression been made possible.

April 23. . . . Have just got through my first hearing of *William Tell*[61] at the Fourteenth Street Opera House with Ellie and Miss Mary Ulshoeffer. The two ladies had a nice time, but this opera doesn't attract one much; and if I didn't know its high repute and take it for granted that it would develop its merits on further acquaintance, I should say it was very heavy, dreary, and dull, without a trace of Rossini's fluency and freshness, without a single sharp-cut, definite musical thought (except the familiar old hand-organ melody in the third act)—without unity, breadth, or even effective contrasts. I don't wonder now that people rejoice over *Lucia* and *Ernani,* if this be a type of the music that preceded them. Handel's *Deborah* [London 1733] would be light and sparkling after this monotony of smooth-spoken commonplace.

April 24. . . . Ellie went to Gottschalk's [fourteenth concert][62] tonight with George Anthon. I couldn't well go, as I ought to have done, and I hate Gottschalk's profanations of music: dirty antics and dexterities that crowded audiences admire and applaud, as if they were manifestations of Musical Art and not mere exhibitions of mechanical skill and muscular strength. They are to Music what an acrostic (or "Peter Piper picked a peck of pickled peppers") is to Poetry and Eloquence.

April 26. . . . Have been with Ellie to Eisfeld's tonight. Decidedly a capital concert. Mozart's Quartette in B-flat, No. 3,[63] was lovely, particularly the clear, melodious first Allegro, built on a few exquisite phrases of simple song, such as nobody but Mozart ever wrote. How different his gaiety is from Haydn's—and Beethoven's![64] Haydn enjoys himself like a man of human cares and ties and interests and sympathies, with

[61] This was the third attraction of Maretzek's season—the second was *Il trovatore,* performed on April 18 and 21 by LaGrange, with Aldini as Azucena (Adelaide Phillips having departed), Brignoli (evidently recovered from his "horseness"), Amodio, and Coletti. The cast of *William Tell,* besides LaGrange, included Bertucca-Maretzek, Bolcioni, Amodio, Coletti, and others.

[62] The assisting artists at Gottschalk's fourteenth concert, as usual an overcrowded triumph, were Mrs. Bostwick and Candido Berti.

[63] Presumably the "Hunt" Quartet, K. 458, number four of the "Haydn set."

[64] Strong increasingly tended to indulge in this little ritual of bestowing comparative character traits upon his favorite composers.

a healthy mind, a sunshiny temper, and a sound digestion. He is the honest, hearty German paterfamilias, almost Philister [Philistine], happy in the work that gives his babies their *butterbrot,* never dwelling on the past, and saying of the future (with [the German poets] Matthias Claudius [1740–1815] or [Gottfried August] Bürger [1747–1794], or somebody), "*therefor let der liebe Herr Gott sorgen.*" It's his normal state to be laughing in a kindly, wholesome, genial way.

Beethoven is self-conscious, earnest, intense, ever thinking of the perished past and the possible future and the infinite abyss that underlies the present moment, and he laughs seldom. When he does, he surrenders himself to the unwonted stimulus and sings a wild dithyrambic, full of power and inspiration, but from which one half shrinks back as if the singer were "fey."

Mozart's good spirits suggest a retiring, thoughtful scholar and poet, who can be joyous and genial but is always a little above the common level of humanity, full of thoughts a little too pure, "too bright and good, for human nature's daily food," and always blending unconsciously with the jest and licence of his most thoughtless hour a little sadness, a little souvenir of the past, a little suggestion of something deeper than mere downright free-hearted fun.

As to Handel, I never heard him laugh, and can't imagine that phenomenon any more than I can conceive of Isaiah and Ezekiel cracking jokes over oysters and Scotch ale. Rossini and Co. laugh as people do in drawing rooms and boudoirs.

Certainly, the hearing of music stimulates the secretion of Bosh.

Besides the Mozart Quartette we had a Trio of Mendelssohn's [in C minor, op. 66 (1845)], the piano part whereof was well played by an amateur, Mrs. Boker, to wit (*née* Miss Oriana Anderson, daughter-in-law of Düsseldorf Gallery Boker).[65] Played with vigor and accuracy, but a heavy, confused, uninteresting composition without breadth, contrast, or salient, definite thought—in short, a bore.[66]

Beethoven's Quintette (for stringed instruments) in C major [op. 29 (1801)][67] was very splendid. Though manifestly written after Beethoven had formed a style of his own, there are phrases in it that suggest Mozart. Probably it belongs in date to the beginning of his second period. The concluding movement was great. This was the best of Eisfeld's concerts for a long while.[68]

Old Badiali was there, in great raptures over the Mozart Quartette. He had attended the morning rehearsal with delight and amusement, for he had never heard any of Mozart's "chamber music" before! Yet he is one of the people whom we call *Artists in Music,* and of a high grade. Think of an eminent literary artist of fifty,[69] or there-

[65] George Henry Boker was the proprietor of the fashionable and successful Düsseldorf Art Galleries, located at 497 Broadway.

[66] "We have never been able to share the common enthusiasm for the [Mendelssohn Trio], probably because we have never been able to understand it," wrote Seymour (*Times,* April 28, 1856).

[67] Announced as its first performance in America.

[68] The remainder of the program included a vocal quartet "A Voice from the Lake," by Eisfeld, and a glee by John Callcott (1766–1821), sung by G. W. Morgan's recently formed (or re-formed) Glee and Madrigal Union, consisting of Mrs. Georgiana Stuart Leach, Maria and Stephen Leach, and John Frazer; solos were sung by Frazer and Mrs. Leach, all excellently accompanied at the piano by Morgan. Joseph Burke played first violin in the Beethoven Quintet.

[69] Badiali was then forty-six years old.

abouts, in ecstacies over the discovery that Milton or Shakespeare had written some charming productions!

May 12. . . . Saturday night [May 10] we heard *Der Freischütz* at the Fourteenth Street Opera House with Mr. and Mrs. S. B. R. LaGrange was Agatha; the other parts were poorly filled, the choruses rickety, and the incantation scene mutilated and its ghosts a second-rate article. But what a lovely opera it is, under every disadvantage![70] And what a perfect embodiment in music of the feeling that underlies German legend and fiction—Tieck, Fouqué, Hoffmann, and Co.[71]

Der Freischütz was the second German opera to be produced at the Academy of Music that season. The first, Flotow's *Martha,* presented on April 26, had been superbly performed by LaGrange,[72] from whose lips the German language "flowed in a manner to be envied by a born *tedesca.*" Indeed, wrote Burkhardt (*Dispatch,* May 4, 1856), she "rattled through the recitatives as if she had been nourished on nothing but gutterals from her infancy."[73] As Lady Harriet, she had been ably assisted by an all-tedescan cast recruited from last year's German opera company: Martini d'Ormy (Nancy), Quint (Lionel), Müller (Plunkett), and a Herr Meissner, a "rugged basso" (the Sheriff); as a special attraction, Madame Bertucca-Maretzek, seated in the orchestra, played the harp part. The *Martha* production was a popular success, receiving generally enthusiastic reviews (barring Hagen's furious indictment of German opera as given in New York).[74] "All young Germany was there," reported *Gamma,* "full of noisy joy, and eager for the opera which would give them once more the beloved songs of their native land" (*Albion,* May 3, 1856, p. 212).

But an angry R. Storrs Willis (formerly a devoted and unquestioning Germanophile) castigated the German members of the audience for their bad manners. Reviewing *Der Freischütz* in the *Musical World* (May 17, 1856, p. 237), he wrote: "Perfectly orderly and manageable at home, the lower-class Germans, until they have been in this country some time, think that it is an element of freedom to be rude, vociferous, and unlicensed in their behavior here." Willis earnestly recommended flogging by a policeman's "locust" to beat some manners into them and form them into "decent citizens. . . . Some of them have painfully needed such a flogging for the last two German nights at the Academy." Not only had they mercilessly hissed an obviously

[70] Not according to Theodore Hagen, in whose opinion the opera's melodic "trivialities" were by now "used up": "Who can listen to the *Laughing* or *Hunting* choruses or that of the young girls, [or] to Max's celebrated air *Durch die Wälder,* without feeling that this music does not answer the views and tastes of the better classes in the present musical world?" (*Review and Gazette,* May 17, 1856, p. 147). Seymour, too, found the melodies, that "for the most part never were vocal, [to] have become a little tiresome from excessive repetition" (*Times,* May 13, 1856).

[71] Ludwig Tieck (1773–1853), Friedrich de la Motte Fouqué (1777–1843), and Ernst Theodor Amadeus Hoffmann (1776–1822) were eminent spinners of nineteenth-century German fantasy.

[72] She appeared in every opera performed at the Academy during this season: besides *Ernani* and *Der Freischütz,* in *I puritani* (April 28), *Lucia* (May 2), *Norma,* with Henriette Behrend as Adalgisa (May 7), and *Il trovatore* (May 9).

[73] Her singing, too, wrote *Gamma,* was "irreproachable, gushing pure as the warbling of a wood-bird—flowery and splendid as a bush of roses" (*Albion,* May 3, 1856, p. 212).

[74] Limited exclusively and redundantly, he charged, to productions of *Martha* and *Der Freischütz* (*Review and Gazette,* May 17, 1856, p. 147).

pick-up chorus of German girls, "who stood faltering and distrustfully there, doing the best they could," but even Madame LaGrange had been the target of their abuse throughout the performance of *Martha*. Such boors, Willis indignantly added, "should be made nearer acquainted with the historical mud-puddles of their native village."

The *Freischütz* performance, however, had been splendid, he wrote. Madame LaGrange, exquisitely attired all in white, with her hair drawn back and her "jauntily arrayed" feet, looked so "girlishly-fresh" as to be unrecognizable until her beautiful voice identified her. The others, too, were excellent, with Madame Siedenburg as Aennchen, Quint as Max, Meissner as Caspar, Müller as Prince Ottokar, and above all, Maretzek, who gave an especially felicitous performance of the overture.

Strong, who did not return to the Academy during the remaining week of the season, makes no reference to the three spectacularly successful guest appearances of Felicita Vestvali on May 12, 14, and 16. Having created a sensation in Mexico, Vestvali was briefly in New York to engage new singers for the Mexican opera, of which she had been made director (and incidentally to pick up a few performances for herself).[75]

[75] "She was five months in the city of the Montezumas and sang sixty-two times," propagandized the *Mirror* (April 26, 1856). "Her benefit [there] netted five thousand dollars, accompanied by presents rich and rare. . . . Young New York is dying to see the queen of hearts, with her incomparable pair of—eyes—once more upon the boards of the Academy."

New-York Historical Society

Vestvali, resplendent in feminine garb.

Maretzek, chronically in need of a contralto, seems to have had no difficulty in letting bygones be bygones (nor did Vestvali); thus, she was welcomed back to the Academy in her old roles of Arsace, Maffio Orsini, and Azucena,[76] being "pelted with entire greenhouses of bouquets" by huge, wildly enthusiastic audiences[77] and eulogized by an all but delirious press. Looking even more resplendently magnificent than before, Vestvali had vocally improved as well. But, as an all-but-overcome R. Storrs Willis put it: "Vestvali is so downright handsome that you have to get a little *accustomed* to her to listen to the music at all" (*Musical World,* May 17, 1856, p. 237).

Encouraged by the increased attendance during the final week of the opera, Maretzek announced a two-week continuation of the season (without Vestvali),[78] reviving during this period *Luisa Miller* on May 23 (with LaGrange as Luisa)—with only moderate success—and *La sonnambula* on May 29 (with LaGrange as Amina). The "positively last performance" of the season was announced for June 2 with Maretzek's benefit, consisting of the complete *Sonnambula* and two acts of *Ernani*—both sung, of course, by LaGrange, with Brignoli, Amodio, Coletti, and others. Following this finale, however, members of the company returned on June 6 for a complimentary benefit to Carolina Vietti-Vertiprach, who appeared (rather pointedly) as Arsace (first act of *Semiramide*) and Azucena (last three acts of *Il trovatore*).[79] And on June 13 the company appeared yet again in a performance of *Ernani,* graciously donated by Madame LaGrange for the benefit of the chorus and orchestra. This performance was portentously advertised as "most positively Madame LaGrange's last appearance in opera prior to her departure" (as it turned out, only on a concert tour with Gottschalk).[80]

Although Maretzek was hailed as a phenomenon—"the man who made the Academy pay"—that edifice now stood in greater financial peril than ever. At a sparsely attended stockholders' meeting on June 16 it was announced that the Academy was in arrears for the interest on its second mortgage (apparently held by Phalen and Coit), to say nothing of other indebtednesses. To escape foreclosure or liquidation

[76] With LaGrange, respectively, as Semiramis, Lucrezia, and Leonora.

[77] Taking direct aim at LaGrange, Hagen stated, as an "unmistakable fact, that Vestvali draws more than any singer in the States" (*Review and Gazette,* May 17, 1856, p. 147).

[78] Who, nothing daunted, collected a company consisting of Costanza Manzini, Luigi Ceresa, Gasparoni, and Barattini, and, much to the delectation of the inhabitants, presented a kind of opera season in Boston, under the excellent conductorship of Jaime Nunó (1824–1908), a recent emigrant from Spain, via Cuba and Mexico (*Dwight's,* June 7, p. 79; June 14, 1856, pp. 86–87).

[79] Despite her recent absence from the opera stage—surprising, considering the recurrent shortage of *prima donna* contraltos—Vietti-Vertiprach was acclaimed a splendid artist, especially as Arsace, a role in which she had been equaled only by Didiée.

[80] Between opera performances and piano *soirées,* LaGrange and Gottschalk had managed to squeeze joint appearances at a number of quickly accessible places: Philadelphia (where Gottschalk was a particularly great favorite), Brooklyn, Newark, and various New Jersey and Westchester County localities. On June 7, LaGrange assisted at Gottschalk's sixteenth and final *soirée,* a brilliant event at Niblo's Saloon; on June 11 he assisted at LaGrange's own "*concert d'adieu,*" again at Niblo's. It had been rumored that Maretzek planned to present them in a series of summer promenade concerts at the Academy, but instead, at the close of the opera season they departed on an early summer tour of upper New York State and Canada. They appeared subsequently, with huge success, at Newport, where LaGrange had taken rooms at the Ocean House for the remainder of the summer.

(or worse—having the Academy fall into "infidel hands"), it was proposed that each stockholder contribute a so-called "loan" of $150, without security or assured repayment (see *Dwight's,* June 14, p. 84; *Leslie's,* June 14, p. 6, June 28, p. 39; *Dispatch,* June 22, June 29, 1856). How they responded to this suggestion remains unreported. Although Maretzek offered to lease the Academy for three years at an annual rental of $22,000—but only if the pernicious free stockholders' tickets for every performance (responsible for "empty seats in crowded houses") were abolished—the building remained closed until September,[81] when a flimsy sort of truce was apparently effected.

Of far greater interest to Strong was an unusual concert at the Academy on May 17, when Eisfeld, with sixty members of the Philharmonic, would perform Beethoven's incidental music to Goethe's drama *Egmont* (1788) for the first time in the United States.[82] An unstaged performance, it would be accompanied by an "explanatory poem," written and declaimed by one Donald McLeod; Maria Brainerd would sing the two songs Beethoven composed for Clara, Egmont's beloved.

May 17. . . . Went with Ellie and her mother at 10 A.M. to the rehearsal of Eisfeld's concert at the Fourteenth Street Opera House. Heard the Overture to *Oberon* for the first time in a long while. It was wonderfully fresh and genial and full of life and beauty. Then a long recitative and aria of Beethoven's (*Ah! perfido,* or some such thing) that was cold and flat as sung by one Miss Brainerd,[83] but seems a very vigorous composition; and then the Adagio and Finale of a piano and orchestra affair of Mendelssohn's [Concerto in G minor, played by Richard Hoffman], which I've heard before (at Castle Garden in the Spring of '46), and which is among the best of its class, combining exquisite melody and well-constructed instrumentation,[84] and intended to convey musical thought, not to show off a pianist's manipulation. At that stage of the performance I came downtown, expecting to hear the rest of the program this evening.[85] . . .

[later] we started for Eisfeld's concert, but before we'd walked a block, poor Ellie's

[81] It was reported in July—apparently erroneously—that Maretzek had been awarded such a lease and that he was momentarily bound for Europe to engage new singers.

[82] Only the overture had so far been heard.

[83] Strong evidently had a selective memory: as we know, Miss Brainerd had sung the *Ah! perfido* at Eisfeld's *soirée* on March 22, at which Strong was present. It was performed on this occasion with an orchestration by Julius Unger (*Review and Gazette,* May 31, 1856, pp. 162–63).

[84] "It is a pity, indeed—indeed a pity," fumed an outraged Burkhardt, "that the so-called critic [Fry] of a respectable daily [the *Tribune*] should exhibit, in the year 1856, such lamentable imbecility as is contained in the following notice of this performance: 'The concerto of Mendelssohn, with piano and orchestra, will hardly bear being touched. The very idea of an orchestra with eighty pieces and an Academy of Music, attached to a pianoforte, is a provoking of most incongruous attachments.'" How could a concerto be performed without an orchestra accompaniment? demanded Burkhardt. And besides, "If Mario's silken-thread head-notes could be heard in every part of the Academy, surely every note of Hoffman on a grand piano could [be], and was, heard and appreciated by all 'whose praise was worth having'" (*Dispatch,* June 1, 1856).

[85] It included Eisfeld's Italianate *Scena* and *Aria, Matilda a me repita,* dedicated to, and sung by, Badiali, who was at last about to return to Europe after some seven illustrious years in the United States and Latin America.

cramps were so sharp that we concluded to come back again.[86] So Beethoven's music to *Egmont* is still unknown to me.[87]

June 29. . . . Heat most oppressive; a *coup de soleil* in each cubic foot of the blazing sunshine. Everybody's devotion at Trinity Chapel this morning seemed languid and limp. Reverend Hobart's sermon was perfectly flaccid, and a very elaborate *Te Deum* by Mendelssohn had plainly perspired till the parts had all run into each other, the musical coloring had got mixed, the melodies lost their outline, and it was all a muddle.

July 2. . . . Kuhn dined with us yesterday, and we went to the [fourth] concert of the Mendelssohn Union [at the City Assembly Rooms].[88] Heard Mendelssohn's music to [Racine's] *Athalie* and to [Goethe's] *Walpurgisnacht* [op. 60 (1832, 1843)] [sung] by a large and capitally drilled chorus, with piano accompaniment. Solo parts well filled also—good voices and evident careful study of the music, rare in these amateur performances.[89] On the whole, the execution of the music was most unusually satisfactory and creditable.[90] The *Walpurgis* affair did not impress me very much, but the *Athalie* must be a very splendid work, of that there can be no doubt, even on a first hearing. I did not think Mendelssohn could sustain himself on a high level through so long a composition, nor that he could write anything so free from manner and so full of beautiful, melodic feeling. I hope I may hear it again.

July 24. . . . One of our civic scourges, an organ-grinder, is putting his broken-winded engine of torture through "St. Patrick's Day in the Morning," just so far off

[86] Ellen Strong was in the final phase of pregnancy: on May 26 she gave birth to George Templeton Strong II, the future composer and watercolorist.

[87] And as well to the Academy stockholders, whose perpetual seats remained noticeably empty. Musically, it was a brave and admirable experiment, albeit a frustratingly fragmented substitute for the staged drama, wrote Willis (*Musical World,* May 24, 1856, pp. 249–50); Hagen, however, defended both the performance and the work in a blaze of chauvinistic ardor (*Review and Gazette,* May 31, 1856, pp. 162–63). Alexander Wheelock Thayer, Dwight's "Diarist," recently returned from two years in Europe, contributed a substantial and informative review-*cum*-essay dealing with the concert and *Egmont* to *Dwight's Journal of Music* (May 24, 1856, pp. 61–62).

[88] Located at 446 Broadway, the new City Assembly Rooms had been opened to the public (for musical purposes) at the grand complimentary concert tendered to John A. Kyle on his retirement, on February 1, 1856 (see following OBBLIGATO). "The large room (divided by a partition) in which the Concert was held is magnificent, and superior, far superior, to anything of the kind in New York, both as regards elegance and capacity," reported the *Times* (February 2, 1856). "The acoustical properties of the building are good, especially for the voice. Indeed, the aggregate superiorities of this *salle de concert* are so obvious that there can be no doubt of its becoming the culminating point of all musical assemblies." Only one fault was noted: poor ventilation resulting in intense heat. (Where was Alexander Saeltzer?)

[89] Scarcely amateurs. The Lyric Odes from *Athalie* were sung by Mrs. Clara Brinkerhoff, Mrs. J. M. Warner, and the Misses C. A. Dingley, M. E. Hawley, Annie Kemp, Hattie Andem, and Maria Leach. In the *Walpurgisnacht,* the soloists were Miss Kemp and Messrs. John Frazer and Stephen W. Leach. Also performed, and highly praised, was Eisfeld's vocal quartet, "A Voice from the Lake." The piano accompaniments were played by George F. Hayter and the conductor was, of course, the admirable G. Washbourn Morgan.

[90] Richard Storrs Willis agreed. "The beautiful music of *Athalie* was given in a manner creditable to any society whatever. The choruses were prompt, true to time, pitch, and shading" (*Musical World,* cited in *Dwight's,* July 19, 1856, p. 127).

that I daren't shy anything at him for fear of stirring up the wrong man. Thank fortune though that it's neither *Casta diva* nor *Ah, non giunge*—both epidemic just now.[91]

Not music but a rigorous commuting schedule occupied Strong's attention for the remainder of the summer—first to Sachem's Head, then to Brattleboro, and finally to Nahant, where Ellen Strong and her sons successively vacationed and Strong spent his weekends. Between weekends he was occupied with duties in Wall Street, at Trinity Church, and at Columbia College. And like all Americans in this crucial election year, he was seriously preoccupied with the mounting sectional strife that increasingly permeated daily life and threatened to rend the nation.

In any case, if Strong suffered from a lack of music, there was little enough to attract him during that sparse season—no Philharmonic, no Eisfeld *soirées,* not even opera. At least, not until September 1, when Maretzek, "the indomitable", once again precariously wrested the Academy of Music from the predatory clutches of its executive committee and launched yet another short season, to end on October 1 (not coincidentally, the shadowy terminal date of Paine's unfortunate lease).

Still lacking a lease of his own—it was allegedly still being circulated among the shareholders for their agreement to his demand that they relinquish their free seats for all performances at the Academy (*Sharps and Flats,* p. 21)[92]—Maretzek again opened his season with *Il trovatore*[93] to so overwhelming an opening-night attendance that "money had to be turned away," wrote the awed reporter for the *Times* (September 2, 1856).[94]

Maretzek had added to his company (consisting of LaGrange, Phillips, Amodio, Brignoli, etc.) two new tenors, Luigi Ceresa and—fresh from Havana—Mario (or Mariano) Tiberini, who was heralded not only as a descendent of the Roman Emperor Tiberius[95] but the desolate survivor of a tragic romance. Tiberini's first sojourn in New York was of short duration. Receiving splendid reviews (except from Hagen)[96]

[91] It was estimated in the press that some 4382 such infernal machines were daily being operated in the summertime streets of Manhattan.

[92] This privilege applied to all performances at the Academy, including opera off-nights, when dramatic performances were given, among them Hackett's celebrated Falstaff in Shakespeare's *The Merry Wives of Windsor.*

[93] "*Il trovatore* has become a perfect rage," wrote Watson (*Leslie's,* September 27, 1856, p. 242). "It has been played four or five nights out of eight, and has attracted audiences numbering thousands. . . . The last performance of *Trovatore* must have netted the manager considerably over two thousand dollars"; $2700, estimated the *Tribune.*

[94] "In the early part of the evening one dollar was freely paid for a chair," reported Watson. "and we heard five dollars offered in vain for a seat for a lady. There must have been at least twenty-five hundred dollars in the house"; according to the treasurers' report it was $2782.25 (*Leslie's,* September 13, p. 210; October 18, 1856, p. 290).

[95] A publicity ploy that aroused a goodly amount of derision among the aggressively democratic, not to say blasé, critics. Following Tiberini's debut, Seymour wrote (*Times,* September 3, 1856): "Last night Signor Tiberini had not only to support a heavy role but a weighty pedigree. Considering the ponderosity of the latter, it is really creditable that a moderate-sized man got through so bravely." Despite his pretensions, however, Seymour found Tiberini to be "an artist of merit," about on a par with Brignoli and Bolcioni.

[96] And from an ambivalent critic for the *Mirror* (September 4, 1856) who reported Tiberini to be "unquestionably a highly accomplished artist [able to perform] wonders with a voice of very lim-

for his Edgardo in *Lucia* (September 3), Tiberini fell into dispute with Maretzek over which roles he would sing and hastily departed for Philadelphia, where he was received with open arms by the sensationally successful Parodi/Strakosch concert company.

The more tractable Ceresa, on the other hand, after enjoying an "unmistakable triumph" as Ernani (September 8), remained with the company, apparently content to sing whatever roles he was assigned. Lacking Tiberini's vocal finesse, Ceresa possessed a powerful and thrilling tenor voice capable of negotiating roles "beyond even Brignoli's powers."

Appearing as the King (in *Ernani*) was the long-absent, unlamented baritone Francesco Taffanelli. "Signor Taffanelli, whose first appearance it was in five years, sang as he did in bygone days at Astor Place, no better, no worse," tersely commented the new *Porter's Spirit of the Times* (September 13, 1856, p. 32).[97] But Madame de La-Grange, the Elvira, reported the *Mirror* (September 9), "looked like a picture, sang like an angel, and acted like a lady."

After a *Trovatore* (September 10) and a *Norma* (September 15)[98] the Academy closed for a week of intensive final rehearsals for Maretzek's major attraction of the season, the mightily ballyhooed American premiere on September 24 of Meyerbeer's opera *L'Étoile du nord* (Paris 1854).[99] Strong heard its second performance.

September 27. . . . *Star of the North* last night with Ellie and George Anthon. Opera admirably put on the stage and all parts well filled.[100] Music generally overworked and elaborated so as to obscure its not very brilliant ideas. It seems viscid and glutinous, and one gets through the opera as a fly through a glue-pot. There are two or three

---

ited compass, and of a thin, hard, and generally unsympathetic quality." Yet, he sang "with such exquisite taste—so much delicacy, feeling, and expression, that one can, to some extent, overlook the shortcomings of his vocal organ."

[97] In February 1856, publication of the *Spirit of the Times* was brought to a close, and on September 5 of that year, with the New York journalist George Wilkes (1817–1885) as publisher, William T. Porter as his associate editor, and John Darcie as theatre and music editor, *Porter's Spirit of the Times* made its first appearance. In September, too, Edward Hodges, "the Nestor of the musical profession," became co-editor with R. Storrs Willis of the *Musical World*.

[98] Intersected on September 11 by a "Mammoth Musical Jubilee" at the Crystal Palace, where, in the brilliant light of 7500 gas jets, Maretzek conducted a "monster orchestra" of some 200 players in a program of favorite opera gems, patriotic pieces, and his own "Tip-Top Polka." It was an electioneering stunt perpetrated by some "would-be Barnum from the South," deprecated Hagen, and as for the performances, the least said about them, the better (*Review and Gazette,* September 20, 1856, p. 284).

[99] Maretzek did not disdain the most blatant of Barnumesque methods in promoting this opera. A few days before its premiere, Broadway pedestrians were reportedly baffled by the appearance on walls and billboards of "large, mysterious posters, which, upon a deep blue ground displayed the *Ursa Major* with an overgrown Polar Star above it." No explanatory text. "Was it a prospectus for lectures on astronomy?" asked the *Musical World* (September 27, 1856, p. 450), or was it intended to draw attention to the predictions of Mme. X, the Astrologer? Only when the opera advertisements began to appear was it revealed that the posters had referred to Meyerbeer's opera.

[100] By LaGrange, Siedenburg, Bertucca-Maretzek, Susan Pyne, Brignoli, Amodio, Coletti, Arnoldi, Quinto, Müller, and Barattini. In Burkhardt's opinion (*Dispatch,* September 28, 1856), the staging at the Academy surpassed the production of *L'Étoile* he had seen in Paris the year before.

points that stand out vividly and may be worth something, but the opera as a whole seems *not* an inspiration.

~

The critics, as usual, expended acres of verbiage upon synopses of the opera's plot. Meyerbeer's *L'Étoile du nord,* with a new libretto by Scribe, was based partly on *Ein Feldlager in Schlesien,* composed for Jenny Lind in 1844. The text had been translated into Italian for the Academy production by one Manfredo Mazziani. An amalgam of the more cherished opera clichés, the opera had to do with a fictional Peter the Great of Russia (Amodio) and how he came to choose Caterina, a lowly Finnish beauty (LaGrange), to be his Empress, but only after she had impersonated her brother (Quinto), a Russian officer who had deserted in order to marry a lowly peasant girl (Bertucca), and after she (Caterina) had gone (temporarily) mad (according to Richard Grant White, "in white muslin") after spying upon Peter (himself disguised as a lowly shipbuilder) in the act of ingesting copious libations while dallying with not one, but two *vivandières* (Mesdames Siedenburg and Susan Pyne).

The critics mostly agreed that the music was "the work of a master hand," and while, as Fry pointed out, not essentially melodic, it would grow on one with further

Music Division, The New York Public Library

acquaintance. But Hagen pronounced the score to be a cut-and-paste job and thus devoid of musical inspiration, excepting only the emotional moment at the end of act two, when Meyerbeer employed an "old German tune, a people's song and march, to genial music, upon which he could build his usual artificial notes" (*Review and Gazette,* October 4, 1856, pp. 306–7) But, as even Hagen admitted, the inimitable LaGrange, in the role of Caterina, surpassed all of her previous achievements. Amodio, a ludicrous choice for Peter the Great, did as well as could be expected in a role for which he was physically and vocally unfitted. The others were generally praised, as was the lavish staging. New Yorkers were advised not to miss this delectable production, for it was by now no secret that opera's days at the Academy were numbered.

Indeed, crowning his triumphant season with a fifth and final performance of *L'Étoile* on September 30—his benefit—Maretzek, on being "called before the curtain" at the end of the first act by an enthusiastic audience, unleashed his anger and frustration with the Academy hierarchy in a bitter speech, quoted in all the papers: "Ladies and Gentlemen: On this day, eight years since, did I for the first time make my appearance before a New York audience. During those eight years I have toiled to earn your approbation . . . but in spite of the public favor and generosity, I have not succeeded in my primary object. This was the establishment of Italian opera in New York. Various reasons have been assigned for the various failures of Italian opera. Sometimes refractory tenors have been accused, at other times the exorbitant prices of prima donnas have been condemned, and occasionally public judgment has been graciously content to censure its own indifference. . . . It is, in my opinion, the utterly wrong and pernicious principles upon which Italian opera has invariably been conducted in New York [that are to blame]—principles not only completely inconsistent with American feelings and sympathies, but inconsistent with those of every capital city at present to be found in continental Europe.

"In every opera house which has been built in New York the privileges of a limited and exclusive body of men have been guaranteed. In the Academy of Music this principle has been carried to its climax. At the Astor Place Opera House the privileged portion of the audience at least secured the rent of the house. But here, in the Academy of Music . . . in addition to the enormous rent demanded, the privileges of a would-be exclusive party are larger—the claims they make upon a manager are more exigent—their terms are harder—their requirements are heavier upon his brain and his body and his sweat and his toil than they have ever before been; not but that I am certain that the stockholders as a body would be glad to grant all just and reasonable demands required by me, were it not that the Executive Committee [Phalen, Coit, and Wolfe] have determined upon enforcing these unreasonable claims.

"As a natural consequence, all former managers have sunken. . . . Even I, a manager by profession . . . have barely been able to secure myself from loss. . . . Prosperous as [the just-ended month] has been, it would not have been worth my while to have continued my management under those conditions which have been imposed upon me. Therefore is it that I have declined becoming the lessee of the Academy."

Whereupon Maretzek, amid "loud cheering," returned to the orchestra pit and completed his final performance at the Academy. A bombshell!

The press, in an eruption of answering editorials, came out strongly in support of Maretzek. Except, that is, the *Herald*. Long quiescent in opera matters, the *Herald* was apparently still in league with Phalen and Wikoff, the latter back from Europe and evidently still a power at the Academy, albeit now behind the scenes. Pretending to provide an impartial forum for the combatants, the *Herald* on October 3 published a letter from Phalen, written from Newport, hotly defensive of the stockholders' legal rights and the purity of their intentions, and condemning Maretzek as a dishonest villain. Wikoff, also writing from Newport, and for once signing his name to what the *Herald* (October 4) chose to call a "Manifesto," assailed Maretzek and his supporters in the press and promised to supply the *Herald* with the shocking facts of the controversy. Together with this "Manifesto" the *Herald* published Maretzek's "Counterblast" to Phalen's letter, supplying a treasurer's report of the receipts and disbursements for the recent "most successful" season at Academy, showing a deficit of $450.

During the "Merry Thirty Days War," as Maretzek refers to the ensuing hostilities, "the 'dailies' in general and the *Herald* in particular [persisted in] egging on the belligerents—apparently enjoying the fun of a 'free fight' among the operatics—and [during that fateful presidential campaign] making no little political capital out of the event by mixing it up with secession, nullification, and the Presidential questions," editorialized *Porter's Spirit* (October 11, 1856, p. 104).

"We learn that the stockholders are extremely wroth with Maretzek," continued the *Spirit,* "and vow [paraphrasing *Othello*] that he shall 'never more be officer of theirs.'" But Maretzek, a man of infinite resource (not to say daring), had by no means burned his bridges. As he writes in *Sharps and Flats* (pp. 21–23), convinced that the terms he demanded would not be granted,[101] he had foresightedly secured the Boston Theatre for an opera season of three weeks and further made arrangements with Don Francisco Martí's New York agent for a season at the Tacón Theatre in Havana, to begin in early 1857. For the present, he announced two "Grand Lyric Concerts," to be performed on October 6 and 8 by his complete company—stars, chorus, and orchestra—at the "handsome and commodious" City Assembly Rooms. He had been induced to give these concerts, he advertised, "in order to give the public an opportunity of hearing these artists, as well as to afford those who do not ordinarily visit the Theatres a means of enjoying the music of *Il trovatore* and *Star of the North* in the Concert Room."

Maretzek's novel "Lyric Concerts," or "Drawing Room Operas" as he alternately billed them, were an instantaneous success.[102] The first part of his first program, reported the *Times* (October 7, 1856), "consisted solely of selections from 'the Trovatore' rendered by Mesdames LaGrange and Adelaide Phillips and Messrs. Coletti, Brignoli, and Amodio, with full chorus and orchestra. These artists have made the reputation of the opera in this country, and it is only necessary to say that they preserved it last night

[101] An ultimatum was formally delivered to him by a sardonically smiling Chevalier Wikoff, who doubted that Maretzek would abandon the Academy, whatever the terms, after the "stupendous success" of *Star of the North*. According to the *Dispatch* (October 19, 1856), the stockholders, at a meeting on October 15, had at last agreed to "waive [their] privileges to free admission to the Opera, with secured seats, [and] on all occasions for which the Academy shall be let for balls, concerts, and lectures, for the term of one year, from October 1, 1856." But that clause had been noticeably omitted in Maretzek's contract, "though verbally promised." It was retained, however, in the agreement with the Philharmonic Society for their forthcoming concerts at the Academy.

[102] By October 6, concurrent with the first concert, Wood's Minstrels advertised a burlesque in blackface of a "Concert *à la* Maretzek, without the aid of the stockholders."

in a creditable manner. A complete and richly-colored sketch of the opera was presented to the audience, and thoroughly appreciated and enjoyed. . . . In the second part we had the Overture to *Masaniello,* excellently played by the orchestra; the 'La-Grange Polka,' vocalized by Madame LaGrange in her usual astonishing manner; the *Brindisi* from *Rigoletto,* sung by Signor Ceresa and deservedly encored, a trio by Beethoven, played by the Brothers Mollenhauer [Edward, Frederick, and the recently arrived Henry, a cellist]; *Casta diva* from *Norma,* sung by Madame LaGrange; *Non più mesta* from *Cenerentola,* sung by Miss Adelaide Phillips, who possesses a delicious concert voice; and the Finale to the third act of *Ernani,* rendered by Madame LaGrange, Signori Ceresa, Amodio, Coletti, and full chorus. . . . We feel sure that nothing superior has ever been heard in a concert room."

At his second "Opera in the Drawing Room" Maretzek added Bertucca-Maretzek, and Siedenburg to his cast and presented "Gems" from *Star of the North* and arias from *Lucrezia Borgia, Rigoletto, Il barbiere,* and *Macbeth.* The inevitable added concert was triumphantly given on Friday, October 10, again with Gems from *Star of the North* and additional arias from *Les Vêpres siciliennes, Ernani,* and *Il trovatore.* As *Porter's Spirit* lamented (October 18, 1856, p. 120): "We cannot but regret that such a magnificent troupe of artists are lost to New York. . . . From all appearances . . . we shall have to do without opera this winter, for both Maretzek and the Academy seem mutually bent on starving each other into submission. . . . For the present, Italian opera is dead in New York, and the songbirds of the sunny South have fled." (But Maretzek had another trick up his sleeve.)

Strong, inhabiting a different sphere, had apparently remained aloof from all this drama. Nor did he pay heed, beyond a single unsatisfactory hearing of two acts of his beloved *Der Freischütz,* to the unpropitious season of German opera that under Bergmann's musical direction precariously hung by a thread at Niblo's during September and October (see following OBBLIGATO).

On October 9, upon the first autumnal stirrings of life at the Philharmonic, Strong joyfully noted: "Next Saturday is the first Philharmonic rehearsal, and they play the *C-minor Symphony*!"

Compelled by the voracious space demands of their mushrooming associate membership, the Society had shifted their concerts and public rehearsals to the greater (but still insufficient) expanses of the Academy of Music;[103] and although the first concert (of the fifteenth season) was not scheduled until November 22, the rehearsals for it commenced in early October. It was widely noted that Eisfeld, replacing Bergmann as conductor for the coming season,[104] subjected the orchestra to uncommonly detailed and rigorous rehearsals, probably to still accusations in the press that the Philharmonic

[103] This auspicious moment was clouded by the shocking lapse of the Philharmonic's treasurer (and future president), Scharfenberg, who absconded to Europe with the Society's sinking fund, amounting to $799.90. The outraged board of directors, at a meeting on November 2, "accepted his resignation" and ruled that he must repay every penny, with interest (Philharmonic Archives). The unseemly episode seems quickly to have blown over.

[104] According to the minutes of the Philharmonic board of directors' meeting (September 16, 1856), Bergmann and Eisfeld tied for the approaching conductorship and Timm cast the deciding vote (Philharmonic Archives). For the coming season Bergmann would thus resume his former seat in the Philharmonic's cello section.

concerts and rehearsals had degenerated into mere social gatherings for the display of clothes, exchange of gossip, and flirtation.

Especially disapproving was Richard Grant White, who attributed the greatly increased Philharmonic associate membership not to "a wider diffusion of musical taste" but to "the discovery that the Society is fashionable,[105] and that associate membership is the cheapest way of enjoying all the privileges which it has to bestow." The subscriber, numbered in the tens, explained White, "receives for his $10 three tickets to each of the four concerts of the season, [while] the associate member [numbered in the hundreds] receives for his $5 one ticket to each of the concerts and one to each of the four public rehearsals." A bargain!

"The throng at these rehearsals has become as great almost as that at the concerts," continued White; the rehearsals "have been adopted as a pleasant lounge or rendezvous for a Saturday afternoon. . . . [They] have become concerts under another name, for it is but natural that both conductor and performers should be less willing to go over a piece, passage by passage, and, if necessary, bar by bar, under the circumstances just alluded to. . . . Against the pernicious influence of these concert rehearsals the Society must struggle if it would attain the eminent position in which we hope to see it" (*Courier and Enquirer,* October 10, 1856). Evidently Eisfeld took these comments too literally with his demanding rehearsal methods—much to Strong's delight, however, when they concerned Beethoven's C-minor Symphony.[106]

October 12. . . . the city has its good gifts, as pure and noble as the keenest and healthiest enjoyment of woods and hills and October sunshine, e.g., Beethoven in C minor. Heard it with Ellie at the Philharmonic rehearsal (Academy of Music, a good change of locale) yesterday afternoon. Brattleboro or Catskill could not have given us that thing. Excellently well done. Frequent pauses and repetitions and retracing of steps are precious when that transcendent work is being rehearsed. You cannot hear it often enough, or enough of it. As each weighty phrase is played, you feel that something you want to dwell on is passing away, and that you have not half fathomed it. You are relieved and delighted when Eisfeld's baton raps and the orchestra tries back again and gives you another chance.

October 25. . . . Philharmonic rehearsal this afternoon—Overture ["In the Highlands,"] by Gade, pleasant and rather suggestive; Cherubini's [Overture] to *Medea* [Paris 1797], very elegant and agreeable—and *The* Symphony—C minor.

What one may call the *third sentence* of that Andante—I don't know how I can better indicate it—the beautiful melodic passage beginning in A-flat and modulating abruptly into C major—is, I think, almost the noblest and loveliest single thought in music. It affects me more strongly than *any other.* The significance and effect of such a thing is not definable in words—one must try to express the way it strikes him in some analogy, and I should say that a painting that showed one a militant angel soaring

[105] "The Philharmonic Society finds nothing undesirable, of course, in the fact that it may have become the fashion," smugly replied the Society's latest Annual Report.

[106] But Eisfeld may have carried a good thing too far. After the concert the *Musical World* (November 29, 1856. p. 651) wondered if "there be such a thing as practicing music too much. . . . The C-minor Symphony has been rehearsed with such fidelity and so often by the Philharmonics, and Mr. Eisfeld, particularly, has been so conscientious with them of late, that while the notes proper have been improved, the soul seems to have flagged somewhat."

victorious through Heaven—full of angelic life and love and strength—would be a *like* creation in Art—that is, if it were truer than positive painting ever was, or can be.

November 8. . . . Heard the C-minor Symphony rehearsed this afternoon with Ellie—part of it twice. The first movement gains on one more than any other. There's nothing like it for intensity and strength. It seems absolutely *dangerous* to hear—like the river below Niagara, with its wiry eddies, or some prodigious steam engine—as if it might hurt you, should you get a little nearer. Surely those first two notes, so often repeated, are not "Fate knocking at the door," or any such nonsense, whatever the *Hirnbesitzer* [brain possessor] Beethoven chose to say, but simply the excellent instrumentation of a long, weary, restless, impatient *sigh*—the sigh of a strong man in prison—within four walls—or rather, unable to find work for his energies and waiting without hope for that which the Andante embodies—free, harmonious development of his power, leading him to the glorious consummation and victory of the final movement.

Or it was meant to be Pathological, perhaps—the first movement is Chronic Dyspepsia, sub-acute inflammation of the coats of the stomach—the gnawing of the gastric juice—accelerated pulse—throbbing head—nausea—megrims—vapors and desperation.[107] The liver begins to act in the Andante; the patient is congratulated by his friends on his looking so much better, and walks the streets convinced that "Radway's Ready Relief"[108] is what he has sought so long. In the Finale he is regenerated and restored—is once more an ornament to Society and makes his home happy.

~

On October 6 the *Herald* announced a momentous event: "The steamship *Africa,* which arrived on Thursday last (October 2), brought to our shores Sigismund Thalberg (1812–1871), undoubtedly the greatest living pianist.[109] Mr. Thalberg's fame has preceded him to the United States, and his name has been a household word in our musical circles for many years.[110] . . . It is gratifying to say that Mr. Thalberg, although standing at the highest position, professionally and socially, assumes none of those disgusting, pretentious airs which have injured many really good artists with our straightforward, democratic people. Mr. Thalberg is about forty years of age; he looks more like an Englishman than a German,[111] speaks English better than a great many Englishmen, is the possessor of an immense fortune, and is married to the daughter of

[107] Strong was probably still suffering the aftermath of a three-day attack of dyspepsia, so severe, he wrote, that it would have taxed the descriptive powers of Dante himself (Private Journal, November 8, 1856).

[108] A widely advertised, all-purpose panacea.

[109] A distinction Thalberg had in fact shared with Franz Liszt for more than two decades: "The world possesses but two great pianists in the present day," wrote Seymour (*Times,* November 11, 1856), "Liszt, who roams the mountains and revels in the wild splendors of the cataract and the volcano, and Thalberg, who treads the peaceful valley and gathers the fragrant flowers which we all know and love."

[110] For more than twenty years, scarcely a pianist had appeared in the United States who had not played Thalberg's compositions, principally his fantasies on themes from the operas.

[111] Thalberg, whose origin is disputed, was then forty-four years old. Reputedly an Austrian of noble, albeit illegitimate, birth, he is generally believed to have been the natural son of the Count (sometimes identified as "Prince") Moritz von Dietrichstein and a Baroness von Wetzlar. The Liszt scholar Charles Suttoni contends, with much corroborative evidence, that Thalberg was in fact the son of Moritz's older brother Prince Franz-Joseph von Dietrichstein (Liszt, pp. 22–23, footnote 1).

Thalberg the Elegant.

Music Division, The New York Public Library

[Luigi] Lablache. He will give a concert here in about two weeks, probably at Niblo's Saloon."

This was no mere puffery. Despite his reputedly illicit birth, Thalberg—brought up as a member of the Austrian aristocracy—had enjoyed all the educational and social advantages of his caste, and thus naturally came by his elegantly understated manners. In an age accustomed to exhibitionism on the concert platform, the quiet, gentlemanly assurance with which Thalberg produced his breathtaking pianistic miracles was in itself a revelation. As Arthur Loesser writes: "Thalberg, perfectly dressed, groomed, and barbered, cultivated an air of perfect poise, an abstention from every superfluous movement, however emotionally apposite, during his most hazardous fingerwork" (Loesser, p. 372).

Indeed, Thalberg's innovative "hazardous fingerwork," had created a revolution in the world of pianism when he introduced it in the early 1830s. A tremendously prolific composer, principally of opera fantasies, Thalberg had devised a unique and ingenious technique for simulating on the piano the melting, "singing" quality of the human voice, by allowing both hands (aided by judicious use of the pedal) to share in stating a melody in the middle register of the keyboard, all the while surrounding it with cascades of arpeggios such as had never before been heard. Only a miraculous "third hand" could have created this effect: "It is not pianism that we listen to," wrote Seymour, "but vocalism, embellished with all that chasteness, elegance, and consummate mechanism can provide" (*Times,* November 11, 1856).

Thalberg came to the United States under the management of the formidable Bernard Ullman, who—perhaps fired by Gottschalk's triumphs—early in the year had abandoned both the publication of *L'Entr'acte*[112] and the hopeless contest for control

Yet another school of thought holds that Thalberg, although a protégé of Count Moritz and educated in Vienna, was the legitimate son of Josef and Fortunée Stein of Frankfurt (see *Baker's*).

[112]According to the *Mirror* of March 10, 1856, Ullman was by then in Paris, busily engaging artists for America; he had left his little theatrical gossip sheet not in the care of his partner John Darcie but of his friend and associate, one Jacob Gosche, a musical handyman who had served in the

of the Academy of Music and had gone to Europe in search of an even greater attraction. Short of bringing Franz Liszt to America, Ullman could hardly have bagged a greater prize.[113]

Arriving during the final month of the fiercely raging presidential campaign of 1856, Thalberg (or Ullman) wisely decided to delay his debut until after election day. In the interim Thalberg went off on a sightseeing junket to Niagara Falls.

To condition the public to Thalberg's understated style, Ullman's promotional efforts, too, assumed an unaccustomed gentility. Thus, welcoming serenades and other such ostentatious rituals of greeting were shunned. In his artfully underplayed newspaper advertisements for Thalberg's first concerts—on November 10 and 11 at Niblo's Saloon, surprisingly not at the larger theatre—Ullman inaugurated a new technique of entrepreneurial seduction. He confidingly explained that "Artists of renown who visit this country are actuated by two motives: the desire to accumulate money and the ambition to extend the dominion of their art-triumphs. The majority—who aim at the first object—select a large building where thousands may obtain admission; the minority are content with the one which appreciation can alone bestow. It is not indelicate to say that Thalberg belongs to the latter class. He desires not merely a pecuniary success, but an art-exposition—an art-success. To obtain this, he has cheerfully relinquished the advantages of a large hall, and in preference has selected a room of limited capacity (such as Niblo's Saloon), in which the nuances, the lights and shadows, the delicate tints and the broad contrasts which impart an individuality to piano-forte playing may be gathered with the ease and comfort of a home circle. In this way Mr. Thalberg hopes to contribute—here as well as in Europe[114]—his share toward the development of music as one of the sister arts, and not unduly to display his capacity as a performer.[115] From the same motive [and here Ullman relapsed into the crassly mundane] the prices of admission have been fixed at a moderate standard[116]—certainly too moderate to afford him that just emolument to which he is entitled, since the highest average of receipts, in a room containing only about 800 seats with standing room for 300 persons more, after deducting the usual free admissions and the proportionately large expenses, will leave him a smaller share of profits than has been gained heretofore

---

promotional campaigns for Lind, Grisi/Mario, Sontag, and Rachel. Gosche was now independently offering his services "as manager to artists."

[113] And not only Thalberg. As Dwight's correspondent ornately announced (October 11, 1856, p. 15): "Ullman, the indefatigable, who flies back and forth over the Atlantic like a shuttle, weaving star after star of European theatre and concert notoriety into the great American web of Art—and speculation—has engaged the famous contralto Mme. [Elena] d'Angri, who has been thought second only to Alboni. Her speedy arrival is looked for. It is not stated whether she is to concertize with Thalberg." She did.

[114] And in Brazil, where Thalberg had toured in 1855.

[115] "Mr. Ullman had a decided talent for advertising, a clever way of putting himself in communication with the public and shaping his announcements like confidential communications of his business affairs," grudgingly conceded Maretzek (*Sharps and Flats,* p. 37).

[116] One dollar admission, reserved seats 50 cents extra. Reserved seats might be purchased two days in advance—uptown at C. Breusing's music store (601 Broadway) and downtown at Van Norden and King's (46 Wall Street). Only tickets of admission would be sold at the door at concert time. By the morning of November 8 the papers reported that all the reserved seats for the first concert had been sold. Shameless humbuggery, countered Burkhardt, who claimed that hundreds of seats had been "kept back for speculators" (*Dispatch,* November 9, 1856).

by artists holding an inferior position in the musical world to that universally conceded to Mr. Thalberg."[117]

As Thalberg's manager, Ullman regained his lost credibility with the better part of the volatile New York press.[118] "The quiet and unpretending way in which [Thalberg's] business matters were managed, under the judicious care of Mr. Ullman," wrote Watson, "forbade any great demonstrative excitement, but the solid and worldwide reputation of Thalberg created that legitimate desire to hear one whose genius had extorted the admiration of the civilized world" (*Leslie's,* November 29, 1856, pp. 370–71).

Indeed, Ullman's genteel tactics were hardly necessary. Even before Thalberg arrived, the music journalists had exhausted their superlatives in recounting the wonders of his achievements as a virtuoso, composer, and gentleman. After hearing him, they reacted with a unanimity that was downright unsettling. Until now, as Watson observed after Thalberg's third concert (November 13): "No artist appeared among us but he had some fault. He had either something too much or too little; there was always a peg upon which to hang an objection.[119] But in the case of Thalberg . . . perfection is conceded—perfection beyond all competition, and beyond all praise. This is the only case in which we can record a perfect unanimity of opinion throughout the New York musical world" (*Leslie's,* November 22, 1856, p. 370).

For example, on November 11, after Thalberg's first concert[120] Richard Grant White wrote: "His accuracy is marvelous to the verge of the miraculous"; William Henry Fry wrote: "He delineates a melody like a dramatic artist and darts his arpeggio spray like an Apollo"; Seymour wrote: "Thalberg is the greatest pianist we have had in America. . . . His performances can only be appreciated, not described"; Watson wrote: "His grasp of the instrument is Titanic"; and the fussbudgety critic of the *Evening Post:* "M. Thalberg performs with a confidence, ease, brilliancy, and perfection quite beyond the power of description. Other and lesser lights have appeared, with all the snobbish paraphernalia of white kid gloves, artistic and abstracted ways of looking up at the ceiling, and [concluding a work] with a demonstrative flourish, as who should say, 'Was that not most remarkably difficult and most wonderfully performed?'" But Thalberg's demeanor was "that of a quiet, unpretentious gentleman, whose life is in his art."

Seymour credited New York's keen appreciation of Thalberg's great piano playing

[117] Thalberg's (and presumably Ullman's) prodigious profits on this tour exceeded those earned by any preceding visiting artist except, perhaps, Jenny Lind (and Barnum).

[118] Except Burkhardt, who—cherishing his old hatred of Ullman—deplored what he called the "shoddy tactics" used to promote the great and matchless Thalberg, unsuitable tactics, he wrote, conceived by "an humble imitator of Barnum, with more than Barnum's impudence, and less than Barnum's wit and brain" (*Dispatch,* November 9, 1856).

[119] Indeed, as we know, even Jenny Lind had her detractors.

[120] At which he performed—on two of the seven Érards purportedly sent from Europe for his use on this tour—his fantasies on *La sonnambula* (op. 46) and on *Masaniello* (op. 52), his Grand Variations on the Barcarole from *L'elisir d'amore* (op. 66), and his spectacular Étude in A minor (op. 45). Although an encore was demanded after every piece, Thalberg merely acknowledged the demand with a courtly bow; only at the end of the concert did he oblige his audience with a sensational performance of his transcription of the Serenade from *Don Pasquale* (op. 67).

in no small measure to the spadework of such splendid American pianists as Gottschalk and Mason. They were excellent artists, he wrote, of whom "the city may be proud—the one with his poetic languor and fitful inspiration; the other with his massive grasp of classic thought and graceful utterance of manly sentiment. Of the two," he added, "we may boast of neither at the present moment, for Gottschalk has surrendered himself to a pirate crew of pupils, and Mason has thrown himself into Chopin and is not likely to appear above the surface for some time to come.[121] We should have forgotten all about the twain, had we not seen their enthusiastic faces at [Thalberg's] concerts, beaming genial reciprocity on the great artist whom they honor with true artist's pride" (*Times,* November 14, 1856).

Throughout Thalberg's first series of seven concerts in New York[122] (astoundingly compressed within a period of twelve days), he played exclusively his own compositions and opera fantasies.[123] His assisting artists were the well-liked, new American soprano Cora de Wilhorst[124] and the esteemed Italian opera baritone Filippo Morelli; they were accompanied at the piano (or "conducted," as the advertisements had it) by Signor (or rather Señor) Jaime Nunó.[125] At the two final concerts of his series (numbers six and seven, on November 20 and 21), Thalberg was joined by Gottschalk at a second Érard in performances of the two-piano version of Thalberg's Fantasie on *Norma* (op. 12). A managerial masterstroke! "To add Gottschalk to Thalberg," gushed Richard Grant White, "is indeed 'to make honey a sauce to sugar.'"[126]

Strong, with his detestation of virtuosos and all things virtuosic, responded with only limited enthusiasm to the Thalbergian excitement. Unable to accompany Ellen

[121] With the advent of Thalberg, Gottschalk apparently decided against resuming his *soirées* and indeed devoted himself to teaching at his popular and profitable "Conservatoire." Mason, after having successfully completed the first series of six Mason/Bergmann matinées on April 29 (see following OBBLIGATO), would, for reasons of his own, not resume his chamber-music concerts until early 1858, by which time Theodore Thomas had taken Bergmann's place as presiding spirit of the group. During the remainder of 1856, Mason engaged in teaching and occasional concert-playing, locally and on short tours of upper New York State and New England—sometimes in collaboration with Adelaide Phillips.

[122] With an additional concert in Brooklyn on November 17.

[123] According to Richard Hoffman: "His repertoire [for his American tour] consisted only of about twelve of his fantasias, but these were played with absolute perfection." Like Gottschalk, "Thalberg was wise enough to avoid all compositions which he felt did not belong to his peculiar genre," writes Hoffman. "He did not encroach [except sparingly] upon the classics. He knew his limitations, but he did not allow others to discover them" (Hoffman, p. 129).

[124] A member of New York's Upper Ten, Madame de Wilhorst (*née* Withers), upon her marriage to a titled German adventurer, had been disowned by her wealthy father. Forced to support herself (and, it was gossiped, her husband as well), Madame de Wilhorst, possessing a well-cultivated, charming voice, was seeking a career as a concert and opera singer. Her recent debut, on September 18, and its follow-up concert (October 2), both at Niblo's Saloon, had been most favorably received in the press.

[125] Among Nunó's achievements must be listed his composition of the Mexican national anthem.

[126] "The performance . . . served admirably to show Thalberg's great excellencies and his solid school and thorough mechanical training [as contrasted with] Mr. Gottschalk's peculiar qualities," wrote Hagen, adding with barbed pen that Thalberg had taught his audiences that "there are far higher excellencies in a pianist than the mere accomplishment of gymnastic tricks, sky-rocket arpeggios, or piccolo whirligigs" (*Review and Gazette,* November 29, 1856, p. 371).

and Charles Kuhn to Thalberg's first concert because he "had to attend to the Church," Strong heard him the following evening (November 11),[127] with, he tersely commented, "more satisfaction than I counted on."

Strong's "satisfaction" was evidently prompted more by Thalberg's gentlemanly manners than his music. On a second hearing Strong unbent only slightly.

November 18. . . . Thalberg's [fifth] concert. Quite satisfactory. It's refreshing to observe the absence of affectation, pretension, and clap-trap in all the man does. People may differ about the value of his work[128] and doubt whether the result is worth the labor of a life, but it is presented to those who choose to hear it in a simple, quiet way, without the faintest flourish of trumpets, and one can't but feel kindly toward the performer. Poor little Madame Cora de Wilhorst (Reuben Withers's rather pretty daughter) didn't do so well as when I heard her before—wasn't liberally applauded and looked savage.[129] Poor little soul, one can't but admire her loyalty to the very dubious man of her choice, for whose sake she is dropped by her pecuniary papa, and has become "professional." Whether he is a Count or a Courier or a Lag[130] at home in his own country is an unsettled question. Anyhow, she supports him, his big dog, and his little baby, by her earnings. So the LaGrange is understood to provide for her husband, the Baron de Stankovitch, with the money he loses to that accomplished cosmopolite, the Duke de Calabrito.[131]

Beyond his prominence as LaGrange's husband, the convivial Baron had suddenly assumed an identity of his own in the iridescent world of opera. Under his unexpected "management," Maretzek's opera company, now renamed the "LaGrange Company," reopened on November 10 (timed to compete with Thalberg's first concert)[132] for a six-week sojourn at the Academy of Music. Just when all had seemed lost, it was the Baron de Stankovitch (in secret collusion with Maretzek) who had at last been able to

[127] At his second concert Thalberg played his fantasies on the Serenade and Minuet from *Don Giovanni* (op. 42), on *Mosè* (op. 33), and on *Lucrezia Borgia* (op. 50); also his Tarentelle (op. 65).

[128] Represented on this occasion by his *Don Giovanni* Fantasie, his Tarentelle, and first performances of his arrangement of the Quartet from *I puritani,* a new Étude, and the solo version of his *Norma* Fantasie.

[129] "Madame de Wilhorst possesses a fine voice and much merit in an artistic point of view," wrote Seymour (*Times,* November 14, 1856), but "she is slightly pettish. She has a number of little ways charming in the family circle, but rather wearisome elsewhere. The most provoking of these is beating time with her foot or her hand for the purpose of instructing the accompanist. . . . Signor Nunó does not need such ungraceful prompting, and in fact less frequently damages the time than Madame Wilhorst." Too, the *Mirror* (September 19, 1856), after her first appearance, observed that "an artist never should recognize individuals among the audience by smiling, or looks, or nods. It interrupts the identity of the actor with the part assumed, and quite destroys the illusion of the scene."

[130] *Lag,* as defined in Partridge, was contemporary slang for a convict sentenced to deportation, or a ticket-of-leave man (parolee).

[131] A recently arrived adventurer, the Duke de Calabrito (or Calibretta), together with his traveling companion, a French count, were raising Upper Ten eyebrows galore with their uncanny aptitude for winning large sums of money at cards (see Haswell, p. 538).

[132] The Ullman/Maretzek hostility still raged. Only a few days earlier, Ullman had accused Maretzek (or one of his henchmen) of having "murderously" attacked him with a slingshot (*Herald,* November 3, 1856). True or false, it was great for business.

extract a lease[133] from the Academy directors, but only on his sacred pledge that the reprehensible Max would not be permitted to enter the Academy portals except as a paying auditor.

On opening night at the Academy, the large and fashionable audience assembled to hear the inevitable *Il trovatore*—with LaGrange, Phillips, Brignoli, and Amodio—witnessed, or rather, participated in an extraordinary drama. As *Porter's Spirit* (November 15, 1856, p. 184) eloquently describes it, no sooner had Kreutzer, Maretzek's bearded replacement, entered the orchestra pit, than "an *émeute* commenced, which evinced a determination on the part of the majority of the audience to preclude Mr. Kreutzer . . . and insist on the restoration of the indefatigable Max, in spite of all the executive committees in New York. Poor Kreutzer (who, to do him justice, bore the infliction like a Teutonic lamb), was saluted with a volley of sibilations of no gentle or mistakable character, and deafening shouts of 'Maretzek,' in every conceivable language, patois, or pronunciation, arose from every part of the house; as if by magic, Maretzek-men, like Clan Alpine's,[134] springing up in every direction. . . . Meanwhile, Mr. Kreutzer remained quietly seated in his chair, and the audience, in order to make him understand that they meant 'no offence in the world' toward him personally, gave him three cheers, whereupon he gracefully bowed, with his hand on—his vest—and smiled, too, but it was a sickly smile and bespoke considerable mental, if not bodily, disturbance.

"Taking advantage of the lull, Kreutzer waved his baton, and the hirsute drummer gave a terrific roll on the tympani, but the malcontents were not to be silenced . . . and the stormy cries of 'Maretzek' were renewed with redoubled vigor. . . . Seeing the inutility of further attempts, [Kreutzer] wisely vacated the conductor's chair; this was the signal for general applause and fresh calls for Maretzek, who [by some coincidence], being convenient to the scene ["white-cravatted, waistcoated, and kid-gloved"] . . . stepped forth and was saluted with immense applause, in which the ladies joined, waving their embroidered handkerchiefs in recognition of the handsome conductor, who smilingly acknowledged the graceful compliment." After a little by-play with Kreutzer, who understandably seemed relieved to be put out of his misery, Maretzek, "in obedience to the people's will," triumphantly resumed his place at the podium, and the wicked directors were foiled.[135]

After the third act Maretzek was called out on the stage, and in response to the storm of applause, he made the following little speech: "Ladies and Gentlemen: I am not prepared for the honor you have done me today. You will excuse me if I tell you, in a few words, that I am very grateful for your kindness. I must abstain from any further remarks, as my last speech made so great an effect. (Roars of laughter.) I shall refrain from further speechmaking. (Renewed applause.)"

Upon a hurried succeeding exchange of letters between de Stankovitch and Paine (apparently still in the picture), the defeated Academy directors, in a sorry attempt to

[133] Consisting, according to the *Herald* (November 13), of an agreement to pay an unspecified "round sum per night, with the understanding that a certain person is not to be employed."

[134] "These are Clan Alpine's warriors true" (Sir Walter Scott, *The Lady of the Lake* [1810], Canto V, Stanza 9).

[135] As part of this elaborate charade, Madame LaGrange had threatened to leave the theatre if Maretzek did not conduct.

Maretzek the Indomitable.

save face, passed a resolution: "That in consideration of M. de Stankovitch's honorable conduct with respect to his lease, that no condition be imposed as to whom he shall employ as conductor."

On the fourth night of the new season, George Templeton Strong attended the opera.

November 17. . . . Opera . . . *L'Étoile du nord*—doesn't improve on acquaintance—very prostrating music. Some talent—dreadful strain and oppressive labor—little sign of genius—nothing but painful effort to be brilliant from introduction to finale. Polished insanity is bad, but Meyerbeer's toilsome struggle to astonish is worse. He's constantly striving to stand on his head after the manner of an eccentric genius, and the result is fatiguing, if only from sympathy with the composer.

November 22. . . . Just from the Philharmonic. . . . Concert was at the Academy of Music. Crowd unprecedented in the annals of that Society.[136] The building was packed full half an hour before Eisfeld rapped for his forces to come to order. We almost abandoned the quest of seats in despair—only the most indefatigable exertions gained them at last.[137] A great change from the old scenes at the Apollo Rooms; not wholly for the better.

Nine-tenths of this assemblage cared nothing for Beethoven's music and chattered and looked about and wished it was over. A smaller audience of appreciative people would have been far more agreeable, even to the orchestra, for it would have applauded with more sympathy and intelligence. However, it's well to bring masses of people into contact with the realities of music; it helps educate their sense of Art, and Heaven knows they need it. Think of this vast congregation listening apathetically to the Fifth Symphony,[138] and their exploding into a demand that LaGrange repeat her "Concert Variations" by Rode, a piece of inane vocalization. Very difficult, "would to Heaven it were impossible," as Dr. Johnson said.[139]

November 28. . . . [visited by his young nephew from Boston, on November 24] took little Nelson Derby to Niblo's, where we saw *Pongo, the Intelligent Ape,*[140] and as

[136] It was "one of the largest audiences ever present at a musical performance in this city," reported the *Courier and Enquirer* (November 24, 1856). The recent growth of the Philharmonic was nothing short of prodigious. "Niblo's was too small last season—the Academy of Music is too small this," wrote the *Times* (November 24, 1856). Indeed, Everybody was there: "Thalberg was there—Gottschalk was there—Mason was there—Maretzek was there—Mlle. d'Angri was there—Mrs. Emma Bostwick was there—the Opera Company was there—while the orchestra included every resident instrumental musician of note in the city. Henry C. Timm, the President of the Philharmonic Society . . . [made] crashing noises, at proper intervals, on the cymbals" (*Dwight's,* November 29, 1856, p. 69).

[137] Indeed, "chairs were brought in and hired to those who were fortunate enough to get them, at the rate of a quarter of a dollar apiece" *(Dwight's, ibid.).* And even so, many ladies were obliged to stand throughout the evening.

[138] Richard Grant White agreed: "We never saw Beethoven's masterpiece fall so flat before a Philharmonic audience before. The performing members of this Society are now erring as much on one side as in former years they did on the other. They now seem to be turning the Association into a money-making concern. This will end in its ruin as a Philharmonic Society. Its tone will inevitably become low—musically first and socially afterward—and then it will be no better than a promenade concert, which, however good, is not a Philharmonic concert. There is not one person in twenty of that vast concourse on Saturday evening who understood or enjoyed the music, or went to the concert for the music's sake" (*Courier and Enquirer,* November 24, 1856).

[139] LaGrange had generously volunteered to replace Bertha Johannsen, the new *prima donna* of the German Opera, who, reported Seymour, had sent advance word to the Society that "she was going to be sick for a few days and could not sing." Besides the Rode Variations, which LaGrange sang sensationally, as usual (despite the vocal wobble, or wiggle, that was becoming more and more noticed), she fared less well with Mozart's *Non mi dir (Don Giovanni).* Two other soloists "afflicted the concert," wrote Seymour, one a violinist, William Doehler, a member of the opera orchestra, who played an excessively long fantasia by Ferdinand David on Schubert's song *Lob der Tränen* ("In Praise of Tears," op. 13.2); the other a pianist, Robert Goldbeck (1839–1908), a recent arrival, via England, from Germany, who played solos by Chopin, Weber, and himself. "They were nice players," wrote Seymour, "but not of sufficient importance to merit individual mention." Besides Beethoven's Fifth, the orchestra played Cherubini's Overture to *Medea* and Gade's "Scotch" Overture, the latter, according to Seymour, a work "well chosen for playing out the audience. The only regret is that it cannot play itself out of the Library of the Society" (*Times,* November 24, 1856).

[140] A popular pantomime performed by the Ravels.

the curtain fell on the dying tableau of that faithful and ill-treated animal at an early hour, we went to the Academy of Music and saw the last act of *Il trovatore.*[141] Nelson thought it not near as good as Pongo. Children often utter profound truths; I agreed with Master Nelson.

Tuesday [November 25] to Eisfeld's first "Classical Soirée" of this (the seventh) season. Mozart's Quartette in C major, no. 6[142] (nice Andante), Schubert [Piano] Trio in B-flat, no. 1 [played by Richard Hoffman, Noll and Bergner], and Beethoven Quartette in F major, op. 18 [no. 1 (1798–1800)].[143] Nothing very salient in any of them. At least one half the "classical" music now extant should be burned with fire and utterly destroyed, under the direction of a competent commission. Mankind would lose some nice things, to be sure, but little extracts might be saved that would include all that is worth having, and then givers of concerts would be obliged to confine themselves to the really great and genial works that would remain, and which we now hear so seldom, "for the sake of variety."[144]

Last night with Ellie to Thalberg's at Niblo's Saloon. First of a new series of [three] concerts with an orchestra,[145] and among the most satisfactory performances (outside the Philharmonic room) I've attended for a long while. Thalberg makes up his programs very judiciously.[146] I'm thankful to any man who gives me a chance to hear the Overture to *Oberon, Non più andrai,* and Beethoven's Concerto in C minor (in part)—even a good scrap from the *Barber* and the Overture to *William Tell.*[147] Thalberg was superb, of course, but played nothing I cared to

[141] Sophisticated fare for a contemporary child!

[142] Probably K. 465, number six of the "Haydn set."

[143] Additionally, Maria Brainerd sang one of Mendelssohn's songs on Goethe's poem "Suleika," either op. 34, no. 4 (1834), or op. 57 (1839), and "The Streamlet" by Kalliwoda, with violin *obbligato* played by Noll.

[144] Strong did not attend Eisfeld's following *soirée,* on December 23, when the program consisted of the String Quartet, op. 16, by the rarely heard Bohemian composer Wenzel Veit; a Nocturne for French horn by W. Lorenz, played by Henry Schmitz; a first performance of the Trio concertant, op. 119, by Spohr, played by Noll, Bergner, and Robert Goldbeck; songs by Kücken and Schubert, performed by Otto Feder; and Beethoven's String Quartet in B-flat major, designated as number six, doubtless his op. 18, no 6.

[145] In the scant week since the brilliant conclusion of his first series Thalberg had given concerts in Albany, Troy, Newark, and Philadelphia; he was now back in New York, and—floating on clouds of mellifluous Ullmanesque promotional prose—was about to launch his second series. Retaining Morelli, Thalberg would be assisted, instead of Wilhorst, by the renowned opera contralto Elena d'Angri (1821–?), the "Cantatrice di camera to the Emperor of Austria," who had arrived in early November, accompanied by her husband and her sister (or daughter) Mathilde d'Angri. Instead of Señor Nunó at the piano, a small orchestra (advertised as a "Grand Orchestra") conducted by Carl Bergmann would henceforth supply overtures and accompaniments, thus providing an exciting new dimension to the concerts (especially satisfactory to Strong) by allowing Thalberg to play the first movement of Beethoven's Piano Concerto, No. 3 in C minor, op. 37 (1800), and later the one in E-flat major, the "Emperor."

[146] Strong was giving Thalberg credit that more likely was due to Bergmann.

[147] Strong chose to ignore the highly acclaimed performances of the debutante Elena d'Angri in arias from *Semiramide* and *La cenerentola* and in an "English Scene, with Recitative," from Alexander Macfarren's "serenata" *The Sleeper Awakened* (London 1851), dedicated to her and the English tenor Sims Reeves. Described by Richard Grant White (*Courier and Enquirer,* November 28, 1856) as "a dark-haired, dark-eyed dame, with a meaning look, a winning smile, and a plenteous person," she was a "vocalist of the first rank," who, in White's opinion, "among the contraltos . . . has had no

hear,[148] save and except Beethoven's lovely concerto.[149] The crowd was dense. Thalberg is achieving a great success and must be making lots of money out of the Gentiles. (His features indicate him to be an Israelite.)

Heat and carbonic gas made the ill-ventilated concert room pestilential and purgatorial.[150] It was fearful to look at the multitude of men and women and of glaring gaslights, and to think of the consumption of oxygen. I tried to imagine carbonic acid a visible vapor, streaming up in columns from the chandeliers to the ceiling and pouring down the walls to mingle with the crowd.[151] . . . Ellie has been at the Opera tonight [to hear *Il trovatore*].

December 1. . . . Went tonight solus (Ellie is at her mother's) to hear the third part of the *Seasons* by the Harmonic Society at Dodworth's, with a piano and string quartet as substitute for an orchestra. Solos poor. Basso sang false enough to give one neuralgia; perhaps he had given it to one of his colleagues, for the cries of the tenor were terrible. But the choruses were very clearly given, particularly the noble "Hunting Chorus," though the light and shade of the orchestra were sadly missed in its grand closing phrases.[152] I thought Haydn's music would have pacified and placidified me, but it didn't.[153]

~

With the opera season suddenly and unexpectedly shortened by two weeks, opera-goers were torn between gloom over its rapidly approaching end and titillation over the impending production of Verdi's morally questionable opera *La traviata* (Ven-

---

equal here, except Alboni." The critics agreed that she was magnificent; in Burkhardt's estimation no less magnificent than Thalberg. Morelli sang an aria from *The Marriage of Figaro* and the *Largo al factotum* from *The Barber of Seville* with his usual artistry. Bergmann, in addition to the overtures to *Oberon* and *William Tell,* closed the program with the March from *Tannhäuser.*

[148] Thalberg's other pieces on the program were his fantasies on *Lucrezia Borgia* and *L'elisir d'amore.*

[149] Like Fry, the *Albion*'s contentious new critic *Raimond,* who had replaced the persistently ailing *Gamma,* categorically disapproved of the concerto as an art form (as he did of the symphony): "For our own part, not even Mr. Thalberg's playing can reconcile us to this unnatural union of the orchestra with the pianoforte," he wrote. (Richard Grant White agreed; Burkhardt disagreed.) "Either the orchestra must savage the pianoforte, or good-naturedly patronize it, or respectfully give way to it," wrote *Raimond.* "Of course, Mr. Bergmann had the good sense to adopt the latter course" (*Albion,* November 29, 1856, pp. 571–72). Neither of these delicately attuned critics demurred, however, nor did Strong, at Thalberg's elaborate cadenza; indeed, it was "no less striking," wrote White, than Beethoven's original.

[150] *Raimond,* too, pronounced the "tropic atmosphere" at this concert "suffocating" and "unendurable," thereby incurring Niblo's wrath and the consequent withholding of the offending critic's press tickets *(ibid.).*

[151] Indeed, for a short period following this concert, theatre ventilation became a hot topic in the press.

[152] The soloists were Mrs. Georgiana Stuart Leach, Miss Behrend, a Miss Rhemmio, and Messrs. Johnson and Wooster; the conductor was Bristow, reinstated after resigning and being replaced by Bergmann for several months; Timm accompanied at the piano. The program included as well Mendelssohn's *Lobgesang* and the *Inflammatus* from Rossini's *Stabat Mater.* The further activities of the Harmonic Society in 1856 are discussed in the following OBBLIGATO.

[153] Perturbed by matters at Columbia College beyond even Haydn's powers to soothe, Strong wrote (December 1): "Confound the College and its concerns. It's perfectly clear that my delightful dream—indulged in for eighteen years—of helping build up a real seat of learning, has vanished and gone."

ice 1853), based on the Alexandre Dumas *fils* novel *La Dame aux camélias* (1848).[154] Recalling last year's controversies over *Rigoletto* and *Il trovatore, Porter's Spirit* expected another "general outcry. . . . Yet what nonsense all this outcry is," reasoned its reviewer (Darcie). "*La Dame aux camélias* has been done in all sorts of ways as a drama,[155] and *La traviata* is but an operatic version of the same subject. . . . We fully expect that the orthodox and religious press will be 'down upon' *La traviata,* but that will not prevent the public from hearing it and judging for themselves" (*Porter's Spirit,* November 29, 1856, p. 216).

Indeed, the outcry had already begun: "In this opera," reported the *Evening Post* on November 18, "Verdi has 'out-Heroded Herod'; and if, as the rule seems to obtain, the greater the complication of horrors presented by the plot, the greater the success of the opera, we may predict for the last abortion of Verdi's muse the most flattering success." And Hagen, in the *Review and Gazette* (November 29, 1856, p. 370): "Verdi's poorest opera, *La traviata,* will be performed at the Academy. Just as we expected, the management has already come out in the *Herald* with an article upon the controversy on the immorality of the piece, which took place in England during the performances. It is the only means to make the trashy, immoral music pay." Upon which Burkhardt commented: "We can well understand what 'trashy' music means (for we have listened to all of Verdi's operas), but are at a loss to know what 'immoral' music means" (*Dispatch,* November 30, 1856).

Strong, who probably had read the Dumas novel, maintained that the plot was no better or worse than that of many a revered classic.

December 3. . . . Ellie has been with the Kuhns to hear Verdi's *Traviata*—first performance. People say the plot's immoral, but I don't see that it's so much worse than many others, not to speak of *Don Giovanni,* which as put on the stage is little but rampant lechery, from Donna Anna's first shriek in *Non sperai* to Zerlina's squeal behind the scenes at the end of the first act.

~

The *Evening Post* critic agreed, writing on December 4, 1856: "Those who have quietly sat through the glaring improprieties of *Don Giovanni* will hardly blush or

[154] In England, wrote Watson, "the heads of the church did their best to put an injunction upon [the opera's] performance; the Queen refrained from visiting the theatre during the performances, though the music, words and all, was not unheard at the palace" (*Leslie's,* December 13, 1856, p. 18). *Raimond,* who identified the hubbub-in-advance as a "ridiculous feeling generated by some of the more absurd members of the London press," sardonically noted, after its first performance at the Academy, that *La traviata* had caused no increase in the crimes reported in the following morning's papers (*Albion,* December 6, 1856, p. 584).

[155] It was hardly unfamiliar as a play. As *Camille, or, The Fate of a Coquette,* it was first locally performed by the celebrated actress Jean M. Davenport at the Broadway Theatre in 1853. In March 1856, although it was proclaimed "among the very worst of the Frenchy dramas," it ran for three consecutive weeks at Laura Keene's Varieties (the former Metropolitan Theatre) with Keene in the title role. Just preceding its premiere as an opera, in November 1856 it was even played for a week at Barnum's virtuous Lecture Room, with Mrs. Mestayer in the title role. In December, as *Camille, or, A Moral of Love,* it was played five times at Laura Keene's Theatre in a revival that now included "musical gems" from *La traviata,* including "the celebrated Waltz," arranged by Keene's music director, Thomas Baker. In 1857 it would be burlesqued as "Camomile."

frown at anything in *La traviata*." As for the score: "We can hardly say too little in its praise. It seemed to us to have neither the force, genuineness, nor originality, either of the composer's former works, or of the other composers most commonly known to us. . . . The composer . . . hardly ever hits an undoubted *aria* and never a good one. . . . The accompaniments wanted power and richness, and the airs (!) were flat and unmusical to a degree.[156] At the same time we were tormented by fleeting reminiscences of better music . . . which, however, never came to anything, so that we felt like one waiting for a sneeze." The critic detected a distinct resemblance in the romance *Di provenza* to Stephen Foster's "Old Dog Tray" (1853), except that it was "not quite so good." Of the singers, Madame de LaGrange (the Violetta) was splendid both vocally and dramatically; Brignoli (Alfredo) was not in very good voice, and Amodio (Germont) "sang finely—his voice was as solid, round, and ripe—as himself."

"The dreadful event took place last night," jocularly wrote Seymour (*Times,* December 4, 1856). "Verdi's improper opera *La traviata* was produced for the first time with humiliating success. A moralist viewing the spectacle of keen enjoyment perceptible in the house could have none but the saddest apprehensions for the future [moral] prosperity of the audience. The thousands who were assembled, in spite of all the warnings . . . seemed to enter into the wicked spirit of the play with the greatest possible delight and to sympathize with the heroine as if she were a most estimable and praiseworthy young person."

Seymour commented particularly on the company's remarkable achievement in preparing the opera so expeditiously and so well: "It is, we believe, exactly a week since the score of this opera was received from Europe. In that brief period the parts have been copied, studied, committed to memory, and repeatedly rehearsed. There was no evidence of hurry. Everyone appeared to be well prepared; the orchestra admirable, the chorus excellent. Madame LaGrange as the heroine, was dressed charmingly and looked bewitching. Her vocalization throughout was all that could be desired.[157] The scene in the first act (it was the finale) was tumultuously encored although the curtain had descended and the artists appeared before it." In this production: "for the purpose of obtaining better wardrobe effects" (or perhaps for "moral" reasons, to distance the plot from the present?) the action was moved back a hundred and fifty years, to take place in Paris of about 1700.

Although Seymour had at first enthusiastically praised the opera's "champagney" score, on rehearing it he voiced some doubts: "The melodies are graceful and moderately fresh, are written with that distinct and fluent emphasis for which Verdi is remarkable, [but] the principal fault of the opera is that the materials are too slight for

[156] *Porter's Spirit* (December 6, 1856, p. 232), on the contrary, found the score to be "full of sparkling melodies which possess all the elements of popularity." Without a doubt, the music would be found on everybody's piano "within a month." To say nothing of the hurdy-gurdies.

[157] Although several reviewers had of late solicitously commented on unmistakable signs of vocal fatigue shown by Madame de LaGrange (and small wonder). Hagen, in his intensely malevolent review of *La traviata,* wrote: "We cannot help . . . giving expression in our sincere regrets at the frightful ravages the voice of Madame LaGrange seems to have undergone in this country. She can hardly sustain a tone longer than for one measure without trembling and shaking. We fear it will very soon seem to be that the deserving, industrious lady will be nothing but a singer of cadenzas" (*Review and Gazette,* December 13, 1856, p. 388).

four acts. Verdi appears to have been lazy, or to have written this work by contract, and with the full determination of using as little labor as possible. If the score were carefully winnowed, it would be found that there were but half a dozen grains of melody to an inordinate quantity of chaff. . . . The effect of a single hearing is decidedly pleasant, for all the leading ideas of the opera are enforced with such pertinacity that the dullest ear catches something, and thickest lips reproduce an echo of the music. Whether this pleasing sensation is increased after several performances remains to be seen" (*Times,* December 8, 1856).

But Hagen, in his review of *La traviata,* unleashed a vitriolic broadside against Paris, Parisian society, both Dumases, Italian opera in general, and Verdi in particular: "After having explored the horrors of the dungeon, prison, rope, poignard, and other delightful attributes of society in the middle ages, and the brains of its modern romantic describers, [Verdi] thought it most proper to do the same business on a more modern scale. He introduced, therefore, the musical treatment of the suffering of consumption[158] and the scenes of the brothel. As the musical illustrator of crime, immorality, and all kinds of operatic nonsense, he was certainly the right man to compose music to a libretto like that of *La Dame aux camélias.*" And musically: "*La traviata* contains the greatest amount of commonplaces ever heaped together in one opera. It is dance music without the genius of a Strauss or a Lanner. . . . In one word, *Il trovatore* compared with this new opera is a perfect jewel, and *Ernani* put together with it appears like Beethoven's *Fidelio.*" Besides, it contained insufficient ensembles; the actors were not up to the required "Bacchanalian spirit" of the work; "The whole thing was done in a heavy, desolate manner; it appeared like champagne-drinking at a funeral" (*Review and Gazette,* December 13, 1856, p. 388).

Fry, disregarding the work's "immorality," devoted his review mainly to a kind of musical synopsis of the opera—piece by piece and performer by performer. *La traviata* had "some fine passages and some exceedingly well-worked-up progressions," he wrote, but it also betrayed a certain hastiness of detail, especially in contrast to "the elaborate miniature painting of Meyerbeer's *Star* [*of the North*]." In Fry's opinion, "some of the airs would bear substitution by others in the author's happier vein."

And Richard Grant White (as reported in *Dwight's,* December 13, 1856, p. 87): "The music is as poor as Verdi can write; that of *Rigoletto,* even, shines by contrast. At the end of the third act there is a careful piece of concerted writing, but as to the rest—*niente, niente, niente.*"

Apparently oblivious to all this hullabaloo, Strong blissfully imbibed Mozart at the first rehearsal for the forthcoming Philharmonic concert on January 10, 1857.

December 6. . . . At Philharmonic rehearsal with Ellie this afternoon. Mozart's "Jupiter" Symphony. Perfectly and transcendently beautiful. No music is beautiful in equal degree with his. Sublimity belongs to Handel. The power of Beethoven is in part

[158] Generally regarded as a particularly objectionable aspect of the work: "Nothing in fact could be more flagrantly absurd," wrote *Raimond* in the *Albion* (December 6, 1856, p. 584), than to "produce a consumptive heroine singing away her soul." It was "too grossly out of nature and too flagrantly false in art to be tolerated upon the lyrical stage." Burkhardt, who found *Traviata* to possess "even less merit than the generality of Verdi's operas," heartily agreed with *Raimond*'s "sensible words" (*Dispatch,* December 7, 1856).

due to the presence of an uncanny kind of intensity and power—a mighty spirit seeking rest and finding none. Haydn owes much to the goodness and healthiness and geniality embodied in his best works. But in hearing Mozart you think only of the purity and beauty of his art—his copious creative faculty. Roses and lilies fall from his lips whenever he opens them. There is wonderful moderation and self-restraint too. He never overworks an idea. It is produced and fairly presented, and then withdrawn for something else. The Spohrs and Wagners and other painstaking mechanics must have been often tempted to swear, by his extravagant and wanton expenditure of thought: "This little lovely phrase: if it had only occurred to *me,* I could have ground it up and elaborated it into a whole symphony, and here this profligate scoundrel has wasted it utterly—used it merely to connect two parts of an air—thrown it away as the mere preface to something else, where it is not noticed till you look for it."

December 11. . . . Went to *Traviata* . . . *Traviata* is utter drivel. I could write as bad an opera myself. To call it bad is to do it more than justice; it has not strength enough to stand alone or to *be* anything. It is definable by the negation of every good quality. Its plot is mere sentimental immorality, of course. But the cultivated, enlightened dilettanti who make up the overwhelming majority of audiences everywhere care nothing for the meaning of the story an opera sets before them, so deep and fine is their appreciation of Dramatic Art; and the common remark that the plot makes no sort of difference is perfectly true, for all practical purposes. One or two people from the country, who solemnly purchase the libretto and make a point of reading and trying to understand it, may be demoralized,[159] but they are served right for coming where they don't belong. To ninety-nine out of the hundred it makes no difference whether the plot of the silly and stupid phantasmagoria that passes before their eyes is taken from the *Memoirs of Casanova* or the *Acta sanctorum.* It is in either case a mere pastime for indolence and imbecility, an unmeaning accompaniment to the music, or in most cases, to the vocalistic tightrope-dancing of certain scurvy Italians. Therefore, I'm surprised that sensible people here and abroad have made such a clamor about the immorality of this opera.

~

The day following this performance of *La traviata,* a farewell benefit for LaGrange,[160] the opera company—LaGrange, Adelaide Phillips, Brignoli, Amodio, Gasparoni, and the Maretzeks—sailed for Havana,[161] leaving the Academy of Music

[159] "As to its impropriety," wrote Richard Grant White, "it would but be known to one in a hundred of the audience, were it not for the translation of the *libretto* which Mr. Darcie has published" (containing eight pages of melodies from the opera arranged by Thomas Baker) (*Courier and Enquirer,* December 4, 1856).

[160] LaGrange was almost unanimously eulogized: "No singer ever worked more faithfully than she in her vocation," wrote *Raimond* (*Albion,* December 6, 1856, p. 584). "She has shrunk from no effort and shied in no undertaking." And Watson (in *Leslie's,* December 6, 1856, p. 7): "LaGrange is undoubtedly the most conscientious, the most honest artist we have ever had with us. She keeps every engagement, and never trifles with or disappoints the public. To her honor this is spoken, and it is a merit which adds to her deservedly brilliant artistic reputation."

[161] A smooth voyage, apparently, for the *Herald* (December 30, 1856) reported their safe arrival in Havana on December 18 and their successful opening at the Tacón Theatre on December 20 with, of course, *Il trovatore.* For their adventures in Havana, see *Sharps and Flats,* pp. 26–36.

dark and silent. Rumors were rife, however, of a speedy reopening early in the New Year, with Parodi, d'Angri, de Wilhorst, and Tiberini to appear under the direction—of Strakosch?[162] of Ullman? of Thalberg?

Thalberg, in the meantime, continued to accrue unprecedented triumph upon triumph. With an intensified schedule (if that were possible), he appeared, between side-trips to Philadelphia and Brooklyn, with d'Angri, Morelli, and Bergmann's orchestra—at Niblo's Saloon on November 29 (repeating the first movement of Beethoven's C-minor Concerto); at Niblo's Garden on the afternoon of December 2 (gratis) for the city's public-school children;[163] on the evening of December 2 at Niblo's Saloon (playing the first movement of Beethoven's E-flat Concerto); again at Niblo's Saloon on December 4; and at Niblo's Garden on December 9 and 11, when the admirable Mme. d'Angri, assisted by Mlle. Mathilde d'Angri and Morelli, gave semi-staged performances in costume of scenes from *Romeo and Juliet, Semiramide,* and *The Barber of Seville.*[164] Then, after a whirlwind tour, which included multiple appearances in Philadelphia, Baltimore, and Washington, Thalberg made a flying trip to New York to assist at Gottschalk's "farewell" concert at Niblo's Saloon on December 26.[165] The feature of the program was Gottschalk's spectacular Grand Duet for Two Pianos, on themes from the ragingly popular *Il trovatore;*[166] according to the advertisements, it had been composed especially for the occasion.[167]

"Bravura pieces of this kind do not invite criticism," wrote Seymour in the *Times* (December 27, 1856). "They are written for a certain purpose, and the test of their excellence is the success they achieve. Judged by this standard, Mr. Gottschalk's duet is an extraordinary production. The audience were electrified with it, and, notwith-

[162] Did the reappearance of Strakosch's name in the *Herald*'s columns, after a long banishment, signify another mysterious declaration of peace similar to the earlier rapprochement with Wikoff? wondered the *Dispatch* (October 16, 1856). But the Chevalier, as the *Herald* (December 26, 1856) solicitously informed its readers, was out of the running as opera director, for his presence was needed in the chancelleries of Europe, "where he has the most important diplomatic schemes in hand."

[163] An event that was principally instigated and engineered by Lowell Mason.

[164] With Elena d'Angri appearing, respectively, as Romeo, Arsace, and Rosina; not equaling Vestvali in looks but far surpassing her in "expressiveness and intelligence of physiognomy" and in "dramatic capacity," "musical culture," and "vocal power" (*Albion,* December 13, 1856, p. 596).

[165] Advertised as "the last given by Mr. Gottschalk prior to his departure for Havana, Mexico, South America, and Europe. It will also be the last appearance of Mr. Thalberg prior to his Eastern tour." Yet, on December 29, three days later, they appeared together in Brooklyn, this time with Gottschalk assisting, in a two-piano performance of Thalberg's *Norma* Fantasie, a work they frequently played together on the road. In all, according to Lott (pp. 639–47), Thalberg and Gottschalk collaborated ten times, appearing together in Philadelphia, Baltimore, Washington, Albany, and Troy, New York.

[166] This *Gran duo di bravura,* as it is listed in Doyle's *Bibliography* (D-97), was apparently never published, nor has its manuscript been found. Richard Hoffman maintains that Thalberg and Gottschalk jointly composed it (Hoffman, p. 130) and indeed, a mysterious "Duo on Verdi's 'Trovatore' (with Gottschalk)" is included in the *Grove's* (5th ed.) list of Thalberg's compositions. See also Offergeld, *Centennial Catalog,* entry 267.

[167] Also announced to appear, but prevented by indisposition, was Madame d'Angri. She was ably replaced by Madame Patania, who had been banished from the opera company early in the year after suing William H. Paine for non-payment of her salary (see *Herald, Mirror,* March 14, 1856).

standing its length and difficulty, demanded an encore.[168] To this it was entitled, not only as a compliment to Mr. Thalberg and Mr. Gottschalk, but by virtue of its effectiveness as a high-pressure concert piece."[169]

Gottschalk, with Thalberg's pupil Emile Guyon at the other piano, would repeat his *Trovatore* extravaganza at the approaching Philharmonic concert.[170] It was a program that Strong would forgo, despite its inclusion of his treasured "Jupiter" Symphony. It was not that he loved Mozart less, but that he loathed Gottschalk more.

[168] Indeed, many who had been present reportedly demanded a repeat of the entire farewell concert.

[169] Richard Hoffman particularly recalled a "remarkable double shake which Thalberg played in the middle of the piano, while Gottschalk was flying all over the keyboard in the 'Anvil Chorus,' [and] produced the most prodigious volume of tone I ever heard from the piano" (Hoffman, p. 131).

[170] Although Gottschalk had been elected an honorary member of the Philharmonic in 1855, this was his first (and apparently only) appearance with the Society.

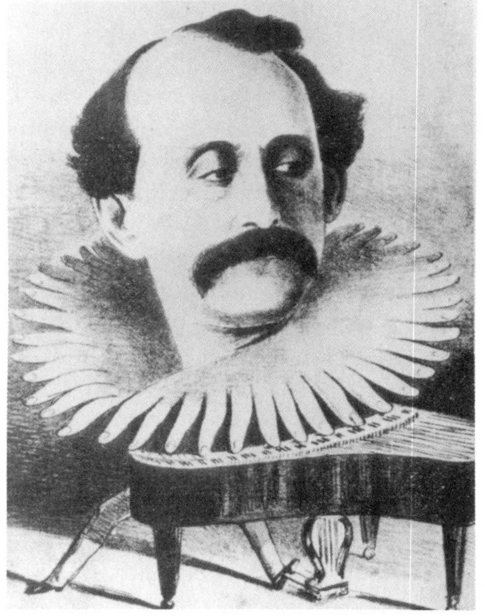

Both: Music Division, The New York Public Library

Thalberg and Gottschalk, the multidigited keyboard marvels.

OBBLIGATO: 1856

There is something in music more than mere amusement. It inspires the imagination with thoughts above the weary round of this working day world; and affords the most delicious balm for toil-worn brains and bruised affections. It is the language of love—of religion—of heaven itself. The happiest death-bed we ever witnessed was that of our good old grandmother, who passed away singing "Vital spark of heavenly flame."

New-York Evening Mirror
February 25, 1855

As the year approached its end, on December 9, 1856, the *Herald* devoted an enlightening and evocative column-and-a-half to a "retrospective and prospective view" of New York's most distinctive commodity, its entertainment business. "The public amusements of a great city are among its most important institutions," began the editorial (doubtless by Wilkins). "They assist in forming the mind of the young, either for good or bad[1]—they influence the trade of the metropolis—they give support, directly and indirectly, to thousands of worthy citizens and citizenesses—they attract strangers from all parts of the country—they make brisk traffic in dry goods, Opera cloaks, lorgnettes, ice cream, fans, jewelry, bouquets, *bon bons,* liquor, oysters, humbugs, and various other considerable and inconsiderable trifles.

"We have now about twenty places of public amusement, aristocratic and democratic—good, bad, and indifferent. Among these we find an aristocratic Opera House, eight regular theatres, and two democratic Ethiopian Opera Houses holding theatrical licenses. Each of these establishments has a style of entertainment particularly its own, and a regular paying audience, which is not often attracted to any other house.

"These theatres are nearly all new, and are the finest in the world; about two million dollars are invested in them, in buildings, lands, decorations, scenery, properties, and costumes. The nightly expenses of the Opera never fall below one thousand dollars, those of the theatres will average three hundred dollars per night; and it is a remarkable fact that while actors' salaries and all kinds of labor have risen from thirty

[1] A statement not without its poignant parallel in the final decade of the American twentieth century.

to one hundred per centum, the public has steadily resisted any attempt to increase the price of admission to the theatres. We have heard that ten years ago the joint salaries of the three most popular artists at Mitchell's Olympic amounted to twenty-six dollars weekly. The same artists now could not be had for less than ten times that amount.

"The theatres have followed the uptown movement. But a short time ago the principal houses were the Park, in Park Row, and the National, in Leonard Street. Neither of these theatres now exist. Downtown we have only the Chambers Street Theatre [formerly Burton's, originally Palmo's] and the Broadway—the last named establishment being closed for repairs.[2] Broadway, between Howard and Amity Streets, now presents one blaze of light on every evening. Here are seven theatres, all within a stone's throw of each other, all new, or nearly new, and all making a tremendous display outside and in.

"The present season commenced auspiciously," continues the *Herald,* "and such is the cosmopolitan character of our population that the theatres suffered but little from the excitement of the Presidential election. Max Maretzek was the first in the field, opening the Academy for Italian Opera on the first of September, continuing through that month—being ruined, of course—snubbing the directors in his memorable speech—then being snubbed by the directors—then going to Boston for three weeks, where he was ruined again—then coming back here with M. le Count de Stankovitch as director—somebody ruined again. . . . The career of this company is about at an end in New York."[3] The combination of Thalberg and the Opera "made too much luxury for the musical public, and it [the public] adhered to Thalberg as the freshest novelty."

The *Herald* neglected to mention the new German opera company who had ingloriously appeared three times weekly at Niblo's Garden during September and October,[4] and were now, in late December, about to resume performances at the Broadway Theatre. Imported from Germany at the instigation of Carl Bergmann, who fondly envisioned a permanent German opera in New York under his direction, the venture had been supported by a group of prosperous local German merchants.[5] It was even rumored that a German opera house was in the planning stages. The company, managed by a Herr von Berkel, consisted of his wife Minna von Berkel *(prima donna),* Anna Picker *(comprimaria),* Messrs. Hugo (or Heinrich) Pickaneser (tenor), Joseph Weinlich (basso), and the local tenor J. B. Beutler. Bergmann was, of course, the conductor and guiding musical spirit and Theodore Thomas his concertmaster.

After months of relentless propagandizing by Hagen on the superior glories of

[2] To restore a wall that had collapsed into an excavation for a building next door to the theatre.

[3] But only temporarily.

[4] Alternating with the Wonderful Ravels, who were enjoying a phenomenal run at Niblo's of some 300 consecutive performances.

[5] And with the encouragement of Theodore Hagen, the quintessential German, who hoped that "our own citizens, or such of them as desire rational opera in America given in some other way than by fits and starts, must also lend their aid to the enterprise. . . . It is a comfort to think that at last we may have something besides Bellini, Donizetti, and Verdi" (*Review and Gazette,* September 6, 1856, p. 273).

Minna von Berkel, prima donna *of the new German opera company.*

German opera and the special wonders of these particular singers, the company at last made their debut at a crowded Niblo's on September 16, with—an inexplicable choice—Meyerbeer's essentially un-German *Robert le diable* as their opening vehicle.[6] An unmitigated disaster, unanimously chorused the critics, except, of course, Hagen, who defensively maintained that, compared with this superb effort, every Italian company that had previously attempted *Robert le diable* in America had "made a complete botch" of it (*Review and Gazette,* September 20, 1856, p. 291).[7] Seymour scornfully retorted that since "the *worst*" previous cast of *Robert the Devil* had consisted of no lesser artists than Steffanone, Bertucca, Bettini, and Marini, and the most recent one of Sontag, Steffanone, Salvi, and Marini: "We are not aware that it has been *botched* by any company except the German one now at Niblo's" (*Times,* September 22, 1856).

Watson was at a loss to conceive how Bergmann, with his uncompromisingly high standards, could have allied himself with so shoddy an enterprise. With hardly "a single redeeming feature," their *Robert* was "nearly the worst opera performance" Wat-

[6] Even Hagen was forced to admit that he would have preferred a "more thoroughly national work" for their opening, but they had their reasons, he extenuated, and besides, he claimed, *Robert der Teufel* possessed more Germanic elements than did Flotow's *Martha.*

[7] Might it have been their misguided intention to outdo Maretzek's elaborate productions of the work that had prompted the German company to make this outlandish choice?

son had "ever witnessed in New York." Madame von Berkel, the Isabelle, despite an adequate voice and apparently earnest effort, tended to "shout unpleasantly," as did Mlle. Anna Picker, the Alice; Herr Pickaneser, the Robert, on the other hand possessed a diminutive, "boudoir voice" that ludicrously belied his heroic build.[8] Only the basso Weinlich, who sang Bertram, showed some small promise, although he, too, was far from being first-class—or even second. Beutler, who as a rule was merely tolerated, absolutely shone in this company (*Leslie's,* September 27, 1856, p. 243).

The troupe fared no better with their following offerings. Despite Hagen's blissful prognostications of a wide-ranging and innovative repertory,[9] they proceeded to reiterate such familiar works as *Alessandro Stradella* (September 20), *Masaniello* (September 27), and, on October 4, *Der Freischütz.*

"Heard two acts of *Der Freischütz* Tuesday evening [October 7] at Niblo's," wrote Strong in his private journal on October 9. "Poorly sung, on the whole. It was sad to hear Agatha [Minna von Berkel] struggling and striving in vain to do justice to that freshet of strong, joyous melody—her Allegro in the second act. She sang her notes, but the contrast between her visible toil and the free, spontaneous inspiration of her music was too manifest. The orchestral business was all admirable, the glorious overture could not have been played with more accuracy or truer feeling. Bergmann is a great leader."

Things at last began to give promise of looking up[10] with the German company's following presentation, on October 9, of Lortzing's charming opera on Fouqué's *Undine* (Magdeburg 1845), and it was hoped that with the new singers momentarily expected from Germany the venture might yet prove successful. And indeed, their prospects considerably brightened with the arrival of Bertha Johannsen,[11] a *prima donna* from the Frankfort opera, who gave superior performances of Agathe in *Der Freischütz* on October 23, Lady Harriet in *Martha* on October 25, and Marie in *The Daughter of the Regiment* on October 28.[12] A tall and personable, if not exactly beautiful, blonde, Johannsen not only possessed a powerful soprano voice of good quality and wide

[8] Although Fräulein Picker and Herr Pickaneser had "made the reverse of a success" in their roles, Burkhardt could not, "under any circumstances," condone the hisses they had received (*Dispatch,* September 21, 1856).

[9] Going far beyond the overworked *Martha* and *Der Freischütz,* Hagen's dream repertory encompassed such "German" works as "Boieldieu's *Die weisse Dame* and Halévy's *Die Judin,*" as well as Lortzing's *Undine, Die beiden Schützen,* and *Zar und Zimmermann;* Flotow's *Stradella* (and *Martha*); Meyerbeer's *Hugonotten* and *Nordstern;* Wagner's *Lohengrin* and *Tannhäuser;* Beethoven's *Fidelio;* Weber's *Oberon* (and *Der Freischütz*); Weigl's *Die Schweizerfamilie;* Nicolai's *Merry Wives of Windsor;* and Mozart's *Figaros Hochzeit;* also such German adaptations from Bellini, Adam, Donizetti, and Auber as the company's repertory might include (*Review and Gazette,* July 12, 1856. p. 209). But Burkhardt hotly objected to any alien intrusion: "Our public goes to Niblo's," he maintained, "to witness *German* opera, not to see translations, already old and worn out by repeated good, bad, and indifferent performances in French, Italian, and English forms" (*Dispatch,* October 26, 1856).

[10] Except, that is, for Pickaneser, who only deteriorated with each succeeding performance and was "guilty of vocal 'false pretences' in holding the rôle of leading tenor in a company aspiring to artistic responsibility," wrote Darcie (*Porter's Spirit of the Times,* October 18, 1856, p. 120).

[11] Madame Johannsen was accompanied by her husband, a Herr Scherer (or Scheerer), a *basso buffo* (or baritone).

[12] At Johannsen's second *Martha* (on October 29) Martini d'Ormy took over the role of Nancy from an ailing Madame von Berkel. An improvement. Also added to the German company were the local baritone Oehrlein and, incongruously, the tenor Giuseppe Guidi (of Astor Place memory), who

range, but knew how to use it with skill and taste; she was, besides, "a practiced actress."

A distinct improvement at the box office was hoped for, as well, with the shift, on October 23, from the original blanket admission price of fifty cents (with no reserved seats) to a more socially selective pricing schedule of one dollar for reserved seats in the parquet and dress circle, fifty cents for unreserved tickets in the family circle, and twenty-five cents for seats in the upper boxes.

With Johannsen bringing new life to the enterprise, ambitious plans were announced for new productions: Lortzing's *Zar und Zimmermann, Die weisse Dame* (Boieldieu's *La Dame blanche*) and even *Fidelio.* But abruptly the premiere of *Zar und Zimmermann,* advertised for November 4, was canceled at the last minute. "Whether that diminutive manager, Mr. von Berkel, has come to a standstill at last, or whether the stoppage is only temporary, caused by sickness in the troupe," Darcie was at a loss to say (*Porter's Spirit,* November 8, 1856, p. 168). And although, concededly, he might regret the permanent loss of Madame Johannsen and Mr. Weinlich (and might even wish to hear Signor Guidi again), the writer regarded the entire enterprise as a cynical "experiment on the credulity of the public," and the sooner the remainder of the company departed for the beer-gardens of the Bowery, the better.

An afflicted Hagen chiefly blamed the fiasco—for such it was—on the joint refusal of Madame Johannsen and her husband Herr Scheerer to perform unless they were paid in advance—a particularly unfair demand since they had been paid a month's salary before embarking for the United States. But, too, Hagen blamed Niblo's exorbitant rental of $300 a night—a staggering $900 a week, due weekly in advance—as a serious factor in the company's financial collapse, to say nothing of the salaries of the other featured singers, the chorus singers, orchestra musicians, and the thousand-and-one other financial demands of opera production, however modest. It was only with the help of the few concerned German/American citizens who came to the rescue that the company had been enabled to survive as long as they did, and only with more such help—and with a more efficient managerial approach (directed by Hagen)—would German opera at last "fulfill its destiny: to complete the musical education of this country" (*Review and Gazette,* November 15, 1856, p. 354).

At the end of the year the German company rose phoenix-like from the ashes and again, under Bergmann's musical direction, commenced a new three-times-weekly season of German opera at the recently restored Broadway Theatre. For their opening, on December 29, they presented Beethoven's *Fidelio,* with Madame Johannsen (as Leonora), Madame von Berkel (Marcellina), Pickaneser (Florestan), Scheerer (Fernando), Weinlich (Pizarro), Oehrlein (Rocco), and Beutler (Jacquino). Theodore Thomas was again the concertmaster, Weinlich did double duty as stage director, the versatile violinist Joseph Mosenthal (of the Philharmonic and the Mason/Bergmann quartet) directed a chorus largely drawn from Bergmann's German singing societies, the sets were designed by George Heister, and the costumes by Hollerman.

---

had apparently acquired enough German to substitute, on October 27, for the inept Pickaneser in the role of Stradella. Rarely praised in the past, Guidi was positively welcomed as a distinct improvement over his predecessor. Not so the other new members of the cast: Mlle. Kronfeld, a frightened, seventeen-year-old debutante with a tiny voice, who attempted the role of Leonore, and a Herr Neufeld, the Barbarino, whom even Hagen hoped never to hear again.

This first German *Fidelio* in America elicited evasive critical double-talk no less murky than had its English forerunner at the Park Theatre in 1839.♪ At that time M. M. Noah had proclaimed it to be "a work of sublime *maestoso* . . . full of imposing combinations, comprehensiveness of thought, and perfect harmony in the instrumental accompaniments." Seymour now chose to describe *Fidelio* as "a classical work [that] in its characteristics betrays the prolific invention of the master of symphonic composition. To a musician," he continued, "it is interesting principally for the variety and originality of its musical forms and for the abundant coloring of its harmonies and orchestral treatment; to the public it is rather heavy; to the artist somewhat laborious. For these reasons *Fidelio* is not what may be termed a popular Opera, although it invariably achieves a temporary success. But it is an Opera which benefits the act to which it belongs, and which in its appointed way prepares the mind for better or worse—thereby resembling the marriage service"[13] (*Times,* December 31, 1856).

Hagen, needless to say, was ecstatic that an authentically German *Fidelio* had at last materialized in this musically benighted land. "An event in the history of musical art in this country," he called it. Yet he, too, sought to justify the failure of this towering masterpiece to achieve popular acceptance. "We daresay a great many of our amateurs, and even artists, who heard this opera for the first time were disappointed. It is so different from the customary operas given in our theatres that to most of the above-named persons the music must have appeared unintelligible.[14] . . . The fact is that in some parts of *Fidelio* Beethoven was so much in advance of his time that even now it can scarcely be named popular with our advanced amateurs and artists." Yet, at his most advanced, Beethoven was closely linked to Mozart, wrote Hagen, giving instances of the Mozartian influences he detected in *Fidelio.* But Beethoven had taken Mozart only as an inspirational point of departure. Using his orchestra as more than mere accompaniment, Beethoven had cast each instrument in a definite role indispensable to the unfolding of the drama. To cope with the demands of this complex orchestration and, moreover, of the spoken dialogue in which the work abounded, the singers were faced with unique difficulties requiring not only superlative vocalization and musicianship, but special declamatory and histrionic skills as well.

Considering these formidable difficulties, the performance had been "pretty satisfactory." The orchestra under Bergmann did commendably, although they might have benefited from more rehearsals, wrote Hagen. Johannsen, like most *prime donne,* sang better than she spoke, and although she evidently had some comprehension of her part, she lacked the physical or dramatic power fully to realize it; besides, the role required a voice of greater compass than Johannsen possessed.

But a euphoric Burkhardt doubted if any living soprano could have surpassed the "magnificent grandeur, earnestness, and largeness of effect" that Madame Johannsen brought to her role. Indeed, he credited what he termed the "triumphant success" of the *Fidelio* production chiefly to her "almost flawless" performance. After his earlier prognostications of disaster, Burkhardt proclaimed that this production of *Fidelio* had at last placed the troupe "upon a firm pinnacle of operatic fame" (*Dispatch,* January 4, 1857). Yet, only a sparse audience attended the following performance of *Der Freischütz*

[13] The work's complete title is *Fidelio, oder die eheliche Liebe (Fidelio, or, Conjugal Love).*

[14] Indeed, the *Courier and Enquirer* (December 24, 1856) recommended that in order to comprehend *Fidelio,* Corbyn's newly issued libretto be read—but *before,* not during, the performance.

on December 31. The German company would continue to eke out their engagement at the Broadway Theatre for most of the following month.

In December, too, the Pyne/Harrison troupe at last returned to Niblo's after a triumphant farewell tour that had extended far beyond their original expectations.[15] Opening on December 15 with an ill-chosen vehicle *Le Val d'Andorre (The Valley of Andorre)*[16] (Paris 1848)—an apparently misplaced attempt at light opera by Halévy—they suffered one of their rare failures. Not only was the work devoid of a single memorable melody, complained Seymour (*Times,* December 16, 1856), but Louisa Pyne, ever a tower of vocal perfection, had betrayed "frequent signs of fatigue, and more than once we missed the finished excellence of this admirable vocalist"; perhaps she had overexerted herself at rehearsals, he wrote. Dramatically, however, Pyne was more delightful than ever. Harrison both sang and acted better than ever before; Charles Guilmette, a newcomer, possessed a baritone voice of limited sonority but delicious quality; he "managed it like an artist" and was a fine actor, besides. But [W.] H. Reeves! "Without a different and more happy set of circumstances," cryptically wrote Seymour, "it is impossible for any man to have been worse than Mr. Reeves, and nothing but the extreme scarcity of tenors in the 'Valley of Andorre' can account for his success with the fair sex" (a reference to the plot, if not the audience). The orchestra, conducted by Anthony Reiff, Jr., aroused Seymour's disapproval as well: "It is little else than insulting to pretend to give operas with an orchestra of twenty-two or twenty-three performers," he stormed. "We are surprised that Mr. Niblo permits the reputation of his theatre to be compromised by such senseless parsimony."[17]

The Valley of Andorre was promptly dropped in favor of a succession of foolproof Pyne/Harrison classics: *The Crown Diamonds, The Bohemian Girl, The Daughter of the Regiment,* and for the holidays, *Cinderella,*[18] all being especially captivating after "Halévy's dull mass of sound," as Darcie remarked (*Porter's Spirit,* December 27, 1856, p. 280).

Thus the Broadway lyric stage in 1856—at least in its higher manifestations. In the domain of popular musical entertainment minstrelsy continued to reign supreme, with Buckley's Serenaders, George Christy and Wood, White's Serenaders, and Bryant and Mallory's Campbell's Minstrels commanding the field. On August 25 both the Buckley and the Christy and Wood companies scooped Maretzek's September 1 opening at the Academy with gala openings of their own. The Buckleys, absent since March,[19] inaugurated their new "beautiful temple" at 585 Broadway with a blackface

[15] During the interim they had stopped off in New York to give two of their typical concerts at Niblo's, on May 26 and 28.

[16] Performed in 1851 at Brougham's Lyceum as a benefit for the actor Henry Lynn and immediately forgotten.

[17] Regretting that the effect of the "gay little French operas" in which this company excelled "should be marred by an insufficient orchestra," Seymour later absolved Reiff, observing that the conductor "appears to be a painstaking man and does the best he can with the small means at his disposal" (*Times,* December 19, 1856).

[18] *Cinderella* was being presented as a year's-end attraction at Barnum's Lecture Room as well.

[19] The Buckleys' long absence from the New York scene suggests possible business difficulties early in 1856, for in January they collaborated with Perham in his "Great Matrimonial and $100,000 Gift Enterprise," an unlikely alliance. At any rate, the Buckleys announced that they would be tour-

At Buckley's New Opera House.

burlesque of *Il trovatore*.[20] As one of "a few invited guests" at a preview of the theatre, the *Mirror* (August 23, 1856) reported on its "many and elegant *coups d'oeil*. . . . It is one of the most compact and complete little theatres we have ever seen, having a regular stage, an ample parquet and gallery capable of seating 1800 persons, an orchestra and proscenium." According to the *Mirror,* it had cost some $30,000 to build—the Buckleys claimed to have spent $50,000. They boasted, too, of its "double places of exit, one on Broadway, the other in the rear, both of which will be opened at the

ing during the construction of their new hall, and that the old locale at 539 Broadway would be available to let from April first on. During the period before their departure the Buckleys presented such novelties as *Richard the Third, or, Shakespeare Murdered in Twenty Minutes; Matrimonial Blessings, or, A Musician's Rehearsal;* and something called *The Court of Ice Burg.*

[20] "There is a band of negro minstrels in New-York which is absolutely cruel in its adaptation of beautiful music to barbarous words and worse acting," ranted Hagen (*Review and Gazette* (November 29, 1856, p. 370). "They lately performed a burlesque of Verdi's *Trovatore,* and we were shocked at the savage cruelty with which they treated the music. Imagine, reader, the beautiful music of the *Anvil Chorus* sung to such words as 'Fill up the lager, fill up the lager' . . . and the duet in the last act composed of the words, 'Spare my darkey, spare my darkey,' and 'Dry up, dry up,' etc. etc. etc., mingled with any number of ancient and terrible negro airs, the very remembrance of which makes

conclusion of the performance." The *Mirror* found the Broadway entrance to be "not well arranged, nor is it so wide as it should have been. But in case of accident, means of egress have been provided under the stage to Mercer Street." Although no music had been heard at the preview celebration, "there were plenty of mirth and wine, the flavor of the latter [of which] a portion of the company seemed to enjoy amazingly."

In September, Caroline Hiffert (who had recently been singing with the Alleghanians)[21] replaced Miss Eleanor as the Buckleys' *prima donna,* appearing in their "new" burlesque operas: *Maritana* (during September and October), *The Bohemian Girl* (November), and *Cinderella* (December).[22] Also in November they presented *The Dismal of the Dread Swamp,* a "Grand, Original, Musical, Quizzical, and Comical Parody" of Harriet Beecher Stowe's new novel *Dred, a Tale of the Great Dismal Swamp* (1856).[23]

On August 25, too, Christy and Wood, after a short summer recess, reopened their newly refurbished "Temple of Negro Minstrelsy" at 444 Broadway, now enlarged to hold 1800 persons. In Barnumesque superlatives they touted their theatre's innovations, the most prominent being a hydrant standing in the middle of the auditorium, "so arranged as to be perceptible to all, with hose attached, so that a full head of water could at any time be turned on by anyone in its vicinity." Not that it would ever be required, since no effort was being spared to guard against fire or any other sort of accident. (Contemporary theatre-goers were perpetually haunted by the specter of fire, and justifiably so.) Christy and Wood's advertisements proudly called attention, too, to the "tasty drawing room, which has been magnificently fitted up for the accommodation of ladies, and we think we may fairly challenge the world to produce the equal to our establishment." Their opening attraction was a revival of the T. D. Rice classic *Bone Squash Diavolo,* featuring George Christy. The major hit of their season was *Weffo, the Sensible Monkey* (presumably an offspring of *Pongo, the Intelligent Ape*), hilariously played by George Christy.

Among the old-timers, early in August Eph Horn, the beloved "Brudder Bones," returned from his triumphs in California, and again joined forces with Charley White and confreres in a show at the Buckleys' former opera house, now again called the Chinese Rooms. There they were followed in September by Dan Bryant and Ben Mallory's "old and original Campbell's Minstrels, consisting of Thirteen Unequalled Performers, the Model Troupe of the World." Announced for "six (only) of their In-

---

us shudder. We shall not visit that 'opera-house' again. If they *must* give burlesques, why can they not select such music as they at least are capable of singing?"

[21] Replacing, together with a Miss Sallie Fletcher, Miriam Goodenow, who had left the group upon her marriage to one T. P. Robb, while on tour in California in 1852. By now the Alleghanians consisted, besides these ladies, of W. H. Oakley alto, J. M. Boulard basso, and J. Fletcher tenor (*Review and Gazette,* February 9, 1856, p. 33; May 17, p. 146).

[22] Reprinted from the *Express,* a lengthy and informative editorial dealing with minstreldom and its history, and particularly eulogizing the Buckleys and their opera travesties, appeared in the amusement section of the *Herald* on September 1, 1856. Masquerading as an unsigned card, it was obviously inserted by the Buckleys as an advertisement.

[23] Mrs. Stowe's novel had recently been seen in three separate adaptations for the legitimate stage: in September at the National Theatre, with little Cordelia Howard as Tom Tit, at Brougham's Bowery Theatre, with T. D. Rice as Old Tiff, and in October at Barnum's Lecture Room, with General Tom Thumb as Tom Tit.

imitable Ethiopian Soirées," they were persuaded to remain a week longer; they then moved into Empire Hall (596 Broadway) for a successful run.

Throughout this minstrel-dominated period, the Franklin Museum (sanctum of Madame Wharton's Model Artistes) boastfully advertised: "Ethiopian Troupes Flung in the Shade by the Female Opera Troupe" and their "Ethiopian singing."[24]

From May through July, model artiste-ism on a presumably higher aesthetic plane was exhibited nightly at Empire Hall (two doors above the now rebuilt Metropolitan Hotel) by Louis Keller, a German entrepreneur.[25] According to his claims, his "Grand Tableaux and Musical Soirées" encompassed "all that is famous and refined in the arts of Painting and Sculpture, either Sacred, Moral, Mythological, or Historical, together with National Subjects of more recent interest,[26] forming at once one of the most beautiful and intellectual entertainments for the approval of an enlightened people."[27] To this commendable end, Keller had engaged—"at great expense"—in addition to his troupe of twenty-seven artistes, a corps of "talented persons in the various departments of Scenery, Machinery, etc., including a full and superior orchestra," conducted by a Mr. Grille (E. Grill, a Philharmonic violinist), intended musically to enhance and complement the stage pictures.

Thus, Keller's opening program, following the performance of the Overture to *Fra diavolo,* offered a tableau, "The Chariot of the Sun," shown to the accompaniment of Lanner's "Life's Pulse Waltz"; Madame Keller's tableau, "Bacchus and Ariadne," paired with Grill's "Pepita Polka"; and Keller's creation "Famine," displayed to background music from *Lucrezia Borgia.* The grand finale of the evening was a "great National Tableau 'The Battle of Bunker Hill,' after Turnbull," musically embellished by a rousing performance of "Hail Columbia."

During his sojourn at Empire Hall, Keller continuously added new, predominantly German, performers to his cast, among them the Germania [vocal] Quartette Club, the Loreley *Männerchor,* the vocalists Kazia Lovarny and her husband Franz Stoepel (xylochordeon virtuoso and sometimes blackface minstrel), Michael Turner, an Austrian zitherist, the growingly popular actress/singer Maria Duckworth, the veteran comic entertainer Doctor Valentine, and "Adonis," an inappropriately named magician to whom Burkhardt vehemently objected. Admission at Keller's was fifty cents.

Among the more pretentious fringe entertainments during the summer of 1856 was a "Grand Literary Concert" at the Tabernacle on June 11 given by Mr. and Mrs. John Cooper Vail, who interspersed their prose and poetry declamations with opera arias and popular songs. They were assisted by Alfred Sedgwick and his eight-year-old son Charles, who collaborated in a duo on themes from *Norma* arranged for treble and bass concertinas. Tickets were fifty cents.

At the City Assembly Rooms, on July 15, a Mr. A. Chartier, "Violinist to the

[24] Their daily three o'clock performance, advertised the Franklin Museum, was "always concluded by half-past four, thereby enabling all to leave by the different steamboat and railroad lines."

[25] In 1855, Keller and his troupe had fleetingly appeared at the Broadway Theatre in *Phanor and Azemus,* an ephemeral production.

[26] As, for instance, in this election year, "A New Tableau of the Election, or, Three Candidates for the Presidency."

[27] And a variable feast, for Keller claimed to possess a "repertoire of upwards of 3,000 pictures."

Emperor of France," announced a "Musical and Terpsichorean Entertainment," with the assistance of Mr. C. B. Vandergucht, Violoncellist to the King of Belgium; Mr. Reiter, Pianist, and Mr. DuBrucq, Oboist, both from the *Conservatoire* of Brussels; Mlles. Ernestine Henrarde, First Dancer from the Royal Theatres of Denmark, Sweden, and Her Majesty's Theatre, London, and Annie Henrarde, from Her Majesty's Theatre. Admission was fifty cents; front seats one dollar.[28]

Musical free lunch was widely dispensed at the scores of plebeian refreshment places that seem to have sprung up like mushrooms in 1856. To name only a few: the Fountain Chop House (167 Walker Street) offered "Hitchcock's Free Concert" as a nightly attraction; the Bowery Free Concert Hall (157 Bowery), described as "the most magnificent place of entertainment of its kind in the world," gave "sacred concerts" on Sunday afternoons and evenings to supplant their more mundane weekday fare; Thomas H. Bell and Co.'s Free Concert Hall (535 Broadway) offered "interesting novelties"; Musical Hall (161 Bowery) featured programs (sacred on Sundays) consisting of "solos, glees, duets, comic songs, burlesques, imitations, dances, etc.," all directed by a Professor Watson (assuredly not our Watson!); and the Arcade Concert Saloon (127 Grand Street) proudly presented "Morris the original, Shaw the quaint, and Riley the humorist," a trio that outranked the "greatest melodists in the United States." At the Arcade, too, parenthetically informed a postscript to their advertisement, "Artists of a superior order of musical talent will always find an opening at this saloon."[29]

Exuberant ethnic entertainments were served up at the myriad convivial German establishments that strewed the Bowery and neighboring streets. And at the Bellevue Gardens, a new, German-oriented, suburban resort at 80th Street and the East River, a series of weekly "sacred" band concerts was launched on Sunday afternoon, June 29, featuring the Washington Band (later succeeded by Shelton's American Band) offering programs ranging from hymn-tunes to opera arias to military quicksteps to polkas, all to the accompaniment of delectable refreshments, and all for the single admission price of 12½ cents. As the season progressed, a weekly concert and ball was added to the schedule on Wednesdays at 6 P.M. The Bellevue Gardens were available besides on weekdays for picnics, "target companies," and school outings; they were easily reached by the Second and Third Avenue (railroad) "cars," which, according to the advertisements, ran every five minutes. (Oh, for the good old days!)

In town, at the Atlantic Garden on lower Broadway, Dodworth's Band resumed their long-established series of Sunday "sacred" concerts on June 1, and continued until autumn. They appeared as well for the duration of the American Institute Fair, again held at the all-but-defunct Crystal Palace in October.

[28]This superior Belgian company did not prosper. Brought from Europe on false pretenses by a group of unscrupulous speculators, they found themselves stranded at Saratoga Springs soon after their arrival. There, a sympathetic Gottschalk came to their rescue with a benefit concert; he subsequently persuaded M. Maillard, the proprietor of an elegant French confectionery establishment at 621 Broadway, to engage them to perform there nightly from 9 to 11:30 (*Dwight's,* August 30, 1856, p. 175).

[29]In vitriolic terms, Hagen describes two kinds of so-called "Free Concerts in New-York" in the *Review and Gazette,* November 29, 1856, pp. 372–73.

Among the more unusual music happenings of this lively summer was the waterborne exhibition of the sensational new steam calliope, puffed (so to speak) as the "greatest invention of the age."[30] At fifty cents a head, intrepid passengers were taken on a cacophonous cruise of New York harbor aboard the steamboat *Union,* then were deposited—depending upon the passenger's aural endurance—at the foot of Robinson, Spring, or Amos Street, ten, twenty, or thirty minutes from the time of boarding. One Jonathan Day, sole agent for the calliope, advertised that although the music, produced by steam, could be heard as far as ten to twelve miles distant, the instrument had to be seen close up to be appreciated; he invited steamboat and railroad agents to inspect the device. (Think of a generation of steam locomotives crisscrossing the nineteenth-century American terrain in tuneful ensemble!)[31]

Also off the beaten track, a more refined form of music machine arrived in New York in October when a Mr. Van Oeckelen exhibited an accomplished automaton clarinetist on whose invention he had lavished a lifetime of labor. So lifelike was the clarinetist, wrote the *Times* (October 18, 1856), that it was only when the garments of this "clockwork troubadour were removed, and the intricate cranks, drums, and levers exposed to view, that the spectator [believed he was] not really being duped. . . . If Mr. Van Oeckelen could develop a few Italian singers on the plan of the clarinet player," slyly added the *Times,* " there would be no more difficulty at the Academy of Music."

Among the popular singing groups, the Hutchinsons swooped in for a single concert at the Tabernacle on March 20, bringing, as they advertised, "New Songs (and old) of the West, of Freedom, of Temperance, of Good Times Coming, etc." The peripatetic Alleghanians, too, after a tour of the Atlantic states, gave a return concert at the Tabernacle on May 16.[32] In September they settled into the Athenaeum (654 Broadway) for a week of nightly performances.

A new and different kind of native singing group, billed as the "Old Folks," enjoyed a flurry. Refreshingly congenial to native tastes amid the surrounding musical exotica, the "Old Folks' Concerts of Ancient Sacred Music" were presented at the Tabernacle by the "New-England Pilgrim Society," a group from Massachusetts consisting of sixteen vocalists and five instrumentalists who, in eighteenth-century dress, and presumably in traditional New England style, intoned tunes by William Billings (1746–1800), Daniel Read (1757–1836), Jacob Kimball (1761–1826), and other early New England composers. "Apart from the interest attaching to the L. M. [Long Meter] and C. M. [Common Meter] tunes which delighted our great-grandfathers," wrote Seymour (whose great-grandfathers had presumably never been within sight of the Western Hemisphere), "there is something perfectly delicious in the quaintness of the costumes and the peep they afford into the coquetry of a past age." Too, the voices were good and the music given "with precision, [although] a greater regard for the lights

[30] Invented in the United States about 1850 by A. S. Denny, the steam calliope was patented in 1855 by one Joshua C. Stoddard.

[31] The calliope received an unfavorable press: "It was enough to strike a cat dumb with amazement and horror," reported the *Mirror* (July 16, 1856).

[32] News had just been received of the untimely death in Chicago, on April 24, of the greatly admired original soprano of the Alleghanians, Mrs. Robb, *née* Miriam Goodenow.

and shades (or softs and louds) would make the L. M. pieces less wearisome" (*Times,* June 3, 1856).

The popularity of the Old Folks' Concerts provoked a particularly virulent response from Hagen, who as a newcomer to these shores was receiving his first taste of this distinctive, if anachronistic, branch of American culture. The group's success, he stormed (*Review and Gazette* June 14, 1856, p. 177), only went to prove that "Mankind in more than *one* thing affords justification of the theory that the race is only an improved order of monkey—without the tail." Catering to the American predilection for "burlesques and exaggerated imitations or caricatures," as evidenced by the national passion for "the peculiarities of the African race as domesticated in America . . . men (so-called) blacked their faces, mimicked the lowest order of negroes, and in so doing found attentive audiences and plenty of silver." Now that the day of loathsome blackface minstrelsy was past, as Hagen wishfully claimed, "our own ancestors . . . are selected as a fitting theme for our ridicule, and their peculiarities of dress are burlesqued by troupes who give uncouth mimicries of the uncouth music of their times." So much for New England psalm singing.

An equally distinctive group of "Mountaineer Singers" from Berne, Switzerland, "famous for warbling complicated orchestral pieces with their voices" (*Dwight's,* May 24, 1856, p. 63), appeared for four concerts at the Tabernacle, assisted by Maria Brainerd, "the brothers L. Dachauer Gaspard," as the duo pianists from the Paris *Conservatoire* were billed, and C. Sage of the New Orleans French Theatre, then went on their way.

Concert-giving prodigiously increased in 1856. As Hagen noted (*Review and Gazette,* February 23, 1856, p. 50): "The concert season of the present winter seems to be as lively and active as that of last year was barren and lifeless. There is a complete rush amongst our artists, or those who bear this name, to exhibit their talents and abilities; everybody seems to be anxious to be heard and appreciated as much as possible." The phenomenon, doubtless encouraged by the extraordinary success of Gottschalk's *soirées,* was largely manifested by the prevalence of concerts given in series rather than singly.

The most significant of these multiple efforts was the massive series of ten weekly "sacred" Sunday evening orchestra concerts (with an eleventh added for the conductor's benefit) inaugurated by Carl Bergmann at the City Assembly Rooms on March 16, 1856 (less than a month before the expiration of Bergmann's present conducting assignment at the Philharmonic and concurrent with the ongoing Mason/Bergmann chamber-music concerts).[33] With his young colleague and protégé Theodore Thomas as concertmaster[34] and a chamber orchestra of twenty-four picked musicians (mostly from the Philharmonic), Bergmann—as he had previously done in Boston with the

[33] Describing Bergmann as "the able director of everything that is worth directing in New-York," the *Times* critic (March 18, 1856) exclaimed, after his first Sunday concert: "How that man's arm must ache when he goes to bed!"

[34] Despite William Mason's imputation of "more or less friction" between Bergmann and Thomas during the time of their quartet collaboration (Mason, p. 196), it is a fact that Bergmann chose Thomas not only to be first violinist of that group, but as concertmaster for his series of Sunday concerts, and later for the German opera at Niblo's and the Broadway Theatre.

Theodore Thomas in his early twenties.

Germania—explored a broad and frequently unfamiliar musical landscape. In addition to the tried-and-true symphonies and overtures by Haydn, Mozart, Beethoven, Mendelssohn, and Spohr, he presented unfamiliar works, many for the first time in the United States, by the contemporary giants Schumann, Wagner, and Berlioz, and also by such lesser moderns as Hugo Ulrich, Julius Rietz, and Wilhelm Tschirch.[35]

Bergmann's vocal soloists—Henriette Behrend, Otto Feder, J. B. Beutler, Oehrlein, and Anna Picker—sang opera arias by Mozart, Mercadante, Donizetti, Meyerbeer, Vaccai, and William Vincent Wallace, but also German songs by Schubert, Fesca, and Robert Franz (1815–1892). Two transitory new pianists, a Miss Lebrecht and a Mr. Emmerth, uneventfully played pieces by Mendelssohn, Chopin, Schumann, Heller, and Thalberg; Theodore Thomas more memorably played Mendelssohn's Violin Concerto; various combinations of Philharmonic musicians played chamber works (largely with French horn) by Beethoven, Cherubini, Weber, Halévy, and Spohr; and Bergmann's two German singing societies, the *Arion* and the *Sängerbund,* performed choral music by Mozart, Beethoven, Cherubini, Mendelssohn, and the idiosyncratically named Tschirch, but principally by Wagner. Indeed, the Bridal Procession from *Lohengrin* and/or the Overture, March, and Pilgrim's Chorus from *Tannhäuser* appeared on

[35] Hugo Ulrich (1827–1872), a protégé of Meyerbeer, was a talented composer whose ultimate achievements did not fulfil his early promise; Julius Rietz (1812–1877), Mendelssohn's successor as conductor at Düsseldorf, was currently the conductor of the *Gewandhaus* concerts in Leipzig; Wilhelm Tschirch (1818–1892) was one of six brothers eminent in literary and musical Germany; he would visit the United States in 1869 to conduct a number of prominent choral groups.

at least six of the eleven programs (and, it was reported, were almost invariably encored).[36]

As might be expected, each of Bergmann's concerts was glowingly praised by Hagen. It was a rare satisfaction, he wrote after the first, to report an attempt to establish instrumental concerts in our city "worth listening to [a palpable stab at the Philharmonic] and within the means of all classes" (tickets were fifty cents). The orchestra, though small,[37] succeeded admirably because "everybody tried his best to make it sound as well as possible" (*Review and Gazette,* March 22, 1856, pp. 83–84). Indeed, following Bergmann's second concert Hagen disingenuously wrote: "We should not wonder if these concerts should prove, after a little while, a dangerous rival to those of the Philharmonic, as in fact they are, if not better, at least equally good" (*Review and Gazette,* April 5, 1856, pp. 99–100).[38] Hagen was indebted to Bergmann, he stated, for the opportunity to hear first performances in America of such transcendent works as Schumann's Symphony No. 4 in D minor, op. 120 (Leipzig 1841, revised Düsseldorf 1851), and to become familiar with the music of Wagner's *Lohengrin* and *Tannhäuser,* albeit in fragments. The Schumann symphony (performed on March 30), wrote Hagen, possessed polyphonic characteristics not unworthy of Beethoven himself—characteristics, however, that rendered its melodic content inaccessible to listeners ignorant of polyphony.

Gamma (who disdainfully noted that Bergmann's audiences consisted predominantly of German males wearing hats),[39] evidently belonged to this underprivileged category, for he wrote in the *Albion* (April 5, 1856, p. 164): "This work of Schumann has no significance whatever. It is impossible to discover a single leading idea, and the only truth to be extracted from so long a musical poem is that the author is sadly deficient in creative spirit. It is in vain that he proves to us how well versed he is in his table of musical logarithms; it is in vain he has recourse to violent explosions of brass instruments, or calls to his aid the most frightful dissonances in order to attract and fix the attention; he will never be able to persuade us that mathematics and music—deafening noise and melody—are all one and the same thing."[40]

Equally harsh judgment greeted the first local performance (on April 27) of Schumann's *Manfred* Overture, op. 115 (Leipzig 1852). As far as Seymour was concerned (*Times,* April 28, 1856), it was "perfectly unintelligible" and unpleasantly flat, especially after hearing Berlioz's exhilarating "Roman Carnival" Overture (played on April 13, April 27, and at the final concert of the series, on June 1), now hailed as a work of genius.

Hagen approvingly noted an increased attendance by ladies at the fourth concert.

[36] In general, Bergmann gave an inordinate number of repeats throughout this series—probably equally for reasons of audience indoctrination and for economizing on rehearsal time.

[37] It was reportedly augmented after the first concert.

[38] Watson echoed the sentiment; he confessed that he looked forward to each of Bergmann's concerts "with as much anticipation of pleasure as in days gone by we waited, longing for the next Philharmonic concert" (*Leslie's,* May 3, 1856, p. 327).

[39] And *Dwight's* New York correspondent ——t—— observed (March 29, 1856, p. 265) that Sunday entertainments were more acceptable to members of the "foreign population" than to natives.

[40] Sentiments not entirely unknown to auditors of twentieth-century music.

Abandoning himself to mighty praises of Beethoven's ineffable *Leonore* Overture No. 3, played on that occasion, he pointedly recalled its venomous first reviews in Vienna in 1806 (probably as an object lesson to his colleagues who were inimical to modern music).

In addition to Schumann's Fourth Symphony and his *Manfred* Overture, Bergmann conducted first performances in America of his Overture, Scherzo, and Finale, op. 52 (1840), and also of Berlioz's early "Waverley" Overture, op. 2 (Paris 1828). Bergmann's firsts included as well Julius Rietz's "attractive" Concert Overture, op. 7; Hugo Ulrich's less attractive *Sinfonie triumphale,* op. 9; Wilhelm Tschirch's ambitious "Grand Dramatic Tone Picture" in ten parts, "A Night on the Sea," for solo tenor and bass (Beutler and Oehrlein), with chorus (the *Sängerbund*) and orchestra; and a Grand Overture by Bergmann himself.

Bergmann warmly championed the compositions of Mendelssohn, widely regarded as an unorthodox composer, who, with the exception of his *Midsummer Night's Dream* music, had not gained great favor among the more conservative of the local cognoscenti. "Bergmann is entitled to much praise," wrote Seymour (*Times,* April 22, 1856), "for his frequent efforts to familiarize our public with Mendelssohn's productions. Since Wagner has been talked of, it has been customary to twaddle about Mendelssohn and try to drag him down to the level of that gentleman. Mr. Bergmann evidently thinks a great deal of Wagner," continued Seymour, "but he has no distrust of Mendelssohn for that reason. The Symphony [the "Scotch"] is a lasting justification of the world's opinion of Mendelssohn's genius. It is a great and perfect work." Furthermore, the symphony had been "really wonderfully performed," as had Beethoven's *Coriolanus* Overture, op. 62 (1807), also a work billed as the Andante from "Mozart's Fantasia, op. 11,[41] and Otto Nicolai's "exceedingly effective" Overture to *The Merry Wives of Windsor* (Berlin 1849).

In his cello-playing persona Bergmann performed for the remainder of the season at the Mason/Bergmann monthly matinées, the third of which took place on January 29 at Dodworth's Hall. On this occasion the program, with Mason at the piano, included Mozart's Piano Quartet in E-flat, K. 493 (Vienna 1786), and the Piano Trio in G minor, op. 15, no. 2, by Anton Rubinstein, a composer who was increasingly performed and admired both in Europe and the United States. Maria Brainerd, as usual accompanied at the piano by her teacher, Dr. Beames, sang the "slumber aria" from *Der Freischütz* (in English) and Cherubini's *Ave Maria,* and Mason played two piano pieces—a Rhapsody on Hungarian themes, by Liszt,[42] and Mason's own *Grande Valse de bravoura.* "Liszt's Hungarian fantasias will never do in a concert-room," breezily remarked Hagen, although they could be quite charming when heard privately in the company of people familiar with Hungary and its ethnic characteristics (*Review and Gazette,* February 9, 1856, p. 35).

For the fourth matinée, on February 26, the program included Beethoven's String

[41] Attempts to identify certain compositions from their current designations are often fruitless, as in this instance.

[42] According to George P. Upton (Thomas, II, 38), it was the Rhapsody No. 12 in C-sharp minor.

Quartet in F minor, op. 95 (1810); a repeat, "by request," of Rubinstein's Piano Trio;[43] a new Tarantelle for piano, op. 87, by that "amiable and able musical thinker" Stephen Heller;[44] and, most venturesomely, the Concerto in D minor for Three Claviers by Johann Sebastian Bach, a composer known in New York chiefly by reputation. Played on three pianos by Mason, Timm, and Scharfenberg, the concerto was accompanied by the string quartet augmented by a double bassist from the Philharmonic.

Attracted perhaps by the novel prospect of a simultaneous performance on three pianos, a great and—much to Hagen's (and Watson's) disapproval—overly noisy crowd of ladies had congregated at Dodworth's, many of whom could not find a seat "although very many extra chairs had been provided." The resulting hubbub worked havoc with Hagen's serene contemplation of the Beethoven Quartet, which opened the program; it was a complex and profound work that exceeded the comprehension of the ordinary listener but offered "great and pure sensations" to the initiated.

But the Bach concerto was a disappointment. Surprisingly, Hagen, no less than his colleagues, found it hopelessly antiquated; it was, he wrote, deficient in the "sweet and melodious music" to be found in some of the same composer's works for voice and orchestra. *Gamma,* who was thankful for the chance to hear Rubinstein's trio again, felt no similar gratitude for the concerto's "resuscitation," and William Henry Fry—certainly no admirer of the music of yesteryear—pronounced the work to be interesting only as an antiquity. "Composed at a time when such music was just emerging from the fugue," he explained, "it has neither passion nor rhetoric to recommend it, nor yet transcendental harmonies. But still, it was proper to play it, [if only] as a relic of the past" (*Tribune,* February 27, 1856).

Watson, who saluted Rubinstein for possessing both "the grit" and "the stuff" needed at this time of precarious musical transition, found the Bach concerto to be not only "suggestive of antiquarianism but of a flavor that to the modern musical palate smacks unpleasantly of the *mummy.* But," he quickly about-faced, "no lapse of time can conceal the clearness and breadth of the design or the purity and consistency of the musical form. Its mathematical precision and its grammatical correctness are at once its beauties and its faults; they are beauties as forming imperishable models in their peculiar style; they are faults to the general hearer, as possessing nothing of human sentiment or passion" (*Leslie's,* March 8, p. 199; March 15, 1856, p. 215).

The fifth Mason/Bergmann matinée, on March 25, began with a Haydn "Overture in G Major," frustratingly listed as "op. 68";[45] Mason, Thomas, and Bergmann played Schubert's beautiful Trio in E-flat for violin, cello, and piano, op. 100 (Vienna 1828);[46] and, with F. Herwig supplying an extra violin, Mendelssohn's String Quintet in A major, op. 18 (1826, 1832). Mason wound up the program with Chopin's Impromptu in A-flat, op. 29 (1837) and one of the waltzes from op. 64 (1846–47).

[43] Fry regarded a trio employing a piano, violin, and violoncello as "a stupid combination, the first interfering with the two last, and the reverse" (*Tribune,* February 27, 1856).

[44] This was Hagen's opinion. To Watson, Heller's Tarantelle "hardly repaid the trouble of studying it." Mason wisely encored it with his own "Silver Spring," a beautiful work "executed *con amore,* so delicately, so gracefully, so poetically, that we . . . felt ourselves giving way to the expression of a delight that was generally felt and expressed, even by the 'lion' Gottschalk himself," who apparently was present (*Leslie's,* March 15, 1856, p. 215).

[45] See preceding footnote 41.

[46] Pronounced by Watson to be "an exceedingly labored and uninteresting composition, very bare of geniality or impulse" (*Leslie's,* April 5, 1856, p. 263).

Before giving the sixth and final matinée of the series, on April 29, the Mason/Bergmann group presented two "Classical *Soirées*," on April 15 and 22 at Dodworth's, intended, it was explained, to serve those unable to attend "morning" concerts.[47] At the first *soirée* Henriette Behrend sang songs by Robert Franz and Proch; Beethoven's String Quartet, op. 95, was repeated, as was Schumann's Piano Quartet, op. 47. At the second, Clara Brinkerhoff sang arias by G. Torrente (a deceased member of the local Italian music community) and Donizetti; Schumann's String Quartet in A, op. 41, no. 3 (1842) was performed;[48] Mason played his *Amitié pour amitié* and Dreyschock's *Zum Wintermärchen;* and the program ended with Beethoven's massive Piano Trio in B-flat (the "Archduke"), op. 97.[49]

At their final matinée they audaciously presented Beethoven's arcane String Quartet in B-flat, op. 130 (1825); a "Grand Aria" from *Robert le diable* and a song by Franz Abt were performed by Madame von Berkel, making her American debut on this occasion;[50] Mason played a group of his own pieces—the popular "Silver Spring," the Lullaby, and an immensely difficult *Étude de concert;* and the series ended with Schumann's Piano Quintet.

In the *Times* (May 1, 1856), Seymour informed his readers that Beethoven's Quartet, op. 130, was generally regarded as one of his "craziest" creations: "It was not a pleasant work to listen to, and did not fill the listener with admiration, either for the genius or science of the great master. The necessity for writing sometimes attacked Beethoven in the most commonplace way," explained Seymour, "and his muse must have been in a singularly dry condition when this quartette was brought forth." It could be of interest only to a student of music. Then, turning to Schumann: "Schumann's Quintette is a pretentious work with a limited number of ideas, magnificently elaborated." And besides: "We have had a little too much of Schumann this winter."

Watson shared Seymour's opinion of the Beethoven quartet: "Anything more dreary and monotonous we never listened to," he wrote. "It seemed to us a mere collection of fugitive pieces strung together without design and regardless of sequentiality or contrast. Long movements and short movements, some of them hopelessly spun out and others prematurely cut short, swelling up, in all, to six parts. Custom and cant commands us to admire it because it is Beethoven," wrote Watson, "but we cannot compel admiration, and in this instance Beethoven has failed to warm us or instruct us. Nothing, we believe, came from Beethoven's mind but contained some germ of beauty, and doubtless this Quartette forms no exception to the general remark, but a needle in a bundle of hay is hard to find." And worse: "We are constrained to say that the performance added little to the merit of the work" (*Leslie's,* May 17, 1856, p. 358).

[47] Among them, surprisingly, George Templeton Strong who, despite their superior programs, seems to have remained aloof from the Mason/Bergmann concerts, as he did of Bergmann's Sunday orchestra performances.

[48] A work judged by the *Musical World* (April 26. 1856, p. 201) to be "destitute of melodic thought" and lacking in "pleasing effects of contrast, light and shade, and harmonic ingenuity."

[49] ". . . one of those instances where Homer sometimes sleeps," wrote the *Musical World* of this trio, "and when he sleeps he is tedious" *(ibid.)*.

[50] "Of the singing on this occasion, the less said the better," commented ——t—— (*Dwight's,* May 3, 1856, p. 37). If Madame von Berkel represented the standard of singing at the principal German opera houses, as she was advertised to do, then woe betide the coming German opera.

But to Hagen, to hear this quartet was to float beatifically upon the topmost cloud of the seventh heaven. To hear it, he wrote, was a privilege rarely granted to the true believer in "the great and beautiful in our art. A few years ago . . . people thought this strange music was sheer madness, and most of the artists joined in this opinion." Since then, however, like Beethoven's formerly uncomprehended Ninth Symphony, "the veil which for so long a time covered the later quartets of Beethoven began to be lifted, the clouds of so-called madness began to pass away, and where formerly the uttermost darkness seemed to prevail, the daybreak of intelligence has come at last, bringing with it glimpses of long-slumbering grandeur." Hagen took the "greatest pleasure," too, in praising the extraordinary qualities of musicianship displayed by the members of the Mason/Bergmann ensemble, not only in their masterly performance of this sublime work, but in everything they undertook (*Review and Gazette,* May 3, 1856, p. 132).

It was announced that they would resume their concerts in the fall, but they did not in fact reappear until early 1858, by which time, despite Bergmann's continuing presence, they had become the "Mason/Thomas Quartet."

In any number of ways Bergmann continued to be New York's most visible musician, On June 16, 1856, he musically officiated at the grand Annual Pic-Nic and Concert of the *Sängerbund,* whose combined forces—on this occasion comprising twenty-one male choral societies accompanied by seven bands of music—marched in well-ordered formation from their headquarters at Mechanics' Hall (160 Hester Street) through the Bowery, Bond Street, and down Broadway to City Hall Park, "where an immense concourse of people assembled to see them pass." Then up Chatham Street, back to the Bowery, to Grand Street and the East River, where they boarded steamers taking them to the festival grounds at the Bellevue Gardens. There, following a ceremonial that included a speech by a Mr. Feldner of Hoboken, Bergmann conducted a concert comprising works for male chorus by Stuntz and Silcher,[51] but also by Mendelssohn, Meyerbeer, and Wagner (the by-now well-rehearsed Pilgrim's Chorus from *Tannhäuser*). Then followed daylong feasting and extempore performances by members of the various choral societies and the seven bands. Three steamboats, for a fare of 8½ cents, plied between lower Manhattan and the Bellevue Gardens at fifteen-minute intervals throughout the day, making their final trip back to town at seven in the evening after a festive day.

Apparently, Bergmann was capable, too, of spreading himself too thin. Among his hundred-and-one other professional activities, he accepted the conductorship of the Harmonic Society upon Bristow's unexplained resignation from that post, as the *Tribune* announced on April 8. On May 12, Bergmann splendidly conducted the Society in Handel's *Judas Maccabaeus.* In a verbose review of the performance, William H. Fry, reverting to the didacticism of his 1852–53 lectures, exhaustively dissected the fugue as a musical form. Although he disapproved of fugues, Fry granted that the Har-

[51]Joseph Stuntz (1793–1859) composed operas and works in a great number of other forms, including choruses for men's voices—among them a *Heldengesang in Walhalla,* presumably in anticipation of Wagner, at least in subject matter. Friedrich Silcher (1789–1869) was a noted folklorist, conductor, and composer of choral music.

monic Society, under Bergmann, had done a creditable job, although "more Italian breadth of delivery—more clear vocal enunciation—was required in certain cases" (*Tribune,* May 14, 1856).

Bergmann conducted the Harmonic Society's final concert of the season at Dodworth's on June 30 in a mixed program ranging from Handel and Haydn to Charles E. Horn and Sir Henry Bishop; the singers were Mr. and Mrs. Stephen Leach, Mrs. Jameson, Messrs. Johnson and Alden, and of course the chorus. As late as October, Bergmann continued to be listed in the *Musical World* as conductor of the Harmonic Society.[52] An error, stormed an irate official of the Society, who demanded a correction in a furious (and somewhat vindictive) letter to the editors, appearing in the issue of November 1 (p. 554): "Mr. G. F. Bristow has been Conductor [again] since the middle of September," he wrote. "Mr. Bergmann made an engagement with us for the season, but finding he neglected us for four successive nights—after promising, within an hour before rehearsal each time, that he would be with us in the evening, we were compelled to dismiss him, as we could not place any dependence upon him. His name was already announced as our conductor for the season, but Mr. G. F. Bristow has been engaged, and under his baton the Society will give several performances, we think, with credit to all concerned."

And so they did. With Bristow in charge, the Harmonic Society once again gave their traditional performance of *Messiah* on Christmas night, this time at the Broadway Tabernacle. The soloists were the Leaches, Mrs. Jameson, and James A. Johnson.

The Mendelssohn Union, now entering their third season under the brilliant guidance of G. W. Morgan, continued to be unequivocally admired for their splendid and polished performances and interesting programs. Their concerts, for which no tickets were sold, were supported entirely by members' subscriptions: for $5 a year, each subscriber received two admissions to each of the Union's four annual concerts and to their thirty-two rehearsals. A high point of this season's offerings was their performance at the City Assembly Rooms, on December 13, of the acclaimed new oratorio *Eli,* by the Italian-born, English composer/conductor Michael Costa. Composed for the Birmingham Festival, where it was first performed in 1855, its prompt local presentation eloquently testified to the "watchfulness and progressiveness" of the Mendelssohn Union's director, observed Seymour, who devoted an enlightening article to the work and its performance (*Times,* December 15, 1856).

Concerning *Eli*'s merits, wrote Seymour, opinions were likely to differ: admirers of the great classic oratorios were not inclined to be pleased with its Italianate/dramatic character, but "those who have advanced with Mendelssohn will perhaps detect an extension of his ideas in *Eli* and hail it as a progressive work of the day—a fresh effort to give to oratorio what it has so much lacked, dramatic force and coloring. . . . In a city like this, where pure church music scarcely exists," continued Seymour, "the operatic bearings of the work will hardly be viewed with disfavor." In its fluent and graceful melodies, and in a great many other admirable characteristics, *Eli* reminded Seymour of Fry's ill-fated *Stabat Mater,* a work he described as "crowded with excellencies, that had been kicked by every foreigner who had asinine strength enough for

[52] Indeed, it was reported that under his direction a performance of Beethoven's Ninth Symphony was being contemplated (*Musical World,* September 13, 1856, p. 421).

the effort."[53] Like Fry, he wrote, Costa was never heavy and he rarely used the "fugue formula, for both of which he is to be thanked." Less admirable were Costa's shameless out-and-out plagiarisms from Mendelssohn.

Outstanding among the generally excellent performers was Giuseppe Guidi, whose "perfectly admirable" artistry Seymour unreservedly praised. The other solo singers were the Misses Hawley, Leach, Andem, the euphoniously named Misses Tingle and Dingley, the Messrs. Hawes, Conkey and Bell. A Miss Emily Hanley deserved special mention for her able harp accompaniments. Less satisfactory was the substitution of a piano for the orchestra; an organ would have been better, especially with "the best organist in the city (Mr. Morgan) present." The difficult piano part, however, was capably played by Berge, a last-minute replacement for Timm.

As we know, Morgan also directed and accompanied the Glee and Madrigal Union (consisting this year of the three Leaches and John Frazer) in an extended series of concerts at Hope Chapel; occasionally Morgan contributed a piano solo.

Almost rivaling Bergmann in the multiplicity of his professional pursuits, Morgan, who in addition to his various choral activities served as organist at Grace Church and doubtless gave music lessons to a great number of its parishioners and their offspring, announced a series of four afternoon piano "recitals" at Dodworth's, ill-advisedly timed to begin on January 8 amid the great initial blaze of excitement over Gottschalk's *soirées*. Perhaps wishing to outdo Gottschalk, Morgan had chosen as his medium a novel—indeed locally unknown—form of musical exhibition, the "recital,"[54] entailing the solo performance of a full program without benefit of assisting artists. Morgan's stated objective in giving this series was pedagogical. According to his prospectus, it was his purpose to "assist the student in the elucidation of the best of the classical and modern schools of Pianoforte compositions." Apparently no paragon of modesty, Morgan planned to accomplish this goal by "various exemplifications . . . of the different styles of playing requisite for the perfect interpretation of the *chef d'oeuvres* of the great masters" as well as "the most celebrated works of the modern composers."[55]

Morgan's "illustrations," he transparently announced, would not, however, include works by "composers resident in this city," because (naming no names) "the public have frequent opportunities for hearing them performed by the authors themselves." Imagine Willis's surprise, then, on seeing Morgan's own name listed in the printed program as the composer of the Variations on "Ye Banks and Braes," with which his first recital concluded.

Morgan's piano playing did not receive the undiluted acclaim he evidently expected. At the first recital, wrote Willis, the last movement of Beethoven's Sonata *pathétique* was rushed beyond the "usual standard tempo." The same was true of Mendelssohn's *Andante* and *Rondo capriccioso,* op. 14, although it was otherwise "cleverly performed." An unidentified movement from Handel's "Harpsichord Lesson" and

[53] The *Stabat Mater* score had in fact recently been published by Oliver Ditson.

[54] Liszt had originated the term in 1840, when he performed the first programs entirely devoted to pianoforte music at the Hanover Square Rooms in London.

[55] A programing plan intended, doubtless, to surpass Gottschalk by including the "classics" that Gottschalk was censured for neglecting.

Bach's Prelude and Fugue in E major from the *Well-tempered Clavier* were, however, splendid, for Morgan excelled in music of the classical school, especially fugue playing. Chopin's "Polonaise from op. 10," although not an interesting piece, was well enough played, but the same could not be said for (Theodor) Döhler's Nocturne or Weber's "Invitation to the Waltz." Perhaps Morgan was by then fatigued by the strain of playing a whole program without assistance. He recovered, however, in time for the last piece, playing it well, "but the modulations, preludes, and the ending seemed [to Willis] of an extemporaneous character—as though composed at the moment" (*Musical World,* January 12, 1856, p. 13).

Watson took great exception to Morgan's claims. To fulfill his intention of providing model interpretations in *all* styles of music required a range of capabilities far beyond Morgan's (or anybody's) scope. Indeed, even Gottschalk, although he came closest to possessing all the qualifications, might not be able to deliver them unconditionally. "No man is universal," wrote Watson. "Some who will render a sonata by Beethoven instinct with life and soul, will possibly gambol as gracefully as an elephant through a mazurka by Chopin or a romance by Henselt; while others, who could interpret all the tortuosities of Listz [*sic*], would utterly fail in rendering the simple, playful tenderness of Mozart or the profound strictness of Bach" (*Leslie's,* January 19, 1856, p. 90).

Morgan, evidently a man ahead of his time, addressed his listeners verbally as well as musically,[56] thereby invoking Hagen's disapproval. Remarking on the small attendance at Morgan's second recital (shifted to the evening of January 24), Hagen advised him in the future to omit "all remarks about the compositions on the program, as the little which is said is mostly unsatisfactory, and with regard to a great many pieces [by Beethoven, Bach, Osborne, Thalberg, Döhler, and again Morgan] even too much" (*Review and Gazette,* February 9, 1856, p. 34).

There was no satisfying the critics. Morgan was a player essentially of classic music, and a fine one, too, wrote an anonymous reviewer for the *Musical World* (February 2, 1856, p. 49), but his attempts to "get on with the romantic and fanciful school" were like "a solid and highly respectable Wall Street gentleman trying to acquire the airs and graces of a Fifth Avenue beau." Surely he must know that "a mere raising of the arms and shoulders is but that visual style of expression of the modern school—something which is seen, but not heard from the fingers—which belongs to the pantomimic moderns, perhaps, but not to the classics and the school of a better taste."

By his third "pianoforte recital" (evening of February 21) the label no longer applied, for Morgan was assisted by the singers Annie Kemp (a star pupil of Mrs. Seguin), John Frazer, and J. W. Alden in a full-fledged miscellaneous *soirée* that consisted predominantly of English glees and ballads and Italian opera arias, and minimally of piano pieces. And at the final event of the series (March 27), the singing cast consisted of Miss Kemp and the members of the Glee and Madrigal Union: Frazer and the three Leaches.[57]

[56] In March, Morgan announced a course of lectures on harmony and composition; he intended, besides, to form elementary classes (*Musical World,* March 22, 1856, p. 135).

[57] At the outset, admissions to Morgan's recitals were 50 cents, $1 for reserved seats; by the second recital (emulating Gottschalk), 50 cents for ladies and $1 for gentlemen; by the final event, a blanket 50 cents.

Undiscouraged by Morgan's failed piano series, and evidently dazzled by Gottschalk's triumphs, the young American pianist T. Franklin Bassford (a protégé of Richard Grant White and probably a pupil of Gottschalk) immediately followed with his own series of four pianoforte *soirées* (not recitals), beginning on April 4 at Dodworth's Hall. In these concerts, wrote Seymour (*Times,* April 5, 1856), Bassford so blatantly attempted to imitate Gottschalk, both as a pianist and composer, that, although he possessed "decided talent" as a pianist, the young man "would have shone to greater advantage had he come before the public" without his compositions. And, even more emphatically, before the advent of Gottschalk, who "with his strong and elegant individuality can entertain an audience for any given length of time simply by playing his own compositions." But Bassford: "As a composer, his talents are equivocal,"[58] wrote Seymour. "He imitates, probably without knowing it, but the imitation is too palpable to escape notice. In his *'Marche du matin,'* and the 'Echo of the Past,' the name of the composer should be Gottschalk, not Bassford."

Bassford's cast of assisting artists for the series consisted of a Miss Louisa Payne (not Pyne); Allan Irving, Dolores Nau's quondam baritone, now settled in New York; "Little Ada," a four-year-old "musical prodigy"; and Candido Berti, who did second-piano duty in performances of Bassford's Triumphal Fantasie (the now-naturalized *Marcha triunfal*) and other items requiring accompaniment. By now Bassford had, alas, nearly run his course. On November 2 he perished at sea when the ship *Le Lyonnais,* bound for France, was wrecked in a collision off Nantucket (see *Dwight's,* December 6, 1856, p. 79; Strong *Diary,* II, p. 310, entry for November 8, 1856).

Gottschalk's dominant presence on the current concert scene included as well—tucked in among his New York *soirées* and lightning out-of-town flights—a diversity of guest appearances at concerts given by colleagues, many of whom assisted in return at his own *soirées.* As we know, this professional reciprocity reached its peak in Gottschalk's joint appearances with Madame de LaGrange and Thalberg. Among the lesser artists to whose concerts he lent his immense drawing power was the splendid harpist Aptommas, at whose *soirée* (January 17 at Dodworth's) he played his *Marche de nuit,* "The Banjo," and part of his *Lucrezia* Fantasie.[59] At Karl Wels's annual concert (Dodworth's, May 23), Gottschalk collaborated in performances of Wels's duos for two pianos—a Fantasie on themes from *Il trovatore* and the provocatively titled *Marche d'Amazone.*[60] On March 8 at Dodworth's, Gottschalk played his *Souvenirs d'Andalousie* and "The Banjo" at the long-delayed debut of the Italian opera tenor Antonio Rosetti, to which Madame di Ferrari and the baritone Vincenzo Morino also contributed their talents. On May 29 at Niblo's Saloon, Gottschalk joined Badiali and Brignoli in assisting Madame Patania at her concert, playing his "Italian Glories" again with

[58] Yet, as we know, on January 31, Gottschalk had opened his Hispanic program (his fourth *soirée*) with Bassford's *Marcha triunfal,* accompanied at a second piano by another young disciple, Candido Berti.

[59] Also appearing on this occasion were Henry C. Timm, Oswald Bernardi, and the Brothers Mollenhauer.

[60] Wels's other assisting artists were Madame Wallace-Bouchelle, Signor Bernardi, Aptommas, and the Brothers Mollenhauer.

Wels at the second piano,[61] and alone his *Marche de nuit* and *Valse poétique;*[62] and, "as a special favor," accompanying Madame Patania in a *Grande Valse* by Luigi Venzano (1814–1878).

Always mindful of his French heritage, Gottschalk played "two of his most popular compositions" at a complimentary event given at the City Assembly Rooms on February 29 for one Gustave Naquet, who lectured in French on "The Life and Genius of Rachel." Alfred de Musset's play *Un Caprice* (Paris 1847) was performed by remnants of Rachel's company, and, with William H. Paine's permission, arias were sung by the Italian tenor Giulio. Admission was fifty cents.

It was, of course, axiomatic that the public idol Gottschalk should be avidly pursued as a teacher, and he was nothing loath to take fullest advantage of this commercially rewarding desirability. In February, in the full heyday of his glory, he informed his adoring public in a card: "Mr. Gottschalk, being unavoidably obliged to postpone his departure to Lima for six or eight weeks, will during this time accede to the request of numerous friends and receive a limited number of pupils on the piano-forte. He has engaged the piano-forte warerooms of Mr. Descombes, No. 766 Broadway, where early application by letter may be made. The term will consist of twelve lessons [of one hour each]. Price $60.[63] Applications may also be left at the piano-forte and music store of William Hall and Son, No. 239 Broadway."

And at the beginning of the new season, on September 22, just before the Thalberg onslaught, the *Times* affably puffed: "Mr. Gottschalk, the Bard of the Piano, as Berlioz calls Litz [*sic*], has returned to New-York and will shortly resume his delightful *soirées* [he didn't]. In the meantime he is making extensive preparations for a hard Winter's work in the teaching way—the only 'way to wealth' for pianists in America. We notice by an advertisement elsewhere that he has started a series of piano classes at a remarkably low figure. The advantages of this system of tuition are manifold, and have been amply demonstrated in the conservatories of Europe. Mr. Gottschalk's transcendent talent cannot fail of exciting the emulation of his pupils, and his art-enthusiasm will, we are sure, push them on vehemently. These classes are worthy of the warmest support."

More explicitly, it was advertised in the general press that on September 20, Gottschalk was opening a *Conservatoire de Piano* at his teaching headquarters, Descombes's piano warerooms, where he would give "a practical and theoretical course of Instruction on the Piano, on the plan of the Conservatoire of Paris. The pupils will be divided into classes of eight each. The course will comprise eight lessons of two hours each; the first hour will be devoted to the study and performance of some symphonic

[61] "Mr. Gottschalk was the instrumental lion of the night and monopolized all the enthusiasm of the audience," wrote the *Times* (May 30, 1856). "He was called out three times after every performance and, inspired by this just appreciation, played with even more than his usual perfection in a duet for two pianos, 'Italian Glories' . . . ably assisted by Mr. Wels."

[62] Published in 1855 as *Sospiro,* subtitled *Valse poétique,* op. 24 (D-148; *Piano Works,* V, 141).

[63] "I see, by the way," ironically commented Dwight's New York correspondent ——t—— (February 23, 1856, p. 165), "that [Gottschalk] announces that 'at the urgent request of his numerous friends' he has *consented* to take pupils during the six or eight weeks that he will remain here, at the modest price of $60 per twelve lessons! I wish him success!"

masterpieces of the great composers, carefully transcribed [by Gottschalk] for eight pianos; the second hour will be devoted to individual instruction, each pupil in turn playing some brilliant piece by a modern piano composer.

"This plan has proved the most successful of any yet attempted in the Conservatoires of Europe, and is almost universally adopted. Each pupil, in this way, gets all the advantage of the instruction given to the others, and a general interest and spirit of emulation is obtained which can follow no other course of instruction.[64]

"Persons wishing to take advantage of this course will please make early application, as Mr. G. wishes to classify the pupils according to their proficiency. He will thus be able to take players less advanced than he has heretofore received, which will obviate the necessity of rejecting many who applied last season. Terms of the course, $20."

That little selectivity was exercised is suggested by an emended subsequent advertisement (October 15): "In order to admit all the pupils who make application, and in order to classify them by their proficiency, Mr. Gottschalk has divided his classes into 'Elementary,' 'Middle,' and 'Superior Class.'" And added: "As applications are made, new classes are formed."[65]

In the meantime, Gottschalk had advertised that he was available as well from September 10 to October 11 for a course of twelve private lessons "on the plan of last season," again for a fee of $60 for hour-long sessions and $30 for half-hours.

Music pedagogy in the public schools continued to be carried on by George Frederick Bristow, who periodically exhibited his pupils' accomplishments at the Tabernacle, sometimes for good causes. On January 31 he conducted a "School Girls' Concert," the proceeds, at twenty-five cents a ticket, being used to purchase a piano for the Girls' Department of Ward School No. 44; on May 21, to raise funds for a piano for the Boys' Department,[66] he conducted "fifteen or sixteen hundred" grammar-school children in a program of solos, glees, and choruses, with, according to the *Evening Post* (May 22, 1856), "a precision and vigor that must have impressed their large audience," estimated at about 4000. "The ease and correctness with which mere children performed difficult music from Mendelssohn, Donizetti, Balfe, and other composers was not a little surprising, and shows that the opportunity alone is wanting to make a musical people of us."

And to top off the year, on December 12 the pupils of Grammar School No. XI appeared at the Academy of Music in a gala performance of G. F. Root's popular cantata *The Flower Queen,*[67] directed by Bristow, accompanied by Shelton's American

[64] As an exalted Watson admonished parents of prospective pupils: "Every word of instruction from Gottschalk is a golden precept whose worth is not to be measured by money" (*Leslie's,* September 20, 1856, p. 227).

[65] It may be that Candido Berti inherited some of the overflow. On September 22 he announced in the papers his readiness to teach pianoforte playing to "young learners as well as to advanced pupils who may wish to acquire a thorough knowledge of the higher branches of pianoforte playing."

[66] Two pianos for Ward School No. 45 were similarly subsidized by some 2500 listeners who attended a pupils' concert at the Tabernacle on October 21, this time conducted by Francis H. Nash, their teacher (*Musical World,* October 25, 1856, p. 579).

[67] As far as Hagen was concerned, the success of *The Flower Queen* offered "more hope of the future dawn of a national opera than all the *Rip Van Winkles, Giovanna di Napolis,* etc., that have seen

Band, and conducted by J. C. Woodman, a teacher of music at the school. To enhance the all-American character of the evening, William Mason performed some of his piano compositions.

Pedagogy, as always, provided the basic bread-and-butter occupation for music practitioners of all grades and varieties, from ex-concert-managers (like Helmsmüller) to ex-actor/singers (like Allan Irving). To the unquenchable Eliza Valentini, teaching—or rather the giving of annual students' concerts—afforded an outlet for the public self-expression for which she eternally thirsted. Thus, at this year's event, given on May 22 at the Academy of Music as a benefit for the Building Fund of the Church for Deaf Mutes, she concluded an overlong program, consisting of some fourteen musical numbers[68] and two declamations—one in sign language—with her own interpretation, or rather superproduction, with orchestra and chorus, of the *Marseillaise* (probably intended to put Rachel's electrifying rendition to shame). "A remarkable specimen of musical buncombe," wrote the *Times* (May 23, 1856), "it consisted of the 'Marseillaise Hymn expressly arranged for this occasion,' with an accompaniment of side drums, cymbals, and Chinese crackers. A scanty supplement in the shape of a French flag was added, in which the fair vocalist endeavored to wrap herself. A more delirious affair we have seldom listened to; such bungling and fumbling and screaming we never wish to hear again."

During the too-frequent intervals between opera seasons at the Academy of Music, many of the idled Italian opera singers turned to concert-giving. Thus, besides Patania and Rosetti, at whose concerts Gottschalk had assisted, the opera singers who gave programs of predominantly Italian opera repertory were, on April 15 at Niblo's Saloon, the tenor Giulio,[69] brilliantly assisted by LaGrange, Morelli, Rovere, Bernardi, and Maretzek, who accompanied at the piano "with delicacy and discretion";[70] on May 22 at Dodworth's, Mariano Manzocchi, introduced in the papers as a "Professor of singing and recently Musical Conductor in the theatres of Paris and Naples," who appeared with Bertucca-Maretzek, Ventaldi, Amodio, Rovere, and Gasparoni; and on June 2 at Dodworth's, an all-but-unknown Italian tenor Antonio Alajmo (or Alaimo), assisted by the all-but-forgotten Zoë Aldini, also by Morelli, Richard Hoffman, and Signor Luciano Albites, another incipiently eminent singing teacher and opera conductor. On June 13, Amodio, assisted by Patania, Brignoli, and Morelli, gave a fine, but "thinly attended," concert at Niblo's Saloon (on the same evening as the thinly attended benefit performance of *Ernani* for the opera orchestra, donated by Madame de LaGrange, was given at the Academy); on June 27, at Niblo's Saloon, Adelaide Ventaldi gave a "Grand Concert," with the assistance of an "eminent," but unnamed, assisting cast.

---

the light of the theatrical stage in the different Atlantic cities" (*Review and Gazette,* April 5, 1856, p. 97).

[68] Performed by her pupils Madame Eugénie de Lussan (mother of the future *prima donna* Zélie de Lussan), and a Mrs. Sheehan; also the forgotten violinist Halma and—of all people—Maretzek, who conducted an orchestra and chorus.

[69] Replacing Brignoli, whose recent "equestrian performance" had rendered him "*hors de combat,*" as the *Mirror* merrily punned.

[70] And less brilliantly assisted by Thalberg's pupil Emile Guyon, an unexciting pianist who made his American debut on this occasion, playing two of his master's opera fantasies.

The high point of these Italian-opera-oriented concerts was the reappearance of Teresa Parodi, whose crowded tour schedule with Maurice Strakosch brought them to New York for two concerts at Niblo's Saloon on October 22 and 27. While the powers at the Academy of Music were ceaselessly engaged in wrangling, Parodi and Strakosch, as the papers unfailingly observed, had been reaping a golden harvest with their brilliantly successful concert tours,[71] taking in the major cities and not ignoring the less traveled byways as well. With programs artfully devised to provide something to suit every taste[72] and a "very strong" supporting cast consisting of Paul Julien, the singers Tiberini, Bernardi, and Morino, and, of course, with Strakosch playing his delicious piano compositions (and presumably the accompaniments as well), Strakosch's Grand Concert Company, as it was called, attracted fashionable, capacity audiences to both their events in New York.

It was Parodi, however, with her superb voice and "bold impulsive method," who was the magnet. Her "vocation for the stage is unmistakable," wrote Watson. "It displays itself even in the concert room. However she may strive to school herself to the cold proprieties of concert singing, the dramatic genius with which she is gifted will betray itself in bursts of powerful declamation and burning passion." In Mendelssohn's "Jerusalem," for instance, although Watson may have disputed its inclusion in a program of secular music, Parodi's "very grand" performance (in English), electrifyingly conveyed "more the threatening of divine vengeance than the warning of divine love" (*Leslie's,* November 1, 1856, p. 323).

Tiberini, it was generally agreed, sounded better at Niblo's than he had at the Academy of Music; he was, in fact, "a beautiful tenor and superior artist," wrote Fry (*Tribune,* October 24, 1856). Julien, now a grown-up young man of fifteen, was, as always, mightily praised,[73] as, in lesser degree, was Bernardi. But Strakosch, despite his widely admired "perception of the popular taste," managed on this occasion to offend his audience by playing as an encore a "mild fantasia on the nigger melody 'Nelly Bly' [(1849) by Stephen Foster]. This is trying to be a little too popular," complained the *Times* (October 24, 1856).

The Strakosch/Parodi visit to New York was strategically timed. As Wilkins disingenuously pointed out (*Herald,* October 28, 1856): Parodi's "full, rich tones, set off with the vivid coloring of a great dramatic artist, are exceedingly welcome in these

[71] And, for Strakosch, successful beyond the concerts. It was rumored, wrote Watson, that in 1852, when Strakosch first visited Chicago on an early tour with Parodi, he had purchased a small piece of land, and at every subsequent visit there had added to it, for a total outlay of about $15,000. The property was now said to have risen in value to about $100,000, a staggering sum! Strakosch, wrote Watson, was on his way to becoming a millionaire (*Leslie's,* August 16, 1856, p. 151).

[72] Parodi's immense repertory spanned the emotional gamut from operatic high drama to the lilt of popular ballads, from solemn oratorio to the intense fervor of the *Marseillaise,* eclipsed only by her even more stirring rendition—as its encore—of "The Star-Spangled Banner."

[73] Julien, of course, played as marvelously as ever, wrote Watson, "but why does he always play the same pieces?" (again and again Vieuxtemps's *Fantaisie caprice* and Hauman's Fantasie on Themes from *Masaniello*). Fearing for Julien's artistic future at this crucial stage of his life, Watson spared no words in his fatherly reproof of the young man. He had some harsh comments as well for Tiberini, who although he had sung the *Spirito gentil* in generally admirable taste, had unfortunately chosen to end it with a cadence that was "hackneyed, unsuitable, and decidedly vulgar" (*Leslie's,* November 1, 1856, p. 323).

days when most of our *prime donne* make up for lack of voice and dramatic power by profuse ornamentation, which, like other sweet things, one may have too much of" (a pointed reference to LaGrange's monopoly of the *prima donna* field). More directly, the *Albion* critic blurted out (October 25, 1856, p. 512): "Parodi is a better singer than LaGrange." (The press was evidently attempting to accelerate the impending end of the Maretzek regime at the Academy of Music.)

The Italian opera singers frequently joined forces as well with their ethnic opposites. Thus, the admired English basso Allan Irving was assisted, on May 25 at Niblo's Saloon, by Felicita Vestvali (a coup!), Badiali, and, with Maretzek's permission, Luigi Ceresa, all of whom sang opera arias to the piano accompaniments of Señor Nunó and William Dressler; Aptommas and W. A. King played solos. Good as it was, grumbled the *Tribune,* the entertainment was too long.

On May 27 at Niblo's Saloon the American soprano Isadora Clark gave a program essentially of Italian opera arias, assisted by Brignoli, Amodio, and Manzocchi, and accompanied by a small but good orchestra conducted by Carl Bergmann. On May 26 and 28 the Pyne/Harrison troupe sang music by Donizetti and Bellini as well as Balfe and Benedict at their two "operatic concerts" at Niblo's.[74]

Indeed, as Wilkins observed in the *Herald* (December 29, 1856), so pervasive had the fad for Italian opera music become that "all the young ladies in the upper strata of New York society are now laboring under a terrible disease—a chronic attack of Italian music. . . . The symptoms of the disease are visible in several amateur concerts—some in the 'large and richly decorated apartments of the aristocracy'—others in fashionable churches—to all of which an admission fee is charged and the proceeds given to the poor. . . . Young ladies were formerly more harmless. They made red worsted puppies and unavailable pincushions for fancy fairs; now, forsooth, they must assault Verdi, Bellini, Donizetti, and a number of other respectable masters, who . . . really do not deserve such treatment."

Wilkins was doubtless referring to the charitable amateur concert given to mark the opening (December 18) of the fashionable new Baptist Church at 35th Street and Fifth Avenue. To enhance the splendors of an edifice that, according to the *Tribune* (December 19, 1856), was "frescoed so with Italian allegory that we thought at first we were in a Roman Catholic chapel," a bevy of demurely anonymous "sirens," decked out in "all the heartrending artillery of the toilette," dauntlessly delivered themselves of a program not only devoted to opera music by Rossini, Donizetti, and Verdi but actually offering "airs from that wicked opera *La traviata,* that heathenish tragedy *Semiramide,* that desperate drama *Il corsaro*—all in a Baptist Church! What would the man of the wilderness say to it? But, *mutatis mutandis;* nothing is fixed. Everything obeys the laws of change, the use of wealth, the spread of art, the vagaries of fashion."[75]

[74] "First rate," reported the *Times* (May 30, 1856), except for the tenor (Harrison), "who seems to progress from bad to worse with remarkable celerity."

[75] Musicales at home, too, were increasingly being given by members of the Upper Ten. The *Mirror* (May 24, 1856) reported a "'Brilliant Matinée Musicale' at the house of a lady in the Fifth Avenue, at which several amateur ladies and gentlemen 'assisted'; and Messrs. Brignoli, Gottschalk, Aptommas, and others also took part. The music was very fine; and the crowd excessive—a regular fashionable Fifth Avenue squeeze, done up *à la mode.*"

Again, among the most active native singers were Maria Brainerd, Georgiana Stuart Leach, and Mrs. Jameson, who, in addition to their guest appearances with the numerous music societies and their official duties in several church choirs, gave concerts of their own, assisted variously by Stephen Leach, J. B. Beutler, Joseph Burke, Jules Hess (a new violinist), Aptommas, Clare Beames, and G. Washbourn Morgan. These ladies contributed their talents, too, to sacred concerts at the different churches and at benefits and complimentary concerts galore, as did Mrs. Bostwick, William Mason, Otto Feder, Theodore Eisfeld, the violinist James W. Perkins (back from his studies at the Paris *Conservatoire*), Dodworth's Band, the German *Liederkranz,* and countless others. Brignoli and Amodio sang "oratorios"[76] to raise funds for a new organ for Dr. Cummings's fashionable St. Stephen's Church, where W. A. King was now in charge of the music.[77] The good causes supported in 1856, among many others, were the German Ladies' Society, the American Widows Relief Organization, the Newsboys' Lodging House, and the Hebrew Ladies' Benevolent Fair.

Madame de LaGrange, together with Brignoli and Morelli, graciously performed for the inmates, 170 in number, of the Institution for the Blind: "Several elaborate pieces were sung by Madame LaGrange to a chorus [extempore] of blind children," reported the *Mirror* (March 28, 1856), "and although no rehearsal had taken place, their voices blended in perfect harmony."[78]

Among the complimentary concerts, the most spectacular of the year was the widely ballyhooed farewell tribute to the eminent flutist John A. Kyle upon his announced retirement from the musical profession. With an imposing list of sponsors and virtually daily communiqués in the gossip columns, the great event finally took place on February 1, 1856 (marking the opening of the City Assembly Rooms). The participants were Maria S. Brainerd, a Miss Ellen Brenen (a highly promising pupil of Badiali's), Carlotta Pozzoni, Badiali, Allan Irving, Beutler, Aptommas, Burke, Hoffman, Kiefer, Meyerhofer, Morgan, C. W. Beames, Henry C. Timm, and Kyle himself. The long program was immeasurably lengthened by innumerable encores, wrote an unusually uncomplaining *Times*.

A Grand Concert (more a memorial) was given at the City Assembly Rooms on June 30 to raise funds to erect a monument in Greenwood Cemetery in tribute to James Shelton, the founder of Shelton's American Band. Among the performers were George F. Bristow, Signor La Manna, J. B. Beutler, one of the Stoepels, and one F. G. Miller.

[76] Chiefly consisting of excerpts from *I Lombardi*.

[77] At the Fifth Avenue Presbyterian Church a magnificent and long-awaited Jardine organ was unveiled on May 25 for an overflow crowd of "gaily dressed and fashionable inhabitants of that aristocratic quarter of the city." Exhibiting the instrument were William Mason, organist of the church, and G. Washbourn Morgan; during the intermission Edward Jardine skillfully demonstrated the organ's capabilities in a solo of his own (*Dwight's,* June 7, 1856, pp. 76–77; also see Ogasapian, pp. 118–19, 245).

[78] On October 2 a concert was given by a quartet of blind singers who had been trained by the Institution's music director, George Frederick Root. As an added attraction, the institute's most illustrious alumna, the blind poetess Fanny Crosby, was scheduled to deliver a "poetical address" especially written for the occasion.

And, with alas unwarranted optimism, the July 2 papers carried a card addressed to the musical public of New York: "It is suggested by a committee of gentlemen to give a concert in the fall of the year for the benefit of Signor Ferdinand Palmo, the first manager of Italian opera in New York [*sic*]. It is sincerely hoped by the committee that the musical profession generally, and the public, will aid in giving their cordial assistance to one of the chief promoters of music in New York, in order to purchase him an annuity, which may secure him from the ills of poverty during the few years he may be with us." Would-be subscribers were directed to communicate with George W. Morgan at 179 East 17th Street. Nothing further was heard of Palmo's annuity.

Meanwhile, back in February, Paul Julien, together with his touring partner August Gockel, had returned to New York for his annual season of "farewell benefits." At the first of two such valedictory events, at Niblo's Saloon on February 8, the unexciting assisting artists had been Mrs. Bostwick, the violinist Julius Meyer, and the pianist/accompanist A. Woeltge. At the second (again with Gockel), at the City Assembly Rooms on March 3, a brilliant assisting cast featured Julien's gifted little friend Adelina Patti, now thirteen years old, and her half-brother Ettore Barili, with whom Julien was about to embark on a new tour that would include two concerts in Havana.

Watson leaves a memorable portrait of the adolescent Patti. Although still only a mere child, he wrote, she was "a most delicious singer, full of impulse and abounding with talent. Her voice is of a rare and beautiful quality, clear, sympathetic, melodious, and flexible in a remarkable degree. Her intonation is as true as steel, and her enunciation clear and unusually distinct. We know not which to admire the most—the brilliant Italian style, the simple English song, or the archly characteristic Spanish ballad.[79] . . . She is a little marvel and sings as involuntarily as the lark carols, and for the same reason, because it is the impulse of her nature, and she cannot help it. If her womanhood bear out the promise of her youth," foretold Watson, "she will set the world crazy and be a thing to marvel at!" (*Leslie's,* March 15, 1856, p. 215.)

Patti's brother, too, deserved the greatest praise, continued Watson, but Gockel, who had apparently not settled down with the passing years, "literally gave the piano fits. How the poor instrument survived that succession of severe spasms, we are at a loss to understand." As for Julien, he played the same pieces at each of these concerts with his usual magnificence,[80] but although he was indisputably a genius, Watson had misgivings about his future progress.

Of the other concert-givers, on January 18 at the Tabernacle, the Brothers Mollenhauer, after several announcements and cancellations, presented a "farewell concert" prior to their return to Europe, assisted by Timm, Aptommas, Bernardi, and a miscellaneous group of players from the Philharmonic. On February 26, still present, they explained in a card that they had been "unavoidably obliged to postpone their departure for some time longer," and in the meantime would resume their teaching of

[79] At this concert Patti sang a Spanish folk song (probably in preparation for Havana), also the *Ah! non giunge* from *La sonnambula,* Jenny Lind's "Echo Song," and, with her brother, a duet from *Il barbiere.*

[80] Again Alard's Fantasy on *La favorita* and Haumann's Fantasy on *Masaniello,* adding, on February 8, Vieuxtemps's *Fantaisie caprice,* and on March 3, a *Jota aragonesa* and Paganini's "Witches' Dance." Assisting at an oration delivered at the Tabernacle on March 7 by Stephen H. Branch, Julien unabashedly repeated Hauman's *Masaniello* Fantasy and Paganini's "Witches' Dance."

Adelina Patti and Paul Julien, teen-aged friends and seasoned professional colleagues.

the piano, violin, cello, and singing. On June 5 the Mollenhauers, now apparently here to stay, presented another concert, this time at Dodworth's, at which they introduced their newly arrived brother Henry, former Violoncellist to the King of Sweden; Madame Bertucca-Maretzek, Adelaide Ventaldi, Signor Quinto, and Carl Bergmann assisted.

Meanwhile, at Dodworth's Saloon on May 15, Frederick and Edward Mollenhauer played their "Siamese Twin" duets at Aptommas's harp *soirée;* also appearing were Miss Brainerd, who, as usual, sang a song by (and with) Beames, and G. F. Hayter, who delivered himself of a transcription for piano of Rossini's *Stabat Mater.*

On December 2, Aptommas introduced an ambitious series of "classical and miscellaneous harp *soirées,*" to be given on the first Tuesday of every month for the duration of the season. Assisting at his opening *soirée* were the opera singers Bertucca-

Maretzek, Minna von Berkel, Brignoli, and Guidi; the pianists Florentine Spaczek (or Szpaczek), Henry C. Timm, and G. W. Morgan (playing both the piano and the new *Orgue Alexandre*);[81] also Henry and Frederick Mollenhauer (cello and violin respectively), and one Hughes, a harpist.

And what, amid all this vast musical activity, had become of the American composer? Although the association for the performance of American music envisioned by Bristow in 1854 had not yet come into concrete being, its concept had evidently been germinating all the while. During the interim, on June 16, 1855, the *Musical World* (p. 74) had published a pseudonymous letter to the editor—in effect an eloquent manifesto—wherein was outlined the purpose and principles of such a society: "I am glad to see," wrote *Justitia* (unquestionably the maverick Charles Jerome Hopkins), "the interest for American music has at last begun to exhibit itself in the proposed organization of an association to be called the *New-York American Musical Union,* for the purpose of encouraging the efforts of young American composers and having their productions performed in a suitable manner—of course, provided they are considered meritorious by a capable committee.

"The association is to consist of an instrumental quartet (to be increased to an octet, if considered expedient), a vocal quartet (to be increased to a sextet under the same conditions), and good amateur vocalists and performers on the different instruments, the desire being to give all kinds of compositions a fair trial and a chance of being properly performed, except those requiring a full orchestra and chorus.

"It is the intention of the gentlemen already interested in this new idea to give a Soirée every month or two months, as may be more acceptable, during the winter season, on which occasions nothing but American compositions will be presented. This idea has already received the sanction of many of our most accomplished and respectable musical amateurs, among whom is Mr. [Richard] Pell, the able conductor of the 'Euterpean Orchestral Society.'[82]

"It has not been considered necessary to confine the privilege of membership to native Americans, but to allow foreigners to belong thereto, provided only their principles are Republican, and their aim be, in common with us, the production of native art. One of this latter description is Mr. Fritz [Frederick] Mollenhauer, the celebrated violinist under whose able direction the instrumental Quartet party belonging to the new association expects to flourish.

"It is the opinion of many, and it has been often asserted, more especially by foreigners, that America can boast of no classical music. Now such an assertion only

[81] The *Orgue Alexandre,* an instrument (essentially a melodion, or harmonium) claiming to combine the capabilities of the piano and organ, was invented in France by the celebrated Alexandres, father and son. It had been introduced at Dodworth's Hall on November 7 by a gifted newcomer, one Ranieri Villanova, with the excellent assistance of a Miss Louisa Boucher of New York (a daughter of Alfred Boucher?). Among their most admired performances had been Gems from *La traviata* and *Souvenirs d'Irving Place,* appropriately consisting of melodies from *Il trovatore* (*Times,* November 10, 1856).

[82] Soon to celebrate their 58th anniversary, the venerable Euterpean Society continued to hold their weekly musical meetings on Tuesday evenings, from October to April, at the Mercer House (Mercer and Broome sreets) (*Musical World,* October 11, 1856, p. 481).

shows the ignorance of the perpetrator thereof, for, as our efforts thus far in collecting American musical compositions have proved, it *does* exist, and to a greater extent than many imagine. But heretofore there has been no chance for a native composer to place his music before the public in such a manner as to have it fairly tried and impartially judged.

"We speak now more particularly with regard to classical chamber music. For example, how often has it been ironically asked, 'Where are your American quartets, quintets, etc.?' We are glad we can answer each question, and inform the inquirer where he can find not only quartets and quintets, but overtures and symphonies for full score of orchestra, all works of native Americans who have never been out of the country.

"But, it may be asked, 'Is all this music good for anything? Is it classic and original?' Suffice it to say that in Philadelphia, where a party has been in the habit of performing some of this 'American music,' and *that* party consisting in a great measure of German professors of music, some of the quartets have been pronounced equal to an Onslow or Spaeth![83]

"Some of your readers may have a little curiosity to know who this composer might be. We answer that it is Mr. Charles Hommann [*c.* 1800–*c.* 1862, a native of Philadelphia], now living in Brooklyn, a gentleman whose retiring disposition and native modesty have been the principal barriers to his having become, long ere this, one of the most celebrated, if not the most so, of American composers.[84]

"We have already in our possession three instrumental pieces from the pen of Mr. Hommann and Mr. George F. Bristow, the talented conductor of the New York Harmonic Society. And we have in prospect many other kinds of compositions from different composers.

"We think it will only be necessary for it to be generally known that there is now a chance for all young Americans who desire to distinguish themselves by musical composition to have their labors rewarded by a fair trial and impartial criticism, to secure the good will and cooperation of many individuals who otherwise would be disposed to throw a bucket of cold water upon the embryo idea of such a thing.

"But to all those who object to it on the ground that American music is not good music, [that] it is unclassical, plagiaristic, or unfit to be compared with German productions, we would say, 'Give it a fair trial.' If Americans do not know how to compose now, it does not follow that they never *will* know how."

When, on February 16, 1856, the fledgling American Music Association, as the society came to be named, at last made their modest debut at Clinton Hall (generously loaned them by the Mendelssohn Union), they did so without benefit of advertising, probably from lack of funds. Other than by word of mouth, it was only through Seymour's rather guarded announcement in the *Times* on the morning of the concert that the extraordinary undertaking was made known to the general public.

"The distinguishing feature of this *soirée*," wrote Seymour, "is that all the music

[83] Andreas Spaeth (1790–1876) was a prolific Swiss composer, popular in the nineteenth century.

[84] Hommann's modesty was apparently more enduring than his music, of which little is known beyond a few published salon pieces for piano and some manuscripts in various musical media, some of which are found at the Library Company of Philadelphia.

is from the pen of native Americans—the performers also being American" (loosely identified as "Maria Brainerd, a quartette party, several pianists, and a host of other native artists"). "We do not mention this fact as a hint that either one or the other will be better than what can be had from sources less local," hedged Seymour, "American music is comparatively a novelty. We do not know whether it is better or worse than what we have been hearing. It is but right, therefore, that we should judge for ourselves."

It was the American Music Association's intention to present a monthly *soirée,* "if present success warrants such an enterprise." The potential boon to unperformed composers was self-evident: "At present there is no encouragement for the struggling American composer," wrote Seymour, expatiating on the native composer's perennial plight. "No matter what his talent, he can only write for his portfolio, unless, indeed, he is content to narrow his capacity to the meager requirements of the music publishers [chiefly for easy-to-read parlor music]. There is no existing medium through which his works can be submitted to the ordeal of public criticism. If there be such a medium, it is closed by prejudice and a dominant musical influence [doubtless a reference to the German-oriented Philharmonic]. There are in our midst men who are capable, we believe, of giving to art a new and national impetus. They have waited their opportunity in vain."

Reviewing the concert, Seymour (*Times,* February 18, 1860) reported a fair-sized attendance, "quite large enough for the limited capacity of the apartment." Of the nine compositions performed he confined his critical comments only to two: Hopkins's "Symphony," rather ambitiously titled "Life," and a violin and piano sonata by Hommann. Both works, of which only separate movements had been played, displayed "good perception of the classic form, but little freshness." Of the two, Seymour inclined to Hommann's sonata: "Like all young writers," he wrote, "Mr. Hommann is open to the charge of reminiscence, his subjects bearing a family likeness to other subjects that may be found in well-known works." This was, however, a good fault, for it testified to the young composer's "vigorous" study of the existing musical literature. The other pieces (alas, unidentified) were "up to Concert pitch, but not beyond it." Indeed, suggested Seymour: "At the next *soirée* of the Association, we hope to hear better instrumental music and see the names of some distinguished volunteers. There are a few eminent musicians in New-York," he pointed out, "who should be associated with this movement."

And having gone so far, Seymour proceeded to take issue with what he considered "an indiscreet and unjust statement" in the Association's perhaps overzealous introductory prospectus: "'We do not wish it to be thought,'" he quoted from the document, "'that the object of our enterprise is an earnest of our total and unreserved renunciation of all except native American music; but we wish it to be clearly understood that we consider the prevalent opinion that the birth of an individual on American soil renders "null and void" his claim to original musical genius a disgrace to the world we live in.'"

Not so, protested Seymour: "Whenever American music has been good for anything, it has met with approbation from the public." Witness the success of Fry's *Leonora* (perhaps an unfortunate choice of example) and Bristow's *Rip Van Winkle;* and witness the successes of William Mason and Louis Moreau Gottschalk. "It is simply unjust to say that Americans do not believe in American genius, or that they are over-eager to run after foreigners." It was the American artists who were at fault because they were not organized: "Every man goes on his own hook. There is no cooperation. The consequence is that the Germans, who do cooperate with each other, have command of all the avenues that lead to the public."

Lacking such organization, "an American finds it difficult to obtain a hearing for his works. He must spend a lifetime in negotiating with Committees. He must submit to the ill will of the executants. He must patiently bear up against unjust comparisons. He must have the maw of an ostrich to digest all the harsh and stupid things that will be said of him. But when he has reached the public he will find no lack of sympathy." Seymour was "anxious to see the American Music Association prosper, in order that fresh facilities may be extended to young composers. It will not teach the public anything," he inconclusively concluded, "but it will benefit the artist; it will not injure foreign music, but it will do good to that of native origin."

R. Storrs Willis, although himself an occasional composer,[85] chose to dismiss this historic event with a nonchalant wave of the hand: "A National effort of a commendable kind has just been made in this city and the first concert of American music given," he casually wrote in the *Musical World* (February 23, 1856, p. 85). "We regretted exceedingly that we were not present—the sudden arrival of friends at the moment having made us oblivious of all else." At least Willis informed his readers that anyone wishing to submit a manuscript to the Association might do so upon paying the membership dues of $5 at the offices of the *Musical World* (257 Broadway), where the manuscripts could be left.

In lieu of a review of his own, Willis reprinted the *Tribune*'s routine notice of the event (February 18, 1856), obviously not by Fry, who remained unaccountably aloof from a cause he might have been expected to support. Although not advertised, reported the *Tribune,* the concert was well attended by an appreciative audience, and "selections from the compositions of our own countrymen were rendered in a manner indicating mature preparations by the artists engaged. Their pleasant *soirée,* the first of a series, has no doubt won for them the favorable opinions which their excellent experiment deserves."

By their second concert, however—at the Stuyvesant Institute on April 3—the press had become somewhat more attentive. This time the *Musical World* (April 12, 1856, p. 173), perhaps not uninfluenced by the inclusion in the program of two parlor songs by Willis, discussed the works heard and the several performances, if not all the performers, in a certain amount of detail: Charles Hommann's String Quintet, a creditable work, employed the instruments efficiently, allowing none to "lie idle and listless during the momentary prominence of others, as they are prone to do in the hands of young composers. There was altogether considerable *swing* to the composition," wrote the critic (apparently not Willis), "showing that Mr. Hommann has got beyond the first hesitating A.B.C. of the art." The performers, still frustratingly unidentified, began shakily but gained confidence as they went on.

Miss Annie Kemp, a charming young contralto, reflected credit on her teacher, Mrs. Seguin, with her fine renditions of Willis's songs "Sleep, the kind angel" and

[85] And in December a three-time lecturer at the Board of Education on the importance of including music as an integral part of "popular education" (*Times,* December 13, 1856).

"Spring Song." "As she stood in Stuyvesant Hall, which is a remarkably unattractive place," remarked the critic, "she looked like a pretty bird in a shabby cage."

Gottschalk's *Galop di bravura*[86] was well played by Candido Berti and duly encored, and the third movement of Hopkins's *Symphony of Life,* evidently played by the string ensemble, was weightily judged to have "expressed well that struggle to which we all are put, to gain an eminence in the world. He [Hopkins] is struggling through Art," the reviewer continued. "His aim is high and pure, and in the language of the German miners in ascending from below to pure air, we will say to him, *Glück auf*!" (An ethnically ill-chosen, if well-meant, sentiment, given the circumstances!)

A pretty song by T. Franklin Bassford was "neatly sung" by Mrs. Brinkerhoff, who only somewhat successfully struggled with the "unvibratory" acoustics of that "wretched music box of a place," and Bassford's Ballade for piano was "fairly composed and executed" by its composer.

At this point, in mid-concert, Gottschalk arrived, and the atmosphere suddenly became charged with electricity as he proceeded to accompany Mrs. Brinkerhoff in his song "Alone," best described, wrote the critic, as "a duet between piano and voice, inasmuch as both talk so expressively to each other. The melody floats a good deal in the upper regions of the *soprano,* and the hall appertaining decidedly to the *lower* regions, it was exceedingly difficult for Mrs. Brinkerhoff to accomplish her task. But an experienced and cultivated voice is not easily foiled in what it has undertaken," and apparently Mrs. Brinkerhoff (and Gottschalk) emerged victorious, for the song was encored. Also encored was "The Gondolier's Serenade," a vocal quartet by William Mason, described as stylistically an instrumental, rather than vocal, piece. And to cap things off, in response to the audience's insistent demand, Gottschalk at last yielded and thrilled everyone present with his brilliant performance of "The Last Hope."

"We trust the American Music Association will go on," the reviewer concluded, but, he lectured, "they should have a regular organization: regular practice, tickets for performing and non-performing members; in short, they should be constituted like the Philharmonic and like Eisfeld's Quartette. Above all, they should secure an attractive and suitable place for their performances and ignore, hereafter, Stuyvesant Institute."[87]

By the third and final concert of their first season, on May 30, at least one of these admonitions had been heeded: the Association shifted to Dodworth Hall, where a crowd assembled to hear them. The program, now reported in the *Musical World* (June 7, 1856, p. 273) piece by piece, if still not title by title, consisted of Hommann's quintet, presumably the same quintet, but this time performed in a manner that was "measurably perfect"; Mr. Wooster, a baritone, gave another song titled "Alone," this one from Bristow's opera *Rip Van Winkle;* Berti, who defaulted, was replaced by an embarrassed but game Mrs. Jameson; Miss Comstock, a pupil of Charles Bassini, despite her enfeebled health delivered "Switzerland," a song by the Baltimore composer James

[86] This was a version for solo piano of the presumably lost *Galop di bravura (d'après Quidant)* for two pianos that Gottschalk had played with Berti on March 20 at his tenth *soirée.* According to Doyle, it was this piece that was published in 1854 by Horace Waters as "Tournament Galop," bearing no credit to Quidant (D-153–153/A; *Piano Works,* V, 235).

[87] And furthermore, in the *Times*'s opinion, they should shorten the waits between pieces, something that was "likely to try the patience of any audience."

Monroe Deems (1818–1901) with "much expression"; Allen Dodworth, despite some occasional blurred notes, played his Cornet Variations with his accustomed mellow tone and finished execution; and a song by Hopkins was beautifully sung by Annie Kemp, despite its ill-advised accompaniment for strings and piano that swamped the singer. "But young composers have to try their hand at a great many things before they settle into their best style," avuncularly philosophized the reviewer.

At last William Henry Fry was represented with a setting for vocal quartet[88] of the popular poem of yesteryear (1823) "Marco Bozzaris,"[89] by the New York poet Fitz-Greene Halleck (1790–1867). "The composer's aim in this piece was apparently to subjugate the musical to the rhetorical effect," to the inevitable detriment of its musical content, wrote the critic. "A piece in this way may either seem good or bad, accordingly as you understand the aim of the composer. Fry is never aimless, he has always a clear intellectual idea of what he is about to accomplish," a quality the reviewer apparently lacked, for, shirking his primary professional responsibility, he lamely concluded: "The task of the public is to discover what this is."

William Mason played his "Silver Spring" with his usual success but pleased the audience less with his encore (unidentified). A fugal work for solo soprano and chorus by Hopkins revealed creditable writing, but the "fugue" was in fact no fugue but only an "imitation" of one. Hommann's Violin and Piano Sonata in D-flat, with a "sufficiently long" Andante, was played by Hopkins and Julius Meyer, and a "neat and pleasing" song by the violinist and piano dealer T. J. Cook was charmingly sung by Miss Kemp. Morgan (a recent American) conducted from the piano.

Explaining that he was withholding his severest barbs in consideration of the commendable cause, Seymour (*Times,* June 3, 1856) pronounced several of these pieces to be "really excellent." Parts of Hommann's quintet were "worthy of any master"; their quality went to show how musical genius in the United States had been ignored and how greatly needed was such a society to make it known. Fry's indifferently sung vocal quartet, although a "very peculiar" work, abounded in "dramatic effects and [was] rich in harmonic resonance." Although the poem was inhospitable to musical treatment, it had been skillfully handled by Fry, another composer who illustrated the need for this kind of organization: "Mr. Fry is a man of unquestionable musical genius," wrote Seymour, "and the only pieces of his composition we have heard this season have been rendered at these concerts."[90]

By December 30, when the New-York American-Music Association, as this innovative society was now hyphenated (to stress their purpose), launched their second season with a matinée at Dodworth's Academy, they had complied with the remainder of the *Musical World*'s admonitions. The existence of this group, reported the *Tribune* (December 30, 1856), at last showing signs of interest, was "due to the enthusiasm of a young and gifted amateur of music, Mr. C. J. Hopkins, son of a very clever man,

[88] Now apparently lost; the work is not listed in William Treat Upton's catalogue of Fry's works.

[89] A work celebrating the heroic death of the Greek patriot Marco Bozzaris (Markos Botsaris) (1788–1823) in the struggle for Greek independence, a cause with which Americans warmly empathized.

[90] Suggesting that a work by Fry might have been performed at the Society's first concert, after all.

New York Sep 10th 1856.

We the undersigned do hereby promise and consent to take part as artists, in the concerts of American Music to be given in this city of New York during the Winter Season of 1856–7 under the name of "the concerts of the New York American-Music Association", or "Society for the encouragement of Native Art."

L. M. Gottschalk.
Candido Berti
Emma G. Bostwick.
Geo. F. Bristow.
T. J. Cook
Wm Mason

Bishop [John Henry] Hopkins [1792–1868] of the Episcopal Church, Vermont." Young Hopkins had by now "engineered his project into the vitalities of a second season, brought out a Constitution and By-Laws, and, in a word, organized a Society." The officers were C. Jerome Hopkins president, T. J. Cook vice-president, and Richard Storrs Willis, George Frederick Bristow, and George Henry Curtis, consulting committee (see *Dwight's,* December 20, 1856, p. 93). According to the *Musical World* (November 20, 1856, p. 651), four concerts were planned for their second season, each to be performed by a chorus of thirty-five voices, an instrumental quartet, a vocal quartet, and one or more eminent soloists. So far, the volunteers included Mesdames Bostwick, Jameson, Sheppard, and Hawley, and Messrs. Gottschalk, Bristow, Mason, and, incongruously, "Signor" Guilmette of the Pyne/Harrison company, now touted as the "late Basso Assoluto to his Excellency Dom Pedro II of Brazil." The programs, too, although their aim was to promote American music, would no longer be limited solely to native composers but to music composed in the United States.

But the *Tribune* (December 30, 1856), now speaking with the unmistakable voice of William Henry Fry, maintained that because "The object is, first, middle, and last, to perform American music, and as nothing can be known of American music unless it is adequately performed, the least that eminent artists from Europe, equally with those of American birth, who are well received here by the public, can do, will be to render their services voluntarily to the young body." The pieces to be performed at the impending concert were composed by G. H. Curtis, C. Hommann, C. J. Hopkins, E. A. Paine, G. F. Bristow, W. H. Walter, G. Godone, and J. N. Pychowski—"all new and American. . . . As the growth of art in any country is, as a general rule, dependent chiefly on the support it receives from the public, the utility of upholding this American Music Association will speak for itself." Then the inevitable Fryism: "Our counsel to the Society is to burn crude works after performing them privately . . . and to have no bad performances in public. The public will not play wet-nurse."

Young Jerome Hopkins had enunciated a more valid credo for an evolving American music:

> *GIVE IT A FAIR TRIAL. IF AMERICANS DO NOT KNOW HOW TO COMPOSE NOW, IT DOES NOT FOLLOW THAT THEY NEVER* WILL *KNOW HOW.*

At least they were on their way.

APPENDIX I

Under the heading, "Father Heinrich and Jenny Lind," the following series of progressively embittered letters appeared in the *Journal of Fine Arts* (December 15, 1851, p. 134);

New York, Dec. 11, 1851

MR. EDITOR: Since you were so kind as to interest yourself in my musical manuscript work, entitled:

The Jenny Lind Maelstrom;[1]
or,
The Shipwreck of a Book, &c.

I send you, with the programme of the piece, an account of the circumstances that led to its composition, involving correspondence on both sides, which I deem it no more than justice to myself, should be made public; the more so, as I hope shortly to be enabled to listen to the performance of this production, together with several of my late works, by artists in New York or elsewhere, who will be possessed of discrimination and independence to prove themselves able and impartial judges, and evincing likewise generosity enough for one who has labored so long and faithfully in the cause of music. Yours respectfully,

[signed] A. P. HEINRICH.

[1] W. T. Upton, *Heinrich,* List of Compositions: see *Jenny Lind and the Septinarian. An Artistic Perplexity: Jenny Lind's Journey across the Ocean,* etc., pp. 279–80.

THE JENNY LIND MAELSTROM;
OR,
THE SHIPWRECK OF A BOOK,
A PHANTASY FOR THE PIANOFORTE
Programme

No. 1. Presentation of the Book:
The Artist's Concert Ouverture
" 2. Council of the Critics: *Preludio pensoroso.*
" 3. Shipwreck of the Book: *Allegro furibondo.*
" 4. Adieu to the Book: *Finale.*
" 5. The Mocking Bird and the Nightingale: *Coda scherzante.*[2]
" 6. The Spirit Bond: A Song.[3]

Composed by
ANTHONY PHILIP HEINRICH

[Letter] No. I

New York, 14 Sept. 1850

MADEMOISELLE JENNY LIND.

Most distinguished Madam:—Your true genius combined with the excellencies of your heart induce me to present you my musical homage on your happy arrival in the New World. I hail you from the bottom of my heart, and wish that your musical fame will brightly illumine the horizon of the Western Hemisphere. Nothing but sympathetic enthusiasm could have tempted me to address you with my cordial dedications, which I hope will be kindly received. I must confess that I should like to know you personally, and to have a chat with you. In my younger days I admired the bright qualities of the Swedish ladies, of whom in *Wraxal's Travels* through the ancient Scandinavian mythological realms of the *"goddess Freya"* and other northern deities such a glowing description is given. Little did I dream then that at so late a period of my life I should be inspired—through the lustre of your name and brilliant debut in the Empire City of America—with some emanations of the muse. I am preparing a selection of my works, which I shall do myself the honor of presenting to you in person. It gives me the greatest pleasure to perceive that such a general warmth of welcome prevails in all hearts towards you. Your most bountiful donations to the various institutions in this city, when I read it in one of the papers, overcame me with such emotions that I wept like a child. May the Great Guardian of every earthly felicity and the angels of

[2] *Ibid.*, p. 282.
[3] *Ibid.*, p. 290.

the sweetest concords accompany the "Empress of Song" wherever she dwells, which wishes sincerely

ANTHONY PHILIP HEINRICH.

No. II

New York, 27th October, 1850

MADEMOISELLE JENNY LIND.

Madam:—On the 14th Sept. I had the honor of addressing you a letter, together with the presentation of my musical dedications. I mentioned then that I would wait on you personally with a selection of my works. I did so at your residence a few days previous to your trip to Boston—Mr. Gjortsberg [Hjortsberg], your secretary, perhaps being prevented by some unforeseen occurrence to keep his appointment with his brother of Brooklyn, from whom likewise I had received a note of introduction—and as moreover your valet at the antichambre could not admit me, I retreated *con molta pazienza e filosofia,* and effected a safe return home, my old arms aching meanwhile from the ponderous weight of the volume. The said book now follows, *sans cérémonie,* for your acceptance. In furtherance of my original design, it only remains to present you my Grand Cantata:

MUSIC, THE HARMONIZER OF THE WORLD.[4]

[Also] "A lone trembling flower"[5] dedicated to your celebrated countrywoman, Miss Fredricka Bremer. I earnestly desire to hear, in one of your concerts, *Jenny Lind's Musical Journey across the Atlantic, &c,* the different parts of which I have given into the hands of the transcriber. This *Divertimento instrumentale* being brief, fluent, and, I trust, pleasing, it would give the orchestra no particular trouble, and if the musicians were willing in their magnanimity to execute on the same occasion, in conjunction, my own *Marcia funerale,*[6] it might produce the effect of my resuscitation, as to all appearances I am considered by the Musical World here dead and gone; and then, perhaps, their hearts would soften towards "Father Heinrich," which title they have kindly deigned to bestow on him, but to whom they, as yet, only proved truant children. I fondly anticipate your kind decision to gratify the Veteran Kentucky Composer,[7] who appreciates all that is said of your moral worth and musical genius. I will only say, concerning the contents of the present book, that no other individual possesses the aggregate amount

[4] *Ibid.,* p. 282.

[5] *Ibid.,* p. 281.

[6] *Ibid.,* pp. 281–82.

[7] Heinrich persisted in identifying himself as a "Kentucky composer," although it was now more than a quarter century since his Kentucky adventure (1818–1823).

of its music. With the exception of divers fugitive pieces, few, indeed, have seen my compositions; I myself cannot any more obtain some of the important copies of the bound book, as several years since [1835] about 500 of my music plates and an entire Opera in manuscript were destroyed by fire. In the pleasing anticipation of your being favorably disposed towards the result of my labors, I have but to add, respected madam, that I hope ere long to enjoy an interview with you. Meanwhile, believe me, tho' unseen, your friend.

A. P. Heinrich.

No. III

New York, 1st November, 1850

Mademoiselle Jenny Lind.

Esteemed Madam:—In consequence of our brief conversation yesterday morning, I have reason to conclude that my various dedications, alluded to in my letters, dated 14th September and 27th October, are of no interest to you, artistically. Had I not thought otherwise before seeing you, I should not have sent you the emanations of my muse, for there is no Prima Donna living to whom I would tender them. I freely confess that I am deeply disappointed at your seeming indifference to my simple *verbal* request to have my descriptive Orchestral Work (*Jenny Lind's Musical Journey across the Atlantic*) performed at one of your *rehearsals*. Presuming, therefore, that the bound book and unbound manuscripts are of trifling value to you, I respectfully request that you will cause them to be sent to my residence, No. 351 Broome Street. As a Bohemian, I intend to have them conveyed, together with the *Partitura* of the above mentioned Orchestra Work, to the Imperial and Royal Museum at Prague, a magnificent National Institution, where everything pertaining to the arts and sciences is deposited, the whole supported and patronized by the Emperor, the nobility, and citizens of the kingdom, outnumbering 4000 subscribers. I may, perhaps, shortly, by way of England, visit my native country, where, at all events, my *Barnum's Museum Polka*[8] will meet a cordial welcome at the Prague Museum. There is a young lady in this city who plays this *Polka di Bravura* in a brilliant and effective manner. Should you wish it, perhaps my young friend (Julia W. Pomeroy, Pianist of distinguished abilities) will favor me, to call on you and perform the Polka for you, after which you may pass your verdict upon it. To speak the truth, the young lady accompanied me the first time I made an ineffectual attempt to see you. Regretting extremely that I have unwittingly caused you any trouble, I remain, honored madam, as ever, your sincere wellwisher,

A. P. H.

[8] *Ibid.*, p. 294.

No. IV

New York, 7th November, 1850

TO MADEMOISELLE JENNY LIND.

ESTEEMED MADAM:—As I have never received a syllable in reply to my letters of 14th Sept., 27th Oct., and 1st November, it astonishes me much, the more so as I hear that you maintain two secretaries, whose duty it should be to look to these things. I have vainly expected every day the return of my bound book and unbound manuscripts, and I again most earnestly and respectfully solicit your promptest attention to my request. It matters very little what you and your coadjutors think of my compositions, provided I only receive them in good order. My compliments, if you please, to the courteous *Mr. Benedict,* though (for reasons unknown to me) he has not thought proper to acknowledge my presentations of music to himself. It is not surprising that that gentleman should have overlooked the orchestral work, entitled *Jenny Lind's Journey, &c,* as its composer, unlike the throng, has not pressed Mr. Benedict sufficiently to obtain a single interview. Unfortunately for myself, I have no orchestras at my command in this country, but would not fear to test my numerous orchestral works of every description before the highest European tribunals. I cannot but express my regret at being compelled to trouble you again on the subject of my music. *The remedy lies with yourself,* for if you do but comply with my reiterated desire and send me the aforementioned book and manuscripts, I promise you henceforth, honored madam, not to make any further application to you, either "in propria persona" or by letter. Trusting that this attempt to sustain my reputation may not prove unsuccessful, believe me, madam, your obedient and humble servant,

A. P. HEINRICH.

No. V

New York, 7th November 1850

MAX GJORTSBERG, ESQ.

My dear sir:—Fearing that my previous letters addressed to Miss Lind may have been lost in the multitude of epistles which she is said to receive daily, I urge upon you the necessity of handing in the enclosed to that lady *yourself.* After its perusal I cannot doubt but that Miss Lind will comply with my request immediately. I wish to be clearly understood. It is not with me a matter of dollars and cents, but that which I value far more highly than any pecuniary consideration, *viz.:* my reputation as a composer. I make this explanation to you, Sir, in order that you may press upon Miss Lind the attention due to my years, independent of my claims musically. Relying implicitly for the satisfactory arrangement which I have proposed concerning my book and manuscripts, I remain, yours respectfully,

A. P. HEINRICH, 351 Broome st.

New-York Hotel, November 8th, 1850

A. P. Heinrich, Esq.

Dear Sir:—You must kindly excuse my long delay in answering your letter. I should long before this have done so, but Miss Lind having expressed her wish to write to you herself has been the cause thereof. As soon as her time will allow her I shall remit to you her answer. In the meantime, believe me, dear sir, yours very truly,

Max Gjortsberg.

APPENDIX 2

From the New York *Herald,* October 7, 1850:

BARNUM, JENNY LIND, AND THE PRESS

We perceive in several exchange papers, attacks upon the New York press in reference to the Jenny Lind excitement, and the *Herald,* as usual, comes in for the principal share of the abuse. It is more than insinuated that "black mail" has been levied, and that the articles about the Swedish Nightingale have been paid for. This must certainly be all very rich to Barnum, who, behind the scenes, enjoys the joke, and pockets his $5,000 net, each concert, $15,000 per week, $780,000, or more than three-quarters of a million per annum, while the papers receive nothing but vituperation for their services, except, indeed, a few free tickets given grudgingly, and very often to the worst part of the house.

There can be no doubt that Barnum is coining Jenny Lind's notes into dollars through the newspapers, but there the matter ends, so far as the press is concerned, unless, indeed, as we except the abuse we must pocket as the reward of generosity.

But how does Barnum turn the press to his account? Just as follows: Being a shrewd Yankee, and once of the press gang himself, he knows the ropes, and having enlarged his experience during his exhibition of Dr. Edson, "the Living Skeleton, Joice Heth, pretended to be the nurse of Washington, General Santa Anna's leg, General Tom Thumb, and the Woolly Horse, he sends paid agents about in all directions to get up an excitement. The papers report the excitement as news; the report produces a new excitement among the readers, more or less in proportion to the extent of the circulation—other papers copy the report, and thus multiply it over the land. Barnum does not so much as thank them for their pains.

For months before Jenny Lind's arrival, he kept up a constant excitement by sending communications to the newspapers about her, all of which were inserted without costing him a dollar. While she is on board the *Atlantic* an excitement is got up by Barnum's agents—a concert is given, and a report is published of it on her arrival. Then, preparations of every kind are made to give her a reception. The reception, with the attendant excitement, is published by the papers at considerable expense and much labor to the reporters, who get no thanks for their trouble.

In the next place, it is given out that the furniture of Jenny Lind's apartments in the hotels cost a mint of money—in Boston so much as $13,000. The furniture is certainly magnificent, and the manufacturer is praised to the skies. This is reported, and stimulates the excitement. But what is the fact? Some of this furniture turns out to be actually second-hand, while the new is lent by the furniture store for the occasion, the proprietor considering himself well paid by the puffs he receives from the press. When Jenny Lind removes from the hotel the furniture is returned, or, perhaps a portion of it is wanted by the establishment. But this is not all.

Barnum, by his agreement, is to pay the hotel expenses of Jenny Lind and *suite*. The unsophisticated reader will say that this must cost an enormous amount, considering the magnificent furniture of the apartments, private board, and gold service. He will perhaps be astonished when we tell him that instead of costing Barnum anything, he makes money by the transaction. The hotels do not charge him a cent, and it is even said that he has been well paid for bringing the Nightingale to these establishments. Now, the report published in the papers of the great expense he incurs for hotels "brings grist to his mill," for it impresses the reader with an idea that such an expenditure necessarily requires very high prices to sustain it. And the hotels, on the other hand, participate in the profits of the excitement from the *éclat* arising from their supposed spirit in making such preparations for Jenny Lind, and by the shoals of fish that consequently fall into their net. Thus, all parties are benefited by the press, except the press itself.

All this time Jenny Lind is unconscious of the use that is made of her name to swell the amount of the receipts. Why, the receipts themselves are exaggerated, in order to produce an effect for the next concert. For example, the Swede, in the benevolence of her heart, devoted the entire of her share of the profits of the first concert in New York to the purposes of charity, but did not wish to have it published. Barnum, thinking it would be a pity to hide the virtues of "the angel" under a bushel, proclaimed the fact at the close of the concert. He announced that $10,000 were her share, and designated the different charities to which that sum had been appropriated. But it turned out that "the chickens were counted before they were hatched," and that instead of $10,000 there was only $7,000 forthcoming. How were the other $3,000 to be made up? Jenny Lind had to put her hand in her pockets and to pay what she never received. This charity, of course, was only "lending to the Lord," as the inscription on the lock of one of her apartments in the Revere House testifies, for whatever is thus given is amply repaid, and Barnum reaps a splendid harvest, though the need which produces it costs him nothing.

Then look at the excitement got up by selling the first choice seat at auction. Before the eventful day comes, Barnum's agents are busy at work and a *furore* is raised; any money will be given for a seat that is sometimes about the worst in the house, as at Castle Garden, and is never better than one that costs $5. The rivalry of pride, or an eye to business, pushes it up to $225, $625, or lastly, as at Providence, to $650. This has its effect, not only upon the other tickets of that concert, and the following concerts in the same place, but on the first ticket in the next city, so that we would not be surprised if the price of that first seat would reach $1,000 at the first concert in New Orleans.

All these results flow from the liberality of the press, which has made one fortune for Barnum, and is now making another for him by thanklessly and gratuitously occupying its space with accounts of the sayings and doings of the Swedish Nightingale.

It is true that the glorious woman is worthy of all the honor and glory and renown the press can give her, but it is well the public should understand that Mr. Barnum is the only gainer in the business. Mademoiselle Lind, of course, shares half the receipts, but then she devotes them to the noble work of education in her native land, and for this, independent of her wonderful musical genius, she has the sympathy of the press, and of two worlds here below, to say nothing of the world to come.

APPENDIX 3

Advertisement for William Henry Fry's lectures appearing in the *New-York Daily Times* (November 17, 1852) and in various other daily newspapers in New York:

> The aim of these lectures will be to present, in a condensed but clear form, an illustrated history of the rise, progress, and present state of all departments of instrumental and vocal music; whether sacred, dramatic, symphonic, classic, romantic, or national, or of those various kinds of music which it would be difficult to class specifically. The manner in which the subject will be treated will enable the hearer to understand the structure of various musical compositions, to form more correct opinions of the performance of vocal and instrumental artists, and to comprehend more clearly the proper terms of musical criticism. In short, the effort of the lecturer will be to give, as minutely and thoroughly as such a course of musical lectures can, a view of the literature, an analysis of the philosophy, and an explanation of the technicalities of music, both as a science and an art. A residence of several years in Europe has enabled the Lecturer to collect a large amount of rare materials for the practical illustration of the historical and critical text.
>
> THE ILLUSTRATIONS
>
> of these Lectures will form one of their principal attractions, and will be so copious and particular as to leave no Historical or Critical passage to the text misunderstood by any hearer who can distinguish the difference between varying sounds. The *present state,* as well as the origin and progress of the
>
> OPERA, THE ORATORIO, AND THE BALLAD
>
> will be illustrated by the performance (by *Artists of distinction,* an ample chorus, and grand orchestra) of the most popular and characteristic passages in the works of

THE GREATEST MODERN COMPOSERS

whose Overtures, Solos, Concerted Pieces, and Choruses will all be made to contribute to the elucidation of the Lecturer's text. And as a condensed History of the Art from the *remotest ages and in all countries* will be given, and every statement sustained and explained by the performances of a musical composition in the style remarked upon, a copious but carefully made selection of

CURIOUS AND RARE MUSIC OF ALL AGES AND COUNTRIES

will be produced. The Lecturer has made researches in the Great Libraries of Europe, and has obtained *an unbroken sequence of musical compositions* commencing at a period *more than a thousand years* distant, and which forms a complete exponent of the development of the art from the time of Charlemagne.

Paintings of antique and barbaric instruments and copies of the Illuminated Music Books of the early ages of the Catholic Church will be exhibited. In the course of the lectures there will be an analysis of *Greek* poetry in its musical relations; likewise an extended view of the application of English poetry to music, indicating the resources of the language and the reforms required. Among the curious music to be performed are: "The Chinese Hymn," sung in the presence of the Emperor at the annual Thanksgiving, and supposed to be the oldest piece of music in existence. Various national and sentimental airs of the same people; the chief religious and secular airs of the East Indians, exhibiting their early efforts in the production of melody; Egyptian music collected during Napoleon's expedition into that country; two ancient Greek hymns rendered into modern notation after Meibomius and Burette; Ode of Boece of the 9th century; Song of the Battle of Fontane [*sic*] of the same era; Song of Eric, Duke of Frioul; Complaint on the death of Charlemagne; *Ut quieant lexis*—the origin of the modern system of *solfeggi*—from the original; Chorus sung anciently in Venice at the ceremony of the marriage of the Doge with the Adriatic; Song of Blondel, the troubadour who accompanied Richard Coeur de Lion; Song of the French Armies in the year 1400; Chants of the Sainte Chapelle, 18th century; Extracts from Hucbald on Harmony of the 9th century, the earliest writer known on the subject; the most ancient piece of music in parts, handed down in England; Selections from the Music Book used by Queen Elizabeth; Palestrina's Original Mass; Gluck's *Orpheus and Euridice;* Extracts from the Works of the Founders and Subsequent Masters of the Chief Schools of Europe.[1]

[1]Marcus Meiboom, or Meibomius (*c.* 1626–1710) was a German (or Danish) music historian; Burette, probably Pierre-Jean (1665–1747) was an authority on ancient Greek music; "Boece," al-

The illustrations having shown the progress of the art thus far, the number of Solos, Duetts, Trios, Quartettes, Choruses, Overtures, and other vocal and instrumental pieces from the works of the greatest

MODERN ITALIAN, FRENCH, AND GERMAN COMPOSERS,

which will be given, are entirely too numerous for mention in a general advertisement. Among them, however, will be extracts from Le Seur's [*sic*] opera *La Caverne,* Spontini's *Vestale.* Félicien David's *Christopher Columbus*[2] and Meyerbeer's *Prophète.* And it may be remarked that some of the Lectures will embrace

GRAND CONCERTS

of Classical and Dramatic Music with Explanatory and Historical Comments; and that for the proper attainment of this object the Musical Illustrations will be given by

TWO HUNDRED PERFORMERS

Including a corps of Principal Operatic and Concert Singers of

the first grade, an Orchestra
of Eighty and a
Chorus of One Hundred.

The design of these lectures being not only different from, but wider in scope and more elaborate in detail than any which have been presented to the public of either Europe or America.

though not of the ninth century, refers to the Roman philosopher Boethius (*c.* 480–534); Sainte Chapelle is a church in Paris; Hucbald (*c.* 840–*c.* 930) is an early Flemish music theorist; Giovanni Pierluigi da Palestrina (1525–1594) is the superb Italian Renaissance composer; Gluck's opera *Orfeo ed Euridice* was first performed at Vienna in Italian in 1762; then at Paris in French in 1774.

[2] *La Caverne* by Jean François Lesueur (1760–1837) was first performed in Paris in 1793; Félicien David's descriptive symphony *Christophe Colomb* was first heard in Paris in 1847.

APPENDIX 4

"In planning the old Academy of Music," writes Alexander Saeltzer in his *Treatise on Acoustics in Connection with Ventilation* (New York, 1872), "I was forced to this arrangement, viz.: the descent of the galleries, as the number of seats required was 5,500, and without it many hundreds of seats would have been useless. This immense drop of 8 feet, never known or executed in any other theatre before, was one of the main causes of the success of acoustics in that house; the great number of seats in the galleries, seven or eight rows in depth on the side alone, demanded a great height of the building; 78 feet was the height from the middle of [the] parquet floor to the ceiling, and this space gave such a volume of condensed air that, without ventilation, even, it would have secured at least for two hours' time a healthy and congenial air for sound; but here I will add that all the walls, ceilings, gallery breast-works, etc., throughout the house were covered with boards tongued and grooved so that every part formed a sound board. The shape of the auditorium ceiling formed part of a circle, its centre point about four feet below the parquet floor; this form is necessary to prevent the rays of sound from concentrating more toward the middle of the building than toward the side walls. The outlines of the old Academy approached more the shape of a funnel with a semicircle at the end; the proportion of the auditorium was beyond any approach to known forms, the depth being about one-third more than the width; a deep proscenium to lessen the proportion, and this very depth of the proscenium proved most excellent for propelling sound" (pp. 19–20).

APPENDIX 5

Programs performed by Louis Moreau Gottschalk in his series of concerts, 1855–56, as listed in the newspapers:

No. 1: Dodworth's Rooms, December 20, 1855

With Joseph Burke, Karl Wels, and Richard Hoffman

I

1. Italian Glories, Fantasia di bravura on themes from *Norma, Lucrezia,* and *Sonnambula,* for two pianos . . . . Gottschalk
   Wels and Gottschalk
2. Fragments of the Fantasia on *Lucia* . . . . Gottschalk
   Gottschalk
3. (a) Ballade . . . . Gottschalk
   (b) Marche de nuit
   (c) Mazurka
4. The Banjo, American Sketch . . . . Gottschalk
   Gottschalk

II

5. Grand Sonata for four hands, E Minor . . . . Onslow
   Hoffman and Gottschalk
6. (a) The Last Hope, Religious Meditation . . . . Gottschalk
   (b) Funeral March . . . . Chopin
   Gottschalk
7. Sonata in A Major, for piano and violin . . . . Mozart
   Burke and Gottschalk
8. Fantasia on *La figlia del reggimento* . . . . Gottschalk
   Gottschalk

No. 2: Dodworth's Rooms, December 27, 1855.

I

With Joseph Burke, Karl Wels, and Richard Hoffman

1. Italian Glories, Fantasia di bravura on themes from *Norma, Lucrezia,* and *Sonnambula* for two pianos . . . . Gottschalk
   Wels and Gottschalk
2. Danse des sylphes (d'après Godefroid) . . . . Gottschalk
   Gottschalk
3. Andante con variazioni and Finale, "Kreutzer" Sonata for violin and piano[1] . . . . Beethoven
   Burke and Gottschalk
4. The Banjo . . . . Gottschalk
   Gottschalk

II

5. Jérusalem, Triumphal Fantasie, for two pianos . . . . Gottschalk
   Hoffman and Gottschalk
6. (a) Ballade . . . . Gottschalk
   (b) Marche de nuit
   (c) Souvenirs d'Andalousie[2]
   Gottschalk
7. Concertstück . . . . Weber
   Gottschalk, accompanied by Hoffman at a second piano.

[1] Not performed.
[2] Not performed.

No. 3: Dodworth's Rooms, January 25, 1856

With Joseph Burke and Richard Hoffman

I

1. Finale of *Lucrezia Borgia* . . . . Gottschalk
   (first time)
   Gottschalk
2. (a) Solitude, ballade (first time) . . . . Gottschalk
   (b) Valse poétique
   (c) Souvenirs d'Andalousie (first time)
   Gottschalk
3. Concertstück, March & Finale (by request) . . . . Weber
   Gottschalk, accompanied by Hoffman

II

4. El Cocoyé, Grand Fantasie on Cuban Dances . . . . Gottschalk
   Gottschalk
5. Sonata for Violin and Piano ("Kreutzer") . . . . Beethoven
   Burke and Gottschalk
6. Septuor [*sic*] from *Lucia* . . . . Liszt
   Gottschalk

No. 4: Dodworth's Rooms, January 31, 1856

Dedicada a los Españoles peninsulares y cubanos

With Candido Berti

Primera Parte—España

1. Marcha triunfal para dos pianos . . . . T. F. Bassford
   Ejecuta por los Señores Berti y Gottschalk
2. (a) Manchega
   (b) La Jota aragonesa
   (c) Recuerdo de Andalusia (Fandango e jaleo)[3]
   Compuestos y ejecutados por L. M. Gottschalk
3. La Marcha real española y fragmentos de la Sinfonia para 10 pianos, "El Sitio de Zaragoza" . . . . Gottschalk
   Ejecutado en uno por el autor

Segunda Parte—Cuba

4. Caprichos sobre danzas de Puerto Principe[4]
   La Caringa
   Maria lancero
   Compuestos y ejecutados por L. M. Gottschalk
5. Recuerdo de la vuelta de abajo[5]
   Zapateado cubano
   Tengue terengue
   Bembo como tá
   Maria la Ho y el tango
   El Cocoyé
   Compuestos y ejecutados por L. M. Gottschalk

No. 5: Dodworth's Rooms, February 14, 1856

With Karl Wels and Aptommas

I

1. Fantasia di bravura for two pianos . . . . Wels
   Gottschalk and Wels
2. Fantasie for Harp, Italian Melodies . . . . Alvars
   Aptommas
3. (a) Sérénade . . . . Gottschalk
   (b) Chant du soldat
   (c) Rayons d'azur
   Gottschalk
4. L'Éternel [*sic*] Carnaval de Venise . . . . Gottschalk
   Gottschalk

II

5. Grand Scherzo, op. 31 . . . . Chopin
   Gottschalk
6. Studio per l'arpa, in imitation of the Mandolin . . . . Alvars
   Aptommas
7. Le Bamboula . . . . Gottschalk
   Gottschalk

No. 6: Dodworth's Rooms, February 22, 1856

With Karl Wels and Aptommas

I

1. Fantasia di bravura (by general request) . . . . Wels
   Gottschalk and Wels
2. Fantasie on *La Fille du régiment* . . . . Aptommas
   Aptommas
3. (a) Solitude . . . . Gottschalk
   (b) Mazurka
   (c) Rayons d'azur (Polka)
   Gottschalk
4. Dance and Study for the Harp . . . . Aptommas
   Aptommas
5. Serment et bénédiction,
   from *Benvenuto Cellini* . . . . Berlioz/Liszt
   Gottschalk

II

6. Impromptu . . . . Chopin
   Valse
   Gottschalk
7. Solo for Harp . . . . Aptommas
   Aptommas
8. Mr. Gottschalk will play any three pieces of his own composition that the audience may select.

No. 7: Dodworth's Rooms, February 28, 1856

With Richard Hoffman and Aptommas

I

1. Jérusalem, Grand Triumphal Fantasie for two pianos . . . . Gottschalk
   Hoffman and Gottschalk
2. Solo for Harp, Italian Melodies . . . . Aptommas
   Aptommas
3. (a) La Danse ossianique . . . . Gottschalk
   (b) Ballade
   (c) La Gazelle, Andante élégant . . . . R. Hoffman
   Gottschalk
4. Solo for Harp: Les Fées . . . . Aptommas
   Aptommas
5. Fantasia on *La Fille du régiment* . . . . Gottschalk
   Gottschalk

II

6. Second Polka de concert . . . . M. V. Wallace
   Gottschalk
7. Solo for Harp, Welsh Melodies . . . . Aptommas
   Aptommas
8. Fragment, Fantasie on *Lucia di Lammermoor* . . . . Gottschalk
   Gottschalk

No. 8: Dodworth's Rooms, March 8, 1856

With Harry Sanderson and Aptommas

I

1. Overture to *La Chasse du jeune Henri* for two pianos . . . . Gottschalk
   Sanderson and Gottschalk
2. Fantasie on *I Montecchi* and *Semiramide* . . . . Aptommas
   Aptommas
3. (a) Serenade . . . . Gottschalk
   (b) La Jota aragonesa
   (c) Souvenirs d'Andalousie
   Gottschalk
4. Scotch Melodies . . . . Aptommas
   Aptommas
5. Finale, *Lucrezia Borgia* (by request) . . . . Gottschalk
   Gottschalk

II

6. (a) La Scintilla (Mazurka) . . . . Gottschalk
   (b) La Danse des sylphes
   Gottschalk
7. Study, in imitation of Mandolin . . . . Aptommas
   Aptommas
8. Serment et bénédiction *(Benvenuto Cellini)* . . . . Berlioz/Liszt
   (by request)
   Gottschalk

No. 9: Dodworth's Rooms, March 13, 1856

With Vincenzo Morino, Candido Berti, and T. F. Bassford

I

1. Grand Duett on *Belisario,* for two pianos . . . . Alexandre Goria
    Bassford and Gottschalk
2. Romance from *Linda de Chamounix* . . . . Donizetti
3. (a) Prière . . . . Gottschalk
    (b) Le Songe d'une nuit d'été
    (c) Fandango
    Gottschalk
4. Song
    Morino
5. Septuor [*sic*] from *Lucia di Lammermoor* (by request) . . . . Liszt
    Gottschalk

II

6. (a) Marche de nuit . . . . Gottschalk
    (b) The Banjo
    Gottschalk
7. Tarantella (a popular Neapolitan song) . . . . Rossini
    Morino
8. Concertstück . . . . Weber
    Gottschalk, accompanied by Berti

No. 10: Dodworth's Rooms, March 20, 1856

With Otto Feder and Candido Berti

I

1. Galop di bravura (d'après Quidant)[6] . . . . Gottschalk
   Berti and Gottschalk
2. Song, from *La favorita* . . . . Donizetti
   Feder
3. (a) Prière (by request) . . . . Gottschalk
   (b) La Savane
   (c) Chant du soldat
   Gottschalk
4. Air, "In Happy Moments," from Maritana . . . . Wallace
   Feder
5. Scherzo (by request) . . . . Chopin
   Gottschalk

II

6. (a) The Water Sprite (Polka) . . . . Gottschalk
   (b) Fragment: Fantaisie héroique sur "God Save the Queen"
   Gottschalk
7. Song, "Hark, Hark, the Lark" . . . . Schubert
   Feder
8. (a) Impromptu . . . . Chopin
   (b) Valse
   (c) Any piece of Gottschalk's that the audience may call for.
   Gottschalk

[6] Alfred (Joseph) Quidant (1815–1893), French composer and pianist. The two-piano version of this work is lost; "Tournament Galop," a version for solo piano, was published by Horace Waters in 1854.

No. 11: Dodworth's Rooms, March 28, 1856

With the Brothers Mollenhauer and Candido Berti

I

1. Grand Fantasie on *Norma,* for two pianos . . . . Thalberg
   Gottschalk and Berti
2. The Mermaids: A Fairy Tale. Picture Characteristique . . . . C. Newman
   (1) Midnight on the Ocean; (2) Waves of the Ocean;
   (3) Approaching the Mermaids; (4) Dance of the Spirits;
   (5) Death of the Wanderer
   The Mollenhauers
3. (a) The Last Hope (by request) . . . . Gottschalk
   (b) Séville à minuit [Minuit à Séville]
   (c) Fandango [Souvenirs d'Andalousie] (by request)
   Gottschalk
4. Andante et Rondo Russe . . . . De Bériot
   Mollenhauer
5. La Rapidité (Étude de concert) . . . . W. V. Wallace
   Gottschalk

II

6. Les Bois: Fantaisie symphonique, for piano and orchestra . . . . Émile Prudent
   Arranged for two pianos by Gottschalk
   Gottschalk and Berti
7. Grand Duet, for two violins . . . . Mollenhauer
   The Mollenhauers
8. Fragment: Fantasia on *Lucia* (by request) . . . . Gottschalk
   Gottschalk

No. 12: Dodworth's Rooms, April 5, 1856

With Henriette Behrend and Candido Berti

I

1. Grand Fantasie on *Norma,* for two pianos . . . . Thalberg
   Gottschalk and Berti
2. Grand Aria, from *Marino Faliero* . . . . Donizetti
   Behrend
3. (a) Solitude . . . . Gottschalk
   (b) Mazurka
   (c) Esquisse
   Gottschalk
4. Ballad, "I Strive to Forget Thee" . . . . W. V. Wallace
   Behrend
5. La Rapidité, Étude de concert . . . . M. V. Wallace
   Gottschalk

II

6. El Cocoyé, Cuban National Fantasia . . . . Gottschalk
   Gottschalk
7. German Romanza, "The Winged Messenger" . . . . A. Fesca
   Behrend
8. Le Mouvement perpetuél (Finale of Sonata in C) . . . . Weber
   Gottschalk

No. 13: Dodworth's Rooms, April 10, 1856

With Karl Wels, Candido Berti, and the Brothers Mollenhauer

I

1. Grand duetto concertando for two pianos on airs from *Il trovatore* . . . . . . Wels
   Gottschalk and the Author
2. Grand duetto for two violins . . . . Mollenhauer
   The Mollenhauers
3. (a) Prière . . . . Gottschalk
   (b) Sérénade
   (c) Forest Glade (Polka de concert)
   Gottschalk
4. Variations brillants for violin . . . . Mollenhauer
   Friedrich Mollenhauer
5. Étude de concert . . . . Goria
   Gottschalk

II

6. Silver Spring . . . . William Mason
   Gottschalk
7. Duetto for two violins . . . . Neumann
   The Mollenhauers
8. Les Bois (by request) . . . . Prudent
   Gottschalk, accompanied by Berti

No. 14: Dodworth's Rooms, April 24, 1856

With Mrs. E. G. Bostwick and Candido Berti

I

1. (a) La Jota aragonesa . . . . Gottschalk
(b) Étude . . . . Goria
Gottschalk
2. Scena ed aria from *I Masnadieri* . . . . Verdi
Mrs. Bostwick
3. (a) The Last Hope . . . . Gottschalk
(b) Si oiseau j'etais . . . . Henselt
Gottschalk
4. Styrian Song: "Awake, sweet Treasure of my Love" . . . . Eckert
Mrs. Bostwick
5. Étude . . . . W. Mason
Gottschalk

II

6. Andante con variazioni for two pianos . . . . Schumann
Gottschalk and Berti
7. Serenade . . . . Schubert
Mrs. Bostwick
8. Serment et bénédiction *(Benvenuto Cellini)* . . . . Berlioz/Liszt
Gottschalk

No. 15: Dodworth's Rooms, May 16, 1856

With E. Wallace-Bouchelle, Richard Hoffman, Karl Wels,
T. F. Bassford, and Emilio Halma

I

1. Fantasia di bravura on *Belisario* for two pianos . . . . Goria
   Bassford and Gottschalk
2. Song, Grand Scene from *Der Freischütz* . . . . Weber
   Mme. Wallace-Bouchelle
3. (a) Solitude . . . . Gottschalk
   (b) Chant du soldat
   (c) Rayons d'azur
   Gottschalk
4. Song, "Go, go, thou Restless Wind" . . . . W. V. Wallace
   Mme. Wallace-Bouchelle
5. The Banjo (by special request) . . . . Gottschalk
   Gottschalk

II

6. Jérusalem, Grand Triumphal Fantasia for two pianos . . . . Gottschalk
   Richard Hoffman and the Author
7. Souvenir du Bosphore . . . . Vieuxtemps
   Halma
8. Song: "The Rapture Dwelling" . . . . Balfe
   Mme. Wallace-Bouchelle
9. Any one piece of Mr. Gottschalk's the audience may call for.

No. 16: Niblo's Saloon, June 7, 1856

With Anna de LaGrange, Oswald Bernardi, and Richard Hoffman

I

1. Jérusalem, Grand Triumphal Fantasy for two pianos . . . . Gottschalk
   Richard Hoffman and the Author
2. Romance and Prayer, from *Otello* . . . . Rossini
   Mme. de LaGrange
3. (a) Rayons et ombres, Serenade[7] . . . . Gottschalk
   (b) Danse des sylphes
   Gottschalk
4. Duet: Là ci darem, from *Don Giovanni* . . . . Mozart
   Mme. de LaGrange and Signor Bernardi
5. Invitation à la valse . . . . Weber/Liszt
   Gottschalk

II

6. Mr. Gottschalk will perform any one of his compositions the audience may select.
7. Variations . . . . Rode
   Mme. de LaGrange
8. Aria, from *Zaïra* . . . . Mercadante
   Bernardi
9. *Lucia,* Finale . . . . Liszt
   Gottschalk
10. Aria, from *Robert le diable* . . . . Meyerbeer
    Mme. de LaGrange
11. Romanza, from *I martiri* . . . . Donizetti
    Bernardi
12. Grand Concerto . . . . Weber
    Gottschalk, accompanied by Hoffman at a second piano

[7] "William Hall and Son have just published . . . the first number of the beautiful *Ballades* of this original composer. The entire collection [of twelve] is entitled *Rayons et Ombres,* and we hope it will have the same merit and success as the well known volume of poetry by Victor Hugo which bears the same title. The first of these little musical poems . . . is a *Sérénade,* written in a soft and impressive minor tone" (*Gamma, Albion,* May 10, 1856, p. 224).

Only four pieces—appearing at various times—are known to have been published under this blanket title: *La Sérénade (Le Mancenillier)* (1856), *Ricordati* (1857), *Reflets du passé* (1858) and *Morte!! (She is dead)* (1869).

BIBLIOGRAPHY

ABBREVIATIONS

IC	Information Coordinators
N-YHSQ	*New-York Historical Society Quarterly*
NYPL	New York Public Library
UMI	University Microfilms International

BOOKS, ARTICLES, AND PAMPHLETS

Aldrich, Richard. *Musical Discourse* (New York, Oxford Univ. Press, 1928).

Anon. *A Brief Memoir of the "Black Swan," Miss E. T, Greenfield, the American Vocalist* [pamphlet] (London, 1853).

Anon. (Julia Glass Byrne). *Gossip of the Century: Personal and Traditional Memories—Social Literary Artistic, etc.* (London, Ward & Downey, 1892).

Anon. *Squints Through an Opera Glass, by a Young Gent Who hadn't any thing else to do* (New York, *Merchants' Day Book*, 1850).

Arditi, Luigi. *My Reminiscences* (New York, Dodd, Mead, 1896).

Arpin, Paul. *Life of Louis Moreau Gottschalk*, trans. Henry C. Watson (New York, n.p., Detroit, IC, *c.* 1853).

Asbury, Herbert. *The Gangs of New York* (New York, Knopf, 1927; rpt. Capricorn, 1970).

Austin, William W. *Susanna, Jeanie, and The Old Folks at Home: The Songs of Stephen C. Foster from His Time to Ours* (New York, Macmillan, 1975).

Barnum, Phineas T. *The Life of P. T. Barnum* (New York, Redfield, 1855).

———. *Struggles and Triumphs; or Forty Years' Recollections of P. T. Barnum* (Hartford, Burr, 1869).

———. *Struggles and Triumphs: or, The Life of P. T. Barnum*, ed. George S. Bryan, 2 vols. (New York, Knopf, 1927).

———. *Selected Letters of P. T. Barnum*, ed. A. H. Saxon (New York, Columbia Univ. Press, 1982).

Barzun, Jacques. *Berlioz and the Romantic Century*, 3rd ed., 2 vols. (New York, Columbia Univ. Press, 1969).

Beers, Henry A. *Nathaniel Parker Willis* (Boston, Houghton, Mifflin, 1885).

Bender, Thomas. *New York Intellect* (New York, Knopf, 1987).

Benedict, Julius. "Jenny Lind" (*Scribner's Monthly Magazine*, May 1881, pp. 120–32).

Berlioz, Hector. *The Memoirs of Hector Berlioz, from 1803 to 1865*, trans. Rachel S. C. Holmes, rev. and ed. Ernest Newman (New York, Knopf, 1932).

A Brief Memoir of the "Black Swan," Miss E. T. Greenfield, the American Vocalist [pamphlet] (London, 1853).

Brown, T. Allston. *A History of the New York Stage, from the First Performances in 1732 to 1901*. 3 vols. (New York, Dodd, Mead, 1903).

Bull, Sara C. *Ole Bull: A Memoir* (Boston, Houghton, Mifflin, 1883).

[Byrne, Julia Glass]. *Gossip of the Century: Personal and Traditional Memories—Social, Literary, Artistic, etc.* (London, Ward & Downey, 1892).

Carse, Adam. *The Life of Jullien* (Cambridge, Eng., W. Heffer, 1951).

———. *The Orchestra from Beethoven to Berlioz* (Cambridge, Eng., W. Heffer, 1948; rpt. Broude Bros., 1949).

Chase, Gilbert. *America's Music: From the Pilgrims to the Present*. Rev. 3rd ed. (Urbana, Univ. of Illinois Press, 1987).

Chorley, Henry F. *Thirty Years' Musical Recollections* (London, Hurst & Blackett, 1862; rpt. Vienna House, 1972).

Clay, Mrs., of Alabama. *A Belle of the Fifties* (New York, Doubleday, Page, 1905).

Curtis, George William. *Early Letters of George William Curtis to John Sullivan Dwight: Brook Farm and Concord*, ed. George Willis Cooke (New York, Harper, 1898).

———. *From the Easy Chair* (New York, Harper, 1891).

———. *The Potiphar Papers* (New York, Putnam, 1853).

Davison, J. W. *Music During the Victorian Era: From Mendelssohn to Wagner* (London, W. Reeves, 1912).

Didimus, H. "L. M. Gottschalk" (*Graham's Magazine*, Jan. 1853, pp. 61–69).

Dizikes, John. Opera in America: A Cultural History (New Haven, Yale Univ. Press, 1993).

Duffy, John. *Sword of Pestilence: The New Orleans Yellow Fever Epidemic of 1853* (Baton Rouge, Louisiana State Univ. Press, 1966).

Elson, Louis C. *The History of American Music* (New York, Macmillan, 1904; rev. ed. Arthur Elson, Macmillan, 1925; rpt. Franklin, 1977).

Epstein, Dena J. *Music Publishing in Chicago Before 1871: The Firm of Root and Cady 1858–1871* (Detroit, IC, 1969).

———. *Sinful Tunes and Spirituals: Black Folk Music to the Civil War* (Urbana, Univ. of Illinois Press, 1977).

Erskine, John. *The Philharmonic Society of New York: Its First Hundred Years* (New York, Macmillan, 1943; rpt. in *Early Histories of the New York Philharmonic*, Da Capo, 1979).

Evans, Henry Ridgely, and Harry L. Clapham. *Melody Magic* (Washington, D.C., Clapham, 1932).

Fay, Amy. *Music-Study in Germany* (Chicago, McClurg, 1880; rpt. Dover, 1965).

Field, Maunsell B. *Personal Recollections, Memories of Many Men and Some Women* (New York, Harper, 1874).

Forbes, Elizabeth. *Mario and Grisi: A Biography* (London, Gollancz, 1985).

Foster, George G. *New-York by Gaslight* (New York, M. J. Ivers, n.d.).

———. *New-York in Slices* (New York, William H. Graham, 1849).
———. *New-York Naked* (New York, R. M. DeWitt, *c.* 1850–61).
Gottschalk, Louis Moreau. *Notes of a Pianist*, ed. Clara Gottschalk Peterson (Philadelphia, Lippincott, 1881).
———. *Notes of a Pianist*, ed. Jeanne Behrend (New York, Knopf, 1964).
Groce, Nancy. *Musical Instrument Makers of New York: A Directory of Eighteenth- and Nineteenth-Century Urban Craftsmen* (New York, Pendragon, 1991).
Harris, Neil. *Humbug: The Art of P. T. Barnum* (Boston, Little, Brown, 1973).
Haswell, Charles H. *Reminiscences of an Octogenarian of the City of New York* (New York, Harper, 1896).
Hegermann-Lindencrone, Lillie de. *In the Courts of Memory* (New York, Harper, 1912).
Herz, Henri. *My Travels in America,* trans. Henry Bertram Hill (Madison, Univ. of Wisconsin Press, 1963).
Hewitt, John Hill. *Shadows on the Wall* (Baltimore, Turnbull Bros. 1877).
Hibben, Paxton. *Henry Ward Beecher* (New York, Doran, 1942).
History of the Liederkranz of the City of New York, 1847–1947, and of the Arion, New York (New York, Compiled by the History Committee, 1949).
Hoffman, Richard. *Some Musical Recollections of Fifty Years* (New York, Scribner's, 1910; rpt. IC, 1976).
Holland, H. S., and W. S. Rockstro, *Jenny Lind the Artist, 1820–1851* (London, J. Murray, 1893).
Hone, Philip. *The Diary of Philip Hone, 1828–1851*, ed. Allan Nevins (New York, Dodd Mead, 1927; rpt. Kraus, 1969).
Hornblow, Arthur. *A History of the Theatre in America.* 2 vols. (Philadelphia, Lippincott, 1919).
Howard, John Tasker. *Our American Music: A Comprehensive History from 1620 to the Present.* 4th ed. (New York, Crowell, 1965).
Huneker, James G. *The Philharmonic Society of New York and Its Seventy-Fifth Anniversary: A Retrospect* (New York, Philharmonic Society, 1917; rpt. in *Early Histories of the New York Philharmonic*, Da Capo, 1979).
Ireland, Joseph N. *Records of the American Stage, from 1750 to 1860.* 2 vols. (New York, T. H. Morrell, 1866; rpt. Blom, 1966).
Kellogg, Clara Louise. *Memoirs of an American Prima Donna* (New York, Putnam's, 1913).
Klein, Hermann. *The Reign of Patti* (New York, Century, 1911).
Krehbiel, Henry E. *The Philharmonic Society of New York* (London/New York, Novello, Ewer, 1892; rpt. in *Early Histories of the New York Philharmonic*, Da Capo, 1979).
La Brew, Arthur. *The Black Swan: Elizabeth T. Greenfield, Songstress: A Biographical Study* (Detroit, 1969).
Ladies of the Mission. *The Old Brewery, and the Mission House at the Five Points* (New York, Stringer & Townsend, 1854).
Lahee, Henry C. *Annals of Music in America* (Boston, Marshall Jones, 1922).
———. *Grand Opera in America* (Boston, L. C. Page, 1902; rpt. AMS, 1973).
Liszt, Franz. *An Artist's Journey (Lettres d'un bachelier ès musique 1835–1844),* trans. and ed. Charles Suttoni, Chicago, Univ. of Chicago Press, 1989).

Loesser, Arthur. *Men, Women, and Pianos: A Social History* (New York, Simon & Schuster, 1954).

Loggins, Vernon. *Where the Word Ends: The Life of Louis Moreau Gottschalk* (Baton Rouge, Louisiana State Univ. Press, 1958).

Lott, Allen R. *The American Concert Tours of Leopold de Meyer, Henri Herz, and Sigismund Thalberg,* 2 vols. Ph.D. dissertation, City Univ. of New York (Ann Arbor, UMI, 1986).

Lowens, Irving. *Music and Musicians in Early America: Aspects of the history of music in early America and the history of early American music* (New York, Norton, 1964).

Lumley, Benjamin. *Reminiscences of the Opera* (London, Hurst & Blackett, 1864).

Maretzek, Max. *Crotchets and Quavers, or Revelations of an Opera Manager in America* (New York, French, 1855; rpt. Dover 1968).

———. *Sharps and Flats* (New York, American Musician Publishing Co., 1890; rpt. Dover, 1968).

Mason, Rufus Osgood. *Sketches and Impressions, Musical, Theatrical, and Social (1799–1885), including a Sketch of the Philharmonic Society of New York, from the After-Dinner Talk of Thomas Godwin, Music Librarian* (New York, Putnam, 1887).

Mason, William. *Memories of a Musical Life* (New York, Century, 1901).

Mathews, W. S. B. *A Hundred Years of Music in America* (Chicago, G. L. Howe, 1889; rpt. AMS, 1970).

Messiter, A. H. *A History of the Choir and Music of Trinity Church, New York* (New York, E. S. Gorham, 1906).

Metcalf, Frank Johnson. *American Writers and Compilers of Sacred Music* (New York and Cincinnati, Abingdon, 1925).

Milne, Gordon. *George William Curtis and the Genteel Tradition* (Bloomington, Indiana Univ. Press, 1956).

Mott, Frank Luther. *A History of American Magazines.* vol. 2 (Cambridge, Belknap Press, 1936).

———. *American Journalism: A History of Newspapers in the United United States through 250 Years, 1690 to 1940* (New York, Macmillan, 1947).

Northall, William Knight. *Before and Behind the Curtain, or Fifteen Years' Observations among the Theatres of New York* (New York, W. F. Burgess, 1851).

Odell, George C. D. *Annals of the New York Stage.* vol. VI (New York, Columbia Univ. Press, 1931–36; rpt. AMS, 1970).

Offergeld, Robert. "The Gottschalk Legend: Grand Fantasy for a Great Many Pianos." Introduction to *The Collected Works of Louis Moreau Gottschalk,* ed. Vera Brodsky Lawrence, 5 vols. (New York, Arno, 1969).

Ogasapian, John. *Organ Building in New York City: 1700–1900* (Braintree, Mass., Organ Literature Foundation, 1977).

Pearse, Mrs. Godfrey, and Frank Hird. *The Romance of a Great Singer* (London, Smith, Elder, 1910; rpt. Arno, 1977).

Pemberton, Carol A. *Lowell Mason, His Life and Work* (Ann Arbor, UMI, 1985).

Pleasants, Henry. *The Great Singers* (New York, Simon & Schuster, 1966).

Pray, Isaac Clark. *Memoirs of James Gordon Bennett and His Times, by a Journalist* (New York, Stringer & Townsend, 1855).

Ridgeway, Thomas. "William Henry Fry, the First American Composer of Grand

Opera" (Philadephia, *Publications of the Genealogical Society of Pennsylvania*, Oct. 1943, pp. 120–35).

Ritter, Frederic Louis. *Music in America*. 2nd ed. (New York, Scribner's, 1890; rpt., Franklin, 1972).

Rockstro, W. S. *A General History of Music* (New York, Scribner & Welford, 1886).

Root, Harvey W. *The Unknown Barnum* (New York, Harper, 1927).

Rosenberg, C. G. *Jenny Lind in America* (New York, Stringer & Townsend, 1851).

Ross, Joel H., M.D. *What I Saw in New-York, or A Bird's Eye View of City Life* (Auburn, Derby & Miller, 1851).

Ryan, Thomas. *Recollections of an Old Musician* (New York, Dutton, 1899).

Saeltzer, Alexander. *A Treatise on Acoustics in Connection with Ventilation* (New York, Van Nostrand, 1872).

Sala, George Augustus. *A Journey Due North* (Boston, Ticknor & Fields, 1858).

Saxon, A. H. *P. T. Barnum: The Legend and the Man* (New York, Columbia Univ. Press, 1989).

Schabas, Ezra. *Theodore Thomas: America's Conductor and Builder of Orchestras: 1835–1905* (Urbana, Univ. of Illinois Press, 1989).

Schmidgall, Gary. *Shakespeare and Opera* (New York, Oxford Univ., Press, 1990).

Schonberg, Harold C. *The Great Conductors* (New York, Simon & Schuster, 1967).

———. *The Great Pianists* (New York, Simon & Schuster, 1963).

Shanet, Howard. *Philharmonic: A History of New York's Orchestra* (New York, Doubleday, 1975).

Smith, Mortimer. *The Life of Ole Bull* (Princeton, Princeton Univ. Press, 1943).

Southern, Eileen. *The Music of Black Americans: A History* (New York, Norton, 1971).

Squints through an Opera Glass, By a Young Gent Who Hadn't Any Thing Else to Do (New York, *Merchants' Day Book*, 1850).

Stendhal (Marie-Henri Beyle). *Life of Rossini* (1824), trans. and ed. Richard N. Coe (New York, Orion Press, 1970).

Still, Bayrd. *Mirror for Gotham: New York as Seen by Contemporaries from Dutch Days to the Present* (New York, New York Univ. Press, 1956).

Stoddard, R. H. *Recollections, Personal and Literary* (New York, A. S. Barnes, 1903).

Strong, George Templeton. *The Diary of George Templeton Strong*, ed. Allan Nevins and Milton Halsey Thomas. 4 vols. (New York, Macmillan, 1952).

Suttoni, Charles. *Piano and Opera: A Study of the Piano Fantasies Written on Opera Themes in the Romantic Era*. Ph.D. dissertation, New York Univ. (Ann Arbor, UMI, 1973).

Thomas, Theodore. *Theodore Thomas: A Musical Autobiography*, ed. George P. Upton. 2 vols. (Chicago, McClurg, 1905).

Thompson, Oscar. *The American Singer: A Hundred Years of Success in Opera* (New York, Dial, 1937).

Toye, Francis. *Rossini: a Study in Tragi-Comedy* (New York, Knopf, 1947).

Trotter, James Monroe. *Music and Some Highly Musical People* (Boston, Lee & Shepard, 1878; rpt. Johnson, 1969).

Upton, George P. *Musical Memories* (Chicago, McClurg, 1908).

Upton, William Treat. *Anthony Philip Heinrich: A Nineteeth-Century Composer in America* (New York, Columbia Univ. Press, 1939; rpt. AMS, 1967).

———. *William Henry Fry: American Journalist and Composer-Critic* (New York, Crowell, 1954; rpt. Da Capo, 1974).

Wagner, Richard, and Franz Liszt. *Correspondence,* trans. Francis Hueffer; rev. W. Ashton Ellis. 2 vols. (New York, Scribner's, 1897; rpt. Vienna House, 1973).

Wallace, Irving. *The Fabulous Showman: The Life and Times of P. T. Barnum* (New York, Knopf, 1947).

Ware, W. P., and T. C. Lockhard, Jr. *P. T. Barnum Presents Jenny Lind: The American Tour of the Swedish Nightingale* (Baton Rouge, Louisiana State Univ. Press, 1980).

Wecter, Dixon. *The Saga of American Society: A Record of Social Aspiration, 1607–1937* (New York, Scribner's, 1937, 1970).

Werner, M. R. *Barnum* (New York, Harcourt, Brace, 1923).

Westervelt, Leonidas. "The Jenny Lind Prize Song" (*N-YHSQ* April 1938, pp. 39–59).

White, Richard Grant. "Opera in New York" (*Century Illustrated Monthly Magazine,* May 1882, pp. 31–43; June 1882, pp. 193–210).

Whitman, Walt. *Specimen Days & Collect* (Philadelphia, R. Welsh, 1882–83).

Willis, Nathaniel Parker. *Hurrygraphs* (New York, Scribner's, 1851).

———. *Pencillings By the Way* (Auburn, Alden, Beardsley, 1853).

———. *Memoranda of the Life of Jenny Lind* (Philadelphia, Robert E. Peterson, 1851).

Winter, William. *Old Friends* (New York, Moffat, Yard, 1909, 1914).

BIBLIOGRAPHIES, BIOGRAPHICAL DICTIONARIES, ENCYCLOPEDIAS, ETC.

Baker's Biographical Dictionary of Musicians. 5th ed., rev. Nicholas Slonimsky (New York, Schirmer, 1975).

Cyclopedia of Music and Musicians, ed. John Denison Champlin and William Foster Apthorp. 3 vols. (New York, Scribner's, 1888–90).

Dictionary of American Biography, ed. Allen Johnson and Dumas Malone (New York, Scribner's, 1928–53).

Dictionary of American Negro Biography, ed. Rayford W. Logan and Michael R. Winston (New York, Norton, 1982).

Doyle, John G. *Louis Moreau Gottschalk 1829–1860: A Bibliographical Study and Catalog of Works* (Detroit, IC, 1983).

Dox, Thurston J. *American Oratorios and Cantatas: A Catalog of Works Written in the United States from Colonial Times to 1985,* 2 vols. (Metuchen, N.J., Scarecrow, 1986).

Grove's Dictionary of Music and Musicians. 1st ed., Sir George Grove, ed. (London, 1878-80); *American Supplement,* ed. Waldo Selden Pratt (New York, Macmillan, 1935); 5th ed., Eric Blom, ed. (New York, St. Martin's Press, 1961); *The New Grove,* ed. Stanley Sadie (London, Macmillan, 1980).

Jones, F. O. *A Handbook of American Music and Musicians, Containing Biographies of American Musicians and Histories of the Principal Musical Institutions, Firms, and Societies* (Buffalo, C. W. Moulton, 1887; rpt. Da Capo, 1971).

Kaufman, Thomas G. *Verdi and His Major Contemporaries: A Selected Chronology of Performances with Casts* (New York, Garland, 1990).

Kutsch and Riemens. *Grosses Sängerlexicon.* 2 vols. (Stuttgart, Franke Verlag, 1987).

Loewenberg, Alfred. *Annals of Opera, 1597–1940.* Rev. 3rd ed. (Totowa, N.J., Rowman & Littlefield, 1978).

Macmillan Encyclopedia of Music and Musicians, ed. Albert E. Wier (New York, Macmillan, 1938).

Marcuse, Sibyl. *Musical Instruments* (New York, Norton, 1975).

Mattfeld, Julius. *A Handbook of American Operatic Premieres, 1731–1962* (Detroit, IC, 1963).

———. *A Hundred Years of Grand Opera in New York, 1825–1925* (New York, NYPL, 1927).

———. *Variety Music Cavalcade: Musical-Historical Review, 1620–1969.* 3rd ed. (Englewood Cliffs, N.J., Prentice-Hall, 1971).

Moore, John W. *Complete Encyclopedia of Music, Elementary, Technical, Historical, Biographical, Vocal, and Instrumental* (Boston, J. P. Jewett, 1854; Appendix, O. Ditson, 1875).

National Cyclopedia of American Biography (New York, James T. White, 1892).

The New Encyclopaedia Britannica (Chicago, Encyclopaedia Britannica Co., 1974–).

The New Kobbé's Complete Opera Book, ed. and rev. the Earl of Harewood (George H. H. Lascelles) (New York, Putnam, 1976).

Nicholl, Allardyce. *A History of English Drama.* 3rd ed., vols. 4–6 (Cambridge, Eng., Cambridge Univ. Press, 1965).

Offergeld, Robert. *The Centennial Catalogue of the Published and Unpublished Compositions of Louis Moreau Gottschalk* (New York, Ziff-Davis, 1970).

Partridge, Eric. *The Macmillan Dictionary of Historical Slang* (New York, Macmillan, 1974).

Redway, Virginia Larkin. *Music Directory of Early New York City: A File of Musicians, Music Publishers, and Musical Instrument-makers listed in New York directories from 1786 through 1835, together with the most important New York Music Publishers from 1835 through 1875* (New York, NYPL, 1941).

Southern, Eileen. *Biographical Dictionary of Afro-American and African Musicians* (Westport, Greenwood Press, 1982).

Weichlein, William. *A Checklist of American Music Periodicals 1850–1900.* Detroit Studies in Musical Bibliography 16 (Detroit, IC, 1970).

NEW YORK DAILY NEWSPAPERS

(Unless otherwise noted, the following newspapers have been read for the years covered in this volume.)

Evening Mirror, ed. Hiram Fuller.
Evening Post, ed. William Cullen Bryant.
Daily Times, ed. Henry Jarvis Raymond. 1851–.
Daily Tribune, ed. Horace Greeley.

Herald, ed. James Gordon Bennett.
Morning Courier & New-York Enquirer. ed. James Watson Webb.

PERIODICALS
(published in New York, unless otherwise indicated)

The Albion, or British, Colonial, and Foreign Weekly, ed. John R. Young. 1850–.

American Monthly Musical Review and Choir Singers' Companion (monthly), ed. Isaac Baker Woodbury. 1850–52.

Merged 1852 with the

Choral Advocate and Singing Class Journal (monthly), ed. Darius E. Jones. 1850; Darius E. Jones and Lowell Mason, Jr. 1851; Lowell Mason, Jr. and Isaac Baker Woodbury. 1852. (to form the)

Musical Review and Choral Advocate (monthly), ed. C. M. Cady. 1853.

Later titles:

New-York Musical Review & Choral Advocate (fortnightly), ed. C. M. Cady. 1854.

New-York Musical Review & Gazette (fortnightly), ed. Theodore Hagen. 1855–.

Dwight's Journal of Music: A Paper of Art and Literature [Boston] (weekly), ed. John Sullivan Dwight. 1852–.

Figaro! or Corbyn's Chronicle of Amusements (weekly), ed. Wardle Corbyn and J. W. S. Hows. 1850; D. Russell Lee and Thomas Powell. 1851.

Frank Leslie's Illustrated Newspaper (weekly), ed. Frank Leslie with Henry C. Watson. 1855–.

Graham's Magazine [Philadelphia] (monthly), ed. George Rex Graham. 1851.

Harper's New Monthly Magazine, ed. Henry J. Raymond. 1850–.

Home Journal (weekly), ed. George Pope Morris and Nathaniel Parker Willis. 1850–.

The Message Bird: A Literary and Musical Journal (fortnightly), ed. anon. 1850.

Later titles:

Journal of the Fine Arts: American and Foreign Record of Music, Literature, and Art, ed. anon. 1851.

The Musical World and Journal of the Fine Arts: An American and Foreign Record of Music, Literature, and Art, ed. Oliver Dyer. 1852. Merged 1852 with *The Musical Times (q.v.)* (to become)

The Musical World and New York Musical Times, ed. Richard Storrs Willis and Oliver Dyer. 1852; Richard Storrs Willis. 1853–54.

Later titles:

Musical World, ed. Richard Storrs Willis. 1854–55.

New York Musical World: A Literary and Fine-Art Paper, ed. Richard Storrs Willis, Dr. Edward Hodges, and Augustus Morand. 1856.

New York Clipper (weekly), ed. Frank Queen. 1853–54.

New York Dispatch (weekly), ed. Charles Burkhardt. 1856.

Parker's Journal: A Weekly Gazette of Literature, Fashion, Art, and Science, ed. William R. Parker and Spencer Wallace Cone. 1850–51.

Philharmonic Journal, ed. Henry C. Watson. March 23, 1854 (only known issue).

Putnam's Monthly Magazine of American Literature, Science, and Art, ed. Charles F. Briggs, with George William Curtis and Parke Godwin. 1853–.

Saroni's Musical Times: A Weekly Journal Devoted to Music, Literature, and the Fine Arts, ed. Hermann S. Saroni. 1850

Later titles:

The Musical Times (weekly), ed. Hermann S. Saroni; D. M. Cole and J. S. Black. 1851. Merged 1852 with the *Musical World and Journal of the Fine Arts (q.v.)* to become the *Musical World and New York Musical Times.*

Sartain's Union Magazine of Literature and Art [Philadelphia] (weekly), ed. John Sartain. 1851.

Spirit of the Times: A Chronicle of the Turf, Agriculture, Field Sports, Literature, and the Stage (weekly), ed. William T. Porter. 1850–56.

Succeeded by:

Porter's Spirit of the Times, ed. George Wilkes and William T. Porter. 1856.

Sunday Times and Noah's Weekly Messenger (weekly), ed. M. M. Noah. 1850–51.

ARCHIVAL MATERIALS

NEW-YORK HISTORICAL SOCIETY LIBRARY

Castle Garden, 1850–51. Day books, contracts, receipts, correspondence, recipes, menus, etc.

Hone, Philip. Diary. 1838–51.

Strong, George Templeton. Private Journal. 1835–75.

NEW YORK PHILHARMONIC ARCHIVES

Minutes of board of directors' meetings; account books; annual reports. 1850–.

INDEX

By Marilyn Bliss

Asterisks designate persons who settled permanently in the United States; "premiere" and "debut" refer to first performances in New York; the term "vocalist" is used to distinguish singers of popular music from performers of oratorio, concert, and opera repertory. Page references in italics refer to illustrations. Alphabetization of titles ignores definite articles in all languages; leading function terms (as, and, of, *etc.*) are also ignored. No distinction has been made between attributed and signed criticism under the critic's name.